Contemporary
Literary Criticism
Yearbook 1993

Guide to Gale Literary Criticism Series

For criticism on	Consult these Gale series
Authors now living or who died after December 31, 1959	*CONTEMPORARY LITERARY CRITICISM (CLC)*
Authors who died between 1900 and 1959	*TWENTIETH-CENTURY LITERARY CRITICISM (TCLC)*
Authors who died between 1800 and 1899	*NINETEENTH-CENTURY LITERATURE CRITICISM (NCLC)*
Authors who died between 1400 and 1799	*LITERATURE CRITICISM FROM 1400 TO 1800 (LC)* *SHAKESPEAREAN CRITICISM (SC)*
Authors who died before 1400	*CLASSICAL AND MEDIEVAL LITERATURE CRITICISM (CMLC)*
Black writers of the past two hundred years	*BLACK LITERATURE CRITICISM (BLC)*
Authors of books for children and young adults	*CHILDREN'S LITERATURE REVIEW (CLR)*
Dramatists	*DRAMA CRITICISM (DC)*
Hispanic writers of the late nineteenth and twentieth centuries	*HISPANIC LITERATURE CRITICISM (HLC)*
Poets	*POETRY CRITICISM (PC)*
Short story writers	*SHORT STORY CRITICISM (SSC)*
Major authors from the Renaissance to the present	*WORLD LITERATURE CRITICISM, 1500 TO THE PRESENT (WLC)*

ISSN 0091-3421

Volume 81

Contemporary Literary Criticism
Yearbook 1993

The Year in Fiction, Poetry, Drama, and
World Literature and the Year's
New Authors, Prizewinners, Obituaries,
and Outstanding Literary Events

James P. Draper
EDITOR

Jeffery Chapman
Christopher Giroux
ASSOCIATE EDITORS,
CLC YEARBOOK

Jennifer Brostrom
Brigham Narins
Janet Witalec
ASSOCIATE EDITORS

 **Gale Research Inc.** • *DETROIT* • *WASHINGTON, D.C.* • *LONDON*

STAFF

James P. Draper, *Editor*

Jennifer Brostrom, Jeffery Chapman, Christopher Giroux, Drew Kalasky, Thomas Ligotti, Brigham Narins, Sean René Pollock, David Segal, Janet Witalec, *Associate Editors*

Deron Albright, Martha Bommarito, Joseph Cislo, Lynn M. Spampinato, *Assistant Editors*

Jeanne A. Gough, *Permissions & Production Manager*
Linda M. Pugliese, *Production Supervisor*
Donna Craft, Paul Lewon, Maureen A. Puhl, Camille P. Robinson, Sheila Walencewicz, *Editorial Associates*

Sandra C. Davis, *Permissions Supervisor (Text)*
Maria L. Franklin, Josephine M. Keene, Michele Lonoconus, Shalice Shah, Kimberly F. Smilay, *Permissions Associates*
Jennifer A. Arnold, Brandy C. Merritt, *Permissions Assistants*

Margaret A. Chamberlain, *Permissions Supervisor (Pictures)*
Pamela A. Hayes, Arlene Johnson, Keith Reed, Barbara A. Wallace, *Permissions Associates*
Susan Brohman, *Permissions Assistant*

Victoria B. Cariappa, *Research Manager*
Mary Rose Bonk, Maureen Richards, *Research Supervisors*
Reginald A. Carlton, Frank Vincent Castronova, Robert S. Lazich, Andrew Guy Malonis, Mary Beth McElmeel, Donna Melnychenko, Tamara C. Nott, Jaema Paradowski, Norma Sawaya, *Editorial Associates*
Laurel Sprague Bowden, Dawn Marie Conzett, Eva Marie Felts, Shirley Gates, Julie A. Kriebel, Sharon McGilvray, Stefanie Scarlett, Dana R. Shleiffers, Amy B. Wieczorek, *Editorial Assistants*

Mary Beth Trimper, *Production Director*
Catherine Kemp, *Production Assistant*

Cynthia Baldwin, *Art Director*
Barbara J. Yarrow, *Graphic Services Supervisor*
C. J. Jonik, *Desktop Publisher*
Willie F. Mathis, *Camera Operator*

Library of Congress Catalog Card Number 76-38938
ISBN 0-8103-4989-2
ISSN 0091-3421

Printed in the United States of America
Published simultaneously in the United Kingdom
by Gale Research International Limited
(An affiliated company of Gale Research Inc.)
10 9 8 7 6 5 4 3 2 1

The trademark **ITP** is used under license.

Contents

Preface vii

Acknowledgments xi

v

IN MEMORIAM

TOPICS IN LITERATURE: 1993

Preface

A Comprehensive Information Source on Contemporary Literature

Scope of the *Yearbook*

*C*ontemporary Literary Criticism Yearbook* is a part of the ongoing *Contemporary Literary Criticism (CLC)* series. *CLC* provides a comprehensive survey of modern literature by presenting excerpted criticism on the works of novelists, poets, playwrights, short story writers, scriptwriters, and other creative writers now living or who died after December 31, 1959. A strong emphasis is placed on including criticism of works by established authors who frequently appear on syllabuses of high school and college literature courses.

To complement this broad coverage, the *Yearbook* focuses more specifically on a given year's literary activities and features a larger number of currently noteworthy authors than is possible in standard *CLC* volumes. *CLC Yearbook* provides students, teachers, librarians, researchers, and general readers with information and commentary on the outstanding literary works and events of a given year.

Format of the Book

CLC, Volume 81: *Yearbook 1993*, which includes excerpted criticism on more than twenty authors and comprehensive coverage of three key issues in contemporary literature, is divided into five sections—"The Year in Review," "New Authors," "Prizewinners," "In Memoriam," and "Topics in Literature: 1993."

- **The Year in Review**—This section consists of specially commissioned essays by prominent writers who survey the year's works in their respective fields. Wendy Lesser discusses "The Year in Fiction," Allen Hoey "The Year in Poetry," Robert Cohen "The Year in Drama," and William Riggan "The Year in World Literature." For introductions to the essayists, please see the Notes on Contributors.

- **New Authors**—This section introduces seven writers who received significant critical recognition for their first major work of fiction or whose work was translated into English and published in the United States for the first time in 1993. Authors were selected for inclusion if their work was reviewed in several prominent literary periodicals.

- **Prizewinners**—This section begins with a list of literary prizes and honors announced in 1993, citing the award, award criteria, the recipient, and the title of the prizewinning work. Following the listing of prizewinners is a presentation of nine entries on individual award winners, representing a mixture of genres and nationalities as well as established prizes and those more recently introduced.

- **In Memoriam**—This section consists of reminiscences, tributes, retrospective articles, and obituary notices on five authors who died in 1993. In addition, an Obituary section provides information on other recently deceased literary figures.

- **Topics in Literature**—This section focuses on literary issues and events of considerable public interest, including AIDS in Literature, the Philip Larkin Controversy, and Revising the Literary Canon.

Features

With the exception of the four essays in "The Year in Review" section, which were written specifically for this publication, the *Yearbook* consists of excerpted criticism drawn from literary reviews, general magazines, newspapers, books, and scholarly journals. *Yearbook* entries variously contain the following items:

- An **Author Heading** in the "New Authors" and "Prizewinners" sections cites the name under which the author publishes and the title of the work covered in the entry; the "In Memoriam" section includes the author's name and birth and death dates. The author's full name, pseudonyms (if any) under which the author has published, nationality, and principal genres in which the author writes are listed on the first line of the author entry.

- The **Subject Heading** defines the theme of each entry in "The Year in Review" and "Topics in Literature" sections.

- A brief **Biographical and Critical Introduction** to the author and his or her work precedes excerpted criticism in the "New Authors," "Prizewinners," and "In Memoriam" sections; the subjects, authors, and works in the "Topics in Literature" section are introduced in a similar manner.

- A listing of **Principal Works** is included for all entries in the "Prizewinners" and "In Memoriam" sections.

- A **Portrait** of the author is included in the "New Authors," "Prizewinners," and "In Memoriam" sections, and an **Excerpt from the Author's Work,** if available or applicable, is also provided. Whenever possible, a recent, previously unpublished **Author Interview** accompanies each "New Author" entry.

- The **Excerpted Criticism,** included in all entries except those in the "Year in Review" section, represents essays selected by editors to reflect the spectrum of opinion about a specific work or about the author's writing in general. The excerpts are typically arranged chronologically, adding a useful perspective to the entry. In the "Year in Review," "New Authors," "Prizewinners," and "In Memoriam" sections, all titles by the author being discussed are printed in boldface type, enabling the reader to easily identify the author's work.

- A complete **Bibliographical Citation,** designed to help the user find the original essay or book, follows each excerpt.

- **Cross-references** have been included in the "New Authors," "Prizewinners," and "In Memoriam" sections to direct readers to other useful sources published by Gale Research. Previous volumes of *CLC* in which the author has been featured are also listed.

Other Features

The *Yearbook* also includes the following features:

- An **Acknowledgments** section lists the copyright holders who have granted permission to reprint material in this volume of *CLC*. It does not, however, list every book or periodical reprinted or consulted during the preparation of this volume.

- A **Cumulative Author Index** lists all the authors who have appeared in the various literary criticism series published by Gale Research, with cross-references to Gale's biographical and autobiographical series. A full listing of series referenced in the index appears at the beginning of the index. Readers will welcome this cumulated author index as a useful tool for locating an author within the various series. The index, which lists birth and death dates when available, is particularly valuable for locating references to those authors whose careers span two periods. For example, Ernest Hemingway is found in *CLC*, yet a writer often associated with him, F. Scott Fitzgerald, is found in *Twentieth-Century Literary Criticism*.

- Beginning with *CLC*, Vol. 65, each *Yearbook* contains a **Cumulative Topic Index,** which lists all literary topics treated in *CLC Yearbook* volumes and the topic volumes of *Twentieth-Century Literary Criticism, Nineteenth-Century Literature Criticism,* and *Literature Criticism from 1400 to 1800.*

- A **Cumulative Nationality Index** alphabetically lists all authors featured in *CLC* by nationality, followed by numbers corresponding to the volumes in which the authors appear.

- A **Title Index** alphabetically lists all titles reviewed in the current volume of *CLC*. Listings are followed by the author's name and the corresponding page numbers where the titles are discussed. English translations of foreign titles and variations of titles are cross-referenced to the title under which a work was originally published. Titles of novels, novellas, dramas, films, record albums, and poetry, short story, and essay collections are printed in italics, while all individual poems, short stories, essays, and songs are printed in roman type within quotation marks. When published separately, the titles of long poems (e.g., T. S. Eliot's *The Waste Land*) are printed in italics.

- In response to numerous suggestions from librarians, Gale has also produced a **Special Paperbound Edition** of the *CLC* title index. This annual cumulation, which alphabetically lists all titles reviewed in the series, is available to all customers and is published with the first volume of *CLC* issued in each calendar year. Additional copies of the index are available upon request. Librarians and patrons will welcome this separate index: it saves shelf space, is easy to use, and is recyclable upon receipt of the following year's cumulation.

Citing *Contemporary Literary Criticism*

When writing papers, students who quote directly from any volume in the Literary Criticism Series may use the following general forms to footnote reprinted criticism. The first example is for material drawn from periodicals, the second for material reprinted from books:

[1]Alfred Cismaru, "Julien Green's 'Journal': A Contemporary Look Backwards," *Mid-American Review* IX, No. 2 (1989), 136-42; excerpted and reprinted in *Contemporary Literary Criticism,* Vol. 77, ed. James P. Draper (Detroit: Gale Research Inc., 1993), pp. 282-84.

[2]George H. Smith, *Atheism, Ayn Rand, and Other Heresies* (Prometheus Books, 1991); excerpted and reprinted in *Contemporary Literary Criticism,* Vol. 79, ed. James P. Draper (Detroit: Gale Research Inc., 1993), pp. 384-89.

Suggestions Are Welcome

The editor hopes that readers will find *CLC Yearbook* a useful reference tool and welcomes comments about the work. Send comments and suggestions to: Editor, *Contemporary Literary Criticism,* Gale Research Inc., Penobscot Building, Detroit, MI 48226-4094.

Acknowledgments

The editors wish to thank the copyright holders of the excerpted criticism included in this volume, the permissions managers of many book and magazine publishing companies for assisting us in securing reprint rights, and Anthony Bogucki for assistance with copyright research. We are also grateful to the staffs of the Detroit Public Library, the Library of Congress, the University of Detroit Library, Wayne State University Purdy/Kresge Library Complex, and the University of Michigan Libraries for making their resources available to us. Following is a list of the copyright holders who have granted us permission to reprint material in this volume of *CLC*. Every effort has been made to trace copyright, but if omissions have been made, please let us know.

COPYRIGHTED EXCERPTS IN *CLC*, VOLUME 81, WERE REPRINTED FROM THE FOLLOWING PERIODICALS:

America, v. 169, July 31-August 7, 1993. © 1993. All rights reserved. Reprinted with permission of America Press, Inc., 106 West 56th Street, New York, NY 10019.—*American Literature,* v. 65, June, 1993. Copyright © 1993 Duke University Press, Durham, NC. Reprinted with permission of the publisher.—*The American Spectator,* v. 26, September, 1993. Copyright © *The American Spectator* 1993. Reprinted by permission of the publisher.—*The Antioch Review,* v. 47, Spring, 1989; v. 51, Spring, 1993. Copyright © 1989, 1993 by the Antioch Review Inc. Both reprinted by permission of the Editors.—*The Atlantic Monthly,* v. 272, September, 1993 for "An Icon of Englishry" by Geoffrey Wheatcroft. Copyright 1993 by The Atlantic Monthly Company, Boston, MA. Reprinted by permission of the author.—*Belles Lettres: A Review of Books by Women,* v. 8, Spring, 1993. Reprinted by permission of the publisher.—*The Bloomsbury Review,* v. 10, July-August, 1990 for "A Crude Instrument, a Little Pigment & Some Stolen Time" by James R. Hepworth. Copyright © by Owaissa Communications Company, Inc. 1990. Reprinted by permission of the author.—*Book World—The Washington Post,* March 27, 1988; March 12, 1989; April 21, 1991; March 22, 1992; April 26, 1992; November 22, 1992; June 13, 1993; June 27, 1993. © 1988, 1989, 1991, 1992, 1993, *The Washington Post.* All reprinted with permission of the publisher.—*Booklist,* v. 89, May 1, 1993. Copyright © 1993 by the American Library Association. Reprinted by permission of the publisher.—*Callaloo,* v. 9, Winter, 1986. Copyright © 1986 by Charles H. Rowell. All rights reserved. Both reprinted by permission of the publisher.—*Chicago Review,* v. 34, Spring, 1984. Copyright © 1984 by *Chicago Review.* Reprinted by permission of the publisher.—*Chicago Tribune,* April 4, 1993 for "Honoring Her Forebears" by Nancy Stetson. © copyrighted 1993, Chicago Tribune Company. All rights reserved. Reprinted by permission of the author./ March 22, 1992. © copyrighted 1992, Chicago Tribune Company. All rights reserved. Used with permission.—*Chicago Tribune—The Arts,* April 25, 1993 for "A Gay Epic" by Hilary de Vries. © copyrighted 1993, Chicago Tribune Company. All rights reserved. Reprinted by permission of the author.—*Chicago Tribune—Books,* March 28, 1993 for "Scenes of Extremity" by Mona Simpson. © copyrighted 1993, Chicago Tribune Company. All rights reserved. Reprinted by permission of International Creative Management, Inc./ February 23, 1992 for "At a Cultural Crossroads" by Madison Smartt Bell; April 19, 1992 for "Singing the Big City Blues" by Michael Dorris; July 25, 1993 for "When Danger, Pain and Imminent Death Pierce Illusion's 'Murky Veil'" by Judith Wynn. © copyrighted 1992, 1993, Chicago Tribune Company. All rights reserved. All reprinted by permission of the respective authors.—*The Christian Science Monitor,* September 4, 1992 for "As Others See the Vietnamese" by Kathleen Kilgore; January 7, 1993 for "Images of Now and Then in Poetry's Mirror" by Elizabeth Lund; March 11, 1993 for "Flowing Moments in Imagined Time" by Simson L. Garfinkel; April 6, 1993 for "A World of Omens and Oracles" by Merle Rubin; May 26, 1993 for an interview with Rita Dove by Steven Ratiner. © 1992, 1993 the respective authors. All rights reserved. All reprinted by permission of the respective authors.—*The Chronicle of Higher Education,* April 14, 1993. Copyright © 1993 *The Chronicle of Higher Education.* Reprinted with permission of the publisher.—*Commentary,* v, 84, December, 1987 for "Toni Morrison's Career" by Carol Iannone. Copyright © 1987 by the American Jewish Committee. All rights reserved. Reprinted by permission of the publisher and the author.—*Contemporary Literature,* v. 15, Autumn, 1974; v. 23,

Feingold. Copyright © News Group Publications, Inc., 1991, 1993. All reprinted by permission of *The Village Voice* and the respective authors.—*VLS,* n. 105, May, 1992 for "Harlem on Her Mind: Toni Morrison's Language of Love" by Jane Mendelsohn; n. 112, February, 1993 for a review of "Martin and John" by Vince Aletti; n. 114, April, 1993 for "Brain Man: Albert Einstein's Twisted Legacy" by Carol Anshaw; n. 114, April, 1993 for "Northeastern Exposure" by Dwight Garner; n. 116, June, 1993 for a review of "The Virgin Suicides" by Katherine Dieckmann. Copyright © 1992, 1993 News Group Publications, Inc. All reprinted by permission of *The Village Voice* and the respective authors.—*The Wall Street Journal,* February 1, 1993. © 1993 Dow Jones & Company, Inc. All rights reserved. Reprinted by permission of *The Wall Street Journal.*—*The Washington Post,* March 23, 1992; January 10, 1993; January 23, 1993; March 25, 1993; April 15, 1993; May 19, 1993; June 29, 1993. © 1992, 1993, Washington Post Co. All reprinted with permission of the publisher.—*The Women's Review of Books,* v. IX, June, 1992 for "Harlem Nocturne" by Deborah A. McDowell; v. X, March, 1993 for "Miss Puppet Lady" by Gabrielle Foreman; v. X, May, 1993 for "Metaphysical Poets" by Elisabeth Frost. Copyright © 1992, 1993. All rights reserved. All reprinted by permission of the respective authors.—*The Yale Review,* v. 80, October, 1992; v. 81, October, 1993. Copyright 1992, 1993, by Yale University. Both reprinted by permission of the editors.

COPYRIGHTED EXCERPTS IN *CLC*, VOLUME 81, WERE REPRINTED FROM THE FOLLOWING BOOKS:

Abé, Kōbō. From *Beyond the Curve.* Translated by Juliet Winters Carpenter. Kodansha International, 1991. Copyright © 1991 Kodansha International. All rights reserved.—Abé, Kōbō. From *The Woman in the Dunes.* Knopf, 1964. Copyright © 1964 by Alfred A. Knopf, Inc. All rights reserved.—Butler, Robert Olen. From *A Good Scent from a Strange Mountain: Stories.* Henry Holt and Company, 1992. Copyright © 1992 by Robert Olen Butler. All rights reserved.—Calasso, Roberto. From *The Marriage of Cadmus and Harmony.* Translated by Tim Parks. Knopf, 1993. Copyright © 1993 by Alfred A. Knopf, Inc. All rights reserved.—Clum, John M. From "'And Once I Had it All': AIDS Narratives and Memories of an American Dream," in *Writing AIDS: Gay Literature, Language, and Analysis.* Edited by Timothy F. Murphy and Suzanne Poirier. Columbia University Press, 1993. Copyright © 1993 Columbia University Press, New York. All rights reserved. Reprinted with the permission of the publisher.—Dasenbrock, Reed Way. From "What to Teach When the Canon Closes Down: Toward a New Essentialism," in *Reorientations: Critical Theories and Pedagogies.* Edited by Bruce Henricksen and Thaïs E. Morgan. University of Illinois Press, 1990. © 1990 by the Board of Trustees of the University of Illinois. Reprinted by permission of the publisher and the author.—Edelman, Lee. From "The Plague of Discourse: Politics, Literary Theory, and AIDS," in *Displacing Homophobia: Gay Male Perspectives in Literature and Culture.* Ronald R. Butters, John M. Clum, Michael Moon, eds. Duke University Press, 1989. Copyright © 1989 by Duke University Press, Durham, NC. All rights reserved. Reprinted with permission of the publisher.—Eugenides, Jeffrey. From *The Virgin Suicides.* Farrar, Straus and Giroux, 1993. Copyright © 1993 by Jeffrey Eugenides. All rights reserved.—Glück, Louise. From *The Wild Iris.* The Ecco Press, 1992. Copyright © 1992 by Louis Glück. All rights reserved.—Gunn, Thom. From *The Man with Night Sweats.* Farrar, Straus and Giroux, 1992. Copyright © 1992 by Thom Gunn. All rights reserved.—Jones, James W. From "Refusing the Name: The Absence of AIDS in Recent American Gay Male Fiction," in *Writing AIDS: Gay Literature, Language, and Analysis.* Edited by Timothy F. Murphy and Suzanne Poirier. Columbia University Press, 1993. Copyright © 1993 Columbia University Press, New York. All rights reserved. Reprinted with the permission of the publisher.—Jones, Thom. From *The Pugilist at Rest: Stories.* Little, Brown and Company, 1993. Copyright © 1993 by Thom Jones. All rights reserved.—Kingsolver, Barbara. From *Pigs in Heaven.* HarperCollins Publishers, 1993. Copyright © 1993 by Barbara Kingsolver. All rights reserved.—Lightman, Alan. From *Einstein's Dreams.* Pantheon Books, 1993. Copyright © 1993 by Alan Lightman. All rights reserved.—Morrison, Toni. From *Playing in the Dark: Whiteness and the Literary Imagination.* Cambridge, Mass.: Harvard University Press, 1992. Copyright © 1992 by Toni Morrison. All rights reserved.—Morrison, Toni. From *Jazz.* Alfred A. Knopf, 1992. Copyright © 1992 by Toni Morrison. All rights reserved.—Muske, Carol. From "Rewriting the Elegy," in *Applause.* University of Pittsburgh Press, 1989. Copyright © 1989 by Carol Muske. All rights reserved. Reprinted by permission of the publisher.—Ng, Fae Myenne. From *Bone.* Hyperion, 1993. Copyright © 1993 Fae Myenne Ng. All rights reserved.—Peck, Dale. From *Martin and John: A Novel.* Farrar, Straus and Giroux, 1993. Copyright © 1993 by Dale Peck. All rights reserved.—Proulx, E. Annie. From *The Shipping News*. Charles Scribner's Sons, 1993. Copyright © 1993 by E. Annie Proulx. All rights reserved.—Richter, David H. From *The Critical Tradition: Classic Texts and Contemporary Trends*. Edited by David H. Richter. St. Martin's Press, 1989. Copyright © 1989 by St. Martin's Press, Inc. All rights reserved. Reprinted by permission of the publisher.—Sherwood, Frances. From *Vindication*. Farrar, Straus and Giroux, 1993. Copyright © 1993 by Frances Sherwood. All rights reserved.—Sontag, Susan. From *AIDS and Its Metaphors*. Farrar, Straus and Giroux, 1989. Copyright © 1988, 1989 by Susan Sontag. All rights reserved. Reprinted by permission of Farrar, Straus and Giroux, Inc. In the British Commonwealth by Wylie, Aitken & Stone, Inc.—Turner, Darwin T. From "Theme, Characterization, and Style in the Works of Toni Morrison," in *Black Women Writers (1950-1980): A Critical Evaluation*. Edited by Mari Evans. Anchor Press/Doubleday, 1984. Copyright © 1983 by Mari Evans. All rights reserved. Used by permission of Doubleday, a division of Bantam Doubleday Dell Publishing Group, Inc.

PHOTOGRAPHS AND ILLUSTRATIONS APPEARING IN *CLC*, VOLUME 81, WERE RECEIVED FROM THE FOLLOWING SOURCES:

PLAYBILL® covers printed by permission of PLAYBILL Incorporated. PLAYBILL® is a registered Trademark of PLAYBILL Incorporated, New York, NY: **pp. 20, 22, 24, 25, 27, 29;** AP/Wide World Photos: **pp. 39, 89, 121, 163, 215;** Jacket of *The Marriage of Cadmus and Harmony,* by Roberto Calasso. Alfred A. Knopf, 1993. Jacket design by Barbara de Wilde. Jacket painting: "Pandora Descending to Earth with Mercury," by Jean Alaux dit le Romain, private collection. Photograph by J. Sassier/Editions Gallimard. Reprinted by permission of Alfred A. Knopf, Inc. and Editions Gallimard: **p. 48;** ©Jerry Bauer: **pp. 53, 61, 71, 81, 101, 274, 283, 412;** Photograph by Fred Viebahn: **p. 131;** Jacket of *Thomas and Beulah,* by Rita Dove. Carnegie-Mellon University Press, 1986. Reprinted by permission of the publisher: **p. 146;** Photograph by Conor Horgan: **p.156;** Photograph by Ander Gunn: **p. 175;** Photograph by Mark Taylor: **p. 190;** Photograph by Joan Marcus: **p. 199;** Photograph by Craig Schwartz: **p. 207;** ©Lutfi Ozkok: **p. 299;** ©Topham/The Image Works: **p. 314;** Photograph by Richard De Combray: **p. 328;** Photograph by Wallace Stegner: **p. 338;** Alon Reininger/Contact: **p. 384;** Photograph by Steve Hamby: **p. 396.**

The Year in Review

The Year in Fiction

by Wendy Lesser

One of the things that might be said to characterize 1993 is the sight of venerable (and some not so venerable) authors trying their hands at new forms. A science fiction novel from a British mystery writer, ghost stories from a Southern realist, a thriller from the author of experimental prose, a highly experimental work from an agricultural feminist—these are some of the adventures that marked the year in fiction. Not all of the radical departures were equally successful, however, and some of the best novels of the year resulted from concerted authorial efforts to return to old terrain.

I am not, I should admit, a big fan of P. D. James's mysteries. With her limited pool of suspects supplying information and misinformation to an overly literate clue-meister, James tends to play narrowly inside the murder-in-a-vicarage rules, creating an atmosphere that is far too airless and secluded to yield the thrill of real death. And something of this cloistered airlessness invades her new science-fiction venture, *The Children of Men,* mainly through the presence of the etiolated narrator, a middle-aged Oxford don named Theodore Faron. Faron is chosen by his author for the same reason he is chosen by the band of conspirators who seek him out: he is the only near relative of the country's seemingly benevolent dictator, the Warden of England, Xan Lyppiatt. Now, if *you* were one of five powerless rebels in a murderously repressive country, and you needed help from someone outside your group, would you choose the dictator's cousin and former advisor? And if you were the cousin, someone who had carefully insulated himself through a lifetime of passive selfishness, would you suddenly risk everything to explore the accusations of a group of strangers? Moreover, if you knew your cousin was the person who governed every detail of the country's operation, would you go directly to him with your suspicions that the nation was not being run entirely on the up-and-up? I doubt it. And yet we are expected to believe in these actions on the part of P. D. James's characters.

Part of the problem, I suspect, is her misunderstanding of the difference between the murder-mystery genre and the science-fiction genre. In the murder mystery, we readers sign a contract at the front end to abandon all notions of plausibility. We have such an investment in a) getting people murdered and b) getting those murders solved that we do not worry if a few normal rules of human behavior get broken. We do not remind ourselves that handfuls of well-to-do country-house visitors are unlikely to get murdered over a weekend; we do not worry about the fact that a murder can rarely be solved merely by asking questions of the suspects; we do not even mind fortuitous coinci-

dences that help the plot along, as long as they steer us toward the ravenously desired solution. The point of the murder mystery, in its polite-vicarage form, is that it inhabits a world that *looks* just like our present world but follows entirely different rules.

The point of science fiction is just the opposite. The settings have been changed, the technology and conventions are different, but familiar principles of human behavior need to prevail for the science fiction's power to work. A science-fiction novel set in the future is almost always a parable about our own time. Its premise is often that something went wrong in the way we were doing things, and that our descendants are suffering the consequences. In working out the solution to their problem and attempting to evade the fate we have willed them, these victims may use scientific tools or social systems we have never heard of, but their basic approach—their relation to cause and motive and coincidence and love and hate and suspicion—will essentially be ours.

Theodore Faron is more like a Martian. We learn in the course of the novel that, earlier in his life, Faron was responsible for the death of his only child, a two-year-old daughter: he apparently ran over her in his car. What P. D. James fails to understand is that she can't bring an event like that into the novel and expect us to get over it when it has ceased to serve its plot function. Whereas death in a murder mystery is an expected and often repeated thrill, death in science fiction is a threat: we can't take the hypothesized worldwide catastrophe seriously without seriously fearing death. A death in a good science-fiction novel (particularly the death of a child) cannot be simply a plot device. But that is exactly how P. D. James uses it—not only in the offstage death of the daughter, but in the gradual diminishment of the hardy band of conspirators, as each in turn gets knocked off by the opposition, leaving only our hero and the woman he has come to love. (I saw movie rights glistening in the wings at this point.)

In *The Children of Men,* P. D. James has wasted an excellent premise: the idea that human beings, for unknown reasons, have suddenly ceased to reproduce. From this promising starting-point she gives us nothing more than an updated rehash of the Christ-child story (complete with birth in a manger—this time assisted by a politically correct black midwife). There is nothing wrong with having religious overtones in a science-fiction allegory; indeed, they are almost indispensable, even for agnostics. (*Especially* for agnostics, for whom science fiction is one of the few available forms of religious indulgence, one of the few channels through which we can imagine a world beyond our perceived reality.) But invoking the spiritual element does not get you off the scientific hook. P. D. James owes us an explanation. How did the siege of barrenness begin, and why did it end? How did this particular woman get chosen to bear the first new child? What were the after-effects of his birth? After all, even the Bible, notoriously mysterious as it is, gives us answers to such questions. The least a modern-day Biblical imitator can do is to live up to the plotting standards of her Predecessor.

Peter Taylor's two previous books—*A Summons to Memphis* (1986) and *The Old Forest, and Other Stories* (1985)— demonstrated that even in his late sixties the author could write at the top of his form. Perhaps these successes encouraged him to feel that he could, with impunity, let down his hair a bit, show us a side of his writing that was a little less masterful, a little less under his control. This he has done, at any rate, in the new book of stories, *The Oracle at Stoneleigh Court.* What unites all the tales in this book is their concern with the idea of ghosts, or witches, or spiritual influences of some kind. Though this hardly sounds like a respectable topic to have attracted an elder statesman of our literature, there are ample precedents. And two of these precedents—Henry James's story "The Jolly Corner" and Ibsen's play *Ghosts*—seem particularly to haunt the present collection, which consists of three one-act plays as well as a selection of stories.

Unlike Ibsen, Taylor is not a master of the dramatic form, and his one-acts are creakily explicit. But this very explicitness, which damns them as literature, is exactly what makes the plays interesting as case studies in authorial psychology. Here we see Peter Taylor's darkest and most vengeful side, unmediated by the rich humor of his usual narrative style. A grown-up brother and sister argue over their dead father's character, after which the father's ghost appears to each of them: to the man as a dilapidated wreck, to the woman as a handsome young lover. An old father, lying on his deathbed, speaks first with the ghost of the beloved daughter he long ago disinherited, and then with her living son, the grandson he has not seen until that moment. A middle-aged couple whose only son has just gone missing in Vietnam see him returned to life, but embodying their worst fears: he is a draft-dodging hippie in the eyes of his father, a coldhearted killer when he confronts his mother. Reading these plays (which couldn't possibly be performed), you feel you're plunging straight into the realm of Taylor's deepest preoccupations. The plays are like unsheathed daggers, instruments of Oedipal revenge.

The fact that Taylor wanted to write plays but couldn't has, perhaps, enriched his fiction in very much the way it did Henry James's. One of the fragmentary stories in this collection, **"The Real Ghost,"** is virtually a re-telling of James's "The Jolly Corner," in suitably Jamesian language. Partly, this is Taylor's attempt to lay claim to his respectable heritage. But it is also something more. The Jamesian style was invented to portray the nuance of individual viewpoint—to suggest that even the barest, most pointed "facts" can be true only from a particular perspective, with all the qualifying subjectivity that implies. This style is thus singularly appropriate to the contemplation

of witches and ghosts, who *only* appear (when they appear at all) to the individual capable of perceiving them.

As James did in "The Jolly Corner," Peter Taylor links the suspicions inherent in ghost-spotting to the suspicions and fears aroused by adult sexual love. James's Spencer Brydon awakens from his spine-chilling bout with his ghostly alter ego to find his head, literally, in the lap of the woman he belatedly loves. No less resistant to the entanglements of sex is Taylor's narrator Roger in *The Oracle at Stoneleigh Court.* An eighty-eight-page novella set during and immediately after the Second World War, *The Oracle* is really a witch story more than a ghost story, chronicling the mystical connection between the narrator's weird old Aunt Gussie and the glamorously sexual Lila Montgomery. Unlike the quieter, "nicer" girls from Roger's home state of Tennessee, Lila chooses to work her way through the war at a high-powered job; in doing so, she remains mysteriously inaccessible to Roger.

Witches and, to a lesser extent, other aspects of spiritualism have traditionally been viewed as primarily female (leading some modern-day feminists specifically to include witches among their oppressed constituencies). Taylor uses and, one might say, abuses this tradition. The witches in *The Oracle at Stoneleigh Court* and **"The Witch of Owl Mountain Springs"** are typical old crones, scary unattached females with no man around to control them. And in **"An Overwhelming Question,"** though there is no explicit witchcraft, the young male protagonist dies a sudden, ghastly death while fleeing the sexual advances of his fiancée. Older sisters, oppressive sisters-in-law, and proprietary grandmothers and aunts are powerful, insistent presences in the bulk of these stories, most of which are told by some hapless male. But Taylor cannot be fully identified with his female-fearing men. As an author, he takes great pains to give us so much distance on his male narrators that we are often left with a feeling of condescension toward them, if not outright contempt. The witches and ghosts who haunt Taylor's stories tell us more about the people who believe in them than they do about themselves; and whether their author is one of those believers is not something he is willing to divulge.

For most of his career, Walter Abish was one of those purposely irritating writers who welcome the label "experimental." A New Directions author, he favored arbitrary and noticeably literary devices, as in one of his early "novels," *Alphabetical Africa,* which consists of fifty-one chapters titled from A to Z and back to A, each chapter relying heavily on words containing the designated letter. "X stands for experimental," one such chapter begins, "and for excretion, that is for plain shit on the trail." The critic is tempted to add: Exactly.

Then, in 1980, came a breakthrough, a sudden and almost violent transformation. *How German Is It,* which won the PEN/Faulkner Award that year, was Abish's gesture in the direction of a wider readership. In contrast to the fragmented and alienated word-clusters he had previously produced, it contained distinct characters, several plots, and a protagonist you could practically identify with. Set in contemporary Germany, the novel reflected persuasively and intelligently on the postwar German mood of denial, with its superficial emphasis on material success and its underbelly of revolutionary politics. This, it seemed, was the novel Abish had been preparing to write all those years, the sources of its irritation now *real* and not merely literary, its imperfections and repetitions justified—more than justified—by the apt critique they conveyed.

And now, thirteen years later, comes *Eclipse Fever,* an even more readable novel, if a somewhat less permanently valuable one. Packaged by Knopf for mainstream consumption, *Eclipse Fever* marks Abish's belated departure from the avant-garde ghetto, his sudden eligibility for reviews in general-interest periodicals. His latest novel can almost be read as a straightforward corporate-conspiracy thriller. To the 1974 readers of the highly convoluted *Alphabetical Africa,* this turn of events would have been inconceivable. It's as if James Joyce had followed up *Ulysses,* not with *Finnegans Wake,* but with *The Ministry of Fear* and then *Our Man in Havana.*

Eclipse Fever is set mainly in Mexico during the period surrounding the recent total eclipse, which remains an off-stage presence toward which events move and around which they finally slither, leaving the eclipse itself ideal, inviolate, undescribed. The central character is a Mexican intellectual, a critic named Alejandro, who is married to the beautiful, probably unfaithful Mercedes; much of the novel consists of Alejandro's imaginings of the suspected affair between Mercedes and a well-known American novelist, Jurud. Woven in with this personal story of betrayal is a political story about the devious machinations of an American corporation, Eden Enterprises, which has plans for Mexico that include construction of an elevator in the historic Pyramid of the Sun. Eden is run by Preston Hollier, whose wife, Rita, is having an affair with Alejandro's best friend, Francisco. The two plots are finally welded together in the person of Bonny, Jurud's runaway teenage daughter, who travels to Mexico with a shady character named Emilio in order to witness the eclipse, and who instead ends up witnessing a murder.

Abish has always been obsessed with geography, with the possibilities of travel, with the foreignness of foreign countries. A refugee himself (his parents fled Austria for Shanghai in 1940, when he was nine), he is the ultimate Displaced Person of literature. No language is natural to him; every language is a screen, a means for artifice. He is a master of the *unheimlich,* not so much in the sense of "uncanny" as in the sense of "unfamiliar": literally, the familiar made strange. Only through purposeful alienation can his characters escape the snares of daily life. And yet, in *Eclipse Fever,* the effect is sometimes the opposite of alienation. Displacement, yes; but not distance. Time and again, reading descriptions of Alejandro's conversations with his editor, his visits to favorite coffee houses with friends, his negotiations about television appearances, I caught myself thinking: Oh, so *this* is what it feels like to be a Mexico City intellectual; *this* is the inside view of what I normally see only from the outside, as an American tourist or a reader of American fiction. And then I would remember that Walter Abish is no more a Mexico City intellectual than I am. But he has the capacity to persuade us that he is.

A literary move in the opposite direction characterizes Janet Kauffman's latest book, *The Body in Four Parts.* Kauffman began her publication history as a Knopf writer, a Gordon Lish discovery. She had all the elements that might seem to add up to the most desirable kind of critical and commercial success: a good ear, a penchant for strong women characters, a knowledge of out-of-the-way lives (such as those of independent farmers or rural wastrels), and—not to be sneezed at—a name publisher and editor. Had she cared above all for literary fame, she could no doubt have crafted these elements into a full-fledged "career."

There is something marvelous about seeing someone take all these benefits, all these useful stepping-stones, and cast them away with wild abandon. There is something heartening about watching a writer who could have had things easy *choose* to be difficult. Or perhaps choice is not the issue. What primarily shaped Janet Kauffman's prose has turned out, in the long run, to be her finely tuned ear, and in *The Body in Four Parts* she has given over everything to the demands of that ear.

This is not to say that the book is entirely plotless, much less characterless. The main character, the narrating sensibility, is a woman who never tells us her name. (She is referred to as "Babe" by someone else, but that is just as likely to be an honorific as a given name.) In the course of the first chapter—the first of the book's four sections—we learn that this woman has three siblings: the watery Dorothea (also called S., for obscure reasons); the fire-filled Jean-Paul; and the air-linked Jack. We also learn, almost by osmosis, that these "siblings" are not actually her brothers and sister but are, rather, elements of herself.

I stress the word "elements" because the book itself does. Its sections are named after the traditional four (the narrator herself is Earth), and the four characters each embody them wholly. Just as our lives partake of all four, so does the narrator's life spring from the four existences she contains. There are other characters as well: Margaretta, the wise local fishwoman; Joseph Blue, a man from another country; and Lucy and Aunt Charlaine, two friends of Joseph Blue. Most of these people appear in the "Earth" section, which is by far the longest in the book. But their role in the narrator's life is never pinned down; they are random and elusive, except for Margaretta. We get the feeling that this meandering quality of the book largely reflects the personality of the narrator, who is—by most of our usual standards—crazy. Harmless, but crazy.

Despite the meandering, things do happen in *The Body in Four Parts.* The narrator and Margaretta go on a car trip, seeking watercress as a present for the submerged Dorothea. Margaretta and Jean-Paul later go in search of Joseph Blue and his female companions. The narrator makes love with Jack. Jean-Paul kisses Dorothea. And so on. In the background of the book lie other plots: Margaretta's poverty-stricken and violent childhood (including a rape); Joseph Blue's experiences in other countries; Dorothea's literary compositions, which are interpolated into the main plot in handwritten pages.

The book has its irritations (among which I would count

those handwritten pages), but they are minor compared to its achievements. It is, for one thing, funny—at least in places. And the language is rhythmically beautiful, with the haunting visual specificity of poetry. The choicest passages of description are, to my mind, worth combing the whole book for. And if you didn't have to comb the book, you wouldn't care as much about them: that's partly the lesson of the women's diligent search for watercress, that leaf which grows only in pure, flowing water. Janet Kauffman's prose is such a plant: it's hard to cultivate, impossible to train (the way one trains ivy) for practical, decorative purposes. It exists in itself, as a common delicacy. It may not be to your taste. But if it is, this book will satisfy.

The Body in Four Parts is a very slim book. At the opposite end of the length spectrum is Vikram Seth's *A Suitable Boy,* which is apparently the second-longest novel in the English language (Richardson's *Clarissa* being the first). Seth is mainly known to American readers as the author of a witty novel-in-verse, *The Golden Gate,* though he has also written several books of poems and a wonderful travel memoir, *From Heaven Lake. A Suitable Boy,* written in the old-fashioned style of a realist novel, is his first fictional visit to his homeland, India. But "visit" is perhaps the wrong word for such monumentality: "prolonged stay" more accurately describes both the writer's experience of this work and the reader's.

The plot revolves around Lata, an upper-middle-class Hindu girl of a somewhat earlier generation, and her family's search for "a suitable boy" for her to marry. Lata herself has her own opinions on the subject (at one point, for instance, she falls unsuitably in love with a Muslim boy), and much of the novel's suspense comes from our wondering which of the three likely suitors she will eventually choose. Along the way we are treated to lengthy disquisitions on an amazing variety of topics, from traditional Indian music to post-Partition politics, from shoe-making to Anglo-American relations, from travel on Indian trains to life in the most rural villages. I myself found some of these excursions tiring, and would have preferred a more Austenian length and focus. (Jane Austen is clearly an influence on Seth, and is respectfully alluded to in the novel itself.) But the book's monumentality has been its major claim to international attention, and people who, unlike myself, have actually traveled to India tell me that the cultural background material is what makes the novel so rich. I do not think *A Suitable Boy* will be Seth's most lasting work, but it is certainly a pleasure to pass the time with.

The same goes for John Le Carré's *The Night Manager.* His latest novel is much better than the recent *Russia House,* though worse than *A Perfect Spy* (but then, what is not?). Even middling Le Carré is more satisfying than the best of almost anyone else, and *The Night Manager* is relentlessly gripping from beginning to end. The eponymous hero is not up to George Smiley (he gets the girl, for one thing, which seems dully swashbuckling), but he will do for the purposes he fills here; and the minor characters are charming, especially the Americans. It is a book that for once departs from Le Carré's Iron Curtain focus (almost necessarily so, since the Iron Curtain itself has departed) and instead takes its villains from the international

drug and arms trade. Characteristically, Le Carré has made the worst of these villains British. And even the British arms dealer is not as bad as his counterpart in British intelligence, who ranks with the worst of Le Carré's insidious establishment figures. But I have already ruined enough of the plot. Suffice to say that in addition to the usual Le Carré pleasures, we are treated in *The Night Manager* to those material joys previously associated more with the work of Ian Fleming—that is, fancy hotels, luxurious yachts, beautiful women, mouthwatering meals, and insanely expensive interior decoration.

Two story collections, one by a newcomer and one by a youngish old hand, are worth significant attention. *The Magic of Blood* by Dagoberto Gilb is the first full-length collection (aside from chapbooks, that is) by this half-Chicano writer in his early forties. Produced by an author who has supported himself and his family primarily through construction work, Gilb's fiction focuses on the lives of those at the bottom end of the economic pile—everyone from the lower middle class on down. But don't expect either social realism or do-good ideology: these little gems haven't a shred of condescension or naiveté. If anything, Gilb's stories about Latino carpenters and corrupt foremen and homeless Los Angelenos and battling neighbors have a Chekhovian delicacy of tone. Nothing much happens in each tale, but what does happen has great impact, on the characters and on us. Gilb is an original, with a voice and a style all his own. He doesn't fit into any cultural or ethnic clichés, which may be why it has taken so long for him to get his first book into print.

Elizabeth Tallent is about the same age as Dagoberto Gilb, but *Honey* is already her fourth book. Though her terrain is only a stone's throw from his (they both focus on the American Southwest), her characters tend to be upper middle class, or getting there soon. Their concerns are less financial than emotional: these are stories of marriages coming together and coming apart, children as the stretched ropes between tug-of-war parents, and houses that, in their decor, reflect the indulged tastes of their owners. Tallent is the mistress of quiet moments of domestic anxiety. She is not after high tragedy or melodrama; when she stabs us with her knifelike prose, we barely even know we've been hurt. *Honey* represents old ground for her—many of the settings and even some of the characters are revisited from earlier work—but it is old ground looked at with new eyes: the eyes of resigned maturity, settling in for the long haul.

Another writer who has used the new year to tread familiar ground is A. S. Byatt. Once again, with *Angels & Insects,* we are in Byatt's favorite period, the latter half of the nineteenth century. In these two novellas, she offers us two complete tales of Victorian love and marriage, along with a seminar on nineteenth-century biology, a study of Swedenborgian spiritualism, a smattering of Poe, a soupçon of Browning, and a semester's worth of information about the Tennyson family circle. Only a writer as profuse as Byatt would think of these as novellas, for *Morpho Eugenia* is nearly 200 pages long and *The Conjugial Angel* over 150. But, committed as she is to the pleasures of the Victorian three-decker, this author would feel she was cheating us if she gave us anything less than a fat book.

The hero of **Morpho Eugenia**—and hero he is, complete with humble but gentlemanly origins, noble aspirations, life-threatening travels, scholarly intelligence, sexual gallantry, and, finally, hard-won emotional wisdom—is William Adamson, a student of South American insect life who finds himself, at the beginning of the 1860s, cast upon the mercy of the wealthy Alabaster family. Ensconced at their country estate, hired to classify Sir Harald's chaotic natural history collection and simultaneously play devil's advocate to the old man's ideas about science and religion, Adamson falls for the eldest Alabaster daughter with Pavlovian speed and predictability. Before he can even get close enough to propose, however, we readers begin to suspect there is something not altogether nice about the beautiful, sorrowful Eugenia's relationship with her half-brother, Edgar. (I had tumbled to the entire plot by page 54; others, more alert, will guess as early as page 6.) But poor William—who, being trapped in the nineteenth century, has not read about the young Virginia Stephen's relationship with her Duckworth half-brother, nor been subjected to decades of newspaper reports and popular fiction about incest—is slower on the uptake. In fact, it's not until he actually finds his beauteous wife in bed with her despicable cad of a brother, three children into the marriage, that he understands how he's been duped. By this time, luckily, he's fallen in love with the local intellectual—not the governess, exactly, but a minion-about-the-manor called Matty Crompton, with whom he has been composing a treatise on the social system of the local ant colonies. On the strength of their publisher's advance, William and Matty dump the odious Alabasters and buy one-way tickets to South America. (This part reminded me of the hilarious moment in *The Bostonians* when Basil Ransom, on the basis of a single essay accepted by a quarterly magazine, resolves to marry on the strength of his literary success. But whereas I know Henry James intended to be funny, I'm by no means sure about Byatt.)

William Adamson is, to the best of my knowledge, a fictional character. Emily Jesse (nee Tennyson), one of the heroines of **The Conjugial Angel,** is not. Sister to the poet Alfred and fiancée of Arthur Hallam, Emily had the unfortunate fate of being the not-yet-married "relic" (as Victorian widows were called) of the mid-nineteenth-century's most famous dead person; for, by composing *In Memoriam* in Hallam's honor, Tennyson both immortalized Arthur's early death and robbed Emily of her exclusive personal stake in it. A. S. Byatt, writing from the perspective of the participants in an 1875 séance, imagines what it would have been like for Emily to survive Arthur, mourn for eight years, eventually marry, have children, grow old, and still continue to pine for her first great love.

In *Possession,* her previous novel, Byatt included long pastiches of Browning, Tennyson, and Christina Rosetti that she had audaciously composed herself; here she mercifully limits herself to quoting mainly from the actual Victorians. But even that technique can wear thin rather quickly. I sympathize with A. S. Byatt's desire to lavish affection on literary gems, to unearth them from their scholarly hid-

ing places and exclaim, "See, what beauties!" Such admiration and wonder have no place in the present-day world of academic criticism, where they are abused as "belletristic connoisseurship." I miss that sense of literary enthusiasm in most academic writing, and I understand Byatt's wish to join it with her novelistic impulses. Nonetheless, my spirits droop when I come across a line like "Sophy Sheekhy knew large runs of *In Memoriam* by heart," and I sense what I'm about to be put through.

People may have loved poetry better and memorized it more in the nineteenth century than they do now. Still, I can't believe they really went around reciting the choicest passages all the time, as Byatt would have them do. Nor, I suspect, did people in the nineteenth century constantly view themselves as characters in a nineteenth-century setting. I'm not saying Victorian authors ignored the intellectual and social trends that are now so apparent to Byatt. But the real nineteenth-century authors didn't spout the theories of their times; they *used* them. And their characters, however well-read or thoughtful they were, didn't spend endless pages quoting from contemporary poetry. They didn't have time to, because they were busy leading the lives that drew on and gave rise to that poetry. This, finally, is what I miss in Byatt: a sense of the lived, daily, textured reality that good poetry and fiction can evoke, but that mere quotation can never capture.

More contemporary versions of love (and failed love) occur in the recent works of three accomplished novelists: Mary Gordon, Sue Miller, and Richard Bausch. Mary Gordon, like A. S. Byatt, has opted this time round for the novella, and her **The Rest of Life** contains three of them. Memory has often been central to Gordon's technique, but here it actually dictates the structure of each work: all three novellas are told to us from the points of view of women who have been deeply in love with a single man. The first woman loves a priest; the second a globe-trotting journalist; the third a young poet who committed suicide when he was sixteen. In the first two cases, the stories are told from the midst of the relationships, but with much casting backward over the past and equally much looking forward to anxiety-prone futures. In the third novella, which gives the collection its title, a seventy-eight-year-old Italian woman, revisiting Turin from America, looks back on the tragedy that has dictated the entire shape of her life and wonders what she could have been thinking or feeling at the time. None of these three works contains much in the way of action, but all three are strikingly rendered portraits of a state of feeling.

Sue Miller, on the other hand, has a great deal invested in plot. This is not to say that there's no emotion in **For Love:** there is plenty, on the part of all sorts of characters, from the middle-aged heroine to her young-adult son to her aging-hippie brother to her estranged husband. But the feeling does not float timelessly in the characters' consciousnesses, the way it does in Gordon; in Miller's work, emotion is a response to event. In **For Love,** the first and most prominent event is a fatal car accident that kills an adolescent girl, a babysitter in one of the secondary households of the novel. The death is conveyed starkly and horrifically, but then it is over, and it is up to the characters to spend the rest of the novel working up to it, and then working it out. Other, more quotidian events—the packing up of an aging parent's home, the attempt to reconcile a troubled marriage, the delivery of a visiting child to an ex-spouse, the encounter with an old rival from childhood—are all presented with Miller's usual skill. She is a strange writer from my point of view, one whose talent as an artist constantly exceeds the parameters she has set herself as a topic-chooser. I fear, every time I pick up a Miller novel, that its obvious subject-matter will overwhelm its fictional artistry; and I am pleasantly surprised every time, never more so than with this book.

Richard Bausch's sixth novel is a testament to his extraordinarily sympathetic powers of narrative. He gives us a book in which memory and contemplation are vastly disproportionate to plot, and he nonetheless manages to make the ending suspenseful. Thomas Boudreaux, whose reconstructed journal takes the form of the book **Rebel Powers,** does not profess to be a literary man. He runs a bookstore on a small island off the coast of Virginia, keeps company with a "wonderful woman" who lives at the other end of the island, and chats with the locals during the off-season. But his present life, as a divorced, rather isolated man in his early forties, is not our major concern. The Thomas we come to know through this novel is the adolescent boy whose military father was dishonorably discharged and sent to prison for stealing equipment and writing bad checks.

Bausch has thus set himself two seemingly insuperable problems: to give us a literary document by a man who is not a writer, and to make the melodrama of adolescent despair into something adults can take seriously. He solves the first problem insufficiently: partly by cheating (some of these gloriously musing sentences could only have been written by a pro), and partly by allowing us to be bored on occasion by the narrator's repetitive obsessiveness. But in regard to the second problem, Bausch succeeds miraculously. He does this largely by creating, in the figure of Thomas's mother Connie, an adult we can deeply care about. Thomas gives us a double vision of his mother—primarily from the point of view of the eighteen-year-old he was when the crucial events took place, but with overlays of an adult's hindsight and enriched understanding. This makes the novel's small tragedies especially painful, because we have to watch the unconscious or unwilled cruelty of a teenager toward his parents, and simultaneously feel the narrator's subsequent regret for that cruel behavior. In a way, the whole novel is Thomas's penance for his failure to understand as a child, his effort to reconstruct what really happened and this time view it correctly.

If several of this year's novelists are resurveying old terrain, none is doing so as willfully and oddly as John Banville. *Ghosts,* the latest novel by this Irish writer is a bit like a Peter Greenaway film: the visual elements are entrancing, the mystery plot is intricate and obscure, and the characters are all faintly (sometimes aggressively) threatening oddballs. Like Greenaway, Banville is particularly interested in humankind's strange mixture of passions for the beautiful and the violent, especially in combination. In *The Book of Evidence,* his previous novel, he gave us a main character who set out to steal a privately owned portrait of a young woman (it sounded, from the description, like a Vermeer), and ended up murdering her flesh-and-blood counterpart, a maid who worked for the portrait's owner. And now, in *Ghosts,* Banville offers us a houseful of eccentric, mainly criminal, sometimes violent characters who are all obsessed with the visual arts.

Ghosts is set entirely on an unnamed island, presumably off the coast of Ireland. Like Shakespeare's *The Tempest,* which it explicitly echoes in places, it begins with a shipwreck. Among those who straggle onto the beach are Sophie, a black-clad photographer; Flora, described as looking like a Modigliani; and Felix, whose shady past includes evil doings in art forgery. They and their companions make their way to a large house inhabited by one Professor Kreutznauer and his assistant Licht, who are engaged in studying the work of the famous painter Vaublin. For some unspecified time past, they have been helped in their research by another art expert, a nameless man recently released from jail, who also serves as *Ghosts'* narrator. "Serves" is not exactly right, for this narrator considers himself the novel's master, the Prospero-like figure who has created the entire cast. "A little world is coming into being," he tells us on the second page of the novel. "Who speaks? I do. Little god."

If you are looking for a plot in any conventional sense, you may as well give up on *Ghosts* right now. Though there are elements of suspense (Why is Kreutznauer afraid of Felix? What happened in the past with a Vaublin painting called *The Golden World?* And what is the narrator's connection to all this?), they are hardly the motivating forces in this novel. The achievement of *Ghosts* is to use words as brushstrokes, to create in language an artwork that has all the appeal of a complex painting. Our eye roves over it and back again, not in linear, chronological order but in a state of suspended time, picking up new details and drawing new conclusions with each concentrated gaze. "They have a presence that is at once fugitive and fixed," the narrator says of his characters when he finally, and explicitly, presents them as characters in a Vaublin painting. "They seem to be at ease, langorous almost, yet when we look close we see how tense they are with self-awareness. We have the feeling they are conscious of being watched . . . " This is the language of sensitive, intelligent art criticism, heightened and transformed into the realm of fiction.

One of Banville's victories in *Ghosts* is to have created a famous painter out of whole cloth. True, Vaublin's work contains elements of the Dutch and Flemish masters—Vermeer's crystalline stillness, Rembrandt's luminous darkness, Breugel's antic figures at play. And with their Pierrots, their cherubs, their allegorical nature scenes, Vaublin's paintings also have affinities with those of French artists like Watteau, Poussin, and Fragonard. But there is no single artist on whom Banville is drawing when he renders his evocative descriptions of Vaublin's work. We cannot simply hunt up the key and insert it in the novel to unlock its mysteries of identity. Instead, we need to give our minds over to imagining Vaublin's paintings, which exist nowhere else but in our imaginations. Banville received a great deal of acclaim for *The Book of Evidence,* which—with its lovingly detailed, self-distanced chronicling of the murderer's deed—was hailed as a worthy successor to Camus's *The Stranger* and Dostoyevsky's *Crime and Punishment.* Such praise is bound to be overpraise, and in fact *The Book of Evidence* struck me as a coy and artificial work, with a narrator who was constantly searching for the highest-priced word on the menu. **Ghosts** is a far better novel, though it is also a more difficult one. Where the narrator in *The Book of Evidence* was always striving for effect, **Ghosts'** narrator quietly achieves it. The deep irony is that they are intended to be the same person. I do not know what people who have not read the previous novel will make of the new one. Many of the central questions in **Ghosts**—such as who the narrator is, and what his crime was, and how he previously dealt with women, and how he knows so much about art—are answered only in *The Book of Evidence.* Hence many of the Greenaway-like mysteries of **Ghosts** dissolve if you've read the earlier book. The plot becomes straightforward rather than contorted, the narrator gains a name and a history, the motivations come clear. But one unresolvable mystery remains. How did the coldly and flagrantly self-dramatizing narrator of the earlier novel become the elusive, evocative artist of the present work? One wants to know if this is the character's moral progress, or Banville's. But, as another Irishman famously remarked, how can you tell the dancer from the dance?

The Year in Poetry

by Allen Hoey

In preparing to review the year in poetry, I find myself struggling against the impulse to launch a full-blown jeremiad deploring triviality, posturing, limitations of craft and imagination, and self-indulgence. All this in a year marked by the publication of new and collected or selected works by quite a few luminaries, yet rarely has a firmament been so dimly lit by so many dull stars. Of the seventeen poets herein reviewed, eleven are (if just barely) in their sixties or seventies, yet those poets in their forties show, on the whole, much stronger work. Symptomatically, the National Book Award has, for a second consecutive year, slighted three nominees of demonstrably higher merit than the winner. (Whatever might be made of it, last year's National Book Critics Circle Award and Pulitzer Prize went to the two volumes singled out here as best: Hayden Carruth's *Collected Shorter Poems* and Louise Glück's *The Wild Iris,* respectively.) With Carruth's *Collected Longer Poems* and Jack Gilbert's new collection, *The Great Fires,* slated for spring release, 1994, at least, is getting off to a promising start.

Readers interested in exploring root causes for the current condition of poetry will find explicit suggestions as well as thoughtful analysis that provides a springboard for inference in Alan Shapiro's **In Praise of the Impure,** subtitled *Poetry and the Ethical Imagination: Essays, 1980-1991.* In essays that range from general topics—narrative, new formalism, and the living tradition, to reduce them to capsule summaries—to balanced readings of individual poets including J. V. Cunningham, Robert Hass, and John Berryman, Shapiro considers poetry not as literary play detached from our lives but regards style as "consciousness in action" and stresses "the second life of poetry" (a term taken from Eugenio Montale), "the life it takes on in us years after our initial reading, when it coalesces with some unforeseen experience, when some occasion suddenly recalls it, and it comes to us bearing its gift of revelation." For a poem to carry that "gift," however, it must be grounded in knowledge of the world; a clear, organic sense of form (not rhyme and meter merely flourished as "a badge of affiliation"); and a willingness to extend the imagination to ethical concerns.

Individual essays on the "ethical imagination" ("Flexible Rule," from which the above quote is taken) and the use of form in poetry ("The New Formalism" and "Some Notes on Free Verse and Meter") are exemplary in their balance; while Shapiro champions specific poets, there is no suggestion that poets treated less flatteringly are victims of grudge-match mentality. Those new formalists whose poems suggest a belief "that the erection of a metrical frame around a subject [is] all the imaginative work

they [have] to do" might disagree, but Shapiro presents a convincing analysis for why so much new formalist poetry seems so shallow: "The crude management of form can render only crude overgeneralized emotions."

Finally, an essay that should be required reading for all students, instructors, and administrators in creative writing programs, "Horace and the Reformation of Creative Writing" goes a long way to explain our current penury. In earlier societies, the education of poets was a lengthy process; Irish master bards, for example,

> had to pass through a very rigorous twelve-year course of training, encompassing not only the study of prosody and the memorization of all the tales and poems of the nation, but also, among other things, the mastery of history, music, law, science, and divination. His was a poetry inextricably bound up with the realities of social and political life.

Against this, Shapiro contrasts contemporary two-year MFA programs with lax, almost non-existent curricular demands, which promote an approach to the teaching of writing—and, one might hazard, the product of such instruction—"in which vagueness and mystification pass for knowledge." Both Donald Hall in "Poetry and Ambition" and Dana Gioia in "Can Poetry Matter?" have covered much of this territory, but Shapiro, writing from an insider's perspective, is both more specific and more lacerating in his assessments. In this unlikely culture medium, what can we expect will grow?

Of the new collections by prominent "elder" poets, Donald Hall's **The Museum of Clear Ideas** seems overall the most satisfying. In this, his eleventh collection in 38 years, he demonstrates a lifetime's mastery of poetic craft. Every poem in the collection is written in syllabics, yet the lines rarely call attention to their strict metric. The form is most visible in the extended sequences "Baseball" and "Extra Innings," where nine-syllable lines accumulate in nine-line stanzas through the first sequence, gaining one syllable per line and one line per stanza in the succeeding three "Extra Innings." Even here, the line breaks do not seem forced or the lines padded to fulfill the form, a frequent failing of syllabic verse. Despite felicities of craft, the volume does not equal Hall's major achievement to date, the book-length *The One Day* (1988), nor is it as emotionally satisfying as either *Kicking the Leaves* (1978) or *The Happy Man* (1986).

In three of four sections, Hall employs strategies of distancing. The two sequences of "Baseball" poems, for instance, are addressed to Dada collagist Kurt Schwitters.

11

The sequences begin from the premise of explaining the sport but piece together fragments of various concerns into a verbal "collage," including daily life on the speaker's farm and, most movingly, the struggles arising from Hall's and Jane Kenyon's medical crises (documented in Hall's marvelous book-length essay, *Life Work,* also published in 1993; it serves as a wonderful companion volume to these as well as earlier poems by Hall). This approach, however, defuses the emotional gain of the material, both through an almost surrealistic juxtaposition of situation and image and the cavalier, almost Ashbery-like tone of the speaker.

The title sequence, subtitled "Or say: Horsecollar's Odes," poses different problems. Each of these poems, an endnote informs us, takes "the number and shape of stanzas in Horace's first book of odes"; names of characters seem derived from the same source (Flaccus, Glaucus, Sabina) or from neo-classical models (Camilla and Julia). Many of the poems conclude with an answering coda, the "Or say" of the subtitle, as with "O Camilla, Is It":

> O Camilla, is it conceivable that
> you feel as ardent as I do—as horny
> as seven goats? Camilla, let us hurry out of these
>   grossly
>
> getting-in-the-way clothes onto a wide bed
> with its covers hurled off to play skin-music
> on bright sheets, slowly increasing the tempo
>   until Eden comes.

                                *

> Or say: At this moment, according to habit,
> Horsecollar interrupts his ode to contradict
> his ode; or calls upon Professor Zero to sneer
> at Horsecollar, at hypocritical humanity, and at
> Professor Zero. Analysands cherish reversals
> in the performance of Heraclitean understand-
>   ing
> achieved after eight years on a Viennese sofa;
> Horsecollar revels in luxuries of antithesis,
> by which any Eden, temperate with blessedness,
> freezes forever in the flames of coldest hell.

In many respects this sequence resembles "Four Classic Texts" from *The One Day;* the bracketing sections of that poem, however, offer a grounding context, and the use of biblical as well as classical models provides a necessary balance and corrective. The problem here seems a question of tone. Horace's odes, like other classical and neo-classical works, rely on a shared sense of social conviction and convention, even if shared only by an elite. Today, such shared sensibility seems impossible, and, without that seedbed, poems in that manner can seem, rather than biting and satirical, merely arch. While some of these poems find the self-deprecating balance requisite for satire ("Let Many Bad Poets" comes to mind), this does not happen consistently enough to make the sequence fully rewarding.

The most satisfying of the sections, "Another Elegy," memorializes a fictional poet who seems a composite of Hall and his contemporaries. Divorce, separation from children, political activity, and reliance on drink surface as generational problems which the fictitious Bill Trout has faced and, in most cases, surmounted. In many ways, the elegy celebrates a generation of poets who succeeded in surviving in ways the previous generation—Jarrell, Roethke, Lowell, and Berryman—never managed. Yet the poem descends into neither self-pity nor self-congratulation, managing an evenness of intimacy and objectivity comparable to that in *The One Day.* Consider this passage from near the end, involving the narrator, Trout, and his third wife, a Bengali dancer:

> Each year
> his death grows older. Outside this house, past
>   Kearsarge
> changing from pink and lavender through blue
>   and white
> to green, public language ridicules "eager pur-
>   suit of honor."
>
> Do I tell lies? " . . . in middle age he fell in
>   love . . . "
> Did he never again tremble from chair to table?
>   At night
> Bill delivered his imagination and study to *Lav-*
>   *erne*
> *and Shirley,* laughing when a laughtrack bullied
>   him
> to laugh—while Reba groaned an incredulous
>   Bengali groan—
> in order not to drink.
>   Yet again he walked in a blue
> robe in detox, love's anguish and anger walking
>   beside him.

The easy shift between the personal and the public, as well as the elegiac and the playful, and the firm sense of line mark the work of a master. Had Hall extended emotional as well as formal satisfaction through the book, he might have equalled or even surpassed his best.

W. S. Merwin uses syllabics, as well as regular stanzas and occasional rhyme, far less successfully in *Travels,* his thirteenth collection; the effect, given his now-typical lack of capitalization and punctuation, is often confusing. Take, for example, these opening stanzas from "Another Place":

> When years without number
> like days of another summer
> had turned into air there
> once more was a street that had never
> forgotten the eyes of its child
>
> not so long by then of course nor
> so tall or dark anywhere
> with the same store at the corner
> sunk deeper into its odor
> of bananas and ice cream
>
> still hoarding the sound of roller
> skates crossing the cupped board floor
> but the sidewalk flagstones were
> cemented and the street car
> tracks buried under a late
>
> surface . . .

And so on for eleven pages. Individual lines and passages are striking, but a reader must redact to make sense of this. In the third line, for instance, is "there" part of the preceding lines or the lines that follow? Line endings bear no particular weight; the first two lines seem clearly self-contained units, and the first stanza itself seems a complete syntactical unit. But what about the radically enjambed first line of the third stanza, and the final line of that stanza which runs over into the next? Extended narrative is equally problematic; as in his early volumes, Merwin seems more interested in the play of language over image than in developing a clear plot to guide through diversion and distraction. Most successful are the handful of short lyrics at the very end, including "Rain Travel" and "After the Spring," which approach the best poems in perhaps his finest collection, *The Rain in the Trees* (1988).

Merwin's struggle to shed the conventional style of his first collections is chronicled in **The Second Four Books of Poems,** which reissues *The Moving Target, The Lice, The Carrier of Ladders,* and *Writings to an Unfinished Accompaniment,* those volumes in which he developed his mature manner. The ability to cast unpunctuated language over lines so that syntactic values are rarely obscured, a facility shared by Gary Snyder and Lucille Clifton, did not come easily to Merwin. This may account for why so many of the poems in this omnibus seem repeated efforts to claim the same material. The bardic, shamanistic mode also seems an uneasy fit. Few of these poems are as satisfying as a handful from his earliest collections— "Burning the Cat," for instance, or "The Drunk in the Furnace"—though his successes are usually brief lyrics, like "For the Anniversary of My Death":

> Every year without knowing it I have passed the
> day
> When the last fires will wave to me
> And the silence will set out
> Tireless traveler
> Like the beam of a lightless star
>
> Then I will no longer
> Find myself in life as in a strange garment
> Surprised at the earth
> And the love of one woman
> And the shamelessness of men
> As today writing after three days of rain
> Hearing the wren sing and the falling cease
> And bowing not knowing to what

Note the clear correlation between line and meaning, stanza and sentence. Yet the pleasures of such delicate lyrics are won by reading through too many pages of poems pitching toward the tone and not quite ringing it. Readers unfamiliar with Merwin's earlier work would be better served by his (at times too) generous *Selected Poems.*

A more rewarding republication, Galway Kinnell's **Three Books** contains revised versions of *Body Rags, Mortal Acts, Mortal Words,* and *The Past.* Kinnell, a notorious tinkerer (rumor has it that *The Book of Nightmares* was extensively revised in galleys), notes in his introduction that most of the revisions are "simply deletions of 'ill-written and extraneous material,'" including ". . . clotted conceits, fanciful elaborations, . . . grandiloquence, redundancies, . . . pointlessly elaborate sound effects, contrived usages, efforts to enliven through heightened language what would have been lively if given straight. . . ." Most poems have been touched, if just a little, with notable gains. Students of Kinnell and of the

poetic process will derive considerable interest and satisfaction in comparing these with the originals, as well as savoring them on their own merits.

Considerably less interesting and satisfying is Mark Strand's **Dark Harbor,** his eighth collection. With some pretensions toward being a longish Stevensesque meditation, it seems instead more neo-surrealist posturing, at its worst descending into silliness, as in section XIX, in its entirety:

> I go out and sit on my roof, hoping
> That a creature from another planet will see me
> And say, "There's life on earth, definitely life;
>
> "See that earthling on top of his home,
> His manifold possessions under him,
> Let's name him after our planet." Whoa!

Did even Pope in "Peri Bathous" imagine such sinking? Strand seems to provide an explanation for the poem in section XXXII: "The idea of being large is inconceivable. . . . The image of a god // . . . [who] brings whole rooms, whole continents to light, / Like the sun, is not for us." Doubtless he intends this to reflect on our social condition, but the poem is so sealed from any clear reference to the external world, the comment reflects nothing but the poem itself. Even in XLI, when Strand's speaker, regarding "the distance of stars," "wonder[s] if the physicist / Sees the same sky I do," this brief and almost moving meditation on "mystery" is cut short with a gesture of hip dismissal: "Ah, who knows! We are already travelling faster than our / Apparent stillness can stand, and if it keeps up / You will be light-years away by the time I speak." Such consistently flip evasion of responsibility marks a failing of ethical imagination, at the very least.

In section 4 of **Garbage,** A. R. Ammons wonders:

> . . . is a poem about garbage garbage
>
> or will this abstract, hollow junk seem beautiful
> and necessary as just another offering to the
>
> high assimilations . . .

Obviously, panelists for this year's National Book Award picked door #2. In the first section, however, Ammons implies a different answer: "why should I // be trying to write my flattest poem, now, for / whom. . . ." And who should hesitate to take him at his word? On the next page, at the end of a long, largely disconnected string of polysyllabics (each section links strings of phrases with colons and commas, only the first beginning with a capital letter, only the last ending with a period), parenthetically—and tellingly—Ammons wonders, "(hey, is the palaver rapping, yet?)." Though he may intend passages like this to seem droll and charming, too much of the poem, in fact, seems self-indulgent "palaver," yakking at great lengths within the width of a spool of adding machine tape (thus the thoughtful line breaks) in order to hear himself think. This pretends to be "a scientific poem" but suffers, instead, from a scientific posturing that has flawed even more successful earlier poems like "Corsons Inlet." Unlike in his best earlier poems, however, one can go pages without meeting anything resembling an image, and what else might one expect from a poet who offhandedly volunteers, 35 pages into a book called *Garbage:*

> . . . I don't know anything much about
> garbage
> dumps: I mean, I've never climbed one: I
>
> don't know about the smells: do masks mask
> scent: or is there a deodorizing mask . . .

For this, they passed over Hall's *The Museum of Clear Ideas,* Mark Doty's *My Alexandria,* and Margaret Gibson's *The Vigil* (both reviewed later).

Although I had not heard of Shirley Kaufman before reading **Rivers of Salt,** her sixth collection of poems, I came away with considerable respect for her lyric ability. While these poems are not lengthy, overly discursive, or ponderously philosophical, their elegantly rendered observations of life in Jerusalem, memories of parents and children, and experiences while travelling contain more depth, detail, heart, and wisdom than Strand or Ammons even glimpse. Most poems set in the Middle East labor under the too easy weight of Importance they presume; a twenty-year resident of Jerusalem and witness to war, Kaufman's point of view is not the political tourist's. The details of "Waiting," the opening poem of the volume, are those of the speaker's daily life, yet even musings on the weather, waiting for an expected season of rain—"A few blurry showers in the north, / not in Jerusalem," or "Last week clouds came, a dark insensible mass / above the hills, but nothing fell"—are heightened by more vaguely menacing passages: "We can't do anything / but wait. Fear sticks to our minds / like the black lice of newsprint." Only toward the end does that fear take solid form:

> There are black rubber masks in our closet.
> When you tighten the buckles
> and smooth the rubber snugly over your face
> and attach the filter according to the printed in-
> structions,
> you can breathe fresh air
> for about six hours. That's what they tell us.

These details, too, are commonplace. No histrionics, no assumed heroism: this is the voice of the Israelis who wait for more than rain to fall.

Along with fear, Kaufman provides tenderness, humor, and an eye for detail. Above all, she has a sense of human strengths and failings, and how the pleasures of one are not necessarily diminished by awareness of the other. In "Cineraria," the speaker visits with an American expatriate while in Delhi and listens to his countercultural adventures on a porch "lined with pots of purple cineraria. / Little imperialist flowers / from my own back yard."

"Once," he tells her,

> he went to visit
> Ginsberg and Orlovsky
> in Benares. He wanted
> to talk about poetry,
> but they kept asking him
> about the Ganges. "Peter
> served tea like a Hindu wife."
> Not exactly, I'm thinking.
> Whatever we're sharing only

seems the same.

In these few lines, Kaufman efficiently presents four characters and an entire milieu. And, however deflating the speaker's assessment of her host, she continues to share a pleasant moment with him. Kaufman's subjects rarely exceed the capacity of her craft, which, though not considerable, carries the necessary weight through an entirely pleasurable book.

Of the many collected and selected volumes published this year, five seem necessary to mention. **The Owl in the Mask of the Dreamer,** John Haines' collected poems, gathers poems from six previous collections and includes, in addition to a section of new poems, a selection of uncollected earlier poems. Haines' early work is less widely known than that of two contemporaries with whom he shared influences and whose work his resembles—James Wright and Robert Bly—and that's too bad, because Haines' poems, while they may not achieve the heights of Wright at his best, do not descend into either the self-pity of Wright or the grating surreal polemics of Bly at their worst. Tu Fu, Li Po, and Georg Trakl are among the influences Haines acknowledges; of them, Trakl's Expressionism colors the earlier poems most; the opening stanzas of "Moons," from *The Stone Harp* (1971), are typical:

> There are moons like continents,
> diminishing to a white stone
> softly smoking
> in a fogbound ocean.
>
> Equinoctial moons,
> immense rainbarrels spilling
> their yellow water.

Mixed with mystical realism are political poems, poems more firmly grounded in the Alaskan landscape, and cleanly detailed poems about wildlife.

Two thirds of the way through the volume, beginning with *New Poems 1980-88* (1990), Haines' canvas enlarges and his style achieves greater variety. These poems draw considerably on art history and refer to the works of such artists as Hieronymus Bosch, Auguste Rodin, Goya, and Michelangelo, as well as to science, literature, and history. Many take the form of monologues in the voices of historical figures and extend his tonal range to the colloquial. The closing stanzas of "Diminishing Credo," a poem addressed to Eugène Delacroix, give a sense of the later work:

> Under your hand for one last time
> the animal torso quickened,
> aroused from sleep to fury;
> and with you also an old dream
> of the barricades flickered
> and the map of history vanished.
>
> It was the time of the photographer
> and his flat, grey field,
> the time of ascending balloons . . .

This poem treats the same sense of diminishment as the section of Strand's **Dark Harbor** quoted above, but Haines' choice of a specific historical moment and figure to embody that sense of loss provides a context that lends depth to the expression of loss—a depth that gains, as well, from the wonderfully ironic image of optimism in the final line. Those unfamiliar with Haines' most recent poems will particularly find this collection frequently rewarding.

Less rewarding is *The Darkness Around Us Is Deep,* William Stafford's selected poems, edited and with an introduction by Robert Bly. Most of the poems here are brief lyrics, built from relatively simple, declarative sentences in Stafford's trademark flat diction. "Near" reveals much about the style:

> Walking along in this not quite prose way
> we both know it is not quite prose we speak,
> and it is time to notice this intolerable snow
> innumerably touching, before we sink.
>
> It is time to notice, I say, the freezing snow
> hesitating toward us from its gray heaven;
> listen—it is falling not quite silently
> and under it still you and I are walking.
>
> Maybe there are trumpets in the houses we pass
> and a redbird watching from an evergreen—
> but nothing will happen until we pause
> to flame what we know, before any signal's
> given.

The first lines describe the style with almost embarrassing accuracy. And, though Stafford is often regarded as a poet of "place," this poem, like many of those selected, despite occasional place names, occurs in a limbo-land of almost-detail ("redbird," not cardinal or scarlet tanager, for instance; "evergreen," not pine or cedar). Even the relationship between speaker and addressed remains undefined. Yet Stafford builds a sense of importance through rhetoric—"it is time to notice this intolerable snow / innumerably touching, before we sink." What makes the snow intolerable? Who or what is innumerably touching? Sink into what?—questions a good writing teacher would ask. Then, he heightens the flat diction through repetition and urgent iteration: "It is time to notice, I say, the freezing snow. . . . " These hardly seem the masterstrokes of a poet whom Bly would name a national treasure.

The limits of Stafford's talent, or at least the modest uses to which he put it, are clearly demonstrated in this volume. Bly's editing, moreover, has done the work no great service. Poems are selected and gathered in sections that seem designed to domesticate Stafford to Bly's usual esthetic agenda, and no apparatus is provided to give any sense of chronology. Hence, readers lose any sense of how Stafford's style has progressed, particularly unfortunate since the poems are similar enough to seem gathered from two books published in close proximity rather than from eight volumes published over thirty years.

In contrast, Robert Bertholf's edition of Robert Duncan's *Selected Poems* provides a brief but useful introduction and gathers both uncollected and previously issued poems chronologically by either date of composition or publication, respectively. He has succeeded admirably, as well, in representing the variety of Duncan's stylistic, prosodic, and thematic concerns in a reasonably sized volume. The extent of Duncan's intelligence, erudition, and formal expertise cannot be demonstrated in a brief notice, and prob-

ably do not need to be. Readers unfamiliar with his work apart from the few anthologized pieces should avail themselves of this fairly inexpensive edition.

Fewer readers will be familiar with the work of Jane Cooper, gathered in *Scaffolding: Selected Poems.* The volume collects work from the late forties and fifties (unpublished until her 1974 collection, *Maps & Windows*) through to 1983 (when the book was originally assembled for British publication). Additionally, she includes an essay, "Nothing Has Been Used in the Manufacture of This Poetry That Could Have Been Used in the Manufacture of Bread," which explains her long delay publishing her earliest poems and offers a revealing glimpse of the social constraints experienced by women writers immediately after the Second World War. These poems are not unusual for the period, characterized by compression of statement, mythical reference, and personal distance, but many are strong examples of the period style, and, at their best, transcend that style. This passage from an unfinished crown of sonnets, "After the Bomb Tests," moves backward from the Bikini atomic tests to consider the origins of the nuclear age in the discoveries of Johannes Kepler:

> I walk out of the house into the still air,
> Moving from circle to circle—hot, cold,
> Like zones of water this October night.
> All the stars are still arranged in spheres,
> The planets stalk serenely. Thinking of Kepler
> I pick a grassblade, chew it up, then spit.
> *Now I have thought,* he said, *the thoughts of God.*

Other poems concern felt obligations of motherhood, made complex in "Mercator's World," wherein a distorted projection map may make navigation easier but blurs a sense of actual distance and proportion, and the tensions of sexual relations in a newly liberated world.

Through the sixties and seventies, Cooper loosened her meter and tightened her language. The most recent poems show considerable formal reach, especially in the sequence involving the incarceration of Rosa Luxemburg, "Threads." Based on Luxemburg's letters to the wife of a fellow political prisoner in World War I Germany, the poem looks at the "threads" of the speaker's concern—political repression and nature—as they twine and ravel, as in the opening passage of the second of three sections:

> Hans is killed
>   Now twilight begins at four
> N "broke the news"
>   Over the great paved courtyard
>   hundreds of rooks fly by with a rowing
>   stroke
> Such a parade of grief! Why can't friends under-
>   stand
> I need solitude to consider? Why not tell me
> quickly, briefly, simply
> so as not to cheapen
>   Their homecoming caw,
>   throaty and muted is so different from
>   their
>   sharp morning caw after food. As if
> metal balls,
>   tossed from one to the other, high in the
>   air,
>   *tinkled* exchanging the day's news

> my last two letters
> addressed to a dead man . . .

As is frequently the case, early schooling in metrics has given her a sharpened sense of how to shape a freer line. The diversity, craft, and attention to detail evinced in Cooper's work, particularly in contrast to that of less practiced but more prominent poets, underscore the question of what standards we use to measure accomplishment.

John Engels' work, fully represented in *Walking to Cootehill: New and Selected Poems, 1958-1992,* demonstrates a level of intelligence and craft similarly under-appreciated. Nearly half of the poems are new, enough to justify a book to themselves, so issuing them as part of a selected poems seems designed to consolidate his work with a new publisher. Given that decision, Engels has chosen to organize the poems thematically in two broad sections, "The Naming" and "The Unnaming," mixing poems from his previous eight collections throughout. Each poem, however, includes the title and date of first book publication, allowing the reader to appreciate the through-lines of poetic concern while registering the ways in which Engels' craft and concern have matured.

Engels' poems are characterized by complexity of thought, reflected in dense, knotty syntax and a frequently Latinate vocabulary—Milton a rather ironic influence for a Catholic poet. Many of his poems also accumulate over considerable length, building detail on detail, but "The Naming," from his 1981 collection, *Vivaldi in Early Fall,* gives a taste:

> This is the kind of night
> on which Yuan Chen cried out
> to his dead wife, *when one
> dreams of another, are both
> aware of it?* the shadows lying close
> in his bed, ice roaring
> in the great river. From such a night
>
> Adam himself awoke, knowing
> none of this had ever been,
> opened his eyes
> onto the glorious mess of the contingent,
> propped himself on one elbow,
> and without astonishment gave names
> to the *bee-orchid, the giraffe.*

The pressure to name the forces of nature, threatening as that roaring ice, which are part of "the glorious mess of the contingent," impels much of Engels' work, whether those forces be fire, rot, underground streams—whatever wreaks havoc with the orderly structures we impose on the universe. Those same forces take the form of the beautiful and exotic, even if commonplace, things of the world: blossoming tomatoes, the colors of flowers in spring or summer, and the necessary if fruitless task Engels undertakes in poem after poem, of trying to cope with the world through language.

Like Engels, Mark Doty brings considerable verbal resources and moral seriousness to bear on his subjects. *My Alexandria,* his third collection, extends the scope of his narratives to engage questions of mortality. Awareness of AIDS pervades the poems, whether they deal directly with the disease or not. Beginning with poems in *Turtle, Swan,*

gay sexuality has been a commonplace of Doty's work. If poems in *Bethlehem in Broad Daylight* provided a glimpse of gay life in the early eighties, this volume looks at the aftermath of that period. The title tacitly recognizes that theme with its allusion to Cavafy, whom Doty describes in "Chanteuse" as a poet of "memory's erotics":

> That was all it took
> to console him, some token of Alexandria's
> anarchic life. How did it go on without him,
>
> the city he'd transformed into feeling?

Although Doty's style is far from Cavafy's, he shares a desire to change the details of life into feeling, and memory is similarly erotic in pull.

Being gay is not the sole focus of the poems, but a sense of living in an age of dying pervades. In "Brilliance," for example, a friend of the narrator is caring for "a man / who's dying," trying to help him remain engaged with a world he knows he will soon be leaving by getting a pet. After first rejecting the idea, the man agrees to goldfish, at which point the narrator segues into a story about "a Zen master who'd perfected / his detachment from things of the world" and

> remembered, at the moment of dying,
> a deer he used to feed in the park,
> and wondered who might care for it,
> and at that instant was reborn
>
> in the stunned flesh of a fawn.
> So, Maggie's friend—
> is he going out
>
> into the last loved object
> of his attention?

So, too, Doty's poems, with all their concern with mortality, remain connected to "the whole scintillant world." The primary problem with this volume is Doty's apparent urge to perfect The Mark Doty Poem, which, as in the example above, braids together two distinct narrative strands to reach a lyrical synthesis. Satisfying as the results of this form may be, it threatens to become formulaic.

An intelligent and eloquent critic, Bruce Bawer demonstrates in some of his poems the leadenness that marks the less successful new formalists discussed by Alan Shapiro. Many poems in *Coast to Coast,* despite considerable heart, labor under excessive literary consciousness; "I'm feeling Dickinsonian tonight—" one otherwise fine lyric begins, and another, "This is a sight Wordsworth never knew." As pervasive are stiffness within the line and unimaginative use of rhyme, as in the opening of "Bookshelves," a sonnet:

> On the industrial fringe of Park Slope
> one hot summer morning, we carried the boards
> that would be our bookshelves onto President
>   Street,
> and tied the long pieces, with a hundred feet
> of rope, onto the roof of my old car.
> Our new home in Manhattan seemed so far,
> I feared the knots would unravel, the cords
> snap in two, the wood break free of the rope.

The presentation of gay relationships, as casual as Doty's,

is Bawer's greatest felicity. The shopworn conceit does not need this elaboration, metrical variations are similarly clumsy, and the rhyme words are all nouns, except for a fairly nominative adjective; varying parts of speech helps avoid the too predictable chime at the line end. As seems the ironic case with some other new formalists, Bawer is at his most engaging when he drops received form.

Jane Kenyon, in **Constance,** her fourth collection, demonstrates admirably what can be achieved in the mainstream poem. She abjures tricky enjambments that call too much attention to themselves and concentrates on condensing language into relatively quiet lines that go about their business. And the business of this book is, to a considerable extent, dealing with her lifelong struggle with clinical depression. Set against the backdrop of childhood recollection and current life on a New England farm, the poems build sets of relationships between children and parents, spouses, friends, and humans and the natural world from the fewest possible details. "Wood Thrush," the ninth section of "Having It Out with Melancholy," moves easily between the internal and external, delineating a careful emotional sequence:

> High on Nardil and June light
> I wake at four,
> waiting greedily for the first
> note of the wood thrush. Easeful air
> presses through the screen
> with the wild, complex song
> of the bird, and I am overcome
>
> by ordinary contentment.
> What hurt me so terribly
> all my life until this moment?
> How I love the small, swiftly
> beating heart of the bird
> singing in the great maples;
> its bright, unequivocal eye.

The tone is fairly restrained, despite the speaker's exultation at discovering a "bird's eye" perspective on her life. Also moving are "Chrysanthemums" and "Pharaoh," both of which apparently grow out of surgery performed on her husband, Donald Hall. "Pharaoh," especially, gains force from its indirect approach to the possibility of death, moving through the awkwardness of adjusting to post-surgical life ("Touch rankles, food / is not good"), to the closing image of the husband under a sheet as "a sarcophagus," surrounded by "the things [he] might need in the next / life . . . comb and glasses, / water, a book and pen."

In her fifth volume of poetry, **The Vigil: A Poem in Four Voices,** Margaret Gibson extends her lyric talent into a book-length poem set over the course of a single day and involving four women who span three generations of a family. The event that draws mother Lila, sisters Sarah and Jennie, and daughter Kate together in October 1986 is the firing of Sarah's kiln, the overseeing of which is the title's vigil. The firing of clay into harder forms provides a central metaphor for the firming of relationships over the course of the poem. All the principals, as well as the relations between them, have been fired by the dysfunction and alcoholic codependence surrounding the father; gath-

ered together, they are quickly "pulled in, watchful," as Sarah observes,

> As if an exacting angel
> turned us inward, away from
> whatever might be
> said or done in truth, or pretense,
> to soften grief
> or give joy

The women take their turns, each of their forms designed to reflect character: Sarah and Lila have long, spindly verses; Jennie speaks in brief prose paragraphs; and Kate delivers her thoughts in long lines divided into one- or two-line units. Such devices are important, for distinguishing between voices through diction or syntax is not one of Gibson's accomplishments, though members of a single family provide considerable challenge in that respect. Plot, also, is not a significant aspect; instead, Gibson teases us forward, revealing through lyric accumulation a shifting complex of believably intimate relationships.

The shifting relationships in **Materialism,** Jorie Graham's fifth collection, are those more often treated in post-structuralist treatises than books of poems: those between concept and object, signifier and signified, text and reader, and even energy and matter, are the central relationships that drive this lyric meditation. In fact, several selections in the volume are "adapted" from prose works by authors as diverse as Plato, Marx, Heidegger, Wittgenstein, Audobon, Stanislavsky, Walter Benjamin, and Benjamin Whorf, concerning physics, mythology, linguistics, and natural history. Individual poem titles, including the repeated "Notes on the Reality of the Self," "Subjectivity," "Invention of the Other," "The Visible World," and "Existence and Presence," point toward Graham's concern with our role in a world of matter. In "Steering Wheel," for instance, she anatomizes the process of backing a car out of a driveway, noting the complexity of observation and interaction usually taken for granted in routine tasks. Each poem acknowledges the difficulty of finding a text to represent the apprehension: "Oh but I haven't gotten it right," she interrupts "Steering Wheel," then guiding the poem closer to the mark.

Real human exchanges are rare. The poems prefer the distance of memory or observation, as in one of the "Notes on the Reality of the Self," in which the speaker watches a man in a bakeshop "who sits, hands folded eyes closed, / above the loaf still entire, and speaks inwardly / huge strange thoughts of thanks." From such detailed observation of others, by implication, can the speaker come to know herself. More often, the speaker grapples with nature, either through a window or, as in "The Visible World," by sorting through by hand:

> . . . If I look carefully, there in my hand, if
> I
>   break it apart without
> crumbling: husks, mossy beginnings and end-
>   ings, ruffled
>   airy loambits,
> and the greasy silks of clay crushing the pinerot
>   in . . .
> *Erasure.* Tell me something and then take it
>   back.

> Bring this pellucid moment—here on this page
> now
>   as on this patch
> of soil, my property—bring it up to the top and
> out
>   of
> sequence. Make it dumb again—won't you?—
> what
>   would it
> take? Leach the humidities out, the things that
> will
>   insist on
> making meaning.

Graham's language is both precise and lyric (apart from unfortunate lapses into Deconstructionist jargon, such as *"Erasure"*), and her lines register subtlety of inflection. The close observation of both nature and action is occasionally thrilling, and her facility with poetic technique often enviable, but at times the book seems overweighted toward the intellect, pleasures of the eye and ear subordinate to the demand of calculated argument rather than the argument with ourselves from which, Yeats said, poetry is made.

Like Graham, Brenda Hillman employs an external system of thought to help structure the poems in *Bright Existence;* unlike Graham's secular sources, however, Hillman grounds her work in gnostic lore, as she did in the companion volume, *The Death Tractates* (reviewed in *CLC,* Vol. 76). Whereas that collection details Hillman's response to the death of a close female mentor, these poems range over details in the daily life of a newly divorced mother, including eating with her daughter in McDonald's, attending therapy sessions, and collecting dry cleaning. Like those in *Materialism,* the poems emphasize a relation between self and the outer world, raising questions about the nature of reality, but they are based in a spiritual tradition that focuses questions inward, to the soul rather than the intellect, seeking to heal the fracture between the spiritual and the material. From the austerities of gnosticism, Hillman makes a poetry surprisingly open to joy, though joy—"Adult Joy," as she titles one poem—is inextricable from sorrow: "The slender vessel used for weddings / was also used for funerals," she begins, concluding that, when "[w]e grow up," "Joy becomes the missing event, / what reaches us unknown / without wisdom." Still, wisdom is what we seek.

In most religious disciplines, the everyday world is the realm of practice. So Hillman's poems grow from mundane chores, from the sights, sounds, and textures of daily life as they reveal both cleft and possibility of healing. At their weakest, particularly in the fourth section, the techniques call too much attention to themselves—parenthetical asides that never close, commas repeated or dropped a line—as well as a kind of word salad reminiscent of some of Roethke's work, with echoes of nursery rhymes and gibberish. The impulse here, however, is to capture the workings of a mind released to the depths of memory or darkness of solitude, occasioned, for instance, by the slight scraping of a branch against a night window which "made the sound / of missingness" ("Branch, Scraping"). In general, however, Hillman develops details across well-heard lines, as in the title poem:

> In spring, the great pines waited a little faster.
> Wildflowers turned
> on their big circles, under the earth
>
> and the orchid, which always came back
> to the same slanty light
> in the forest floor
> pushed toward the edges of itself.
>   . . . . .
>
> The oak moths,
> holding pale tomorrows,
> dropped on invisible threads before the flower,
>
> the part that wasn't ready
> stayed inside a little longer
> and the part that was ready to be something
> came forth—

While neither as fully satisfying or consistently well crafted as Louise Glück's *The Wild Iris,* **Bright Existence** similarly reaches toward the base of our lives. In Hillman's poems, overbearing darkness, though returning each night, every morning grows lighter. Two strong collections in as many years mark Hillman as a promising poet.

The Year in Drama

by Robert Cohen

Given the brilliance of the previous year, it is not too surprising that 1993 looked a little dim by comparison. Except for the New York premieres of **Angels in America** and, to a lesser extent, *The Kentucky Cycle,* both of which (or all four of which—as each of these colossi consists of two full evenings of Theatre) were reviewed in these pages last year, 1993 had few thrills and an unnerving number of disappointments. The year was also marked by a severe narrowing of themes, at least in New York, so that at times plays seemed to be speaking to each other more than the public at large. Rare was the play that did not treat— or at least extract a chuckle from—Jewish concerns, gay concerns, the Theatre itself (in particular, American musical comedies), or all three of these in combination. (Male) characters in two different plays dated chorus boys from *Cats,* at least three plays cited lines from *A Streetcar Named Desire,* and culled quips from Shakespeare and songs snatches from Broadway musicals seemed to float from play to play. More than half of the plays on Broadway, by rough count, had at least one gag in Yiddish; any theatregoer who didn't know what *shtupping* means probably does now. I'm afraid the New York theatre suffered this year from an excess of audience-to-stage familiarity, if not a cozy complicity.

I was supposed to review Wendy Wasserstein's **The Sisters Rosensweig** in these pages last year, but the play was such a hit—at the smallish Mitzi Newhouse Theatre—I couldn't get in. Seen this year at Broadway's much larger Barrymore Theatre, where it is still (February 1994) enjoying a long run, it's a very solid piece of serio-comic workmanship, and, apart from the previously reviewed **Angels in America** and *Kentucky Cycle* (see the penultimate paragraph of this essay for an update on **Angels**), was probably the best straight (i.e. non-musical) production of a generally weak Broadway season. The eponymous sisters are Jewish-American versions of the three Prozorovs—the title characters in Chekhov's great play, *The Three Sisters*—and Chekhov's famous Three are openly referenced by the Rosensweigs during the course of Wasserstein's work. Like the Prozorovs, one of the sisters Rosensweig is married, two are not, and all three have attracted an odd assortment of male suitors and hangers-on. Wasserstein sets her play abroad, in London at a stately drawing room in Queen Anne's Gate where Sara, the elder sister, makes her home. Sara (née Sadie) is a much-divorced international executive; she has become wholly Englished and assimilated ("I'm a cold bitter woman who's turned her back on her family, her religion and her country," she says), and is now celebrating (actually ruing) her 54th birthday by having a reunion with her younger sisters. These are Pfeni (née Penny), a world-traveling journalist just in from India, and the delightful "Dr. Gorgeous," who's neither a doctor nor gorgeous but Mrs. Henry Teitlebaum (she's the married one), an advice-filled yenta-mama who doubles as a London tour guide, and triples (incongruously) as a Boston talk-show pseudo-psychiatrist. The men in town these days include, as sort of the Vershinin of the group, one Mervyn Kant (né Kantlowitz), a New York furrier who is now into synthetics, widowerhood, and—he hopes—a second time around. He's pursuing Sarah, while a bi-sexual theatrical type, Geoffrey, is—if inconstantly—in pursuit of Pfeni. As in the Russian play, people are coming and going (from Bombay, Boston, and Brooklyn, to Dublin, Lithuania, and Tajikistan—this is decidedly NOT a provincial scene), but hardly anything actually gets done. Merv woos Sara with a grown-up and pragmatic ardor ("I still believe there can be happiness in life, Sara. Brief, but a moment or two . . . "), and Pfeni gets unceremoniously dumped by Geoffrey ("I miss men," laments Geoffrey. "It's all right," Pfeni replies, "I do too!") Dr. Gorgeous, by far the liveliest of the three, is escorting the ladies of her Temple Beth El Sisterhood around town; when they give her the Chanel dress she's always wanted, it's the emotional high point of the play. This, however, sets a rather limited dramatic parameter. Most of the play's talk—which is unflaggingly erudite, witty, topical, and delightful—is about the pros and cons of going Home: to Jewishness, to New York, and to Marriage, Mom, and Family. A return, in other words, to some remembered sense of normalcy. That's what all the née-ing's about: everybody (but Geoffrey, the sole gentile) was born as somebody else, and as Wasserstein says (in the preface to the published edition), "most of the characters in the play are struggling with who they are." As well they should: the nées have it, it seems.

Although the performances and direction are superb, and the comedy fairly unstinting (Madelaine Kahn's right-on-the-edge portrayal of Dr. Gorgeous will be the great memory of this production), I enjoyed reading this play more than seeing it; Wasserstein's main lines—and main one-liners—are just too perfect to come out of real mouths. Sara's iciness and Brit-brittleness, Merv's utilitarian romanticism, Pfeni's sexual/geographical wanderings, and Dr. Gorgeous' Jewish-mama ministrations are all programmatically effective—they add up to a neat construction and some good comic confrontations—but they're far too shallowly drawn to support the sort of ontological struggle Wasserstein attempts: broad cultural clashes (Jewish *v.* Gentile, homey *v.* peripatetic, gay *v.* straight) substitute for the personal crisis (or investigation) from which personal identity actually emerges. And if identity isn't personal, then what is it? The play also lacks an essential carnality; it's virtually impossible to get behind Sara and Merv's—or Pfeni and Geoffrey's—couplings, since there is nothing remotely sensual about any of them. Nor is this posed as a matter of the characters' maturity; the relationship between Sara's 17 year-old daughter Tess and her boyfriend, which founders on political activism, is equally antiseptic in the passion department. Sexy words are spoken, and the performers are suitably warm-blooded and attractive, but the play keeps everybody at a frigid distance; these are ideographic rather than human characters, and they don't sweat. As a result, we don't really care if Sara and Merv get together, or if Pfeni and Geoffrey fall apart; and Dr. Gorgeous, brashly (and ethnically) enticing as she may be, can't really hold the play together. In her preface, Wasserstein credits a debt to George S. Kaufman, Moss Hart, Noel Coward, and Chekhov: the first three have respectively tutored her well in Broadway comic structure, Broadway Jewish nostalgia, and flit-Brit wit; but I'm afraid the Russian doctor needs to be called in for further consultation.

On the flip side of **Rosensweig** was Frank Gilroy's **Any Given Day,** a true Chekhovian construction which, lacking the Broadway snap of the Wasserstein work, closed

very shortly after opening. Though not a success, Gilroy's play was intermittently affecting, and a welcome reminder of what at least some good plays used to be like. That the play appeared at all came as something of a shock: Gilroy made his stunning Broadway debut way back in 1965, with *The Subject Was Roses* which captured the Pulitzer Prize along with the Tony and Critics Circle Awards of that year. But the talented dramatist, though continually productive, has made little national impression since. His re-emergence on Broadway was made doubly nostalgic inasmuch as a couple in this play are the younger versions of the couple from the earlier one: clearly this is a family—presumably fictive—that Gilroy has been tracking for thirty years.

Like **Rosensweig,** the play is a New York drawing-room family drama, this time we're in the Bronx during the early 1940s, in the turbulent historical cusp as the Great Depression was moving into all-out World War. Again we have three grown children to deal with, two sisters and a brother this time, plus a suitor and a straying husband for the sisters; there are also some interesting fringes: a too-tippling, Jewish family (and friend-of-family) doctor, an autistic and wheelchair-bound son, and an unhappily clairvoyant grandmother. As with the Wasserstein play, the plot is relatively incidental and doesn't bear retelling; the specific familial (and putatively dramatic) occasions that Gilroy creates instead comprise a quietly simmering Chekhovian stew. Gilroy's themes are honest ones: love and neglect, work and marriage, duty and passion, and the persistence of longstanding rivalries (spousal, sibling, and parental); while nothing that happens in the play is particularly noteworthy, there is a credible and generally engaging integrity in the ensemble of family troubles and disillusions. The only note that jarred—and jarred mightily—was the prescient matriarch, woodenly played by Sada Thompson. The surreal conceit by which grandma knows the future adds nothing to the play's dramatic or theatrical values, and seriously diminishes its otherwise appealing qualities of familial homeostasis and naturalism. It's a dramaturgical mis-*coup* of the first order.

I shouldn't suggest, though, that **Any Given Day** is in Chekhov's league even apart from this. While faithful to its time and characters, finely-textured in its details, and smoothly performed, Gilroy's play is barely intriguing, rarely funny or moving, and almost totally absent of dramatic momentum. What it lacks is hope, spirit, and adventure; it's not just set in the pre-war Bronx, it's mired there. The failure of naturalism, when in fact it does fail, is that it gives us nothing that we can't see on our own, and sets nothing into motion that we want to track; it has no more fascination than somebody else's family dinner. What gives Chekhov's *Three Sisters* (and Gilroy's *Subject Was Roses*) their dramatic dynamism is the captivating and near-palpable forces of human aspiration, all the more poignant because it turns out to be unproductive: a hope always deferred. **Any Given Day,** well-formed as it is, lacks the force of (even misguided) enthusiasm, and runs dry from a sheer lack of anticipation. Wasserstein's play may want more Chekhovian depth; Gilroy's needs more Great White Way pizazz.

If Gilroy has been rarely represented on our stage, Lanford Wilson has been one of the great—if often unheralded—dramatists of our time: *The Rimers of Eldritch, The Hot l Baltimore, The Gingham Dog, Talley's Folly,* and *The Fifth of July* are brilliantly structured and beautifully carved portraits of inner America. **Redwood Curtain,** however, is as distant from those achievements as one can imagine: it's an arch metaphysical melange of Vietnam angst, environmental assaults, aesthetic confusions, and young/old, male/female, east/west, reality/fantasy dialectics. "Geri," an Amerasian love child, follows a man she believes to be her father into the redwood-and-marijuana fields north of Arcata, California. "Lyman," the man, is a burly, half-deafened Vietnam veteran; he first evades Geri so as to lure her deeper in the wood, and then stalks her when she's gone so far she can't turn back. But this is no mere stalking tale; both characters, it develops, are in fact seeking their ancestral and biological roots among the tall trees. And their taller tales: most of what both of them tell us (and each other) is lies.

There is just too much play here; every time Wilson's central plot ("who is Geri's Dad?") loses itself down a blind alley (or forest trail), Wilson simply widens the map: now suddenly Geri's a concert pianist; now she's a faery spirit who controls the thunderclaps; now everything we've heard up to this point is shown to be untrue. By the play's midpoint we've lost track of the initial action (or we're no longer concerned with it) and when Wilson returns to his initial theme he's left us somewhere in the next dimension.

Wilson has a gift for poetic dialogue unmatched in our theatre since Tennessee Williams, but in **Redwood Curtain** it's all self-conscious and effete. "I could will it to rain or thin the turbulence, send the clouds out over the ocean and inform the sun to burn through the fog and warm the earth," says Geri, (and the lights change to prove that she means it), "I can tell the birds to fly to the trees that surround the vineyards across the valley and leave the woods to the two of us." This is not the language we really want—or need—to explore the world of Asian war orphans, or West Coast anti-environmentalism, or even the agonies of piano prodigies; nor does it lead us into the realms of profundity or epiphany; it's just persiflage. Wilson has a great subject, a great set—magnificent towering redwoods by John Lee Beatty—and he's received a fine performance from Debra Monk in an adjacent role (as Geri's adoptive aunt), but the play goes off in too many directions, none of them (like Lyman) worth following into the woods. The all-but-amateur actor playing Geri was an absolutely inexplicable choice for a Broadway show. The play has its supporters—Frank Rich at the *New York Times* gave it a rave—but I think they're honoring the author, not the work. I continue to look forward to Wilson's work, of course, but please let this be a solitary lapse.

Athol Fugard continues to probe deeply into his continent's troubles (and, seemingly as a byproduct, into the human condition), and he makes the most of just two actors in his newest work, **Playland,** which employs (for the most part) a conventional format to explore issues ranging from personal and social to theological and cosmic. Set outdoors, at a night watchman's camp adjacent to a run-down amusement park in the South African Karoo district, a (white) park visitor encounters the park's (black) watchman at twilight on New Year's Eve: it is 1989, in the waning years of official apartheid. But the park's opening has been delayed until the generator gets fixed and the lights go on, so the white man ("Gideon le Roux") strikes up a conversation with the Black watchman ("Martinus"). When the park opens, Gideon soon goes in, but he returns to Martinus' camp, once, twice, and once again. The play, performed without intermission, spans the night: by dawn, when the two characters depart (together), they have plunged deeply into their pasts, their souls, their culture(s), and each other. Both have been killers, and both have been—and are now—decent men; the manner in which these conflicting realities are reconciled brings them (and us) face to face with war, justice, race, religion, guilt, and the vast uncertainties of the South African future—itself a microcosm of the world's. This is Fugard's most penetrating disquisition—and "disquisition" describes the play's weakness as well as its strength—of the human predicament in its current forms. Gideon is a victim of his victories: in South Africa's ruinous Border War ("South Africa's Vietnam," Fugard calls it in a program note), Gideon had killed dozens of enemy troops (one assumes they were troops); in a single horrific ambush he machine-gunned an entire unit of twenty-seven men. Martinus had only killed once—it was a white boss man who had raped Martinus' fiancée—but he continues to kill the man over and over in his mind. Hovering over both of them is the Bible's "Number Six." To Martinus, "Thou Shalt Not Kill" is holy gospel, but to Gideon it's just Church cant; still, it stokes the Hellfires buried deep in his mind and he strikes out blindly for absolution. "That's why you keep coming back tonight: Forgiveness!" cries Martinus. "That's too big for me, white man," he continues, "I'm just a night watchman. Go ask God for that forgiveness!" Gideon answers: "Forget about Him man. He's forgotten about us. It's me and you tonight. The whole world is you and me. Here! Now!"

There are obvious parallels with Samuel Beckett and *Waiting for Godot,* here, and a striking use of the carnival metaphor has proved powerful for many European writers and filmmakers in recent decades. "They wait for Playland and the happiness machines," says Martinus, "and when we switch on the lights and the music, they come. Like moths they come out of the night—the old uncles with the fat aunties, the young boys and the pretty girls, even the little children. They all come to play because they all want to forget." But of course we've come to Playland as well: Fugard's Playland, and we've not come to forget. Both universal and particular, Fugard's world is sublimely humanistic and boldly unsentimental, with its optimism sharply limited but unerringly focused. This play strikes few dramatic chords—it is largely a philosophical dialogue with little exterior action or event—and it reaches its emotional climaxes through thematic (and even theological) rather than personal dialectics. Though **Playland**'s characters are detailed, they remain impersonal, unlike the folks in, say, the same author's *A Lesson from Aloes* or *"Master Harold"* . . . *and The Boys.* This is at least partly because the conversation between these total strangers is a contrivance to begin with; while we accept it as such, this places us on a strictly abstract plain, despite the naturalistic details of setting, costume, incident, and dialect. No two people have ever had such a conversation, any more than any two men, in real life, have spoken Beckett's Gogo-Didi duologue. Dramatic force at the South Coast production, therefore, was largely achieved through an outsized (and sometimes amazing) acting intensity on the part of the play's two performers, Kene Holliday (as Martinus) and Richard Doyle.

Another play from and about South Africa this year appeared under the name of newcomer Tug Yourgrau. Yourgrau's a Jewish South African actor/filmmaker living in Massachusetts, and his play, *The Song of Jacob Zulu,* was nominated for six 1993 Tony awards, including Best Play. It was perhaps the most unusual Broadway venture of the year. Set in a Zulu village in 1985, the work is a conscious effort to apply classic Greek tragic dramaturgy to the contemporary horror of African apartheid. The story is a true one: a well-educated young black man, an apolitical pacifist raised in a devout Christian household, is radicalized by racist violence and commits an act of intentional political terrorism, killing four innocent people in a suburban shopping mall. Caught, he is tried, convicted, and executed by hanging. Yourgrau's play, created in a series of workshops and improvisations with Chicago's celebrated Steppenwolf Company in 1992, treats the young man—here renamed Jacob Zulu, perhaps combining the author's Jewish and African roots—as he seeks to defend the indefensible, and explain the inexplicable. During the course of the action Jacob confesses, repudiates his confession, defends his action, repudiates his defense, and finally capitulates to his own hanging. What gives the work its majesty is neither plot intrigue nor character development—although the treatment of a defense attorney is impressive—but the near-Aeschylean choric presence of Joseph Shabalala and the all-male all-African singing group, Ladysmith Black Mambazo, which Shabalala founded and heads. Slowly marching toward us from the back wall at the play's opening, this swaying "chorus line" sweeps relentlessly forward, a singing black tidal wave that keeps us in awe—and in tow—for the rest of the evening. Ladysmith is the group that backed up Paul Simon in his *Graceland* album; here it more than backs up *Zulu:* it seizes and dominates the foreground as well, alternately celebrating life and lamenting catastrophe; calling for struggle and retreating into reflections. Joseph Shabalala, as it turns out, was not incidental to the play's creation; much of the play was written around his music, and some of the lyrics are his too. Indeed, it's the plot "incidents" that are truly incidental here. And is not this how the great Aeschylean tragedies were written? We don't know, of course—none of the original Greek music or choreography survives—but the events of Yourgrau's written script are neither more nor less fully developed than those in, say, Aeschylus' *Suppliants,* and the music not only enthralls the audience but advances a powerful political aesthetics. Apartheid ended, I suspect, more because of poetics than politics, and this is but one example. A great performance by Ladysmith Black Mambazo, and K. Todd Freeman as Jacob helped things along tremendously. *The Song of Jacob Zulu* is not a major play, but its appearance

on Broadway is a major event, and was a major (if not commercial) success.

Will somebody please give Neil Simon a year off? This great writer—clearly the second most commercially successful playwright in history, with 27 Broadway shows, all hits or near-hits, and his own Broadway theatre to play in or rent out—now seems to have pretty much run out of gas. It is perhaps symptomatic of his stall that the high point of BOTH of his 1993 Broadway ventures—*The Goodbye Girl* and *Laughter on the 23rd Floor*—are parodies of Shakespeare (who is, of course, the MOST commercially successful playwright in history). I'm afraid this ended up as Simon's "I Hate Hamlet" year, and one begins to be concerned with authorial envy—of Paul Rudnick (writer of *I Hate Hamlet*) as well as the Avon Bard himself.

In *The Goodbye Girl,* Simon has picked up the pieces of his memorably charming 1977 film of the same name, in which Richard Dreyfuss, playing an underemployed actor, comes into New York to essay the title role in a gay-themed off-Broadway *Richard III,* while at the same time negotiating a nasty sublease dispute with some unexpected and unwanted roommates: a dumped mom (played by Marsha Mason) and her daughter. The film's highlight was Dreyfuss' screaming, queening Duke of Gloucester

("Now ithah wintah of owah dithcontent . . . ") which won him the year's Oscar; the (considerably reduced) highlight of the 1992 stage play, which is ostensibly a musical, was Martin Short's politically-cleaned-up reprisal of this same scene, converted (prior to Broadway, after protests from the gay community) to the actor's playing the role as "a man playing a woman playing a man." Still a good scene, if hopelessly un-outrageous. But what utterly vitiates the current Broadway production is that all the film's bite is altogether gone: Simon has pulled his punches along with his incorrectness, and the delicious and sweaty sexual fencing of Dreyfuss and Mason that fueled the film is replaced here with a bland, tongue-in-cheek banter that's shared winkingly between its two pleasant (and *too* pleasant) romantic leads—and with the audience. This is a feel-happy Broadway musical; the couple (Bernadette Peters plays opposite Short) is obviously headed to communal bliss from their first feintings, the messy relationship angst (and artistic despair) of the earlier work is gone, and the only tension remaining is what to do with little Lucy, the dumped mom's daughter. Scenes which in the film advanced the struggle for urban (and professional) survival here merely outline an exhausted sitcom formula of boy gets girl, loses girl, becomes girl, gets girl: cycled once for Mom and once again for Lucy. Neither Marvin Hamlisch's music nor, regrettably, David Zippel's lyrics measurably raised the level of these mechanical stage episodes into anything that held one's attention; indeed, the musical numbers themselves seemed randomized throughout the play, inserted, as it were, because the format required them. Dance numbers, which were justified (or rationalized) by the expedient of having Peters play a TV choreographer (for PBS of all things), were utterly unrelated to the plot's goings-on, as were the out-of-nowhere pop gospels of an otherwise extraneous landlady (Carol Woods) who sang only to advance the minute hand. This was a mishmash throughout, and, but for the generally winsome (and occasionally too winsome) performances, all but an embarrassment for the justly celebrated author, composer, and lyricist. Short, making his Broadway debut, received exceptional reviews for his affability and charm, but his role (and the play) would have been far more effective if he had also excited our disgust. When he brazenly sits in Peters' apartment, wearing only his guitar, it's not *cute:* we should feel violated, like she does.

The other Simon play of 1993 was **Laughter on the 23rd Floor,** which promised somewhat more than it delivered; at one time said to be about Sid Caesar and the legendary writing team that put together TV's Golden Age "Your Show of Shows," it turned out to more closely portray Jackie Gleason and a host of lesser lights. Here is a show with no plot at all: it's three different gatherings of the team: the comic "Max Prince" (Caesar/Gleason, as played by Nathan Lane) with his seven adoring writers and a bimbo secretary. To give it some tone, if not storyline, Simon has placed it at the end of the Caesar/Prince era (1953), when the networks have cut Max from ninety to sixty minutes, and are pushing him towards material that will play in Pocatello. "They want shit!" growls Max, whose taste runs to more intellectual fare such as a take on Marlon Brando doing *Julius Caesar.* Like the gender-bispecific Richard performance in **Goodbye Girl,** this Shakespearean parody

a la Tennessee Williams is the highlight of the current play, but its comic delight is leavened by the fact that the material surrounding it—Simon's own—is, if anything, even more self-conscious than the send-up.

What Simon has failed to do in **23rd Floor** is show his comics doing what they do best: creating comedy. Instead, they merely trade gags—testily and relentlessly—finding each other's humor, and Max's in particular, considerably less than amusing. It's sort of throw and kvetch. While the text touts the 23rd floor office (it's on 57th Street—numerologists can have a field day here) as a comic nirvana (a young neophyte, presumably the adolescent Simon himself, blandly narrates—mostly from the side), on stage it actually seems like a miserable place to work, sort of a wisecracking Hades: here, Hell is other people's gaglines. There's a sustained nastiness to the humor, too, which eventually numbs the proceedings. Max regularly punches his fist through the wall (that's the Gleason in the character: "pow, right in the kisser" we almost hear him say), he's enraged at Joe McCarthy, the networks, the Rosenberg's electrocution, and the ignorance of the TV audience in roughly equal measure; we don't know enough about any of this—through the play at least—to share his feelings or to appreciate his ironies. Much of the jokiness is ancient and forced: Polish jokes, Jewish jokes, ageist jokes, and infinitely long-winded vulgarisims: the proper pronunciation of the word fucking—"fahking" says the Russian emigré—generates at least a dozen laughs, but they're increasingly hollow as the evening wears on and the audience wears out; we are all trying hard to help Max's gang (and Simon's play) out of a jam, rather than enjoying ourselves, and we are ultimately embarrassed by the mirthless crudities.

Clearly, Simon is locked in a time warp. If *Lost in Yonkers* and *Broadway Bound* were successes, and I think they were, it's because Simon's memorial reconstructions of his youth touched tender chords of childhood and discovery; old comedy routines, however, even dressed up in current clothes (and language) are only stale bread. The actors are as hardworking here as any on Broadway, and they are largely successful; there ARE a lot of laughs, and probably enough to keep the show running for the season. And Nathan Lane is simply spectacular: eye-popping, cheek-bursting, heart-thumping. Lane soars in **Laughter on the 23rd Floor,** but the play is stuck deep in the basement.

Paul Rudnick wrote the real *I Hate Hamlet,* which enjoyed a mild success on Broadway last year; his new play, **Jeffrey,** which is NOT about Shakespeare, is even better: it's a light romantic comedy about sexual attraction and its attendant woes. The woes, in this case, are basically medical, as the sexual attraction is (in the key situations) between infected and uninfected men. Rudnick's play is both sadly piquant and regularly delightful. The horror of AIDS notwithstanding, (gay) life goes on, the author reports, and can even get better.

Rudnick is a very nimble farceur, and his opening scene, with a gaggle of boys (and one girl) popping out of a queen-sized bed center stage, is a little gem of lying-down stand-up. Rudnick's comedy—which essentially concerns a young man meeting a potential flame just after taking a vow of celibacy—is wry, rolling, and sage; it's *Love's Labor's Lost* with a double twist. The serious parts of *Jeffrey* deliver truths of no particular depth (it's anti-abstinence, but with precautions), yet the integrity is wholly trustworthy, the humor genuine and for the most part good-spirited, and the romance goofy and sentimental: the play ends atop the Empire State Building with "Embraceable You" overlaid; is this a Gershwin year or what? *Jeffrey* is a play that the audience likes, and I liked. A cross-over work, it has excited more resistance in gay quarters than in the straight community, but Rudnick has done a near-perfect job of being mildly offensive (i.e. mildly daring) in both directions. It is quite splendidly acted by the New York cast, particularly John Michael Higgins in the title role, who is both wonderfully relaxed and acidly vivacious at the same time.

The bravest play in New York this year (it actually opened at the end of 1992) was Frank McGuinness' *Someone Who'll Watch Over Me,* an import from the Hampstead Theatre in London. McGuinness' play is set in a dingy Lebanese prison cell where three hostages—an Irishman, an Englishman, and an American—are each chained by an ankle to separate cinderblock walls. The enforced stasis of this environment—which is unchanged throughout the play's nine scenes, but for one early arrival and two late departures—is numbing, as it must be. McGuinness, however, all but overcomes it.

Much of the play, naturally, consists of the actors (characters) coming to terms with this grim environment. They tell stories, argue, joke, sing, curse, recite, reveal their dreams, drive imaginary cars, direct imaginary movies, narrate historic steeplechase races, and re-enact the 1977 Ladies' Wimbledon Finals. Mostly they torment each other. "Who's the piece of shit? You are!" says the Irishman. "I want to crack your fucking face open. I'm going to fucking kill you," says the American. "You both scare the shit out of me," says the Englishman. It's the world of *No Exit,* where Hell is Other People: "These guys don't need to tear us apart. We can tear each other apart," the Yank concludes.

The Beckettian gallows humor ("That's the idea, let's abuse each other!" cries Didi to Gogo as they wait for Godot) is rarely forced, and covers a rich topical gamut: sexual, ethnic, religious, and social/political; there may be no atheists in foxholes, but there's a lot of class struggle and gender reidentification. And the comedic vein is deeply grounded in the barely imaginable boredom of the Beirut prison, which we know to be a true one. What has been endured? And what measures made it endurable? McGuinness gives us credible answers, and continually forces us back upon our own imaginations. This does not completely satisfy, however, as the play's fundamental situation steadfastly resists any sort of structured response or dramatic momentum. "Jesus, the boredom, the boredom, the bloody boredom!" cries the Irishman in the first scene, and by the end of the play we have long since agreed with him. How we could take it for two years, instead of two hours, is hardly a question we want to dwell on. The title paraphrases a Gershwin song which, illuminated by some fairy starlight between scenes, implies a world elsewhere,

but does not promise it. The three performances (the guards remain offstage)—by Stephen Rea as the cocky Irishman, Alec McCowen as the fey Englishman, and James McDaniel as the (black, in this case) American—were magnificent, as they had to be.

If McGuinness' play was the bravest of the season, Frank Pugliese's *Aven' U Boys* was the toughest. Set under an elevated railway track in the racially-tense Bensonhurst section of Brooklyn, and performed by an exceptional cast of young performers, *Aven' U Boys* is a depiction of nearly relentless juvenile violence—only the juveniles have ostensibly grown up; two have gotten married and one even has kids. The story of the three "boys"—Ed (a racist assassin and masochist), Rocky (an alluring but inconstant pretty-boy), and Charlie (a wimp who turns wife-beater and child abuser) begins with them pummelling each other into submission; not too long after this they start pummelling others as well. Most of the play's action is various forms of torture-for-fun, which we generally euphemize as "abuse." The boys' story is narrated by their three "girls," who sometimes respond with generosity, always with trepidation, and—towards us at least—with a welcome sense of irony: they can speak our language too, even if their "boys" cannot. Not the least of the play's points is that the characters, while verging on sociopathy, still pursue the most ordinary of middle-class American "virtues" of marriage, work, and religious worship. So what has gone wrong? Everything. A grimly brilliant set by Kurt Lundell, featuring curb-to-curb squalor beneath the roaring trains, corrugated iron shutters sealing off the abandoned storefronts, and ubiquitous grime and graffiti leavening all, makes the point (as does the play's title) that it is the brutalizing urban environment itself that centers this play: this is our "Street Scene" for the 90s, and the "villain" is Avenue U itself; the "boys," though this is no excuse (and the "girls" are proof of this), are simply locked in its thrall.

In its superb performance (at the John Houseman Theatre off-Broadway), *Aven' U Boys* is a hugely powerful work; it was not a commercial success, however, and closed much too soon to be seen widely. Nor has it been published as of this date (February 1994). A shame: this play is riveting and important; it's also well-constructed and in some scenes exquisitely detailed. I suspect Mr. Pugliese will favor us with more of his talent in the coming years, at which time *Aven' U Boys* will be brought back to the stage: it's a wake-up call, and a lot more besides.

Three important plays this season were composed essentially in monologues. This is not exactly a novelty—Brian Friel's outstanding *The Faith Healer* of a few seasons back is only one of the form's predecessors—but it seems to be a growing trend, possibly in response to economics among other things. I will discuss them in what is, in my opinion, descending order of importance.

Sherry Glaser's *Family Secrets,* which opened first in Los Angeles in 1993 and then in New York early in 1994 (where I saw it), comprises five sequential monologues delivered by five characters, all performed by Ms. Glaser, who makes her minimal costume and wig changes on stage without missing a beat. The altogether admirable text is by Glaser and her husband, Greg Howells, who also directs. The family that we see in *Family Secrets* is a father (Mort), his wife, their two daughters, and finally Mort's aged mother, all in that order; each has about twenty minutes to tell us his or her hopes, peeves, afflictions, miseries, and (occasionally) affections. Most of all this is played cozily right to the audience, though there are a few screams played straight to God, and most of the play (and it is a play) is hilarious—right to the unsentimental but deeply touching and life-affirming conclusion. The play and Ms. Glaser's performance have been widely compared to the Jane Wagner/Lily Tomlin *Search for Signs of Intelligent Life in the Universe* and, while it lacks the edginess of that other (and perhaps more brilliant) one-woman work, it delivers as powerful a "goose bump moment" at its end, and a more whole-bodied storyline in the preceding process. To talk of Glaser's play is to talk of her characters: particularly the women: Bev, the would-be Perfect Mom, who had a ten year nervous breakdown while trying to live up to her mother's expectations (and who eventually emerges flooded with tears as she digs her hands into her mother's ashes); Fern, the elder daughter and would-be free spirit, who experiences (while delivering her baby at home) an apocalyptic and all-but-unbearable catharsis; Sandra, the would-be punk teenager and blow-job champ, chafing in-

stead at the old parental bit; and now-widowed Grandma Rose, trembling, twinkling, and occasionally incontinent, in love again, and winsomely leading us in singing "Sunrise, Sunset" as she invites us over for Passover dinner. "Are you all Jewish" she asks us, amazedly, peering past the proscenium. Even the *goyim* want to say yes.

Who is Sherry Glaser? Or Greg Howells for that matter. All the program tells us is that she's a Bronx-born college drop-out with a background in improvisational comedy, and that he likes to be considered "the world's greatest substitute teacher." From such lean beginnings genius seems to be flowering: let it reach full bloom! Nothing is exactly startling here, but it's all first-class professional work, funny and moving, often inspired, and generally right in your face. Glaser's performance in the five roles, which she inhabits from top to bottom and from inside to out, is extraordinary.

Just three monologues suffice for the most intelligent American play of the season, and also one of the most successful. Jon Robin Baitz is one of America's most exciting young dramatists, and his *Substance of Fire,* though not one of my favorites, received a good deal of attention in 1991. His *Three Hotels* from the current season, though brief, is a small masterpiece. Set in an Edwardian suite in Tangier, a beachfront cabana in St. Thomas, and a corner

room in the Hotel Principal in Oaxaca, the 80-minute drama traces the breakup of a career and marriage, and the breakdown of two lives, with exquisite dramatic economy and intellectual finesse. The play is heartbreaking but brutally unsentimental.

Kenneth Hoyle (né Hirshovitz—Jewish assimilation is the theme of the year, it seems) is an ex-Peace Corpsman, now toughened into an international baby formula executive; his job is marketing the white stuff in the third world where it apparently does more harm than good, as his company is up there with Union Carbide and the Dalkon Shield on the *60 Minutes* hit list. Ken's particular specialty is firing staffers that don't live up to the company's corporate bloodthirst with the requisite enthusiasm; he's deliciously good at it as the play begins in the African suite. Quick cut to the Virgin Islands, where Barbara, Ken's Company Wife, is at her hubby's trade convention—"a sort of baby formula summit"—where she has just given a speech to the "Wives of Executives Stationed in the Third World." "Be Careful" was the title of her speech: Barbara and Ken's teenage son was murdered for his new Rolex six years ago on Copacabana Beach. Barbara's speech is infiltrated by feelings of guilt, loss, resentment and despair; as she sits in her cabana post-speech, she drifts into deeply worried incoherence. Quick cut one last time to the heart of Mexico: Ken's now been fired himself—three hours after Barbara's inchoate and overrevealing speech in St. Thomas—and she's subsequently disappeared; Ken's now hoping against hope to find her at their former honeymoon and favorite vacation spot. It's the Day of the Dead. "And in Mexico," Ken writes to his mother, "they don't look at death as a loss. It's an occasion for rejoicing." But he finds little to rejoice about as the play winds down.

The brevity and simplicity of this tale should not obscure the wondrous brilliance of its construction and the deep penetration of its perusal: these two characters have as full a life as any we are likely to see on a modern stage, and their breakup and breakdowns are symptomatic (and paradigmatic) of far larger conflicts. No mere indictment of capitalism (or marriage), *Three Hotels* is a powerful and compelling study of the most crucial and contemporary of free world dialectics; Baitz seamlessly mixes political, marital, economic, geographic, and social themes in a wholly human, profoundly moving nexus. Though a short play, every single line both adds to the story and cuts into its characters; Baitz' pen must have a diamond nib. The hotels of the title ("I came of age in hotels," Ken says, "in a hotel, nothing sticks") form a tragic counterpart to the home that corporate (and, often, contemporary) life denies. It's his mother who had a home and who has one now—the Jewish home for the Aged in Baltimore. Ken writes to her "Casting about for a history. Now. At this late date. Silly." Not silly at all. Though there is no interaction between characters, this is one of the most strongly plotted (one of the ONLY plotted) plays of 1993.

The third and possibly least successful play of monologues was *Life Sentences,* by Richard Nelson, an American living in England where he is often showcased by the Royal Shakespeare Company. Nelson was recently represented in New York by the excellent *Some Americans Abroad* and *Two Shakespearean Actors.* Like **Three Hotels, Life Sentences** portrays a tenuous couple, boyfriend-girlfriend in this case, with the "boy" a fortyish and rather mousy professor (Burke), and the "girl" his twenty-years-younger, slightly simple-minded live-in companion (Mia). Here the action takes place in and around Burke's house and office; in the first act Burke talks to us, in the second Mia does, and in a brief finale they both talk to us, and say a few words to each other as well. A third but non-appearing character—a Polish novelist and unkempt roué (sort of a Slavic Dylan Thomas) that Burke has invited as guest lecturer—centers much of the action by proving the object of Burke's and Mia's envy, admiration, ire, and desire. One can pretty well guess the slender story that unfolds, which has a depressing inevitability. The first part of the play premiered on public television a couple of years ago (as did **Three Hotels**—TV is of course a medium of monologues), and it has a quiet and intelligent domesticity throughout; unlike **Hotels,** however, it's more a vignette than a study, and more satiric than sad, with Nelson skewering, as in his *Americans Abroad,* feckless (male) academics and the dim-witted young women who (at first) idealize them. **Life Sentences** is continually apt, engaging and diverting, and it has a quiet but inexorable spiral of inner action which is no less attractive for being predictable. Its monologic form, moreover, gives a postmodern gloss to a premodern structure (essentially, this is a comedy of adultery), making its characters' self-consciousness a deliberate virtue. It's a nice play, but a slight one; I hope it spawns few imitators.

I'm going to add one more collection of monologues here, though there's little pretense that this one is a play at all. This is Eric Bogosian's persuasively violent **Pounding Nails in the Floor with my Forehead,** which like Glaser's work made it to New York in early 1994 after earlier appearances in L.A. (where I saw it) and elsewhere. Bogosian ends this piece exactly where you'd expect him to: kneeling on the stage, his forehead pounding the planks, his voice screaming for "Silence!" It is the epiphanic moment of the performance: a cry to still his own creativity, to wipe out the human pollution with which Bogosian sees the planet (and his own brain) violated, a pollution which he seems madly driven to personify.

For those not yet familiar with Bogosian's extraordinary work, which he writes as well as performs, it has—so far at least—largely comprised serial monologic presentations of characters drawn from a wide spectrum of (male) American life: human life, loosely considered. What Bogosian gives us is a modern-day (or postmodern-day) "Our Town," except that his town is New York, not Grover's Corners, and "the way we were, the living and dying" is nauseatingly contemporary: it's a world of thugs, racists, rapists, phone whores, drug dealers, con men, and corrupt practitioners of the once-nobler arts: medicine, law, even the arts of (postmodern) performance. Near-duplicate monodramas *Drinking in America* and *Sex, Drugs, Rock & Roll* preceded this one, but **Pounding Nails . . .** is Bogosian's best to date. On the surface, it is more of the (brilliant) same: a "dirty homeless bum from New York;" "Phil," a tormented solipsist nurturing his "inner baby" ("I have the tee shirts and the tote bags to prove my commitments"); "Red," a wildly inductive dope peddler; "Eric," a recovering male; and a savagely-observed over-prescribing physician, whose numbing list of side-effects is drolly dispensed to a terrified patient afraid even to question this patronizingly-cheery, white-coated abuse of every right known to man or woman. We, of course, are the patient, and we swallow hard between our bursts of laughter. Like its predecessors, **Pounding Nails . . .** is richly comic and deeply scary; it's at times virtually cathartic. But Bogosian has reached something of a pinnacle of mimicry by now: his voices are superb; they're virtually perfect replicas of persons we encounter rarely but recall acutely. What's more, the mimicry goes far beyond vocal sounds and gestures, it extends deep behind the actor's eyes: Bogosian replicates the gaze in which Our Town (New York—or Altoona) all too often fixates us and makes us tremble. He is one of the most truly frightening performers alive, no less so for being seductively funny. "I'm an animal; I eat, sleep, fuck and bite. All the rest is extra." says Bogosian, and he and we are equally implicated—and violated.

1993 was not a banner year for new musicals; one failure (**Goodbye Girl**) is noted above, and one immediately below, another (**Red Shoes**) closed immediately and two foreign imports (**Cyrano** and **Blood Brothers**) had receptions so cool I didn't get around to seeing them— particularly at $65 a ticket. Peter Townsend's *Tommy* was a certifiable hit, and a terrific show, but I reviewed its La Jolla opening in these pages last year, and have nothing to add at this point. So I am left to remark only about **Kiss of the Spiderwoman** for 1993 musicals; fortunately, **Kiss** is indeed quite remarkable. The piece, which began its life as a work-in-progress at the State University of New York, Purchase, four years ago, is adapted from the well-known political/sexual novel by the Argentinean Manuel Puig; the also-well-known adapters include Terrence McNally (book), John Kander (music), Fred Ebb (lyrics), and Harold Prince (director). Set in a Latin American jail, "sometime in the recent past," the play treats two cellmates, one (named Valentin) a political prisoner, and one (Molina) who's homosexual; basically the story traces the relationship—at first grudging and finally loving—that develops between them. Valentin is a neo-Marxist (or just a plain Marxist—we never get into these worrisome details, it's a musical, after all); he's been toughened rather than weakened through horrible torture. Molina has been jailed for pederasty; his prison preoccupation is recounting and recreating the roles of Aurora, his favorite movie star—in all roles but that of the Spiderwoman, whose kiss is death. The Spiderwoman has a life of her own in this jailhouse fantasy, however. Valentin appreciates the diversion of Molina's storytelling, but insists on drawing a demarcation line down the middle of their cell that Molina may not cross; by play's end, however, Molina (a spiderwoman in his own right) draws Valentin over the line, and they become not just cellmates but cell mates.

This is not an easy show to like: the torture scenes are unsparing and relentless, even if high-styled, and criminality is as ubiquitous even as it is official. An intentional case of food poisoning leads to an on-stage pants-soiling (and an attendant on-stage shit-clean-up); there are also on-stage beatings, deafenings, murder, and lots of blood. Photographs of the brutal regime's "disappeared" enemies, paraded by the cast in a powerful musical number, are woefully timeless, and obviously not limited to Latin America or past decades. Even the play's central sexuality—between a gay and a straight man—is skewed; it's prison sex, *No Exit* sex, and it's patronizing at best, betrayal and whoring at worst (Valentin submits to Molina, essentially, to get a note passed over the wall after Molina's release.) Sartre called this Hell fifty years ago, McGuinness show's it's Hell in **Someone Who'll Watch Over Me,** yet it's all we can point to as Love in the **Spiderwoman**'s world. And, as with Prince's signature work, *Cabaret,* there is no happy ending at the ending, only the forecast of much, much more of the same. Indeed, the strongest thing this show has going for it is neither its music nor its staging but it's reality: this is an Amnesty International musical and it works primarily on that level—as it must.

Plus it has a giant theatrical energy—one stemming as much from innovation as show-bizzy-ness—that has always been Prince's trademark. Spiderwebs sweep the stage, corpses dangle from electric fences, and jail doors clang open and shut with well-cadenced percussion. Projections limn the outside Latin world, and Chita Rivera, highstepping and cantilevering at age 60 or thereabouts in

the role of Aurora/Spiderwoman, carries us into escapism and fantasyland with an aplomb as sure as Joel Grey's MC in *Cabaret* thirty years ago. All in all, *Kiss of the Spider-woman* creates a uniquely entertaining sensationalism, with some stirring songs (including the *Les Miz*-inspired, revolutionary-heroic barricade-stormer, "The Day After That"), some sharp ironic sexual humor, and a good half-dozen fetching fantastical jailhouse reveries. And it's probably a good thing that the political debate is left to generalities; there's little audience support these days for neo-Marxist terrorism (even as up against neo-fascist tyranny), no matter how well sung.

The best musical premiering in America in 1993 will not be in New York until late next year. *Sunset Boulevard,* which opened in Los Angeles, is as close as one can come to a pseudo-baroque melodrama these days, and it's an absolutely wonderful one-of-a-genre, plopped down—as it seems to be—half-way between Hollywood and Beverly Hills, and only a few blocks from the eponymous Avenue itself.

The Andrew Lloyd Webber opus was put together by a great team of Broadway and British (West End/RSC) prize-winners, including Webber himself (music), Christopher Hampton and Don Black (book and lyrics), Trevor Nunn (direction), Bob Avian (musical staging), John Napier (sets), Anthony Powell (costumes) Andrew Bridge (lights) and Glenn Close (star); Lloyd Webber (who also produced) additionally managed to negotiate a $5 million renovation of the L.A. Shubert Theatre, pulling the mezzanine four rows closer to the action, and providing backstage space for what has been called the biggest set in the history of theatre (one unit alone—a palatial, Gothic-Rococo-Victorian two-story living room—is 32 feet high, weighs 30,000 pounds, and astonishingly it FLIES up, with Close and a few others still scrambling around inside it). Unlike other extravaganzas of this sort—including some under Webber's control—every artist and every dollar pulls his/her/its weight: *Sunset Boulevard* is a seamless and enthralling experience, fully justifying its record-setting (for L.A.) $65 ticket price.

L.A. is, of course, an ideal town for the American opening of this show; not only do the events take place in the geographical vicinity but in the local mindset as well: L.A. is a company town (it's really E.H.: Extended Hollywood) that all but dines on celebrity sex scandals; reprocessing them as movies-of-the-week, if not of-the-minute. And when the scandals come from show-biz itself, all the better. *Sunset Boulevard* is, of course, the hoary tale—initially a 1950 Billy Wilder film—of a silent film star ("Norma Desmond") forced into wealthy but lonely retirement when the movies turned to the talkies. Alone but for her faithful butler Max (whose own story eventually emerges), Norma has an accidental encounter with a disillusioned and penniless young writer, "Joe Gillis," who happens upon Norma's fabled mansion while fleeing a pair of thuggy creditors. Norma and Joe quickly fall into a rather pathetic symbiosis: Joe agrees to collaborate in a comeback script for Norma; Norma keeps Joe in a style to which he had never become accustomed. Champagne flows, music plays, and the bedroom beckons: Symbiosis

inevitably leads to a deepening—and deeply corrupting—sexual liaison, and Norma and Joe gradually raise the stakes from mutual employment, to exchanged gifts, to escalating threats of desertion, violence, and suicide. What really binds them, however, is not money or sex but the fantasy of the comeback (and, for Joe, the breakthrough); it's the eternal myth of The Big Star and The Big Picture. "Everyone needs new ways to dream," says (sings) Norma, but the real dreamers are the dream merchants themselves. "Animals, actors: two kinds of hell," says one of the film people early on: its a sentiment the L.A. audience knows and shares, and they're lapping it up.

The Big Star of the Big Play is Glenn Close, and she's stunning: an almost-Kabuki make-up job makes her facial language something of a perpetual close-up in the 2,000 seat house, and her fingers tell a story every moment she's on stage; it takes a star to play a star, and she's got it. Close has a resilient and capable voice, too, though it lacks the subtle dynamic control that could give more contours to her mid-level range; at very loud and very soft, however, she's terrific, and she's acceptable in all registers. Alan Campbell is appealingly sour as Joe Gillis, and George Hearn is also terrific as the sadly elegant, tuxedoed-and-white-gloved Max. Webber's score is sharper and more distinct than in recent outings, with some actual spoken text for punctuation this time, and some underscored recitative (some lifted directly from Wilder's film) that gives this play a more realistic (and American) feel than anything of his since *Evita*. There are also some real comedy numbers, and they work; rare in a Webber spectacle. The real star of the show, however, is John Napier, whose settings are TRULY breathtaking. In forty years of theatregoing, I have never said "Wow!" out loud during a scene shift; I did so at the Shubert Theatre, though, and I'm still THINKING "Wow!" as I write this down. And yet the effect that elicited this gasp was absolutely on thematic target: it was an airborne juxtaposition of the reel and the real, illusion (cinematographic) and delusion (personal), a magically enabling moment of super-scenography. Thanks to Webber, and director Nunn, too, for the commitment to expand our technological horizons at whatever cost. Few people have worked harder or more effectively to make the billion dollars or so they'll be getting from this.

John Patrick Shanley's *Four Dogs and a Bone* is this season's other satire of Hollywood filmmakers and how they ravage young actors and playwrights—and while it's generally witty and diverting, and occasionally harsh (verbally at least), it has none of the theatrical charisma of the grandiose *Sunset Boulevard,* nor the penetration of David Mamet's *Speed-the-Plow.* Rather, it's a brutal, brittle sequence of two-person dialogues that take place, over a day and night and morning after, between a film producer, a writer, a would-be ingenue, and a would-still-be ingenue. Notably (and predictably), the writer has his ideals to be sacrificed, the actresses compete to place their eternally-renewable virginities at fame's and fortune's disposal, and the producer, suffering from a giant cyst on his rectum, has only his "principles or demi-principles" to fall back on. The dialogue is bright, pointy, and tense. "I need a friend," chirps one character. "If you had a friend, you'd eat him," chirps back another. It matters little who said which (in fact, I can't even remember), but the irony is fetching, though the characters and story are limp. "Why do you hate Mark so much?" "Because he gave me pleasure when all I wanted was to be deeply disappointed." BRRRRONNNG goes the Brechtian rim shot: but where is Kurt Weill when we need him? What we have here is sort of a (mildly) wickeder Saturday Night Live, with fellatio jokes.

Shanley is one of our most promising playwrights and filmwriters, with a large following in the small theatre circuit (Manhattan Theatre Club, Circle in the Square, Ensemble Studio Theatre), and a much larger general public for his wondrous movie, *Moonstruck.* Here he is too obviously going for the easy laughs, and though he gets them he loses what is strongly appealing in his other works: the delicious agony of heartsickness. At the performance I saw, only Peter Jacobson, the understudy playing the producer, had any emotional momentum.

Two entirely lighthearted works appeared on Broadway without impacting theatre history in the slightest. ***Ain't Broadway Grand*** ("No, it ain't!" was the first line of *Variety*'s review) epitomized the sort of empty-headed do-nothing go-nowhere musical that has become all too common on New York's Entertainment Row in the past de-

cade or so. This is the story of the real Mike Todd (né Avrom Goldbogen; are we tired of this yet?) and how he dumbed down a (fictitious) 1948 Broadway musical from a pretentious avant-garde (well, Yalie-written, anyway) failure to a brainless, tits-and-ass commercial success. Which allows the current producers to palm off tits and ass as historically (and therefore apolitically) correct, and to rake in the proceeds in the process. But it is no go; stultifying (and continually-reprised) music, paste-on grins for acting, and a horribly embarrassing double-entendre scene in which we get the gags THE FIRST TIME, leaving nothing to entendre the second time around. A 1.0 on the Richter scale.

Fool Moon, however, was a true delight, though not dramatic at all; this is a two-part silent vaudeville with inspired mimists David Shiner and Bill Irwin. As they mercilessly cavort through and to the audience, dragging people onstage with them from time to time, the Richard Rogers Theatre virtually rocks off its foundations with massed convulsive laughter. There is little reason to describe the terrific production here—it has little place in "The Year in Drama" except for taking place in a legit New York theatre—but to suggest that a viewing might help anyone more fully understand the potentials—comic, violent, and epistemological—of pure mimesis.

In my end is my beginning: ***Angels in America*** remains the best play of the year, as it was the best play of last year when I initially reviewed it based on the Los Angeles production. Opening in New York in May, ***Millennium Approaches,*** the first half, walked off with the Tony and a Pulitzer (as predicted in these pages); ***Perestroika,*** the second half which is now somewhat rewritten, opened later in the Fall to mixed but still electrifying acclaim ("The broadest, deepest, most searching American play of our time," said *Newsweek*'s Jack Kroll). Cast changes from the L.A. production were in one case a strong plus and in no cases a debit; and even though I somewhat favored the earlier L.A. stage design, the N.Y. production was superb throughout and is surely not to be missed; the best new play I've seen in many years. An exhausting ritual, though, for cast as well as audience. At the preview I saw, Ron Liebman, performing in one play while still rehearsing the other, FELL ASLEEP on stage, right in the middle of one of his own scenes. No one in the audience did, however.

But the predominance of gay and Jewish themes (both of which figure in ***Angels,*** and one or both found their way into at least 16 plays reviewed above this year) certainly has some worrisome aspects for the theatre's future. So does the situation where nearly half of Broadway's plays cite earlier Broadway plays; some even end with characters singing songs from them. The extent to which gay and Jewish and theatrical preoccupations respond to the concerns of traditional theatre audiences—and theatre practitioners—is a measure of how much theatre has retreated from larger social issues, and indicates an unresponsiveness, in our mainstream theatre, to wider political fronts. The theatre is certainly not dying: its current fiscal health is remarkable. But there are limits to which the traditional theatre crowd attract a general public wholly on its own terms; and there are dangers in the theatre's becoming a solely fraternal, or sororal congregation of like-thinking and like-worshipping theatre buffs. "Are you all Jewish?" Rose asks the audience in *Family Secrets.* It's good for the play, but bad for the future of theatre (and I say this as a Jew myself), when most everyone laughingly nods yes.

The Year in World Literature

by William Riggan

The year 1993 was an excellent one in world literature, both in the quantity of significant works produced and in the quality of those works. Particularly impressive were the efforts of writers from India, China, Egypt, and Central Europe.

Asia

India's Vikram Seth created what was literally the year's biggest literary sensation with the publication of *A Suitable Boy,* the 1,350-page tale of a nice, quiet nineteen-year-old North Indian girl named Lata and her quest to find a husband in 1950 as the world's largest and youngest democracy prepares for its first general election and tries to decide on a suitable course for its future. Stately, conservative in style and temperament, kindly and charming in disposition, all-encompassing in its social and geographic reach, and using Jane Austen (with a touch of Tolstoy) as its model and inspiration, the work is major accomplishment by any measure and possesses the fullness of life of the great nineteenth-century novels it so well emulates.

In her carefully constructed novel *A River Sutra* Gita Mehta follows the experiences of a naïve and nameless Indian bureaucrat, "little brother," who retires to run a government rest house in the jungle along the sacred Narmada River, only to discover that the river's teeming traffic of people, stories, and passions makes it the last place on earth where he should have expected to be able to withdraw into contemplative solitude. Monks, teachers, executives, courtesans, and musicians all figure prominently in the many stories that unfold in the course of the narrative, stories whose sources, like those of the river itself, are the rich, deep founts of Indian mythology, archeology, and anthropology.

The grand old man of Indian letters, R. K. Narayan, issued three novellas under the title *The Grandmother's Tale.* The lead story involves a young bride's search for the child-groom who deserted her shortly after their arranged marriage, thus depriving her of all status and value. Over the course of the story she manages to locate him (he has remarried and resettled in a distant city), and—with the aid of the occult arts she has acquired—she reestablishes her position and name in his family. Her story takes a decidedly Gothic twist at its conclusion, when, upon her death, the husband again abandons his family and takes up with a seventeen-year-old girl from a nearby village. The second novella features a small-town official and petty racketeer in a tale of paranoid comedy, greed, and self-deceit. The third charts the comic and serendipitous course of a would-be romance novelist and her gourmet cook of a husband, whose many recipes and descriptions of banquets and feasts ultimately supplant the silly love story in which they are inserted; when the romance is finally jettisoned, the resulting cookbook becomes a runaway bestseller.

In *Red Sorghum* Mo Yan weaves five novellas into a seamless family portrait covering three generations in a township of China's Shandong Province. Concentrating on the lawless 1930s and the Japanese occupation but also touching on the Cultural Revolution and the post-Mao reform movements of the 1980s, the portrait that emerges is one of a society teetering on the edge of anarchy; with no central government left and every village practically forced to fend for itself, both the horror and the humor of the brutal, barbarous prewar and interwar years are brought to life in vivid detail. Mo's countryman Su Tong reissued his novella *Wives and Concubines* with two other narratives under the title *Raise the Red Lantern,* capitalizing on the fame of the Academy Award-winning film of that name by Zhang Yimou (who, incidentally, debuted in the early 1980s with a film version of *Red Sorghum*); the rechristened title story traces the fortunes of a young female student forced to give up her studies and marry into the household of an aging merchant, where her presumption and sensuality spark a series of intrigues and developments that lead inexorably to tragedy.

Japan's wildly successful and critically acclaimed novelist Haruki Murakami (famous abroad for *A Wild Sheep Chase* and *Hard-Boiled Wonderland and the End of the World*) brought out the first collection of his short stories in translation, *The Elephant Vanishes.* The book is comprised of seventeen first-person tales set not so much remote from ordinary life as hidden within it, in undiscovered alleyways, surreal corners of the most ordinary suburbs, and ever-so-efficient but slightly sinister factories that mass-produce elephants in assembly-line fashion. One narrator escapes from the "muddle" of his life through an elaborate twelve-step shirt-ironing ritual; another discovers that she no longer requires sleep and begins to spice up her routine days as a homemaker with daring nocturnal adventures; and an elephant-factory worker specializing in ears finds his dreams invaded by a dwarf who invites him to dance. In the title story the closing of a suburban zoo forces the community to make a painful decision regarding the old, unwanted elephant that was its main attraction; however, the affection between the animal and his longtime keeper is so profound that the two are rendered equal in size, allowing the beast to slip its chains and vanish with the keeper. So it goes in Murakami's inventive, dreamlike world.

Near East

Naguib Mahfouz, Egypt's 1988 Nobel Prize winner, saw his 1960s novella *Adrift on the Nile* make its belated appearance in translation; a slight but charming work that seeks to deal seriously with the spiritual anomie of the educated but powerless middle class, the rather static tale centers on the evening gatherings of a group of complacent and superfluous older men and their *kif*-clouded, self-indulgent discussions on all manner of social, cultural, and political topics. The invasion of the group by a woman journalist who does not share their torpor and cynicism and who plans to write a play about the circle shakes them out of their complacency and even leads them to abandon their houseboat for a foray into the city and the urban realities they have so long been denying; when tested, however, they of course fail miserably.

In the novellas *The Well of Life* and *The Thread,* published together in a single volume, Nawal El Saadawi, Egypt's most celebrated woman writer, presents two quasi-surreal narratives about oppressed women struggling to emancipate themselves from the control of men, whether husbands or fathers; in both stories everything that occurs is cast as strange and inexplicable, all actions unfold with the compulsive necessity of nightmare, and the reader is constantly made aware of a didactic message.

The Jordanian-born writer Abdelrahman Munif completed his epic *Cities of Salt* trilogy in 1993 with *Variations on Night and Day.* Where *Cities of Salt* and *The Trench* traced the development of the Sultanate of Mooran (a thinly disguised Saudi Arabia) from the discovery of oil in the 1930s by British and American groups through the 1950s, *Variations* returns to the opening decades of this century to reveal how the Sultan Khureybit consolidated his power and created Mooran as a modern nation-state. The detailed portrait of palace life, with its multiple intrigues among the Sultan's wives, sons, and adjutants, is as fascinating and revealing as the sweeping depiction of governments' and business leaders' machinations involving the emerging country and its vast economic potential.

In *Fima* Israel's Amos Oz takes us into what seems at first the depressingly squalid and chaotic life of fiftyish Efraim (Fima) Nisan, a lowly receptionist at a gynecological clinic. Fima has the messiest imaginable personal life and an obsession with such matters of the mind as politics, sex, guilt, metaphysics, ethical obligations, and questions of suffering and evil. Evidently emblematic of his generation of Israelis—idealistic, but reduced now to reading newspapers and arguing with the radio—Fima engages one's sympathy over the course of his nonstop monologue. Thus, when the "sad event" warned of in the novel's very first sentence actually occurs, Fima begins to draw on hitherto untapped resources of common sense, generosity, and purposefulness, and we witness with growing satisfaction the transformation of an individual into something larger and more fully human than he was at the outset.

In *Unto the Soul* Oz's countryman Aharon Appelfeld produces one of his most enigmatic tales yet. As in most of the author's earlier works, the setting is a world in ruins (nominally Ruthenia, in the western Ukraine)—austere, bleak, and almost claustrophobic in its sense of further impending doom. As a brother and sister charged with tending the Cemetery of Martyrs drift into forgetfulness, dissipation, incest, and sickness unto death, the allegory of resignation, disintegration, and imminent cataclysm becomes terrifying in its absoluteness and power.

Elsewhere in the Middle East, Latife Tekin, one of Turkey's finest young writers, made her debut in translation with *Berji Kristin: Tales from the Garbage Hills,* a largely plotless but wholly provocative and enjoyable novel that uses humor, fantasy, and playful exaggeration to depict the plight of migrants from the countryside struggling to survive in Istanbul.

Central and Eastern Europe

From the outstanding Czech novelist Ivan Klíma comes *Judge on Trial,* an emotionally wrenching epic tale of justice and conscience and memory set in the aftermath of the 1968 Soviet invasion. Handed a spectacular murder trial by government and party officials, the apostate jurist Adam Kindl finds his conscience, loyalties, and career suddenly thrown under an intense scrutiny every bit as rigorous as that of the actual defendants. The resulting turmoil—Kindl tries to sort out the many contradictions of his family and love life and balance the will of the party against his own personal and juristic convictions—is evoked with both wit and passion. Originally issued in *samizdat* form in 1978 but only now finding sanctioned publication, the work is generally regarded as Klíma's masterpiece, a vivid and compelling portrait of a generation forced to witness the dissolution of its ideals and the destruction of its accomplishments.

In *The Little Town Where Time Stood Still* Klíma's countryman Bohumil Hrabal offers a more easygoing, low-key, and seemingly effortless account of two family histories: one in "a far-off country of which we know nothing" but which closely resembles the interwar Czech republic, and the other in postwar Czechoslovakia dominated in all aspects by communism. These stories were heavily cut and radically "adjusted" by Writers Union censors when they were originally submitted for publication in 1973; invoking one (usually mundane and unheroic) reality to ridicule the political situation, Hrabal enraged officials. The stories now stand fully restored both in the original and in the new English translation. No overt antitotalitarian blasts here, just the charmingly idiosyncratic creation of a minutely examined, matter-of-fact provincial world broken by constant ripples of amusement.

The Slovak writer Martin Šimečka was honored with the Mobil Corporation's 1993 Pegasus Prize for his novel *The Year of the Frog,* originally issued in the mid-eighties as an underground "padlock" series of three novellas, then commercially published as a complete book in 1990 after the fall of the communist government. The story concerns the coming of age of a young man, the son of a famous dissident, in an oppressive society that severely limits his options. The narrative mirrors the author's own experience as the son of a leading historian who was imprisoned by Communists for his outspoken views but who later became an adviser to Václav Havel during the "velvet revolution."

In *The Inner Side of the Wind* the Serbian novelist Milorad Pavić produced another of his imaginatively inventive fictional experiments, recasting the ancient story of Hero and Leander in a double narrative beginning literally at opposite ends of the book and set simultaneously in the seventeenth and twentieth centuries. The Leander figure is now an illiterate stonecutter-turned-monk in Belgrade of the 1600s whose picaresque story is alternately hilarious and horrifying. Hero is Heronea Bukur, a struggling university student in the 1930s who suffers through several misadventures in Belgrade and has a passionate love affair in Prague that ends tragically—at least according to one of the versions given by others in the tale. Little is ever fully conclusive in Pavić's fiction.

The Hungarian Péter Lengyel's 1988 novel *Cobblestone* became available to a worldwide audience in English translation in 1993, presenting "a philosophical mystery for the millennium" (i.e., 1896's thousand-year celebration of the founding of the Magyar nation). The novel is a fascinating suspense tale about a polyglot gang of safecrackers in fin-de-siècle Austria-Hungary and a richly informative lesson in Central European history chronicling the glory days of the Habsburg empire in the late nineteenth century, the Stalinist era of the 1950s, and the moral and social morass of the Kadar regime's "gulash communism." The Romanian émigré author Norman Manea followed up his dual success of 1992, represented by the essay volume *On Clowns* and the short story collection *October, Eight O'Clock,* with another volume of short fiction, *Compulsory Happiness;* its four novellas present an appalling panorama of human cruelty and suffering, including one of the most horrific and prolonged prison interrogations yet recounted. Albania's Ismail Kadare saw his controversial 1990 fable on totalitarianism, *Palace of Dreams,* rendered into English at the same time that he brought out a new work, *Claire de Lune.* This brief novel of manners and morals revolves around the efforts of a modern-day Virgin Mary to clear her name and honor in the face of calumnious lies told by her neighbors and acquaintances. She must also deal with the mysterious birth of a child.

In the starkly titled *Fear* the Russian novelist Anatoly Rybakov presents a stunning account of the Stalinist purges through the story of a young school-newspaper editor whose one casual, impolitic remark sends him to prison and Siberian exile. The novel is set during an era of mass arrests, torture, sham trials, terror, and death on an unimaginable scale, and the direct rendering of Stalin's mind and personality is the most profound and deft since Solzhenitsyn's memorable chapter in *The First Circle* over twenty years ago. Viktoria Tokareva, long known to her Russian compatriots for her filmscripts and slightly zany tales of ordinary people, at last reached a wider audience with *The Talisman, and Other Stories.* Making the best of a passable marriage, escaping a really bad one, surviv-

ing divorce, avoiding loneliness at all costs, and finding someone decent (or at least good-looking) are the predominant themes here; there is almost no intrusion of ideology, religion, or current affairs. True to the spirit of her model, Chekhov, Tokareva overcomes any sentimental tendencies with a healthy dose of cynicism, a sharp eye for the ridiculous, and a clear conviction that common decency is the very least one should expect in relations with one's fellow human beings. The equally popular novelist Sergei Zalygin was introduced to the West in 1993 through the translation of his tragic and compelling 1975 novel *The Commission.* Concerning a group of village leaders charged with guarding and maintaining a valuable forest near their Siberian home in 1918, the story takes place just after Russia withdrew from World War I and before Lenin and the Bolsheviks had firmly established Soviet power over many parts of Russia. Though politically correct for the 1970s USSR in its portrait of strong, wise, incorruptible peasants standing firm against greedy *kulaks* and various enemies of the Revolution, the novel nevertheless possesses considerable impact and vitality.

Africa and the West Indies

South Africa's André Brink brought out the English version of his captivating 1988 novella *Cape of Storms,* a mythic tale told from the nominally native perspective of the fabled giant T'kama (a reincarnation of the untamed giant Adamastor alluded to by Rabelais and developed later by the Portuguese poet Camões), about the first encounter between Europeans and Africans five centuries ago when Vasco da Gama sailed around the Cape of Good Hope. In his even newer novel *On the Contrary* Brink again moves far afield from his earlier angry antiapartheid novels. Here he returns to the South Africa of the early eighteenth century to tell the story of the French-born adventurer Estienne Barbier's three eventful journeys into "the dark heart of Africa" and his emergence as an unlikely leader of rebel Afrikaner colonists in their struggles with the corrupt East India Company.

In *The Powers That Be* Brink's countryman Mike Nicol recounts the story of Enoch Mistas, a black youth with a Bible chained to his wrist and strange voices in his head who leads a messianic uprising against an imperious and bewildered government. Born immediately following a period of severe drought and plague, Mistas becomes the anointed redeemer of his downtrodden people, gathering unto him the poor and the disenfranchised in such numbers that the mere rumor of their existence incites unrest throughout the land and precipitates an apocalyptic confrontation with governmental forces. In the aftermath the fate of Mistas remains uncertain, clouded over by official lies, journalistic speculation, and an ever-growing layer of folklore.

The young Nigerian author Ben Okri, winner of England's prestigious Booker Prize a couple of years back for his novel *The Famished Road,* returned in 1993 with *Songs of Enchantment,* at least nominally a sequel to its predecessor. Drawing extensively on Yoruba mythology, Okri creates an African town in which spirits interact freely with humans, bringing miracles but also cataclysmic disasters. The narrator Azaro, for instance, is an *abiku,* a child destined to die young, be reborn, and return quickly to the spirit world in a heartbreaking cycle, "unable to come to terms with life." The world depicted is such a surreal, capricious, and phantasmagoric one, however, that many readers and admirers of Okri have come away disappointed, finding mainly repetition and synesthetic overload where enchanted fantasy and mythic flights of imagination were evidently intended.

Caryl Phillips of St. Kitts in the Caribbean followed up his successful books *Higher Ground* and *Cambridge* with *Crossing the River,* which presents four interrelated narratives involving, respectively: an American tobacco planter who sets out for West Africa in 1841 in search of his former slave who is now a missionary; a series of letters from this missionary to his former master describing his life since liberation; the log of a slave ship in Africa in 1752; and an interracial love affair in besieged Yorkshire during World War II. All four strands, like the author's earlier novels, "derive their structure from the forced relocations of the slave trade and their moral power from a depiction of human goodness surviving degradation." In this case the degradation concerns slavery, particularly the sale of children, and *Crossing the River* succeeds as another extremely forceful performance from Phillips.

In his twenty-first novel, *Resurrection at Sorrow Hill,* Guyana's Wilson Harris creates an imaginary realm at the confluence of three rivers in his native land where an "asylum for the greats" has been established, including among its inmates Monty the Venezuelan (Montezuma), Len the Brazilian (Leonardo da Vinci), Socrates, Buddha, and Marx. There is also Hope—who scripts the entire comedy we are reading, edited by "Wilson Harris"—and his adversary Christopher D'eath. They are all attended by Doctor Daemon, who encourages them to play out parables of human dilemmas, notably those emphasizing both the desire for revenge and the need for compassion in the wake of such violations as the Conquest. As always with Harris, his newest work requires, in his own terms, "the closest attention to density" in order to navigate the ambivalence and flux of its tone and the obstinate difficulty of its language and images.

Harris's countryman Roy Heath, in *From the Heat of the Day,* charts his typical "downward path to wisdom," here focusing on the vicissitudes in the marriage of a middle-class woman and a once-ambitious provincial who settles for the dull but steady life of a postal clerk. The charting of the slow shifts over time in the couple's feelings for each other is subtle and supple, and the brief epiphanies that punctuate their lives are lyrical and often dryly comic, with darker and more tragic currents coursing at least one or two levels below the surface.

France

Of the many fine works of fiction and poetry published in French in 1993, perhaps none had a more powerful impact than the late Hervé Guibert's *Paradise,* a novel in which fiction is progressively replaced by autobiography as the protagonist and his female companion both take ill during one of their frequent foreign jaunts with what seems at first only some inconvenient infection. Slowly, inexorably, tragically, however, the illness is revealed to be AIDS as it robs him more and more of vitality, strength, memory, lucidity, and finally life.

Another very different work which appeared posthumously in 1993 was *Conte bleu,* a surrealistic prose poem by the late grande dame of French letters, Marguerite Yourcenar, about mysterious jeweled treasures, an exotic slave girl, avaricious European traders, ruthless pirates, and fantastical sea creatures. The conte was issued together with two other short tales: "The First Evening," written with her father and first published in 1929; and "Maleficence," a curious piece involving tuberculosis and exorcism and first issued in 1933.

Le secret (*The Secret*) by Philippe Sollers bends the conventions of the spy thriller into what one perceptive critic has termed "a static but highly combative analytic novel" that takes off from a lengthy foray into an assassination plot against the pope and expands its circle of attention to encompass such disparate activities as narcotics trafficking, sperm banks, genetic engineering, the international media, and ethnic cleansing. In *Olivier et ses amis* (*Olivier and His Friends*) Robert Sabatier presents a gentle, colorful, and picturesque narrative set in Montmartre a generation ago. Daniel Boulanger's *Ursacq* offers a tale of quiet desperation and painful solitude in the story of the seventyish manager of a provincial auction house who seeks out the company of academics and prostitutes and ultimately succeeds in getting the memoirs of one of his "ladies" published shortly after her death, only to be forced into retirement over the resulting scandalous publicity. Chantal Chawaf uses the myth of Demeter and Persephone to undergird the haunting story told in *Vers la lumière* (*Toward the Light*) of a woman drawn ineluctably by the ghostly illuminated figure of her late mother toward her own death by drowning.

Germany

Following *Die Verteidigung der Kindheit* (*The Defense of Childhood*), his 1991 magnum opus on the tragic absurdity of the two former Germanies, Martin Walser returned in 1993's *Ohne einander* (*Without Each Other*) to his lifelong topics of human frailty, the artificiality of marriage, and the inability of hearts and minds to come to terms with love. Set amid the literary and journalistic community—and readable as a roman à clef for those privy to that world in any degree—the novel is an excruciating and excoriating examination of the infinite ways in which lovers, marriage partners, parents, and offspring constantly and unavoidably disappoint, injure, demean, and betray one another. Enormously entertaining despite its depressing subject, the book has become the year's biggest bestseller in Germany.

In *"Ich"* (*"I"*) Wolfgang Hilbig draws from today's headlines and the continuing revelations of the past four years for his account of a writer and *Stasi* (State Security) informant in East Germany prior to the collapse of the Wall; the story winds back upon itself when "Reader," the object of "I's" scrutiny, turns out to be a *Stasi* snitch as well, and again when Feuerbach, the *Stasi* contact, reveals his own literary aspirations. Written with the aid of several actual informants, the book is a significant document on the abuse of power, the corruption of language, and the distortion of essential human values within the former Democratic Republic.

The Swiss-German novelist Adolf Muschg took a loftier road in **Der Rote Ritter** (*The Red Knight*). A thousand-page recasting of the Parsifal story, the novel follows its hero from his youth as a "guileless fool," to his knightly adventures and his journey from ignorance and confusion to wisdom and grace, through to his attainment of the Holy Grail. The result is a marvelous epic of self-development and self-perfection, a bildungsroman par excellence that has been drawing comparisons to such revered classics as Thomas Mann's *Joseph* tetralogy and Goethe's *Wilhelm Meister* volumes. A stunning, edifying, and truly monumental achievement.

Other

Dacia Maraini produced perhaps the year's best-received and best-selling novel in Italy, **Isolina,** which fleshes out the true story of a poor but fun-loving and attractive young girl whose body was found floating in the river at Verona in January 1900, the victim of a botched abortion. The Basque novelist Bernardo Atxaga (nom de plume of Joséba Irazu Garmendia) enjoyed worldwide success with **Obabakoak,** a wildly imaginative set of tales revolving primarily around the Basque town of Obaba but ranging widely in space and time and in styles of writing; the book was described by one reviewer as "a delicious literary paella." Brazil's grand old man of letters, Jorge Amado, saw his twenty-first and newest novel, **The War of the Saints,** rendered into English and distributed worldwide in celebration of his eightieth birthday; set amid the mulatto culture of the northeastern Bahia province, the story is a typically lively, carnivalesque narrative infused with magic realism, in which statues come to life and rescue young lovers from the clutches of puritanical elders and in which many a sacred cow—whether political, religious, academic, or ideological—is brilliantly skewered. It is a wholly joyous and vibrant creation. And lastly, from Mexico came Elena Poniatowska's **Tinísima,** a massive but vividly readable portrait of Tina Modotti, an Italian-born photographer, social militant, and communist who lived in Mexico in the 1920s and participated actively in the country's cultural, intellectual, and political life. Through Tina's story the author composes a vivid picture of Mexico in the first half of this century, depicting its culture, ideals, political machinations, revolutionary struggles, hopes, and illusions from the unique perspective of a foreign woman.

Notes on Contributors

Robert Cohen is professor of Drama at the University of California, Irvine, and the author of *Acting in Shakespeare.* He has written several highly-regarded theater books and treatises, including *Theatre Giraudoux: Three Faces of Destiny; Acting Power: An Introduction to Acting; Acting One; Acting Professionally: Raw Facts about Careers in Acting; Creative Play Direction;* and *Theatre.* He contributes essays to various academic and theater journals and has reviewed "The Year in Drama" for *Contemporary Literary Criticism* since 1986. A professional stage director as well, Cohen is co-artistic director of Theatre 40 in Los Angeles and a regular guest director at the Colorado and Utah Shakespeare Festivals. He holds a Doctorate in Fine Arts from the Yale School of Drama and has lectured widely on theatrical topics in the United States and abroad.

Allen Hoey is the author of *A Fire in the Cold House of Being,* a verse collection chosen by Galway Kinnell for the 1985 Camden Poetry Award. An Associate Professor in the Department of Language and Literature at Bucks County Community College outside of Philadelphia, Hoey has contributed poems and essays to such journals as the *Georgia Review,* the *Hudson Review,* the *Ohio Review, Poetry, Southern Humanities Review,* and the *Southern Review.* He holds an M.A. and a D.A. from the English Department of Syracuse University. *What Persists,* his most recent collection of poetry, was published in 1992.

Wendy Lesser is the founding editor of the *Threepenny Review.* She is also the author of three books of cultural criticism: *The Life Below the Ground: A Study of the Subterranean in Literature and History, His Other Half: Men Looking at Women Through Art,* and most recently, *Pictures at an Execution.* A regular contributor to the *New York Times Book Review,* the *New Republic,* and other periodicals, Lesser holds a Ph.D. in English from the University of California, Berkeley, an M.A. from King's College, Cambridge, and a B.A. from Harvard University.

William Riggan is Associate Editor of *World Literature Today* and an expert on Third World, Slavic, Anglo-American, and smaller European literatures. The author of *Picaros, Madmen, Naïfs, and Clowns: The Unreliable First-Person Narrator,* Riggan has written extensively on the history of both the Nobel and the Neustadt International Prizes in Literature. He also regularly reviews new foreign poetry and fiction for several journals and newspapers.

New Authors

Roberto Calasso

The Marriage of Cadmus and Harmony

Calasso is an Italian novelist, nonfiction writer, essayist, and publisher, born in 1941.

INTRODUCTION

The first of Calasso's works to be translated into English and published in the United States, *Le nozze di Cadmo e Armonia* (*The Marriage of Cadmus and Harmony*) delineates the ancient Greek myths that have influenced Western culture. The work opens with the abduction of Europa by Zeus, chronicles the complex interwoven myths concerning their descendants, and concludes with the marriage of Cadmus and Harmony, which was supposedly the last time the gods interacted with mortals. In retelling these tales, Calasso examines their focus on rape and other acts of violence which characterized the relationship between humanity and the gods. Calasso also illuminates the influence of the ancient myths on Western thought and language. Although most critics have noted that *The Marriage of Cadmus and Harmony* resists placement in a single literary genre, the work is most frequently classified as a novel, with many commentators attributing the book's success to the author's lucid and engaging approach to storytelling. Simon Schama commented: "Calasso has not been content to describe or analyze this rich garment of myth. He has spun and woven it from new yarn, so that we experience its power as we are learning its complexity. His is a book rich in anthropological insight, but it will be read and re-read not as treatise but as *story:* one of the most extraordinary that has ever been written of the origins of Western self-consciousness."

CRITICISM

Mary Lefkowitz   (review date 14 March 1993)

[*Lefkowitz is an American professor of Greek and Latin whose critical studies include* The Lives of the Greek Poets *(1981) and* Women in Greek Myth *(1986). In the following review, she praises Calasso's "vivid and entertaining" rendering of ancient Greek myths in* The Marriage of Cadmus and Harmony.]

There were no mythology books in fifth-century Athens.

Everyone knew the stories. Boys were taught to recite Homer's accounts of Achilles' anger and the return of Odysseus, and other epic poems recounted the myths of the love affairs of the gods and the adventures of the famous heroes. Myths were related to women working at their looms, and male citizens could watch how the dramatists would tell the same stories in new and exciting ways.

But after the mid-fourth century, when King Philip of Macedon defeated Athens, and his son Alexander, through his conquests, spread Greek culture throughout the Mediterranean area, the first Greek mythology books were written for the many people who did not know the stories. Perhaps the most influential surviving example of this genre is the epic *Metamorphoses* or *Transformations,* by the Roman poet Ovid, which recounts in Latin verse how certain mortals were turned into animals or plants as a result of their encounters with the gods.

Christian writers usually preferred to tell the old stories in bowdlerized form, with oblique references to sex and

39

emphasis on whatever moral lessons might be learned from the myths: do not boast that you are better than a god unless you want to end up as a rock, like Niobe, or as a spider, like Arachne. Do not try to emulate the gods or, like Tantalus, throughout eternity you will hunger after food that is always being snatched away from you. When rewriting accounts of abductions of women by gods, Victorian mythology books emphasized romance and adventure. Readers could learn how Europa rode off happily on a beautiful white bull, without reflecting how she felt when she discovered that her new pet was, in fact, the god Zeus, and what exactly it was that Zeus did to her so that she became the mother of Minos, King of Crete.

How different is the vivid and entertaining narration of the same tales offered by the Italian author and publisher Roberto Calasso in *The Marriage of Cadmus and Harmony,* first published in Italy in 1988 and now translated by Tim Parks. Like Ovid, Mr. Calasso is fascinated by metamorphosis and the processes by which changes of shape and status occur. But Ovid's account is restrained by comparison. In Mr. Calasso's re-creation of the myths, desire is the key to the most significant action, and he makes it abundantly clear why Zeus was attracted to Europa, or why Dionysus came to the rescue of Ariadne after she was abandoned by Theseus, or why women seem to figure in, and ruin, the life of every famous hero.

The women and goddesses in the stories are equally affected by passion and hardly innocent of where their desires will lead them. Mr. Calasso makes it easy for us to understand why Theseus so appealed to Ariadne that she was willing to show him how to kill the Minotaur and get out of the labyrinth, even though it meant betraying her father, Minos, and leaving her palace home.

Like Ovid, Mr. Calasso has a distinct authorial presence; he offers judgment on both characters and stories, and on their relationship to the modern world. But where Ovid treats his characters with mild condescension and some irony, Mr. Calasso treats them with the kind of respect believing pagan writers like Homer and Callimachus might have given them. Also unlike Ovid, Mr. Calasso often provides several different versions of a story, so that his readers can see the various potential meanings a myth can have.

His book begins with the story of Europa and the bull. Mr. Calasso tells the story several times over, each time offering the reader more interesting details culled from the original narrative. And then, as if by association, he takes us through virtually all the other myths, until eventually we get to the title story, the marriage of Cadmus and Harmonia, here called Harmony to emphasize the meaning of her name. Cadmus found Harmony while searching for his sister Europa, who had disappeared from Sidon while gathering flowers with other girls of her age. Zeus had taken her to Crete, and from there she gave her name to the whole continent of Europe. As Mr. Calasso sees it, Cadmus' marriage marks the beginning of the cycle of the myths that laid out the basic patterns for later European fiction.

This conscious choice of a frame to his narrative suggests

that Mr. Calasso has written a work designed explicitly for the culture of the 1990's. Other myth books, even Ovid's, begin with an account of the origins of the world, the birth of Earth from the Void and Earth's marriage with Heaven. But Mr. Calasso is writing for an audience that is more interested in the interaction of gods with men and (especially) women than in rehashings of the origins of gods who in its opinion never really existed. As a result of this disbelief, Mr. Calasso's gods seem more like powerful human beings than the slow but relentless enforcers of justice in whom the ancient Greeks for centuries believed.

But along with the absence of morality in Mr. Calasso's narrative comes a refreshing absence of moralizing that modern readers are certain to appreciate. Instead, he pauses to explain how the stories are connected with the lands and the natural world in which they are set. Like Ovid, he is not particularly interested in the connection of these myths with actual religious practice, and like most ancient writers of mythology he assumes that the way in which the stories were told did not change over time. Occasionally he offers some very general reflections on the meaning of the myths, which do not so much challenge his readers to think hard about what they have been reading as reassure them that they have without real effort experienced something deeply significant.

This desire to remain at a respectful distance from the ancient world keeps Mr. Calasso's book, for all its real learning, from being a work of scholarship. But neither was Ovid's *Metamorphoses.* Rather, it was a serious entertainment, meant to be enjoyed in the process, but to leave the reader with some lingering sense that what seemed remote and forgotten is in some way part of his own very different world.

> *Mary Lefkowitz, "A Zeus for the 90's," in* The New York Times Book Review, *March 14, 1993, p. 12.*

Merle Rubin   (essay date 6 April 1993)

[*In the following essay, Rubin describes Calasso's delineation of ancient Greek myths as "one of the most comprehensive and comprehensible modern attempts at re-creating this vanished world" of classical antiquity.*]

What is at once so familiar and so strange as the world of the Greek myths? The nightly skies are strewn with planets and constellations bearing the Greek or Roman names of mythical gods and heroes: Jupiter, Venus, Mars, Orion, the Pleiades. English literature glitters with allusions to Apollo, Pan, Odysseus, Troy, the Muses, Helen, Leda and the Swan.

Classical values are woven into the fabric of Western culture. Classical ideals of self-government informed the thought of America's founding fathers and also inspired the authors of the French Revolution. Concepts of athletic competition, geometry, metaphysics, and aesthetics also owe much to classical models.

Yet, how alien and archaic this vanished world sometimes seems: a world of omens and oracles, where the sacred and the profane mingled close at hand and a polytheistic pantheon of gods and goddesses seemed to spend most of their time acting out a lurid soap opera of passion, jealousy, revenge, seduction, and abduction, with a hefty measure of metamorphosis thrown in to keep things moving. Nor is there any single source or sacred text, like the Bible or the Koran, to which the reader can turn to study Greek mythology.

As the Italian author and editor Roberto Calasso points out in *The Marriage of Cadmus and Harmony,*

> The Greeks were unique among the peoples of the Mediterranean in not passing on their stories via a priestly authority. They were rambling stories, which is partly why they so easily got mixed up. And the Greeks became so used to hearing the same stories told with different plots that it got to be a perfectly normal thing for them.

What we know of Greek mythology comes from many sources: statues, temples, coins, inscriptions, and of course literature—from the solemn works of Homer to the playful writings of Ovid and the disbelieving satires of Lucian.

Calasso draws on a vast array of variant myths and stories and molds them into a single text, which—though scarcely definitive—may still be one of the most comprehensive and comprehensible modern attempts at recreating this vanished world.

Part narrative, part meditation, this marvelously engrossing book plunges the reader right into the thick of the mythological action with its opening scene, in which Zeus, disguised as a bull, carries off a girl called Europa from the coastline of Asia to the island of Crete. There, her descendants, the lonely, monstrous Minotaur and his sister Ariadne, will play their parts in the story of Theseus, founder of Athens.

Meanwhile, Europa's brother Cadmus, sent to search for his abducted sister, ends up founding the city of Thebes, saving Zeus himself from a primordial monster, and marrying the lovely Harmony, daughter of Ares and Aphrodite.

Winding his way through the maze of these and other stories with clarity and brio, Calasso illuminates the twists and turns of plot linking one myth to another, while elucidating the underlying themes and patterns that give each myth a ghostly resemblance to other myths. Again and again, there are heroes who slay monsters, heroines who betray their countries to bestow themselves on monster-slaying heroes from afar. Everywhere, one finds abandoned women who hang themselves, youths and maidens who transform themselves into trees and flowers to avoid the pursuit of gods who, in turn, transform themselves into snakes, bulls, swans, eagles, and wolves to seduce their human lovers.

Calasso's concise, straightforward style of storytelling untangles the most complicated plots, while his pithy comments on Greek culture and politics provide substantive food for thought. In the eternal shenanigans of the Olympian deities, he recognizes the human spirit's desire for a world of greater freedom and playfulness.

The Olympians, he reminds the reader, realized the over-whelming power of Ananke, or Necessity. Yet "they preferred to make believe that they were subject to Eros just as much as to Ananke, though all the time aware that . . . this was just a blasphemous fraud." Ananke's inescapable net of circumstance is camouflaged by Aphrodite's brightly hued girdle of romantic illusion, because if "Ananke commands alone, life becomes rigid."

Many of Calasso's insights are not new: the idea of Greece as an aesthetic culture, the notion of Sparta as a forerunner of the modern totalitarian state, and the linking of Apollo and Dionysus as interrelated opposites. Minds as diverse as Matthew Arnold, Friedrich Nietzsche, and I. F. Stone have explored similar terrain, often more brilliantly and more thoroughly.

But Calasso's emphasis on telling the stories rather than analyzing them—or, more accurately, telling them with just enough analysis to make them more lucid and intriguing—is a refreshing approach. It differs from Mary Renault's approach. Whereas the author of *The Bull from the Sea, The King Must Die,* and other books, wrote full-fledged novels making imaginative use of modern fictional techniques to capture the flavor of an archaic sensibility, Calasso's work is closer to an anthology, albeit one in which the collected stories are sinuously intertwined. It is a work of power and grace. These qualities are apparent even in the rather clumsy English translation by Tim Parks.

> *Merle Rubin, "A World of Omens and Oracles," in* The Christian Science Monitor, *April 6, 1993, p. 11.*

The New Yorker (essay date 12 April 1993)

> [*In the following article, the critic describes a panel discussion in which Calasso and several prominent writers commented on* The Marriage of Cadmus and Harmony.]

The gods of literature are on a first name basis, and this was never more in evidence than last Friday night, when Joseph, Susan, and Simon gathered on the second floor of the Italian Consulate, at Park Avenue and Sixty-ninth Street, to pay homage to a new book by Roberto. The book is *The Marriage of Cadmus and Harmony,* a heady but crowd-pleasing meditation on Greek mythology, which is just coming out in this country, from Knopf, after several prize-winning years in Europe; Roberto is Roberto Calasso, the publisher of Adelphi Edizioni, which is the Knopf of Milan; Joseph, Susan, and Simon are, of course, Joseph Brodsky, Susan Sontag, and Simon Schama. Leon Wieseltier, of *The New Republic,* who was the moderator, said, simply, "I won't introduce the panelists. You know who they are." Derek—that's Walcott to ordinary mortals—was there, too, sitting off to the right in the front row; Oliver (Sacks) was way in the back; and the dapper gentleman chewing his pipe was greeted by everyone, in the one exception to the first-name rule, with kisses on both cheeks and an Italian-inflected cry of "Professor Eco!"

If the number of laureates and luminaries gathered to hear readings from Roberto's work suggested that the evening was an occasion for international glittery hobnobbing, or that the book is sexy because of his reputation as a jet-setting publisher, this impression was corrected—or at least substantially revised—when Leon Wieseltier started talking soberly about how long it's been since myths were valued as truths, as real explanations for the governing principles of nature and human life. He asserted that, in spite of having given up belief in myths, we still look for meaning in them. "Think of meaning as the poor man's truth," he said. From that moment on, the evening was one of high-velocity intellectual traffic—as tough as a grad-school seminar, but grander, and more entertaining. Joseph claimed that the tone of *The Marriage of Cadmus and Harmony* is godly, because, like the gods, it is intimate and highly impersonal at the same time, and he proposed that Roberto himself had been invaded by one of the gods—or, at least, become the mouthpiece for one of them. Susan explained what makes a book "noble"—it must invoke something from the past, some historic milestone or ancient struggle—and Simon discoursed on the schism between the poetic and the rational in the study of history, the two poles personified originally by the fanciful historian Herodotus and the facts-are-facts historian Thucydides. He praised Roberto for uniting the poetic and the rational voices, and then, as illustration, read a favorite passage from Roberto's book, on the implications of Sparta.

The Marriage of Cadmus and Harmony is not fiction, history, or literary criticism, not a collection of aphorisms or rhapsodic Cliffs Notes on the classical, but a little of all these; like the deities themselves, it is constantly changing form.

—*The New Yorker*

Roberto himself, dressed in a publisher's elegant blue suit, but with a writer's flash in his eye and stray lock of hair on his brow, sat in the first row listening intently. He joined the panelists after their tributes, and when a member of the audience asked him if his book was postmodern he replied fervently, "I never felt in my life the need of using the word 'postmodern.' " Then he smoked pensively and sparred with Susan about whether or not the fact that he is a man had any impact on his approach to the ancient gods and heroes. "Susan, do I need to remind you that literature is genderless?" he demanded. The discussion that followed was nothing like the usual polite and politically correct panel chat at New York literary events; it was more like a rarefied argument between Talmudic scholars long familiar with each other's biases, or—to take a prototypical debate much analyzed by the panelists—the argument between Zeus and Hera over who gets more pleasure from sexual intercourse, the man or the woman.

Neither Susan nor Simon nor Joseph could quite define what kind of book *The Marriage of Cadmus and Harmony*

really is, and it was this that seemed to delight them most. Apparently, it is not fiction, history, or literary criticism, not a collection of aphorisms or rhapsodic Cliffs Notes on the classical, but a little of all these; like the deities themselves, it is constantly changing form. Joseph said, "It combines—well, God knows what! Sometimes it lurches into poetry." He gave an example, declaiming a few lines about the isle of Leuke in his sonorous Russian accent:

> It's an island for castaways and people who want to offer up a sacrifice. No one has ever dared stay there after sundown. . . . The temple guards are sea gulls. Every morning they wet their wings in the sea and sprinkle water on the stones. And with their wings they sweep the floor.

Joseph also said, waving an unlit cigarette and sounding refreshingly mortal, "Second only to the pleasure of reading this book is the pleasure of writing it—and I'm a little mad at my friend Roberto for depriving me of the opportunity to do it." (pp. 32-3)

> *"Word from Olympus," in* The New Yorker, *Vol. LXIX, No. 8, April 12, 1993, pp. 32-3.*

Jasper Griffin   (review date 22 April 1993)

[*In the following review, Griffin praises Calasso's departure from the tenets of modern scholarship to present a nonacademic interpretation of Greek culture and myth in* The Marriage of Cadmus and Harmony.]

The gods of ancient Greece are dead, but the myths will not lie down. The peculiar quality which marks them off from the other mythologies of the world is their concentration on human beings of a definite period of the mythical past: the heroes and heroines. Closer to the gods than we can be, descendants in fact of sexual unions between gods and mortals, they were also brighter, more beautiful, more clearly visible and intelligible in their brilliant outlines; the limits of human aspiration and fragility are marked out luminously by their aspirations, loves, and disasters. That intoxicating combination has given them a power over the Western imagination which in one way or another appears in creative artists as varied as Botticelli, Titian, Monteverdi, Marlowe, Gluck, Keats, Hölderlin, Tennyson, Joyce. They also have inspired many systematic treatments which resemble creative writing: Charles Kingsley's *The Heroes* (chivalrous *gestes*), Robert Graves's *Greek Myths* (avatars of the White Goddess), Sir James Frazer's *Golden Bough* (ritual of the dying god).

The Italian writer Roberto Calasso is in that tradition. His extraordinary book [*The Marriage of Cadmus and Harmony*] is the work of an amateur—in the best sense—not a professional scholar. It draws on the whole range of classical literature, and it has six hundred footnotes giving the ancient sources, mostly of course poets, beginning with Homer and Hesiod, from whom his versions of the myths are drawn. Modern scholarship is on the whole ignored. That means that there is no mention of the connections, spectacularly worked out by Walter Burkert, between Greek myth and the sacred stories of the ancient Near East; no discussion of the Indo-European inheritance which underlies it, about which the school of Georges Dumézil has done so much; no mention, even, of the fact that half a millennium before Homer the Linear B tablets, Greek documents of the second half of the second millennium BC, record most of the names of the gods who are familiar to us, but omit some and include others whom later Greeks had forgotten—Dopota, Manasa, "Drimios the son of Zeus." Greek myth of the classical period had behind it a long and complex history. But for that you must go to the professionals.

Calasso's book is something different: an exposition and explanation of Greek myth from within its own world. He enters into that world and writes as a creative mythographer, learned but also daring. He also gives an interpretation of Greek culture in mythical terms. He describes, with energy and a kind of love, the mythical creation of the world, the monstrous creatures who preceded the Olympian gods: fabulous serpents; a cosmic egg; Protogonos the First-Born, with four eyes, four horns, golden wings, three animal heads, and two sexes. Finally Zeus becomes supreme. Monstrous deities give place to the transfigured humanity of Olympus.

Most of the book is concerned with that last period, the rule of the world by gods characterized by beauty and by sexual desire. In pedantic fact, many of the myths had origins which had nothing to do with love; but with the passing of time they came increasingly to be seen as a great repertoire of erotic tales, tales of lustful pursuit, flight, rape, and the transformation of lovers, beloveds, and offspring into all the features of the world—animals, birds, flowers, trees, fountains. In that world Calasso is at home, and his book is in part a modern version of the *Metamorphoses* of Ovid. But it is also in part an imaginative history and recreation of the nature of animal sacrifice and the origins of eating and of guilt, the beginning of totalitarianism in Sparta, the mythical way of seeing the world, and the nature of contact between human creatures and the divine: how we once possessed it, and how we lost it.

It plunges at once into the middle of things:

> On a beach in Sidon a bull was aping a lover's coo. It was Zeus. He shuddered the way he did when a gadfly got him. But this time it was a sweet shuddering. Eros was lifting a girl onto his back: Europa. Then the white beast dived into the sea, his majestic body rising just far enough above the water to keep the girl from getting wet. . . .

Four hundred pages later the book ends almost where it began, with the wedding of Europa's brother Cadmus to the goddess Harmony, the disasters brought by the gods on his daughters and their sons; and Cadmus' own exile, in which he meditates on his original coming from Asia to Greece, in search of his abducted sister.

Calasso begins at the same point as the first European historian, Herodotus. The name of Europe is that of an abducted girl; the alphabet was brought to the West by her brother in vain quest of her. And the abduction of Europa, as Herodotus tells us and Calasso follows with gusto, was a link in a chain of reciprocal abductions of princesses, Europe and the Orient alternately avenging rape with rape.

First Io, beloved of Zeus, was driven eastward in the form of a cow by the jealous Hera, then Europa, beloved of Zeus, was carried westward on the back of a bull. Then men take a hand, imitating the ways of gods with other mortals, and Medea is stolen by Jason from the East, and Helen by Paris from the West. After that, says Herodotus, the Trojan War caused enmity between West and East, and so in the fullness of time the great kings of Persia, King Darius and King Xerxes, invaded Greece with all the countless hordes of the Levant. And now we are in the daylight of history. Myth leads to history and explains it; and history begins with the violent erotic onslaught of the gods on mortal women.

The Greeks remembered that there was a time when men and gods feasted together. That closeness fitted with the momentous decision of the deities of Olympus, their great innovation in the history of the world, as Calasso puts it, to aim, not at power, but at perfection. This decision becomes central to his own personal meditation on the myths. The gods were very close to mortals and very like them, separated most vitally by the fact that mortals must eat, and so must destroy—the guilt of eating (deeper than that of eating meat rather than vegetables) marked us off from the radiant self-sufficiency of the Olympians. The Olympians gave up eating food and subsisted instead on ambrosia—"immortality"—and nectar—"conquest of death." Their perfection made itself perceptible to mortals as an aesthetic experience. The mortal heroes and heroines existed for a brief period of time, one marked by "the supremacy of the visible," when the unseen powers of the world consented to fashion themselves according to the rules of the visible, so that the most anthropomorphic of gods resembled the most splendid of men.

But the shared meals of human and divine diners led, in the mortal world, to disasters. When the mortal Cadmus married the goddess Harmony, the gods gave her a necklace; its fatal splendor caused crimes and catastrophes, husbands betrayed, mothers murdered. When Peleus married the goddess Thetis, who was to bear him Achilles, the goddess Discord, left off the list of invitations, produced the golden apple "for the most beautiful," which caused the Judgment of Paris and the Trojan War (and Achilles' death). Tantalus, father of Pelops, lost his head when he had the privilege of dining with the gods, and served up to them the flesh of his own son. This began a long hereditary curse which worked its destructive way through the generations of his family, right down to the death of King Agamemnon at the hands of his wife and hers at those of her son.

So the gods turned away, and the connection between divine and human took another form, that of rape:

> This is the sign of the overwhelming power of the divine, of the residual capacity of distant gods to invade mortal minds and bodies. . . . With the old convivial familiarity between god and man lost, with ceremonial contact through sacrifice impoverished, man's soul was left exposed to a gusting violence, an amorous persecution, an obsessional goad. . . .

The stories of abduction, rape, violent possession keep recurring with different names and different details. Not only does one heroine's story resemble another's, even to the suicides and metamorphoses; each myth has many forms.

> Mythical figures live many lives, die many deaths, and in this way they differ from the characters we find in novels, who can never go beyond the single gesture. But in each of these lives and deaths all the others are present, and we can hear their echo.

The novel, restricted to a single version, makes it more dense, more detailed—to compensate for its lost variants. Calasso might have observed that some modern novels, for example David Lodge's *Changing Places* or Italo Calvino's *If on a winter's night a traveller,* struggle to reclaim that openness, to regain indeterminacy; in the novel such antiquarianism is regarded as experimental, avant-garde. The reader is dizzied by the variants, just as "the mythographer lives in a permanent state of chronological vertigo."

It is somehow in keeping with this that elsewhere in his book Calasso presents another set of mythical events, another portentous fall. This time, sexual union of gods and men came first:

> Hierogamy: it was the first way the gods chose to communicate with men. The approach was an invasion, of body and mind, which were thus impregnated with the superabundance of the divine. . . .

Why weren't men able to go on with hierogamy?

They could not do so because of the crimes of Prometheus, who stole fire from heaven and gave it to man, and who also cheated the gods and established the ritual of animal sacrifice as the sole way of communicating with the gods. Men slaughtered animals and feasted on the meat; to the gods they offered burnt sacrifice, roasting on the altar the thigh-bones wrapped in fat. The reason for this strikingly uneven division was that Prometheus once upon a time succeeded in tricking Zeus into choosing a bundle containing the bones of a slaughtered animal, and the gods have received this ever since. It seems here like a different story from the one which Calasso has previously told. Was it the momentous trick of Prometheus, or was it the sin of the gods' guests, which ended the shared meals?

And that, of course, is the point. Calasso is not a scholar but a mythographer. It suggests indeed a curious loss of nerve that in the six hundred or so footnotes which give the ancient sources for his myths—an array of some erudition—he refers to ten works of modern scholarship, quite eccentrically chosen. There is an immense mass of modern scholarly writing on myth, some of it very illuminating, and it would seem more rational to pass it by in complete silence than to make so half-hearted a gesture toward it. Why bother to refer to fewer than a dozen fairly recherché articles, when most of the book is written with such self-confident zest? Being a mythographer, Calasso is not held to the rules of coherence and consistency which harry more academic writers. As he says himself,

> If, out of some perversity of tradition, only one version of some mythical event has come down to us, it is like a body without a shadow, and we must do our best to trace out that invisible shadow in our minds.

Calasso writes in language drawn from the myths themselves, and partly in consequence his work has, from moment to moment, an air of chronological progression. Children succeed parents, divine and human; different stages of the world succeed one another. But he finishes where he began, like the mythical serpent which swallows its own tail. He gives his own quasi-mythical explanations of the development of things—how metamorphoses flourished and ceased, how meat-eating was essential to the foundation of civic society, how the Spartans secularized the sacred band of initiates and so invented the Stalinist type of society. Other Greeks chose perfection as opposed to power; Sparta chose power for itself and institutionalized terror.

> Sparta is surrounded by the erotic aura of the boarding school, the garrison, the gymnasium, the jail. Everywhere there are *Mädchen in Uniform,* even if that uniform is a taut and glistening skin.

Responsibility and guilt, too, present themselves in mythological shapes: . . . the gods invade the mind, and human agents cannot be wholly responsible. Calasso also deals in the timeless and the aphoristic. Thus he points out that the Greek gods give no commandments, and writes that Greek rules of moderation and injunctions to "know thyself " are "maxims elaborated by man to defend himself from the gods." The classical is "a hybrid between the barbaric and the neoclassical." Zeus fathered Helen on the goddess Nemesis; this shows that "the greatest exploit of Zeus's reign [was] that of having forced necessity to bring forth beauty." Erichthonius, ancestor-hero of Athens, was born when Hephaestus attempted to rape Athena; his seed fell to earth and engendered a man whose body ended in the earthy form of a serpent. Athena reared the baby, and that is why the Athenians, "fruit of a craftsman's not-to-be-satisfied desire for a goddess," are close to the goddess, to her quality of detachment, and to the quest for perfection of form. Greek myth "escapes from ritual like a genie from a bottle." After the regime of "commensality," convivial meetings of men and gods, came, as we have seen a second time, that of rape. But there also came

> the third regime, the modern one . . . that of indifference, but with the implication that the gods have already withdrawn, and hence, if they are indifferent in our regard, we can be indifferent as to their existence or otherwise. Such is the peculiar situation of the modern world.

Calasso's book is brilliant, dazzling to read, a labyrinth lit by a fire. The whole of Greek mythology is simultaneously present from Homer to Nonnus at the very end of pagan antiquity, the strange figure who versified (in forty-eight books!) the exploits of the god Dionysus, and who also versified the Gospel according to Saint John. The book winds and retraces a complex path, through a world in which temporal succession is not a firm rule, and in which human sexuality, desire, pursuit, flight, possession, underlie and explain everything, from the rules of cult to the

An excerpt from *The Marriage of Cadmus and Harmony*

Whenever their lives were set aflame, through desire or suffering, or even reflection, the Homeric heroes knew that a god was at work. They endured the god, and observed him, but what actually happened as a result was a surprise most of all for themselves. Thus dispossessed of their emotion, their shame, and their glory too, they were more cautious than anybody when it came to attributing to themselves the origin of their actions. "To me, you are not the cause, only the gods can be causes," says old Priam, looking at Helen on the Scaean Gate. He couldn't bring himself to hate her, nor to see her as guilty for nine bloody years' fighting, even though Helen's body had become the very image of a war about to end in massacre.

No psychology since has ever gone beyond this; all we have done is invent, for those powers that act upon us, longer, more numerous, more awkward names, which are less effective, less closely aligned to the pattern of our experience, whether that be pleasure or terror. The moderns are proud above all of their responsibility, but in being so they presume to respond with a voice that they are not even sure is theirs. The Homeric heroes knew nothing of that cumbersome word *responsibility,* nor would they have believed in it if they had. For them, it was as if every crime were committed in a state of mental infirmity. But such infirmity meant that a god was present and at work. What we consider infirmity they saw as "divine infatuation" (*átē*). They knew that this invisible incursion often brought ruin: so much so that the world *átē* would gradually come to mean "ruin." But they also knew, and it was Sophocles who said it, that "mortal life can never have anything great about it except through *átē.*"

Thus a people obsessed with the idea of hubris were also a people who dismissed with the utmost skepticism an agent's claim actually to *do* anything. When we know for sure that a person is the agent of some action, then that action is mediocre; as soon as there is a hint of greatness, of whatever kind, be it shameful or virtuous, it is no longer that person acting. The agent sags and flops, like a medium when his voices desert him. For the Homeric heroes there was no guilty party, only guilt, immense guilt. That was the miasma that impregnated blood, dust, and tears. With an intuition the moderns jettisoned and have never recovered, the heroes did not distinguish between the evil of the mind and the evil of the deed, murder and death. Guilt for them is like a boulder blocking the road; it is palpable, it looms. Perhaps the guilty party is as much a sufferer as the victim. In confronting guilt, all we can do is make a ruthless computation of the forces involved. And, when considering the guilty party, there will always be an element of uncertainty. We can never establish just how far he really is guilty, because the guilty party is part and parcel of the guilt and obeys its mechanics. Until eventually he is crushed by it perhaps, perhaps abandoned, perhaps freed, while the guilt rolls on to threaten others, to create new stories, new victims.

Roberto Calasso, in his The Marriage of Cadmus and Harmony, *translated by Tim Parks, Alfred A. Knopf, 1993.*

to us the sky and its stars do not suggest order and a human history, but, Calasso writes,

> The truth is it is the [Greek] myths that are still out there waiting to wake us and be seen by us, like a tree waiting to greet our newly opened eyes.

(pp. 25-6)

Jasper Griffin, "Alive in Myth," in The New York Review of Books, *Vol. XL, No. 8, April 22, 1993, pp. 25-6.*

Peter Green   (review date 10 May 1993)

[*Green is a British translator, critic, and professor of classics whose historical and critical studies include* The Laughter of Aphrodite *(1966),* Armada from Athens: The Failure of the Sicilian Expedition, 415-413 B.C. *(1970),* The Shadow of the Parthenon *(1972),* A Concise History of Greece to the Close of the Classical Era *(1973), and* Ovid: The Erotic Poems *(1981). In the following review, he faults Calasso's approach to ancient myths in* The Marriage of Cadmus and Harmony *as an example of the "suburbanization of myth," in which ancient beliefs are revised and diluted to appeal to modern sensibilities.*]

The suburbanization of myth has a long and depressing history. Already by the sixth century B.C., Xenophanes of Colophon was complaining about the improprieties that Homer and Hesiod attributed to the Olympian gods and taking rationalist sideswipes at divine anthropomorphism, pointing out that Thracian gods had red hair and blue eyes, while the black gods of the Nubians had snub noses and woolly hair—and if oxen could draw, he added, guess what their gods would look like. Attacked on one flank by sexual *pudeur,* and on the other by sophistic reason, the old myths suffered serious censorship and secularization even before they got clear of antiquity and into the tender allegorizing hands of medieval Christianity. Roberto Calasso's [*The Marriage of Cadmus and Harmony*] shows that this process is still going strong.

Emergent middle-class mores found the miscegenetic habit of Zeus or Pasiphaë embarrassing, the muscle-bound swillings and murders of Heracles somewhat vulgar and the ecstatic rending and devouring of raw flesh practiced by Dionysiac devotees plain scary. Euripides took the whole archaic smorgasbord of divine cannibalism, rape, incest and absolute power and turned it into a deadly theatrical device with which to shock bourgeois sensibilities by serving up raw myth as a framework for social realism. The sophist Protagoras, as is well known, made man the measure of all things, and the Hellenistic age took the process one step further by bringing the gods down into the marketplace and making them behave uncommonly like market shoppers. Thus the divine beings in Apollonius Rhodius's *Argonautica,* for all their immortality and their omnipotence, soothe middle-class sensibilities by aping the speech and the manners of the Alexandrian *lumpenbourgeoisie.*

In the political arena, Protagoreanism was neatly adapted to the ambitions of Alexander's heirs by the fabulist Eu-

pattern of the stars and the color of the flowers. We have lost the ability to see the world in those mythical terms;

hemerus, who opened up the field of dynastic self-invention by proclaiming that the Olympian gods had started life as great kings or generals whose noble deeds had won them deification: a new kind of enskyment through merit. Alexander's exploits, after all, had arguably eclipsed those of Heracles and Dionysus, and Heracles (as everyone knew) had bridged the gap between earth and heaven. Besides, there were distinct advantages to be had from this kind of God Manifest, who was a good deal more accessible to petitions than the Olympians. When Demetrius the Besieger entered Athens in 290 B.C., he was greeted by a chorus praising his beauty and extolling him as the one true god, since "the other gods are far away, or cannot hear, or are nonexistent, or care nothing for us; but *you* are here, and visible to us, not carved in wood or stone, but real, so to you we pray." No wonder the Epicureans sidelined the Olympians into a remote and ineffectual Elysium.

This erosion of faith in the Olympians—with a corresponding upsurge of interest in foreign cults, preferably violent and visceral, that promised a good deal more emotional bang for the drachma—was bound to have an impact on the attitude toward Greek myth, since the genesis of the latter had been intimately bound up with the Bronze Age development of the old Indo-European pantheon, not least in its uneasy assimilation to indigenous Mediterranean cults such as the Mistress of Beasts or the Mother-Goddess. As the numinous quality drained out of mythic narrative, as urbanism began to defuse the old life-and-death cycle of the year, as meteorology and astronomy curtailed the privileges of weather-gods such as Zeus (no divine bolts, no angry thunder, not even an eclipse), what remained came to be more and more seen as a series of often indecent *contes drolatiques,* as anachronistic material suitable for literary exploitation or philosophical allegorizing. And for escapism, too: all those Euripidean choruses wishing they were far away and quite different, preferably turned into birds, had their logical culmination in Ovid's *Metamorphoses,* where the arbitrary urges (more often sexual than not) of Apollo or Zeus could at least be thwarted by the dissolution and the reconstitution of the object as tree or river; while those with divine aspirations could envisage a splendid starry future in the sky, revamped as a constellation.

We end *The Marriage of Cadmus and Harmony* with the comforting thought that the gods are really only outsize funny human beings and that it's sex-and-symbolism that makes the world go round.

—*Peter Green*

What got left out was the archaic sense of terror and helplessness in the face of the unknown, a world in which gods behaved like outsize versions of the patriarchs and the viragoes on whom they were unconsciously modeled: pow-

ers of nature endowed (because one begins from what one knows) with a human face and human attributes, yet immortal, ageless, untrammeled by even rudimentary morality in the human sense, and as touchy and self-absorbed as the small children whom in so many ways they resembled. To cross them was rather like touching a high-voltage cable: you fried. No canting nonsense about virtue or good intentions could save you.

Science and sophistry got the intellectuals of the Greco-Roman world away from this primal terror but left them with a psychological problem that proved remarkably persistent. (It is still with us today.) Their inherited beliefs were not amenable to sweet reason; their heads told them one thing, their hearts another. An epigram by Callimachus debriefs a dead man: Hades is a fable, he tells his questioner, who cries out in horror, "We are undone!" They desperately needed the myths in which they could no longer believe—not only for psychological comfort, but as a source of moral and social validation. It is extraordinary how often even a rational, ironic intellectual like Ovid will appeal to myth for what today would probably be called empowering precedent. The old platitude about Homer being the Bible of the Greeks is more precisely true than many people realize.

What is even more surprising is the magnetic pull that ancient myth still retains today. Freud, Jung and his epigones Joseph Campbell, Cassirer, Lévi-Strauss: all have dug deeply into various aspects of the mythic tradition (incest seems to be a constant), and each has his devoted followers. The stories that evolved, partly aided by Near Eastern borrowings, among the warring baronies of Mycenaean Greece display universal elements: they have a kind of epidemic appeal, even (or especially) to people with only the haziest notion of the Bronze Age itself. They are, as Jung said, archetypal.

Roberto Calasso is only the most recent fisher to throw a baited hook to this myth-hungry audience. To judge by the publicity since his book's original appearance in Italy in 1988, the hook is well and truly in. So how does he go about it? What are his assumptions, what ingredients has he put together to form his bait and what kind of person does he have in mind as his captive listener? Not someone like me, that's for sure. By the time I'd slogged my way through nearly 400 pages I felt like the wedding guest pinned down by an unstoppable and archly loquacious Ancient Mariner. Calasso has two styles: jocose but leaden narrative fiction when retailing the myths themselves, and explicatory discourse heavy with assertive aphorisms. The opening words alone almost stopped me: "On a beach in Sidon a bull was aping a lover's coo. It was Zeus." We get the Aeschylean version, the Herodotean version, the Apollodoran version, all refracted through Calasso's suburban eye and platitudinous manner. At times I began to hope that he was putting us on: "Ariadne has been left behind. The clothes fall from her body one by one." But no. What she's in for is Dionysus, "bursting with youth, his Bacchants buzzing all around him."

As for the aphorisms, I began to collect them in a kind of bemused incredulity: "Dionysus's phallus is more hallucinogenic than coercive." "Heracles is contaminated by the sacred, it persecutes him his whole life." "Every notion of progress is refuted by the existence of the *Iliad.*" "Since Olympia is the image of happiness, it could only have appeared in the Golden Age." "The dense green in the Peloponnese has a hallucinatory glow to it." "The crown was a mobile *templum,* bringing together election and danger." "What we call Homeric theology was a reckless interval in the lives of the gods." "In Greece, myth escapes from ritual like a genie from a bottle." It's not that these statements are nonsensical; there is a kind of perception at work here. But it is random, arbitrary and self-indulgent.

Calasso has read all the ancient sources and a good deal of the modern scholarship. This makes what he does with his research even more of an anticlimax: all we get is his playful rehashing of various well-known myths as pseudo-fiction, interspersed with obiter dicta on the human condition. Thus, paradoxically, it isn't so much Calasso's scholarship that is at fault, which is the usual trouble with works of this kind. The problem is a lack of creative imagination, the very thing for which Gore Vidal sings his praises on the dust jacket. But then there's enough kinky sex in this book to keep the author of *Myra Breckenridge* happy.

To take the measure of Calasso's inadequacy one need only compare, say, his account of the Minotaur with that given by Michael Ayrton in *The Maze Maker* (1967), which is perhaps the most brilliant re-creation of the ancient mythic mind ever achieved in a modern language. "Asterius has a bull's head," Calasso announces brightly, "because his father was the big white bull Pasiphaë fell in love with." Ayrton, by contrast, goes straight and more radically to the heart of the matter, which is the terrible cloudy inner tension in the Minotaur's mind between beast and man: "Cud gags, cud gags, mounts in his mouth, gags speech, man's speech, cud, cud, no man makes cud, no man near man no man, no man . . . "

Calasso takes as the epigraph to his book a quotation, slightly mistranslated, that he gives as "These things never happened, but always are" and ascribes to "Sallust, *Of Gods and of the World,*" an author whom the unwary may identify (as I suspect the translator did) with the Roman historian best known for his monographs on Catiline and Jugurtha. In fact, this Sallust—more correctly, Saloustios—was a Greek Neoplatonist of the fourth century A.D., a friend of the Emperor Julian; and I cannot help wondering whether Calasso took to heart also the opening words of Saloustios's treatise: "Those who would learn about the gods need to have been well educated from childhood and must not be bred up among foolish ideas; they must also be good and intelligent by nature, in order that they may have something in common with the subject." It's somehow of a piece with the rest of his book that he should try and argue for the universalism of his theme from an essay that is a string of Neoplatonic platitudes. Perhaps he was encouraged by the thought that Saloustios, like Julian, was trying to rehabilitate the old gods in the face of Christianity. Perhaps this is even what appealed to Vidal, though I doubt it.

As the comparison with Ayrton shows, there is a funda-mental superficiality about Calasso's approach to his subject. This is partly due to his quest for universality, which leads him to treat all his sources, from Homer to Lucian, from Hesiod to the Byzantine mythographers, as essentially comparable. It is true that he did not set out to write a work of history; and yet his technique robs his presentation of a complicating historical perspective. It also prevents him from remarking upon his own position, which is a little like that of the Hellenistic *littérateurs,* who were full of nostalgia for past tradition, hell-bent on retrieving primal innocence, busy trawling among ancient testimonial for some key to the human condition: etiologizing magpies whose academic taste for obscurity was only equaled by their determination to explain every odd myth and ritual in sight. *These fragments I have shored against my ruins:* Pound and Eliot, too, have contributed to what in many ways presents an uncomfortably similar mise-en-scène to that of the Hellenistic age. Calasso is riding a trend.

Which brings me back to his potential audience. Here we have these artfully selected retellings of myth, mainly concerned with sexual goings-on, the gods in human, non-threatening, hot-tubbish mode, with the additional advantages of magical stamina and transformation scenes, Everyman and Superman in one, plus a few pseudo-profundities for cultural uplift that (as Mary Lefkowitz recently observed with great politeness) "do not so much challenge [Calasso's] readers to think hard about what they have been reading as reassure them that they have without real effort experienced something deeply significant." Insofar as Calasso's book is premised on just such passive and credulous readers, and satisfies them that it has done all their work for them, it is a kind of classicizing kitsch. Just who is going to swallow this synthetic pabulum? Much the same people, I suspect, as those of the well-heeled Hellenistic middle classes (with a smattering of intellectual pretensions) who watched the plays of Menander. Calasso has produced a *Tanglewood Tales* for our times, which will please the cultural yuppies of Europe and, now, America.

Worse, the book gets one thoroughly depressed, after a while, with Greek myth as such. This is primarily due to Calasso's emphasis on tabloid sex ("With a little girl's infatuation, she described Cadmus's body, fantasized his hand boldly touching her round breasts," and so on) and resolute avoidance of the numinous or truly terrifying (Dionysus becomes a comic stud, Prometheus and his eagle are wisely ignored). Still, it remains true that the ubiquity of rape as a motif ("the sign of the overwhelming power of the divine," Calasso pontificates), the self-absorbed narcissism of these deities, the endless incidents of cannibalism, incest, murder and betrayal do not exactly enhance the bright dawn of Western civilization. It is not the duty of a mythographer, of course, to make the gods look good, or to cheerlead for their culture; but Calasso, while cheerleading with the best of them, still manages to turn his Olympians into comic cutouts.

Calasso leaves us on the verge of literate history ("no one could erase those small letters, those fly's feet that Cadmus the Phoenician had scattered across Greece"), but when forced to face the various nastinesses of Tantalus, Pelops,

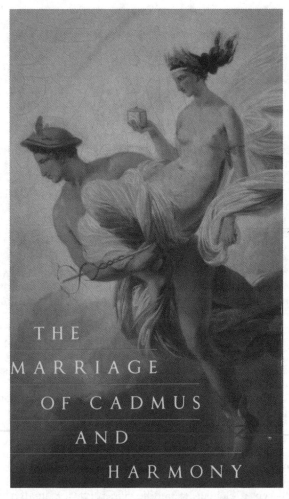

Book jacket for The Marriage of Cadmus and Harmony.

Thyestes and the rest, he can only argue that "to invite the gods ruins our relationship with them but sets history in motion. A life in which the gods are not invited isn't worth living. It will be quieter, but there won't be any stories." *Parturient montes, nascetur ridiculus mus.* (A mountainous parturition, giving birth to a ridiculous mouse.) Then, as though to disprove his own findings, he throws in long anecdotal digressions on Athens and Sparta in historical times, again chiefly predicated on sex (Athenian pederasty, the sodomization of Spartan brides before marriage). At one point he picks up the idea of reasoned thought (Anaximander, Heraclitus) overriding the paratactic particularities of myth ("like the cipher, like the arrow of Abaris, the *logos* transfixes in the merest atom of time what the rhapsodies had strung together and repeated over and over for night after smoky night . . . the resulting thrill was without precedent"). But, thrill or no thrill, we end with the comforting thought that the gods are really only outsize funny human beings and that it's sex-and-symbolism that makes the world go round. Baby boomers will buy this book in droves. (pp. 50-2)

> Peter Green, "Olympic Games," *in* The New Republic, *Vol. 208, No. 19, May 10, 1993, pp. 50-2.*

Peter Conrad   (review date 30 May 1993)

[*In the following review, Conrad focuses on the dichotomy between pagan and Christian thought in Western civilization and views* The Marriage of Cadmus and Harmony *as "an apologia for paganism."*]

The death of God, according to a character in an Iris Murdoch novel, has set free the angels (and, he adds, they are terrible). But the death of God has also more benignly set free the gods—the multiple, metamorphosing deities of Olympus so different in their morals from the austere and solitary occupant of the Christian heaven.

Roberto Calasso's extraordinary book [*The Marriage of Cadmus and Harmony*] begins as a retelling of Greek myths and ends as a vindication of mythic thinking and a critique of the spectral, abstracted Christian worldview. The fables of Homer or Ovid, which send the gods among men to assist favoured warriors or to ravish available nymphs, recognise the convivial interdependence of the human and the divine; the Christian gospels reject the lures of this world and establish the supremacy of the invisible. Calasso's compendium, itself a myth, ventures like all myths to explain the depradations of history and to atone for our loss of paradise.

Calasso begins with the question 'But how did it all begin?' The query is cyclically repeated, and answered in different, always provisional, ways. Myth disdains the notion of certainty. It is a mode of conjecture and a licensing of fiction: Calasso's epigraph from Sallust warns: 'These things never happened, but are always.'

Western culture has two competing accounts of creation. In the Greek version, Uranus rowdily, seamily copulates with Ge, Mother Earth. In the Christian alternative, a disembodied spirit moves on the face of the waters and impregnates them without recourse to sex.

Art and literature have for centuries temporised between these incompatible theological systems. In the Renaissance, Ovid was moralised, so that the lustful rampages of the gods could be read—by hypocritical or self-deceived clerics—as allegories of the indefatigable Holy Spirit. The romantics attempted, like Shelley in *Prometheus Unbound* or Keats in *Hyperion,* to reconcile Hellenic hedonism with Hebraic morality. The effort persists in modernism: Eliot treats the blind, ambisexual Tiresias as a Christian prophet, and Joyce converts Odysseus to Judaism.

Calasso beautifully and ingeniously contributes to this tradition of commentary on our schizophrenic heritage. His book is an apologia for paganism. By contrast with the Christian decalogue, he remarks: 'The Greek god imposes no commandments. How could he forbid anything, when he has already done it all himself?'

There is, as Calasso sees it, more wisdom in this riotous indulgence than in the Christian policy of abstinence: 'The Greeks had no inclination for temperance. They knew that excess is divine, and that the divine overwhelms life.'

The absence of commandments also means that there can be no authorised version of a Greek myth. Christianity certifies one truth and disqualifies all others: hence Milton's purging of errant stories in *Paradise Lost.* But Calasso's serial recitations, doubling back to the beginning to tell a variant of the same fable, celebrate the imaginative freedom bequeathed to us by the Greeks: 'No sooner have you grabbed hold of it,' he comments in a characteristically vivid metaphor, 'than the myth opens out into a fan of a thousand segments.'

The Greeks did without sacred texts. Instead, to answer questions like Calasso's about ultimate origins, they consulted Homer. Calasso notes the bemusement of Herodotus, wondering where the *arriviste* gods of Olympus had come from. 'Homer is the real scandal', he writes admiringly, because *The Iliad* shamelessly invented a cosmogony.

Homer imagined the gods and quite arbitrarily assigned powers to them. Yet despite this supreme bluff, as Calasso comments when noting how the Homeric heroes derive the causes of their actions and emotions from the gods, 'no psychology has ever gone beyond this: all we have done is invent, for those powers that act upon us, longer, more numerous, more awkward names'. Freud, mythically personifying the belligerent energies of the mind, merely lodged Olympus inside us and retold the stories of Oedipus or Electra as cases for clinical treatment.

Calasso beautifully and ingeniously contributes to the tradition of commentary on our schizophrenic heritage in *The Marriage of Cadmus and Harmony.* His book is an apologia for paganism.

—Peter Conrad

The myths are factories for the imagination, endlessly producing facsimiles. Calasso is intrigued by the Greek obsession with shaping moulds, which 'could be applied to an extremely wide range of materials'. Plato gave the name of 'demiurge', appropriated from the humble guild of Athenian mould makers, to 'the artificer of the whole world'.

But there is a danger to this almost industrialised process of manufacture, since the cast may eventually forget the mould which gave it form and meaning. Hence our debasement of the obliging, adaptable Olympians: Nike, the winged and sandalled goddess of victory, survives only as a brand name for running shoes.

The crux of Calasso's many-stranded narrative, prophesying the obsolescence of the gods, is just such a case of substitution, when the myth begins to deal in phantom copies of itself. This is the story of the Egyptian Helen, according to which the innocent Helen remained in Egypt while the Trojan war was fought over a ghostly simulacrum of her. (The legend is treated by Richard Strauss and Hugo von Hofmannsthal in their opera *Die Aegyptische Helena;* one of the incidental revelations of Calasso's book is that opera

may be the artistic form with the longest memory of the ostracised classical gods, and the one responsible for their survival into the modern world.)

Homer kept teasingly quiet about the unreality of the Trojan Helen, because his heroes could not be allowed to fight over a replica. He foresaw, Calasso surmises, 'his great future enemy: Plato, evoker of copies, of unstoppable cascades of copies that would flood the world'. The Platonic idea scrupulously removed itself from profuse, meretricious reality; 'the power of the abstract' was asserted, allowing Christianity to call for the suppression of that visible, carnal world where the gods had flourished.

The press in his native Italy, scenting bad blood, has nicknamed Calasso 'l'anti-Eco'. Yet his imaginative endeavour is the same as Umberto Eco's in *The Name of the Rose,* where the medieval monks who destroy Aristotle's treatise on the profane, lubricious art of comedy are defending their own prudish religion against paganism.

Calasso shares Eco's grand ambition for cultural synthesis, although Eco's novel is modelled on the strict interpretative science of scholasticism, while Calasso adapts the more anecdotal, casually fantasticated form of Ovid in the *Metamorphoses.* Rather than preferring one to the other, we should be grateful we have both. *The Marriage of Cadmus and Harmony* is enlivening, enthralling, essential: a classic.

Peter Conrad, "The Gods in Their Element,"
in The Observer, *May 30, 1993, p. 3.*

Patrick Parrinder   (review date 5 August 1993)

[*Parrinder is an English educator and critic who regularly reviews contemporary fiction. Below, he examines the changing role of ancient Greek myths in Western culture and praises Calasso's attempt to revitalize the fables as "a primary source of aesthetic experience."*]

Mythology was once defined by Robert Graves as the study of whatever religious or heroic legends are so foreign to a student's experience that he cannot believe them to be true. Mythical stories are disturbing and invite disbelief; but our own myths are so taken for granted as to be largely invisible. Conventional encyclopedias of mythology exclude Biblical narratives. 'Religious knowledge' remains a compulsory school subject, while instruction in traditional mythology is normally a by-product of some more reputable form of training. In English culture one might think that the Greek myths have been exploited largely for decorative effect. The myths are domesticated and trivialised in modern intellectual and popular culture: we speak of the Oedipus complex, Cupid's arrows and Pandora's box. But the dissemination of the Greek myths in England since the Middle Ages, so far from being an accidental or casual affair, was a direct result of the pedagogical revolution embodied in the rise of the universities and grammar schools.

For hundreds of years the Greek myths played a central, if unacknowledged, part in the curriculum which was the common possession of the English educated classes. Yet the myths' entitlement to a place in any curriculum has been controversial since the very beginnings of speculation about curriculum design. The fact that Christianity could be regarded as a mythology did not become apparent in Europe until sometime in the 19th century; its official position in the English school system has not been seriously questioned until our own time. In ancient Athens, however, fewer than two hundred years separate Pisistratus, who established the text of Homer and prescribed it for study in the schools, from Plato, whose ideal curriculum banished mythological study.

Plato argues in the *Republic* that, since only good can come from the gods, the traditional tales of the Greek gods and heroes cannot be true; and even if they were true they would corrupt the young. Among the crimes committed by the gods which young people ought not to know about, lying, laughter and rape are prominent—though Plato's views on lying and laughter possibly do not bear investigation. He maintains, for example, that the future Guardians of the Republic should not be exposed to tales or instances of lying, but he also says that the Guardians themselves are the only citizens who should be allowed the privilege of lying when reasons of state demand it. Rape, however, is different. Plato unequivocally condemns the tales of heroes like Theseus, not to mention Zeus himself, 'going forth to perpetrate a horrid rape'. Plato is not alone in being shocked and disturbed by the prevalence of rape in the tales.

Roberto Calasso's evocation of the corpus of Greek mythology [in *The Marriage of Cadmus and Harmony*] begins with a rape, and returns to the theme with numerous reflections on the metaphysics—not the ethics—of rape. In ethical terms we will not get very far with the Greek myths if outrage is our only response to stories of rape. Calasso quotes Herodotus's relaxed, man-of-the-world view that to abduct women is generally considered to be the 'action of scoundrels', but to worry about abducted women is the 'reaction of fools'. 'Had they not wanted to be abducted, they would not have been,' Herodotus observes. In Greek mythology there is little point in distinguishing between rape and abduction, and had women not been raped there would have been no history, or even perhaps no world.

There has, of course, been no shortage of allegorical interpretations of the divine rapes and other crimes which litter the Greek myths. Plato was already conscious of the possibilities of allegorical reading, though he found them irrelevant since a young person cannot distinguish between what is allegorical and what is not. The story of Europa and the bull, which Calasso recounts on the first page of *The Marriage of Cadmus and Harmony,* has obvious allegorical possibilities, since the bull was the emblem of Minoan civilisation. The story might conceivably have less to do with female violation than with the magic of naming, which is central to our modern experience of the myths since they continue to provide us with so much of our vocabulary. Europa stands for Europe, we may wish to say, just as Narcissus is the original narcissist and Harmony is harmony.

The divine rapes (and much else) in Greek myth have been interpreted as figuring military invasions. At a more gen-

eral level, they can be seen as a projection of the supposed triumph of patriarchal over matriarchal forms of society. Such explanations appealed to Robert Graves, whose two-volume collection of *The Greek Myths* first appeared in 1955. For all his reputation as a hierophant of the White Goddess, holding court in his Majorcan retreat like some minor god in exile, Graves was strongly attracted to political and sociological readings of the myths. He brought to them the same taste for multi-layered interpretation that had earlier made him a pioneering critic of Modernist verse. A story revealing the creative essence of humanity and the cosmos could, at another level, be decoded as the ideological glossing-over of a military victory. At the same time, like the grand mythographical theorists of earlier generations to whom he is plainly indebted, Graves ultimately believes that all myths are the same myth. His brief introduction to *The Greek Myths* modestly advances a near-universal explanation of the myths in terms of moon and sun-worship and fertility-ritual—in effect, the Key to All Mythologies for which George Eliot's Mr Casaubon had so fruitlessly sought. Frazer's *The Golden Bough* had shown how such a key could be announced to the world: not as a poetic revelation, but in the secular modern form of a scholarly treatise.

In *The Greek Myths,* Graves suppresses his poetic flamboyance and offers a sober and methodical translation of the myths in an orderly scientific setting. Text and commentary remain rigidly separate. (The commentaries, which have been found idiosyncratic, could be updated by an editor in the light of new knowledge.) Graves's indispensable reference-work could not be more different from Roberto Calasso's elegiac and evocative reinterpretation of the myths and their world. *The Marriage of Cadmus and Harmony* is not a work of reference. It has neither chapter-titles nor index and—bizarrely, because it is in no sense a novel—it appears in the fiction section of Cape's catalogue. Its aphoristic and oracular style owes much to Nietzsche, whose collected works Calasso (a Milanese publisher) has brought out in Italian. Where Graves respects and observes the generic boundaries, Calasso deliberately blurs them.

The densely-woven prose and elliptical narrative make this a difficult book to read through, though it repays the effort. It both retells the Greek myths, loosely following the same chronological sequence as Graves, and makes them the subject of an intricately-wrought essay in cultural theory. Yet its matter will infuriate the cultural theorists, being the record of a single-minded absorption in the Greek inheritance and of a lofty refusal of any kind of commitment to modernity. Since Umberto Eco is Italy's leading cultural theorist-cum-novelist, it is not for nothing that Calasso has been dubbed the 'anti-Eco'.

He begins with an epigraph from Sallust—'These things never happened, but are always'—and there is more to this than a Freudian or Nietzschean anthropological view of the Greek myths as the sources of primordial truths about the human psyche. Calasso writes of seduction as 'the invincible impulse', of possession as 'the highest form of knowledge, the greatest power', and of the sacrifice of virgins as 'the origin of every dark eros'. This litany of essences, ultimates and origins is tied to particular stories—of Zeus and his women, of Apollo and Dionysus, of Agamemnon and Iphigenia—and we may feel that it is vouched for by the very words used to assert it. Thus the permanence of the Greek eros can be made to sound self-evident by the mere repetition of the concept of the erotic and of the word *eros*. Part of the purpose of Calasso's narrative and expository method is to recapture the magical dimensions of mythical language.

For Calasso it took divine interference in human affairs to set history in motion, and history is inherently Hellenic or post-Hellenic. This book acknowledges nothing or almost nothing that is outside the sequence of the Greek ages, and its real theme is perhaps to rewrite this sequence of ages in the light of a nostalgia for Calasso's own version of the Golden Age. *The Marriage of Cadmus and Harmony* stands or falls by its re-creation of the Golden Age when the gods appeared and reappeared on earth, and could pick and change their shapes at will. Rape was, as often as not, the purpose of such metamorphoses. In some cases the consequence of rape was the birth of a god or a hero, in others the birth of a monster. Then in no more than two or three generations the heroes made themselves redundant by killing off all the monsters, before slaughtering one another beneath the walls of Troy. After the age of heroes comes the alphabetical age, when all that remains is to keep telling the old stories. Soon we can perceive the beginnings of the modern condition in which gods and men become indifferent to one another, and societies embodying a principle of godlessness are set up.

The monsters that the heroes set out to kill were among the last vestiges of the age of metamorphosis. They survived into the period when temples were built, when statues took the place of the presence of the gods, and when transformations were sought by artificial means. Pasiphae had to crouch inside a wooden cow when she became enamoured of a bull, and her son the Minotaur was trapped (like Lucius in *The Golden Ass*) inside his incongruous shape. Daedalus, the architect of Pasiphae's insemination, designed the first pair of wings so that he and his son could escape across the sea like birds. The wooden horse the Greeks built to enter Troy was a rational stratagem depending for its effect on the Trojans' credulity and readiness to believe that the age of metamorphoses and divine manifestations was not past. After that, the Greek statues would suffice to preside over the temples whose absent deities could, at best, be placated by offering sacrifices.

The Marriage of Cadmus and Harmony is haunted by the possibility of an imaginative return to the moment when gods and human beings shared the world with one another. 'A life to which the gods are not invited isn't worth living,' Calasso declares in conscious or unconscious parody of Oscar Wilde on the subject of utopias. But the necessary consequences of inviting the gods were rapes, abductions, sacrifices and the beginning of history. The gods for their part were gratifyingly interested in human beings but could not help regarding them as clockwork toys, playthings that in no time became the focus of Olympian squabbles. The story of the sorceress Iynx is all too charac-

teristic. Part of the story may be guessed by anyone familiar with *Jynx Torquilla,* the wryneck.

Iynx (the daughter of Pan and Echo) was a sorceress who made up love potions. One day she offered a drink to Zeus. The god drank the potion, and the first woman he set eyes on was Io, wandering about in Hera's sanctuary in Argos. Zeus was possessed by love for Io, and jealous Hera turned Iynx into a wryneck as punishment. Later, Aphrodite bound a wryneck to a little wheel, making a sort of perpetual motion machine in which the jerky twisting of the bird's neck would help to keep the wheel revolving. She gave this toy to Jason, who used it to seduce Medea. Medea became infatuated with Jason and helped him to seize the Golden Fleece. Thus the maker of love potions becomes a wryneck, but the wryneck when tamed and harnessed as a divine plaything possesses the properties of a love potion. At one level this story exhibits the simple constitutive magic that was to be recaptured by Kipling in the *Just So Stories.* Another level is more disturbing, since it speaks of a time when creation was still reversible, before a love potion was clearly and irretrievably a love potion, and a wryneck a wryneck. This was a time when everything still hung suspended on the whims of the gods.

Once history had begun, men could only approach the gods by making sacrifices and through initiation into the occult mysteries. As *The Marriage of Cadmus and Harmony* progresses, it not only tells of the death of the heroes and the foundation of the Greek cities, but dwells more and more on the Mysteries and the 'vertigo' that they inspired in their devotees. Perhaps this book itself should be seen not so much as a recital and reconsideration of the myths but as the record of an initiation process. One stage of this initiation is for the reader to learn to accept and revel in the multiple variants of each mythical story. A myth which survives in only one version is 'like a body without a shadow', Calasso observes. (More than this, the mythical narratives sometimes seem to change their shapes as freely as the gods themselves.) The most puzzling and most paradoxical variants are often the best. A second stage of initiation brings us to see the mythical narrative as a kind of deconstructible dream-text, in which Apollo and Dionysus or the hero and the monster may be one and the same, and in which Helen of Troy was a phantom or simulacrum of the real or bodily Helen, who was left behind in sanctuary in Egypt after Paris abducted her, so that the ten years' war need never have been fought.

When Heinrich Schliemann excavated the ruins of Troy, he astonished his contemporaries by proclaiming that the Homeric epics had pinpointed the site of an actual fortified city. In Calasso's hands, archaeology and ancient history recede, as if Schliemann and his successors had never held a spade. Pride of place is given instead to speculative anthropology and psychohistory, with the aim not of revealing the key to all mythologies but of reviving and reinvigorating the Greek myths as a primary source of aesthetic experience. But there is no such thing as an aesthetics without content—an aesthetics, that is, shorn of ethical and political implications. For this reason Calasso counterposes the world in which the gods were present with the awful example of a godless society—that of Sparta.

In Sparta the traditional cults were superseded by a single temple, built close to the communal dining hall: the temple of Fear. Under its utopian ruler Lycurgus ('he who carries out the works of the wolf') Sparta continues to be associated with ideas of Puritanical nobility and virtue—Plato's Guardians were based on the *ephors* or overseers of the city. But Calasso's virulent critique shows how the Spartans, having abolished the old gods, set out to ape the Olympian deities and to repeat their worst crimes. The most revealing legend about the *ephors*, according to Calasso, is the story of Skedasus, an outsider who made the mistake of trying to report the rape of his two daughters by the Spartan soldiery. The overseers took no notice of Skedasus's allegations, and the poor man committed suicide.

In Calasso's eyes, however, indifference to the gods rather than indifference to rape is the heart of the Spartan tyranny. Once the gods were banished, the poets and storytellers (as we see from Plato) would soon follow. The poetic view of rape seems to say that what is odious if performed by a mere man takes on an air of sublimity if performed by a god or a hero. The gods came down to earth in a moment of annunciation, violent, brutal and brief, leaving behind them the 'sign of the overwhelming power of the divine'. The annunciation is also an insemination. *The Marriage of Cadmus and Harmony* is the powerful expression of a writer who is himself enraptured by the Greek myths, which he sees as anything but historical relics. Would a less metaphysical and more sceptical approach to this body of myth 'but take its greatness with its violence', to misquote Yeats? Calasso does not risk this, preferring to fan the embers of the old stories, and to exchange our supposed enlightenment for their afterglow. This all too seductive study is the book Walter Pater might have written, if he had turned his attention to the Greek myths and had read up on Nietzsche, Freud and modern scholarship. Calasso's readers may have come to understand the Greek world better—they have certainly been possessed by it. (pp. 15-16)

Patrick Parrinder, "Rapture," in London Review of Books, *Vol. 15, No. 15, August 5, 1993, pp. 15-16.*

FURTHER READING

Lee, Andrea. "The Prince of Books." *The New Yorker* 69 (26 April 1993): 43.
   Discusses Calasso's literary background, his life in Italy, and his career as a publisher.

Jeffrey Eugenides
The Virgin Suicides

Born in 1960 (?), Eugenides is an American novelist and short story writer.

INTRODUCTION

Set in an affluent suburb of Detroit, Michigan, *The Virgin Suicides* revolves around the suicides of five teenage sisters and the community's reaction to their deaths. The daughters of strict Roman Catholics, the Lisbon sisters led sheltered lives despite their beauty and popularity with boys, and the mystery surrounding their deaths only served to increase their status with their male classmates and neighbors. Employing a first-person plural narrative, the novel is told in retrospect by several anonymous men who have been fascinated with the Lisbon girls since childhood. As youths, the narrators fantasized about the sisters, briefly dated them, and later collected artifacts used by or belonging to the girls in an attempt to explain why they killed themselves. Commentators have praised *The Virgin Suicides* as an insightful and lyrical commentary about adolescence, teenage suicide, obsession, community life, and the role of women in contemporary society. Nicci Gerrard observed that "*The Virgin Suicides* triumphs precisely because of its juxtaposition of exact verbal wit and wild strangeness. Its subject is the American suburb undomesticated, and the banal American Dream gone estatically wrong."

CRITICISM

Publishers Weekly (review date 15 February 1993)

[*In the following review, the critic offers a laudatory assessment of* The Virgin Suicides.]

Eugenides's tantalizing, macabre first novel [*The Virgin Suicides*] begins with a suicide, the first of the five bizarre deaths of the teenage daughters in the Lisbon family; the rest of the work, set in the author's native Michigan in the early 1970s, is a backward-looking quest as the male narrator and his nosy, horny pals describe how they strove to understand the odd clan of this first chapter, which appeared in the *Paris Review,* where it won the 1991 Aga Khan Prize for fiction. The sensationalism of the subject matter (based loosely on a factual account) may be off-putting to some readers, but Eugenides's voice is so fresh and compelling, his powers of observation so startling and acute, that most will be mesmerized. The title derives from a song by the fictional rock band Cruel Crux, a favorite of the Lisbon daughter Lux—who, unlike her sisters Therese, Mary, Bonnie and Cecilia, is anything but a virgin by the tale's end. Her mother forces Lux to burn the album along with others she considers dangerously provocative. Mr. Lisbon, a mild-mannered high school math teacher, is driven to resign by parents who believe his control of their children may be as deficient as his control of his own brood. Eugenides risks sounding sophomoric in his attempt to convey the immaturity of high-school boys; while initially somewhat discomfiting, the narrator's voice (representing the collective memories of the group) acquires the ring of authenticity. The author is equally convincing when he describes the older locals' reactions to the suicide attempts. Under the narrator's goofy, posturing banter are some hard truths: mortality is a fact of life;

teenage girls are more attracted to brawn than to brains (contrary to the testimony of the narrator's male relatives). This is an auspicious debut from an imaginative and talented writer.

A review of "The Virgin Suicides," in Publishers Weekly, *Vol. 240, No. 7, February 15, 1993, p. 188.*

Michiko Kakutani   (review date 19 March 1993)

[*In the following mixed assessment of* The Virgin Suicides, *Kakutani discusses the novel's narrative structure and voice.*]

Jeffrey Eugenides's piercing first novel [*The Virgin Suicides*] begins with a startling and horrible event: a 13-year-old girl hurls herself out of a window and impales herself on the iron fence that runs around her family's house.

"It didn't matter," Mr. Eugenides's narrator recalls,

> whether her brain continued to flash on the way down, or if she regretted what she'd done, or if she had time to focus on the fence spikes shooting toward her. Her mind no longer existed in any way that mattered. The wind sound huffed, once, and then the moist thud jolted us, the sound of a watermelon breaking open, and for that moment everyone remained still and composed, as though listening to an orchestra, heads tilted to allow the ears to work and no belief coming in yet. Then Mrs. Lisbon, as though alone, said, "Oh, my God"

On her second try, her daughter Cecilia had succeeded in "hurling herself out of the world."

This terrible event, along with the subsequent suicides of Cecilia Lisbon's four pretty sisters, feels like something out of a Greek tragedy. It's not at all the sort of thing one expects to find in a coming-of-age story set in the leafy Detroit suburbs of the 70's; and as related by Mr. Eugenides, the deaths of the five Lisbon sisters take on the high, cold shimmer of myth. Their suicides become a symbol of the innocence lost as adolescents are initiated into the sad complexities of grown-up life, and the lost, dying dreams of a community that finds its collective dreams of safety spinning out of reach.

With its incantatory prose, its fascination with teen-age tragedy and its preoccupation with memory and desire and loss, *The Virgin Suicides* will instantly remind readers of Alice McDermott's fine 1987 novel, *That Night.* Not only are the themes of the two books similar, but so also are their structures and narrative methods. Both novels focus on events that fracture the consciousness of an entire community into a before and after. And both are narrated by observers who recall the larger-than-life events of their youth from the vantage point of middle age. In their recollections, actual experiences blur together with the distortions of nostalgia; events are re-imagined, extrapolated and heightened in an effort to memorialize and make sense of the past.

In the case of *The Virgin Suicides,* the narrator is a collective "we," a group of young men who speak in one voice.

They were once in love with the Lisbon girls, and are now, some 20 years later, trying to piece together the story of their deaths. These men, now balding and weary and a bit disappointed with their humdrum lives, serve as the book's Greek chorus, stitching together the story of the Lisbon sisters' tragedy, as they meditate upon its meaning.

Through this narrator, we catch a series of intriguing glimpses of the enigmatic Lisbon sisters: the saintly 13-year-old Cecilia, and her older siblings, the sexually precocious Lux, who at the age of 14 sleeps with men on the roof of her family's house; the skittish romantic, Bonnie, who dreams of going on dates; fastidious Mary, who spends hours gazing at herself in a lighted mirror; and brainy, 17-year-old Therese, who grows fluorescent sea horses in a drinking glass in her room.

Beautiful and eccentric, the sisters have captured the imagination of the neighborhood boys, who spend hours spying on them and collecting souvenirs of their lives: snapshots taken by neighbors, cosmetics stolen from the garbage, a brassiere filched one night from the house. What is the girls' magical allure? In an ordinary suburban world of lawnmowers and barbecues, they represent the extraordinary: the odd, the inexplicable, the romantically extreme.

Under the thumb of their domineering mother—who never allows them to date, and who insists they wear baggy, ridiculous clothes—the Lisbon girls lead strangely hermetic lives, defined by church and school. Though their ineffectual father seems vaguely sympathetic to their plight, he never stands up to their tyrannical mother.

Eventually the boys succeed in taking the Lisbon sisters on a single group date, but Lux breaks her mother's curfew and the girls are permanently grounded. They are pulled out of school and locked in the house. In one memorable scene, their suitors make a last-ditch effort at communication. Having managed to get the girls on the phone, they begin playing them their favorite songs: "You've Got a Friend," "Wild Horses" and "Time in a Bottle." The girls respond by furtively playing some of *their* favorite songs: "Alone Again, Naturally," "Where Do the Children Play?" and "So Far Away."

Nothing, however, impedes the girls' withdrawal from the world. "The house receded behind its mists of youth being choked off," Mr. Eugenides's narrator recalls, "and even our own parents began to mention how dim and unhealthy the place looked." Leaves pile up on the lawn, garbage collects by the curb, and at night, raccoons prowl its yard. Sour, unpleasant smells seep out of the house, and grime and dust soon cover over its windows and doors.

The reader repeatedly wonders why the girls don't rebel. Why don't they reach out to friends, or run away from home? Why don't the authorities insist that they go to school? What has driven their mother to impose such a strict regime in the first place?

Such obvious questions are never addressed by Mr. Eugenides, and his willful ignoring of these issues can grate on the reader's nerves, momentarily breaking the spell of his tale.

Gradually, however, the narrator's hypnotic voice succeeds in transporting us to that mythic realm where fate, not common sense or psychology, holds sway. By turns lyrical and portentous, ferocious and elegiac, *The Virgin Suicides* insinuates itself into our minds as a small but powerful opera in the unexpected form of a novel.

> *Michiko Kakutani, "Of Death in Adolescence and Innocence Lost," in* The New York Times, *March 19, 1993, p. C23.*

> **When I began writing [*The Virgin Suicides*], I would lie in bed and try to imagine one of my family members committing suicide and how betrayed and angry I'd feel.**
>
> **—*Jeffrey Eugenides, in an interview with Joseph Olshan, in* People Weekly, *19 April 1993.***

Suzanne Berne (review date 25 April 1993)

[*In the review below, Berne provides a mixed assessment of* The Virgin Suicides, *analyzing Eugenides's use of detail, language, and narrative structure.*]

When a bewildered student asked him to explain his famous short story "A Rose for Emily," William Faulkner declared that he was simply writing about a "young girl with a young girl's normal aspirations to find love" who was "repressed" by her selfish father, with tragic results. Typically, he never mentioned the story's most complex feature: a collective narrator pieces together the ghoulish story of proud, love-famished Miss Emily, isolated in her crumbling antebellum mansion, who eventually murders her Yankee lover and sleeps for a generation beside his moldering corpse.

It seems fitting to mention "A Rose for Emily" by way of introducing Jeffrey Eugenides's first novel, *The Virgin Suicides,* because Mr. Eugenides is not only writing about tragically repressed young girls but also using a collective narrator to tell their story. And as in Faulkner's tale, that narrator serves both as a device for emphasizing the girls' isolation and finally as the novel's true protagonist. The reader becomes even more interested in why this "we" persists in its fascination with the five Lisbon sisters of suburban Grosse Pointe, Mich., than in why each of the girls "took her turn at suicide."

Like Miss Emily, the teen-age Lisbon girls are forbidden to date or fraternize with boys by a possessive parent, in their case a rigidly Roman Catholic mother. Of course, being taboo makes the girls wildly desirable. In the dazzling first chapter (which as a short story won *The Paris Review*'s Aga Khan Prize), a gang of neighborhood boys attempt to understand the initial suicide attempt of the youngest daughter, Cecilia, while also documenting their obsession with all "five glittering daughters in their home-made dresses, all lace and ruffle, bursting with their fructifying flesh." These same boys, we gradually realize, have

---

An excerpt from *The Virgin Suicides*

We know portions of the diary by heart now. After we got it up to Chase Buell's attic, we read portions out loud. We passed the diary around, fingering pages and looking anxiously for our names. Gradually, however, we learned that although Cecilia had stared at everybody all the time, she hadn't thought about any of us. Nor did she think about herself. The diary is an unusual document of adolescence in that it rarely depicts the emergence of an unformed ego. The standard insecurities, laments, crushes, and daydreams are nowhere in evidence. Instead, Cecilia writes of her sisters and herself as a single entity. It's often difficult to identify which sister she's talking about, and many strange sentences conjure in the reader's mind an image of a mythical creature with ten legs and five heads, lying in bed eating junk food, or suffering visits from affectionate aunts. Most of the diary told us more about how the girls came to be than why they killed themselves. We got tired of hearing about what they ate ("Monday, February 13. Today we had frozen pizza . . . "), or what they wore, or which colors they favored. They all detested creamed corn. Mary had chipped her tooth on the monkey bars and had a cap. ("I *told* you," Kevin Head said, reading that.) And so we learned about their lives, came to hold collective memories of times we hadn't experienced, harbored private images of Lux leaning over the side of a ship to stroke her first whale, and saying, "I didn't think they would stink so much," while Therese answered, "It's the kelp in their baleens rotting." We became acquainted with starry skies the girls had gazed at while camping years before, and the boredom of summers traipsing from back yard to front to back again, and even a certain indefinable smell that arose from toilets on rainy nights, which the girls called "sewery." We knew what it felt like to see a boy with his shirt off, and why it made Lux write the name Kevin in purple Magic Marker all over her three-ring binder and even on her bras and panties, and we understood her rage coming home one day to find that Mrs. Lisbon had soaked her things in Clorox, bleaching all the "Kevins" out. We knew the pain of winter wind rushing up your skirt, and the ache of keeping your knees together in class, and how drab and infuriating it was to jump rope while the boys played baseball. We could never understand why the girls cared so much about being mature, or why they felt compelled to compliment each other, but sometimes, after one of us had read a long portion of the diary out loud, we had to fight back the urge to hug one another or to tell each other how pretty we were. We felt the imprisonment of being a girl, the way it made your mind active and dreamy, and how you ended up knowing which colors went together. We knew that the girls were our twins, that we all existed in space like animals with identical skins, and that they knew everything about us though we couldn't fathom them at all. We knew, finally, that the girls were really women in disguise, that they understood love and even death, and that our job was merely to create the noise that seemed to fascinate them.

> *Jeffrey Eugenides, in his* The Virgin Suicides, *Farrar Straus Giroux, 1993.*

stayed obsessed into adulthood. The novel is framed by their collective determination "nearly two decades later" to comprehend what happened to the luscious, stifled Lisbon sisters. These amateur investigators interview people who knew the family, re-examine remembered incidents and overheard conversations, and review suitcases of "exhibits" pertaining to the girls, ranging from Cecilia's diary to a brassiere to a cache of old cosmetics, all of which they regard as "sacred objects."

That a large group of men in their 30's should remain so captivated by a teen-age fixation that they've kept a "refurbished tree house" in the neighborhood to warehouse these exhibits is something that taxes the most willing imagination. And yet the reader's skepticism is often disarmed simply by the evocative, carefully observed detail of the novel. Take, for example, this description of the boys' hotly awaited visit to the Lisbon basement for the one party the girls are allowed to give: "The steps were metal-tipped and steep, and as we descended, the light at the bottom grew brighter and brighter, as though we were approaching the molten core of the earth. . . . The green and red linoleum checkerboard flamed beneath our buckled shoes. On a card table, the punch bowl erupted lava." Mr. Eugenides is blessed with the storyteller's most magical gift, the ability to transform the mundane into the extraordinary.

But the novel's lyrical charm can't conceal its increasingly intrusive framework. The Lisbon sisters, the narrator claims, "have scarred us forever, making us happier with dreams than wives." While we can imagine *one* man feeling that way, a whole crowd of permanently broken hearts seems unlikely. Whereas Faulkner used his collective narrator to implicate an entire community in one woman's destruction, Mr. Eugenides employs the same narrative device to tantalize, to heighten the drama, without ever really answering the question of why those poor girls have stayed so mesmerizing, for so long, to so many people.

> Suzanne Berne, "Taking Turns at Death," in The New York Times Book Review, *April 25, 1993, p. 13.*

Katherine Dieckmann   (review date June 1993)

[*In the following review, Dieckmann examines Eugenides's treatment of obsession, suicide, and social issues in* The Virgin Suicides.]

This season's buzziest book, **The Virgin Suicides,** is a smartass yet sensitive fiction about the self-immolation of five attractive teenaged sisters in a vanishing suburbia of yesteryear. (Given the references to bongs and Bread, let's say mid-'70s.) *Rolling Stone* has declared Jeffrey Eugenides's debut the "Hot First Novel" in its annual celebration of sizzling cultural trends. The same issue contains another, strangely related item, separated from the Eugenides mention by nine pages. Under "Hot Dates" we find a color photo of Al Gore's trio of tall daughters, a triumph of long blond hair and perfect posture. The accompanying copy reads, "You've watched them. You've felt your pulse quicken. You've imagined calling them on the phone: 'Hi, it's me. What are you wearing? What about the others?'

You know it could never be. . . . Still, that spun-silk hair, those perfect teeth, the fact that there's three of them. . . . "

Body count aside, this smug, voyeuristic prose could easily serve as jacket copy for **The Virgin Suicides.** The book is so creepily dead-on about a certain form of male obsessiveness that you almost can't slag it. Almost. Because this "hot" novel fosters the very condition it pretends to rise above: one where pretty girls become fetishes for boys to such a degree that the girls' fundamental well-being (in this case, their sanity and survival) is less essential than if they're wearing blue or have just gone up a cup size.

Such scrupulous attention to bodily goings-on reaches a degree of absurdity in **The Virgin Suicides,** where the movements of the five aloof, vaguely witchy Lisbon sisters—Therese, Mary, Bonnie, Lux, and Cecilia—are studied by a gang of boys who live in their neighborhood. The girls are dominated and squashed by hyperreligious, old-fashioned parents, who foist wholesomeness on their daughters in a vain attempt to stave off normal teenage desires: "Mrs. Lisbon thought the darker urges of dating could be satisfied by frolic in the open air—love sublimated by lawn darts."

The way such control can backfire and literally drive an adolescent crazy is the overt message of this narrative. "We just want to live," complains Therese on the one occasion the Lisbons let their progeny out on a group date. "If anyone would let us." But that "anyone" includes the boys, who rhapsodize over the girls' musty body odors and rifle the family's garbage to retrieve a used Tampax (of course the sisters all get their periods at the same time), "spotted, still fresh from the insides of one of the Lisbon girls."

Yuk, right? Still, **The Virgin Suicides** is an incredibly entertaining read, for many of the same reasons *Heathers* (clearly the novel's black comedy prototype) is a great movie. Eugenides recreates small-town teenage rites with meticulous fervor and unspools them in a diction both lyrical and inflated. The man is nothing if not a clever writer, spiking his trickier emotional moments with brilliant barbs. He describes the Lisbon sisters, or the four that remain after the fifth has offed herself early in the narrative, moving through school like amorphous angels: "They passed beneath the great school clock, the black finger of the minute hand pointing down at their soft heads. We always expected the clock to fall, but it never did, and soon the girls had skipped past the danger, their skirts growing transparent in the light coming from the hall's far end, revealing the wishbones of their legs." Eugenides is also given to descriptive masterstrokes: a Trans Am becomes an "aerodynamic scarab."

But this guy may be too bright for his own good. He constructs **The Virgin Suicides** around a gimmick that eventually collapses on itself: the book is collectively narrated by the neighborhood boys, now in midlife and looking back on their teenage years, with all the requisite layers of nostalgia. These boy-men have spent their entire adult lives obsessed with the Lisbon girls, poring over the Lisbon-related effluvia they've collected and catalogued, interviewing key players in the drama, trying to piece together why Cecilia slit her wrists in the tub and why, when that failed, she leapt out a window only to be cleanly impaled on the family fence (a virginal death), and why the four other sisters followed suit some months later with varying degrees of suicidal ingenuity. So, why?

Eugenides unwittingly provides the answer in the closing sentence of his book: "It didn't matter in the end how old they had been, or that they were girls, but only that we had loved them, and that they hadn't heard us calling, still do not hear us, up here in the tree house, with our thinning hair and soft bellies. . . . " Obviously the fact that the Lisbon sisters were ripening into young women *did* matter, as did the fact that they were kept cloistered in the house—had they been boys, the story would no doubt have read differently. But what resonates most is the image of pudgy, middle-aged men sitting around getting woodies over memories of spotted panties, never having accepted the fact that the girls died before they had a chance to fuck them. The fascinating and unacknowledged subtext of **The Virgin Suicides** is that the girls recognized just how vile being a female in this culture can be, and decided to nip the possibility for further violations in, as they say, the bud.

> *Katherine Dieckmann, in a review of "The Virgin Suicides," in VLS, No. 116, June, 1993, p. 5.*

Nicci Gerrard   (essay date 6 June 1993)

[*In the excerpt below, Eugenides discusses suicide, his upbringing and literary aims, and* The Virgin Suicides.]

He seems like a cross between a portrait of a Renaissance prelate—high forehead, slightly hooked nose, large eyes yellowy-brown like walnuts—and a thoroughly modern New York literary type, with his black shirt and blue jeans, his talk of creative writing schools, publishing parties and writing techniques, his mirthful parrying of questions and ironic self-deprecation. The real Jeffrey Eugenides—serious, anxious and soft—hides like a hermit crab in its protective shell.

Eugenides is 33, half-Greek from his father's side, half-Anglo-Irish from his mother's ('but all-American') and since he left college he has been describing himself as a writer. 'It was getting a little uncomfortable at cocktail parties', he admits, 'when people asked me what I had published, and I had to tell them: nothing.' The embarrassment is over ('perhaps that's the best thing about having completed a novel'). With his extraordinary, ferociously lyrical **The Virgin Suicides** Eugenides is being talked about as one of the most original new voices in the American literary world. He's given up his secretarial day-job. He's a writer.

The Virgin Suicides is set in the clipped-lawn respectability of suburbia (actually Grosse Pointe, in Detroit, where Eugenides grew up), which it transforms into a baroque and swampy kind of dream. Fish flies swarm in foamy layers over dress-hems and darken windows, unrecognisable stars rise in the night sky over the neat rooftops, naked women copulate on balconies. Precisely-identified small-town America is invested with extreme strangeness, suffused with obsession and desire.

At the centre of this familiar-abnormal world are the five Lisbon sisters (Therese, 17; Mary, 16; Bonnie, 15; Lux, 14; and Cecilia, 13). We learn in the first paragraph—and indeed from the novel's title—that they will all kill themselves. In 250 pages, and in just over a year, the sisters are dead. First pale Cecilia, wearing a cut-off, carrot-stained wedding dress, who leaps from her bedroom onto an iron fence, then the other four: overdosed, hung from the house beams, gassed in the garage; all gone.

The five teenage girls—forever fixed in their pubescent and slightly grubby beauty, forever desirable, forever offering themselves up to the gaze of the town and forever unavailable—are remembered 20 years later by **The Virgin Suicides**'s narrator. The narrator is Eugenides's bold romantic conceit; a memorial collective voice, a bit like a Greek chorus, of the boys in the neighbourhood, who grew up with the girls, lusted after them, spied on their womanly rituals, kissed their strawberry-lip-sticked mouths at parties, tried to save them—and who now cannot forget them.

The Lisbon girls have become the essence of mysterious femaleness, particularly promiscuous Lux, who unbuttoned so many of the boys' straining belts, stroked so many of them into a state of permanent desire. We never know why the sisters have to die, only that their deaths seep through the atmospherically-glutted book like a kind of desire.

How on earth did Eugenides create such a beautifully bizarre, nearly-offensive tale? His answer—at first—is functional and almost dismissive (the voice of the graduate of Stanford University writing course): 'I was at my brother's house and fell to talking with my nephew's babysitter; she told me that she and all her sisters had once tried to kill themselves. She couldn't tell me why. I played around with the idea, at first having the whole town as narrator. Gradually, the narrative focus became adolescent, unreliable, obsessed.'

He wasn't, he insists, concerned with themes or symbols. 'I learnt nothing about myself from the book—except that I could finish a book.' I ask him if he's ever considered suicide. 'No' (except in a teenage, now-you'll-be-sorry way). I ask him about his own childhood with his two elder brothers, banker-father and 'home-making' mother, which took place among those very lawns and porches. 'Perfectly happy in every way.' I ask him about his own adolescence—was it as humidly obsessive as in the novel? 'No.'

Later, abruptly, he talks about his youthful religious longings. He read Zen books and books by Catholic monks; he dreamed of converting, of becoming a monk or priest himself. Travelling through Europe, he became fascinated by the weight of religious history, so solid after the absence of religious upbringing in his own life. He went to India and (for one week only) worked alongside Mother Teresa: 'I was so unformed in my personality and was trying on different personas; being a saint was a bit tight on my shoulders, though. At 20 you can really change your philosophy of the world by reading a single book, or by one chance meeting.'

I ask if maybe his 'perfectly happy' childhood had a few gaps that he was searching to fill. He admits (the trendy literary type all gone now) that he felt 'forces of fear', and that his panicky heart would pound uncomfortably at night; that he was searching for 'systems of happiness'; that he was afraid of his own body and sexuality then; that even today he feels that 'if you merge with your body that means dying with your body—and I still hope that I won't.' Then he ducks back into his shell: 'I'm happier with my body, though, now that I lift weights and play basketball!'

Jeffrey Eugenides has always wanted to be a writer ('except for one week when I thought I'd like to become a doctor. I told my mother and she just laughed; if even your mother laughs then you know you'd better forget it'). He wrote in high school, he wrote at college. His drawers are filled with short stories and with three unfinished novels. Success, after so many years, is 'a bit like a dream'.

Now he spends his days writing, working out and giving interviews. He shares his New York flat with a friend ('I want it to go on record that we pay the same rent and he has the better room') and thinks one day he'd like to marry and have children. But not right now.

In many ways he is a very American second-generation-Anglo-Irish-Greek. His style is East Coast irony, and New York 'is where I feel most at home'. When he comes out from behind his smiling defences, however, he is an altogether more mysterious mix of control and vulnerability. And *The Virgin Suicides* triumphs precisely because of its juxtaposition of exact verbal wit and wild strangeness. Its subject is the American suburb undomesticated, and the banal American Dream gone ecstatically wrong.

*Nicci Gerrard, "Five Sisters Stun Suburbia,"
in* The Observer, *June 6, 1993, p. 61.*

I wanted to play up the role of the obsession of the boys, to make it a mystery they're trying to piece together with evidence that won't prove anything. It's 20 years later and they're still not over it. It's the idea that it's still going on, and they're finally able to write about it and try to put it in the past.

—Jeffrey Eugenides, in an interview with Scott Martelle, in The Detroit News, 3 April 1993.

Kristin McCloy   (review date 20 June 1993)

[*In the following review, McCloy provides a favorable assessment of* The Virgin Suicides.]

In the hands of someone else, the story of five teen-age girls, all from the same family, taking their own lives might be a dreadful tale, dark and depressing. But despite the ghoulish nature of his subject, or perhaps because of it, Jeffrey Eugenides never loses his sense of humor [in his debut novel *The Virgin Suicides*]. Mordant to be sure, and always understated, Eugenides' sense of the absurd is relentless (he describes one of the girls, Bonnie, as being "a foot taller than any of her sisters, mostly because of the length of her neck which would one day hang from the end of a rope"). After the first suicide, in which the youngest sister, Cecilia Lisbon, leaves a party in the rec room to hurl herself out of a window and onto the standard white picket fence below, one of the invited guests remembers to call across the lawn, "Thank you for the party, Mr. and Mrs. Lisbon."

The other outstanding feature of Eugenides' novel is its voice: first person plural. The narrator speaks, always, as a collective "we," a pronoun that stands for all the neighborhood boys who witnessed the Lisbon girls' lives, and deaths, from the vantage point of their lawns, treehouses, attic and bedroom windows. As the anonymous-boy-next-door, that "we" manages both an exacting and fascinating account of every possibly relevant detail, with no witness' account deemed too trivial. It recalls a suburban community that no longer exists, in which everybody takes his turn as informant, from Skip the plumber's assistant who finds Cecilia's diary "by the toilet," to Peter Loomis, who delivers the funeral flowers for FTD.

From the beginning, we are told of the sisters' impending suicides; the mystery of this book lies not in when, where or how they did it, only in why, and this story is told as recollection by the group of boys, now grown into men. Still obsessed with the Lisbon girls, they determine for once and for all to gather all the available data for this ultimate analysis.

In the investigation that follows, the book traces a history of adolescence; it's a little like thumbing through a yearbook with someone who adds brief postscripts to faded faces, such as Mike Firkin's, "who later became a missionary and died of malaria in Thailand." We hear about Trip Fontaine, who loses his virginity to a 37-year-old blackjack dealer named Gina Desander while on vacation in Acapulco with his father and his father's boyfriend. He comes back a different creature. "When [Trip] returned we heard his new deep voice sounding a foot above our heads, apprehended without understanding the tight seat of his jeans, smelled his cologne and compared our own cheese-colored skin to his."

Transformed into the school dreamboat and later interviewed at a drying-out rehabilitation center somewhere in the desert, Trip Fontaine's claim to relevance is the brief love affair he had with Lux, the Lisbon sisters' erotic siren. One night after he has contrived to spend the evening at the Lisbons', watching television under Mrs. Lisbon's strict tutelage, Lux attacks him in his car. "Years later he was still amazed by Lux's singleness of purpose, her total lack of inhibitions, her mythic mutability that allowed her to possess three or four arms at once."

He never finds out if this episode is the cause, but Lux is thereafter immediately grounded. It is around this time that the neighbors begin to chart the growing disrepair of the Lisbons' house, as if the ever-increasing captivity of those four remaining girls were the cause of its decay. "The blue slate roof . . . visibly darkened. The yellow bricks turned brown. Bats flew out of the chimney in the evening. . . . Other than to school or church, the Lisbon girls never went anywhere."

At this point, there is a movement at the high school to somehow acknowledge the tragedy of Cecilia Lisbon's suicide, and thus ensues the Day of Grieving. "Teachers passed out mimeographs related to the day's theme, which was never officially announced, as Mrs. Woodhouse felt it inappropriate to single out the girls' tragedy."

Again and again, the adults in the book emerge as an incompetent, embarrassed presence in the face of trauma (after Cecilia's first, unsuccessful attempt at suicide, psychiatrist Dr. Hornicker's advice to her parents is that they allow the 13-year-old to wear makeup).

Determined in the way that only the lust-stricken can be, Trip Fontaine finally takes matters into his own hands and asks Mr. Lisbon's permission to take Lux to the Homecoming. In the face of Mr. Lisbon's inevitable denial ("he and his wife had certain rules, and he couldn't very well change them now for the younger ones, even if he wanted to his wife couldn't let him, ha ha"), Trip comes up with a brainstorm. "What if it was a bunch of us guys?" he asks. "And we took out your other daughters, too, like in a group?"

Thus he sets in motion the only unchaperoned date the Lisbon girls ever had. In many ways, this date is the climax of the book. The Lisbon girls, outfitted in homemade dresses purposely sewed several sizes too big, are finally brought into the light, and the mostly random group of boys chosen to escort them are "overwhelmed by the Lisbon girls' volubility. Who had known they talked so much, held so many opinions, jabbed at the world's sights with so many fingers?"

The girls dance, they kiss their dates and drink Peach Schnapps beneath the bleachers, and when Trip and Lux are voted King and Queen of the prom, "even girls in $100 dresses applaud." When one of the boys asks Mary Lisbon if she's having a good time, she seems to be speaking for all of them when she answers, "I'm having the best time of my life."

Unfortunately, as the 11 o'clock curfew rolls around, Trip and Lux are nowhere to be found. According to drunken Uncle Tucker, who lives across the street, Lux arrived two hours later, alone, in a taxi.

After this episode, the Lisbon girls are taken out of school, and Mrs. Lisbon shuts the house "in maximum-security isolation." The story takes on a certain poignancy here, as it details attempts at communication with flashing lights and songs played over the phone. It's girls and boys, the eternal duet.

When the boys finally receive a written note that says only, "Tomorrow. Midnight. Wait for our signal," they're ready. Armed with Chase Buell's mother's car keys, they sneak over to the Lisbon house and make Lux their offer: They'll take the girls to Florida. She seems to accept, but shushes them and asks them to wait for her sisters. "We've got a lot of stuff," she says.

They wait and wait, but the house only grows increasingly silent. Finally, they sneak down to the basement, which hasn't been touched since the ill-fated day when Cecilia killed herself. "A brownish scum of punch lay caked in the cut-glass bowl, sprinkled with flies. . . . A profusion of withered balloons hung from the ceiling on thin ribbons. The domino game still called for a three or a seven."

It's only when Buzz Romano begins to dance, kicking up a sewage smell from the inch of floodwater covering the basement floor, that the boys see "the only thing that had changed in the room since we left it a year before. Hanging down amid the half-deflated balloons were the two brown-and-white husks of Bonnie's saddle shoes. She had tied the rope to the same beam as the decorations."

Like the rest of her sisters in the house above her, Bonnie has committed suicide. "We had never known her," the author writes. "They had brought us here to find that out."

In the end, despite the constant thread of humor woven throughout, what this book captures is the utter bewilderment of those left behind—the painful inconclusiveness of medical explanations or psychological diagnoses (the ever-lame Dr. Hornicker's hypothesis that the girls all suffered from Post-Traumatic Stress Disorder following Cecilia's suicide).

"It didn't matter how old they had been," Eugenides writes, "or that they were girls, but only that we had loved them, and that they hadn't heard us calling."

In the end, the author seems to be saying, suicide is only a testimony to love wasted. (pp. 2, 5)

Kristin McCloy, "Highbrow Horror," in Los Angeles Times Book Review, *June 20, 1993, pp. 2, 5.*

Jeffrey Eugenides with Jennifer Brostrom, *CLC Yearbook* (interview date 17 December 1993)

[*In the following interview, Eugenides discusses* The Virgin Suicides *and his writing career.*]

[*Brostrom*]: *What is your writing process like?*

[Eugenides]: When I was writing **The Virgin Suicides** I had a nine to five job so I strove to maintain a schedule of writing for two hours each night and then four hours on Saturday and Sunday. Since the publication of that book I've been able to write full-time—I begin each morning and generally write for a full day.

Can you discuss any works-in-progress?

I'm working on a book that chronicles the journey of a mutated gene as it passes down through five generations of a Greek family. The book begins in the 1860s and comes into our own period, as the gene, inevitably, ends up in my own midwestern backyard.

Did you plan **The Virgin Suicides** *as a form of social commentary?*

I suppose there are themes of urban decay that are present in the narrative, but I didn't set out to write a form of social commentary.

Do you have any comments on the portrayal of women in the novel?

[**The Virgin Suicides**] is written from a collective male, and largely fallible, point of view. The boys are fascinated with the girls, but they clearly don't understand them, and there is a sense that the narrative voice is complicit—as is the entire community—in the suicides [of the Lisbon sisters]. While the narrative voice is quite obsessive, my sympathy was with the girls.

Do you have any comments on the novel's critical and popular reception?

Before the book was published I was a little worried that the obsessiveness—and the fact that all the girls die and are victimized—might be misinterpreted. But in general, that hasn't been the case. Most readers seem to feel for the girls' plight. I've received a lot of letters from teenage girls who tell me that they identify with the novel and that I understand exactly what it's like to be a girl of that age. To me, this is heartening, but also strange given that the narrative is written from a male, and clearly obsessive, perspective. . . . It makes me wonder if they're projecting part of their own experience onto the sense of blankness that surrounds the Lisbon sisters in the novel.

What are your primary goals as a writer?

Bellow says that "the humanities will be called upon to choose a wallpaper for the crypt," as the end of civilization draws near. Sometimes it feels that way. My goal, in that case, would be to come up with a wallpaper that was totally mesmerizing, with levels upon levels of action—the kind of wallpaper Bosch might choose for his home. Decorate the crypt, in other words, to escape it. . . .

I suppose my goal for myself is to satisfy my own desire for freshness while at the same time keeping in mind the traditional pleasures of literature. My grandparents came from Smyrna. So did Homer [according to one legend]. I can't give up telling stories, no matter how much I might want to deform them.

FURTHER READING

Gates, David. Review of *The Virgin Suicides,* by Jeffrey Eugenides. *Newsweek* CXXI, No. 16 (19 April 1993): 64.

> Positive assessment of *The Virgin Suicides.* Gates writes: "Eugenides is one of those rare writers who can manage sympathy and detachment simultaneously—and work small wonders with words while he's at it."

Offill, Jennifer. "Death Becomes Them." *San Francisco Review of Books* 18, No. 6 (November-December, 1993): 17-18.

> Mixed review in which Offill classifies *The Virgin Suicides* as an "ingenious detective story in which the most intriguing clues are the ones that lead nowhere." Offill finds, however, that the book is both humorously entertaining and disappointing in its themes.

Prince, Tom. "Good Grief: Jeffrey Eugenides and His Drop-Dead First Novel, *The Virgin Suicides.*" *New York* 26, No. 17 (26 April 1993): 54, 56-8.

> Combines discussion of Eugenides's upbringing, education, and work experiences with a brief review of *The Virgin Suicides.*

Rubin, Merle. "Boys Trying to Make Sense of Girls." *The Wall Street Journal* (26 April 1993): A10.

> Mixed review of *The Virgin Suicides,* in which Rubin states: "[Eugenides] tends, perhaps, to rely too heavily on style as a substitute for depth and substance, but his deadpan prose and keen sense of intonation carry the day."

Thom Jones
The Pugilist at Rest

Born in 1945(?), Jones is an American short story writer.

INTRODUCTION

Nominated for a 1993 National Book Award, *The Pugilist at Rest* concerns embattled individuals struggling with what the narrator of the title story calls the "violence, suffering, and the cheapness of life." Such stories as "Break On Through" and "The Black Lights" focus on Vietnam veterans and former prizefighters trying to cope with the psychological and physical wounds they have both inflicted and suffered. Other embattled protagonists in the collection include an elderly woman dying of cancer, an amnesia victim wandering around Bombay after surviving a car crash, a macho doctor trying to liberate his henpecked brother, and a retarded janitor fighting the social system and his unfaithful ex-wife. Noting Jones's emphasis on pain and suffering, his frequent references to the philosophical writings of Arthur Schopenhauer and Friedrich Nietzsche, and his use of self-absorbed characters, critics have praised *The Pugilist at Rest* as a pessimistic document on the bleakness of existence and the emotional costs of survival. Robert O'Connor observed: "The stories show, unapologetically, the gritty side of life as a man, not only in our time but throughout time. By courageously confronting not only the how but the why of life and war and love, Thom Jones offers not redemption, but understanding."

CRITICISM

Publishers Weekly (review date 12 April 1993)

[*In the review below, the critic praises Jones's narrative voice and references to twentieth-century American history in* The Pugilist at Rest.]

One might have to reach back to Raymond Carver's *Will You Please Be Quiet, Please?* (which copped the National Book Award for fiction in 1976) to find a debut collection that is so compelling and original. There are instant classics here [in Thom Jones's *The Pugilist at Rest*]: the title story, which soars from the horrors of Vietnam to the besplattered arenas of amateur boxing to disquisitions on war and madness and God; **"Unchain My Heart,"** about a magazine editor's love affair with a deep sea-diver—"He smells of sea salt, tobacco, and musk. Barechested, his muscles are taut, hard and slablike . . . His hands are blue from the cold of hanging idle at his recompression stops. . . . When Bocassio arises from the floor of the ocean, his lovemaking is out of this world. There's a reason for this. He's breathing heavy concentrations of nitrogen and it gives him a hard-on that won't quit." Throughout these stories, memories of fear and violence in late 20th-century America propel narratives that flash and burn and reconstitute themselves in unfailingly stunning fashions: an amnesiac ad executive from L.A. reels from a bus crash onto the edge of the Arabian Sea in Bombay and works to revive a dying horse in the surf; after a bout, a young boxer—with a "sinister set of reddish-black stitches bristl[ing] under the curve of each eyebrow"—drives his dead-drunk trainer to detox where they will talk about Nietzsche. "Soak your face in brine twice a day," says the trainer, "and read the man."

Jones's voice, no matter the persona, is irresistible—sharp, angry, poetic. His characters—among them a struggling special-ed student, a rebel physician, and a woman suffering through chemotherapy—are scarred, spirited survivors of drug abuse, war and life's cruel tricks. With references ranging from rock 'n' roll to Schopenhauer, from Dostoyevski to Joe Louis, Jones is sure to command a mighty audience—not only of literary readers, but also of people who did not know their stories could be told.

> *A review of "The Pugilist at Rest," in* Publishers Weekly, *Vol. 240, No. 15, April 12, 1993, p. 47.*

John Mort (review date 1 May 1993)

[*In the following, Mort favorably assesses* The Pugilist at Rest.]

[The roughly sequential stories collected in Thom Jones's **The Pugilist at Rest**] begin in Vietnam, where Jones demonstrates a nice ability to interweave grueling combat scenes with surreal discussions of Archie, Veronica, and Jughead. **"Break on Through"** is the heartbreaking tale of a man who can function only in combat; when he is sent home he barricades himself in his house and kills both his wife and himself. **"The Black Lights"** is about a marine who goes 'round the bend after losing a boxing match. When his psychiatrist requires him to keep a journal, he decides to prove how normal he is, so he writes: "A good day. Read. Played volleyball and had a good time smoking with the brothers. Picked up a lot of insight in group. Favorite breakfast: shit on a shingle. Two hundred push-ups. Happy, happy, happy!" Later, Jones' soldier persona becomes a surgeon who is devoted to treating the homeless but who wrecks the home of his brother; another time, he's a pickup artist whose attitude toward sexual encounters is so shrewd and self-mocking that it seems odd he even bothers. Jones' manic characters find a brief comfort in action, whether it's combat, boxing, or deep-sea diving; burdened with high sensitivity and intelligence, they find ordinary routines to be insane. Jones is funny, affecting, and never sounds a false note.

> *John Mort, in a review of "The Pugilist at Rest," in* Booklist, *Vol. 89, No. 17, May 1, 1993, p. 1570.*

Jones's characters—an epileptic vet, a woman dying of cancer, a boxer preparing for a fight—are seen working toward Truth by any means necessary. It's too early to call him Champ. But there's no doubt that he's already a contender.

—Jeff Giles, in his "He Could Be a Contenda," in Newsweek, **21 June 1993.**

Thomas McGuane (review date 13 June 1993)

[*McGuane is an American novelist, scriptwriter, short story writer, essayist, and journalist. In the review below, he discusses the themes and characters in* The Pugilist at Rest.]

Writers as good as Thom Jones appear but rarely. The original poetry of his fictional world is irresistible, and the sense that he knows this world absolutely has cleansed his prose and produced an affectless sheen.

The Pugilist at Rest, Mr. Jones's first book, is a collection of 11 stories arranged in four sections, bound thematically as well as by philosophical references that provide a sometimes sardonic and antithetical context for the excruciating clarity and vividness of the writing. The tone is one of almost unremitting pessimism. In these eventful and grim, thoroughly active tales, Americans find themselves enslaved to what one is tempted to call destiny, in view of the sweeping determinism with which the author portrays war, narcotics, bureaucratic oppression and bad luck. Many of these stories are written in the first person, and "I" is such a slippery individual that the thought police are going to have their work cut out for them separating the author from his narrators.

The stories in the first section are about the war in Vietnam, primarily, and about its aftermath in injured lives. I frankly wonder whether anyone has written better about this war or better caught its terrifying otherness. The common voice of these soldiers and of the author himself is not what we have become accustomed to: the soldier as bystander, paralyzed by ambivalence, or the soldier as mourner. The men of these stories are outright warriors. They don't really understand the national story that placed them here, but they buy it. These men were, and in some cases will again be, ordinary citizens in ordinary American towns. But for now the heart of darkness has become the self of darkness, and the American capacity for efficient violence is raised to a shock wave of perception. After reading Mr. Jones's accounts of men on reconnaissance in Southeast Asia, you look at your countrymen differently.

His assertion, in the title story, that a kind of sadism springs from grief is one that lingers:

> There was a reservoir of malice, poison and vicious sadism in my soul, and it poured forth freely in the jungles and rice paddies of Vietnam. I pulled three tours. I wanted some payback. . . . I grieved. . . . I grieved for myself and what I had lost. I committed unspeakable crimes and got medals for it. It was only fair that I got a head injury myself.

None of this would work without the author's absolute authority, and it does work, despite the somewhat familiar terrain of rock 'n' roll, drugs, unspecific fear, horrible wounds viewed with detachment, that all-consuming Vietnam zombieism that is so very different from the out-of-focus injuries and encoded behavior of other wars. For Mr. Jones, death in Vietnam is grotesque and ignominious: recently living, dreaming men turned into kitsch statues or glistening semisolids, sometimes becoming projectiles themselves. Such horrors are the perfect backdrop for the narrator's cynical quotations from Schopenhauer or twisted historical views ("It is thought that St. Paul had a temporal-lobe fit on the road to Damascus"). Out of the languor of killing come such cries from the heart as "I wanted to give my buddies a good show!"—that is, produce a "stunning body count."

Here, our rangers yearn for the "purple field" of heightened perception and trancelike power, a thoroughly dehumanized predatory state that will lead, they hope, to their survival and necessarily to the death of the enemy. Yet there is merriness in the face of stated gloom and, born of pain and reflection, a survivor's rakishness.

Boxing, as a subject, resembles war for Thom Jones, not just because of its violence but also because of the way its practitioners, even its champions, are victimized by absurd, external and, finally, deterministic forces. His boxers, like his soldiers, seem to be involved in some crazy experiment the intention of which lies well outside their understanding. Or they imagine themselves enacting a Nietzschean will to power. It is often most useful for them to assume they are the subject of a joke and that, while it may offer them small consolation, at least someone, unknown to them, is enjoying it. Even the enjoyment of others is heartening to these beleaguered people, who are reduced like true primitives to putting their faith in medical mumbo jumbo or dreams of eventual peace.

In stories like **"Wipeout,"** sex and love offer a kind of politics of cruising, with abstract goals like "action," "breaking hearts" and "dumping" resulting in the familiar outcome of extreme isolation. In another story, **"Mosquitoes,"** a Los Angeles emergency-room doctor, ruled by his fascistic, Darwinian social views, dreams of solitude and indulges his own version of the Robinson Crusoe story. As with other of Mr. Jones's *isolatoes,* he will bring his dogs, as well as a case of mosquito repellent with which, the reader imagines, he intends to banish the Eumenides.

In **"Unchain My Heart,"** a smart and attractive woman— an editor condemned to mining the slush pile at some magazine, stomach aching from licking the mucilage of envelope flaps for rejected manuscripts, surrounded by hip, teasing, negligible co-workers—falls in love with the grossest possible male, a black-bearded deep-sea diver who drives a mortgaged Ferrari, a violent man whose bones are dissolving from residual nitrogen bubbles trapped in his marrow. Death, abortion and a suiting up for new follies are the available reiteration.

In fact, one day this intelligent woman may well join the prizefighters and war heroes in Mr. Jones's vividly described psychiatric hospitals. She herself might have been the product of the nightmarish tension within unhappy homes where children are sick or are praying for a parent's death. Mr. Jones doesn't say which of his seemingly universal situations applies.

One may, as millions do, simply lose one's health. In some of Mr. Jones's stories, religion seems to have been replaced by nutritional fanaticism. Surgical crises loom. From the nose job in Thomas Pynchon's *V.* to the angioplasty in

> Writers as good as Thom Jones appear but rarely. The original poetry of his fictional world is irresistible, and the sense that he knows this world absolutely has cleansed his prose and produced an affectless sheen.
>
> —*Thomas McGuane*

John Updike's *Rabbit at Rest,* the medical procedure has come to be a numinous, almost celebratory rite of our literature. In Mr. Jones's work, ill health is a mania. In the astounding story **"I Want to Live!"** the author's penchant finds its apotheosis in a kind of medical *Walpurgisnacht* in which a blameless and simple woman suffers and dies from cancer. This inescapable depiction of misery refurbishes the author's pessimism at a stroke. I finished this story and ran out of my house to stare in blind hope at the sky.

Some of Mr. Jones's seekers look to their visions, whether drug-induced or epileptic premonitions, to break into everyday, even picayune, life, writing advertising copy or enjoying the weather. Indeed, they dream of being ordinary. In the hellishness of their plights, their dreams have given them a kind of heroism.

Will Mr. Jones's indomitable pessimism produce an eventual artistic limitation, a kind of radar beneath which must fly much of what we cherish as human? I don't know. Thom Jones is a wonderful writer: I'll take what I get.

> *Thomas McGuane, "Unhappy Warriors," in* The New York Times Book Review, *June 13, 1993, p. 7.*

Robert O'Connor   (review date 29 June 1993)

[*An American educator and novelist, O'Connor is the author of* Buffalo Soldiers *(1993), which concerns an American soldier searching for redemption. In the following review, he examines the philosophical aspects of* The Pugilist at Rest.]

Nietzsche, in one of his aphorisms, wrote, "If we have our own why of life, we can get along with almost any how." The problem is that invariably the how arrives first and without explanation. Thom Jones, in his outstanding debut collection, *The Pugilist at Rest,* makes a connection between the how and the why—the parallel universes of feeling and mind—in stories about men and how they come to terms with their most ancient adversaries.

"The Pugilist at Rest," the title story, concerns the induction into the art of war of its unnamed narrator. At Marine Corps boot camp, he assaults and fractures the skull of a bully who is bothering one of his friends, a soldier named Jorgeson. Later, in Vietnam, Jorgeson saves the narrator's life before being killed by the North Vietnamese. The narrator runs from the field but takes credit for Jorgeson's heroics. It releases something in him, though: "a reservoir of malice, poison, and vicious sadism in my soul . . ." He winds up pulling three tours of duty, learning to love war as he tries to live up to his image as a hero. When he arrives stateside he returns to boxing, transporting the war onto his own shores and into the ring, where he is finally seriously injured. This is all rendered in powerful, gritty detail, with an authentic voice that recalls the best scenes of Tim O'Brien and Michael Herr.

But what sets Jones apart is his interest in the why of life. In the middle of the story, the narrator thinks of Schopenhauer, Dostoevsky—and Theogenes, the great slave gladiator of ancient Rome, where the contestants

> were strapped to flat stones, facing each other nose-to-nose. When the signal was given, they would begin hammering each other with fists encased in heavy leather thongs. It was a fight to the death. Fourteen hundred and twenty-five times Theogenes was strapped to the stone and fourteen hundred and twenty-five times he emerged a victor.

It is an audacious move in an audacious collection. The narrator, himself a pugilist forced to retire due to his injuries, is attempting to make sense of his life, connecting himself to other men in times past. It is these stunning leaps over time and history that move this collection past the mimetic concerns of rendering a moment and into the larger concerns of rendering a culture.

Men make war not only upon each other, but upon women, particularly those they profess to love. **"Wipeout,"** the story of one heel's progress through life, is a virtual Sun Tzu's guide to the art of dating. The narrator, unnamed as many of Jones's narrators are, discourses quite entertainingly on maintaining dominance over the opposite sex. But underneath, he realizes his facility with women dooms him to an empty life. Winning isn't everything, Jones implies, and in any case, it's a lonely thing. But he doesn't sentimentalize: "You have to be true to yourself. What I did sprang from my deepest instincts. The scorpion stings, it can't help itself. There are no choices."

Giving voice to the deepest instincts of man is what Thom Jones is after. His characters, having bought into the Hemingwayesque code of violence, excitement, misogyny and danger, are hard up against it and are looking for some new answers to the old questions. Even the woman narrator of **"Unchain My Heart"** can't get around this paradigm. After her deep-sea diving lover is killed in an accident, she takes up with a Marine Corps fighter pilot. "I've learned deep," she informs us, "now I want to learn speed."

Readers who marvel at the often inexplicable behavior of men will no doubt recognize the people in this collection. In the final two stories, **"A White Horse"** and **"Rocket Man,"** Jones taps into something magical, something symbolic, something to finally explain that shimmering thing for which men will sacrifice all. In **"Rocket Man"** a fighter named Billy Prestone is about to take a match where he will surely be beaten. He seeks advice from his guru, a broken-down alcoholic ex-boxer, who invokes Gurdjieff and

Nietzsche and tells Prestone that the other fighter will see "that you have something that goes far beyond what fighters call *heart.*"

One of the things Thom Jones won't stand accused of is not having heart. These stories show, unapologetically, the gritty side of life as a man, not only in our time but throughout time. By courageously confronting not only the how but the why of life and war and love, Thom Jones offers not redemption, but understanding.

> *Robert O'Connor, "The Fight for the Meaning of Life," in* The Washington Post, *June 29, 1993, p. D4.*

Judith Wynn (review date 25 July 1993)

[*In the following laudatory review, Wynn provides a thematic analysis of* The Pugilist at Rest.]

Thom Jones takes the events of what seems to have been a rough-and-tumble life and sets them to the deeper rhythms of reflection and self-insight. *The Pugilist at Rest* is the debut of an impressive new talent.

—Judith Wynn

"You may rely on it," Henry David Thoreau once told an admirer, "you have the best of me in my books." The same could be said of former marine, ex-boxer, ex-advertising executive and one-time high school janitor Thom Jones, whose ***The Pugilist at Rest*** is a collection of hard-hitting short fiction about former marines, ex-boxers and other men and women at grips with life's major ordeals: war, sex and disease.

In the title story a veteran contemplates the medals he won in Vietnam. Were his deeds heroism or farce? Did his slaughtered best friend do all the work and leave him all the glory? Some 20 years later, he's epileptic, thanks to head injuries sustained in a drunken boxing match that he fought after getting home. "I wanted to give my buddies a good show," he recalls.

But epilepsy is "the sacred disease." Dostoevsky had it. Other visionaries—St. Paul, Joan of Arc and Muhammad—were said to have had it. "Each of these in a terrible flash of brain lightning was able to pierce the murky veil of illusion which is spread over all things."

Piercing that veil is the driving force behind these 11 strife-ridden, often grimly comic stories. Meanwhile, the brooding specters of Nietzsche and Schopenhauer loom above the fray to lend meaning and self-renewal to some of the most beleaguered characters this side of Robert Stone and Larry Heinemann.

"We are like lambs in a field," wrote Schopenhauer,

"disporting ourselves under the eye of the butcher. . . ." And who was this Schopenhauer? "A crank, a guy with an axe to grind, a hypochondriac, a misogynist, an alarmist who slept with pistols under his pillow," thinks the nameless cancer patient in the book's most heart-rending story, **"I Want to Live!"**

But Schopenhauer begins to make sense to the patient as her illness grinds her down. Then a childhood memory of a scrappy pet rooster on her parents' farm puts the dying woman in touch with the ruthless old German's celebrated "life force" and boosts her over the final barrier.

Danger, pain, and imminent death open the doors to super-rational perception in Jones' world. The soldier-protagonist of **"Break on Through"** taps into a psychic "field of purple" on night maneuvers in Vietnam and has a terrifying vision of the American eagle as a satanic Humphrey Bogart, complete with trench coat and talons. In **"Rocket Man"** a boxer whose face has been pulverized by his opponent gets a miraculous "third wind" that carries him to victory.

The same principle operates on the field of erotic combat. **"Unchain My Heart,"** convincingly narrated from a woman's point of view, tells how an ambitious editor plays hooky from her job to go deep-sea diving in shark-infested waters with her ultra-macho lover and gets stoned on nitrogen. "I don't see God," she says, "but it's not bad." Back at work and subsequently dumped, the narrator faces vengeful colleagues and an unwanted pregnancy. How she pulls a victory out of this mess is a tribute to human resilience.

Not all the characters are winners. In **"Silhouettes,"** a young janitor wins and loses a destructive woman while a comical chorus of his co-workers' useless good advice plays on. The rambunctious emergency-room surgeon of **"Mosquitoes"** tries in vain to break up his henpecked brother's depressing marriage. **"Wipeout"** thrusts us into the mind of a promiscuous stud who plays off one girlfriend against another so that we see—perhaps against our better judgment—how much fun it might be to get away with that particular kind of murder.

The poisonous side effects of sex flare up again in **"As of July 6th, I Am Responsible for No Debts Other Than My Own."** The combat veteran of the title story is a teenager in this one and must deal with his mother's sensual bondage to a man he despises. Only his grandmother's stoical love keeps him from going after his stepfather with a butcher knife: "She warned me about the futility of life . . . and because of this I'm still on the streets, not in some psycho ward or jail, or dead from a heroin overdose or an alcoholic street fight."

An amnesiac ad writer in **"The White Horse"** gets a whiff of the abyss when he sees a dying, abandoned circus horse in India and can't rest until American wealth and optimism (plus the help of an efficient old German doctor) get the wretched nag back on its feet.

The knockout tale is **"The Black Lights."** A savage amateur boxing match lands a Marine sergeant in the neuropsych ward at Camp Pendleton. Jones nimbly marches us through a pocket-sized inferno of broken, cast-off soldiers as the sergeant undergoes psychotic "black light" seizures.

It's a kill-or-cure dilemma, and the sacred vision arrives—as epiphanies do—via the mundane. A troupe of frightened, elderly square dancers comes to entertain the patients, and the sergeant is jolted out of his stupor by their artistry: " . . . their sufferings and miseries vanished in their dancing, as they fell into the rhythm of the music and the singsong of the caller's instructions."

Thom Jones takes the events of what seems to have been a rough-and-tumble life and sets them to the deeper rhythms of reflection and self-insight. *The Pugilist at Rest* is the debut of an impressive new talent.

> *Judith Wynn, "When Danger, Pain and Imminent Death Pierce Illusion's 'Murky Veil',"* in Chicago Tribune—Books, *July 25, 1993, p. 6.*

Ted Solotaroff   (review date 6-13 September 1993)

[*Solotaroff is an American editor, critic, and educator. In the following review, he focuses on Jones's descriptions of embattled individuals coping with loss, violence, and suffering, and claims that the battle-weary soldier of "The Pugilist at Rest" is the typical Jones protagonist.*]

The hangups of the life load the opportunities of the writer. Load as with guns, and load as with dice. There are several interactive furies in the writing persona of Thom Jones, the much-vaunted new fiction writer; propelled by his talent for dramatizing them, they make [*The Pugilist at Rest*] seem like a three-car collision in the Indy 500. Lots of power and lots of wreckage pile up as each situation races along its violent or otherwise "wired" premise to its baleful destination.

Jackknifed at the front is the Vietnam experience. As told in three stories, in his own words and reflections, they center on the training, recon operations and post-combat crackup of a Marine hero, champion boxer and romantic philosopher: i.e., a deep brute. A victim of his own bravado, he expresses, often inadvertently, the special destructiveness that hovered over the war itself and that lives on in a half-life of psychological and moral radiation. A recent article in *Rolling Stone* estimated that at least a tenth of the men who fought in Vietnam are now homeless and that half suffer from chronic seizures of violence and despair known euphemistically as post-traumatic stress disorder. Along with the walking wounded is the righteous brutality, the Ramboism that the Vietnam War, both in our conduct and defeat, continues to reinforce. (This point is lost upon the idiot moralist at *The Wall Street Journal* who blamed the civil disobedience of the anti-war movement for the murder of David Gunn, the Florida obstetrician who performed abortions, by a member of Operation Rescue. Yet whose legacy is Operation Rescue if not that of the Moral Majority and the other cultural warriors of the right? Weren't any of the managers of *The Wall Street Journal* listening to Patrick Buchanan and his shock troops at the Republican Convention?)

Which is not to say that Thom Jones is a fictionist of the radical right. Though at times he comes close. As another of his protagonists, a surgeon, explains himself: "We are diluting and degrading the species by letting the weaklings live. I am guilty of this more than anyone. I took the Hippocratic oath and vowed to patch up junkies, prostitutes, and violent criminals and send them back out on the streets to wreak more havoc and mayhem on themselves and on others." Even in his less truculent stories, Jones's recurrent narrator shows pretty much the same macho elitism, though sensitized by a heroic wound, a Jake Barnes who still has his balls but suffers from epileptic seizures—as well as an ambiguous moral lesion. The title story is emblematic of the "attitude" of the others.

Jones's self-hero is not given a name in **"The Pugilist at Rest,"** but in the following story about combat experience he is called "Hollywood," which I'll use here for convenience and, to some extent, for appropriateness. Hollywood preps for fighting in a people's war—perhaps the main reason the war was so anomalous and so morally destructive for Americans—by fracturing the skull of a fellow recruit in boot camp. The event is more chilling in its matter-of-factness than in its performance. His platoon is running to the drill field, rifles held at port arms:

> I saw Hey Baby give Jorgeson a nasty shove with his M-14. Hey Baby was a large and fairly tough young man who liked to displace his aggressive impulses on Jorgeson, but he wasn't as big or as tough as I. . . . I set my body so that I could put everything into it, and with one deft stroke I hammered him in the temple with the sharp edge of the steel butt plate of my M-14. . . . I was a skilled boxer, and I knew the temple was a vulnerable spot; the human skull is otherwise hard and durable, except at its base. There was a sickening crunch, and Hey Baby dropped into the ice plants along the side of the company street. . . . To tell you the truth, I wouldn't have cared in the least if I had killed him. . . . Jorgeson was my buddy, and I wasn't going to stand still and let someone fuck him over.

Behind the all-but-lethal excess of the payback lurks a suggestive conflict. Jorgeson's unusually beautiful and powerful "cobalt-blue eyes" as well as his beatnik ways both attract and bug Hollywood, who is drilling himself in the *Semper Fi* attitude, and he resolves this ambivalence by an act of violence whose magnitude affirms both his protectiveness and his toughness. "Hey Baby was a large and fairly tough young man who liked to displace his aggressive impulses on Jorgeson, but he wasn't as big or as tough as I." The style is the man. In this assertion of butch psychology, complete with the clinical jargon and fussy grammar, lies much room for narcissistic havoc.

Jones is not unsubtle. **"The Pugilist at Rest"** begins with Hey Baby being humiliated after he is caught writing a letter to his girlfriend in the midst of a lecture on the muzzle velocity of the M-14. So there is a kind of chain reaction of conflict between the male self as "hard-core" and human that continues to explode throughout the story. For reasons left unexplained, Jorgeson becomes even more combative than Hollywood and they both end up in an

elite recon unit, where Jorgeson dies heroically, surrounded by enemy dead, his eyes in "a final flash of glorious azure." From there on the way is open to equivocally remembered mayhem.

> Hey Baby proved only my warm-up act. There was a reservoir of malice, poison, and vicious sadism in my soul, and it flowed forth freely in the jungles and rice paddies of Vietnam. . . . I wanted some payback for Jorgeson. I grieved for myself and what I had lost. I committed unspeakable crimes and got medals for it.

What's he saying? A novelist of steadier moral vision kept his Kurtz distinct from his Marlow in dealing with "the horror, the horror" of colonialism, which the United States entered belatedly in a big way to ring down its curtain. As perpetrator, explainer and judge, Thom Jones has his hands full, and the right sometimes seems to knoweth not what the left is doing. Even so, this conflict between self-images of sensitivity and virility provides much of the tone and narrative rhythm that lift his Vietnam stories off the ground of banality and also reflects the moral dilemma of the Vietnam vet caught between the pride of having fought in and survived the Green Hell and the guilt over what it took to do so. Since his fellow citizens provide little reinforcement for the first and much for the second, the Vietnam veteran is thrown back on comradeship with the fallen and with the Corps or the Army, just as he was during the fighting itself, to lift his conduct off his conscience. This is why the Vietnam Memorial, unlike those of previous wars, remains so emotionally active, and why the most effective rehab facilities for Vietnam vets are ones run by themselves with the discipline of boot camp.

It's only "fair," as Hollywood remarks, that his own payback should be a head injury delivered by a fellow Marine at a boxing smoker after the war. Medical opinion is unclear about the consequent damage and treatment, but Hollywood prefers to regard it as "Dostoyevsky's epilepsy," which puts him in the company of St. Paul, Muhammad, Black Elk and Joan of Arc. "Each of these in a terrible flash of brain lightning was able to pierce the murky veil of illusion which is spread over all things. Just so did the scales fall from my eyes."

For Hollywood there are two sets of scales: one that blocks the transcendent, another that prevents us from seeing that all of us mostly live in a "world of shit," as the expression went in Vietnam. For this, Hollywood draws his authority from Schopenhauer, who has taught him about the will to power and its grievous consequences as well as *"how hollow and unreal a thing is life, how deceitful are its pleasures, what horrible aspects it possesses."*

All of this—the machismo, the suffering, the terminal resignation—coalesces for Hollywood into the figure of "The Pugilist at Rest"—a Roman statue copied from the early Greek, perhaps of the famous Theogenes, who, 1,400 fights to the death behind him, waits for the next with a world-weary perspicacity in his eyes beneath the scar tissue.

The statue is the only figure, pugilist or otherwise, at rest in these stories: the sight of the shore for a man struggling in an undertow. In **"Break on Through"** the tutelary figure is Satan himself, who visits Hollywood one night in the jungle and leads him into "the purple field"—the zone of the sixth sense that separates the killer from the killed, whose most memorable inhabitants are an elegant Indian who specializes in torture and a Navy Seal who has already fragged an officer and is more scary to his unit than are the Vietcong. **"The Black Lights"** shifts the devastation to a Marine psycho ward where Hollywood is under the care of Eagle Hawkins, a manic psychiatrist with a prosthetic nose, his own having been bitten off by a recovering catatonic. It is Hawkins who gets the narrator to keep a journal in whose entries one can see the premises of the striking persona that dominates this collection ("I am a boxer dog of championship lineage. . . . Once my jaws are clamped on something it cannot escape. . . . I do not have that liquid, soft expression you see in spaniels, but rather assertive eyes that can create a menacing and baleful effect. . . . Before my accident . . . I had been a great hero of the circus—the dog shot from cannons"). Striking in its being as overbearing as it is tormented: Ayn Rand meets Dostoyevsky.

In civilian life, the Thom Jones narrator is no less hardcore. In **"Wipeout"** he still keeps a body count, though now it is female. During the course of an affair with a superior woman, "a Zen chick," he comes down with a serious flu: "I was suddenly vulnerable, a tenderhearted sentimentalist. I was on the verge of turning human and having feelings and so on." But luckily for both of them, she gets pregnant and he throws her out. "I couldn't believe the cruel words that spat from my vicious filthy mouth. There was this sense of unreality." But again, it's hard to know where contrition ends and boasting begins. First he is plagued with longing and self-loathing. Then he realizes, "But you have to be true to yourself. The scorpion stings, it can't help itself. There are no choices. Besides, the action gets even better when the word gets around."

Several of the other stories are similar documents of a licensed id and a fragile ego taking comfort from reading Nietzsche. In **"Rocket Man"** the former is embodied in a rising light heavyweight and the latter in an alcoholic corner man who instructs him in the positive side of "the will to power." In **"Mosquitoes,"** they come together again in a trauma surgeon who intervenes in his brother's pretentious marriage by getting it on with his cheating but beautifully breasted wife. Or the persona shifts genders in **"Unchain My Heart,"** the story of an affair with a dominating and singularly priapic scuba diver, formerly a bank robber, as told by an extraordinarily macha, so to speak, New York editor.

That Thom Jones has been so quickly bumped up the line of new writers makes, I guess, a point that corroborates Christopher Lasch's view of a culture of narcissism. It should be said, though, that Jones is more than just another talented young writer who is a pushover for himself and muscular male values. What he understands deeply as well as clinically is pain and mortality, the validating elements of his balefulness. The only other stories as intense as the military ones are a close account of a woman's struggle with a particularly rapid form of cancer, a kind of Tet of-

---

An excerpt from "The Pugilist at Rest"

Theogenes was the greatest of gladiators. He was a boxer who served under the patronage of a cruel nobleman, a prince who took great delight in bloody spectacles. . . . It was the approximate time of Homer, the greatest poet who ever lived. Then, as now, violence, suffering, and the cheapness of life were the rule. . . .

Perhaps it is Theogenes who is depicted in the famous Roman statue (based on the earlier Greek original) of "The Pugilist at Rest." I keep a grainy black-and-white photograph of it in my room. The statue depicts a muscular athlete approaching his middle age. He has a thick beard and a full head of curly hair. In addition to the telltale broken nose and cauliflower ears of a boxer, the pugilist has the slanted, drooping brows that bespeak torn nerves. Also, the forehead is piled with scar tissue. As may be expected, the pugilist has the musculature of a fighter. His neck and trapezius muscles are well developed. His shoulders are enormous; his chest is thick and flat, without the bulging pectorals of the bodybuilder. His back, oblique, and abdominal muscles are highly pronounced, and he has that greatest asset of the modern boxer—sturdy legs. The arms are large, particularly the forearms, which are reinforced with the leather wrappings of the cestus. It is the body of a small heavyweight—lithe rather than bulky, but by no means lacking in power: a Jack Johnson or a Dempsey, say. If you see the authentic statue at the Terme Museum, in Rome, you will see that the seated boxer is really not much more than a light-heavyweight. People were small in those days. The important thing was that he was perfectly proportioned.

The pugilist is sitting on a rock with his forearms balanced on his thighs. That he is seated and not pacing implies that he has been through all this many times before. It appears that he is conserving his strength. His head is turned as if he were looking over his shoulder—as if someone had just whispered something to him. It is in this that the "art" of the sculpture is conveyed to the viewer. Could it be that someone has just summoned him to the arena? There is a slight look of befuddlement on his face, but there is no trace of fear. There is an air about him that suggests that he is eager to proceed and does not wish to cause anyone any trouble or to create a delay, even though his life will soon be on the line. Besides the deformities on his noble face, there is also the suggestion of weariness and philosophical resignation. *All the world's a stage, and all the men and women merely players.* Exactly! He knew this more than two thousand years before Shakespeare penned the line. How did he come to be at this place in space and time? Would he rather be safely removed to the countryside—an obscure, stinking peasant shoving a plow behind a mule? Would that be better? Or does he revel in his role? Perhaps he once did, but surely not now. Is this the great Theogenes or merely a journeyman fighter, a former slave or criminal bought by one of the many contractors who for months trained the condemned for their brief moment in the arena? I wonder if Marcus Aurelius loved the "Pugilist" as I do, and came to study it and to meditate before it.

Thom Jones, in his The Pugilist at Rest: Stories, *Little, Brown and Company, 1993.*

fensive within the body, and of an American advertising man undergoing an "epileptic fugue" of amnesia on a fetid beach in Bombay, whose "loathing for everything on the face of the earth, including himself," is lifted by a local physician whom he gets to save a dying horse.

It will be interesting to see what happens to Jones. Most serious matters are closed to the hard-boiled, as Saul Bellow once remarked, and unless you're a Jonathan Swift it's hard to sustain interest in a point of view that prefers pedigreed boxers and horses to humans. There's a lot of tangled family distress aching at the back of these stories about angry people and their power trips, which begins to be addressed in a recent *New Yorker* story, where Jones's sentiment flows to a psychotic sister rather than to the familiar, enraged narrator. If I were his editor, I'd suggest he keep going in that direction. As a Vietnam veteran, he needs Nietzsche like a hole in the head. (pp. 254-57)

> Ted Solotaroff, " 'Semper Fi', Nietzsche," in The Nation, *New York, Vol. 257, No. 7, September 6-13, 1993, pp. 254-57.*

Brooke Horvath   (review date Fall 1993)

[*In the review below, Horvath positively assesses* The Pugilist at Rest.]

The eleven stories comprising [*The Pugilist at Rest*] have an impressive history: within the space of a year, eight of them appeared in the *New Yorker, Esquire, Harper's, Story,* and elsewhere, and the volume's title selection deservedly took first place in the 1993 O. Henry Awards and was also reprinted in *Best American Stories 1992.* The dust jacket boosts are equally deserved, John Barth dubbing Jones "a remarkable new American writer" and Michael Herr praising the book's exploration of "the codes and rituals of what we call American manhood." Herr's comment targets one of the collection's thematic centers; another can be found in the remark of one of Jones's narrators: "human behavior, ninety-eight percent of it, is an abomination." Indeed, these two thematic points of reference often come together as the "codes and rituals" of American manhood prove responsible for many of life's abominable moments.

Organized into sections, the first three stories deal with Vietnam and conjure a "funny universe where God couldn't keep the faithful alive but the Devil could." A boxer and member of a Marine recon team, Jones's narrator—and many of the collection's stories feature essentially the same protagonist—finds in war as in boxing "the science of controlling fear" and a test of manhood that involves both taking and dishing out pain through the commission of "unspeakable crimes." Part two—which many readers will find hopelessly misogynistic—presents three stories of men (one from the woman's point of view) whose code of masculinty defines women as bitches to be seduced and left, often with their compliance. The three stories of part three are a more diverse group, turning to look through a son's eyes at his mother's rocky love life, a special-ed student whose limited life as a school janitor almost disappears when he falls for and marries the town

slut, and a widow dying of cancer (this last almost too horrific in its details and bleak in its vision to bear). The two stories concluding *The Pugilist at Rest* tell of an ad man suffering, like the narrator of the Vietnam stories, from left-temporal-lobe epileptic seizures and a prizefighter's friendship with his washed-up trainer.

These are bleak, violent, crazed, butt-kicking stories of men and women—but mostly men—seeking psychic/spiritual balance in extreme, character-testing experiences. They are stories whose trying-to-get-straight vision of life comes out of Schopenhauer and Nietzsche, whose work is quoted several times. Through it all, Jones's characters pay heavy prices to learn hard lessons: that, in or out of the jungle, in Vietnam or back in the World, the "best feeling" is that heady rush of the "primal man" who knows that it all boils down to "kill or be killed," that the best one can hope for is a tenacious hold on one's will to live despite the odds, despite the lack of good reasons to do so. If these stories are more than vaguely autobiographical, as I suspect them to be, they spring from a life I would not have wished on anyone, but it is one mark of Jones's power that he has been able to face up to and stare down that life and to connect with these eleven body blows. In *The Pugilist at Rest* readers will learn what Melville meant about shouting "No! in thunder" and what Leonard Cohen means when he talks about something that "looks like freedom but feels like death." (pp. 224-25)

> Brooke Horvath, in a review of "The Pugilist at Rest," in The Review of Contemporary Fiction, *Vol. XII, No. 3, Fall, 1993, pp. 224-25.*

Thom Jones with Jennifer Brostrom, *CLC Yearbook* (interview date 18 November 1993)

[*In the following interview, Jones discusses his writing career and* The Pugilist at Rest.]

[Brostrom]: *Please describe your writing process.*

[Jones]: I simply write what comes to me. . . . Often I will hear something in passing, perhaps as I walk through a room, and then a couple weeks later I'll remember the line. I often begin that way, with just a single line of speech which I write, and then a story begins to take shape. I don't really plan it, I just get the first draft out, which seems to flow automatically. . . . The stories in *The Pugilist at Rest,* for example, are partly autobiographical, about people who meant a great deal to me. I was writing from the heart with a lot of emotion—they were magical stories that just seemed to pour out. . . . I'm working on a new story right now, and I know it's good—I'm really happy with it. At this point it's really an ecstatic experience, but I know that when I'm done with it, I'll be sick of it, and even hate it.

Is this a pattern that happens in all of your writing?

I believe you need to feel a bit manic as an artist if you're going to do something *different,* authentic, and not just another story that you see in a lot of the journals in which people are just trying to be safe. I tried to do that, and I never even got to first base. Finally I decided, "I hate those stories—they're boring. . . . I want to write something that *I* like." As soon as I did that, it became easy.

Do you perceive that sense of unoriginality or "safeness" as a problem in contemporary literature and publishing?

Oh no. I think there are many marvelous writers being published today. I don't even like to read some of them when I'm writing. . . . The classical writers can also make you feel as if you haven't got any business writing. The artists that have endured have lasted for a reason.

Is this a goal of yours—to create a work that endures in American literature?

For the sake of readers—not for the sake of self-aggrandizement. I just love to *read* and I feel that it's an honor to be able to write and have an audience. . . . Writing is more important to me than my own life—I never really wanted to do or be anything other than a writer. And yet, as I mentioned, I was lazy about it. I suppose if you're serious about something and you fail, then you have to acknowledge that you're a failure. By being lazy, you can excuse yourself—there's always the possibility that you *could* be successful if you really tried.

Do you plan to continue writing short stories?

I love writing short stories because you can sit down and complete a draft in one day. If it isn't working—if there's something artificial about it, you can sense it. With a novel, it's difficult to maintain your perspective and maintain a consistent voice. If you have to go to work, it's nearly impossible to keep track of the whole project. In the past I also thought there wasn't much use in writing short stories because I didn't know that you can make a fairy good living at it if you're successful. The story I'm currently writing may become a novel. It's set in Africa, so I'll probably have to do some travelling and research.

What lifestyle would you advocate for a developing writer?

Carson McCullers wrote *The Heart is a Lonely Hunter* when she was twenty-five years old and Hemingway wrote *The Sun Also Rises* when he was twenty-six, but that seldom happens—most first novelists are forty. I would tell a young writer that he or she should go out and have experiences—see the world, learn as much as you can. Writers have to know more about life in general terms than anyone anywhere. . . . A writer has to know human nature, to be a psychologist as well as a craftsman.

Did you write the stories in **The Pugilist at Rest** *with a collection in mind?*

The stories were written over a period of years—one of the stories was originally written when I was nineteen years old. My first literary sale was to *The New Yorker* [**"The Pugilist at Rest"**] and it won the O. Henry award. The next story was **"I Want to Live!"**, which just got into *Best American Short Stories 1993*.

Had you previously attempted to publish your work?

Yes, but in fits and starts. I never *really* tried until about two years ago. I felt that I was getting older and needed to make a decision about my life. I also got a computer, which made revision much easier. I used to write a forty-

page story and then decide "well, this is good enough," but it wasn't, I needed to do thirty drafts. I was basically lazy. But once I was published and had that initial success, things became very easy. I immediately received calls from agents and book publishers wanting to know if I had a book.

Who are your primary literary influences?

The first writer that really excited me was J. D. Salinger. Then I began reading Dos Passos, Mailer, the British "Angry Young Men" like John Osborne. . . . Kingsley Amis's *Lucky Jim* was a strong influence. V. S. Naipaul's *A House for Mr. Biswas* is probably my favorite book—I read it every year.

Some critics have emphasized the strongly masculine quality of the stories in **The Pugilist at Rest.** *Can you comment on this?*

A critic in the *Nation* commented that all this Nietzsche and Schopenhauer and machismo is a bit much—that a little goes a long way. I agreed with him and thought that it was a good review even though it wasn't particularly favorable. . . . The strange thing is that I really don't like Nietzsche that much. My background probably also influenced the concern with masculinity in those stories. As a child I had conflicts with my father and stepfather, and I've never liked people—particularly men—pushing me around. This is probably why I got into boxing. I got fired from jobs because I refused to take orders and if I felt threatened, I was prepared to react in an extreme manner. A lot of those emotions and conflicts are revealed in the writing—I suppose it was kind of cathartic to write those stories. Recently, since I've received some recognition, the tone of my work has been shifting, becoming a bit more positive and upbeat.

How were you influenced by the experience of temporal lobe epilepsy?

I had several seizures as the result of an injury. The fits were often like spiritual trances, a kind of spiritual ecstasy. At the time of the fits I had a certainty that God existed, and I saw the world as a kind of necessary theater in which everything has a role. It seemed to be a heightened vision in which common things you never notice like pieces of furniture seemed interconnected and of equal importance—I felt at peace with the world, and confident that all things have a purpose. I do consider myself a strongly spiritual person, even obsessed with a search for God. I have intense empathy and concern for all people and living things, and I think this is what inspires my writing.

FURTHER READING

Birkerts, Sven. Review of *The Pugilist at Rest,* by Thom Jones. *Boston Review* XVIII, No. 5 (October-November 1993): 30.
    Comparative analysis of *The Pugilist at Rest* and Denis

Johnson's *Jesus' Son*. Birkerts places both of these works within the tradition of Raymond Carver's short fiction.

Alan Lightman
Einstein's Dreams

(Full name Alan Paige Lightman) Born in 1948, Lightman is an American novelist, nonfiction writer, and educator.

INTRODUCTION

A professor of physics and writing at the Massachusetts Institute of Technology, Lightman has written numerous essays and books on astronomy, cosmology, and theoretical physics. *Einstein's Dreams,* his first work of fiction, purports to be a record of the dreams that Albert Einstein had from mid-April to late June 1905, when he was working as a clerk in the Swiss Patent Office and formulating his theory of relativity. Composed of thirty chapters, with vignettes from Einstein's life interspersed among them, *Einstein's Dreams* opens at 6 a.m. with Einstein waiting at his desk for the arrival of a typist and ends over two hours later when he gives his manuscript on his theory of time to the typist. Each fable depicts human behavior in a world in which time operates under different rules. In one chapter, for example, time passes more quickly at lower altitudes, prompting the rich to build their homes on stilts high in the mountains in order to prolong their lives. In another fable, cause and effect have no relationship to time. As a result, people act impulsively, knowing that their actions will not have future consequences. In describing his book, Lightman has stated his "hope that each of the fantasy worlds has some grain of truth in it about our world and the way we behave and the way time shapes our world."

Critical reaction to *Einstein's Dreams* has been overwhelmingly positive. Commentators have favorably compared Lightman's book to the work of Jorge Luis Borges as well as to Jonathan Swift's *Gulliver's Travels* (1726) and Italo Calvino's *Le città invisibili* (1972; *Invisible Cities*). Others have praised Lightman's innovative examination of philosophical and existential concepts of time, the radical nature of Einstein's ideas, and the imaginative, intuitive, and mysterious aspects of scientific discovery. In praising *Einstein's Dreams,* Dennis Overbye has written that "Lightman spins these fantasies with spare poetic power, emotional intensity and ironic wit. . . . If time is a burden, he implies—too often—the attempt to escape it is an even deadlier burden."

CRITICISM

Dennis Overbye (review date 3 January 1993)

[*Overbye is the author of* Lonely Hearts of the Cosmos: The Scientific Quest for the Secret of the Universe *(1991). In the following review, he compares* Einstein's Dreams *to the work of George Gamow and Italo Calvino, and notes that Lightman's fables are grounded in scientific theory.*]

Albert Einstein, in one of the many remarks that have endeared him to writers seeking epigrams, said that what really interested him was whether God had any choice in how to create the world. Of all the attributes God might have chosen for the universe, surely among the most poignant and mysterious is time. To a physicist time is what a clock measures. To most of the rest of us it is irregular—like a current, sometimes swift, sometimes slow, carrying us along. Despite the efforts of the Einsteins and Newtons of the world, the dichotomy between objective and subjective time still remains.

These two facets of the temporal have rarely been as slickly and delightfully joined as they are in this tiny novel—which reads like a collection of playful fables—about time and its inhabitants. *Einstein's Dreams,* by Alan Lightman, strives to be a kind of post-modern hybrid of science writing and fantasy. It stands partly in the tradition of a series of books written in the 1940's by George Gamow, an astrophysicist and a founder of Big Bang cosmology. Gamow's tales are about a bank clerk named C. G. H. Tompkins, whose dreams and adventures involve the wonders of relativity and quantum mechanics. But Mr. Lightman, a physicist with a decidedly poetic bent, also owes much to fabulists like Italo Calvino, whose book *Invisible Cities* seems to be the model for *Einstein's Dreams.*

Mr. Lightman's conceit is that on the nights leading up to Einstein's formulation of the special theory of relativity—which forever transformed our notions of time—the young scientist, then a 26-year-old patent clerk in Bern, Switzerland, dreamed about time, conjuring up notion after notion of how God might have chosen to construct things.

On each frenzied night a new dreamlike, cartoony picture of Bern lurches into motion, the lives of shopkeepers and lovers arranged and rearranged to adapt to the temporal exigencies and opportunities of each new vision. In one dream, a woman swept back into the past by a stray current of time huddles in a doorway trying not to kick up dust that could alter history. In another vision, time moves in a circle and history keeps repeating itself; some unhappy people, sensing they are doomed to endless repetitions of their mistakes, fill the night with their moans. In still another dream, cause and effect become disjointed: a woman's heart leaps and a week later she meets a suitor.

Mr. Lightman spins these fantasies with spare poetic power, emotional intensity and ironic wit, although he often veers toward sentimentality. If time is a burden, he implies—too often—the attempt to escape it is an even deadlier burden. In his scheme, the only happy people are those who have surrendered to the moment. Thus the scientists are always grumpy, and the artists are always joyous. In the acausal world, he gushes, "each kiss is a kiss of immediacy."

There is a sly method to this madness, though; many of these dreams are based on real physics. Playing off the relativistic idea that people in motion would appear to age more slowly, Mr. Lightman offers a caricature of special relativity—a dream in which all the houses and offices are on wheels, constantly zooming around the streets (with advanced collision-avoidance systems). In another fantasy, people go to the center of time in order to freeze their lovers or their children in century-long embraces; this place is clearly reminiscent of a black hole, where, theoretically, gravity would stop time.

Mr. Lightman's vision of a woman's heart leaping before she has met the man she will fall for is likewise based in science; acausality is a feature of quantum mechanics, a revolution 70 years old and still snowballing through physics. And even the fantasy of a world where time has three dimensions instead of one, where every moment branches into three futures, has a scientific antecedent; one view of quantum theory, known as the "many worlds" interpretation, has been espoused by Stephen Hawking, among other physicists.

It's no wonder that the fictional Einstein is tired enough to spend most of this book sleeping. He dreams not of many worlds, but rather of the many exhausting facets of our own.

> *Dennis Overbye, "A Kiss Is Just a Kiss of Immediacy," in* The New York Times Book Review, *January 3, 1993, p. 10.*

Michiko Kakutani   (review date 5 January 1993)

[*Kakutani is a regular contributor to the* New York Times. *In the following review, he favorably assesses* Einstein's Dreams, *praising Lightman's precise prose and attention to detail.*]

If Alan Lightman's first novel, *Einstein's Dreams,* were a painting, it would have been painted by Magritte. Its images are beautiful but disturbing, meticulously rendered trompe l'oeil exercises with a haunting philosophical subtext.

In one chapter, men and women rush about frantically, trying to capture time, which takes the form of a nightingale, under a bell jar so they can make their lives stand still. In another, people seem unable to go forward with their lives; they sit about languorously, trapped in a moment of time, endlessly repeating the same rituals over and over.

The sonorously named Mr. Lightman, who teaches physics and writing at the Massachusetts Institute of Technology, has begun this captivating book with a simple premise: he purports to set down what Einstein dreamed during the late spring and early summer of 1905 when he worked in the Swiss Patent Office in Bern and published several papers that would revolutionize 20th-century physics. The papers would begin to define Einstein's theory of relativity and set forth important new principles about the nature of space and time.

The dreams Mr. Lightman has given his fictional Einstein also deal with the mysteries of space and time, but they have little to do, for the lay reader anyway, with the technicalities of quantum theory and everything to do with the human condition and its time-ridden existence.

In each dream, Mr. Lightman postulates a different world in which time obeys different rules, rules that have a direct impact on human psychology and behavior. In an acausal world, where cause and effect are not connected through time, artists are joyous because "unpredictability is the life of their paintings, their music, their novels." Everyone here lives in the moment, and since the present has little effect on the future, few people pause to think about the consequences of their actions.

"Rather, each act is an island in time, to be judged on its own," writes Mr. Lightman.

Families comfort a dying uncle not because of a likely inheritance but because he is loved at that moment. Employees are hired not because of their résumés but because of their good sense in interviews. Clerks trampled by their bosses fight back at each insult with no fear for their future. It is a world of impulse. It is a world of sincerity. It is a world in which every word spoken speaks just to that moment, every glance given has only one meaning, each touch has no past or no future, each kiss is a kiss of immediacy.

A similar situation obtains in a world in which there is no future: one year before the scheduled end of the world, schools close their doors, and one month before the end, businesses shut down. A sense of liberation envelops everyone. People pay their bills with a smile, because money is losing its value, and they settle their differences with a shrug because there is nothing to worry about anymore. "They do not seem to mind that the world will soon end," writes Mr. Lightman, "because everyone shares the same fate. A world with one month is a world of equality."

In Mr. Lightman's other imaginary worlds, people react in wildly different ways to the existential exigencies of their condition. In a world in which everything is predestined, some people grow passive and complacent, accepting that what will be will be; others rail against their lot in life, furiously trying to reinvent their futures, despite the impossible odds.

The world in which people live forever is divided into two populations: "the Laters" and "the Nows." The Laters, who argue there is plenty of time for everything, dawdle over coffee in cafes and pass their days rearranging their furniture, reading magazines and discussing the possibilities of life. The Nows, in contrast, "move through a succession of lives, eager to miss nothing." To make the most of their infinite existence, they are constantly reading new books, studying new trades, learning new languages.

"The Nows and Laters have one thing in common," Mr. Lightman writes.

> With infinite life comes an infinite list of relatives. Grandparents never die, nor do great-grandparents, great-aunts and great-uncles, great-great-aunts, and so on, back through the generations, all alive and offering advice. Sons never escape from the shadows of their fathers. Nor do daughters of their mothers. No one ever comes into his own.

By turns whimsical and meditative, playful and provocative, **Einstein's Dreams** pulls the reader into a dream world like a powerful magnet. As in [Italo] Calvino's work, the fantastical elements of the stories are grounded in precise, crystalline prose. As in Jorge Luis Borges's ficciones, carefully observed particulars open out, like doors in an advent calendar, to disclose a magical, metaphysical realm beyond. In moving from science writing to fiction, Mr. Lightman has made an enchanting, delightful debut.

Michiko Kakutani, "Imagining How Time Might Behave Differently," in The New York Times, *January 5, 1993, p. C16.*

When writing, I live in the moment and it's timeless. I go into a glorious mental state and that's when I'm happiest of all.

—Alan Lightman, as quoted by Kate Kellaway, in her "A Book of Hours and Years," in The Observer, 31 January 1993.

Richard Eder   (review date 10 January 1993)

[*An American critic and journalist, Eder received the Pulitzer Prize for criticism in 1987. In the review below, he praises Lightman for describing the possible forms of time as well as the links between its philosophical and existential meanings.*]

It is 6 a.m. at the Swiss Patent Office in Bern in the year 1906. A gray light begins to reveal the contents of the room: the desks, which appear "soft and shadowy like large sleepy animals"; the shelves containing patent applications for a better drill, a quieter typewriter and a host of other things. "It is a room full of practical ideas."

Except for those of the employee dozing at one of the desks. His trousers are too big, and his head is shaggy and contains no practical ideas at all. It is used for dreams and calculations based upon the dreams; it belongs to Albert Einstein, who has fallen asleep after completing his paper on the nature of time.

Alan Lightman, a physicist who teaches at MIT and writes about what might be called the mind of science and the minds of scientists, has turned to a fictional form to suggest the strange intuitive light that flickers at the frontiers of discovery. What the Einsteins do is not resolve our mysteries but enlarge them.

Einstein's Dreams is 30 brief fables that imagine the subconscious seed bed from which the thinker's theory of time—part of his work on relativity—emerges. For example, Lightman's Einstein has been an insomniac dreamer. Each dream has evoked an alternative world in which time moves in a different way. On that gray Bern morning, in 20 crumpled sheets of paper, he has chosen the one he will build his work upon.

Lightman invents the others worlds where time runs backward, stops suddenly dead, starts up suddenly, or moves in eddies, in jerks, or in three different dimensions at once. There is time that goes terribly slowly, time that goes at different speeds in different towns, time that is sticky and time that runs a perpetual loop.

The author plants each of these notions in vignettes about hypothetical realms like those of Gulliver or perhaps of Italo Calvino. His tiny Lilliputs and Laputas, no longer than 500 or 600 words each, are entrancing. They are set in 30 alternative Berns or sometimes in an alternative Zurich or Fribourg. Alternative Swiss move through them in patterns governed by 30 alternative versions of time. They are miniature people, improbable people, fragile people with the intensified humanity and comical poignancy of a puppet theater that time works as it tries out its alternative stories.

In one, time's flow has eddies that circle backward. Those who are carried back into the present wear dark suits, talk softly and have to be very careful. One woman cowers in the bushes so as not to be seen or to kick up dust. Dust would get on a passerby's shoes, he would stop to clean them, he would forget an errand for his wife, she would grow pettish and cancel a lake excursion, thereby failing to make the acquaintance of the young woman who was to become their son's wife and the grandmother of a man crucial to the signing of a European treaty in 1979. So the time-drifters have to make a point of doing nothing to interfere with the present as they wait to be eddied back where they belong.

In another world, time moves more slowly the farther you get from the planet's center. In order to delay aging, people build their houses on the tops of mountains; the more privileged mount theirs on stilts half a mile above the peaks. They despise their lower-down neighbors, and they especially despise the improvident who insist on enjoying the meadows and valleys. But at such rarefied heights, they grow thin and dry, and age faster, in fact.

Lightman's lovely irony is at work. His time variations are never merely conundrums. In a world where time moves in three dimensions, a man stands on his balcony and gazes at a red hat lying in the snow. He thinks of visiting a fascinating but difficult woman in Fribourg. In the first dimensions, he stays home, meets a nicer woman and lives in peaceful happiness. In the second, he goes, stays with the enchanter and lives in passionate happiness. In the third, he goes, stays an hour, returns inconclusively and stands on the balcony gazing at the red hat. That he does all three things is the conundrum; the emotion of this oddly moving story is in the red hat.

In another world, the inhabitants are divided into two groups. The first lives by schedules and clocks, by a mechanical time that never varies. The second lives by the rhythms of their bodies and their emotions. Intergroup encounters can be perilous, but Lightman pulls back from the notion's agreeable dryness to something more haunting. A bargeman moves his craft along the river, measuring off fathoms and minutes. Through the evening mist, a pair of lovers awake to the lights going by in the dark, and are surprised to see it is night.

At one level, **Einstein's Dreams** is a provocative exploration of time's illusive nature and polymorphous possibilities. It sketches aspects of relativity with a light allusiveness that makes its astonishment, if not its entire meaning, as clear to the non-scientific reader as words alone can manage.

But Lightman does far more than that. He is an artist who paints with the notion of time; he makes a delicate link between its philosophical and its existential meanings. Time weeps and laughs in the perplexed inhabitants of his fables, and it glitters in the radiant mountaintops and painted sky that suddenly overshadow their humanity in a story about time ending. What ends, of course, is time as the marker of what passes. What remains, with the mountains, is time as what lasts.

The author has a winning sense of place, of the look and smell and feel of things. Time, however variously it moves, frets and chivvies his towns and townspeople. The solace they get from a plate of smoked beef, or a glass of beer or an embrace, is palpable. Whatever time may do in any of the alternative worlds, Lightman is on the side of the universally present moment.

Here and there, in interludes, he gives us homely glimpses of Einstein and his friend Besso. At one point, Einstein tells Besso that he wants to understand time in order to get to "the Old One." Besso points out that the Old One may not be interested, and, besides, knowledge is not the same as closeness. In another interlude, they go fishing, and when Einstein laughs and jiggles the boat, "the clouds rock with his laughter." The universe varies with its observer.

Lightman has done much more than make relativity visible by seeding it with human stories. He makes his human stories more deeply visible by seeding them with relativity. The delightful and disconcerting surprise when we finish reading about his 30 alternative worlds of time is to realize how many of them—slowness, expansion, contraction, speed, standstill, jerkiness, even reversibility—trouble and distract the spirit in our very present non-alternative one. (pp. 3, 9)

> Richard Eder, "Time and Time Again," in Los Angeles Times Book Review, *January 10, 1993, pp. 3, 9.*

Roz Kaveney   (review date 22 January 1993)

[*In the following review, Kaveney compares* Einstein's Dreams *to Italo Calvino's* Le città invisibili (*1972;* Invisible Cities) *and compliments Lightman's depiction of Einstein.*]

Albert Einstein, a young clerk in Switzerland, drowsy but unable to sleep, waits for the patent office typist to arrive early to type up his Special Theory of Relativity. For months he has been considering time; his meditations have taken over his dreams, dreams which form the bulk of the novel and which are interrupted only occasionally by memories of ordinary moments. Outside the office, around Einstein, haunting his dreams of time, is the provincial, inward-looking city of Berne. This excellent first novel [**Einstein's Dreams**] is a double homage to Einstein and to Italo Calvino, whose *Invisible Cities* it imitates in form. All the cities portrayed by Calvino's Marco Polo are ways of looking at Venice; all the relationships between humanity and time dreamed by Lightman's Einstein are ways of looking at Berne.

Contrary to the cartoonists' idea of a blackboard full of equations climaxing downwards to a succinct point, Einstein's method made crucial use of reverie, "thought experiments" of which those featuring twins, one on a rocket and one earthbound, are perhaps the best known. Einstein was one of the most poetically creative of scientists, and the variations on time this novel uses—causal time, time as a sense, time as a function of gravity—might have amused him.

Each variation is worked out in human terms. Einstein's radicalism is reflected in his invention of a world in which the rich live in stilt houses among the-mountains to avoid the swifter time of valleys; the orderliness of bourgeois society is mocked in another, in which time is absolutely pre-ordained.

A slight sentimentality is one of the things Lightman has learned from both his masters. The framing narrative

---

An excerpt from *Einstein's Dreams*

In this world, it is instantly obvious that something is odd. No houses can be seen in the valleys or plains. Everyone lives in the mountains.

At some time in the past, scientists discovered that time flows more slowly the farther from the center of earth. The effect is until later, will not wrinkle until later, will not lose the urge for romance as early. Likewise, a person looking down on another house tends to dismiss its occupants as spent, weak, and shortsighted. Some boast that they have lived their whole lives high up, that they were born in the highest house on the highest mountain peak and have never descended. They celebrate their youth in their mirrors and walk naked on their balconies.

Now and then some urgent business forces people to come down from their houses, and they do so with haste, hurrying down their tall ladders to the ground, running to another ladder or to the valley below, completing their transactions, and then returning as quickly as possible to their houses, or to other high places. They know that with each downward step, time passes just a little bit faster and they age a little more quickly. People at ground level never sit. They run, while carrying their briefcases or groceries.

A small number of residents in each city have stopped caring whether they age a few seconds faster than their neighbors. These adventuresome souls come down to the lower world for days at a time, lounge under the trees that grow in the valleys, swim leisurely in the lakes that lie at warmer altitudes, roll on level ground. They hardly look at their watches and cannot tell you if it is Monday or Thursday. When the others rush by them and scoff, they just smile.

In time, people have forgotten the reason why higher is better. Nonetheless, they continue to live on the mountains, to avoid sunken regions as much as they can, to teach their children to shun other children from low elevations. They tolerate the cold of the mountains by habit and enjoy the discomfort as part of their breeding. They have even convinced themselves that thin air is good for their bodies and, following that logic, have gone on spare diets, refusing all but the most gossamer food. At length, the populace have become thin like the air, bony, old before their time.

Alan Lightman, in his Einstein's Dreams, *Pantheon Books, 1993.*

---

presents Einstein as a secular saint. The little parables are worked out logically, to a point where they sometimes become merely cute. The logic, though, is part of the point; Lightman is a physicist as well as a fluent writer, and in these witty fabulations, for a moment, the Two Cultures are as one.

Roz Kaveney, in a review of "Einstein's Dreams," in The Times Literary Supplement, *No. 4686, January 22, 1993, p. 19.*

Lee Lescaze   (review date 1 February 1993)

[*In the following review, Lescaze positively assesses* Einstein's Dreams, *noting that "Lightman renders the dreams with the clarity and grace of a fabulist."*]

The 26-year-old Albert Einstein wasn't good dinner company. Nor was he a good husband. Nor a good father. His thoughts were elsewhere. He was a man possessed by one of history's astonishing bursts of mental creativity.

The extraordinary 1905 output of the Bern patent clerk, which launched him as one of the defining intellectual figures of this century, is the springboard for Alan Lightman's amusing, thought-provoking and charming novel, *Einstein's Dreams.*

Relativity-averse readers who regret that Einstein exploded the easier-to-understand Newtonian universe should be particularly happy with this novel. Time has rarely been so engagingly put on display.

In the short chapters of this very short novel, the dreaming Einstein imagines 30 different worlds, distinguished from one another by the nature of time. These worlds aren't described in abstract terms. Instead, Mr. Lightman presents each one in a brief scene complete with real people carrying on the tasks of ordinary lives. Lovers meet. Children chase each other down the streets. Shopkeepers roll down their shutters at the end of day.

Mr. Lightman renders the dreams with the clarity and grace of a fabulist, but he also knows that the true study of time can be confusing and all-absorbing, even for an Einstein. "His dreams have taken hold of his research. His dreams have worn him out, exhausted him so that he sometimes cannot tell whether he is awake or asleep."

If these dreams exhaust their dreamer, they are a delight to read. What happens if time is a circle in which people caress each passing moment, oblivious to the fact that each will repeat itself again and again? Or, how does a world function in which some people have been transported backward in time, where they cower, hoping not to disturb their futures?

Suppose that people have no memories and therefore passion is ever-fresh. Or, what if each life is but a single day, one session of light and one of darkness? How different are those born into light from those who spend their first half-life in darkness?

Imagine that time is rigid, the future predetermined. Since all is predestined in such a world there is no choice and hence no freedom, no right and no wrong.

Einstein also dreams silly worlds in which people believe that time slows at high altitudes and therefore, in pursuit of longevity, they not only move to mountaintops but build their homes on stilts. The richest live highest.

The dreaming young physicist also considers a world in which time slows not at high altitudes but at high speeds. People build houses, offices, entire cities on wheels and keep them racing around in an effort to defeat time.

The ultimate defeat of time has been accomplished in another of Einstein's 30 dreams. In a world where people live forever, society splits between people who would do everything later and those who would act now. If there is infinite time, the Laters ask, why rush? If there is infinite opportunity, say the Nows, seize it all. But immortality has its drawbacks. If everyone is immortal, everyone forever has a father, a mother, a grandfather, a grandmother and so on. No one comes into his own. All questions provoke endless deliberation. There is no individual freedom.

Mr. Lightman, who teaches physics and writing at Massachusetts Institute of Technology, makes the concept of time both accessible and full of wonder. He gives each dream world a date between mid-April and late June 1905, the period in which Einstein was working on his theory. In occasional interludes between the dreams, Mr. Lightman provides glimpses of Einstein's life at the time. Einstein had started out to write about electricity and magnetism, but he suddenly announced to a friend that this would require a reconception of time.

The friend is dazzled by Einstein's ambition and thinks his mind is capable of anything. At the same time, he worries that, lost in his thoughts, Einstein will forget to eat, will take sick.

The novel opens with Einstein at his patent-office desk at 6 a.m., waiting for the typist. He has written his theory of time. Other schemes of time may exist in other worlds, but Einstein has chosen what strikes him as the most compelling explanation of this world. The novel ends with the typist's arrival. It is 8:06 a.m. when he hands her his manuscript, which she will type in her spare time. He looks out the window. He feels empty.

Einstein's Dreams is, of course, hardly a novel. No plot. No character development. No characters except Einstein.

It is a meditation, a fable and a pleasure. Its appeal is a tribute to the enduring power of the mystery of time—even in a post-Einstein world.

Pantheon has further enhanced the book's charm by publishing it in a small format suited to its brevity. The book fits easily into a pocket. In a spare moment one could pull it out. To read one dream takes little longer than the blink of an eye.

Lee Lescaze, *"Time and Time Again: A Novel Experience,"* in The Wall Street Journal, *February 1, 1993, p. A8.*

Simson L. Garfinkel (review date 11 March 1993)

[*Garfinkel is an American writer who specializes in science and technology. In the following, he favorably reviews* Einstein's Dreams, *observing that "above all, Lightman is fascinated with love and love lost."*]

Imagine what would happen if time passed slower in the mountains than in the valleys. In such a world, would not every person seek to live among the clouds in order to prolong their lives as long as possible? Would not height become status, with the truly wealthy building their homes upon stilts in order to squeeze additional seconds loose from the cosmos?

The world in the clouds is just one of many suggested by Alan Lightman in his first book of fiction, ***Einstein's Dreams.*** Lightman, who teaches physics and writing at the Massachusetts Institute of Technology, is best known for books that explore science and technology, such as *A **Modern-Day Yankee in a Connecticut Court: And Other Essays on Science*** (1986).

Einstein's Dreams is a collection of short stories, each taking place in Switzerland during the first decade of this century. Each story is a psychological investigation of how people would be changed by distortions in the way time flows.

After setting each stage, Lightman conjectures about the lives, passions, and loves of the people who inhabit that particular world. He does so with a lively and touching prose, rich and full of vitality.

In one story, time flows in a circle, and each person knows that he or she is destined to repeat every smile, laugh, and cry again and again for an eternity.

In another story, time continually stops and restarts itself in spurts, giving rise to uncertainty and a certain arbitrariness. In a third story, time flows at different rates in different cities: Few people in this world write letters to friends in distant lands.

Above all, Lightman is fascinated with love and love lost. In one world, people cannot remember the past; each person must carry a diary telling his or her personal history. Some couples retire eagerly to their beds, he writes, for each night has all of the excitement of the first. Others spend their time obsessively reading and rereading their books, repeatedly rejoicing in their accomplishments and crying over their losses.

The stories are the fictional reveries of Albert Einstein himself, who in 1905 was a Swiss patent clerk struggling to create a new theory of time and space—his theory of Special Relativity. In one of the fictional glimpses of Einstein's life that pepper the book, the scientist tells his friend Michele Besso, "I want to understand time because I want to get close to The Old One."

The era and places Lightman writes about impart a touch of nostalgia to the stories; his attention to details such as the kiss of lovers and the embrace of parents adds to the sense of melancholy. Charming and thought-provoking, this hand-sized book makes for good, albeit brief, reading.

Simson L. Garfinkel, "Flowing Moments in Imagined Time," in The Christian Science Monitor, March 11, 1993, p. 12.

Carol Anshaw (review date April 1993)

[In the following excerpt, Anshaw criticizes some of Lightman's fables as weak but contends that Lightman succeeds in capturing "the intellectual playfulness of Einstein."]

It is [a] young, febrile Einstein that Alan Lightman recreates in his small, well-crafted piece of fabulism, **Einstein's Dreams.** The conceit goes like this: It is 1905. Einstein is in Bern.

> In the long, narrow office on Speichergasse, the room full of practical ideas, the young patent clerk still sprawls in his chair, head down on his desk. For the past several months, since the middle of April, he has dreamed many dreams about time. His dreams have taken hold of his research. His dreams have worn him out, exhausted him so that he sometimes cannot tell whether he is awake or asleep.

And as the nights progress, so does the pageant of various versions of time. "Suppose time is a circle, bending back on itself. The world repeats itself, precisely, endlessly." In another world, "the passage of time brings increasing order." Yet another is a "world without memory," which is, de facto, "a world of the present." "In a world where time is a sense, like sight or like taste, a sequence of episodes may be quick or may be slow, dim or intense, salty or sweet, causal or without cause, orderly or random, depending on the prior history of the viewer."

Perhaps the loveliest is the "world in which there is no time. Only images." The collage that follows begins, "A child at the seashore, spellbound by her first glimpse of the ocean. A woman standing on a balcony at dawn, her hair down, her loose sleeping silks, her bare feet, her lips."

In between (although too infrequent) are interludes with Einstein and his friend Michele Besso.

> I want to understand time because I want to get close to The Old One.
>
> Besso nods in accord. But there are problems, which Besso points out. For one, perhaps The Old One is not interested in getting close to his creations, intelligent or not.

In his best moments, Lightman, who teaches physics and writing at MIT, brushes the heights of Calvino. In other stretches, though, his conceit creaks; its walls show themselves to be not terribly weight-bearing (worlds where time runs backward or people live for only a day). But as a whole, this tiny volume approaches the intellectual playfulness of Einstein, who is said to have worked more like an artist—by imagination and intuition—than a scientist. (p. 23)

Carol Anshaw, "Brain Man: Albert Einstein's Twisted Legacy," in VLS, No. 114, April, 1993, pp. 22-3.

Lightman on the interrelation of art and science:

I believe there's an external reality independent of our minds which we as scientists attempt to discover, truths about nature independent of our prejudices—art is separate from that. But then scientific pursuit is also a human activity so to that extent humanity does affect scientific enterprise . . . I think we are all both scientists and artists.

Alan Lightman, as quoted by Kate Kellaway, in her "A Book of Hours and Years," in The Observer, 31 January 1993.

David L. Wheeler (essay date 14 April 1993)

[In the following essay, based on an interview with Lightman, Wheeler discusses Lightman's science background and the writing of Einstein's Dreams.]

It feels odd to ask Alan Lightman, a man who has written a best-selling novel exploring the nature of time, if he has some time on Friday. "Yes," he says, "I have some time."

Getting to Mr. Lightman's office from the main entrance of the Massachusetts Institute of Technology involves a walk up some broad steps, between ponderous Ionic columns, and into a dark lobby that leads to MIT's "infinite corridor."

Rollerblading was recently banned in the corridor, so students and faculty members must walk down the hall that connects a seemingly endless string of buildings and divides a seemingly endless series of departments and their bulletin boards. A notice tacked on one board reads:

DO YOU LOSE TRACK OF TIME? LEARN HOW TO CONTROL IT!!!!

A right turn twists the path past a row of five-foot-high, barrel-shaped tanks for liquid nitrogen that sit outside the Cryogenics Laboratory. A left turn, a brief stroll past glass walls and the glare of light up from snow, and then white lettering over a small case on the left side of the wall announces: "Department of Humanities." An alcove by the case leads to two small, wire-laced glass windows set in two slender elevator doors, which stand like a secret entrance to another world.

Mr. Lightman is on the third floor of Building 14, in an office tucked behind the reception area for the Program in Writing and Humanistic Studies, which he directs. In a temple of technology, Mr. Lightman leads a band of writers—poets, biographers, historians, and novelists.

A clock that runs counterclockwise sits over his desk. If the clock, a gift from a friend, is held up to a mirror, it can be more easily read. A tiny painting by Mr. Lightman's wife, an artist, hangs on the opposite wall, a picture of a man rowing alone in the fog.

In his novel, **Einstein's Dreams,** Mr. Lightman describes a series of dreams that Einstein had in 1905 while he was working as a patent clerk and developing the theory of relativity, which would change 20th-century physics. The fictional dreams, which have no biographical basis, describe different possibilities for what time could be. Rather than dwelling on theoretical details, Mr. Lightman describes how the novel's characters experience time in these alternate worlds.

Mr. Lightman seems to have struck a sympathetic note with many readers. His book has been edging up *The New York Times Book Review*'s list of best sellers for two months, and occupied fifth place [the week of April 14, 1993].

Mr. Lightman himself is no stranger to time. Aside from living in it, like everybody else, he has thought about it as a theoretical physicist. In essays for such magazines as *Harper's, The New Yorker,* and the now-defunct *Science '86,* he has introduced the general public to physics, astronomy, and cosmology, in which time is an essential element. His most recent books are *Great Ideas in Physics,* an introductory college textbook; *Ancient Light,* a summary of what is known about the origin and evolution of the universe; and *Origins: The Lives and Worlds of Modern Cosmologists,* a book of interviews with 27 cosmologists.

Mr. Lightman is a reserved man who measures his words as carefully in speech as he does in writing, and he leaves the impression that he means what he says. His humor often has the deadpan, dry quality of someone from Maine, where he spends his summers. A Yankee could get the impression that Mr. Lightman himself is a Yankee, but he was actually born and brought up in Tennessee, and he occasionally stretches a vowel in the Southern manner.

"First of all," he begins, "I don't know where ideas come from. But I'm pretty sure that the first thing that came to me was the title. The two words 'Einstein' and 'dreams' together represent a wonderful tension between the physical and the psychological."

"Einstein connotes for us a rational, logical, detached notion of the physical world," he says, "whereas our dreams emerge from a more ambiguous world, an inner world where all kinds of possibilities constantly open up to us, where we can fly, where we're vulnerable, where we take chances."

Gradually, Mr. Lightman says, his professional writing has evolved from scientific papers, to essays about the human side of science, to experiments with fictional techniques in those essays by telling stories with a point. He began *Einstein's Dreams,* his first novel, in the spring of 1991, after the title "dropped down from the sky." He finished it eight months later.

He finds writing fiction both exhilarating and terrifying. The frightening part, he says, is when the characters come alive.

"The novel, or whatever you are writing, starts flopping around like a fish," he says. "You don't have complete control of it. I have learned you shouldn't try to sit on the fish. You should let it flop a little bit."

He banned any of the usual explanatory science-for-the-public prose from the novel because, he says, "it would have killed the book."

"I think my background as a physicist was essential for imagining the many different ways that time might behave," he adds. "But once I conceived a particular dream world, I resisted the strong temptation to make that world scientifically plausible."

He does hope that readers may come away with the impression that the scientific process can sometimes be mysterious. "When a scientific idea is emerging in the mind of a scientist," he says, "and before it gets distilled into an equation, that process is very similar to any creative process, artistic or literary."

Mr. Lightman's own life as a scientist has largely been squeezed out by his writing and administrative duties. He became the head of the writing and humanistic-studies program a year and a half ago. "I felt I owed MIT some service," he says of the job. "But I don't think I was cut out to be an administrator. It is completely antithetical to creative activity."

From boyhood, Mr. Lightman says, he has always had a strong interest in both science and the humanities. As a teen-ager he wrote poetry and built model rockets. He studied at Princeton University and the California Institute of Technology, then taught physics and astronomy at Harvard and conducted research at the Smithsonian Astrophysical Observatory. MIT attracted him with a position as a professor of science and writing, an appointment that spanned two colleges.

He still considers himself partly a scientist, even if he is not now active in research. He remembers watching a boat pull a water-skier wearing a wing-like parachute up into the air last summer and feeling compelled to calculate what determined the angle of the rope. "I think I will always have that love of science—to try to figure things out," he says.

He slipped an inside joke for scientists into *Einstein's Dreams.* One of the chapters describes a world in which time passes more slowly for people traveling at high speeds. As a result, people put their houses and offices on wheels and propel the buildings with the most powerful engines they can devise. Everyone is trying to move faster than anyone else, so that time will pass more slowly for them. The concept behind the chapter is the theory of relativity.

"This particular fantasy world is at least as fantastic as the other worlds," he says. "So unless you knew, you wouldn't be able to pick it out and say, 'Aha, there's the correct theory of time.'"

"Modern physics has uncovered a view of the world that is utterly fantastic and non-intuitive and incredible."

When Mr. Lightman finished the book he sent it to his agent in New York. He also sent it, with some nervousness, to a dozen or so writers he admires, a mixture of poets, science writers, and novelists, including Oliver Sacks, a neurologist who has written about brain disorders, and Doris Lessing, the fiction writer.

Mr. Lightman also sent a manuscript to Salman Rushdie, whom he had never met but whose work he admires. "There are similarities in the fantasy elements that he has used in his writing and what I have used," says Mr. Lightman. (He sent the book to Mr. Rushdie through a series of agents, since Mr. Rushdie is still in hiding as a result of having been sentenced to death by Iran's Ayatollah Khomeini for writing the novel *The Satanic Verses,* which many Muslims found sacrilegious.)

"Sending the book to Salman Rushdie was like sending a note off in a bottle," he says. "It was a million-to-one long shot that he would ever get the book and 10 million to one that he would ever look at it."

In a letter that Mr. Rushdie sent back, he told Mr. Lightman that he found *Einstein's Dreams* "at once intellectually provocative and touching and comic and so very beautifully written." Mr. Lightman says he was looking for criticism, not a blurb, but the sentence wound up on the book's jacket anyway.

The responses he got from Mr. Rushdie, Mr. Sacks, Ms. Lessing, and other writers were among the most meaningful reactions he has received, Mr. Lightman says. "At that point I was completely satisfied," he says, "It didn't matter to me what else happened." The reviews have been mostly admiring—"an elegant wisp of a novel" (*The New York Times*), "amusing, thought-provoking, and charming" (*The Wall Street Journal*), and "so magical, so beautiful, so *shining,* that it immediately transports you back to childhood" (*Chicago Sun-Times*). Not every dream world Mr. Lightman constructed works for all readers, however. A writer for the *Voice Literary Supplement* found that sometimes Mr. Lightman's "conceit creaks."

In public appearances that Mr. Lightman made on a 10-day book tour last month, he preferred reading from the book to talking about it. "Fiction should stand on its own," he told an audience at Chapters, a Washington bookstore. In that reading, he sat before rows of shelves at a large oak table. With a crystal pitcher of water and a glass at his elbow, he cracked open his small, black-and-gold book and began to read:

> In this world, the passage of time brings increasing order. Order is the law of nature, the universal trend, the cosmic direction. If time is an arrow, that arrow points toward order. . . .

> In such a world, people with untidy houses lie in their beds and wait for the forces of nature to jostle the dust from their windowsills and straighten the shoes in their closets. People with untidy affairs may picnic while their calendars become organized, their appointments arranged, their accounts balanced. Lipsticks and brushes and letters may be tossed into purses with the satisfaction that they will sort themselves out automatically. Gardens need never be pruned, weeds never uprooted. Desks become neat by the end of the day. Clothes on the floor in the evening lie on chairs in the morning. Missing socks reappear.

> If one visits a city in spring, one sees another wondrous sight. For in springtime the populace

become sick of the order in their lives. In spring, people furiously lay waste to their houses. They sweep in dirt, smash chairs, break windows.

An audience of 50 or so people listened intently. A gray-haired man smiled at Mr. Lightman's description of one world in which time slowed down as distance increased from the center of the earth. To avoid aging, people lived at the highest elevations possible and put their houses on stilts.

After reading a few selections, Mr. Lightman took a few questions, signed some books, and then flew back to Boston. He had to teach his course—"Introduction to Astrophysics and Astronomy"—the next day.

In his office, Mr. Lightman elaborates on what he hopes the novel will accomplish.

"I would hope that each of the fantasy worlds has some grain of truth in it about our world and the way we behave and the way time shapes our world."

"The psychological dimensions of time are very rich," he continues. "A number of readers have told me they think about things differently now."

Maybe time is a spiral, like the tape in a tape recorder, recording motion and life, then winding down to a halt. In blue jeans, white sweater, and leather work boots, Mr. Lightman sits with his hands clasped in his lap. The tape recorder on his desk clicks off. Outside his office window, the snowflakes stop in mid-air. (pp. A6, A13)

> *David L. Wheeler, "Exploring the Nature of Time in Physics and in Fiction," in* The Chronicle of Higher Education, *April 14, 1993, pp. A6, A13.*

Alan Lightman with *CLC Yearbook* (interview date 7 August 1993)

[*In the excerpt below, Lightman discusses* Einstein's Dreams, *his aims as a writer, and his literary influences.*]

[*CLC Yearbook*]: *What are your primary aims or goals as an author?*

[Lightman]: To convey the mentality and culture of the world of science, which is as foreign to most people as India is to an American.

Please discuss any background research you conducted for **Einstein's Dreams.**

Research on the geography and culture of Switzerland, 1900.

Are your personal experiences incorporated into **Einstein's Dreams?** *Were you inspired by any specific events or people?*

I used my personal experiences and understanding of people to imagine how people would behave if time behaved differently.

Who are your primary literary influences, and why?

Italo Calvino, Gabriel García Márquez, Luis Borges, Salman Rushdie, Michael Bulgakov—I love writers who distort reality in order to see reality more clearly; these writers also write beautifully.

Do you currently have any works-in-progress? Do you foresee a departure or continuation of the style/themes of your writing in future works?

Einstein's Dreams is my first work of fiction, after many books of nonfiction. I am currently working on a second novel.

Fae Myenne Ng

Bone

Ng is an American novelist, born in 1957(?).

INTRODUCTION

Set in San Francisco's Chinatown, *Bone* focuses on the effects of cultural assimilation on Chinese Americans. Told by Leila, the eldest daughter of the Leong family, the novel provides a provocative account of the humiliation and discrimination many immigrants and first-generation Americans endured. *Bone* details the superstitions and prejudices perpetuated by and inflicted upon the Leongs, the conflicts that arise within the confines of Chinatown and their home, and Leila's feelings of guilt, resentment, and alienation. Central to the family's history are the tenuous marriage of Mah and Leon Leong and each daughter's reaction to the assimilation process and immigrant experience: Leila works as a liaison between the Chinese community and San Francisco's English-speaking public school system; Nina escapes to Manhattan and travels to the Orient as a tour guide; and Ona remains in Chinatown where she eventually commits suicide. Critics have praised the sparse prose of *Bone* which, according to Ng, reflects the frugality of the lives of Chinese immigrants. Commending the novel's prose style, Michiko Kakutani stated: "Blessed with a poet's gift for metaphor and a reporter's eye for detail, Ms. Ng writes with grace, authority, and grit."

CRITICISM

Cristina Garcia   (review date 10 January 1993)

[*Garcia is a Cuban-born American fiction writer and editor whose first novel,* Dreaming in Cuban, *was nominated for the 1992 National Book Award. In the review below, she offers a mixed assessment of* Bone.]

In Fae Myenne Ng's delicately wrought first novel, one senses the profound loneliness at the heart of the immigration experience, of the immigrant family itself—a cutting off from the past, a furious remaking of the present, febrile hopes for the future. "Family exists only because somebody has a story, and knowing the story connects us to a history," says Leila, the narrator of *Bone* and the eldest

daughter of a Chinese-American family in San Francisco. "To us, the deformed man is oddly compelling, the forgotten man is a good story, and a beautiful woman suffers."

In *Bone,* the deformed man is Leila's stepfather, Leon Leong, a dreamer and schemer with a hopeful heart and the merchant seaman's lust for adventure. The forgotten man is Lyman Fu, her father who migrated to Australia years ago, leaving his wife and daughter to fend for themselves in America. And the beautiful women are Leila's mother, Mah, whose good looks have been ravaged by years toiling in a Chinatown sweatshop, and Ona, the middle daughter, who jumped off the 13th floor of a Chinatown housing project, leaving her family behind to fathom why.

Ng assembles her characters' varied histories much the way Mah pieces together culottes and party dresses at her sewing machine, one seam, one story at a time. In the end, Ng has fashioned a spare, elegant book embedded with small fireworks of imagery and insight. When the "sewing ladies" came to comfort Mah after Ona kills herself, they "pushed in with their hello smiles, their arms full of food. Colored threads trailed in under their slippered feet." Leila, considering her stepsister's suicide, says:

> I want to sweep over her whole life and comb out all the sadness that made her do it. Like Leon and Mah, I went over every moment I had with Ona and tried to find my own moment of failure.

> Fault. In English or Cantonese, that was the word we were all afraid of. I held it like a seed in my mouth.

The portrait Ng paints of contemporary Chinatown is not particularly picturesque, but it is honest, fresh, beguiling. Her characters curse and gamble and fight, drive fast American cars, use recreational drugs. They have names like Zeke, Priscilla and Mason. They work in fast-food joints and mechanics' garages. They get drunk on Tom Collinses, get married in Reno, rebel against seeming "too Chinesey." They watch a lot of *I Love Lucy*.

Unfortunately, there is a hollowness at the core of the novel. Ona, the middle daughter, the daughter who killed herself, remains a cipher throughout. Despite all the family suffering and the pointed analysis by stepsister Leila, Ona remains a mystery, barely convincing even as a memory. With few exceptions, details about her life seem vague, almost generic, and her ill-fated love affair with a half-Peruvian, half-Chinese boy named Osvaldo Ong seems more the stuff of distraction than tragedy.

Sadly, the most salient description of Ona is of her fascination with numbers:

> Ona was a counter. She counted the one hundred and forty times our pet rooster crowed in his short life; she tried to keep count of the number of culottes Mah sewed one summer (Mah sewed faster than Ona could keep count). She counted off the days till Leon was coming home, and then she stood at the mouth of the alley, counting the cabs that went by.

Furthermore, Leila, on whom we depend to tell her step-sister's story, seems oddly removed from her death. She relies on shorthand psychology and aphorisms to summarize Ona's life. Leila burdens the story with obvious explanations, and yet despite this, Ona somehow still eludes her—and us.

Perhaps Ng's point is partly this: that we live among ghosts, that we hardly know those we think we love, that the human heart is ultimately unknowable. But with so much of *Bone* dependent on the messy aftermath of Ona's death, so much regret and soul-searching wracking Ona's family, the fact that we don't know her better, cannot care more for her, leaves us emotionally frustrated as readers.

Happily, though, like the dried plums Leila and her step-sisters loved to suck on as children, there is much else to savor in this novel: the cultural collisions and unlikely juxtapositions that claim all new immigrants; the growing sense of a new "vocabulary of feeling" that is swelling and enriching the English language; the mysteries and rhythms of adaptation.

Leila's stepfather told his daughters once that "sorrow moves through the heart the way a ship moves through the ocean." Despite its shortcomings, Fae Myenne Ng's fine, moving novel leaves a bittersweet wake in the heart.

> *Cristina Garcia, "Reading Chinese Fortunes," in* The Washington Post, *January 10, 1993, p. 8.*

Richard Eder   (review date 14 January 1993)

[*Eder is an American journalist and Pulitzer Prize-winning critic. In the following review, he favorably assesses* Bone, *considering it "a gritty and moving story" about the immigrant and assimilation experience in America.*]

In each national variation on the American novel of ethnic assimilation and estrangement, there is the battering of the old country by the new, the pains and gains of the young and the cleavages and dilutions in the family traditions. In none of them does the family loom so large as in the work of Chinese-American writers.

More than with Irish-American, Italian-American or Jewish-American stories, the emphasis is on what is lost or sacrificed. In different ways and to different degrees, we find in the fiction of Amy Tan, Gish Jen and David Wong Louie something much graver than simply a wry, a difficult or even painful adjustment.

The edifice of tradition is more complex and redoubtable, and it collapses in dangerous shards. What goes on inside the Chinese-American protagonists can approach a deranging displacement. Most distinctively, the displacement is registered not just in the old but in the young as well.

Fae Myenne Ng's *Bone* is in this tradition. Its story of an old San Francisco couple and their three grown children gives a sense of the wildness underlying the changes that the two generations go through. Tragic things happen, although the book is not a tragedy, nor is it written in tragic tones. The voices of the narrator—oldest of the three children—and of the others are terse and percussive. They shift abruptly from the emotional to the matter-of-fact with an effect that is sometimes comic and often coolly illuminating.

Leila tells her family's story. Mah and Leon, her mother and stepfather, are immigrants who have struggled all their lives to survive. Mah sewed long hours in a Chinese sweatshop and, after hours, at home; more recently, she opened a modest Chinatown clothes shop.

Leon shipped out for months at a time as a merchant seaman; in between, he took a variety of grueling shore jobs. Leila is a social worker in the Chinese community; Nina, the youngest, lives in New York and works as a tour guide for American groups visiting China. The middle sister, Ona, kills herself by jumping from the upper floor of a San Francisco housing development.

Ona's death is the shattering of the family vessel. Leila's account portrays the pressures that led to it and the secondary explosions that followed. She tells it as a series of vignettes that range back and forth between past and present.

Ona is not really the focus. We learn relatively little about her or, for that matter, about her death. As a child she was Leon's pet. Later he threw her out for going around with the son of a business partner who had swindled him. She was, in that sense, a rebel against her family's ways and means.

But what we gradually see, in Ng's lively and artful unfolding of the story, is that they all were. Nina has kept her distance, although she stays in touch and returns for Ona's funeral. Leila has stayed in San Francisco to mediate between Mah and Leon, who are stormily apart as much as stormily together. But she lives with her kind, handsome and—ethnically speaking—liberated Chinese-American boyfriend, an auto mechanic. Both sisters feel insufficient.

"She thought I had the peace of heart, knowing I'd done my share for Mah and Leon," Leila says of Nina. "And I thought she had the courage of heart, doing what she wanted."

Solicitous and impatient, guilty and pluckily inquisitive by turns, Leila reveals herself as well as her story. Nina, more distant, is drawn with less detail and equal sharpness. "I know about *should*. I know about *have to*," she replies when Leila refers to their parents' emotional neediness. "We want to do more, we want to do everything. But I've learned this: I can't."

The book's strength and surprise, however, lie in its portraits of Mah and Leon. For a while, these are amusingly colorful characters, warring with each other and with America. Mah seems to be the traditional Chinese matriarch: bossy, emotional and continually deserted by Leon. He goes to sea or flees periodically to a downtown hostel, littering his room with half-finished repair projects and mooching around with his old Chinatown cronies.

Amid this agreeable picturesqueness and a lively Chinatown scene, Ng inserts a deeper story. It is Mah and Leon, in fact, who are the real rebels. Immigrating to America was a leap into peril; it meant two lifetimes of punishing labor and social humiliation. It meant settling for the "bone" of the title. It meant that their children could live with more choices—and with burdens of guilt and cultural confusion.

But Mah and Leon are rebels against their own choices as well. Leon's flights are part of it. So was Mah's affair with her sweatshop boss. So was her unexpected agreement to go on a Hong Kong vacation with Nina shortly after Ona's death, while Leon, the apparent freebooter, stays home to take care of things.

Bone, although it can be facile and sentimental—Leila's boyfriend is too much of a perfect prince, for example—tells a gritty and moving story. Inside their cantankerousness and traditionalism, the two old people are as impulsive and unconstrained as children, free spirits in their yokes.

Richard Eder, "A Gritty Story of Assimilation," in Los Angeles Times, *January 14, 1993, p. E5.*

An excerpt from *Bone*

I sipped again: a long bitter taste. And it was Ona. That's the thing that was in my head. Everything went back to Ona. And beyond Ona there was the bad luck that Leon kept talking about. What made Ona do it. Like she had no choice.

Leon blamed himself. He had this crazy idea that our family's bad luck started when he broke his promise to Grandpa Leong. Grandpa Leong was Leon's father only on paper; he sponsored Leon's entry into the country by claiming him as his own son. It cost Leon. Each time he told us, his eyes opened wide like he was hearing the price called out for the first time. "Five thousand American dollars." Of more consequence was the promise to send Grandpa Leong's bones back to China. Leon was away when Grandpa Leong died. Leon worried about the restless bones, and for years, whenever something went wrong—losing a job, losing the bid for the takeout joint, losing the Ong and Leong Laundry—Leon blamed the bones. But in the end the bones remained here.

Then Ona jumped and it was too late. The bones were lost, like Ona was lost. That's why Leon shipped out on a cargo voyage. Cape Horn was as far away as a ship could go. Forty days to the bottom of the world.

Mah thought it was the bad choices she made. My father, Lyman Fu. Her affair with Tommie Hom. She thought all the bad luck started with her.

Nina blamed us, this family. Everybody. Everything. Salmon Alley. The whole place. That's why she's in New York now. Getting pregnant didn't have to be a problem—I told her to keep the abortion a secret. It was her business. Nobody had to know. Telling was her way out. For a long time she didn't call me, and even now she only half tells me what she does, who she sees. I hear it from other people. My own sister. The way I see it, she's afraid to let us know too much. I used to think she was ashamed of us: the way Leon has turned into an old-man bum, and how bitter Mah is now.

Who knows what she thinks of me? Somehow Nina thought the problem was a combination of us together, cooped up on Salmon Alley. We stirred up the bad luck.

I thought I knew Ona. She was the middle girl, the in-between one. I thought she was some kind of blend of Nina and me, but I had no idea it was such a dangerous mix. Now I feel that I should have known, that I should've *said* something that might have anchored her.

Nina gets mad at me when I keep on about it. "Let it go," she said. "Ona had her own life. It was her choice."

Maybe Nina's right. Too much happened on Salmon Alley.

Fae Myenne Ng, in her Bone, *Hyperion, 1993.*

Michiko Kakutani   (review date 29 January 1993)

[*In the review below, Kakutani praises Ng's convincing use of memory and realistic depictions of Chinese immigrant life in America.*]

"Remembering the past gives power to the present," says Leila Leong, the narrator of Fae Myenne Ng's incantatory first novel [*Bone*]. "Memories do add up." Our memories, she continues, can't bring back the dead, "but they count to keep them from becoming strangers."

Moving backward in time like Harold Pinter's *Betrayal* or the Stephen Sondheim musical *Merrily We Roll Along*, *Bone* is a memory-novel, a novel composed of Leila's memories of her family, and her family's memories of their past lives in China and their new lives in the United States. It is a meditation upon the circumstances surrounding the mysterious suicide of Leila's sister Ona and the endless reverberations that that death has had on the entire Leong clan.

As Leila tells us, she is the oldest of the three Leong daughters: Ona was the middle sister; Nina, the youngest. Leila's own father disappeared before her birth, and she regards Leon—her mother's second husband, and the father of Ona and Nina—as her own father.

All of the Leongs blame themselves for Ona's death. Leon thinks he's brought bad luck on the family by failing to honor a promise he made to his adoptive father to return his bones to China. Mah, the mother, worries that her own sins—having an affair with her boss, Tommy Hon—have doomed the family to unhappiness. And Leila berates herself for not having paid more attention to Ona's problems, for not figuring out that something was wrong.

All three sisters, we learn, have had a difficult time straddling their parents' circumscribed world in San Francisco's Chinatown and the bustling, contemporary world beyond. They feel at once suffocated by Mah and Leon's provincialism and guilty about the freedoms and luxuries they take for granted as young American women; at once resentful of their parents' enslavement to the past and wistful about the history that eludes them here in the United States.

"We're lucky, not like the bondmaids growing up in service, or the newborn daughters whose mouths were stuffed with ashes," Leila says.

> The beardless, soft-shouldered eunuchs, the courtesans with the three-inch feet and the frightened child brides—they're all stories to us. Nina, Ona and I, we're the lucky generation. Mah and Leon forced themselves to live through the humiliation in this country so that we could have it better. We know so little of the old country. We repeat the names of grandfathers and uncles, but they have always been strangers to us. Family exists only because somebody has a story, and knowing the story connects us to a history.

Each of the Leong daughters has tried to make her own separate peace with her past. Leila has remained at home, working as a counselor at a local school and keeping a watchful eye on her parents. Nina has fled Chinatown altogether: she has moved to New York and taken a job as an airline flight attendant. Ona has found herself stuck midway between the old world and the new: she works as a hostess at Trader Vic's, and dates Osvaldo, the son of her father's former partner and current nemesis. Under fierce pressure from her parents, she breaks off with Osvaldo, an event that will play a pivotal role in her eventual suicide.

The Romeo and Juliet story of Osvaldo and Ona isn't the only melodrama in the Leong family saga. As Leila unpeels the layers of her family's past, we learn that her parents' lives, too, have been fraught with passion, anger and sadness. Summarily abandoned by her first husband, Mah married Leon, knowing his job as a merchant sailor would keep him traveling a good part of the time: such a marriage, she reasoned, would enable her to calibrate her emotional commitment and protect herself from further hurt. Instead, there were loneliness and days and weeks of waiting, and Mah soon fell into an affair with her employer.

When Leon discovered the affair, he moved out of the house on Salmon Alley and took a shabby room at a nearby boarding house. There, he passes the time dreaming up get-rich-quick schemes and silly new inventions: electric sinks, cookie-tin clocks, cash registers with intercoms.

Though a rapprochement of sorts had been arranged, Leon and Mah have recently been estranged again by the very losses that should have made them partners in grief: their life savings in a failed business venture, and Ona, who leaped off the 13th floor of a nearby housing project.

Having grown up in San Francisco's Chinatown herself, Ms. Ng conjures the immigrant world of Mah and Leon with the affectionate knowledge of an insider and the observant unsentimentality of an outsider. She conveys to the reader the incredible hardship of these characters' lives: the long years spent in sweatshops and kitchens and laundry rooms, the hours and hours spent waiting in lines for Social Security and unemployment compensation. We are made to see, through the eyes of Leila, both the remarkable perseverance of her parents in the face of so much difficulty, and the degree to which that perseverance has been built, in equal parts, on naïveté and genuine courage.

Blessed with a poet's gift for metaphor and a reporter's eye for detail, Ms. Ng writes with grace, authority and grit. The reader eagerly awaits her next book.

> *Michiko Kakutani, "Building on the Pain of a Past in China," in* The New York Times, *January 29, 1993, p. C26.*

Louis B. Jones   (review date 7 February 1993)

[*Jones is an American novelist. In the review of* Bone *below, he commends Ng's prose style and lauds her depictions of the assimilation process faced by Chinese Americans.*]

In Fae Myenne Ng's sophisticated first novel, *Bone*, the prose has the sort of profound restraint that first strikes the reader as deceptively simple; but on closer inspection, it seems an example of that rarer quality, simplicity itself. In the way that a single stroke of an inked brush can cause a horse's solid leg to pour out onto the page, so Ms. Ng touches negative space to bring up three-dimensional people. The first lines are a good example:

> We were a family of three girls. By Chinese standards, that wasn't lucky. In Chinatown, everyone knew our story. Outsiders jerked their chins, looked at us, shook their heads. We heard things.

> "A failed family. That Dulcie Fu. And you know which one: bald Leon. Nothing but daughters."

> Leon told us not to care about what people said. "People talking. People jealous." He waved a hand in the air. "Five sons don't make one good daughter."

Bone is a novel about the younger generation in San Francisco's Chinatown—the girls in nice sweaters, their boyfriends in freshly washed Trans Ams or BMW's—and their parents, in black cloth shoes, who may still have only fragments of English; to their children, they have perhaps begun to seem mean or stingy, their circumstances indefinably sticky. *Bone* is a novel about getting out of Chinatown—or, rather, about whether one should want to get out—and all the unforgivable disloyalty of "assimilation," as entering mainstream culture is referred to, in an unfortunate metaphor of digestion.

The story takes the form of an inward-spiraling meditation by Dulcie Fu's oldest daughter, Leila, on a single event: the death of the family's middle sister, Ona, who jumped or fell from the 13th floor of a big pink apartment building on the edge of Chinatown, stoned on Quaaludes. The novel is plotless in the sense that no other crucial event takes place, but the reader feels pushed forward by the diagnostic motive that floods all suicide narratives. On the occasion of self-slaughter, one of the most taboo of human deeds, we all join in asking the same pressing question: "Why?"

Unluckily for readers of *Bone,* the question can't be answered, because not enough is known of the circumstances surrounding Ona's death. Nobody was with her at the time. This element of mystery is one of the things that makes Ms. Ng's book feel more like reality than fiction; it has reality's exasperating pointlessness. Ona died for no apparent "reason" in the moral etiology that a work of fiction usually provides. The best guess, on the evidence in the book, is that her death was accidental: she was sleepy on downers; she had too much to live for; she had made an appointment for the following day. But if Ona's death is intended as a symbol for the book's larger theme, it's definitely a case of suicide.

This theme is the difficulty of cultural assimilation. And Leila implies in several misty passages that jumping was Ona's only escape from being "stuck" in Chinatown. The youngest sister, Nina, had already escaped, to New York City. Leila also has saved herself by moving across town to live with her boyfriend, Mason Louie, a provider of an-

esthetics like drugs, fast cars and sex (for, in the book's one sex scene, physical love is construed as a rubbing toward numbness, toward forgetfulness of Chinatown). When Leila joylessly, almost furtively, marries Mason, the event is treated within her family almost as (like suicide) a form of self-erasure, an application for a foreign visa.

In America, a magical injustice reigns. "In this country, paper is more precious than blood," Leila's stepfather, Leon, tells his friend You Thin Toy. In order to get to California, Leon had to invent "paper" ancestors; his wife married him only for his green card; when he tries to visit a grave, he discovers that it can only be done with the proper documents. Families are destroyed in the scramble to cross the impossible ocean, and then they are reassembled out of severed pieces in America's Chinatowns, mysterious sovereign colonies where the census taker doesn't go and a social security number is merely a strange token of a civic religion.

America is still a distinctly abstract country to those who live here. It's still an idea, a sort of project. The Jeffersonian notion is that yes, in a way, paper *is* more important than blood. And so waves of immigrant literature continue to announce the birth of new middle classes, the transcendence of the ghetto. We novelists practice a bourgeois art form, and scholars like to say that the novel as a literary form evolved along with the bourgeoisie, to tell that most self-conscious class what to do and to illuminate what it already is doing, the theory being that the upper and lower classes don't need (or care) to be given such instruction. The wonderful efflorescence in Chinese-American fiction seems to inform a robust new class, naming ambivalence and ambiguities far removed from the good-against-evil moral structure one finds in the traditional tales of older societies throughout the world. Ambiguity and ambivalence, after all, are expensive luxuries. Leila is a modern woman; her problem is that her parents have started to look like peasants to her, and she doesn't know how to feel about these new perceptions.

As a matter of fact, the reader doesn't know how to feel about them either. The literature of assimilation lives uncomfortably—and sometimes, therefore, humorously—on a lively, anxious boundary line. On the one hand, we mourn the departure from an ancient culture; on the other, we're occasionally asked to see that same culture in its absurd or even harmful aspects. In *Bone,* Ms. Ng has provided no attitudinal clues to keep the reader morally comfortable, and what results is an authentic journey into a mysterious place. Leila says of her husband: "Sure, I went for Mason for his looks, his long, lean build and his car. But he's got plenty of other qualities: he has a job and he finishes whatever he starts." And of her mother and stepfather: "She married Leon for the green card. . . . He didn't care; he knew his card was good forever." As we listen to Leila, we suddenly find ourselves a little bit closer—closer than we in the middle class ordinarily prefer—to a certain steady pulmonary connection between love and money.

Bone, which reportedly took 10 years to compose, is written in a perfectly clear, undecorated prose that stops the eye at every sentence. Simply by telling the unadorned facts of the story, Ms. Ng makes it clear that moving across town to a new neighborhood can be, in its own way, as hard as crossing the Pacific Ocean. (pp. 7, 9)

> *Louis B. Jones, "Dying to Be An American," in* The New York Times Book Review, *February 7, 1993, pp. 7, 9.*

Ng on writing *Bone:*

My test as a fiction writer was to create a whole landscape—a place and people that express everything I learned growing up in that world.

Fae Myenne Ng, in Abby Tannenbaum's "Getting to the Marrow," in New York, *25 January 1993.*

Diane Yen-Mei Wong   (review date Spring 1993)

[*Wong was coordinating editor for* Making Waves: An Anthology by and about Asian American Women *(1989). In the following review, she lauds the stylistic aspects of* Bone.]

Readers who choose to spend the night with Fae Myenne Ng's **Bone** must accept the all-too-clear conclusion of the plot, which Ng presents in one paragraph at the beginning of the first chapter: "Mah and Leon are still married, but after Ona jumped off the Nam, Leon moved out. It was a bad time. Too much happened on Salmon Alley. We don't talk about it. Even the sewing ladies leave it alone."

There it is: the entire plot. Don't expect surprises, because the novel's strength is not the plot. And the reverse chronological order of the book can sometimes be annoying: Ng litters her pages with portents of suicide and death.

Having written that revealing paragraph, though, Ng can then use her nonstop staccato brush to paint a vivid picture of the real Chinatown, a stark ghetto that exists behind tourist facades and above the import/export shops lining crowded streets—a community struggling to survive economically and culturally.

Ng develops multidimensional Chinese Americans and presents them through the eyes of an insider, Leila, through whom we discover complexity and humanity. As the oldest daughter and the child to whom her parents turn for help in interacting with the white world, Leila must look for proof of her stepfather's age to help qualify him for Social Security. She searches through his old suitcase and finds a treasure chest containing photos and other mementos that make up his life:

> A scarf with a colored map of Italy. Spanish pesetas in an envelope. Old Chinese money. Dinner menus from the American President Lines. The Far East itinerary for Matson Lines. A well-used bilingual cookbook. . . . Selections from newspapers.

Leila's mother, a garment worker, has spent all her life at a job that pays little and demands much in an industry that absorbs the life force of many immigrants. Ng's description disturbs and moves:

> She said she was ready to quit the sewing shops. I was glad to hear it. I'd watched the years of working in the sweatshops change her body. Her neck softened. Her shoulders grew heavy. Work was her whole life, and every forward stitch marked time passing. She wanted to get out before her whole life passed under the stamping needles.

With the plot's outline already clearly defined, Ng takes time to play with words. From the beginning, the rhythm of each phrase cannot be ignored. The quick beat and minimal phrasing used to describe Leila's time with lover Mason reflect the pace of their interaction, which is constantly interrupted by her parents' unending demands: "We dozed and woke up starved. It was dark by the time we finished our burritos at the taqueria down the block. We stopped at the corner bodega for some groceries: juice and milk and bread for morning, chips and beer for that night."

As the story progresses, the reader discovers that Ng's love of language does not stop with rhythm: it extends to alliteration ("I signed where the policeman pointed. Pen. Paper. Press down.") and onomatopoeia ("I love the tuck-perfect fit of the drawers, and the *tock!* sound the brass handles make against the hard wood"). Playful language does not, however, mask the book's serious nature.

Bone is a book about survival and the price it exacts on immigrants and their children: Leila survives by remaining attached to her family; the youngest survives by cutting ties; the middle child despairs because she cannot find a path that allows her to be herself and her parents' child.

Leon, the stepfather, once told Leila that there was a Chinese tradition of honoring paper and treating all writing as sacred. Ng's writing may not be sacred, but it is worthy of respect.

> *Diane Yen-Mei Wong, "Survival," in* Belles Lettres: A Review of Books by Women, *Vol. 8, No. 3, Spring, 1993, p. 21.*

Nancy Stetson   (essay date 4 April 1993)

[*In the essay below, Ng discusses her prose style and the autobiographical and realistic nature of* Bone.]

When author Fae Myenne Ng was growing up in San Francisco's Chinatown, she saw how people in the community would send relatives' bones back to China for burial. She was so impressed with this tradition that she made it an important element in her debut novel, **Bone.**

"I was very moved by this bone ritual when I was a child," Ng says in a telephone interview. The "old-timers," she explains, saw America as a place to work and China as home. They always intended to return home, but couldn't, due to the Chinese revolution and American laws.

"This is the generation of men that inspired my life as a writer and this book in particular," Ng says. "They came to this country to make a living and to bring it home and to raise their families, but in the end they couldn't do that. The working class . . . find themselves at the end of their lives in these SRO [single room occupancy] hotels with only their pennies.

"It was very important to make this journey back home after death. They talked about it. It was dreamed of. That moved me. I call the book *Bone* to honor that tradition. I'm not able to send bones back to China, to send this generation of men, to give them back what they missed out on in their lives. But somehow, creating this book . . . was a way of giving a resting place to my memories of them."

Bone, narrated by the eldest of three daughters, focuses on the struggles and conflicts within one Chinese family in San Francisco. The mother, Mah, marries Leon in a marriage of convenience. Leon, a merchant seaman, leaves the family for weeks at a time to escape his tumultuous marriage. An unrealistic schemer, he loses the family's money in a business failure. The youngest daughter moves across the continent to the East Coast to escape. The middle daughter escapes permanently by jumping off a building.

Those who are left struggle with questions and guilt. Leon believes he brought all this upon the family because he neglected to send the bones of his paper father to China. (The man was not a blood relative; the relationship existed only on paper, so the Immigration and Naturalization Service would allow Leon into the country.)

Critics and readers praise the book. "Readers understand the anger," says Ng. "They understand being in many of the different predicaments: having parents that you have to take care of, having sisters that you don't know, wanting to be closer to people that you can't understand. We all have parents that we have to leave on different levels, and we all have to leave something in our lives. The book in many ways is about that desire to escape."

Ng's own parents are unable to read their daughter's book because it's in English. "I've been able to tell them that the heart of the book celebrates the kind of hard work immigrants have put into this country as a way and an effort of setting up a foundation, a place for us to stand," Ng says. "I think that gives them comfort, because it helps them to understand that their labor and their sacrifices are appreciated."

Ng, 36, now lives in Brooklyn with her husband, writer Mark Coovelis. She spent 10 years writing *Bone,* supporting herself as a waitress and by doing temporary work. She also received fellowships from foundations such as the National Endowment for the Arts.

In *Bone,* Ng says, "I worked very hard at creating a very simple and honest and bare language, because I wanted the language to reflect the frugality of these people's lives, of hard-working classes of people who have very little but don't waste anything. . . .

"I think my study of the Chinese poets really gave me a very good discipline, because there is a simplicity in Chinese poetry. But there's something very rich, and I wanted that quality of richness and the simplicity . . . Their images were just wonderful, [the language is] very precise, [and] has a way of exploding your imagination."

Just like Ng's own sentences. The old-timers would be proud.

Nancy Stetson, "Honoring Her Forebears," in Chicago Tribune, *April 4, 1993, p. 3.*

Fae Myenne Ng with Jennifer Brostrom, *CLC Yearbook* (interview date 4 January 1994)

[*In the following interview, Ng discusses Chinese-American culture and her novel* Bone.]

[*Brostrom*]: *What are your primary goals as an author?*

[Ng]: I want to write about true life. *Bone* was inspired by the Chinese bachelor society—the generation of laborers who came to America to work the gold mines, to build the transcontinental railroad, and to help develop California agriculturally; and who, because of many factors—the Chinese exclusion laws, the anti-miscegenation laws, the revolutions in China—lived out their lives in this country, many dying without the comfort of family.

Are your characters fictional or based on actual people you knew?

I took real conditions in Chinese-American history and created a fictional landscape in which to explore the effects of the exclusionary legislation. I was moved by the hard lives of the old-timers I knew, and the characters in *Bone* are created out of my witness of their hardships and my sadness at their passing.

Would you talk about your theme of emigration in **Bone?**

I wanted to explore the desire to escape—a place or condition, a community or a relationship—and I wanted to look at the courage it takes not only to leave, but to remake another world. In *Bone,* Mah's first marriage to Lei's father helps her escape war-torn China; her second marriage to Leon allows her to stay in America. In her infidelity, she hopes for true love. Leon buys his way out of China with a promise he cannot keep. The price for Lei's choice to stay close to the family is the constant negotiation between her sense of duty and her desire for independence. Nina believes that the problem is in the place, Chinatown, and flies to the far coast, but ironically, from New York, she takes tours to China, where she begins to find a way to reconcile her conflicted sense of loyalty.

Several critics commented on the novel's treatment of the subject of Chinese assimilation into American society. Can you comment on this?

Assimilation is often the first filter used to look at literatures of communities outside of the mainstream, the Other Americans. The world the sisters in *Bone* inhabit is clearly defined and culturally specific, but it is a world in the remaking. An old world is being broken down and a new world is to be created. None of the sisters want to enter Middle America. Each sister has a heroic dream of remaking her world with hope and courage, in the tradition inherited from their old-timer ancestors. *Bone* hopes to describe that journey, the personal and spiritual cost of leaving one life in order to make another.

Some reviewers wanted an explanation for Ona's suicide in **Bone.**

Suicide was another metaphor to speak about departure. My point was not why Ona committed suicide. The point was to suggest that there is a way to honor her decision.

Could you talk about the structure of the novel?

The backward-moving structure came from life. From the old-timers, I often heard the phrase, "Things were better back in China . . . back home . . . back then. . . . " The Chinese exclusionary laws provided another odd source of inspiration. These exclusionary laws taught people to taunt at us "Go back to China!" The desire to go home, the belief that home was "back there," and the exclusionary curse all influenced the question I started with: what was "back there?" Where was home?

The narrator Leila was in part my response to the damage caused by these exclusionary laws—I wanted the intimacy of her voice to invite the reader into a seemingly closed world. Creating this "welcome" in Leila's voice was a great challenge. This invitatory tone is a gesture that counteracts the damage of this country's exclusionary legislations.

What kind of research was involved in writing **Bone?**

An old-timer who worked the graveyard janitorial shift at the Fairmont used to bring me all the newspapers the guests left behind, a gesture that sparked my love for reading and for learning about current events. While thinking about and planning my novel, I read the *Records of the Grand Historian of China,* Lu Chi's *Art of Letters,* Sun Tzu's *Art of War,* Lao Tze's *Treatise on Response and Retribution.* While writing, I read books on philosophy, cultural anthropology, the history of food and festivity, ancestral worship, and death and mourning rituals. I also read literature and archival material on Chinese-American immigration history. Of course, I also listened to any stories the old-timers wanted to share.

Can you discuss the language in **Bone?**

I wanted to create a language that reflected the frugality of the Chinese working class. The English had to be lean, unsparing, even brutal in its bareness because it was meant to reflect honestly the harshness of immigrant livelihood. But I also wanted the English to have a unique cadence that suggested the vitality and vibrancy in the Chinese language.

Bone seems to me to be the best metaphor for the enduring quality of the immigrant spirit. The book's title honors the old-timer's desire to have their bones sent back to China for proper burial. I wanted to remember the old-timers buried here against their wishes. As I wrote **Bone,** I was conscious of their regret, so I wanted to create in the language of the book, an English that could serve as the fertile and final resting place for my memories of the oldtimers.

In a New York Times *interview, you commented that the discipline of learning to sew helped you learn to write.*

What I learned from the sewing ladies is what you can learn from any laborer—stamina.

FURTHER READING

Mahin, Bill. "A Fine First Novel of a Chinese Girl's Coming of Age." *Chicago Tribune* 158, No. 56 (25 February 1993): Sec. 5, p. 3.

> Favorable assessment of *Bone,* focusing on Ng's portrayal of the Leong sisters and their reaction to the assimilation process.

Marcus, James. Review of *Bone,* by Fae Myenne Ng. *VLS,* No. 112 (February 1993): 5.

> Laudatory review of *Bone.* Marcus praises Ng's prose style and examines the title's relevance to the story.

Dale Peck
Martin and John

Born in 1968(?), Peck is an American novelist.

INTRODUCTION

Martin and John centers on John, a young gay man trying to cope with memories of childhood trauma and the death of Martin, his AIDS-infected lover. This work, which was published in Great Britain as *Fucking Martin,* is comprised of two interwoven narratives, both told by John. In one John recounts how he came to meet and fall in love with Martin. The other is a series of episodic short stories, each featuring a different pair of fictional lovers named Martin and John. Throughout the course of the novel, these narratives coalesce to form the narrator's identity. John explains, "I tell myself that by reinventing my life, my imagination imposes an order on things and makes them make sense. But sometimes I think that horror is all I know and all I'll ever know." Acclaimed by some critics for its candid exploration of such themes as child abuse, familial relationships, and victimization, *Martin and John* has been described by Michiko Kakutani as "a story about the cycles of pain and grief that spiral through people's lives, and the efforts an artist makes to reorder and transcend that hurt."

CRITICISM

Richard Eder   (review date 24 January 1993)

[*Eder is an American journalist and Pulitzer Prize-winning critic. In the review below, he praises Peck's unconventional depiction of the psychological aspects of homosexuality in* Martin and John.]

If there were a Lenin for the revolution in attitudes that recognizes homosexuality as an alternative normality, Dale Peck would be in Siberia. Not for right-wing obstructionism but for left-wing deviation. Once a revolution gets under way, its literature tends to be conservative in form and upbeat in outlook, like the primer about an amiable two-mother household that has caused such a furor in some of the New York schools.

Martin and John will never get into the schools. Not just because of its stylistic complexity and sometimes its diffi-culty, or its graphic renderings of homosexual acts ranging from tender to savage, or its grim detailing of the physical horrors in the last stages of AIDS.

Peck's first novel has a dark brilliance and moments of real beauty, but it is a book that is shocking, hard to accept fully, and hard to ignore. It is impassioned in its identification with the gay condition, yet it rides fiercely athwart any common notion of political correctness.

It is a *de profundis* that in some ways comes full circle once more to suggest the homosexual as ill, and AIDS as his scourge. But the older belief holds that homosexuality is a disease in a healthy world. *Martin and John* seems to imply that it is a flaming reaction—not healthy, exactly, but authentic and uncontainable—to a diseased one.

This is not explicit, and perhaps it is not quite the author's intended message. It is this reader's sense of the implications of a book that is a dazzling explosion of voices and stories that hide behind and emerge out of each other. It is a book of theatrical quick changes. Costumes are flaunted and removed to reveal other costumes, or to flash glimpses of what may be either flesh or a body stocking.

Peck has created two parallel sets of narrations. One is about John, who flees his prosperous and abusive widower father in Kansas, spends some time as a male hustler in New York, falls in love with Martin, who contracts AIDS, moves him back to Kansas where he nurses him until he dies, and then, HIV-positive, begins to write.

The second narrative is a string of episodes in which John and Martin move through a series of fictions about gay life, changing their own roles and identities in each one. Although typographically distinct, the two sets of narratives bleed into each other. By the end, after a woman in one of the episodes calls him Dale, it is clear that both the "real" and the "fictional" John largely represent the author, while the two Martins stand in different ways for the author's loves, needs and fantasies.

It can be hard to make out, and I had to go back over it a second time; and it changed color and shape somewhat when I did. But the darkness, glitteringly backlit or spotlit—it is impossible to get away from theatrical images—prevails almost entirely.

At first, and recurringly, it is in variations on the abusive father and the mother who dies, leaves or is destroyed. Later, it takes up a sexual chiaroscuro: promiscuous rough trade, a pseudo-masochistic episode, an old pimp who brutally initiates the "fictional" John, introduces him to physical ecstasy, cares for him lovingly, and then is nursed by him when he is dying. There are the different Martins, with brief moments of happiness and then the long despair and degradation of AIDS. There is, above all and through both sets of narratives, John's vertiginous sense of horror and unstable identity.

"I tell myself that by reinventing my life, my imagination imposes an order on things and makes them make sense," he tells us at the end, alone and trying to write. "But sometimes I think that horror is all I know and all I'll ever know. . . . "

The darkness has many variations. Some are stagy, for example a scene in which John gets a customer to penetrate him with a rifle and then scares him away by insisting that he pull the trigger. Others are pure agony: an episode in which John helps the dying Martin bathe as a stream of blood and feces washes down the drain. John imagines it contaminating the entire earth so humanity will die.

There is a comically campy fantasy in which Martin—rich, charming and talented—squires John around New York and spirits him off to Jamaica and Paris. When Martin performs at the piano, "the most masculine looking men rolled their eyes like queens. . . . The women leaned to one another and whispered 'Oh, if only . . .'" It is impure, demented Cole Porter. There is a breakfast before Martin falls ill. "Love is in the morning"—there had been sex the night before—Martin says, and for a moment, we get a sense of happiness that is universal.

One of the finest stories has John and Martin, already ill, working as night watchmen in Kansas and befriended by

what, in their sectarian universe, is the equivalent of the Righteous Gentile. Charlie, an old watchman, asks John about his girlfriends and then, silently understanding, invites them both to dinner. Too tactful to give direct advice, he manages to urge John to get in touch with his father. "When people are dead, that's not a good time to get acquainted, you know?"

It will not happen. The deepest darkness in *Martin and John* is about fathers. The "real" John's father drinks and seems to feel a mixture of love and resentment. Once, when John was a child, the father found him making a mess out of trying to fix a faucet. With who knows what mixture of anger and, possibly, widower's despair, he trod brutally on the boy's hand, maiming it. He was abjectly apologetic and avoided violence until, years later, when John was 14, he took offense at a snippy remark and slapped him. John was goaded into boasting about details of a homosexual encounter. Taunted and outraged, his father beat him up.

> *Martin and John* has a dark brilliance and moments of real beauty, but it is a book that is shocking, hard to accept fully, and hard to ignore. It is impassioned in its identification with the gay condition, yet it rides fiercely athwart any common notion of political correctness.
>
> —Richard Eder

The fictional episodes have all kinds of variations on the theme. A fictional father rapes John's quadriplegic mother; another half-strangles her, and a third father beats Martin with a pine log while his mother, dressed in sequins, calmly sips a drink. "She looked like an ice cube in rum." There is longing as well as hatred. In one episode, Martin is John's middle-aged stepfather. Not only is he loving and supportive, as a real father should be, but he carries support to the extreme of having sex with the boy.

Lasting abuse can consist of a single blow, however much apologized for, the book suggests. Sometimes abuse consists simply of a father being a man and having sex with his wife. Sometimes, John writes, "I feel like a bird that has just succeeded in its struggle to break from the white blindness of its shell and confronts for the first time the overwhelming red plumage of its father and the first shadows of the night, and wants only to crawl back."

Estrangement from the father and the world, not necessarily by abuse but by the very nature of the gay condition: It is a chilling, even despairing vision. So is a passage in which John is seduced by a young woman friend, only to find his arousal withering when she mentions having had a baby. "She made sex seem unerotic, less like fantasy, more like life."

The sadness behind the horrors of Peck's troubling book

is this suggestion that in some deep and perhaps irremediable way, homosexuals are barred from any enduring relationship with life and must settle for a fugitive, ill-fated affair with it. AIDS plays a part, but Peck seems to see a darkness beyond it. On the other hand, his may be a vision not of separation but of reunion in a darkness that is universal in different ways to all of us. (pp. 3, 7)

Richard Eder, "Beyond AIDS, a Darkness," in Los Angeles Times Book Review, *January 24, 1993, pp. 3, 7.*

Vince Aletti   (review date February 1993)

[*In the following review, Aletti praises* Martin and John *for its intensity while criticizing its excessively abstract narrative structure.*]

"It's like I've taken a puzzle, a jigsaw puzzle, and put it together all wrong, so that none of the pieces fit into each other, but are forced together or merely laid end to end. I look down on the picture that is supposed to be rectangular, but is circular." Coming at the end of Dale Peck's episodic, fragmented debut, *Martin and John*—an antinarrative fabricated from a slew of little narratives—this description of a work in progress seems to sum up the enterprise.

The words belong to John, an apparently autobiographical writer stand-in, whose italicized first-person accounts are the book's frail chronological spine. Alternating with these brief segments are the longer stories he's written, each of which is told by a character named John, who, like the puzzle maker, scrambles pieces from his life in an obsessive, delusional reordering of events and people. Attempting to transform his history into fiction—something healing, revealing, and "true"—John can only shuffle things around. And no matter how many times he reinvents his story, he keeps coming back to a few ugly, sad facts: abuse, abandonment, lost love, death. Beneath their weight, his elaborately constructed personal mythology crumbles.

Peck seems to have a similar problem. Teasing his story every which way—whipping up raw tragedy, offhand comedy, and lots of hallucinated melodrama with a very small constellation of characters—he's playing author in a showy, postmodern way. Reality is mutable, truth shifts from chapter to chapter. Life history dissolves and recombines as if in a dream. But Peck isn't like Robbe-Grillet or his late '60s New Novel posse, fracturing narrative so that only pure, cold phenomena remain. When Peck's done shredding autobiography in *Martin and John,* what remains is messy, inchoate emotion. He goes over and over the material, telling and retelling it in different versions, not just because he's reluctant to pin it down, but because he can't let it go.

Like so many writers who've worked with deeply personal stories—Dorothy Allison, David Wojnarowicz, and Gary Indiana come to mind—Peck seems possessed by his material. John isn't inspired by his life to make up stories, he's trapped by his history and repeats it compulsively. Not every episode goes dark with pain and grief, but those

are the novel's ruling emotions, along with a kind of desperate love, and they're planted early on. He might imagine himself in a suburban home or a family farm, in Kansas or on Long Island, but his father, always named Henry, nearly always gets drunk and beats him up. (Significantly, Henry is also the name John gives to his first older lover and the man he picks up at a leather bar who keeps him in bondage for a weekend.) His mother, always Beatrice, might be an intimidated housewife or a widowed lush in a trailer or a stepmother now divorced and busy in her garden, but she's never capable of shielding him, never really there when the boot comes down. His lover, Martin, might be a runaway boy hiding in the hayloft, a man his mother picked up one night in a bar, or a wealthy dilettante who showers him with jewels, but he always disappears or dies.

Martin is the book's love object and blind spot. Alternately protective, indulgent, seductive, aloof, sympathetic, and withdrawn. Martin—in all his guises—is the lover as cipher. Fascinating but ultimately unknowable, he's John's fantasy fuck doll/father figure: "He's rich, nice-looking, has a remarkably affectionate personality, and he loves me." Even when he's not rich and perfect—when he's working night shift at a warehouse in a small Midwestern town—Martin has no life of his own outside John's obsession. With no fixed identity except the loved one, Martin shines only in reflected light, a fogged mirror for John's narcissism and confusion.

"Martin has become something abstract," notes Peck, stepping back to a writerly remove, toward the book's end. "A symbol." That's fine for the novelist, perhaps, but a real stumbling block for the reader. The romance of Martin and John is apparently a very brief one. According to one version of the story: Martin succumbs to the first ravages of AIDS less than six months after their affair starts, and the novel's most vivid scene is a description of his sudden, hideous death in the shower. John's grief permeates the remainder of the book, but it, too, is abstract and impossible to share.

If Martin is to have any emotional weight as the beautiful, terrible icon of AIDS death, he needs to be more than a phantom or a figment of a figment of someone's imagination. Shuffling his cards of identity, Peck keeps the reader at a distance and leaves him stranded there when the writing (usually coolly, unremarkably accomplished) turns flaccid or flat. *Martin and John* is the novel as multiple choice, flooded with emotion only to be drained of feeling, heartrending and heartless, compelling and deadening. Peck's right: the puzzle doesn't fit. But the pieces are hard to put down. (pp. 5-6)

Vince Aletti, in a review of "Martin and John," in VLS, *No. 112, February, 1993, pp. 5-6.*

Michiko Kakutani   (review date 9 February 1993)

[*In the following review, Kakutani favorably assesses* Martin and John, *noting Peck's sincere renderings of emotionally brutal scenes.*]

On its simplest level, *Martin and John,* Dale Peck's astonishing first novel, recounts the story of a young man's flight from his abusive, homophobic father and his later efforts to come to terms with his lover's death from AIDS. But if this fiercely written novel offers an indelible portrait of gay life during the plague years, it also opens out to become a universal story about love and loss and the redemptive powers of fiction. It is a story about the cycles of pain and grief that spiral through people's lives, and the efforts an artist makes to reorder and transcend that hurt.

A succession of overlapping and sometimes contradictory episodes, *Martin and John* is made up of two elliptical narrative lines. The first relates the story of how John left Kansas, became a hustler in New York City, fell in love with Martin and eventually became a writer. The second consists of tales written by John, tales in which he reimagines Martin, himself and his parents as an assortment of other characters. At times, what's real and what's invented seem to blur together; fantasies, nightmares and memories converge, producing strange new echoes and reverberations.

"I remember making up my first stories at night, kept awake by the sound of my parents fighting in the other room," John tells us.

> Every fiction is always opposed to some truth, and the opposition in these stories was easy to spot, for they were about a happy mother, happy father, happy John. But this changed. Soon the stories I imagined were as horrible as the one I lived. I found a power in it, and that power increased as the imagined horror became more and more like the events of my life. You can search for a meaning in that. I tell myself that by reinventing my life, my imagination imposes an order on things and makes them make sense. But sometimes I think that horror is all I know and all I'll ever know, and no matter how much I try to loose my mind from the bonds and the boundaries of the events of my life, it returns to them always, obsessively, like a dog sniffing for a bone it buried too deep and now can't find.

Indeed, many of the stories John relates are so devastating the reader can only shudder. In one, his mother contracts a mysterious, debilitating disease, and her doctor warns her that pregnancy would fatally accelerate it. Her husband, however, reminds her that he has always wanted a large family and forcibly takes her to bed. Months later she has a bloody miscarriage (witnessed by a shocked 10-year-old John) that leaves her paralyzed and unable to talk. Unable to cope with his guilt, John's father packs her off to a nursing home to "finish dying," while he and John set off for Kansas to try to start a new life.

In some versions of this story, John's father becomes a soppy drunk who constantly tries to recreate his late wife's presence by donning her apron, cooking her recipes, fondling her favorite trinkets. He babbles on endlessly about the guilt he feels for her illness, the remorse that colors his every thought and action. In other versions, John's father emerges as a violent drunk who kicks John in the head when he learns of his homosexuality and crushes the boy's hand.

As for Martin, he surfaces in John's stories in a variety of guises, a chameleonlike figure defying easy definition. In one telling, he's a runaway discovered hiding in John's father's barn. In another, he's John's mother's lover, who secretly seduces her son. One version depicts Martin as a charming and enormously wealthy New Yorker who courts John with expensive presents. Another portrays him as blue-collar worker, assigned to the night shift at a Kansas warehouse.

Six months after meeting John, Martin discovers he has AIDS. His illness progresses as rapidly and as horrifically as that of John's mother: the radiant young man is soon a 6-foot-2-inch skeleton weighing 80 pounds, poked full of catheters, his life leaking away even as John learns that he, too, has tested positive for the virus.

Many of the scenes in *Martin and John*—from the awful, shattering deaths of Martin and of John's mother, to the violent, sadomasochistic sex acts engaged in by John—are graphic in their emotional brutality. They are meant to be: John is someone who says he knows only "love and hate, rage and joy, terror and numbness"; for him, "there is no center to any of these spectra, only north and south poles which I sway between like a pendulum which exists only at its two high points."

At times Mr. Peck's language grows a little too poetic and portentous: "I read my body now," he writes, "not as often as I did then, when each bruise was a new book I couldn't quite understand no matter how many times my hands returned to it." For the most part, however, he maintains remarkable control of his material, investing potentially melodramatic scenes with a sense of earned emotion. His wisdom about human feelings, his talent for translating those feelings into prose and his sophisticated mastery of literary form all speak to a maturity that belies his 25 years. In short, a stunning debut.

> *Michiko Kakutani, "From Gay Themes, a Universal Story of Love," in* The New York Times, *February 9, 1993, p. C15.*

Catherine Texier   (review date 28 February 1993)

[*Texier is an American novelist and critic. In the review below, she describes* Martin and John *as "unflinchingly honest" and considers Peck a "brave and very talented writer."*]

In his daring debut novel [*Martin and John*], Dale Peck has written an unflinchingly honest, dark coming-of-age story about a young gay hustler who goes from Kansas to New York and back again to nurse his dying lover.

Mr. Peck takes a lot of chances in *Martin and John,* most obviously with its structure. Italic sections, presumably episodes of the narrator's life, are interwoven with a series of stories, each featuring a different pair of lovers called Martin and John. The earlier stories show John growing up in Kansas with his father, Henry, and his mother or stepmother, Bea, in different settings and circumstances, discovering his homosexuality. Each family depicted is dysfunctional or broken. Sometimes it's the mother who dies, sometimes it's the father. The fathers are construction workers, prone to drinking and violence in the home; the mothers are victims of the fathers. In the later stories, all the Martins eventually die of AIDS.

There is a certain awkwardness to this structure as though the writer couldn't settle on a set of characters. It initially seems confusing and might even turn gimmicky, if not for the lyrical power of Mr. Peck's writing. But as the stories unfold, a kind of slippage of identity occurs. Maybe this John is really the same narrator under different guises, who keeps reinventing himself and his life, if we take our clue from small, telling, recurrent details dropped throughout the book: a crescent-shaped scar that curls around John's eye, John lifting his legs up from a bed and spreading them in front of Martin's face, Martin playing the piano, John bringing him a rose.

In the end, even the italic episodes that punctuate the book mesh with the actual stories, responding to them like fugues played in different keys, creating a flow of narration seething with life. By breaking the story line and blurring the identity of his characters and the hard boundaries between the stories, Dale Peck succeeds in exploring the experience of being gay with a remarkable complexity and depth of feeling.

At the heart of *Martin and John* is John's anger at his father and hopeless longing for his love. In the first story, "Blue Wet-Paint Columns," John's mother is a quadriplegic who goes to live in a hospice when he is a teen-ager. Overwhelmed with guilt and grief, John's father tries to keep her memory alive by literally taking her place: he dons her apron to cook her old recipes, and in one stunning and deeply disturbing scene, John finds him wearing her blue satin gown and high heels, a wig sitting crookedly on his head, his face heavily made up. "He wore her underwear, and the pale fabric stretched so tightly across his buttocks that I could see the split between them as if he were naked. . . . A few crumpled pieces of toilet paper fell to the floor when he took the bra off."

The rage that John feels at that instant echoes the rage that John, the hustler, feels when his father smacks him for being insolent and John blurts out that he has had sex with another man ("It was strange, but it made me feel so good . . . the way I'd made *him* feel good"), provoking the father into beating him up until John tastes blood on his lips. "Shut up!" the father shouts. "The words," John realizes, "are filled not with anger but with pain, and I close my eyes then, and my mouth. I've won."

It's an amazing feat for any writer, in particular a male writer, to expose so nakedly the need for closeness with a father that lies underneath a son's rage. In the story "Three Night Watchmen" John tells the guard with whom he shares the night shift that he's had a falling-out with his father. The other man, speaking of his estranged son, gives this advice to John: "I've got this feeling he's going to miss me one day, and maybe I'll be dead by then, and so what can he do? . . . Say something, John, don't wait that long." *Martin and John* reads like this "something" John needs to tell his father, about his homosexuality, about his love, about the unbearable pain of being John.

The women in *Martin and John* do not fare as well. Pathetic victims, they are quickly disposed of. An early scene shows the mother caught by her young son in the middle of a miscarriage in her kitchen: "A damp bloody mass pushed at her crotch, staining a maroon patch of darkness on sky-blue pants. . . . She seemed both empty and full, like a tube of toothpaste squeezed from the middle." A powerful metaphor, it's nevertheless a grotesque and unlikely image, a nightmare vision of pregnancy and miscarriage fantasized by a man deeply scared of the female body. In a later story, the father drops this line about his wife: "She stopped getting her period, you know, and after that, she just dried up." Even Susan, a friend of John's, is a ready and willing victim, as she chooses to make love with John, even though he is H.I.V. positive, in order to become pregnant.

Ultimately, though, *Martin and John* is a love poem from the "gay boy in off the farm from Kansas" to Martin, and perhaps all the Martins he has loved in his life.

From Martin the first lover, a farm boy from Kansas appearing out of nowhere in a haystack, to Martin the last lover, whom John takes back to Kansas and nurses until he dies, there is Martin the night watchman who makes John dream about the gay scene in New York; Martin the romantic piano player; Martin the rich New Yorker who covers John with precious gems and invites him to an apartment done up like the land of Oz, complete with a yellow brick path leading to the Emerald City, "an oval room with walls covered in softly gleaming, lazily wandering tubes." It's Martin the multi-headed lover, everygayman, sexy, poignant, irresistible, funny, sly, provocative, lustful, until the illness undoes him and he turns into a bitter, impotent queen who eventually hemorrhages to death in the bathtub.

The pain is finally too much for John to bear. Rage at the father has turned into rage at the illness: he asks an unnamed sick lover to penetrate him with a .22 rifle. "I try to think about the gun. . . . I imagine I see . . . a little flash of death as the bullet takes off and starts its hundredth-of-a-second hurtle toward my body, where it will . . . leave behind nothing but numbness. And then quietly, so quietly, I whisper, "Pull the trigger.' " But the man drops the gun and flees.

When, having peeled off the stories like so many onion skins, we finally discover John, the narrator, writing in his little room in Kansas where he has sequestered himself for a year after Martin's death, trying to recapture his life, a bottle of AZT on the shelf waiting for him to get sick, the circle is complete. There is but one John, alone, spinning those tales in the face of death, a Scheherazade buying his time by keeping the master spellbound, "gathering the colored strands of the rainbow and braiding them together into white light," as Martin told him to do.

In this short book, Dale Peck has managed to pack the density and the depth of a human life. He is a brave and very talented writer. (pp. 12-13)

Catherine Texier, "Loves of a Young Hustler,"
in The New York Times Book Review, *February 28, 1993, pp. 12-13.*

David Kaufman   (review date 15 March 1993)

[In the review below, Kaufman deems Martin and John *"one of the more inspired and brilliant novels that deal not only with AIDS but the grief and bereavement that are inescapably a part of every life."]*

A dozen years into the epidemic, perhaps the tragedy of AIDS has become too relentless a factor in our lives to sustain, unrelieved, a conventional, direct approach without lapsing into mawkishness and sentimentality. But what of the writers who feel that humor in any guise is an inappropriate response to so serious a topic? When it comes to their novels concerned with AIDS, maybe something other than narrative coherence is prescribed. The reality of AIDS may be too *virulent,* in a sense, to be captured through customary fictional devices.

Such is one inference that might be drawn from *Martin and John,* a willfully confusing new AIDS novel by Dale Peck that keeps altering its narrative terms and eschewing conventional tools—including humor—before it arrives at the *beginning* of its story. Long before it becomes clear that "John," the quasi-autobiographical narrator, took up writing after his lover "Martin" died of AIDS, each of these two figures is represented by numerous, contradictory backgrounds.

It's not one Martin that we or John meet but many. Nor is it a single John who's recalling their respective relationships. In what amounts to a Cubist approach, all the Martins and all the Johns are somehow different yet at once the same, connected by emotional truths that betray their alikeness. The episodic fictions that contain them can best be categorized as a fugue, in which both figures evolve through the different characters they embody.

There's nothing particularly new about first-person narrators who seem to be creating and reinventing themselves as they go along. Postmodern literary games have come in and out of fashion as regularly as designers' lines, with Vonnegut, Barthelme, Calvino and Roth quickly springing to mind. But with life-and-death stakes that seem so urgent and vital, Peck transcends the experimentation and novelty that often seem ends in themselves.

"I usually read over what I've written," says John as he nears the conclusion of his quixotic memoir. "I see it differently the second time around. It's like I've taken a puzzle, a jigsaw puzzle, and put it together all wrong, so that none of the pieces fit into each other, but are forced together or merely laid end to end. I look down on the picture that is supposed to be rectangular, but is circular."

In this stunning but difficult work, which marks the auspicious debut of its 25-year-old author, the permutable personalities and shifting perspectives are inflicted on the reader like shots of Novocain, with a numbing effect on all that came before, without really preparing us for where we're headed. Only in retrospect do they appear to be what they are: inchoate fragments of aborted stories or scenarios that seem to resemble or relate to one another while they mutate in startling ways. They tend to focus on dramatic, frequently violent, life-changing moments, and they reveal more through their details even as they obscure any larger picture. But somehow the larger picture

manages to emerge. It tells of the universal conditions of love, loss, grievance, death and bewilderment.

The first John we meet is 10 years old when he returns from school one day to discover his mother collapsed and hemorrhaging as she miscarries what would have been her second child. She's placed in a Long Island hospice where she will die of a progressive muscle disorder twelve years later, when she's 44. In the meantime, John and his father move to Kansas. "I hadn't known where we were going when we left, and I didn't know we'd arrived when we got there." This pathetic refrain becomes a haunting motif that could describe any of the various Johns whose stories are related, or the single first-person narrator who, magically, represents all of them.

It's only after John and his father have settled in Kansas that he begins to understand the tragedy of his parents' marriage, as he matures and his father emotionally deteriorates: Although the doctor had advised against a second pregnancy, John's father had insisted on having a larger family, and now blames himself for his wife's protracted dying. He also becomes an alcoholic, and even takes to wearing his wife's clothes and makeup in some bizarre enactment of his grief. "My father the drag queen: his stage name, I suppose, would be Miss Communication."

When John next appears, in a chapter titled "Driftwood," there is suddenly a reference to an older brother, Justin, who drowned. Even more startling, John's now-healthy mother, Bea, lives in Kansas with him and his father, Henry. Rather than being the guilt-ridden father, this Henry has always blamed Bea for their other son's death.

Martin is introduced in the narrative to this second, doppelgänger John, who discovers him in a barn with a wound near his eye and brings him into the family home, where his parents nurse him back to health. Evidently a runaway from an abusive situation, Martin initiates John in the ways of sex, but eventually he leaves as mysteriously as he arrived. "We only really met in little ways: a line of sweat, muddy trails of water, a traced scab, a kiss," says John of Martin.

> My mother cooked him food, my father tried to boss him around. I don't think we were ever quite aware of how we depended on him, but he filled a space in our lives, the space created by Justin's death. That's obvious. But we labored for too long under the idea that we knew him better than he knew us, when all we really knew was what we wanted him to be. So in the morning, when he was gone, the house seemed incredibly vacant, and we realized that we didn't know what had left it this time, nor what to use to fill the space left behind.

No matter which John we meet, there is always a vacancy that is at first filled through love by a Martin, then created again by his loss or disappearance. And it's the same for the other figures that course through the narrative like phantoms: All the mothers, named Bea or Beatrice, are longing for a lost child or deceased husband. All the fathers, named Henry, are aching for the wife or child who died or abandoned them. And both parents usually turn to alcohol to deal with their anguish. By constantly shuffling their fictional backgrounds, the overriding conceit of *Martin and John* goes a long way toward making its two central characters emblematic of an entire generation forced to grapple with its mortality prematurely. John number three is 13 or so when he loses his virginity to his stepfather, named Martin, "on my mother's double bed during the afternoon's heat while she was at work." In keeping with the progressive age of the characters, which is a device to suggest they're the same even while remarkably different, the fourth John is older still, and his circumstances far more complex. Yet another John, who had arrived in New York via Port Authority when he was almost 16 and become a hustler, could be describing Peck's own novelistic technique:

> I had run away, arrived here only hours before. . . . I'd abandoned my past, poured it from my life like liquid from a bottle. I ignored what I already knew—that a bottle is never as important as what fills it—and I also tried to ignore the details which began to pile up in me like separate ingredients waiting to be mixed together.

Throughout the narrative, John consciously wrestles with the slippery difference between fiction and truth. It's part of a larger phenomenon he refers to when he says, "Sometimes I don't know what I remember, what's real and what's been transformed with time."

But no matter how "fictional" it may or may not be, it's the last version of the story that seems the most solid and reliable. It is certainly the most sustained and extensive, spanning a number of chapters, as opposed to the discrete, episodic ones preceding it. It is here, we detect, well through the book, that the "true" story begins.

With slightly more than a third of the narrative remaining, the opening chapter, "Always and Forever," starts off with a revealing epigraph taken from [Henry] James's "The Real Thing" that implicitly justifies the fictional games Peck has been playing until then:

> They saw a couple of drawings that I had made of the establishment, and Mrs. Monarch hinted that it never would have struck her that he had sat for them. "Now the drawings you make from us, they look exactly like us," she reminded me, smiling in triumph; and I recognized that this was indeed just their defect.

The ultimate John moves in with the independently wealthy Martin in a matter of months after arriving in New York. With Peck emphasizing the committed love between them, their relationship is conveyed through vivid descriptions of their lovemaking and various outings they enjoy together. There are also violent recollections of Martin's physically abusive upbringing, which parallels John's, as well as a mugging episode on the Upper West Side and a confrontation with a group of gay-bashers in a Brooklyn subway station.

But no passage in the book is as vivid or as fraught as the lengthy one that describes Martin's grotesque death in the bathtub, after a long period contending with AIDS. The traumatic scene is relived in one of a number of italicized chapters, where it intermingles with John's apparent fan-

tasy of a graphic S&M act in which he compels his sex partner to shove a gun up his ass.

The final Martin is a writer, though he's never tried to publish. "His story, a long, perhaps unending narrative, floats at me from off the page," comments John, "defying the cramped letters that frame it, spilling out into life. There is much of Martin in it; there are things I hadn't thought of before, but after reading him, I ask myself, Is this real? and then answer, Yes."

John digs through Martin's journal and later reflects that "this isn't a story, some would say, because there is no conflict within it; this is an account, long and flawless, multifaceted like a jewel, but forever the same thing." And of course, all of John's perceptions of Martin's writing could be applied to the novel we're reading.

Though Peck feels acutely the inadequacy of words for expressing anguish, he has nevertheless managed to do precisely that, by conveying his story obliquely and circuitously, by creating a circle instead of a rectangle. The result, *Martin and John*, is one of the more inspired and brilliant novels that deal not only with AIDS but with the grief and bereavement that are inescapably a part of every life.

—*David Kaufman*

Peck can be accused of a sophomoric use of symbols and of being self-consciously "profound," but one senses that he decided only enigmatic conclusions and a cloying naïveté would suffice for relating a grief that might otherwise defy description. His scrupulous avoidance of humor makes *Martin and John* seem distinctive from other novels with AIDS as a central concern, and certainly from the more recent popular ones. In a number of respects, one is bound to be reminded of Michael Cunningham's *A Home at the End of the World,* another exquisitely written novel, albeit one that deals with AIDS only peripherally. Both Peck and Cunningham focus on the childhood of their respective characters, perhaps to show that nothing could prepare them for the pain they will know as adults.

What Peck is finally left with is the futility of his ambition to pay Martin homage by writing this novel: "How can this story give Martin immortality when it can't even give him life?" he asks with agonizing frustration. "Now I wonder, Has this story liberated anything but my tears? And is that enough? I want to ask. To which I can only answer, Isn't that enough?" At the very end, after an omniscient narrator takes over and Peck's own name, Dale, becomes interchangeable with John's, he also writes,

> The sum of life isn't experience, I realize, isn't something that can be captured with words. Inevitably, things have been left out. Perhaps they appear in others' stories. Perhaps they were here

once and John's forgotten them. Perhaps some things he remembers didn't really occur.

Like the protagonist of "The Real Thing," Peck detects the "defect" in approaching his subject directly or realistically. Though he feels acutely the inadequacy of words for expressing anguish he has nevertheless managed to do precisely that, by conveying his story obliquely and circuitously, by creating a circle instead of a rectangle. The result, **Martin and John,** is one of the more inspired and brilliant novels that deal not only with AIDS but with the grief and bereavement that are inescapably a part of every life. (pp. 347-49)

> *David Kaufman, "Heroes with a Thousand Faces," in* The Nation, *New York, Vol. 256, No. 10, March 15, 1993, pp. 347-49.*

Gregory Woods   (review date 26 March 1993)

[*In the following mixed review, Woods examines Peck's narrative technique in* Fucking Martin, *which is the British title for* Martin and John.]

Gay American fiction has developed its own versions of what, in African-American writing, have been called "ascent" and "immersion" narratives. The gay version of "ascent" chronicles the move away from family life and the restrictions of small-town morality towards liberation and coming-out in the big city. In the converse "immersion" narrative, largely developed in response to HIV and AIDS, a gay man becomes HIV positive and returns to his origins, either nostalgically, to revisit the scenes of his adolescence, or, if already ill, simply to die out of sight of the social and sexual whirl.

Dale Peck's first novel, [**Fucking Martin**], involves both types of narrative and more. Its narrator, John, and his lover, Martin, reappear in various guises, but always as lovers, in stories written by John both during their affair and after Martin's AIDS-related death. The title of the American edition consisted only of the two lovers' names. Its British title—a calculated risk on the part of both author and publisher—seems even more to the point. It works as both the name of a favourite activity and the exasperated naming of a favourite man.

John grows up with a violent and abusive father, an ailing mother and a succession of stepmothers. He finds relative escape from this background by selling his body in New York. There, in 1982, he meets Martin. When they find that Martin is HIV-positive, they move out of the city to Kansas. Martin dies. John writes his stories. In the closing pages, to further complicate matters, John refers to himself as Dale. What one has suspected for most of the book is thereby endorsed: this is a species of autobiography. The publishers have provided reviewers with a lurid and illwritten account of the author's life, which confirms that the childhood passages, at least, are based on his own experiences.

So the book moves disturbingly through degrees of reality, now laying claim to mimetic authenticity, now foregrounding its own fictionality, but never losing sight of its central obsessions. These meet on a cusp between pain and

delight, whether physical or in the mind. Peck writes with passionate intensity. On the negative side, he starts out with the common American male writer's difficulty, when narrating a boy's transition from childhood, of trying not to sound like Holden Caulfield. Once that tendency has been overcome, he occasionally overwrites, at times sounding as if he had just been given a thesaurus. But these are minor faults in a fascinating first novel.

> *Gregory Woods, "Ascent of Men," in* The Times Literary Supplement, *No. 4695, March 26, 1993, p. 20.*

Mona Simpson   (review date 28 March 1993)

[*Simpson is an American novelist and critic. In the following review of* Martin and John, *she praises Peck's powerful depictions of pain, violence, love, and passion.*]

Dale Peck, in his first novel, **Martin and John,** gives me what I look for most when I open a new book: a world that is our world and also full of things I didn't know, characters in scenes that are at once recognizable and indelible.

Peck favors extremity. We first hear John, the narrator, describing the day he came home to discover his mother, Bea, miscarrying.

> This is not the worst thing I remember: coming home from school one day to find my mother in a chair, collapsed. Her skin was the color of wet ashes, her head sat like a stone on her right shoulder, and a damp bloody mass pushed at her crotch. . . . Her legs were spread wide, and more blood, pooling on the yellow vinyl of the chair, showed up like the red speck in a spoiled egg yolk.

John was ten years old, and his first thought was, "Is she still alive?"

The first long chapter, titled "Blue Wet-Paint Columns" traces John's recognition of his father's violence, which caused his mother's pregnancy, miscarriage and eventual death. He remembers when his mother told him "I went to the doctor today. He told me I can't have another baby." That night, he heard his parents arguing.

" 'But we want a big family,' my father says again and again.

" 'That doesn't matter now,' my mother answers each time."

After an ambulance took her away to a hospice on Long Island, John's father, Henry, drove his son to Kansas, where they would live together alone on the prairie. This chapter introduces many of the book's themes: the father's violence, intimately connected with sex, a sweet but ultimately fallow connection with a woman John's own age, an older man's sexual incursions on John, as a child.

There is a strange, cool sex scene with a girl named Susan. They walk through waist-high prairie grass, shivering from the cold wind, and then slide down red cliffs, lifting clouds of dust. Their sex, though, leaves John feeling nothing for the girl who straddles him and remembering, with guilt, that he had sometimes felt this same absence of emotion towards his mother.

His mother is dead, by the end of the story, and John goes back to the Long Island Hospice, to collect her things. He understands only then that his father

> raped her and he killed her. There was something he wanted more than he wanted to believe that his wife could die if she became pregnant again, so he raped her. He didn't beat her, didn't rip her clothes off; chances are that all he did was hide her birth control pills or refuse to wear a condom. . . . These facts settled around me not with the surprise of discovery, but the familiarity of acknowledgement. But then, it was never really a question of clues but a simple matter of admitting something that I'd known for a long time; it was kind of like coming out. . . .

The novel is constructed in a way that seems natural and almost inevitable, though I've never seen it before. Short, italicized chapters that stand up as very brief short stories alternate with longer narratives. With the exception of the first, very short monologue, delivered by John's mother, the book is told in the first person. Several narrative threads continue, but the book feels less like a novel than a collection of short stories, all related, all exploring the different dramatic possibilities offered to one keen sensibility.

Peck lets his narrator play with the differences between what really happened and what is made up. While some of the later chapters cohere with the events and characters introduced in the seminal "Blue Wet-Paint" chapter, others read like variations on the initial theme, with several imagistic threads connecting what may originally have been disparate stories.

In a perfect and tiny short story, set on a beach, we see the father lying on a blanket between his wife and son while he holds down his son with one hand and fondles his wife with the other. John imagines seeing this odd crucifixion from far above, as the father hurts both him and his wife, almost drowning them both, with sex.

In another story, it is John's father who dies, and Martin is the man Bea remarries and who eventually takes John's virginity. This Martin habitually runs his hand through John's hair, echoing a gesture the father made in an earlier chapter. In yet another version, both mother and father live in Kansas, and Martin, a strange incandescent boy with whom John feels the first stirrings of romantic love, appears in the barn.

"Have you ever ridden in a limousine? Have you ever looked at the world from the top of a sixty story building?" Martin asks from the hayloft—questions that evoke the mythic New York that the gay young Midwestern men in the book share. John has a scar and Martin, he discovers, does too. "Who did this?" John asks. Martin answers, "Someone I loved for a little while."

Certain things endure through the plot's transformations. Martin is always the name of the man John loves. Susan is the name of first girl John sleeps with and later, in the New York chapters, Susan is the friend with whom he has

sex in order to impregnate. All the fathers are named Henry, all mothers and stepmothers, Bea.

A recurrent image is John's hand, which his father deformed by stepping on it when drunk so that it is no more than a fixed claw. When John runs away to New York, he meets a young boy his own age, with a scar: " 'My father,' the boy said wearily, 'A broken Coke bottle.' " They share a cab and each boy discovers the other's hand. "It was pretty ruined. His I mean," John says.

These images and threads of action connect the book, which doesn't observe the common unities of character and circumstance, while allowing a great amount of play.

In one incarnation, John's father is rich. We learn that John ran away from Kansas and became a hustler, living with an older man named Barclay in New York, who bathed him between each trick and cleaned his toenails with a brush.

In another chapter, Martin is John's young lover, who works the night shift at a plant and tells John about New York. "Men everywhere . . . Their own apartments, their own cafes, their own clubs. They hold hands even."

In this version, John's first lover was Henry, who was either "an old lech who took advantage of a little kid" or a man "so gentle he'd always treat me like it was my first time."

Martin tells John a story about a party in New York, where a beautiful man playing the piano fell in love with another man who sat down next to him on the bench. In a later chapter, Martin and John are those two men. Several chapters toy with the idea of money, with Martin as a rich lover; and both these versions turn on an incident of urban homophobic violence.

Peck is at his best in scenes of extremity, such as the one in which Martin, dying of AIDS, bleeds and defecates in the bathtub and John feels his own face fall into itself like a rotten orange.

> I cry only for my self, and if any thought of Martin remains, or of my mother, or of my father, they founder in a sea of other names, and nameless faces, and in the faces of hundreds of men whom I remember by a common name, a name that remains unconnected to any identity no matter how many times it is assumed. And that name, I must remind myself, is my own: John.

Or the scene, after Martin's death, when he goes to a bar and meets Henry.

> It was not, I think, in Henry's nature to hurt anyone. When I stroked his slick-leathered thigh in the taxi, he moaned; there was nothing dominant about it. If he'd had his way, we probably would have had sex normally, with perhaps a few accoutrements: a leather harness, latex gloves. But I insisted, and he knew what to do. We both did, we all did; we'd been taught, by people now mostly dead.

Twenty-five-year-old Dale Peck has written a powerful first novel, a book to be read not only for its promise of an impressive career also but for its own stark and violent beauties.

Mona Simpson, "Scenes of Extremity," in Chicago Tribune—Books, *March 28, 1993,* p. 5.

An excerpt from *Martin and John*

I divide my life in two: before Martin, and after Martin. There are many places I could make the division: before my mother's death and after, before I ran away from home and after. Before, and after. But Martin. I loved him. That's nothing—if someone is weak enough, or strong enough, I'll love them. But he loved me back. Now, I feel the lack of him every day. Oh, he hated me at the end. Every day he wished aloud that I would get sick and die before he did. But I never stopped loving him. I won't say he didn't hurt me. There were times when I got picked up and stayed away for two or three days, so that when I came home Martin would clutch me and beg for forgiveness. The sight of him always filled me with guilt. Within minutes Martin picked up on this and turned cold on me. Now, if I think about him for too long, I get tired. I go to the bedroom then, and I use only one pillow and I ball up the blanket and I hold it in my arms, and I tell myself the only thing I know: that my life is divided in two now, irrevocably, by a chasm as wide and deep and unfillable as any canyon. But I still can't decide if that chasm is Martin's life, or if it's his death.

Dale Peck, in his Martin and John, *Farrar, Straus, Giroux, 1993.*

Laurence O'Toole (review date 2 April 1993)

[*The following is a positive review of* Fucking Martin.]

Fucking Martin is a rare first novel, with a rare title to match. Dale Peck's most wounding tale is written in response to a pained and violent childhood. This is fiction as exploration, therapy, exorcism. And fiction is most definitely the word: not autobiography dressed up and thrown down on the page, but a life's raw material rigorously and thrillingly transformed.

The narrative is complex, fragmented, and any kind of signposting is in short supply. It takes a while to figure out how two versions of Martin and John run in parallel: one "real", the other "made up". The real John—Peck's fictional counterpart—grows up inside a broken-down Kansas family, with a frail mother and extremely brutal father. At the turn of the 1980s, he leaves for New York to enrol as a teenage hustler. He falls in love with Martin who soon after takes sick with Aids. There follow scenes of Martin's physical disintegration. This closing-in on death as the last frontier of meaning is in keeping with much recent US art: the body and its workings are ineluctably real, and not just another postmodern simulation.

John writes a journal, a series of "useful fictions" about a couple called Martin and John. The tales may always be different but the themes remain the same: of desire and seduction, turbulence, over-ripeness and the high cost of loving. Peck's delivery is controlled and laconic. It bites best of all when the terrain turns visceral, in treating illness and hurt, or in graphic scenes of heavy duty SM involving hot wax and nipple clamps.

The starkness of Peck's gaze helps to keep the odour of cleverness from settling. This is formal invention with a purpose. John writes in order to figure out how he got where he is. Straight autobiography merely ties him in knots. So he writes things that never happened and finds the horrors he writes down are as horrible as those he experienced. Except for one crucial difference: that imagination has the power to "impose order on things and make them make sense".

Throughout *Fucking Martin,* Dale Peck is mediating his life through fiction, feeding the former through the latter to show off its complex workings and meanings. This understanding is revealed surely and slowly, and can be dazzling. It's like getting to the end of a very good, very taut, emotional detective story and having more secrets laid bare than you ever guessed it contained. Out of density rises real communication. And it is only the best fiction that has anything to say.

Laurence O'Toole, "Costs of Loving," in New Statesman & Society, *Vol. 6, No. 246, April 2, 1993, p. 25.*

Dale Peck with Jennifer Brostrom, *CLC Yearbook* (interview date 7 December 1993)

[*In the following interview, Peck discusses* Martin and John, *AIDS and literature, and his goals as a writer.*]

[*Brostrom*]: *Did you conduct any background research in preparation for writing* **Martin and John***?*

[Peck]: The geographical settings—the experience of life in Long Island, New York, and Kansas—came from my personal experiences of living in these settings at various times. I was also a member of ACT UP for about three years. This organization was primarily a direct action group that held public demonstrations about AIDS issues and distributed an enormous amount of the most recent AIDS medical information to its members each week including updates on experimental treatments that were being done in the United States and abroad. This medical information appears in a sort of "by the way" manner in *Martin and John.* I worked as a volunteer for ACT UP and spent six months handing out clean needles to injection drug users on the lower east side of New York. This was a form of civil disobedience and it was also a service to try to keep these people from sharing needles and passing HIV along. I was arrested three different times—twice for disrupting traffic in the streets and one time for raiding the set of the CBS evening news with Dan Rather and forcing it off the air. The primary goal of these demonstrations was AIDS awareness, forcing AIDS into the national discourse.

Did this activism directly influence your writing?

Yes, although I don't write directly political fiction in the sense of strongly political writers such as Gore Vidal or

Sarah Schulman, who are often explicitly concerned with politics. My political concerns are there in the subtext of my writing, but I'm not a particularly skilled writer on overtly political themes, so I don't write that kind of literature.

Do you have any comments or perceptions concerning the portrayal of AIDS in contemporary art and literature?

I suppose I'm still amazed at how strongly AIDS in literature has remained a gay theme despite, in demographic terms, its effect on the rest of the population. Virtually all the art I've seen [with AIDS as the subject] has also been informed by homosexuality, and it's surprising to me that this limitation still continues. While it's gratifying to see that gay people are continuing to find original ways of dealing with the disease, I think there's also, after about thirteen years into the epidemic, a very boring kind of AIDS artwork that is being produced. The form has been established over the past seven or eight years and people are simply recycling it. But then there are also some highly original artists and writers—Tony Kushner with *Angels in America,* for example—who are finding original ways of dealing with AIDS.

You used the word "boring." What kind of art or literature do you consider boring?

I have what I think are fairly unreasonable expectations for art. If it doesn't stun me, if it doesn't cut me to the bone, then I'm not interested in it at all. If I feel that a work of art is just saying the nice or expected things, the things that won't upset anyone; to me that all falls under the term "boring."

Richard Eder commented positively that your novel was not "politically correct." Do you have any response to this?

Since writing **Martin and John** I've become very much against the notion of "politically correct." I think the entire concept of political correctness was more or less a reactionary concept invented by the right wing. In the past "politically correct" was just a term, even a joke, that was used in left wing circles until the right wing very skillfully seized upon the term and gave it fearsome and negative connotations.

I think that art that has that sense of sameness that can become boring is most often a result of a deficiency in the artist rather than a deficiency in the artist's politics. I'm not as much concerned with a novel's overt political statements as its covert political statements. . . . I'm interested in things that are not said as opposed to things that are said; the kinds of things that people choose not to talk about.

Richard Eder also perceived a theme of "darkness" associated with homosexuality in **Martin and John.** *Was this your intention?*

There is a tendency for the heterosexual critics to view literature that includes homosexual characters as literature about homosexuality. It is true that as a gay writer I have a strong following within that community, for which I'm very grateful. A writer couldn't ask for a more loyal or challenging audience. However, it is never my intent to write exclusively about homosexuality—I'm concerned with portraying emotional truths. I also want to write for a broad audience.

How autobiographical is **Martin and John?**

There are autobiographical themes in the book but no autobiography. The only "real life" aspects of the novel are the settings based on places I've lived. . . . There are similarities in the character of the father to my father, there are similarities in the character of John to my own character, and there are similarities in the female characters to my stepmothers—my father has been married four times. None of them, however, are actually based on real people.

Many reviewers commented on the novel's experimental form. Did you plan to use this structure, or did it evolve as the novel progressed?

The novel originally began with a short story—the story "Transformations" was the first Martin and John story I wrote. Then, when I wrote another story dealing with the same issues, I couldn't think of character names and so I used the [names Martin and John again]. After writing those two stories, I conceived of the whole project of **Martin and John.** I worked on the book for about four years, and when it was finished I had five hundred pages of manuscript from which I cut 300 pages of stories.

Do you currently have any works-in-progress?

I'm just over a third finished with a new novel called *The Law of Enclosures.* The title is derived from the sixteenth century British law of agrarian reform which required peasants to fence in property with fences which they could not afford to build. Consequently, they were herded off the land into the cities where they became the basis for the modern capitalist proletariat, while the countryside was consolidated into the hands of the nobles.

The story is set in America and focuses on Beatrice and Henry, who were the parents in **Martin and John. Martin and John** is the first of a planned seven-book series which are linked only in a minor way by characters and strongly linked by common themes. Some characters from each book will be carried into the next book. . . .

A section of *The Law of Enclosures* will be a true biography of my father and his four wives. . . . (Usually when I want to write about real people, I simply write realistically about them rather than turning them into fiction.) I believe that the story will be tragic because of their experience of violence, poverty, domestic strife, hatred, and breaks between every single generation. For example, my father's father died when he was very young, my mother's parents abandoned her. I want to write about these terrible experiences but also offer a happy alternative, so I'm writing what is essentially a high melodrama about Beatrice and Henry and setting it up in contrast with the actual tragedy of my own parents.

Many reviewers seemed to view **Martin and John** *as a thinly-disguised autobiography.*

There's a common feeling that when you write in the first person and you're as young as I am, you can't have had much experience of things beyond your own life. Particularly when you're writing about a character who is writing a confessional account of his own life. The character John was essentially my double in *Martin and John*, and I've tried to make it clear that although there's probably not an emotion that John felt that I haven't felt, there are any number of experiences that he had in the book that I haven't had.

The same is true for all the other characters—they are literary creations. Certainly my experience in families has been marked by violence, but in vastly different ways than John's was. My experience of homosexuality has also been marked by violence and by AIDS, but I myself don't have AIDS. . . . If my entire experience of homosexuality is in some way colored by AIDS, it's not because I'm HIV positive myself; it's just the way the world is today.

Was there a relationship or experience of death in your life that mirrors that in the novel?

I've lost a few close friends, but this has happened during the past year and a half. . . . When I was in college AIDS was really just an idea without any reality for me. It was when I moved to New York City that I decided to face the situation by joining ACT UP, because I thought something needed to be done. Very quickly, at least half the people I was meeting, if not more, were HIV positive largely because I was meeting them through activist circles. I do have a lot of friends who are [HIV] positive and I have some friends who are ill, and I've lost friends—but I don't want to say that my experience of AIDS has been defined by the life or death of a single individual because I think the disease is much more complex than that.

What do you hope to accomplish in the future with your writing career?

I'm hoping to expand my writing from what was read as a personal text to one that is much more sociological. I would like to be seen as a strongly American writer. . . . I've always felt that my experience was very much an American experience—I'm solidly a product of lower-middle-class American life. My father was a self-employed plumber and I grew up first on Long Island and then in the midwest. I want to express this in a way that is considered not just a cultural record, but also highly literary.

Frances Sherwood
Vindication

Sherwood is an American novelist and short story writer, born in 1940.

INTRODUCTION

Vindication is a fictional biography of Mary Wollstonecraft, the eighteenth-century author of *The Vindication of the Rights of Women* (1790) who is widely considered to be one of the first voices of the feminist movement. Blending historical detail with a modern narrative voice, Sherwood chronicles Wollstonecraft's troubled childhood, her struggles to write while supporting herself as a single parent, her relationships with her literary contemporaries, and her ultimate success as the most famous female author of her time. Many critics have applauded Sherwood's characterization of Wollstonecraft as a woman of contradictions whose desire for independence was sometimes compromised by passionate love affairs, and whose success was frequently tainted by feelings of self-doubt and instability. Some reviewers, however, have expressed concern that readers who are unfamiliar with the facts of Wollstonecraft's life will be misled by Sherwood's fictional portrait which incorporates such imaginary events as the protagonist's confinement in the mental institution Bedlam following the breakup of a love affair with the artist Henry Fuseli. *Vindication* is nevertheless considered an entertaining novel of historical interest and contemporary relevance, particularly for its treatment of women's issues. Sherwood has commented: "Most of all, I wanted to popularize Mary . . . to make every woman in America know about her, because even though we are separated by 200 years, her struggle to be a complete person intellectually and emotionally is still our struggle."

CRITICISM

Gayle Feldman   (essay date 12 October 1992)

[*In the following essay, based on a conversation with Sherwood, Feldman relates background events leading to the writing and publication of* Vindication.]

Frances Sherwood's first encounter with Mary Wollstonecraft took place about seven years ago. As Sherwood, an associate professor of English at Indiana University's South Bend campus recalls, "I was very impressed by a plate in artist Judy Chicago's installation *The Dinner Party,* which depicted Mary on her death bed. It was obvious she had had such a hard life!" Other encounters followed, until a book just had to be written.

The result—a fictional fantasy on the life of the 18th-century author of *A Vindication of the Rights of Women* (and mother of *Frankenstein's* literary begetter, Mary Shelley)—will be published under the title **Vindication** by Farrar, Straus & Giroux next May. Already, rights have been sold to Orion (Britain), Mondadori (Italy), Krüger (Germany), Bonniers (Sweden), Cappelens (Norway) and Lindhardt od Ringhof (Denmark), and the novel has garnered a six-figure paperback floor and been selected by the Book-of-the-Month Club.

However, the book's life, like its heroine's, did not start out all that smoothly: Sherwood was rejected by four literary agents and despaired of ever getting the novel published. But late last year, she decided to give it one more try.

Speaking to [*Publishers Weekly*] from Indiana, she recalled, "I read an article about Jonathan Franzen, in which there was a quote from his editor which I liked very much. I took a wild chance and sent the manuscript to that editor, to Jonathan Galassi. I was preparing myself for rejection when one day last winter the telephone rang. It was Jonathan, and he said he was interested in my book. I started to cry on the phone, then and there. It was the third best day in my life, the first two being the birthdays of my children." To make the obvious pun, it was vindication indeed.

Sherwood, as Galassi points out, is not a complete novice to print. She has received two O. Henry short story awards—for **"History"** (published in the *Greensboro Review*) in 1989 and **"Demiurges"** (published in the *Sonora Review*) this year—and brought out a collection of stories, ***Everything You've Heard Is True,*** with Johns Hopkins in 1989. She was also a Stegner fellow at Stanford back in the mid '70s, and received a grant from the National Endowment for the Arts in 1990, which helped fund the research for ***Vindication.***

But why travel back to the 18th century? Why Wollstonecraft, and why a novel rather than straight biography? Sherwood explains: "When I had to write the NEA grant proposal, I thought at first that I would do a scholarly work. But I'm a fiction writer. Also, my research turned up all this juicy stuff about the period that I wanted to be free to use. I was fascinated by the history of underwear, plumbing, food. . . . I was interested in the history of Bedlam, so I placed Mary there, even though she was never there. In the novel, Mary's first love is gay, but in reality she didn't fall in love with him. But that gives me the opportunity to talk about discrimination against gays. The book is full of fabrications, but I also hope it is authentic."

"Most of all, I wanted to popularize Mary," Sherwood continues, "to make every woman in America know about her, because even though we are separated by 200 years, her struggle to be a complete person intellectually and emotionally is still our struggle. The biographers have always been perplexed about the discrepancy between Mary's personal life and what she wrote—emotion and chaos versus emancipated rhetoric. But I could understand that combination perfectly from my own life. My reaction to her poverty and her struggle to be educated was visceral. I didn't consider myself very well educated, and I have known economic hardship. I feel like a sister to her."

Sherwood's life certainly has taken some curious turns. The daughter of a very liberal family, she was born in Washington, D.C., spent part of her childhood in Brazil, and was the only white undergraduate student at Howard University in 1960. She married a fellow student, a West Indian, and left school after one year to start a family. Eventually she was able to get a masters degree, but "writing was always a luxury." In fact, she only settled down

to novel writing more than two decades later, after she left the marriage.

The book pictures the 18th century as being anything but enlightened: child abuse, brutality, poverty, all inhabit the world that Sherwood conjures up. At times it requires a rather strong stomach. Galassi agrees: "It's a very unpretty vision, but I'm sure it's very real, and I think every age is the age of brutality. One of the points of the book is that a lot of human behavior that we think of as modern and degraded has always been there—it was just covered up. Remember, this is a fantasy about this person; it uses an 18th-century character but talks about her in a modern way, and is as much about modern life as it is about life then."

Galassi promises a "substantial" printing, although plans will not be finalized for some time. Sherwood, meanwhile, is hard at work on a second novel, this time set in Northern California during the Beat period. But be they set in the 18th or the mid-20th century, she muses, "We read novels for their secrets, for the things that are not written up in the history books. The truth of the human heart can, after all, only be hinted at."

Gayle Feldman, "FSG's 'Vindication' of the Slush Pile," in Publishers Weekly, *Vol. 239, No. 45, October 12, 1992, p. 20.*

Publishers Weekly   (review date 1 March 1993)

[*Below, the critic offers a positive assessment of* Vindication.]

Sherwood's heralded debut [***Vindication***] is an arresting and convincing portrayal of Mary Wollstonecraft, the 18th-century author of *The Vindication of the Rights of Woman* and perhaps the first feminist.

Lending her subject a modern sensibility, Sherwood describes Mary's wretched childhood, and follows her through the humiliation of demeaning jobs and chronic poverty. Eventually, via the publication of *Vindication* and other books, Wollstonecraft becomes the most famous female author of her times. Wisely, Sherwood resists romanticizing Mary's complex personality. While she portrays her as intelligent, witty, idealistic and courageous, she also acknowledges the difficult edges of her character: Mary is impetuous, nervous, wildly passionate and subject to melancholy; she is self-destructive and full of self-doubt. In fact, her life is a series of ironies and contradictions: the crusader who writes that "marriage is legalized prostitution" finally finds safe harbor in a union with a man she had scorned; and, tragically, having survived a stint in Bedlam and a suicide attempt, Mary dies just when she has achieved the unimpeded means to write.

In meticulously rendered background detail, Sherwood describes the brutal realities of the 18th century: public hangings, maimed children, abused women; the excesses of the French Revolution are acutely observed through Wollstonecraft's eyes. There are also droll and vivid portraits of publisher Joseph Johnson and the habitués of his salon, including firebrand Tom Paine, artist Henry Fuseli and a most eccentric William Blake. Boldly conceived and

An excerpt from *Vindication*

Mary remembered the first time she was hurt. She was in a small circle at the end of the road. The strange half cast of the evening light made it seem like an arena. The dust was rising up in a cone of light and the rose petals were falling down. Her nose was clogged and she could not breathe. Stop, stop, she wanted to shout, but it would not stop. The bad boys continued to throw dirt balls at her.

Waking from her dream of death on the shore of the Thames, Mary had been seized with a sharp sense of joy. All her senses awoke and her awareness of herself was poignant and painful. The smell of decay emanating from her wet clothes reminded her of being on the punt in the river at Bath, of the estuary at Laugharne. The sound of the people mumbling in the background, the heavy, swinging dirge of concern was reminiscent of Paris during the Revolution. Mary saw lights from across the Thames that night as if they were the bobbing fishing boats lighting up in the Bay of Lisbon. Lisboa, they called it. She sank back onto the sand.

The London rain had stopped, and the moon rising bright and full promised Mary that she would do great things someday. She *had* done great things. Yet it did not seem to matter, the great things. It was the someday. That was what mattered. She had a someday.

Why had she done it, they whispered on the riverbank. Why did she try to kill herself?

For love, somebody said.

Ah, love.

The lack of it.

Where is her mother?

Where is her father?

Where is her husband?

They say she used to dress in black all the time.

A pity and a shame.

They say she is a famous writer.

Then she is rich.

If I were rich, I would not kill myself. I would spend my money. And a woman rich on her own work? She must be lonely. She must be a man in disguise.

Midwives babble.

Slop-carriers smell.

Seamstresses have a way of looking in their laps.

Coachmen whistle. . . .

The boatmen who saved Mary rowed her downstream to Blackfriar Stairs, with two boatloads of men and women following behind. They carried her up Ludgate Hill to Joseph's place, swinging her in a blanket done up like a hammock. It was a procession, torches aloft with swirls of flame bleeding into the night. Occasionally a face was illuminated—skewed mouths, a narrow sweep of cheek, red eyes, a crumpled row of teeth.

Frances Sherwood, in her Vindication, *Farrar, Straus and Giroux, 1993.*

adroitly paced, the narrative builds in dramatic power. There is one cavil, however: by embroidering the facts of Wollstonecraft's life, interjecting some imagined experiences into a narrative that otherwise hews to the facts as we know them, Sherwood may confuse readers into thinking that everything here is true. But her virtuosity succeeds in rendering the torments of a brilliant mind struggling against hypocritical and punitive social codes.

A review of "Vindication," in Publishers Weekly, *Vol. 240, No. 9, March 1, 1993, p. 36.*

Catherine Texier   (essay date May 1993)

[In the following essay, Texier praises Sherwood for depicting Mary Wollstonecraft's life from a twentieth-century perspective.]

Mary Wollstonecraft was our first modern feminist. The author of the flamboyant 1792 manifesto *A Vindication of the Rights of Woman,* she demanded no less than total equality between the sexes—a revolutionary thought at the time and, apparently, even now.

First-time novelist Frances Sherwood first encountered Wollstonecraft in a textbook she was teaching to a high school class. In a sidebar, Virginia Woolf described little Mary sleeping in the hallway outside her mother's bedroom door to protect her from her father's beatings. The scene was unforgettable, but it would be years before Sherwood would use it in *Vindication,* her sexy, irreverent romp of a novel loosely based on the life of the renowned English radical.

And what a remarkably modern life it was. Coming of age in literary London, Wollstonecraft was weaned on the ferment of the French and American revolutions. Dubbed by her fellow writer Horace Walpole "a hyena in petticoats," she was a single mother who actually supported herself through her writings. Born into a downwardly mobile middle-class family, she had left her home to make a living as a governess, teacher, and writer. In 1792, at the start of the Reign of Terror, she moved to Paris to join the revolutionary intelligentsia. There, she had a passionate and destructive affair with an American businessman, Gilbert Imlay, which produced a daughter, Fanny. Her subsequent marriage with the philosopher William Godwin was unfortunately short-lived. Within months of the wedding Wollstonecraft, then 38, died after giving birth to her second daughter, also named Mary, who survived. (And Mary would later equal her mother's notoriety by eloping with the poet Percy Bysshe Shelley and writing the classic *Frankenstein.*)

Frances Sherwood's life, with its dramatic turns of fortune, is also the stuff of novels. So maybe it was natural for her to recognize herself in Mary Wollstonecraft's torments. The 52-year-old author describes her own childhood during the McCarthy era as stimulating—full of music and books and ultra-liberal parents. But it suddenly fell apart when she was 17. Sherwood's father, a Jewish lawyer-biochemist-linguist, committed suicide the day before he was to appear before the House Committee on Un-American Activities. Soon thereafter, Sherwood started on a rocky path that would take her through two difficult marriages, a stint as the only white student in an all-black college, and three children. Seven years ago, she egan to write fiction. Two of her short stories won O'Henry awards.

You'd think that after such an auspicious literary beginning, Sherwood's career would be launched, but getting *Vindication* published was an adventure in its own right. Unable to find an agent, Sherwood took a wild chance and sent the manuscript to [Farrar, Straus & Giroux,] where it was unearthed from the slush pile by Jonathan Galassi, the editor who first published Scott Turow. Sherwood's foray into the 18th century it seems, was just as accidental. On a grant from the University of Indiana, she went to Europe to study the English feminist's work. At first she was thinking along the lines of a biography, but "I wanted to research clothing and furniture and toys and food and recipes and the history of makeup, and I realized that I was researching a novel."

Sherwood has stuffed her book with juicy details that make the revolutionary period come alive with all its warts and—literally—dirty underwear: the puppies brought to suckle Wollstonecraft's painfully engorged breasts when she is dying after childbirth; the lice living in dirty wigs and in the cracks of the gorgeous puffed dresses sewn tightly on women's bodies for a month; or the leather "plumpers" inserted in the mouth to pad out cheeks sagging from the loss of teeth.

One of Sherwood's first, and most important, decisions was to drop any pretense of period style. "I just knew that I couldn't do it," she says. "So better not try. I decided arbitrarily that I was going to write about the 18th century in a 20th-century way." There is a freedom in the way Sherwood weaves the pungent historical facts with her contemporary imagination that brings to mind Jeanette Winterson's *The Passion* or A. S. Byatt's *Possession*. She acknowledges her debt to the "new historicism," which she defines as bringing into the mainstream the histories of marginal people and minorities, questioning what really did happen.

After reading *Vindication,* I plunged into a couple of Wollstonecraft biographies, trying to find out what Sherwood had made up. Less than I expected, it turns out. Mary's jealousy, her fits of depression, her suicide attempts, her father's violence, her mother's indifference to her, were all there. Sherwood's major twist is her characters' eroticism. Mary's infatuations are turned into full-fledged sexual liaisons, and her love affair with Imlay becomes a kinky fantasy of S&M games and cross-dressing. "I made their relationship evil to match the political environment," she says.

As a result, *Vindication* reads like a fast-paced, literary bodice-ripper. When asked why she had given Mary—who, apparently, was a virgin until her affair with Imlay at age 34—the free sexuality of a modern woman, Sherwood laughs: "For good reading!" adding, "Along with the prudery of the period, there was a whole lot of sexual undercurrent. Take underwear, for instance. Corsets were designed to make the female figure more appealing—push out the breasts and pull in the waist—yet the women wore no underpants."

One of *Vindication's* most startling scenes shows Mary visiting her friend William Blake on a hot summer day in his lush, tropical garden. Blake's wife is naked, and pretty soon, good wine helping, Blake and Mary join her, and here they are, sitting around a table, discussing God's perfection, kissing each other like a bunch of hippies high on grass.

"I wanted people to identify with the '60s," the author explains, "the idea of people cavorting, and the opium and the sherry. But there was also a '50s feeling to the French Revolution," adds Sherwood, who, because of her own life, sees a real connection between the horrible betrayal of the Reign of Terror and that of communism. Still, what stays with the reader is an exuberant ride through a heady and experimental time. (pp. 70, 72)

> Catherine Texier, "18th-Century Fox," in Harper's Bazaar, No. 3377, May, 1993, pp. 70, 72.

Richard Eder (review date 9 May 1993)

[*An American critic, Eder received the 1987 Pulitzer Prize for criticism and a 1987 citation for excellence in reviewing from the National Book Critics Circle. In the following review, he praises Sherwood's ability to write convincingly about the past.*]

There are a number of gifted novelists who write about the past in what is virtually a future tense. They do not use the assurance of history to tell us that this is how it was; instead, they project themselves and their readers, as if by time machine, back into a different place where everything is still uncertain and to be discovered. The voices and thoughts of their characters have unfamiliar timbres and associations. Rather than moving confidently backward out of the clarity of Now, we move uncertainly forwards out of the fogginess of Then.

Marguerite Yourcenar's *Memoirs of Hadrian* worked that way. Russell Hoban's *Riddley Walker* and Jim Crace's *The Gift of Stones* took us into the constriction and immediacy of a Stone Age society which, being prehistoric, lacked the calm foreshortening of historical perspective. Adam Thorpe's *Ulverton* gave us the voices of a dozen generations of an English village as if each generation were a separate national identity struggling to resolve itself.

Such fiction is light-years away from the traditional historical novel. We are only truly in the past when we feel lost in it. Of course we still perceive the characters, even if strangely; but we no longer feel, as we do somehow in the work of such conventional historical novelists as Gore Vidal, that the characters perceive us. They couldn't; we have not been invented. This is oddly unsettling, but once unsettled we are up for a real journey.

Frances Sherwood's *Vindication* plunges us into a brush fire of nerves, longings, weaknesses, passions and intelligence to make a portrait of Mary Wollstonecraft, an early

English feminist. She loosens the blue stockings and comes up with a swirl of colors, only one of which is blue.

Wollstonecraft comes down to us as one of a circle of late 18th-Century radical thinkers and artists that included such figures as Thomas Paine, William Blake, William Godwin, Henry Fuseli, the dissenting minister Richard Price and others. She wrote the scandalously successful *Vindication of the Rights of Women,* which argued that women must cultivate their intellectual powers and independence, and exercise citizenship and the vote. She claimed that she could love man only as a fellow being and only as justified by the dictates of reason. Horace Walpole pronounced her "a hyena in skirts."

So much for the tidy picture in the history books. True, there were some disheveled footnotes. Wollstonecraft was the lover of a flamboyant American writer and political adventurer named Gilbert Imlay, by whom she bore an illegitimate daughter. She made several attempts at suicide. She married Godwin, by whom she was pregnant, and died giving birth. The child was Mary, who eloped at 17 with Shelley, and wrote *Frankenstein.*

Footnotes are what you use when you don't want to disarrange the text. Sherwood shatters the text. She does nothing so simple as write a novel about the "real"—e.g. colorful, passionate and reckless—Wollstonecraft inside the blue stockings. That would be another form of tidiness. *Vindication* makes the feminist as real as the woman; something that Camille Paglia also aims at, in a way, except that Paglia is a polemicist, not an artist. Sherwood, the artist, yokes two battling souls in a personage as bright and unstable as the blue light and red shift of a quasar.

Sherwood's accomplishment is to give her Mary, with whom she takes various historical liberties, a voice and a mind that dart erratically as if released from a dark room into the light. Daughter of a vain and brutal father, terrified at having to make her penniless way in a time when a woman faced the choice between male protection and literal destitution, she has no plan. Her growing notion of what women should be comes in dizzy flashes, like stars from a blow to the head. Her growing up is a series of blows: her father beating her mother, her mother's terrible death, service under a tyrannical old woman, with boils whose scabs flutter like "pot-lids."

She and her two sisters start a school for girls based on serious book-learning and no physical punishment. When the school fails she goes as governess to an aristocratic family in Ireland. Her early writing comes to the notice of a radical London publisher, Joseph Johnson. He takes her in, gives her a job writing and brings her into his lively and eccentric circle. There is the publication of *Vindication,* a disastrous affair with the painter Henry Fuseli, a breakdown, a stay in France to report on the Revolution, her liaison there with Imlay who eventually abandons her, her return to London, marriage to Godwin and early death from childbirth fever, the decimator of women up into this century.

Sherwood's Mary is mercurial, valiant and needy, and her peregrinations light up the variety of the times. There is

> **Sherwood does nothing so simple as write a novel about the "real"—e.g. colorful, passionate and reckless—Wollstonecraft inside the blue stockings. *Vindication* makes the feminist as real as the woman; something that Camille Paglia also aims at, in a way, except that Paglia is a polemicist, not an artist. Sherwood, the artist, yokes two battling souls in a personage as bright and unstable as the blue light and red shift of a quasar.**
>
> **—*Richard Eder***

her stay in the broken-down Irish mansion of Lady Kingsborough, a place of dogs, dirt and eccentricity. Her employer urges her to beat her two little girls, and the girls cheerfully demand it as well. Mary resists, but succumbs to the family's gentle, funny, crippled 16-year-old son. In their mutual innocence, their passion is confined to what she later describes as "rubbing."

There is a ripple of comedy throughout. Mary participates in Johnson's boisterous Thursday dinners, at which Blake, Godwin and the other great men talk and eat expansively but she has to shout to get herself listened to, while fending off assorted inquiring feet under the tablecloth. Visiting Blake and his wife in their overgrown garden, she finds herself part of a not-entirely innocent Song of Innocence. Her middle-aged, roly-poly hosts strip naked and talk of angels; soon she is tipsy and naked herself, and being patted.

There are terrible scenes. Her agonizing death after the birth of little Mary is the more horrifying for the resignation with which she and the grief-swollen Godwin accept the medical helplessness of the time. Even among the enlightened, women had not only a different freedom but a different fate. A scene in Bedlam, where she is taken after a breakdown, is grisly but relatively pat. There is a prodigious storm at sea. The passengers huddle in the hold and Sherwood, whose phrases jar to Mary's fierce and tremulous rhythms, writes: "The rain pelted, pelt, pe, p the deck, stopped."

Sometimes the author introduces a deliberately factual touch, with data about women's employment and wages. Sometimes, particularly in the comedy, she uses Dickens-like contrasts of light and dark. This is particularly true of a few shining benevolences who light up Mary's persistent but uncertain pilgrimage. Joseph Johnson, her rescuer and mentor, is one of the book's most distinctive characters; eccentric, nurturing and gay in both senses. Mary's movement from shock over the revelation to acceptance is told quite magically. So is her susceptible sexiness in which ardor and a protesting puzzlement are finely joined.

Vindication's darting course through Mary's poignant contradictions makes it uneven and disjointed at times. Occasionally we lose sight of her, as she loses sight of herself; we are becalmed as she is. But Sherwood has taken us to a past that is not so much another country as white-capped headwaters that do not yet know their river. (pp. 3, 9)

> Richard Eder, "The First Feminist," in Los Angeles Times Book Review, *May 9, 1993, pp. 3, 9.*

Hilary Mantel   (review date 21 May 1993)

[*Mantel is a British novelist. In the following review, she finds* Vindication *to be an accomplished but ultimately disappointing novel.*]

Mary, a child in a disorderly household, works out what girls should be: "Girls must be smart . . . and strong, a whole host of things, but not dutiful or obedient, for that assumed a mother and father who were intelligent and rational."

Mary is Mary Wollstonecraft, or her fictional shadow; Frances Sherwood has used Wollstonecraft's career as the starting-point for an imaginative exploration of the London of William Blake and the Paris of Dr Guillotin [in **Vindication**]. She handles ideas deftly, and emotions with conviction; her tone is arch and funny, slightly throw-away, and quite free from cramping reverence.

Her heroine has a poor start in life, a victim of a violent family and her own blossoming, unfeminine cleverness. We meet her in Bath at the age of twenty-two, a lady's companion; follow her home to nurse a mother dying of breast cancer, and then into the household of her married sister Eliza. She helps Eliza run away from a bad marriage—for which Eliza is not grateful—and with her other sister, Everina, sets up a school for girls. She meets the dissenting minister, Richard Price, who encourages her to write; goes to Ireland to be a governess, and is sacked because her charges soon prefer her to their mother.

Like the historical Mary, she returns to London, and becomes a scribbler under the patronage and roof of Joseph Johnson, the printer; Sherwood offers a lively and convincing version of a man whom Claire Tomalin, in her biography of Wollstonecraft, calls "wary, self-effacing and remarkably efficient at obscuring his own tracks". At Johnson's dinner-table, she meets Tom Paine, William Blake and the egotistical painter Fuseli, with whom she has an affair. In a fever of passion and idealism, she produces her great work, *Vindication of the Rights of Women;* travels to revolutionary Paris, survives the Terror, bears a child to Gilbert Imlay, an American adventurer; marries William Godwin, dies horribly after a protracted labour. The novel does not distort Mary Wollstonecraft's career, but rather simplifies and shapes it; Sherwood has blended motifs and references from Mary's own books into her fictionalized life. But why sensationalize? Wollstonecraft's real life, with its fugues and suicide attempts, needs little enhancement. A Bedlam scene, here, though well-written, is *de trop.*

Sherwood provides her own commentary on the action, its coolness a contrast with the busy, tactile world that Mary inhabits. Her idiom is fluid and responsive; the dialogue is plain, sharp and sardonic. What impresses most is the central portrait, which accommodates all the complexities and inconsistencies which make up human personality. "I must learn", Mary says, "how to tread the middle ground between loneliness and freedom"; and it is on that precarious middle ground the author hovers, necessarily wise after the event, but able to convince us that she comprehends Mary's troubled head and heart. Mary is a vulnerable and dangerous creature, a high-principled woman desperate for love; Sherwood understands how, once hurt by the world, human beings go on hurting themselves. She and Mary between them locate a problem generations of feminists have faced: "I advocate a life I do not live. . . . I turn around and betray myself. . . . I am a fraud."

Sherwood's portrait of the exterior world is hardly less successful, though the sections set in France during the revolution are not free from error and have a predigested feel. The book ends with what seems like an odd misjudgment—a love-scene for Shelley and Mary Godwin (who was the baby who killed Mary Wollstonecraft). Temptation got the better of Frances Sherwood, one feels; but if she wanted to write of the next generation, she should have devised a new tone. The book's intimate quality seemed shaped by some quality in its heroine; but what appeared to be empathy is simply technique. It is disillusioning; the thread of sympathy, held taut between the writer and her subject, turns out to be nothing finer than the puppetmistress's string.

> Hilary Mantel, "A Troubled Heart," in The Times Literary Supplement, *No. 4703, May 21, 1993, p. 23.*

Loraine Fletcher   (review date 4 June 1993)

[*In the following review, Fletcher evaluates Sherwood's treatment of historical and biographical themes in* Vindication.]

"She is alive and well. She lives, my dear, in your heart, in your mind," Percy Shelley says to Mary Wollstonecraft's daughter in the epilogue to **Vindication.** Yes, this does get a bit like Consequences, as the well-known names keep turning up. He's asserting a community of experience from one generation of women to another. It's Frances Sherwood's point as well, and governs the techniques of this fictional biography.

Her Wollstonecraft's sensibility feels very modern, give or take an empire-line dress or two, and Sherwood wisely makes no attempt at 1790s talk. Her characters speak and think in 1990s American. The clever heroine with her bullying father and exploitative lovers would feel at home in any mildly literary circle now, English or American. The strengths of Sherwood's writing lie in her sense of a feminist continuous present.

But if we are Wollstonecraft, then she is us, and the conclusion is somehow much more presumptuous than the premise. As a child of the Enlightenment, she is more remote, in her response to religion or natural landscape, for instance, than we probably like to think.

When she came to London after a disastrous term as a

governess, the radical publisher Joseph Johnson gave her space in *The Analytical,* found her somewhere to live and introduced her to his authors: Paine, Blake, Bage, Godwin and others. This is an ambitious book, and Sherwood can't do (nobody could) Johnson's Thursday dinners. Paine says, "I am the Revolution" a lot, and everyone worries about Blake seeing God's face in a tree, but there's not much to back the sense they all had, especially Wollstonecraft, of their power to make the world anew. Sherwood quickly moves her heroine from these scenes to the brutal or duplicitous courtships of Fuseli and Imlay; commoner ground.

For the English setting, we have to fall back on headlice, proletarian women sewn into their clothes from Christmas to Easter, Tyburn hangings. It's authentic, but applicable to any decade of the 18th century. In Paris, though, the guillotine is author-friendly as usual. Sherwood tries to escape the reductivism inherent in all biography by ample quotation and by making her heroine conscious of the disparity between the real Wollstonecraft's authoritative writing and her own messy emotions. It's a disparity the real Wollstonecraft may have felt too, of course.

At the end of *Vindication,* the punitive medics arrive, the labour goes on interminably, the baby who will write *Frankenstein* 20 years later is removed and replaced by two puppies in a last nightmare effort to dislodge the afterbirth by suckling. Sherwood's fanciful impressionistic style is more indecorous here than earlier, and Claire Tomalin's austere 1974 version remains the only way to do it. But Sherwood could write a better novel without the peg of biography.

Wollstonecraft's mind resists novelistic embroidery. She fictionalised her own life twice, more competently and passionately than anyone could do it for her, in *Mary: a Fiction* and *The Wrongs of Woman,* and we need to turn to these to meet her uncomfortable genius.

> *Loraine Fletcher, "Unholy Mary," in* New Statesman & Society, *Vol. 6, No. 255, June 4, 1993, p. 40.*

Laura Shapiro (review date 7 June 1993)

[*In the following review, Shapiro lauds Sherwood's convincing blend of fact and fiction in* Vindication.]

It's impossible to sum up this novel with any neatness or dispatch. Frances Sherwood's *Vindication* is startling, depressing, enlightening and unforgettable, and that doesn't begin to do it justice. Start with her daring: for the heroine of this, her first novel, Sherwood chooses Mary Wollstonecraft (1759-1797), the British feminist whose *A Vindication of the Rights of Woman* was one of the most radical documents of its time (and its time included the American and French revolutions). Even the relatively genteel account of Wollstonecraft's life in *The Dictionary of National Biography* is hair-raising: she grew up wretchedly with an alcoholic father, got fired as a governess, ran a small school until it collapsed, lost her dearest woman friend to an early death, attempted suicide when one of her great loves rejected her and died at 36 after giving birth to her

second child. She also became a celebrated writer dining and debating with some of the liveliest men around, including Thomas Paine, William Blake and the philosopher William Godwin, whom she married chiefly because she was pregnant with their child. This needed fiction?

But Sherwood doesn't try to outdo the facts; she plunges into them, discovering (or creating—it hardly matters) a horribly mistreated child, a tormented woman, an angry feminist, a passionate writer. Sherwood's Wollstonecraft is a lurid creation, subject to horrors piled on horrors, not only beaten by her father but rejected by her mother *and* sexually abused by her nurse. As an adult she is pathetic, often infuriating, constantly falling in love with men who humiliate her, renewing her degradations over and over. Worst of all, she cannot love her child any better than she herself was loved. Her memories of childhood beatings are vivid, and she despises violence; yet once, in despair, she throws the infant against a wall. The publication of *A Vindication* makes her famous, but she struggles helplessly to live up to its message: that strength, wisdom and independence are the noblest virtues for women as well as men.

> **Sherwood's Wollstonecraft is a lurid creation, subject to horrors piled on horrors.**
>
> **—*Laura Shapiro***

As for literary London in the 18th century, the London that so entranced Boswell and Dr. Johnson—Sherwood's view is a little different from theirs. She sees the underside, the crowds rushing to watch the hanging of a 12-year-old thief, the gutters overflowing with human waste, the children crippled that they might become more successful beggars. "The port was in a tall decanter," she writes, describing a dinner party of radical intellectuals in a home outfitted with Wedgwood and cut glass. "There was mincemeat pie on the table; a line of ants clustered around the strawberry tarts and pie crumbs on the white cloth. Some mice were running along the baseboards."

Despite the unremitting muck and the heroine who refuses to act like one, *Vindication* isn't totally gruesome. There are pleasures and triumphs in Wollstonecraft's life, and they thread their way quietly through the narrative, especially a profound friendship with her publisher, Joseph Johnson. Thrown out of her job as a governess, Wollstonecraft turns up on his doorstep penniless and bedraggled, hoping that since he has agreed to publish her work he will give her a small advance. Instead he takes her in, asks her to write for the journal he publishes and gives her a home. Sherwood describes this friendship wonderfully, tracing it all over the house, from Wollstonecraft's attic bedroom—where she writes and suffers—down to the kitchen, where she likes to sit and talk with the housekeeper.

In the end, the tale told in *Vindication* is deeply convincing, not just because Sherwood knows the 18th century but because she knows how to write a novel. It's as if she has lifted a corner of history and exposed the life beneath, fact and fiction swarming together like the ants about the crumbs. This astonishing first novel exerts a grip on the imagination that can't be shaken off. Watch out, we may be in for a Wollstonecraft craze to rival the one for Frida Kahlo.

Laura Shapiro, "By Feminism Possessed," in Newsweek, Vol. CXXI, No. 23, June 7, 1993, p. 64.

Wendy Smith (review date 27 June 1993)

[*Smith is an an American journalist and critic. In the following review, she characterizes* Vindication *as an ambitious but flawed novel.*]

In her ambitious first novel [**Vindication**], O. Henry Award-winning short story writer Frances Sherwood weaves a tangled web of themes around a complex heroine with mixed success. Her reimagining of pioneering feminist Mary Wollstonecraft's life suffers from an uneven tone and bumpy pacing, yet this flawed work is more stimulating than many novels that have greater polish simply because they attempt less.

Sherwood, by contrast, has attempted a lot. She touches on topics as diverse as English radicals' excitement about the French Revolution and differing approaches to childbirth as she recreates the society in which Wollstonecraft lived, and readers unfamiliar with 18th-century history may find the references somewhat confusing. Yet for the most part, the author skillfully integrates these external details with the more personal, existential dilemma at the novel's heart: the painful contradiction between the power and control displayed in Wollstonecraft's intellectual endeavors and the miserable turbulence of her emotional life.

In a sensitive portrait that accords with the known facts, Sherwood depicts Wollstonecraft as a clever, angry woman who early in life rejects men's power over her sex as unjust, whether it consists of her father getting drunk and beating her mother, her brother mocking her for wanting to read books, or male authors writing "too many novels with submissive women." The young Mary, desperately longing to be "intelligent and rational," concludes that "most of what is written, what is, what exists in the world does not include me." She sets out to be included, by joining a circle of radical London intellectuals who believe as she does in reason and equality, and by writing books that claim those concepts for women as well as men.

Yet, as Wollstonecraft tells her friend and publisher Joseph Johnson, "I advocate a life I do not live . . . I am not independent. I am a fraud." The author of *A Vindication of the Rights of Woman,* who has the audacity to write in 1792, "I love man as my fellow, but his sceptre, real or usurped, extends not to me," in fact loves men who hurt her. In the same year as those brave words, the breakup of her affair with painter Henry Fuseli leads to Wollstonecraft's confinement in Bedlam. Rescued by Johnson and journeying to France to view the Revolution, she becomes

involved with an American, Gilbert Imlay, who likes rough sex and abandons her after their daughter, Fanny, is born in 1794, prompting Wollstonecraft to twice attempt suicide.

"The contrast between her accomplishments and her feelings about herself . . . quite amazing," says Johnson—one of several instances in which a character offers psychological analysis that reflects the assumptions of an age imbued with Freud's insights rather than the 18th century's more mechanistic views. Several ironic references to Wollstonecraft as "the most famous woman in the world" also seem too knowing for the period, and Mary's bitter rejoinder, "That was for five minutes, years ago," inappropriately echoes Andy Warhol. Sherwood may have intended to create a modernist prism refracting the past through a contemporary sensibility, but that is not the novel she has written. In her essentially conventional narrative, which immerses readers in the events and ideas of Wollstonecraft's age, these 20th-century musings are as jarring as the occasional intrusions of an authorial voice into a story told primarily from the protagonist's point of view.

The awkward lurching between historical and modern attitudes, subjective and objective points of view, is symptomatic of **Vindication's** overall lack of coherence. The book has wonderful moments: a moving explanation of actress Sarah Siddons's impact on the young Mary; talks with her first mentor, dissenting minister Richard Price, that show a starved mind hungrily grasping at intellectual nourishment; nice scenes of boisterous interactions among a crew of visionary misfits that includes William Blake, Thomas Paine and William Godwin; clever use of a single conversation to distill the process by which Godwin, initially disliked by Wollstonecraft, wins her respect and affection; Mary's heartbreaking cry on her deathbed (after giving birth to the daughter who would become Mary Shelley): "Women have been dying of [childbed fever] forever. What kind of progress has been made, and for whom?"

But these moments just don't add up to a satisfying whole—indeed, scenes seem to be strung together arbitrarily rather than following one another naturally in a thoroughly worked out progression of ideas and emotions. There is little growth or change in the novel: Wollstonecraft never achieves her self-proclaimed goal, to "learn how to tread the middle ground between loneliness and freedom," and Sherwood seems content to describe her destructive love affairs in excruciating detail—rather scanting the books that made her reputation—without ever illuminating the emotional needs that drove her to abusive men. **Vindication** aims high but, regrettably, fails to live up to its considerable aspirations.

Wendy Smith, "In a Man's World," in Book World—The Washington Post, June 27, 1993, p. 9.

Margaret Forster (review date 11 July 1993)

[*Forster is a British novelist, biographer, and critic. In the following review, she finds* Vindication *entertaining and well-crafted, but expresses concern that the novel misrepresents Mary Wollstonecraft's life.*]

Novels based on the lives of real people, even long dead people, are always dangerous enterprises. Dangerous because they tamper with received truth, dangerous because their avowed aim is to lie, all in the name of satisfying unsatisfied curiosity. Is this sort of distortion right, is it fair?

Frances Sherwood will have to face up to these kinds of questions rather more seriously than other historical novelists simply because *Vindication,* her novel about Mary Wollstonecraft, deviates so *wildly* from the known facts. But controversy is something she obviously anticipated since she has taken care to state, in a note at the beginning of the book, that she realizes her story bears only a surface resemblance to the actual history on which it is based— "there are many deviations." But the crux of the matter is: are these deviations important or not?

Immediately, there is a problem, or rather two, both quite different. On the one hand this novel will attract those who know nothing about Mary Wollstonecraft (1759-97), the feminist author of *A Vindication of the Rights of Women* and the mother of Mary Wollstonecraft Shelley; such readers will therefore gain powerful first impressions of Wollstonecraft from it. On the other hand there will be readers who know a lot about her and want to know more. I would suspect this second group will be larger and more strongly affected by these harmless sounding deviations.

These deviations fall into several categories but only one is disturbing. It seems to me perfectly acceptable that Ms. Sherwood, who is also the author of *Everything You've Heard Is True,* a volume of stories, should try to illuminate the dark corners of Wollstonecraft's life about which we know little and suspect much—that, surely, is the function of historical fiction. We know, for example, that she was a sensual woman but we have no real knowledge of her intimate love life. One of the best things about this novel is that it persuasively imagines what Wollstonecraft's sexual feelings might have been. As far as these kinds of deviations go, there is no quarrel.

But others cause a distinct queasiness. There are instances where Ms. Sherwood is not simply filling in gaps but inventing events that never happened and that are alien to the spirit of Wollstonecraft. After the breakup of her relationship with the artist Henry Fuseli, she was distressed, as we know from Claire Tomalin's biography of Wollstonecraft, but never mad. Ms. Sherwood, however, has her "bundled . . . up in a blanket and [taken] away as fast as they could to Bedlam." There follows a harrowing description of Bedlam, an experience that haunts her for the rest of her (imagined) life.

Even more curious is a scene in which Mary's lover, Gilbert Imlay, whips her with her consent. Mary Wollstonecraft? Whipped? It's just as likely that she would have snatched the whip and turned it on him. But the most objectionable of all the deviations Ms. Sherwood concocts is a moment when Wollstonecraft hates her first baby, Fanny, so much that she throws her against a wall. Imlay, too, contrary to what we know, is depicted as having no interest whatsoever in his daughter. The reader familiar

with Wollstonecraft is likely to be appalled; the reader who is not, and who may never take trouble to find out, will have absorbed an interpretation of her that is utterly disloyal to her memory.

If this is a good novel otherwise (which it is) does the falsification matter? Yes, I think it does. Mary Wollstonecraft was a remarkable woman. She was the only woman in a group of brilliant radical intellectuals that included Thomas Paine; her *Vindication of the Rights of Women* made her internationally known; she lived through the Reign of Terror in France. With all that, who needs deviations?

Yet Ms. Sherwood is devoted to her subject. The pages of her novel exude enthusiasm. She writes in a clipped and terse style and constructs a great deal of dialogue that conveys Wollstonecraft's sense of urgency. The wealth of personal detail—clothes, domestic settings—is impressive. If I had known nothing about Mary Wollstonecraft I would have loved this novel. As it is, I worry. Can I beg all readers not already acquainted with Ms. Tomalin's biography, *The Life and Death of Mary Wollstonecraft,* to read it immediately after finishing *Vindication*? It is, I assure you, a necessary corrective.

> Margaret Forster, "This Is Sort of Your Life, Mary Wollstonecraft," in The New York Times Book Review, *July 11, 1993, p. 21.*

Frances Sherwood with Jennifer Brostrom, *CLC Yearbook* (interview date 10 November 1993)

[*Below, Sherwood discusses* Vindication *and her writing career.*]

[*Brostrom*]: *Please discuss any background research you conducted for* **Vindication.**

[Sherwood]: I made several trips to England, and went to practically every place Wollstonecraft had lived and travelled. I studied the history of all aspects of life during the eighteenth century including the history of clothing, the history of makeup, the history of food, and the origin of common slang phrases. . . . It took about four years to complete the research and writing.

Some critics have praised your use of historical detail but expressed concern that readers will be misled by the fictional events depicted in **Vindication.** *Can you comment on this?*

There are fictional events in the book. I had Wollstonecraft attend a hanging she may have never seen, I had her go to Bedlam . . . in part because in my research I discovered these fascinating historical details and events, and I wanted to write about them. I wanted to create an authentic sense of what life was like during this time, and I also wanted to write a really juicy book that people would want to read—a real page-turner. Some reviewers have stated, "I've read Tomalin's biography, and this is where you should turn for the truth on Wollstonecraft." My response is that in preparation to write *Vindication* I read six biographies, researched numerous additional sources, and completely immersed myself in Wollstonecraft's life. I feel confident that I was true to her spirit.

Can you comment on the parallels between history and modern events portrayed in **Vindication***?*

In my research I began to see parallels between historical events of the time and events that have occurred during the 20th century. . . . For example, I perceived a possible similarity between the disillusionment experienced by the intellectuals and radicals during the Reign of Terror of the French Revolution and the disillusionment of idealists after the exposure of Stalin. There is also a scene in the novel with characters based on William Blake and his wife that is reminiscent of the hippie era during the 1960s.

How did your personal experiences influence the writing of **Vindication***?*

The book is in part an expression of my inner life. I am a manic depressive and could relate to the turmoil of Wollstonecraft's emotional life and also to her often painful experiences within personal relationships. The more I became involved with her writings, the more I could sense the effect of extreme emotional ups and downs in her life. Wollstonecraft, of course, would not have been diagnosed as a "manic depressive" in those days, but the evidence exists that she suffered from a depressive disorder. . . . Also, I didn't feel comfortable using period language because I knew I couldn't do it accurately, and I decided I had to associate the book with something I know well— and I thought "what do I know better than myself?"

What are your primary aims as a writer?

To earn a place in American literary history—to be remembered as an American writer, which is a pretty lofty goal. I'm not particularly interested in literary prizes, but I do want to be read and appreciated by as many readers as possible.

What is significant to you about being an American writer?

I think it's the American tradition of individualism and innovation that has existed from the beginning in American literature with writers like Melville, and even Hawthorne, for example.

Who are your primary literary influences?

I can't isolate my literary influences, since each has served its purpose at a particular time. For example, at one point during my youth I read Kafka extensively, but I never read him now. . . . The Brontës, Jane Austen, and Louisa May Alcott were all female role models I turned to, and who influenced my own belief in my capabilities as a writer. I grew up during the 1950s, so I had very few positive women for role models. . . . Also, Richard Price has

been a recent influence, as well as Russell Banks, Janet Hobhouse, and Jorge Luis Borges.

Do you advocate any particular lifestyle or employment for the contemporary artist?

I currently have a university position, which allows me to make a living. I've previously had numerous experiences and nine-to-five jobs, but find that teaching is the first position that allows the time and freedom to write. At this point, I can't imagine holding down a nine-to-five job and also trying to write. I do think I'm approaching the point at which I can support myself solely by writing. . . . I don't advocate any particular lifestyle for writers—simply talk to everyone, read everything you can get your hands on, and live as fully as possible. Reclusiveness is necessary for the actual writing, but you need life experience to be a mature writer.

Do you consider yourself a feminist writer?

Yes I do. I think feminist themes are important to any work that deals with human values. People think of our society as advanced, but issues concerning human care such as child abuse and the treatment of women really have not progressed much over the past two hundred years, and I wanted to show this in the novel. I'm currently working on a book that focuses on women in the 1950s, but feminist and historical themes are not exclusive to my work.

How do you perceive yourself in relation to the larger picture of contemporary literature and publishing?

I do not perceive myself as a marginal writer—I want to write for the largest audience possible. I do believe that certain aspects of publishing can be challenging for women writers who do not have a certain marketable popular image, however. . . . Many aspects of the publishing business do run on an "old boys club" mentality. For example, I was recently at a booksellers convention where the women booksellers informed me that they had read the book and that it was selling quite well, while most of the men said that they hadn't read it, and that the sales were poor. The attention and interest of booksellers as well as publishers is of vital importance to whether books are bought and read by the public.

What do you consider the fundamental goal of **Vindication***?*

To present a strong woman who overcame serious difficulties and did not compromise in her work or passion. To show that this was happening two hundred years ago, so it can happen today.

Prizewinners

Literary Prizes and Honors
Announced in 1993

Academy of American Poets Awards

Fellowship of the Academy of American Poets
Awarded annually to recognize distinguished achievement by an American poet.

Gerald Stern

The Lamont Poetry Selection
Established in 1952 to reward and encourage promising writers by supporting the publication of an American poet's second book.

Rosanna Warren
Stained Glass

Peter I. B. Lavan Younger Poets Award
Established in 1983 to annually recognize three accomplished American poets under the age of forty.

Thomas Bolt
David Clewel
Christopher Merrill

Walt Whitman Award
Secures the publication of the first book of a living American poet.

Stephen Yenser
The Fire in All Things

American Academy and Institute of Arts and Letters Awards

Academy-Institute Awards
Given annually to encourage creative achievement in art, music, and literature.

Ellen Akins, Rich Bausch, Vance Bourjaily,
Deborah Eisenberg, Rolf Fjelde,
Tina Howe, Denis Johnson, A. G. Mojtabai

Witter Bynner Foundation Prize for Poetry
*Established in 1979 and awarded annually to recognize
an outstanding younger poet.*

Patricia Storace

Sue Kaufman Prize for First Fiction
*Awarded annually to the author of the best first fiction published
during the preceding year.*

Francisco Goldman
The Long Night of White Chickens
(see *CLC*, Volume 76)

Richard and Hilda Rosenthal Foundation Award
*Awards given annually for accomplishment in art and literature. The literature award recognizes
a work of fiction published in the preceding year which, while not a "commercial
success," is considered a literary achievement.*

Robert Olen Butler
A Good Scent from a Strange Mountain
(see entry below)

Morton Dauwen Zabel Award
*Presented in alternating years to poets, fiction writers, and critics, to encourage progressive,
original, and experimental tendencies in American literature.*

James Purdy

James Tait Black Memorial Book Prize
*Sponsored by the University of Edinburgh and awarded annually for the best
work of fiction published during the previous year.*

Rose Tremain
Sacred Country

Booker Prize for Fiction
Britain's major literary prize is awarded annually in recognition of a full–length novel.

Roddy Doyle
Paddy Clarke Ha Ha Ha
(see entry below)

Booker Russian Novel Prize
Established in 1992 and awarded annually to recognize the best new Russian novel.

Vladimir Makanin
The Baize-Colored Table

Georg Büchner Prize
Awarded annually, the Georg Büchner Prize is considered Germany's
most prestigious literary award.

Peter Rühmkorf

Commonwealth Writers Prize
Awarded annually to promote new Commonwealth fiction of merit outside
the author's country of origin.

Githa Hariharan
The Thousand Faces of Night
(first novel)

Goncourt Prize
Awarded annually in France by the Academie Goncourt *to recognize a prose work*
published during the preceding year.

Amin Maalouf
Le rocher de Tanios

Governor General's Literary Awards
Honors writing that achieves literary excellence without sacrificing popular appeal. Officially known
as the Canadian Authors Association (CAA) Literary Awards, awards are given annually
for works written in both English and French in the categories
of fiction, nonfiction, poetry, and drama.

Nancy Huston
Cantique des plaines
(fiction)

Carol Shields
The Stone Diaries
(fiction)

Denise Desautels
Le saut de l'ange
(poetry)

Don Coles
Forests of the Medieval World
(poetry)

Daniel Danis
Celle-là
(drama)

Guillermo Verdecchia
Fronteras Americanas
(drama)

Hugo Awards

Established in 1953 to recognize notable science fiction works in several categories.

Connie Willis
Doomsday Book
(novel)

Vernor Vinge
A Fire upon the Deep
(novel)

Lucius Shepard
Barnacle Bill the Spacer
(novella)

Janet Kagan
"The Nutcracker Coup"
(novellette)

Connie Willis
"Even the Queen"
(short story)

Ruth Lilly Poetry Prize

Awarded annually to an outstanding American poet.

Charles Wright

Los Angeles Times Book Awards

Awards are given in various categories to honor outstanding technique and vision.

Mark Doty
My Alexandria
(poetry)

Barbara Kingsolver
Pigs in Heaven
(fiction)
(see entry below)

Lenore Marshall/*Nation* Poetry Prize

*Established in 1974 to honor the author of the year's outstanding collection of poems
published in the United States.*

Thom Gunn
The Man with the Night Sweats
(see entry below)

National Book Awards

Established in 1950 to honor and promote American books of literary distinction in various categories.

E. Annie Proulx
The Shipping News
(fiction)
(see entry below)

A. R. Ammons
Garbage
(poetry)

Gore Vidal
United States: Essays 1952-1992
(nonfiction)

Clifton Fadiman
(distinguished contribution to American letters)

National Book Critics Circle Awards

Founded in 1974, this American award recognizes superior literary quality in several categories.

Cormac McCarthy
All the Pretty Horses
(fiction)

Hayden Carruth
Shorter Collected Poems 1946-91
(poetry)

Nebula Awards

Established in 1965 to honor significant works in several categories of science fiction published in the United States.

Connie Willis
Doomsday Book
(novel)

Connie Willis
"Even the Queen"
(short story)

New York Drama Critics Circle Award

Awards are presented annually in several categories to encourage excellence in playwriting.

Tony Kushner
Angels in America: Millennium Approaches
(best new play)
(see entry below)

Nobel Prize in Literature
Awarded annually to recognize the most distinguished body of literary work of an idealistic nature.

Toni Morrison

Obie Awards
Awards in various categories are given annually to recognize excellence in off-Broadway and off-off-Broadway theater productions.

Harry Kondoleon
The Houseguests

Larry Kramer
The Destiny of Me

Jose Rivera
Marisol

Paul Rudnick
Jeffrey

PEN American Center Awards

Faulkner Award for Fiction
Annually recognizes the most distinguished book-length work of fiction by an American writer published during the calendar year.

E. Annie Proulx
Postcards
(novel)

Edgar Allan Poe Award
Presented annually for outstanding achievement in mystery writing.

Michael Connelly
The Black Echo

Pulitzer Prizes

Awarded in recognition of outstanding accomplishments by American authors in various categories within the fields of journalism, literature, music, and drama. Literary awards usually recognize excellence in works that concern American life.

Robert Olen Butler
A Good Scent from a Strange Mountain
(fiction)
(see entry below)

Louise Glück
The Wild Iris
(poetry)
(see entry below)

Tony Kushner
Angels in America: Millennium Approaches
(drama)
(see entry below)

Rea Award

Presented annually to recognize outstanding achievement in the short story genre.

Grace Paley

Tony Awards

Officially titled the American Theatre Wing's Antoinette Perry Awards, prizes are presented in recognition of outstanding achievement in the Broadway theater.

Tony Kushner
Angels in America: Millennium Approaches
(best play)
(see entry below)

United States Poet Laureate

Created in 1986 by an act of Congress to honor the career achievement of an American poet.

Rita Dove
(see entry below)

Whitbread Literary Awards

Awarded annually in several categories to encourage and promote English literature.

Jeff Torrington
Swing Hammer Swing!
(novel)

Robert Olen Butler

A Good Scent from a Strange Mountain

Award: Pulitzer Prize for Fiction

(Full name Robert Olen Butler, Jr.) Born in 1945, Butler is an American novelist and short story writer.

INTRODUCTION

A collection of fifteen short stories, *A Good Scent from a Strange Mountain* chronicles the experiences of Vietnamese immigrants who settled in suburban New Orleans, Louisiana, following the Vietnam War. Butler, who served in the war as a translator, integrates Vietnamese myths and folklore with contemporary American culture to address such themes as cultural assimilation, displacement, loss, and memory. In the story "Snow," for example, the narrator laments the loss of Vietnamese traditions: "There are other Vietnamese here in Lake Charles, Louisiana, but we are not a community. We are all too sad, perhaps, or too tired. But maybe not. Maybe that's just me saying that. Maybe the others are real Americans already." In "Mid-Autumn" a pregnant Vietnamese woman compares her passion for a boy she knew in Vietnam with the ambivalence she feels for the American soldier who married her and brought her to the United States. As she relates these feelings to her unborn child, she suggests that Vietnam will live on in her memory even though she can never return to her native country. Critical reaction to *A Good Scent from a Strange Mountain* has been positive, with reviewers praising Butler's compassionate and realistic depiction of the Vietnamese people, language, and culture. Richard Eder has stated: "It is the Vietnamese voice that [Butler] seeks and that, in these stories, he has so remarkably and movingly found. . . . Butler writes essentially, and in a bewitching translation of voice and sympathy, what it means to lose a country, to remember it, and to have the memory begin to grow old. He writes as if it were his loss, too."

PRINCIPAL WORKS

The Alleys of Eden (novel) 1981
Sun Dogs (novel) 1982
Countrymen of Bones (novel) 1983
On Distant Ground (novel) 1985
Wabash (novel) 1987

The Deuce (novel) 1989
A Good Scent from a Strange Mountain (short stories) 1992
They Whisper (novel) 1994

CRITICISM

Publishers Weekly **(review date 20 January 1992)**

[*In the following review, the critic praises* A Good Scent from a Strange Mountain.]

Set in the Vietnamese enclaves of suburban New Orleans, [the 15 stories in *A Good Scent from a Strange Mountain*] capture the voices of people who have lost their homeland and are trying to adapt to an alien culture. Butler (*On Dis-*

121

tant Ground), who served in Vietnam as an Army linguist, affords readers a sense of the Vietnamese spirit through diverse narrators: Buddhists and Catholics, repatriated businessmen from the North and housewives native to the South. Integrating the elegiac quality of memories with the cadences of folklore, the characters tell of their experiences during the war and their attempts to make sense of its bewildering aftermath. Their adopted land has contributed its own exotica: in **"Love,"** a former spy turns to voodoo to eliminate his wife's lover. The title piece is a magical realist tale of a man nearly 100 years old who imagines he is visited by Ho Chi Minh, whom he had known as a youth when they worked together in London and Paris. Now they discuss the divergent paths each has taken. When languages are different, perceptions collide; in **"Fairy Tale"** the narrator relates how her American boyfriend, unfamiliar with the proper intonations of Vietnamese, turns a beautiful compliment into an absurdity. In writing sensitively and eloquently of a culture struggling to survive, Butler also shows us the prevailing society through fresh eyes. (pp. 46-7)

A review of "A Good Scent from a Strange Mountain," in Publishers Weekly, *Vol. 239, No. 4, January 20, 1992, pp. 46-7.*

Madison Smartt Bell   (review date 23 February 1992)

[*In the following review, Bell discusses Butler's use of language and metaphor in* A Good Scent from a Strange Mountain.]

With *A Good Scent From a Strange Mountain,* Robert Olen Butler reveals his discovery of a pocket of cross-cultural peculiarity, which has become, for him, a sort of writer's paradise. The place is Lake Charles, La., but the people are all Vietnamese, immigrants who came there in the aftermath of the war, Northerners and Southerners, Buddhists and Catholics, drawn by a climate similar to that of their lost nation. The community they form in the new world gives the 15 stories of Butler's collection a sort of novelistic unity, enhanced by his sharp insight into their ways, their beliefs and their reactions to life among strangers in a strange land.

Each of the stories is a monologue told in a Vietnamese voice, and Butler, who served in Vietnam as an Army linguist, can reproduce these voices with a beautiful fidelity. With his mastery of the language comes understanding of various Vietnamese ways of thought. This book offers a rare and privileged glimpse of what the Vietnamese in the U.S. think of each other and also what they think of the rest of us.

"Fairy Tale," the story of a Saigon bargirl who comes to America as the wife of an American diplomatic functionary, turns on subtleties of language. As in many Oriental languages, a shift of tone in Vietnamese can change meaning altogether, a factor that leads to many strange utterances from the mouths of maladroit foreigners.

Miss Noi describes how she fell for her husband:

> He wanted to say in my language, "May Vietnam live for ten thousand years." What he said,

very clear, was, "the sunburnt duck is lying down." Now if I think this man says that Vietnam should live for ten thousand years, I think he is a certain kind of man. But when he says that a sunburnt duck is lying down—boom, my heart melts.

Miss Noi makes a myth for herself around the idea of the sunburnt duck. But because of the misunderstanding, the myth is false, the marriage fails and she becomes a bargirl again, in New Orleans, this time. It isn't exactly a life of suffering but a deadening plenitude of sex and unaccustomed luxury, represented to her by a surfeit of apples, which in Vietnam were a significant treat that only her GI lovers could provide. "In New Orleans, there are apples in the store and I buy them and I eat too many. The taste is still good but it is not special anymore."

Land of plenty! There are enough European-Americans who have foundered on it too. Miss Noi meets one of them, Fontenot, an ugly, awkward, tongue-tied man who, oddly enough, was so happy in Vietnam he cannot readjust to life back home. In Fontenot her fable of the sunburnt duck is reanimated:

> Once upon a time there was a duck with a long neck and long beak like all ducks and he lives in a place all alone and he does not know how to build a nest or preen his own feathers. Because of this, the sun shines down and burns him, makes his feathers turn dark and makes him very sad. When he lies down to sleep, you think that he is dead, he is so sad and still. Then one day he flies to another part of the land and he finds a little animal with a nice coat and though that animal is different from him, a nutria, still he lies down beside her. He seems to be all burnt up and dead. But the nutria does not think so and she licks his fingers and makes him well. Then he takes her with him to live in Thibodaux, Louisiana, where he fixes cars and she has a nice little house and she is a housewife with a toaster machine and they go fishing together in his little boat and she never eats an apple unless he thinks to give it to her. Though this may not be very often, they taste very good to her.

Many of the stories work similarly, by mapping a Vietnamese legend onto an American situation. This technique is aided by Butler's ability to extend a metaphor or motif to the level of a metaphysical conceit. Sometimes the conceit becomes comic, as in **"Relic,"** where a successful businessman acquires as his most prized possession one of the shoes John Lennon was wearing the day he was killed. But behind the amusing incongruities there's always a poignancy.

This mixture appears most prominently in **"The American Couple,"** narrated by a quite sober Vietnamese woman who has trained herself to wiggle and squeal like a successful game show contestant and has won a trip for herself and her husband Vinh to a hotel in Puerto Vallarta, full of other such winners. Her expertise in American pop culture helps them befriend an American couple. It turns out, however, that the husbands are both veterans, compelled finally to re-enact the war between themselves in a silly but savage way. The bitterness of the mock combat forces both Vinh and his wife to consider just how far, and to what effect, they've been absorbed by the culture into which they've immigrated.

"The American Couple" takes up the issue of assimilation more directly than some of the other stories and also reveals its own doubleness more plainly. Butler's achievement is not only to reveal the inner lives of the Vietnamese but also to show, through their eyes, how the rest of us appear from an outside perspective, one more objective than our own. Any reader of this book will feel a strange and perhaps salutary sense of exposure, and be made to wonder, among other things, just who are the "real" Americans.

> *Madison Smartt Bell, "At a Cultural Cross-roads," in* Chicago Tribune—Books, *February 23, 1992, p. 3.*

I had no warning [that *A Good Scent from a Strange Mountain* was going to win the Pulitzer Prize]. It came as a total surprise, something remarkable and wonderful that hit with the abruptness of a bolt of bayou lightning.

—Robert Olen Butler, in the New York Times, *20 April 1993.*

Jon Anderson   (review date 22 March 1992)

[*In the review below, Anderson discusses how Butler's upbringing and experiences in Vietnam influenced his writing.*]

Robert Olen Butler once was asked what he thought of being labeled as "a Vietnam novelist." He recoiled from the phrase. "Artists get at deeper truths," he explained. "It's like saying Monet was a lily-pad painter." Such specifics are metaphors, backdrops and starting points for writing, in his case, about the nature of kinship, of nostalgia, of longing, of love.

More to Butler's liking was being told that the stories in his new book, *A Good Scent From a Strange Mountain,* are so delicately phrased that they sound as if they had been written in Vietnamese and later translated. "I'm glad they catch people that way," he said in a telephone interview from his home in Louisiana. "That was a hard effect to achieve." . . .

[Butler] has written about Vietnam before, notably in his much-praised first novel, *The Alleys of Eden.* Published in 1982, it told of an Army deserter and a bar girl who escape from the rough back alleys of Saigon just before the North Vietnamese take over, and are reunited, unhappily, in a suburb of Chicago.

After that, Butler wrote five more novels. All sold comfortably well. "I almost convinced myself that I was not

a short-story writer," he said. But not quite. Writing his sixth novel, *The Deuce,* a kind of extended dramatic monologue, "I got a handle on how to write first-person stories." It also meant plugging back into lessons learned at Northwestern University.

Born in Granite City, Ill., Butler landed on the Evanston campus in 1963 as a theater major. With considerable enthusiasm, he played major roles in four of the six campus productions that year. Midway through his sophomore year, encouraged by such mentors as the late Dr. Robert Breen and Lilla Heston, Butler transferred to oral interpretation, an approach to literature through performance, based on the premise that every piece of writing has an implicit narrative person whose personality can be deduced from textual clues, such as choice of words, sentence structure and rhythm.

"That turned out to be my best training in literature," Butler said, "and ultimately found expression in this book of stories."

Butler also needed time to digest what he had experienced in Vietnam. "I went there in 1971, right after I received my master's degree from the University of Iowa [where he will teach this June at the Iowa Summer Writing Festival]," he said. "I went to language school for a year, learned Vietnamese, went over first in intelligence, then was assigned to Saigon City Hall as an administrative assistant to the American counterpart to the mayor.

"I made dozens and dozens of very close friendships with all sorts of people, from street beggars to upper-level bureaucrats. I loved to go out at 2 in the morning, wander back alleys, talk to people. Warm, open, welcoming people."

Butler filled many notebooks, but "I almost never refer to them," he said. "The fundamental reality of fiction writing is always sensual," he said. There was "a kind of moment-to-moment sensuality" in Vietnam, though few of the 3 million U.S. soldiers sent there showed any interest in understanding it.

Still, "Vietnamese culture, even when they resisted it, had a deeper effect on them than we realize. They had an encounter with their own sense of what is family, what is connected, what is not."

What Butler has captured now, critics have said, is a step beyond that, a sense of lost Vietnam drawn from its emigrants.

"Butler's achievement," noted reviewer Madison Smartt Bell in the *Tribune,* "is not only to reveal the inner lives of the Vietnamese but also to show, through their eyes, how the rest of us appear from an outside perspective, one more objective than our own."

> *Jon Anderson, "Inside Stories," in* Chicago Tribune, *March 22, 1992, p. 3.*

Larry Brown   (review date 23 March 1992)

[*Brown is an American novelist whose works include* Dirty Work *(1989) and* Joe *(1991). In the review below, he offers a favorable assessment of A Good Scent from a Strange Mountain, praising in particular Butler's compassionate depiction of the Vietnamese people.]*

It would be a scary thing to leave your homeland and never be able to return to it, but for the thousands of Vietnamese who have relocated to the United States, that scariness is a reality. The lives of some of those people are eloquently portrayed by Robert Olen Butler in [*A Good Scent from a Strange Mountain,* a] collection of 14 stories and one novella. Mixing deep heartbreak with humor and stoicism, these stories are sometimes woven of myth, and legend, sometimes simply out of the sheer inventiveness of a good writer's art. Butler has an obvious love for the country of Vietnam, and his descriptions of its rivers, mountains, jungles and cities form a backdrop to the stories that is visible to the mind's eye and very beautiful.

He writes of soldiers and citizens, prostitutes and grandfathers, sons and fathers and mothers and daughters, and of children left behind. The reader is left overwhelmed by the compassion in his voice, which is the voice of many people, and by the intimate details of lives that American readers have not been privileged to glimpse much before now, since most of the published literature about Vietnam has been told from an American point of view. Even though most of these stories take place in the United States, specifically around New Orleans, Vietnam is always there, always reminding us of what these people have lost.

The stories in this book make the lives of these people real, inform us of their concerns and give us a much-needed understanding of their culture and the enormous hardships they have endured. So many of them lost so much, yet, in these stories at least, their strength of character and their hopes for a good future come through.

In **"Mid-Autumn,"** a pregnant woman talks to the unborn baby girl floating in the silent sea inside her, telling her of the young man she was betrothed to, and of how he was killed in a battle in the mountains, but assuring her that her father is a good American man and that she will love him. Next comes **"In the Clearing,"** in which a man talks through distance and time to the son he was forced to abandon as the troops streamed into Saigon, when the only hope for his own safety was a boat fleeing down the Saigon River.

There is a wildly funny story, **"Love,"** told by a man who was a spy in Vietnam, whose job was to call in coordinates for attacking U.S. bombers. He is married to a very beautiful woman 10 years younger. In his home country, whenever another man started to pay a little too much attention to his wife, who often walked along with the top two buttons of her blouse undone, he would send the man a message, warning him that he could call down "fire from heaven" upon him. Now in New Orleans, he is forced to seek out the help of a "low-down papa" to put a curse upon the Vietnamese restaurant owner who has his eye on her. The voodoo man, whose shingle says "DOCTOR JOSEPH. HARD PROBLEMS SOLVED," gives him a hog bladder that must be filled with blood and the excrement of a he-goat, tied up with a lock of his wife's hair and thrown over the roof of his enemy. He is obliged to go to a petting zoo

and undergo the indignity not only of having an entire class of schoolchildren watch him trying to scoop up the goat pellets in a popcorn box, but of being caught high in a tree above the house of his enemy when his wife and her lover come out and see him, with the result that he falls out of the tree and breaks both legs and one arm. "The man who once could bring fire from heaven now could only bring [excrement] from the trees."

There is a story of an ancient parrot brought over who misses his old master and longs for death; a story of a bar girl in New Orleans who had American lovers in Vietnam and wishes for fairy-tale dreams to come true; a ghost story intermingled with the escape from Saigon, when the last U.S. helicopters were leaving the roof of the embassy; and stories about the lives of the new generations that are being raised in America and whose parents fear they are losing their heritage.

In all these stories, we see the profound sadness of a people displaced, of men and women and children who seem oddly without bitterness. The people in these stories have accepted their fate and have made the most of it.

Larry Brown, "Vietnam through Wistful Eyes," in The Washington Post, March 23, 1992, p. D2.

Butler on writing *A Good Scent from a Strange Mountain*:

I started with a little bit of Vietnamese folkway . . . that had to do with Vietnamese boys who capture crickets, get them riled up, put them at opposite ends of a paper tunnel and watch them fight, usually to the death. . . .

Seven hours later I had a short story. . . . Twenty-four hours after that, I had ideas for two dozen more stories. The first-person voice and being compelled to write that little story somehow unlocked something, and I suddenly had access to all these voices. Suddenly dozens of voices flooded into my head, and I told Allen Peacock, my editor, about it, and he said: "Great. Let's do a book."

Robert Olen Butler, in the New York Times, *20 April 1993.*

Richard Eder (review date 29 March 1992)

[*An American critic and journalist, Eder received the Pulitzer Prize for Criticism in 1987. In the review below, he offers a stylistic and thematic overview of A Good Scent from a Strange Mountain.]*

For the Vietnamese immigrants in Robert Olen Butler's stories, distance is sentient. It buzzes inside them like a crossed telephone line, a haunting syncopation under the forthright American rhythms they are trying to learn.

Butler's Vietnamese live, for the most part, in waterside communities in Louisiana: Lake Charles, Gretna, Versailles. The author himself lives and teaches in Lake Charles. Ever since he went to Saigon in 1971 as an Army linguist, he found his personal and literary vocation—unlike other writers there—less in exploring what it felt like to be an American in Vietnam than in what it felt like to Vietnam to have Americans there.

It is the Vietnamese voice that he seeks and that, in these stories, he has so remarkably and movingly found. What it means for these expatriates to come to a new country and function in it is more the setting than the theme. Butler writes essentially, and in a bewitching translation of voice and sympathy, what it means to lose a country, to remember it, and to have the memory begin to grow old. He writes as if it were his loss, too.

The 15 stories in *A Good Scent From a Strange Mountain* differ considerably in weight and complexity. One or two are brief lyrics. In **"Mid-Autumn,"** a mother speaks to her unborn baby about a village boy she passionately loved and who was killed; and of the calmer love she feels for her husband, an American soldier who brought her to the United States. She tells a fairy tale about a prince who came down from the moon, who longs to get back and cannot, but who finds the Earth good in its own way.

There is the romance of a New Orleans bar girl and an American who fell in love with Vietnam during the war. His passion for her memories allows her to become a contented American housewife. Another romance takes place between a waitress and an older man, a Polish Jew who becomes her mentor in overcoming the strangeness of America.

These stories are graceful but a little too easy in their emotional movements and their lessons. Others are harsher and more effective. In **"Open Arms,"** the Vietnamese narrator recalls serving as translator in an American-Canadian program to turn captured Viet Cong into informants. One day, they bring in Thap. He is a man of tragedy; his wife and children were killed in a Viet Cong raid on a village. His burning devastation contrasts with the sleek South Vietnamese major who takes part in his interrogation.

"If I was the major," the narrator recalls, "I'd feel very nervous because the man beside him had the mountain shadow and the steady look of the ghost of somebody his grandfather had cheated or cuckolded or murdered 50 years ago and he was back to take him." Thap's tragedy is too big; his first allegiance had betrayed him. Now his new allegiance betrays him in a different way, a casual, pragmatic American way.

The sense of loss among the expatriates is played out in different fashions. In one story, the narrator has become a successful businessman, and put aside his memories of Vietnam to concentrate on his American future. The price he pays is emotional blankness. He dearly loves his wife, who lives closer to her memories, but when he embraces her, she is no more real to him than the itch in his ankle or his agenda for the next day.

The wife's grandfather arrives for a visit. She remembers how he used to carry her on his back; he represents all the tradition she left behind. Her excitement is dashed when he fails to remember her or to take any interest in anything except their new car. Her desolation spurs the husband to a redeeming leap of imagination; he hoists her up on his back and gallops around their garden.

There is poignancy in many of the stories, but, except perhaps in one or two, Butler avoids sentimentality. A principal reason for this, and one of his main strengths, is his ability to speak in his characters' voices—an almost perfect English but with odd strains and inflections—and to discover what they discover without foreknowledge or patronage.

One story is pure comedy. The narrator is a solemnly insignificant man with a beautiful and restless wife. In Vietnam, he ran a network of informants for the Americans. He used his position to warn off potential rivals; if they paid no attention, the Americans would receive a report of Viet Cong activity just where the rival worked or walked. An aerial attack would follow.

In America, of course, the narrator has no such power. So when a Vietnamese rival begins paying court to the wife, the reprisal has to be different. It is hilariously elaborate and utterly effective.

In a collection so delicate and so strong, the title story stands out as close to magical. It is narrated by Dao, an expatriate who is nearly 100 and lives with his daughter. His thoughts wander between past and present; he will die any day.

"Ho Chi Minh came to me again last night, his hands covered with confectioners' sugar," the story begins. Dao, so near death and with an unquiet memory of the past, receives visits from the ghost of Vietnam's founding leader. They had been roommates in Paris during World War I. Both had worked in the kitchen of the great chief Escoffier, Ho Chi Minh as an apprentice pastry cook. Ho's passion was his country's liberation; Dao remembers him putting on an ugly and ill-fitting bowler hat—and furious at having to do it—to go out to Versailles where the Peace Conference was taking place, and try to get the ear of Woodrow Wilson.

The two men went their different ways. The narrator became a Hoa Hao Buddhist, a sect of austere unworldliness. Its meditations take shape around the phrase: "A Good Scent From a Strange Mountain." Ho, of course, chose revolution.

Ghost and dying man are now together, each with his own sense of incompletion. The narrator has lived spiritually apart from his country's tragedy. And Ho? He was never able to make a successful pastry glaze. Thinking of politics, he failed to listen properly to Escoffier. He used confectioners' instead of granulated sugar.

Through the words of Dao, Butler holds the two failures in equilibrium. To neglect a revolution and to neglect a glaze are two aspects of human limits. "I was only a washer of dishes but I did listen carefully when Monsieur Escoffier spoke," Dao says. "I wanted to understand everything. His kitchen was full of such smells that you knew you had to understand everything or you would be incomplete forever." (pp. 3, 7)

Richard Eder, "Seeing the Vietnamese," in Los Angeles Times Book Review, *March 29, 1992, pp. 3, 7.*

David Streitfeld   (review date 26 April 1992)

[*In the following excerpt from a review of* A Good Scent from a Strange Mountain, *Streitfeld comments on Butler's narrative voice and his familiarity with Vietnamese language and culture.*]

[Butler's] seventh book and first collection of stories, *A Good Scent From a Strange Mountain,* is getting enthusiastic reviews and, equally important, did by publication day something none of his previous books ever did: made it into a second printing.

The stories in the book are unified by a common subject matter: They are about Vietnamese expatriates living in America, and are told in their voices. On the dust jacket, Philip Caputo claims that Butler's "depictions of Vietnamese-Americans are as moving as Amy Tan's of Chinese-Americans; and Butler's is the greater artistic achievement because he had to exercise far more imagination to enter the minds and hearts of his subjects."

It's not always considered acceptable these days to write in the voice of another. Sometimes it's seen as a form of cultural imperialism, and sometimes it simply provokes arguments as to whether it's effective. . . .

Butler says he hasn't got any flak yet, nor did he with his previous novel, *The Deuce,* which was told from the point of view of an Amerasian youth. On the other hand, several of his short stories were rejected by the *New Yorker*—not for reasons of quality, Butler says an editor there explained, but because the magazine has a policy of not publishing stories where the voice of the narrator is different from that of the author. (This isn't true, says *New Yorker* Fiction Editor Daniel Menaker. "We find such stories, which I call 'literary transsexuals,' don't work very well, but we don't have a policy against them.")

Butler's defense: "I know the language and culture intimately. I know the Vietnamese people probably better than I knew most of the people I grew up with. But beyond that, it's an article of faith for the artist—that we can leap in our imaginations into the minds and hearts and souls of people quite different from ourselves."

Vietnam's appeal for Butler—which has yielded, in addition to *A Good Scent,* three novels that form a loose trilogy—came about completely by accident. He was on the verge of being called up in '68 when he was told that, if he enlisted for three years instead of being drafted for two, he'd likely be assured of a particular occupational specialty. He wanted counterintelligence, which would have meant working stateside.

Instead, he learned Vietnamese in Crystal City for a year and ended up working as an administrative assistant connected to the Saigon mayor's office. This meant free time to wander around the city and fall in love—not with a particular woman, but the whole city, people and civilization.

"The Vietnamese have an extraordinary capacity to take people one at a time. Many if not all of them would have good reason to be very resentful or suspicious of me, just because I was American. But at the tiniest gesture of respect they responded with extravagant warmth and openness."

An excerpt from "Mid-Autumn"

We are lucky, you and I, to be Vietnamese so that I can speak to you even before you are born. This is why I use the Vietnamese language. It is our custom for the mother to begin this conversation with the child in the womb, to begin counseling you in matters of the world that you will soon enter. It is not a custom among the Americans, so perhaps you would not even understand English if I spoke it. Nor could I speak in English nearly so well, to tell you some of the things of my heart. Above all you must listen to my heart. The language is not important. I don't know if you can hear all the other words, the ones in English that float about us like the pollen that in the spring makes me sneeze and that lets the flowers bear their own children. I think I remember from our country that this is a private conversation, that it is only my voice that you can hear, but I do not know for sure. My mother is dead now and cannot answer this question. She spoke to me when I was in her womb and sometimes, when I dream and wake and cannot remember, I have the feeling that the dream was of her voice plunging like a naked swimmer into that sea and swimming strongly to me, who waited deep beneath the waves.

And when you move inside me, my little one, when you try to swim higher, coming up to meet me, I look at the two oaken barrels I have filled with red blooms, the hibiscus. They have no smell to speak of, but they are very pretty, and sometimes the hummingbirds come with their invisible wings and with their little bodies as slick as if they had just flown up from the sea. I look also at the white picket fence, very white without any stain of mildew, though the air is warm here in Louisiana all the time, and very wet. And sometimes, like at this moment, I look beyond this yard, lifting my eyes above the ragged line of trees to the sky. It is a sky that looks like the skies in Vietnam. Sometimes full of tiny blooms of clouds as still as flowers floating on a bowl in the center of a New Year's table. Sometimes full of great dark bodies, Chinese warriors rolling their shoulders, huffing up with a summer storm that we know will pass. One day you will run out into the storm, laughing, like all the children of Vietnam. . . .

Please understand that I love you, that you are a girl. My own mother never knew my sex as she spoke to me. And I know that she was a Vietnamese mother and so she must have been disappointed when she came to find out that I was a girl, when she held me for the first time and she shared the cast-down look of my father that I was not a son for them. This is the way in Vietnam. I know that the words she spoke to me in the womb were as a boy; she was hoping that I was a boy and not ever bringing the bad luck on themselves by acting as if I was anything else but a son. But, little one, I am glad you are a girl. You will understand me even better.

Robert Olen Butler, in his A Good Scent from a Strange Mountain, *Henry Holt, 1992.*

This reaction probably wasn't entirely due to Butler's knowledge of the language, but it certainly didn't hurt. "If a G.I. speaks the language," he believes, "it's taken as an automatic sign of respect. It's one of those self-perpetuating things: if the Vietnamese get respect, they give it back. Then the Americans are less likely to respond with callousness, and so forth."

> David Streitfeld, "The Commuter's Tale," in Book World—The Washington Post, *April 26, 1992, p. 15.*

George Packer   (review date 7 June 1992)

[*In the following review, Packer praises Butler's portrayal of the Vietnamese in* A Good Scent from a Strange Mountain *but faults some of the stories as melodramatic.*]

For three decades Vietnamese have played the foils in an American psychodrama. We venture, we kill, we dream, we regret, we make peace; they smile their innocent or sinister smiles. One of the Vietnamese characters in Robert Olen Butler's first collection of short fiction gives a bitter self-portrait through distorting American eyes: "We were fascinating and long-suffering and unreal or we were sly and dangerous and unreal."

A Good Scent From a Strange Mountain goes a long way toward making the Vietnamese real, and its method is bold: each of the 15 stories is told in the first person from the viewpoint of a Vietnamese transplanted from the Mekong Delta to the Louisiana bayou. The Americans have become foils; it's the Vietnamese who are now at the center, haunted by the past, ambivalent about their hosts, suffering sexual torments, seeking a truce in their various wars.

This reversal makes for a less hyperbolic kind of story than most American fiction and film about the war in Vietnam and its aftermath. In their new home on the Gulf Coast these Vietnamese are often visited by old ghosts and legends, but the war itself is on the periphery, a given. Unlike Americans, they don't pick at the horrors they've survived and there's hardly a word of politics. Their memories are dominated instead by bittersweet sense experience: in **"Preparation"** a woman readying her friend's corpse for burial combs and envies the beautiful hair she combed and envied when they were girls in Saigon.

Vietnam, where Mr. Butler served as an Army linguist fluent in the language, is the setting for two of his six novels—*The Alleys of Eden* and *On Distant Ground,* which share common characters. They are the work of a writer who is intoxicated by Vietnam and the Vietnamese, who loves what has alienated so many other Americans, including novelists: the strange lingual tones, the ambiguity of relations in an ancient and complex society, the teeming nighttime streets of Saigon. The heroes of both novels withdraw from the war—one as a deserter, the other as a traitor of sorts—in favor of personal ties, to a South Vietnamese woman and a Vietcong prisoner. Vietnam is where these Americans become more compassionate, not more cruel, and the memory of Vietnam keeps them in the grip of a powerful nostalgic longing for the smell of market food, the flesh of a lover or the face of a lost child.

In his stories Mr. Butler confers this longing on his Vietnamese characters. And in doing so he manages to make them completely original, with quirky interests and odd obsessions, as distinct from one another as from the Americans they brush against.

In **"Fairy Tale"** a bar girl, remembering what a delicacy apples were in Saigon, thinks how, like apples in America, sex has become too abundant for her to savor it: "You take a bite now and you can make yourself remember that apples are sweet, but it is like the apple in your mouth is not even there. You eat too many apples and all you can do is remember them." In **"Snow,"** a spinster with little hope of ever marrying expresses a different shade of melancholy: "There are other Vietnamese here in Lake Charles, Louisiana, but we are not a community. We are all too sad, perhaps, or too tired. But maybe not. Maybe that's just me saying that. Maybe the others are real Americans already."

Probably not. These Vietnamese—even the businessman in **"Relic"** who swears that "America is the land of opportunity"—seem to live their real lives in the past and the supernatural. In the title story, an old man preparing for death is visited by the ghost of Ho Chi Minh in search of memories. Ho's hands are covered in the sugar he baked with when the two men worked at a [Paris] hotel in 1917. In spite of the Communist victory, Ho's ghost confesses: "I am not at peace."

The dying man, whose relatives have brought Vietnamese political murder to New Orleans, asks Ho, "Are there politics where you are now, my friend?" The implicit answer is that there are only memories, that it's the burden of the dead to recover them all, that sugar is as important as war. The dying man finally understands Ho's restlessness:

> He has used confectioners' sugar for his glaze fondant and he should be using granulated sugar. I was only a washer of dishes but I did listen carefully when Monsieur Escoffier spoke. I wanted to understand everything. His kitchen was full of such smells that you knew you had to understand everything or you would be incomplete forever.

To become complete, these dislocated men and women return in memory and imagination to Vietnam, where folk tales narrated within the stories often illuminate their present condition. An expectant mother who lost her first lover in Vietnam tells her unborn American child a fairy tale: an emperor went to the moon and found happiness there, but after returning to earth he could never go back; he could only remember. A South Vietnamese soldier is saved from Vietcong ambush by a beautiful woman's ghost; later, when he finds the ghost to thank her; she devours him; and the man telling the story on a Greyhound bus feels devoured, too, in his uneasy American exile.

The intricacy of these stories, and of most of the collection, lies in their motifs, not in psychological insight. Mr. Butler uses the narrative surprises and symbolic imagery of folklore, and as in folklore his meanings can be both simple and opaque. The longest and most ambitious of the stories, **"The American Couple,"** comes much closer to the familiar terrain of contemporary fiction. But to do so it has to give its Vietnamese woman narrator an essentially American consciousness. In the shifting tensions of two couples spending a day together at a Mexican resort—one Vietnamese, one American, of whom the husband is an obsessive Vietnam vet—Mr. Butler loses in focus and compression what he gains in complexity. Nothing in **"The American Couple"** is quite as vivid as the sugar on Ho Chi Minh's ghostly hands.

But there are risks in the simpler tales. They sometimes tend toward melodrama: large, obvious emotions are generated by manipulations of plot. And Mr. Butler can't always resist sentimental endings. Since these weaknesses also show up in his two war novels, they're more than just functions of taking on so many convincingly Vietnamese points of view. But in the absence of sophisticated, familiar, telling ironies, and within the limits of what even this most sensitive American writer *can* know about his Vietnamese characters, he's often left with crude resolutions. At least three stories end happily ever after in at long last love.

One of the strongest stories, **"The Trip Back,"** shows Mr. Butler's art at its most moving and problematic. A businessman drives to the Houston airport to pick up his wife's grandfather, just emigrated from Vietnam. On the way home, the old man expresses interest in little other than the businessman's car, which has induced a memory of driving from Saigon to Hanoi years before. "This man beside me was rushing along the South China Sea," the businessman thinks. "Right now. He had felt something so strong that he could summon it up and place himself within it and the moment would not fade." The grandfather has returned so vividly to the deep past that he has no memory of the granddaughter he's about to be reunited with. And the businessman begins to dread that when his own time comes he won't "die well," that his own life will be reduced to "the faint buzz of the alarm clock beside my bed," that "I may be prepared to betray all that I think I love the most." He's afraid that he'll end up remembering even less than the grandfather—without his homeland, without his wife.

In the end, he overcomes his wife's grief at being forgotten with a simple gesture, meant to be poignant, that seems inadequate to the profundity of his crisis. It takes a little away from an almost perfect story. But *A Good Scent From a Strange Mountain* is remarkable not for its flaws, but for how beautifully it achieves its daring project of making the Vietnamese real.

> *George Packer, "From the Mekong to the Bayous," in* The New York Times Book Review, *June 7, 1992, p. 24.*

Kathleen Kilgore   (review date 4 September 1992)

[*Kilgore is an American editor, biographer, and nonfiction writer. In the excerpt below, she praises Butler's humanistic depiction of the Vietnamese people in* A Good Scent from a Strange Mountain.]

Robert Olen Butler's *A Good Scent From a Strange Mountain* makes deeper and truer sense of the bittersweet life of exiled Vietnamese. He concentrates on Westernized families who escaped in 1975. The only American fiction writer who has delved deeply into the lives and psyches of these new Americans, Butler is fluent in Vietnamese, and it shows. It's refreshing to see this ancient and subtle language used with respect instead of GI pidgin.

Each of Butler's stories forms a poignant monologue. The Vietnamese characters take center stage and speak as if justifying their existence. Sometimes this didacticism is intrusive, but it may be unavoidable; the world view of the characters differs so greatly from that of the audience. Butler's characters appear to have adapted well to American life, but they nonetheless bear an overwhelming sense of loss.

In their nostalgia, guilt, and pain, they are no different from Westerners who have experienced wrenching traumas. But Vietnamese traumas find their outlet in a spirit world—a mental universe of unseen, powerful forces. This alternative reality occasionally intrudes at moments of stress and dislocation: A translator in the war wonders if a turncoat Viet Cong is really a demon; a lonely housewife discovers that her grandfather's soul has transmigrated into a parrot; an elderly, dying man converses nightly with the ghost of his old comrade Ho Chi Minh.

Though Butler's book excels in presenting Vietnamese life, he is an outsider. It's too soon for the Vietnamese themselves to tell their stories. Like all immigrants, the first generation is preoccupied with survival. The next generation of Vietnamese-Americans will produce anthropologists, sociologists, and journalists with a foot in both cultures.

> *Kathleen Kilgore, "As Others See the Vietnamese," in* The Christian Science Monitor, *September 4, 1992, p. 12.*

> **The irony of it, the thing that's fitting about it, is that this book that seems to be fully and completely about the Vietnamese, is every bit as much about American culture as it is about the Vietnamese.**
>
> **—Robert Olen Butler, in the New York Times, *20 April 1993.***

Pat C. Hoy II   (review date Fall 1992)

[*In the following review, Hoy examines the themes in* A Good Scent from a Strange Mountain.]

Robert Olen Butler's haunting poignant stories [in *A Good Scent from a Strange Mountain*] do what war books rarely do: they bring us face to face with the people we fought for and the people we fought. In that strange war in Vietnam it was hard to tell the difference.

Most of Butler's characters are Vietnamese-Americans living in southern Louisiana on flat bayou land that resembles the country they left behind. They are, nevertheless, uneasy culture straddlers struggling for assimilation—some too easily becoming "one of us," others clinging to a past they do not fully understand. Through them we experience the effects of war, effects continuing long past the putative end of hostilities.

The men fare less well than the women, but the differences are slight. In **"Love"** a diminutive Vietnamese man struggles to hold on to his beautiful wife. As an "agent handler" during the war he could call for firepower to destroy rocket locations. "The United States Air Force would come in and blow those coordinates away," he tells us. "You can see how this might be a great help to a seemingly wimpy man with a beautiful wife."

After the war, in America, his wife falls again for another Vietnamese, this time "a former airborne ranger, a tall man, nearly as tall as an American." The little man elicits help this time from a "black man with a fire of a different kind." Doctor Joseph's voodoo concoction ultimately sends the little fire-bringer up a tree "in a fit of rage," and even though he injures himself in a fall, his strange bomb finds its mark. Recovering in a hospital room, the man tells his wife stories about the "ways the Vietnamese were becoming a part of American society." She sits by his bedside, ministering silently to his needs.

Other men in Butler's stories yearn for and often rediscover the importance of the fire-bringer's madcap persistence. In **"Crickets"** a Vietnamese father tries to reach his American-born son through a game from his "own childhood in Vietnam." But his son shows no lasting interest in crickets fighting to the death. Besides, America produces only the "very large and strong" charcoal crickets that are "slow and . . . become confused." Missing are the small brown "fire crickets" that were "precious and admirable" among the kids in Vietnam.

Even American men who seemed to bring the fire back from Vietnam lose it on the home front. **"Letters from My Father"** recounts the disappointment of a war child whose American father finally rescues her and her mother from Ho Chi Minh City. But, after a year in Louisiana with her father, she yearns for the man she finds in a packet of his old letters, written on her behalf "when he was so angry with some stranger he knew what to say."

In **"The American Couple"** a Vietnamese-American wife on vacation with her husband in Puerto Vallarta discovers, as she watches him in a mock battle with another veteran, that there is "passion still inside him." The men, she figures, had "shared something once, something important—rage, fear, the urge to violence, just causes, life and death. They'd both felt these things in the same war. And neither of them wanted to let go of all that." Observing

them, she realizes that she had "embraced this culture with such intensity that it isolated [her] from him, made it impossible for him to find a way to touch [her] anymore." But Vinh in his grey suit, studying spreadsheets, flying here and there with his leather briefcase, is also American. America subverts their passions.

These stories pointing past the war are matched by others looking back long before it in which the old ways are recalled. The confrontational narrator of **"A Ghost Story"** challenges us to listen to his tale of Miss Linh, a beautiful young woman who had "passed into the spirit world." Miss Linh once saved a Vietnamese major from the Viet Cong only to crush him later in her jaws. The narrator, insisting on the truth of that story, tells his own. He too encountered Miss Linh. On the last day of the war as he ran for asylum in the U.S. Embassy, she saved him once from instant death and then again, giving him access to a "limousine with American flags." But as he drove away in the vehicle that would take him to safety in America, he "looked out the window and saw Miss Linh's tongue slip from her mouth and lick her lips, as if she had just eaten [him] up." He reminds us in closing that "indeed she has."

There are other ghost stories, each powerful and distinct in its own right: **"Open Arms"** about a Viet Cong deserter who awakens in a fellow countryman from the South all that he need ever remember about a wife who abandoned him for a cripple during the war; **"Relic"** about a wealthy Vietnamese-American who acquires one of the shoes John Lennon wore the day he was murdered and discovers with that shoe on his foot something of the "lightness" of a martyr's death; and **"A Good Scent from a Strange Mountain"** about a man's enlightening "visitation" from his old friend Ho Chi Minh who helps him clarify his own obligation to establish harmony in the Vietnamese family before he dies.

In **"The Trip Back,"** the most powerful of these ghost stories, a man struggles to recover the memory of his senses, rather than the memory of his mind. Coming back from the Houston airport with his wife's ageing grandfather, the narrator learns that the old man cannot remember his granddaughter. Yet he remembers vividly the two-day trips he used to make between Saigon and Hanoi in his Hotchkiss. The wind through the window of the Acura evokes that memory, but standing in America, face to face with his granddaughter, the old man remembers nothing about her. Neither can the narrator, apart from his wife, recover her "forgotten gestures." He can reconstruct her face. "But the image did not burn there," he tells us, "did not rush upon me, did not fill me up with the feelings I genuinely felt for her." And so, in his "slump of grief," he wonders if in the end he may "deep down, secretly, . . . be prepared to betray all that I think I love most."

Looking in on these stories from the outside, we see a touch of lunacy: ludicrous plots, bizarre games; far-fetched men and women their southern neighbors might consider a bit touched. But inside the stories, inside the lives Butler creates, we experience loss and need. We learn about the suffering that comes from desire, and just for an instant we look into things so deep we can't deny them. (pp. cxvi-cxviii)

Pat C. Hoy II, "Suffering and Desire," in The Sewanee Review, *Vol. C, No. 4, Fall, 1992, pp. cxvi-cxviii.*

Additional coverage of Butler's life and career is contained in the following source published by Gale Research: *Contemporary Authors,* **Vol. 112.**

Rita Dove

United States Poet Laureateship

(Full name Rita Frances Dove) Born in 1952, Dove is an American poet, short story writer, and novelist.

For further information on Dove's life and works, see *CLC*, Volume 50.

INTRODUCTION

Best known for *Thomas and Beulah*, which received the 1987 Pulitzer Prize in poetry, Dove is considered one of the leading poets of her generation. In her work she draws on personal perception and emotion while integrating an awareness of history and social issues. These qualities are best evidenced in *Thomas and Beulah*, which commemorates the lives of her grandparents and offers a chronicle of the collective experience of African-Americans during the twentieth century. In awarding her the United States poet laureateship, James H. Billington praised Dove as "an accomplished and already widely recognized poet in mid-career whose work gives special promise to explore and enrich contemporary American poetry."

Dove was born in Akron, Ohio, into a highly educated family. An excellent student, Dove was a "Presidential Scholar," ranking nationally among the best high school students of the graduating class of 1970. After obtaining a bachelor's degree from Miami University of Ohio in 1973 and then studying in Germany, Dove enrolled at the Iowa Writers' Workshop. She published her first full-length collection of poetry, *The Yellow House on the Corner,* in 1980. She currently teaches at the University of Virginia.

Dove's poetry is characterized by a tight control of words and structure, an innovative use of color imagery, and a tone that combines objectivity and personal concern. Although many of her poems incorporate black history and directly address racial themes, they present issues, such as prejudice and oppression, that transcend racial boundaries. Dove has explained: "Obviously, as a black woman, I am concerned with race. . . . But certainly not every poem of mine mentions the fact of being black. They are poems about humanity, and sometimes humanity happens to be black." In *The Yellow House on the Corner,* for example, a section is devoted to poems about slavery and freedom. "Parsley," a poem published in *Museum,* recounts the massacre of thousands of Haitian blacks because they allegedly could not pronounce the letter "r" in *perejil,* the Spanish word for "parsley."

Dove also combines racial concerns with historical and personal elements in *Thomas and Beulah.* Loosely based on the lives of Dove's maternal grandparents, this work is divided into two sections. "Mandolin," the opening sequence of poems, is written from the viewpoint of Thomas, a former musician haunted since his youth by the death of a friend. "Canary in Bloom," the other sequence, portrays the placid domestic existence of Thomas's wife, Beulah, from childhood to marriage and widowhood. Through allusions to events outside the lives of Thomas and Beulah—including the Great Depression, the black migration from the rural South to the industrial North, the civil rights marches of the 1960s, and the assassination of President John F. Kennedy—Dove emphasizes the couple's place in and interconnectedness with history. Dove remarked: "I'm always fascinated with seeing a story from different angles, but also, in the two sequences, I'm not interested in the big moments. . . . I was interested in the thoughts, the things which were concerning these small people, these nobodies in the course of history."

Grace Notes contains autobiographical poems that delineate Dove's role as mother, wife, daughter, sister, and poet. "Pastoral," for instance, describes Dove's observations and feelings while nursing her daughter, and "Poem in Which I Refuse Contemplation" relates a letter from her mother that Dove received while in Germany. Like her previous works, *Grace Notes* has been favorably reviewed by critics. Sidney Burris observed that *Grace Notes* "might well be [Dove's] watershed because it shows her blithely equal to the ordeal of Life-After-A-Major-Prize: she has survived her fame."

Dove's first novel and most recent work, *Through the Ivory Gate,* incorporates elements often considered typical of her poetry. The story of a young black artist named Virginia King, *Through the Ivory Gate* has been praised for its unique structure, which incorporates the characters' memories and storytelling abilities. Documenting the protagonist's acceptance of her black identity in a society that devalues her heritage, the novel relates Virginia's attempts to reconcile herself to events and prejudices experienced and learned in her childhood, adolescence, and early adulthood.

Dove holds the distinction of being the first African-American as well as the youngest individual to hold the post of United States poet laureate. In this new role Dove hopes to make poetry more appealing and accessible to the general public. She has stated: "Given the choice between watching television and reading a book, it is a difficult battle. You have to find ways to show people the pleasure of reading, and that it is something continual and deepening—not a quick bite." Dove subsequently hopes "to break down the ivory tower, . . . I want to reduce the anxiety that people have about poetry."

PRINCIPAL WORKS

Ten Poems (poetry) 1977
The Only Dark Spot in the Sky (poetry) 1980
The Yellow House on the Corner (poetry) 1980
Mandolin (poetry) 1982
Museum (poetry) 1983
Fifth Sunday (short stories) 1985
Thomas and Beulah (poetry) 1986
The Other Side of the House (poetry) 1988
Grace Notes (poetry) 1989
Through the Ivory Gate (novel) 1992

OVERVIEWS

Arnold Rampersad   (essay date Winter 1986)

[*Rampersad is an African-American educator, critic,* *and the author of the highly respected two-volume biography* The Life of Langston Hughes *(1986-88). In the excerpt below, he praises Dove as one of the most important black writers of the late twentieth century and admires her poetic voice, technique, and wide range of subjects.*]

For the past few years Afro-American poetry has been in a state of inactivity not unlike a deep slumber. Ten or fifteen years ago, black poets stood so very close to the center of the movement for civil rights and black power that they seemed almost to defy W. H. Auden's celebrated lament that poetry makes nothing happen. Then, slowly but steadily, much of the air went out of their practice of the genre. Although the times are hard for all black artists, the losses in this particular area have far exceeded the rate of attrition, so to speak, in fiction or even in drama—for all of the many onerous demands of the stage. Not only is one hard pressed to come up with the name of a black poet of any consequence today who did not first make his or her reputation during the late sixties and very early seventies, it is also very difficult to assert that any of the poets of that period have grown *as poets* in any remarkable way since then. Although writers such as Audre Lorde, June Jordan, and Mari Evans have continued to be effective and influential, no poet, as far as I can tell, has built on his or her beginnings in the late sixties in anything like the way that Toni Morrison, Alice Walker, John Wideman, Gloria Naylor, and David Bradley, for example, have built on their own starts in fiction during the same period.

If one looks at *male* poets, as a separate category, the contrast is perhaps even more severe and puzzling. Unlike the leading role and the plentiful number of male poets, such as Amiri Baraka, Don L. Lee, and Etheridge Knight, at the height of the movement, impressive young black male poets seem to have all but disappeared from the scene. There are exceptions, of course—but my sense is of a particular dearth of black men as poets today; it seems to be almost unfashionable now to be both a black male and a poet. However, the weak performance by young male writers is probably only a token of the general decline in the art of verse in recent years within black culture, especially as compared to what has happened in fiction.

Now, on the other hand, with the consistently accomplished work of thirty-three year old Rita Dove, there is at least one clear sign if not of a coming renaissance of poetry, then at least of the emergence of an unusually strong new figure who might provide leadership by brilliant example. Thus far, Rita Dove has produced a remarkable record of publications in a wide range of respected poetry and other literary journals. Two books of verse, **The Yellow House on the Corner** (1980) and **Museum** (1983), have appeared from Carnegie-Mellon University Press. A third book-length manuscript of poetry, **Thomas and Beulah,** is scheduled to be published early in 1986 by the same house. Clearly Rita Dove has both the energy and the sense of professionalism required to lead other writers. Most importantly—even a first reading of her two books makes it clear that she also possesses the talent to do so. Dove is surely one of the three or four most gifted young black American poets to appear since LeRoi Jones ambled with deceptive nonchalance onto the scene in the late nineteen fifties, and perhaps the most disciplined and technically accomplished black poet to arrive since Gwendolyn Brooks began her remarkable career in the nineteen forties.

These references to the sixties and early seventies are pointed. Rita Dove's work shows a keen awareness of this period—but mainly as a point of radical departure for her in the development of her own aesthetic. In many ways, her poems are exactly the opposite of those that have come to be considered quintessentially black verse in recent years. Instead of looseness of structure, one finds in her poems remarkably tight control; instead of a reliance on reckless inspiration, one recognizes discipline and practice, and long, taxing hours in competitive university poetry workshops and in her study; instead of a range of reference limited to personal confession, one finds personal reference disciplined by a measuring of distance and a prizing of objectivity; instead of an obsession with the theme of race, one finds an eagerness, perhaps even an anxiety, to transcend—if not actually to repudiate—black cultural nationalism in the name of a more inclusive sensibility. Hers is a brilliant mind, reinforced by what appears to be very wide reading, that seeks for itself the widest possible play, an ever expanding range of reference, the most acute distinctions, and the most subtle shadings of meaning.

In what I take to be Dove's determination to break new ground and set fresh standards in relation to the black writers of the half-generation before her, there are some dangers. The most subtle of these she may not have completely avoided: some of her work seems to have been conceived and written, however unconsciously at times, in a spirit of reaction. This is almost to be expected, since Dove must be acutely aware of herself as a poetic reformer, one with great potential as a leader, even if she hardly ever condescends to expose her indignations. One must assume, however, that her hostility to the "black arts" tradition is at least in part behind her astonishing poem **"Upon Meeting Don L. Lee, in a Dream,"** from *The Yellow House on the Corner:*

> . . . Moments slip by like worms.
> "Seven years ago . . ." he begins; but
> I cut him off: "Those years are gone—
> What is there now?" He starts to cry; his eye-
>   balls
>
> Burst into flame. I can see caviar
> Imbedded like buckshot between his teeth.
> His hair falls out in clumps of burned-out wire.
> The music grows like branches in the wind.
>
> I lie down, chuckling as the grass curls around
>   me.
> He can only stand, fists clenched, and weep
> Tears of iodine, while the singers float away,
> Rustling on brown paper wings.

Dreaming or awake, Dove in her art certainly confronts Lee in his own once dominating, or domineering, version of the poet's role. Her opposition may be couched in this poem in highly personal terms (neutralized by the idea that the perception of Lee here is in a dream), but it is in fact mainly philosophical. Dove sees poetry, its dignity, nature, and functions, in a way quite different from most of

the writers who came just before her. These writers sometimes used poems the way a Jacobin mob used cobblestones—because there was nothing more destructive at hand. Not so Dove, who clearly comes to verse with a profound respect and love, and an appropriate solicitude for its tradition and future. For some people, such an approach is hopelessly retrograde; for Dove, I suspect, it is as necessary as life itself.

As a poet, Dove is well aware of black history. One of the five sections of *The Yellow House* is devoted entirely to poems on the theme of slavery and freedom. These pieces are inspired by nameless but strongly representative victims of the "peculiar institution," as well as by more famous heroic figures (who may be seen as fellow black writers, most of them) such as Solomon Northrup, abducted out of Northern freedom on a visit to Washington ("I remember how the windows rattled with each report. / Then the wine, like a pink lake, tipped. / I was lifted—the sky swivelled, clicked into place"), and the revolutionary David Walker ("Compass needles, / eloquent as tuning forks, shivered, pointing north. / Evenings, the ceiling fan sputtered like a second pulse. / *Oh Heaven! I am full! I can hardly move my pen!!!*"). In these works and others such as **"Banneker"** in the later volume, *Museum,* Dove shows both a willingness and a fine ability to evoke, through deft vignettes, the psychological terror of slavery. She is certainly adept at recreating graphically the starched idioms of the eighteenth and early nineteenth centuries, at breathing life into the monumental or sometimes only arthritic rhythms of that vanished and yet still echoing age. Her poems in this style and area are hardly less moving than those of Robert Hayden, who made the period poem (the period being slavery) virtually his own invention among black poets. Dove's special empathy as a historical poet seems to be with the most sensitive, most eloquent blacks, individuals of ductile intelligence made neurotic by pain, especially the pain of not being understood and of not being able to express themselves. The scientist Benjamin Banneker:

> What did he do except lie
> under a pear tree, wrapped in
> a great cloak, and meditate
> on the heavenly bodies?
> *Venerable,* the good people of Baltimore
> whispered, shocked and more than
> a little afraid. After all it was said
> he took to strong drink.
> Why else would he stay out
> under the stars all night
> and why hadn't he married?
>
> But who would want him! Neither
> Ethiopian nor English, neither
> lucky nor crazy, a capacious bird
> humming as he penned in his mind
> another inflamed letter
> to President Jefferson—he imagined
> the reply—polite, rhetorical . . .

Dove writes few poems about racism today. One might say that she apparently declines to dwell on the links between past history and present history. Sensitive to the demands of her art, she perhaps is wary of what she perceives as the trap set by race for the black writer. She writes of black experience, but mainly in the course of "ordinary" things—where a given human situation is recognizably black but not defined even in part by the tension that many of us see as ever-present between the races. The situations she describes that involve blacks are almost always very close to the poet's private experience, part of her personal and family history; both inside and outside of this tight little circle there is little sense of racial identification even in the objective sense of the term. Such meagerness of racial feeling may have curious, even dubious roots—a question that surfaces disturbingly when one searches for the final meaning of a poem such as **"Nigger Song: An Odyssey":**

> We six pile in, the engine churning ink:
> We ride into the night.
> Past factories, past graveyards
> And the broken eyes of windows, we ride
> Into the gray-green nigger night.
>
> We sweep past excavation sites; the pits
> Of gravel gleam like mounds of ice.
> Weeds clutch at the wheels;
> We laugh and swerve away, veering
> Into the black entrails of the earth,
> The green smoke sizzling on our tongues . . .
> In the nigger night, thick with the smell of cab-
>   bages,
> Nothing can catch us.
> Laughter spills like gin from glasses,
> And "yeah" we whisper, "yeah"
> We croon, "yeah."

Further complicating the matter are poems that indicate that Dove, who sometimes poetically masks herself as a shy, withdrawing spirit, knows something about rage inspired by political and social injustice. **"Parsley,"** the last poem in **Museum,** is a chilling evocation of the madness that led General Trujillo allegedly to order the massacre of thousands of Haitian blacks in the Dominican Republic apparently because they could not pronounce the letter "r" in *perejil,* the Spanish word for "parsley." The Haitians speak, to open the poem:

> There is a parrot imitating spring
> in the palace, its feathers parsley green.
> Out of the swamp the cane appears
>
> To haunt us, and we cut it down. El General
> searches for a word; he is all the world
> there is. Like a parrot imitating spring,
>
> we lie down screaming as rain punches through
> and we come up green. We cannot speak an
> R— . . .

As a theme in verse, Dove seems to say, indignation at social injustice has a place but one that should not be too prominent; *racial* indignation must be even more discreet. Indignation tends to destroy art itself, she apparently believes, especially black art; a confrontation with racism appears to open the world but often only opens a void that gapes deceitfully between the poet and her possession of the wide world. Dove wishes nothing less than possession of that wide world; she longs for the complete freedom of her imagination:

> I prove a theorem and the house expands:

the windows jerk free to hover near the ceiling
the ceiling floats away with a sigh.

> As the walls clear themselves of everything
> but transparency, the scent of carnations
> leaves with them. I am out in the open
>
> and above the windows have hinged into butter-
> flies,
> sunlight glinting where they've intersected.
> They are going to some point true and unproven.

"The house expands"—but Dove's expansions begin, as they should, with the familiar. The reader can easily be distracted by the many sophisticated or even arcane references in *The Yellow House on the Corner* and *Museum* from seeing the extent to which the poet, for all her ambition, breathes an affection for the homely and the familiar that is signalled in the title of her first book before being countered (as if one purpose, in fear of too much familiarity?) in the title of her second. I referred earlier to the mask of a shy, withdrawing spirit she sometimes wears; nevertheless, that spirit ("My heart, shy mulatto," as she puts it in one place when she writes of her adolescence), as a transcended part of her psychological history, remains authentic in its way. Many of her most affecting poems take us back to those years when romantic doubt, intimidation by the complex newness of life, and a survivor's gift for fantasy stepped in spontaneously between emotion and calm intelligence. So uncompromising is Dove's later, adult intelligence that we cling to some of these "softer" poems in relief.

In *The Yellow House,* one finds **"A Suite for Augustus"** and the three-part **"Adolescence"** grounding the larger work and then sanctioning Dove's more ambitious flights; the same is true for the beautiful section "My Father's Telescope" in *Museum.* **"A Suite for Augustus"** sketches the passage of years between a knob-kneed virginity and the arrival of womanhood, between nervous black adolescences, male and female, and the final "making" of the cool world. With deft wordplay, an excellent dramatic sense, and a sure ability to choose just the right fragment of experience and expose it to precisely the correct amount of light, Dove takes us—within the space of relatively few lines—on a historical tour of a sensibility. The suite opens with **"1963":**

> That winter I stopped loving the President
> And loved his dying. He smiled
> From his frame on the chifforobe
> And watched as I reined in each day
> Using buttons for rosary beads.
>
> Then tapwater rinsed orange through my under-
> wear.
> You moved away . . .

Adolescent waywardness, its haunted, quixotic eye and self-absorbed, self-caressing languor of temperament, merge gradually with the will towards monumentality of a gifted, ambitious persona who eventually will look back mainly to help her chart the way ahead. Unafraid of temporary obscurity, of the surreal half-note, but always seeking finally the representation of clear vision, Dove moves stylishly from effect to effect. [She writes in] **"Planning the Perfect Evening":**

. . . Stardust. The band folds up
resolutely, with plum-dark faces.
The night still chirps. Sixteen cars

caravan to Georgia for a terrace,
beer and tacos. Even this far south
a thin blue ice shackles the moon,

and I'm happy my glass sizzles with stars.
How far away the world! And how hulking
you are, my dear, my sweet black bear!

As a poet, Dove loathes sentimentality; she is so hypersensitive to false sweetness that her work will sometimes seem far too demanding to the reader who takes honey with his poetry. Perhaps this general principle, as much as anything else, also explains her tough-minded attitude to race. Certainly she is only modestly sentimental about her own past; she insists on looking back with dancing irony and a disciplined will to understand, and not simply evoke or indulge. Dove's aim in her evocations of her past, her "roots," is a glistening but really scrubbed and unvarnished remembrance of lost time. **"Grape Sherbet,"** from "My Father's Telescope":

The day? Memorial.
After the grill
Dad appears with his masterpiece—
swirled snow, gelled light.
We cheer. The recipe's
a secret and he fights
a smile, his cap turned up
so the bib resembles a duck.

　　　　　　　. . .

Everyone agrees—it's wonderful!
It's just how we imagined lavender
would taste. The diabetic grandmother
stares from the porch,
a torch of pure refusal . . .

Dove insists on a more austere governance of intimacy than many poets, and most people, are willing to concede. Even when she looks back with affection on the memory of growing up with her father, her manner is one of mock chastisement. The stars are *not* far apart, as he had taught her. No; with passing time

. . . houses
shrivel, un-lost,

and porches sag;
neighbors phone

to report cracks
in the cellar floor,

roots of the willow
coming up. Stars

speak to a child.
The past

is silent. . . .

Between father and daughter, now man and grown woman, "Outer space is / inconceivably / intimate."

As much as she values home, Dove ranges widely as writer; it is an essential part of her commission to herself as a poet. Europe, as the prime example, is a neighboring field to be mastered like the field of home. The composer Robert Schumann, a German woman who has lost her man in war and lives thereafter crazed by grief ("She went inside, / fed the parakeet, / broke its neck"), the age-old science and mystery and ritual of making champagne— Rita Dove sees everywhere a continuity of human experience. Africa and Asia come more lightly within her frame of reference, but nowhere is she a perfect stranger. The past, too, for her is everything in human history of which she can be made aware, not least of all in the antiquity of Europe and Asia, or the Middle Ages. Dove's approach is neither panoramic nor political; still less is it for cultural genuflection. Cerebral, skeptical, and yet at the same time intensely human, she looks on the wide world and the fallen centuries, with the same essentially ironic consciousness, the same shrewd intelligence that does not absolutely forbid love, but conditions it, that marks the recreation of her own private past. **"Catherine of Alexandria"** memorializes a celebrated would-be martyr of the early Christian church:

Deprived of learning and
　　the chance to travel,
No wonder sainthood
　　came as a voice

in your bed—
　　and what went on
each night was fit
　　for nobody's ears

but Jesus'. His
　　breath of a lily.
His spiraling
　　pain. Each morning

the nightshirt bunched
　　above your waist—
a kept promise,
　　a ring of milk.

Dove's imaginative flights are tacked down again and again by homey details: "the woolens stacked on cedar / shelves back home in your / father's shop," in **"Catherine of Siena"**; the "two bronze jugs, worth more / than a family pays in taxes / for the privilege to stay / alive, a year, together," in **"Tou Wan Speaks To Her Husband, Liu Sheng."** On the patina of dust obscuring the humanity of the past from our eyes Rita Dove quietly traces a finger. She writes in a colloquial, familiar idiom that subdues the glittering exotic and makes the ultimate effect of most of these "foreign" poems to be nothing less than a documentation of her claim to the whole world as her home.

The absence of strain in her voice, and the almost uncanny sense of peace and grace that infuses this wide-ranging poetry, suggest that Dove has already reached her mature, natural stride as a poet. I suspect that this judgment might be premature in itself. Both volumes are so tightly controlled, so guarded against excess, that some readers may find them in certain places—perhaps even as a totality— too closely crafted, too reserved, for unqualified appreciation. I think that what we may have in these two books— although they already outclass the complete works of many other poets, and virtually all black poets of Dove's generation—is in fact only the beginning of a major career. In which direction will Dove's great talent take her? I believe that, paradoxically for someone so determined to be a world citizen, she may yet gain her greatest strength by returning to some place closer to her old neighborhood.

Very carefully, I do not say her, "home"—much less her "real home" or her "true home." Such terms, made shabby by the hucksters, are millstones to a poet like Dove; for her, a house is not necessarily a home. In the end, she may yet as a poet redefine for all of us what "home" means. Dove herself would probably benefit in her own way as an artist from this active redefinition. Then one should perhaps see in her work a loosening of rhythms and a greater willingness to surrender to improvisational and other gifts that she has kept in check but certainly earned the right to indulge. I would expect a vision growing more and more—again paradoxically—into narrower focus and consistency, with the emphasis shifting from irony and learning and calm intelligence towards the celebrations of the more wayward energy that springs naturally out of human circumstance. (pp. 52-60)

Arnold Rampersad, "The Poems of Rita Dove," in Callaloo, *Vol. 9, No. 1, Winter, 1986, pp. 52-60.*

I want to break down the ivory tower. . . . I want to reduce the anxiety that people have about poetry.

—Rita Dove, in "Lovely Meter, Rita-Made," in People Weekly, 31 May 1993.

Robert McDowell (essay date Winter 1986)

[*McDowell is an American critic, educator, and poet whose work, like Dove's, is known for its lyrical quality. In the following excerpt, a portion of which previously appeared in* Contemporary Literary Criticism, *Volume 50, he presents an overview of Dove's poetry up to the publication of* Thomas and Beulah *and discusses her development as a poet.*]

Rita Dove has always possessed a storyteller's instinct. In *The Yellow House on the Corner* (1980), *Museum* (1983), and . . . *Thomas and Beulah* [1986], this instinct has found expression in a synthesis of striking imagery, myth, magic, fable, wit, humor, political comment, and a sure knowledge of history. Many contemporaries share Dove's mastery of some of these, but few succeed in bringing them together to create a point of view that, by its breadth and force, stands apart. She has not worked her way into this enviable position among poets without fierce commitment.

Passing through a graduate writing program (Iowa) in the mid-seventies, Dove and her peers were schooled in the importance of sensation and its representation through manipulation of The Image. The standard lesson plan, devised to reflect the ascendancy of Wallace Stevens and a corrupt revision of T. S. Eliot's objective correlative, instructed young writers to renounce realistic depiction and offer it up to the province of prose; it promoted subjectivity and imagination-as-image; it has strangled a generation of poems.

How and why this came to pass is less important, really, than admitting that it is so. Literary magazines are gorged with poems devoid of shapeliness and scope. Imagistic, cramped and confessional, they exist for the predictably surprising, climactic phrase. An historically conscious reader, aware of literary tradition, might understandably perceive an enormous cultural amnesia as the dubiously distinguishing feature of such poems. Such a reader will rue the fact that the writing and interpretation of poetry has diminished to a trivial pursuit, a pronouncement of personal instinct. If this is the dominant direction of a discouraging Moment, then Rita Dove distinguishes herself by resolutely heading the other way.

Unlike the dissembling spirit indicted above, Dove is an assembler who gathers the various facts of this life and presents them in ways that jar our lazy assumptions. She gives voice to many positions and many characters. Like the speaker/writer of classic argumentation, she shows again and again that she understands the opposing sides of conflicts she deals with. She tells all sides of the story. Consider the titles of her books, their symbolic weight. The personal turning point *House on the Corner* evolves, becoming the public Museum (symbol of preserved chronology); that, in turn, gives way to the names of two characters whose lives combine and illustrate the implicit meanings of the personal House and the public Museum.

The Yellow House on the Corner, first of all, is a showcase for Dove's control of the language. This is our first encounter with the powerful images we have come to associate with her work:

The texture of twilight made me think of
Lengths of dotted Swiss.

As the sun broke the water into a thousand needles
tipped with the blood from someone's finger . . .

This nutmeg stick of a boy in loose trousers!

These are the observations of original sight.

There is also the rich and heavily symbolic use of color—red, orange, blue, yellow, and black and white. They usually appear as adjectives, but her adjectival preoccupation comes across with a difference. For example, while repeatedly employing *black* as an adjective ("black place," "black table," "prune-black water," "horses black," "black tongues," "my black bear"), she never settles for quick agreement based on obvious connotations. Instead, she injects the adjectives with tantalizing ambiguity and new meanings based on their relationships to other words. She redefines our connotative relationship to them. She outdistances most poets simply because she understands that adjectives enhance nouns by better defining them; they are part of the equations we are born to cope with, not substitutes for weak noun counterparts.

The Yellow House also introduces the poet's devotion to

myth, her determination to reveal what is magical in our contemporary lives. (pp. 61-2)

In [**"This Life"**], **"The Bird Frau," "The Snow King," "Beauty and the Beast,"** and others, she echoes, distorts, and revises ancient myths; in **"Upon Meeting Don L. Lee in a Dream"** and **"Robert Schumann, Or: Musical Genius Begins with Affliction,"** she focuses on characters whose actual lives have been the stuff of myths.

These and a number of short love poems comprise one side of Dove's Grand Equation. Travelogue poems (consistent throughout her work) erect a transitional bridge between her myth-making component and the historical, public side of the equation: poems examining race relations in America. At their best, poems from the myth-making category are lyrical and mysterious; poems from the latter category are heartbreakingly honest and inescapable. Though these last poems are placed throughout the volume, the third section is made up entirely of them, a fact which makes it the most relentless and coherent segment of the book.

In these poems, Dove makes the reader aware of the relationship between private and public events. **"The Transport of Slaves from Maryland to Mississippi,"** for example, is based on an incident of 1839 in which a slave woman thwarts the escape of a wagonload of slaves by helping the driver regain his horse. The narrative point of view shifts three times, revealing the complexity of the incident and of the characters involved in it. No prescriptive strategy limits expression, as the woman's opening monologue makes clear. Describing the driver she says, " . . . his eyes were my eyes in a yellower face. . . . He might have been a son of mine." The justification of her act is poignant even though its consequences are disastrous for her fellows.

This section of *The Yellow House* is bold and beautifully elegiac, presenting the motives and gestures of all of the dramatic players. The poet's wise utterance peels back the rhetorically thick skin of injustice and exposes Man's inhumanity for what it is: unbearable, shameful, unforgettable.

> Well,
> that was too much for the doctor.
> Strip 'em! he ordered. And they
> were slicked down with bacon fat and
> superstition strapped from them
> to the beat of the tam-tam. Those strong enough
> rose up too, and wailed as they leapt.
> It was a dance of unusual ferocity.
>
>   **("Cholera")**

That final grim understatement intensifies the reader's outrage.

Dove's synthesis of an historical consciousness, devotion to myth, and virtuoso manipulation of parts of speech convey us into the world of her major thematic preoccupation. In one poem she writes "My heart, shy mulatto," which informs the closing lines of a later poem like **"Adolescence—III."**

>   . . . I dreamed how it would happen:
> He would meet me by the blue spruce,

A carnation over his heart, saying,
"I have come for you, Madam;
I have loved you in my dreams."
At his touch, the scabs would fall away.
Over his shoulder, I see my father coming toward us:
He carries his tears in a bowl,
And blood hangs in the pine-soaked air.

This poem, and this volume's cumulative thrust, redefines the poet's need to reconcile the conventional, Romantic American wish (that life be a fairy tale) with the cruel facts of Black America's heritage.

Museum begins with travelogues, which prepare the reader for travel poems that eclipse the personal by introducing overlooked historical detail. **"Nestor's Bathtub,"** a pivotal poem in this respect, begins with the lines "As usual, legend got it all wrong." This announces a dissatisfaction with the conventional ordering of events and an intention to rejuvenate history by coming up with new ways of telling it. In successive poems (**"Tou Wan Speaks to Her Husband, Liu Sheng," "Catherine of Alexandria," "Catherine of Siena," "Boccaccio: The Plague Years,"** and its companion piece, **"Fiammetta Breaks Her Peace"**), Dove adopts a variety of personae that bear witness to the struggles of victimized women in societies in which men are dubiously perceived as gods.

This strategy continues into the book's second section, though the subjects and personae are primarily male (**"Shakespeare Say," "Banneker," "Ike"**). Here is the narrator in **"Reading Holderlin on the Patio with the Aid of a Dictionary"**:

> The meaning that surfaces
> comes to me aslant and
> I go to meet it, stepping
> out of my body
> word for word, until I am
> everything at once.

As in *The Yellow House,* in *Museum* Dove focuses on characters, and chooses characters to speak through, from the historical rosters of those whose lives have been the stuff of fable. Toward the end of this section, her identification with historical and mysterious male-female consciousness is most complete in **"Agosta the Winged Man and Rasha the Black Dove."** In this poem she tells the story of a pair of German circus performers, an inscrutable deformed man and an equally inscrutable black woman who dances with snakes. These characters are performers, who like the poet, look at the world in unique ways.

>   Agosta in
> classical drapery, then,
> and Rasha at his feet.
> Without passion. Not
> the canvas
>   but their gaze,
>   so calm,
> was merciless.

The poem that follows, **"At the German Writers Conference in Munich,"** examines and exploits this preoccupation from another angle. In the poem another art—

another way of performing—is described. The calm, stiff characters of a tapestry are not outwardly grotesque as are the characters in the preceding poem. Nevertheless, they appear to be out of step with their woven environment, existing as they do in a world of flowers. The two poems, together, illustrate a brilliant shifting of focus, a looking out of the eyes of characters, then a merciless looking into them.

The third section of *Museum* contains a focusing down of this strategy in a tight group of Family poems in which the father is the dominant character. He is perceived by the innocent narrator as the teacher, the bearer of all that is magical in the world.

> I've been trying
> to remember the taste,
> but it doesn't exist.
> Now I see why
> you bothered,
> father.
>
>   ("Grape Sherbet")

Whether he is making palpable an impalpable taste or miraculously rescuing roses from beetles (**"Roses"**), or deftly retrieving what is magical from a mistake (**"My Father's Telescope"**), he is clearly the narrator's mentor, inspiring a different way of meeting the world:

> this
> magician's skew of scarves
> issuing from an opaque heart.
>   ("A Father Out Walking On the Lawn")

But even in this tender, celebratory section, Dove includes one poem, **"Anti-Father,"** which satisfies her self-imposed demand that she tell all sides of the story.

> Just between
>
> me and you,
> woman to man,
>
> outer space is
> inconceivably
>
> intimate.

The innocent narrator, now a knowledgeable woman, reverses roles here, contradicting the father but offering magical insight in doing so.

The closing section of Rita Dove's second volume summarizes all that has preceded it, and in two remarkable poems, anticipates *Thomas and Beulah.*

The narrator of **"A Sailor in Africa"** spins off from a Viennese card game (circa 1910) and unravels the adventures of the characters in the game. A black slave, who is actually a sea captain, outwits his captors and takes over their ship. He is shipwrecked later, only to discover great wealth in his isolation. This effortless storytelling combines Dove's great strengths—memorable images, wit, travelogue, fable, complex representation of motive and gesture, historical awareness—and is a groundbreaking poem.

It is balanced and rivaled by **"Parsley,"** the book's concluding poem, which tells the story of a dictator who orders the annihilation of 20,000 blacks because they cannot pronounce the letter "r." The poem is constructed in two parts. The first, a villanelle, presents the entire drama; it is all the more terrifying because the facts smash against the stark and beautiful container of the form itself. In the second part of the poem, a third person narrator examines the dictator's relationship to his mother, who can "roll her 'r's' like a queen."

> As he paces he wonders
> who can I kill today . . .
>
>   Someone
> calls out his name in a voice
> so like his mother's, a startled tear
> splashes the tip of his right boot.
> *My mother, my love in death.*

As she often does, Dove unerringly combines private and public political history in this and in many other poems in *Museum.* It is a direction that flourishes on a book-length scale in *Thomas and Beulah.*

"These poems tell two sides of a story and are meant to be read in sequence." So begins *Thomas and Beulah.* Their story is told twice: from Thomas's point of view in the twenty-three poems of "Mandolin," and from Beulah's point of view in the twenty-one poems of "Canary in Bloom." The time, according to an extensive Chronology at book's end, covers the years 1919-1968. Most of the story takes place in Akron, Ohio, a city, which the Chronology also tells us, had a Negro population of 11,000 (out of a total population of 243,000) in 1940.

The chief narrative method employed, the story twice-told, does not rely so much on action; it relies on reactions of characters to events and circumstances that affect them even though they are wholly beyond them. The questions generated by this approach are chilling and clear: if two characters, deeply involved with one another, interpret events (inner and outer, private and public) so differently, what does this suggest about our manipulation of history; what does it say about our reliability as witnesses, as teachers of successive generations; what is true?

Truth in *Thomas and Beulah* is found in the characters themselves. In **"The Event,"** the first poem in the section entitled "Mandolin," Thomas leaves Tennessee for the riverboat life. He travels with a good friend, Lem, and a magical symbol, a talisman which gathers pain and wards it off—his mandolin. In a turn that explodes the deliberate echo of Mark Twain's *Huck Finn,* Lem dives overboard to collect chestnuts on a passing island and drowns. This tragedy, at the outset of his journey, will haunt Thomas for the rest of his life. We observe his arrival in Akron in 1921, deftly and desperately playing his mandolin for pay. He is a driven figure, confronting his guilt and his second-class citizenship in a racially divided country. His half-hearted attempts to sell himself in such a country will drive the more sheltered Beulah to find fault in him. It is a key element of his tragedy that he faults himself for it, too:

> He used to sleep like a glass of water
> held up in the hand of a very young girl.

and later,

> To him work is a narrow grief
> and the music afterwards
> like a woman
> reaching into his chest
> to spread it around.
>
>   **("Straw Hat")**

After their marriage, the promise of equality and upward mobility is profoundly betrayed. The world is threatening, malicious after all. In **"Nothing Down,"** they buy a new car for a trip to Tennessee, but the symbol and the dream it represents are destroyed when they're passed by a carload of jeering whites; in **"The Zeppelin Factory,"** Thomas lands construction work, laboring on the largest building in the world without interior supports (another appropriate, unforgettable symbol for the world we make) and hates it; Thomas ponders the impending birth of a third daughter against the backdrop of union violence (**"Under the Viaduct"**); Thomas walks out of a movie house to witness a splendid natural phenomenon (**"Aurora Borealis"**), but even this double barreled symbolic magic is overpowered by the grim facts of the world around him. Finally, he finds even his oldest companion, his mandolin, estranged:

> How long has it been . . . ?
> Too long. Each note slips
> into querulous rebuke, fingerpads
> scarred with pain, shallow ditches
> to rut in like a runaway slave
> with a barking heart. Days afterwards
> blisters to hide from the children.
> Hanging by a thread. *Some day,*
> he threatens, *I'll just*
> let go.
>
>   **("Definition in the Face of Unnamed Fury")**

Only in his own good heart is Thomas vindicated, and the physical manifestation of his goodness is his family. In **"Roast Opossum,"** he spins two tales for his grandchildren: hunting opossum for Malcolm, a tale of horses for the girls. This tender poem makes a case for salvation implicit in one generation's nurturing another by gathering and making palpable history and myth, fact and fiction. In such ritual we discover our one defense against the inhuman things we do to one another.

The section concludes with three elegiac poems covering the events of Thomas's declining health and eventual death. **"The Stroke"** contains a lovely memory of Beulah during pregnancy and his certainty that the pain he feels is Lem knocking on his chest. In the end, Thomas appropriately suffers his final heart attack behind the wheel of his car (**"Thomas at the Wheel"**).

Whereas Thomas's life is a perpetual scramble toward definition, Beulah's, as presented in "Canary in Bloom," is pre-ordained. She will marry; she will bear children. These restrictions force her to develop an inward, private life. For example, her fear and distrust of male figures is established early in **"Taking in Wash."** Her father comes home drunk:

> Tonight
> every light hums, the kitchen arctic
> with sheets, Papa is making the hankies
> sail. Her foot upon a silk
> stitched rose, she waits
> until he turns, his smile sliding all over.

This is the seed of her reaction to her suitor and future husband. She would prefer a pianola to his mandolin; she hates his yellow scarf. When they marry, "rice drumming / the both of them blind," she sees Thomas as "a hulk, awkward in blue serge." Her father places her fingertips in Thomas's hand, and men in collusion have delivered her up to her fate.

From this point on, Beulah's story seeks the form, the shape, of meditation. In **"Dusting"** she fondly remembers a boy at a fair, comparing that magical location and meeting with the hard news of her life. In **"Weathering Out"** she daydreams through her seventh month of pregnancy, glad to be rid of Thomas as he daily hunts for work. In the sad **"Daystar"** she reclines in the backyard while the children nap and dreams of a place where she is nothing. In **"The Great Palace of Versailles"** she works in a dress shop, frequents the library, and temporarily loses the facts of her own life in the magic of lords and ladies.

Beulah's development of a rich inner life is the result of meditation with an outward eye. Throughout her long battle with the prescribed role she was born to play, she continues to cope admirably and compassionately with the world outside. She manages her family; she feeds transients during the Depression; she shows kindness to the daughter of a prejudiced neighbor. As the poems progress her wisdom deepens. Her attitude toward Thomas softens, too. While sweeping she recalls the drive to Tennessee, how

> Even then
> he was forever off in the woods somewhere in
>   search
> of a magic creek.
>
>   **("Pomade")**

And later, addressing him in **"Company"**:

> Listen: we were good,
> though we never believed it.

If she does not change her life, Beulah through wisdom comes to understand it. She also comprehends the lives of her daughters. At their husbands' company picnic—a segregated picnic—Beulah remembers the march on Washington and its effects on the lives of her children. Her meditative impulse blossoms. Her preferred inner life squares off against the world of iniquity, and the succeeding generation is better off for it.

When I consider the discouraging Moment I mentioned at the beginning of this article, when I despair of it, I turn to only a few poets of my generation and am revitalized. Rita Dove's development through three volumes reminds us of the necessity for scope in poetry. A wide range of talent in service to an assembling vision is the tonic we need for discouragement. (pp. 63-70)

Robert McDowell, "The Assembling Vision of Rita Dove," in Callaloo, Vol. 9, No. 1, Winter, 1986, pp. 61-70.

AWARD ANNOUNCEMENTS

Irvin Molotsky (essay date 19 May 1993)

[*In the excerpt below, Molotsky discusses Dove's appointment to poet laureate, her new responsibilities, and critical reaction to her appointment.*]

Rita Dove, a Pulitzer Prize-winning writer whose works evoke the history of her country and memories of her family, was named today the nation's next poet laureate. Ms. Dove is the first black poet to hold the position; at 40, she is also the youngest to be chosen.

In choosing Ms. Dove, the Librarian of Congress, James H. Billington, remarked on her relative youth. "I take much pleasure in announcing the selection of a younger poet of distinction and versatility," he said. "Having had a number of poet laureates who have accumulated multiple distinctions from lengthy and distinguished careers, we will be pleased to have an outstanding representative of a new and richly variegated generation of American poets."

Among predecessors of Ms. Dove, who will take over in the fall, are Robert Penn Warren, Richard Wilbur, Joseph Brodsky and the current laureate, Mona Van Duyn.

Ms. Dove, who teaches poetry at the University of Virginia, won the 1987 Pulitzer Prize in poetry for **Thomas and Beulah,** a collection loosely based on her maternal grandparents. The critic Helen Vendler said that Ms. Dove, a writer noted for the leanness of her work, had "planed away unnecessary matter: pure shapes, her poems exhibit the thrift that Yeats called the sign of a perfected manner."

Ms. Dove often brings the black experience into her work, which relies heavily on autobiography and history. In an interview today, she described her poem **"Mississippi,"** for example, as "almost a meditation on the Mississippi River and what it has meant in American history." And when a black person reads it, she said; the description of going downriver conveys the experience of "falling deeper into slavery."

In **"Mississippi,"** part of the collection, **Grace Notes,** published in 1989 by W. W. Norton, she writes:

> In the beginning was the dark
> moan and creak, a sidewheel
> moving through. Thicker
> then, scent of lilac,
> scent of thyme; slight hairs
> on a wrist lying down in sweat.
> We were falling down
> river, carnal
> slippage and shadow melt.

> We were standing on the deck
> of the New World, before maps;
> tepid seizure of a breeze
> and the spirit hissing away . . .

Ms. Dove was recently appointed Commonwealth Professor of English at the University of Virginia, which is close enough to Washington for her to contemplate spending at least a part of every week in the capital.

When asked whether she might have an impact in this city, with its large black population, she said by telephone from her home in Charlottesville, Va., "It's exciting to think about what I can do to make a difference in the Washington area and throughout the country."

Today's young people, white as well as black, she said, see mostly the limousines and luxury hotels of athletes and entertainers as signs of success, often not noticing intellectual achievement.

"If only the sun-drenched celebrities are being noticed and worshiped," she said, "then our children are going to have a tough time seeing value in the shadows, where the thinkers, probers and scientists are who are keeping society together."

Ms. Dove was born in Akron, Ohio, and is a graduate of Miami University of Oxford, Ohio, and the University of Iowa. She is also the author of a collection of short stories, **Fifth Sunday** and a novel, **Through the Ivory Gate.**

In discussing the use of her grandparents' lives in **Thomas and Beulah,** she said, "I took liberties, but they would recognize themselves."

Something of Ms. Dove's approach can be seen, perhaps, in the very title of the book. Her grandfather's name was Thomas but her grandmother's was Georgianna, changed to Beulah for reasons of poetry.

" 'Georgianna' is a beautiful name, but it is too long and takes over a line," she said. Besides, it is a masculine-based name and she wanted a feminine one.

Rod Jellema, a retired professor of poetry at the University of Maryland and now a teacher at the Writers Center here, noted the way Ms. Dove "gets so far into the consciousness of those people."

As an example of her concise but evocative style, Mr. Jellema cited this excerpt from **"Ars Poetics,"** which appeared in her collection **Grace Notes:**

> What I want is this poem to be small,
> a ghost town
> on the map of wills
> Then you can pencil me in as a hawk
> a traveling x-marks-the-spot.

Of Ms. Dove's selection as poet laureate, Mr. Jellema said: "It's such a good idea to have a black poet in that position. She is the premiere black poet, living or dead." (pp. C15, C18)

From 1937 until 1986, the Library of Congress appointed consultants in poetry. In 1986 the position was elevated to poet laureate, taking its name from the British model. Unlike her British counterpart, however, Ms. Dove will have no obligation to compose a poem to mark an event of joy or mourning. The American poet laureate can do just about as she pleases, for which Ms. Dove will be paid $35,000 for the one-year term and be given an office in the Library of Congress.

"If a poem were to occur," Ms. Dove said, she would write it. But she added: "Occasional poems are not as powerful as those that come out of a deep need or conviction. Those poems that come out come out because they have to come out." (p. C18)

> *Irvin Molotsky, "Rita Dove Named Next Poet Laureate; First Black in Post," in* The New York Times, *May 19, 1993, pp. C15, C18.*

[My appointment] sends a message that the laureate is in the true American tradition and there are many kinds of that tradition.

—*Rita Dove, in "Lovely Meter, Rita-Made," in* People Weekly, *31 May 1993.*

David Streitfeld   (essay date 19 May 1993)

[*In the following essay, Streitfeld discusses the obstacles Dove will be facing as poet laureate as well as her duties and aims.*]

In a surprise move intended to give new life to the job of U.S. poet laureate, Librarian of Congress James Billington selected University of Virginia professor Rita Dove for the position yesterday. By picking the 40-year-old Dove as the successor to Mona Van Duyn, 72, Billington is making clear that the post no longer merely caps a career.

"This will ruin my life, but it's an incredible honor and I'd be crazy not to accept it," Dove said yesterday from her home in Charlottesville. She was already full of ambition and plans—two of the things the library administrators are hoping for.

"There's an awareness we've not been successful in reaching a large segment of a potential audience for poetry," acknowledged Prosser Gifford, the library's director of scholarly programs and its poetry czar. "Some of the themes which Rita Dove treats, as well as her own personality, may indeed help in this respect."

Translation: She's not only a good poet, but energetic, female and black, and thus a good candidate to do more than draw the usual 200 hardy souls to the Library of Congress readings. The lesson of Maya Angelou, whose poem for President Clinton's inauguration received mixed reviews (at best) from the poetry establishment but thrilled millions of ordinary folk, has not been lost.

Dove's appointment, which takes effect in October, comes at a moment when poetry is undergoing a bit of a boom. The urban phenomenon of poetry slams, the versifying

neo-beatniks, the increased cash prizes, the awarding of a Nobel Prize to poet Derek Walcott last year—all are feeding the fires.

While Dove said that being the first black laureate didn't make much difference to her personally, "it is significant in terms of the message it sends about the diversity of our culture and our literature, which is just vibrant now. That's something which should be a cause for rejoicing, rather than fear or anguish."

The post of laureate has its origins in that of poetry consultant, which began in 1937. In 1986 the position was upgraded, assuming the grand title of laureate. By design, duties are rather vague—in order, the library says, "to afford each incumbent maximum freedom." The laureate, who with a single exception has stayed for only a year, advises the library, answers mail about poetry and schedules an annual series of readings. The actual production of poetry is not mandatory.

David Lehman, editor of *The Best American Poetry* annual anthology, said the selection of Dove is a pretty daring choice. Everyone expected the laureate to be someone in his or her fifties, at a minimum.

She'll have a great opportunity to either be as frustrated with the office and its lack of real responsibility and real purpose as the previous laureates or, with her intelligence and vitality, to make the position one that might expand the audience for poetry—which we all fervently hope for."

Dove, an Ohio native who is married to the German novelist Fred Viebahn, has written four books of poems. The third, **Thomas and Beulah,** won the Pulitzer Prize in 1987. She's also done a book of stories, **Fifth Sunday,** as well as a novel, **Through the Ivory Gate,** which appeared last year to good reviews, and a forthcoming play. But verse is her first and truest love.

"Poetry is language at its most distilled and most powerful," she said yesterday. "It's like a bouillon cube: You carry it around and then it nourishes you when you need it."

Her work ranges from the pastoral to the intimate, touching humorously on modern times ("Here's a riddle for Our Age: when the sky's the limit, / how can you tell you've gone too far?") and probing racial issues. From **"Genetic Expedition":**

> . . . My child has
> her father's hips, his hair
> like the miller's daughter, combed gold.
> Though her lips are mine, housewives
> stare when we cross the parking lot
> because of that ghostly profusion.

Dove, who will receive a $35,000 stipend, said she will commute to Washington. She is the sixth laureate to follow Robert Penn Warren, who got the first title at age 80.

Among the previous laureates, only Joseph Brodsky and Mark Strand moved to Washington for their stints, and both became caustic about the limitations of the post. While signing on for a second year is a negotiable option, only Nemerov has done so. Mona Van Duyn said two weeks ago that "if someone did ask me [to serve a second year], I would scream and run as far as possible in the other direction."

The typical cycle for a laureate, said anthologist Lehman, has gone like this: "There's the initial splendor of being appointed, a flurry of attention, a buildup of expectations. Then you show up in Washington, and find out everyone is obsessed with politics. Poetry probably ranks with ballet in the yawn-provoking department."

It gets worse, he continues, "There's this bureaucracy at the library, but on the other hand there isn't very much of a staff for the laureate. The best of them wonder why they're there. It's easy for the poet to disappear, and poetry itself to be entirely eclipsed."

Dove said she understood the frustrations of the laureates. "In the last 12 years, there has been an uneasy relation between the federal government and the arts. It's gone so far that the arts, including literature and poetry, have been considered suspect and even subversive. I'm hoping that with the new administration this will change."

Acknowledging the slight surge in poetry's popularity, Dove said: "You have to be vigilant and keep pushing. This is a country that operates on stardom. We love our stars. It seems very important to keep poetry in the public eye, so people feel comfortable with it."

The entertainment media, she noted, tend to celebrate the seductive, easy answer. "Given the choice between watching television and reading a book, it is a difficult battle. You have to find ways to show people the pleasure of reading, and that it is something continual and deepening—not a quick bite."

The laureateship, she figures, "is an honor, but it's also a job. It's an honor with strings and thorns attached, probably. But so be it. It's a challenge, and I'll try to be ready."

Failing all else, it will be an adventure. As a poem in her collection **Grace Notes** has it:

> The first time
> for anything is the best,
> because there is no memory
> linking its regrets to drop
> like bracelets in the grass . . .

(pp. A1, A14)

David Streitfeld, "Laureate for a New Age," in The Washington Post, *May 19, 1993, pp. A1, A14.*

INTERVIEWS

Rita Dove with Steven Schneider   (interview date Fall 1989)

[*In the following interview, Dove discusses the writing of*

Thomas and Beulah, *receiving the Pulitzer Prize, and the writing process.*]

[*Schneider*]: *How does it feel to be the first black woman poet since Gwendolyn Brooks to win the Pulitzer Prize?*

[Dove]: My first reaction was quite simply disbelief. Disbelief that first of all there hasn't been another black person since Gwendolyn Brooks in 1950 to win the Pulitzer Prize in poetry, though there certainly have been some outstanding black poets in that period. On a public level, it says something about the nature of cultural politics in this country. It's a shame actually. On a personal level, it's overwhelming.

Did you feel you had written something special when you completed **Thomas and Beulah?**

I felt I had written something larger than myself, larger than what I had hoped for it to be. I did not begin this sequence as a book; it began as a poem. The book grew poem by poem, and it wasn't until I was about a third of the way through that I realized it would have to be a book. So I grew with it and I had to rise to it. I started with the Thomas poems because I wanted to understand my grandfather more—what he was like as a young man, how he grew up and became the man I knew. To do that though, I realized pretty early on that I could rely neither on my memories of him nor on the memories of my mother or her sisters or brothers, but I had to get to know the town he lived in. What was Akron, Ohio like in the '20s and '30s? It was different from the Akron I knew. That meant I had to go to the library and read a whole bunch of stuff I never counted on researching to try to get a sense of that period of time in the industrial Midwest. On other levels, I had to enter male consciousness in a way which was—well, I knew I could do it for one or two poems but this was an extended effort. I was really, at a certain point, very very driven to be as honest as I could possibly be. Also, I didn't want to impose my language or my sensibility upon their lives. And things got—

Things got very complicated?

That's right.

Did you have a different kind of satisfaction about finishing this book than your other two books?

It was different. I am not going to say I was more satisfied; I don't think I have a favorite book of mine. But there was a feeling of relief because I had made it through.

How long did it take you to write **Thomas and Beulah?**

About five years. I was working on the **Museum** poems in the middle of that, too. So, altogether five years.

You've mentioned to me that your life has been quite hectic since you won the Pulitzer. How does this affect your life and your writing?

First of all, the act of writing is such a private, basic matter. It's you and the poem, you and the pencil and the paper in a room under a circle of lamplight. And that is the essence of writing. A public life, then, becomes schizophrenic; on the one hand, you have to extend yourself and talk to people about your writing, an experience which you cannot really articulate. To talk about private experience to total strangers is very schizophrenic. Once in a while it's good to get out and do readings because the shadows on the wall grow large when you are writing. But in this past year and a half, I sometimes feel I have been a little too public—or let's just say I feel the public encroaching on the private time.

Are things getting back to normal now? Do you find you are able to work on a regular schedule?

Things are getting back to normal for several reasons. One of them is that I think I've learned a little bit how to live with the public life and not let it affect the private sector. Also how not to feel guilty about saying "No."

For some writers, winning such a prize so young can block their creative output for years to come. How do you respond creatively to the pressures of fame?

I remember when I first got the Pulitzer, the question that came up in every interview was: "Does this put pressure on you now for your next book?" And in those first weeks afterward, the question always hit me out of left field. What did they mean?

You didn't feel pressured until they started asking you.

Exactly. I didn't feel it at all. So in a way, it is an artificial pressure. It's particularly artificial if one really sits down and thinks about the number of people who have gotten Pulitzers and how many of them stayed "famous." If you look at the list, it's very interesting. Nothing's guaranteed.

So some Pulitzer winners have declined in reputation?

Sure, some Nobel Laureates as well.

So that takes some pressure off?

Right. And taking that further, what does it mean? I mean it's wonderful, but in the end, what is important to me? When I go into the room and try to write a poem, the Pulitzer doesn't mean a thing. I am still just as challenged by the blank page.

Much has been said about the number of black writers who seem to have been ignored by the literary establishment. This surfaced again recently when James Baldwin died. Do you think the literary establishment has been unfair to black writers?

Of course it has been unfair—this is true not only for black writers, but for other minorities as well. It is outrageous that James Baldwin never got a Pulitzer Prize. It's outrageous that Ralph Ellison didn't get every literary award around for *Invisible Man.*

There have been recent attempts to revise the canon and to give more attention to women writers and to minority writers in America. Are you gratified by these attempts? Are they going far enough?

I think they are absolutely necessary. I can't say whether they are going far enough: it depends where, in what context. But it's important to try to round those things out. Let's face it: if Gwendolyn Brooks or Toni Morrison are not on the reading lists for Ph.D. dissertations, students aren't going to read them.

So what do you think your winning the Pulitzer Prize for poetry means to other young black American writers?

When I was growing up it would have meant a lot to me to know that a black person had been recognized for his or her writing. **Thomas and Beulah** is a book about black Americans, and two very ordinary ones at that. Nothing spectacular happens in their life. And yet this "nonsensational" double portrait is awarded a prize. That's what is important.

You mentioned you talked recently with some South African writers. Does winning the Pulitzer Prize give you more political leverage and visibility?

The Pulitzer does carry international credentials. In the past year and a half I have had increased opportunities to talk and to meet with writers of other countries and to see how they live. Because of the Pulitzer, I got the chance to do a conversation via satellite with some South African writers. I may have the chance of going there, which is certainly not going to be a pleasure trip. I feel the need to see the situation there for myself if it's possible.

Let's talk about **Thomas and Beulah.** *Your interest in these characters resulted from a story your grandmother told you as a child. Is that right?*

Yes. That story actually became the first poem in the book. I was about ten or twelve when she told me about my grandfather coming north on a river boat; it seems he had dared his best friend to swim the river, and the friend drowned. This was, for me, a phenomenal event. My grandfather had been a very gentle and quiet man. Frankly, I couldn't see how he could have carried that kind of guilt around all those years. I found it incredible that I had never heard the story before. In the writing, I had to confront several problems: How could he have borne it? How does anyone bear guilt that is irretrievable?

Did you set out consciously on a quest to reclaim your roots?

No. Not consciously. Though it was a conscious attempt to understand someone who had meant a lot to me, who was part of me. And in doing that I got drawn more and more into my family history which was perfectly fine and kind of wonderful. It gave me a doorway into my history. I had a hinge, something that I could work on and through. I ended up talking to a lot of people about my grandparents; I learned a lot about my roots that doesn't even appear in the book.

Certainly that knowledge becomes meaningful to you and who you are today.

Yes, exactly. I think I was always working toward that. Now, when I look back on the three books that I have done and see how they move, I understand that old adage about coming back to your own backyard. But it is almost as if I started out in **The Yellow House on the Corner** with a very domestic scene, a real neighborhood. The second book, **Museum,** was much more about art and artifact, and attempts to register personal human experience against the larger context of history.

There are some family poems in **Museum** *too.*

Yes—but the family poems in that book constitute one section only; the overwhelming majority are portraits of individuals in their particular historical context.

How did you go about recreating the era of Thomas and Beulah's migration?

I read everything I could get my hands on about the migration from the rural south to the industrial north. The WPA books that were done on each state were especially invaluable.

So there were lots of details you had to track down.

Exactly the stuff that will drop out of the next edition of the *Encyclopedia Britannica,* right? I was trying to get that feeling, that ambiance, so I talked to my mother an awful lot about what it was like growing up at that time. She was remarkable. At first she asked, "What do you want to hear?" But I didn't know what I wanted to hear. I just wanted her to talk, and that's what she did. I amassed so much material; then I had to kind of forget it all in order to write the poems.

You have said of **Thomas and Beulah** *that "less and less did it become based on my grandparents because after a while I was after a different kind of truth." What is the larger truth you were after?*

I was after the essence of my grandparents' existence and their survival, not necessarily the facts of their survival. That's the distinction I'm trying to make. So when I said it became less and less about them, I meant I was not so concerned about whether Thomas in the book was born the same year as my grandfather (he wasn't, incidentally) or whether in fact it was a yellow scarf he gave Beulah or not. What's important is the gesture of that scarf. One appropriates certain gestures from the factual life to reinforce a larger sense of truth that is not, strictly speaking, reality.

Is there something especially significant about a generation like Thomas and Beulah's which had to uproot itself—in this case, from the South, in order to work in northern cities?

Yes, of course. Only very recently have historians begun to explore that entire era in any depth and what impact the great migration, as they call it now, had on not only southern communities and northern communities but a host of other things. So much has been done or talked about the uprooting of the black family through slavery, but this was a second uprooting and displacement. It's the first time that blacks in this country had any chance, however stifled, of pursuing "the American dream." Obviously not with the same advantages as whites, not even as the otherwise ostracized European immigrants, and so it is a very poignant era. I never heard very much about it when I was a child. I wondered why my cousins from Cleveland spoke with a southern accent, but we didn't. It wasn't that unusual that entire communities were brought up and resettled around each other. It's a major population movement in our country that just went largely unrecorded.

Did you begin with the notion of writing such a closely knit sequence where many of the poems depend upon previous ones?

As I said earlier, when I started out I did not think in terms of a book. I did start out with a single poem. Then I thought, "This isn't enough," and I went on. I thought I was going to have a suite of poems, a group of six or seven. At that point I did want them narrative; I thought there must be a way to get back into poetry the grandness that narrative can give, plus the sweep of time. Lyric poetry does not have that sweep of time. Lyrics are discrete moments. On the other hand, a lot of narrative poems can tend to bog down in the prosier transitional moments. I didn't see very many long narrative poems that really weren't smaller poems linked together. So one of the things I was trying to do was string moments as beads on a necklace. In other words, I have lyric poems which, when placed one after the other, reconstruct the sweep of time. I wanted it all. I wanted a narrative and I wanted lyric poems, so I tried to do them both.

Some of the poems seem more capable of standing alone than others—"*Jiving*" *and* "*Lightning Blues*" *for example. Many others depend on our reading of the previous ones.*

At the beginning of the book I warn that these poems are meant to be read in sequence. I put that in there because the poems make most sense when read in order. But even though some of the poems are absolutely dependent on others, in the writing I was still trying very hard to make each poem wholly self-sufficient, of a piece. In other words, a particular poem may be dependent on an earlier poem for its maximum meaning, but in itself it is a complete poem. It just happens to need another beat to make the best connection.

A few of the poems have italicized song-like rhymes that sound like they might derive from southern minstrels or gospels. I am especially thinking of "*Refrain.*" *Let me just read you a few of these. This is the one I really love.*

> *Take a gourd and string it*
> *Take a banana and peel it*
> *Buy a baby blue Nash and wheel and deal it.*
> *Count your kisses sweet as honey*
> *Count your boss' dirty money.*

What's the origin of those lyrics?

I made them up. They are in the spirit of country blues. They are also influenced by spirituals and gospels. The poem "**Gospel**" begins as a takeoff on "Swing Low Sweet Chariot." It starts off: "Swing low so I / can step inside." Both "**Refrain**" and "**Gospel**" are written in quatrains, and I think there's quite a kinship between them. The roots—no, let's say the connections—between gospel and blues are very close.

Were you listening to recent blues recordings?

No. Mostly older blues recordings though I have listened to recent ones too. While I was writing this book I was playing a lot of music, everything from Lightnin' Hopkins to older ones like Larry Jackson or some of the recordings that Al Lomax made of musicians, all the way up to Billie

Holliday, stopping about in the '50s. It seemed to be the music for the book.

Let's talk about Akron, Ohio, the town where Thomas and Beulah lived. Your book serves as a commentary and history of that place with its zeppelin factory and Satisfaction Coal Company, and its impoverishment during the Depression. This kind of social realism in your work seems striking and in some ways a departure from your earlier work.

At some point in the writing, I knew the poems needed background; I realized that I had to give a history of the town. I can't say I approached this task with joy. After all, Akron is not a tourist attraction. Let's face it: few of us were born in beautiful places. Yet I remember Akron, Ohio as a place of beauty. Rilke says in his *Letters to a Young Poet,* that if you cannot recount the riches of a place do not blame the place—blame yourself, because you are not rich enough to recall its riches. When I read that again, I realized that I'd be doing Akron an injustice if I would just dwell on its industrial ugliness, and if I could not explain or bring across some of its magic or make it come alive to others, then it was my problem, certainly not Akron's.

*Does **Thomas and Beulah** feel like a different book from your earlier ones?*

I think it is a departure from my other work—rather, I came home.

And, rather than a collection of poems, each working out a discrete universe, **Thomas and Beulah** is a string of moments that work together to define a universe much in the way a necklace defines the neck and shoulders. In my first book, **The Yellow House on the Corner,** there was an entire section dealing with aspects of slavery; **Museum** is somewhat of a hodgepodge of various social and political realities and how individuals work within them. **Thomas and Beulah** is the first sustained effort at sequence.

*It seemed to me that especially in **Yellow House** and in places in **Museum** there is more of a surrealistic feeling to some of the poems. In **Thomas and Beulah** we don't get as much of that. It seems much more grounded in the place and in the time and in the people.*

The word "surrealistic" has been used quite often in describing my work, and I must say I have always been amazed by it. I never thought of myself as being surrealistic.

Maybe "deep image."

No. Obviously, though, this is what people think of it. So now I kind of smile; I'm not going to escape this world. I mean, I accept it as a fair judgment. To me magic, or the existence of an unexplainable occurrence, is something I grew up with. One shouldn't try to explain everything. I learned to live with paradox, to accept strange happenings. I listened to older people talking about, for example, a person who refused to die easy and came back to haunt. In terms of memory and guilt, that makes a lot of sense to me. Now I'm not talking about ghost stories; I'm talking about how to live with strangeness. And for a minori-

ty, particularly black people growing up in America, a lot of surreal things are going on all the time.

One interesting thing about the Thomas section of the book is that Lem really haunts Thomas throughout. I find that very moving. Is this based on the story you referred to earlier from your grandmother?

Yes, yes. And you know the only facts that I had in the story were that my grandfather had come up the river with a good friend and that the friend had died. I knew nothing about the man. In fact, my grandfather never mentioned the story to us as children. The idea of Lem haunting him grew out of the poems—it actually grew out of the character of Thomas and what I felt he would have done.

Another question about Thomas. He comes across in some ways as a real lady's man. How did Beulah tie him down?

I don't know! I mean I think that . . . he might come across that way, but his being a lady's man was constrained by the death of his friend. In a way, he is trying to play his way out of hell.

Of course, the other side of it is he is very dedicated to his family.

He's a classic case in that he mourns the youth he had, but he can't get back to it anyway. I think it would be untrue for any of us to say we haven't felt that at some point. You feel you want to let go of all the stuff that starts attaching itself to you as you grow up, but you can't do it anymore.

The bills have to be paid. What is it that you admire about Beulah? And what is it you would like to honor in her?

I think of Beulah as being a very strong woman who still has no way of showing how strong she could be. She is the one who really wants to travel, to see the world. She is curious; she is intelligent; and her situation in life does not allow her to pursue her curiosity. If there is anything I want to honor in her, it is that spirit.

The sense of sacrifice?

Certainly that too, but lots of people make sacrifices. It's the way one handles sacrifice that's crucial.

She did it gracefully.

She did it gracefully, but not too gracefully—that is, not without spunk. It's important that people know there's a struggle involved, that the sacrifice is being made. You have to learn not to be crushed by what you can't do.

Both Thomas and Beulah seem relatively free of gnawing bitterness towards their environment, towards whites, despite some difficult circumstances, very difficult circumstances. Is there a lesson in this?

A lesson? Let me take a different tack. We tend to forget that there were generations upon generations of black Americans who did not have the luxury of bitterness. I don't mean to suggest that there was no bitterness, just that you had enough to do with surviving. You had to eat first. This drive for survival above all else could lead to a certain autism; one's personality freezes.

The civil rights movement and the rise of black consciousness in the 1960s made the release of emotion—anger, elation, fury, righteousness—possible. One could get emotions out without being poisonous and so still be able to go on with life. But Thomas and Beulah came from a different generation, from an era when there was no point in talking about what white people had and black people did not. That was a fact of life—it didn't mean they liked it, it didn't mean they thought it was right. But there were a few more pressing matters to talk about. Inequality was a given. I know how impatient we became with our grandparents in the '60s and our great aunts, when we would call ourselves Afro-Americans or black and they would continue to say "colored" and we'd go: "AHHHHH, come on." The impatience of youth. Why aren't Thomas and Beulah furious? Well, they were, but they had a different way of expressing it.

Both Beulah and Thomas grow old together, and sadness overtakes the readers as we read of their health problems and their demise. But they stick together and support each other. Is there a commentary on aging here for a society which is accused of neglecting its elderly?

Yes. Certainly one of the things I learned in writing **Thomas and Beulah** is that all of us are guilty at one time or another of not assigning other people their full human

Dust jacket for Dove's award-winning Thomas and Beulah.

worth, for whatever reasons—men having preconceived ideas of women or vice versa, racial prejudice, misconceptions about the young and the old. In order to be able to understand my grandfather, or how my grandmother could be the woman she was, I had to go back and revision their youth. It was a humbling experience for me. And there are certain satisfactions with age that we tend not to think about.

Thomas and Beulah are there for each other to the very end. That kind of commitment through thick and thin, as sappy as it may sound, is a striking part of the book.

I received essays written in the form of letters from students at Brown University. One student thought Thomas and Beulah didn't like each other at all, that the marriage was very sad. I was absolutely amazed at that notion. It must have something to do with our concept of love—that if we are young it is going to be romantic all the way through. In the poem **"Company"** Beulah said: "Listen: we were good, / though we never believed it." I remember that absolutely calm feeling that my grandparents had, a sense of belonging together. Today I see young lovers struggling to find earth-shattering ecstasy in every second. That's a part of love, but it's a small part.

There is a kind of ripeness about their love that is unusual and that only comes with age.

Absolutely.

What does the future hold for Rita Dove? Do you plan on writing more poetry or trying a novel?

More poems, of course, and I definitely plan to write more fiction. I'm writing a novel right now. Why not?

Will you be doing a lot more teaching? Or traveling in the next couple of years?

I have this year off, but I will be going back to teaching in the fall. I enjoy teaching. Travel is always in my life. I'm always traveling, it seems.

*We mentioned fiction and you do have that one book of short stories (**Fifth Sunday**). Do you find the two activities—writing fiction, writing poetry—mutually supportive or do you think of them as separate, unrelated activities? Is there any kind of schizophrenia about it? Or is it just natural?*

I think that they are part of the same process. It's all writing; there are just different ways of going about it. I don't find them compatible in the sense that when I am writing poetry I am not usually going to start a story. If I'm writing a story I am in a slightly different mode. I can't explain what it is—it's not as severe as speaking another language. Still, I think the notion of prose writing and poetry writing as separate entities has been artificially created, partly as a result of fitting writing into the academic curriculum where it is easiest to teach them separately. That's valid pedagogical methodology, but there is no reason for them to exist separately outside the workshop. One of the things I deplored when I was in graduate school was just how separate the two were kept; fiction writers and the poetry writers didn't even go to the same parties.

This is the final question. It's actually two. Does writing poetry enable you to be more fully aware of who you are? Is it the bliss of writing that attracts you?

(After some hesitation) No. It isn't the bliss of writing but the bliss of unfolding. I was hesitating with the question because I wanted to consider how to go about making my answer clear without making it sound corny. I don't think poetry is going to make anyone a better person, and it is not going to save you. But writing is a constant for me. There's an edge that needs to be explored, the edge between being unconscious and then suddenly being so aware that the skin tingles. Let me be more precise. There is that moment in the writing of a poem when things start to come together, coalesce into a discovery. This is sheer bliss, and has something to do with discovering something about myself. It doesn't mean I understand myself; in fact, the more I write the less I know of myself. But I also learn more. Territory is being covered—excursions into the interior. I write for those moments of discovery really, but there are two steps in this process: one is the intimate revelation, and the second step is to take that revelation and to make it visible—palpable—for others.

It's one thing to experience strong emotion; it's another thing to communicate it to others. I do believe that an experience inarticulated will be lost; part of my task as a writer, one of the things I take on and want to do, is to articulate those moments so they won't be lost. I think there is no greater joy than to have someone else say, "I know what you mean." That's real corny, but it's what literature does for all of us, the reader as well as the writer. An active reader longs to be pulled into another's world and to comprehend that world, to get into another's skin utterly and yet understand what's happening at the same time. That's an immensely exciting thing. And that's what I work for. (pp. 112-23)

> Rita Dove and Steven Schneider, in an interview in The Iowa Review, *Vol. 19, No. 3, Fall, 1989, pp. 112-23.*

It is perplexing that poetry seems to exist in a parallel universe outside daily life in America.

—Rita Dove, in Felicity Barringer's "A Poets' Topics, Jet Lag, Laundry and Making Her Art Commonplace," in The New York Times, *20 June 1993.*

Rita Dove with Steven Ratiner   (interview date 26 May 1993)

[*In the interview below, Dove comments on the role of history and music in her poetry.*]

[*Ratiner*]: *One of the central features in your poetry and fic-*

tion is the power of history and memory. Where does that drive to tell the story originate in your life?

[Dove]: Well, it begins really with two things: One of them, that I wasn't represented in history . . . either as a female or as a black person. And also the sense that ordinary people are not represented in history, that history gives you the tale of heroes, basically . . . . You are right, it is certainly something that has not only fascinated me, I'd almost say haunted me all these years. Also because I think that history is a very powerful weapon. If you can edit someone out of history then the next generation, the one who doesn't have a memory [of certain events] anymore, won't have anything to go on. And cultural memory is remarkably short in our day and age because communities are disintegrating, so there is no oral or communal sense of carrying on a tradition.

As a poet, are you a carrier of history?

A carrier of history of a particular sort. I think that in **Thomas and Beulah** what I was hoping to hand down [to the next generation] was a sense of two very normal people living through a period of incredible change in the United States . . . . But also I am interested in recovering a sense that we, as individual human beings, can connect to the universe.

What I love in your writing is your astounding sense of the particular, as if we were living through the experiences. Some provide us with a small glimpse of a black America we'd otherwise never see.

Well, that is just marvelous, because I think if we can, as human beings, enter those worlds even for an instant, then it makes it a little more difficult to hate someone else because they are different, to treat them badly or to kill them.

Your poems portray the lived experience of history. Two examples from **Grace Notes** *come to mind: "Summit Beach" seems to bring back the figure of your grandmother Beulah again, and "Crab Boil" centers on a girl I took to be a young Rita Dove.*

In each poem, a small personal experience is depicted center stage with just a hint of the larger historical forces churning in the background. The phrase "the Negro beach" is enough to conjure the racial climate in the 1920's. But Beulah seems hardly aware of this when she "climbed Papa's shed and stepped off / the tin roof into the blue / with her parasol and invisible wings." If not the tide of history, there must be something else that supports this woman, gives her the confidence to take that brave step.

I think the "something else" in that poem particularly is a sense of self, a sense of love, that comes from family and the community. I keep coming back to the community. . . . What will always keep you going is that sense of being buoyed up by others, others who understand, others who care, who are maybe going through the same things. The girl in **"Crab Boil"** doesn't quite understand the segregated beach business but she has learned, even at that age, to look and pay attention to her elders.

But you create an interesting tension between the commu-

nal sway and the will of the individual. The girl keeps on questioning. She almost empathizes with the crabs captured in the pail, especially with Aunt Helen's comment, "Look at that— / a bunch of niggers, not / a-one get out 'fore the others pull him / back." They tell the girl the crabs will feel no pain, and she finally accepts their claim. "I decide to believe this: I'm hungry."

But you have the feeling that she goes with their wisdom, yet she doesn't believe it totally. I think, really, she bows to the exigency of the situation. But I think that is the best of all possible kinds of relationships between individuals and the community, because I am not advocating that we be subsumed by some kind of group. We are all individuals who may share in various groups certain things that make us feel that we have a community. But the individual should never be obliterated or even blurred by that connection with the community. Even Beulah in **"Summit Beach"**—she wants to fly!

You've talked about the intellectual discipline in your household, the knowledge that your parents tried to "armor" you with as a girl.

Absolutely. It wasn't that rules were laid down, except in terms of television, which was a certain number of hours a week . . . but a feeling in the household was that the only ticket you have to a happy life is to do the best you can in whatever you do.

And the one place we were allowed to go practically any time was the library, but we had to read all the books that we got . . . .

And I remember coming back from the library once nearly in tears, I was about 11 or 12 or so, because they wouldn't let me check out Françoise Sagan. And I had read something in a magazine about this young girl who had written a risqué novel, and I wanted to read it. I think it was *Bonjour, Tristesse,* and they said, "No, you can't read it, you are not an adult." And it was the first time someone had told me I couldn't read anything, so I came home and my mother wrote a note that said, "Let her check out any book she wants." I think they felt if it was too old for us then we would get bored quickly.

That made a great impact on me; I think it was one of those moments when I realized that they trusted me.

Knowing how you feel about this, I thought it was curious how often you touch on the sense of "forbidden experience" in your writing. In one poem, there are Uncle Millet's stories, which you weren't supposed to hear but somehow memorized. There is the sense of unbridled fantasy in another, but you say "it's not the sort of story / you'd tell your mother."

Forbidden stories are powerful stories. They are forbidden for reasons, and there are different reasons. But forbidden stories are those that can somehow change your life. . . . And as wonderful as my childhood was, there certainly was a sense that they were watching over us and they were not going to let us stray from a certain kind of path. . . . That kind of dreaming that takes you out of the influence of the family is not something you tell your mother, because you instinctively know . . . they will start tighten-

ing the reigns. It is also the feeling of the individual's imagination being a dangerous thing for the community. I'm not trying to say communities are all about this: This is a give-and-take thing. There are good things, and there are things that are confining.

In the last several years, we've had an experience where the larger community wants to censor art and individual imagination. Society is not willing, as were your parents, to turn over complete responsibility to the individual.

It is extremely dangerous. It is dangerous for the spiritual health of the world. You cannot keep a mind sequestered, you know; it will break out some way. It is offering people trust that they will be humane. The idea is that if one has grown up in an honest, compassionate kind of way, a disciplined way, then no knowledge is dangerous, because a person will take that knowledge and be able to think about it and be able to figure out what is wrong or right.

Music is another pervasive presence throughout your writing. Was that also something inherited from your parents?

Records were always being played in our house, very different kinds of records. There was a Bessie Smith and Josh White, but there were also Fauré sonatas. My paternal grandparents did play instruments, the mandolin and the guitar. My parents, though, did not play instruments. It's odd, but when we were 10, it was time to pick an instrument, so I learned cello, as [one of my characters] Virginia does, and played cello all through college and even beyond. . . . But I think music was one of those first experiences I had of epiphany, of something clicking, of understanding something beyond, deeper than rational sense.

*In the novel [**Through the Ivory Gate**], when the character of Virginia plays the cello for the first time in years, you write that "the high notes in each phrase insinuated themselves into her blood: above the treadmill of chordal progressions a luminous melody unscrolling and floating away, high in the upper ether, where there was no memory or hurt." How does music or art accomplish such transformation?*

If I knew how music did that, I would be one up on everybody. I think that is one of the magical things about music—and you're right it is not just music, but any art—when the pleasure of its making, or the pleasure of the journey that it takes you on transcends [not only] the memories of pain you might have, but even the pain that might be contained in what it is talking about. An incredibly sad piece can make one exhilarated. I think this is one of the secrets of art, how it can help us, not digest the pain, but in a certain way take in that pain or hurt in our life and still prevail. It lifts you up over it but it doesn't let you forget it.

Let me ask you about the music of your writing—not just "music" as a motif but the musical textures you create with your words. There's one passage where Thomas was speaking: "How long has it been . . . ? / Too long. Each note slips / into querulous rebuke, fingerpads / scored with pain, shallow ditches / to rut in like a runaway slave / with a barking heart." It almost feels like a tenor sax belting out a be-bop phrase.

The music is so important to me, I can't really emphasize that too much. I think that one of the ways that a poem convinces us is not just the words, the meaning of the words, but the sound of them in our mouths, the way they increase our heartbeat or not, the amount of breath it takes to say a sentence, whether it will make us breathless at the end or whether it gives us time for repose or contemplation. It's the way our entire body gets involved in the language being spoken. And even if we are reading the poem silently, those rhythms exist.

There are times when, in fact, the sound, the music, leads me as much as any sense. In that section of Thomas's, I wanted to get across some of the frustration he was feeling as he tries to go back to the mandolin and he is rusty and he can't make it work the way he wants to. It's one thing to say that in plain old language, but to make the rhythms jagged and back-and-forth and full of stops and starts and aggravations, that then kind of explode in, as you said, a sax riff, a little bit of blues—this was for me a way of conveying that more deeply than saying he was "frustrated."

When you make a poem, what good is it in your life, and what good do you hope it might be when a reader receives it?

As human beings, we are endowed with this incredible gift to articulate our feelings and to communicate them to each other in very sophisticated ways. And writing a poem in which the almost inexpressible is being expressed is almost the pinnacle of the human achievement. So in that sense it is silly to ask what good is *that*, to reach the pinnacle.

The other thing is that when a reader reads a poem—I know that every time that I write a poem . . . I try to remember or try to imagine that reader—the reader that I was—curled up on the couch, the moment of opening a book and absolutely having my world fall away and entering into another one and feeling there was one other voice that was almost inside of me, we were so close.

In writing a poem, if the reader on the other end can come up and say: "I know what you meant, I mean, I felt that too"—then we are a little less alone in the world, and that to me is worth an awful lot. (pp. 16-17)

> *Rita Dove and Steven Ratiner, in an interview in* The Christian Science Monitor, *May 26, 1993, pp. 16-17.*

REVIEWS OF RECENT WORKS

Judith Kitchen   (review date Spring/Summer 1990)

[In the following excerpt, Kitchen praises Dove's "feminine sensibility" and the ways in which it leads to fresh perceptions in Grace Notes.*]*

Rita Dove is both a woman and black but her poems are not "about" being a woman, or being black; those facts are simply the context in which her poems occur. That does not mean she shrinks from issues related to being black or being female, and many of the poems in Dove's *Grace Notes,* her fourth collection, speak directly to the marginality of blacks and women in the larger culture. Clearly she cares about these issues, but she doesn't assume that dealing with them makes her a poet. She is a poet because of her fine ear, her keen perception, her love of the individual word. If there is a unity in this book, it is not the unity of theme or of character; it is the unity of an incisive mind applying itself to a particular life.

Grace Notes is a complex weave of personal experience, memory, dialectic, and visual imagination. Each poem adds a layer of experience or insight so that the whole is experienced much as a piece of music; one senses its shape long before one has words to describe it. It is nearly impossible to cite any single poem as exemplary of a specific thematic concern; instead, they overlap, giving the book a dense, luxurious structure. She has arranged the poems to resist categorization. For example, each of the five sections begins with an epigraph, but the epigraph does not necessarily apply to the section it heads. Dove did something similar in *Museum,* but here this displacement becomes part of the way in which the book must be read. The reader, in effect, must make the connections—and there are myriad connections to be made.

> **Rita Dove is both a woman and black but her poems are not "about" being a woman, or being black; those facts are simply the context in which her poems occur.**
>
> **—Judith Kitchen**

Dove resists ideology in all guises, preferring the inquisitive mind that discovers meaning rather than shapes it. And her strong sense of self allows room for such discovery. Because of the individual nature of the poems—ranging from childhood in Ohio to instances of black suppression, from Eugene's soliloquy under the sink to Dove's memory of her daughter's conception and her father-in-law's death, from landscapes in the Southwest to an old folk's home in Israel—it is nearly impossible to label them, even in terms of theme. Instead, they become parts of the larger picture, each offering up a small moment of observation or insight which, in turn, sheds light on another. The overall effect of the book is that of an interior voice dealing with the exterior world, often intruding on the act of observation with reflective comment. This happens from poem to poem, but the method of the book is reproduced in microcosm in **"Ozone,"** which is my personal favorite. In this twenty-nine-line poem, the poet alternates her own "take" on the hole in the ozone layer with an italicized, running response to a quote from Rilke. The effect is that of both seeing through the poet's eyes and simultaneously hearing her interior voice. The poem begins:

> . . . *Does the cosmic*
> *space we dissolve into taste of us, then?*
> —Rilke, *The Second*
> *Elegy*

> Everything civilized will whistle before
> it rages—kettle of the asthmatic,
> the aerosol can and its immaculate awl
> perforating the dome of heaven.

> We wire the sky for comfort:
> we thread it through our lungs for a perfect fit.
> We've arranged this calm, though it is constant-
>   ly
> unraveling.

> *Where does it go then,*
> *atmosphere suckered up*
> *an invisible flue?*
> *How can we know where it goes?*

The poem continues with a series of associative leaps until Rilke's cosmic question is contemplated on practical, present-day terms, and today's ecological issues merge with a spiritual quest: *"Rising, the pulse / sings: / memento mei."* What is the significance of the individual in the face of global destruction?

Rita Dove's female sensibility is the underpinning of the book. She is mother, wife, daughter, sister—but she lets none of these roles substitute for individual consciousness and imaginative exploration. Her womanly roles are the means to new understanding of the world. In **"Pastoral,"** she describes the ultimate feminine act of nursing her infant in such a way that she, in fact, discovers a truth about male perception. Male and female experiences merge in the act of mutual understanding that constitutes a poem:

> I liked afterwards best, lying
> outside on a quilt, her new skin
> spread out like meringue. I felt then
> what a young man must feel
> with his first love asleep on his breast:
> desire, and the freedom to imagine it.

At the same time, Dove celebrates her womanhood. **"After Reading Mickey in the Night Kitchen for the Third Time Before Bed"** shows her daughter discovering "facts" about the vagina. It ends with an acknowledgement of their basic individuality, and their shared womanhood: "How to tell her that it's what makes us— / black mother, cream child. / That we're in the pink / and the pink's in us." Women are celebrated. They did not make the nuclear silos which rise above the plains. "They were masculine toys. They were tall wishes. They / were the ribs of the modern world." Significantly, the book begins with a poem that stands alone, **"Summit Beach, 1921,"** in which a young girl sits on the Negro beach, not dancing with the others, but fingering a scar and remembering her great moment of childish imagination:

> She could wait, she was gold.
> When the right man smiled it would be
> music skittering up her calf
>
> like a chuckle. She could feel

> the breeze in her ears like water,
> like the air as a child when
> she climbed Papa's shed and stepped off
> the tin roof into blue,

> with her parasol and invisible wings.

Rita Dove seems, in **Grace Notes,** to be offering today's adult women, and today's blacks, those same invisible wings—the faith to step into blue. Why should we reserve the territory of imagination for childhood? Poetry, then, is one of Dove's answers; it is, as in **"Ars Poetica,"** a "traveling x-marks-the-spot." She zeros in on what is important by a faithful, close observance of the world. She gives us its particulars, and she makes it mysterious and fluid:

> **"Mississippi"**

> In the beginning was the dark
> moan and creak, a sidewheel
> moving through. Thicker
> then, scent of lilac,
> scent of thyme; slight hairs
> on a wrist lying down in sweat.
> We were falling down
> river, carnal
> slippage and shadow melt.
> We were standing on the deck
> of the New World, before maps:
> tepid seizure of a breeze
> and the spirit hissing away . . .

The line breaks highlight words, demonstrate their own carnal slippage, layering the poem with black history, with individual experience, with a sense of the overall importance of this New World in which we all, male and female, black and white, share a future.

The jacket cover claims that grace notes are musical embellishments, but I like to think of them as the almost invisible thread that holds a piece together. Certainly the grace notes of this collection—the lyric poems that shimmer with a music all their own—are suggestive of the larger shape behind their singular subjects. "What are music or books if not ways / to trap us in rumors? The freedom of fine cages!" *Grace Notes* is such a fine cage—golden and filigreed, showing the boundaries of our vision at the same time that it offers us freedom of imagination, the possibility of soaring beyond the bars. (pp. 268-71)

> *Judith Kitchen, in a review of "Grace Notes,"*
> *in* The Georgia Review, *Vol. XLIV, Nos. 1 &*
> *2, Spring-Summer, 1990, pp. 268-71.*

Helen Vendler   (review date 1991)

[*Vendler is regarded as one of America's foremost critics of poetry. Her* Part of Nature, Part of Us: Modern American Poets *(1980) is considered a vital work in the study of contemporary poetry. In the following excerpt, she examines a selection of poems from* Grace Notes, *admiring their lyricism and tension.*]

[Rita Dove] looks for a hard, angular surface to her poems. She is an expert in the disjunctive, often refusing the usual discursive signs of "the meditative." Crosscutting and elliptical jumps were her chief stylistic signature

even in her first volume, *The Yellow House on the Corner.*
Grace Notes is her fourth book, and represents both a return to the lyric from her successful objective sequence
Thomas and Beulah, and an attempt to make her poems
weigh less heavily on the page. Her poems are rarely without drama, however, and she has done a remarkable thing
in making even the routines of motherhood become dramatic, in the best poems in this volume, a sequence occupying Part III of *Grace Notes.* Here is **"The Breathing, the
Endless News":**

> Every god is lonely, an exile
> composed of parts: elk horn,
> cloven hoof. Receptacle
>
> for wishes, each god is empty
> without us, penitent,
> raking our yards into windblown piles. . . .
>
> Children know this: they are
> the trailings of gods. Their eyes
> hold nothing at birth then fill slowly
>
> with the myth of ourselves. Not so the dolls,
> out of the count, each toe pouting from
> the slumped-over toddler clothes:
>
> no blossoming there. So we
> give our children dolls, and
> they know just what to do—
> line them up and shoot them.
> With every execution
> doll and god grow stronger.

This is at once mock-horrific (the angelic daughter lines
up her dolls and shoots them) and culturally unnerving.
The actors: the gods and ourselves; the godlike children
and their not-godlike dolls; the picture of life as the successive killing of successive "dolls" by emergent "gods"; the
declining parents; the fetishistic nature of consciousness
and its gods (part noble elk horn, part indecent cloven
hoof)—all these are immensely suggestive without ever
becoming quite explicitly allegorical.

In **"Genetic Expedition,"** Dove (a black married to a
white husband) contrasts her own looks to those of her
blond daughter, with a frankness that sentimentality
would blush at:

> Each evening I see my breasts
> slacker, black-tipped
> like the heavy plugs on hot water bottles;
>
> . . . . .
>
> My child has
> her father's hips, his hair
> like the miller's daughter, combed gold.
> Though her lips are mine, housewives
> stare when we cross the parking lot
> because of that ghostly profusion.
>
> *You can't be cute,* she says. *You're big.*
> She's lost her toddler's belly,
> that seaworthy prow. She regards me
> with serious eyes, power-lit,
> atomic gaze
> I'm sucked into, sheer through to
>
> the gray brain of sky.

The disturbing ending—an atomic extinction of the parent
back into the mind of the universe—draws the sensual immediacy of the opening into its component gray quanta,
raw material for the next invention of the sky.

As these poems suggest, Dove's lines and stanzas are carefully aligned into dovetailed wholes. (The pun, unintended, seems legitimate.) Her **"Ars Poetica"** doesn't deal with
the making of poems, only with the stance from which
they are made. This is contrasted to the large ambitions,
presented satirically, of two male straw men:

> What I want is this poem to be small,
> a ghost town
> on the larger map of wills.
> Then you can pencil me in as a hawk:
> a traveling x-marks-the-spot.

This doesn't get to the heart of Dove's talent. Her true *ars
poetica* in this volume is a harsh poem called **"Ozone,"**
which is about arrangement and what it yields—which is
precisely nothing (if you choose to see it that way). Life,
says the poem, is "suckered up / an invisible flue"; it "disappear[s] into an empty bouquet." The maddening aspect
of art is that life disappears into it once you've cleared out
the space for life to fit into it. The weirdness with which,
as [Wallace] Stevens said, "Things as they are / Are
changed upon the blue guitar," is both the despair and the
triumph of artists. Thinking to express feeling, they make
a hole in reality:

> Everything civilized will whistle before
> it rages—kettle of the asthmatic,
> the aerosol can and its immaculate awl
> perforating the dome of heaven.
>
> We wire the sky for comfort;
> we thread it through out lungs for a perfect fit.
> We've arranged this calm, though it is constant-
>   ly
> unraveling.
>
>   . . . . .
>
> The sky is wired so it won't fall down.
> Each house notches into its neighbor
> and then the next, the whole row scaldingly
>   white,
> unmistakable as a set of bared teeth.

Dove hasn't always this angry fatality, but there is an electricity (whistling, raging) about this wiring and notching
and scalding and perforation that makes **"Ozone"** unforgettable. The poem speaks to the pain underlying Dove's
work: the barely contained nervous tension which can
only be appeased by notching one bared tooth into the
next, carefully blowtorching a hole in the sky with awl-like
precision, fixing the hole like "a gentleman [who] pokes
blue through a buttonhole." Dove's combination of the
domestic kettle, the artisanal awl, the aesthetic bouton-
niere, and the passional bared teeth convinces a reader
that Dove's inner factions are in intense communication
with each other.

Dove is interested by intransigency and its discontents. In
one of the lesser poems here, a set of students respond to
what they (and Dove, their teacher) take to be racism in

a (white) lecturer (who may be William Arrowsmith; the poem is called **"Arrow"**):

> . . . We sat there.
> Dana's purple eyes deepened, Becky
> twitched to her hairtips
> and Janice in her red shoes
> scribbled [a note of rage]. . . .
>
>   My students
> sat there already devising
>
> their different ways of coping:
> Dana knowing it best to have
> the migraine at once, get the poison out quickly
> Becky holding it back for five hours and Janice
> making it to the evening reading and
> party afterwards
> in black pants and tunic with silver mirrors
> her shoes pointed and studded, wicked witch
>   shoes:
> Janice who will wear red for three days or
> yellow brighter
> than her hair so she can't be
> seen at all

Janice's way, we suspect, is Dove's way; anger and tension are released in the scribbling of a note, the flaunting of color, the disappearance of self into raiment. The comparative slackness and "realism" here are a mode Dove carries off less well than she does her fierce and laconic "symbolic" mode. Here is her splendidly suggestive **"Medusa"**:

> I've got to go
> down where my eye
> can't reach
> hairy star
> who forgets to shiver
> forgets the cool suck
> inside
>
> Someday long
> off someone will
> see me
> fling me up
> until I look
> into sky
>
> drop his memory
>
> My hair
> dry water

Resistant though this is to analysis, it feels right, at least to me. That "hairy star," the eye, forgets (because of its visual and cerebral way of being) the shiver and the suck of the passional life. By descending into her subaqueous realm, Medusa gains the snaky locks that symbolize her knowledge. When another eye sees her, she is stellified and turned into the "dry water" of art. The beholder forgets his other life, stands rooted. This too is an *ars poetica*, though not only that.

I admire Dove's persistent probes into ordinary language, including the language of the black proletariat. Here, the most successful experiment in that genre is **"Genie's Prayer under the Kitchen Sink"**—a monologue by a grown son (Eugene, the "Genie" of the title) summoned by his mother to unclog the kitchen sink. The touch be-

comes uneasy here and there, though, as Dove wants a decorativeness in her poem that the voice can't sustain:

> . . . I came because I'm good at this, I'm good
> with my hands; last March I bought some 2 by
>   4s
> at Home Depot and honed them down
> to the sleekest, blondest, free-standing bar
> any mildewed basement in a cardboard housing
>   tract
> under the glass gloom of a factory clock
> ever saw. . . .

One can believe in the first four lines of this, but not the last three.

Dove's youth, in this volume, is already shadowed, and one can see her trying to peer out of her present emotional riches into a savorless future. She visits an old poet in **"Old Folk's Home, Jerusalem"**:

> So you wrote a few poems. The horned
> thumbnail hooked into an ear doesn't care.
> The gray underwear wadded over a belt says So
>   what. . . .
>
> Valley settlements put on their lights
> like armor; there's finch chit and my sandal's
> inconsequential crunch.
>
> Everyone waiting here was once in love.

The flatness of "my sandal's inconsequential crunch" betokens a Dove to come, looking at intransigency become inconsequential, though still held in the unyielding principle of her angular stanzas. (pp. 396-401)

> *Helen Vendler, "A Dissonant Triad," in* Parnassus: Poetry in Review, *Vol. 16, No. 2, 1991, pp. 391-404.*

Geoff Ryman   (review date 11 October 1992)

[*Ryman is a Canadian science fiction and fantasy writer. In the review below, he praises Dove's emphasis on storytelling and use of memory in* Through the Ivory Gate.]

Rita Dove is a poet whose volume of work **Thomas and Beulah** won a 1987 Pulitzer Prize. Yet the strength of her first novel, **Through the Ivory Gate**, is her prose, her ability to describe and suggest. The novel's heroine, Virginia King, is a gifted musician and actress. She takes up a temporary post in an elementary school in her hometown of Akron, Ohio, a homecoming that provokes a flood of memories. As Virginia helps the schoolchildren to develop a puppet show, she remembers her own childhood—the early days in Akron, her family's move to Arizona, her university studies, her love for a fellow student called Clayton.

The story is gentle and the style plain, at its best describing the sky over Lake Erie, a neighbor's homemade pastries, the décor of a restaurant or the face of a long-lost aunt. It is a happy book, about the pleasures of living. The author has a talent for sanguine observation.

The novel moves, as does memory, through association.

I think so many of our young people feel that poetry is something they're going to be tested on and not going to know the right answer. Those are small but practical things that could reduce the anxiety level when it comes to the notion of poetry. It would be a great public service on TV or radio, if they would set aside just 20 seconds, 30 seconds, 40 seconds for a short poem.

—*Rita Dove, in Felicity Barringer's "A Poets' Topics, Jet Lag, Laundry and Making Her Art Commonplace," in* The New York Times, *20 June 1993.*

One chapter starts in Akron, with Virginia playing the cello. She remembers events in class that morning, and is reminded of her own childhood. She remembers lying on a bed and listening to the Arizona rain. She thinks about the children's puppet show, with its magic football and drum majorettes. This cues different memories of becoming the only black drum majorette in her high school. We get flashbacks within flashbacks.

There are also narrative currents. We meet Clayton in the first chapter, and we want to meet him again. We see that he is beautiful and that Virginia still loves him. What went wrong? We know that Virginia has an Aunt Carrie living in Akron. Virginia sees her in dark dreams and avoids visiting her. Why? The father of one of her pupils takes a romantic interest in her. Is he the man to replace Clayton?

As in Jane Austen, the heroine's quest for a male partner has a larger social dimension. When an early high school beau turns out to be illiterate, Virginia's mother, usually so distant, comforts her. "How many black male students does Arizona State have—20, 30? . . . It's simple arithmetic. The more education you get, the fewer black men you'll meet on the way."

The book deals sparingly but effectively with the issue of race. Virginia becomes a mime artist and puppeteer partly because there are few parts for black actresses. When she gets her first straight-A report card, a white school friend pushes her over and calls her a nigger. The book begins powerfully with the young Virginia's first encounter with a Sambo doll and the confusions this causes her.

Throughout the novel, dolls and puppets are a recurring motif. Virginia is called the Puppet Lady, and she has a puppet alter ego through whom she can talk more easily to the children. As a child, she visits a Hopi reservation, sees a kachina doll and is told, "Hopi parents hang kachinas up on the walls so that their children learn to recognize their gods."

"Funny how fantasy works. And memory," muses Virginia on her first day back in Akron. Fantasy in the form of theater, puppetry and dreams is juxtaposed with recollec-

tion—perhaps unfairly, as the memories in this book are so appealing and vivid. The ivory gate of the title is Homer's—the gate through which false dreams come. Fantasy is both good and bad, a means of liberation and a means of control. In fantasy, there is Sambo.

These themes of fantasy, childhood and oppression are brought together, perhaps a touch too explicitly, in a scene toward the end. Virginia dreams she is lecturing on the subject of Sambo to an audience of adult heads screwed onto children's bodies. "The first thing to bear in mind about Sambo," she begins, "is that Sambo is all of us. We all want to make merry, to wear bright colors and sing in the sun all day." The oppression of a race is seen in the context of the oppression of children and of joy.

Through the Ivory Gate is a first novel that has problems. It is tentatively structured and compromises its attractive restraint to achieve drama at the end. Aunt Carrie tells Virginia of a secret grief at the heart of her family; a child is so fixated on Virginia that she attempts suicide.

Descriptions of sex retreat into airy metaphor—"Their bodies merged into one long, yearning curve and the sea rose up to meet them." At times the book also seems to shy away from pain. Virginia relegates playing the cello to a hobby, after years of work, without apparent anguish. We are told about strain between her and her mother, but see only normal mother-daughter bickering.

Virginia gets straight A's, does well in her university, is an accomplished actress and ends the book by being offered a part in an Off Broadway play. All this success gets wearying. The children adore her, their parents adore her, her colleagues adore her. She receives heartwarming tributes from most of the characters in the book: for her looks, her intelligence, her achievements. It comes as a relief when she finally does something wrong. "Boy, are you young," says the mother of the girl who has tried to throw herself off the top of a staircase because of Virginia. Even here, the unpleasantness is over quickly. After telling Virginia a few home truths, the mother smiles and takes her in to see the child.

Through the Ivory Gate is mature in its telling of little stories—Virginia's recollections of life with a troupe of puppeteers, of visiting the rubber factory where her father worked, of neighborhood boys daubing a house so that it looked as if it had measles. Virginia's grandmother and aunt lean back in their chairs and tell us stories that reach even farther back to a more collective past. The book aims to present the richness of a life and its connections to family and friends, culture, place, seasons and self. In this it succeeds. (pp. 11-12)

Geoff Ryman, "Nothing Succeeds Like Virginia," in The New York Times Book Review, October 11, 1992, pp. 11-12.

Gabrielle Foreman   (review date March 1993)

[*In the following mixed assessment of* Through the Ivory Gate, *Foreman lauds Dove's descriptive powers, but faults the novel's structure and negative portraits of African-American men.*]

I should begin by confessing that I just don't like novels about children. They remind me too much of children's books without the charm of great illustrations—and even as a child I didn't much care for those. Reading Rita Dove's first novel, *Through the Ivory Gate,* I get the sneaking suspicion that I'm back on my weekly fourth-grade trip to the library, this time with Ntozake Shange's "woman in yellow"—and she gets Toussaint L'Ouverture, adventure, resistance and the Adult Reading Room, while I get Dove's puppeteer heroine, Virginia King, instead.

I group Dove and Shange together for more than the reference to the vignette from *for colored girls.* . . . They are both consummate poets in a line of African American women—Gwendolyn Brooks, Margaret Walker, June Jordan, Audre Lorde and Alice Walker, for instance—who begin with verse and reach out to prose. Dove, Shange, Brooks and Jordan belong to a smaller subset still: Jordan's *His Own Where* (1970) is an adolescent love story, while Brooks' *Maud Martha* (1952), Shange's two novels *Sassafrass, Cypress and Indigo* (1982) and *Betsey Brown* (1985), all are coming-of-age stories of memory, pain and discovery with young Black girls at their centers.

Dove extends Brooks' legacy even further. *Thomas and Beulah* (1987) made Dove the second African American poet ever to win a Pulitzer Prize; Brooks was the first (1949). *Through the Ivory Gate* arches back to revise Brooks' *Maud Martha,* and to give its heroine more flexibility and independence, while at the same time it highlights their protagonists' surprisingly similar fluster and angst. Imploded, almost claustrophobic spaces, narrative snatches that show Black women dealing with regular, ordinary, everyday troubles of color, childhood and romance—nothing magical, nothing loudly tragic or grand—this is what the two novels share.

Dove's novel is the story of Virginia King as she rattles "around the emotional furniture of her childhood." With drama degree in hand and a stint with a political troupe called "Puppets & People" just folded, she comes back to the Ohio city of her youth as "Miss Puppet Lady," a visiting artist in the Akron primary schools. Through flashbacks we get glances of Clayton, her college friend and lover, who turns out to be gay; her distanced and dehydrated parents Ernie and Belle, who move the family out to Arizona to save their marriage; selected family stories and secrets; her childhood racial and romantic traumas; her "majorette days" and her love of the cello and mime. In the narrative present Dove describes Virginia's interchanges with the fourth-grade class she teaches and their parents, including an affair with a too well-groomed and scented Black single father who, in her Grandma Evans' words, is "too good-looking to do good" but tries nonetheless.

Dove's strengths come through most forcefully when she describes, or when the narrative is in the mouths of, its older characters. Her father's impulsive family-minus-mother jaunts out of the stultifying heat of his home, their drives to Hopi mesas and his lectures about Papago and Pima culture, bring him to life. Grandma Evans' nursing-home recollections of her courtship capture a character as charming as Hurston's Tea-Cake. "I remember how your grandpa said [my name] when he first got a conversation going with me," she explains:

> Set his guitar down real slow. "Miss Virginia," he said, "you're a fine piece of woman." Seems he'd been asking around. Knew everything about me. Knew I was bold and proud and didn't cotton to no silly niggers. Vir-gin-ee-a, he said, nice and slow. Almost Russian, the way he said it. Right then and there I knew this man was for me. That's how you pick 'em, honey. Listen how they say your name. If they can't say that right, there's no way they're going to know how to treat you proper, neither.

"A truth for all times," nod those of us attuned to wooing, grandmotherly advice, or the importance of orality, names and naming in the African American tradition. Dove captures a cadence and urgency in Aunt Carrie's voice as well. I don't understand why Dove seems to want Carrie's story to be pivotal to the novel itself, but while Carrie's telling it, I certainly understand why it's important to *her.*

One might argue that Dove patterns her narrative structure after a collage; she chooses bits and pieces that come together, not to make a whole but to make an impression. Flashes from present to past and vignettes made of memories (one could go on) work like pregnant pauses, inviting us to fill in gaps and become participatory readers. Yet most of her breaks act more like interruptions. Confronted with Mrs. Voltz, the neighbor with Wonderbread arms who makes Virginia tea and discourses on birds, I'm tempted to ask, as Dizzy Gillespie might, "So what?" When the plot builds to what the jacket cover describes as a revelation that threatens "to shatter the healing [Virginia's] memories bring," one is left not knowing the characters intimately enough to understand why it matters so much. As gorgeous as Dove's language is in this section, I must wonder why Carrie's confession is important enough to Virginia to claim such a central location in the novel.

I have similar problems with *Through the Ivory Gate*'s other vignettes. The pouting tantrums of a Black girl who wants blond playthings rather than African American dolls, the replayed memories of the actual yellow-coiffed classmate who, incited by her darker friend's second-grade success, feels compelled to call her "nigger," the ubiquitous part-Indian grandmother Zora teased us about: they ring true but, well, tired. More importantly, Dove's treatment of Black men also seems rehearsed. *For colored girls* . . . and *The Color Purple* focused on self-awareness and the collective empowerment of Black women. "This is not an attack on you," we've told our brothers and fathers, our lovers and friends; "it's about us and you just can't stand being ignored." Yet Dove's gratuitous treatment of too-smooth straight Black men—wooden lines like "heavy, sister" glide out of more than one "brother's" mouth—and Virginia's compulsion to lie about her name and where on campus she's heading when she runs into some friendly Black male students, are only topped off by her mother Belle's lecture on "suitable" Black men.

Virginia the high-school majorette has met a young man

whose "diction [is] perfectly proper," is charming and is melt-away *fine* at that, only to discover through a love-note that he just can't spell—and the thrill is gone. Now I'm a notoriously bad speller myself; and, at fifteen, I left just such a note on a boy's doorstep, only [to] have his mother find it and its spelling errors, "fallic" of all words among them, so I'm sensitive. Still, Belle brings us to this story's pregnant pause: "as she read, [she] sucked in her tongue, then her outrage dimmed and a cold, set look took its place . . . 'It's going to be a problem you know.' " Belle goes on to contemplate the numbers of Black men in college, half of whom "head for white girls first chance they get": "it's simple arithmetic. The more education you get, the fewer black men you'll meet on the way." I can feel my brother cringe, and I too resent the invited response to Dove's narrative pause: Don't teach this boy who can talk about everything and treats women well *how* to spell; drop him, that'll take care of the "problem." Dan Quayle can't spell, and that's certainly not what makes him unsuitable.

1992 was a rich year for African American women writers: *Jazz, Bailey's Cafe, Possessing the Secret of Joy*—all deal with memory and highlight form; and God knows *Waiting to Exhale* adds pace to the everyday trials and tribulations of Black women not much older than Virginia King. Some might find *Through the Ivory Gate* charming, its structure challenging, its treatment of Black men unimportant or inoffensive, and its musings and memories the stuff of our literary tradition. Rather, I see this as the first novel of an accomplished poet whose second novel might take off from *Through the Ivory Gate*'s stronger moments.

> Gabrielle Foreman, "Miss Puppet Lady," in The Women's Review of Books, *Vol. X, No. 6, March, 1993, p. 12.*

FURTHER READING

Interview

Rosenberg, Judith Pierce. "Rita Dove: Judith Pierce Rosenberg Interviews Our New Poet Laureate." *Belles Lettres* 9, No. 2 (Winter 1993-94): 38-41.

Dove discusses her "life as a writer, thinker, mother, and teacher."

Additional coverage of Dove's life and career is contained in the following sources published by Gale Research: *Black Writers; Contemporary Authors,* Vol. 109; *Contemporary Authors New Revision Series,* Vol. 27; *Contemporary Literary Criticism,* Vol. 50; *Dictionary of Literary Biography,* Vol. 120; and *Poetry Criticism,* Vol. 6.

Roddy Doyle
Paddy Clarke Ha Ha Ha

Award: Booker Prize for Fiction

An Irish novelist and screenwriter, Doyle was born in 1958(?).

INTRODUCTION

Set in 1968 in a working-class neighborhood of Northern Dublin, Ireland, *Paddy Clarke Ha Ha Ha* is told from the viewpoint of a ten-year-old boy. Chronicling the title character's daily routines and mischievious antics, which include starting fires with his magnifying glass, writing his name in wet cement, and fighting with his schoolmates, the novel addresses such themes as friendship, religion, and familial relationships. While some critics have faulted *Paddy Clarke Ha Ha Ha* for its lack of introspection, episodic plot, and reliance on anecdotes, most have praised the work's realism, effective use of dialect, and engaging descriptions of boyhood and working-class Ireland. Peter Kemp has stated: "[In] its fiesty comedy, unsentimental nostalgia and vivid realizing of a young boy's take on life, *Paddy Clarke Ha Ha Ha* makes an impressive and likeable addition to a line of Irish writing that got memorably under way with the opening scenes of [James] Joyce's *A Portrait of the Artist as a Young Man.*"

PRINCIPAL WORKS

The Commitments (novel) 1987
The Snapper (novel) 1990
The Commitments (screenplay) 1991
The Van (novel) 1991
Paddy Clarke Ha Ha Ha (novel) 1993
The Snapper (screenplay) 1993

The Commitments, The Snapper, and *The Van* are collectively referred to as *The Barrytown Trilogy.*

CRITICISM

Peter Kemp (review date 11 June 1993)

[*In the following review, Kemp discusses Doyle's depiction of boyhood in* Paddy Clarke Ha Ha Ha.]

With *Paddy Clarke Ha Ha Ha,* the novelist who wrote *The Snapper* has produced a book whose alternative title could well be *The Nipper.* Paddy, its boisterous narrator, is just ten years old—as was Roddy Doyle in 1968, the time at which the novel is set. Heightening the autobiographical feel, Paddy patrols that patch of North Dublin working-class suburbia which—fictionalized as Barrytown—Doyle has already roped off as his own.

Period colour, in this first of Doyle's books to look back at the past, is unobtrusively but atmospherically touched in. Paddy munches Toffo and muses about the Americans fighting "gorillas" with helicopters in the Mekong Delta. Crazy about George Best, he is given for Christmas *A Pic-*

torial History of Soccer, inside which his da has faked the footballer's signature. On the Clarkes' recently purchased record-player revolve the sole three LPs they possess: *South Pacific, The Black and White Minstrels* and *Hank Williams The King of Country Music.*

Skillfully enough, Doyle resurrects 1960s Ireland in *Paddy Clark Ha Ha Ha.* But his book's real feat is its uncannily immediate bringing back to life of the responses and routines of a boy in that place and period. Paddy's headlong enthusiasms whoop and bounce across the pages.

—Peter Kemp

Skillfully enough, Doyle resurrects 1960s Ireland. But his book's real feat is its uncannily immediate bringing back to life of the responses and routines of a boy in that place and period. Paddy's headlong enthusiasms whoop and bounce across the pages. Sentences fall over themselves in their eagerness to communicate his keenness for William books or his liking for running through big concrete pipes on building sites, starting fires with his magnifying glass or writing the names of himself and his best friend Kevin in wet concrete workmen have just spread.

Doyle agilely itemizes the jumble of data flickering through the boy's brain—especially the numerical odds and ends that fascinate him. The life expectancy of a mouse is eighteen months; there are thirty-five billion corpuscles in your blood; of the fifty-four houses already built in Barrytown, seventeen have Venetian blinds.

Around these pieces of mathematical precision swirls a welter of inventive supposition. A schoolmate killed by leukaemia is rumoured to have died either from drinking sea water or swallowing a gobstopper. The demise of Mr Quigley up the road is attributed—after a thought-provoking episode of the crime series, *Hitchcock Presents,* to Mrs Quigley's having added powdered glass to his omelette ("It made a lot of sense"). Viewed from Paddy's angle, death seems less an absence than a weird kind of presence: "Liam and Aidan had a dead mother, Missis O'Connell was her name." Life—a matter of careering down "our road" and knowing exactly which meal will be waiting on the table ("shepherd's pie on a Tuesday")—seems unbreakably fixed and secure.

The near-tribal loyalties and rituals of the ten-year-old boys in their virtually girl-less world are conveyed with spot-on punchiness: the standardized bouts of jeering, the formalized scuffles, the vowings to "get" intruders such as the newcomers from the "Corporation houses". Together, Paddy and his gang seem like a pack of small mammals whose fits and starts of recklessness and aggression are just about curbed by chastening clouts from adjacent adults.

Under the group-toughness, though, Doyle shows you something more sensitive that gets privately expressed. Paddy's feelings for his mother are registered with un-mawkish care—as are his sensuous and aesthetic reactions to domestic pleasures. The patterned moquette of the family sofa puts him in mind of grass that's just been mown or the back of his head after a haircut. In the steamy wet-walled kitchen on washing day, he watches as sheets shiny with huge bubbles rise out of the water "like a whale being caught" as they are reeled into the mangle.

Another everyday factor stirring Paddy's imagination is Catholicism. Among the statistics he pores over are the estimated millions of years to be spent in Purgatory expiating such sins as "robbing" magazines or aniseed balls from cornershops. One of his games, whose lingo is comically concocted from Catholic Truth Society pamphletese, is an idiosyncratic re-play of Fr Damien's experiences with lepers in the Congo.

Catholicism is, meanwhile, the reader discerns, impinging less amusingly on the lives of Paddy's parents and gradually helping to prise them apart. Despite its cock-a-hoop opening gusto, the novel slowly moves towards a sombre destination. In this, it resembles Doyle's last book, ***The Van,*** an initially jaunty chronicle of male working-class matiness which sours into a bitter depiction of camaraderie breaking apart. As his parents row, Paddy's boyish scrappings take on an uglier aspect. His friendship with Kevin turns out to be less fixed than it looked. The takingly candid, ingenious, rowdy and joyful creature the reader first meets has clenched and hardened into guarded, lonely premature adulthood.

The transition to this bleak ending is a bit uncertain—just as, occasionally, Doyle's expert ventriloquism wavers: it seems improbable, for instance that, as he bawls the grossest treachery he can think of at his former friend, Paddy should note, novelist-like, "I saw it, the hurt, pain, the rage charge through his face in a second." But, in its feisty comedy, unsentimental nostalgia and vivid realizing of a young boy's take on life, ***Paddy Clarke Ha Ha Ha*** makes an impressive and likeable addition to a line of Irish writing that got memorably under way with the opening scenes of Joyce's *A Portrait of the Artist as a Young Man* and was recently given a macabre twist in Patrick McCabe's *The Butcher Boy.*

Peter Kemp, "A Barrytown Boy," in The Times Literary Supplement, *No. 4706, June 11, 1993, p. 21.*

Brian Morton (review date 18 June 1993)

[*In the review below, Morton compares* Paddy Clarke Ha Ha Ha *to other novels told from a child's viewpoint.*]

Before the last of the jokes were taken out of *Punch,* there was a feature inspired by a news item about a school essay of Graham Greene's having been auctioned at Christie's. *Punch* claimed to have dug up several more by the literary great-and-good, of which by far the most convincing was a "What I did on my summer holidays" by the ten-year-old Samuel Beckett. It was a litany of bleak, small-voiced *non sequiturs:* "and then . . . and then . . . and then" (and then, just to please the literary truffle-hogs, there was a disembodied head—someone's sleeping da, presumably—poking up out of Dun Laoghaire strand).

As Ur-Beckett it was perfect, and it came to mind again as exactly the tone Roddy Doyle has found for ten-year-old Paddy Clarke [in *Paddy Clark Ha Ha Ha*]. Paddy's da, a quiet, imaginatively accommodating man, is sinking into a soft marital quicksand, but the tensions between da and ma are no more than subliminal quivers round the edges of Paddy's consciousness.

Doyle is never tempted to tell more than the boy understands. Paddy's life is persuasively compounded of the weird peace that comes from self-imposed rites of passage and meaningless challenges: knick-knack, three-and-in, relievio, popping tar bubbles with lolly sticks to trap bees in the hot goo, regular initiations by the Gaelic god of silence Ciùnas (actually the poker-wielding Kevin, Paddy's best friend) at which the boys adopt a scatological persona for the week ahead. Most are, of course, forgotten within the day, but to be known as Shite or Fuck for seven days is no mean magic.

Doyle has a good ear for the sort of howlers teachers like to swap in staff rooms—" 'I had two bloodshot eyes and one black one', 'Three eyes, eh, Clarke?' "—but they are delivered with complete innocence and without a whiff of irony. Writing through the eyes of children, it is always tempting to bank up a huge mass of "objective" information at the edges of their field of vision, and to intrude heavy-handed "awakenings" or even, in Doyle's part of the country, "epiphanies".

Where Paddy's life differs utterly from the child's-eye-view of *A Portrait of the Artist as a Young Man* is the complete absence of a backward glance. There is none of the stream-of-consciousness "moo-cow" nonsense, nor of Faulkner's "tale told by an idiot" stuff; none of the contrived scenarios in Laing's *Conversations with Children*, and none of Joyce's frankly dishonest psychologising.

Paddy's is not a *stream* of consciousness, but a sequence of disconnected drips. Denied the warm bath of absorption in the mother (and ma seems increasingly detached, lost in her worries), "innocence" is a kind of torture to be mitigated by elaborate games.

At first glance, *Paddy Clarke Ha Ha Ha* is the novel Roddy Doyle might have been expected to write first, the autobiographical warm-up for the *Barrytown Trilogy* of *The Commitments, The Snapper,* and *The Van.* The setting is the same, but Paddy Clarke's is a more constrained and threatened world, one in which humour works at a lower, less outgoing level. The obvious parallel is with Jim Kelman, the only other contemporary writer who can inhabit a non-ironic consciousness so absolutely and convincingly. There is, though, none of Kelman's sandbagging proletarianism.

Where Paddy differs from his Barrytown predecessors is that (accusations of "showing off" aside) he has not yet fully developed that characteristically self-protective Irish instinct for display, in which a joke or a story is a cake or

a bottle to be divvied up and passed round. Its other side is, of course, the unself-conscious clownishness of *Waiting for Godot,* in which it is virtually impossible to share, where awareness is trapped and enclosed, buzzing hopelessly like those bees in melted tar, or simply engulfed in sand.

Brian Morton, "Tar Baby," in New Statesman & Society, Vol. 6, No. 257, June 18, 1993, p. 39.

Liz Heron   (review date 2 July 1993)

[*In the excerpt below, Heron praises Doyle's blending of comedy and realism in* Paddy Clarke Ha Ha Ha.]

Even childhood memoirs intimate that world events are never entirely peripheral to biography. In Roddy Doyle's *Paddy Clarke Ha Ha Ha* the Vietnam War and the Arab-Israeli conflict are among the furniture of boyhood memory. This is 1968 in Dublin's working class Barrytown, and since Paddy Clarke is 10, the age of his creator at that time, we can infer that a lot of the novel's zest comes from Doyle's remembrance of things experienced—though that's a long way from making fiction the same thing as autobiography.

> *Paddy Clarke Ha Ha Ha* starts off as callous comedy and ends up making painful reading, without once sliding into sentimentality.
>
> —*Liz Heron*

There is almost a surfeit of episodic rough and tumble, classroom antics, thieving and pervasive bullying. These ring true enough, and what is funniest is what is most recognisable, but only much later is the comedy subdued and childhood disquietingly established as a narrative of conundrums. It is not just the world out there on the TV news that is perplexing, but the unpredictability and mysteriousness of adults, the contradiction between the tyranny of boyhood, with all its macho cruelties, and the little boy's neediness for friendship and the love of siblings and parents. *Paddy Clarke Ha Ha Ha* starts off as callous comedy and ends up making painful reading, without once sliding into sentimentality.

Liz Heron, in a review of "Paddy Clarke Ha Ha Ha," in The Times Educational Supplement, No. 4018, July 2, 1993, p. 18.

Diane Turbide   (essay date 30 August 1993)

[*In the excerpt below, Turbide provides a brief overview of Doyle's career and discusses the author's depiction of working-class Ireland in* Paddy Clarke Ha Ha Ha.]

The second of four children of a printer and a homemaker,

Doyle has created a literary landmark with his fictional Barrytown, a working-class area of his native Dublin. His first three novels, known as the *Barrytown Trilogy,* centred on the Rabbittes, a family of eight whose lives are a mixture of high comedy, depressing poverty and domestic chaos. The first, *The Commitments* (1987), is the raucous story of a group of fractious, foul-mouthed teenagers who form a "Dublin Soul" band that performs black Motown music. A movie version, with a screenplay by Doyle and directed by American Alan Parker, became one of the surprise hits of 1991.

The saga continues with *The Snapper,* a grimly hilarious account of unmarried Sharon Rabbitte's unexpected pregnancy. The film version, directed by Britain's Stephen Frears, will be a gala presentation at Toronto's Festival of Festivals next month. Doyle also recently completed the screen-play for his 1991 novel *The Van,* which was short-listed for Britain's Booker Prize, and will co-produce the movie version.

It has been a heady six years since Doyle and a friend formed a company called King Farouk to publish *The Commitments* (they dissolved it the next year, when a British publisher picked up the book). "I still find it hard to believe that there are Japanese and Czech versions of *The Snapper,*" Doyle mused. "I don't actually know anyone who reads Japanese well enough to know if it's a good translation."

Any translator would have a daunting job with Doyle's work. Written almost entirely in dialogue, the books are full of hilarious slang, colloquialisms, vulgarisms and cursing that is so vibrant and charged that it is almost musical. Expressions like "f—in' eejit," "shite," "yeh bollix" and "ridin' " (for sexual intercourse) turn up on almost every page. But, in fact, the foul language is so eloquently precise that it can be regarded as highly refined. And it does not disguise the affection among the Rabbittes. Despite the unemployment, poverty, alcohol abuse and limited social mobility that beleaguer them, they embody their own brand of family values.

Paddy Clarke Ha Ha Ha is also set in Barrytown, but it departs radically in style and tone from his previous works. Told from the point of view of 10-year-old Paddy, it depicts his daily life as a round of mock and real fights, school lessons, garbled religious musings, athletic games and thoughts about new ways to torment his younger brother, Sinbad. Underlying the whimsy is the increasing tension between his mother and father, which gives the novel a melancholy flavor as it moves towards its sad but inevitable conclusion. While the book is not autobiographical, its emotional inspiration, Doyle says, came from the birth of Rory, 2½, the first of his two sons with his wife, Belinda. "It just opened up the floodgates of my own past," he explained. And referring to the book's strong sense of place, he said, "It's not my life, but it's my geography."

In the past, Doyle's unvarnished portrayal of working-class Ireland has garnered as much censure as praise in his native country. "I've been criticized for the bad language in my books—that I've given a bad image of the country," said Doyle. "There's always a subtle pressure to present a good image, and it's always somebody else's definition of what is good." The author's own view is that his job is simply to describe things and people as they really are. And in Doyle's world, the lives are tough, the language is rough—and beauty and tenderness survive amid the bleakness. As Jimmy Rabbitte would say: "Fair play to 'im."

> *Diane Turbide, "Dublin Soul," in* Maclean's *Magazine, Vol. 106, No. 35, August 30, 1993, p. 50.*

Nicci Gerrard   (essay date 31 October 1993)

[*In the excerpt below, Gerrard offers praises for* Paddy Clarke Ha Ha Ha.]

Ha Ha Ha! So it's all over for another year. No one can be cross that Roddy Doyle's beguiling novel about growing up won this year's Booker. Narrated by the Paddy Clarke of the title, it's quick and funny and sad: bristling with dialogue and not a word out of place; eager and cynical as only the tumbling mind of a ten-year-old boy can be.

Paddy Clarke Ha Ha Ha is a wonderful portrayal of pre-adolescence. Paddy and his mates spend their days strutting and bragging and internally cowering; they set themselves tests of daring, beat each other up, mock each other's sorest secrets (a dead mother, a small penis, a wet bed), pretend to be adult. Scabs, farts and shit fill their conversation. Tears must never be seen. Cigarettes must be smoked with ease. Babies are silly, so are hugs, and love is a dirty word—though in the dark nights Paddy listens to his parents fighting and longs for the tenderness of safety. One is left with a sense of melancholy fondness. Childhood is a dark place in this bright book, and laughter not so funny.

> *Nicci Gerrard, "A Useful Little Prize," in* The Observer, *October 31, 1993, p. 18.*

Paul Gray   (review date 6 December 1993)

[*In the following review, Gray compares* Paddy Clarke Ha Ha Ha *to James Joyce's* A Portrait of the Artist as a Young Man *(1916), faulting Doyle's work for its lack of plot and reliance on anecdotes.*]

James Joyce's *A Portrait of the Artist as a Young Man* famously begins, "Once upon a time and a very good time it was there was a moocow coming down along the road . . . " Roddy Doyle's *Paddy Clarke Ha Ha Ha* opens this way: "We were coming down our road." The echo sounds intentional, as if Doyle, with fine Irish fatalism, knows that all books about Dublin's seedy, seething street life carry the curse of invidious comparison with the works of the master. Why not invoke it at the top and then get on with the story?

This maneuver may be unduly superstitious, particularly since Doyle, 35, has been thriving in Joyce's shadow. His first three novels earned impressive reviews and sales, and two of them—***The Commitments*** and ***The Snapper***—have received successful screen adaptations. And in October, ***Paddy Clarke Ha Ha Ha*** won the Booker Prize, Britain's most highly trumpeted literary award. Thanks to the publicity attendant upon the Booker, U.S. readers get the chance to buy Doyle's fourth novel now instead of next April, when it was originally scheduled to cross the Atlantic.

Some people, inevitably, will wonder what the Booker judges could possibly have been thinking. For ***Paddy Clarke,*** while intermittently funny, fresh and affecting, is ultimately frustrating. Its hero serves as its narrator, a 10-year-old boy trying, with his gang of schoolmates and other pals, to wreak mischief in their Dublin neighborhood, circa the mid-1960s. Graffiti, whether spray-painted or gouged in wet cement, constitute a major offensive strategy. Another is invading forbidden turf, such as walled-off backyards, where the prospect of a pair of ladies' knickers on a clothesline drives the lads into a frenzy of guilty glee.

Much energy goes into plans for annoying their schoolmasters. The boys make noises when supervisory backs are turned. At the Friday movie showings, a popular game is projecting hand images onto the screen. "That was the easy part," Paddy notes. "The hard bit was getting back to your seat before they turned the lights back on. Everyone would try to stop you, to keep you trapped in the aisle."

Although he has a photograph of Geronimo, "the last of the renegade Apaches," on his bedroom wall and likes to think of himself as a renegade too, Paddy piously believes the conventional wisdom shared by his friends: "When you were doing a funny face or pretending you had a stammer and the wind changed or someone thumped your back you stayed that way forever." And juvenile humor naturally appeals to him: "Did you hear about the leper cowboy? He threw his leg over his horse."

Unfortunately, after 50 or 60 pages of this, the realization dawns that anecdotes and strung-together incidents are all the novel offers in the way of plot. Doyle's impersonation of young Paddy may be too accurate, prompting readers to recall that history is not replete with examples of successful 10-year-old novelists. Joyce's *Portrait* takes its hero through adolescence; Paddy's self-portrait remains stuck somewhere past the moocow stage.

Paul Gray, "Making Mischief in Dublin," in
Time, *New York, Vol. 142, No. 24, December 6, 1993, p. 82.*

John Gallagher   (review date 12 December 1993)

[In the review below, Gallagher praises Doyle's use of comedy, sorrow, and irony in Paddy Clarke Ha Ha Ha.*]*

Like childhood itself, Roddy Doyle's novel of Irish schoolboys [***Paddy Clarke Ha Ha Ha***], begins lightheartedly but grows ever more serious.

Doyle's first novel, ***The Commitments,*** became a hit movie a couple of years ago, but few Americans read the slangy Dublin novel itself. Two more novels won acclaim in Ireland and Britain for the Dublin-born writer but little notice on this side of the Atlantic.

But when Doyle recently received the Booker Prize—Britain's equivalent to the Pulitzer Prize—for ***Paddy Clarke Ha Ha Ha,*** he seemed destined to win many more American readers.

And he should. From a humorous beginning, ***Paddy Clarke Ha Ha Ha*** matures into an unforgettable portrait of troubled youth.

Paddy, a high-spirited 10-year-old, narrates his story; or, more accurately, he blurts it out in a child's breathless stream of consciousness. Doyle's loose, slangy style may put off some readers; he uses no chapter divisions, and sets off dialogue with dashes instead of quotation marks. But this book is worth the effort.

At first Paddy is any precocious boy, one who happens to live on the outskirts of Dublin in the 1960s. He plays cowboys but thinks kissing is stupid. He hates his little brother. He and his best friend, Kevin, start tiny fires in vacant fields near his house. He idolizes his soccer heros.

On the telly, he and his family watch American shows like "The Virginian" and "Daniel Boone," and they wonder at the distant conflict in Vietnam. In school, Paddy plays boyish pranks, while adults try to teach the boys a smattering of Gaelic.

But there's a disturbing note in this life, and it's the casual cruelty of Paddy and his mates. At first it's just boyish, if rough, bullying of smaller boys, especially Paddy's brother. But this theme of undeserved suffering will swell to much more tragic import.

Even in those cruel moments, though, Doyle celebrates life. Richly comic, the book doesn't soften or glamorize the years of childhood. Ten-year-old boys are often more monster than angel, and Paddy and his friends are true to their animal spirits.

But Paddy—and the reader—gradually hear more clearly the ominous sounds swelling in the background. The bickering of his parents comes to sound less like occasional spats to Paddy, more like rounds of a long-running bout.

Paddy, with the innocence and ignorance of childhood, blames himself for his parents' unhappiness. Even when his father slaps his mother and storms out of the house, to return drunk, Paddy feels that he ought to be doing more to make his folks whole again.

He can do nothing, of course. And by the end of the novel, Paddy had taken the first steps from innocent youth toward sullen adolescence.

Indeed, the irony of the title remains hidden until the very end. And when we finally do perceive its meaning, we see that the only laughter in Paddy's life hereafter is the sort that hides the tears.

John Gallagher, "Tale of Troubled Irish Lad Lures American Audience," in Detroit Free Press, *Sec. G, December 12, 1993, p. 7.*

Christopher Lehmann-Haupt (review date 13 December 1993)

[*Lehmann-Haupt has served as chief daily book reviewer for the* New York Times *since 1969. In the review below, he provides an overview of* Paddy Clarke Ha Ha Ha *and discusses the title character's psychological development.*]

"We were coming down our road. Kevin stopped at a gate and bashed it with his stick. It was Missis Quigley's gate; she was always looking out the window but she never did anything." So begins *Paddy Clarke Ha Ha Ha,* the fourth novel by the Irish writer Roddy Doyle, whose previous books include *The Commitments, The Snapper* and *The Van,* together known as Mr. Doyle's *Barrytown Trilogy.*

And so, with echoes of [James] Joyce's *Portrait of the Artist as a Young Man* ("there was a moocow coming down along the road"), the reader enters the mind of 10-year-old Patrick Clarke. Paddy is a bright, inquisitive child who is trying to negotiate a world that he sees with the utmost clarity and comprehends almost nothing about.

Paddy's world is divided into extremes of danger and safety, which attract him equally. On warm, sunny days, he, his pals and his younger brother, Francis (nicknamed Sinbad) enjoy poking the tar bubbles in the road that runs through Barrytown: "You burst the bubble and the clean soft tar was under there; the top was gone off the bubble— it was a volcano. Pebbles went in; they died screaming.

"No no, please—! —don't—! Aaaaaaaahaaah——"

Paddy is the bravest at exploring the open underground pipes of a new sewerage system:

> Running through the pipe was the most frightening brilliant thing I'd ever done. . . . You judged by the sound of your breath and feet— you could tell when you were swerving up the side of the pipe—until the dot of light at the end that got bigger and brighter, out the end of the pipe, roaring into the light, hands up, the winner.

Yet Paddy seeks security:

> Under the table was a fort. . . . I'd sit in there for hours. . . . I fell asleep in there; I used to. It was always cool in there, never cold, and warm when I wanted it to be. The lino was nice on my face. The air wasn't alive like outside, beyond the table; it was safe. It had a smell I liked.

And: "My hot water bottle was red, Manchester United's color. Sinbad's was green. I loved the smell off the bottle. I put hot water in it and emptied it and smelled it; I put my nose to the hole, nearly in it. Lovely."

Paddy's daily rounds of school and playtime are frightening tests of possibility, endurance and pain. In a horrifying passage he describes torturing his little brother.

> Sinbad's lips had disappeared because he was pressing them shut so hard; we couldn't get his mouth open. Kevin pressed the fuel capsule against his mouth but it wouldn't go in. I pinched Sinbad's arm; no good. This was terrible; in front of the others, I couldn't sort out my

little brother. I got the hair above his ear and pulled it up; I lifted him: I just wanted to hurt him. His eyes were closed now as well but the tears were getting out. I held his nose. He gasped and Kevin shoved the capsule halfway into his mouth. Then Liam lit it with the match!

> We said we'd get Liam to light it, me and Kevin, just in case we got caught.

> It went like a dragon.

Is this the act of psychopaths? You have to wonder, even though Paddy is capable of committing clumsily loving acts toward his brother as well as ones of extreme cruelty. What you eventually conclude is that Paddy is reacting to some pressure in his life of which he is not entirely aware. Perhaps this comes from the children in the public housing projects who increasingly encroach on Paddy's world. Perhaps it is the international unrest of the late 1960's that prompts one local tabloid to announce in headlines that "World War Three Looms Near." Or perhaps it is something going on in Paddy's home.

Mr. Doyle's novel, which won the 1993 Booker Prize in England, evokes the details of a child's everyday life with unusual intelligence and humor. Here is Paddy being taught by his father to ride a bike he has got for Christmas: "He held the back. He said nothing. I pedaled. We went down the garden. I went faster. I stayed up; he was still holding. I looked back. He wasn't there. I fell over. But I'd done it; I'd gone a bit without him. I could do it. I didn't need him now. I didn't want him."

And here is Paddy watching his mother do the laundry.

> The sheets were shiny with huge wet bubbles and my ma put a corner up to the mangle and turned the handle and the sheet rose out of the water like a whale being caught. The water ran down the sheet and the bubbles were crushed as the sheet was pulled through the rolls and came out flat, looking like material again, the shininess all gone.

Eventually, despite how the randomness of Paddy's daily experiences mirrors the reality of childhood, the formlessness threatens to pall. Almost precisely at this point, whatever is unconsciously troubling Paddy at last reveals itself:

> It wasn't lots of little fights. It was one big one, rounds of the same fight. And it wouldn't stop after fifteen rounds like in boxing. It was like one of the matches from the olden days where they wore no gloves and they kept punching till one of them was knocked out or killed. Ma and Da had gone way past Round Fifteen; they'd been fighting for years—it made sense now—but the breaks between the rounds were getting shorter, that was the big difference. One of them would soon fall over.

With remarkable sensitivity, Mr. Doyle dramatizes the effects of this discord on Paddy's demeanor. He shows how trouble at home propels Paddy from the warm, familiar comforts of childhood into a cold, indifferent world where the laughter of the novel's title finally echoes hollowly.

Christopher Lehmann-Haupt, "A Window

Into the Mind of a 10-Year-Old Irish Boy," in The New York Times, *December 13, 1993, p. B2.*

Louise Glück
The Wild Iris

Award: Pulitzer Prize for Poetry

(Full name Louise Elisabeth Glück) Born in 1943, Glück is an American poet.

For further information about Glück's life and career, see *CLC*, Volumes 7, 22, and 44.

INTRODUCTION

In *The Wild Iris* Glück uses biblical and mythical allusions, extended metaphors, and introspective language to examine her ambivalence about religion, mortality, and faith. The poems in this collection are written from three distinct perspectives: those of God, the poet, and the flowers in a garden that the poet and her husband tend. Through a series of interwoven dramatic monologues, the poet engages in a dialogue with God, during which she challenges God's apparent mercilessness and detachment, while God attacks the self-indulging and self-pitying nature of humans. In one poem, for example, the poet laments: "You must see / it is useless to us, this silence that promotes belief." God later responds: "If you hate me so much / don't bother to give me / a name: do you need / one more slur / in your language?" The flowers similarly reproach the poet for needing to believe in a higher power and for failing to recognize the interconnectedness of all life-forms. In "Scilla," for example, the flowers chide: "Why do you look up? To hear / an echo like the voice / of god? You are all the same to us, / solitary, standing above us, planning / your silly lives: you go / where you are sent, like all things, / where the wind plants you." While some critics have faulted *The Wild Iris* for being too personal, cryptic, and pessimistic, most have praised the work's emotional and intellectual intensity and Glück's individualistic, daring, and honest approach to difficult themes. Noting the collection's unusual narrative structure, David Baker has stated: "[The] poems of *The Wild Iris* are representations of our hunger for what we have named God, nature, love, self. . . . After all, the flowers don't really speak in *The Wild Iris,* nor is God exactly peering at Louise Glück from behind the trees. Rather, these poems carry out a dramatization of the processes of birth and growth and of those habits of mind which must be exposed and conversed with in order to be better known."

PRINCIPAL WORKS

Firstborn (poetry) 1968
The House on Marshland (poetry) 1975
Teh (poetry) 1976
Descending Figure (poetry) 1980
The Triumph of Achilles (poetry) 1985
Ararat (poetry) 1990
The Wild Iris (poetry) 1992

CRITICISM

Publishers Weekly (review date 11 May 1992)

[*In the following review, the critic provides a positive assessment of* The Wild Iris.]

The award-winning author of *The Triumph of Achilles* looks here at relations between heaven and earth. More than half of the poems [in *The Wild Iris*] address an "unreachable father," or are spoken in a voice meant to be his: "Your souls should have been immense by now, / not what they are, / small talking things. . . . " This ambitious and original work consists of a series of "matins," "vespers," poems about flowers, and others about the seasons or times of day, carrying forward a dialogue between the human and divine. This is poetry of great beauty, where lamentation, doubt and praise show us a god who can blast or console, but who too often leaves us alone; Gluck, then, wishes to understand a world where peace "rushes through me, / . . . like bright light through the bare tree." Only rarely (in **"The Doorway,"** for example) does the writing fail. But when dialogue melds with lyricism, the result is splendid. In **"Violets"** the speaker tells her "dear / suffering master": "you / are no more lost / than we are, under / the hawthorn tree, the hawthorn holding / balanced trays of pearls." This important book has a powerful, muted strangeness.

A review of "The Wild Iris," in Publishers Weekly, *Vol. 239, No. 22, May 11, 1992, p. 58.*

Fred Muratori   (review date 15 May 1992)

[*In the review below, Muratori offers praise for* The Wild Iris.]

Glück's [*The Wild Iris*] presents a series of spare, somber lyrics on the predicament of mortality. Through the ostensible medium of prayer—many of the poems are titled either "Matins" or "Vespers"—she gives tongue to both voiceless creations (the short-lived snowdrops who say they are "afraid, yes, but among you again / crying yes risk joy / in the raw wind of the new world") and to Creator ("you are worth / one life, no more than that"), as well as to her own ambivalence toward a higher power ("In what contempt do you hold us / to believe only loss can impress / your power on us"). Though the poems glimmer more than gleam, repeated readings unveil subtle reversals and shadings, evoking the ghostly consciousness that has always invested Glück's best work.

Fred Muratori, in a review of "The Wild Iris," in Library Journal, *Vol. 117, No. 9, May 15, 1992, p. 96.*

Constance Hunting   (review date Summer 1992)

[*Below, Hunting discusses the language, allusions, and themes in* The Wild Iris.]

In her sixth collection of poems, [*The Wild Iris*] Louise Gluck speaks in the accents of the creation which is Creation. She attains pure tonality as she speaks not for but in the voices of natural phenomena, man in the term's generic sense, and God (or Creator). As person, she is absent; as poet she is, basically, everywhere, answering question with question, seeking, proposing, disposing. Her language is of the simplest and highest, gaining unusual beauty and authority. Yet so fresh is her vision that we seem to hear the words as for the first time. What could be simpler than the voice of **"Retreating Wind"**: "When I made you, I loved you. / Now I pity you," or the voice of the title poem which recapitulates the Resurrection: "Hear me out: that which you call death / I remember"? Further, these and the other voices resonate with unspoken allusions, Biblical, mythical, even lightly Miltonic and Keatsian. Each voice is individual; that of the morning glory (**"Ipomoea"**) could never be mistaken for that of blue squills (**"Scilla"**). Dimension is added by such titles as "Matins" and "Vespers," whose repetition hints at the mornings and evenings of Genesis. With the exception of one or two poems which do not fit seamlessly in, the book becomes not a mere collection but a fully unified work. Its combination of simplicity, daring, and thematic quality ensure *The Wild Iris* a place unique in current American poetry.

Constance Hunting, in a review of "The Wild Iris," in Small Press, *Vol. 10, No. 3, Summer, 1992, p. 54.*

An excerpt from "Trillium"

When I woke up I was in a forest. The dark seemed natural, the sky through the pine trees thick with many lights.

I knew nothing; I could do nothing but see.
And as I watched, all the lights of heaven
faded to make a single thing, a fire
burning through the cool firs.
Then it wasn't possible any longer
to stare at heaven and not be destroyed.

Louise Glück, in her The Wild Iris, *The Ecco Press, 1992.*

Phoebe Pettingell   (review date October 1992)

[*In the excerpt below, Pettingell discusses the principal themes in* The Wild Iris.]

In her previous five books, Louise Glück honed a spare, pessimistic, faintly mystical tone of voice. Its notes of lamentation rarely altered. Nevertheless, there was something compelling about its eerie, childlike timbre. Characteristically, Glück's poems probed the thin line between a desire to kick back at life's rottenness and the impulse to turn tail and retreat into immobility. "Birth, not death, is the hard loss," one of her earliest lines exclaimed, and that cry continued to reverberate through subsequent work. Sometimes the bleakness became numbing. Yet there were also tantalizing flashes of dialogue with an absent god, and a furtive sense of magic wonder directed toward nature.

These intimations have blossomed into *The Wild Iris.* The

entire book develops the conceit of a garden as it progresses from the first spring bulbs to push stalks through the newly thawed soil to fall's hardiest daylilies as they await the first frost. The poet has been told that

> depressives hate the spring, imbalance
> between the inner and outer world. I make
> another case—being depressed, yes, but in a
>   sense passionately
> attached to the living tree, my body actually
> curled in the split trunk, almost at peace in the
>   evening rain
> almost able to feel
> sap frothing and rising: Noah says this is
> an error of depressives, identifying
> with a tree, whereas the happy heart
> wanders the garden like a falling leaf, a figure for
> the part, not the whole.

It is true that Glück identifies with whole landscapes, sometimes, and readily takes upon herself the pain of others. In this book, she turns each flower into a persona to express a separate aspect of her emotional experience. Some give tongue to her depression. **"The Wild Iris"** complains that "it is terrible to survive / as consciousness / buried in the dark earth." In **"Red Poppy"** that flower, as it loses its petals after a single day's blooming, confesses, "I speak / because I am shattered." But other blossoms work through this reluctance to face life, and discover affirmation: "afraid, yes, but among you again / crying yes risk joy / in the raw wind of the new world."

This poetic universe of talking flowers recalls the *unheimlich* world of *Grimm's Fairy Tales,* where animals and inanimate objects converse with humans. In this primitive, enchanted landscape, Glück opens herself to communication with its creator. Many of the book's final poems report a dialogue between the poet and God. In **"Sunset,"** he chides:

> You have no faith in your own language.
> So you invest
> authority in signs
> you cannot read with any accuracy.
>
> And yet your voice reaches me always,
> And I answer constantly,
> my anger passing
> as winter passes. My tenderness
> should be apparent to you
> in the breeze of the summer evening
> and in the words that became
> your own response.

I take this as Glück's affirmation that her own poems represent a "response" to despair. Her eloquent denizens of a primal garden and their deity push back the pall of hopelessness to assure us that "creation has brought you great excitement." (pp. 114-15)

> *Phoebe Pettingell, in a review of "The Wild Iris," in* The Yale Review, *Vol. 80, No. 4, October, 1992, pp. 114-15.*

David Biespiel   (review date 22 November 1992)

[*Below, Biespiel examines Glück's treatment of pain and despair in* The Wild Iris.]

There are a few living poets whose new poems one always feels eager to read. Louise Gluck ranks at the top of the list. Her writing's emotional and rhetorical intensity are beyond dispute. Not once in six books has she wavered from a formal seriousness, an unhurried sense of control and a starkness of expression that, like a scalpel, slices the mist dwelling between hope and pain.

For most of her career, Gluck has been grappling with one problem: how to transform into beauty what she perceives to be a hostile world and, at the same time, remain honest to her own feelings of confusion and hostility towards it. Her verse reminds you of another poet whose great pain, and the formal feeling that came of that pain, reinvented American poetry a century ago: Emily Dickinson. It's evident now that Louise Gluck is the heir to Dickinson's lyric empire of despair and sensation. Plainly said, if you read any new book of poems before the year is out, read **The Wild Iris**.

The Wild Iris challenges the bulk of recent American poetry that has extolled the virtues of the quotidian and of self-revelation—the very subjects of Glück's own previous work. But here Glück asks: "Is it enough / only to look inward?" Or mustn't poetry also "force clarity" upon eternity and the whole of existence? In its visionary manner, *The Wild Iris* affirms the latter.

—*David Biespiel*

A book-length conversation in three voices, **The Wild Iris** is a cross between the Book of Job and the Davidic Psalms. The voices, which appear in a series of dramatic monologues, are those of the poet, the Creator, and the summer garden Gluck and her husband tend throughout the book's time frame. Resembling Dante's *Divine Comedy,* the book opens with the poet both at the "end of my suffering" and in the "center of my life." Immediately, she asserts that speech, inherently, is "full of grief." To speak, she tells us, is to be sorrowful; and she blames the silent Creator, whom she addresses as the "Unreachable father."

In a series of poems entitled "Matins," she challenges God's existence: "You must see / it is useless to us, this silence that promotes belief." "To be one thing," she cries in **"Scilla,"** is to be "next to nothing." But the creator pities her, retorting through the witchgrass's voice:

> If you hate me so much
> don't bother to give me
> a name: do you need

one more slur
in your language?

And so it goes, poem after poem, until some understanding is reached. It's then that a lonely Creator can, with subtle irony, address the poet as "my poor inspired / creation," and the poet can be more conciliating in ["**Parousia**"] addressing the Creator as "Love of my life."

This book challenges the bulk of recent American poetry that has extolled the virtues of the quotidian and of self-revelation—the very subjects of Gluck's own previous work. But here Gluck asks: "Is it enough / only to look inward?" Or mustn't poetry also "force clarity" upon eternity and the whole of existence? In its visionary manner, **The Wild Iris** affirms the latter.

> *David Biespiel, in a review of "The Wild Iris,"*
> *in* Book World—The Washington Post, *No-*
> *vember 22, 1992, p. 8.*

Elizabeth Lund   (review date 7 January 1993)

[*In the following excerpt, Lund discusses the theme of religion in* The Wild Iris *and calls the work a turning point in Glück's career.*]

Louise Glück's **The Wild Iris** tries to answer the questions "Who am I?" and "What is the nature of God?" Most of the poems use a flower as both metaphor and indirect subject, yet the collection is more like a record of the speaker's prayers. Readers unfamiliar with Glück's crisp, sparse language may have difficulty finding their way into these poems.

The first few pages do not provide enough of a narrative, and it would be easy to conclude that the writer's vision is too personal and cryptic for others to share. Glück begins her first poem, **"The Wild Iris,"** with the assertion that, "At the end of my suffering / there was a door." It's a fascinating lead, yet the second stanza reads, "Hear me out: that which you call death / I remember." Such assertions are hard for readers to grasp and are a risky move at the beginning of a book.

What's interesting about **The Wild Iris** is the way Glück tries to define the nature of God. As she states in the [sequence "Matins"] " . . . I cannot love / what I can't conceive, and you disclose / virtually nothing. . . . " At times the reader may feel that the poet is spiritually immature or is missing obvious answers, but it is rewarding to see her work out of one mindset where she refers to God as "unreachable father" and into another where she is grateful because " . . . this one summer we have entered eternity."

The Wild Iris is indeed a turning point for its author, a woman known for both her thematic obsessions and her distinctive use of language. Perhaps more important, the book tackles questions that need to be addressed both in the artistic community and in society at large.

Glück's conclusion, at least in regard to the frailties of the physical world and the garden she cultivates with her husband, is found in her poem **"The White Lilies"**:

Hush, beloved. It doesn't matter to me
how many summers I live to return:
this one summer we have entered eternity.

I felt your two hands bury me to release its
splendor.

> *Elizabeth Lund, "Images of Now and Then in*
> *Poetry's Mirror," in* The Christian Science
> Monitor, *January 7, 1993, p. 14.*

Daniel McGuiness   (review date Spring 1993)

[*In the following review, McGuiness praises the honest and sincere tone in* The Wild Iris.]

David Letterman summarized the Madonna phenomenon recently by turning to the camera that is his life and saying, in mock astonishment, "You know, I think she wants to shock us." Despite something resonant in such anecdotes, one looks in vain in each of Glück's six books for the self-conscious pose, the poet voguing for the camera, the artist peering from inside this creation, just for a second, to remind us of her manipulation. This may be because this is a seamless career, each swerve and veer not calculated by her but calculated for her by whoever, near the third millennium, will write the definitive study of poetry in America near the second millennium. Whether you like it or not, Louise Glück will be in that book.

So, for the record: [**The Wild Iris**] is a short book. The scene and players: a garden, a god. The arrangement: a growing season from spring to winter, the flowers blooming as their hour strikes, morning to night, the family tending their acres, and eternity, showing itself in the movement of air across ground that we call weather. Eighteen poems titled with the names of flowers; the flowers speak in character. Twenty-one poems, in the book's first half called "Matins," in the second half called "Vespers," in which the gardener prays in character. Fifteen poems, with various, mostly meteorological, titles, in which the overarching presence responds. Everybody seems grumpy: the flowers because the humans aren't listening, aren't paying enough attention to their beauty and their anagogic lessons; the gardener because the overarching presence isn't listening, isn't moved by her poems, by her pleas so pleasingly presented; the overarching presence because he or she is tired of listening, tired of the incessant ego of his creation: "I gathered you together; / I can erase you / as though you were a draft to be thrown away / an exercise / / because I've finished you, vision / of deepest mourning." Not gorgeous. Not hermetic. Ironic. Anger muted. Almost funny. And it is all so carefully constructed we could take it for an epic (if epics can be lyrics or lyrics epical) like Dante's or Derek Walcott's (if epics can eschew the macho or the macho epics).

In **Ararat** Louise Glück tried on other voices, abandoned the vatic stance, surprised us all. She's done it again. (pp. 311-12)

> *Daniel McGuiness, in a review of "The Wild*
> *Iris," in* The Antioch Review, *Vol. 51, No. 2,*
> *Spring, 1993, pp. 311-12.*

Judith Kitchen   (review date Spring 1993)

[*In the excerpt below, Kitchen offers a favorable assessment of* The Wild Iris, *praising Glück's focus on nature, the human condition, and religion.*]

[Louise Glück's **The Wild Iris** is an] innovative, demanding new work by one of our most important poets. **The Wild Iris** returns to the distanced voice of Glück's early poetry—and to its restrained, meticulous observation of the natural world—but this volume is not recapitulation. It is a foray into new territory, from which emerges a personal mythology giving rise, in turn, to theology.

The Wild Iris weaves three essential voices. The first is the singular, solitary cry of the supplicant. Sometimes devotional, sometimes chaste, sometimes ecstatic, this voice is found in the seven poems entitled "Matins" and the ten called "Vespers"—all of which present the human condition. These poems contain both praise and query, comprising a one-sided debate with the concept of god. The second voice is that of the earthly garden—of flowers both tended and wild, the anthropomorphized world speaking as from within some innate wisdom. The third voice is a dispassionate divinity as he declares himself, either as a presence in the natural world or as an absence. Together, these fifty-four poems form a single braid; the reader senses both the individual strand and the combined strength.

The poems of **The Wild Iris** are intellectual, wholly realized within the rational mind, and yet they depend not only on an intimate knowledge of nature but also on a respect for (and passionate love of) the natural world. In narrative time, the book's duration is from early spring through early fall—a garden's visible cycle. By giving the garden a voice, Glück forces us to see ourselves as the plants might see us—silly, foolish creatures obsessed with our mortality. Glück does not really describe the plants (description alone being of no interest to her); she speaks from *inside* the flowers, giving each a voice and unearthing new knowledge of human behavior by examining the particularities of each variety, whether it is the lamium's predisposition toward shade ("living things don't all require / light in the same degree") or the snowdrop's surprising revival ("I didn't expect / to waken again, to feel / in damp earth my body / able to respond again . . . "). The garden asks of us the most demanding questions, as in **"Field Flowers"**:

> Is it enough
> only to look inward? Contempt
> for humanity is one thing, but why
> disdain the expansive
> field, your gaze rising over the clear heads
> of the wild buttercups into what? Your poor
> idea of heaven: absence
> of change. Better than earth? How
> would you know, who are neither
> here nor there, standing in our midst?

The garden recognizes a collective experience. In contrast, the human voice here is isolated, almost monastic, tinged with loneliness. It searches for more than the immortality of words: for an order in the silence, a way to put the solitary life into a larger perspective. The morning prayers—the "Matins" poems—are optimistic in the sense that they are still asking devout questions. The "Vespers" are darker, more ready (in the absence of a spiritual sign) to discern a message in the natural world. Thus they are more likely to shock with their unexpected insight. For example, by following the implications of her own argument, Glück is able to speak of human responsibilities *and* to discover something of the nature of eternity:

> You who do not discriminate
> between the dead and the living, who are, in consequence,
> immune to foreshadowing, you may not know
> how much terror we bear, the spotted leaf,
> the red leaves of the maple falling
> even in August . . .

Human beings bear a double burden. We can see the red leaves and know winter will follow; we *are* the red leaves which will drop from the branches. And god—whoever or whatever—does not differentiate between *knowing* and *being*.

The Wild Iris divides neatly into "morning" and "evening" sections, folding on the hinge of two central poems which must be seen as representing yet another (a fourth) voice—that of the poet, wholly conscious of herself in language, speaking of her ordinary life: in **"Heaven and Earth"** there is a fully realized present-tense moment while she watches her husband in the garden at sunset; in **"The Doorway"** she looks to the past, recognizing in herself the wish to recover the moment before her body flowered into the betrayal of womanhood, "the epoch of mastery / / before the appearance of the gift, / before possession." Because the reader has become accustomed to the particular tones and nuances of the three predominant strains, this intrusion comes as a surprise. On careful examination, though, each half contains one other poem (**"Love in Moonlight"** and **"Presque Isle"**) also in this private, secular voice. In addition, there are occasional external interruptions that provide a balanced, healthy skepticism—and an ability to live comfortably in the world. In **"Song,"** this received wisdom provides an ironic counterpoint to the poet's visionary state: "But John / objects, he thinks / if this were not a poem but / an actual garden, then / the red rose would be / required to resemble / nothing else . . . "

This honesty finds its more detached counterpart in the "deity" poems. Steeped in pertinent detail, and with such titles as **"Clear Morning," "End of Winter," "Retreating Wind," "End of Summer," "Early Darkness,"** and **"September Twilight,"** these poems fix chronological time even while moving toward abstract concepts. As they accumulate, the godhead emerges as a bit annoyed at his own creation. "You were not intended / to be unique," he announces in **"Midsummer,"** and then refers to "your incidental souls / fixed like telescopes on some / enlargement of yourselves.' Having given us life and tragedy and the means to turn it into story, he is tired of our "chaos." We are flawed "distractions." He retreats. In **"September Twilight"** (the final poem of this sequence), he declares his experiment complete—we have become his "vision of deepest mourning."

This is a book that should be read at one sitting. The

voices combine to create an intense religious experience—even if the god proves to be nonexistent. The effect is one of dazzling austerity, as in the final lines of **"End of Summer"**:

> If you would open your eyes
> you would see me, you would see
> the emptiness of heaven
> mirrored on earth, the fields
> vacant again, lifeless, covered with snow—
> then white light
> no longer disguised as matter.

It is a privilege to watch as a poet breaks new ground. In *The Wild Iris,* Louise Glück has applied a stringent mind to nature in order to understand not only the self but the definition of faith and/or acceptance. (The acceptance, though, is a dark one: we are given one brief life.) Like [Robert] Frost, Glück looks for the moment she will see *beyond* and *through.* The poems are simultaneously passionate and remote, as though written with the white heat of a distant star. Their visionary mode may even provide an entry into the snowy fields. (pp. 156-59)

> *Judith Kitchen, "The Woods Around It," in* The Georgia Review, *Vol. XLVII, No. 1, Spring, 1993, pp. 145-59.*

David Mason   (review date Spring 1993)

[In the following excerpt, Mason compares The Wild Iris *to Glück's previous poetry collection,* Ararat.]

Louise Glück's two most recent collections are a study in contrasts. Her 1990 book, *Ararat,* now out in paperback, is to my mind a disaster, so dull and solipsistic that, reading it, I felt as though I had been cornered at a party by a bore moaning interminably about her rotten family. When she writes "Long ago, I was wounded"—a line that frames the book—I want to say, "Get over it, for crying out loud! Read some Roger Fanning! At least when families fail him he can look at lizards and roadside cafes!" This is Glück's idea of profundity: "I'll tell you something: every day / people are dying." In an earlier poem she writes, "I was born to a vocation: / to bear witness / to the great mysteries." Well, human psychology is a great mystery, but Glück's problems don't amount to a hill of beans.

After *Ararat* I dreaded reading Glück's latest, *The Wild Iris,* but it's a far better book, perhaps her best. These poems are Rilkean meditations on the things of this world, especially those found in a garden, and on God. More often than not the focus is on large issues and the vision is more generous than in her earlier books. Here, for example, is a fine poem called **"Field Flowers"**:

> What are you saying? That you want
> eternal life? Are your thoughts really
> as compelling as all that? Certainly
> you don't look at us, don't listen to us,
> on your skin
> stain of sun, dust
> of yellow buttercups: I'm talking
> to you, you staring through
> bars of high grass shaking

> your little rattle—O
> the soul! the soul! Is it enough
> only to look inward? Contempt
> for humanity is one thing, but why
> disdain the expansive
> field, your gaze rising over the clear heads
> of the wild buttercups into what? Your poor
> idea of heaven: absence
> of change. Better than earth? How
> would you know, who are neither
> here nor there, standing in our midst?

It's the perfect indictment of everything she wrote in *Ararat.*

The Wild Iris is not by any means a perfect collection. Glück's Rilkean posture, reinforced by the publishers when they report that she wrote the book "during a ten-week period in the summer of 1991," sometimes seems too obvious, and there are bad poems like **"Love in Moonlight"** side by side with good ones like **"The Hawthorn Tree."** Nevertheless, it signals a refreshing change in a poet who desperately needed a new direction. (pp. 226-27)

> *David Mason, in a review of "The Wild Iris," in* The Hudson Review, *Vol. XLVI, No. 1, Spring, 1993, pp. 226-27.*

An excerpt from "September Twilight"

> You come and go, every one of you
> flawed in some way,
> in some way compromised: you are worth
> one life, no more than that.

> I gathered you together;
> I can erase you
> as though you were a draft to be thrown away,

> an exercise

> because I've finished you, vision
> of deepest mourning.

Louise Glück, in her The Wild Iris, *The Ecco Press, 1992.*

Henry Taylor   (review date May 1993)

[In the following excerpt, Taylor praises The Wild Iris's *ambitious themes but faults the work's didactic tone.]*

Readers will vary in their readiness to accept the premise of Louise Glück's sixth collection, [*The Wild Iris*], a sequence in which many voices address profound questions arising from a recognition of earthly beauty and human mortality. The setting is a garden. In poems mostly titled either "Matins" or "Vespers," a person not easily distinguishable from the poet asks divinity to reveal itself. (Seven poems are titled "Matins," and ten are titled "Vespers." This may discourage anthologists, but the device is not ineffective as the sequence establishes itself.) In poems mostly titled by the names of plants, other voices address existence and divinity. On the face of it, the poems are in the voices of the plants, but it is somehow unfair to leave it at that: could a poet of Glück's gifts truly expect us to suspend our disbelief so far above the rocks? Say rather that the device is a trope, that the poet's voice imagines assorted vegetable conditions. Finally, in poems mostly titled with phrases establishing seasons or times of day, there come some answers to some of the questions, in a voice that is to be taken as that of the divine.

It is noteworthy when a poet of Glück's accomplishments undertakes a project of such ambition, so fraught with obvious chances to appear foolish or pretentious. Even if it should prove unsuccessful, the effort can hardly be ignored; this is a bid for major achievement, and a number of extravagant claims have already been made for it. I am grateful for several poems in this book, and grateful, too, that I can admire them without feeling obliged to claim that Glück is the reincarnation of Emily Dickinson.

The poems in the voice of the poet, or someone who shares some facts of her life, are the least evidently strained, and out of their questions and observations come occasional triumphs of perception, as at the end of the second "Matins":

> We never thought of you
> whom we were learning to worship.
> We merely knew it wasn't human nature to love
> only what returns love.

Furthermore, most of the speaker's poems are capacious enough to include unusually direct treatment of abstraction. The sixth "Matins" begins concretely:

> What is my heart to you
> that you must break it over and over
> like a plantsman testing
> his new species? Practice
> on something else.

The prayer proceeds to compare the speaker's isolated condition with that of the roses and aphids; the infested rose is not separated from the healthy ones, and the aphids are free to go from one to another. The ending is a moving statement of the central problem:

> Father,
> as agent of my solitude, alleviate
> at least my guilt; lift
> the stigma of isolation, unless
> it is your plan to make me
> sound forever again, as I was
> sound and whole in my mistaken childhood,
> or if not then, under the light weight
> of my mother's heart, or if not then,
> in dream, first
> being that would never die.

The book opens, however, with the title poem, which very gradually reveals its hovering, simultaneous status as the voice of a wild iris and the voice of the poet speaking through a wild iris. The voice is self-conscious and portentous from the outset:

> At the end of my suffering
> there was a door.
>
> Hear me out: that which you call death
> I remember.

> Overhead, noises, branches of the pine shifting.
> Then nothing. The weak sun
> flickered over the dry surface.

The effect, unfortunately, is similar to that of an ambitious and largely successful high-school production of a Greek tragedy: through elaborate papier-mâché masks, on which talented students have lavished considerable artistic skill, come the words of a nearly adequate public-domain translation, in well-rehearsed but finally uncomprehending voices. In such a context a minor slip-up is dangerously obtrusive. **"Love in Moonlight"** plunges immediately into an awkwardness of pronoun reference: "Sometimes a man or woman forces his despair / on another person. . . ." And even in a setting, tone, and atmosphere so remote from the everyday world of the newspapers, **"The Red Poppy"** cannot but evoke Dan Quayle; it begins, "The great thing / is not having / a mind."

The poems spoken by the divinity sometimes transcend theatrical beginnings, though almost all of them are heavy with bald statements of wisdom. **"Retreating Wind"** starts with portentous flatness: "When I made you, I loved you. / Now I pity you." It goes on, however, to distinguish between the cyclical lives of many plants, and the single lives of humans:

> your lives are the bird's flight
> which begins and ends in stillness—
> which *begins* and *ends,* in form echoing
> this arc from the white birch
> to the apple tree.

That is not only convincing, it is consoling: the echo of an earthly loveliness takes on qualities suggestive of the hereafter, even as the statement denies the possibility.

Very rarely, the poems display mild humor to good effect, deepening and enriching the portrayal of spiritual search. The second "Vespers" poem is not lighthearted, but the speaker's intelligent humanity comes through partly as a result of a few seconds of exasperation:

> I must report
> failure in my assignment, principally
> regarding the tomato plants.
> I think I should not be encouraged to grow
> tomatoes. Or, if I am, you should withhold
> the heavy rains, the cold nights that come
> so often here, while other regions get
> twelve weeks of summer.

Throughout the book, this seeker's voice is generally plausible and emotionally satisfying. If the other voices had been developed with a more delicate touch, this book would have been more important, and less self-important. (pp. 96-99)

> *Henry Taylor, "Easy Listening (Part II)," in* Poetry, *Vol. CLXII, No. 2, May, 1993, pp. 96-110.*

Elisabeth Frost   (review date May 1993)

[*In the following excerpt, Frost provides a mixed assessment of* The Wild Iris, *discussing Glück's use of voice and focus on the human condition.*]

Louise Glück's *The Wild Iris* begins with a voice seemingly beyond death: "At the end of my suffering / there was a door. / Hear me out: that which you call death / I remember." The voice is that of the wild iris, in the title poem to the collection. It initiates the theme of human mortality, always in opposition to seasonal death and resurrection, that gives the volume its shape. . . . *The Wild Iris* needs to be read as a whole, for it moves through the seasons, and from dawn to evening, with all the elegance and inevitability of a Renaissance sonnet. The journey along the way, however, records a maddening absence of revelation depicting a tragic world in which the search for union is futile, even as the act of speech is inevitable. The wound of existence can never be healed, and yet all life yearns to speak. As **"The Red Poppy"** attests to its human observers, "I am speaking now / the way you do. I speak / because I am shattered."

Glück's short, intense lyrics transcribe three types of voice: those of the humans at work in the garden (often in the form of prayers—"Matins" and "Vespers"), those of other natural objects (**"Trillium," "Violets," "Witchgrass"**) and that of the distant deity regarding his creation. Adopting the traditional pronoun, Glück represents the creator as male. This "unreachable father" bears some likeness to the Old Testament God who rules by law, not love. He is frequently mystified and disappointed by those below:

> Do you suppose I care
> if you speak to one another?
> But I mean you to know
> I expected better of two creatures
> who were given minds . . .

Beyond anger and outrage, he cultivates sheer force. **"Clear Morning"** opens with an assertion of power: "I've watched you long enough, / I can speak to you any way I like—." And the poem closes with a brutal resolution:

> I cannot go on
> restricting myself to images
>
> because you think it is your right
> to dispute my meaning:
>
> I am prepared now to force
> clarity upon you.

"Images," representations that the human mind can understand, seem paltry to the higher power of the creator. This gap—this inability to talk the same language—is the tragedy *The Wild Iris* plays out.

For all Glück's speakers, ancient wounds underlie facades of bravura and accusation. The God of **"Early Darkness"** argues that suffering is the human condition, one that precedes even sin: "You are not suffering because you touched each other / but because you were born, / because you required life / separate from me." Did we ask to be born, to be separate? And is our "rebellion" the source of God's own wounds? Even if it is, the fundamental gap cannot be bridged, and, as human beings, our losses hardly matter. The speaker of "Matins" is baffled: "We never thought of you / whom we were learning to worship. / We merely knew it wasn't human nature to love / only what returns love." These solitary workers of the garden offer

up their prayers to a "father" who can only respond narcissistically: "you are / too little like me in the end / to please me."

Given these disjunctions, it is all the more painful that the voices rarely answer each other, that isolation is seldom broken. "What are you saying? That you want / eternal life? Are your thoughts really / as compelling as all that?" demand the "Field Flowers" of the humans at their margins, seeming at least to maintain a dialogue, however hostile. And yet, in the forward rush of the utterances that comprise *The Wild Iris,* each challenge yields to another. Each voice contributes its own unanswered monologue.

[Glück] confines herself to the mythic. She rarely butts heads with the contemporary, maintaining instead the purity of image and voice that characterizes the timeless high lyric. There are some moments, though, when a "real" speaker seems evident. Especially toward the middle of the sequence, the garden is that of the poet's Vermont home, and the "John and Noah" of the dedication appear, clearly not biblical allusions. These poems explore a struggle with liminal states represented by spring and fall, as well as the frightening responsibility of tending any living thing, whether human being or growing vine. Yet, in their very realism, they seem to be culled from a different garden. *The Wild Iris,* like Glück's previous powerful books, raises the art of lyric to new heights. Yet Glück has less success in uniting lyric speculation with the here-and-now. (p. 25)

Elisabeth Frost, "Metaphysical Poets," in The Women's Review of Books, *Vol. X, No. 8, May, 1993, pp. 24-5.*

Helen Vendler   (essay date 24 May 1993)

[*Vendler is an American educator and critic who has contributed numerous articles on poetry to such journals as the* New York Times Book Review *and the* New Yorker. *She has also written book-length studies on W. B. Yeats, George Herbert, Wallace Stevens, and John Keats. In the following essay, Vendler provides a thematic and stylistic analysis of* The Wild Iris.]

Louise Glück is a poet of strong and haunting presence. Her poems, published in a series of memorable books over the last twenty years, have achieved the unusual distinction of being neither "confessional" nor "intellectual" in the usual senses of those words, which are often thought to represent two camps in the life of poetry. For a long time, Glück refused both the autobiographical and the discursive, in favor of a presentation that some called mythical, some mystical.

The voice in the poems is entirely self-possessed, but it is not possessed by self in a journalistic way. It told tales, rather, of an archetypal man and woman in a garden, of Daphne and Apollo, of mysteriously significant animal visitations. Yet behind those stories there hovered a psychology of the author that lingered, half-seen, in the poems. Glück's language revived the possibilities of high assertion, assertion as from the Delphic tripod. The words of the assertions, though, were often humble, plain, usual;

it was their hierarchic and unearthly tone that distinguished them. It was not a voice of social prophecy, but of spiritual prophecy—a tone that not many women had the courage to claim.

It was something of a shock, therefore, when Glück's recent book **Ararat** turned away from symbol to "real life," which was described with a ruthless flatness as though honesty demanded a rock-bottom truth distilled out of years of reflection. In that book Glück restrained her piercing drama of consciousness, and reined in her gift for poetic elaboration. It was clear that some sort of self-chastisement was underway.

Now, reversing course, she has written a very opulent, symbolic book, full—of all things—of talking flowers. [**The Wild Iris**] is really one long poem, framed as a sequence of liturgical rites: the flowers talk to their gardener-poet; the poet, who is mourning the loss of youth, passion and the erotic life, prays to a nameless god (in Matins and Vespers, many times repeated); and the god, in a very tart voice, addresses the poet. As the flowers are to their gardener-poet, so is she to her gardener-god; the flowers, in their stoic biological collectivity, and their pathos, speak to her, sometimes reproachfully, as she speaks, imploringly, to her god. The god has a viewpoint both lofty and ironic, and repeatedly attacks the self-pity or self-centeredness of the poet. These are dangerous risks for a late twentieth-century poem to take, but Glück wins the wager of her premises. The human reader, too, is placed in "this isthmus of a middle state" (Pope) between the vegetatively animate world and the severe spiritual world, and shares the poet's predicament.

She is here returning to an earlier sequence of hers called "The Garden," which rewrote the myth of Eden. As **The Wild Iris** progresses, we see that Eden has collapsed. The opening mood of the book reflects the absolute pointlessness of living when one can think of nothing to hope for. Despair prompts the liturgical addresses to the god (seven Matins by day in the first half of the sequence, ten Vespers by night in the second half). Most of the other titles in the sequence are names of flowers, beginning with the wild iris and ending with the silver lily, the gold lily and the white lilies.

Glück links herself in these flower-poems to her two chief predecessors in using flowers as images of the soul, George Herbert and Emily Dickinson. In spiritual deprivation, the soul is like a bulb hidden underground. In spring, it finds its season of flowering and renewal. Here is Herbert:

> Who would have thought my shriveled heart
> Could have recovered greenness? It was gone
>   Quite underground, as flowers depart
> To see their mother root, when they have blown;
>   Where they together,
>   All the hard weather,
>   Dead to the world, keep house un-
> known. . . .
>
>   And now in age I bud again,
> After so many deaths, I live and write;
>   I once more smell the dew and rain,
> And relish versing; O my only light,
>   It cannot be

>   That I am he
> On whom thy tempests fell all night.

And here, to bridge the gap of time between Herbert and Glück, is Dickinson:

> Through the dark Sod—as Education—
> The Lily passes sure—
> Feels her white foot—no trepidation—
> Her faith—no fear—
>
> Afterward—in the Meadow
> Swinging her Beryl Bell—
> The Mold-life—all forgotten—now—
> In Ecstasy—and Dell—

In a more effortful moment, closer to the more despairing Glück poems, Dickinson wrote about the helpless religious pleading of the seed "That wrestles in the Ground, / Believing if it intercede / It shall at length be found."

But the lessons that the soul was taught in the seventeenth century and the nineteenth century have to be rescripted for the late twentieth century. No longer convinced of the preciousness of each individual soul, are we to grieve over our individual losses? In one of Glück's poems, the bed of scilla reproaches the poet for her focus on the erotic self, and urges her to abandon herself to collective biological being, to be one of an undifferentiated bed of human flowers. The collective wisdom of the scilla bed is one way of looking at one's fate: to say of oneself and others, "We go where we are sent by the wind of Fate, take root by water, and hear the mingled musics of life's current and its songs." Here is **"Scilla,"** as the flowers reprove the poet:

> Not I, you idiot, not self, but we, we—waves
> of sky blue like
> a critique of heaven: why
> do you treasure your voice
> when to be one thing
> is to be next to nothing?
> Why do you look up? To hear
> an echo like the voice
> of god? You are all the same to us,
> solitary, standing above us, planning
> your silly lives: you go
> where you are sent, like all things,
> where the wind plants you,
> one or another of you forever
> looking down and seeing some image
> of water, and hearing what? Waves,
> and over waves, birds singing.

The poem **"Scilla"** is arranged on a few strings: one is the necklace of "-ing"'s (thing, nothing, standing, planning, things, looking, seeing, hearing, singing)—nine of them in seventeen short lines. The four successive questions comprise another string, and yet another is linked by water: "waves of sky blue," "some image of water," "waves," "waves." Even the word "echo" brings up the myth of Narcissus bending over water; we "look up" to hear the echo, and "look . . . down" to see an image. The sharp reproof of **"Scilla"** asks whether it should not be enough for us to see waves and hear birdsong. What, after all, do we need the post-reproductive erotic life for? And why should we lament its absence so bitterly?

Just when we might begin to believe in the scilla-solution

and try to live like plants, Glück's god enters with *his* correction of the scilla's point of view:

> Whatever you hoped,
> you will not find yourselves in the garden,
> among the growing plants.
> Your lives are not circular like theirs:
>
> your lives are the bird's flight
> which begins and ends in stillness—
> which *begins* and *ends,* in form echoing
> this arc from the white birch
> to the apple tree.

And would the poet want, in any case, to relive the erotic life? Glück answers with a picture of the archetypal young couple in the Garden:

> I couldn't do it again,
> I can hardly bear to look at it—
>
> in the garden, in light rain
> the young couple planting
> a row of peas, as though
> no one has ever done this before,
> the great difficulties have never as yet
> been faced and solved.

By the next poem, the garden is being called "the poisonous field," and the couple, fallen into mutual recrimination, are sharply chidden by the god, who reminds them that they suffer equally and should rise in spiritual stature through grief. As the man and the woman sink in self-pity, each saying, *"No one's despair is like my despair,"* the god retorts,

> Do you suppose I care
> if you speak to one another?
> But I mean you to know
> I expected better of two creatures
> who were given minds: if not
> that you would actually care for each other
> at least that you would understand
> grief is distributed
> between you, among all your kind, for me
> to know you, as deep blue
> marks the wild scilla, white
> the wood violet.

Glück's god is here voicing the Keatsian belief that individual grief creates personal identity, the "colors" of character. The ravishing musicality of Glück's ending emphasizes the surprisingly consonant nature of various identities: the *violet* is *white,* the scilla is *wild,* and *wild* and *white* and *violet* in the *woods* make for a phonetic beauty that stands for natural and moral beauty.

I have gone through this much of Glück's narrative simply to show its didactic and dialectical nature, its dimensions, its mythical means. The sequence is constantly surprising as it moves along, since we have no idea who will speak next, in what tone, with what spiritual argument. There is an exquisite defense, for instance, in **"Love in Moonlight,"** of all that the erotic life has meant, could mean, did mean. Outside, we see a summer evening, "a whole world thrown away on the moon":

> and in the dark, the gold dome of
> the capitol

> converted to an alloy of moonlight, shape
> without detail, the myth, the archetype, the soul
> filled with fire that is moonlight really, taken
> from another source, and briefly
> shining as the moon shines: stone or not,
> the moon is still that much of a living thing.

Surely this fifteen-line "sonnet" in elegiac memory of the borrowed light of passionate love will hold its own against the strictures of scilla or the scilla's god.

And how does the story end? It has several endings. One is the poet's; she blossoms in spite of herself (the last Vespers). Three are the god's: the tender **"Sunset,"** the stern **"Lullaby"** and the pitiless **"September Twilight,"** as the god erases his work. Two are poems spoken by a single flower: **"The Silver Lily"** reassures the poet about the end, while **"The Gold Lily"** is full of terror and abandonment. Finally **"The White Lilies"** offers a colloquy between two lovers, as one calms the fear of the other with the old paradox that temporal burial is the avenue to imaginative eternity:

> Hush, beloved. It doesn't matter to me
> how many summers I live to return:
> this one summer we have entered eternity.
> I felt your two hands
> bury me to release its splendor.

These old reciprocals—burial and permanence, mortality and eternity—are lyric standbys. But Glück's white lily, unlike Dickinson's and Herbert's flowers, will not rise from its "mold-life" except on the page.

What a strange book *The Wild Iris* is, appearing in this fin-de-siècle, written in the language of flowers. It is a *lieder* cycle, with all the mournful cadences of that form. It wagers everything on the poetic energy remaining in the old troubadour image of the spring, the Biblical lilies of the field, natural resurrection. It depends, too, on old religious notions of spiritual discipline. It is pre-Raphaelite, theatrical, staged and posed. It is even affected. But then, poetry has a right to these postures. When someone asked Wallace Stevens's wife whether she liked his poems, she answered, "I like Mr. Stevens's poems when they are not affected. But they are so often affected." And so they were. The trouble lay, rather, in Elsie Stevens's mistrust of affectation. It is one of the indispensable gestures in the poet's repertory. (pp. 35-8)

> *Helen Vendler, "Flower Power," in* The New Republic, *Vol. 208, No. 21, May 24, 1993, pp. 35-8.*

Claudia Keelan   (review date October-November 1993)

[*Keelan is an American poet whose works have appeared in numerous literary journals. In the excerpt below, she provides a brief overview of Glück's poetry and discusses the poet's treatment of feminism and religion in* The Wild Iris.]

For twenty years, Louise Gluck has written stunning, post-tragic lyric poetry. Her largest contribution to the canon has consisted in her revisioning of myth, if not in feminist then in feminine terms, her version of women's less empowered sexuality, a reification of Freudian psychology. Hers is a poetry which unabashedly affirms Freud's notion of biology as destiny, and it is the painful brevity with which she negotiates that arena that affirms her gift:

> **"Palais des Arts"**
> Love long dormant showing itself:
> the large expected gods
> caged really, the columns
> sitting on the lawn, as though perfection
> were not timeless but stationary—that
> is the comedy, she thinks,
> that they are paralyzed. Or like the matching
>   swans,
> insular, circling the pond: restraint so passionate
> implies possession. They hardly speak.
> On the other bank, a small boy throws bits of
>   bread
> into the water. The reflected monument
> is stirred, briefly, stricken with light—
> She can't touch his arm in innocence again.
> They have to give that up and begin
> as male and female, thrust and ache.
>   (from *Descending Figure*)

Glück's poetry has often examined a conventional dynamic between girlhood and sexuality, the painful mirror her mother's body holds up to her own, defining one extreme of the dialectic. An argument with the silent god/father/lover—"his hand over her mouth"—(**"Dedication to Hunger"** from *Descending Figure*) is the antithetical trope. Gluck's power has partially derived from her momentary struggles with this victimized ideology:

> Then the shutter snapped,
> the rabbit went free. He flew
> through the empty forest
>
> that part of me
> that was the victim.
> Only victims have a destiny.
>
> And the hunter, who believed
> whatever struggles
> begs to be torn apart:
>
> that part is paralyzed.
>   (from **"Liberation,"** *The Triumph of Achilles*)

This temporary annihilation of self, however frightening, reaches towards a language not yet made, a poetry which will resist the objectification of noun by verb, which will confound the conventional closure of lyric in expectation of a language of liberation. It is an expectation still luminous in *The Wild Iris*. In her most recent book, Gluck continues to define the relationship between the silent, male principle and the vocable suffering of the female, in a world where "bond cannot be proven . . . " (*Descending Figure*).

Written alternately in the voices of a garden, God, and the poet at her devotions, the poems in *The Wild Iris* ask "do you know who I was, how I lived . . . " (**"Snowdrops"**) of a God weary of "speaking through vehicles only . . . as you prefer . . . " (**"Clear Morning"**). Here is a God who asserts "human beings must be taught to love / silence and darkness . . . (**"Lullaby"**). Though the garden

and the elements that pass through the garden are the main vehicles for prayer in *The Wild Iris,* there is very little description of the garden; the poet chooses instead to use flowers and other natural objects as screens through which she whispers her lack:

> This is how you live when you have a cold heart.
> As I do: in shadows, trailing over cool rock,
> under the great maple trees.
>   (from **"Lamium"**)

To her credit, Gluck acknowledges her constant use of the pathetic fallacy:

> Like a protected heart,
> the blood-red
> flower of the wild rose begins
> to open on the lowest branch,
> supported by the netted
> mass of a large shrub:
> it blooms against the dark
> which is the heart's constant
> backdrop, while flowers
> higher up have wilted or rotted;
> to survive
> adversity merely
> deepens its color. But John
> objects, he thinks
> if this were not a poem but
> an actual garden, then
> the red rose would be
> required to resemble
> nothing else . . .
>
>   (from **"Song"**)

It is her honesty, her acknowledgement of the predetermined and unvarying way in which she sees the world that accounts for her trademark beauty and strength of voice; on the other hand, it may also be what keeps the language from the freedom it seeks. Gluck's use of the colon, not only in *The Wild Iris,* but throughout her oeuvre, seems an urgent demand for an equational reality, a reality, if we are to believe the requests of the praying figure in *The Wild Iris,* her God continually confounds:

> When I made you, I loved you.
> Now I pity you.
>
> I gave you all you needed:
> bed of earth, blanket of blue air—
>
> As I get further away from you
> I see you more clearly.
> Your souls should have been immense by now,
> not what they are,
> small talking things—
>
> I gave you every gift,
> blue of the spring morning,
> time you didn't know how to use—
> you wanted more, the one gift
> reserved for another creation.
>
> Whatever you hoped,
> you will not find yourselves in the garden,
> among the growing plants.
> Your lives are not circular like theirs:
>
> your lives are the bird's flight
> which begins and ends in stillness—

which *begins* and *ends* . . .
(from **"Retreating Wind"**)

I find myself wondering what new place might be made if Gluck were to cut every like and as, every colon. Though the God in *The Wild Iris* speaks primarily in the voice of season, what is said is conventionally Christian. Fittingly, then, the series entitled "Matins" and "Vespers" relying as it does upon the canonical hours comprises the most effective speech in the book:

"Matins"

The sun shines; by the mailbox, leaves
of the divided birch tree folded, pleated like fins.
Underneath, hollow stems of the white daffodils,
   Ice Wings, Cantatrice; dark
leaves of the wild violet. Noah says
depressives hate the spring, imbalance
between the inner and the outer world. I make

another case—being depressed, yes, but in a
   sense passionately
attached to the living tree, my body
actually curled in the split trunk, almost at
   peace, in the evening rain
almost able to feel
sap frothing and rising: Noah says this is
an error of depressives, identifying
with a tree, whereas the happy heart
wanders the garden like a falling leaf, a figure for
the part, not the whole.

By reclaiming the autonomy of individual utterance, the poet of *The Wild Iris* ultimately makes a claim for the sanctity of the temporal. Like Job, Gluck moves through protest to reconciliation. Having lost all, she still demands her right to argue with God. (pp. 4-5)

Claudia Keelan, "That Which Is Towards," in Poetry Flash, *No. 247, October-November, 1993, pp. 1, 4-5, 14-15.*

Additional coverage of Glück's life and career is contained in the following sources published by Gale Research: *Contemporary Authors,* Vols. 33-36, rev. ed.; *Contemporary Authors New Revision Series,* Vol. 40; *Contemporary Literary Criticism,* Vols. 7, 22, 44; and *Dictionary of Literary Biography,* Vol. 5.

Thom Gunn

The Man with Night Sweats

Award: The Lenore Marshall/*Nation* Poetry Prize

(Full name Thomson William Gunn) Born in 1929, Gunn is an English poet, critic, editor, and essayist who resides in the United States.

For further information on Gunn's life and career, see *CLC,* Volumes 3, 6, 18, and 32.

INTRODUCTION

The Man with Night Sweats has been praised for its unsentimental examination of AIDS, death, and neglected members of contemporary American society. Written between 1982 and 1988, the poems comprising the collection range widely in style—including both free and traditional verse—and are grouped into four sections. In the first, Gunn celebrates the emotional ties of friends, homosexual lovers, and brothers in such poems as "The Hug" and "An Invitation." The second section contains one poem, "A Sketch of the Great Dejection," in which the narrator momentarily rests in a graveyard to contemplate life and death, which he likens to a journey through "a sea of raw mud." The next group of poems provides commentary on animals, nature, and homeless people. For example, "Cafeteria in Boston," which fluctuates in tone between fascination and repulsion, depicts a beggar eating leftovers. The poems in the last section confront death and the AIDS epidemic. "The Man with Night Sweats," for instance, describes the fear of a man who wakes with the first symptoms of AIDS, while "Lament" chronicles the physical decline of a friend suffering from the disease and the various worldviews he adopts as his symptoms worsen.

Critics note that although the collection's subject matter grows progressively darker, *The Man with Night Sweats* concludes on a hopeful note. In "A Blank," the final poem, Gunn depicts a single, homosexual male walking with his adopted son, an image that such commentators as Hugh Haughton interpret as a celebration of "the individual's power to shape his life on his own terms." Praising Gunn as a "poet without vanity" who strives to discover truth through poetry, Henri Cole has written that "what Gunn is continually attempting to grasp or understand in this book is the condition of those around him, strangers and lovers alike, and we treasure his tone of brotherly forbearance as he makes his way."

PRINCIPAL WORKS

Fighting Terms: A Selection   (poetry)   1954; revised edition, 1958
The Sense of Movement   (poetry)   1957
My Sad Captains, and Other Poems   (poetry)   1961
Selected Poems [with Ted Hughes]   (poetry)   1962
Positives [with Ander Gunn]   (photography and poetry) 1966
Touch   (poetry)   1967
Poems, 1950-1966: A Selection   (poetry)   1969
Moly   (poetry)   1971
Jack Straw's Castle, and Other Poems   (poetry)   1976
Selected Poems, 1950-1975   (poetry)   1979
The Occasions of Poetry: Essays in Criticism and Autobiography   (essays)   1982; enlarged edition, 1985
The Passages of Joy   (poetry)   1982
The Man with Night Sweats   (poetry)   1992

CRITICISM

William Scammell   (review date 7 March 1992)

[*In the following review of* The Man with Night Sweats, *Scammell faults Gunn's poetry for lacking emotional intensity.*]

Thom Gunn's early poetry was an engaging mix of up-to-the-minute subject matter and formal propriety, and that is the formula he has stuck to ever since. Elvis and other 'rebellious' figures rode out of neat 17th-century stanzas, or Popean couplets, all black leathers and come-on menace, striking postures for combat, riding the youth cult happily to the top of the pops. At one time he was bracketed with Ted Hughes, Cambridge's other outstanding poet of the Fifties, but the link was entirely fortuitous. Hughes's rebellion against welfare stateism of the spirit and the neutering of instinct was real, deep, and lasting, finding its utterance in forgotten rhythms and gutturals, whereas Gunn's was more akin to the burgeoning pop culture he celebrated—'the disobedient / who keep a culture alive / by subverting it.' What was catchy about it was the Tribe-of-Ben sparkle and polish elicited from an apparently boring time given over to Tommy Steele, coffee bars and trad jazz. He never wrote as badly as Hughes sometimes can, trusting to craftsmanship rather than to inspiration, but neither did he ever write as well. On the credit side, however, he stayed well clear of gentility and of the dubious paths trodden by those other Fifties revolutionaries, Amis and Osborne.

The move to America, in the Sixties, might be thought to have signalled a loosening-up of his interests and techniques, but the influence of Yvor Winters, the sternly rational poet-critic, seems to have easily outweighed that of Beats, Black Mountaineers, and those other free-versers endlessly rocking in Whitman's cradle. San Francisco gave him plenty to write about, as did the wider American scene, and Gunn is never less than thoughtful, lucid, compassionate; but in reading him you often had the feeling that he was simply versifying the passing scene, and the end result wasn't so very different from what any sensitive commentator might have said in prose. Even the gay poems were freighted more with humanism than with the raw pleasures and pains of existence. Doubtless this is all to his credit as a citizen but it doesn't make for that enlargement of the self we look for in the best poetry. The disturbing, near-'fascist' (as it is sometimes dubbed) element in Eliot and Yeats and Lowell is precisely that ability to corner the ego thrashing about in all its tumid excess. I suppose what is at stake here is poetic sincerity, that worrying space which opens up between proclamation and performance, the 'mannered solemnities' (as Gunn says himself) of the style and the substance it drills into submission. A short elegy for J. V. Cunningham, in [*The Man with Night Sweats*] gives us his credo:

> He concentrated, as he ought,
> On fitting language to his thought
> And getting all the rhymes correct,
> Thus exercising intellect
> In such a space, in such a fashion,
> He concentrated into passion.

But where is the passion or the sense in this smooth, Augustan distinction between 'language' and 'thought', long since exploded by a host of philosophers and critics? 'And there's no such thing / as an insincere / erection is there?' asks **'Tenderloin'**, reaching for what seems an incontrovertible piece of hard evidence, but this erection is so intent on doing its forensic duty that it forgets its prior obligation to be real, fleshly, unaxiomatised.

By 'proclamation' above I mean the string of signals this book puts out about Gunn's programmatic spontaneity: 'my body insisted on restlessness', 'I live and live / my body's fear', 'that knack / of opening my settled features', 'I sought to extend the body's education', 'I adored / The risk that made robust', 'The hedonistic body', 'A role your need for it had half-defined', 'crude itch of evergreen', etc. The message is loud and clear, and banal too unless redeemed by quiddity, thisness, irrefutable particulars of feeling, which is always disinclined to be well-behaved. The poems aren't helped either by the odd Yeatsian and Eliotic inflection, and though **'Well Dennis O'Grady'** is enjoyable, it's pure W. C. Williams, just as the movement of later pentameters, crowded with auxilliaries, owes much of their interest to Frost.

Perhaps I'm making overmuch of what seems to me archaic and low-pressure. The contemporaneity of the book's presiding evil angel, Aids, is undeniable, and there are moving tributes to many of Gunn's friends, brutally killed by the epidemic. **'Improvisation'** is enjoyable, partly because it questions and discards his usual 'un-rigid, liberal' postures as being inadequate to the no-hoper he tries to help, one whose street-corner existence is 'paved with specifics like an Imagist epic'. Best of all is **'Cafeteria in Boston'**, which again celebrates a down-and-out (like Wordsworth and Hughes, Gunn has a tender eye out for tramps), this time a 'black scavenger' who wolfs down the greasy leftovers of dishes which were revolting even when first served. There's the odd cliché still (eyes 'studiously turned away') and preachy line, but here thought and feeling are galvanised into memorable confusion, the moral exordium fully earned. Nonetheless, I can't help thinking that Gunn needs to break out of his niceness and find a way down inside the rag and bone shop he draws such elegant plans and elevations of.

William Scammell, "Not Quite Concentrating into Passion," in The Spectator, *Vol. 268, No. 8539, March 7, 1992, p. 32.*

Hugh Haughton   (review date 1 May 1992)

[*In the following review of* The Man with Night Sweats, *Haughton remarks on the evolution of Gunn's poetry and discusses the volume's focus on physical and emotional intimacy and desire.*]

It is ten years since Thom Gunn's last book, and if *The Man with Night Sweats* has taken a long time to write, it also, for all its sometimes scaresome lucidity, takes a long

The project of *The Man with Night Sweats* has a stunning imaginative symmetry. In it, Gunn returns to the iconic images of his early poems—to the soldiers, the lovers, the emblems of male strength—and re-writes them as images of suffering, of bodily weakness, of the ravages of disease and the cost of sexual pleasure.

—*Eavan Boland, in his "A Mirrour for Poets," in* PN Review, *November-December 1993.*

time to read. This is not because there is anything the least obscure about the poetry, but that its very translucency, its plainness, tends to conceal the scale of the poet's involvement in his material.

Gunn's verse has always been marked by a strange combination of intimacy and detachment. Whether he writes in the shapely stanzas and traditional metres with which he began, or in the looser-seeming improvisatory notations learned from William Carlos Williams and other American poets, Gunn's lyrics hold experience and the reader at arm's length. For all their distinctiveness, they are strangely voiceless, faceless; though they explore intimate feelings, they adopt a protective intellectual decorum that is almost anonymous, a masculine armour that shields at the same time as it expresses the poet's inveterate amorousness. The magnificent first poem of his first book, *Fighting Terms* (1954), established the terms. It is a poem of convalescence set in the aftermath of the Trojan war, and in it the poet asserts both existential independence ("I was myself; subject to no man's breath") and the need for formal protection ("I called for armour"). In the title-poem of the new collection, Gunn still carries his armour ("my flesh was its own shield") and is still on the track of his own elusive identity ("I . . . catch myself instead"), but here and in the book as a whole, his defences and identity are under siege as never before. The result is perhaps his most wary, moving, personal book to date. It is a forceful reminder that Gunn, though strangely neglected in England, is one of the most singular and compelling poets in English during the past half-century.

In one of his few autobiographical essays, Gunn writes that his "life insists on continuities—between America and England, between free verse and metre, between vision and everyday consciousness". Since his move to the United States, his verse has moved freely between open and closed forms, yet, though his essays and poems show the liberating effects of Williams and LSD, Gunn's improvisatory lyrics have a curious stiffness about them—as if he always had Yvor Winters (or Samuel Johnson) breathing down his neck. Nevertheless, it has been the challenge of American subject-matter, and the great Williamsian receptivity to new forms of experience, which have shocked his rhythmic intelligence into new shapes of recognition.

Gunn's essays on the poets he admires are haunted by such unmisgiving notions as "honesty" and "accuracy", and he is one of those poets for whom the truest poetry is the least, not the most, feigning. As he puts it in the thoroughly Americanized poem **"Autobiography"**, about his English childhood, "the sniff of the real, that's / what I'd want to get".

The "sniff of the real" is everywhere in evidence in *The Man with Night Sweats*—the sniff of an unglamorized California, of gay America, the messed-up urban America of Reaganomics. Yet so is Gunn's admiration for the tough vernacular traditions of sixteenth-century verse and his taste for such traditional lyricists as Fulke Greville and Ben Jonson. Unlike other would-be restorers of and returners to earlier poetic modes in the post-war years—unlike Winters, Donald Davie, or C. H. Sisson, for example, unlike even Robert Lowell or Geoffrey Hill—Gunn's choice of traditional lyric norms and forms has (almost) nothing in it of historical pastiche—no cultural nostalgia for the "antique drum". Gunn's appetite for couplets and stanzaic metres, epigrams and epitomes, the kind of repertoire available to a Ben Jonson, is everywhere at work in his new poems, but it has nothing arch or archaizing about it. It is never a sign of historical homesickness or cultural conservatism but an instrument for recording a new ethos. He writes of and from the modern climate, as if wholly at home here; these new poems have a claim to be some of the most authentic occasional poems of our time (like those of that very different gay American poet, Frank O'Hara).

In an essay on Ben Jonson, Gunn claims "all poetry is occasional". What he likes about Jonson is not the propaganda for literary and social hierarchy or faded Penshurstiana but "plainness of statement", "the absence of showiness", "the effort to get things straight". What we find in Gunn's low-key Jonsonian reports from San Francisco in crisis are attempts to find a public speech that will make room for the definition of new kinds of friendship, grief and affinity. Gunn's instinct for tough, objectively realized lyric forms is a response to new social formations—new ways of organizing and living lives in a culture based not on familial or professional structures, but on desire, "neighbourhood" and affinity.

In an earlier sequence, "Misanthropos", Gunn wrote about an imaginary survivor of an atomic holocaust. In the new poems he writes as the intelligent survivor and surveyor of his own life in the era of AIDS—**"In Time of Plague"**, as one poem puts it. The poems give the sense of someone cautiously reconnoitring the small-scale world of individual lives lived in the shadow of the epidemic, just trying to "get things straight". Gunn's early poem on Caravaggio's painting of the conversion of St Paul (**"In Santa Maria del Popolo"**) spoke with existentialist magniloquence of "the large gesture of solitary man, / Resisting, by embracing, nothingness". The new poems by contrast offer small but decisive gestures, amorous rather than metaphysical, of resistance to nothingness by a plainly sociable man. The first poem, **"The Hug"**, registers his partner's embrace on a particular night with the anatomical precision of a Leonardo drawing ("Your instep to my heel,

/ My shoulder-blades against your chest"), only to turn it into a bodily emblem of their intertwined lives:

> It was not sex, but I could feel
> The whole strength of your body set,
>   Or braced, to mine,
>   And locking me to you
> As if we were still twenty-two
> When our grand passion had not yet
>   Become familial.
> My quick sleep had deleted all
> Of intervening time and place.
>   I only knew
> The stay of your secure firm dry embrace.

The flexed, flexible rhyme-scheme and the asymmetrical but shapely metrical pulse—picked up, no doubt, from the occasional Horatian lyrics of Ben Jonson—give lyric body to his lover's "secure firm dry embrace". Gunn's words, too, seek to be secure, dry, firm—and the "embrace" they celebrate is "braced" by his unobtrusive and unsentimental verbal musculature.

"The Differences" records a different kind of intimacy—and embrace. It begins with a delicious view of a boy walking a street:

> Reciting Adrienne Rich on Cole and Haight,
> Your blond hair bouncing like a corner boy's,
> You walked with sturdy almost swaggering gait,
> The short man's, looking upward with such
>   poise. . . .

The poise of the dead-pan iambic pentameter has been hijacked for a moment of low camp epiphany. As the poem goes on, however, the tone deepens; having celebrated exuberant sensual pleasures, the speaker calls up Cavalcanti on Love and shifts to another erotic tableau of intimate interlinking between males:

> Opaque, yet once I slept with you all night
> Dreaming about you—though not quite embraced
> Always in contact felt however slight.
> We lay at ease, an arm loose round a waist,
> Or side by side and touching at the hips,
> As if we were two trees, bough grazing bough,
> The twigs being the toes or fingertips.

The lovely vague reciprocity suggested by the indefinite articles here ("an arm . . . a waist"), and the tactful Ovidian metamorphic play of "bough grazing bough" give this a delicately adjusted, erotic precision ("not quite embraced"), making it a faithful monument to a casual encounter.

As so often in Gunn, the poem is alive above all to the aftermath of excitement, the repercussions of intimacy—compare **"The Bed"** in *Jack Straw's Castle,* with its lovers "loose-twined across the bed / Like wrestling statues". This is most vivid at the close when: "We woke at times and as the night got colder / Exchanged a word, or pulled the clothes again / To cover up the other's exposed shoulder, / Falling asleep to the small talk of the rain."

"Philemon and Baucis" imagines another such embrace. Reworking the traditional Ovidian story, Gunn condenses the relationship between the classical arboreal couple into

one plastic sculptural image of "Two trunks like bodies, bodies like twined trunks / Supported by their wooden hug":

> Truly each other's, they have embraced so long
> Their barks have met and wedded in one flow
> Blanketing both.

Most of the poem is devoted to expounding the unstable "flow" that ends up in this ungendered arboreal interlacing of bodies, but it is the balancing out of two lives in one permanent intertwining which interests Gunn in this commemoration of fidelity within a gay "marriage".

The poems I have mentioned all come from the first of the book's four sections—that devoted to celebrations of closeness and exchange between friends, lovers, brothers. It includes **"An Invitation"**, a laid-back Horatian verse letter in couplets in which Gunn invites his brother to stay in San Francisco "With my household where they all excel: / Each cooks one night, and each cooks well"—a celebration of new forms of sociability, set against the terrible failure of social provision in Reagan's America, where you can "watch the jobless side by side with whores / Setting a home up out of doors". This well-organized, easygoing gay household is, in its way, as much an emblem of hospitality for Gunn, and for our time, as Penshurst was to Jonson.

[The book's second section is composed of the one poem entitled] **"A Sketch of the Great Dejection"**—an exercise

Caricature drawing of Gunn, by David Levine. Reprinted with permission from The New York Review of Books. *Copyright (c) 1993 Nyrev, Inc.*

in psychological allegory set in "a desert of raw mud", uneasily reminiscent of Bunyan, Eliot, maybe Duncan—and thereafter, the tone of the whole book darkens. The third section puts together an uneven patchwork of social observations and bleak sketches of social derelicts, many taken from Gunn's earlier pamphlet, *Undesirables* (1988). It offers portraits of "Tow Head on Skateboard / perfecting himself ", **"Old Meg"**, a deranged down-and-out, a "black scavenger" eating leftovers in a **"Cafeteria in Boston"**, the "lethargic conviviality" of an alcoholic on the streets, a young beggar "wholly employed / with scrounging cigarettes, drugs, drink", whose existence the poet notes is "paved with specifics like an Imagist epic", and others. The mode of such poems is harsh, externalized, almost self-punishing—and most are marked equally by repulsion and fascination towards their subjects and sitters. If they seem more grimly sociological than the best poems in the book—angry commentaries on political indifference and urban brutality—they also bear upon the crisis of corporeality, of bodily identity and sociability, which the more compelling poems address in more personal terms. The most vivid of them are explorations of the shadowy borderland between physical and social disgust. The horrific vision of sexual infection in **"Tenderloin"**, of junk meat in **"Meat"**, of "abandoned platefuls crusted stiff / like poisoned slugs" in **"Cafeteria in Boston"**, of an "enzyme's cruelty" in **"Yellow Pitcher Plant"**, represent grotesque instances of bodily abuse, travesties of appetite and desire.

It is in the final section of the book, launched with the title poem (which offers us an image of the unsettled poet's vision of his own death) that Gunn's vision of bodily crisis—and of the AIDS epidemic—comes most movingly to the fore. **"The Man with Night Sweats"** takes us into the new but already too familiar nightmare of waking to fears about having the first symptoms of AIDS:

> I wake up cold, I who
> Prospered through dreams of heat
> Wake to their residue,
> Sweat, and a clinging sheet

The poem speaks in the language of physical terms and symptoms, but again as incarnations of a way of life. Though scared of their possible consequences, Gunn remains true to the "dreams of heat", the 1960s West Coast dreams of sexual and hallucinogenic liberation explored in earlier poems such as **"The Geysers"** and **"Moly"**. Even as he faces up to the cracking of the "shield" of his body, he remains faithful to its promise:

> I grew as I explored
> The body I could trust
> Even while I adored
> The risk that made robust

The interplay between physical and imaginative growth is the crux here; he doesn't say "I explored as I grew up", but "I grew as I explored"; he still trusts the kinds of imaginative enfranchisement involved in exploring "the body" and "the risk" it carried with it—even in time of plague, when sexual "risk" (especially for "high-risk" groups) is a matter of life and death. The poem ends with a self-embrace. "I have to change the bed", he says, "but catch myself instead"

> Stopped upright where I am
> Hugging my body to me
> As if to shield it from
> The pains that will go through me,
>
> As if hands were enough
> To keep an avalanche off.

Poignantly facing his physical vulnerability, the speaker constructs a kind of bounding shield out of the tightly interlaced alternating rhymed couplets and quatrains. Of all the emblematic embraces consummated in the book, this shielding self-embrace is the most primary.

The best of the poems in *The Man with Night Sweats* rely, like much of Gunn's work from first to last, on the limiting embrace of rhyme, but they are also explorations of a profoundly amorous, companionable commitment to the world of bodily intimacy.

—*Hugh Haughton*

The bulk of the poems confront the deaths of particular friends—the crisis of individuals locked in their wasting bodies. **"Lament"**, about the illness and death of a particularly close friend, is written in an unflinchingly secular idiom that even in the face of death refuses to give up on the Horatian sociability of Gunn's California, with its "normal pleasures of the sun", "hedonistic body", "summer on the skin" and "moderate taste of tea". In such a culture it is perhaps only the poet who can make out of such brutally shortened lives something like completeness:

> Your own concerns were not
> Long-term precisely, when they gave the shot
> You made local arrangements to the bed
> And pulled a pillow round beside your head.
> And so you slept, and died, your skin gone
> grey,
> Achieving your completeness, in a way.

Such "local arrangements" are all there are, and the poem is impressively true to them—without seeking further reassurance than the local arrangements of the couplets which are used to describe the "difficult, tedious, painful enterprise" of the death. **"The J Car"**, written about another friend's death, adopts the same stoically secular form; it ruefully admits to feeling "if they believe everything might / Still against likelihood come out all right", though of course it doesn't. The poem admits to the need for reassurance and "neat arrangement" but refuses to reassure.

"The Reassurance" describes a dream in which the same dead friend returns and embraces his living friends ("You hugged us all round then"), leading the poet to say "How like you to be kind", only to return upon himself ironically, "And, yes, how like my mind / To make itself secure". Yet what is impressive about these "terminal" poems is the poet's unsettling refusal to make himself secure by such false reassurances. **"Memory Unsettled"** grimly celebrates an embrace which offers genuine reassurance—to a dying man in hospital, not the survivors ("You climbed in there beside him / And hugged him in plain view"). In **"The Missing"**, a poem about the "progress of the plague", Gunn explores the shock to his own bodily identity caused by the wasting away of his friends. Seeking to define his need for solidarity, he adopts another very different image of an "embrace":

> I do not like the statue's chill contour,
> Not nowadays. The warmth investing me
> Led outward through mind, limb, feeling, and
>   more
>
> In an involved increasing family.
>
> Contact of friend led to another friend,
> Supple entwinement through the living mass
> Which for all that I knew might have no end,
> Image of an unlimited embrace.

Of course the "supple entwinement" of that "unlimited embrace", the source of his sense of belonging within the "increasing family", has, cruelly, become the source of his crisis, leaving the poet precariously "unsupported" and "incomplete". AIDS threatens not only his life and the lives of his friends but a larger communal homosexual identity of which they are all part.

"Death's Door", the penultimate poem of the book, is a kind of palinode or contrary to **"My Sad Captains"**, the early lyric in which Gunn imagines dead friends and heroes in orbit, "turn[ing] with disinterested / Hard energy, like the stars". Now he imagines the outnumbering dead as terrible "recruiting armies", "an archaic host" gradually "weaned / From memory". Four dead contemporaries, in some posthumous limbo watching television in a grim travesty of their ordinary lives, are caught too in a benumbed travesty of a friendly embrace ("Arms round each other's shoulders loosely, / Although they can feel nothing"). Gradually they lose interest in the life they leave behind, and "They break themselves of touch"—this is the ultimate image of death for the author of *Touch.* What he calls "the perfect discipline" of the dead offers a nightmare vision of solidarity—the opposite of the erotic "supple entwinement of the living mass". When he sees the dead "break apart at arm and hip", the phrase suggests that their individual physical dissolution is inseparable from their mutual separation—the "edging apart" which ends all possibility of further embrace.

The last poem ["A Blank"] sets against all these deaths an anecdote to counterpoise a "year of griefs". Gunn catches sight of a past lover of his through a bus window, "A four-year-old-blond child tugging his hand, / Which tug he held with a slight smile". For the deep-dyed emblem-shaper this poet has always been, the young single father becomes an emblem of admirable "self-permission", the individual's power to shape his life on his own terms—which here means opting "To educate, permit, guide, feed, keep warm, / And love a child" and so transpose the erotic "expectations he took out at dark" into "another pitch" but based on "the same melody". It is a tribute to the in-terlocking mesh of images which gives Gunn's vision its conviction in these poems that what strikes us about the moment (and about the relationship between man and boy) is an equivalent of the various erotic and companionable embraces fleshed out within the book as a whole.

What moves Gunn's moral imagination is the physical bond between father and son, the muscular bond enacted in the father's holding "against" the child's "tug" and offering him his "countering pull":

> The blank was flesh now, running on its nerve,
> This fair-topped organism dense with charm,
> Its braided muscle grabbing what would serve,
> His countering pull, his own devoted arm.

The best of these poems rely, like much of Gunn's work from first to last, on the limiting embrace of rhyme, but they are also explorations of a profoundly amorous, companionable commitment to the world of bodily intimacy. They bear out the claim made in one of his essays that in poetry "Rhythmic form and subject-matter are locked in a permanent embrace". In a recent poem (**"Saturday Night"**) not printed here, remembering the "sexual New Jerusalem" of the 1960s, Gunn reflects, "The embraces slip, and nothing seems to stay / In our community of the carnal heart". In Gunn's work, art seeks to render permanent the transitory embraces through which we play out our need for each other and shield ourselves. (pp. 12-13)

Hugh Haughton, "An Unlimited Embrace,"
in The Times Literary Supplement, *No. 4648,*
May 1, 1992, pp. 12-13.

Henri Cole   (review date 31 August-7 September 1992)

[*Cole is a Japanese-born American educator, poet, and critic. In the following excerpt, he compares Gunn's poetry to that of the Elizabethans and offers praise for the collection's focus on the AIDS crisis.*]

Even our "best" poets can sometimes seem like discreet neighbors: We hear them only distantly, coming and going, passing through life, until one day we find they've moved inexplicably away. Hence, one is doubly grateful, after a ten-year silence, to have this new collection [*The Man With Night Sweats*] by Thom Gunn, whose title announces itself soberly, without adornment.

Gunn is a defiantly unsituatable poet—a formalist who often writes in free verse, an Englishman living in America, an autobiographical poet whose subjects elude the self. He was born in 1929; his is the generation of James Merrill and Adrienne Rich. One might, in fact, think of him as a kind of hybrid of the two, humane in every way, employing a calm, metaphysical surface (like Merrill) while addressing sex and sexuality with candor (like Rich). Perhaps "metaphysical" is the more operative word here, for some of the poems in *The Man With Night Sweats* unfashionably recall Shakespeare and Donne, those Elizabethans still bearing upon contemporary poets.

Take, for example, a love poem like **"The Hug,"** which opens this various collection. Irregularly rhymed, in iambic meter, it begins:

It was your birthday, we had drunk and dined
  Half of the night with our old friend
    Who'd showed us in the end
To a bed I reached in one drunk stride.

The rhythms here, like Donne's, are colloquial, and the language, instead of being weighty in the manner of Milton or sweetly mellifluous in the manner of Spenser, has the rougher music of everyday speech. And like Donne, Gunn enjoys twisting his metrics and grammar cleverly down the page, as in these lines continuing **"The Hug"**:

I dozed, I slept. My sleep broke on a hug,
  Suddenly, from behind,
In which the full lengths of our bodies pressed:
  Your instep to my heel,
My shoulder-blades against your chest.
  It was not sex, but I could feel
The whole strength of your body set,
  Or braced, to mine,
    And locking me to you
As if we were still twenty-two
When our grand passion had not yet
  Become familial.

This book, divided into four sections, begins with poems boldly erotic and ends at "death's door," where "the dead outnumber us" and "their recruiting armies grow!" Such a darkening evolution of theme is not so surprising from a gay man writing during the years of epidemic, when desire and death are irreconcilably bound. As Gunn states sorrowfully in **"In Time of Plague"**:

My thoughts are crowded with death
and it draws so oddly on the sexual
that I am confused,
confused to be attracted
by, in effect, my own annihilation.

One thinks of Donne and the two distinct poets he was: a bawdy cynic of love unafraid of addressing his mistresses in his poems, but also a grave and witty religious poet. Gunn has written that poetry can be "an instrument for exploring the truth of things, as far as human beings can explore it" (something he learned from the Stanford professor, poet and critic Yvor Winters), and his new poems seem a solemn testament to this. It would have seemed to Winters, as it does to Gunn, an insult to the poem that it could be used as "an exercising ground for the ego." Here is a poet without vanity—that aberration afflicting so many of us—whose poems consider instead those lives that, like branches, crisscross his own. "Writing poetry has in fact become a certain stage in my coping with the world," he tells us, "or in the way I try to understand what happens to me and inside me. Perhaps I could say that my poetry is an attempt to *grasp,* with grasp meaning both to *take hold of* in a first bid at possession, and also to *understand.*"

What Gunn is continually attempting to grasp or understand in this book is the condition of those around him, strangers and lovers alike, and we treasure his tone of brotherly forbearance as he makes his way. There are Brad and John, whom he meets on a bench, "fiercely attractive men" who want him to stick their needle in his arm. Seeking to enter their minds, Gunn reflects:

. . . am I a fool,
and they direct and right, properly
testing themselves against risk,
as a human must, and does,
or are they fools, their alert faces
mere death's heads lighted glamorously?
                  ("In Time of Plague")

And there's the dear friend whom he addresses in **"Lament"**:

You never thought your body was attractive,
Though others did, and yet you trusted it
And must have loved its fickleness a bit
Since it was yours and gave you what it could,
Till near the end it let you down for good,
Its blood hospitable to those guests who
Took over by betraying it into
The greatest of its inconsistencies
This difficult, tedious, painful enterprise.

With gravity and candor, a kind of distillation of knowledge about death emerges: Death is something rigid, defining "an absence with its cutting line." The deaths of others leave us less defined, for "it was their pulsing presence" that made us clear. "Death is so plain!"

Writing poetry has in fact become a certain stage in my coping with the world or in the way I try to understand what happens to me and inside me. Perhaps I could say that my poetry is an attempt to *grasp,* with grasp meaning both to *take hold of* in a first bid at possession, and also to *understand.*

—Thom Gunn

Yet amid all this astringent life experience, astonishingly, a profound hope emerges. We see it first in the presence of the love poems that open this book, and we see it in the final poem, **"A Blank,"** in which the narrator encounters on the street a former lover with "a four-year-old blond child tugging his hand." Gunn remembers:

A sturdy-looking admirable young man.
He said 'I chose to do this with my life.'
Casually met he said it of the plan
He undertook without a friend or wife.

Now visibly tugged upon by his decision,
Wayward and eager. So this was his son!
What I admired about his self-permission
Was that he turned from nothing he had done,
Or was, or had been, even while he transposed
The expectations he took out at dark
—Of Eros playing, features undisclosed—
Into another pitch, where he might work

With the same melody, and opted so
To educate, permit, guide, feed, keep warm,
And love a child to be adopted, though
The child was still a blank then on a form.
The blank was flesh now, running on its nerve,
This fair-topped organism dense with charm,

Its braided muscle grabbing what would serve,
His countering pull, his own devoted arm.

This is a human story unwritten in American poetry to date. It is a gay poem, of course, though the experience remains non-gender specific. And how rare that hopefulness should set one apart, even from the likes of Herbert, who asks himself in "The Pilgrimage," after his remarkably foul allegorical journey, "Can both the way and end be tears?" Gunn would seem to dissent cautiously; though his journey has brought him restlessness, it has also brought self-knowledge and, after a while, a gladdening recuperation:

> My body insisted on restlessness
>   having been promised love,
> as my mind insisted on words
>   having been promised the imagination.
> So I remained alert, confused and uncomforted.
> I fared on and, though the landscape did not
>   change,
> it came to seem after a while like a place of recu-
>   peration.
>   **("A Sketch of the Great Dejection")**

One danger in writing poems as open to feeling—whether erotic or angry or contemplative—as these are, and so vigorously structured (often in pentameter), is that occasional free-verse pieces, like some of those collected in the third section of this volume—about nature, animals or San Franciscans living off the streets—can seem a bit improvised or slight, lacking the energy of more compressed verse. Perhaps nonmetrical verse seemed to invite these earthly subjects more than poems of mortality, where metrical patterns help control elegiac emotions, like the steady drum tap accompanying a coffin to its cemetery.

Not long ago *New York Times* music critic Bernard Holland, discussing the contemporary American composer John Corigliano, whose First Symphony has already come to be known as the "AIDS Symphony," remarked that responses to great human events and plagues "can be created only later, when the phenomenon is no longer so horrifyingly and distortively close," as is the case with AIDS. Otherwise, he argued, the result "speaks in the language of a *New York Daily News* or *New York Post*"—as opposed, I presume, to the high art of *The New York Times.* Such empty cant is a bad excuse for avoiding judgment on the art at hand—whether symphony or poem or etching. And it offers no explanation for Shostakovich's Leningrad Symphony No. 7 (composed during the 900 days of Leningrad's blockade by the Germans in World War II, when more than 600,000 died of starvation), or Yeats's political poems (about Yeats, Auden wrote, "mad Ireland hurt you into poetry"), or Goya's etchings suggested by the Napoleonic invasions (in which the painter indicted human evil and corruption), to name but a few examples of art produced at the historical moment it depicts and standing as a monument to the human spirit in the face of appalling suffering. The literature of AIDS does not lie in the future. It is everywhere around us, extracted, like all art, from lives as they are lived, contemplated, perhaps even understood. It may speak the language of violent contrasts, but that is not to say it is unmeasured truth. Those who follow decades from now will write well-researched historical ac-

counts. But while the artist creates, the historian assembles, sometimes aspiring to what the artist achieves, but more often settling for a near-cousin to it. (pp. 221-23)

> *Henri Cole, "Sketches of the Great Epidemic,"
> in* The Nation, *New York, Vol. 255, No. 6, August 31-September 7, 1992, pp. 221-23.*

An excerpt from "Lament"

>   Meanwhile,
> Your lungs collapsed, and the machine, un-
>   strained,
> Did all your breathing now. Nothing remained
> But death by drowning on an inland sea
> Of your own fluids, which it seemed could be
> Kindly forestalled by drugs. Both could and
>   would:
> Nothing was said, everything understood,
> At least by us. Your own concerns were not
>
> Long-term, precisely, when they gave the shot
> —You made local arrangements to the bed
> And pulled a pillow round beside your head.
>   And so you slept, and died, your skin gone
>   grey,
> Achieving your completeness, in a way.

> *Thom Gunn, in his* The Man with Night Sweats, *Farrar
> Straus Giroux, 1992.*

William Logan   (review date 15 November 1992)

[*Logan is an American poet and critic. In the following excerpt, he presents a mixed assessment of* The Man with Night Sweats.]

The aloofness of Thom Gunn's poetry has never welcomed the warming emotions. His departure from England almost 40 years ago stranded him between two cultures, and within his insulating privacy he has written of America without being of America. His poems are wry, self-consumed, a little eaten up with their advantages, charmingly stiff in an Old World way. A few are contingent, unlovely affairs about contingent, unlovely affairs. His poems of homosexual desire seem staged in their seductive bravado, like pornographic movies shot on home video. He often tries to be with it without being of it; his slighter poems have an irritating, smug triviality. In *The Man With Night Sweats,* a poem of empty-headed couplets [**"An Invitation"**] (an invitation to a visit) drags in San Francisco's homeless and hungry as if they were part of a Cook's tour, the local flora and fauna, and then snugly turns to praise the cooks in the poet's household ("Each cooks one night, and each cooks well").

In many poems his aversion to the serious seems a pocket-sized pathology, but his allegorical or classical poems (**"Odysseus on Hermes"**) are cruel as marble; if they were to come to life, like the Commendatore in *Don Giovanni,* the reader would die of shock. Mr. Gunn's best poetry is a resistance to the beautiful, a withholding or withdrawing in the formality of the verse movement, where his slightly elevated phrasing is that of a man who must be won over.

A poet of such instincts often suffers failures of sympathy. He is therefore most attractive when being unpleasant, neither requiring sympathy nor soliciting it. **"Looks,"** about a poet uglier in mind than in body, is a pitiless *fin de siècle* portrait of decadent desire, of the failure of art to rescue the artist from his moral ugliness. The more inhuman Mr. Gunn's poems, the richer and more fretful the imaginative resources. The more difficult the observation, the more complicated the implication.

Mr. Gunn's grimmest and most guarded poems are witnesses to the death of friends from AIDS, a plague that has risen into metaphors of plague. Here his formal distances, his comforts in the methods of literary detachment, give him a purchase not available to poets more weakly personal. The poems are written in a measured voice of despair, every word a vain effort of memory, a memory that is the only memorial to these abbreviated lives.

> Your dying was a difficult enterprise.
> First, petty things took up your energies,
> The small but clustering duties of the sick,
> Irritant as the cough's dry rhetoric.
> Those hours of waiting for pills, shot, X-ray
> Or test (while you read novels two a day)
> Already with a kind of clumsy stealth
> Distanced you from the habits of your health.

The tired and scarcely achieved rhythms become part of the weary tone. It has taken great effort to compose the feeling in these elegies, especially for a poet uncomfortable with feeling. No one could fail to be troubled by them, even when they are not convincing as poetry—at some level even Mr. Gunn's imagination has flinched in its melancholy offices. He has rarely recovered the deftness or speed that drove him through the metrical register of *Fighting Terms* or *The Sense of Movement,* his earliest books; but in some poems here he has crossed into a harrowed maturity. (p. 16)

Gunn on *The Man with Night Sweats*:

[*The Man with Night Sweats*] consists of my poems from 1982, when my last book was published, to 1988. I stopped there and put it in the drawer. I find increasingly that it's very difficult for me to write poetry after the publication of a new book. This has been my way of cheating it. I finished the book, I put it in a drawer, and I decided I wasn't going to publish it until ten years from the date of the previous book. I've just gone on writing, which is what I planned to do, so I guess my little game has worked. (On the other hand, when it gets published, maybe I'll dry up then. But meantime I've gotten a certain amount of the book after next written.)

Thom Gunn, in an interview with Jean W. Ross, in Contemporary Authors New Revision Series, *Volume 33, 1991.*

William Logan, "Angels, Voyeurs, and Cooks," in The New York Times Book Review, *November 15, 1992, pp. 15-16.*

Alfred Corn   (review date February 1993)

[*Corn is an American poet and critic. In the following excerpt, he comments on the evolution of Gunn's poetry and some of the strengths of* The Man with Night Sweats.]

Yvor Winters had many students, a number of whom published poetry, but seldom with much success. In the instances of J. V. Cunningham and Thom Gunn, though, master was surpassed by disciples. Accepting Winters meant shouldering the discipline of meter and rhyme, which for Gunn, as for his teacher, was closer to a passion than to a technique. That much granted, how then do we understand Gunn's ability to write equally passionate *unmetered* poetry? Whatever the psychological forces or aesthetic strategies involved, the experiment has worked. To the by-now-boring question of whether or not contemporary poets should write in rhyme and meter his books implicitly answer, either: depends on the poem in question. (Even so, until poets can compose in meter very, very well, better not publish early attempts at all, since iambs and rhymes dispassionately and unmistakably expose anything second-rate.) Traditional prosody has in most cases fit Gunn's subjects the way a cuirass fit a Roman soldier: the protected torso is represented in a leather sheath with sharply defined musculature. Form of this kind follows a generalized human pattern, reinforcing function by adding a slightly idealized strength and symmetry that would almost justify the package by itself. When we get to Gunn's unmetered poems, though, a better comparison would be a pair of jeans that have stretched and conformed to the body underneath without imposing much in the way of their own structure. Part of his special status in poetry is Gunn's dual allegiance to the formality of European classicism and the informality of American romanticism. He has an audience both here [in the United States] and in England, but neither country has offered him approval at its most resounding, almost as though neither trusts him to be entirely loyal. Meanwhile his loyalties go to something else besides nationality.

Gunn's early poetry, written in England, adopted a soldierly stance, as *Fighting Terms,* his first title, clearly suggests. His models included Shakespeare's history plays and Roman tragedies, Stendhal's ironic, French version of *espagnolisme,* and the hard-edged disillusion of Camus's *L'Étranger,* or at least the first half of that book. This is a poetry where at high noon or midnight ignorant armies clash, the unignorant poet in their midst taking the sting out of prevailing absurdity by describing it in intelligently disillusioned blank verse. He doesn't grieve, doesn't long for transcendence or an afterlife, doesn't ask for a world without death and rattlesnakes: he simply takes the rattlesnake and milks it into a tumbler, safely downs the venom, and, not so much high as exhilarated, waits for verses to arrive.

It's a little easier to be a stranger abroad than at home, and

Gunn's second book, *The Sense of Movement,* marks his transfer to American ground, more specifically, California, his new emblematic figure someone like Marlon Brando of *The Wild One,* and his motto, "One is always nearer by not keeping still." The Fifties English literary faction known as The Movement, of which Gunn was a charter member, must have felt that it had somehow been set on end, and the question is whether English poetry has ever really forgiven him for his choices. Auden would have understood. There have been seven later books, including a *Selected Poems,* all of which track Gunn's assimilation of American realities to his European perspective, and, among these, undisguised poems about his life as a gay man and his participation in California counterculture of the late Sixties and early Seventies. LSD, sex, leather, weight lifting—it's all told with a faith more American than present-day America itself that the heavy yoke of oppressive conformity can be tossed aside by anyone willing to risk a quick gesture of unself-righteous honesty. The poetry public has traditionally been on the prudish side, though, particularly where gay sexuality was concerned (witness the storm clouds over Whitman once people stopped to look at what he was actually saying); and it's fair to speak of an actual eclipse of Gunn's reputation not really dispelled by the appearance of his Selecteds nor by *The Passages of Joy,* his excellent volume published ten years ago.

The Man With Night Sweats may change the situation, either because the public is more receptive to poems with gay subject matter than it once was, or, with more justice, because the excellence of the poems is inescapable. I can go a step further and point out that many of the gay poems also involve AIDS, a topic that has seemed to rally interest and support, and not in the poetry world alone. So much so that the attitude sometimes seems to be: It's OK to be gay (or lesbian) so long as you have AIDS. Thom Gunn doesn't, but many of his friends have died from AIDS-related illnesses, and it has been an inevitable theme in his recent poetry.

This new book, like the earlier ones, has its militancy, but it is less military. It opens with **"The Hug,"** a poem about transformation of feeling in a relationship from early fieriness to the family-style loyalty characteristic of love after several decades have tempered it.

> It was your birthday, we had drunk and dined
>   Half of the night with our old friend
>   Who'd showed us in the end
>   To a bed I reached in one drunk stride.
>   Already I lay snug,
> And drowsy with the wine dozed on one side.
>
> I dozed, I slept. My sleep broke on a hug,
>   Suddenly, from behind,
> In which the full lengths of our bodies pressed:
>   Your instep to my heel,
>   My shoulder-blades against your chest.
>   It was not sex, but I could feel
>   The whole strength of your body set,
>   Or braced, to mine,
>   And locking me to you
>   As if we were still twenty-two
>   When our grand passion had not yet

> Become familial.
> My quick step had deleted all
> Of intervening time and place.
>   I only knew
> The stay of your secure firm dry embrace.

This twenty-two-line poem is iambic throughout, line lengths that extend from dimeter to pentameter. Variant feet are introduced expressively, as in, "The whole strength of your body set, / Or braced, to mine," where a trochee in second position adds emphasis to the strength described and anticipates the bracing action mentioned in the next line. Every line is rhymed, but not according to a recurrent pattern, and the poem is broken into two stanzas of six and sixteen lines each. Reading it gives the sensation of formal control not in the least like a straitjacket or even a suit of armor. The "secure firm dry embrace" described (and enacted) is neither the clench of hand-to-hand combat nor the lovers' ecstatic union: it is a warm gesture of solidarity. As such, a good emblem for the entire volume, where we find love, but not *la folie d'amour;* sex, but not in an anguishing or ecstatic mood; and form without what might be called the gadgetry of form. **"The Hug"** takes place at night and is aware of the connection between night, sex, and death. In his sixties, and especially after what might be called the decade of necrology, Thom Gunn is able to contemplate the end as it approaches, but at a manageable distance.

Less lucky is the person portrayed in **"To a Friend in Time of Trouble,"** who has AIDS and is beginning to lose his strength. Gunn shows him strolling around the cabin in the woods he built in earlier days, surveying his handiwork and by extension his life. This is the first in a series of portraits that account for some of the best writing in the book, the most harrowing and maybe even the best poem, one titled **"Lament,"** which charts the decline of a friend's health along with a series of different stances he adopts as symptoms worsen. At first Gunn sees his friend "In hope still, courteous still, but tired and thin, / You tried to stay the man that you had been." But the struggle eventually comes to an end, and the poem concludes this way:

> You never thought your body was attractive,
> Though others did, and yet you trusted it
> And must have loved its fickleness a bit
> Since it was yours and gave you what it could,
> Till near the end it let you down for good,
> Its blood hospitable to those guests who
> Took over by betraying it into
> The greatest of its inconsistencies
> This difficult, tedious, painful enterprise.

The word "hospitable" resonates gratingly with the prospect of purely medical residence, a dwelling where this friend is himself a "guest." I was reminded also of [Sylvia] Plath's "Dying / Is an art, like everything else. / I do it exceptionally well." The difference here is that death is involuntary, the "art" involved a matter of transforming something not chosen into a new pattern of meaning as little discordant with the sufferer's earlier life as he was able to make it.

There isn't room here to cover the full range of Gunn's portraiture, his memorable rendering of friends (not all of them with AIDS, by the way, and not all the gay men entirely admirable) or characters encountered only tangentially. Still, I won't omit mentioning several poems about street people that, without sentimentality, bring characters usually overlooked into the ambit of poetry. These and the other portraits will disprove the claim we hear so often that poets are blind to life outside artistic and academic ghettoes. Subject is never enough, of course. The poems succeed mainly because Gunn avoids the falsifications of sentimentality—even as he draws on more of the sympathetic imagination than was once typical of his poetry. This book is far from the adamant and steel of *Fighting Terms.* According to your views, Gunn's new warmth is a striking improvement or a capitulation to more familiar patterns of feeling. Is that the result of age? The humanizing process of bereavement? A purely aesthetic choice? Maybe all of these. Whatever the cause, I would like to cast a vote in favor, without falling back on critical sentimentality in the form of blurbese like "deeply moving" or "brilliant." The other common form of critical sentimentality is condemnation enjoyed for its own sake. (pp. 291-95)

> *Alfred Corn, in a review of "The Man with Night Sweats," in* Poetry, *Vol. CLXI, No. 5, February, 1993, pp. 291-95.*

Gunn's testimonies [in *The Man with Night Sweats*] resist bitterness or formless tirades against fate. His poems ultimately defy emptiness and loss in the realm of art, if not in life. As Blake would put it, he "builds a Heaven in Hell's despair."

> *—Phoebe Pettingell, in her "Poetry in Review," in* The Yale Review, *October 1992.*

Michael Wood (review date 27 May 1993)

[*Wood is an English educator and critic. In the following excerpt, he favorably reviews* The Man with Night Sweats.]

There is a good deal of implied narrative in Thom Gunn's verse [in *The Man With Night Sweats*]—one poem is called **"Autumn Chapter in a Novel"**—but the fictional worlds are not parodied or played with, and are rarely whimsical. They serve as a backdrop, provide busy, complicated scenes full of battles, wounds, courts, palaces, cities, crime, addiction. "It was a violent time," Gunn writes of Shakespeare's and Jonson's age. "Wheels, racks, and fires / In every writer's mouth, and not mere rant." But it's always a violent time in Gunn's work; and a difficult one. He is a writer "against contentment." Lazarus, in a remarkable early poem, decides to stay dead because he doesn't like the look of the world he is to return to.

Hence Gunn's sympathy for dropouts, rebels, fighters, drunks, who recur constantly in his work as figures of ex-

clusion and awkwardness, marks of what troubles all personal and social relations, and are occasionally flagged a little too obviously for the meaning we are supposed to see in them: "the disobedient / who keep a culture alive." They appear in poems, though, where there is not the least sense of awkwardness of form or language, where an uncluttered continuity of literary tradition seems to reign— as if the poetry were an answer to a world it couldn't reach or correct. More, as if giving up on poetry, especially the poetry which tackles the apparently barbarous, were to yield to barbarism. In a work dedicated to Yvor Winters, Gunn insists that "Continual temptation waits on each / To renounce his empire over thought and speech." He also says, in a later work, that he tries "to render obscure passages into clear English," where "passages" can take as many murky or literary (murky and literary) meanings as we want.

This gap between topic and tone offers very striking ironies—the best-known example is probably **"On the Move,"** from *The Sense of Movement* (1957), where a group of bikers forms an elegant, almost metaphysical image of restlessness, as if Empson or Auden had taken to the highway.

> On motorcycles, up the road, they come:
> Small, black, as flies hanging in heat, the
>   Boys . . .
>
> It is a part solution, after all.
> One is not necessarily discord
> On earth; or damned because, half animal,
> One lacks direct instinct, because one wakes
> Afloat on movement that divides and
>   breaks . . .
>
> At worst, one is in motion; and at best,
> Reaching no absolute, in which to rest,
> One is always nearer by not keeping still.

But there was always a risk that the irony would turn into a remoteness from the very persons or scenes to be held in view—those slightly too tidy rhymes, the very English and now rather dated "one"—and in later work Gunn has negotiated this risk with consummate care and tact. He needs a distance for his most powerful and thoughtful effects; but he needs to confess an involvement too, and has found increasingly effective, and witty, and moving ways of doing this. As in this evocation of Elvis Presley, where the language manages a subtle mixture of intimacy and sadness and grandeur. **"Fatty,"** especially, suggests slippage and ill-health but also sounds like a schoolkid's nickname.

> The King of rock 'n roll
> grown pudgy, almost matronly,
> Fatty in gold lamé,
> mad King encircled
> by a court of guards, suffering
> delusions about the assassination,
> obsessed by guns, fearing
> rivalry and revolt . . .

Similarly, this song of a wino has an almost Brechtian bitterness about it, the lilt of the verse mocking the misery of the situation, but we experience the indignity and the anger with the man rather than from a comfortable, observer's distance:

> I stand here in the cold
> in a loose old suit bruised and dirty
> I may look fifty years old
> but I'm only thirty . . .
>
> I need some change for a drink
> of sweet wine Sir a bottle of sherry
> it's the sugar in it I think
> will make me merry . . .
>
> The bastard passed me by
> fuck you asshole that's what I say
> I hope I see you cry
> like Sparrow one day . . .

In *The Man With Night Sweats,* his first volume of verse in ten years, Gunn finds new registers of intimacy, and new ways of combining formal elegance with an attention to change. **"To Isherwood Dying,"** for example, weaves ancient tropes about love and death into a genuine delicacy on a terrible occasion, portrays death as the reward for a fidelity to desire, a loyalty to old, unsentimentalized longings. Everything depends here on the grace and fluidity of the first long sentence, the quiet echoing of "crumbled," and the lift offered by the repeated "could be":

> It could be, Christopher, from your leafed-in
>   house
> In Santa Monica where you lie and wait
> You hear outside a sound resume
> Fitful, anonymous,
> Of Berlin fifty years ago
> As autumn days got late—
> The whistling to their girls from young men who
> Stood in the deep dim street, below
> Dingy façades which crumbled like a cliff.
> Behind which in a rented room
> You listened, wondering if
> By chance one might be whistling up for you.
> Adding unsentimentally
> "It could not possibly be,"
> Now it's a stricter vigil that you hold
> And from the canyon's palms and crumbled
>   gold
> It could be possibly
> You hear a single whistle call
> Come out
> Come out into the cold,
> Courting insistent and impersonal.

There are moments in this volume, particularly toward the beginning, where Gunn's formality, even in interplay with beautifully noted personal and sexual situations, seems a little bland, as if Auden had taken not to the highway but to the drawing room. But this effect quickly vanishes—notably in **"Odysseus on Hermes,"** where the man sees the boy-god as the instrument of disturbance and power, of disturbance *as* power, "The astonishing kiss and gift / of the wily god to the wily man"—and the later parts of the book constitute a tour de force of self-scrutiny and compassion. Even the most attractive old themes are tested and found wanting: "I said our lives are improvisation and it sounded / unrigid, liberal, in short a good idea." It *is* liberal, and a good idea, but it is also, as the poem shows, a luxury unknown to the real down-and-outs, the "ugly

young man," for instance, to whom Gunn always carefully gives a quarter:

> Mostly
> he perches on the ungiving sidewalk, shits
> behind bushes in the park, seldom weeps,
> sleeps bandaged against the cold, curled
> on himself like a wild creature,
> his agility of mind wholly employed
> with scrounging for cigarettes, drugs, drink
> or the price of Ding Dongs, with dodging knife-
>   fights,
> with ducking cops and lunatics, his existence
> paved with specifics like an Imagist epic,
> the only discourse printed on shreds of newspa-
>   per,
> not one of which carries the word improvisation.

The ungiving sidewalk is a rebuke to the giver, since it seems curiously uncomplicated, hard but not tricky; and the Imagist epic is like a zoom out of the young man's world into classy literature, a measure of the distance words and people can and may need to travel. In another poem Gunn explores the appeal of two young men pushing drugs, attractive not in spite of the danger they represent, but because of it,

> I love their daring, their looks, their jargon,
> and what they have in mind,
>
> Their mind is the mind of death.

Gunn's mind at this stage is itself close to death—to the death of all the friends and acquaintances who have succumbed to AIDS, which he calls a "plague," and "the largest gathering of the decade"—and the last section of the book comprises an extraordinary sequence of poems about dying and watching others die; about the exclusion and guilt of health itself when the gathering is as large as it has become. The man in [**"The Man With Night Sweats"**] has adored risk, he says, and has trusted his body: cannot regret his life in "a world of wonders" but equally "cannot but be sorry" to contemplate the ruin of his physical person, and the harassing of his mind; "My mind reduced to hurry / My flesh reduced and wrecked."

"I was delivered into time again," Gunn says in **"Lament,"** a remarkable poem detailing with patience and horror the death of a friend; and finally, however "crowded with death" his thoughts are, however much he may be drawn to the risks and daring of the dying generations around him, his own mind is the mind of life. The volume ends with the glimpse of a former lover who has decided, "without a friend or wife," to adopt a child. What Gunn admires about this decision is not an abstract kindness or zeal, but the man's ability, as Gunn sees it, to be faithful to the spirit of his homosexual adventures while finding the music of parenthood; transposition rather than denial.

> . . . he turned from nothing he had done,
> Or was, or had been, even while he transposed
> The expectations he took out at dark—
> —Of Eros playing, features undisclosed—
> Into another pitch, where he might work
> With the same melody, and opted so
> To educate, permit, guide, feed, keep warm,
> And love a child . . .

At this point the civility which seemed bland at the start of the volume has turned into a miniature form of civilization itself; a refusal to abandon either our vulnerability or our virtues, a final moral elegance. (pp. 33-4)

> *Michael Wood, "Outside the Shady Octopus Saloon," in* The New York Review of Books, *Vol. XL, No. 10, May 27, 1993, pp. 32-4.*

I wrote the poems [in *The Man with Night Sweats*] one by one, and I wasn't aware of what was connecting them, which was the almost heroic way in which people die. . . . On the whole, the people I've known have accepted their deaths with tremendous strength, even politeness.

—*Thom Gunn, as quoted by John Gallagher, in his "Top Gunn," in* The Advocate, *10 August 1993.*

Robert Pinsky (essay date 6 December 1993)

[An American poet and critic, Pinsky was one of the judges responsible for awarding the 1993 Lenore Marshall/Nation Poetry Prize. In the following essay, in which he explains why Gunn was chosen, Pinsky offers a stylistic and thematic analysis of The Man with Night Sweats.*]*

Readers and reviewers have made Thom Gunn's *The Man With Night Sweats* one of the most admired poetry books of recent years. Affirming that response, the judges for the Lenore Marshall/*Nation* Prize have selected it unanimously from more than 200 books published in 1992.

The book's unusual acclaim recognizes, in part, Thom Gunn's distinctive genius—clear, direct but always with something in reserve, generous toward weakness, dryly deflating of cant, a purely focused flame of perception. It has always been a spirit that regards human imperfection without sourness or sentimentality and that finds redeeming grace in a variety of places: in San Francisco street life or in a sixteenth-century tomb; in an LSD trip or in European history or both at once. That eclectic freedom of attention is paralleled by Gunn's ability to write either in sinuous, etched formal stanzas or in free verse, and to make the two modes fit together in each of his books.

Now, in Gunn's most recent book, that genius rises triumphantly to new circumstances. These poems have two notable strengths related to subject matter: First, many of them are about the AIDS epidemic, as seen from inside San Francisco's gay community; and second, the poems avoid stereotype and cliché. They are moving and richly detailed and they do not behave predictably. This inwardness, not mere topicality, gives the book its particular urgency. These are not poems of anyone-at-all, and because they are infused with Gunn's peculiar nature as an artist,

they encompass more than any "issue" or feature story. The individual character of the poet, by resisting the confines of expectation, enlarges the work.

For example, the poems related to AIDS in *The Man With Night Sweats* are not lugubrious: Even when it has the power to make a reader weep, the writing itself is not dabbing righteously at its eyes. Celebrated poems like **"Lament," "In Time of Plague"** and **"Courtesies of the Interregnum"** have so much dignity along with their force that they do credit to the readers who have made them something like classics already. And this is by no means an "AIDS book." The poems about the plague and its victims are all the stronger by being collected along with poems of the same sensibility that deal with matters like domestic love (**"The Hug"**), the life of street derelicts (**"Improvisation"**), the reinvention of old genres for contemporary life (**"An Invitation"**) or lowly, surreptitious kindness (**"Cafeteria in Boston"**). Though death may color everything in this book, the emotions of elegy and *timor mortis* are also colored in return by the rest of life.

Sometimes Gunn's meditations on death are even somewhat funny, as in his vision of the afterlife in **"Death's Door,"** which imagines the dead—including "My mother archaic now as Minos / She who died forty years ago"—watching the living on celestial television:

> These four, who though they never met
> Died in one month, sit side by side
> Together in front of the same set,
> And all without a *TV Guide.*

At first, having "unlearned their pain" and freed of sensation too, the dead watch their friends and relatives conduct mortal lives, which are to them "repetitive / As situation comedies." But there is attrition of a kind in that other world, too:

> With both delight and tears at first
> They greet each programme on death's stations,
> But in the end lose interest,
> Their boredom turning to impatience.
>
> 'He misses me? He must be kidding
> —This week he's sleeping with a cop.'
> 'All she reads now is *Little Gidding*.'
> 'They're getting old. I wish they'd stop.'

Gunn's peculiar variations of what is kept private and what is made open, with intimacy braiding a subtle course through the impersonal, govern such matters as the specific, unelaborated "these four"—who go unnamed. Gunn's balance between what he specifies and what he withholds is idiosyncratic, and beautifully calculated. In a parallel way, while the surface of Gunn's writing often conveys welcome to the reader, an alert rhetorical readiness, there is always an inward, subjective current in the opposite direction, toward dark sources in the poet's subjectivity. In this poem, under the comedy of two-syllable rhymes like "kidding" / "Gidding," and behind the absurd, cinematic fantasy, a severe drama takes place. The dead forget:

> The habit of companionship
> Lapses—they break themselves out of touch:
> Edging apart at arm and hip,
> Till separated on the couch,

They woo amnesia, look away
As if they were not yet elsewhere,
And when snow blurs the picture they,
Turned, give it a belonging stare.

The image of snow blurring the television screen takes a turn that is startling yet logical, a quiet surprise that exemplifies another characteristic of Thom Gunn's work, an understated brilliance of invention that makes remarkable strokes of imagination seem almost commonsensical. Here, the poem simply flips the metaphorical sense of a word back over:

Snow blows out toward them, till their seat
Filling with flakes becomes instead
Snow-bank, snow-landscape, and in that
They find themselves with all the dead,

Where passive light from snow-crust shows
   them
Both Minos circling and my mother.
Yet none of the recruits now knows them,
Nor do they recognize each other,

They have been so superbly trained
Into the perfect discipline
Of an archaic host, and weaned
From memory briefly barracked in.

Unrelieved yet compassionate, good-humored although it is quite fatalistic, Gunn's sense of the world has an austere humanity, a stoicism that has learned to live with grim assumptions.

—Robert Pinsky

The poem's vision, at bottom, has less to do with a fancied objective afterlife than with the poet's own meditation on oblivion. This individual or subjective basis for what is imagined is related to the poet's cliché-proof quality, the capacity that uniquely suits him for this book's great, variously elegiac poems about AIDS. Unrelieved yet compassionate, good-humored although it is quite fatalistic, Gunn's sense of the world has an austere humanity, a stoicism that has learned to live with grim assumptions.

This steady, underlying tough-mindedness enables Gunn to risk sentimentality and defy it. Because he does not strike the conventional poetic poses associated with the "bleak" in one direction or the "compassionate" in another, he can write poems as plain and direct as **"Memory Unsettled."** The power to cut through to emotion without using much in the way of metaphor or image, in language that is the equivalent of flour and water, recalls the great poems of Ben Jonson:

Your pain still hangs in air,
Sharp motes of it suspended;
The voice of your despair—
That also is not ended:

When near your death a friend
Asked you what he could do,
'Remember me,' you said.
We will remember you.

Once when you went to see
Another with a fever
In a like hospital bed,
With terrible hothouse cough
And terrible hothouse shiver
That soaked him and then dried him,
And you perceived that he
Had to be comforted,

You climbed in there beside him
And hugged him plain in view,
Though you were sick enough,
And had your own fears too.

Such writing recalls the principle that Ezra Pound attributes to Anatole France, of searching for the least possible variation that will make something ordinary and journalistic become distinguished. This poem's formal mastery—the all but imperceptible rhymes and the syntax stretched across them like supple, resilient cable—gives a simple anecdote the mysterious form of art.

That mode, style as a fine, penetrating oil, is only one of this volume's resources. The denser language of its longer poems builds layers of narrative intensity, for example. And there is another, imagistic kind of poem in free verse: As in **"Yellow Pitcher Plant,"** where the insect drawn to the "small honeyed warts" of the carnivorous plant becomes an epitome of desire heeded past recovery:

till grazing downhill
the fly finds the underbrush
of hairs casually pushed through
has closed behind—
a thicket of lances—sharkteeth—

or in **"Outside the Diner,"** where the wino who sleeps in an abandoned car with "blackened sole and heel / jammed against the side windows" is compared implicitly to the city weed that grows "marginal to the grid / bearded face turned toward light."

The Man With Night Sweats is more various than quotation can demonstrate, with the variety unified by a presiding passion, a grave and complicated witnessing that refuses paraphrase. The book speaks to readers without compromising the stubborn, particular qualities of the writer and his experience. The sinister, alluring gavotte of death and desire that takes place in the bar of **"In Time of Plague,"** for instance, seems to come from a region beyond all prose explanations. What creates the possibility of such speech, clear and inexhaustible, firm and fluid, is the art of poetry, worked by a master. (pp. 701-02)

Robert Pinsky, "The Lenore Marshall/ 'Nation' Poetry Prize—1993," in The Nation, New York, Vol. 257, No. 19, December 6, 1993, pp. 701-02.

Additional coverage of Gunn's life and career is contained in the following sources published by Gale Research: *Concise Dictionary of British Literary Biography, 1960 to Present; Contemporary Authors,* Vols. 17-20, rev. ed.; *Contemporary Authors New Revision Series,* Vols. 9, 33; *Contemporary Literary Criticism,* Vols. 3, 6, 18, 32; *Dictionary of Literary Biography,* Vol. 27; and *Major 20th-Century Writers.*

Barbara Kingsolver
Pigs in Heaven

Award: *Los Angeles Times* Book Award for Fiction

Born in 1955, Kingsolver is an American novelist, short story writer, nonfiction writer, and poet.

For further information on Kingsolver's life and career, see *CLC,* Volume 55.

INTRODUCTION

Pigs in Heaven is the sequel to *The Bean Trees,* Kingsolver's critically acclaimed first novel. *The Bean Trees* introduces Taylor Greer, a young woman who leaves Kentucky and travels west in search of a more fulfilling life. En route, she becomes guardian to Turtle, a young Cherokee girl who has been abused and abandoned by her parents. Set three years later, *Pigs in Heaven* centers on Taylor's discovery that she has no legal claim to Turtle because she did not obtain approval from the Cherokee nation before initiating the adoption process. Asking that the girl be returned to her reservation, Cherokee lawyer Annawake Fourkiller argues that only the tribe, a dwindling minority group and a tight-knit cultural community, can properly provide for Turtle and instill in her an understanding of her heritage and identity. Relating Taylor's attempts to retain custody of Turtle, initially by fleeing their home, the novel chronicles Taylor's search for a solution that meets the best interests of all three parties. Although faulted for its sentimental predictability, eccentric characters, and focus on popular social issues, *Pigs in Heaven* has been praised for its insightful examination of the bond between parent and child and of the rights of Native Americans, children, the working class, and single mothers—groups that have traditionally lacked political power. Karen Karbo has asserted: "Possessed of an extravagantly gifted narrative voice, [Kingsolver] blends a fierce and abiding moral vision with benevolent, concise humor. Her medicine is meant for the head, the heart and the soul—and it goes down dangerously, blissfully, easily."

Homeland, and Other Stories (short stories) 1989
Animal Dreams (novel) 1990
Pigs in Heaven (novel) 1993

PRINCIPAL WORKS

The Bean Trees (novel) 1988
Holding the Line: Women in the Great Arizona Mine Strike of 1983 (nonfiction) 1989

CRITICISM

Wendy Smith (review date 13 June 1993)

[*An American critic, editor, and journalist, Smith is the author of* Real Life Drama: The Group Theatre and America, 1931-1940 *(1990). In the following review, she provides a highly favorable assessment of* Pigs in Heaven.]

There is no one quite like Barbara Kingsolver in contemporary literature. She writes about working-class lives with an exhilarating combination of grit and joy that only Lee Smith among her peers can match, and Smith's work is more firmly rooted in a specific region (Appalachia), while Kingsolver engages the whole of American culture in novels and short fiction—*The Bean Trees, Homeland and Other Stories, Animal Dreams*—that sympathetically explore the worlds of people from many different backgrounds. She is the equal of any bestselling author in her gift for engaging, accessible storytelling, and she illuminates her themes through imagery woven into her plots with a technical aplomb that would delight any English professor. Her dialogue sparkles with the sassy wit and earthy poetry of ordinary folks' talk; her descriptions have a magical lyricism rooted in daily life but also on familiar terms with the eternal. Her political sophistication is as impressive as her knowledge of the human heart. It seems there's nothing she can't do.

Pigs in Heaven, her third novel, resoundingly reinforces that impression. Even the ungainly title, at first glance a startling lapse for someone as careful with words as Kingsolver, turns out to be a key metaphor, drawn from a Native American myth about the stars we know as the Pleiades, that encapsulates the book's most important theme: the delicate, often painful balancing act any society must perform between the needs of the community and the rights of the individual. But that's a dry way of describing an issue Kingsolver has embodied in a dramatic, emotionally complex story that sets up a powerful situation—a mother threatened with the loss of her child—and proceeds to gently thwart our preconditioned response to it.

Taylor Greer, heroine of Kingsolver's first novel, returns here with her adopted daughter, Turtle, the Indian girl who was abandoned in Taylor's car in *The Bean Trees.* While visiting Hoover Dam, the 6-year-old sees a man fall into the spillway; the ensuing nationwide media coverage of his rescue attracts the attention of Annawake Fourkiller, a lawyer for the Cherokee Nation in Oklahoma, who travels to Taylor's home in Tucson to warn her that the adoption of a Native American child without the consent of her tribe is illegal.

The reader's sympathies, of course, are immediately with Taylor, who rescued a girl who had been tortured and sexually abused. Smart, angry Annawake comes across as obsessed with the desire to avenge the disastrous adoption of her twin brother by a white family; her explanation of the 1978 Indian Child Welfare Act appears abstract compared with Taylor's love for Turtle. When the panic-stricken adoptive mother takes off with her daughter to avoid submitting to the Cherokee Nation's judgment, it appears that *Pigs in Heaven* will be a tale of a courageous individual defying interfering authorities.

But Kingsolver would never make things so simple. People's hunger for a meaningful place within a loving community has been a central subject in all her books; she has a working-class person's understanding of the ways in which the ideal of individualism can be twisted into a justification for the strong to oppress the weak and the victims to blame themselves. In her perfectly calibrated narrative, which juggles several simultaneous storylines, she prompts us to see the need for collective justice as well as personal fulfillment—not, as Annawake misguidedly does, by making blanket statements, but by showing how these issues work themselves out in particular lives.

Taylor's mother, Alice, goes to visit a cousin on Annawake's reservation (it's typical of Kingsolver's craftsmanship that this development was set up in *The Bean Trees*), allowing the author to give emotional weight to the Cherokee Nation's claim on Turtle by painting an attractive portrait of a neighborly environment in which everyone looks out for each other and by bringing to light the girl's grieving grandfather. Even the forbidding Annawake becomes human when viewed through Alice's shrewd, tolerant eyes.

At the same time, Taylor's life on the run with Turtle heartbreakingly demonstrates how impossible it is to be a good mother when you're totally cut off from any support system. Barely scraping by in a series of low-paying jobs, forced to leave Turtle with a flaky, larcenous ex-waitress named Barbie who is hardly the ideal babysitter, Taylor finally despairs when she learns the milk she's been urging her daughter to drink is actually making Turtle sick; like many Native Americans, she's lactose intolerant.

Those who see political correctness lurking behind every bush will doubtless be irritated by Kingsolver's careful, warmhearted denouement, which asserts that conflict between the individual and the collective can be resolved to everyone's benefit. But within the context of her sensitive story replete with appealing people who deserve to find happiness, her conclusion is both dramatically and emotionally satisfying. Like all of Kingsolver's fiction, *Pigs in Heaven* fulfills the longings of the head and the heart with an inimitable blend of challenging ideas, vibrant characters and prose that sings.

Wendy Smith, "The Mother and the Tribe,"
in Book World—The Washington Post, *June 13, 1993, p. 3.*

Kingsolver on the theme of poverty in *Pigs in Heaven*:

It has to do with our mythology in this country . . . that if you are smart enough and work hard enough, you will make it. It allows us to perpetuate this huge gulf between the well-off and the desperately poor. If you fall through the cracks you must be stupid or lazy or both. It's a trap because poverty is viewed as shameful. In this culture, it's more honorable to steal than to beg.

Barbara Kingsolver, in an interview in The New York Times Book Review, *27 June 1993.*

Rhoda Koenig　(review date 14 June 1993)

[*In the following review, Koenig offers a negative assessment of* Pigs in Heaven, *faulting the novel's political implications and reliance on tidy resolutions.*]

The six pigs in Heaven, explains a character in Barbara

Kingsolver's [*Pigs in Heaven*], are the American Indian version of the Pleiades, or the seven sisters (one more example of Indians' being shortchanged). Originally six naughty boys who complained about being punished, they were turned into a constellation by the gods as a warning to other children. But if the moral of that story is the novel's stated theme—"Do the right thing"—the title unfortunately suggests its tone, a cute, dreamy mindlessness that subverts the issues of conflict and choice it propounds. Starting with charm, Kingsolver drifts into ingratiation.

Two years into a dismal second marriage, Alice feels she has made another mistake. Her silent, uncompanionable husband "has no words for Alice—nothing to contradict all the years she lay alone, feeling the cold seep through her like cave air, turning her breasts to limestone from the inside out." Ripe for flight, Alice takes off when she gets a call from a daughter in distress. Taylor has adopted a little Indian girl, Turtle, who had been sexually molested, beaten, and abandoned. Turtle's help in saving a life gets her on the *Oprah Winfrey Show,* where she attracts the attention of Annawake Fourkiller, an aggressive defender of Indian rights. Annawake tells Taylor that Turtle was improperly adopted, since the necessary tribal consent was never obtained, and that she is bringing an action to return Turtle to the Cherokee. Taylor's response is to scoop up her kid and head, with her mother, for the open road.

Barbara Kingsolver has a lovely eye (and nose) for details: the "face-powder" scent of peonies, a "quilt-cheeked" crowd pushing against a wire fence. In Alice and Taylor she creates women who are decent and good-natured, with a sisterly camaraderie and a tart sense of reality (though suspiciously articulate for, respectively, a housecleaner and an auto-parts saleswoman). But television seems to provide not only the motor for Kingsolver's plot but the tone of her characterization and prose. A sticky cloud of niceness soon envelops all but one of the main characters and most of the minor ones, too. I would be far more interested in Annawake's determination to take a child from the woman who has mothered her for half her life if she were envious or demented or pursuing the case out of a desire for personal gain. But Annawake is merely the kind of character we can easily forgive (and patronize): A Bright Girl Who Is Too Hard on Herself.

The prevailing coziness dissolves any chance of suspense: Who can envision a tragic ending for any of these sweet people, all of them terribly concerned about doing the right thing? (The ramshackle narrative, with characters roaming here and there and settling down for picnics and Kaffeeklatsches, doesn't help, either.) Split between real life and literature on one hand and soap opera and sitcom on the other (the dialogue is part honest talk, part TV banter), *Pigs in Heaven* introduces a number of serious problems (failed marriage, child abuse, ethnic identity), then resolves them with a dopey benignity and a handful of fairy dust.

The one rotten apple is Barbie, a waitress who has legally changed her name to match the doll's and has a Barbie hairstyle as well as an identical wardrobe of "thirteen complete ensembles and a lot of the mix-and-match

parts." Barbie is fired for her obsession ("They say I tell people too much about my hobby. This is, like, so stressful for me, that choice of words. Barbie is not a hobby, do you understand what I mean? This is a *career* for me, okay?") and goes off with Turtle and the two women for a while, eventually proving to have not only the mental equipment of a Mattel toy but the morals of Klaus. But why, one wonders, would the sensible Alice insist on taking up with someone who is clearly inflammable plastic from the neck up? (It is perhaps best not to think about such things as consistent characterization in a novel like this; you might then start thinking, Why, if Alice is so nice, does she abandon a husband merely for being dull, and why does he make no attempt to find her?)

An excerpt from *Pigs in Heaven*

Turtle seems spent. She lies across the front seat with her head on Taylor's right thigh and her tennis shoes wagging idly together and apart near the passenger door. The low greenish lights of the dashboard are reflected in her eyes as she looks out at the empty space of her own thoughts. Beside her face Turtle cradles Mary, her square utility flashlight. It's the type that people take deer hunting, large and dark green, said to float if dropped in water. She never turns it on; Turtle doesn't even particularly care whether it has batteries, but she needs it, this much is clear. To Taylor it seems as incomprehensible as needing to sleep with a shoebox, and just as unpleasant—sometimes in the night she hears its hollow corners clunk against Turtle's skull. But anyone who's tried to take Mary away has found that Turtle is capable of a high-pitched animal scream.

Taylor squints through the windshield wipers. She's driving toward the blaze of lights she knows has to be Las Vegas, but she can barely see the sides of the road. The storm moving north from Mexico has caught up to them again.

Turtle shifts in her lap and looks up at Taylor. "Am I going to have to go away from you?"

Taylor takes a slow breath. "How could that happen? You're my Turtle, right?"

The wipers slap, slap. "I'm your Turtle, right."

Taylor takes a hand off the wheel to stroke Turtle's cheek. "And once a turtle bites you, it doesn't let go, does it?"

"Not till it thunders."

Turtle seems cramped, and arches her back, pushing herself around with her feet. When she finally settles, she has crawled out of her seat belt and curled most of her body into Taylor's lap with her head against Mary. With one hand she reaches up and clenches a fist around the end of Taylor's braided hair, exactly as she used to do in the days before she had any other language. Outside, the blind rain comes down and Taylor and Turtle flinch when the hooves of thunder trample the roof of the car.

Barbara Kingsolver, in her Pigs in Heaven, *HarperCollins, 1993.*

What is most dismaying is that Kingsolver, clearly a nice, well-meaning woman herself, with a large and affectionate public, has no idea of the appalling implications of her work. Having seen what passions Turtle inspires, Taylor decides to marry her adoring live-in boyfriend, who thinks she's "the Statue of Liberty and Abbey Road and the best burrito of your life." She has come to realize that children feel more secure if their parent figures are married and, come to think of it, heck, she would feel things were more permanent herself. ("When you never put a name on things, you're just accepting that it's okay for people to leave when they feel like it.") After a generation of the greatest freedom and opportunity women have ever known, we're supposed to feel a warm glow at one of them emotionally reinventing the wheel? I don't know about the pigs in Heaven, but the naïve self-congratulation here is enough to make the angels weep. (pp. 99-100)

> Rhoda Koenig, "Portrait of the Artists' Friend," in New York Magazine, Vol. 26, No. 24, June 14, 1993, pp. 99-100.

Karen Karbo   (review date 27 June 1993)

[Karbo is a novelist. In the review below, she praises Kingsolver's blending of political commentary and emotional insight in Pigs in Heaven.]

Barbara Kingsolver's terrific new novel, **Pigs in Heaven,** picks up where her highly acclaimed first novel, **The Bean Trees,** left off. In this heart-twisting sequel, her feisty young heroine, Taylor Greer, is faced with the possibility of losing her 6-year-old daughter, Turtle. Taylor, an outspoken, self-professed hillbilly from Kentucky, had headed west to avoid the poverty and despair that were snagging her former schoolmates. Passing through Oklahoma, she was snagged instead by a child.

In the offhand way that can lead a person in a whole new direction, Taylor stopped at a bar on the edge of the Cherokee Nation; there, an Indian woman deposited a little girl on the front seat of Taylor's Volkswagen and promptly disappeared. The tiny, silent toddler, whom Taylor called Turtle for her fierce snapping-turtle grip, had been beaten and abused. Taylor kept on driving, and when the car broke down in southern Arizona, she decided just to stay put. Thus Taylor Greer became a single mother.

When **Pigs in Heaven** opens, three years have elapsed since Taylor officially adopted Turtle. Not surprisingly, their household in Tucson is a happy specimen of the kind of family life that could never be described as traditional. Taylor has found love of sorts with a musician named Jax, who plays keyboard for a group called the Irascible Babies. Turtle is doing well, considering her devastating past. Together, the three live in a dilapidated stone house at the Rancho Copo, an eccentric low-rent community owned by a local artist. This is deep Kingsolver territory, familiar to readers of her previous novels and short stories, a frowzy stretch of desert where modern-day absurdity, occasional beauty and grinding injustice (usually perpetrated against Indians and Central Americans) intersect.

Early in the book, when Taylor and Turtle are on a visit to the Hoover Dam, Turtle is the only witness to a freak accident: reaching over a wall to grab a soda can, a man falls off the dam and into a concrete spillway. When he's rescued as a result of their efforts, Turtle and Taylor make national headlines and are asked to appear on *Oprah,* as part of a program called "Children Who Have Saved Lives."

It goes without saying that *everyone* watches *Oprah,* even a brilliant, beautiful attorney for the Cherokee Nation, Annawake Fourkiller, who begins a campaign to investigate Turtle's adoption. According to the Indian Child Welfare Act, if an Indian is adopted without the consent of the tribe, the adoption is invalid. Soon thereafter, Annawake pays a visit to Tucson, where she has an awkward conversation with Taylor's boyfriend:

> "You think Taylor's being selfish," he states.
>
> Annawake hesitates. There are so many answers to that question. "Selfish is a loaded word," she says. "I've been off the reservation, I know the story. There's this kind of moral argument for doing what's best for yourself."
>
> Jax puts his hands together under his chin and rolls his eyes toward heaven. "Honor the temple, for the Lord hast housed thy soul within. Buy that temple a foot massage and a Rolex watch."
>
> "I think it would be hard to do anything else. Your culture is one long advertisement for how to treat yourself to the life you really deserve. Whether you actually deserve it or not."

Annawake is right, of course. Still, when I read this, visions of the long-suffering Cherokee who knows the value of kith, kin, sacrifice and every other noble thing missing in American society trudged through my head. And when it turned out that Turtle has relatives in a town on the reservation called Heaven, Okla., I almost despaired, foreseeing a thinly disguised morality play in which Taylor would be forced to give up Turtle simply because Taylor's skin color was politically incorrect.

I couldn't have been more wrong, which attests to Ms. Kingsolver's resounding achievement. For as the novel progresses, she somehow manages to maintain her political views without sacrificing the complexity of her characters' predicaments.

Ms. Kingsolver not only respects Taylor; she also understands a single mother's greatest fear—that her lack of resources can be used against her in an effort to take her child away. (When Annawake Fourkiller visits Taylor's house, she notes that it "is truly rundown by social-service standards . . . and accepts that this could be used to her advantage.") But Ms. Kingsolver also respects the virtues that Annawake sees in the Cherokee Nation: the rare sense of really belonging and, even rarer, the privileged place held by young girls in the spiritual life of the community.

If the novel falls short, it is in its consideration of the people who gave Turtle away in the first place. This child has, after all, suffered a great deal, yet even though Taylor repeatedly attests to the abuse inflicted on Turtle before she came into her care, the actual perpetrators remain off-stage, dismissed as alcoholics who left the reservation and moved to Tulsa. Near the end of the novel, one of Turtle's relatives, acknowledging his suspicions that the little girl was being beaten, admits that "I should have gone and got her. But my wife was dead and I didn't have the gumption." To which Taylor replies, "I've let her down too." But this exchange seems pat and perfunctory.

On the other hand, the solution to the question of whether Turtle would be better off with her mother or her people, while answered in a way that is fanciful, is also satisfying and just. That it is gained by way of a few suspiciously happy coincidences does little to diminish the many pleasures of Ms. Kingsolver's novel. Possessed of an extravagantly gifted narrative voice, she blends a fierce and abiding moral vision with benevolent, concise humor. Her medicine is meant for the head, the heart and the soul—and it goes down dangerously, blissfully, easily.

> Karen Karbo, "And Baby Makes Two," in The New York Times Book Review, *June 27, 1993, p. 9.*

Laura Shapiro   (review date 12 July 1993)

[*In the following positive review, Shapiro provides a thematic analysis of* Pigs in Heaven.]

Turtle Greer, 6 years old, with a lifetime of memories her adoptive mother can only guess at, got her name from the way she holds on. She has a grip like a clamp, and when she clutches Taylor's hand, or her hair, or her sleeve, there's no dislodging those fingers. Turtle was shoved into Taylor's car three years earlier while she was parked by a highway in Oklahoma. Later, Taylor saw that the little Cherokee girl had been beaten and abused. "This child is the miracle Taylor wouldn't let in the door if it had knocked," writes Barbara Kingsolver in her fine new novel *Pigs in Heaven.* "But that's what miracles are, she supposes. The things nobody saw coming."

> **For all its political dimensions, *Pigs in Heaven* is no polemic but a complex drama in which heroes and villains play each other's parts—and learn from them.**
>
> **—Laura Shapiro**

Pigs in Heaven is full of miracles, especially the kind that start out—like Turtle's life—as disasters. At the beginning of the novel, Turtle and Taylor are on a trip to the Hoover Dam, where Turtle is the only person to see a man fall over the side. Taylor finally persuades someone to believe her daughter, and the rescue makes Turtle a heroine. But becoming a heroine, which culminates in an appearance on *Oprah,* engenders a new disaster. Annawake Fourkiller, an Indian-rights lawyer, sees the white mother with her Cherokee daughter on TV and decides the child must

be returned to the Cherokee Nation. Fourkiller has a personal stake in the issue: years earlier her brother was adopted by a white family. She also has the law on her side, for according to a recent Supreme Court ruling, no Indian child can be adopted out of the tribe without its consent. But Taylor isn't about to let go of the little girl who clings to her mother's hand as if to life itself. They pack up and run.

Kingsolver's fans will remember Taylor and Turtle from her wonderful first novel, *The Bean Trees* (1988). Her equally wonderful second novel, *Animal Dreams* (1990), took up a different cast of characters—two visionary sisters from tiny Grace, Ariz.—but retained the savvy wit, the political edge and the unabashed sentiment that make her books so satisfying. With *Pigs in Heaven* Kingsolver takes a risk she hasn't taken before: she challenges her own strong, '60s-style politics by pitting its cultural correctness against the boundless love between a mother and child. For all its political dimensions, this is no polemic but a complex drama in which heroes and villains play each other's parts—and learn from them. Fourkiller, though passionate in her belief that Turtle belongs with her own people, understands the damage that would be done if the law had its way. And Taylor, for her part, begins to understand the power of Turtle's connection to her past.

There are no perfect solutions to the conflict Kingsolver sets up here, and the denouement relies on a somewhat unwieldy coincidence. But while it is less deftly plotted than her first two novels, *Pigs in Heaven* succeeds on the strength of Kingsolver's clear-eyed, warmhearted writing and irresistible characters. There's Barbie, for instance, a waitress obsessed with Barbie dolls. She even dresses like one, in grown-up doll clothes she makes herself. And Alice, Taylor's mother, who has gone through two marriages wondering if there are any men at all who talk. Her current husband is so devoted to silence that he not only ignores her, he watches TV all day with the sound off. And there's Taylor, as smart and funny this time around as she was in *The Bean Trees* but with a new vulnerability born of her devotion to Turtle. Taylor is wonderfully tough-minded—too much so for her own good, perhaps, but she doesn't know how to be any other way until Turtle teaches her. Very few novelists are as habit-forming as Kingsolver, so if her work is new to you, go ahead and get all three books. Read them in any order; they bloom no matter what.

> Laura Shapiro, "A Novel Full of Miracles," in Newsweek, *Vol. CXXII, No. 2, July 12, 1993, p. 61.*

Merrill Joan Gerber   (review date 31 October 1993)

[*An American novelist, short story writer, educator, and author of children's books, Gerber was one of the judges on the committee that awarded Kingsolver the 1993* Los Angeles Times *Book Award for Fiction. In the following, she offers a stylistic and thematic analysis of* Pigs in Heaven.]

Talk shows have recently made their way to the center of

our culture: the media has declared the media its subject—we hear and read impassioned debate about talk show hosts, their guests, their content. These shows are not just a reflection of our times but have become a major force—a public forum, a judge, a hanging jury. While there used to be a respectful separation between subjects and categories, we now see presidential candidates and heads of state on the same couch and in the same setting where only the day before sat cross-dressers and male exotic dancers. In an excess of democracy, we have allowed issues to become mixed up, we don't quite know what attitude to take toward any issue. Is this serious stuff, or entertainment?

Early in Barbara Kingsolver's energized novel, *Pigs in Heaven,* Turtle, the adopted Cherokee child of Taylor, a single mother, finds herself on the Oprah Winfrey show. She has saved the life of a man who tumbled into Hoover Dam. Her appearance seems an innocent enough moment of recognition: Turtle appears as one of a group of "Children Who Have Saved Lives." The talk show, seen by millions, turns out to be the instrument not of Turtle and Taylor's happy notoriety, but of their possible ruination. As soon as Turtle is noticed by Annawake Fourkiller, a Cherokee Indian activist/attorney, the talk show provides the stage on which the electronic village meets the Indian village. When Annawake Fourkiller is alerted to the fact that the child may have been illegally adopted by Taylor, who found Turtle in her car (details of this discovery are told in Kingsolver's earlier novel, *The Bean Trees*) she becomes determined to wrest Turtle from her mother and return her to her tribe.

The subject of the novel coincides with what brings high ratings to talk shows: adoption, ethnicity, child abuse, single motherhood (you name it, *Pigs in Heaven* has it). In fact, the "talk show" concept becomes a metaphor for the book's structure. On a talk show, people with Big Problems get to tell their stories straight from the heart. We hear their voices, see the tears on their cheeks, can judge firsthand the sincerity of their confessions, listen to the logic (or illogic) of their reasoning. By then we're thoroughly invested in the outcome and are willing to stay tuned through the commercials, the arguments of the experts, the prissy righteous statements or the passionate and sometimes violent outbursts of those who have been wronged—or feel they have been. Finally, the bit players come in, the speakers from the audience step forth and add

their opinions, interpretations, their judgments and their praise. In fact, every character in *Pigs in Heaven* stands for some philosophical point of view, some political idea, some standard of behavior, and many of the situations operate, likewise, on a symbolic level.

Because Taylor and Turtle are soldered together by an accident of fate, by love, by a powerful psychic bond and by the rightness of their union, we want it to come out right for them. In *Pigs in Heaven,* Kingsolver asks us to hear everyone out, wait till all the evidence is in. We're happy to. She's an expert entertainer, is supremely able to command our attention, involve our opinions, arouse our sense, engage us—and what better combination of responses can a novel call forth in any reader?

Pigs in Heaven is that rare combination of a dynamic story told in dramatic language, combined with issues that are serious, debatable and painful. Kingsolver knows the world well, she's compassionate, she's smart, she can get into the skin of everyone from the airhead baby-sitter to the handicapped air-traffic control worker, to Taylor's mother who is having a late-in-life romance.

On a recent radio interview, I heard Kingsolver discussing *Pigs in Heaven.* She said that in 11th grade she learned what fiction had to be about: "Man against Nature, Man against Man, and Man against Himself." "Why all this against-stuff?" she said, suggesting how puzzled she was about this way of looking at the world. It certainly wasn't her way. Barbara Kingsolver is for, not against, and her fiction is about getting people together, getting them to live in the global village (not just the Indian village or any other exclusive fenced and guarded fort). When the interviewer asked her if her ability to understand all her characters was something like Flaubert's saying "Madame Bovary, *c'est moi,*" she replied: "I think he knew what she felt like and it wasn't like female-anatomy-stuff. It was the human heart."

That's what *Pigs in Heaven* is about—the human heart in all its shapes and ramifications. (pp. 10, 12)

Merrill Joan Gerber, "Those Ideas in the Air,"
in Los Angeles Times Book Review, *October*
31, 1993, pp. 10, 12.

Additional coverage of Kingsolver's life and career is contained in the following sources published by Gale Research: *Contemporary Authors,* **Vols. 129, 134; and** *Contemporary Literary Criticism,* **Vol. 55.**

Tony Kushner
Millennium Approaches

Awards: Pulitzer Prize for Drama, Tony Award for Best Play, and New York Drama Critics Circle Award for Best New Play

Born in 1957(?), Kushner is an American playwright.

INTRODUCTION

Millennium Approaches comprises the first half of Kushner's two-part drama *Angels in America: A Gay Fantasia on National Themes.* Although it features over thirty characters—including the oldest living Bolshevik, the ghost of Ethel Rosenberg, a black drag-queen, and an elderly rabbi played by a young Gentile woman—*Millennium Approaches* has five main protagonists: Roy Cohn, the infamous, real-life prosecutor and the former henchman of Senator Joseph McCarthy; Prior Walter, a young man who has been diagnosed with AIDS; Louis Ironson, a Jewish homosexual who is Prior's lover; Joe Pitt, an ambitious, bisexual Mormon who works for Cohn; and Harper Pitt, Joe's wife. Concerned with the characters' relationships with one another as well as the interconnections within America's pluralistic society, the play contains numerous subplots that chronicle the characters' reactions to AIDS, the breakdown of their relationships, and the subsequent formation of new bonds. One storyline, for example, revolves around Cohn's relentless and absurd pursuit of political power in the Reagan era. The personification of evil and self-interest in the play, Cohn attempts to place Joe Pitt as "his man" inside the Justice Department. Upon learning that he has contracted AIDS, Cohn denies his own homosexuality and continues with his machinations; believing that homosexuals lack political power, he subsequently argues that because he has power he is not gay—he is simply a heterosexual who has sex with men. Another subplot revolves around the grief that Prior and Harper experience when their respective mates, Louis and Joe, desert them. As Louis and Joe become more involved with one another, both Prior and Harper experience loneliness and various hallucinatory visions: Prior sees himself dancing with Louis while Harper fantasizes about being in Antarctica. At the conclusion of *Millennium Approaches,* an angel appears to Prior and pronounces him a prophet. In *Perestroika,* the second half of *Angels in America,* the partners learn to accept the losses and changes that occurred in the first half of the play and to transform them into positive experiences while Cohn, who refuses to learn, dies of AIDS. Prior proclaims his own unique gospel and

in the final scene directly addresses the audience, extending the play's message to the entire human community.

Critical reaction to *Angels in America* has been overwhelmingly favorable. Commentators laud it as the proverbial "great American play," claiming it addresses such topics as the value and inevitability of change, the nature of self-interest and community, and the major political issues of the 1980s: gay rights, the end of the cold war, the place of religion in modern society, and the ideological struggle between conservatism and liberalism. Critics have also praised Kushner for avoiding the sentimentality that characterizes most dramas that deal with AIDS. As Don Shewey has stated, "*Angels in America* is a landmark not just among AIDS plays or gay dramas but in American theater—partly because Kushner has the audacity to equate gay concerns with the fate of this country."

PRINCIPAL WORKS

A Bright Room Called Day (drama) 1985
The Illusion [adaptor; from the drama *L'illusion co-
    mique* by Pierre Corneille] (drama) 1990
*Millennium Approaches (drama) 1991
*Perestroika (drama) 1992

*These works are performed as parts one and two of the two-part
drama entitled *Angels in America: A Gay Fantasia on National
Themes.*

CRITICISM

Don Shewey (review date 30 July 1991)

[*In the following review, Shewey examines the apocalyptic and spiritualistic themes of* Angels in America *and
praises the play as a "landmark" in American theater.*]

The words *apocalypse* and *millennium* have gotten so
drenched in dread, anxiety, and surrender-to-the-end-of-
the-world that it's shocking to consult American Heritage
and discover the benignity of the dictionary's literal definitions: "a prophetic disclosure or revelation" and "a
hoped-for period of joy, serenity, prosperity, and justice."
In his two-part AIDS epic, *Angels in America,* Tony Kushner acknowledges decay and deterioration as the operative
metaphor for our apocalyptic era: the eroding ozone layer,
collapsing immune systems, governments corroded by individuals' self-interest, evanescent faith. Yet, holding to
the essential meaning of apocalypse, Kushner locates the
opportunity for revelation in the saga of Prior Walter, a
30-year-old man with AIDS, who steps into the role of unlikely prophet and sweeps along with him his Jewish
word-processor boyfriend, his black drag-queen best
friend, a gay Mormon, his missionary mother and pill-
popping wife, a lesbian night nurse, and, oh yes, Roy
Cohn.

The play's eight acts take place between January and August 1986 in New York City (the epilogue jumps to 1990),
with side trips to Salt Lake City, Moscow, and Heaven
(said to be "a lot like San Francisco"). Part One, *Millennium Approaches,* focuses on two couples in crisis, one gay
and one Mormon. Terrified by sickness, Lou abandons
Prior after his diagnosis; as a reward for years spent writing a doddering appeals-court judge's opinions, Joe gets
a Washington job offer that forces him to confront the
problems in his marriage to the hapless Harper. Domestic
drama isn't Kushner's goal, though. Things get flippy
right away. Harper, who takes Valium "in wee fistfuls,"
hallucinates herself into a daydream of Prior's, and they
bond as soul sisters. Because of their deficiencies (mental
and immune), they can see into other worlds through "the
threshold of revelation."

Their mates have a lot in common, too: Smart, handsome,

likeable, they work in the same building, meet cute in the
men's room, and share a weakness for power. In one not-
so-subtle split scene, Joe's political godfather, Roy Cohn,
sweet-talks him into going to Washington to be his butt-
boy at the Justice Department while Lou gets brutally
plowed by a stranger in Central Park. The two couples,
portrayed in complicated and intimate detail, form a canvas on which Kushner sketches the widening implications
of love and betrayal. But the stage is dominated by Roy
Cohn, a tour de force role: flagrantly unpleasant, shrewdly
seductive, the Devil incarnate.

The first play ends with the arrival in Prior's bedroom,
amid ceiling plaster and otherworldly lighting ("So Steven
Spielberg!"), of the Angel who reveals his destiny as a
prophet. The second play, *Perestroika,* is dominated more
by Prior and the Angel and departs almost entirely from
what little semblance of naturalism the work had previously clung to. For one thing, we are suddenly greeted
with a crew of Politburo denizens (including Aleksii An-
tedilluvianovich Prelapsarionov, the world's oldest Bolshevik), who begin each of the play's five acts with a scene
of comic cacophony that somehow recalls both Chekhov's
vaudevilles and Robert Wilson's knee plays. Harper takes
to spending her days at the Mormon Visitors Center
watching mannequins reenact the church's founding when
they're not lapsing into scenes of her husband's affair with,
you guessed it, Lou. Prior's drag buddy, Belize, gets hired
as private duty nurse for Roy Cohn, who on his deathbed
encounters the ghost of Ethel Rosenberg; after Roy dies,
Ethel and Lou say Kaddish over his body while Belize
steals for Prior the stash of AZT acquired for Roy by his
friend Nancy Reagan.

Meanwhile Prior, given a gospel to espouse called "The
Anti-Migratory Epistle," travels to Heaven to fling it back
at the tribunal of angels and demand more life for himself.
They offer him hope, which he settles for, and returns to
earth to help found Queer Nation, but not before counseling the angels to sue God for abandonment. They do, and
guess which Defense Attorney from Hell God retains?

Commissioned by the Eureka Theatre Company (San
Francisco's most politically astute theater), workshopped
at the Mark Taper Forum and the Sundance Institute, and
produced with the help of a special grant from the NEA
and the Fund for New American Plays, *Angels in America*
(subtitled "A Gay Fantasia on National Themes") takes
more than seven and a half hours over two evenings. This
is a play with impressively, dangerously high ambitions.
I walked away exhilarated, not quite sure what I'd seen
but willing to get all opinionated about two things. *Angels
in America* is a landmark not just among AIDS plays or gay
dramas but in American theater—partly because Kushner
has the audacity to equate gay concerns with the fate of
this country. And although it's only his third produced
play (following *The Illusion* and *A Bright Room Called
Day*), *Angels in America* establishes the 34-year-old
Kushner as the most important American playwright to
emerge since David Mamet—a poet and moral visionary
in love with the theater yet awake in the world, who aspires to combine history, sex, and politics with the density
of Caryl Churchill or John Guare.

Unlike, say, *Torch Song Trilogy,* which bravely and unapologetically revealed gay life to the straight world, *Angels* takes in the whole world from the specific, peculiar, privileged viewpoint of homosexuals. Privileged because the gay world has been living with AIDS for more than a decade, and as the enormity of AIDS as a medical, political, economic, and spiritual crisis has sunk in, the gay community continues to provide moral leadership. And unlike other AIDS plays, *Angels* dares to seriously treat the epidemic as divine instruction. Not as a "blessing" or "an opportunity for growth"—the platitudes by which the healthy try to protect the afflicted from the terrifying shadow of death—but as a planetary challenge to bring about a spiritual transformation *or else.*

Needless to say, in a time and society as deeply suspicious of overt spirituality as our own, it takes beaucoup de courage to write a play that addresses these matters openly. Kushner gets away with it by treating the material not as tragedy but as divine comedy. Whether pondering the Tao of AIDS or debating with Talmudic intensity the relationship of man's law to divine justice, his characters almost compulsively undercut their emotions with campy gay humor and Jewish vaudeville shtick. The playwright makes excellent use of the epic form, which provides a narrative structure on which to hang ideas like punching bags for the characters to batter from all sides. Like Wally Shawn, Kushner rarely uses characters as his own mouthpiece; rather than having someone say the right thing, he lets attractive characters speak in favor of Reagan's social policy or "tough love" and (as Brecht advised) leaves it to the audience to talk back.

I can hardly do justice in the space allotted to David Esbjornson's first-rate production or the generous, frequently astonishing acting ensemble. For various reasons, the Eureka mounted a full production of *Millennium Approaches* and presented *Perestroika* as a work in progress. (Kushner is apparently still working on the final version of the play, which will be seen in more complete form next season at the Taper in Los Angeles; it may be seen in New York at the Public Theater or New York Theater Workshop.) Certain scenes were almost fully staged, others read from chairs with scripts in hand, and still others not performed at all but simply summarized ("Scene 12: The Angel appears in black, Prior ascends to Heaven, and the Angel gives Hannah an orgasm"). The cabaret informality turned out to be not just a happy accident but an inspired touch that future productions might wish to retain. Rather than detracting from the play, it reinforced *Angels in America*'s most millennial qualities. When some revelation is surely at hand, it's time to stop looking at the scenery. (pp. 91-2)

> *Don Shewey, "Revelations," in* The Village
> Voice, *Vol. XXXVI, No. 31, July 30, 1991, pp.
> 91-2.*

John Lahr   (review date 23 November 1992)

[*Lahr is an American critic, nonfiction writer, playwright, and novelist. In the following excerpt, Lahr comments on the first full performance of* Angels in America *and discusses the play's themes, characterizations, and tone.*]

High on a hill in downtown Los Angeles, the thirty-six-year-old playwright Tony Kushner stood watching an usher urge the people outside the Mark Taper Forum to take their seats for the opening of *Angels in America,* his two-part "gay fantasia on national themes." It was the première of the play's long-awaited second segment, *Perestroika,* which was being performed, together with the first part, *Millennium Approaches,* in a seven-hour back-to-back marathon. "I never imagined that this was going to come out of sitting down in 1988 to write what was supposed to be a two-hour play about five gay men, one of whom was Mormon and another was Roy Cohn," Kushner said. "The level of attention that's being paid to the plays is completely terrifying." On the first day the Taper opened its box office for Kushner's twin bill, it took in thirty-two thousand eight hundred and four dollars, far exceeding the previous record in the theatre's distinguished history; and just last week *Millennium Approaches,* which ran for a year at the Royal National Theatre in England, won the London *Evening Standard's* award for best play. Driving to the Taper for his opening, Kushner said, he had thought, If I have a fiery car crash, the play will probably be really well received and no one will dare trash it, and it would be this legendary thing. Now Kushner was experiencing the actual rush of first-night terror: he couldn't feel the pavement under his feet. "I feel like I'm walking on some cushion, like dry sponge," he said. "Unsteady. Giddy." (p. 126)

The occasion felt more like a feeding frenzy than like a first night. Robert Altman was there, checking out the play as movie material. A good proportion of the New York theatre's high rollers seemed to be there, too, eager to get a piece of Kushner's action: JoAnne Akalaitis, of the Public Theatre, with whom Davidson will produce the cycle in New York in February; Rocco Landesman, of Jujamcyn; the Broadway producers Margo Lion and Heidi Landesman; and a host of critics, including Frank Rich, of the *Times,* and Jack Kroll, of *Newsweek.* As the houselights dimmed, [Gordon] Davidson [the Mark Taper Forum's artistic director] found his seat and glanced at the copy of *Moby Dick* that Kushner had given him as an opening-night present. "I felt it was appropriate for the occasion," Kushner's inscription read. "It's my favorite book, by my favorite writer, someone who spent years pursuing, as he put it in a letter to Hawthorne, 'a bigger fish.'"

Just how big a fish Kushner was trying to land was apparent as the lights came up on John Conklin's bold backdrop of the façade of a Federal-style building, leached of color and riven from floor to ceiling by enormous cracks. The monumental design announced the scope and elegant daring of the enterprise. It gave a particular sense of excitement to the evening, and bore out one of Kushner's pet theories.

> The natural condition of theatre veers toward
> calamity and absurdity. That's what makes it so
> powerful when it's powerful. . . . The greater
> the heights to which the artists involved aspire,

the greater the threat of complete fiasco. There's a wonderfully vibrant tension between immense success and complete catastrophe that is one of the guarantors of theatrical power.

From its first beat, *Angels in America* exhibited a ravishing command of its characters and of the discourse it wanted to have through them with our society.

Kushner has not written a gay problem play, or agitprop Sturm und Schlong; nor is he pleading for tolerance. "I think that's a terrible thing to be looking for," he told me. Instead, with immense good humor and accessible characters, he honors the gay community by telling a story that sets its concerns in the larger historical context of American political life. "In America, there's a great attempt to divest private life of political meaning," he said.

> We have to recognize that our lives are fraught with politics. The oppression and suppression of homosexuality is part of a larger political agenda. The struggle for a cure for AIDS and for governmental recognition of the seriousness of the epidemic connects directly to universal health care, which is connected to a larger issue, which is a social net.

Set in 1985, at the height of the Reagan counterrevolution, *Millennium Approaches* maps the trickle-down effect of self-interest as Kushner's characters ruthlessly pursue their sexual and public destinies. Louis, unable to deal with illness, abandons his lover, Prior, who has AIDS; Joe, an ambitious, bisexual Mormon Republican legal clerk, abandons his dippy, pill-popping Mormon wife, Harper ("You, the one part of the real world I wasn't allergic to," she tells him later); and Roy Cohn, in his greed, is faithless to everybody. "There are no angels in America, no spiritual past, no racial past, there's only the political," Louis says, in one of the idealistic intellectual arabesques meant to disguise his own moral and emotional quandary, which Joe Mantello's droll characterization both teases and makes touching. Louis invokes Alexis de Tocqueville, and it's Tocqueville who put his finger on that force of American democracy whose momentum creates the spiritual vacuum Kushner's characters act out. "Thus not only does democracy make every man forget his ancestors, but it hides his descendants and separates his contemporaries from him," Tocqueville wrote. "It throws him back forever upon himself alone and threatens in the end to confine him entirely within the solitude of his own heart."

This isolation has its awesome apotheosis in the dead heart of Roy Cohn. "Hold," Cohn barks into the phone—his very first word. Turning to Joe (Jeffrey King), whom he's singled out as a potential "Royboy," he says, "I wish I was an octopus, a fucking octopus. Eight loving arms and all those suckers. Know what I mean?" This is a great part, which calls out of Ron Leibman a great performance. Roaring, cursing, bullying, jabbing at the air with his beaky tanned face and at the phone with his cruel fingers, he incarnates all that is raw, vigorous, and reckless in Cohn's manic pursuit of power. "Love; that's a trap. Responsibility; that's a trap, too," he tells Joe while trying to set him up as his man inside the Justice Department and

Roy Cohn as depicted in Millennium Approaches.

spell out the deep pessimism behind his rapacity. "Life is full of horror; nobody escapes, nobody; save yourself." With his rasping, nasal voice swooping up and down the vocal register, Leibman makes Cohn's evil incandescent and almost majestic. ("If you want the smoke and puffery, you can listen to Kissinger and Shultz and those guys," he confides to Joe at one point. "But if you want to look at the heart of modern conservatism you look at me.") Cohn is the king of control and the queen of denial. He tells his doctor when he learns he has AIDS, "Homosexuals are men who in fifteen years of trying cannot get a pissant anti-discrimination bill through City Council. Homosexuals are men who know nobody and who nobody knows. Does this sound like me, Henry?"

But Cohn's hectoring gusto doesn't overwhelm the piquancy of the other stories. Kushner's humor gets the audience involved in the characters, and the play works like a kind of soap opera with sensibility, whose triumph is finally one of design rather than depth. Kushner doesn't impose personality on ideas but lets ideas emerge through careful observation of personality. He listens to his characters and, with his percolating imagination, blends the quirky logic of their voices with their hallucinatory visions. Prior (played by Stephen Spinella) dances with

Louis in a dream. In her lovelorn grief, Harper (Cynthia Mace) fantasizes herself in the Antarctic, and later Joe comes hilariously alive, stepping out of a pioneer tableau, during Harper's vigil in the Diorama Room of the Mormon Visitors' Center in New York City. Ethel Rosenberg, who owed her execution to Cohn's single-handed, improper intervention with the presiding judge, appears at Cohn's bedside. These hauntings are sometimes dramatized as projections of parts of the self that have been murdered in order to survive. "Are you a ghost?" Prior asks Louis as he sways in the arms of his guilty lover to the tune of "Moon River." "No," Louis says. "Just spectral. Lost to myself." The final, ambiguous image of *Millennium Approaches,* which brings the play to a halt, if not to a conclusive end, is the appearance of an angel to Prior while he languishes in his sickbed. "*Very* Steven Spielberg," Prior says as the set parts and the angel (Ellen McLaughlin) swings down on wires, to proclaim him Prophet and tell him tantalizingly that his great work is about to begin. With the help of jets of smoke, Pat Collins' evocative lighting, and the strong directorial hands of Oskar Eustis and Tony Taccone, the audience is brought bravoing to its feet. The production is far superior in every scenic and performing detail to the celebrated English version.

Perestroika is the messier but more interesting of the two plays, skillfully steering its characters from the sins of separation in the eighties to a new sense of community in the embattled nineties. Though *Perestroika* should begin where *Millennium Approaches* breaks off, it opens instead with an excellent but extraneous preamble by the oldest living Bolshevik, bemoaning this "sour little age" and demanding a new ideology: "Show me the words that will reorder the world, or else keep silent." Kushner can't keep silent; but, while his play refuses ideology, it dramatizes, as the title suggests, both the exhilaration and the terror of restructuring perception about gay life and about our national mission. The verbose Angel that appears to Prior now turns out in *Perestroika* to be the Angel of Death or, in this case, Stasis. She takes up a lot of time broadcasting a deadly simple, reactionary message of cosmic collapse. "You must stop moving," she tells Prior. "Hobble yourselves. Abjure the Horizontal, Seek the Vertical." But, once the characters get back on the narrative track of the plot, *Perestroika* finds its feet and its wisdom.

The real drama of *Perestroika* is the fulminating, sometimes funny battle the characters wage in trying to deal with catastrophic loss. Here, as in *Millennium Approaches,* Cohn, the fixer, is shrewdly placed at the center of the argument. Cohn will not accept loss, always stacking life's deck to maintain his fantasy of omnipotence. "I can get anyone to do anything I want," he tells his black male nurse, Belize (played with panache by K. Todd Freeman), before picking up the phone to blackmail an acquaintance for the drug AZT. "I'm no good at tests, Martin," he tells the acquaintance. "I'd rather cheat." And later, with his stash of AZT in a locked box in the foreground, he crows at his nurse like a big winner: "From now on, I supply my own pills. I already told 'em to push their jujubes to the losers down the hall." All change requires loss, and Cohn's power is a mighty defense against change. His

emptiness is colossal. Significantly, Cohn dies mouthing the same words that introduced him in *Millennium Approaches.* Kushner shows his other characters growing through an acceptance of loss. "Lost is best," Harper says, refusing to take Joe back after his fling with Louis, and going with the flow of her aimlessness. "Get lost. Joe. Go exploring." Prior, too, has finally wrestled control of his life and what remains of his momentum from the Angel of Stasis. "Motion, progress, is life, it's—modernity," he says, unwilling to be stoical. "We're not rocks, we can't just wait. . . . And wait for what? God." His task is to make sense of death and, as he says, "to face loss, with grace."

Part of this grace is humor, the often heroic high-camp frivolity that both acknowledges suffering and refuses to suffer. When Cohn brags to his nurse, "Pain's . . . nothing, pain's life," Belize replies, sharpish, "Sing it, baby." Kushner uses laughter carefully, to deflate the maudlin and to build a complex tapestry of ironic emotion. He engineers a hilarious redemption for the politically correct Louis, who is forced by Belize to say Kaddish over Cohn's dead body in order to steal the remaining AZT to prolong Prior's life. Louis prays with Ethel Rosenberg's ghost over the body, and they end the Hebrew prayer with "You son of a bitch." And at another point in his emotional turmoil Prior turns to Louis and accuses him of having taken a Mormon lover. "Ask me how I knew," Prior says. Louis asks, "How?" Prior rounds on him: "Fuck you. I'm a prophet." Even Cohn gets off a cosmic joke, making a last-minute appearance from Purgatory as God's lawyer. "You're guilty as hell," he growls at the Deity. "You have nothing to plead, but not to worry, darling, I will make something up."

Perestroika ends by celebrating community, not individualism, arguing with eerie serendipity the spirit of the new Clinton era. Even the monstrous Cohn is acknowledged as a fallen victim by the brotherhood. "The question I'm trying to ask is how broad is a community's embrace," Kushner says. "How wide does it reach? Communities all over the world now are in tremendous crisis over the issue of how you let go of the past without forgetting the crimes that were committed." In the play's epilogue, which jumps to 1990, Kushner confronts the audience with the miraculous. Prior has lived four more years. He sits in Central Park in animated conversation with his friends. Then, turning the conversation up and down at his command (Kushner's homage to the ending of *The Glass Menagerie*), Prior steps out of the play world to talk directly to us. It's an extraordinarily powerful (if haphazardly staged) moment, in which the community of concern is extended by the author to the human family, not just the gay world. "Bye now," Prior says. "You are fabulous, each and every one, and I love you all. And I bless you. *More life.* And bless us all."

Backstage, Kushner stood dazed and rumpled among a crowd of well-wishers. "I've been working on this play for four and a half years," he said. "Tonight, a whole era in my life comes to an end. It's been an incredibly strange ride." His exhaustion and the happy fatigue of the cast members, who lingered in doorways, seemed to bear out part of Kushner's opening-night message, which was pinned to the stage-door bulletin board. "And how else should an angel land on earth but with the utmost difficulty?" it read.

> If we are to be visited by angels we will have to call them down with sweat and strain, we will have to drag them out of the skies, and the efforts we expend to draw the heavens to an earthly place may well leave us too exhausted to appreciate the fruits of our labors: an angel, even with torn robes, and ruffled feathers, is in our midst.

Kushner and the excellent Taper ensemble had made a little piece of American theatre history on that cloudless California night. *Angels in America* was now officially in the world, covered more or less in glory. It was a victory for Kushner, for theatre, for the transforming power of the imagination to turn devastation into beauty. (pp. 127-30)

> John Lahr, "Beyond Nelly," in The New Yorker, *Vol. LXVIII, No. 40, November 23, 1992, pp. 126-30.*

[*Angels in America* is] about a decade and a *Zeitgeist* which you just can't discuss without discussing the plague. So it's not a melodrama, like *The Normal Heart,* which I greatly admired, or a rant like *As Is,* which I greatly didn't. It's a meditation.

—Tony Kushner, as quoted by Christopher Hitchens, in his "Angels over Broadway," in Vanity Fair, March 1993.

Hal Gelb   (review date 22 February 1993)

[*In the following excerpt, Gelb assesses the strengths and weaknesses of* Angels in America.]

In *Angels in America* (most recently at the Mark Taper Forum in Los Angeles), a two-part, seven-hour workup of the nation's fin-de-millennium health, Tony Kushner has written an enormously entertaining play while at the same time treating important matters seriously. Kushner de-ghettoizes the AIDS play, placing the disease, like the destruction of the ozone layer or Americans' flight from mutual responsibility in the Reagan era, at the heart of a national and planetary collapse. Mixing realism, fevered hallucination and otherworldly theatrical effects, he pulls back from the tight close-up of so much American drama to underscore a connection between public destiny and love and responsibility in personal relationships. *Angels in America* stands as a kind of lighthouse on the coast of a new era, signaling renewed feelings of hope and longing for community.

The characters—who are both types and not types, and that's the point—include the revenant Ethel Rosenberg,

a saintly gay black nurse and a Jewish cappuccino intellectual named Louis who is endlessly opinionated about democracy, revolution and other big topics but falls apart when illness and death strike close to home. Early in *Millennium Approaches,* Prior Walter, his lover—so well-born he can trace his roots to the Bayeux Tapestry—announces he has AIDS and Louis flees.

Meanwhile, on the other side of the political spectrum, a repressed Reaganite attorney, Joe Pitt, also struggles with responsibility. He wavers between accepting his homosexuality and conforming to his Mormon upbringing by remaining with his wife, Harper (who, suffering Joe's indifference, has turned into a Valium visionary). The play's paradigm of Reaganesque evil is Roy Cohn, who denies he's subject to the same laws of nature and society as everyone else, and who crows, "They say terrible things about me in *The Nation.* Fuck *The Nation."* Strangely, considering Kushner's condemnation of Reagan-era selfishness, his conservatives are intent only on social order and moral decency. They don't talk about deregulation or keeping more of what they've got.

Cohn, who views responsibility and love as a trap—and is represented here without his real-life loyal-to-the-end lover, Peter Fraser—attempts to install Pitt in the Justice Department so he can influence Cohn's disbarment hearing. During the course of the play, Cohn also discovers he has AIDS. These events, along with the disintegrating relationships, Joe and Louis's affair and an attempt to check the unraveling of God's grand design by an angel who flies in, Mary Martin-style, are the play's core.

Yet, despite Kushner's daring theatricality, endlessly fertile imagination and ambitious sense of form, *Angels in America* has its problems, some of them serious. The "angels" plot itself, for one, isn't as fully imagined or its tone as clear as the earthbound narratives, and the angels' cause—anti-migration, cessation of relentless human movement—isn't compelling. A still more obvious flaw is the way Kushner hits the same points over and over. For a good long stretch in the middle section, you feel he's taken the angels' enjoiner to heart: Nothing moveth. And in *Perestroika,* particularly, Kushner generates enough irrelevant material to keep what he's talking about from standing out clearly. The play also conflates different kinds of self-interest. Louis's abandonment of Prior comes from his gut fear of mortality; he can be faulted for spinelessness and betrayal, but not selfishness in the same sense as Reaganite greed. Yet his action comes in for the play's greatest moral heat.

But as Woody Allen movies used to, *Angels in America* generates so much good will that you don't care about its flaws. When it flies—which is much of the time—it *flies.* That has a lot to do with the play's attempt to heal divisions and its penetrating description of the gulfs between us. Kushner's dialogue is remarkable in the way it reveals the love the characters are requesting, requiring, giving and withholding, and I found myself hurting for them in a way I don't for characters in other plays. He also supplies them with a flood of laugh lines. (pp. 246-47)

[The original San Francisco] production in the spring of

1991, at the Eureka Theater . . . offered a fully mounted *Millennium Approaches* and a staged reading of *Perestroika.* (The Taper's was the first full-scale production of both.) At that time, with Reagan/Bush still apparently invincible, the play's apocalyptic vibrations were more than a little disquieting, particularly in the scene where Cohn and a crony picture a conservative dominion lasting well into the next century. Whether it's the new context or rewrites that reshaped the play's outlook, *Angels in America* now seems more optimistic. In front of John Conklin's Federalist facade with its enormous, jagged fault line, Kushner reasserts the interconnectedness of our multicultural, sexually and politically diverse populace. And in an ending that, unfortunately, probably says more about the sweetness of Kushner's heart than about the future, he points to a metaphorical *perestroika* of our own, a passing away of old enmities (well, sort of) and the disappearance of old divisions, with tolerance not just for gays but for Mormons too. Unlike many playwrights on the left, Kushner does a good job of allowing the characters on the right their humanity—except for Cohn, whom he uses for the most part as a focus of conservative evil. But he needs to address the further prejudice of the left— the one that makes the black nurse saintly and the Jewish intellectual the object of greatest moral heat—if the old divisions are to be dealt with. (pp. 247-48)

> Hal Gelb, "Angels in America, Part I: Millennium Approaches, Part II: Perestroika, Mad Forest," in The Nation, New York, Vol. 256, No. 7, February 22, 1993, pp. 246-48.

Richard Hornby   (review date Spring 1993)

[*Hornby is an American educator and critic. In the following review of* Angels in America, *he praises Kushner for deftly avoiding sentimentality in his representation of the effects of AIDS.*]

A seven-hour play about AIDS! What could be less promising? True, Tony Kushner's *Angels in America* has been earning awards and rave reviews, but it is hard to trust plaudits, given the subject matter. Who would want to seem unsympathetic to AIDS victims? I therefore attended the marathon production at the Mark Taper Forum in Los Angeles with about the same enthusiasm as I felt for an ongoing root canal operation, expecting something painful and boring but nonetheless unavoidable. For once, however, the other critics were right; *Angels in America* is a lavish, satirical, morally challenging, wildly imaginative, compelling drama.

The play is set in the mid-1980s, during the depths of the Reagan era. It is rare for an author to be able to capture the essence of a period so recent, but Kushner makes its hypocrisies seem bizarre and distant, as pious statements about family values and free enterprise justify graft, corruption, greed, callousness, and social decay. In most AIDS plays, the disease is exploited for cheap sympathy, but in *Angels* it embodies the realities of desire and death in an unfeeling, escapist society.

Despite its length, the play focuses on just five individuals, over a period of about eighteen months (plus a brief epilogue set in 1990): a gay male couple, a Mormon husband and wife, and, most amazingly, the real-life figure of Roy Cohn. This Republican big shot, former aide to Joseph McCarthy, crony of several Presidents, right-wing ideologue (he actually influenced the judge to sentence the Rosenbergs to death!), died of AIDS in August of 1986. He is portrayed here as a brutal, manic, lying manipulator, a Richard III without the hump. He denies being a homosexual, not out of any moral compunction, but because "homosexuals are men who know nobody and nobody knows. Who have zero clout," insisting that he is a heterosexual who has sex with men. Such is his power (especially as depicted in a bravura performance by Ron Leibman) that you actually swallow this meaningless distinction.

Cohn's protégé, Joe Pitt, is an ambitious young Mormon lawyer, whose wife Harper is addicted to tranquilizers. Their plot deals with their growing realization that straight-arrow Joe is actually gay. The fact that Mormons combine a conservative lifestyle with an outlandish theology is yet another contradiction that Kushner explores. The Mormon's belief in angels is the source for the play's title, and a basis for several funny, wild fantasy scenes, while the connection with Judaism (Mormons believe that the lost tribes of Israel emigrated to America) links the Pitts with Cohn, and with Louis Ironson, an anxiety-ridden Jewish intellectual who has left his lover, Prior Walter, because he is unable to cope with Prior's AIDS.

Kushner spares us no clinical details of the illness, but the focus on Louis' *reaction* to them rather than on the disease per se prevents the play from becoming maudlin. The trouble with AIDS as a subject for drama is the very compassion it evokes, which destroys conflict. What can be said in favor of AIDS? (I did actually read of a right-wing preacher who thanked God for the disease, which he saw as righteous punishment for homosexuals, though he did not make it clear why the Almighty seems to have it in for hemophiliacs too.) Depictions of endless pathos, where the only suspense is in how long the author can forestall the inevitable ending, are hardly dramatic. Thus successful plays involving disease—Sophocles' *Philoctetes,* Chekhov's *Uncle Vanya,* Ibsen's *Ghosts*—focus not on the victims but on the repercussions on those around them. Louis' dilemma is one that ultimately engages us all: How far do the obligations of love take us? Is a committed relationship supposed to be a suicide pact?

Kushner deftly uses other techniques to destroy sentimentality. At one point, the two couples have intense emotional episodes that could easily become maudlin if they were not staged *simultaneously,* in a split scene showing both homes at once; each scene comments on the other, distancing it from us. Kushner also has a wicked sense of humor, which he employs at the most emotionally intense moments; when Prior shows Louis his dark red lesions of Kaposi's Sarcoma, for example, which are literally the mark of death, he jokes, "I am a lesionnaire. The Foreign Lesion. The American Lesion. Lesionnaire's disease. My troubles are lesion." The jokes defuse the obvious melodrama of the scene, but at the same time make it more truly moving, recalling Mercutio mocking his own death in *Romeo and Juliet.*

By the end of the play, nothing much has happened. Joe and his groggy wife have at last separated; Cohn is dead; Prior ironically hangs on, reunited with Louis. The focus has not been on plot, but on witty dialogue, perceptive satire of sexual and political attitudes, plus exuberant spectacle, the last inspired by the cool dreams of drugged Harper and the contrasting fevered ones of Prior. "God almighty," he cries, as one of the dreams begins, "*Very* Stephen Spielberg!"—both justifying and comically deflating an extraordinary, angelic light show. (pp. 189-90)

Angels in America drags a bit in the second half, which includes scenes in Moscow, and an inept episode set in heaven, where both the satire and the spectacle fall flat. Kushner has admitted that the second part needs extensive rewriting, so that the version that arrives in New York will probably be tighter. (pp. 190-91)

> *Richard Hornby, "Dramatizing Aids," in* The Hudson Review, *Vol. XLVI, No. 1, Spring, 1993, pp. 189-94.*

Tony Kushner's epically ambitious play [*Angels in America: A Gay Fantasia on National Themes*] is many things: fantasy, sitcom, philosophical discussion, weeper, vision. But most of all it's a dissection of power, of "clout," in American society—who has it, who doesn't, how things might change.

—*Lloyd Rose, in his* "Angels in America, on *Wings of Power," in* Washington Post, *5 May 1993.*

Don Shewey   (essay date 20 April 1993)

[*In the first part of the following excerpt, Shewey discusses the merits of* Angels in America, *the publicity surrounding the play, and Kushner's early work. In the second part, which is based on a conversation with Kushner, the playwright comments on spirituality, homosexuality, the meaning of* Angels in America, *and aspects of the play's Broadway production.*]

When *Millennium Approaches,* the first half of Tony Kushner's seven-hour epic *Angels in America,* opens April 29 at the Walter Kerr Theatre, it will represent, among other things, a triumph of American theater production. The long list of producers includes the two most powerful not-for-profit theaters in the country (the New York Shakespeare Festival and Los Angeles's Mark Taper Forum), a bunch of hip Hollywood moneybags, and a veritable Who's Who of Broadway's baby-boomer power brokers, led by Rocco Landesman and Jack Viertel of Jujamcyn Theaters. Collectively, they have on their hands the closest thing to a surefire hit this side of Andrew Lloyd Webber. After all, Frank Rich—surrogate for the Almighty in the Broadway firmament—has raved about the

play not once but twice (London and Los Angeles). And for Broadway, the show has acquired a new director in George C. Wolfe, who—as director of the hit musical *Jelly's Last Jam* and newly named producer of the New York Shakespeare Festival—is unquestionably the hottest rising star in American theater.

This is the kind of story the New York press just hates. It's too good to be true. "The play's reputation is dangerously overblown coming into New York," says Mr. Savvy, my insider pal who knows everyone in the theater and their secrets. "Although the good reviews are sewn up, it can never live up to people's expectations. Nothing could. *Hamlet* couldn't. *Oedipus Rex* couldn't. It really is the play that everybody's been looking for—the political play with huge social resonances, the play that speaks for the society in a big way. What's disturbing is that there's a huge vacuum it has to fill simply because it's a play that attempts so much—and succeeds."

There's the rub. Much as we love to cheer something good, New Yorkers like to have a hand in the anointing. Inheriting someone else's success stories makes for attitude. *The New Yorker's* James Wolcott wasn't just speaking for himself when he complained, on Charlie Rose, that he'd read so much about *Angels in America* that he felt like the event had already come and gone. In the absence of discovery ("Such-and-Such Mania!"), the media prefers conflict ("Such-and-Such Wars!"). Sure, there's curiosity about the play, but the real story must be the behind-the-scenes drama—the competition among producers and directors and actors, the backbiting and the betrayals, the winners and the losers, who made what deal, and who got screwed.

"Everyone will review the phenomenon of the play," Mr. Savvy adds. "Everybody's forgotten that it's about a bunch of faggots."

"A Gay Fantasia on National Themes" is what Tony Kushner subtitles *Angels in America,* and he's not kidding. It's not a cosmic coincidence that the play opens on Broadway the same week a million queers descend on Washington, on the heels of the Senate teach-in on gays in the military, as President Clinton gets his first crack at reversing the conservative majority on the Supreme Court, as the media embrace a six-and-a-half-foot-tall black drag queen named RuPaul as pop's newest ministar, almost exactly 10 years and 100,000 deaths after French scientists isolated the human immunodeficiency virus thought to cause AIDS. Kushner's play grew out of that ferment and speaks directly to it.

Plenty of plays and TV shows and a few movies have dealt with AIDS since *As Is* and *The Normal Heart* appeared in 1985, but not many have advanced our thinking about the epidemic. Most portray AIDS within a personal or family context, content to replay the emotional drama of sorrow and courage through which the AIDS crisis becomes real for most of us. By contrast, *Angels in America* turns the telescope around and asks: What does AIDS tell us about ourselves? What does it tell us about the warring factors of the human soul, the part whose first instinct is to comfort a sick person and the part that would run away yelling

"Eee-uw"? Is there a pattern linking our neglect and abuse of people with AIDS, people without homes, our environment, our relationships, our innate longing for faith? Does the renewed subterranean interest in chanting and meditation, shamanism and angelology signify a genuine New Age of enlightenment, or does it mean we've taken too many drugs? In its outward-exploding, everything's-connected vision, *Angels in America* refuses to see AIDS as anything less than the central experience of our apocalyptic time. (pp. 29-30)

I first encountered Tony Kushner as a playwright when I was on a panel compiling an anthology of children's plays. Some theater in Minneapolis submitted Kushner's script *Yes Yes No No,* 12 pages of free verse that struck me as the maddest piece of kid-lit I'd read since Ionesco's story for toddlers in which all the characters are named Jacqueline. Next, I reviewed the premiere of *The Illusion,* his very free adaptation of a 17th-century play by Corneille. Then someone slipped me a bootleg manuscript of this massive play about AIDS and drag queens and Mormons and Roy Cohn, which even in readings and workshops in 1989 was acquiring the reputation of the Great American Play of Our Time. I finally met Kushner himself on the way to a barbecue dinner at a theater conference in Massachusetts. I remember him as shy, smiling, skinny, the only person in the crowd wearing a SILENCE ⅔ DEATH button. Eclectic, erudite, political, theatrical—fascinating combo.

Nothing prepared me for the experience of sitting through *Angels in America* at the Eureka, though. Yeah, it was sprawling, repetitive, dense, demanding, unfinished, but you left the theater grateful to this playwright for confirming that the things you think matter do matter—love, justice, AIDS, spiritual life—and for refusing to compact this urgent material into a tidy two-hour format complete with resolutions. This is not the time for tidy packages but a time for questioning and cracking open. I loved that the main characters were five completely different gay men (a Jewish intellectual, a black private-duty nurse, a 30-year-old caterer with AIDS, a Mormon closet case, and Roy Cohn), none of them drawn with a halo. Even AIDS-ridden Prior, to whom an angel appears declaring him a prophet, fights his destiny all the way, although every time the angel visits, she leaves him with a hard-on.

My favorite thing about the play was that it hewed to no party line. The characters argue and discuss endlessly, and there's no idea so brilliant that it can't be forcefully contradicted or challenged. And the characters are never sexier than when they're discussing the relationship of man's law to divine justice at bedtime or stirring up white privilege and black anti-Semitism over cappuccino. Like no other playwright I can think of, Kushner locates the most vital human interactions at the crossroads of eros and ethics.

When we rendezvous for a breakfast interview at Lox Around the Clock, my respect for Kushner has doubled since our first meeting. . . . He arrives slightly late and immediately launches into a conversation that's exactly as erudite and paradoxical as his writing would lead you to expect.

Kushner's game to share theater dish, at least until you mention George Wolfe's pulling out of another commitment to direct *Angels in America,* which makes him snap, "Don't pick the scabs, please." His hobby is Russian history and his religion is dialectical materialism, so he loves to talk politics and welcomes disagreement. Once you get him going, the references start flowing to Gramsci and Luxembourg and Hannah Arendt and the Frankfurt School and Raymond Williams and Louis Althusser's essay on ideological apparatuses and the state. Just when you're about to murmur, "Girl, you do go on," he'll energetically assert, "Of course, RuPaul is God," or swoon to the table—eyes to heaven, fanning himself with his hand—at the memory of spotting John Kennedy Jr. in the audience. He frequently throws his hands in the air like Al Jolson singing "Mammy," and in the evolution of post-Ludlam gay theater, he proudly places himself and David Greenspan at the forefront of what he calls Theater of the Fabulous.

On the two main questions posed by *Angels in America:*

"Do you cry for Roy Cohn? Part of the impulse to write *Angels in America* came from the way this man who I hated got an obituary in *The Nation* by Robert Sherrill that was completely homophobic. The question of forgiveness may be the hardest political question people face. If there isn't something called forgiveness, if there isn't a statute of limitations on crime, if political movements proceed primarily driven by revenge, there will never be peace and progress. But foregiveness, if it means anything, has to be incredibly hard to come by. These plays are about, among other things, love, justice, and ambivalence. Ambivalence is a very big issue. Forgiveness can never be unambivalent. But how else do we set ourselves free from the nightmare of history?

"The other question is community and collectivity. How do you define community? I don't think community can simply be defined as like-minded individuals banded together for common cause. That's a political movement, a cadre. Those things exist within a context of collectives of people who are wildly disparate. One of the mistakes of Stalinism and possibly Leninism is assuming that the collective has to be tortured into some spirit of homogeneity. For gay people, of course, heterogeneity is necessary.

"I'm frightened, though, by the new tribalism, the new nationalism. I don't like the name Queer Nation. I guess I like the word *community* because it's a civic term. It privileges the notion of collectivity over something more neutral like society, which doesn't tell you anything. To say something's a community is to imply there's something that is called the communal good and there's a way the individuals within this group behave in service to the communal good. I do think it's important to make a distinction between political groups like ACT UP, which are consciously created for a purpose, and what I'm talking about. Community is an entity that is much slower moving, more diffuse, and by its nature harder to define. Within that community, organizations like ACT UP and the Log Cabin Club exist. That is, in a sense, what the American project is.

"Again, life has a rude way of reminding us of the difficulties that poses. I was at the GLAAD awards in LA and there were all these people in the military. I absolutely believe for my own political purposes that we should force them to let us in to serve. On the other hand, it's the military. If we told them to march into Baghdad, they'd do that. I mean, who are these guys like Tracy Thorne and Joe Steffan? Sure, they're cute. Adorable! But Tracy Thorne goes on *Nightline* saying, 'We're not here saying, "We're here, we're queer, get used to it." We just want to serve our country.' Gag me with a spoon! I feel more comfortable with Chuck D than I do with this little twit."

On spirituality: "Since I was a very little kid, I've always had an affinity for the supernatural. That's the side of me that's attracted to the theater. I've always had some sense of God. I find deep spiritual faith enormously attractive. People I've been involved with always turn out to be religious in one way or another. After my mother died, I really began to feel connected to something not bounded by the temporal world. I don't know if that's an ardent desire for her that can't accept her real loss.

"On some very deep level, I find repugnant the idea that there is such a thing as the eternal and the unchanging. The biggest intellectual breakthrough of my life was my last year at Columbia when I read Brecht and Marx and took a class in Shakespeare with a professor who was really into dialectical analysis. Suddenly, the world made sense to me. Almost all deep religious thought is dialectical that way. It's never monolithic. It contains subtlety and sophistication, which only fundamentalist morons read out of it. But I'm also enough of a Marxist and a humanist to believe that the material world is of tremendous consequence and there is nothing that overrides it or is free of it. If there is a spiritual dimension, it's in constant interaction with the material.

"Which is why I feel very comfortable expressing a certain kind of spirituality in the theater. Because of course that angel has all those wires attached to her, and you can see them, and you see Pat Collins's amazing lighting behind her. You see that it's unreal and hokey and rigged up at that same time that it feels like a vision. The cloud of unknowing has to be part of the deal of spirituality. You have to be willing to live in the unknowing. Part of faith is leaping over the chasm of doubt. If you're not afraid, you're not brave."

On going to Broadway: "I never thought the play was going to go to Broadway. Rocco and Jack approached us before Frank Rich's review of the London production, and at the time I figured maybe eventually the play will get to the Minetta Lane Theater and they'd put up the money for that. Up to the last minute, there was always the possibility of going to the Public. I love the Public Theater. It's an honor to have something there. It's the most important theater in the United States. It would have sold out for close to a year. But the stage is really small; we had trouble getting it to work at the Taper. The other big consideration was George [Wolfe], who wanted to take it to Broadway.

"I was nervous about the $60 top price. It was important for me to know you can see the play for less than that. When I said in the *Times* that I wanted the downtown community to see the play, Rocco and Jack kept saying, 'Who are you talking about?' It's the audience that goes to the Wooster Group and the Public. People my age, without a lot of money, academics, people in school. An audience that's interested in serious theater and doesn't want to waste its time with stuff that isn't going to be challenging. I'm a firm believer in preaching to the converted. The purpose of left-political theater isn't to speak to Reagan and his friends.

"So I am guaranteed, in my contract, that after the Tony Awards, 800 seats a week will be available at between $19.50 and $30 apiece—the same price as the Public. In the orchestra and front balcony, too, not in the nosebleed section. The problem we're having now is how to distribute them. I would like to do a Quicktix line, like at the Public. It does separate the rich people, who'd rather call Ticketron than stand in line, from the not-rich people. Anyway, it will happen, if I have to stand in a booth and sell the tickets myself. And they're giving a dollar from every ticket sold to Broadway Cares / Equity Fights AIDS.

"Was it easy to get that provision? Yes. They were very anxious to get the play. They've been completely honorable about it. I also get a billboard in the Village."

On George Wolfe: "In mid November, when we knew we were going to look for a new director, my agent said, 'You know who should direct this? George Wolfe.' It didn't seem plausible to me. I assumed George was busy for the next 6000 years. I hadn't seen much of his work. We hadn't spent more than 20 minutes talking ever. When Rocco called and said George would make himself available, I met with him feeling somewhat skeptical. In the space of an hour's conversation, I was blown away. He'd seen the play in Los Angeles, never read it, had incredibly complicated, subtle, challenging things to say about it and detailed and incredibly exciting thoughts about all the characters. And he had this energy that was completely exhilarating.

"As I began to work with Rocco and Jack and the Shuberts, I realized I had to have a director who knew that arena and how to handle it. I could tell their attitude toward George was a healthy mixture of love, respect, and fear. You don't fuck around with George. He describes himself as a warrior, and he is.

"The fact that George is gay is a plus for me. He brings a certain fabulousness to his work. After the run-through last week, I went up to Robin Wagner's studio with him because he said, 'I'm going to go look at fabric.' They were up there discussing different kinds of chintz for the pillows on Roy's sofa. George picked this incredible combination. He has this phenomenal eye. Every single thing about the production is tremendously important to him. I love that kind of director.

"We both have reputations for being difficult in different ways. People who knew us both were scared there would be some kind of nuclear explosion. So far it's been a complete love affair."

On his own place in the gay community: "When I was 21 or 22 in the late '70s, I remember walking past the Saint and seeing this line of clones waiting to get in, and I thought, 'These people don't look so bad. I'd like to sleep with most of them. Why am I hiding like this?' I've spent most of my life dealing with being overweight. I got very angry when I saw David Drake's piece, when he talks about going to the gym to turn himself into a warrior. There's a way in which I've always felt radically disaffected with the gay community, feeling on a very personal level not attractive and devalued as a result of that. I have a great deal of anger about it. I love Paul Monette's work, but I was reading a novel where this guy with AIDS falls in love with this man who's 50. I thought, 'Thank God, a novel that isn't about Joe Twinkie and John Twinkie who meet at the gym doing their 50th rep of whatever.' The guy takes his clothes off, and the guy with AIDS looks at him and says, 'There's not an ounce of fat on him.' And it's like, 'At 50? Please!' I thought at least when I was 50 . . .! Why don't I just kill myself now?

"I've been arrested with ACT UP three times, and the most recent was the first time in that situation when I didn't feel like a wallflower. People knew who I was. I guess they saw the Gap ad or something. It was like the cool people in high school being nice to me. That's what ACT UP has felt like to me."

On gay spirituality: "I don't know that I believe in archetypes. I have a big problem with anything that smacks of the essentialist or the eternal. I don't believe that gay people have the role of shamans or priests or artists. There have been times when gay people were honored, when difference and otherness was sacred rather than satanic. That's an important thing. But are we really less well-represented in the banking community than in the arts community?

"I don't believe we have a mystical function. I do believe the oppressed hold the truth in the society. The slave knows what the master can't know. You can approach that from the mystical-spiritual or the materialist position and believe the same thing. It's what Walter Benjamin calls the earthworm action of the oppressed. The people who are really making history are those tilling the soil of time and who understand how it works from a molecular, chemical point of view. That's the people at the bottom. That's what was deeply evil about Reaganism—there's no such thing as trickle-down."

On inclusiveness: "Prior used to have a section in his final speech where he said these very confrontational things: 'We won't die for you anymore, and fuck you if you can't accept it.' I changed it because all the straight people in the cast came to me and said, 'We feel hurt by this. You ask us to go on this journey with you, and we go, and at the end you turn it into us-and-them.'

"I felt very angry at first. 'Come on, grow up.' Like, 'I haven't seen you getting arrested on any ACT UP demos. You don't get beaten up because you walk down the street with your boyfriend or girlfriend. I love you and you're not homophobes, but you're not exactly on the barricades, either.' It felt like that whiny American thing of, 'We're one big family. We are the world. We are the children. Don't discourage that.'

"On the other hand, these were political, deeply decent people who were feeling something I did not want people to be feeling at the end of the play. That kind of political note would only work if it could be understood in the context of an embracing gesture the play is making that I want the play to make."

On millennial art: "I was a medieval studies major most of the time I was at Columbia. The year 1000 was a fascinating time. In Europe there was a huge wave of religious fervor. Everyone was convinced that the year 1000 would be the end of history. The building of churches everywhere. Big social turmoil. Lots of shifting property around, in part because the nobility became obsessed with the idea that God doesn't like rich people. They were breaking up estates, giving their money away, fleeing to the Syrian desert to live on top of pillars, trying to recapture the mystical ecstasy of the desert fathers from the 2nd and 3rd century. Which contributed to an increasing exchange of knowledge and resources between Europe and the East.

"From what I learned about medieval notions of the millennium—and 18th- and 19th-century ideas and today's as well—the one thing that meant the most to me was that the end of the world and the end of history is figured as both the arrival of the kingdom of God on earth and the day of wrath. You're not allowed to know which. It's going to be both. It's a profoundly ambiguous event. If you read the minor prophets of the Holy Scriptures, they're constantly going back and forth between this ecstatic vision of the world returned to a state of paradise and the world being completely scorched and destroyed by God's terrible judgment on his wicked creations.

"What I love about the end of *Millennium Approaches* is that people in the audience think Prior is dead, but they also feel this great joy. There are great Romanesque and even Celtic representations in medieval art of people in a state of awe. And you understand how awe is etymologically connected to awful. Their eyes are like dinner plates. They look like they've died of terror. Yet they're also completely ecstatic." (pp. 30-32, 36)

Don Shewey, "Tony Kushner's Sexy Ethics,"
in The Village Voice, *Vol. XXXVIII, No. 116,*
April 20, 1993, pp. 29-32, 36.

Hilary de Vries   (essay date 25 April 1993)

[*In the following essay, de Vries discusses the themes of* Angels in America *and Kushner's views on community, religion, and homosexuality.*]

Four years ago, when Tony Kushner began to write *Angels in America,* he was a relatively unknown playwright attempting to address "some of the issues I felt about being gay in America at the time."

It was a modest, if timely, ambition, and given Kushner's brief resume, one might have expected similarly modest results. His only previously produced work, *A Bright*

The angel appearing to Prior Walter at the end of Millennium Approaches.

Room Called Day, a drama about Weimar, Germany, had received a single professional production—a run at London's Bush Theatre that the playwright called "a catastrophe."

That *Angels in America,* opens May 4 at New York's Walter Kerr Theatre, as possibly the most anticipated play of the year and its 36-year-old author is regarded as the most talented American dramatist since David Mamet is testimony to Kushner's immodest vision.

The play—in two parts, *Millenium Approaches* and *Perestroika*—is a seven-hour examination of Reagan-era ethics that addresses such topics as AIDS, Mormonism and the fall of communism. Critics have hailed it as a significant step beyond the usual kitchen sink concerns of much contemporary American drama. (The first part, *Millenium,* which won the Pulitzer Prize for Drama earlier this month, opens [in May], with *Perestroika* scheduled for later in the year.)

At first reading, *Angels in America* is a complex, and complicated, interweaving of wildly divergent protagonists, real and imagined—a homosexual couple; a married couple; Roy Cohn, the infamous New York defense attorney;

the ghost of Ethel Rosenberg, the convicted Cold War traitor; and Mr. Lies, a travel agent who just might be the product of a Valium-induced hallucination. Also making an appearance are the angels alluded to in the title, who lend an apocalyptic tone to the play's otherwise unholy alliances.

But on a deeper level, Kushner's work, which is subtitled "A Gay Fantasia on National Themes," is a clear-eyed, insightful examination of the political, social and moral forces shaping America during the latter half of the 20th Century—namely the decline of communism and the rising political power of the gay movement, two events that demonstrate what the playwright has called "the end of containment as ideology."

"It's not exactly about the fall of the right," says Kushner. "But to a certain extent it is about the end of a particular kind of political evil, one that is completely hegemonic. Unlike the problem of the Weimar Republic, by 1986 [Perestroika] had begun to happen and that would transform our political landscape.

"You don't want to be stupidly optimistic about it, and I have a great temptation that way. But it was like this miracle happened.

"Of course," he adds, with a slightly apologetic smile, "It is never that simple."

Not that anyone would ever accuse Kushner of being simple. Despite a slightly owlish demeanor and bland, GAP-style wardrobe—gray T-shirt, black jeans, grey cotton cardigan—the playwright retains an aggressive, lawyer-like intelligence that reflects his years as the star of the Lake Charles High School debate team in Louisiana. "I was this incredibly obnoxious debater; now I'm just incredibly obnoxious," he says with a flash of his self-deprecating wit.

Although he was born in New York City and currently lives in Brooklyn, Kushner was raised in Louisiana, the middle of three children born to two classical musicians. It was a highly literate, culturally sophisticated and politically aware household, an ideal environment in which Kushner—white, Jewish, gay and coming of age in the South during the turbulent '60s—developed both a healthy respect and skepticism for the idea of community, a conceit that would come to earmark his work as a dramatist.

"One of the things I wanted to explore was how legitimate is the notion of community," say Kushner. "It is a fundamental American question because that's what this country is—a community comprised of not only different [constituencies] but hostile ones and irreconcilably so."

For Kushner, who has been open about his own sexual preferences since his post-graduate days at New York University, the nation's gay and lesbian community is not only one with which he is intimately familiar, but it serves as an exceptionally apt metaphor for his examination of America as a whole. "Because the demarcation line is sexual preference, the homosexual community is also a very disparate group of people of all races, cultures and political persuasions," says Kushner. "It is synthetic and artificial."

Within these cobbled communities, Kushner ponders man's proclivity for both xenophobia and compassion. As he writes in *Millenium Approaches:* "AIDS shows the limits of tolerance . . . [and that] underneath tolerance is intense, passionate hatred."

It is a different thematic attitude from what Kushner exhibited in his first work, *A Bright Room Called Day,* in which he somewhat pessimistically explored the failure of the left "when confronted with a triumphant right."

The play tracked what Kushner describes as "a group of leftists in Germany in 1932, the friendship of which disintegrates as Hitler comes to power."

The reasons? "There is no simple answer," he says. "Failure of ideology, terror" and most significantly, "the idea that progressive people, in my opinion, are deeper and more sensitive than people on the right and consequently they are more conflicted."

Although *A Bright Room Called Day,* was produced by the New York Theater Workshop after its London run, the play was largely dismissed by critics as agitprop. Kushner concedes his play's weaknesses. "Instead of leaving the whole thing implicit," he says. "I stuck in this character—a performance artist type—who overtly draws the parallel between Hitler and Reagan and that freaked some people out."

One of the people decidely not alarmed by Kushner's dramaturgical excesses, was Oskar Eustis, a resident director at the Mark Taper Forum who was then an adviser to San Francisco's Eureka Theater. After seeing an earlier workshop production of the play, Eustis produced *Bright Room* at the Eureka where it had its first successful run.

"*Bright Room* just knocked me out," recalls the director. "Tony has a combination of political, intellectual and true poetic vision that is unique among American writers."

Kushner, Eustis decided, was the perfect dramatist to write a play about the impact of AIDS on San Francisco's gay community—the play that would become *Angels in America.* For Kushner, who had been disturbed by the "homophobic reaction" to Roy Cohn's AIDS-related death and had decided to write a play about that, Eustis' offer was oddly prescient.

They applied for a special National Endowment for the Arts grant, certain that given the conservative political climate in 1987 they would be rejected.

The result is a leap ahead of *Bright Room.* Says Eustis: "Tony took a deep breath and wrote about what was closest and scariest to him and that unleashed a complexity that is representative of our own lives."

"*Angels* is about pairs of people," says Kushner, who describes his original story line "as sort of inchoate—Roy Cohn, a person with AIDS, a troubled Jewish clerk and a Mormon."

In *Millenium Approaches,* the couples are drawn so that "they make overt sense," he continues. "Republicans are with Republicans, Mormons are with Mormons, gays are with gays and straights are with straights. It is all neatly set up, but then it doesn't work because of all sorts of internal stresses: the Mormon who is married is also gay, and one of the gay couple has AIDS and the other one can't deal with it. So within that seemingly homogenous unit there is enormous conflict and potential for eruption."

Which brings Kushner to Part II, *Perestroika,* in which he takes his cue from Gorbachev's policy of reform in the summer of 1988, the year in which Kushner wrote *Angels,* "to show the couples regrouping in preposterous but productive alliances that may be short-lived and unstable but catalytic of change."

That change, says Kushner, mirrors larger social shifts—namely the decline of the conservative Right, the resurgence of liberalism, and the growing political clout of the gay movement.

Although Kushner in person voices specific, even controversial, political views, *Angels in America,* says Eustis, is not an exercise in easy polemics. Rather, the director says, it is a meditative, deeply felt examination of "how people change and how historically it is necessary that people change."

Indeed, one of the play's main themes—played out as dialectic between Judaism and Mormonism—is an examination "of how theoretical religion exists in a pluralistic society," as one character puts it in *Perestroika.*

"One of the things the play is saying is that [religious] theory is incredibly important to us and that without it, we don't know where we are going," says Kushner. "On the other hand, as systematic approaches to ethics age, get passed up by history, the rules and laws which they had laid down become irrelevant and impossible and we distort ourselves terribly trying to adhere to those beliefs. It is a life and death matter to hang onto your beliefs, but it can also be a life and death matter to know when it's time to say they aren't working anymore."

Kushner credits much of his interest in religion to his family background as part of the little known but thriving Jewish community in Louisiana.

"It wasn't a great place to grow up gay," he says, "but the Jewish community was large." In high school, Kushner was a top student and the leading member on the debate team, but he was also gay, a fact that he says he's known "since as long as I can remember."

Any parental support Kushner received was decidedly toward assimilation. "My father had figured it out and he was upset," says Kushner. "He wasn't a monster about it, but he wanted me to be straight and I wanted him to love me. I also didn't want to hurt my mother and I wanted to have a family."

So Kushner entered psychoanalysis in an attempt to become a heterosexual. It was a futile, but not short-lived, experiment. He spent his undergraduate years at New York's Columbia University in analysis "with a wonderful straight male analyst who started out by saying 'People's sexual orientation doesn't change under analysis.'"

It took four years of analysis, and another three years hiding his sexuality before Kushner, like one of the characters in *Angels in America,* was able to call his mother from a pay phone to tell her he was gay.

"One of the things I learned from being in the closet and then coming out is how much stronger and more fun life can be," says Kushner, citing the writer Hannah Arendt and once again invoking his theme of community. "It is better to embrace your pariah-hood than to try to assimilate." (pp. 6-7)

Hilary de Vries, "A Gay Epic," in Chicago Tribune—The Arts, *April 25, 1993, pp. 6-7.*

The pedigree [of *Angels in America*] runs from Bertolt Brecht through the British playwrights of the 1950s like John Osborne and his inheritors like Edward Bond and David Edgar and Caryl Churchill. They mean a certain tradition and continuity to me, since political art was wiped out for over a decade in America by McCarthyism.

—*Tony Kushner, as quoted by Christopher Hitchens, in his "Angels over Broadway," in* Vanity Fair, *March 1993.*

Michael Feingold   (review date 18 May 1993)

[*Feingold is an American critic and translator. In the following review, he remarks on the political, sexual, and religious themes of* Angels in America.]

Vast, sprawling, inclusive, and wordy, *Angels in America* instantly announces itself as American. Its eccentric, catchall bigness, its lofty appeals to end-of-the-world millennial panic, and the cold water it throws on them with flip jokes and blunt biological talk, couldn't have been assembled anywhere but here, in "the melting pot where nothing melted," as the prologue puts it. Trying to shape a work that includes everything, Kushner doesn't hesitate to turn it all upside down as well: The speaker of this prologue is an elderly Orthodox rabbi, played by a younger and distinctly Gentile actress. The blasphemy and gender subversion, like the flip jokes, stave off pomposity, guaranteeing that every notion advanced will also contain its opposite.

Though a discomfiting character to Kushner's audience, the rabbi is what elderly Jews usually are in works with epic claims, a fount of wit and wisdom; the absurd casting (asked for in the script) implies, not that he is absurd, but that he and the actress are in some respect identical, that as Americans they share some indefinable essence. And this essence fills Kushner's approach, privileging all the characters with his mellifluous turns of speech and brightness of perception, from the Valium-dazed Mormon wife to the compulsively knowing political fixer Roy Cohn.

In that respect, *Angels in America* is the best kind of polit-

ical play. Rather than take an orderly stance on a specific set of issues, it treats politics as a connected and conflicting set of impulses, a moral soup in which we find ourselves swimming. Every move we make, or fail to, defines our position more clearly, but any choice might be unexpectedly disastrous: We're all in the soup together, and it would take a miracle to get us out. Appropriately, Part One of *Angels* ends with a miracle, the appearance of a heavenly messenger to a gay man dying of AIDS. What comes next to fulfill Kushner's vision, I can't say: It's a confirmation of his gifts that he's made people stand up and scream bravos at the end of what is essentially a three-hour-long first act.

The defining ingredient in Kushner's version of the American soup is gayness, a quality to which America grants extra imaginative license as a reward for accepting outcast status meekly. Our institutions are straight, white, and male, but there isn't any straight white male culture; this is the only Western country where ruling-class traits are assumed to include an inability to imagine. Significantly, none of Kushner's gay characters is an artist; homosexuality is only a condition of their lives, a prism through which they inevitably view the world. And there are no straight male characters, except perhaps the functionaries (rabbi, doctor) of whose private lives we get no glimpse, and who are all played by women. Though *Angels* is constructed like a classical double-plot play, and written in the naturalistic, jokey tone traditional on Broadway, it eschews "normality," implying that gay is no less normal than any other way of not-melting in our nonmelting pot.

Louis, the character most like the author—a gay Jew with a gift for verbal pyrotechnics—has a long, circular speech attempting to prove that, logically, America shouldn't be a racist nation, since it has no dominant cultural pattern, and therefore no monolithic sense of nationhood. "It's really just a collection of small problems, the monolith is missing." As the speech winds down its convoluted path, he finds himself declaring, "There are no gods here, no ghosts and spirits in America, there are no angels in America, no spiritual past, no racial past, there's only the political."

This is a joke, of course: Louis is gabbling to avoid admitting that he's abandoned his dying lover, Prior—and Prior, who comes from an old WASP family, is the chosen prophet to whom an angel will shortly appear. Louis, after a failed attempt to blot out his guilt with anonymous sex in the park, links this story with its counterplot by taking home Joe Pitt, the closeted Mormon and Roy Cohn protégé who has just confessed to his mother and wife that he's gay. Prior's apotheosis, balancing Joe's fleshly apostasy, is a parody update of Joseph Smith's vision of the angel Moroni, the founding event of Mormonism.

Both Prior's vision and Lou's betrayal are mirrored in Joe's story when Cohn, a self-hating gay man dying (like Prior) of AIDS, is visited by the ghost of Ethel Rosenberg, whose execution he abetted—a Jew badgering another, the judge ("that timid Yid nebbish"), to kill a third for America's sake. (Perplexed Lou, in contrast, is linked to his Jewish roots by his kinship with the elderly rabbi; but Lou is also weak and vacillating where Cohn is firm and decisive.)

Jews, gays, Mormons, blacks—there aren't any "real" Americans in *Angels* except Prior, just as there aren't any "straight" white males except Joe. Everyone in Prior's previsions of the angel, including his Anglo-Saxon ancestors, speaks Hebrew. It's as if our whole civilization were collapsing into some dialectical final tussle with its Judeo-Christian origins. AIDS, the inexplicable plague that reveals men's sexual proclivities, becomes a symbol for the parts of its own reality America refuses to accept, a habit it acquired from people like Prior's ancestors: One of the two who appear to him beats a quick retreat when he learns that Prior's a "sodomite"; another, in a story Prior tells Louis, jettisoned his passengers as ballast when his ship was sinking.

The parable's ominous resonance implies the presence of bigotry, but the only homophobia we see onstage is the gay internalized kind: Cohn yelling that he has "cancer," Pitt's ulcerating angst. (Another tiny irony, against the bigots who babble about gay "education": Joe found his gayness through the Bible story of Jacob's struggle with the angel.) Newly empowered as a political group, gays and lesbians are seeing their issues become the decade's central themes: equal rights, AIDS funding, gays in the military, rainbow curricula.

This agenda, of course, won't save America; it merely adds another to the pile of "small problems" that make up the monolith. But it makes *Angels* the right play at the right time. Its materials are familiar from a flood of other plays on gay themes; its techniques (overlapping scenes; dreams and fantasies cracking the realistic surface) are standard fare Off-Off-Broadway. What's new is its remix of the old elements in a big, bold way that speaks to our current condition. More than that can't be said, really, till Part Two's onstage and we see what shape Kushner's monolith takes.

Still, the main point is that half of *Angels in America* is finally here: the messenger has arrived, though we haven't yet heard the whole message. Meanwhile, Kushner has clearly fulfilled at least some of his big ambitions. Those of us who took *A Bright Room Called Day* seriously always knew he could, and those who know the downtown theater from which so much of *Angels's* sensibility is drawn will take strength from its popularity, and not fret about the inane uptown hullabaloo that treats it as the only play ever written in America. (pp. 111-12)

> Michael Feingold, "Building the Monolith," in The Village Voice, Vol. XXXVIII, No. 20, May 18, 1993, pp. 111-12.

Robert Brustein (review date 24 May 1993)

[*Brustein is an American educator, critic, and actor. In the following excerpt, he comments on the extensive publicity* Angels in America *has attracted and praises Kushner's balanced and unsentimental treatment of his characters and the AIDS crisis.*]

Tony Kushner's *Angels in America*—or rather the first of its two parts, *Millennium Approaches*—may very well be the most highly publicized play in American theater history. It is certainly one of the most peripatetic. Originally planned for a 1989 opening at San Francisco's Eureka Theater, then performed in full workshop at the Mark Taper in Los Angeles, later produced by the Eureka Theater in 1990, still later by the Royal National Theatre in London in early 1992, then staged along with its second part by the Mark Taper in Los Angeles in late 1992, and now mounted on Broadway after bypassing one of its scheduled sponsors (the New York Public Theater), *Angels in America* has received unanimous praise at every step in its journey.

Meanwhile its author, and latterly its Broadway director, George C. Wolfe, have been inspiring feature stories in countless newspapers and magazines. Awarded a Pulitzer Prize before it even opened in New York, the play will doubtless win multiple Tonys, the Critics Circle Prize, next year's Outer Circle Award and any other honors still being stamped by theatrical trophy factories. A hungry media machine collaborating with a desperate industry has turned the second dramatic effort of a relatively young playwright into that illusory American artifact, The Great American Play.

In short, *Angels in America* is being regarded less as a work of the imagination than as a repository of high cultural hopes and great economic expectations. And burdened with such heavy baggage, it virtually invites close scrutiny at the customs desk, which is to say, a classic critical debunking. This will surely come, but don't expect it from me. I have a few reservations about the script and more about the New York production. But for all the hype and ballyhoo, and granted that one is judging an unfinished work, I would rather join in welcoming the authoritative achievement of a radical dramatic artist with a fresh, clear voice.

Indeed, the real question is how such a dark and vaguely subversive play could win such wide critical acceptance. (Wide audience acceptance is not quite as likely.) Compare how long it took Mamet to find success on Broadway, and consider how many gifted writers such as Sam Shepard, David Rabe, Maria Irene Fornes, Christopher Durang, Wallace Shawn and Craig Lucas, among others, have still not achieved majority status.

As noted, Kushner's new play satisfies special extra-dramatic needs. More intrinsic appeals are suggested in the subtitle, "A Gay Fantasia on National Themes." *Angels in America* is, first and foremost, a work about the gay community in the Age of AIDS—an urgent and timely subject fashionable enough off-Broadway, now ripe for the mainstream. It is also a "national" (that is, political) play in the way it links the macho sexual attitudes of redneck homophobes in the '80s with those of red-baiting bullies in the '50s. It is a "fantasia" not only in its hallucinated, dreamlike style but in the size and scope of its ambitions. (O'Neill, among others, has accustomed us to associate greatness with epic length and formal experimentation.) And it is a very personal play that distributes blame and responsibility as generously among its sympathetic gay characters as among its villains.

In short, despite its subject matter, *Angels in America* is not just another contestant in the Theater of Guilt sweepstakes. Compare it with any recent entry on the same subject and you will see how skillfully Kushner navigates between, say, the shrill accusations of Larry Kramer's *The Destiny of Me* and the soggy affirmations of William Finn's *Falsettos*. It is Kushner's balanced historical sense that helps him avoid both self-righteousness and sentimentality. His balanced style helps as well—angry but forgiving, tough-minded but warmhearted, ironic but passionate, mischievous and fantastical. Kushner is that rare American thing, an artist-intellectual, not only witty himself but the gauge by which we judge the witlessness of others. His very literate play once again makes American drama readable literature.

Kushner takes his title from one of his more memorable lines, "There are no angels in America, no spiritual past, no racial past." But if our country offers few figures of saintly virtue to satisfy our hopes for history, the author provides plenty of hallucinations, dreams, apparitions, ancestral ghosts. There is even a mute tutelary deity, garbed like a figure in a grammar-school pageant, who comes crashing through the ceiling at the conclusion of the play, to the sound of beating wings. (Sam Shepard's unfinished *War in Heaven* is about another angel who crashes onto an American landscape.)

While they are no angels, most of Kushner's characters have their positive side. What he wishes to celebrate is the joy and courage with which they explore their sexuality in a dangerous world. His main subject is how people display, discover and affirm the fact that they are gay. (Only one of his major characters isn't homosexual and she's having a nervous breakdown.) But despite Kushner's sense that America is essentially a queer nation in every sense of the phrase, his dramatis personae are a fairly representative grouping of contemporary American types: Joseph Pitt, a Mormon lawyer; Harper, his Valium-addicted wife; Louis Ironson, a Jewish computer technician; Prior Walter, his Brahmin lover now dying of AIDS; Belize, a former transvestite now turned male nurse—and Roy Cohn.

The presence of this malignant conservative icon heightens the political dimension of the play. As Joe McCarthy's former henchman, Cohn proudly assumes credit for the execution of Ethel Rosenberg (a phantom who appears near the end). But although he identifies homosexuality with subversion, he suffers from Karposi's sarcoma himself. Cohn stubbornly refuses to admit he is gay ("Roy Cohn is not a homosexual. Roy Cohn is a heterosexual man . . . who fucks around with guys"), mainly because gays have no political power. But it is another sign of Kushner's achievement that he is almost able to make this monster appealing (the warmhearted, totally confused Joe Pitt even expresses love for him). Roy Cohn is a classical dramatic villain who remains the play's most fascinating figure, a feat worthy of Racine, who, tradition tells us, wrote his *Phédre* in order to prove he could make an audience sympathize with a criminal character.

Alternating between intellectual debates and feverish dreams, *Angels in America* lacks an animating event or ac-

tion, which is a major structural flaw in such a long (three-and-a-half-hour) work. The compensation is a gallery of wonderful characters, thirty in all, played by eight actors. The pivotal figures are Cohn and Prior, two men dying of AIDS, with two other men, the married Mormon Joseph Pitt, discovering his own sexuality, and Louis, discovering his own cowardice, revolving around these contrasting poles in various attitudes of guilt and sympathy. Louis abandons Prior when his disease reaches an advanced stage, though he seeks a pickup in Central Park in punitive disregard for his own physical health. And it is Louis, deploring the marginality of gays, who reflects on the difficulty of love in a country on the edge of a serious nervous breakdown. ("In the new century, I think we will all be insane.")

This ominous premonition regarding the new century, the expectation of divine retribution, sends shivers through this play. The sense of fatality is Greek but the prediction belongs to Ibsen, who believed that "all mankind is on the wrong track" and that the ghosts of the past and the future would retaliate for all our failed ideas and broken promises. As the ghost of Ethel Rosenberg says to the dying Cohn, "History is about to break wide open. Millennium approaches." *Angels in America* foreshadows these future schisms in the form of radical and sexual strife, the failures of liberalism, the absence of a genuine indigenous culture—and at the same time, curiously, manages to offer a trace of redemption. One redemptive feature, certainly, is a strong-voiced, clear-eyed dramatic artist capable of encapsulating our national nightmares into universal art. (pp. 29-30)

For me the central concern is . . . how [Kushner] will cope with all our deadly critical embraces and still continue his creative development. To be frank, the signs thus far are not exactly promising. The moment commercial interest surfaced for *Angels in America,* there were enough personal betrayals, expedient decisions, fractured loyalties and postponed promises to confirm the playwright's conviction that there are no angels in America—only angles. The Broadway producers, risking millions on a problematic venture, are of course expected to protect their investments. But very few of the creative people involved acted with much honor in this undertaking, not the director who broke his commitment to another theater in order to take the assignment, nor the author who agreed to drop his original designer, members of the original cast and the original director (also his close friend) after *The New York Times* signaled some displeasure with the L.A. production. The decision to bypass the Public Theater may even have hastened JoAnne Akalaitis's departure.

Perhaps to compensate for all the shattered friendships and broken agreements, Kushner has insisted that Wednesday matinee tickets be sold at cheap prices (thus passing the moral debt to his producers in the form of reduced revenue). But one suspects that for all his professed loyalty to nonprofit theaters and "downtown audiences," he is rationalizing for the sake of a Broadway splash. We have had enough theater history (notably, Tennessee Williams's career after *Cat on a Hot Tin Roof,* when he reluctantly allowed Kazan to soften the ending) to tell us that personal deception is not compatible with artistic development. Still, I have enough faith in Kushner's intelligence and self-knowledge (after all, he created Louis Ironson) to believe he won't deceive himself long, and may even turn this experience to creative advantage. The great theatrical subject, which O'Neill pursued all his life and only captured when he created James Tyrone, is how the bitch goddess success blights the life of the American artist. Who is presently learning more about this theme—and is more qualified to write about it—than the author of *Angels in America?* (pp. 30-1)

> Robert Brustein, "Angles in America," in The New Republic, *Vol. 208, No. 21, May 24, 1993, pp. 29-31.*

The power of *Angels in America* is in the combination of Kushner's wise heart and shrewd narrative. Here, teeming with good talk and good humor, is that almost forgotten ingredient of contemporary American theatre—good story. Instead of doing "political theatre," Kushner does theatre politically.

—*John Lahr, in his "Angels on Broadway," in* The New Yorker, *May 31, 1993.*

Donald Lyons   (review date June 1993)

[*In the following review, Lyons criticizes* Angels in America *as derivative, didactic, and an unconvincing espousal of a liberal political agenda that is "brutally and artlessly familiar."*]

The name of the thing is *Angels in America: Millennium Approaches: A Gay Fantasia on National Themes* and that ain't the half of it. What is now at the Walter Kerr Theatre is only the *first* three and a half hours; a further three and a half hours, called *Perestroika,* will arrive in the fall. It is the brainchild of Tony Kushner, whose earlier play, *A Bright Room Called Day,* was an explicit and loud attempt to equate Reagan's America with Hitler's Germany. So one kind of knows what to expect from this cumbrously titled opus. It has been hailed with a rapture unheard in decades. It got the Pulitzer. "The finest drama of our time," said *The New York Observer,* "It asks: Where is God? And yearns for an answer, a prophet, a messiah, or salvation. It is, in its searing essentials, about love." Golly. This language might be thought excessive for the *Oresteia.* Cleverer in expression but no less smitten was Frank Rich of the *Times,* who spoke of "the most thrilling American play in years."

As will perhaps become clear, the huzzas occasioned by *Angels* are not really about this slender, derivative, and vulgar play; they are rather victory chants in celebration of the takeover of a culture. But first, the play. It is direct-

ed by George C. Wolfe, new head of the New York Shakespeare Festival, where *Angels* was scheduled to open until Mr. Kushner thought better of that arrangement (surely not, however, out of Eighties, Reaganite greed) and took it to more lucrative pastures uptown. Mr. Wolfe is the ideal director for a weak script like this: he knows how to keep things moving, how to milk every laugh, how to dramatize every beat. Set in 1985 and 1986, the story centers on the parallel dissolution of two couples: a yuppie Mormon lawyer and his wife; a Jewish clerk and his lover. The Mormon couple is torn asunder by the husband's growing inability to stop cruising parks for men at night and by the wife's consequent paranoia, loneliness, and pill-popping. By the end of *Millennium,* the husband has still not quite accepted his gaiety but is doing mucho hand-holding in bushes. The wife is having hallucinations in which she is transported to Kingdoms of Ice by unorthodox travel agents. This narrative seems unable to settle on an attitude toward the wife: it is, of course, the hubby's duty to embrace his homosexual impulses and thus to wound this woman; it is her duty to suffer, and suffer is about all she does here. The atmosphere is drearily reminiscent of 1950s melodramas of repressed longings à la *Cat on a Hot Tin Roof.* Maybe, of course, the wife will get a lesbian mate in *Perestroika;* it seems the only solution in Kushnerland.

One half of the other couple is a Woody Allen whiner and would-be epigrammatist given to utterances like "Catholics believe in forgiveness, Jews believe in guilt" and "You're nice, I can't believe you voted for Reagan" and "Jeane Kirkpatrick, what does the word freedom mean when she talks about it?" And this guy is the most articulate and cutting spokesman for Kushner's political wit. His lover, a man called Prior Walter, contracts AIDS and declines throughout the play, dying at the moment of the close. Funny, flamboyant, campy, Prior is at least a character within Kushner's creative range. As played by Stephen Spinella, he owes a lot to the bravura style of Charles Ludlum's Theater of the Ridiculous and similar companies. In his illness, Prior is deserted by the politically correct lover and is left to suffer alone. These scenes of pathos, in and out of hospital rooms, are affecting, but their affectingness is more a function of the horror they are signifying than of any special power in Kushner's writing.

The character of Prior is called on to do more than to die bravely and merrily. He must somehow intimate the coming of "another America of truth and beauty" (in Frank Rich's words) or indeed the coming of a messiah of some kind. Of *what* kind we cannot guess, for Kushner's toying with religious imagery and rhetoric is both frivolous and (since he is an admitted Marxist) insincere. *Perestroika* will doubtless offer details of the redemptive scenario (have I read or did I dream that Gorby and Prior join hands to redeem everybody?).

But we get a glimpse of things to come in a huge kitsch angel that hovers over Prior at the finale proclaiming, "the great work begins, the messenger has arrived." "Very Steven Spielberg," quips the moribund but ever-sharp Prior at the sight of this tacky apparition, in allusion to the descent of the spaceship in *Close Encounters of the Third*

Kind. He might better have said, "Very Andrew Lloyd Webber" or "Very Cameron Mackintosh," for this campy angel is really the bastard child of the saucer in *Cats* or the chandelier in *Phantom* or the helicopter in *Miss Saigon.* It is only the glitzy imagery of a degenerate Rialto that Kushner is able to wield when attempting to convey his notion of spiritual beauty or significance.

But, if Kushner's gestures toward utopia and love are singularly unconvincing, he *is* able to hate. Roy Cohn figures as the all-purpose villain in **Angels,** trying to convince the Mormon lawyer to join the Meese Justice Department, sophistically redefining homosexuality and AIDS so as to exclude himself (the best of this stuff is cribbed right from various biographies), being forced to accept succor at the moment of death from the ghost of Ethel Rosenberg (whose death sentence he had declared his proudest achievement). Despite Ron Liebman's Volpone-like energy in the role, the Cohn character becomes in fact less interesting and less coherent as it goes along; his first appearance—a virtually unideological manipulation of power and influence on simultaneous phone lines—is his best. Like Prior—but in an antithetical sense—Cohn is loaded with too much symbolic weight by the clumsy dramaturgy of Kushner; he must be McCarthyism, closetedness, Reaganism, conservatism, and ultimately meanness and not-niceness in general. (Mr. Kushner has said that "progressive people, in my opinion, are deeper and more sensitive than people on the right.") Frank Rich, employing an unsavory locution, dubbed this Cohn "an Antichrist" and also spoke of this Cohn's "shamelessness worthy of history's most indelible monsters." Roy Cohn was an unlovely character, but this is hysterically and tendentiously disproportionate language to use about him in a time that witnessed Hitler and Stalin (Ethel Rosenberg's master).

The fineness of Mr. Kushner's moral judgment may be best gauged neither by his handling of the dead Cohn nor even by his refusal to distinguish between Cohn and Jeane Kirkpatrick but by his solicitation of a nasty and homophobic laugh from the complaisant Broadway audience at the expense of President Reagan's son. In a word, Tony Kushner is someone no wise person would choose as a guide to utopia. His agenda is brutally and artlessly familiar: to indict conservative governments of the United States for the sins of anti-Communism and (don't ask how, please) responsibility for AIDS.

And there is, as many commentators have noted, a new glow of triumphalism around **Angels** since the Democratic election victory. The play is seen as the very voice of the New Age. And in its ludicrous pretensions to greatness that barely mask a corrupt cynicism and a smug didacticism, it does seems exquisitely Clintonian to me. Come to think of it, that descending female angel may have a health-care scheme tucked up her wing. (pp. 56-8)

Donald Lyons, "The Trouble with 'Angels',"
in The New Criterion, Vol. 11, No. 10, June,
1993, pp. 56-9.

FURTHER READING

Christiansen, Richard. "*Millennium* Fits Times: Drama Treats AIDS, Homosexuality with Sensibility." *The Chicago Tribune* (5 May 1993): 30.
　　Favorable review of *Millennium Approaches.* Christiansen remarks that "no recent American drama . . . has come close to approaching the grandeur of language, the complexity of construction and the scope of invention that Kushner displays here."

Feingold, Michael. "Epic Assumptions." *The Village Voice* XXXVIII, No. 49 (7 December 1993): 93.
　　Mixed review of the Broadway production of *Perestroika.*

Kroll, Jack. "A Seven-Hour Gay Fantasia: A Daring and Dazzling Play for Our Time." *Newsweek* CXX, No. 21 (23 November 1992): 83.
　　Positive review of the world premiere of *Angels in America* at the Mark Taper Forum in Los Angeles.

————. "A Broadway Godsend: *Angels in America,* an Epic of AIDS and Homosexuality, Is a Big Ticket." *Newsweek* CXXI, No. 19 (10 May 1993): 56-8.
　　Comments on the Broadway production of *Angels in America* and states that Kushner's play "is unapologetically bold in moving the theme of gay sensibility from the margin to the center of American culture."

————. "Heaven and Earth on Broadway." *Newsweek* CXXII, No. 23 (6 December 1993): 83.
　　Favorably reviews the Broadway production of *Perestroika.*

Kushner, Tony. "Is It a Fiction That Playwrights Create Alone?" *The New York Times* (21 November 1993): Section 2: 1, 30-1.
　　Discusses the writing of *Angels in America.*

Pacheco, Patrick. "How Well Did *Angels* Fly on Opening Night?" *Los Angeles Times* (6 May 1993): F1, F7.
　　Discusses the Broadway opening of *Angels in America* and notes that "as revolutionary as *Angels in America* promises to be for the theater . . . it also appears, on the other hand, to support the most traditional of Broadway's values: spectacle, riveting drama and rich characters."

Richards, David. "*Angels* Finds a Poignant Note of Hope." *The New York Times* (28 November 1993): Section 2: 1, 27.
　　Favorably reviews the Broadway production of *Perestroika,* praising the play as hopeful and compassionate.

Simon, John. "Of Wings and Webs." *New York* 26, No. 20 (17 May 1993): 102-03.
　　Mixed review of *Millennium Approaches,* part one of *Angels in America.*

Stayton, Richard. "An Epic Look at Reagan-Era Morality." *Los Angeles Times* (13 May 1990): 45-6, 48.
　　Discusses Kushner's background and the development of *Angels in America.* The essay is based on an interview with Kushner and director Oskar Eustis.

Weber, Bruce. "Angels' Angels." *New York Times Magazine*
CXLII, No. 49,312 (25 April 1993): 27-31, 48, 50, 52, 54, 56,
58.

 Surveys the on- and off-Broadway productions of *Angels
in America*.

Toni Morrison

Nobel Prize in Literature

(Born Chloe Anthony Wofford) Born in 1931, Morrison is an American novelist, editor, critic, essayist, and playwright.

For further information on Morrison's life and career, see *CLC,* Volumes 4, 10, 22, and 55.

INTRODUCTION

Considered one of the foremost figures in contemporary American fiction, Morrison has won international acclaim for works in which she examines the role of race in American society. Using unconventional narrative structures, poetic language, myth, and folklore, Morrison addresses such issues as black victimization, the emotional and social effects of racial and sexual oppression, and the difficulties African Americans face in trying to achieve a sense of identity in a society dominated by white cultural values. In her explorations of such complex social, political, and philosophical concerns, Morrison acknowledges that reality is ambiguous and that truth is frequently impossible to apprehend. Catherine Rainwater, in addressing the principal themes in Morrison's works, has stated that "[Morrison's] novels are strategic attacks on 'innocent' readers, who assume that art (or any other form of human communication) carries reliable messages to or from the obscure territory of the inner self." In awarding Morrison the Nobel Prize for Literature, the Swedish Academy praised her for giving "life to an essential aspect of American reality" in novels "characterized by visionary force and poetic import."

Morrison was born and raised in Lorain, Ohio. As a child, she became well acquainted with the myths and folklore which figure prominently in her works. Her parents frequently told her ghost stories, and her grandmother kept a journal in which she documented her dreams, believing they could foretell the future. Morrison read avidly as an adolescent, with her interests ranging from classic Russian novels to the works of Jane Austen to Gustave Flaubert's *Madame Bovary* (1857). Morrison later commented: "These books were not written for a little black girl in Lorain, Ohio, but they were so magnificently done that I got them anyway—they spoke directly to me out of their own specificity. I wasn't thinking of writing then . . . but when I wrote my first novel [*The Bluest Eye*] years later, I wanted to capture that same specificity about the nature and feeling of the culture *I* grew up in." After graduating from Howard University with a bachelor's degree in 1953, Morrison earned a master's degree in English from Cornell

University in 1955. She began working as an editor for a textbook subsidiary of Random House in Syracuse, New York, in 1966 and a few years later obtained an editorial position at Random House in New York City. She was instrumental in publishing the autobiographies of such figures as Muhammad Ali and Angela Davis as well as the fiction of such African-American authors as Toni Cade Bambara, Henry Dumas, and Gayl Jones. Morrison left Random House in 1987 to focus on teaching and writing. She has taught at such institutions as Yale University, Bard College, and Princeton University.

The Bluest Eye focuses on Pecola Breedlove, an eleven-year-old black girl who believes she is ugly and longs for blue eyes. Her fixation turns to insanity, however, after she is raped by her father and subsequently gives birth to a premature baby who later dies. Pecola eventually withdraws into a world of fantasy, believing that no one has eyes as blue as hers. In this work Morrison addresses the conflicts between black identity and white cultural values, the social repercussions of marginalizing impoverished members of American society, and the psychological and emotional effects of victimization. At the end of the novel, the narrator observes that Pecola was "all the waste and beauty of the world. . . . All of our waste which we dumped on her and which she absorbed. And all of our beauty, which was hers first and which she gave to us. All of us—all who knew her—felt so wholesome after we cleaned ourselves on her." Reaction to *The Bluest Eye* was positive, with critics praising Morrison's exploration of complex themes, her accessible narrative, and her use of poetic language.

Nominated for a National Book Award in 1974, *Sula* traces the lives of two black women from childhood to maturity. Nel, the more conventional of the two, marries and has children, while Sula goes to college and travels. Although considered an inspiring symbol of freedom by some members of her community, Sula is also perceived as evil because her actions suggest that she can be violent, heartless, and malicious. During the course of the story, for example, she drops a young boy to his death, watches with interest as her mother dies by fire, and seduces Jude, Nel's husband. While some reviewers maintain that Nel and Sula represent good and evil, others interpret the relationship between the characters as representative of an intrinsic conflict experienced by black women: the conflict between the desire to rebel and the urge to conform. Morrison herself states in the novel: "Because [Nel and Sula] had discovered . . . that they were neither white nor male, and that all freedom and triumph was forbidden to them, they had set about creating something else to be." Some critics found the novel's apparent amorality disturbing— Jerry H. Bryant, for instance, perceived something "ominous" in "the chilling detachment" with which Morrison drew her characters—but most were impressed with Morrison's complex characterization.

Song of Solomon, which won the National Book Critics Circle Award in 1977, chronicles Milkman Dead's search for self-identity. At the beginning of the novel, Milkman is torn between the altruistic values of his aunt and the materialism of his father who, being the richest black man in a Michigan town, advises his son: "Own things. And let the things you own own other things. Then you'll own yourself and other people, too." Feeling confused and dissatisfied, Milkman embarks on a journey during which he discovers the richness of his African-American heritage, the importance of community, and the nature of love and faith. Dorothy H. Lee, describing Milkman's spiritual transformation, has stated: "Figuratively, [Milkman] travels from innocence to awareness, i.e., from ignorance of origins, heritage, identity, and communal responsibility to knowledge and acceptance. He moves from selfish and materialistic dilettantism to an understanding of brotherhood." In addition to praising Morrison's portrayal of Milkman's spiritual transformation, critics lauded her blending of fantasy and reality and her adept use of myths and folktales. *Song of Solomon* was the first of Morrison's works to become a bestseller and is generally considered to be the work which established her as a major American writer.

Set on the isolated West Indian island of Isle de Chevaliers, *Tar Baby* focuses on the relationship between Jadine and Son. Jadine, a black model who was educated in Paris, is vain, materialistic, and alienated from African-American culture and her parents, who work as servants. Son is a young drifter from Florida who shuns social hierarchies and is critical of the corruption associated with wealth and power. As the novel progresses, Jadine must decide between Son, to whom she is passionately attracted, and a wealthy white man who has proposed to her. Critics generally interpret *Tar Baby* as an examination of the conflicts that can arise when one attempts to deny one's past. Elizabeth B. House, for example, has stated that Morrison "suggests no easy way to understand what one's link to a heritage should be, nor does she offer infallible methods for dealing with power. Rather, with an astonishing insight and grace, she demonstrates the pervasiveness of such dilemmas and the degree to which they affect human beings, both black and white." Although some commentators found *Tar Baby* obscure and claimed its characters lacked motivation, most praised it for its provocative themes and complex symbolism.

Set in a small Ohio town in the years following the American Civil War, *Beloved* explores the hardships endured by a former slave woman, Sethe, during the Reconstruction Era. Mistakenly believing that she will be taken back to slavery, Sethe murders her infant daughter, Beloved, to spare the girl a life in bondage. Morrison based this scenario on an article she read in a nineteenth-century magazine while editing *The Black Book,* a history of blacks in America. According to the article, Margaret Garner was a runaway slave who was tracked by her owner to Cincinnati. Faced with imminent capture, Garner attempted to murder her four children but only succeeded in killing one. "I just imagined the life of a dead girl which was the girl that Margaret Garner killed," Morrison explained. "And I call her Beloved so that I can filter all these confrontations and questions that she has . . . and then to extend her life . . . her search, her quest." In *Beloved,* Sethe's daughter returns from the grave after twenty years, seeking revenge for her death. Through the use of flashbacks, fragmented narration, and myth, Morrison details the events that led to Sethe's crime and her refusal to seek expiation from the black community. While some critics have contended that Morrison's depictions of violence and humiliation in *Beloved* are melodramatic, most regard her rendition of slavery and its psychological manifestations as among the most affecting in contemporary American literature.

Beloved became a source of controversy several months after its publication. When the novel failed to win a 1987 National Book Award or National Book Critics Circle Award, forty-eight prominent black writers and critics signed a tribute to Morrison's career and published it in the 24 January 1988 edition of the *New York Times Book Review.* The document suggested that despite the international acclaim Morrison had garnered for her works, she had yet to receive sufficient national recognition. The writers' statement prompted heated debate within the New York literary community, and some critics charged Morrison's supporters with racist manipulation. When *Be-*

loved was awarded the 1988 Pulitzer Prize for Fiction, Robert Christopher, the secretary of the Pulitzer board, stated: "[It] would be unfortunate if anyone diluted the value of Toni Morrison's achievement by suggesting that her prize rested on anything but merit."

Jazz chronicles the tempestuous relationship between Joe and Violet Trace, a black couple from Virginia who move to Harlem in 1906. While the novel is set twenty years later when Joe and Violet are settled and content, Morrison uses flashbacks to reveal that Joe once shot and killed an eighteen-year-old girl with whom he had had an affair. In this work Morrison addresses such themes as jealousy and forgiveness, and depicts 1920s Harlem as a symbol of freedom and excitement for many African Americans. Michael Dorris has stated that *Jazz* is "a novel about change and continuity, about immigration: the belongingness you leave behind and the tied-together suitcase you carry under your arm. It's about coping with arrival in a destination that doesn't let you stay the same person." While critical reaction was generally positive, some commentators found Morrison's improvisational narrative structure disjointed and confusing.

Playing in the Dark: Whiteness and the Literary Imagination, Morrison's first work of literary criticism, was first presented as a series of lectures at Harvard University. Maintaining that black characters in classic American novels have been marginalized by literary critics, Morrison seeks to expand the study of American literature through an area of study she calls American Africanism. Morrison explains in the work's preface: "[Until] very recently, and regardless of the race of the author, the readers of virtually all of American fiction have been positioned as white. I am interested to know what that assumption has meant to the literary imagination. When does racial 'unconsciousness' or awareness of race enrich interpretive language, and when does it impoverish it? What does positing one's writerly self, in the wholly racialized society that is the United States, as unraced and all others as raced entail? What happens to the writerly imagination of a black author who is at some level *always* conscious of representing one's own race to, or in spite of, a race of readers that understands itself to be 'universal' or race-free? In other words, how is 'literary whiteness' and 'literary blackness' made, and what is the consequence of that construction?" Critics have praised *Playing in the Dark* as a thoughtful and original examination of how literary criticism has both perpetuated and ignored the racism inherent in American society.

PRINCIPAL WORKS

The Bluest Eye (novel) 1970
Sula (novel) 1973
The Black Book [editor] (nonfiction) 1974
Song of Solomon (novel) 1977
Tar Baby (novel) 1981

Dreaming Emmett (drama) 1986
Beloved (novel) 1987
Jazz (novel) 1992
Playing in the Dark: Whiteness and the Literary Imagination (essays) 1992

OVERVIEWS

Cynthia A. Davis (essay date 1982)

[*Davis is an American critic and educator. In the following essay, which was originally published in* Contemporary Literature *in 1982, she examines Morrison's treatment of identity, society, and myth in* The Bluest Eye, Sula, *and* Song of Solomon.]

Toni Morrison's novels have attracted both popular and critical attention for their inventive blend of realism and fantasy, unsparing social analysis, and passionate philosophical concerns. The combination of social observation with broadening and allusive commentary gives her fictions the symbolic quality of myth, and in fact the search for a myth adequate to experience is one of Morrison's central themes. Because her world and characters are inescapably involved with problems of perception, definition, and meaning, they direct attention to Morrison's own ordering view and its implications.

All of Morrison's characters exist in a world defined by its blackness and by the surrounding white society that both violates and denies it. The destructive effect of the white society can take the form of outright physical violence, but oppression in Morrison's world is more often psychic violence. She rarely depicts white characters, for the brutality here is less a single act than the systematic denial of the reality of black lives. The theme of "invisibility" is, of course, a common one in black American literature, but Morrison avoids the picture of the black person "invisible" in white life (Ellison's Invisible Man trying to confront passersby). Instead, she immerses the reader in the black community; the white society's ignorance of that concrete, vivid, and diverse world is thus even more striking.

The constant censorship of and intrusion on black life from the surrounding society is emphasized not by specific events so much as by a consistent pattern of misnaming. Power for Morrison is largely the power to name, to define reality and perception. The world of [*The Bluest Eye,* ***Sula,*** and ***Song of Solomon***] is distinguished by the discrepancy between name and reality. ***The Bluest Eye*** (1970), for example, opens with a primer description of a "typical" American family: "Here is the house. It is green and white. It has a red door. It is very pretty. Here is the family. Mother, Father, Dick, and Jane live in the green-and-white house." And so on. Portions of that description reappear as chapter headings for the story of black lives, all removed in various degrees from the textbook "reality." ***Sula*** (1973) begins with a description of the black neighborhood "called the Bottom in spite of the fact that it was up in the hills": another misnamed, even reversed situation, in this case the result of a white man's greedy joke. The same pattern is extended in *Song of Solomon* (1977): for example, the first pages describe "Not Doctor Street, a name the post office did not recognize," and "No Mercy Hospital." Both names are unofficial; the black experience they represent is denied by the city fathers who named Mains Avenue and Mercy Hospital. And *Song of Solomon* is full of characters with ludicrous, multiple, or lost names, like the first Macon Dead, who received "this heavy name scrawled in perfect thoughtlessness by a drunken Yankee in the Union Army." In all these cases, the misnaming does not eliminate the reality of the black world; invisibility is not non-existence. But it does reflect a distortion. Blacks are visible to white culture only insofar as they fit its frame of reference and serve its needs. Thus they are consistently reduced and reified, losing their independent reality. Mrs. Breedlove in *The Bluest Eye* has a nickname, "Polly," that only whites use; it reduces her dignity and identifies her as "the ideal servant." When the elegant Helene Wright [in *Sula*] becomes just "gal" to a white conductor, she and her daughter Nel feel that she is "flawed," "really custard" under the elegant exterior.

To some extent this problem is an inescapable ontological experience. As [Jean-Paul Sartre has pointed out in *Being and Nothingness* (1966)], human relations revolve around the experience of "the Look," for being "seen" by another both confirms one's reality and threatens one's sense of freedom: "I grasp the Other's look at the very center of my act as the solidification and alienation of my own possibilities." Alone, I can see myself as pure consciousness in a world of possible projects; the Other's look makes me see myself as an object in another perception. "The Other as a look is only that—my transcendence transcended." If I can make the other into an object in my world, I can "transcend" him: "Thus my project of recovering myself is fundamentally a project of absorbing the Other." The result is a cycle of conflicting and shifting subject-object relationships in which both sides try simultaneously to remain in control of the relationship and to use the Other's look to confirm identity. The difficulty of such an attempt tempts human beings to Bad Faith, "a vacillation between transcendence and facticity which refuses to recognize either one for what it really is or to synthesize them." What that means can be seen in the many Morrison characters who try to define themselves through the eyes of others. Jude Greene [in *Sula*], for example, marries Nel so that he can "see himself taking shape in her eyes;" and Milkman Dead [in *Song of Solomon*] finds that only when Guitar Bains shares his dream can he feel "a self inside himself emerge, a clean-lined definite self." Such characters are in Bad Faith not because they recognize other viewers, but because they use others to escape their own responsibility to define themselves. The woman who, like Mrs. Breedlove, feels most powerful when most submerged in flesh, most like a *thing*, similarly falls into Bad Faith: ". . . I know that my flesh is all that be on his mind. That he couldn't stop if he had to. . . . I feel a power. I be strong, I be pretty, I be young." Milkman complains that he feels "used. Somehow everybody was using him for something or as something." Many of Morrison's charac-

ters learn to like being used and using in return. They collaborate in their own reification so that they can feel that it is "chosen."

Such characters can fall into Bad Faith not only by dependence on one other, but also by internalizing the "Look" of the majority culture. The novels are full of characters who try to live up to an external image—Dick and Jane's family, or cosmopolitan society, or big business. This conformity is not just a disguise, but an attempt to gain power and control. There is always the hope that if one fits the prescribed pattern, one will be seen as human. Helene Wright puts on her velvet dress in hopes that it, with "her manner and her bearing," will be "protection" against the reductive gaze of the white other. Light-skinned women, already closer to white models, aspire to a genteel ideal: green-eyed Frieda "enchanted the entire school," and "sugar-brown Mobile girls" like Geraldine "go to land-grant colleges, normal schools, and learn how to do the white man's work with refinement." The problem with such internalization is not that it is ambitious, but that it is life-denying, eliminating "the dreadful funkiness of passion, the funkiness of nature, the funkiness of the wide range of human emotions" [*The Bluest Eye*]. One who really accepts the external definition of the self gives up spontaneous feeling and choice.

Morrison makes it clear that this ontological problem is vastly complicated in the context of a society based on co-ercive power relations. The individual contest for "transcendence" allows, in theory, for mutually satisfying resolutions, as [Simone de Beauvoir points out in *The Second Sex* (1974)]: "It is possible to rise above this conflict if each individual freely recognizes the other, each regarding himself and the other simultaneously as object and as subject in a reciprocal manner." But that relation is unbalanced by social divisions of power. Helene cannot defy the white conductor; on at least the level of overt speech and action, his Look is unchallengeable. Thus she tries to accept the Look, and his power to give it, by becoming a more perfect object for his gaze: she gives him a "dazzling smile." The temptation to Bad Faith is immensely greater in a society that forcibly assigns subject-power, the power to look and define, to one person over another. In such a context, even willed or spontaneous choices can be distorted to serve the powerful. Mrs. Breedlove's channeling of her own need for order into the duties of "the ideal servant" is a milder version of what happens to Cholly Breedlove, forced to turn his spontaneous copulation into performance before the flashlights of white hunters. Most perversely, even the attempt at rebellion can be shaped by the surrounding culture. The change from "Doctor Street" (as blacks originally called Mains Avenue) to "Not Doctor Street," for example, shows a lingering reluctance to accept white naming, but also a recognition of the loss of the original power to name. More profoundly, "the Days," who take revenge for white violence, are also reactive, still achieving second-hand identity and initiative:

> . . . when a Negro child, Negro woman, or Negro man is killed by whites and nothing is done about it by *their* law and *their* courts, this society selects a similar victim at random, and they execute him or her in a similar manner if

they can. If the Negro was hanged, they hang; if a Negro was burnt, they burn; raped and murdered, they rape and murder.

The adoption of a rigid role, the withdrawal from life, is for Morrison as for Sartre a failure; but her condemnation is tempered by the recognition of the unnatural position of blacks in a racist society.

Power relations can have a similar effect on the community as a whole. The Look of white society, supported by all kinds of material domination, not only freezes the black individual but also classifies all blacks as alike, freezing the group. They become a "we-object" before the gaze of a "Third":

> It is only when I feel myself become an object along with someone else under the look of such a "third" that I experience my being as a "we-object"; for then, in our mutual interdependency, in our shame and rage, our beings are somehow mingled in the eyes of the onlooker, for whom we are both somehow "the same": two representatives of a class or a species, two anonymous types of something . . . . [Fredic Jameson, *Marxism and Form: Twentieth-Century Dialectical Theories of Literature* (1971)]

Again, the basic problem may be ontological, but the institutionalization of the relation, the coercive power of the Third, exacerbates it. This is the reason for all the misnaming: a whole group of people have been denied the right to create a recognizable public self—as individuals or as community. Given that combination of personal and communal vulnerability, it is hardly surprising that many characters choose the way of the least agony and the fewest surprises: they *"choose" their status as objects, even fiercely defend it*. Helene and Geraldine increasingly become perfect images rather than free selves. In this retreat from life they are abetted by a community so dominated by white society as the Third that order and stability are its primary values. In *The Bluest Eye*, narrator Claudia comments that the worst fear is of being "outdoors": "Being a minority in both caste and class, we moved about anyway on the hem of life, struggling to consolidate our weaknesses and hang on, or to creep singly up into the major folds of the garment." Any "excess" that might challenge the powerful Look and increase their isolation is terrifying. And so the images that caused the alienation, excluded them from the real world, are paradoxically received and imitated as confirmations of life.

Claudia is very conscious of the perversity of this position and of its roots in racist society. As a child, she says, she hated Shirley Temple, "Not because she was cute, but because she danced with Bojangles, who was *my* friend, *my* uncle, *my* daddy, and who ought to have been soft-shoeing it and chuckling with me." She recognized the diversion of feeling from her self and world into white values, emphasized by repeated references to white dolls, babies, and movie stars. She was fascinated by those images because they were "lovable" to everyone but her. She tried to "dissect" them, to discover or possess the "magic they weaved on others," but finally learned "shame" at her lack of feeling. Claudia knew, even as a child, the force of alien cultural images. She knew that white "ideals" denied her reality by forcing it into strange forms of appearance and experience. Her first reaction was appropriate: she could feel only "disinterested violence" for what, without relevance to her life, still regulated it.

The child Claudia learns false "love" rather than cut herself off from the only model of lovableness she is offered. But Claudia the adult narrator sees that Shirley Temple cannot really be loved or imitated because she is just a doll, an image without a self behind it. The crime of the racist society is not only the theft of black reality; it is the substitution of dead, external classifications for free self-definition. A society based entirely on the Look, on the absolute reification of the Other, reifies itself. If blacks are defined as slaves, whites are defined as masters; the Third is not a person at all, only an abstraction. There is finally a Look with no one behind it, because the freedom to define the self is denied. The movie stars and pinup girls of the white culture are not models of selfhood. The message they carry is that human life is being and appearance, not choice. To model oneself on them is to lose one's responsibility to create oneself in a world of others; to "love" them is to deny the equal freedom of others.

Life in this depthless world of images is constantly threatened; the problem of Bad Faith is that one must evade the knowledge of what one has done, to keep the illusion of freedom without the risk. This means that one must somehow justify, even collaborate with, the Look of the Other or the Third. Sartre says that one way to handle the gaze of the Third is to "ally myself to the Third so as to look at the Other who is then transformed into *our* object." The internalization of white values is one such act. The choice of a scapegoat goes further, displacing onto the Other all that is feared in the self, and so remaining "free." So the genteel ladies escape "funkiness" in others, as in themselves, of disorder or aberration. Geraldine rejects in Pecola the "waste" that will "settle" in her house. Helene Wright tries to reshape her daughter's nose; Milkman Dead casts off the clinging Hagar.

That displacement is parallel to the white attribution of rejected qualities to blacks. But the position of the black woman is doubly difficult. Black women in Morrison's fictions discover "that they [are] neither white nor male, and that all freedom and triumph [are] forbidden to them" [*Sula*]. Womanhood, like blackness, is Other in this society, and the dilemma of woman in a patriarchal society is parallel to that of blacks in a racist one: they are made to feel most real when *seen*. Thus the adolescent Sula and Nel, parading before young males who label them "pig meat," are "thrilled" by the association of voyeurism with sexuality. But their role as image is complicated by their blackness. They are not just women in a society that reduces women to such cold and infantile images that Corinthians Dead can think that "She didn't know any grownup women. Every woman she knew was a doll baby." They are also *black* women in a society whose female ideal is a *white* "doll baby," blonde and blue-eyed Shirley Temple. Even if they accept their reification they will always be inadequate; the black woman is [as William H. Grier and Price M. Hobbs state in their *Black Rage* (1968)] "the antithesis of American beauty." No efforts at disguise will make them into the images they learn to admire. Defined as the Other, made to be looked at, they can never satisfy the gaze of society.

Because they are doubly defined as failures and outsiders, they are natural scapegoats for those seeking symbols of displaced emotions. Morrison shows the Look taking on monstrous proportions as the humiliated black male allies himself with the Third by making the black woman the object of his displaced fury. So Cholly Breedlove, in his sexual humiliation, looks not at his tormentors, but at his partner, with hatred:

> Never did he once consider directing his hatred toward the hunters. Such an emotion would have destroyed him. . . . For now, he hated the one who had created the situation, the one who bore witness to his failure, his impotence. The one whom he had not been able to protect, to spare, to cover from the round moon glow of the flashlight.

Prevented from looking outward at the oppressor, he displaces blame onto the Other who "saw." That she too is image in the white man's eye is so much worse, for he had counted (as Jude did with Nel) on her existing only for him, seeing him as he wanted her to, being *his* object and *his* subject. The desire to "protect" her was the desire to create himself as her protector. All he can do to restore his selfhood is to deny hers further. In the recurring scene of black male resentment at black women's submission to oppression (the soldiers' stony stares at Helene and the conductor, Guitar's hatred of his mother's smile and of Pilate's "Aunt Jemima act"), Morrison shows the displacement of male humiliation onto the only person left that a black man can "own"—the black woman. Beauvoir remarks that woman in a patriarchal society is "the inessential who never goes back to being the essential, . . . the absolute Other, without reciprocity." The black woman—doubly Other—is the perfect scapegoat.

It is not only men who look for scapegoats. Barbara Smith points out [in her "Toward a Black Feminist Criticism," *Women's Studies International Quarterly* (1979)] that not only "the politics of sex" but also "the politics of race and class are crucially interlocking factors in the works of Black women writers." Morrison shows the subject-object pair and the triad created by the Third operating within a society so dependent on exclusion and reification that it creates "interlocking" systems to define individuals in multiple ways. So even black women can find scapegoats. The prime example is Pecola, black and young and ugly. Claudia says,

> All of us—all who knew her—felt so wholesome after we cleaned ourselves on her. We were so beautiful when we stood astride her ugliness. . . . And she let us, and thereby deserved our contempt. We honed our egos on her, padded our characters with her frailty, and yawned in the fantasy of our strength.

Pecola is the epitome of the victim in a world that reduces persons to objects and then makes them feel inferior as objects. In this world, light-skinned women can feel superior to dark ones, married women to whores, and on and on.

The temptations to Bad Faith are enormously increased, since one's own reification can be "escaped" in the interlocking hierarchies that allow most to feel superior to someone. Only the very unlucky, or the truly free, are outside this system.

Pecola is so far "outside" the center of the system—excluded from "reality" by race, gender, class, age, and personal history—that she goes mad, fantasizing that her eyes have turned blue and so fitted her for the world. But not all outsiders go mad or otherwise surrender. There are Morrison characters who refuse to become images, to submerge themselves in a role. These characters are clearly existential heroes, "free" in the Sartrean sense of being their own creators. But Morrison's treatment and development of this type in the social context she has staked out raise important questions about the nature of heroism and the place of external "definitions" in it.

The characters who are "outdoors," cut off from reassuring connection and definition, are profoundly frightening to the community, especially to a community dispossessed and "peripheral"; it responds by treating the free person as another kind of scapegoat, using that "excess" to define its own life. For example, Sula's neighbors fear and condemn her refusal to fit a conventional role, but her shapelessness gives them shape:

> Their conviction of Sula's evil changed them in accountable yet mysterious ways. Once the source of their personal misfortune was identified, they had leave to protect and love one another. They began to cherish their husbands and wives, protect their children, repair their homes and in general band together against the devil in their midst.

Displacing their fear and anger onto Sula, as onto Pecola, they can define themselves as "better." Sula, unlike Pecola, can bear that role, having chosen to be "outside"; it is then tempting to argue [as Chikwenye Okonjo Ogunyemi does in "*Sula:* 'A Nigger Joke,' " *Black American Literature Forum* (Winter 1979)] that this kind of hero is "a catalyst for good in the society." But Morrison has clear reservations about this situation. In a sick and power-obsessed society, even freedom can become distorted. For one thing, these characters are "freed" by traumatic experiences. Cholly goes through abandonment, sexual humiliation, desertion and rejection: "Abandoned in a junk heap by his mother, rejected for a crap game by his father, there was nothing more to lose. He was alone with his own perceptions and appetites, and they alone interested him." Similarly, Sula is "freed" by her mother's expressed dislike of her and her own part in Chicken Little's drowning: " . . . hers was an experimental life—ever since her mother's remarks sent her flying up those stairs, ever since her one major feeling of responsibility had been exorcised on the bank of a river with a closed place in the middle." The whores in *The Bluest Eye* are also freed by exclusion from society; Morrison's suggestion that such freedom is more deprivation than fulfillment helps to explain their link with Pecola.

Further, their isolation makes such free characters so unable to connect with others that they often act cruelly, out of cold detachment or fleeting impulse. Sula humiliates others "because she want[s] to see the person's face change rapidly" or watches her mother burn because she is "thrilled." Cholly rapes his daughter because he feels no "stable connection between himself and [his] children. . . . he reacted to them, and his reactions were based on what he felt at the moment." Claudia says of Cholly's act, "the love of a free man is never safe. There is no gift for the beloved. The lover alone possesses his gift of love. The loved one is shorn, neutralized, frozen in the glare of the lover's inward eye." That is, "total" freedom is another version of the Look; the hero "transcends" others. This conception of freedom bears some resemblance to Sartre's heroes, who commit outrageous acts in rejection of social prescriptions; but the cruelty of these heroes forces remembrance of the other side of freedom, which they neglect, the recognition of their own "facticity," their existence in the world of consequences. Morrison says that Sula has "no ego"; that is, she is not able to imagine herself as created by her choices. She simply defines herself as transcendence. Similarly, Milkman wrenches free from those "using" him, and sees this as self-assertion: "Either I am to live in this world on my terms or I will die out of it." But to achieve heroism in these terms is to accept the white-male model of heroism as conquest, to make oneself a subject by freezing the Other, to perfect one's image by forcing others to see it. Transcendence on those terms is related to—the other side of—the flight into facticity that Sula sees all around her. The interdependence of the two kinds of Bad Faith, the relation between the transcendent hero and the reified victim, is suggested by the fact that both Sula and Mrs. Breedlove love the "power" of the "position of surrender" in sex. It also explains the collapse of the order Sula makes possible in her town; the community falls into a self-destructive orgy on Suicide Day after she dies. A hero defined solely by exclusion from the community reinforces Bad Faith by showing not a clear choosing self, but a lack of self. That is why Sula finally says, "I never meant anything."

When Sula meets another free person, Ajax, she is unable to sustain the relation; she lapses into the possessiveness she scorned in Nel. But when she recognizes her failure, she sees it as rooted not in Nel's conformism but in her own isolation: "I didn't even know his name," she thinks: "It's just as well he left. Soon I would have torn the flesh from his face just to see if I was right . . . and nobody would have understood that kind of curiosity." The subject as detached self that can only dissect is what Claudia as a child feared to become: "When I learned how repulsive this disinterested violence was, that it was repulsive because it was disinterested, my shame floundered about for refuge. The best hiding place was love." Claudia first thought the only alternative was to become the object, to "love" and emulate received images. But she learns another way. She is not fully heroic: her attempts to act on her feeling (flowers to bless Pecola's pregnancy) are thwarted by an "unyielding" world; and as an adult, she can only tell Pecola's story, "too late" to change it. But she does meet her responsibility to see (not just look), to grasp the existence of herself and others without the evasions of Bad Faith, and she acts on what she sees. Freedom defined as total transcendence lacks the intention and significance that can come from commitment; "freedom," as Sartre comments, "is meaningful only as engaged by its free choice of ends."

Milkman Dead, in Morrison's third novel, finally completes the heroic mission. Morrison makes his status clear by depicting him in clearly mythic terms. Milkman's life follows the pattern of the classic hero, from miraculous birth (he is the first black baby born in Mercy Hospital, on a day marked by song, rose petals in the snow, and human "flight") through quest-journey to final reunion with his double. And Milkman largely resolves the conflict between freedom and connection. At first the familiar cold hero, he comes to ask the cost of the heroic quest— "Who'd he leave behind?" He learns not only that the hero serves a function for society, the exploration of limits it cannot reach, but also that it serves him: his great-grandfather Shalimar left his children, but "it was the children who sang about it and kept the story of his leaving alive." More, he finds that his quest is his culture's; he can only discover what he is by discovering what his family is. By undertaking the quest, he combines subjective freedom with objective fact and defines himself in both spheres. Sartre says that one may respond to the gaze of the Third not by scapegoating and identifying with the Third, but by "solidarity" with the Other, which can allow for common transcendence of the outside definition. By conceiving himself as both free individual and member of the social group, the hero unites his free and factitious natures and becomes part of the historical process by which the struggle for self-definition is both complicated and fulfilled. Thus at the end of **Song of Solomon,** Milkman has restored the names of his family, recovered their song; and he can "fly." But he does not fly away; he flies toward Guitar, his wounded "brother": "For now he knew what Shalimar knew: If you surrendered to the air, you could *ride* it." Only in the recognition of his condition can he act in it, only in commitment is he free.

Roger Rosenblatt has remarked [in *Black Fiction* (1974)] that much Afro-American fiction tends toward myth because of its "acknowledgment of external limitation and the anticipation of it." Morrison has always offered mythic possibilities in her emphasis on natural cycle, bizarre events, and narrative echoes. The mythic sensibility does seem to fit her view of the difficulties of freedom. But there are dangers in the use of myth that are especially acute for writers trying to combine the mythic sense of meaning with the concrete situation of the oppressed. Susan L. Blake has pointed out some of those problems in Ralph Ellison's combination of myth with black folklore [in "Ritual and Ritualization: Black Folklore in the Works of Ralph Ellison," *PMLA* 94 (1979)]. She suggests that the myth and the social situation described in the folklore "do not have compatible meanings," that in fact the correlation to "universal" Western myth "transforms acceptance of blackness as identity into acceptance of blackness as limitation. It substitutes the white culture's definition of blackness for the self-definition of folklore." This question is obviously crucial for Morrison, whose fictions try to combine existential concerns compatible with a mythic presentation with an analysis of American society. But her work resolves some of the problems Blake sees in Ellison's use of myth.

First, Morrison's almost total exclusion of white characters from the books allows her to treat white culture as "necessity" without either mythicizing specific acts of oppression or positing present necessity as eternal. Blake suggests that Ellison's "ritualization" of white brutality—e.g., in the adolescent Battle Royal—suggests a reading—adolescent rites of passage—that contradicts the social reality and almost justifies the event. Morrison avoids such a situation by exclusion of whites. White brutality and insensitivity are part of the environment the black characters must struggle with, but they are most often conditions, institutionalized and often anonymous, rather than events with ritualistic overtones. This allows Morrison to focus attention not on the white characters' forcing of mythic rites—as if they were gods—but on the black characters' choices within the context of oppression. In fact, when coercion is exercised by whites in these works, it is depicted as *anti*-mythic. It does not force boys into manhood (the hunters, for example, discovered Cholly in the act of copulation), or cause a tragic hero's cathartic recognition (the first Macon Dead was blown off the fence in a sudden anonymous act). It destroys the myth and denies characters entrance into it: it forces Cholly to dissociate himself from his own acts; it prevents Jude from growing into manhood and denies Nel the identity with her mother essential to a female myth; it destroys the links between generations that are the foundation of a mythos. The finding of a myth in these novels is a choice that is made in spite of a dominating culture that would deny it. Morrison's allusions to traditional Western myth, then, correct it by showing how far the dominant culture has come from its roots, and emphasize the denial of responsibility in the faceless anti-myth.

But showing the myth coming from inside the black culture is not enough to correct it. Its very form must be adapted to reflect the new sense of reality, the new definition of heroism. Morrison's version of the Icarus story shows her approach. The Icarus tale offers a tempting pattern for a black writer interested in myth and folklore, since it ties in with folk tales of blacks flying back to the homeland; but its limitation, as Blake points out, is that it seems to carry a "moral" incompatible with the concrete situation of blacks, suggesting the failure of the son to be the result of *hubris* rather than oppression. Morrison plays variations on the story that correct that perspective. One version of it has Shalimar flying away and trying to take his son, as did Daedalus. But Shalimar's son is a baby, and Shalimar drops him, unable to soar with him. That version emphasizes, first, that the son's "fall" is the result of a situation beyond his control; second, that the father's desire for freedom and his family ties are in conflict. That second aspect is central to Morrison's analysis and reconstruction of the myth. In the Icarus tale, freedom is available to the characters—they can fly. If they fail, it is because they want an impossible kind of freedom. To transfer that pattern to the black situation would be to suggest that blacks must accept an inferior social position. Morrison's version of the tale shifts the emphasis to divided loyalties. Shalimar is free to return to Africa—totally free. But that kind

of freedom is problematic, not because in itself it is wrong, but because in the particular context he is in—family and children—it involves denial of social and personal bonds. He does not destroy himself by soaring, but he wounds others because not everyone can take that way. The conflict is not between *hubris* and common sense, but between "absolute" freedom and social responsibility. Milkman resolves the conflict when he leaps, flying *toward* his "brother," finding freedom in "surrender" to the air—not in acceptance of his situation as right or as eternal, but acceptance of it as real. Morrison rewrites myth so that it carries the power of natural ties and psychic meaning but also speaks to a "necessity" in the social order.

She is therefore very concerned with the sources of myth, with mythos and personal myth. All the novels try to show the machinery of myth, the ways that meaning can modify experience. Morrison distinguishes between false "myths" that simply reduce, misinterpret, and distort reality—from Shirley Temple to the view of Sula as "evil," from Smith's failed attempt at flight to Macon Dead's obsession with Pilate's hoard—and true myths that spring from and illuminate reality. She insistently raises questions about mythic or symbolic readings of life, often showing even the best-intentioned attempts at meaning going astray. She shifts point of view so often in her fictions that the limitation of the individual view is obvious, and the attempt to make one view into the myth, one person into the hero, is seen for the reductive act that it is. For example, Milkman's early view of himself as the hero besieged by "users" is partly confirmed by the possessiveness of others; his mother realizes that "Her son had never been a person to her, a separate real person. He had always been a passion." But her need is explained by her personal history, and closely parallels Milkman's own selfishness. Thus the multiple perspectives not only qualify the myth by showing that any specific situation may be a different myth for each of the characters involved, since each sees himself at the center of it; they also make the myth's relevance clear by showing the same problems manifested in many cases, so that Milkman's solution is for all. As the myth emerges from the multiplicity of daily lives, finally the mythic hero's estimate of his own significance is confirmed both by his centrality in other views and by his parallels to other lives. Morrison sees quite clearly the danger of myth as existentialist tract abstracted from real situations, and she adapts the myth to the black historical context, reconciling freedom with facticity on both individual and collective levels. But there is another area in which she does not adapt the myth so completely—the area of gender. She is quite able to show black women as victims, as understanding narrators, or even as "free" in the sense of disconnection. But when the time comes to fulfill the myth, to show a hero who goes beyond the independence to engagement, she creates a male hero. Her own emphasis on the effect of particulars on meaning raises questions about that choice.

The use of a male hero does not, of course, necessarily imply the subjugation of women, and Morrison has the tools to correct the male slant. Her use of multiple perspectives has always allowed her to show a number of subjects as comments and variations on the central character.

And her early alternation between male and female versions of the "free" character shows that she does not exclude women from subjective life or choice. She even offers explicit commentaries on Milkman's sexism—from his sister Lena, for example—and parallels to women characters that make his quest a surrogate for theirs. That might seem sufficient: this is Milkman's story, so the other characters, male and female, are secondary. He is everyone's surrogate. To some extent, women are displaced because of the problem Morrison has studied all along—central versus peripheral perceptions—and she makes it clear that concentration on his life is not a denial of others'. But, as with the racial question, mere admission of multiple perspectives does not correct the mythic bias: the structure of the male-centered myth carries certain implications about gender that Morrison could disarm only by changing the story. Because she does not, her version of the hero-tale seems to allow only men as potential heroes. Thus Milkman is a surrogate for women in a very different way than for men.

The epigraph to *Song of Solomon* is, "The fathers may soar / And the children may know their names," and the heroic quest is as male as those words imply. Milkman seeks his forefathers; other than his mother, his female ancestors are nearly irrelevant. Even his grandmother Sing is barely defined, and her role in self-definition is questionable: she convinced the first Macon Dead to keep his grotesquely mistaken name, and her family changed their Indian names to "white" ones. Milkman "proves" himself in struggle with other men, from his father and Guitar to the male community at Shalimar. They reward him by telling him about the heroes who are his ancestors and models, by taking him on an all-male hunting trip, by giving him the name of a compliant woman. And he ends in the heroic leap toward his male alter ego, Guitar. From first to last, women exist for Milkman, and in the plot development, as functions: mother, wife, lover, sister. That narrative concentration in itself weakens Morrison's careful multiple perspectives: we understand Hagar, for example, as a subject in the sense that we see her point of view, but ultimately her story is subsumed in Milkman's search for male models.

Indeed, all the models available to Milkman are male—all the characters, however flawed, who assert independence and become inspirations to the community. Milkman learns what both Macon Deads "say" to observers with their lives:

> See what you can do? Never mind you can't tell one letter from another, never mind you born a slave, never mind you lose your name, never mind your daddy dead, never mind nothing. Here, this here, is what a man can do if he puts his mind to it and his back in it.

There are no women who so focus individual and social awareness in Morrison. Most of the women are the "doll babies" of a dead culture. Those who learn to be free are led to the decision by a man, as Corinthians Dead is by Porter. The myth of heroism traced through the male line allows women to benefit but not to originate.

Milkman does have a female guide figure, his aunt Pilate,

and she might further disarm the androcentric myth. She balances in her character the freedom and connection that Milkman must learn:

> . . . when she realized what her situation in the world was and would probably always be she threw away every assumption she had learned and began at zero. . . . Then she tackled the problem of trying to decide how she wanted to live and what was valuable to her. . . . she knew there was nothing to fear. That plus her alien's compassion for troubled people ripened her and . . . kept her just barely within the boundaries of the elaborately socialized world of black people.

Further, Pilate performs a social function by recognizing the same balance in others. At Hagar's funeral, Pilate sings and speaks to each mourner, "identifying Hagar, selecting her away from everybody else in the world who had died." She pulls the individual into the group and recognizes individuality at the same time. Later, she forces Milkman to face his responsibility for Hagar's death. Her own dying words are, "I wish I'd a knowed more people. I would of loved 'em all. If I'd a knowed more, I would a loved more." That free commitment to others is just what Milkman learns; it is no wonder that he answers by wishing for a mate like Pilate, saying, "There's got to be at least one more woman like you."

In these ways, Pilate too is like the hero, and the importance of her role should not be underestimated. But the terms of her life keep her from really fitting the heroic mold. It is important to the mythic conception that the hero understand what he is, and Pilate does not quite reach that point. She does have the independence and compassion of the hero, but her sense of mission is oddly garbled. She misinterprets her dead father's messages, mistakes his bones for someone else's, cannot complete her "quest" without Milkman's explanation. She does the right thing, but from intuitive rather than conscious knowledge. Thus, while she embodies Morrison's values, she is not the complete hero that Milkman is, for she lacks his recognition of meaning. By contrast to his final state, she seems intuitive, personal, and rather passive.

This distinction is bothersome because it comes so close to the old active-man/passive-woman stereotype. It is quite clearly rooted in the myth structure. It seems fitting that Pilate dies and Milkman is left only with his *imagination* of a woman like her, for in the myth, woman gets meaning from or gives meaning to man; she does not both live and know the meaning as he does. Toni Morrison commented that *Song of Solomon* is about "dominion," and about "the way in which men do things or see things and relate to one another." What the novel shows is that the "universal" myth of Western culture is just such a male story; and the parallels and discrepancies between Milkman and Pilate further show the difficulty of the heroic mode for a woman. By living out the myth, Milkman both finds his own identity—chooses and corrects the myth by free participation in it—and finds a connection to society, an "image" he can be to others that leads and inspires them, that is rooted both symbolically and historically in his community. Former heroes aid that combination of social role and selfhood by becoming suggestive but not confining models. Thus Milkman attains a "definition" of the self that explodes the flat alienating images of the anti-mythic white society. But the woman seems to lack the possibilities available to the man. As a woman, Pilate cannot model herself totally on the male line, though all her meaning derives from it; and she has no true female line, only vague references to women defined by their mates. She acts out her duty to her father but she will never *become* him, as Milkman can, and so understand him from within. Beauvoir says that women "still dream through the dreams of men"; that problem is illustrated perfectly in Pilate, the strong and independent woman who still waits in dreams for messages from her dead father, messages she misreads until corrected by his male descendant.

Morrison often shows women denying their mothers, in the "matrophobia" Adrienne Rich has described [in *Of Woman Born: Motherhood as Experience and as Institution* (1977)] as a rebellion against the imposed female image, an attempt to be "individuated and free." The problem with such a rejection is that it is a "splitting of the self," a denial of facticity that can produce a centerless hero like Sula. Milkman's break from his father is a parallel rebellion; but Milkman is finally reconciled with his forefathers, understanding their intent as well as their actions, grasping the mythic experience from inside and out, and he can do so because of the historical reconstruction that puts their acts in context. That sense of history is not available to women, and without it they have neither the models nor the contextual information to make themselves whole. Until women like Pilate recover their heroic female line, they cannot replace false images with true ones, and they will be left in a world, as Morrison shows, where mothers and daughters reject one another, female friendships are difficult to sustain, the dominating models of female selfhood are baby dolls and pinups, and even heroic women like Pilate cannot pass on their values to their children and grandchildren. Morrison's women can free themselves, like Sula, and be self-defined and disconnected; they can come close to a heroic life. But to serve the heroic integrative function, they need a new myth, in which women too are central, in which it is as important to know why Sing lived her life as why Macon did, and in which Sing's legacy to her descendants is also traced. Morrison has, quite consciously, depicted the male mode of heroism in *Song of Solomon;* it will be interesting to see whether and how she conceives of the female mode.

Morrison's use of mythic structure, more and more overtly as her work develops, is central to her existentialist analysis. The heroic quest for identity achieved by conquest in and of the outer world embodies the human need for transcendence and self-definition; at the same time, the mythic sense of fate and necessity corresponds to the experience of facticity, both as irrevocable consequence and as concrete conditions for choice. Between those two poles—free heroism and determined role—move Morrison's characters. Further, mythic patterns are especially appropriate to her social concerns, since the mythic hero by nature both embodies and transcends the values of his culture. These connections would be significant in most presenta-

tions of existential themes, but the special situations with which Morrison is concerned further complicate her use of myth. On the one hand, traditional myths claim to represent "universal" values and experiences; on the other, they clearly exclude or distort minority experiences by offering inappropriate or impossible models (e.g., Shirley Temple). This contradiction produces the special treatment of myth that Chester J. Fontenot, Jr. ["Black Fiction: Apollo or Dionysus?" *Twentieth-Century Literature* (Spring 1979)], sees in black American fiction, turning on "the tension between the universal order and that produced by mankind for Black people." The myth of what may seem the "universal cosmos" in the majority view is so patently untrue to the black experience that from that perspective it is not mythic, but "linear," demanding denial of past and present reality in favor of "an obscure vision of some distant future" (e.g., the struggle to become Shirley Temple). Meanwhile, the mythic consciousness adequate to the minority experience is in danger of becoming an imprisoning view of oppression as "fated." Morrison, then, must capture "universal" aspirations without denying concrete reality, construct a myth that affirms community identity without accepting oppressive definitions. In the process, she must take the outline of the mythic structure, already so well suited to the existentialist quest for freedom and identity, and adapt it to the historical circumstances that surround this version of the quest. She values the myth as a way to design, not confine, reality; it remains to be seen how much further she can carry that notion. (pp. 7-24)

Cynthia A. Davis, "Self, Society, and Myth in Toni Morrison's Fiction," in Toni Morrison, *edited by Harold Bloom, Chelsea House Publishers, 1990, pp. 7-26.*

Morrison on black women writers:

I think there's something very special about women writers, black women writers in America and those that I know of in any real sense in Africa—Bessie Head, for example, in Africa or Gloria Naylor here. There's a gaze that women writers seem to have that is quite fascinating to me because they tend not to be interested in confrontations with white men—the confrontation between black women and white men is not very important, it doesn't center the text. There are more important ones for them and their look, their gaze of the text is unblinking and wide and very steady. It's not narrow, it's very probing and it does not flinch. And it doesn't have these funny little axes to grind. There's something really marvelous about that.

Toni Morrison, in an interview in Présence Africaine, *1988.*

Darwin T. Turner   (essay date 1984)

[*Turner is an American poet, critic, and editor who has published numerous works on African-American literature. In the following essay, he examines theme, charac-*

terization, and style in The Bluest Eye, Sula, Song of
Solomon, *and* Tar Baby.]

In four novels published between 1970 and 1981—*The
Bluest Eye* (1970), *Sula* (1973), *Song of Solomon* (1977),
and *Tar Baby* (1981)—Toni Morrison has earned a reputation as a gifted storyteller and masterful stylist who has
created haunting images of humans isolated by their failures in love and their problems with identity. Less obviously lyric in her fourth novel than in her first, she continues to demonstrate her artistic skill in memorable, sometimes startling, but always illuminating metaphors, vivid
and credible dialogue, and graceful syntax. In less than a
decade, Morrison has expanded from *The Bluest Eye's*
thematic cameos of young girls confused by love and identity to a gallery of men and women in conflict with parents, children, relatives, social class, social values, community, and themselves. Above all, she commands the storyteller's skill to persuade a reader to suspend disbelief by
discovering credibility in the magic of the tale.

In her first novel, *The Bluest Eye,* Morrison's lyricism
creates an effective mood for the narrator's recollection of
a seemingly innocent world in which she, only nine years
old, naïvely observed the trauma of a pubescent Afro-
American girl forced to find love in incest and to define
beauty as the possession of blue eyes. At the beginning of
the novel, Claudia, the narrator, lives in that innocent and
idyllic world revealed in elementary school primers whose
simple and orderly view of life Morrison mocks in her prologue: "Here is the house. It is green and white. It has a
red door. It is very pretty. Here is the family. Mother, Father, Dick, and Jane live in the green-and-white house.
They are very happy." Despite the Depression, Claudia's
idyll is marred only by the fact that her house is old and
green and that relatives insist on giving her pink-skinned,
blue-eyed dolls which she destroys because she hates
them. Nevertheless, the occasional pain is mild because
"Love, thick and dark as Alaga syrup, eased up into that
cracked window [of her house]. I could smell it—taste it—
sweet, musty, with an edge of wintergreen in its base—
everywhere in that house." By the end of the novel,
Claudia has begun to be aware of the jumble of the real
world: "Hereisthehouseitisgreenandwhiteitthasareddoor
itisveryprettyhereisthefamilymotherfatherdickandjane
liveinthegreenandwhitehousetheyareveryhappy. . . . "
She overhears gossip about adultery and sees her parents'
roomer flirting with three prostitutes whom townspeople
call wicked women. She quarrels with a pretty Afro-
American schoolmate who feels superior because of her
family's wealth and her light skin and long hair; and she
learns that her father has beaten the roomer because he
fondled the budding breasts of her sister. Above all, she
learns that Cholly Breedlove has impregnated his daughter, Pecola, a playmate of hers. And now that she is older,
she knows that the reason the marigolds did not bloom in
that year of 1941 is that certain seeds—like Pecola's
child—could not grow.

Because Claudia's perspective is distorted as a result of her
having been sheltered by love and youth, Morrison tells
the novel's grimmer story through an omniscient narrator.
It is primarily the story of dark-skinned Pecola, who,
knowing that people consider her ugly, believes they
would like her if she had blue eyes. It is the story of Pecola,
who, raped by her father the first time, welcomes his second advance as an unaccustomed demonstration of his
love. But it includes a portrait of Pecola's mother, who,
having lost the romance in her marriage and having identified with her white employers, gives their child a love she
withholds from her own; of Pecola's father, who, abandoned by his parents, bewildered by the routine of his marriage, takes interest only in drinking. It even offers cameos
of Geraldine, a migrant from the South, who fiercely
guards her new social status from any sullying by Blacks
of a lower-class; and of Elihue Whitcomb, a mulatto West
Indian dilettante who has done nothing more useful with
his life than give Pecola the delusion that she has blue
eyes.

Lorain, Ohio, the setting of the novel, is a world of grotesques—individuals whose psyches have been deformed
by their efforts to assume false identities, their failures to
achieve meaningful identities, or simply their inability to
retain and communicate love. The novel ends with an ambiguity characteristic of Morrison's visions of her characters and their world. Morrison suggests that perhaps Pecola, insanely believing in her blue eyes, is nobler than the
townspeople who achieved a false superiority by presum-
ing themselves to possess the opposites of her ugliness, her
guilt, her pain, her inarticulateness, her poverty. "We
honed our egos on her, padded our characters with her
frailty, and yawned in the fantasy of our strength," the
narrator concludes.

The lyric expository style of *The Bluest Eye*—evidenced
in such memorable phrases as "Nuns go by as quiet as
lust" and "Winter tightened our heads with a band of cold
and melted our eyes"—is less obvious in *Sula,* which focuses on two Black girls as they mature in the 1920s and
1930s in a world as barren as that of *The Bluest Eye.* Repressed by her class-conscious mother, Nel Wright matures into an unimaginative woman ("Her parents had
succeeded in rubbing down to a dull glow any sparkle or
splutter she had") whose affection for her friend, Sula
Peace, is stronger than the emotion she feels for her parents or—later—her husband. The more imaginative Sula
consciously rebels against her family, the community, and
a world apparently dominated by men. She watches with
curiosity when her mother burns to death, institutional-
izes her grandmother so as to gain control of the family
home, carelessly takes and abandons men—including
Nel's husband—to satisfy her sexual curiosity, and defies
the community, which considers her a monstrosity.

Superficially, the bland, society-conscious Nel contrasts
with Sula, the vivid rebel. In actuality, they resemble each
other.

> [Their] friendship was so close, they had difficul-
> ty distinguishing one's thoughts from the
> other's. During all her girlhood the only respite
> Nel had had from her stern and undemonstra-
> tive parents was Sula. . . . They never quar-
> reled, those two, the way some girlfriends did
> over boys, or competed against each other for
> them. In those days a compliment to one was a

compliment to the other, and cruelty to one was a challenge to the other.

The most startling resemblance, however, is their emotional isolation from other people. Although Nel Wright consciously seeks to avoid any behavior that will arouse the displeasure of society whereas Sula defies society, neither has close attachment to family. Since childhood, Nel has hated the memory of her mother's having provoked a hostile reaction from Black soldiers when she responded obsequiously to a white train conductor's insulting behavior. As has been stated previously, Sula demonstrates seemingly monstrous indifference or hostility to her mother and grandmother.

Their distancing themselves from their families, however, seems merely to imitate the pattern established by older family members who either felt no love for each other or could not communicate it in traditional ways. Helene Wright, a migrant from the South, has adopted the excessively puritannical standards of middle-class life in a deliberate reaction against her mother, a beautiful Creole prostitute. Love is even more grotesque in Sula's family. Eva Peace, Sula's grandmother, loves her children so much that she sacrifices a leg to feed her children (town gossip says that she deliberately stuck it under the wheels of a train so that she could sue the railroad) and that she instinctively throws herself through an upper-story window in a hopeless effort to rescue her daughter, who is burning to death. But Eva's love does not impress her daughter, Hannah, or her grandmother. Hannah wonders whether Eva ever loved her children, for Hannah believes that she never showed love; and Sula cannot comprehend that Eva thought that she was demonstrating love when she burned her son to death rather than see him continue to suffer as a drug addict.

The relationships of Nel and Sula with men seem no stronger than their relationships with their families. Granddaughter of a prostitute who sold her "love," daughter of a self-conscious social leader who is content with her sailor husband's absence thirteen days out of every sixteen, child of women who do not need men, Nel marries a man because she pities his pain; but when she loses her husband to Sula's careless seduction, she knows that she will have no other men. Granddaughter of a woman abandoned by her husband, daughter of a woman who gives men her worldly possessions as generously as she gives her body, child of women exploited by men, Sula contemptuously uses Black men and white men until she is deserted by the one man she loves. Nel and Sula live in a world in which women must survive without men. It matters not whether the woman accepts love and marriage as a convention of society, as Nel does, or whether she is surprised by the discovery that she can love at least one man, as Sula is. In either instance, a woman will be deserted by the man she loves.

Nel and Sula have no close relationship to the society about them. Whereas Nel listlessly observes the conventions of the society, Sula flouts them. She attends college but discovers no use for her education; she takes white lovers; she insults Black women by taking their men with a contempt implying that they are not worth having.

Strangely, however, the community needs Sula. Just as the Blacks in Lorain needed Pecola so that they could nurture a sense of their superiority, so the Blacks in Medallion, Ohio, hating and fearing Sula, improve their behavior in an unconscious effort to prove their goodness in contrast to her wickedness. Thus, the theme of a communal scapegoat links Morrison's first two novels.

In *Sula,* even more than in *The Bluest Eye,* Morrison demonstrates her ability to conjure the reader into suspension of disbelief. A woman cuts off her leg to feed her children and sets fire to her drug-dazed son; three boys of different sizes and ages become physically indistinguishable; Sula cuts off the tip of her finger to intimidate white boys into believing her fearlessness; a community not only accepts the tradition of Suicide Day (that day on which people should have the right to kill one another or themselves) but even follows the day's deranged creator into accidental death. One is tempted to say that events like these do not occur, but Morrison narrates them so vividly that readers accept them.

In *Sula,* Morrison evokes her verbal magic occasionally by lyric descriptions that carry the reader deep into the soul of a character. For instance, in "1937" from Part Two of *Sula,* she describes Nel's loneliness after her husband Jude has left; a loneliness that does not scream its pain but hovers over her—a "quiet, gray, dirty . . . ball of muddy strings, but without weight, fluffy but terrible in its malevolence"—that forces her to seek comfort in her children's bed, that makes her aware of her empty, dead thighs and her comprehension of women who must never look at men again, that destines her to life "with no thighs and no heart, just her brain raveling away."

Similarly, in describing Sula's sexual intercourse with Ajax, Morrison does not focus on the physical activity except to set the scene. Instead, she lyrically evokes the thoughts of Sula, who—to delay her physical fulfillment—imagines herself an artisan probing through Ajax layer by layer to reach his core: rubbing, scraping, chiseling to reveal the gold leaf beneath the Black skin, then the alabaster beneath the gold, and finally the pure, fertile loam that she will garden.

Equally effective, however, is her art of narrating action in a lean prose that uses adjectives cautiously while creating memorable vivid images. Consider her description of Hannah's death in "1923" of Part One of *Sula.*

Like *The Bluest Eye, Sula* ends with an ambiguity that startles the reader into reevaluating the characters. Early in the novel Sula, while teasing a young boy, accidentally threw him in the river, where he drowned. Readers are easily persuaded to find the fault in Sula's behavior and to feel only compassion for Nel's efforts to comfort her friend. In the final chapter, however, just as Eva had accused Sula of remaining inactive while watching her mother burn—"not because she was paralyzed, but because she was interested," so Eva accuses Nel of watching while Sula killed the boy. Momentarily Nel admits to herself that she had felt good when the boy's hands slipped. "[W]hat she had thought was maturity, serenity and compassion was only the tranquillity that follows a joyful stimulation. Just as the water closed peacefully over the turbulence of Chicken Little's body, so had contentment washed over her enjoyment." Who is the greater sinner, one must ask, the individual who commits a crime and must experience the shame and guilt of the action, or the individual who can enjoy a crime committed by another while maintaining a sense of moral superiority? Unlike Claudia, who, looking back, accepts guilt for the manner in which she and other Blacks deluded themselves into a sense of superiority over Pecola, Nel quickly retreats into her protective delusion by reassuring herself that Eva is merely an old woman who says and does mean things.

In *Song of Solomon,* her most widely acclaimed novel, Morrison shifted her focus from female friends to male friends, expanded her gallery of images, and evoked a folk myth as she continued to focus on themes of a world in which love is deformed and social class clashes with social class.

In her previous novels, centered on women, males were little more than nonentities, disruptive influences on women, or grotesques. The pallid fathers of Claudia and Nel function only as faintly visible stabilizers of the family income. The lovers—Cholly Breedlove, Jude, Ajax—disrupt life by rape or desertion. Others—Elihue and Shadrack—preach strange religions. In *Song of Solomon,* however, Morrison centered her attention on Macon Dead III and Guitar Baines, who, like the female friends in the earlier novels, discover the superiority of intrasexual friendship over heterosexual romance.

Morrison uses the protagonist, Macon Dead III ("Milkman"), to demonstrate the inadequacies of human love in all conceivable relationships. Milkman's father, Macon Dead, Jr., did not want him to be born; but, with the fact of birth a reality, the father wants to mold Milkman into a materialistic, class-conscious replica of himself. Having used him to sublimate her sexual urges by nursing him far past the usual age of weaning, Milkman's mother submissively slips into the role of servant to a young prince, even though his older sisters object to the fact that they are required to act in a comparable role. Maturing, Milkman exploits his female cousin sexually and tries to rob the aunt whom his father has taught him to condemn. Adventuring in search of the treasure of his grandfather, the original Macon Dead, Milkman begins to learn the foibles of pride in materialistic possession. He discovers love in family and community as he basks in the townspeople's memory of his grandfather and as he abandons his sense of class superiority in his desire to immerse himself in a community of Black men. Ironically, Milkman believes his love of family to be strongest when he discovers that his great grandfather—Solomon or Shalimar, a flying African—escaped from slavery by flying back to Africa. Enchanted with the myth of individualistic strength, Milkman does not perceive the irony in idolizing a man who, abandoning his wife and children in order to free himself, perhaps proved himself to be no less selfcentered than Milkman's father.

Milkman's closest friend, Guitar Baines, believes that he has discovered love, but readers may question his wisdom. Relinquishing love for individuals, Guitar embraces a race—his Black race. Joining the Days, Black men sworn to retaliate against oppressive violence by whites, Guitar isolates himself from women and men; for association with either group may cause him to betray the secrets of the Days. He even proposes to kill Milkman because he believes that Milkman has betrayed the Days. Nevertheless, it is Guitar whom Milkman would embrace in friendship and love. Just as Nel Wright Green perceives that she loves Sula more than she loved her husband, so Milkman finds love only in his asexual friendship with Guitar.

Love is rewarding for few Blacks in the arid North of this novel. Innocent of the significance of her actions, Milkman's sexually frustrated mother practices incestuous acts with her father and her son. Reared to believe themselves socially and intellectually superior to Black men of the community, Milkman's sisters age listlessly until one breaks the social barriers by taking a lover. Lonely in the isolation of his devotion to the Days, a sexually starved Black man threatens to jump to his death unless he can have intercourse with a woman; but the listening women merely taunt him. In a home reminiscent of that of the three generations of Peace women in *Sula,* Pilate Dead generates more love than can be found elsewhere; but, even in her home, love exists without permanent support from men. Pilate has no husband because men feared her uniqueness (she has no navel). Her daughter Reba, like Hannah Peace, gives herself so freely to men that they do not need to consider marriage. Reba's daughter, Hagar, gives her love to Milkman; but, when he wearies of her, she first tries to kill him, then dies insane in a vain effort to make herself sufficiently beautiful to win his love.

If Morrison stretched the imagination of readers by creating credible grotesques in earlier novels, she strains the imagination in *Song of Solomon.* Yet again she succeeds. An African who can flap his arms and fly away from oppression; an Afro-American woman who dangles from her ear a box containing her name—her identity; an Afro-American who foolishly believes that he can fly; children named Pilate, First Corinthians, or Magdalene because of the family tradition of blindly selecting names from a Bible: such people seem improbable, but Morrison's art invests them with life.

In earlier novels, Morrison merely hinted at white oppression of Blacks. For instance, in *The Bluest Eye,* she mocked the fact that Blacks in Lorain call their arid hilltop "the Bottom" because whites, who promised to give them fertile bottom land, assured them that the hill was the bottom of heaven. The theme of white oppression, however, is expanded in *Song of Solomon.* Solomon's son, Jake, is renamed Macon Dead by a drunken Union soldier who ignores the importance of a Black man's name and identity. The original Macon Dead is killed by whites who covet his property. In *Song of Solomon* Blacks take vengeance. A Black servant, Circe, cherishes the realization that, in a decaying mansion polluted and destroyed by dogs, she has outlived the white owners who thoughtlessly abused Blacks. The Days avenge the destruction of Black people. Whereas Morrison earlier restricted her canvas to depictions of the intraracial problems of Blacks, in *Song of Solomon* she presents more fully the interracial problems of Blacks.

The Bluest Eye and *Sula* end on notes of deliberate ambiguity that cause the reader to reevaluate the characters. The ambiguity of the ending of *Song of Solomon* is even more significant because it causes the reader to question the theme. Admiring his great-grandfather who knew how to fly and his aunt who could fly "without ever leaving the ground," Milkman confronts Guitar on opposite sides of a crevasse:

> "You want my life?" Milkman was not shouting now. "You need it? Here." Without wiping away the tears, taking a deep breath, or even bending his knees—he leaped. As fleet and Wright as a lodestar he wheeled toward Guitar and it did not matter which one of them would give up his ghost in the killing arms of his brother. For now he knew what Shalimar knew: If you surrendered to the air, you could ride it.

What is certain about the scene is that a man like Milkman's father could never ride the air. But will Milkman? Have his new love for his aunt and his reaffirmation of love for Guitar so fortified his soul that he can magically ride the air? Will he discover, in a startled moment as he falls, that his faith could not sustain him? Is he consciously relinquishing his life because he wants to rid himself of the materialism of his mortality? At the beginning of the novel, a Day jumped to his death because he believed that he could fly. Does the ending pessimistically affirm that flight is mere delusion, or does it affirm the theme that one may learn to fly?

Although Morrison's style continues to appear as one of the admirable qualities of her art, the lushness of *The Bluest Eye* seems transformed into a vivid but leaner prose exhibited not only in authorial description but even in dialogue—especially in the interior monologues of Milkman. Consider, for example, Morrison's skillful development of tension through Milkman's contrasting visual and olfactory impressions as he approaches and enters a house where Circe's sudden appearance recalls his childhood's terrifying yet erotic nightmares about witches.

In *Tar Baby,* however, Morrison seems to return to her earlier style to tell the story of two young Afro-Americans whose love cannot overcome their cultural differences. Educated at the Sorbonne through the financial assistance of millionaire Valerian Street, for whom her aunt and uncle are servants, Jadine lives in and embraces the cultural values of cosmopolitan centers such as Paris and New York. Hers is the sophisticated world of fashion and film. In contrast, Son, a deserter from a ship, is an uneducated, violent man who disdains the wealthy and feels comfortable only in the Black community of his Florida home. Unable to remain contentedly in the Street household on a Caribbean island, Son insists that Jadine return to America with him. But there he cannot endure the people and activities of her New York world; and she cannot endure the communal ghosts who torment her in his Florida home. She leaves, to return to the island and then to Europe. Son follows her to the island where perhaps he loses himself among the ghostly chevaliers who nightly race their horses through the rain forest.

When one compares *Tar Baby* with Morrison's earlier

Tribute to Morrison that appeared in the January 24, 1988 edition of the *New York Times Book Review*:

Despite the international stature of Toni Morrison, she has yet to receive the national recognition that her five major works of fiction entirely deserve: she has yet to receive the keystone honors of the National Book Award or the Pulitzer Prize. We, the undersigned black critics and black writers, here assert ourselves against such oversight and harmful whimsy.

The legitimate need for our own critical voice in relation to our own literature can no longer be denied. We, therefore, urgently affirm our rightful and positive authority in the realm of American letters and, in this prideful context, we do raise this tribute to the author of *The Bluest Eye, Sula, Song of Solomon, Tar Baby* and *Beloved:*

Alive, we write this testament of thanks to you, dear Toni: alive, beloved and persevering, magical. Among the fecund intimacies of our hidden past, and among the coming days of dream or nightmares that will follow from the bidden knowledge of our conscious heart, we find your life work ever building to a monument of vision and discovery and trust. You have never turned away the searching eye, the listening ear attuned to horror or to histories providing for our faith. And freely you have given to us every word that you have found important to the forward movement of our literature, our life. For all of America, for all of American letters, you have advanced the moral and artistic standards by which we must measure the daring and the love of our national imagination and our collective intelligence as a people.

Your gifts to us have changed and made more gentle our real time together. And so we write, here, hoping not to delay, not to arrive, in any way, late with this, our simple tribute to the seismic character and beauty of your writing. And, furthermore, in grateful wonder at the advent of *Beloved,* your most recent gift to our community, our country, our conscience, our courage flourishing as it grows, we here record our pride, our respect and our appreciation for the treasury of your findings and invention.

Robert Allen, Maya Angelou, Houston A. Baker Jr., Toni Cade Bambara, Amina Baraka, Amiri Baraka, Jerome Brooks, Wesley Brown, Robert Chrisman, Barbara Christian, Lucille Clifton, J. California Cooper, Jayne Cortez, Angela Davis, Thulani Davis, Alexis De Veaux, Mari Evans, Nikky Finney, Ernest J. Gaines, Henry Louis Gates Jr., Paula Giddings, Vertamae Grosvenor, Cheryll Y. Greene, Rosa Guy, Calvin Hernton, Nathan Irvin Huggins, Gloria T. Hull, Gale Jackson, June Jordan, Paule Marshall, Nellie McKay, Louise Meriwether, Louise Patterson, Richard Perry, Arnold Rampersad, Eugene Redmond, Sonia Sanchez, Hortense Spillers, Luisah Teish, Joyce Carol Thomas, Eleanor Traylor, Quincy Troupe, Alice Walker, Mary Helen Washington, John Wideman, Margaret Wilkerson, John A. Williams, and Sherley Anne Williams, in a letter to the editor, New York Times Book Review, 24 January 1988.

works, Jadine and Son seem too ordinary, too stereotypical—created solely to demonstrate the clash of class and culture. Even the other characters seem strangely stereotypical: a benevolent but paternalistic millionaire who never learns the actual names of the natives who work for him; his wife, who has never matured beyond the seventeen-year-old girl whom he married for her beauty; dignified and docile Black servants.

One must wonder why Morrison created such polar opposites as Jadine and Son. Their worlds differ so significantly that compatibility seems impossible. Their cultural and class differences, however, may conceal Morrison's emphasis on a more significant difference—that of their sexes. In Morrison's works, Black men and women—regardless of class or culture—never sustain harmonious relationships in heterosexual love. Men can love male friends; women can love female friends; parents can love children; but men and women cannot love each other permanently either in wedlock or outside it.

Although she has written only four novels, Morrison has already achieved status as a major novelist—an artful creator of grotesques destined to live in worlds where seeds of love seldom blossom. (pp. 361-69)

> *Darwin T. Turner, "Theme, Characterization, and Style in the Works of Toni Morrison," in* Black Women Writers (1950-1980): A Critical Evaluation, *edited by Mari Evans, Anchor Press/Doubleday, 1984, pp. 361-69.*

Carol Iannone   (review date December 1987)

[*Iannone is an American educator, editor, and critic. In the following excerpt from a review of* Beloved, *she provides an overview of Morrison's career and a mixed assessment of the novel under review.*]

Miss Morrison calls her novels "village literature," "peasant literature," and they do indeed portray an exotic, fantastical world, derived from her childhood, in which even the everyday black life of ordinary Midwestern towns comes alive in folklore, magic, superstition, fable, poetry, song, and myth; in odd, quirky characters colorfully nicknamed or named from the Bible; in vibrant, flavorful, and frequently humorous dialogue and bizarre, extraordinarily conceived situations; and in Miss Morrison's clear, seamless language.

In classic plight-and-protest style, Miss Morrison's novels do also present the "trauma" (in [Irving] Howe's word) of black life, with blacks as much the victims of black cruelty as of white, and by no means always in the male-upon-female pattern that has been much noted of late. To be sure, the trauma is implicitly or explicitly set within the oppression of a racist society, but the picture that emerges of black life is nevertheless frequently "harrowing" (as Diane Johnson has observed).

The Bluest Eye attempts to show the terrible consequences for blacks of internalizing the values of a white culture that both directly and indirectly rejects them. The novel is set in the years just before World War II in Lorain, Ohio. Eleven-year-old Pecola is a poor ugly black girl who prays to have blue eyes in the poignant, wistful hope that this will bring her the love she longs for and also somehow alleviate the multiple miseries of her hate-filled,

quarrelsome, violent family, ironically named Breedlove. Pecola becomes the victim of one after another in a chain of black people in this book, including her own mother and father, who have been twisted and perverted by the false, empty, and often vicious standards of the white world. (The "humiliations, defeats, and emasculations" of her father are described in one long, almost expressionistic sequence that culminates in his rape of Pecola, an act described as a manifestation both of hatred and of a love horribly distorted by inchoate wretchedness.)

Much of the novel is narrated by another black child, Claudia MacTeer, whose family is poor, harried, and struggling, but basically stable and loving. The voice of this sassy, bright black girl renders the texture and details of her existence with curiosity, freshness, astringency, and humor. But at the end of the novel, a more mature Claudia indicts the entire black community for its part in Pecola's degradation, for failing to love her and instead despising her for her extreme poverty and ugliness.

The strengths of *The Bluest Eye*—purity of language, economy of structure, strong narrative voice, and a sensitive yet surgical delineation of some of the miseries of black life—in some measure compensate for many of its weaknesses, which include an insistence on an ethic of total victimization and a sometimes relentless pathos. But the virtues cannot overcome the flaws in the novel's vision. Miss Morrison crudely manipulates the assignment of judgment and blame in this book, refusing to transcend black and white as categories of good and evil. The icy scorn she levels at the black middle class, especially exemplified in a certain type of black woman who destroys her natural "funkiness" in the interest of "thrift, patience, high morals, and good manners," is itself but a variant of her scorn for the white world, whence such falsely "good" values supposedly derive. Instead of exploring the universal theme which she herself has set into play—the fatal and terrifying lapses of love in the human heart—Miss Morrison sticks doggedly to her shallow dichotomies.

The Bluest Eye is hardly the only place where Miss Morrison has registered her objection to the "push toward middle-class respectability" in which blacks have "abandoned the past and a lot of the truth and sustenance that went with it." To be sure, such sentiments often go hand-in-hand with complaints of a different nature against the black-is-beautiful idea—which is to say that Miss Morrison's feelings on this matter are somewhat complicated, if not downright contradictory. There is, for example, a strain in her thought which seems not only not to condemn but even to endorse certain pathological elements in black life, in an echo, ironic to say the least, of Norman Mailer's essay "The White Negro."

Thus, remarking on the "tremendous possibility for masculinity among black men," Miss Morrison concedes that "They may end up in sort of 20th-century, contemporary terms being also unemployed. They may be in prison." But, she insists, "they are adventuresome." Of what is "described as a major failing of black men—they do not stay home and take care of their children"—she observes that "that has always been to me one of the most attractive features about black male life . . . the fact that they would split in a minute just delights me. It's part of that whole business of breaking ground." And in general, she observes:

> This special lack of restraint, which is a part of human life and is best typified in certain black males, is of particular interest to me. It's in black men despite the reasons society says they're not supposed to have it. Everybody knows who "that man" is, and they may give him bad names and call him a "street nigger"; but when you take away the vocabulary of denigration, what you have is somebody who is fearless and who is comfortable with that fearlessness. It's not about meanness. It's a kind of self-flagellant resistance to certain kinds of control, which is fascinating. Opposed to accepted notions of progress, the lock-step life, they live in the world unreconstructed and that's it.

An ingrained repugnance for the "lock-step" life and a steady if formless fascination with the "unreconstructed" are a frequent motif in Miss Morrison's work, and they inform the structure of her second novel, *Sula*. Here she traces the lives and families of two black women, from their close childhood friendship to their estranged maturity.

Nel Wright is the offspring of a black woman who has ironed out all the wildness of her nature and of her part-Creole background in order to achieve a tight, starched refinement. Sula Peace comes from a "woolly house" of many rooms in which the restraints of the civilized world are very thin. Sula's grandmother, Eva, abandoned with three small children years before by her young husband, is an ambiguous figure who is shown to be capable of devotion but who sets her grown son Plum afire in his bed rather than witness his drug-induced deterioration. Eva's daughter and Sula's mother, Hannah, is a beautiful, sensuous widow who keeps a steady sequence of lovers, "mostly the husbands of her friends and neighbors." Sula's own life is cut loose from any moorings when she overhears her mother's remark to friends that she loves her daughter but does not like her, and when she herself carelessly but unintentionally causes the drowning of a local boy. "The first experience taught her that there was no other that you could count on; the second that there was no self to count on either."

Nel takes the traditional route of marriage and family while Sula goes on to college, travel, sex, and a quest "to make myself." When she returns to town years later she puts her grandmother Eva in a wretched old folks' home, indulges in casual promiscuity, and offhandedly seduces and discards Jude, Nel's husband, thereby wrecking the marriage. Sula begins to feel the pull of possessive love herself when she falls for the smooth, sexy Ajax, but he departs the moment he detects the "scent of the nest." Nel never remarries but lives a dry, lonely, duty-filled existence until, years later and long after Sula's death at the age of thirty, she realizes that her unhappiness stems from missing not Jude, with whom she had a relationship of mutual dependency, but Sula, who alone aroused in her the "sparkle or splutter" of her nature, the richer, deeper potential of her unfulfilled character.

Some critics have balked at the sensational level of physical and emotional violence in *Sula*, but what is really disturbing is the author's determination to take no clear stand on the appalling actions she depicts. *Sula* turns into a parody of *Wuthering Heights*, especially of its ultra-intense Latinate rendition in the film version by Luis Buñuel. Both works oppose the tamed complacencies of civilization to the raw, fanged passions of nature, but *Sula* never achieves the genuine resolution of *Wuthering Heights*. It would seem that Miss Morrison wants things both ways: although we have in *Sula* some of the trappings of a feminist novel—a matriarchy of women alone, two young black girls who have to face life in the realization that they are "neither white nor male," a sketch of Sula as a frustrated artist, a deliberate effort to portray female friendship—in Sula's doomed search for unconditioned freedom the novel also appears to criticize feminist doctrine. Similarly, when Ajax leaves Sula, there is a perceptible feeling of sadness at the failure of love, one of Miss Morrison's usual themes, and yet also a kind of endorsement of his right to roam and remain unattached.

Miss Morrison attempts to resolve the tensions in her novel with what amounts to an aesthetic evasion. Her horrendous portrait of people cutting and bruising and burning each other and themselves in fits and flails of wild, thoughtless willfulness ends with Nel's sudden belated awareness of her love for Sula. But even if a proper union of their differing temperaments could have occurred, how would that heal, dispel, balance, offset, or even make comprehensible the frightening picture of black life that Miss Morrison has presented? The moral issues the novel raises are left hanging, not so much unanswered as answered in a number of self-canceling or mutually canceling ways.

In *Song of Solomon*, Miss Morrison at last permits herself to work her material through, and the novel, although more diffuse than the tightly crafted *Sula*, is more satisfying. Macon Dead II is the richest black man in his Michigan town ("Own things," is his motto), but so empty is life in his company that his wife gains her pleasure by nursing their youngest child Macon III until he is four years old, thus earning him the nickname Milkman. Macon II has a sister, Pilate, poor but independent, uneducated but wise in the deep things of life, in touch with all that her brother has left behind of their strange, sad, eventful childhood. In her dark, pleasantly odorous, and cluttered shack, where she lives with her daughter Reba and granddaughter Hagar, Milkman begins to discover the richer and more remote dimensions of black life that his father has drained from their home.

Increasingly dissatisfied with his soft, limited life and his dependency on his father (who, as bad as he is, is nevertheless portrayed with a degree of sympathy), Milkman decides to set out on a search through the South for a purported bag of gold that is connected to his father's and Pilate's childhood, and which he hopes will make him more independent. He soon realizes that he is really on a search for his family history, which is a far greater treasure, full of strength and joy as well as suffering and pain. This quest in turn becomes a spiritual journey of great energy, depth, and exhilaration as Milkman learns for the first time of the underlying coherence of life, the capacities and contingencies of human existence.

As in classical quest myths, Milkman's journey requires him to face danger and loss and hardship and progressively to shed the trappings of his former life. He must learn to know and respect a wide assortment of black people, including many he would once have arrogantly overlooked. Through various depredations, he comes to empathize with his mother, his neglected sisters, and his cousin Hagar whom he had carelessly discarded after a twelve-year affair.

In a sense Milkman is like Sula, unable at first to understand or to trust the fitful patterns of love and hate, involvement and abandonment that seem to inform human relationships; but unlike Sula he is allowed to work beyond this, as what he learns of his past gradually illumines and orders his present. Milkman's ability to see imaginatively into other people's lives grows greater and greater as his self-regard dissolves. When his aunt Pilate murmurs her last words—"I wish I'd a knowed more people, I would of loved 'em all. If I'd a knowed more, I would a loved more"—he is able to comprehend at last the nature of such a generous, unconditional love and to be moved by it to the threshold of genuine attachment himself.

Song of Solomon has its flaws—some sections remain flat, and there is some undigested protest—but the line of Milkman's journey is quite pure. To this point in her career Miss Morrison had not shown much real interest in the spiritual dimension that the Bible has brought to black life, beyond using its bountiful, sonorous names for her characters, or beyond the occasional indictment of Christian values for stunting and distorting lives. And *Song of Solomon,* despite its biblical title, is itself constructed not as a Christian tale but out of the folklore of slavery. Still, at the end of the hero's quest he has clearly learned that he who loses his life shall save it—or as Milkman puts it, "If you surrendered to the air, you could *ride* it."

In her next work, *Tar Baby,* a racist novel designed to show the natural superiority of blacks, Miss Morrison, as if running from the expansive implications of *Song of Solomon,* returns to all her crabby grievances with a vengeance. Worse, since *Tar Baby* is the only one of her novels largely set in the present, it is deprived of the narrative energy that is released in her when she is dealing with the more exotic black characters and environments of previous decades.

Set in a splendid house on an isolated Caribbean island, *Tar Baby* has the trappings of those erotically charged women's novels in which frigid, raven-haired beauties are surprised in their bedrooms by dark sensual men who pin their wrists together and startle them into a troubled awareness of their unsatisfied longings. In fact, the frigid raven-haired heroine of *Tar Baby,* appropriately named Jadine, *is* surprised in her bedroom by a sensual black man who pins her wrists together and startles her into a troubled awareness of her unsatisfied longings. This embarrassing book is hardly worth discussing save to note that it asserts once again the need for blacks to keep themselves unspotted from the white world and leaves its hero, Son,

with the choice of chasing after the irredeemably white-tainted Jadine or of returning to his primitive black past, even more amorphously presented here than ever before in Miss Morrison's novels. (pp. 60-2)

[In] *Beloved,* Miss Morrison turns back to the history of slavery. Set near Cincinnati around 1873, *Beloved* chronicles the fortunes of Sethe, once a slave on the Sweet Home plantation in Kentucky. Sethe and her husband had belonged to a "good" master—one who treated his property well—but on the pattern of *Uncle Tom's Cabin,* they had come at their master's death under the charge of a singularly cruel man known only as schoolteacher [*sic*].

Because of gross mistreatment, a number of the Sweet Home slaves plan to escape. Sethe sends her three children ahead, then gets through herself after great hardship. A child is born to her en route with the assistance of a poor white girl after whom the baby is named, Denver. Sethe's husband Halle fails to join her; later she discovers that, shortly before he was to leave, his spirit had been broken when he secretly witnessed her being forced by schoolteacher to give her milk to grown white boys. Sethe attempts to make a life for herself with her husband's mother, Baby Suggs, a strong, big-hearted woman who becomes an "unchurched preacher," telling her fellow blacks that they must learn to love themselves in a world where no one else does. But finally Baby Suggs's sorrows overcome her; she announces one day that "there was no bad luck in the world but white-folks," takes to her bed, and begins slowly to die.

Suspended in her own grief, Sethe stays on in the house with Denver, a withdrawn and lonely child. The house is haunted by the ghost of "Beloved," a baby daughter Sethe had killed one month into freedom in the mistaken belief that she and her children were all about to be dragged back into slavery. When another former Sweet Home slave by the name of Paul D arrives, gets rid of the ghost, and begins to take up life with Sethe and Denver, Sethe almost lets herself believe that happiness is possible. But then the ghost returns in the flesh as a young woman at the age she would have been had the baby lived. The reunion with Beloved is at first joyous, but soon she turns malevolent, destroying whatever life Sethe and Denver have made, and contributing to Paul D's departure. Finally Denver seeks help, the now-pregnant Beloved is finally exorcised by a group of neighborhood women, Denver begins life anew, and Paul D returns to Sethe in a spirit of love and acceptance.

There are many compelling elements in *Beloved,* including the delineation of the psychological and emotional effects of being owned—of having no sense of self, of fearing to trust or to love when anything can be taken away at any time. The portrayal of the very limited consciousness of the slaves and ex-slaves, and of their painful slow growth toward damaged self-awareness, is also effective, although sometimes the halt and hesitant nature of their thoughts makes the novel almost catatonic. A couple of scenes in which Sethe begins to feel the rush of life are well and affectingly done.

But the book grows massive and heavy with cumulative

and oft-repeated miseries, with new miseries and new dimensions of miseries added in each telling and retelling long after the point has been made and the reader has grown numb. The graphic descriptions of physical humiliation begin to grow sensationalistic, and the gradual unfolding of secret horror has an unmistakably Gothic dimension which soon comes to seem merely lurid, designed to arouse and entertain.

Still, while far from successful as a work of art, **Beloved** is fascinating to view in the progression of Toni Morrison's work, in which a tropism for simplistic plight-and-protest has done fitful battle with the more capacious demands of a functioning moral imagination. True, Miss Morrison does not display a really sure hand in her treatment of the moral dimensions of Sethe's initial act of child murder, yet unlike the almost offhand treatment of similar crimes in **Sula,** she does make the deed stand as a matter of great gravity and consequence. Sethe is defiant about what she has done, but then later on she must undergo the trial of Beloved's return and vengeance, must suffer the torment involved in confronting and overcoming the past, before she can be free to live. Interesting too is the way in which **Beloved** can almost be read as Miss Morrison's own effort to exorcise the burden of history, to be free in her work of what Howe called the "defining and crippling" violence that has been the subject of the black protest novel. (pp. 62-3)

> Carol Iannone, "Toni Morrison's Career," in Commentary, *Vol. 84, No. 6, December, 1987, pp. 59-63.*

Morrison on black-white relations in the United States:

I feel personally sorrowful about black-white relations a lot of the time because black people have always been used as a buffer in this country between powers to prevent class war, to prevent other kinds of real conflagrations.

If there were no black people here in this country, it would have been Balkanized. The immigrants would have torn each other's throats out, as they have done everywhere else. But in becoming an American, from Europe, what one has in common with that other immigrant is contempt for *me*—it's nothing else but color. Wherever they were from, they would stand together. They could all say, "I am not *that.*" So in that sense, becoming an American is based on an attitude: an exclusion of me.

Toni Morrison, in an interview in Time, *22 May 1989.*

Catherine Rainwater   (essay date Spring 1991)

[*Rainwater is an American educator, editor, and critic. In the following essay, she examines the narrative strategies Morrison employs in her novels.*]

Toni Morrison's narrators consistently try to formulate or adopt a system of values appropriate to African American experience. Their search leads only to a keen sense of the complexities of human existence and so provokes at least

one fairly recent critic [Cynthia Dubin Edelberg, in her "Morrison's Voices: Formal Education, the Work Ethic, and the Bible," *American Literature* (May 1986)] to complain that Morrison fails to defend the values that she apparently endorses. Morrison's novels certainly do *seem* to vacillate on an array of important social and moral issues, including the question of whether Christianity and formal education help or hinder black people and of whether the problems of family violence and incest stem from pathological hatred or pathological love. However, rather than assume that Morrison unwittingly reveals her own uncertainties through her fiction, we need to consider another more plausible explanation: Morrison's narrators and characters (not the author) are the locus of various kinds of uncertainty that become a subject of her fiction. Thus, we might appreciate better the complexity of her narrative management.

Morrison's narrational strategies are traditional, yet her novels undercut the traditional kinds of authority in which such narrative forms are usually grounded. This technique might be treated as a commonplace postmodern gesture if not for the fact that these same novels, in their thematic messages about art, register strong disapproval of postmodern "games"—even (and perhaps especially) serious philosophical "games" with readers concerning truth, meaning, and value. In earnest pursuit of some unambiguous truth that she might convey to readers, Morrison, through her fiction, challenges basic assumptions about aesthetics as a trustworthy epistemological category. Her novels are strategic attacks on "innocent" readers, who assume that art (or any other form of human communication) carries reliable messages to or from the obscure territory of the inner self.

A key element of Morrison's authorial identity derives from her apparent need to expose and eradicate the "sin" of "innocence." Innocence derives from naive assumptions about one's ability to know the truth. In its most insidious form, such innocence allows a person to refuse responsibility for "misreading" a situation, as when in **Tar Baby** (1981) Valerian Street realizes without sufficient guilt that he had ignored the signs of Michael's suffering. Considering such an authorial mission, Morrison's preference for omniscient narrators seems puzzling at first. After all, the moral and epistemological authority such narrators usually embody is a focus of Morrison's attack. However, Morrison sometimes employs a Jamesian technique: she temporarily merges the narrator's point of view with that of a character, but later undercuts or problematizes this point of view by presenting its alternatives. Such a strategy finally reiterates her thematic message that there is no reliable ground or "mooring" from which to know or tell the "true" version of any story. Morrison's omniscient narrators, whose points of view only intermittently imply her own apparent authorial point of view, are ultimately as bereft of certainty as Milkman Dead when in **Song of Solomon** (1977) he tries to locate the original version of his family history within the variants of it that tease him into acts of interpretation.

A prominent theme in Morrison's work concerns the absence of reliable authority, the inscrutability of one human being to another and, concomitantly, the lack of definitive meaning in phenomenal events. This theme is elaborated in a variety of ways—through character interaction as well as through numerous formal mechanisms, especially the "mask" motif that appears throughout Morrison's fiction. Her novels suggest that problems of knowledge occur partly owing to differences in human perception and, thus, in the "versions" of "reality" people espouse. Her works also demonstrate, however, that even when we share common perceptions and agree upon facts, human motives and inner life remain obscure to the observer.

For example, in *Song of Solomon,* Macon Dead wonders about his sister, Pilate, whose inner life is not revealed by her outward appearance. Giving voice to Macon's thoughts, the narrator tells us that "he [Macon] knew her face better than he knew his own." But her face is often "like a mask." And "she chewed things, [so] if you were close to her, you wondered if she was about to smile or was she merely shifting a straw from the baseline of her gums to her tongue. Perhaps she was dislodging a curl of rubber band from inside her cheek, or was she really smiling? From a distance she appeared to be whispering to herself, when she was only nibbling or splitting tiny seeds with her front teeth." Many of Morrison's characters likewise behave in ways difficult, sometimes impossible, for an observer to interpret. At times her characters' motives remain hidden even to themselves and so invite the reader's skepticism toward others' interpretations. Moreover, the narrator employs the pronoun "you"—"if *you* were close to her, *you* wondered"—a rhetorical strategy that suggests the responsibility of the reader-participant in the narrative to recognize his or her own uncertain interpretive position. As the narrator of *Tar Baby* concludes, individuals are "formed, fleshed, thick with a life which is . . . not accessible."

In light of such a theme concerning the inscrutability of people and experience, a reader of Morrison's fiction begins to see that she also erodes reader confidence in the conventional narrative patterns that she employs in the novel. The bildungsroman, the "initiation" story, and other similar genres, characterized by certain kinds of closure and narrated by conventional first- and third-person narrators, usually presuppose accessible "truth" about experience. Morrison uses these and other narrative forms that generate in the reader a variety of premodern expectations, including faith in the narrator's access to truth or, allowing for limitations of the narrator, at least a faith in the accessibility of truth through the overall work of art. She also draws from a variety of African folktale patterns in her work; however, again she evades closure, which is a primary structural feature of such models.

Morrison develops ideas about art at a thematic level, and briefly considering these ideas leads to a better understanding of the more complex issues of her narrative technique. First, her novels emphasize the magical power of art (indeed, several of her characters possess magical powers). Like magic, art reveals a destructive as well as a constructive use. The destructive power resides for Morrison's characters particularly in seductive popular art such as blues songs and movies. Popular art invites people to enter into fantasy worlds where they may seek escape from reality, or they might also learn, inappropriately, to apply the interpretive norms of fiction to life. In *The Bluest Eye* (1970), Pecola's mother, Pauline, despairs because she cannot meet the (white) standards of beauty that she learns from the movies: "The onliest time I be happy seem like was when I was in the picture show. . . . [T]he screen would light up and I'd move right on in them pictures." Eventually, however, she complains that the movies just "made coming home hard." In *Tar Baby,* Jadine likewise falls victim to illusions fostered by pop art. She nearly dies in a bog when she wanders into an attractive landscape that reminds her of "something by Bruce White or Fazetta—an elegant comic book illustration." In *Song of Solomon,* another effect of art, or at least of storytelling, is enchantment or narcosis. When the witchlike Pilate tells Milkman and Guitar the story of her life, they sit "in a pleasant semi-stupor, listening. . . . [A]fraid to say anything . . . and afraid to remain silent lest she not go on with its telling."

Art carries dangerous power that is controlled by artists who, according to Morrison, bear great responsibility to those affected by their creations. Sula is an irresponsible artist in the novel named for her. She often speaks and acts merely to see her effects on people. Though usually not intentionally cruel, she is detached; her idle imagination and "gift for metaphor" lead her to do harm. At this particular point in the story, the narrator seems to speak from Morrison's implied authorial point of view and pronounces judgment: "Like any artist with no art form, she [Sula] became dangerous." Another misguided artist is Valerian Street (a horticulturist) in *Tar Baby,* who escapes through imagination the ugly fact that his wife abuses their son Michael. Safe in his fantasies, Valerian comfortably misinterprets his son's "messages" of distress. He "ma[kes] up . . . information" to fit his pleasant world view and thus becomes "guilty . . . of innocence. Was there anything so loathsome as a willfully innocent man?" asks the narrator, who also answers the question from viewpoint of the implied author. "Hardly. An innocent man is a sin before God. . . . No man should live without absorbing the sins of his kind."

Within the context of Morrison's fiction, Valerian's sin exemplifies the sin of any artist who uses creative power to escape rather than to alleviate, or at least to confront, human suffering. He shirks his duty to "receive" and "deliver" the "message" that Michael sends, and he bears the responsibility to do so even though the baby's face and words are difficult to interpret. Instead of realizing and ending the child's as well as the wife's suffering (she is tortured with guilt), Valerian escapes into his greenhouse. The narrator's judgment of him thus applies to any artist, who must hear and deliver the messages of humanity: "A real messenger, a worthy one, is corrupted by the messages he brings . . . even if it . . . wilt[s] rows of angel trumpets and cause[s] them to fall from their vines." This narrator's judgment of the artist's responsibility does not vacillate, even though on the issue of child abuse the narrator sometimes takes on the point of view of the abuser and thus seems alternately to condemn and to sympathize with the victimizer. In this way Morrison's narrators frequently equivocate on questions of human motivation and intent, and consequently, they seem to avoid authoritative moral judgments. Such equivocation does not suggest that all human behavior is justified; it only suggests that since we cannot finally know *why* a person acts evilly, we are better off deferring judgment and understanding that we are all capable of wrongdoing, whatever our motives. However, her narrators always *insist* that an artist cannot be forgiven for "innocence"—for encouraging or allowing partial or naive points of view and the moral judgments that accrue to them. To dispel such grievous "innocence" is the writer's moral duty.

Complicating this moral imperative is the problem central to Morrison's art—the inaccessibility of truth or complete knowledge. Valerian, for example, never knows with certainty of Michael's abuse until the boy has grown up and left home. Only after he learns the facts does he suddenly pause to reenvision past events that were, when they transpired, quite ambiguous. How, then, does one carry "messages" when phenomena resist our efforts to grasp their final significance? Precisely this question is fundamental to Morrison's narrative management. Her works display a gradually diminishing faith in generic forms; as these forms appear increasingly inadequate, the reader must confront their breakdown and within it discover Morrison's essential "message." As her narrators gradually renege on the type of authority that the reader traditionally invests in them, a different sort of narrator-reader relationship develops; the narrator and the reader are simultaneously "corrupted by the messages" of human experience. Depriving us of the comforts of form, the text also deprives us of "innocence"—an easy escape from knowledge that is too easily encoded, enclosed, and managed within a form.

Tempting readers to make this escape, Morrison's narrators assume the role of the detached, omniscient observer who is often equated with "authorial presence." Three of the novels feature Olympian, third-person narrators of unknown origins and identity. The narrator in *The Bluest Eye* strikes the same detached, omniscient pose although she tells her story from the first-person point of view as an adult who recalls her childhood. Finally, omniscient narration in *Beloved* (1987) alternates with lyrical narrative passages spoken by the title character that the narrator (and other characters) try to interpret. (Two chapters toward the end are narrated in first-person by Sethe and Denver, respectively; both try to account for Beloved's apparent disembodied existence.) Invariably, however, Morrison's omniscient narrators emerge bereft of the truth and clarity that are traditionally theirs. Yet they are not "unreliable" narrators; Morrison's novels conspicuously avoid attempts to outwit, deceive, or engage the reader in intellectual games that involve subtle flaws in the narrators' perceptual or moral faculties. Especially at those moments in the texts when narrators temporarily assume a particular character's point of view, Morrison encourages the reader to understand that such empathy itself diminishes one's certain hold on the truth. Her narrators want to tell us the truth, but cannot find it. In *Song of Solomon,* the narrator speaks from Ruth's perspective as she looks for a "mooring, a checkpoint, some stable visual object that

assured . . . the world was still there; that this was life and not a dream." However, with Ruth the narrator concedes that "there was nothing you could do with a mooring except acknowledge it, use it for the verification of some idea you wanted to keep alive." Ensconced within traditional generic forms, Morrison's narratives themselves embody a search for moorings—generic norms that "keep alive" the "idea" of authority and extant truth—even as the novels display a kind of reverse epistemology: all moorings are gradually lost as characters, narrators, and readers discover what and how they do not know about experience.

One type of narrative mooring lost in the novels is the conventional circular pattern. Such patterns traditionally suggest closure or the availability of complete knowledge. For example, the rise-and-fall pattern of many nineteenth-century novels implies a full-circle structure of human destiny, and the "initiation" story and the bildungsroman imply a logical progression from youth to maturity that coherently reconciles origins with endings. In Morrison's novels some type of circular narrative pattern attempts but conspicuously fails to enclose a "completed" story. The "idea" of closure is kept "alive" as an ideal, but the origins and endings of the various strands of the stories remain elusive, a narrative feature for which Morrison has been criticized. The characters, together with their stories, evade closure. Pecola Breedlove "step[s] over into madness" and isolation; Sula dies misunderstood; Milkman Dead flies away; Son gallops off to join the mythical Haitian horsemen of the Isle des Chevaliers; Beloved's ontological status is unclear from the outset of the novel; and the narrator concludes by telling us that she is "disremembered and unaccounted for," at last.

Pecola's story in *The Bluest Eye* is conveyed through strategies of encirclement, as if drawing smaller and smaller rings around a center could somehow force "truth" to appear there. The seasonal chapter headings of the text compose the outermost circle of the narrative. However, the narrator's disclaimers that appear at the beginning and end of the text declare that the "harvest" of truth is not forthcoming, just as literally in the novel the harvest of marigolds fails: Pecola's baby dies, and the marigolds do not germinate. At the beginning of the novel, the narrator says she cannot explain "why" any of the events happened as they did, and at the end of the text, she reveals that neither she nor any of the other townspeople ever really felt empathy for Pecola. They merely used her life as we use a story; her failure was a means of assessing their own imagined success; her weakness, an index to their "fantasy of . . . strength." Perhaps the narrator's telling of Pecola's story could be viewed as an attempt to atone for the sin of "innocence." If so, Morrison's management of the narrative prevents the "sin" from being committed twice, for the narrator's attempt to "harvest" the truth of the past is fraught with breakdowns of which the narrator herself is aware.

Within the circular narrative pattern of seasons that implies but does not yield a "harvest" or closure with truth, there are smaller circlings. The narrator's mind turns, for example, upon childhood memories of people who were, paradoxically, both monstrous and kind. Memories of child molesters, including Pecola's father, Mr. Henry, and Soaphead Church, motivate the narrator to discover "what got into people" to account for such crimes. Searching for the origins of their behavior, she searches their personal histories, only to arrive again at the shocking fact of their deeds, now surrounded by a host of possible explanations, none definitive. She cannot completely, fully know these characters nor discover the secrets at the center of their being. Essentially, the adult narrator is no better able to understand human behavior now than when she was a child on the outer "edges" of a confusing swirl of adult conversations. "Their conversation is like a . . . dance: sound meets sound. . . . Another sound enters but is upstaged by still another: the two circle each other and stop. Sometimes their words move in lofty spirals. . . . We do not, cannot, know the meanings. . . . So we watch their faces, their hands, their feet, and listen for truth in timbre."

Circular patterns apparently compose some inherent choreography of the mind but do not describe experience itself. In this and subsequent novels, Morrison's texts develop circular patterns and simultaneously demystify them as authoritative narrative devices. Her fiction destroys the illusion of discoverable, containable truth and insists that history, personal or collective, neither accounts for particular tragedies nor proffers lessons for the future. The text allows no escape from the story through encoded order and explanation, and it so confronts the reader with something akin to immediate experience. Such narrative management destroys the reader's "innocence" because it interferes with some basic habits of interpretive response. We cannot gain comfortable distance from these characters by considering them different from us because their lives are different from ours; nor can we "use" their stories the way the townspeople used Pecola's, to gain some complacent sense of our own moral or intellectual superiority. *Beloved* ends with the same, perhaps more strongly stated message. The narrator says of Beloved, "They forgot her like a bad dream. After they made up their tales, shaped and decorated them, those that saw her that day on the porch quickly and deliberately forgot her." And anyway, says the narrator, "It was not a story to pass on." This statement implies that not only is Beloved's story too painful to remember by retelling but also that her experience, like that of so many of Morrison's other characters, is uncontainable, untotalizable in a form that affords distance from what is told.

Morrison's second novel, *Sula* (1974), likewise displays a circular narrative pattern that the narrator demystifies as it proceeds. *Sula* recalls *The Bluest Eye* in implying that the yearly cycles of life produce repetitions but not completeness or closure. The narrative begins and ends with an account of the dying black neighborhood outside Medallion. This narrative circle records more than forty years' history of the area, from 1919 to 1965. Each year is itself a circle: the people mark passing time with local annual rituals such as National Suicide Day. Although time passes in *Sula,* the narrative erodes any notion of history as coherent accumulation of knowledge. The years pass. The same figures appear and disappear in the town, but with different names: in one passage, Nel remarks how some of the young boys in 1965 seem to be replicas of the youths of the 1920s and 1930s. Each passing year brings more and more old people to fill up the retirement homes. Although these people have lived through the same yearly cycles, their shared pasts do not unite them. Indeed, their pasts are not really shared. For example, the narrator informs us, "Shadrack and Nel moved in opposite directions, each thinking separate thoughts about the past. The distance between them increased as they both remembered gone things." However circular, time does not enclose people within temporal or historical community; instead, it apparently drives them apart, as it does Nel and Sula, who were once best friends. With the black community destroyed, with Sula and many others dead—their stories finished but not completed—Nel remains isolated; all the separate stories crowd together in concentric but separate "circles." She cries: "It was a fine cry—loud and long— but it had no bottom and it had no top, just circles and circles of sorrow."

As in *The Bluest Eye,* repetitive cycles and narrative circles do not yield fullness of knowledge or closure but merely reveal the human need for knowledge and closure. *Sula* leaves Nel stranded without moorings, with burdensome knowledge, and in need of revising her vision of the past. Nel realizes she has missed Sula since their estrangement, which occurs after Sula seduces Nel's husband, Jude. Nel never fully comprehends Sula's reasons for having an affair with Jude, nor does she understand the source of her own bitterness until very much later: "All that time, all that time, I thought I was missing Jude." Thus the past cannot be explained, encircled and dismissed, because with each new insight obtained in the present the past begins anew to rearrange itself; a new "circle" forms. A narrative begun as a circumscribed history reveals its own task as unfeasible.

Circularity, as well as a kind of incremental repetition, characterizes *Song of Solomon,* Morrison's third novel. Like the previous two books, it implies but never actually establishes closure. The narration begins and ends with the stories of two otherwise unrelated characters who take "flight." The narrator finishes telling without completing the life of Milkman Dead, who is born when his mother witnesses a "flight" from an upstairs window and who perhaps dies in his own "flight" from the top of a cliff. As a bildungsroman, *Song of Solomon* traces the life of a young man from youth to adulthood, but the attempt to tell his story suggests that the story cannot really be told, indeed, cannot really be known. The fabric of Milkman's life unravels as he grows, and so at the end his life seems only arbitrarily contained by the framing device or "mooring" that surrounds it.

Milkman's story—like that of all human beings but especially paradigmatic of African American experience— cannot be told partly because his African origins are unrecoverable. The narrator tells us that Milkman's father's stories of the past "explained nothing." So he becomes obsessed with discovering his identity and ancestry. His obsession revolves around several key incidents in his life, but these incidents, the more they are pondered, yield less and less of any reliable or verifiable truth. Repeated incrementally in the novel, these incidents serve only to generate infinite possible versions of Milkman's past. In tracing these possibilities, the narrator conspicuously refrains from finally authorizing any one of them and thereby circumvents whatever closure the overt, circular narrative structure implies.

One of these incrementally repeated passages from Milkman's life concerns the alleged incest between his mother and her father. Milkman's father, Macon, and his mother, Ruth, tell Milkman two completely different versions of a single incident that occurred shortly after Dr. Foster's death. Macon swears he caught Ruth naked next to the body, with the old man's fingers in her mouth, while Ruth swears that, clad in a slip, she stood near the body, respectfully kissing the old man's hand. Milkman has no idea which version to believe, and his knowledge of both parents alternately corroborates both accounts. Possessed of "unwanted knowledge" as well as "a responsibility for that knowledge," Milkman struggles to figure out the "truth." However, each time his mind revolves on the subject, he only adds to his already burdensome knowledge some new and equally unwelcome piece of information, until all hope of "truth" is lost in a welter of proliferating versions.

A second incrementally repeated obsession in Milkman's life involves a folksong that he believes holds clues to his heritage. All his life he hears the song about "Sugarman" who "done fly away / . . . cut across the sky / . . . gone home." When he travels as an adult back to his father's hometown, Shalimar, he hears an apparent version of the same song. Through a series of quite imaginative interpretations and alterations of the song lyrics, he concludes that the song was originally about "Solomon," an African ancestor who flew away; moreover, he decides that Shalimar, the town, was once "Solomon," the name altered through oral tradition. The song becomes for Milkman an oral history of his family. In short, each time Milkman hears the song, he alters it and his past until he constructs a new version of his life that pleases him. This invented past is even less verifiable than his father's stories, dismissed earlier because they "explained nothing."

Milkman's treatment of the song as key to the elusive "truth" mirrors the textual patterns of Morrison's novel itself. Each time Milkman returns to the song as a source, he adds to, subtracts from, and transforms the source itself until, far from reaching any definitive truth, he has simply made up a new possible story to consider alongside the other possible stories. Likewise, Morrison's narrator purports to tell Milkman's life story but instead reveals the ways in which any single definitive story eludes us. As in *The Bluest Eye* and *Sula,* the story cannot be contained within narrative boundaries. The outermost circle of the narrative seems arbitrarily imposed, since Milkman's life story extends back before his birth into myth and, the narrator implies, continues beyond his physical death, when he joins the ghosts of his ancestors. Moreover, no single story of his life is verifiable; there are only numerous possible versions. *Song of Solomon,* like Morrison's other novels, unmoors our confidence in diachronic progression and posits instead a synchronic model of experience that, be-

cause of the limitless proliferation of versions, eludes containment within narrative form.

Tar Baby likewise exhibits a circular narrative pattern without closure. The novel begins and ends with Son traveling toward the Isle des Chevaliers, and within this outermost narrative circle, his and the other characters' lives circle around nodal points without any resolution. The narrative is presented as an initiation story, but the initiation effects no real changes in the characters' lives. Indeed, all variously end up where they started. Jadine, despite what she has learned from Son about being true to her black heritage, returns to her old life among white, fashion-conscious sophisticates and to a white boyfriend. Sidney and Ondine, her stepparents, reconcile with their employers, the Streets, despite serious disagreements; Valerian Street lapses into a state of powerlessness and paralysis even more profound than before; and Margaret continues her old life, awaiting the grown-up Michael's calls and visits that never come.

Son, the focal character in the novel, returns to the Isle des Chevaliers to reclaim Jadine, whom he loves. He is willing to give up his convictions and do anything, want or believe anything she wants. However, Marie-Therese Foucault (a Haitian witch) tricks him into approaching the island from the far side, where he encounters the blind horsemen of Haitian myth. Like Milkman in *Song of Solomon,* Son disappears into some realm completely inaccessible to narration. His fate there is not verifiable; he is simply gone, escaped from the narrative circle.

Between the two trips to the island, Son's life is narrated in circles. Indeed, his entire adult existence revolves around the search for his "original dime," a circular object and Son's metaphor for the satisfaction he achieved only once in his life when he earned his first money. He looks for this satisfaction in all experiences, including his relationship with Jadine and his return with her to Eloe, Florida, where he grew up and where he now tries to recapture the past. Like the other characters, Son leads a life that never resolves but only revolves; the narrative circles do not provide closure but expose fruitless cycles. His escape at the end, if indeed it is truly an escape, places him outside these cycles but also outside the reach of the narrative.

If Morrison's characters' lives do not cohere, and if they defy attempts to structure them, Morrison's narratives themselves frustrate the reader who seeks patterned, appropriate responses to disturbing material. The reader shares with the narrator the problem of "what . . . to do with . . . information." Despairing of language to render truth, the narrators often hope that some other medium, especially music, will be more successful. As the narrator of *The Bluest Eye* declares concerning Cholly Breedlove's life, "The pieces . . . could become coherent only in the head of a musician." Thus, Morrison suggests that reading is much like Claudia and Frieda's earlier-mentioned experience of listening to adult conversation and grasping only the "edges," the "timbre." Her narrators' apparent distrust of language implies Morrison's own view of narrative as obstructing a more elemental encounter with experience. However, the music affording this encounter (if such exists) would have to be instrumental, since Morrison's fiction shows how song lyrics mislead characters.

Circular structures are not the only conventional narrative mooring that Morrison's works gradually demystify. Her narrators also constantly backtrack in pursuit of elusive points of origin, even as they attempt to pursue forward, linear development. Morrison's novels suggest that there is never enough available information to complete the narrated moment; the narrator must constantly begin again at some new place, as if to force the various discontinuous sequences to converge upon the truth. If one cannot tell a single diachronic story, these texts imply, then one must tell many stories that, held together synchronically in the reader's mind, might consequently illuminate one another.

One variety of narrative regression involves attempts to account for the present moment in a character's life by sifting backward through the lives and memories of contingent characters. In none of the novels, however, are origins historically recoverable. Morrison's latest novel, *Beloved,* makes this point perhaps most emphatically in its insistence that memory is both an evasion and a re-creation of the past, not a record of it. The narrator's efforts to clarify Beloved's past fail, first, because, as a ghost, Beloved herself is ontologically different from characters with traceable human connections and, second, because her family ties were severed (during her life) by slave traders. Like Beloved's relationship with her mother—defined primarily through incremental repetitions of her mother's disappearance—Beloved's relationship to all the characters in the novel is defined by absence not presence, of clear linkages. Indeed, the several phases of Beloved's own life (as she narrates it in the lyric portions of the novel) are separated by gaps of unrecoverable memory. The linkages between one part of her life and another are as unclear as her linkages to others' lives. For example, how Beloved ends up near Sethe's house and thus becomes a part of Sethe's life is unclear. One character, Stamp Paid, ventures an explanation that Sethe also considers and tells Denver: "Beloved had [probably] been locked up by some whiteman for his own purposes. . . . [S]he must have escaped to a bridge or someplace and rinsed the rest out of her mind." Thus, her life as narrated is a pastiche of her own and other peoples' dubious accounts of it. In **Beloved,** efforts to know one human being through her past relationships to others fail because of the unrecoverable nature of the past, as well as to differences in human perception, memory, and explanation of experience.

In *The Bluest Eye,* which searches for the truth about Pecola Breedlove's tragic life, the narrator actually amasses more information about Pecola's parents and her final betrayer, Soaphead Church, than about Pecola herself. Although the narrative opens in the autumn of 1940 and purports to account for events through the summer of 1941, the narrative dwells often in years prior to 1940, as if the life stories of Cholly, Pauline, and Soaphead (and, in turn, the lives of their precursors) could somehow explain Pecola's, which eludes full explanation. Morrison's technique here is not that of the traditional family saga, in which the lives of many characters, do, in fact, illuminate

one another. For Morrison's characters, the thread of origins disappears in the backward expanse of generations, and the story is prefaced by a statement of failure: "There is really nothing more to say—except why. But since *why* is difficult to handle, one must take refuge in *how.*"

The Bluest Eye conveys how history, like individual lives, is ultimately incoherent. The narrator implies that we are wiser to examine the incoherence, the points of breakdown and fracture in experience, rather than to look for consistency. For example, the deprivations and fractures in Cholly Breedlove's life more plausibly account for his treatment of Pecola than do any of his experiences that can be narrated. Abandoned on a garbage heap as an infant, and alone in the world since age thirteen, Cholly is primarily shaped by what is absent from his experience. According to the narrator, "The aspect of married life that dumbfounded him and rendered him totally disfunctional was the appearance of children. Having no idea of how to raise children, and having never watched any parent raise himself, he could not ever comprehend what such a relationship should be."

The same type of narrative regression in pursuit of origins characterizes *Sula.* Like *The Bluest Eye, Sula* features a forward-moving, chronological organization—chapter titles are dates, from 1919 to 1965. However, the narrator searches the histories of the focal characters. From this search intriguing patterns emerge that, upon close scrutiny, fail to disclose the types of explanations usually expected from such patterns. For example, Sula is a cruel woman, who even as a child could watch dispassionately while others died. In fact, she earns her reputation as pariah when she merely watches her own mother burn in a fire. Sula's grandmother, Eva, likewise was capable of similar inhuman acts. She burns her own son to death after she discovers he is an incurable drug addict. However, Eva's past reveals a compassionate and fiercely protective side to her nature that Sula conspicuously lacks. Whereas one can infer compassionate motives (however barbarously manifested) from Eva's behavior, such motives are absent in the granddaughter, who instead seeks out new experiences because she is bored and curious. Thus, the grandmother's life does not explain the granddaughter's, despite the narrator's exploration of similarities between the two that invite us to compare them. Moreover, such likenesses do not unite the two women. Sula and Eva dislike each other, and Eva becomes to some extent one of Sula's victims. Without connections, Sula lives in a "center of silence . . . and a loneliness so profound the word itself had no meaning."

Song of Solomon likewise follows a pattern of forward motion through time. It traces the life of Milkman Dead from birth to death. However, this novel, even more than the others, reveals serious difficulties in maintaining this straightforward pattern. The narrator not only backtracks through personal histories and circles back onto pivotal obsessions of the characters but also fractures the diachronic process by variously beginning again, as if there were no logical place to pick up the strands of the story in order to advance it.

Milkman Dead is obsessed with the past; indeed, his daily

personal habits reflect this compulsion to look backward. As a child he kneels in the front seat of the car and looks backward at the passing scenery as it retreats. As a man he is constantly looking behind him, as if to discover something there that would explain his current situation. Despite Milkman's interest in continuity, the narrator tells us that he is "incoherent"; his face "lacked . . . a coming together of the features into a total self." Part of the narrative quest in this novel is to discover the "total sel[ves]" of the characters, and like Milkman the narrator often looks backward to discover the linkages and to escape the fear that "at any time, anyone might do anything."

The narrator in *Song of Solomon* often disrupts the flow of the story with chapters and subsections that begin in a new place, not chronologically subsequent to what has come immediately before. Chapter 4, for example, skips to Milkman's adulthood, some twelve years after the events of the previous chapter. However, almost immediately, the narrator begins to search backward through time to account for the present. This attempt, however, laterally deflects attention onto the stories of other characters. Before the chapter concludes, the narrative has taken at least four different directions in an effort to amass information convergent upon and, apparently explanatory of, Milkman's life. Morrison's story continues to branch and to open out, a narrative technique that recalls the conventions of the family saga; however, much unverifiable information accrues that never ultimately coheres. In fact, the reader sometimes ponders whether ties of kinship account for anything except human desire for continuity. The narrator suggests that there is finally no accounting for Milkman's boredom, aimlessness, and lack of vital connections and coherence. In various ways each of the chapters replicates this narrative process of a backward motion, new beginnings, without recovery of origins or continuity. When Milkman finally invents his past from the "Sugarman" folksong, the gaps in the song as well as the gaps in his life are the focal points. As in *Beloved* the past does not elaborate upon the present, but revisions, embellishments, and "readings" of the past can be used to fill in what is always missing in the present. Still, no definitive explanations are available.

Tar Baby follows a similar process of backtracking, especially in the life of Son, the main character. Thematically, the novel insists, like *Song of Solomon,* on the impossibility of anyone's knowing anyone else. Indeed, Son does not really know himself. He creates for himself many identities, yet none contain his total self. He feels incomplete, as if he does not "have a real life, like most people. I've missed a lot." As in the other novels, the narrative continuously ebbs into contingent lives but fails to locate connections. Each of Son's invented identities, in fact, seems discretely separate from the others, as his final escape into the spirit realm seems disconnected from all parts of his earthly existence. Like Milkman and Beloved, Son is incoherent, and the pieces of his life do not add up in a way to account for the effects of his apparent origins.

In all of Morrison's novels, narrative regressions betoken incomplete and unverifiable knowledge. Moreover, the narrators of these works tend sometimes to grant the authority of whatever version is currently the center of interest, and this habit reinforces the reader's impression that Morrison vacillates on pivotal issues. The best example of inconsistent attribution of authority occurs in *Song of Solomon* and concerns whether or not Ruth and her father have actually committed incest. When the narrator tells us that Dr. Foster himself admits discomfort with his daughter's affection for him, the reader suspects Ruth, and not her father, of inappropriate feelings. When Macon accuses the two of incest, the reader will recall that Ruth secretly breast-fed her son until he was much too old, and again suspect her. But when the narrator tells Ruth's story, Ruth's explanation is equally plausible, and the reader then should remember Macon's meanness as well as Dr. Foster's tendency to isolate his family from the community. Such isolation (as Ruth's reported thoughts reveal) could easily have forged an inappropriately close but innocent bond between father and daughter. Moreover, the question grows even more complex when we recall that standards of normalcy vary—a fact emphasized by the narrator's habit of entering each character's consciousness and temporarily seeming to justify his or her standards. Precisely what constitutes an "inappropriate" bond varies among individuals. Macon, a cold and mean person, might suspect any display of affection between parent and child. In short, each "version" bears some authority, and the narrator will not ultimately pass judgment on any one of them because the inner life of humans remains obscure and "inaccessible." The narrator's avoidance of traditional authority thrusts responsibility outward onto the reader, who must "do [something] with this information"; the reader may not, however, expect the narrator to help by pointing to a particular character's culpability. This narrative method causes the reader to join the narrator in pondering "what got into people," and simultaneously, it prevents readers from using the characters' failures to generate their own "fantasy of strength" [*The Bluest Eye*]. Without a final explanation of behavior, we cannot assume our own superiority and exemption.

A final narrative strategy that Morrison employs to unmoor the reader from traditional expectations of order is her use of biblical analogues as apparent structuring devices. Morrison subverts these biblical paradigms just as she subverts generic norms—to deprive readers of one more "innocent" alternative. Morrison will not allow her works to be interpreted as Christian allegory or parable. Biblical allusions and character names occur often throughout all of Morrison's novels. Generally speaking, her works vex even the most loosely applied typological readings. In fact, many of her characters named for biblical figures seem completely opposite to their prototypes. Morrison implies that biblical allusions, like circular patterns and other narrative devices, generate expectations of order that life itself does not fulfill. *Song of Solomon,* for example, is anything but a neatly arranged allegory of God's love for a people.

Like Christian paradigms, the paradigms of African folk legend and myth also fail to convey the structure of phenomenal experience. Morrison employs religion and myth just as she employs the conventions of narrative: to show

how all external "moorings" and "authorities" fail to explain human tragedy; they merely "keep alive the idea" that it can be explained. In their repudiation of the conventional authority they usually wield, her narrators destroy the reader's traditional avenues of escape into innocence, and by refusing to explain, her texts immerse the reader in perplexing experience. Thus, Morrison becomes a "worthy messenger." Her stories "corrupt" because they cannot become, like the people's story of Pecola, a morally smug arrangement "of lies . . . called truth." Pecola's neighbors ostracize her as a scapegoat and infer their own blessedness from her apparent damnation. But Morrison teaches that we cannot "see . . . in the new pattern of an old idea the revelation and the Word" [*The Bluest Eye*] because in the world of Morrison's fiction there is no Revelation and no absolute Word. There are only words and a world in which we are isolated interpreters without absolute moorings. (pp. 96-111)

> Catherine Rainwater, "Worthy Messengers: Narrative Voices in Toni Morrison's Novels," in Texas Studies in Literature and Language, Vol. XXXIII, No. 1, Spring, 1991, pp. 96-113.

REVIEWS OF RECENT WORKS

Wendy Steiner   (review date 5 April 1992)

[*Steiner is a Canadian-born American educator, translator, editor, and critic. In the following review, she praises* Playing in the Dark, *as a "self-help project meant both to map out new critical territory and to rearrange the territory within."*]

Toni Morrison is both a great novelist and the closest thing the country has to a national writer. The fact that she speaks as a woman and a black only enhances her ability to speak as an American, for the path to a common voice nowadays runs through the partisan. In her novel *Beloved,* for example, Ms. Morrison restores to the collective memory a particular strand of its emotive past, turning a story of former slaves into what amounts to a national epic. Though it is "not a story to pass on," she offers everyone—not just those injured—the chance to feel the pain, the injustice and the need for healing.

Playing in the Dark: Whiteness and the Literary Imagination was first presented as a series of lectures at Harvard University. Here, Ms. Morrison invites literary scholars to carry on her generous task of making the black experience resonant for all Americans. Black characters in classic American novels, she maintains, have been as marginalized as their real-life counterparts. The "shadow" darkening American fiction, in her view, has been a critical nontopic because "the habit of ignoring race is understood to be a graceful, even generous, liberal gesture." But "excising the political from the life of the mind is a sacrifice that has proven costly. . . . A criticism that needs to insist that literature is not only 'universal' but also 'race-free'

risks lobotomizing that literature, and diminishes both the art and the artist," she says. "All of us, readers and writers, are bereft when criticism remains too polite or too fearful to notice a disrupting darkness before its eyes."

Toni Morrison calls this proposed area of study "American Africanism." White American fiction, she states, has fabricated a black persona that is "reflexive," a means for whites to contemplate their own terror and desire without having to acknowledge these feelings as their own. Such characters thus operate like vaudeville blackface, indicating "the sycophancy of white identity." In texts by the most canonic of American writers, Poe's *Narrative of Arthur Gordon Pym,* for example, the death or oppression of a black character is followed by the apparition of a "closed and unknowable white form." "These images of blinding whiteness," Ms. Morrison says, "seem to function as both antidote for and meditation on the shadow that is companion to this whiteness—a dark and abiding presence that moves the hearts and texts of American literature with fear and longing."

The black "shadow" has, paradoxically, allowed white culture to face its fear of freedom, Ms. Morrison continues. Though Pilgrim, colonist, immigrant and refugee embraced America for its promise of freedom, they were nevertheless terrified at the prospect of becoming failures and outcasts, engulfed by a boundless, untamable nature. It was not surprising, then, that writers explored American identity in the most anxiety-ridden genre of literature—the romance. There they could fill in the romance's "power of blackness," as [Herman] Melville called it, with the figure of the slave, whose lack of freedom and whose blackness confirmed his contrast to the master. Africanism, the culture's construction of black slavery, stood, therefore, not only for the "not-free" but also for the "not-me."

Given the proliferation of African-American studies programs and, more generally, the politicization of literary scholarship, Ms. Morrison's charge that academics have ignored the topic of blacks in literature may seem surprising. At a time when conservative scholars and commentators are hammering the humanities for allegedly coercive political correctness, she can hardly fault criticism for reticence about race. Equally surprising is her claim that *Playing in the Dark* is apolitical:

> I want to draw a map . . . of a critical geography and use that map to open as much space for discovery, intellectual adventure, and close exploration as did the original charting of the New World—without the mandate for conquest. I intend to outline an attractive, fruitful, and provocative critical project, unencumbered by dreams of subversion or rallying gestures at fortress walls.

Chiding liberal critics for their discrete neglect of darkness, she sets out to map this political minefield without engaging in conquest or subversion or rallying cries. The question is whether someone of even Ms. Morrison's sensitivity can carry this off.

As Ms. Morrison delves ever deeper into Africanism, the neutrality of her mapping disappears. She considers Bernard Bailyn's study of William Dunbar, a Scotsman who left sophisticated London to find his true identity as a wealthy planter in Mississippi. Dunbar's sense of his individualism, innocence, heroism and manliness shades into the archetype of the solitary, alienated American. "What, one wants to ask, are Americans alienated from?" Ms. Morrison asks.

> What are Americans always so insistently innocent of? . . . Answers to these questions lie in the potent and ego-reinforcing presence of an Africanist population. . . . This new white male can now persuade himself that savagery is "out there." The lashes ordered . . . are not one's own savagery; repeated and dangerous breaks for freedom are "puzzling" confirmations of black irrationality; the combination of Dean Swift's beatitudes and a life of regularized violence is civilized. . . . These contradictions slash their way through the pages of American literature.

Ms. Morrison's anger at these slashing contradictions becomes steadily more apparent. She quotes Harry Morgan's remark in Hemingway's *To Have and Have Not* that "having" a "nigger wench" is "like nurse shark." Ms. Morrison explains the phrase as meaning "the furthest thing from human, so far away as to be not even mammal but fish. . . . Harry's words mark something so brutal, contrary, and alien in its figuration that it does not belong to its own species." By making a black woman "not even mammal," nor even of "its own species," "nurse shark" commits the same crime that Bethe suffered in *Beloved.* Pregnant and nursing another child, she was held down in a barn by the white "Schoolteacher" and his boys, who sucked her milk and contrasted, in neat columns, her human and her animal traits.

Much as Ms. Morrison claims to "take no position . . . on the quality of a work based on the [racist] attitudes of an author," the moral and emotional force of her explorations is apparent. If the American identity is formed against this black shadow, it is a sign of abject weakness and a cause for shame. Ms. Morrison's gesture of standing back, judgment-free, as the indictment of white American identity mounts seems disingenuous. And though she says dispassionately enough that her aim "is to avert the critical gaze from the racial object to the racial subject; from the described and imagined to the describers and imaginers; from the serving to the served," this shift of focus is not innocent of moral impact. How could it be? The genius of Ms. Morrison's approach is to enlist those very describers and imaginers—white men of letters—in an investigation that can end only in their self-indictment.

This is the least generous reading of *Playing in the Dark,* but also the most obvious. One could argue, too, that the book's depiction of criticism as a "whitewashing" of American literature is much overstated. Leslie Fiedler's classic *Love and Death in the American Novel* dealt long ago with the partnership of black and white characters in [James Fenimore] Cooper and [Mark] Twain, as they headed out into the wilderness together. Scholars of Gertrude Stein have not ignored the fact that Melanctha, one of the protagonists of *Three Lives,* is black, that her name

means "black earth" and that as a poor, black, sexually ambivalent women she served Stein as an unthreatening surrogate for exploring love triangles, promiscuity and lesbianism. Evidence for Ms. Morrison's Africanism, in fact, turns up everywhere in literary criticism, though piecemeal, seldom expressed with the eloquence and fervor of *Playing in the Dark.* If no systematic study exists of the role black characters play in forming white identity, one could still see a good part of research in black studies and postcolonialism as working toward just this goal.

Yet the healing power of Toni Morrison's fiction makes one search for a more positive reading of her proposal. She outlines four topics for American Africanist research, three of which are lacerating in their import: how the construction of blackness in America buttresses whites against their fears of enslavement, powerlessness and wrongdoing; how black idiom signals difference and, in time, was linked with the outrage of modernity; and how it allows whites to explore their own bodies through the surrogacy of a debased Other.

But the fourth topic is somewhat different. It concerns the use of stories of slavery and rejection

> as a means of meditation—both safe and risky— on one's own humanity. Such analyses will reveal how the representation and appropriation of that narrative provides opportunities to contemplate limitation, suffering, rebellion, and to speculate on fate and destiny . . . ethics, social and universal codes of behavior, and assertions about and definitions of civilization and reason.

Though I would not want to sentimentalize Ms. Morrison's project, in this last topic is a hint of the generosity that marks her fiction. She presents Sethe's problem in *Beloved* as not only the cruelty of white slave owners but Sethe's own guilt and lack of self-esteem as well. Despite her crossing the Ohio border to emancipation, Sethe cannot become free until she frees herself, until she realizes that she is "her best thing."

In *Playing in the Dark* Ms. Morrison, in effect, takes the next step of imagining the white Schoolteacher who treated her heroine like an animal in that barn. She looks to see how his culture constructed him in literature, and finding the task unmanageable all on her own, she suggests it for the critical community at large. Ms. Morrison's Africanism is meant to teach a black author about white motivation. It should also teach whites about how they have constructed not only black but white identity, and how they have contemplated their own humanity by observing the dehumanization of others.

For one who has been dehumanized, now or in the historical past, this quest into the mind of the oppressor must be supremely painful. But how much more painful and important is it for those who have forged their own identity out of others' degradation to confront this fact and start again! If *Playing in the Dark* is not the innocent research project she pretends, it is also not a mere denunciation of white culture. Instead, it is a self-help project meant both to map out new critical territory and to rearrange the territory within. (pp. 1, 25, 29)

Wendy Steiner, "The Clearest Eye," in The New York Times Book Review, *April 5, 1992, pp. 1, 25, 29.*

Michael Dorris   (review date 19 April 1992)

[*An American educator, nonfiction writer, novelist, and critic, Dorris specializes in Native American studies. His works include* The Broken Cord *(1987) and* The Crown of Columbus *(1991), a collaborative effort with his wife, Louise Erdrich. In the following review of* Jazz, *he lauds Morrison's use of first-person narration and describes her portrait of 1920s New York as "one of Morrison's finest and most acutely drawn creations."*]

It's often said of opera divas, "The voice is her instrument." The same can be true of a writer, particularly when she lets her protagonists speak in turn, each an "I" addressing us boldly as if we were listening and interested in the argumentative explanation of his or her life. There's a challenge to this method, a demand for great skill. Somehow, in a brief space of paragraphs, an individual, sharply edged and unique, must be created and sustained. We must recognize these men or women by tone and context, be moved to indulge them their vanities, their justifications, see through their self-delusions, permit them to duck under the blanket of our empathy and confide, in that safe and timeless place, secrets that they would never trust to another soul.

In *Jazz,* her brilliant, daring new novel, Toni Morrison proves herself once again to be a master of this challenging technique. One by one, a procession of characters, past and present, young and old, step up to an intimate podium—or, rather, grab us by our lapels—and tell their side of the story. And what a story it is.

Joe Trace, long married and deeply attached to Violet through shared history and experience, strays. The object of his attentions is Dorcas, a vain, fickle teenager who later throws him over for Acton, a boy whom she loves for being young and good looking and for treating her badly. Dorcas is shot, dies, and Violet attempts to stab her body in her casket. Then, over time, jagged resentments are soothed; the business of human interaction returns to something like normal. Maybe better than normal.

But *Jazz* is much more than "story." It is the drawn and exhaled breath of a city, sometimes sweet as morning and sometimes smoky harsh. It is the blues song of people who understand suffering and survival. It is the complicated labyrinth that stretches from slavery to the Manhattan of the 1920s, the legacy of a race caught between rage and politeness, relief and frustration. It is a tight entwinement of love stories. It is a marvel.

Morrison has a knack for replicating a cadence of idiomatic language that's both hypnotic and mesmerizing. One character's fantasy of revenge was "the dream that plumped her pillow at night." Dorcas is described as having "all the ingredients of pretty," but she "just missed." She's a high school girl who revealed by her walk that "her underclothes were beyond her years."

Joe, on the other hand, is

a sample case man. A nice, neighborly, everybody-knows-him man. The kind you let in your house because he was not dangerous, because you had seen him with children, bought his products and never heard a scrap of gossip about him doing wrong. . . . He was the man who took you to your door if you missed the trolley and had to walk streets at night. Who warned young girls away from hooch joints and the men who lingered there. Women teased him because they trusted him. He was one of those men who might have marched down fifth Avenue—cold and silent and dignified—into the space the drums made. He knew wrong wasn't right, and did it anyway.

Every voice amazes, not only in its distinctiveness but also in its power, its conviction. The long dead speak as emphatically as the living, as the various participants and observers, antecedents and beneficiaries of the Violet-Trace-Dorcas triangle elbow each other for our ear, each tale syncopating into the next with the beat of a word or idea.

But amid all the comings and goings, underlying all the passion, fueling all the turmoil is the city itself—a place that arguably stands as one of Morrison's finest and most acutely drawn creations. *Jazz,* after all, is a novel about change and continuity, about immigration: the belongings you leave behind and the tied-together suitcase you carry under your arm. It's about coping with arrival in a destination that doesn't let you stay the same person.

"I messed up my own life," Violet tells Felice, Dorca's beautifully nuanced girlfriend. "Before I came North I made sense and so did the world. We didn't have nothing but we didn't miss it."

Joe is equally the victim of his urban environment.

Take my word for it, he is bound to the track. It pulls him like a needle through the groove of a Bluebird record. Round and round about the town. That's the way the City spins you. Makes you do what it wants, go where the laid-out roads say to. All the while letting you think you're free; that you can jump into thickets because you feel like it. You can't get off the track a City lays for you. Whatever happens, whether you get rich or stay poor, ruin your health or live to old age, you always end up back where you started: hungry for the one thing everybody loses—young loving.

Joe and Violet were part of a great wave, a flood of refugees. And

however they came, when or why, the minute the leather of their soles hit the pavement—there was no turning around. Even if the room they rented was smaller than the heifer's stall and darker than a morning privy, they stayed to look at their number, hear themselves in an audience, felt themselves moving down the street among hundreds of others who moved the way they did, and who, when they spoke, regardless of the accent, treated language like the same intricate, malleable toy designed for their play. . . .

Like the others, [Joe and Violet] were country

people, but how soon country people forget. When they fall in love with a city, it is for forever, and it is like forever. As though there never was a time when they didn't love it. The minute they arrive at the train station or get off the ferry and glimpse the wide streets and the wasteful lamps lighting them, they know they are born for it. There, in a city, they are not so much new as themselves: their stronger, riskier selves. And in the beginning when they first arrive, and twenty years later when they and the City have grown up, they love that part of themselves so much they forget what loving other people was like.

The City is the club, the precinct of activity, the arena, the percussion to which the dramas and lyrics of *Jazz* are played. And, as Toni Morrison has imagined it, the City is omniscient and forgiving, elegiac and cruel, a sly whisper one moment and a low rumbling laugh the next.

This is a novel that has all the ingredients of wonderful, and it doesn't miss. It is. (pp. 1, 5)

> Michael Dorris, "Singing the Big City Blues," in Chicago Tribune—Books, *April 19, 1992, pp. 1, 5.*

Richard Eder   (review date 19 April 1992)

[*Eder is an American critic who has won a citation for excellence in reviewing from the National Book Critics Circle and a Pulitzer Prize for criticism. In the review below, he praises the thematic breadth and narrative complexity of* Jazz.]

Jazz is a half-waking dream on a lumpy corncob mattress. Its voices shift, almost in a single sentence, from down-to-earth to intensely poetical. It alternately asserts, and transforms what it asserts. Each shift—each page, virtually—begins with a tangible jolt of discovery, and dissolves, making way for the next shift and dissolution. It can be difficult to follow, yet immensely exhilarating. We raft down Toni Morrison's white water, get mired when it sinks into passages that run too deep underground, and float off when it breaks into the open.

Jazz has fewer undergrounds than did *Beloved,* its predecessor. To my mind—many may not agree—it surpasses it. Nearly as heart-stopping in its intensity, it is on the whole a freer and sunnier book.

In part, this is because of its theme, a kind of sequel to that of *Beloved.* From the darkness of slavery and its nightmare aftermaths, it moves into the glitter, the exaltation and the pain of the turn-of-the-century migration of black people from the rural South to the cities of the North.

The theme is played out principally in the story of Joe and Violet Trace, a Harlem couple who moved north in 1906. Set 20 years later, when they are in their settled and comfortable 50s, it tells how they shatter and heal after an act of passion and violence.

Morrison stories, like the blackbirds that fly through Joe's memories, never come singly. *Jazz* ranges back into the

> With *Jazz* Morrison has written a book that ruminates and discourses, that wanders into climaxes and wanders out of them, that follows its riffs through pain and celebration, that moves all the time while neither leaving the past nor disappearing into the future; that is, in her word, jazz.
>
> —*Richard Eder*

haunted and still blood-stained Virginia countryside of the 1890s. It relates death and disappearance, and the struggle of black people to survive and scratch out a living under a brutal white hegemony. And yet it is *their* struggle and *their* living, and that is the difference from the times of *Beloved.*

Freedom is a banked ember for the abused sharecroppers but, among other things, it is freedom to get on a train. And when, at 30, Joe and Violet finally do; and when, north of Delaware, the Jim Crow green curtain that divides the dining car is pulled open, the ember flares into a blaze. *Jazz* is the story of the blaze, of its magnificence. These were the years when Harlem meant hope, excitement, empowerment, choice, the material flash and glisten of city life and a modest prosperity—and the destruction it brings about at the same time. Joe and Violet partake of both.

Everything bleeds into everything else. Morrison's events all father ghosts, and by no means are all of them tragic. The suicide of Violet's mother after white men break up her home lives on in the long state of depression she goes through later. Her grandmother's fierce, life-defying smile lives on in a fierce smile of her own. The disappearance of Joe's mother "without a trace"—the neighbors use the phrase; child Joe assumes that *he* must be "Trace" and adopts it as his surname—erupts in his middle age as he desperately pursues a teen-age lover. But the laborious will to survive he learned as a young farm worker, and the moral strength, imparted by an old black hunter, come with him as well, and enable him to survive his tragedy.

So much for the theme and, very vaguely, the story. But even if developed in 10 times the detail, they would barely be the skeleton. They would be an opera's libretto without the music. *Jazz* is no arbitrary title, and not simply a motif. Jazz is the world of Joe's young lover, and musicians play it in the cool evenings on Harlem's rooftops. But much more than that, it is the very form, voice and core of this wonderful book. Here is the first paragraph; it sums up the story of Joe and Violet, but it does it as a trumpet will blare a theme that is then unwoven, rewoven, tickled and teased, built up and tossed around for as long as anyone still feels like playing:

> . . . I know that woman. She used to live with a flock of birds on Lenox Ave. Know her husband, too. He fell for an 18-year-old girl with

one of those deep-down, spooky loves that made him so sad and happy he shot her just to keep the feeling going. When the woman, her name is Violet, went to the funeral to see the girl and to cut her dead face they threw her to the floor and out of the church. She ran, then, through all that snow, and when she got back to her apartment she took the birds from their cages and set them out the windows to freeze or fly, including the parrot that said, "I love you."

Each of those phrases is expanded, elaborated, improvised upon. Each links up with a story and its larger themes. Morrison's vision of the city as joyful liberation—standing in the north-bound railroad car, Joe and Violet dance to its jolts—is coupled with its denaturing, destructive power. For love, Joe ruminates, the city substitutes desire; for air, it substitutes breath.

Take the birds. Freed from the South's back-breaking cycle of labor—in both senses—Violet refuses to have children. While Joe earns a good living as a waiter in a downtown hotel, and sells cosmetics on the side, she bustles around Harlem as a home hairdresser. Then childlessness catches up with her, sending her into silent depression. At home she talks only to her birds and a doll she keeps under the bed.

When her silence, the city's offer of easy pleasure and Joe's own demons drive him to take up with Dorcas, the teenager, and then to shoot her, Violet's despair sends her on a rampage that ends with her birds. The parrot goes out on the window ledge, but since he can't fly he stays there, looking in. Day after day, he squawks "Love you" through the windowpane until he topples off and dies.

There is sharp grief there, the fall of a world in the fall of a parrot. Morrison can play grief this small; she can play it much larger. In 1880 or so, Violet's mother, Rose, sits in her cabin clutching her empty coffee cup while bailiffs remove the furniture piece by piece. They remove the table at which she is sitting, then they slowly tip her chair forward until she topples onto the floor. The cup rolls away. And the neighbors come consoling:

> He ain't give you nothing you can't bear, Rose. But had He? Maybe this one time He had. Had misjudged and misunderstood her particular backbone. This one time. This particular spine.

Amid the pain, there is a beauty that Morrison achingly conveys: of the countryside and the deep loyalty of the black farmers to the land and each other; and of Harlem in its glory days. There is a humor that braids into the pain and goes as deep.

The black sharecroppers are burned out to free them to harvest the white man's cotton, a bumper crop after years of drought: "Softer than silk and out so fast the weevils, having abandoned the field years ago, had no time to get back there." Young Violet, an itinerant cottonpicker, sleeps out in the fields one night. Something falls from the tree beside her. "The thump could not have been a raccoon because it said Ow." It was the first meeting with Joe, who had been sleeping in the branches.

The stories fan out through Harlem at a time when drink, sex, disrespecting the elders, and the knife fight were the measure of social decay; when church groups held bridge parties, and neighbors strolled and sat out on the stoops. They fan back to the ghosts in the South. There is a young man brought up as white by his rich mother, who learns his father is black and goes to confront him. There is Joe's wandering mother who takes to the woods, lives in a cave and is attended by flights of blackbirds.

An excerpt from *Jazz*

Pain. I seem to have an affection, a kind of sweettooth for it. Bolts of lightning, little rivulets of thunder. And I the eye of the storm. Mourning the split trees, hens starving on rooftops. Figuring out what can be done to save them since they cannot save themselves without me because—well, it's my storm, isn't it? I break lives to prove I can mend them back again. And although the pain is theirs, I share it, don't I? Of course. Of course. I wouldn't have it any other way. But it is another way. I am uneasy now. Feeling a bit false. What, I wonder, what would I be without a few brilliant spots of blood to ponder? Without aching words that set, then miss, the mark?

I ought to get out of this place. Avoid the window; leave the hole I cut through the door to get in lives instead of having one of my own. It was loving the City that distracted me and gave me ideas. Made me think I could speak its loud voice and make that sound sound human. I missed the people altogether.

I thought I knew them and wasn't worried that they didn't really know about me. Now it's clear why they contradicted me at every turn: they knew me all along. Out of the corners of their eyes they watched me. And when I was feeling most invisible, being tight-lipped, silent and unobservable, they were whispering about me to each other. They knew how little I could be counted on; how poorly, how shabbily my know-it-all self covered helplessness. That when I invented stories about them—and doing it seemed to me so fine—I was completely in their hands, managed without mercy. I thought I'd hidden myself so well as I watched them through windows and doors, took every opportunity I had to follow them, to gossip about and fill in their lives, and all the while they were watching me. Sometimes they even felt sorry for me and just thinking about their pity I want to die.

So I missed it altogether. I was sure one would kill the other. I waited for it so I could describe it. I was so sure it would happen. That the past was an abused record with no choice but to repeat itself at the crack and no power on earth could lift the arm that held the needle. I was so sure, and they danced and walked all over me. Busy, they were, busy being original, complicated, changeable—human, I guess you'd say, while I was the predictable one, confused in my solitude into arrogance, thinking my space, my view was the only one that was or that mattered. I got so aroused while meddling, while finger-shaping, I overreached and missed the obvious. I was watching the streets, thrilled by the buildings pressing and pressed by stone; so glad to be looking out and in on things I dismissed what went on in heart-pockets closed to me.

Toni Morrison, in her Jazz, *Knopf, 1992.*

And the story of Joe and Violet, which starts gentle and then turns bloody and dark, turns gentle once more. After the shooting, a turbid, confused affair, nobody cares to identify Joe to the police. For weeks, he sits in his room weeping and inert; and it is Violet, after her rampage and roused from her lethargy, who begins to rouse him and mend their life.

Their story could have been either a tragedy or a melodrama, with appropriate climactic endings. But Morrison has written a book that ruminates and discourses, that wanders into climaxes and wanders out of them, that follows its riffs through pain and celebration, that moves all the time while neither leaving the past nor disappearing into the future; that is, in her word, jazz. (pp. 3, 5)

> Richard Eder, "Those Nights on the Harlem Rooftops," in Los Angeles Times Book Review, April 19, 1992, pp. 3, 5.

Jane Mendelsohn   (review date May 1992)

[*In the following review, Mendelsohn examines the themes in* Jazz *and* Playing in the Dark.]

Imagine a world in which love never dies, only fades in and out like a musical phrase, varying and deepening with each return. This is the place Toni Morrison has created in her latest novel, *Jazz,* a supple, sophisticated love story which explores the possibilities of romance as both a natural phenomenon and a literary form. Filled with the familiar elements of a Morrison book—mournful, vivid characters, natural and unnatural disasters, an operatic (occasionally soap-operatic) orchestration of history and myth—*Jazz* nevertheless takes a different direction from Morrison's earlier works. Less controlled, more improvisational, it picks up her favorite subject, human freedom, and spins out of it not only an inventive story but also a new way to write. Whereas in her other books she has sometimes been too possessive of her characters, hovering over their movements, explicating their every thought, in *Jazz* she loosens up and lets her inventions soar. She does this in part by giving herself a persona. Half gossip, half visionary, her nameless narrator interrupts the story, re-imagines whole passages, draws attention to herself one moment, then casually returns to her tale the next. In the process, Morrison realizes her own limits, and sets her characters free.

Jazz tells the story of Violet and Joe Trace, married for over 20 years, residents of Harlem in 1926, "when all the wars are over and there will never be another one." Violet works as an unlicensed hairdresser, doing ladies' hair in their own homes, and Joe sells Cleopatra cosmetics door to door. They live in an apartment building on Lenox Avenue "where the sidewalks, snow-covered or not, are wider than the main roads of the towns where they were born." When the novel opens, Joe has shot his 18-year-old lover, Dorcas, and Violet has disfigured the dead girl's body at her funeral in a fit of rage. Joe, who was not caught, is in mourning, crying all day in his darkened apartment, and Violet has taken on the task of finding out whatever she

can about Dorcas. As the narrator says, "Maybe she thought she could solve the mystery of love that way. Good luck and let me know."

Instead of solving the mystery of love, Violet finds that "not only is she losing Joe to a dead girl, but she wonders if she isn't falling in love with her too." She befriends Dorcas's Aunt Alice and borrows a photograph, which she places on the mantelpiece and visits in the middle of the night. Like Sethe in *Beloved,* Violet gradually loses herself to the memory of a dead girl, in this case not actually her daughter, but a substitute for the child she and Joe never had. The "private cracks" in Violet's personality, which had begun to show before Joe's affair, deepen after Dorcas's death; Violet has been unhappy for a long time, drowning her sorrows in Dr. Dee's Nerve and Flesh Builder and the empty *I love you*s of her domesticated parrot. Joe, too, has been searching for something; convinced that he alone remembers the days when he and Violet were happy, he is "hungry for the one thing everybody loses— young loving." *Jazz,* which skips around temporally, sometimes sending notes drifting through the narrative before we can understand them, basically moves backwards in time, revealing in the history of Violet and Joe's relationship, and in the relations of their ancestors, how they came to be in the strange predicament of the present, isolated from each other, themselves, and their dreams.

The novel's present is a time of overwhelming energy, confusing to some, enlivening to others, a moment in history when blacks, having streamed into New York from the South at the end of the 19th century, call Harlem their own, and their music has "dropped on down, down to places below the sash and the buckled belts." "Just hearing it," one of the book's characters thinks, "was like violating the law." Everyone in the story is moved by jazz in one way or another; it's always playing, always pouring down from windows or up from nightclubs. It inspires Dorcas's Aunt Alice to raise her niece with the puritanical strictures that later cause her to rebel into the arms of Joe Trace. It moves Dorcas to yearn for the kind of love Joe can't give her. It is what the girl hears, and what she thinks about, when she dies.

Morrison's New York embodies the spirit of jazz. Free, but frightening in its freedom, it's a place where the night sky "can empty itself of surface, and more like the ocean than the ocean itself, go deep, starless":

> A colored man floats down out of the sky blowing a saxophone, and below him, in the space between two buildings, a girl talks earnestly to a man in a straw hat. He touches her lip to remove a bit of something there. Suddenly she is quiet. He tilts her chin up. They stand there. Her grip on her purse slackens and her neck makes a nice curve. The man puts his hand on the stone wall above her head. By the way his jaw moves and the turn of his head I know he has a golden tongue. The sun sneaks into the alley behind them. It makes a pretty picture on its way down.

New York is a character in *Jazz,* always referred to, respectfully, as "the City," and it becomes a metaphor for the book itself, a way for Morrison to talk about the novel as she's writing it: "All you have to do," she says of the City, "is heed the design—the way it's laid out for you, considerate, mindful of where you want to go and what you might need tomorrow." New York, like jazz, and like *Jazz,* has an uncanny way of describing itself in the act of being. I once heard someone say that walking the gridded streets of Manhattan was like walking inside an architectural drawing. Similarly, *Jazz* contains stories within stories, and within these, or outside them, "everywhere and nowhere," is the voice of the nameless narrator, endlessly commenting on her imaginings and then disappearing into them herself.

As the novel shifts back in time, Morrison gives us the stories of Violet and Joe's childhoods, and even further back, the unresolved love story of Joe's mother, Wild, and the white man, Golden Gray, whom Violet's grandmother raised. Violet and Joe, both born in the South, met picking cotton in Palestine, Virginia, when Joe fell out of a walnut tree in the middle of the night, practically into Violet's lap. Morrison leads us to believe that there is something inevitable, almost mythically necessary in their meeting. Without pressing the point too hard, she makes it clear that strains in their personalities and their pasts determine their dreams, and therefore their tragedies.

Violet, whose mother, Rose Dear, threw herself into a well, was raised by her grandmother, True Belle, a former slave who moved to Baltimore (leaving Rose Dear behind) when her owner, Vera Louise, moved there to have the baby she had conceived with a black man. By the time True Belle entered Violet's life, she had spent most of her own raising a little boy, half black but white-skinned, named Golden Gray, and she filled Violet's head with stories of this perfect, unattainable prince. "My own golden boy," Violet later remembers, "who I never saw but who tore up my girlhood as surely as if we'd been the best of lovers."

At the center of the novel is the story of Golden Gray's journey to find his black father. It's told with the dreamy, fablelike quality of a parable. Morrison has to strain to fit it into the rhythm of the rest of the book, but in the end it reveals so much about her project that it seems essential. On his way to find and kill his father, the spoiled, self-satisfied Golden Gray passes a pregnant black woman collapsed and bleeding on the road, and after much deliberation, decides to bring her to his father's house. In Morrison's description of the event, which she tells from several points of view, including, momentarily, that of the horse Golden Gray is riding, the incident takes on the exalted power of a myth, but it's a myth told with a certain tentativeness, in a voice that admits its own limitations.

Telling the story of Golden Gray's encounter with the woman, the narrator interrupts herself several times, remarking on her own unreliability, hesitating to go forward, as if the story were too painful to recount. "Now I have to think this through," she says, "even though I may be doomed to another misunderstanding." She explains:

> Not hating him is not enough; liking, loving him is not useful. I have to alter things. I have to be a shadow who wishes him well, like the smiles of the dead left over from their lives. I want

> to . . . [l]ie down next to him, a wrinkle in the sheet, and contemplate his pain and by doing so ease it, diminish it. I want to be the language that wishes him well, speaks his name, wakes him when his eyes need to be open. I want him to stand next to a well . . . and while standing there in shapely light, his fingertips on the rim of stone. . . . There then . . . from down in it, where the light does not reach . . . some brief benevolent love rises from the darkness.

This passage expresses a remarkable amount of compassion for a character whose arrogance prevents him from wiping the caked blood from a black woman's face. The language in which Morrison couches her compassion is subtle: the way "wishes him well" becomes a wishing well, the way the wishing well turns into the page we are reading, and the reader becomes "him," the rider, looking into the darkness of words and seeing a brief benevolence rise to the surface, wrinkling the sheet of the page. The poetry of this paragraph is shifting, vulnerable, easily overlooked. *Jazz,* which contains other passages as carefully wrought as this one, can be at times almost painfully exciting to read.

It can also be disjointed, unconvincing, even irritatingly repetitive, but afterwards the poetry of the book stays in the mind, while the rest drifts into the background, like incidental music. *Jazz* replays the old plot of rupture and reconciliation, and still it surprises, lifting at the end to a moment of beauty. Morrison, who usually tells us at the beginning of her novels what will happen, here lets her characters come into their own, confident enough to surrender them to the mysteries of romance. It's a novel that you wish you could read for the first time twice, but one that asks for second and third readings, the kind that come from knowing something about the nature of the work. Similarly, Violet and Joe have to accept that they can live their story for the first time only once. Then they will be able to find each other, to be, in the book's words, "inward toward the other." In imagining Joe and Violet's adult love, Morrison reaches to find a language that will harmonize doubt and desire. The voice she discovers is sumptuously incomplete, quavering between happiness and despair. It is enough simply to listen.

. . . . .

In *Playing in the Dark: Whiteness and the Literary Imagination,* Morrison again reaches for a new language, only here she seeks to expand the vocabulary of literary criticism. This slim volume, consisting of three straightforward, illuminating essays, argues for the expansion of the study of American literature to include an investigation of the ways in which "the major and championed characteristics of our national literature" are "responses to a dark, abiding, signing Africanist presence." Seeking to look at American racism in a new way, to consider its impact not on its victims but on those who perpetuate it, Morrison calls for a criticism that will explore the way Americans have chosen to talk about themselves through the reflexive use of a fabricated Africanist persona. In other words, as Morrison puts it, "The subject of the dream is the dreamer." The Africanist persona in American literature is a projection, and to investigate it as such reveals a great deal about that literature and the nation that produced it.

Morrison makes two major points in the book, but they are really two ways of saying the same thing. The first, that the championed characteristics of American literature— "individualism, masculinity, social engagement versus historical isolation; acute and ambiguous moral problematics; the thematics of innocence coupled with an obsession with figurations of death and hell"—are responses to an "Africanist pressence" which predates our national literature, seems to me useful but limited, because it is impossible to prove. (It is also unclear whether Morrison means to include a Native American presence.) The second point, that "American writers were able to employ an imagined Africanist persona to articulate and imaginatively act out the forbidden in American culture," can be demonstrated and deepened.

Morrison does this through close readings of classic American writers—Cather, Twain, Hemingway—and their texts burst open at her touch. Discussing *Sapphira and the Slave Girl, Huckleberry Finn, To Have and Have Not,* and others, she explores the ways in which Africanist personas have been used by others to engage in "power without risk," "a *safe* participation in loss, in love, in chaos, in justice." Morrison takes this investigation even further in her second essay, in which she traces the American romance with romance. Looking at 19th century American literature, she observes that "for a people who made much of their 'newness,'—their potential, freedom, and innocence—it is striking how dour, how troubled, how frightened and haunted our early and founding literature truly is." As Morrison goes on to explain,

> Romance . . . made possible the sometimes safe and other times risky embrace of quite specific, understandably human, fears: Americans' fear of being outcast, of failing, of powerlessness; their fear of boundarylessness, of Nature unbridled and crouched for attack; their fear of the absence of so-called civilization; their fear of loneliness; of aggression both external and internal. In short, the terror of human freedom—the thing they coveted most of all.

Writers writing about other writers tend to write about themselves, and here Morrison is no exception. While this explicates the underside of American romanticism, it also describes Morrison's central concern as a novelist. The terror of human freedom and its consequences—for blacks, whites, men, women, anyone who has been denied it or afraid of it—is as much the subject of *Playing in the Dark* as it is of *Jazz.*

Joe and Violet are both trapped in dreams of their past— nightmares, really—which cause them to hurt each other and prevent them from believing that they have power over their own lives. In *Playing in the Dark,* Morrison explores how the temptation to enslave others instead of embracing freedom has shaded our national literature, and how an acceptance of this truth will enable us to see that literature's struggles and fears, and so better understand its exuberance. In both works her wisdom is to locate strength in what appears to be weakness. She sees in Vio-

let, in Joe, in Huck, and in Jim dangerous and thrilling urges toward surrender and escape, and she loves them as much as she chastises them for this. They are contradictory characters, like people. In subjecting them to her generous attention, she doesn't so much set them free as acknowledge that they already are. (pp. 25-6)

Jane Mendelsohn, "Harlem on Her Mind: Toni Morrison's Language of Love," in VLS, No. 105, May, 1992, pp. 25-6.

Jane Miller   (review date 14 May 1992)

[In the review below, Miller examines Morrison's treatment of African-American life in Jazz.*]*

Within the first half-page of Toni Morrison's novel, [*Jazz*], an 18-year-old girl has been shot dead by her middle-aged lover, and his wife has been manhandled from the funeral after attempting to cut the dead girl's face with a knife. Both events are witnessed and kept secret by a community which has reason to distrust the police and to look kindly upon a hitherto gentle, childless couple, whose sudden, violent sorrows they recognise and are able to forgive. And as the spring of that year, 1926, bursts a month or two later upon the 'City' of this extraordinary novel, its all-seeing gossip of a narrator is moved to declare—if only provisionally—that 'history is over, you all, and everything's ahead at last.'

The novel's theme tune is spun out from these contrasts and whirled through a series of playful improvisations by a storyteller who admits to being—and, as it turns out, expects the reader to be too—'curious, inventive and well-informed'. It is impossible to resist the seductions of this particular narrative voice as it announces its own fallibilities, mourns its distance from some of the events it will therefore need to invent, boldly revises its own speculations, even as it recalls, replays, retrieves them for us before our very eyes and with our assumed complicity. For, of course, this voice also undertakes to guarantee both tale and telling as truth, history, music known and shared by all who have roots in the black urban communities of America in the Twenties. And for readers with quite other roots? Well, the voice is no more prepared than Morrison is herself to 'footnote the black experience for white readers'. As she put it in a recent interview: 'I wouldn't try to explain what a reader like me already knew.'

There are obscure sentences in this novel as in earlier ones, dense and elliptical passages, the consequence, perhaps, of a language drenched in speech and therefore off-hand at times with its secrets and avowals. Yet the lyricism and elasticity of Morrison's writing come in part from her absolute faith in the fruits of a tension between what it is she knows and what she believes other people know or could know if they used their heads. Readers are 'curious, inventive and well-informed' too, as she knows. All Morrison's novels have been crucially concerned with readers and with manipulative uses of literacy in racist societies. Her characters' reading of newspapers, letters, 'other people's stories printed in small books', are watched as signs of a politics, a whole way of reading the world. Her narrators are always conscious of their readers, and in this novel its musical elaborations are composed around the most flagrant toying with readerly expectations. At one moment there is a shameless revelling in what an imagination, forged through the minutest observation of physical detail and by the ordinary repetitiveness of life, can come up with; followed at once by a refusal to yield to the pull of either the inevitable or the apocalyptic. The novel's quietly happy ending comes as a triumphant countering to the imagination's more clamorous tendencies as, in a final aside, the narrator shrugs off the characters' evasion of authorial vigilance as they put 'their lives together in ways I never dreamed'.

Joe (the murderer), Violet (his wife) and Dorcas (the murdered girl) are all, though differently, orphans and people collected by the City through a series of migrations from the 1870s onward. Joe and Violet, the grandchildren of slaves and themselves members of a generation which shared a repertoire of horrors (torchings, evictions, riots, near-starvation) while rarely if ever choosing to talk about these things, are driven by the poverty and violence of their rural Southern lives, not just to Baltimore, but further, to the City. The journey they make there by train in 1906 may be cramped and occluded by a 'green-as-poison curtain' from the obsequious services lavished on the white passengers. Yet Joe and Violet experience it all as a dance of the most exhilarating anticipation and release, prefiguring the promise of the City itself: 'They were hanging there, a young country couple, laughing and tapping back at the tracks, when the attendant came through, pleasant but unsmiling now that he didn't have to smile in this car full of coloured people.' Most aspects of their lives are characterised by a similar doubleness. Names and nicknames become witty creations in the teeth of a history which actually deprived people of names. Joe's second name is Trace, the mistake he made as a child on hearing that his parents had 'disappeared without trace', and Violet is quickly renamed Violent by her astounded neighbours.

The dead girl, Dorcas, was orphaned by the riots of 1917 in East St Louis. Now she listens to the City's siren songs of glamour and sexual bliss from the locked and neat apartment of her guardian aunt, who dreads above all for her niece the provocations of black music and the dancing it inspires. Dorcas bides her time. She has not yet flowered into beauty, and now never will. Her skin is still bad, tiny hoofmarks speckling her lower cheeks. If Joe is by no means what her dreams are made of, but a cosmetics salesman in his fifties with a wife, he loves her hopelessly, hoofmarks, callowness and all, and he showers her with gifts and promises. Even Dorcas's disbelieving friend is bound to concede that 'I think he likes women, and I don't know anybody like that.' Dorcas, however, longs for Acton, the cool young man who lets her dance with him. She dies marvelling at Acton's fastidious attention to his jacket, now spattered with her blood.

The novel dwells less on the reasons for the murder, or even on the grief suffered in its wake by the murderer and his wife, than on a past which might be thought to have foretold these events. Spirited and consolatory lamentation provides an accompanying counterpoint, rich in echoes, remembered if unrecorded, of similar moments of desperation, pain, incomprehension. Joe has been haunted all his life by thoughts of his mother. He had grown up thinking her dead, but discovered at 18 that she is the wild woman who lives alone in the woods, an animal he has learned to laugh at and even torment. Violet, the third of the five children of a woman who drowned herself in a well, suppresses this and other terrors in her vigorous determination to survive in the City. But neither she nor Joe wants children. They have good memories too: a grandmother who laughed in the face of disaster, a friend called Victory, who listened. Like the City that they come to accept and even love, for its skies, its noise, its people, the past is alive with contradictory energies, with kindnesses as astonishing as the cruelties.

In one prefiguring episode a young man, golden in beauty and in name, learns that his father was black and goes in search of him. Golden Gray, as his Southern belle of a mother has named him, stumbles upon the wild woman, just as she is giving birth to Joe. When he recoils from her, Morrison's narrator wavers:

> That is what makes me worry about him. How he thinks first of his clothes, and not the woman. How he checks the fastenings, but not her breath. It's hard to get past that, but then he scrapes the mud from his Baltimore soles before he enters a cabin with a dirt floor and I don't hate him much anymore.

Racism is the accumulation of particular moments for her characters, experienced from earliest childhood, never an abstraction. For Joe there is the memory of 'two whitemen . . . sitting on a rock. I sat on the ground right next to them until they got disgusted and moved off.' Golden Gray is learning about this through his own well-tended finger-tips, and he is forgiven for the moment.

Apart from the briefest stutter at the very beginning of her writing life in the early Seventies, Toni Morrison's career as a novelist has been greeted with gathering superlatives. It is true that one or two 'serious' journals have published mean-spirited pieces arguing against her eligibility for Great American Writer status on the grounds that her concerns are too parochial. Yet even the most limiting and patronising reviews of her novels have acknowledged that they are ambitious achievements of exceptional originality and power. This, her sixth, is likely to be received with the same sort of enthusiasm. It may also be that it will be thought slighter than **Beloved** (her most recent novel) in some respects. It is shorter and its beauties are more contained. Readers report finding **Beloved** so unbearably painful to read at times that they needed to gather strength to go on. If the pain is less intense here, that may be because it is absorbed into the poetry, in a way that the blues reverberations make possible. **Jazz** seems to me to represent an advance in Morrison's work; it is as subtly reliant on the processes of history as **Beloved,** and a novel of urban life to rival any other. A voice which hears the chorus of 'slow moving whores, who never hurried anything but love' chronicles the human part of the city beneath skies which separate and join the visible and the invisible.

Daylight slants like a razor cutting the buildings

in half. In the top half I see looking faces and it's not easy to tell which are people, which are the work of stone masons. Below is shadow where any blasé thing takes place: clarinets and love-making, fists and the voices of sorrowful women.

It is a poetry grounded in fact. Violet dresses real heads of hair and feels a shift in the demand for her services like a draught directed at the nape of her neck. The watching, listening narrator is beguiled by more than music and light. People's lives are very much their own business as well as other people's. They have money to earn, meals to cook, apartments to furnish and clean. They think as actively while they wash as while they read. The details of a particular life are only to be understood as part of the pitfalls and aspirations of whole communities, even in the City. More than in any other novel I know of, the connections between country and city are preserved, as history, memory and loss.

Violet, it turns out, has had other lapses, or 'cracks'. She once took someone else's baby, though she returned it before any harm was done. The narrator explains:

> I call them cracks because that is what they were. Not openings or breaks, but dark fissures in the globe light of the day. She wakes up in the morning and sees with perfect clarity a string of small, well-lit scenes. In each one something specific is being done: food things, work things; customers and acquaintances are encountered, places entered. But she does not see herself doing these things. She sees them being done.

Morrison has addressed all her novels to the need for black people to see themselves within a culture which does not encourage them to do so. Later in the novel, Dorcas's young friend remembers the love scenes the two girls used to invent together and discuss, and she tells Violet:

> Something about it bothered me, though. Not the loving stuff, but the picture I had of myself when I did it. Nothing like me. I saw myself as somebody I'd seen in a picture show or a magazine. Then it would work. If I pictured myself the way I am it seemed wrong.

Jazz is a love story, indeed a romance. And romance and its high-risk seductions for young women come with special health warnings when it is poor young black women who might succumb to it. For romance has always been white, popular, capitalistic in its account of love as transactions voluntarily undertaken between class and beauty and money. But the romance which is a snare and a delusion has also spelled out a future for young women, a destiny, significance and pleasure—and particularly when there was little enough of those possibilities for them or for the men they knew. The older women of Morrison's novels know that sex can be a woman's undoing, that men, 'ridiculous and delicious and terrible', are always trouble. The narrator in *Jazz* is generous with warnings: 'The girls have red lips and their legs whisper to each other through silk stockings. The red lips and the silk flash power. A power they will exchange for the right to be overcome, penetrated.'

Morrison's writing of a black romance pays its debt to

blues music, the rhythms and the melancholy pleasures of which she has so magically transformed into a novel. More than that, she has claimed new sources and new kinds of reading as the inspiration for a thriving literature.

> Jane Miller, "New Romance," in London Review of Books, *Vol. 14, No. 9, May 14, 1992, p. 6.*

Ann Hulbert   (review date 18 May 1992)

[*Hulbert is an American editor and critic whose works include* The Interior Castle: The Art and Life of Jean Stafford *(1992). In the following review, she offers a mixed assessment of* Jazz *and* Playing in the Dark, *stating that "Morrison is determined to shake up not just her readers, it seems, but also herself. She intends to challenge our assumptions about race and literature, and to question her own instincts, which she admits toward 'romanticizing blackness' and 'vilifying whiteness.'"*]

Toni Morrison is the compleat black American writer. She has the rare distinction in our balkanized cultural landscape of being both academically and popularly canonized: her books claim a high place on college reading lists as well as on best-seller lists; she holds a prestigious professorship at Princeton University, and is a prominent spokeswoman on racial questions, large and small. Now, in her sixth novel and her first book of criticism, a series of lectures about American literature that she recently delivered at Harvard, she has evidently set out to do what such well-established authorities rarely dare: change her mind and some of her methods.

Morrison the critic, whose indictments of what she has termed "whitemale" culture have been extreme, here steps forth as an apolitical, anachronistic scholar. She declares herself committed to patiently exploring the white imaginative perspective. In fact, from the project that she outlines in *Playing in the Dark,* you wouldn't guess that she is ensconced at the forefront of the politically correct, multicultural academy. She maintains that her colleagues in literature departments simply refuse to address race in their readings of the works that have shaped American culture and identity. And she promises that the study she urges of "the Africanist presence" in those works offers a non-ideological opportunity "to comprehend the resilience and gravity, the inadequacy and the force of the imaginative act." The fruit of such an endeavor, she announces, "is delight, not disappointment." Rather than a call to subvert the canon, it is a reminder of "the treasure trove that American literature is." The old-fashioned celebratory tone is disorienting. What country, which decade, are we in?

In *Jazz,* there's no need to ask either question. We are in Harlem in the mid-1920s, eavesdropping on an unhappy triangle involving a middle-aged couple, Joe and Violet Trace, and Joe's 18-year-old lover, Dorcas. But the novel, which is narrated by an obtrusively mysterious voice, poses another question: Who is talking? What authority lies behind this intimate portrait of a black community at the height of the black cultural renaissance of the Jazz

Age? As if Morrison's aim of tolerantly exploring white writers' depictions of blackness weren't unexpected enough, her novel embarks on what looks like the ultimate mission of self-sabotage: she is questioning a black writer's efforts to penetrate the heart of a black world.

Morrison is determined to shake up not just her readers, it seems, but also herself. She intends to challenge our assumptions about race and literature, and to question her own instincts, which she admits tend toward "romanticizing blackness" and "vilifying whiteness." In both books, a self-conscious effort at sympathetic examination confronts a reflexive impulse to portray exploiters and victims. The struggle sometimes looks like genuine self-division, sometimes like a strategy to have it both ways. But it rarely bears much resemblance to the daring iconoclasm that Morrison aspires to offer.

Her critical project is most notable, in fact, for being highly derivative. What heresy it contains lies in its lack of originality: Morrison's real accomplishment is to recall, without acknowledging it, the work of the true pioneers who first approached questions about race and imagination with urgency and rigorous open-mindedness. Those predecessors are a hard act to follow, which is perhaps part of the reason that they don't figure in her lectures. In an essay in *The New Negro* (1925), the definitive anthology of the Harlem Renaissance, the black poet and critic William Stanley Braithwaite predicted that "The Negro in American Literature," as he titled his piece, would prove a "magnificent theme" for the literary historian:

> It will be magnificent not because there is any sharp emergence of character or incidents, but because of the immense paradox of racial life which came up thunderingly against the principles and doctrines of democracy, and put them to the severest test that they had known.

Ralph Ellison took up the theme in "Twentieth-Century Fiction and the Black Mask of Humanity," an essay written in 1946 and published in 1953, and he made clear, in terms remarkably similar to Morrison's, that he was not interested in compiling a catalog of white stereotypes of blacks. He elevated the figure of the black to a more important role than manipulated victim: he was the essential "other" in relation to whom American character and American ideas of freedom and individualism were defined and greatly complicated. "I propose that we view the whole of American life as a drama acted out upon the body of a Negro giant, who, lying trussed up like Gulliver, forms the stage and the scene upon which and within which the action unfolds." Ellison set out not to attack the distortions in the portraiture of blacks, but to examine them as clues to the dilemma of the white imagination, "the dilemma arising between his democratic beliefs and certain anti-democratic practices."

Some thirty years after Ellison's piece, treatments of race in American literature had become the cutting edge of scholarship. But you would never guess it from Morrison, who inexplicably laments that on campus "the habit of ignoring race is understood to be a graceful, even generous, liberal gesture." In fact, plenty of professors have aggressively scrutinized the racial attitudes of Faulkner, Mel-ville, Poe, Twain, Hemingway, and others. To take just one current and rather mainstream example, Joan Dayan's essay "Romance and Race" in *The Columbia History of the American Novel* (1991) covers much the same ground that Morrison claims to explore for the first time, down to discussing, in much the same terms, the same passage about "whiteness" in Poe's *The Narrative of Arthur Gordon Pym.*

At first Morrison's blissful ignorance of the politicized academic climate is refreshing. It inspires her to convey a crusading excitement and inclusiveness about her undertaking—not exactly staples of scholarship these days. Where other contemporary critics have inclined toward self-conscious theorizing and political posturing—countering the New Critical reading of Faulkner as a defender of Southern community, for example, with a portrait of Faulkner as politically correct spokesman for the oppressed—Morrison sounds eloquent and free of theoretical baggage. She emphasizes that she is a writer, reading from the inside, not a critic applying interpretive preconceptions; she expects to find ambiguity, not ideology, in serious American fiction.

Morrison's willingness to approach the literary imagination with awe, rather than with an ax to grind, is on display in the first section of the book, where she introduces her enterprise. Following Ellison, she explains that what she labels "American Africanism," the literary fabrication of black figures and associations, "provides a way of contemplating chaos and civilization, desire and fear, and a mechanism for testing the problems and blessings of freedom." Her assumption is that this experiment in "entering what one is estranged from" is mostly a liberating challenge to the ideology of "whiteness."

The result, she announces, is "an astonishing revelation of longing, of terror, of perplexity, of shame, of magnanimity." She finds all of those responses in Willa Cather's efforts to probe the "power and license" of a white mistress over her slave in *Sapphira and the Slave Girl.* What have generally been regarded as problems in the novel she usefully reads as clues to Cather's attempt to understand the precariousness of white female identity.

But as the lectures proceed, Morrison's spirit of patient exploration wears thinner. Having assured us at the outset that, "Yes, I wanted to identify those moments when American literature was complicit in the fabrication of racism, but equally important, I wanted to see when literature exploded and undermined it," she becomes more intent on indictment. As she outlines "some topics that need critical investigation," Morrison the subtle reader is often overwhelmed by a doctrinaire interrogator.

As long as she's speaking in generalities—which she does frequently and repetitiously—Morrison manages to maintain her air of literary curiosity. But the social adversary takes over when she breaks down her sweeping enterprise into more specific critical projects. The first three of her four rather arbitrarily divided topics sound like reductive efforts to demonstrate literature's complicity in crude racism: a consideration of the "Africanist character as surrogate and enabler," of the "way an Africanist idiom is used to establish difference," and of the "ways in which an Africanist character is used to limn out and enforce the invention and implications of whiteness." Those "astonishing revelations" of white ambivalence that Morrison welcomed at first have now vanished. Instead black figures have become tools of a thoroughly unmodulated ideology of white superiority:

> Africanism is the vehicle by which the American self knows itself as not enslaved, but free; not repulsive, but desirable; not helpless, but licensed and powerful; not history-less, but historical; not damned, but innocent; not a blind accident of evolution, but a progressive fulfillment of destiny.

As if slightly taken aback at her own rising rhetoric, Morrison formulates her fourth topic in her more general and generous vein, resisting the easy temptation to vilify whiteness. Once again she proposes a subtler examination of the Africanist narrative "as a means of meditation—both safe and risky—on one's own humanity," and opportunity "to contemplate limitation, suffering, rebellion, and to speculate on fate and destiny." But even such meditations have a way of getting simplified, as it becomes clear when Morrison turns to a particular text, in this instance *Huckleberry Finn.*

Morrison's contribution to the debate over the perplexing ending of Twain's book, when Jim is subjected to mock liberation and captivity at the instigation of Tom Sawyer, shows her divided instincts at work. She calls for a "close examination of the interdependence of slavery and freedom" in the novel, as if it had never been done, but her own assessment is sweeping, not subtle. According to her reading, the book is about "the parasitical nature of *white* freedom" (my emphasis); the lesson is that "neither Huck nor Mark Twain can tolerate, in imaginative terms, Jim freed. . . . Freedom has no meaning to Huck or to the text without the specter of enslavement."

But this is to miss Twain's more ambitious scrutiny of freedom, and to skirt tensions that Ellison, to take one example, carefully examined. Jim, Ellison observed, "is not simply a slave but a symbol of humanity . . . a man . . . who expressed his essential humanity in his desire for freedom," and Huck, like Jim, "is limited in circumstance but not in possibility." Whatever the inadequacies of the end, Twain had confronted the real tragedy of American life in having Huck simultaneously internalize and rebel against the racial assumptions of his society. Trapped by the parasitical nature of white freedom, he nonetheless had a larger vision of freedom; at the same time that he decided not to report on runaway Jim, he assumed that he would go to hell for it.

This muddled but moral sense of responsibility, Ellison believed, was at the heart of the best literary confrontations with race. Still, he emphasized in closing that his essay was not a plea to white writers to define black humanity; it was a call to them "to recognize the broader aspects of their own." Morrison ostensibly shares that aim, which she invokes over and over. But as her ambivalent lectures unfold, it yields again and again to the less imagi-native urge simply to indict white writers for their inhumanity.

Defining black humanity, Ellison reminded his readers, is a task that belongs to black writers, who face "the responsibility of having their ideals and images recognized as part of the composite image which is that of the still forming American people." With great energy and success, Morrison has for two decades shouldered that responsiblity. In *Playing in the Dark,* she characterizes the dilemma of the black writer as a burdensome variation on the predicament of the white writers she examines in her lectures. They have unconsciously assumed an "unraced" audience; she is "a black author who is at some level *always* conscious of representing one's own race to, or in spite of, a race of readers that understands itself to be 'universal' or race-free." In *Jazz,* she explores that situation and its difficulties more self-consciously than ever before.

Unlike Morrison the critic, who is eager to declare her aloofness from academic political fashion, Morrison the novelist works hard to demonstrate her awareness of the current preoccupation with textual "signs" and narrative indeterminacy. The epigraph of *Jazz,* though it comes from the ancient Gnostic Gospels, echoes the terms of reigning critical discourse: "I am the name of the sound / and the sound of the name. / I am the sign of the letter / and the designation of the division." This immodest incantation is the first, none too subtle nudge to be skeptical about the claims of imaginative prowess made by the novel's garrulous narrative "I" (whose identity, the jacket flap informs us, "is a matter of each reader's imagination").

Morrison's narratives have usually been supremely confident. At her best, as in *Song of Solomon,* she imagines her way with seeming effortlessness into the most obscure corners and eccentric souls of the rural or small-town black worlds that she maps in abundant detail. She then intertwines her discoveries in plots that trace her protagonists' quests for self-understanding. Her explorations in empathy, she has said, are meant to be invitations to white readers to undertake their own: "To read imaginative literature by and about us is to choose to examine centers of the self and to have the opportunity to compare those centers with the 'raceless' ones with which we are, all of us, most familiar."

In *Jazz,* however, she has evidently decided to challenge her readers with a less penetrable story. She wants to derail expectations of anything like a linear narrative, and to raise doubts about the possibility of imaginative empathy. This novel is not supposed to be a romanticized, well-rounded portrait of black tribulations, and the blues are Morrison's guide to the rawer, less symmetrical chronicle that she aims to offer instead. As she observed in an essay four years ago, "A modernity which overturns pre-war definitions ushers in the Jazz Age (an age *defined* by Afro-American art and culture), and requires new kinds of intelligences to define oneself." Efforts to shape identity became newly "complex, contradictory, evasive, independent, liquid."

Yet Morrison's riffs on her disoriented characters have a

way of ending up flat and faint, even when the opening notes are true. The improvisatory course of a jam session is the evident model for the gnomic narrator who recounts Joe Trace's affair with teenaged Dorcas, its fatal end (Joe hunts her down in a club with another boyfriend and kills her), and Violet and Joe's bewildered recovery of balance. But the performance is almost too predictably meandering: now coolly surveying, as if from above the rooftops, the Harlem of the 1920s where the story is set; now intimately swooping in to report on characters' lives and thoughts; now rushing the rhythm to anticipate events that have not yet transpired; now slowing down to circle back and cover the ground again, and then to dip dreamily even further back to the past and the South in an effort to explain why violence erupts in the Traces' lives in the City in 1926.

What starts out lyrical quickly becomes labored. In particular, the bird's-eye view celebrations of the heady tempo and daring temper of black life in Harlem during the Jazz Age have a tendency to lapse into cliché. "I'm crazy about this City," the narrator exults, and then proceeds to slip from picturesque images into platitudes: "Below is shadow where any blasé thing takes place: clarinets and lovemaking, fists and the voices of sorrowful women. A city like this one makes me dream tall and feel in on things. Hep." Similarly, the vignettes of Southern life around the turn of the century, for all their fresh details, verge on the formulaic—people dreaming small and feeling out of things.

Against these rural and urban backdrops, the characters in *Jazz* struggle to define themselves in all their complex, contradictory, evasive, independent, liquid selfhood, only to end up seeming one-dimensional. The outlines of Joe and Violet's story at first suggest a predictable drama of brutalizing black man and brutalized black women. Both protagonists, and Dorcas as well, have known the devastating jolt of dispossession that is the familiar legacy of Morrison's characters: Joe the crushing rejection of him by his wild mother; Violet the suicide of her mother and the unsteady loyalty of her grandmother; Dorcas the death of both her parents in riots in East St. Louis.

Yet Morrison clearly intends to make them more than mere victims at the mercy of a cruel world. The trouble is that her efforts to endow her characters with will become steadily more willful and intrusive as the novel progresses. Idiosyncratic motives are scattered in the digressive narrative, but they're rarely developed, and in the end the characters are barely more than sketchy stereotypes. Quiet Joe, a door-to-door salesman of cosmetics, at first seems stirred up by complicated memories, but finally he's little more than a man with a midlife crisis, who's briefly deranged by jealousy.

Similarly, the maternal longings that lurk in Violet's obsessive thoughts of young Dorcas (whose corpse she tried to stab during the funeral), and of the daughter she wishes she had, are left dangling. Instead, we swerve off into a long account of her grandmother's obsession with the golden-haired boy she raised, which reads like an old-fashioned fairy tale. And there's a pat modern coming-of-age story in the orphan Dorcas's discovery of large and selfish appetites despite the admonitions of her straightlaced aunt: the girl is another rebel with the customary cause—hormones and "the dirty, get-on-down music the women sang and the men played and both danced to, close and shameless or apart and wild."

At the end of the novel Morrison resorts to the most heavy-handed device to liberate her characters from predictability. The implication, carefully fostered from the outset, has been that Dorcas's murder will be followed by another act of violence; the suspense of the wandering story has consisted in guessing who will end up killing whom. But Morrison instead stages a manipulative about-face in the plot: Joe and Violet end up living happily ever after in a new and calm intimacy born of their troubles. The narrative voice confesses that it is to blame for failing to foresee the unexpectedly anti-climactic turn of events:

> I was sure one would kill the other. I waited for it so I could describe it. I was so sure it would happen. That the past was an abused record with no choice but to repeat itself at the crack and no power on earth could lift the arm that held the needle. I was so sure, and they danced and walked all over me. Busy, they were, busy being original, complicated, changeable—human, I guess you'd say, while I was the predictable one, confused in my solitude into arrogance, thinking my space, my view was the only one that was or that mattered.

The mistake has been to overdramatize and to trust in an imagination that has conceived the world and the characters too broadly and luridly: "What, I wonder, what would I be without a few brilliant spots of blood to ponder?" the narrator muses, "Without aching words that set, then miss, the mark?"

Morrison has charged her narrator with the duty to avoid the weakness that she herself has acknowledged—an inclination to romanticize black lives. But it's a warning that the presiding voice heeds too late, admitting in closing that "it was loving the City that distracted me and gave me ideas. Made me think I could speak its loud voice and make that sound sound human. I missed the people altogether." The verdict is uncomfortably close to the mark, and the fact that the narrator renders it and then ruminates at some length about the many obstacles to sympathy doesn't retroactively deepen the characters or tighten the plot.

Nor does the final confession of self-doubt really succeed in deromanticizing the portrait. Morrison has very purposefully veered away from a saga of melodramatic suffering, but the novel ends up arriving at sentimentality by a different route. Instead of a bitter cycle of pain, readers are presented a sugary tableau of peace between Joe and Violet: "They eat breakfast then and, more often than not, fall asleep. . . . The rest of the day goes however they want it to. After a hairdressing, for example, he meets her at the drugstore for her vanilla malt and his cherry smash."

In the preface to *Playing in the Dark,* Morrison emphasizes what her novel and lectures make abundantly clear: that an acute self-consciousness unites her fiction and her criticism.

Writing and reading are not all that distinct for a writer. Both exercises require being alert and ready for unaccountable beauty, for the intricateness or simple elegance of the writer's imagination, for the world that imagination evokes. Both require being mindful of the places where imagination sabotages itself, locks its own gates, pollutes its vision. Writing and reading mean being aware of the writer's notions of risk and safety, the serene achievement of, or sweaty fight for, meaning and responseability.

It can indeed seem the height of responsibility to pursue "response-ability" so assiduously, especially when dealing with matters of race and literature. But Morrison's new books suggest that perhaps it is possible to be too mindful of the ways of the imagination, too intent on demystifying it—scrutinizing, assessing, and second-guessing. Her relentless vigilance, rather than issuing in creative sympathy, leads her toward the double dead end of indicting other writers for failures of vision and apologizing for her own. (pp. 43-8)

Ann Hulbert, "Romance and Race," in The New Republic, Vol. 206, No. 20, May 18, 1992, pp. 43-8.

Deborah A. McDowell (review date June 1992)

[*In the review below, McDowell discusses Morrison's use of language and experimental narrative techniques in* Jazz *and notes the similarities between this work and Morrison's previous novel,* Beloved.]

> In the beginning was the sound, and they all knew what that sound sounded like.
>
> —*Beloved*

"Sth." The beginning of *Jazz* is a sound, the sound of the narrator sucking her tooth. "Sth." Following on the heels of this first note, which print makes momentarily unfamiliar, is that common mark of the familiar: "I know." "I know that woman. She used to live with a flock of birds up on Lenox Avenue. Know her husband too. He fell for an eighteen-year-old girl with one of those deepdown, spooky loves that made him so sad and happy he shot her just to keep the feeling going."

As the narrator lays out these pieces of the plot's bare bones, we quickly recognize the strumming of a familiar chord. Indeed, we do all know what that sound sounds like. It is the sound of an adulterous love triangle; of the drama and intensity of romance; of the fleeting pleasures of erotic love; of passion's often violent recompense. It is the sound of a thick, hungry, obsessive love that hurls lovers to the brink of insanity or drives them to the eccentricities of control. It is a melancholy sound of the search for the "magical best thing," that someone out there somewhere that we are sure to find if we just keep looking.

But as her masses of faithful readers will attest, Morrison imparts even to the familiar her own distinctive ring—much like Satchmo gave to "Hello Dolly," or Ella to "A Tisket a Tasket," or Coltrane to "My Favorite Things." Morrison's riff on a timeworn tale features a triangle with a dead woman on one of its sides. In the first few pages

of a novel filled with bizarre events and uncanny juxtapositions, Violet, the second side of this triangle, has stabbed the corpse of Dorcas, her husband's lover, freed from their cages a flock of birds no longer able to fly, and snatched a baby while its sister ducks back inside their house to get a recording of "The Trombone Blues."

The sound that drives the sister to misjudgment and forgetfulness is the sound that holds much of Harlem tightly in its grip. "It's the dirty, get-on-down music [that] made you do unwise disorderly things. Just hearing it was like violating the law. . . . Songs that used to start in the head and fill the heart had dropped on down, down to places below the sash and the buckled belts." Such descriptions seem to reinforce what Marshall Stearns terms the "semi-sordid sexual connotations" that surrounded the controversial beginnings of jazz. But while the "jazz" of Morrison's *Jazz* suggests its share of sex, the novel's angles on desire lie far beyond the "frail [and] melty tendenc[ies] of the flesh." This is the desire that "grown people whisper to each other under the covers," a desire "way, way down underneath tissue." This is not the Devil's music that 1920s Progressive reformers made it out to be. And if, as Amiri Baraka puts it, "jazz was collected upon the numerous skeletons the middle class black . . . kept locked in the closet of his psyche, along with watermelons and gin," then Morrison wants to open the door to that closet to let the skeleton rattle around; but not before she re-members its bones.

Morrison's entire *oeuvre* has involved a studied effort—to invoke *Ezekiel*—to make the dry and disconnected bones of the black historical past live. Though set in 1920s Harlem, *Jazz* traces the movements of its characters back to the near and distant past. Here is a lyrical story of the Great Migration—that twentieth-century Exodus—that carried waves of black people into Northern cities, buoyed on the hope of shelter from violence and want. Black Harlem as "city of refuge" has no meaning without those pockets of the rural South where blacks faced the racism of economic hardship, dispossession and lynch law. In *Jazz,* these pockets are set mainly in Virginia, where many trod the paths from Goshen, to Vienna, to Palestine, witnessing and suffering their own holocaust. In naming these fictive cities of the pre-Migration past, Morrison forges her connection to that link the slaves made between themselves and the Israelites under Egyptian bondage, suggesting that even in Jazz Age Harlem the footprints of slavery have not been lost to time.

One is inspired to read the traces of *Beloved* on the face of *Jazz,* and not simply because Morrison has spoken in interviews of the novels as the first two parts of a projected trilogy and promised that Beloved's life and quest would be a part of *Jazz.* One wants to pair these novels because the workings of Memory—of change, of loss, of grief, of abandonment, of being "junk-heaped," as Sethe puts it in *Beloved*—are so central to them both.

Joe Trace, side three of *Jazz*'s triangle, is born in Vesper County, Virginia, in 1873. *Beloved* opens in 1873, the same year that the ghost turned vengeful woman enters and destroys the tenuous calm at 124 Bluestone Road, forcing Sethe to surrender to the dreaded labor of remembering, repeating and working through. It is remembering her "disremembered and unaccounted for" lost child, and analogously her own missed mothering, that both creates Sethe's pain and makes for its release; and it is memory of the lost mother that is the motor force of *Jazz.*

It is as if the object of each person's desire is, at base, an unconscious substitute for a missing mother—a substitute recalling Freud, or, more poignantly, the lyrics of the spiritual "Sometimes I Feel Like a Motherless Child." (Morrison's decision to make Harlem the Promised Land works resonantly with this motif, for Harlem as metropolis— "mother-city"—has figured so prominently in the black cultural imagination as the icon of racial plenitude.) Violet's mother, Rose Dear, commits suicide after she and her children are dispossessed of house and land in Virginia. Years later, Dorcas watches as her mother is burned alive in her house in East St. Louis, along with Dorcas' cherished dolls, a mere five days after her father's murder. She "never said a word" about her double orphaning until she meets Joe Trace and they trade their painful stories in the twilight privacy of a rented room.

The case of Joe's missing mother seems the most haunting of the three. (Could she even be that "devil child" who "take[s] the shape of a pregnant woman" before vanishing at *Beloved*'s end?) Before he leaves Virginia for the migration North, Joe stalks the countryside looking for his mother, whom he believes to be a wild "playful woman who lived in a rock," a woman "too brain-blasted to do what the meanest sow managed: nurse what she birthed." Joe has been traveling around for 25 years with an "inside nothing" that Dorcas helps to fill—because "she had it too"—until she seeks a different "Paradise" in Alton, a lover closer to her age. She pays for this shift in her affections with her life.

These details must be ferreted from the thicket of this novel's very intricate plot. The reader must cultivate the art of waiting—waiting for details to unfold, for fugitive metaphors to be pinned down—and after waiting, must refract from the richest of narrative matter a linear pattern and sequence that Morrison's novels—like all good modernist texts—are reluctant to provide. Here, as in *Beloved*, the narrator circles the subject, knowing, as Sethe knows, "she could never close in, pin it down."

Jazz is likely to vex and frustrate those who seek the familiar satisfactions of a fast and easy read, to alienate those who do not share the novel's assumption that there is more to reading than tracing characters and plot. If (to quote Susan Sontag in a different context) the reader insists that the ending of the reading experience must coincide ideally "with full satisfaction of one's desire to know, to understand what happened and why," Morrison writes another contract. And what she "gives up" demands a quid pro quo. Although the personal biographies of these characters have been embedded in the events of a collective history—grand and small—the reader is left with narrative gaps and missing pieces all along the way.

Morrison has frequently spoken in interviews of her desire to create in all her work the missing spaces that allow the reader to emerge as co-creator. For example, here on the

pages of the *Women's Review* (March 1988), she explained to Marsha Darling that

> the whole point is to have these characters . . . move off the page and inhabit the imagination of whoever has opened herself or himself to them . . . It's very important to be as discreet as possible in order to make a complex and rich response come from the reader.

Jazz is both lean and discreet and the response it arouses, though eminently satisfying, stirs the mind more than the heart. It is demanding, full of haunting turns and teasing references, beginning with the enigmatic epigraph excerpted from "Thunder, Perfect Mind," a poem from the *Nag Hammadi* gnostic writings:

> I am the name of the sound
> and the sound of the name.
> I am the sign of the letter
> and the designation of the division.

Negotiating the complex relation between words and sounds, words as sounds, and sounds as words is one of the many challenges Morrison has set for herself and for her readers, and her effort to exploit the expressive potential of music for letters places her in such diverse and stellar company as Sterling Brown, Margaret Walker, Langston Hughes, Michael Harper, Amiri Baraka, Ralph Ellison, Ntozake Shange and, just lately, Xam Cartier, to name but a few from the modern African American pantheon. But in selecting jazz as mode and inspiration, Morrison runs up against problems of transliteration, against the stasis that print almost inevitably effects on sound.

If the whole of *Jazz* as narrative experiment falls, in places, just shy of the sum of its parts, the sound of music can be heard throughout, as in this beautifully sensuous passage evocative of an imagist poem: "Motor cars become black jet boxes gliding behind hoodlights weakened by mists. On sidewalks turned to satin figures move shoulder first, the crowns of their heads angled shields against the light buckshot that the raindrops are."

The novel's language is often so prepossessing that I forget Joe and Violet and Dorcas and those who touch their lives. Not only does the sheer virtuosity of much of the novel's language distance me from its characters and their cares; so does its ambitious effort to straddle several artistic media all at once. Photography is just one. Looked at from one angle, *Jazz* is the novel as photo-collage, dealing, to quote Henri Cartier-Breson, in "things which are continually vanishing, and when they have vanished, there is no contrivance on earth which can make them come back again. We cannot develop and print a memory."

In his many pictures of the dead, the famous photographer James Van der Zee certainly appreciated "continually vanishing" subjects, but chased them nonetheless. Morrison incorporates descriptions of many of his photographs that students of the Harlem Renaissance will quickly recognize, but the nucleus of the novel is a photograph from his *Harlem Book of the Dead* of an eighteen-year-old girl lying in her coffin. Morrison sets to narrative the story behind the photograph: the girl's murder by a jealous lover. In an interview with Gloria Naylor, Morrison admitted to being fascinated by this story of "a woman [who] loved something other than herself so much," and wondered "what it is that really compels a good woman to displace the self, her self." The lover escapes punishment because the dying woman will not speak his name. As Morrison continued, "she kept saying, 'I'll tell you tomorrow,' because she wanted him to get away. And he did, I guess; anyway she died."

"Anyway she died." At the end of the novel, that sound lingers in the ear whether we've read Morrison's comment or not. Again, we "all know what that sound sound[s] like," because as students of narrative and culture and of culture's narratives, we've heard it countless times before. It is the sound of a woman's sexual transgression laid to rest. Is it any wonder that it is Dorcas who "lay on a chenille bedspread" thinking of the somebody close by who was "licking his licorice stick . . . blowing off his horn while a knowing woman sang ain't nobody going to keep me down you got the right key baby but the wrong keyhole you got to get it bring it and put it right here . . . "

But Dorcas is not the "knowing woman" of the blues she sings. The snatches of the lyrics in her medley speak of desire without its often violent consequences. Her older, hungrier lover wants not just to fill that "inside nothing," but to preserve the intensity of the kick, the feeling that language diminishes and time erodes. It is Joe who knows and laments "that you could replay in the brain the scene of ecstasy, of murder, of tenderness, but it was drained of everything but the language to say it in." Here, the scene of ecstasy and the scene of murder share a common ground, giving aid and reinforcement to the knowledge we almost always fear to own: that the zone of the erotic is often the zone of violence. And violence begets violence as the "wronged wife" (her shadow side named "Violent") exacts a grotesque revenge on the "other woman's" corpse.

But who will exact revenge in the name of Dorcas killed softly by Joe Trace's gun? Not her aunt, who had failed to control her niece's unruly passions, and who knows, in any case, that when blacks kill blacks justice is seldom sought or won. And if justice can be jettisoned, can compassion take its place? Not in this envious narrator's reckoning. It is almost as if Dorcas' murder is a fitting end for one who courted danger and flaunted the errant ways of youth. It is almost as if her sacrifice enables Joe and Violet to get back the love they'd lost, and the process of that revival is faintly necrophiliac at its core. It is Dorcas' face that helps them make it through the night—this "photograph of a bold, unsmiling girl staring from the mantelpiece," the "only living presence in the house."

But, paradoxically, this living presence is a dead presence—doubly so, for as Roland Barthes and Susan Sontag have well suggested, the "thing" ineradicably there in every photograph is the return of the dead, even when the subject is yet alive. The photograph immortalizes the "missing being" at the same time that it serves as emblem and allegory of desire. Violet and Joe each read on the face of Dorcas the substance of their own desires, and the reader reads the evidence of their self-deceptions. While Violet sees a "greedy, haughty, lazy" face, Joe sees one "absen[t]

of accusation," of "finger point[ing], of lips . . . turn[ed] down in judgment."

We, too, easily discern on the face of this novel the absence of "lips turn[ed] down in judgment." As in almost all of Morrison's novels, concepts like "justice" and "moral retribution," conventionally understood, have little place, as acts of violation and destruction (witness Cholly's rape of Pecola in *The Bluest Eye* and Eva's burning Plum alive in *Sula*) acquire the subtle force of reason and the seeming inevitability of "natural" fact.

But, again, why am I so detached from something that should make me cringe: the unpunished murder of a woman who dares to desire? Because, in the process of "enlarging" herself, Morrison's narrator has reduced Dorcas to the dimensions of a snapshot—a motionless image, fixed, aestheticized, frozen. And I apprehend the horror of her murder mainly at the level of the intellect, finding it fascinating to ponder but difficult to feel.

Jazz stretches taut a tension between the language of the intellect and the language of the heart, a tension captured graphically in Violet's two separate efforts to give sense to her mother's suicide and voice to her own pain: "Might it have been the morning after the night . . . When longing squeezed, then tossed her before running off promising to return and bounce her again like an India rubber ball?" And again more plaintively, "Mama? Is this where you got to and couldn't do it no more? The place where you know you are not and never again will be loved by anybody who can choose to do it?"

The second passage moves me as the first does not. Morrison's deftly created narrator helps me understand the difference, a difference she incorporates into her final and self-conscious assessment of her own narrative drives and desires: "It was loving the City that distracted me and gave me ideas. Made me think I could speak its loud voice and make that sound sound human. I missed the people altogether." That the narrator confesses to living "too much in [her] own mind" to be able to hear and respond to a human sound gives me only momentary satisfaction. But if, in the final analysis, *Jazz* is all "about" this mysterious narrator who finds it easier to aestheticize her people than to feel their pain—which is her pain, her own unmet desires—then Morrison has taken giant steps here, big risks.

On the other hand, if I am left contemplating this narrator and what she "can't say . . . aloud," I am still caught within the labyrinth of her narrative and its seductive designs. My desire to know these people more fully still lingers well after I close the book. Although the narrator understands and censures herself for failing to make them real, I'm still not satisfied. Somehow I want to know more about why Violet stops speaking and starts sleeping with a doll in her arms; more about why Joe Trace kills what he loves. But above all, I want to know more of his beloved and to mourn her loss, as I do his. The narrator's silence about Dorcas' murder, a failure of language, cannot undo its horror.

But *Jazz* succeeds in "saying" much—and with sounding brass—about storytelling in the post-modern age. With sharp breaks and swift chord changes, it riffs on the language of feeling, the transliteration of sound, the violence of language and, most of all, the metaphysics of desire. That I want more at novel's end is a testament to Morrison's knowing genius, for that wanting bespeaks the very essence of desire, which is by definition perpetual want. Want for satisfaction. Want of satisfaction that is floating forever in the distance (or just down the road a piece), left to take its form in endless substitutions, never to be fully known or named. (pp. 1, 3-5)

> *Deborah A. McDowell, "Harlem Nocturne,"
> in* The Women's Review of Books, *Vol. IX,
> No. 9, June, 1992, pp. 1, 3-5.*

An excerpt from *Playing in the Dark: Whiteness and the Literary Imagination*

Race has become metaphorical—a way of referring to and disguising forces, events, classes, and expressions of social decay and economic division far more threatening to the body politic than biological "race" ever was. Expensively kept, economically unsound, a spurious and useless political asset in election campaigns, racism is as healthy today as it was during the Enlightenment. It seems that it has a utility far beyond economy, beyond the sequestering of classes from one another, and has assumed a metaphorical life so completely embedded in daily discourse that it is perhaps more necessary and more on display than ever before.

I am prepared to be corrected on this point insofar as it misrepresents the shelf life of racism in social and political behavior. But I remain convinced that the metaphorical and metaphysical uses of race occupy definitive places in American literature, in the "national" character, and ought to be a major concern of the literary scholarship that tries to know it.

Toni Morrison, in her Playing in the Dark: Whiteness and the Literary Imagination, *Harvard University Press, 1992.*

Michael Wood (review date 19 November 1992)

[*In the following review, Wood discusses the principal themes in* Jazz *and* Playing in the Dark.]

The facts are simple and brutal, you can read them any day in the newspapers. If you read them and if you feel they are published for you. The suggestion that news in America is often just white news, or news for whites, occurs again and again in Toni Morrison's work, nowhere more strongly than in her novel *Beloved* (1987), where a former slave knows that the mere presence of a black face in a paper is the sign not only of disaster but of more than customary horror:

> A whip of fear broke through the heart chambers as soon as you saw a Negro's face in a paper, since the face was not there because the person had a healthy baby, or outran a street mob. Nor was it there because the person had been killed, or maimed or caught or burned or jailed or whipped or evicted or stomped or raped or

cheated, since that could hardly qualify as news in a newspaper. It would have to be something out of the ordinary . . .

Of course, this man's reaction belongs to Cincinnati in 1873, and the news itself is eighteen years older; but it is a theme both of Morrison's new novel, *Jazz,* and of her lectures given at Harvard in 1990 and published as *Playing in the Dark,* that things may not have changed as fast or as much as we think or hope.

"A newspaper can turn your mind," the narrator of *Jazz* says, but Alice Manfred, the character she is worried about, seems to have her mind fairly straight. Alice reads about the violence of the world, and also, between the lines, finds an angry resistance to it.

> Every week . . . a paper laid bare the bones of some broken woman. Man kills wife. Eight accused of rape dismissed. Woman and girl victims of. Woman commits suicide. White attackers indicted. Five women caught. Woman says man beat. In jealous rage man.

Are these broken women mere victims? "Natural prey? Easy pickings?" "I don't think so," Alice repeats. Some are, no doubt, and the novel tells us the story of one of them, Alice's niece Dorcas, a girl who likes to push people into "something scary," and who, when shot by a man she has driven too far, allows herself to die. But other black women in *Jazz* are arming themselves, physically and mentally, and in this they have caught a current of the times, a not always visible indignation that says enough is enough. It is an indignation that is glimpsed in new forms of protest and political organization and heard in the freedom and sadness and hunger of jazz. There are extended flashbacks in the novel, but its main "times" are the 1920s, or rather a period which Morrison dates from 1917, the year of major riots in East Saint Louis and a commemorative march in New York. The novel's most intimate, violent events occur in January 1926. There was a jazz age behind the Jazz Age.

The simplest of public incidents, of the kind that make it into the newspapers, arise from complicated private stories, and such stories, connecting blunt or bitter fact with its riddling context or history, have always been Morrison's business as a novelist. And not only as a novelist. In her introduction to an interesting volume of essays on the Anita Hill-Clarence Thomas affair [*Race-ing Justice, Engendering Power* (1992)], Morrison distinguishes between "what took place" and "what happened," where the former is what can be briefly stated in a newspaper, say, and the latter is what we might, after patient thought and considerable investigation, actually understand. We live in a world of what the narrator of *Jazz* calls "a crooked kind of mourning,"—crooked as a path may be crooked, unavoidably indirect—and the phrase takes us a good way into Morrison's moral landscape.

The mourning is often for a factual event or the fictional version of a factual event, for what suddenly and undeniably took place: a shooting, a rape, the killing of a child. Its "crookedness" comes from its also being part of what happened and keeps happening, and it is one of the special provinces of the imaginative writer. In *Playing in the*

Dark, Morrison speaks of "places where the imagination sabotages itself, locks its own gates, pollutes its vision," and her fiction is largely concerned with the geography and (possible) redemption of such places. The mind, for Morrison, could be a friend but is often an enemy, as we learn in *Beloved,* for instance, where an escaped slave, the woman whose face is in the newspapers, is imprisoned in the horrors of memory:

> She shook her head from side to side, resigned to her rebellious brain. Why was there nothing it refused? No misery, no regret, no hateful picture too rotten to accept? Like a greedy child it snatched up everything.

Even the physical beauty of the real world compounds the problem, disguising the pain and disgrace of the remembered slave farm: "It never looked as terrible as it was and it made her wonder if hell was a pretty place too."

It is horrifying, of course, that history should show such quantities of material cruelty; no less horrifying, perhaps, that the long legacy of such a history is an imagination too often dedicated to self-sabotage, unable even to mourn except in "crooked" ways that displace or deny the full horror of the death and injury being mourned.

Morrison's lucid and eloquent first novel, *The Bluest Eye* (1970), portrays a poor black family who live in a rundown storefront in Lorain, Ohio. There is an important difference, Morrison's narrator insists, between living there and staying there.

> They lived there because they were poor and black, and they stayed there because they believed they were ugly. Although their poverty was traditional and stultifying, it was not unique. But their ugliness was unique. . . . You looked at them and wondered why they were so ugly; you looked closely and could not find the source. Then you realized it came from conviction, their conviction. It was as though some mysterious all-knowing master had given each one a cloak of ugliness to wear, and they had each accepted it without question.

Each member of the family interprets and acts out his or her ugliness differently, but none of them understands that the all-knowing master is not God but only history and habit; the projection of their own benumbed collusion with the mythology of beauty and ugliness that oppresses them beyond their already grim social oppression. Throughout Morrison's novels—those already mentioned, but also *Sula* (1973), *Song of Solomon* (1977), and *Tar Baby* (1981)—variously trapped and bewildered characters fight against similar mythologies, alluring versions of what it means to be black or female or poor or free or respectable or Southern. They fight with energy and dignity but usually without much success. The best they get is release from pain or haunting, or an understanding of the life they are about to lose.

The strongest moments in the novels represent what we might call the paradoxes of crookedness: rape, as a form of love *in extremis;* infanticide as the deepest expression of a mother's care. The ugly father of the ugly family in *The Bluest Eye* rapes his daughter but at least, the narra-

tor bleakly says, he "loved her enough to touch her." For the chief character in *Beloved* the killing of her baby in order to save her from a return to slavery is both simple and unforgivable, what she had to do and what she cannot forget, the direct result of a deformed history. "If I hadn't killed her," she says, "she would have died": and the tangle of the thought is the exact image of the tangle of her heart and mind.

In sharply evoked crookedness of this kind, tender, horrifying, passionate, and violent, Morrison resolves the dilemma which David Brion Davis identified in ["The American Dilemma," *The New York Review of Books* (16 July 1992)]: How can one register the effects of oppression without making the victims seem merely "dehumanized and incapable," precisely the passive, inferior beings their oppressors like to think they are?

In *Jazz* for the first time in Morrison's fiction, there is a genuine escape from crookedness and sabotage, a defeat of mythology, and Morrison herself seems at a loss to describe what has happened—even if she knows precisely what has taken place. Perhaps Morrison is only miming disarray, and in one sense she must be. She has her narrator declare her surprise at her characters' behavior, as if they just got away from her, as if they managed to end up happy without her permission. "I was so sure, and they danced and walked all over me. Busy, they were, busy being original, complicated, changeable—human, I guess you'd say. . . . " I guess we'd rather not say, and of course we can't linger too long over this tired trope. When writers (or their surrogates) say their characters have a life of their own, we wonder both what they are actually up to and why they think this faded metaphor still works.

But while Morrison's narrator is sentimentalizing her characters (it is human to be original and changeable, but no less human, alas, to be blinkered and monotonous), something more interesting is also happening, and to see what it is we need to return to the "facts" of the novel, what the newspapers might have reported for January 1926 on Lenox Avenue and thereabouts.

Middle-aged man shoots and kills an eighteen-year-old girl, they might have said. Wife attempts to slash the face of the girl's corpse. Joe and Violet Trace have been living happily enough in New York City since they came up from Virginia in 1906, more happily (at first) than they ever expected to. They had heard a lot about Baltimore and Violet at least was afraid New York might be "less lovely":

> Joe believed it would be perfect. When they arrived, carrying all of their belongings in one valise, they both knew right away that perfect was not the word. It was better than that.

The narrator, a garrulous, intelligent, unnamed Harlem local ("Sth, I know that woman," she begins), has the same wide-eyed view of the excitements of the (always eagerly capitalized) City. "I'm crazy about this City," she says. "I like the way the City makes people think they can do what they want and get away with it"; and she likes the way it allows people to become "not so much new as themselves: their stronger, riskier selves."

The City is smart at this: smelling and [sic] good and looking raunchy; sending secret messages disguised as public signs: this way, open here, danger to let colored only single men on sale woman wanted private room stop dog on premises absolutely no money down fresh chicken free delivery fast.

The City is one of the main characters of the novel, a strangely cheerful urban home for the "wildness" which in Morrison's other novels has a rural location. "When I see this wildness gone in a person, it's sad," she said in an interview [from Barbara Hill Rigney's *The Voices of Toni Morrison* (1992)]. Wildness is a "special lack of restraint," clearly a virtue in those whose lives have been nearly all restraint. And indeed in *Jazz,* too, there is a rural wild zone, to be found in the Virginia the Traces have abandoned but not forgotten.

Yet of course you can't become your riskier self without taking risks, and even your stronger self may not be strong enough. Joe and Violet, in their different ways, have got lost among the City's enchantments. Their happiness trickles away into aging, they scarcely speak to each other. Violet begins to think of the children she hasn't had, and the meanings of her mother's long-ago suicide. What the narrator calls "cracks" begin to develop in Violet's consciousness, "dark fissures in the globe light of the day," moments when she loses her words and her meanings. And Joe, more traditionally, has a male mid-life crisis, looks for his youth in a young girl; but then also, in rather too novelistic a contortion perhaps, he seems to see in the girl a substitute for the mother he never knew. The girl herself finds a handsome, arrogant boyfriend of her own age, clumsily dismisses Joe, and Joe kills her without knowing which piece of his life he is trying to erase or rearrange. He is not arrested, not even accused, "because nobody actually saw him do it, and the dead girl's aunt didn't want to throw money to helpless lawyers or laughing cops when she knew the expense wouldn't improve anything." Joe and Violet go on living together, miserable, silent, baffled.

All this matches the narrator's expectations. She has meanwhile been imagining the lives of these people and others, giving them pasts, lending them voices: Joe, Violet, their courtship and life in Virginia; the girl, Dorcas, whose parents have been killed in the riots in East Saint Louis; Dorcas's aunt, Alice Manfred, who after her niece's death strikes up an oddly austere and tender friendship with Violet; Dorcas's friend Felice, who gets to know and like the Traces, in spite of their strangeness and their sorrow. But the narrator is imagining all or most of this. She is a novelist within the novel, happy with her performance, and doesn't stint on self-praise.

> Risky, I'd say, trying to figure out anybody's state of mind. But worth the trouble if you're like me—curious, inventive and well-informed. . . . It's not hard to imagine what it must have been like.

It's not hard to imagine, but it's hard to get it right, and this is what our chastened narrator learns at the end of the novel. Not before she changes her personality (or at least

her style) a couple of times, and has a spell as a sort of highbrow Faulknerian memorialist. The prose gets worryingly close to parody here, and signals a frank shift into a grander literary gear—or signals perhaps the writer's need of the freedom to make such a shift. The chatty narrator saying, "I know just how she felt," and "Good luck and let me know," becomes a theorist saying, "I want to be the language that wishes him well, speaks his name." And starts to devise sentences like this one:

> When he stopped the buggy, got out to tie the horse and walk back through the rain, perhaps it was because the awful-looking thing lying in wet weeds was everything he was not as well as a proper protection against and anodyne to what he believed his father to be, and therefore (if it could just be contained, identified)—himself.

"He" is a young mulatto Violet has heard about from her grandmother. He has discovered (from his white mother) that his father was black, and he has gone in search of him. The "thing" he meets on the way is a pregnant young black woman, who may or may not be Joe Trace's mother-to-be. The narrator has a fine time evoking this ripely resonant stuff of the past, but does herself seem caught up in one of the very mythologies Morrison keeps trying to get her characters out of: race as trauma, suffered by the character, but weirdly relished by the teller of the tale. Here as in certain moments in *Song of Solomon* and *Tar Baby,* but not, as far as I can see, in the other novels, a certain talkiness in Morrison's language reflects an abstraction in her thought, a move to diagrams about color rather than the working-through of particular painful experiences.

Fortunately, the diagrams are never there for long, and the talkiness is more than compensated for by something like its reverse: a fine willingness on the novelist's part to inhabit language, to let it do the talking, to see it as itself a freighted form of history rather than a mere means of making statements. The characters in *Jazz* are said by the narrator to treat language like an "intricate, malleable toy designed for their play," and to enter a Toni Morrison novel is to enter a place where words and idioms tease each other, and where what is said is richly shadowed by what is not. This is why she doesn't need to have her narrator announce, "I want to be the language," etc.

When a character in *Song of Solomon* promises to "fly from Mercy," he literally means he is going to try to fly from the roof of Mercy Hospital in a city which I take to be Detroit, but we can hardly miss the suicidal sadness of his project, and mercy is what other characters in the novel long for, sing for, and (occasionally) find.

The very names of Morrison's characters are a mark of their history, in slavery or out, and the jokes they make about their names are a way of remembering that history and fighting it. [In a footnote, Wood states that "the point is well made in Trudier Harris, *Fiction and Folklore: The Novels of Toni Morrison*" (1991).] "Names they got from yearnings, gestures, flaws, events, mistakes, weaknesses," we read in *Song of Solomon.* "Names that bore witness." A list of names follows, starting inside the fiction and moving into the public record: Macon Dead, First Corinthians Dead, Railroad Tommy, Empire State, Ice Man, Muddy

Waters, Jelly Roll, T-Bone, Washboard, Gatemouth, Staggerlee, many others. Joe Trace, in *Jazz,* names himself on the basis of the story he hard about his parents disappearing "without a trace": he decides he is the Trace they disappeared without.

It is in the flowing, personal language of her conclusion that the narrator expresses her new-found humility about what she knows and doesn't know, but it is not exactly in language that she discovers it. What she learns is not only that her characters have cheated her expectations but that they have lived and continue to live in ways she needs to know more about: that they are kinder and wiser and more resilient than she is. "I lived a long time, maybe too much, in my own mind," she says early on, but she is not really apologizing. Her story is skewed not because her mind is where she lives but because her mind has appetites she has not properly considered. "Pain," she says finally, "I seem to have an affection, a kind of sweettooth for it. Bolts of lightning, little rivulets of thunder. . . . What, I wonder, what would I be without a few brilliant spots of blood to ponder? Without aching words that set, then miss, the mark?" Morrison's narrator, like the narrator of Nabokov's *Pnin,* has thought harm is the norm, that unhappy endings are both true and what we want. She has seen her characters as "exotic" and "driven," that is, as characters.

> I was sure one would kill the other [she says of Joe and Violet]. I waited for it so I could describe it. I was so sure it would happen. That the past was an abused record with no choice but to repeat itself at the crack.

As Morrison knows, and has mostly shown in her novels, the past is such a record for many people, and their present is only this cracked repetition of the past. Yet Joe and Violet Trace finally walk away from misery and remorse into an ordinary settled happiness and affection, a "whispering, old-time love." What Morrison is saying through this development, and through the defeat of her narrator's plausible if too lip-smacking narrative predictions, is that forgiveness is (just) possible, and self-forgiveness too. The crooked cannot be made straight but can be survived, left behind. The odds of this happening are not good, of course; they are poor in fiction, and worse in fact. But the odds are there, harm is not everything. *Beloved* was about the pain and necessity of remembering and forgetting; *Jazz* is about remembering all we can and yet knowing, when the time is right, how to change the record.

Talking to Dorcas's friend Felice some time after the murder, Violet Trace asks, "What's the world for if you can't make it up the way you want it?" She can't make it up entirely, but she can make it again, and she has understood that your mind can be your friend as well as your enemy. Violet has messed up her life so far, she thinks, because she "forgot it":

> "Forgot?" [Felice asks].
>
> "Forgot it was mine. My life. I just ran up and down the streets wishing I was somebody else."
>
> "Who? Who'd you want to be?"

> "Not who so much as what. White. Light. Young again."
>
> "Now you don't?"
>
> "Now I want to be the woman my mother didn't stay around long enough to see. That one. The one she would have liked and the one I used to like before."

To be the woman her mother would have liked: it seems a modest enough goal, but it is precisely the goal so few of Morrison's earlier characters can reach. An old freed slave in *Beloved* asks, "If my mother knew me would she like me?" We need to hear the measure of loss in such a question—in the possibility of such a question being asked—if we are to understand the strength of Violet's new confidence, and what the narrator (and we) can learn from her.

The black community in *Beloved* thinks of the erratic behavior of white people as "a far cry from what real humans did," neatly inverting the stereotype Morrison chooses to pursue in *Playing in the Dark,* in which whiteness, in North American literature, is what is human, and blackness is a deviance, exciting, regrettable, or unmentionable. "Until very recently," Morrison says, "and regardless of the race of the author, the readers of virtually all of American fiction have been positioned as white." We know a character in *To Have and Have Not* is white, for instance, "because nobody says so." We would, if we were in any doubt, know he is a man for the same reason, and we may not have progressed as far as we think since 1937.

This, I assume, is how we are to understand Morrison's otherwise puzzling objection to the "graceful, even generous, liberal gesture" of "ignoring race." She herself does not say anything explicit about the race of her readers but that is not the same as ignoring it, and an imaginative understanding of cultural difference, a regard for differently traced histories, will surely take us further than discretion or mere tolerance. "All of us," Morrison says at the end of her lectures, "are bereft when criticism remains too polite or too fearful to notice a disrupting darkness before its eyes." And we are still bereft when darkness is all we see, even if the darkness is a romance rather than a phobia.

Morrison recalls a moment in Marie Cardinal's autobiographical book *The Words To Say It,* where a Louis Armstrong concert is said to provoke an anxiety attack in the white woman who is the main character. Morrison says she smiled at the passage when she read it, partly in admiration of the clarity with which the experience of the music was evoked, and partly because she (mischievously) wondered what Armstrong was playing that could have had such a wild effect ("gripped by panic at the idea of dying in the middle of spasms, stomping feet, and the crowd howling, I ran into the street like someone possessed"). Of course, as these lectures suggest and as the tone of Cardinal's language makes clear, it wasn't Armstrong or the music that released the anxiety, but the way jazz and improvisation expressed a submerged myth of otherness. "Would an Edith Piaf concert or a Dvorak composition have had the same effect?" Morrison agrees they could have. But they didn't and she must be right in feeling that Armstrong's color and the black origins of jazz have a part to play in this version of the myth.

No doubt even sympathetic white constructions of myths of blackness are alarming, and one can only admire the mildness with which Morrison says she doesn't have "quite the same access" to these "useful constructs," because "neither blackness nor 'people of color' stimulates in me notions of excessive, limitless love, anarchy, or routine dread." But in her eagerness to demonstrate the pervasive presence of the myth in North American life, Morrison loses, it seems to me, the myth's real dangers and contours, and replaces them with a supposedly buried, infinitely denied power which is just too easy to find.

Morrison calls Africanism a "trope" and a "virus"; it is the way white Americans take over and mystify the life of the "unsettled and unsettling population" they can neither accept nor ignore. Thus American slaves, who all but disappear in white literature as historical victims, reemerge as "surrogate selves for meditation on problems of human freedom."

There is a "thunderous, theatrical presence of black surrogacy" in American writing which generations of critics have somehow contrived to miss. Morrison finds some interesting, although rather obvious, instances in Twain, Cather, and Hemingway, but she has a harder time with Henry James, and "thunderous" seems loud in any event. The trouble is not the idea of the surrogacy but the tremendous amount of work Morrison wants the idea to do.

> How could one speak of profit, economy, labor, progress, suffragism, Christianity, the frontier, the formation of new states, the acquisition of new lands, education, transportation (freight and passengers), neighborhoods, the military—of almost anything a country concerns itself with—without having as a referent, at the heart of the discourse, at the heart of definition, the presence of Africans and their descendants?

The presence of Africans and their descendants is a referent in all this, or ought to be, and it's an important and too often forgotten one. But what sort of referent is it, and don't the most important questions get mislaid here? The image of the heart seems to blur what Morrison most needs to keep in focus; it makes the argument vast and indefinite and sentimental all at once.

Morrison's case in these lectures is not angry and partial, as some have thought, but global and rather wishful. "Africanism is inextricable from the definition of Americanness," she says. It probably should be, on the grounds that a fudged acceptance of historical responsibility is better than a blank refusal. But is it? The proposition assumes that the guilt of whites with respect to slavery is as large as it ought to be, and that the secret power of blacks bears a real relation to their suffering. This is a noble story, but it isn't a story Morrison tells in any of her novels.

The story she does tell in *Jazz* has a similar generosity, but it has a nuance and a complication the lectures lack. This is not only because good fiction says more than even the most intelligent discursive prose. The story itself is different. It concerns not the black haunting of white minds, but

the slow and difficult liberation of black minds from black and white oppression, from complicity with the all-knowing master of ugliness.

Morrison's chief metaphor for this movement is in her title. This is not a novel about jazz, or based on jazz, and I think reviewers' comments about the improvisatory quality of the writing underestimate what feels like the careful premeditation of the work. Each chapter after the first, for example, picks up an image or other cue from the preceding one, and takes it into new territories: caged birds, hot weather, a hat, spring in the city, the phrase "state of mind," a look, a person, the words "heart" or "pain." This is musical and elegant, as if a tune were to be shifted into a new arrangement, but what it borrows from jazz is a sense of flight and variation, not a method of composition.

The novel is dedicated to the taste and the air of jazz, to what jazz says to people who care for it. No one in this book would have an anxiety attack at a Louis Armstrong concert, even supposing they got to a concert. "Race music," as jazz used to be called, and as a character once calls it here, is the recognizable music of their desire, the sound of their hopes and their dangers. Jazz is risky, like the city, but its risk is its charm. Dorcas's severe aunt hears "a complicated anger in it," but also an "appetite," a "careless hunger." "Come," she hears it saying, "Come and do wrong." Later in the book the narrator listens to young men on the Harlem rooftops playing trumpets and clarinets, and gets a different, easier feeling: "You would have thought everything had been forgiven the way they played." You would have thought: only an impression, no doubt, but one of jazz's real gifts to us. (pp. 7-8, 10-11)

Michael Wood, "Life Studies," in The New York Review of Books, *Vol. XXXIX, No. 19, November 19, 1992, pp. 7-8, 10-11.*

AWARD ANNOUNCEMENTS

William Grimes   (essay date 8 October 1993)

[*In the following excerpt, Grimes provides an overview of Morrison's life and career.*]

Toni Morrison, the author of **Song of Solomon, Beloved, Jazz** and other lyrically narrated novels of black American life, has won the 1993 Nobel Prize in Literature. The announcement was made yesterday in Stockholm by the Nobel Committee of the Swedish Academy, which stated that Ms. Morrison "gives life to an essential aspect of American reality" in novels "characterized by visionary force and poetic import."

Calling Ms. Morrison "a literary artist of the first rank," the academy statement went on to say: "She delves into the language itself, a language she wants to liberate from the fetters of race. And she addresses us with the luster of poetry."

Ms. Morrison, 62, is the 90th winner of the prize, which carries a monetary award of $825,000. She is the eighth woman; the last was Nadine Gordimer in 1991. She is the first black woman to receive the prize. Other Americans who have won the prize in the last two decades are Joseph Brodsky, Isaac Bashevis Singer and Saul Bellow.

In a telephone interview from her office at Princeton, N.J., Ms. Morrison said: "This is a palpable tremor of delight for me. It was wholly unexpected and so satisfying. Regardless of what we all say and truly believe about the irrelevance of prizes and their relationship to the real work, nevertheless this is a signal honor for me."

Ms. Morrison, who has taught creative writing at Princeton University since 1989, published her first novel, *The Bluest Eye,* in 1970. Set in her Ohio hometown, it describes a black girl's painful coming of age in a white society.

In her five subsequent novels, she established herself as one of America's leading fiction writers, a gifted, popular storyteller whose troubled characters and their struggles expose the fault lines of a society built on racial prejudice. In her most recent novel, *Jazz,* she left behind the small-town world of her previous novels to tell, using a complex, polyphonic technique, a tale of passion and violence set in Harlem in the 1920's.

Her novel *Beloved,* was an enormous commercial success and won the Pulitzer Prize for fiction in 1988.

"This is a great day for African-Americans, and for Americans in general," said Henry Louis Gates Jr., the chairman of the Afro-American studies department at Harvard University and the co-editor of [*Toni Morrison: Critical Perspectives Past and Present* (1993)] a collection of essays on Ms. Morrison's work.

"Just two centuries ago, the African-American literary tradition was born in slave narratives," he said. "Now our greatest writer has won the Nobel Prize."

Ms. Morrison said: "I was thrilled that my mother is still alive and can share this with me. And I can claim representation in so many areas. I'm a Midwesterner, and everyone in Ohio is excited. I'm also a New Yorker, and a New Jerseyan, and an American, plus I'm an African-American, and a woman. I know it seems like I'm spreading like algae when I put it this way, but I'd like to think of the prize being distributed to these regions and nations and races."

Ms. Morrison was born in Lorain, Ohio, a steel town about 25 miles west of Cleveland. She was named Chloe Anthony Wofford.

She earned a bachelor's degree in English from Howard University in Washington in 1953 and a master's degree in English from Cornell University in 1955. At Cornell, she wrote her thesis on the theme of suicide in the works of William Faulkner and Virginia Woolf.

After leaving Cornell, she embarked on an academic ca-

reer, teaching English at Texas Southern University in Houston and at Howard. While at Howard, she married Harold Morrison, an architect, by whom she has two children, Harold and Slade. The couple divorced in 1964.

In 1965, Ms. Morrison became a textbook editor for a subsidiary of Random House in Syracuse, and two years later she became a trade-book editor at Random House in New York City. She also taught at the State University College at Purchase, N.Y., and at the State University at Albany. In 1987, she was named the Robert F. Goheen Professor in the Humanities Council at Princeton.

In the early 60's, while at Howard, she began writing fiction as part of an informal group of poets and writers who met to discuss their work. She went to one meeting with a short story about a black girl who longed to have blue eyes. The story later evolved into her first novel.

She followed up *The Bluest Eye* with *Sula* (1973), which was nominated for a National Book Award; *Song of Solomon* (1977), which won the National Book Critics Circle Award, and *Tar Baby* (1981).

These works were followed by *Beloved* (1987), the story of a runaway slave who, when captured, cuts her daughter's throat rather than see her grow up in slavery. The book met with enormous popular and critical success.

The novel's failure to win the National Book Award sparked a protest by 48 black writers and critics, who signed a statement published in *The New York Times Book Review* lamenting the fact that Ms. Morrison had been overlooked for the award and had not yet received a Pulitzer Prize. Shortly afterward, Ms. Morrison won the Pulitzer Prize for *Beloved.*

Ms. Morrison has also written many essays and a play. Her most recent work of nonfiction, published last year, is *Playing in the Dark: Whiteness and the Literary Imagination.*

"I think she got the Nobel Prize for two books, essentially, *Beloved* and *Jazz,*" Mr. Gates said. "*Jazz* is a truly brilliant post-modern book. Imagine combining Ellington, Faulkner and Maria Callas. That's the voice that emerges.

"She's a masterful craftsperson, which people tend to overlook. She is as great and as innovative as Faulkner and García Márquez and Woolf. That's why she deserved the Nobel Prize."

Calling Ms. Morrison "a literary artist of the first rank," the Swedish Academy statement went on to say: "She delves into the language itself, a language she wants to liberate from the fetters of race. And she addresses us with the luster of poetry."

—William Grimes

The announcement that Ms. Morrison had won the Nobel Prize came as something of a surprise. Speculation in the Swedish press had swirled around four possible candidates: Seamus Heaney, the Irish poet, who has been considered a front-runner for several years; Hugo Claus, a Belgian poet, playwright and film maker who writes in Flemish; Bei Dao, an exiled Chinese poet, and Ali Ahmed Saeed, a Syrian-born Lebanese poet who writes under the name Adonis.

American writers whose names have surfaced from time to time are Joyce Carol Oates and Thomas Pynchon.

Ms. Morrison said she had risen about 4:30 A.M. yesterday to write and was startled to hear the phone ring a few hours later. "I knew it was terrible news," she said. "And when a friend of mine on the other end said 'Did you hear?' then I knew it was something awful. It took a long time for me to accept it."

Some hours later, the permanent secretary of the Swedish Academy called her to confirm that she had won the prize and told her that a letter would be on its way.

"I said, 'Why don't you send me a fax?' " Ms. Morrison said, laughing. "Somehow, I felt that if I saw a fax, I'd know it wasn't a dream or somebody's hallucination. I'll tell you one thing: we're going to have a big party here tonight." (pp. A1, B10)

William Grimes, "Toni Morrison Is '93 Winner of Nobel Prize in Literature," in The New York Times, *October 8, 1993, pp. A1, B10.*

The Observer (essay date 10 October 1993)

[*In the following essay, the critic discusses the Swedish Academy's motives in awarding Morrison the Nobel Prize and provides a brief overview of the author's career.*]

'Pain I seem to have an affection, a kind of sweet tooth for it,' says the narrator of Toni Morrison's last novel, *Jazz.* 'Remembering seemed unwise,' says the central character in Toni Morrison's *Beloved,* who struggled each waking day to blot out 'unspeakable' past.

America regards itself as a new and innocent country, without memory or guilt, but the black American winner of the 1993 Nobel Prize for Literature—first African-American ever to win the award—is a long-memoried writer. In each of her six novels she excavates the past, tunneling through atrocities and griefs to reach back into an American history that has been long buried. The denied past becomes a ghost that haunts the present; old bones won't stay safely underground.

Toni Morrison's fierce resistance to racism, which informs all of her writing, has led critics to dub her racism's 'avenging angel'. She is treated by many admirers as the representative of a whole section of society; readers worship her; critics abandon judgment for superlatives. Friends and colleagues describe her in terms of excess—'awe inspiring, she looks like a mountain and laughs like Whoopi Goldberg' (writer and Princeton colleague Paul Watkins); 'magnificent, utterly magnificent' (Morrison's

overjoyed editor Carmen Callil); 'sweet and powerful' (Walter Mosley, the black detective novelist and President Clinton's favourite writer).

This adoration is double-edged, a curse as well as a gift. As Salman Rushdie points out (and he should know better than anyone), elevating Morrison into a flawless representative of black suffering allows us to undervalue her importance as a great writer. Already, the announcement of the Swedish Academy's Nobel Prize has produced a flurry of confused reactions.

Christopher Bigsby, Professor of American Studies at East Anglia and an admirer of Morrison's work, said that the award smacks of 'political correctness'. Per Wästberg, the senior Swedish critic, ex-chair of Pen (the international writers organisation), and antiapartheid activist, is anxious that the Nobel award is 'opportunist and populist' since the two winners before Morrison, West Indian Derek Walcott and South African Nadine Gordimer, also write about racial oppression. He reports that the unofficial shortlist included Belgium's Hugo Claus, South America's Carlos Fuentes, America's John Ashbery and John Updike, Ireland's Seamus Heaney, and Japan's Kenzabore Oe ('Japan will be furious; they always think it is their turn').

The joyless spectre of political correctness may haunt this award, but Toni Morrison stands clear of the debate like a boulder in a fast, shallow stream. She recently dissociated herself from the National Association for the Advancement of Colored Peoples' attempt to censor *Huckleberry Finn* (principally for its repeated use of the word 'nigger'), chastising their literal reading of a classic book.

She edited a collection of essays [*Race-ing Justice, Engendering Power* (1992)] about the Clarence Thomas/Anita Hill affair, in which she herself took up an awkwardly complicated position, confounding both sides. She's been criticised by some feminists for an alleged lack of commitment to female solidarity—she has famously argued with a black American writer, June Jordan, over the conflict between anti-racism and feminism.

Her novels defy both the PC lobby and its opponents. Although they deal with situations bound to appeal to a facile liberal imagination (especially slavery, racism and sexual abuse), they never sag with the political freight of their themes. Morrison says that black writers no longer have to rely upon the patronage of white readers. She explicitly writes for black people ('people like me'), but is nevertheless a national writer. Carmen Callil says that 'she writes magnificently about obsessive love, children, parents, husbands and wives—and it doesn't actually matter whether or not she's black or she's a woman.'

Her two latest novels, *Beloved* and *Jazz* (and her next, *Paradise*), rewrite the imaginative history of America. In each, the grief of the past is forever treading on the heels of the present. In *Beloved,* slavery is the scratch in the groove which condemns the characters endlessly to replay their terrible history. A mother, Sethe, is haunted by the ghost of the child she has killed (because in this white world death becomes the safest place for it). In *Jazz,* set in 1926 Harlem where on every corner musicians beat out the improvising music of high hopes, the replays of sexual obsession and betrayal come to stand for black urban uprootedness and submerged black anguish. *Paradise* will be set in the Seventies and Eighties; at its centre will be Vietnam, the war fought by an army in which America's blacks were so disproportionately represented.

As both Salman Rushdie and the critic Lorna Sage point out, Morrison has invented a new language which is both demotic and rhapsodically poetic—colloquial, biblical, full of the rhythms of gospel music and curdling charm of the blues, swooping from domestic to tragic without a catch. As Rushdie insists, she has really won the award for her writing, 'which she created out of black experience but which enriches the whole of literature'. And Lorna Sage adds: 'On her pages, you can hear many different voices; she draws on oral traditions, folk tales, ghost stories, and in her last novel the improvisations of jazz.'

Carmen Callil, who spoke to Morrison one minute after the prize announcement, just before she turned on her answering machine, said that she sounded 'very very very happy'. Through her New York publishers, Morrison told the waiting world that the award had made her 'unendurably happy' (a typical congruence of pain and joy),—and added that she was glad her mother was 'alive to see this day'.

Morrison's family has been very important to the 62-year-old writer. She was born, the second child in a family of four, Chloe Anthony Wofford (and has told journalists that she remains Chloe Wofford in her heart) in the steel town of Lorain, Ohio.

She was a child of depression and segregation, whose father 'distrusted every word and every gesture of every white man on earth'. But her mother, who would write to President Roosevelt if there were maggots in the flour, believed in the possibility of change. Morrison has said that she grew up with 'more than a child's contempt for white people'. An old blues song refrain goes: 'If it weren't for bad luck I'd have no luck at all', but one of the characters in her novel, *Song of Solomon,* simply says that 'there is no bad luck but white folks'. She pulled herself up through the academic route of the all-black University, Howard, and Cornell (where she did a study of the works of William Faulkner, the southern writer who has had a strong influence on her writing) and then went on to teach English at Princeton.

Compared with the literary brat pack of America, Morrison started writing late. She was nearly 40, with two degrees, two children, and a failed marriage when she published her first novel, *The Bluest Eye.* In 1978, *Song of Solomon* won the National Book Critics Circle Award. In 1988, *Beloved* won the Pulitzer Prize.

Her course has been slow and steady. Whereas Alice Walker, another black American woman writer, has succumbed to New Ageist, politically correct psychobabble and Maya Angelou has indefatigably turned her extraordinary life into an epically self-dramatising autobiography, Morrison remains an essentially private writer.

When she is not writing, she teaches at the Ivy League university of Princeton (alongside Russell Banks and Joyce Carol Oates). One colleague has said that Morrison's fellow Princeton writers are not unanimously delighted: as Gore Vidal once wrote, 'if a contemporary succeeds, a little part of me dies'. Morrison has said that she wants her work to be 'a private thing for public consumption', and unlike many African-American writers, she resists the literature of self-revelation. Hers is a historically-based imagination—although she has said that she feels the suffering of others in her bones. . . .

[In] the glare of success, [Morrison] seems likely to stand firm: a big woman with a quiet voice who has looked with open eyes at things from which most of us turn away—and transformed them into literature that most of us cannot put down.

> *"Laureate-poet of America's Pain," in* The Observer, *October 10, 1993, p. 23.*

David Gates, Danzy Senna, and Lynn James (essay date 18 October 1993)

[*In the essay below, the critics discuss the thematic and political implications of Morrison's works.*]

Toni Morrison got the news last Thursday when a friend called at 7 a.m. "I couldn't figure out what she was trying to tell me," says Morrison. "I thought she was hallucinating." No writer of Morrison's stature and age (62) can help feeling a twinge this time of year. But the 1993 Nobel Prize in Literature seemed likely to go to one of the light heavyweights who've been touted for years: V. S. Naipaul, Doris Lessing, Seamus Heaney or perhaps even Margaret Atwood, Thomas Pynchon or Joyce Carol Oates. In retrospect it's odd that Morrison, probably the chief literary heir of William Faulkner (Nobel Prize, 1949) and unquestionably the most distinguished black American novelist since Ralph Ellison and James Baldwin, wasn't talked about as a contender. But never before had an African-American won the Nobel Prize, nor had any American woman since Pearl S. Buck in 1938. Morrison's surprise that the daughter of one-time Alabama sharecroppers had become a Nobel laureate rings true; so does her insistence that this is more than a personal victory. "I hope it says something about the evolution of African-American writing," she says, "that it's no longer outside the central enterprise, that it speaks about things that matter to anyone."

The Nobel Prize should be more than ample recompense for the prize Morrison is famous for *not* getting: the 1987 National Book Award, which went to Larry Heinemann's *Paco's Story,* rather than to Morrison's *Beloved.* Forty-eight black writers and critics signed a statement protesting the neglect by major awards panels; later that year *Beloved* won the Pulitzer Prize. Morrison, in fact, has long had at least a modest place in the literary establishment: she's been a graduate student at Cornell (her 1955 master's thesis was on Faulkner and Virginia Woolf), a trade-book editor at Random House and, since 1987, a professor of humanities at Princeton. Her six novels, from *The Bluest Eye* (1970) to *Jazz* (1992), reflect the scholarship of the academy and the craftsmanship of the publishing house as well as an outsider's outrage. Morrison is above all a great synthesizer: in her novels the sensibility of the African diaspora melds with the mainstream of American literary tradition.

But the undeniable political significance of Morrison's work—and now, of the Swedish Academy's imprimatur—tends to obscure its literary significance. "The Nobel Prize in Literature is not awarded for gender or race," says Nadine Gordimer, the last woman to win the prize, in 1991. "If it were, many thousands of mediocre writers might qualify. The significance of Toni Morrison's winning the prize is simply that she is recognized internationally as an outstandingly fine writer." While Morrison writes about black women with ferocious reverence, her rhapsodic novels don't traffic in uplift; in *Beloved,* for instance, a mother kills her child rather than have her live in slavery. For Morrison, liberation comes in the act of writing. "Our silence has been long and deep," she told *Newsweek* last week. "In canonical literature, we have always been spoken for. Or we have been spoken *to.* Or we have appeared as jokes or as flat figures suggesting sensuality. Today we are taking back the narrative, telling our story."

It's arguable, of course, that on the brink of the 21st century, narratives are no longer worth appropriating, by women of color or anybody else; that they're being sound-bitten, hypertexted and MTV'd into irrelevance. But don't argue that with Morrison. "The narrative line is the way we understand the world," she says. "So all these announcements about the diminished need or importance of novels are premature."

Now that Morrison has the Nobel, she can start worrying about less theoretical problems—like what to do with the $825,000 that goes with it. "This is new to me, having to decide what to do with money," she says, laughing. "I have no history of having to make such decisions." A more insidious concern is how heavily the world's highest literary honor, heaped on top of the fame she already has, will weigh on her when she sits down to write. "That's a real fear," she says, "but I'm fortunate because I had begun something extremely important to me last year—a new novel that has engaged me thoroughly." If there's any doubt that Toni Morrison can survive even the Nobel Prize, consider her answer when asked which of her books she loves most. She says, "The one I'm not talking to you about."

David Gates with Danzy Senna and Lynn James, "Keep Your Eyes on the Prize," in Newsweek, *Vol. CXXII, No. 16, October 18, 1993, p. 89.*

INTERVIEW

Toni Morrison with Elissa Schappell   (interview date Fall 1993)

[*Schappell is an American educator and free-lance writer. In the excerpt below, Morrison discusses such subjects as her writing technique, how she became a writer, and African-American culture.*]

[*Schappell*]: *You have said that you begin to write before dawn. Did this habit begin for practical reasons, or was the early morning an especially fruitful time for you?*

[Morrison]: Writing before dawn began as a necessity—I had small children when I first began to write, and I needed to use the time before they said, "Mama"—and that was always around five in the morning. Many years later, after I stopped working [as an editor] at Random House, I just stayed at home for a couple of years. I discovered things about myself I had never thought about before. At first I didn't know when I wanted to eat, because I had always eaten when it was lunchtime or dinnertime or breakfast-time. Work and the children had driven all of my habits . . . I didn't know the weekday sounds of my own house; it all made me feel a little giddy.

I was involved in writing *Beloved* at that time—this was in 1983—and eventually I realized that I was clearer-headed, more confident and generally more intelligent in the morning. The habit of getting up early, which I had formed when the children were young, now became my choice. I am not very bright or very witty or very inventive after the sun goes down.

Recently I was talking to a writer who described something she did whenever she moved to her writing table. I don't remember exactly what the gesture was—there is something on her desk that she touches before she hit the computer keyboard—but we began to talk about little rituals that one goes through before beginning to write. I, at first, thought I didn't have a ritual, but then I remembered that I always get up and make a cup of coffee while it is still dark—it must be dark—and then I drink the coffee and watch the light come. And she said, well, that's a ritual. And I realized that for me this ritual comprises my preparation to enter a space that I can only call nonsecular. . . . Writers all devise ways to approach that place where they expect to make the contact, where they become the conduit, or where they engage in this mysterious process. For me, light is the signal in the transition. It's not being *in* the light, it's being there *before it arrives.* It enables me, in some sense.

I tell my students one of the most important things they need to know is when they are their best, creatively. They need to ask themselves, What does the ideal room look like? Is there music? Is there silence? Is there chaos outside or is there serenity outside? What do I need in order to release my imagination?

What about your writing routine?

I have an ideal writing routine that I've never experienced, which is to have, say, nine uninterrupted days when I wouldn't have to leave the house or take phone calls. And to have the space: a space where I have huge tables. I end up with this much space (*she indicates a small square spot on her desk*) everywhere I am, and I can't beat my way out of it. I am reminded of that tiny desk that Emily Dickinson wrote on, and I chuckle when I think, "Sweet thing, there she was." But that is all any of us have—just this small space and no matter what the filing system or how often you clear it out, life, documents, letters, requests, invitations, invoices just keep going back in. I am not able to write regularly. I have never been able to do that—mostly because I have always had a nine-to-five job. I had to write either in between those hours, hurriedly, or spend a lot of weekend and predawn time.

Could you write after work?

That was difficult. I've tried to overcome not having orderly spaces by substituting compulsion for discipline, so that when something is urgently there, urgently seen or understood, or the metaphor was powerful enough, then I would move everything aside and write for sustained periods of time. I'm talking to you about getting the first draft.

You have to do it straight through?

I do. I don't think it's a law.

Could you write on the bottom of a shoe while riding on a train like Robert Frost? Could you write on an airplane?

Sometimes something that I was having some trouble with falls into place, a word sequence, say, so I've written on scraps of paper, in hotels on hotel stationery, in automobiles. *If* it arrives you *know.* If you know it *really* has come then you *have* to put it down. (pp. 86-8)

Do you ever read your work out loud while you are working on it?

Not until it's published. I don't trust a performance. I could get a response that might make me think it was successful when it wasn't at all. The difficulty for me in writing—*among* the difficulties—is to write language that can work quietly on a page for a reader who doesn't hear anything. Now for that, one has to work very carefully with what is *in between* the words. What is not said. Which is measure, which is rhythm and so on. So, it is what you don't write that frequently gives what you do write its power.

How many times would you say you have to write a paragraph over to reach this standard?

Well, those that need reworking I do as long as I can. I mean I've revised six times, seven times, thirteen times. But there's a line between revision and fretting, just working it to death. It is important to know when you are fretting it; when you are fretting it because it is not working, it needs to be scrapped.

Do you ever go back over what has been published and wish you had fretted more over something?

A lot. Everything.

Do you ever rework passages that have already been published before reading them to an audience?

I don't change it for the audience, but I know what it ought to be and isn't. After twenty some years you can figure it out; I know more about it now than I did then. It is not so much that it would have been different or even better; it is just that, taken into context with what I was trying to effect, or what consequence I wanted it to have on the reader, years later the picture is clearer to me.

How do you think being an editor for twenty years affected you as a writer?

I am not sure. It lessened my awe of the publishing industry. I understood the adversarial relationship that sometimes exists between writers and publishers, but I learned how important, how critical an editor was, which I don't think I would have known before.

Are there editors who are helpful critically?

Oh yes. The good ones make all the difference. It is like a priest or a psychiatrist; if you get the wrong one then you are better off alone. But there are editors so rare and so important that they are worth searching for, and you always know when you have one.

Who was the most instrumental editor you've ever worked with?

I had a very good editor, superlative for me—Bob Gottlieb. What made him good for me was a number of things: knowing what not to touch; asking all the questions you probably would have asked yourself had there been the time. Good editors are really the third eye. Cool. Dispassionate. They don't love you or your work; for me that is what is valuable—not compliments. Sometimes it's uncanny: the editor puts his or her finger on exactly the place the writer knows is weak but just couldn't do any better at the time. Or perhaps the writer thought it might fly, but wasn't sure. Good editors identify that place, and sometimes make suggestions. Some suggestions are not useful because you can't explain everything to an editor about what you are trying to do. I couldn't possibly explain all of those things to an editor, because what I do has to work on so many levels. But within the relationship if there is some trust, some willingness to listen, remarkable things can happen. I read books all the time that I know would have profited from, not a copy editor, but somebody just talking through it. And it is important to get a great editor at a certain time, because if you don't have one in the beginning, you almost can't have one later. If you work well without an editor, and your books are well received for five or ten years, and then you write another one, which is successful but not very good, why should you then listen to an editor?

You have told students that they should think of the process of revision as one of the major satisfactions of writing. Do you get more pleasure out of writing the first draft, or in the actual revision of the work?

They are different. I am profoundly excited by thinking up or having the idea in the first place . . . before I begin to write.

> I tell my writing students one of the most important things they need to know is when they are their best, creatively. They need to ask themselves, What does the ideal room look like? Is there music? Is there silence? Is there chaos outside or is there serenity outside? What do I need in order to release my imagination?
>
> —*Toni Morrison*

Does it come in a flash?

No, it's a sustained thing I have to play with. I always start out with an idea, even a boring idea, that becomes a question I don't have any answers to. Specifically, since I began the **Beloved** trilogy, the last part of which I'm working on now, I have been wondering why women who are twenty, thirty years younger than I am, are no happier than women who are my age and older. What on earth is that about, when there are so many more things that they can do, so many more choices? *All right,* so this is an embarrassment of riches, but so what. Why is everybody so miserable?

Do you write to figure out exactly how you feel about a subject?

No, I know how I *feel.* My feelings are the result of prejudices and convictions like everybody else's. But I am interested in the complexity, the vulnerability of an idea. It is not: "This is what I believe," because that would not be a book, just a tract. A book is: "This may be what I believe, but suppose I am wrong . . . what could it be?" Or, "I don't know what it is, but I am interested in finding out what it might mean to me, as well as to other people."

Did you know as a child you wanted to be a writer?

No. I wanted to be a reader. I thought everything that needed to be written had already been written or would be. I only wrote the first book because I thought it wasn't there, and I wanted to read it when I got through. I am a pretty good reader. I love it. It is what I do, really. So, if I can read it, that is the highest compliment I can think of. People say, "I write for myself," and it sounds so awful and so narcissistic, but in a sense if you know how to read your own work—that is, with the necessary critical distance—it makes you a better writer and editor. When I teach creative writing, I always speak about how you have to learn how to read your work; I don't mean enjoy it because you wrote it. I mean, go away from it, and read it as though it is the first time you've ever seen it. Critique it that way. Don't get all involved in your thrilling sentences and all that . . .

Do you have your audience in mind when you sit down to write?

Only me. If I come to a place where I am unsure, I have the characters to go to for reassurance. By that time they are friendly enough to tell me if the rendition of their lives is authentic or not. But there are so many things only I can tell. After all, this is my work. I have to take full responsibility for doing it right as well as doing it wrong. Doing it wrong isn't bad, but doing it wrong and thinking you've done it right is. I remember spending a whole summer writing something I was very impressed with, but couldn't get back to until winter. I went back confident that those fifty pages were really first-rate, but when I read them, each page of the fifty was terrible. It was really ill-conceived. I knew that I could do it over, but I just couldn't get over the fact that I thought it was so good at the time. And that is scary because then you think it means you don't know. (pp. 89-94)

When did it become clear to you that your gift was to be a writer?

It was very late. I always thought I was probably adept, because people used to say so, but their criteria might not have been mine. So, I wasn't interested in what they said. It meant nothing. It was by the time I was writing **Song of Solomon,** the third book, that I began to think that this was the central part of my life. Not to say that other women haven't said it all along, but for a woman to say, "I am a writer" is difficult.

Why?

Well, it isn't so difficult *anymore,* but it certainly was for me, and for women of my generation or my class or my race. I don't know that all those things are folded into it, but the point is you're moving yourself out of the gender role. You are not saying, "I am a mother, I am a wife." Or, if you're in the labor market, "I am a teacher, I am an editor." But when you move to "writer" what is that supposed to mean? Is that a job? Is this the way you make your living? It's an intervention into terrain that you are not familiar with—where you have no provenance. At the time I certainly didn't personally know any other women writers who were successful; it looked very much like a male preserve. So you sort of hope you're going to be a little minor person around the edges. It's almost as if you needed permission to write. When I read women's biographies and autobiographies, even accounts of how they got started writing, almost every one of them had a little anecdote which told about the moment someone gave them permission to do it. A mother, a husband, a teacher . . . somebody said, "Okay, go ahead—you can do it." Which is not to say that men have never needed that; frequently when they are very young, a mentor says, "You're good," and they take off. The entitlement was something they could take for granted. I couldn't. It was all very strange. So, even though I knew that writing was central to my life, that it was where my mind was, where I was most delighted and most challenged, I couldn't say it. If someone asked me, "What do you do?" I wouldn't say, "Oh I'm a writer." I'd say, "I'm an editor, or a teacher." Because when you meet people and go to lunch, if they say "What do you do?" and you say, "I'm a writer," they have to think about that, and then they ask, "What have you written?" Then they have to either like it, or not like it. People feel obliged to like or not like and say so. It is perfectly all right to hate my work. It really is. I have close friends whose work I loathe.

Did you feel you had to write in private?

Oh yes, I wanted to make it a private thing. I wanted to own it myself. Because once you say it, then other people become involved. (pp. 96-7)

You mentioned getting permission to write. Who gave it to you?

No one. What I needed permission to do was to succeed at it. I never signed a contract until the book was finished because I didn't want it to be homework. A contract meant somebody was waiting for it, that I *had* to do it, and they could ask me about it. They could get up in my face, and I don't like that. By not signing a contract, I do it, and if I want you to see it, I'll let you see it. It has to do with self-esteem. I am sure for years you have heard writers constructing illusions of freedom, anything in order to have the illusion that it is all mine, and only I can do it. I remember introducing Eudora Welty and saying that nobody could have written those stories but her, meaning that I have a feeling about most books that at some point somebody would have written them *anyway*. But then there are some writers without whom certain stories would never have been written. I don't mean the subject matter or the narrative but just the way in which they did it—their slant on it is truly unique.

Who are some of them?

Hemingway is in that category, Flannery O'Connor. Faulkner, Fitzgerald . . .

Haven't you been critical of the way these authors depicted blacks?

No! Me, critical? I have been revealing how white writers imagine black people, and some of them are brilliant at it. Faulkner was brilliant at it. Hemingway did it poorly in places and brilliantly elsewhere.

How so?

In not using black characters, but using the aesthetic of blacks as anarchy, as sexual license, as deviance. In his last book, *The Garden of Eden,* Hemingway's heroine is getting blacker and blacker. The woman who is going mad tells her husband, "I want to be your little African Queen." The novel gets its charge that way: "Her white white hair and her black, black skin" . . . almost like a Man Ray photograph. Mark Twain talked about racial ideology in the most powerful, eloquent and instructive way I have ever read. Edgar Allan Poe did not. He loved white supremacy and the planter class, and he wanted to be a gentleman, and he endorsed all of that. He didn't contest it, or critique it. What is exciting about American literature is that business of how writers say things under, beneath and around their stories. Think of *Pudd'nhead Wilson* and all these inversions of what race is, how sometimes nobody can tell, or the thrill of discovery? Faulkner in *Absalom, Absalom!* spends the entire book tracing race, and you can't find it. No one can see it, even the character who *is* black can't see it. I did this lecture for my students that took me forever, which was tracking all the moments of withheld, partial or disinformation, when a racial fact or clue *sort* of comes out but doesn't quite arrive. I just

wanted to chart it. I listed its appearance, disguise and disappearance on every page, I mean every phrase! Everything, and I delivered this thing to my class. They all fell asleep! But I was so fascinated, technically. Do you know how hard it is to withhold that kind of information but hinting, pointing all of the time? And then to reveal it in order to say that it is *not* the point anyway? It is technically just astonishing. As a reader you have been forced to hunt for a drop of black blood that means everything and nothing. The insanity of racism. So the structure is the argument. Not what this one says, or that one says . . . it is the *structure* of the book, and you are there hunting this black thing that is nowhere to be found, and yet makes all the difference. No one has done anything quite like that ever. So, when I critique, what I am saying is, I don't care if Faulkner is a racist or not; I don't personally care, but I am fascinated by what it means to write like this.

What about black writers . . . how do they write in a world dominated by and informed by their relationship to a white culture?

By trying to alter language, simply to free it up, not to repress it or confine it, but to open it up. Tease it. Blast its racist straitjacket. I wrote a story entitled **"Recitatif,"** in which there are two little girls in an orphanage, one white and one black. But the reader doesn't know which is white and which is black. I use class codes, but no racial codes.

Is this meant to confuse the reader?

Well, yes. But to provoke and enlighten. I did that as a lark. What was exciting was to be forced as a writer not to be lazy and rely on obvious codes. Soon as I say, "Black woman . . ." I can rest on or provoke predictable responses, but if I leave it out then I have to talk about her in a complicated way—as a person. (pp. 99-102)

You must have read a lot of slave narratives for **Beloved.**

I wouldn't read them for information because I knew that they had to be authenticated by white patrons, that they couldn't say everything they wanted to say because they couldn't alienate their audience; they had to be quiet about certain things. They were going to be as good as they could be under the circumstances and as revelatory, but they never say how terrible it was. They would just say, "Well, you know, it was really awful, but let's abolish slavery so life can go on." Their narratives had to be very understated. So while I looked at the documents and felt *familiar* with slavery and overwhelmed by it, I wanted it to be truly *felt*. I wanted to translate the historical into the personal. I spent a long time trying to figure out what it was about slavery that made it so repugnant, so personal, so indifferent, so intimate and yet so public.

In reading some of the documents I noticed frequent references to something that was never properly described—*the bit*. This thing was put into the mouth of slaves to punish them and shut them up without preventing them from working. I spent a long time trying to find out what it looked like. I kept reading statements like, "I put the bit on Jenny," or, as Equiano says, "I went into a kitchen" and I saw a woman standing at the stove, and she had a brake, (b-r-a-k-e, he spells it) "in her mouth," and I said,

"What is that?" and somebody told me what it was, and then I said, "I never saw anything so awful in all my life." But I really couldn't image the thing—did it look like a horse's bit or what?

Eventually I did find some sketches in one book in this country, which was the record of a man's torture of his wife. In South America, Brazil, places like that, they kept such mementos. But while I was searching, something else occurred to me, namely that this bit, this item, this personalized type of torture, was a direct descendant of the inquisition. And I realized that of course you can't buy this stuff. You can't send away for a mail-order bit for your slave. Sears doesn't carry them. So you have to make it. You have to go out in the backyard and put some stuff together and construct it and then affix it to a person. So the whole process had a very personal quality for the person who made it, as well as for the person who wore it. Then I realized that describing it would never be helpful: that the reader didn't need to *see* it so much as *feel* what it was like. I realized that it was important to imagine the bit as an active instrument, rather than simply as a curio or an historical fact. And in the same way I wanted to show the reader what slavery *felt* like, rather than how it looked.

There's a passage in which Paul D. says to Sethe, "I've never told anybody about it, I've sung about it sometimes." He tries to tell her what wearing the bit was like, but he ends up talking about a rooster that he swears smiled at him when he wore it—he felt cheapened and lessened and that he would never be worth as much as a rooster sitting on a tub in the sunlight. I make other references to the desire to spit, to sucking iron and so on; but it seemed to me that describing what it *looked* like would distract the reader from what I wanted him or her to experience, which was what it *felt* like. The kind of information you can find between the lines of history. It sort of falls off the page, or it's a glance and a reference. It's right there in the intersection where an institution becomes personal, where the historical becomes people with names.

When you create a character is it completely created out of your own imagination?

I never use anyone I know. In **The Bluest Eye** I think I used some gestures and dialogue of my mother in certain places, and a little geography. I've never done that since. I really am very conscientious about that. It's never based on anyone. I don't do what many writers do.

Why is that?

There is this feeling that artists have—photographers more than other people, and writers—that they are acting like a succubus . . . this process of taking from something that's alive and using it for one's own purposes. You can do it with trees, butterflies or human beings. Making a little life for oneself by scavenging other people's lives is a big question, and it does have moral and ethical implications.

In fiction, I feel the most intelligent, and the most free, and the most excited, when my characters are fully invented people. That's part of the excitement. If they're based on somebody else, in a funny way it's an infringement of a copyright. That person *owns* his life, has a patent on it. It shouldn't be available for fiction.

Do you ever feel like your characters are getting away from you, out of your control?

I take control of them. They are very carefully imagined. I feel as though I know all there is to know about them, even things I don't write—like how they part their hair. They are like ghosts. They have nothing on their minds but themselves and aren't interested in anything but themselves. So you can't let them write your book for you. I have read books in which I know that has happened—when a novelist has been totally taken over by a character. I want to say, "You can't do that. If those people could write books they would, but they can't. *You* can." So, you have to say, "Shut up. Leave me alone. I am doing this."

Have you ever had to tell any of your characters to shut up?

Pilate, I did. Therefore she doesn't speak very much. She has this long conversation with the two boys, and every now and then she'll say something, but she doesn't have the dialogue the other people have. I had to do that, otherwise she was going to overwhelm everybody. She got terribly interesting; characters can do that for a little bit. I had to take it back. It's *my* book; it's not called *Pilate*.

Pilate is such a strong character. It seems to me that the women in your books are almost always stronger and braver than the men. Why is that?

That isn't true, but I hear that a lot. I think that our expectations of women are very low. If women just stand up straight for thirty days, everybody goes, "Oh! How brave!" As a matter of fact, somebody wrote about Sethe, and said she was this powerful, statuesque woman who wasn't even human. But at the end of the book, she can barely turn her head. She has been zonked; she can't even feed herself. Is that tough? (pp. 103-07)

> In fiction, I feel the most intelligent, and the most free, and the most excited, when my characters are fully invented people. That's part of the excitement. If they're based on somebody else, in a funny way it's an infringement of a copyright. That person *owns* his life, has a patent on it. It shouldn't be available for fiction.
>
> —*Toni Morrison*

Why do writers have such a hard time writing about sex?

Sex is difficult to write about because it's just not sexy enough. The only way to write about it is not to write much. Let the reader bring his own sexuality into the text. A writer I usually admire has written about sex in the most off-putting way. There is just too much information. If you start saying "the curve of . . ." you soon sound like a gynecologist. Only Joyce could get away with that. He said all those forbidden words. He said *cunt,* and that was shocking. The forbidden word can be provocative. But after a while it becomes monotonous rather than arousing. Less is always better. Some writers think that if they use dirty words they've done it. It can work for a short period and for a very young imagination, but after a while it doesn't deliver. When Sethe and Paul D. first see each other, in about half a page they get the sex out of the way, which isn't any good anyway—it's fast, and they're embarrassed about it—and then they're lying there trying to pretend they're not in that bed, that they haven't met, and then they begin to think different thoughts, which begin to merge so you can't tell who's thinking what. That merging to me is more tactically sensual than if I had tried to describe body parts.

What about plot? Do you always know where you're going? Would you write the end before you got there?

When I really know what it is about, then I can write that end scene. I wrote the end of *Beloved* about a quarter of the way in. I wrote the end of *Jazz* very early and the end of *Song of Solomon* very early on. What I really want is for the plot to be *how* it happened. It is like a detective story in a sense. You know who is dead and you want to find out who did it. So, you put the salient elements up front, and the reader is hooked into wanting to know, How did that happen? Who did that and why? You are forced into having a certain kind of language that will keep the reader asking those questions. In *Jazz,* just as I did before with *The Bluest Eye,* I put the whole plot on the first page. In fact, in the first edition the plot was on the cover, so that a person in a bookstore could read the cover and know right away what the book was about, and could, if they wished, dismiss it and buy another book. This seemed a suitable technique for *Jazz* because I thought of the plot in that novel—the threesome—as the melody of the piece, and it is fine to follow a melody—to feel the satisfaction of recognizing a melody whenever the narrator returns to it. That was the real art of the enterprise for me: bumping up against that melody time and again, seeing it from another point of view, seeing it afresh each time, playing it back and forth.

When Keith Jarrett plays "Ol' Man River," the delight and satisfaction is not so much in the melody itself but in recognizing it when it surfaces and when it is hidden and when it goes away completely, what is put in its place. Not so much in the original line as in all the echoes and shades and turns and pivots Jarrett plays around it. I was trying to do something similar with the plot in *Jazz.* I wanted the story to be the vehicle which moved us from page one to the end, but I wanted the delight to be found in moving away from the story and coming back to it, looking around it, and through it, as though it were a prism, constantly turning.

This playful aspect of *Jazz* may well cause a great deal of dissatisfaction in readers who just want the melody, who want to know what happened, who did it and why. But the jazz-like structure wasn't a secondary thing for me—it was the raison d'être of the book. The process of trial and error by which the narrator revealed the plot was as important and exciting to me as telling the story.

You also divulge the plot early on in **Beloved.**

It seemed important to me that the action in *Beloved*—the fact of infanticide—be immediately known, but deferred, unseen. I wanted to give the reader all the information and the consequences surrounding the act, while avoiding engorging myself or the reader with the violence itself. I remember writing the sentence where Sethe cuts the throat of the child very, very late in the process of writing the book. I remember getting up from the table and walking outside for a long time—walking around the yard and coming back and revising it a little bit and going back out and in and rewriting the sentence over and over again . . . each time I fixed that sentence so that it was exactly right, or so I thought, but then I would be unable to sit there and would have to go away and come back. I thought that the act itself had to be not only buried but also understated, because if the language was going to compete with the violence itself it would be obscene or pornographic.

Style is obviously very important to you. Can you talk about this in relation to **Jazz?**

With *Jazz,* I wanted to convey the sense that a musician conveys—that he has more but he's not gonna give it to you. It's an exercise in restraint, a holding back—not because it's not there, or because one had exhausted it, but because of the riches, and because it can be done again. That sense of knowing when to stop is a learned thing, and I didn't always have it. It was probably not until after I wrote *Song of Solomon* that I got to feeling secure enough to experience what it meant to be thrifty with images and language and so on. I was very conscious in writing *Jazz* of trying to blend that which is contrived and artificial with improvisation. I thought of myself as like the jazz musician: someone who practices and practices and practices in order to be able to invent and to make his art look effortless and graceful. I was always conscious of the constructed aspect of the writing process, and that art appears natural and elegant only as a result of constant practice and awareness of its formal structures. You must practice thrift in order to achieve that luxurious quality of wastefulness—that sense that you have enough to waste, that you are holding back—without actually wasting anything. You shouldn't overgratify, you should never satiate. I've always felt that that peculiar sense of hunger at the end of a piece of art—a yearning for more—is really very, very powerful. But there is at the same time a kind of contentment, knowing that at some other time there will indeed be more because the artist is endlessly inventive.

Were there other . . . ingredients, structural entities?

Well, it seems to me that migration was a major event in the cultural history of this country. Now I'm being very speculative about all of this—I guess that's why I write novels—but it seems to me something modern and new happened after the Civil War. Of course, a number of things changed, but the era was most clearly marked by the disowning and dispossession of ex-slaves. These ex-slaves were sometimes taken into their local labor markets, but they often tried to escape their problems by migrating to the city. I was fascinated by the thought of what the city must have meant to them, these second and third generation ex-slaves, to rural people living there in their own number. The city must have seemed so exciting and wonderful, so much the place to be.

I was interested in how the city worked. How classes and groups and nationalities had the security of numbers within their own turfs and territories, but also felt the thrill of knowing that there were other turfs and other territories, and felt the real glamor and excitement of being in this throng. I was interested in how music changed in this country. Spirituals and gospel and blues represented one kind of response to slavery—they gave voice to the yearning for escape, in code, literally on the underground railroad.

I was also concerned with personal life. How did people love one another? What did they think was free? At that time, when the ex-slaves were moving into the city, running away from something that was constricting and killing them and dispossessing them over and over and over again, they were in a very limiting environment. But when you listen to their music—the beginnings of jazz—you realized that they are talking about something else. They are talking about love, about loss. But there is such grandeur, such satisfaction in those lyrics . . . they're never happy—somebody's always leaving—but they're not whining. It's as though the whole tragedy of choosing somebody, risking love, risking emotion, risking sensuality, and then losing it all didn't matter, since it was their choice. Exercising choice in who you love was a major, major thing. And the music reinforced the idea of love as a space where one could negotiate freedom.

Obviously, jazz was considered—as all new music is—to be devil music; too sensual and provocative, and so on. But for some black people jazz meant claiming their own bodies. You can image what that must have meant for people whose bodies had been owned, who had been slaves as children, or who remembered their parents being slaves. Blues and jazz represented ownership of one's own emotions. So of course it is excessive and overdone: tragedy in jazz is relished, almost as though a happy ending would take away some of its glamour, its flair. Now advertisers use jazz on television to communicate authenticity and modernity; to say "trust me," and to say "hip."

These days the city still retains the quality of excitement it had in the jazz age, only now we associate that excitement with a different kind of danger. We chant and scream and act alarmed about the homeless; we say we want our streets back, but it is from our awareness of homelessness and our employment of strategies to deal with it that we get our sense of the urban. Feeling as though we have the armor, the shields, the movie, the strength, the toughness and the smarts to be engaged and survive encounters with the unpredictable, the alien, the strange and the violent is an intrinsic part of what it means to live in the city. When people "complain" about homelessness they are actually bragging about it: "New York has more homeless than San Francisco"—"No, no, no, San Francisco has more homeless"—"No, you haven't been to Detroit." We are almost competitive about our endurance, which I think is one of the reasons why we accept homelessness so easily.

So the city freed the ex-slaves from their history?

In part, yes. The city was seductive to them because it promised forgetfulness. It offered the possibility of freedom—freedom, as you put it, from history. But although history should not become a straitjacket, which overwhelms and binds, neither should it be forgotten. One must critique it, test it, confront it and understand it in order to achieve a freedom that is more than license, to achieve true, adult agency. If you penetrate the seduction of the city, then it becomes possible to confront your own history—to forget what ought to be forgotten and use what is useful—such true agency is made possible.

How do visual images influence your work?

I was having some difficulty describing a scene in **Song of Solomon** . . . of a man running away from some obligations and himself. I used an Edvard Munch painting almost literally. He is walking, and there is nobody on his side of the street. Everybody is on the other side.

Song of Solomon *is such a painted book in comparison with some of your others like* **Beloved**, *which is sepia toned.*

Part of that has to do with the visual images that I got being aware that in historical terms women, black people in general, were very attracted to very bright colored clothing. Most people are frightened by color anyway.

Why?

They just are. In this culture quiet colors are considered elegant. Civilized western people wouldn't buy blood red sheets or dishes. There may be something more to it than what I am suggesting. But the slave population had no access even to what color there was, because they wore slave clothes, hand-me-downs, work clothes made out of burlap and sacking. For them a colored dress would be luxurious; it wouldn't matter whether it was rich or poor cloth . . . just to have a red or a yellow dress. I stripped **Beloved** of color so that there are only the small moments when Sethe runs amok buying ribbons and bows, enjoying herself the way children enjoy that kind of color. The whole business of color was why slavery was able to last such a long time. It wasn't as though you had a class of convicts who could dress themselves up and pass themselves off. No, these were people marked because of their skin color, as well as other features. So color is a signifying mark. Baby Suggs dreams of color, and says, "Bring me a little lavender. . . . " It is a kind of a luxury. We are so inundated with color and visuals. I just wanted to pull it back so that one could feel that hunger and that delight. I couldn't do that if I had made it the painterly book **Song of Solomon** was.

Is that what you are referring to when you speak about needing to find a controlling image?

Sometimes, yes. There are three or four in **Song of Solomon**, I knew that I wanted it to be painterly, and I wanted the opening to be red, white and blue. I also knew that in some sense he would have to "fly." In **Song of Solomon** it was the first time that I had written about a man who was the central, the driving engine of the narrative; I was a little unsure about my ability to feel comfortable inside him. I could always look at him and write from the out-side, but those would have been just perceptions. I had to be able not only to look at him but to feel how it really must have felt. So in trying to think about this, the image in my mind was a train. All the previous books have been women-centered, and they have been pretty much in the neighborhood and in the yard; this was going to move out. So, I had this feeling about a train . . . sort of revving up, then moving out as he does, and then it sort of highballs at the end; it speeds up, but it doesn't brake, it just high-balls and leaves you sort of suspended. So that image con-trolled the structure for me, although that is not some-thing I articulate or even make reference to; it only mat-ters that it works for me. Other books look like spirals, like ***Sula***.

How would you describe the controlling image of **Jazz**?

Jazz was very complicated because I wanted to re-represent two contradictory things—artifice and improvi-sation, where you have an artwork, planned, thought through, but at the same time appears invented, like jazz. I thought of the image being a book. Physically a book, but at the same time it is writing itself. Imagining itself. Talking. Aware of what it is doing. It watches itself think and imagine. That seemed to me to be a combination of artifice and improvisation—where you practice and plan in order to invent. Also the willingness to fail, to be wrong, because jazz is performance. In a performance you make mistakes, and you don't have the luxury of revision that a writer has; you have to make something out of a mistake, and if you do it well enough it will take you to another place where you never would have gone had you not made that error. So, you have to be able to risk making that error in performance. Dancers do it all the time, as well as jazz musicians. ***Jazz*** predicts its own story. Sometimes it is wrong because of faulty vision. It simply did not imag-ine those characters well enough, admits it was wrong, and the characters talk back the way jazz musicians do. It has to listen to the characters it has invented, and then learn something from them. It was the most intricate thing I had done, though I wanted to tell a very simple story about people who do not know that they are living in the jazz age, and to never use the word.

One way to achieve this structurally is to have several voices speaking throughout each book. Why do you do this?

It's important not to have a totalizing view. In American literature we have been so totalized—as though there is only one version. We are not one indistinguishable block of people who always behave the same way.

Is that what you mean by "totalized?"

Yes. A definitive or an authoritarian view from somebody else or someone speaking for us. No singularity and no di-versity. I try to give some credibility to all sorts of voices each of which is profoundly different. Because what strikes me about African-American culture *is* its variety. In so much of contemporary music everybody sounds alike. But when you think about black music, you think about the difference between Duke Ellington and Sidney Bechet or Satchmo or Miles Davis. They don't sound any-thing alike, but you know that they are all black perform-

ers, because of whatever that quality is that makes you re-alize, "Oh yes, this is part of something called the African-American music tradition." There is no black woman pop-ular singer, jazz singer, blues singer who sounds like any other. Billie Holiday does not sound like Aretha, doesn't sound like Nina, doesn't sound like Sarah, doesn't sound like any of them. They are really powerfully different. And they will tell you that they couldn't possibly have made it as singers if they sounded like somebody else. If some-one comes along sounding like Ella Fitzgerald, they will say, "Oh we have one of those . . ." It's interesting to me how those women have this very distinct, unmistakable image. I would like to write like that. I would like to write novels that were unmistakably mine, but nevertheless fit first into African-American traditions and second of all, this whole thing called literature.

First African-American?

Yes.

. . . rather than the whole of literature?

Oh yes.

Why?

It's richer. It has more complex sources. It pulls from something that's closer to the edge, it's much more mod-ern. It has a human future.

Wouldn't you rather be known as a great exponent of litera-ture rather than as an African-American writer?

It's very important to me that my work be African-American; if it assimilates into a different or larger pool, so much the better. But I shouldn't be *asked* to do that. Joyce is not asked to do that. Tolstoy is not. I mean, they can all be Russian, French, Irish or Catholic, they write out of where they come from, and I do too. It just so hap-pens that that space for me is African-American; it could be Catholic, it could be Midwestern. I'm those things too, and they are all important.

Why do you think people ask, "Why don't you write some-thing that we can understand?" Do you threaten them by not writing in the typical western, linear, chronological way?

I don't think that they mean that. I think they mean, "Are you ever going to write a book about white people?" For them perhaps that's a kind of a compliment. They're say-ing, "You write well enough, I would even let you write about me." They couldn't say that to anybody else. I mean, could I have gone up to André Gide and said, "Yes, but when are you going to get serious and start writing about black people?" I don't think he would know how to answer that question. Just as I don't. He would say, "What?" "I will if I want" or "Who are you?" What is be-hind that question is, there's the center, which is white, and then there are these regional blacks or Asians, or any sort of marginal people. That question can only be asked from the center. Bill Moyers asked me that when-are-you-going-to-write-about question on television. I just said, "Well, maybe one day . . ." but I couldn't say to him, you know, you can only ask that question from the center. The center of the world! I mean he's a white male. He's asking a marginal person, "When are you going to get to the center? When are you going to write about white people?" I can't say, "Bill, why are you asking me that question?" or "As long as that question seems reasonable is as long as I won't, can't." The point is that he's patronizing; he's saying, "You write well enough. You could come on into the center if you wanted to. You don't have to stay out there on the margins." And I'm saying, "Yeah, well I'm gonna stay out here on the margin, and let the center look for me."

Maybe it's a false claim, but not fully. I'm sure it was true for the ones we think of as giants now. Joyce is a good example. He moved here and there, but he wrote about Ireland wherever he was, didn't care where he was. I am sure people said to him, "Why . . .?" Maybe the French asked, "When you gonna write about Paris?" (pp. 108-20)

Do you read your reviews?

I read everything.

Really? You look deadly serious.

I read everything written about me that I see.

Why is that?

I have to know what's going on!

You want to see how you're coming across?

No, no. It's not about me or my work, it's about what is going on. I have to get a sense, particularly of what's going on with women's work, or African-American work, contemporary work. I teach a literature course. So I read any information that's going to help me teach.

Are you ever really surprised when they compare you to the magic realists, such as Gabriel García Márquez?

Yes, I used to be. It doesn't mean anything to me. Schools are only important to me when I'm teaching literature. It doesn't mean anything to me when I'm sitting here with a big pile of blank yellow paper . . . what do I say? I'm a magic realist? Each subject matter demands its own form, you know. (pp. 121-22)

Some people say, "Oh I can't write a book until I've lived my life, until I've had experiences."

That may be—maybe they can't. But look at the people who never went anywhere and just thought it up. Thomas Mann. I guess he took a few little trips. . . . I think you either have or you acquire this sort of imagination. Sometimes you do need a stimulus. But I myself don't ever go anywhere for stimulation. I don't want to go anywhere. If I could just sit in one spot I would be happy. I don't trust the ones who say I have to go do something before I can write. You see, I don't write autobiographically. First of all, I'm not interested in real-life people as subjects for fiction—including myself. If I write about somebody who's an historical figure like Margaret Garner, I really don't know anything about her. What I knew came from reading two interviews with her. They said, Isn't this extraordinary. Here's a woman who escaped into Cincinnati from the horrors of slavery and was not crazy. Though she'd killed her child, she was not foaming at the mouth. She

was very calm, she said, "I'd do it again." That was more than enough to fire my imagination.

She was sort of a cause célèbre?

She was. Her real life was much more awful than it's rendered in the novel, but if I had known all there was to know about her I never would have written it. It would have been finished, there would have been no place in there for me. It would be like a recipe already cooked. There you are. You're already this person. Why should I get to steal from you? I don't like that. What I really love is the process of invention. To have characters move from the curl all the way to a full-fledged person, that's interesting.

Do you ever write out of anger or any other emotion?

No. Anger is a very intense but tiny emotion, you know. It doesn't last. It doesn't produce anything. It's not creative . . . at least not for me. I mean these books take at least three years!

That is a long time to be angry.

Yes. I don't trust that stuff anyway. I don't like those little quick emotions, like, "I'm lonely, *ohhh*, God . . ." I don't like those emotions as fuel. I mean, I have them, but . . .

. . . they're not a good muse?

No, and if it's not your brain thinking cold, cold thoughts, which you can dress in any kind of mood, then it's nothing. It has to be a cold, cold thought. I mean cold, or cool at least. Your brain. That's all there is. (pp. 123-25)

> *Toni Morrison and Elissa Schappell, in an interview in* The Paris Review, *Vol. 35, No. 128, Fall, 1993, pp. 82-125.*

THE NOBEL LECTURE

John Darnton   (essay date 8 December 1993)

[*An American journalist, Darnton received a Pulitzer Prize for international reporting in 1982. In the following essay, he discusses Morrison's Nobel lecture.*]

In her lecture as the recipient of the 1993 Nobel Prize in Literature, Toni Morrison, the American author, delivered a lovingly wrought paean to language and to the sublime vocation of "word work."

In a half-hour address that brought the crowd in the Swedish Academy here this evening to a standing ovation, she spoke of the value of language: not official language or the censoring language of the state or the trick language of journalism, but language as words, with the magic they contain when they are learned by children.

It is words, she suggested, that empower meditation, that fend off "the scariness of things with no names" and that ease the burden of oppression. And in the end, it is words that enable us to make some sense of our existence by allowing us to stand aside to narrate it.

"We die," she said. "That may be the meaning of life. But we do language. That may be the measure of our lives." In concluding remarks by Sture Ahlen, the secretary of the academy, which bestows the literary award, Ms. Morrison's speech was called a "prose poem" that has a profound message for our time. (p. B1)

Ms. Morrison, 62, is the 90th person, the eighth woman and the first black woman to win the prize, which will be presented on Friday [December 10] and now carries a monetary award of $825,000. In selecting her two months ago, the academy noted: "She delves into the language itself, a language she wants to liberate from the fetters of race. And she addresses us with the luster of poetry."

The author certainly did that this evening. Dressed in a black gown with sequins that reflected light from 13 chandeliers in the Grand Hall above the 18th-century Bourse in Stockholm's Old City, she spoke calmly and in measured cadences, as if reciting verse to the crowd of 400 or so spread before her.

In recounting a story that exists "in the lore of several cultures," Ms. Morrison, the author of *Song of Solomon, Beloved, Jazz* and other novels, began with what she called "the first sentence of our childhood that we all remember": "Once upon a time. . . ."

An old woman, wise and blind—"in the version I know the woman is the daughter of slaves, black, American," the author said—is visited by young people who seem bent on mocking her clairvoyance. One of them says: "Old woman, I hold in my hand a bird. Tell me whether it is living or dead." The old woman refrains from answering at first, but eventually says: "I don't know whether the bird you are holding is dead or alive, but what I do know is that it is in your hands. It is in your hands."

The customary interpretation, Ms. Morrison said, is that the old woman is reprimanding the youths. Whether the bird is dead or alive, the woman is turning their act of mockery back upon them, into an assertion that they are responsible one way or another for the small bundle of life they hold.

Ms. Morrison then offered her own interpretation. The bird, she said, is language. The blind woman, who "draws pictures with words," is a writer. "She is worried about how the language she dreams in, given to her at birth, is handled, put into service, even withheld from her for certain nefarious purposes."

Language can die, Ms. Morrison said. It can be killed. It can be drafted into the army of the oppressors, become an instrument of domination: "Oppressive language does more than represent violence; it is violence; does more than represent the limits of knowledge; it limits knowledge."

Language, she continued, can even be abandoned altogether, through "tongue suicide." She observed, "In her country, children have bitten their tongues off and use bullets instead to iterate the voice of speechlessness."

But used faithfully and correctly, language can "limn the actual, imagined and possible lives of its speakers, readers, writers." There are, however, limits. It "can never 'pin down' slavery, genocide, war," she said. "Nor should it yearn for the arrogance to be able to do so. Its force, its felicity is in its reach toward the ineffable."

Turning the allegory inside out and making the metaphor soar and swoop like the bird that is at the center of the conceit, Ms. Morrison had the young people challenge the blind old woman. They entreat her to impart her wisdom. But she is silent. They demand it of her. They berate her. "Make up a story," they insist finally. But still she is silent and so they begin to tell the story for her:

"Tell us about ships turned away from shorelines at Easter, placenta in a field. Tell us about a wagonload of slaves, how they sang so softly their breath was indistinguishable from the falling snow. How they knew from the hunch of the nearest shoulder that the next stop would be their last. How, with hands prayered in their sex, they thought of heat, then suns. . . ."

The wagon stops at an inn and while the wagon master goes inside, a boy and a girl step from the inn into the wagon. "The boy will have a gun in three years, but now he carries a lamp and a jug of warm cider. They pass it from mouth to mouth. The girl offers bread, pieces of meat and something more: a glance into the eyes of the one she serves. One helping for each man, two for each woman. And a look. They look back. The next stop will be their last. But not this one. This one is warmed."

The children finish speaking and the old woman breaks the silence. "I trust you now," she says. "I trust you with the bird that is not in your hands because you have truly caught it. How lovely it is, this thing we have done—together." (pp. B1, B6)

> *John Darnton, "Accepting Nobel, Morrison Proves the Power of Words," in* The New York Times, *December 8, 1993, pp. B1, B6.*

FURTHER READING

Bibliography

Alexander, Harriet S. "Toni Morrison: An Annotated Bibliography of Critical Articles and Essays, 1975-1984." *CLA Journal* XXXIII, No. 1 (September 1989): 81-93.
    Lists critical essays and interviews.

Middleton, David L. *Toni Morrison: An Annotated Bibliography.* New York: Garland Publishing, 1987, 186 p.
    Standard primary and secondary bibliography.

Criticism

"Toni Morrison: A Special Section." *Callaloo* 13, No. 3 (Summer 1990): 471-525.
    Includes critical articles on Morrison's works through *Beloved.*

Dyson, Michael Eric. "Urgent Reflections on Race and Writing from Toni Morrison." *Tribune Books (Chicago)* (3 May 1992): 7, 11.

> Review of *Playing in the Dark* in which Dyson states: "Morrison's book helps expose the fallacy of viewing race exclusively through the lens of biology by maintaining that race has become 'metaphorical.'"

Erickson, Peter. "Canon Revision Update: A 1992 Edition." *The Kenyon Review* XV, No. 3 (Summer 1993): 197-207.

> Compares *Jazz* to novels written by other African-American women writers, including Thulani Davis, Rita Dove, Gloria Naylor, and Alice Walker.

Jones, Bessie W., and Vinson, Audrey L. *The World of Toni Morrison: Explorations in Literary Criticism.* Dubuque, Iowa: Kendall/Hunt Publishing Company, 1985, 158 p.

> Examines the "themes, settings, motifs, symbolism, characters, and style" of *The Bluest Eye, Sula, Song of Solomon,* and *Tar Baby.*

Leonard, John. "Her Soul's High Song." *The Nation* 254, No. 20 (25 May 1992): 706-08, 710, 712, 714-16, 718.

> Compares *Jazz* to Morrison's previous novels and praises the work as a book of "dispossession and haunting."

Middlebrook, Diane. "Western Literature's Underside." *Los Angeles Times Book Review* (24 May 1992): 2, 7.

> Provides an overview of *Playing in the Dark* and calls the book "a major work by a major American author."

" 'Word Work' in Stockholm." *The New Criterion* 12, No. 5 (January 1994): 1-3.

> Faults the Swedish Academy's decision to award Morrison the Nobel Prize for Literature as being politically motivated. Questioning the aesthetic quality of Morrison's œuvre, the critic argues that "Morrison has made a magnificent literary career out of left-wing sermonizing and sentimentality."

O'Brien, Edna. "The Clearest Eye." *The New York Times Book Review* (5 April 1992): 1, 29-30.

> Mixed assessment of *Jazz.*

Ruas, Charles. "Toni Morrison." In his *Conversations with American Writers,* pp. 215-43. New York: Alfred A. Knopf, 1985.

> Two-part interview conducted in 1981 in which Morrison discusses such topics as why she became a writer, her narrative techniques, and African-American culture.

Stuart, Andrea. "Blue Notes." *New Statesman & Society* 5, No. 200 (1 May 1992): 39-40.

> Dual review of *Jazz* and *Playing in the Dark.*

Sundquist, Eric J. "The Blackness of the Whale." *The Virginia Quarterly Review* 69, No. 1 (Winter 1993): 183-88.

> Discusses the strengths and weaknesses of Morrison's theory of "American Africanism" presented in *Playing in the Dark.*

Additional coverage of Morrison's life and career is contained in the following sources published by Gale Research: *Authors and Artists for Young Adults,* Vol. 1; *Black Literature Criticism,* Vol. 3; *Black Writers; Concise Dictionary of American Literary Biography, 1968-1988; Contemporary Authors,* Vols. 29-32 (rev. ed.); *Contemporary Authors New Revision Series,* Vol. 27; *Contemporary Literary Criticism,* Vols. 4, 10, 22, 55; *DISCovering Authors; Dictionary of Literary Biography,* Vols. 6, 33; *Dictionary of Literary Biography Yearbook 1981; Major 20th-Century Writers;* and *Something about the Author,* Vol. 57.

E. Annie Proulx

The Shipping News

Prize: National Book Award for Fiction

(Full name Edna Annie Proulx) Born in 1935, Proulx is an American novelist, short story writer, and journalist.

INTRODUCTION

The Shipping News is the story of Quoyle, an awkward, unsuccessful man who attempts to escape feelings of personal failure by leaving his unhappy past in New York City and moving to his ancestral home in a remote coastal village in Newfoundland. Settling in the rustic atmosphere of Killick-Claw with his two daughters, Quoyle finds a job writing for an odd local newspaper called *The Gammy Bird* which specializes in reporting sexual abuse cases and whose editor uncannily matches reporters with assignments that play on their personal fears. Proulx depicts Quoyle's gradual attainment of self-worth and happiness while creating a portrait of a community in which eccentric lives are intricately connected with the severe natural environment of Newfoundland. Critics have lauded Proulx's inventive use of language, her artful incorporation of local dialect and folklore, and her vivid descriptions of the landscape. Nicci Gerrard commented: "Newfoundland is the real subject of Proulx's stunning novel, in which the reader is assaulted by a rich, down-in-the-dirt, up-in-the-skies prose full of portents, repetitions, bold metaphors, brusque dialogues and set pieces of great beauty. The characters are radiant with life, but, flung against the drumrolls of rain, the cracking floes and dark skies of an elemental landscape, they are also emblematic." In addition to winning the National Book Award for *The Shipping News* in 1993, Proulx received the PEN/Faulkner Award for *Postcards* and the *Irish Times* International Fiction Award in recognition for her work as a novelist.

PRINCIPAL WORKS

Heart Songs, and Other Stories   (short stories)   1988
Postcards   (novel)   1992
The Shipping News   (novel)   1993

CRITICISM

Dwight Garner   (review date April 1993)

[In the following review, Garner comments on the characters, writing style, and major themes in The Shipping News.*]*

For the Vermont novelist E. Annie Proulx, composing sentences isn't an indoor sport. "The most fun thing about writing," she told an interviewer last year, "is jumping in my pickup truck and taking off—stop along by a graveyard, write some, and then sleep in the truck." Proulx's restlessness rubs off on the men and women in her books—she's interested in what happens to people when the rugs are yanked out from under them. In her first novel, ***Postcards*** (1992), her doomed protagonist careers across the country on a 40-year road trip. In her new novel, ***The Shipping News,*** Proulx uproots a hack journalist and his family from upper New York State, and drives them northward. In both books, her up-country rednecks filter the world through bleary eyes and crippling cultural jet lag.

For her readers, too, Proulx can provide hard traveling. Her talent is enormous but ungainly. You bounce along her sentences—which teem with huge inventories of arcane objects and natural phenomena, and words that don't appear in dictionaries—the way you do along rutted, washboard dirt roads. Even the disclaimer that appears on the title page of *The Shipping News* bears Proulx's idiosyncratic stamp:

> No resemblance is intended to living or dead persons, extant or failed newspapers, real government departments, specific towns or villages, actual roads or highways. The skiffs, trawlers and yachts, the upholstery needles, the logans, thumbies, the plates of cod cheeks, the bakeapples and those who pick them, the fish traps, the cats and dogs, the houses and seabirds described here are all fancies. The Newfoundland in this book, though salted with grains of truth, is an island of invention.

Behind Proulx's information-choked prose is a mind with an uncanny affinity for the antiquated, hardscrabble, and obscure. Before she published her first book of fiction, the lean and tough-minded *Heart Songs and Other Stories* (1988), Proulx wrote *Back to Barter,* which argued for the return of the "Yankee trader," and a popular how-to book, *The Art of Salad Gardening.* Her unlikely knowledge infuses the disheveled farmhouses, mobile homes, and dairy barns her characters occupy with a radiance that other writers about New England's rural poor—Maine's Carolyn Chute, New Hampshire's Ernest Hebert—can't quite muster. And her encrusted sentences and unslaked appetite for regional nuance add weight-of-the-ages heft to the theme that's central in all of her fiction—heredity's crushing burden.

Proulx's men and women can't hide their burdens for a nanosecond. "There's something truly fucked up about you," a near-stranger says, out of the blue, to Loyal Blood, the protagonist of *Postcards.* "I don't know what it is, but I can smell it. You're accident-prone. You suffer losses. You're tilted way far off center." What tilts Blood, and the rest of Proulx's characters, is a Faulknerian tangle of old familial wounds—incest, petty hatreds, long-standing feuds. People are forever exacting retribution for slights they can barely recall. The body count—murders, suicides, maimings—piles up and up.

The harrowing *Postcards* moved in five or six directions at once. It chronicled the slow, grinding despoilment of the Bloods, a Vermont farm clan, when their oldest son flees after killing his wife. The men end up as suicides, or in prison; the women become local freaks, or are forced into factories. Proulx's ambivalence about family and home gives the book its complexity. The Bloods may be at each other's throats when they're together, but separately they're utterly lost.

The Shipping News turns Loyal Blood's flight from home on its head. The book's protagonist, Quoyle, runs not away from but toward his past, abandoning a disastrous

life in upper New York State to move with his two young daughters to his family's ancestral coastal home in Newfoundland. Like Loyal, Quoyle is saddled with a hellish amount of centuries-old shit, notably the inherited weight of his "chief failure, a failure of normal appearance." Proulx sketches Quoyle's tortured childhood in "dreary upstate towns" with broad, indelible strokes:

> [He had a] great damp loaf of a body. At six he weighed eighty pounds. At sixteen he was buried under a casement of flesh. Head shaped like a crenshaw, no neck, reddish hair ruched back. Features as bunched as kissed fingertips. Eyes the color of plastic. The monstrous chin, a freakish shelf jutting from the lower face.

Other children aren't sympathetic. "[They] hissed 'Lardass, Snotface, Ugly Pig, Warthog, Stupid, Stinkbomb, Fart-tub, Greasebag,' pummeled and kicked until Quoyle curled, hands over head, sniveling, on the linoleum."

Quoyle's troubles don't ease with adulthood. Proulx recounts his manifold torments in excruciating detail. He fails at love: His wife, an addled sex-addict named Petal Bear, dumps him and their children and then dies in a car crash. He fails at his career: As a newspaper man, he's a mediocre talent with "a fatal flair for the false passive" and a fear of "all but twelve or fifteen verbs." He's ruinously impressionable: "If [a friend] suggested he leap from a bridge he would at least lean on the rail." His looks give people the screaming meemies; even those close to him concede that the "part of Quoyle that was wonderful was, unfortunately, attached to the rest of him."

Proulx's characters are caught in a Faulknerian tangle of old familial wounds—incest, petty hatreds, long-standing feuds. People are forever exacting retribution for slights they can barely recall.

—Dwight Garner

Throughout *The Shipping News,* Proulx focuses almost solely on Quoyle and his furious, lurching protest against pain, and thus this narrative isn't the broad canvas that *Postcards* was. And because Quoyle is on a search for a better life, and not on the lam, *The Shipping News* lacks the earlier book's onrushing inevitability. But it is easier, in American fiction at least, to write about running than it is to write about the consequences of taking irreversible stands, and Proulx's description of the life Quoyle carves for himself in Newfoundland is full of nuance.

In some respects, *The Shipping News* is an elaboration of "Stone City," one of the longer stories in *Heart Songs.* The story unspools what Proulx calls "the intricate ropes of blood relationship"—it's about a tainted family and the land that carries its curse. Proulx picks up the idea of territorial curses in *The Shipping News,* in which her imagery has even more to do with knots, of the literal and figurative sort. Quoyle—the name is an antiquated spelling of "coil"—and his relationship to the ocean provide much of the book's literal and metaphorical tension. Quoyle can't swim, and Proulx describes the water that's constantly crowding him as a menacing, pitiless thing—"The ocean twitched like a vast cloth spread over snakes," "The bay crawled with whitecaps like maggots seething in a broad wound." Worse, Quoyle finds that his ancestors were a clan of half-wits and pirates who lured unsuspecting ships onto rocky shallows and then "murdered the ship-wrecked, drowned their unwanted brats, fought and howled, beards braided in spikes with burning candles jammed into their hair."

In less capable hands, Quoyle's eventual reconciliation with the ocean and his past could have become a long string of saccharine bummers. But although Quoyle is decidedly melancholy, the book's tone is anything but dolorous. There's something pleasantly off-kilter about Quoyle's hit-and-miss interactions with the women in the book. He carries around "an injected vaccine against the plague of love" from his first marriage, and he doesn't seem to know quite what his daughters, aunt, and lover want from him. When he thinks he's figured it out, they usually tell him to get lost, and he wanders off to scratch his noggin. Proulx has rarely written from a woman's point of view—although there is a wonderful segment in *Postcards,* in which a woman gets her first driver's license late in life and learns the joys of burning down an open road—and she tends to write about women from a remove that renders them puzzling.

Proulx smuggles a fair amount of manic humor into *The Shipping News.* Part of her achievement here is the construction of an elaborate social whirl that Quoyle enters in maritime Newfoundland. Misfits and miscreants swim around Quoyle like tidal currents around a half-submerged buoy. But Proulx isn't just getting her ya-yas out; she doesn't write throwaway scenes. She extracts a good deal of comic fuel, for example, from Quoyle's tenure as the shipping news columnist at *The Gammy Bird,* the town's lurid weekly, whose editors put a car crash on the cover each week even if there hasn't been any. But scenes involving Quoyle and *The Gammy Bird* also draw a lot of blood. The paper is a magnet for hard-luck cases, and each reporter winds up on a beat that taps into his or her inner fears; it's like therapy on a deadline. For Quoyle, that means racing out to car wrecks to "get pictures while the upholstery is still on fire and the blood still hot," and spending time with his jaw muscles bunched up, staring out to sea.

The comic edge Proulx forces on Quoyle's saga can sometimes grate. The fanciful names she gives her characters—Sparky Fudge, Al Catalog, Diddy Shovel, Wavey Prowse—turn too many important moments into cartoon panels. And her abiding love of maps and place names occasionally leads to sentences like "Stole a bicycle in Lost All Hope, rode it eleven miles to Bad Fortune, there he stole a motorcycle and made it to Never Once."

Quoyle's plight, however, doesn't feel trivialized or exaggerated. Rarely in contemporary fiction has a writer so knowingly explored what Nietzsche described, in his chilling aphorism, as the brute recognition that "terrible experiences give one cause to speculate whether the one who experiences them may not be something terrible." In Proulx's earlier work, such haunting speculation drives her characters to violent ends, leaving us abuzz with helpless sympathy and horror. If *The Shipping News* is a more affirming and less astringent saga, its picture of a man wracked by his demons lives frighteningly in the mind. That Quoyle survives his contaminants seems a small and real gift. When the grotesque sins of the father are visited upon this son, he gives, heartily, as good as he gets.

Dwight Garner, "Northeastern Exposure," in
VLS, *No. 114, April, 1993, p. 29.*

Howard Norman   (review date 4 April 1993)

[*Norman is an American translator, novelist, short story writer, and children's literature writer. In the following review, he discusses the plot of* The Shipping News *and praises Proulx's inventive use of language.*]

An early traveler's account of the Maritime Provinces says, "After but a year's visit, one is convinced that the sea has a savage appetite for Newfoundlanders." In E. Annie Proulx's vigorous, quirky novel *The Shipping News,* set in present-day Newfoundland, there are indeed a lot of drownings. The main characters are plagued by dangerous undercurrents, both in the physical world and in their own minds. But the local color, ribaldry and uncanny sorts of redemption of Ms. Proulx's third book of fiction keep the reader from slipping under, into the murk of loss. The novel, largely set in the village of Killick-Claw, along Newfoundland's foggy, storm-battered coast, displays Ms. Proulx's surreal humor and her zest for the strange foibles of humanity.

The protagonist is Quoyle, who almost drowns once. Back in New York State, his marriage to Petal Bear had "a month of fiery happiness. Then six kinked years of suffering." Quoyle, however, was smitten to the end. When Petal is killed with a lover in a car wreck, one of Quoyle's first acts of mourning is to stick his head into the sudden cold weather of the refrigerator to cry. Quoyle, a third-rate newspaper hack with a "head shaped like a crenshaw, no neck, reddish hair" and "features as bunched as kissed fingertips," is left with two daughters, Bunny and Sunshine, ages 6 and 4½. Soon Bunny is plagued with nightmares (of a snarling white dog) that match in intensity her father's hallucinatory re-enactments of Petal's grisly death. Life seems stripped of hope until Quoyle's Aunt Agnis Hamm arrives. The aunt, as she is often referred to, regales Quoyle with stories of their Newfoundland ancestors; at once mesmerizing and disquieting, they draw Quoyle in, albeit with some hesitation. "Quoyle hated the thought of an incestuous, fit-prone, seal-killing child as a grandfather, but there was no choice. The mysteries of unknown family." The grandfather had drowned at age 12, having already sired Quoyle's father.

Quoyle sets out for Newfoundland to find the ancestral house. Once there, Quoyle, his aunt and daughters find the dilapidated place, isolated miles down a barely passable road from Killick-Claw, where Quoyle eventually finds work on *The Gammy Bird,* the local newspaper.

Happily for the reader, Ms. Proulx keeps returning to the offices of *The Gammy Bird.* As Quoyle's gypsy family moves from house to trailer, the office becomes his home base. There he meets the staff, true brigands of outback journalism. It is also where the pitch of Ms. Proulx's writing is most finely tuned. There are, among others, Nutbeem, who steals foreign news from the radio; Tert Card, an estimable rewrite man; and Jack Buggit, the belligerent editor. Their spontaneous monologues, when spiced with the local patois, are wonderfully performed riffs of nostalgia, anecdote, indictment and complaint that strike us as Newfoundland's most rollicking oral literature.

The Gammy Bird specializes in sexual-abuse stories, and we get a file of them a mile high. Quoyle is assigned two beats. There is shipping news: a ship's home port, time of arrival, time of departure, cargo, occasionally the antics of captain and crew. In a region of chronic unemployment, just to have these facts of commerce reported seems a kind of optimism. Ms. Proulx's Killick-Claw is barely hanging on to the second half of the century. Far more disturbing is Quoyle's other beat. As it is put to him by Jack Buggit: "We run a front-page photo of a car wreck every week, whether we have a wreck or not. That's our golden rule. No exceptions."

Nutbeem observes:

> Have you noticed Jack's uncanny sense about assignments? He gives you a beat that plays on your private inner fears. Look at you. Your wife was killed in an auto accident. What does Jack ask you to cover? Car wrecks, to get pictures while the upholstery is still on fire and the blood still hot. He gives Billy, who has never married for reasons unknown, the home news, the women's interest page, the details of home and hearth—must be exquisitely painful to the old man. And me. I get to cover the wretched sexual assaults. And with each one I relive my own childhood. I was assaulted at school for three years, first by a miserable geometry teacher, then by older boys who were his cronies. To this day I cannot sleep without wrapping up like a mummy in five or six blankets. And what I don't know is if Jack understands what he's doing, if the pain is supposed to ease and dull through repetitive confrontation, or if it just persists, as fresh as on the day of the first personal event. I'd say it persists.

Claustrophobic winter arrives, locking in Killick-Claw, icing over the coves. As the harsh months go by, it seems that Quoyle is digging out from his own past. He deals compassionately with the last of his disreputable clan, a demented old cousin living in a hut "crammed with the poverty of another century," by securing him in a rest home. Still fending off visions of Petal, he begins to court the all but silent Wavey Prowse, herself widowed by a drowning. He gets his children ensconced in school and deepens his knowledge and delight as a father. He seems for the first time calm in his heart. The children and aunt

undergo difficult, healing transformations as well. Our sympathies are strongly invested in all of them, as well as in the village itself.

Throughout *The Shipping News,* the sinuousness of E. Annie Proulx's prose seems to correspond physically with the textures of the weather and sea. Her inventive language is finely, if exhaustively, accomplished. If I have any complaint it is that at times she carries her own brand of poetic compression too far: "Billy's worn shape down to the bones, cast Quoyle as a sliding mass." Weather offshore or overland can often seem chokingly imbued with portentousness. Near the novel's end, Jack Buggit sits up in his own coffin, spouting water, having both drowned and not drowned; it is a forced invention in a novel otherwise replete with wonderfully natural ones.

Ms. Proulx is never too showy with her research, though *The Shipping News* is almost an encyclopedia of slang and lore. The way her Newfoundlanders talk, the most factual account seems as high-spirited as gossip over a supper of snow crab, cod cheeks, lobster salad and seal-flipper stew.

Eventually, the actual house of Quoyle is blown into the sea, a drowned house. Yet by spring's open water, Quoyle himself has not only survived but also drummed out some of his demons. In the end, it seems triumph enough that neither Quoyle nor Wavey has drowned.

> *Howard Norman, in a review of "The Shipping News," in* The New York Times Book Review, *April 4, 1993, p. 13.*

Walter Kendrick   (review date October 1993)

[*Kendrick is an American critic and journalist. In the following excerpt, he comments positively on the language and characters in* The Shipping News.]

E. Annie Proulx's second novel, *The Shipping News* is in some ways a quirky, postmodernly fragmented performance. Like her 1992 debut, *Postcards,* it consists of many short chapters (thirty-nine in this case), most with pictorial headings, this time drawings from Clifford W. Ashley's "wonderful 1944 work," *The Ashley Book of Knots,* which Proulx "had the good fortune to find at a yard sale for a quarter." I can't say exactly what knots have to do with the novel, except that, as tools for fishermen and other boaters, they are indispensable on the shores of Newfoundland, where most of *The Shipping News* is set. It tells the lurching, episodic story of Quoyle (no praenomen), a child so unlovely that his own brother calls him "Lardass, Snotface, Ugly Pig":

> A great damp loaf of a body. At six he weighed eighty pounds. At sixteen he was buried under a casement of flesh. Head shaped like a crenshaw, no neck, reddish hair ruched back. Features as bunched as kissed fingertips. Eyes the color of plastic. The monstrous chin, a freakish shelf jutting from the lower face.

Quoyle is Caliban, Benjy, Lenny, the Elephant Man, any monster baby with a loving heart. After his cruel wife's death (the only part of him she loved was his heroic penis), he flees north with his two little daughters, Bunny and

Sunshine, returning to the Quoyles' origin, Killick-Claw, a dead-end town on "the most utterly desolate and miserable coast in the world."

He goes to work for *The Gammy Bird,* the unaccountably profitable local newspaper, which devotes most of its space to wire-service reports of rapes and child molestations in other parts of the world. Quoyle's beat becomes "the shipping news," reports of ships coming and going at Killick-Claw and nearby ports. It's an inauspicious assignment, but to everyone's surprise, including his own, Quoyle scores a rousing success—the first time in his life he's ever done something right. In the process, he joins a community (another first), uncovers several family secrets, and wins the love of Wavey Prowse, a "Tall and Quiet Woman." At the end, Quoyle and Wavey marry, and Proulx points a magical moral:

> Water may be older than light, diamonds crack in hot goat's blood, mountaintops give off cold fire, forests appear in mid-ocean, it may happen that a crab is caught with the shadow of a hand on its back, that the wind be imprisoned in a bit of knotted string. And it may be that love sometimes occurs without pain or misery.
>
> (pp. 133-34)

Not only does [Proulx's depiction of love] entail no weeping and gnashing, it also flowers in full view of family and friends, all of whom have stories of their own. *The Shipping News* reverberates with voices, each possessing a distinctive twang that Proulx exuberantly sings along with. They are hard-edged voices, like the jagged northern names that speak them: Agnis Hamm, Tert Card, Jack Buggit, B. Beaufield Nutbeem. Proulx takes Dickensian delight in reeling them off, as she does Newfoundland's dire place names: Lost All Hope, Bad Fortune, Never Once, Go Aground. She loves dense, chewy, presumably local words: *stribbled, streeling, skreel, marl, scrawn, thunge, drenty, glutch,* and many more that you'll find nowhere outside a Newfoundlandish phrase book. People, landscape, and language fit together like rocks in an unhewn wall, forming a marvelous composite portrait of North America's last margin—which, given death-dealing winters and the madness they induce, it is likely to remain. (pp. 134-35)

> *Walter Kendrick, in a review of "The Shipping News," in* The Yale Review, *Vol. 81, No. 4, October, 1993, pp. 133-35.*

Nicci Gerrard   (essay date 14 November 1993)

[*In the following essay, based on an interview with Proulx, Gerrard focuses on Proulx's colorful and meticulously researched depiction of the landscape and people of Newfoundland in* The Shipping News.]

> Eight years ago, I was looking for canoeing waters and I unfolded an old map of Newfoundland. Each place-name had a story—Dead Man's Cove, Seldom Come Bay and Bay of Despair, Exploits River, Plunder Beach. I knew I had to go there, and within 10 minutes of arriving, I'd fallen in love. I am pulled by the harshness of the weather, the strength of the land-

scape which is dark and stormy and rough, the impenetrability of the tangled Tuckamoor shrubs, the sense of a land holding its own against people.

E. Annie Proulx (E is for unused Edna) went back and back to Newfoundland. She explored the island 'where liquid was solid, where solids dissolved, where the sky froze and light and dark muddled'. She experienced the weather, sharp seasons, walls of milky fog, June icebergs ramming the shore, 50-foot waves that sucked up the grey-green water into spumes, the mild days of summer grace, scudding clouds and the winds that howled over the horizon, tipping ships like bath toys, bringing death. She met the kind, tough Newfoundlanders who gave her their stories; visited the boatyards and fisheries; went out in little fishing boats; ate fried bologna and squid; snooped on lives that are lived in the teeth of the elements.

Out of it came her extraordinary second novel, *The Shipping News,* which has won the *Irish Times* International Fiction Prize and America's National Book Award. *The Shipping News,* which opens in urban America but quickly decamps to the bleak wilds of Newfoundland, tells the story of Quoyle—a tender-hearted, wretched man with 'a damp loaf of a body', head shaped like a crenshaw, no neck, features 'as bunched as kissed fingertips' and an immense jutting chin. His parents show him no love, his brother bullies him, peers taunt his misshapen unhappiness, and he marries a small, pert, frenetic slut—Petal—who mocks him with her infidelities and tramples with sharp shoes over his besotted emotions.

But Quoyle is the soul of submission ('butter of fair spreading consistency') and he sits like a soft lump in a life which is destroying him—until Petal's slender neck is snapped in a car crash. Then, with his two disturbed daughters and his aunt, he runs from modern America to a Newfoundland on the brink of change—'the hard old days are giving way to new soft days', says Proulx, 'but there's a price to pay. It still has the qualities of kindness, civility, co-operation, but the ferocious twentieth century is beginning to encroach.' The unravelling Quoyle is knitted together in Newfoundland. He finds a kind of happiness (happiness as the absence of pain).

Newfoundland is the real subject of Proulx's stunning novel, in which the reader is assaulted by a rich, down-in-the-dirt, up-in-the-skies prose full of portents, repetitions, bold metaphors, brusque dialogues and set pieces of great beauty. The characters are radiant with life, but, flung against the drumrolls of rain, the cracking floes and dark skies of an elemental landscape, they are also emblematic.

Their names—Wavey Prowse, Beety, Nutbeem, Tert Card, Bill Pretty, Diddy Shovel, Bayonet and Silver Melville, Sunbeam—summon up archetypes (Proulx works hard at her names: she reads telephone directories, lists of officials from the fisheries and gas works, roll calls from the mortuaries, in order to have the flavour of Newfoundland in the strange names that she chooses). They look hewn from Newfoundland rock, too—stubbled, callused, reddened; worn into sharp angles or blunted smooth. They have big laps, hands, hearts.

At 58, Proulx herself has this same weather-worn, life-worn appearance, as if she too has spent years walking against wind. She is a pioneer spirit, a writer from the frontier. When she laughs, she looks surprised by her own jollity; she has a big, spare frame, a cap of dark grizzled hair, capable hands, a shrewd brown gaze that arcs over me but then settles on middle-distance, and a long stride. Indeed, she loves being outside. From her house in the Vermont countryside, she canoes, skis cross-country, hunts (for grouse mainly), walks, bikes, searches for woodland flowers and mushrooms, fishes, gardens.

Mainly, however, she writes. 'I came to writing late, and I'm racing against the clock to get everything down. My head is jammed with stories; they are pushing to get out.' She was born in Connecticut in 1935 (the oldest of five girls, in a family of millworkers, inventors and artists) but has spent most of her life in Vermont. She had two 'terrible' marriages (her mouth, the subject, closes); struggled against 'single-mother-with-two-sons poverty'; took a doctorate in history (both her first novel, *Postcards* and *The Shipping News* are meticulously-researched histories of an area—half-joking, she describes *Postcards* as 'the account of rural electrification disguised as a story').

As a 'brutally poor' freelance journalist with, by then, three sons, she wrote on cider, lettuce, architecture, horticulture, lions, mice, weather, beadwork. 'That was my bread and butter; my dessert was to write one or two stories a year, for which I was paid about $10.'

Now she writes full time, but her stories are crammed with odd facts, curiosities which she still picks up avidly like a collector. While researching *The Shipping News,* she lurked in library stacks, reading history and sociology books; she studied maps, tracked down local music and songs; she learnt about boat-building and fishing; she read a year's worth of local newspapers; she took photographs and made sketches; she collected litter from the beaches and sorted through it.

Every month or so, she visits a medical library to browse through the latest research (she's rather keen on trench-foot at the moment). Now she's working on a novel called *The Accordion Crimes* which revolves round different kinds of—'guess what, accordion music': Cajun, French Canadian quadrilles, Polish and Czech music, zadico.

Annie Proulx has three sons (tall and musical) who have now all left home. She lives by herself ('oh it's luxury') down a dirt track, in 'a small tall house' with a hill at the back, and trees and fields around it. She starts work at first light, writing by hand. Hanging from the doorway is a thick cord on which she practises complicated knots (*The Ashley Book of Knots* is tied into *The Shipping News,* a knot introducing each chapter, and even at times carrying the story onward). In the afternoon, she transfers words onto the computer. Each evening she skis or bikes or fishes.

She makes her own bread, likes to cook (her novel is full of food: baked apples, cod cheeks, rubbery squid, bread soaking up juices, the slip of over-cooked pasta round a plate rim). She decorates (on the staircase of her house she has painted a row of 15-feet-high poplar trees), and is a

---

An excerpt from *The Shipping News*

Quoyle woke in the empty room. Grey light. A sound of hammering. His heart. He lay in his sleeping bag in the middle of the floor. The candle on its side. Could smell the wax, smell the pages of the book that lay open beside him, the dust in the floor cracks. Neutral light illumined the window. The hammering again and a beating shadow in the highest panes. A bird.

He got up and went to it. Would drive it away before it woke the aunt and the girls. It seemed the bird was trying to break from the closed room of sea and rock and sky into the vastness of his bare chamber. The whisper of his feet on the floor. Beyond the glass the sea lay pale as milk, pale the sky, scratched and scribbled with cloud welts. The empty bay, far shore creamed with fog. Quoyle pulled his clothes on and went downstairs.

On the threshold lay three wisps of knotted grass. Some invention of Sunshine's. He went behind the great rock to which the house was moored and into the bushes. His breath in cold cones.

A faint path angled toward the sea, and he thought it might come out onto the shore north of the new dock. Started down. After a hundred feet the trail went steep and wet, and he slid through wild angelica stalks and billows of dogberry. Did not notice knots tied in the tips of the alder branches.

Entered a band of spruce, branches snarled with moss, whiskey jacks fluttering. The path became a streambed full of juicy rocks. A waterfall with the flattened ocean at its foot. He stumbled, grasping at Alexanders, the leaves perfuming his hands.

Fountains of blackflies and mosquitoes around him. Quoyle saw a loop of blue plastic. He picked it up, then a few feet farther along spied a sodden diaper. A flat stick stamped "5 POINTS Popsicle Pete." When he came on a torn plastic bag he filled it with debris. Tin cans, baby-food jars, a supermarket meat tray, torn paper cajoling the jobless reader.

. . . perhaps you are not quite confident that you can successfully complete the full program in Fashion Merchandising. Well, I can make you a special offer that will make it easier for you. Why not try just Section One of the course to begin with. This does not involve you in a long-term commitment and it will give you the opportunity to . . .

Plastic line, the unfurled cardboard tube from a roll of toilet paper, pink tampon inserters.

Behind him a profound sigh, the sigh of someone beyond hope or exasperation. Quoyle turned. A hundred feet away a fin, a glistening back. The Minke whale rose, glided under the milky surface. He stared at the water. Again it appeared, sighed, slipped under. Roiling fog arms flew fifty feet above the sea.

E. Annie Proulx, in The Shipping News, *Charles Scribner's Sons, 1993.*

carpenter in her spare time. She enjoys friends and goes to bed alone.

Being on her own is what she chooses: writing, for her, means that she cannot participate in intimate domesticity. 'I back away from life; I observe it. The jolly family circle and loving husband: those things are not for me.' It is a solitary life, but a fortunate one. However, Annie Proulx's small tall house by a hill is for sale now: 'It's time for a change, and I like to shift my ground'. Home is where the words are—and wherever she is, there will be words, stories to untangle. As it says in her beloved *Ashley Book of Knots,* 'There are still old knots that are unrecorded, and so long as there are new purposes for rope, there will always be new knots to discover.'

Nicci Gerrard, "A Gale Force Winner," in The Observer, *November 14, 1993, p. 18.*

Roz Kaveney   (review date 3 December 1993)

[*In the following review of* The Shipping News, *Kaveney praises Proulx's ability to convincingly depict bizarre events.*]

Novels of small-town life are an American genre that continually generates fine work. For a society obsessed with individual identity, America has a surprising love of those virtues that emerge only in a collective context. A British novel about returning to roots would be a theodicy, re-establishing hierarchies and fitting the protagonists into their preordained rank. But the best American novels of return show people creating, rather than finding, the niche that best fulfills them.

[In *The Shipping News*], E Annie Proulx's lumbering hero Quoyle was never much liked by his parents or siblings. He married Petal, who humiliated him with affairs, and has only become a halfway competent journalist because his best friend Partridge saw potential in him. When his parents die, he loses his job, and Petal dies in a car crash after selling their children to a child abuser, from whom they are retrieved physically untouched. Quoyle is open to suggestions about how he should endure the rest of his life, and his aunt drags him off to the family roots in Newfoundland.

It will already be apparent that Proulx is not above throwing in the odd extreme. What follows includes storms at sea, premonitory dreams, decapitations, rescues and the resuscitation of a drowned man during his own wake. Perhaps even more improbably, the battered Quoyle acquires genuine dignity and worth by hard work at a job that he learns to love—turning the shipping news of a small local paper into a column taken seriously by other journalists.

Proulx's triumph is that she makes us swallow all of this. Her work not only describes, but is imbued with, a chancy decency that looks us forthright in the eye and challenges disbelief. This is an artful novel. Proulx takes us to a land of myth—Quoyle is at one level the Holy Fool who does not know how to ask the right questions—and urban legend, full of the things we want or fear to believe in.

What risks being mere whimsy has steel behind it, because there is passion here and a real potential for tragedy. Petal died and was horrid, for all that Quoyle tried to love her. One of editor Buggit's sons drowned and the other is obsessed with the sea even though he has nearly drowned once. Aunt Agnes lost her woman lover years ago to cancer and does not feel able to tell even Quoyle about it.

There is precise intelligence, a sense of how small communities work and of how power is divided within them. Quoyle grows into responsibility because there is a vacuum in the community that needs him to fill it. The chapter heads come from a catalogue of knots; Proulx has the good sense not to avoid this potential crudity in her description of the ties that bind her hero to happiness.

Roz Kaveney, "Local Hero," in New Statesman & Society, *Vol. 6, No. 281, December 3, 1993, p. 39.*

In Memoriam

Kōbō Abé

March 7, 1924—January 22, 1993

(Born Kimifusa Abé; also transliterated as Kobo Abe and Abe Kobo) Japanese novelist, short story writer, playwright, theater director, essayist, screenwriter, and photographer.

For further information on Abé's life and works, see *CLC,* Volumes 8, 22, and 53.

INTRODUCTION

Abé was the foremost Modernist writer in Japan and an international literary figure who was frequently considered a candidate for the Nobel Prize. Sometimes referred to as the "Japanese Kafka," Abé wrote many tales depicting ordinary people in absurd, nightmarish situations. He is best known in the West for *Suna no onna* (*The Woman in the Dunes*), an allegorical, metaphysical novel about an entomologist who becomes trapped in a sand pit by a strange primitive tribe; the awarding-winning film based on this novel, *The Woman in the Dunes,* directed by Hiroshi Teshigahara and scripted by Abé, brought him international acclaim. Critics note that much of Abé's fiction explores the loneliness of modern existence and the tenuous nature of identity, posing questions and describing events designed to undermine the reader's complacency and stimulate reflective thought. He wrote that in his novel *Daiyon kampyoki* (*Inter Ice Age Four*) he wanted "to make the reader confront the cruelty of the future, produce within him anguish and strain and bring about a dialogue with himself." Unlike his contemporary Yukio Mishima, whose uniquely modern fiction incorporated numerous elements from traditional Japanese culture, Abé scrupulously avoided culturally specific details in an effort to address a worldwide audience and underline the universality of his themes. Hisaaki Yamanouchi has written that Abé's "works provide a picture of life in which man is utterly lonely, deprived of communication with his fellow men and determined by physical reality. And yet what Abé intends to prescribe in his works is not despair but tough reasonableness with which to accept the inescapable reality of life; only by doing so can man justify his own existence."

PRINCIPAL WORKS

Owarishi michi no shirube ni (novel) 1948

S. Karuma-shi no hanzai (novel) 1951
Daiyon kampyoki (novel) 1959
  [*Inter Ice Age Four,* 1970]
Suna no onna (novel) 1962
  [*The Woman in the Dunes,* 1964]
*Suna no onna (screenplay) 1964
  [*The Woman in the Dunes,* 1964]
Tanin no kao (novel) 1964
  [*The Face of Another,* 1966]
Moetsukita chizu (novel) 1967
  [*The Ruined Map,* 1969]
Tomodachi, enemoto takeaki (drama) 1967
  [*Friends,* 1969]
Bo ni natta otoko (drama) 1969
  [*The Man Who Turned into a Stick,* 1975]
Abé Kōbō gikyoku zenshu (collected dramas) 1970
Uchinaro henkyo (essays) 1971
Abé Kōbō zensakuhin. 15 vols. (dramas, essays, novels, poetry, and short stories) 1972-1973
Hako otoko (novel) 1973

[*The Box Man,* 1975]
Han gekiteki ningen   (lectures)   1973
Mikkai   (novel)   1977
   [*Secret Rendezvous,* 1979]
Hakobune sakura maru   (novel)   1984
   [*The Ark Sakura,* 1988]
†*Beyond the Curve*   (short stories)   1991

*The film was directed by Hiroshi Teshigahara.

†A collection of previously untranslated stories written between 1949 and 1966, it includes "The Crime of S. Karma," an excerpt from Abé's second novel, *S. Karuma-shi no hanzai.*

INTERVIEW

Kōbō Abé with Nancy S. Hardin   (interview date November and December 1973)

[*In the following interview, which was conducted at various intervals during November and December 1973, Abé discusses his plays, novels, and artwork. Hardin prefaces the interview with an examination of the main themes of Abé's work.*]

A scientific education and a keen and lively imagination underlie the creativity of Abé Kobo. As a writer of novels, essays, plays, as a director of films and theater, and as a photographer, he seems to have an uncanny ability "to contemplate the unimaginable." By examining the nightmarish atmosphere of modern life, Abé alters attitudes toward reality much as Lewis Carroll dealt with complicated nonsense in order to make sense. Whereas the dreaming Alice's confrontations with "a land / Of wonders wild and new" shifted her perspective of reality, so too can one veer out of the endless flow of people on a Tokyo sidewalk and drop down, down a steep underground parking ramp—down into another reality of the Abé Kobo Studio. If one arrives during the rehearsal of a play such as *The Fake Fish* or *The Briefcase,* one feels as did Alice that the world has become curious. Indeed, one's observation of the world can never again be limited to the simplicity of the purely rational, but must hereafter incorporate a more complicated vision, much as that reflected by the compound eyes of insects.

In his plays Abé relies not only on words, but also on a physiological mode of communication that draws from the temporality of dance and movement itself. It is through drama, a combination of words and dance, that Abé is able to bridge the more conventional time/space art forms. For example, one of Abé's techniques of acting which aids in this endeavor is found in what he calls "neutral position."

To achieve "neutral position" an actor is encouraged to choose a place and pose that is comfortable. He then listens to the sounds around him, erasing one after the other until finally he is concentrating on only one sound. When he concentrates on this single sound, other parts of his body are released from tension. In this state the actor is then open to all forms of expression. He may imagine himself, for example, being watched by someone who is holding a gun while standing behind him. His concentration on the original sound is then modified as his attention alerts to the danger behind him. He thus moves from the "neutral position" to a position of tension—reaction to an enemy. That tension is suddenly broken and he must return to an awareness of the original sound. Through the sense of repetition evoked in his mind as he moves back and forth between the extremes of tension and neutrality, the actor is able to experience the depths of a given time/space situation.

Abé uses this technique in his own plays which are frequently characterized by the theme of man's tragicomic situation and his inability to transcend it. At times the humor of Abé is that of psychological manipulation and the dramas become games people play with one another. But Abé also uses a sometimes surreal humor to counterbalance the irrational fear that is so much a part of his world. This humor includes metamorphoses in which people are changed into insects, briefcases, and fish. Closely aligned with the humor associated with change is a sense of terror: "The most fearful of monsters is the well-known friend slightly altered." On this score Abé has been compared to Kafka, for both writers deal with a changed reality; Abé's protagonists, however, do not experience horror to the same extent as Kafka's characters. Moreover, the Abé adversary is known, whereas the Kafka adversary is not.

In both his drama and his novels Abé's characters know no specific nationality. They are contemporary men in contemporary times, confronting problems that have yet to be afforded solutions. Abé crosses cultural boundaries to deal with universal themes; his mind is not limited by the rigidities of a given cultural framework. One looks in vain for the influences of the more traditional Japanese literary forms such as the *Noh.* When asked about this, Abé responded: "You know I have an education in the scientific fields, so I haven't had much education in literature. I think, of course, I have an unconscious influence from traditional works." Neither does he seem to be influenced by Zen Buddhism: "The Japanese rediscovery of Zen was introduced by Americans."

Abé's novels draw much of their imagery from detailed descriptions of the properties of sand, of the varying characteristics and adaptations of insects, of the workings of computers, of the precise measurements of a potassium alginate mold to make a skin-like mask, of the mazes and labyrinths of the city, and of exact instructions for making and existing in a box. All of these images, selected out of a realistic as well as a psychological scrutiny of life, are interrelated with themes that pertain to those moments of crisis when the loneliness and terror which erode the lives of contemporary man, particularly urban contemporary man, become the total reality. In "a world where people were convinced that man could be erased like chalk marks from a blackboard," Abé's characters accept this loneliness and fear as essential realities in their lives and then move on to questions of mystery and ambiguity beyond the facts themselves.

Love in Abé's world is either nonexistent, not to be trusted, or of slight duration. If an emotion resembling love exists, it is perverted by either rage or fear.

—Nancy S. Hardin

For human relations in the Abé novel are, if not bankrupt, frequently suspended "like some algebraic equation that does not include such diverse items as name, occupation, and address." His characters for the most part find themselves "periodically overwhelmed . . . by an unspeakable sense of loneliness." Abé charges modern man with such crimes as that

> of having lost one's face, the crime of shutting off the roadway to others, the crime of having lost understanding of other's agonies and joys, the crime of having lost the fear and joy of discovering unknown things in others, the crime of having forgotten one's duty to create for others, the crime of having lost a music heard together—these are crimes which express contemporary human relations, and thus the whole world assumes the form of a single penal colony.

Because of these losses and the emptiness that accompanies them, the fate of the Abé character is frequently as bizarre as the situation that leads to it. For example, in *The Crime of S. Karma,* the protagonist's emptiness is of such magnitude that when feeling a sense of affinity with a picture of a desert plain, he sucks it into his body simply by looking at it. Later he is arrested when a camel at the zoo, smelling the desert within him, wants to come into his eyes and into that arid landscape he senses there. Undergoing an irrational trial which is as distorted as that of Carroll's King and Queen of Hearts, and having lost all his badges of identity, as well as his name, an exhausted hero is no longer a human shape but something changed into a wall: "The plain extended as far as eye could see. On it I am a wall growing endlessly and serenely." In *The Woman in the Dunes,* Niki Jumpei, while defined by society as a missing person, by enforced confinement in a sand hole redefines his life and becomes a more authentic individual: "The change in the sand corresponded to a change in himself. Perhaps, along with the water in the sand, he had found a new self."

Meaning in the protagonist's existence can be found only in moments of creativity; his loneliness is otherwise unrelieved. Love in this world is either nonexistent, not to be trusted, or of slight duration. For Abé's study of human relations reveals a world wherein individuals cannot truly believe in one another, so that if an emotion resembling love exists, it is perverted by either rage or fear. The protagonist of *The Face of Another* finds his isolation compounded by a facial disfigurement that encourages his am-

bivalence toward his wife: "Thus both the desire to restore the roadway between us and vengeful craving to destroy you fiercely contended within me. At length I could not distinguish between them, and drawing the bow on you became a common, everyday thing; then suddenly in my heart was graven the face of a hunter." In *The Ruined Map* the hunter becomes the hunted and the quest for a meaningful relationship ends in a denial—a surreal dissolution of self into an unknown and impersonal world: "Nothing would be served by being found. What I needed now was a world I myself had chosen. . . . She searched; I hid. . . . I began walking in the opposite direction from her . . . perhaps in order to reach her. I would forget looking for a way to the past." *Inter Ice Age 4* focuses on the constancy and impersonality of change. Dr. Katsumi, the principal character, must acquiesce in the success of a computerized society over the older human values, of the future over the present: "The most frightening thing in the world is discovering the abnormal in that which is closest to us." The packaged protagonist's alienation of *The Box Man* is almost total, yet he manages to survive by his own form of creativity, the notes that he scribbles inside his box. Of love he comments:

> I think we had simply abandoned hope from the beginning. Passion is the urge to burn oneself out. . . . We were afraid of stopping loving before burning out, but we were not sure we wanted to go on the way people usually do. We could not imagine things so far as a half year in the future, as when the room would be full of garbage. . . . Words themselves had already begun to lose their meaning. Time had stopped. Three days, three weeks were all the same. No matter how long our love goes on burning, when it is burnt out it is over in an instant.

Questions put to Abé about his past are not always answered. He grew up in Mukden, Manchuria which he describes as "a frightening place in many ways. There was no law in the streets, where sometimes children were sold as slaves. It was nonetheless a fascinating city, a maze, a labyrinth with very dirty buildings made of black bricks. Outside the city, if one took the train which was very slow, the scenery was endlessly empty and monotonous. There were only a few trees scattered here and there." Abé now lives in the suburbs of Tokyo, commuting to his studio in the center of the city. It is not surprising to find the theme of labyrinthine mazes so prevalent in his works. Nor is it unusual to find him describing and writing of the city so vividly: "The first beat of the city's heart is a signal; within a five-minute period hundreds of filing cabinets are unlocked at one click and swarms of different but indistinguishable workers, like a wall of water released from the floodgates of a dam, suddenly throng the streets. . . ." Abé is an M.D., as was his father, although he has never practiced. His wife, Machi, is a talented artist who has illustrated several of Abé's novels. She is also a successful stage designer who is very much in demand in Tokyo theatre. She does the stage settings for all the Abé plays.

The following interview took place at different intervals in November and December 1973 in Tokyo. Serving as interpreters were Hagihara Nobutoshi, a historian, and Hamada Tomoko, a graduate student in sociology. Abé himself is a warm and gentle person who laughs often. Our conversation ranged over topics including his reading interests, which are international. Of American writers he is particularly interested in Bernard Malamud (*Pictures of Fidelman*) and Susan Sontag (*Death Kit*). But our literary discussions varied from Mayakovsky (*Bed Bug*), Chekhov (*The Cherry Orchard*), Beckett (*Happy Days*), Vian (*L'Automn à Pékin*), and Henry Miller (*Dark Spring*) to mention but a few. Talking with Abé is full of surprises, for his mind is constantly making imaginative associations. His creative virtuosity only begins with writing, for he has as well that rare ability to stimulate and provoke creative growth and excellence in the people around him.

There is one description from out of his past that captures the love of movement that one sees so much in his theater:

> The Japanese, you know, learned how to ride horses from the Mongolians and it was also the Mongolians who expanded the local culture to a world wide one. Have you ever seen real Mongolians? They are very tall, stout, physically strong men. Once I saw some Mongolian soldiers on horseback. It was at the end of the war in 1945 when I was in Manchuria that I have that memory. It was in winter and the road was frozen so that one could ice skate on it. But the Mongolians on horseback opened their legs and dashed. It was spectacular and very frightening. With one hand, they handled the horse; with the other, they carried a rifle. Some crows were flying in the sky and the Mongolians started shooting. With legs wide apart, the soldiers balanced. When their horses suddenly stopped, the men stopped with them. The horses and the men rode as one. It was unbelievable.

Abé Kobo's agility as a creative artist is equally as spectacular.

• • • • •

[*Hardin*]: *Before I came to Japan, I had thought of you primarily as a novelist. One of the most delightful surprises has been watching you direct the actors in the Abé Kobo Studio. How did you become interested in drama?*

[Abé]: To direct human beings is a kind of pleasure. It is fun to handle various personalities. It is something like the sense of driving a powerful sports car. As a director one has the same feeling that a professional racer has when he controls a fantastic machine perfectly. Because, you see, all actors are mad.

The striking thing to me is that your theatrical world relies not only on words, but also on a physiological mode of communication—on dance and movement itself. How exactly does this work?

Simply speaking, there are two types of art: one is spatial and the other one is of time. For example, in order to make time objective, we use a watch. That is to say, we make time into something spatial. The act of making time a spatial entity and the act of verbalizing are very similar. For example, people read a novel and after they finish they can repeat that experience again in themselves.

There are, however, other types of art where people recognize time itself directly. While listening to music, they are experiencing that art. It is a form of "-ing" being. When the music ends, for instance, they cannot reenact that experience.

There is a tremendous gap between spatial art and time art. Drama is the bridge that crosses between them. On the one hand, when one concentrates on the dialogue, he is doing something akin to reading a novel. Yet really to experience drama, it is necessary for the audience to watch the stage where the movements of the actors are ephemeral. There are two ways that drama can affect the reader or the audience. One involves the actor's words and the other his body to express some meaning as an "-ing" form. In this sense drama is dance as well as music, for dance can also be music using the human body. I am very much interested in drama and as a result I ask physiological things from the actors.

This certainly would appear to be true from three of your most recent plays: **The Eyeglass of Love Is Colored Glass, The Briefcase,** *and* **The Fake Fish.** *In* **The Eyeglass of Love,** *for example, it seems that you are rejecting any kind of interpretation or even any pretense of knowing what makes the characters act or feel in a certain way. One of the main points would seem to be that there are no clear distinctions between what is real and what is not. One is left wondering who is sane—the actors or the audience? Or even perhaps what sanity is?*

When we practiced the play I gave different situations to each actor. In one sense it is like a technique of montage so it has a kind of double effect. The audience somehow gets some kind of story or plot, but nothing exact. It is a rather whimsical way of treating the audience. As for an answer, it does not come until the very end of the play. I don't know either who is sane or insane. [Laughter]

Could you tell me something about how you conceived **The Eyeglass of Love Is Colored Glass?**

The title is sheer nonsense. It might lead one to expect a romantic love play. A person with such expectations will get a headache; I am amused by his getting sick and going home in confusion. This is what I really want. It is just like Boris Vian's *L'Automn à Pékin,* a book in which he writes all about Africa and nothing about Peking.

I know that in the Abé Kobo Studio you produce only your plays and those of Harold Pinter. Why Pinter?

Because first of all Pinter's plays require the most effort from the actors. They are all demanding.

Would you mind elaborating? Does it, for example, have something to do with Pinter's use of nonverbal levels of communication? His use of silences?

Partly this is true, yes. However, according to my interpretation of Pinter's plays, it is difficult to separate silence and nonsilence. Both are treated as equal. What interests me is that the world created by Pinter is very different from the world of traditional acting. Pinter's world is impossible to express by conventional means. The actors are quite at a loss about how to perform Pinter's plays.

For instance the relationship between being watched and

watching something is changed. In a traditional play the actor is a man to be watched. But now in Pinter's play, the actors cannot perform in the same conventional manner—just to be watched. So I, as director, cannot produce Pinter's plays just to be watched either.

I'm not sure I follow you.

Perhaps I could begin by saying that one characteristic of Pinter is that in his dialogue time does not flow. Rather time is a spiral. The relationship between time and space is changed. From that concept of time as a spiral, and how it affects the actors, arises the problem. For the conventional actor who plays the conventional way, this aspect of time is not a problem.

Take music for instance. The basic element for music is rhythm because this indicates time in the "-ing" energy form. When one adds to that sense of time spatial elements, then one has created a melody. Melody was very much required in a conventional dramatic technique. But when one wants to perform Pinter's plays or those of Beckett, actors are required to express themselves as more than just a melody.

As for the relationship between seeing and being seen, strictly speaking "to be seen" is an abstract concept. We imagine the situation that we are seen. The consciousness of being seen is very human. If there are two dogs and one dog watches the other being operated on, unless there is a rapid movement, the watching dog never shows any response to the operation. That implies very important things between the relationship to see and to be seen. The dog never recognizes itself as the other. In that operating room the dog to be seen should be the dog on the operating table. People, however, can never separate to be seen and to see. Only one combined entity exists. There is always to see *and* to be seen together. That is the principle.

But we often tend to regard "to be seen" as a kind of concept or idea. On TV or in a movie, there is an actor who is seen. But those of us watching him recognize that concept "to be seen." Therefore we understand to be seen as a kind of stereotype. And as such we don't allow ourselves to be seen literally. We wear armor. Conversely, abandoning that stereotype, we are able to be seen literally. It is necessary to give up this pretense only once, in order to gain the true position of being seen. All this is closely related to the idea of space and spiral time.

Watching and being watched, seeing and being seen, peeking and being peeked at seem to be important motifs in several of your works. In particular I am thinking of **The Woman in the Dunes, The Ruined Map,** *and* **The Box Man.**

Yes, there are passages in *Woman* and *Map*. It is true that in *Box Man* peeking is a very important subject. A man is in a box and has no personality. He just peeks at the world from inside, and the people outside consider him to be just a box and not a human being. So the relationship between to be seen and to see is a very important motif here.

Critics say that in this work you have murdered the novel

form—*perhaps even that the end of the book signifies the death of literature.*

I do admit **The Box Man** is an unconventional novel. The structure is quite unique. There are many tricks, but I don't think they can be understood, even by the careful reader.

What do you mean?

Loosely speaking, **The Box Man** has the structure of a suspense drama or a detective story.

In the same sense as **The Ruined Map** *or* **The Face of Another?**

Yes, but this time it is an extreme case. I think I committed a crime to write that novel because the man who writes that novel is the man who committed the crime. But people never know who that man is. I tried in **The Box Man** to give people an idea of what it is like to live in a box. I even gave directions on how the box is made in case people wanted to build one for themselves.

Aren't you afraid people will write to you with all their problems about making and living in boxes?

Well that actually happened. I got a letter from a man from one of the poorer sections of Tokyo. He said a friend of his has been wanting to live inside a box and he was quite at a loss what to do with him. What this man wanted to know was how I had heard about his friend and how I could have written about him. [Laughter]

Did you reply?

I didn't. What if the man inside the box actually came to see me.

While we are talking about **The Box Man,** *perhaps you would say something about the eight photographs that accompany the book.*

The photographs are a kind of montage. They are rather difficult to explain.

I like their ambiguous and hazy quality. They are moments captured in time and they offer, as well, a sense of "found art." You seem particularly attracted to impersonal places, to objects discarded by society, and to people regarded as outsiders. It seems to me that the music of such photographs is sad and lonely. I am reminded of a passage in **The Face of Another:**

> *True, I must make special mention of this music. Ornamental neon lights, blanched night skies, girls' legs that expanded and contracted with their stockings, forgotten alleys, corpses of dead cats in trash cans, tobacco ashes, and then . . . and then—I cannot name them all—every one of these scenes made its own particular music, its own particular noise. And for the sake of this music alone, I wanted to believe in the reality of the time I was anticipating. . . .*

Praise of my photographs makes me happier than praise of my novels.

Certainly they are intriguing and unexpected photographs.

Each in its own way is a lonely scene, indicating a melancholy reality of a particular time.

I took them at lonely times, and yes, of lonely people. The photograph of the family with the child in the wheelchair was taken in front of the Russian pavilion at Expo in Osaka. I took the family taking photos of a memorable family gathering.

One is of a man looking at a lottery poster for a lottery that has already been drawn. He is an honorable, respectable gangster. It was taken at about six o'clock in the morning. A very lonely time of the day.

One is of a man pushing a bicycle. He is a beggar and he carries all of his property with him.

That photograph is particularly blurred and ambiguous. Its caption says: "Here is a town for box men. Anonymity is the obligation of the inhabitants, and the right to live there is accorded only to those persons who are no one. All those who are registered are sentenced by the very fact of being registered." How do the poetic captions relate to the accompanying photographs?

The captions are not really relevant. These poems only emphasize that I think the photograph as a whole should be a poem.

Is there then any particular reason for the order of the photographs or that the one of the discarded trucks comes last?

Whether there is meaning or not I have forgotten. Each photograph resembles a poem. As for the gangster, he is just a typical gangster. The mirror at the street corner shows a clubhouse of the navy officers in the fashionable style of the 1930s. The freight train is just a freight train. The room is a special one for critical TB patients to be examined and to have emergency oxygen. In that ward on the walls there is a sign: "No Smoking." The photograph of the public urinal with the men urinating was taken at Ueno Station, one of the largest and bleakest stations in Tokyo. I have not talked about these photographs to anyone. The only one I have told before is the editor of Knopf, Harold Strauss, who is a semiprofessional with a camera. But he didn't like them. Maybe you could explain them to him. [Laughter]

Certainly there is a poetic quality in your novels as well as the photographs. Have you written poems as such?

I think there is a tendency toward poetry in my works, but I am hesitant to say that I am a poet. There is a kind of contradictory element in the novel as compared with poetry. It is the function of the eye of the novel to observe the area between those things which are poetic and nonpoetic.

Do you mean realistic?

No, I don't mean that nor do I mean objective. On the one hand, the object passes easily through the mind and, on the other hand, it is often hindered from doing so. There comes a time when one can see it as a kind of identifying object of one's own. At other times, one sees the object as an obstacle against one's mind. It is the function of the novel to see between these two extremes.

I've wondered if Rilke has been a poet that you've been interested in?

When I was young I read Rilke. During the war I was very much interested in him—his poems of course, and *The Notebooks of Malte Laurids Brigge,* as well. I liked the *Notebooks,* but found his philosophy too egotistic. I do think that Rilke has a genius for seeing the object between things poetic and things antipoetic.

I have also been fascinated by your use of images, such as mazes, labyrinths, cages, boxes. Certainly a sense of poetry emerges from these objectified images that happen before our eyes on the stage and in the novels.

Compared with the feudalistic society of the middle ages, we now have an open society. But in another sense we have made for ourselves a cage, or a kind of prison. As a writer one of my efforts is how to deal with an object as object itself. If I try to use these objects as means to express a philosophy, then the story becomes extremely dull. The important thing is *to think into the object,* to allow the object to be an obstacle to the mind and not, as most people do, allow it to pass easily through the mind. Once one thinks into the object, he gets a kind of surprise. Let me say again that Rilke has a true genius for doing this kind of thing. I don't like his philosophy, but I feel his power, his ability as an artist.

Sometimes I think of Lewis Carroll's Alice in Wonderland *when I read your novels or see your plays. Not that the content is the same, but there is something about the approach that gives me the sense of a world turned upside down.*

I like Lewis Carroll very much, perhaps next to Edgar Allan Poe.

Perhaps one thing that reminds me of Carroll is the fact that you use so many mathematical references throughout your novels. You do seem to have an intriguing knowledge of pure mathematics which one finds in your poetic usage of mathematical concepts. I choose at random: "Where in God's name should he start on this equation filled with unknowns?", and "In mathematics there are 'imaginary numbers,' strange numbers which, when squared, become minus. They have points of similarity with masks, for putting one mask over another would be the same as not putting on any at all."

Your point is a pleasant surprise. Although I went to medical school, I might have gone into pure mathematics. **The Crime of S. Karma** was written under the influence of Lewis Carroll—not under the influence of Kafka as so many thought. Although Carroll was a mathematician, *Alice in Wonderland* was written in a nonmathematical way, just as my books may use mathematical terminology in a poetic sense.

I am curious to know how you go about writing. What are your sources of energy? At one point in **The Face of Another** *you say, "For the act of writing is not simply replacing facts with arrangements of letters; it is a kind of venturesome trip. I am not like a postman on a preordained route. There is danger, and discovery, and satisfaction." Isn't writing, or for that matter anything creative, a matter of energy? How do you create your energy? What are its sources? You are* *a man of so many talents: novelist, playwright, director, photographer, mathematician. . . .*

Always I think I have a sense of amazement about myself. Afterwards, I wonder how I was able to create what I did. I judge other novelists by only one standard: the author's control over his material and his ability to give it a life beyond himself. In other words if a certain work surpassed its author, I regard it as very good.

I can say the same thing about my own work. During the time I am writing a novel I remember everything that I write. I remember even on what part of the paper I wrote that paragraph or phrase. But at the moment I finish writing, I forget everything and then I get depressed. On the other hand, if I then read that work again five years later, I am often happily surprised by what I've written. That doesn't mean all my works are superior. Let's put it this way, in case my work is good, just in case, I don't think the author is that good. What I mean to say is that a work should be at least better than himself.

But how do you create the energy for so many things . . . photography, directing, writing?

I really don't know. I don't think in actuality I have that much energy. It may be wrong, but the creativity seems to come out of a sense of scarcity—something like the sense of a "shortage of oil." It is a negative pressure, a sort of emptiness. To make it perhaps more concrete for you I can name two authors, Edgar Allan Poe and Franz Kafka, who seem to me to have the same negative feeling. It is not, you see, entirely a matter of myself, but it is more a matter of what others want. I feel that everyone has a hole, a kind of emptiness. And if I can, I want to fill up the hole.

Will you elaborate on Poe and Kafka as meaningful writers for you?

Poe was really the first person to inspire me to write. I was about fifteen years old at the time. This is a story I don't usually tell. I was born in Manchuria where the winters were very cold. When I was a mere school boy it was so cold that I was unable to go out during recess and I had to stay in the classroom. I read Poe's stories and I told them to my classmates. I had to read one story a day in order to maintain my standing, and there was still a demand even after I had finished all the translations. I then found myself having to invent stories during the whole cold winter. That was the first time I began to write the kind of story that could entertain other people.

I read Kafka after I had become a writer. I was really shocked when I read him for the first time. I felt a sense of relatedness, of someone very close to me. Kafka's way is different from the ordinary way of approaching ideas. Both he and Poe disclosed to me how to share something with other beings, outside the conventional pattern. It seems to me that Kafka's search has to do with how two absolutely lonely, solitary beings can make conversation with each other. In that sense Poe and Kafka create a sense of being in accord, each sounding the same note. It is a question that I concern myself with—this theme of loneliness.

Yes, it is true that in each of your works your protagonists seem lonely, isolated, alienated personalities. . . .

I think first of all that loneliness is universal. Rilke's basic theme is loneliness. And it is one of my central concerns. But you know, as a matter of fact, it is a new theme for the Japanese. The reason is that the concept of loneliness appeared in the urban mode of life. The oldest examples in literature must come from England where urbanization began the earliest. Also in China. Unless the cities were established, the theme would never have emerged. I have discussed this in **Itan no Passporto (Pagan Passport)**.

Do you consider yourself an existentialist?

Perhaps so. I remember that when I was in high school during the war, I was a pacifist. At that time I read such people as Jaspers, Heidegger, Husserl, all of whom undoubtedly influenced me to some extent. I was spiritually and intellectually supported by Dostoevsky.

Have you also read Sartre and Camus?

I did not like Camus at first. Only now do I understand what he is suffering from. I do wish, however, that he had more of a sense of humor. I don't like Sartre at all. He doesn't have any sense of humor. Without humor we cannot bear reality.

The reason that I was so attracted by existentialism initially was quite simply that I was persuaded that "existence precedes essence." In the case of militarism, essence precedes existence. Perhaps the idea of fatherland or motherland really belongs to the category of essence. So from the existentialist's point of view such an idea is really a sort of subordinate one.

Could you apply this to any of your novels in particular?

I am not Sartre. When I write I can't be so analytical. When I am preparing to write I can be analytical and detached. But once I start writing I am not. It is strange but I become subordinate to what I am writing, and I can no longer dominate the work I am writing. After a certain stage I lose a certain control.

A good example of the nonphilosophical workings of my mind has to do with **The Ruined Map.** To tell the truth the opening scene appeared in my dreams and I continued to write. Just before ending I was unable to finish. I struggled for a few months and finally the ending scene appeared in my dreams, and I transcribed it. After all a novel is not so logical a thing.

Could you comment on the fact that, in the end of **Fake Fish,** *the man isn't able to come from out of his dream. He dies within the dream.*

He died in his dream, that is to say before he got out of it. He cannot get out of the dream because he is still in the dream, forever as it were.

Is this like Sartre's "bad faith"? That is to say, are you dealing with a person who does not live his life in an authentic way?

Fake Fish is a kind of black comedy, British style. One man dreams of being a fish, simply speaking, and dreaming of being a fish he dreams too deeply. He makes every effort to get out of that dream, but as I've said during those efforts he dies, and therefore he dreams forever. On a beach after a storm there are many dead fish. Maybe among these dead fish some of them are dreaming men who couldn't get out of their dream. All this, I suppose, is total nonsense.

Then what will you do next?

I always ask myself. What next? I am scared just to think of it.

Do you get frightened before you begin to write?

The most enjoyable time is when I suddenly get the idea for my work. But when I start writing it is very, very painful.

Many people ask why a writer commits suicide. But they don't know the vanity and the nothingness of writing. I think it is very usual and natural for a writer to commit suicide, because in order to keep on writing he must be a very strong person.

—Kōbō Abé

I can believe it.

To write or to commit suicide. Which one will it be? [Laughter]

Better to write.

Many people ask why a writer commits suicide. But I think the people who ask don't know the vanity and the nothingness of writing. I think it is very usual and natural for a writer to commit suicide, because in order to keep on writing he must be a very strong person.

I have noticed that in your work the individual is frequently sacrificed for the good of the group.

You are right. I don't want to lecture, so I will keep this to the point. Writing a novel is very different from thinking something through logically. Whereas now we operate under new social relationships, our inner selves still cling to the older values. Thus there is a conflict between the self who seeks a new social relationship and the self who tries to maintain the older form. Regardless of what one wants, one still must face the new relationship, although the older self rejects it. I suppose that this has been a common literary theme forever. Whether man will survive or not is also an eternal subject, though more pronounced in our time. I think that a characteristic of modern literature is this uneasiness regarding human existence which has been superimposed on a desire for new human relationships. That is to say, there is an uneasiness as to whether the quest for new relationships is meaningful or whether human relationships are worth seeking at all. They might simply disappear altogether. That is what I am facing now. Say, for example, in Beckett's play, *Happy Days,* all human relationships are stagnated. But Beckett put that theme in a play and a play in itself is a means of communication.

Although your own plays may deal with some levels of non-communication, they do communicate.

Yes, I think that is a characteristic modern theme. Pinter also pursues it. Thus we communicate the theme that we are unable to communicate with each other. We terminate our communication. And that's self-contradictory.

One novel we haven't mentioned at all is **Inter Ice Age 4.** *You say at the end that one of your purposes is "to make the reader confront the cruelty of the future, produce within him anguish and strain and bring about a dialogue with himself."*

One word for explaining it. I am not against revolution, but would emphasize that revolution frequently takes a form that kills or hurts the people who want it. As long as a revolutionary recognizes that he will suffer for the sake of the revolution rather than for his own happiness, I agree with the revolutionary in his wish for revolution. Unless one has the confidence to take his life at risk, to be killed in revolution, he cannot make revolution. On the other hand, if one has that strong belief, one should do it. That is the theme of *Inter Ice Age 4.*

Earlier, I was extremely interested in what you were saying about space and time. You spoke mostly of time, however. Could you comment on your use of space in novels such as **The Woman in the Dunes?** *It seems to me that you use space differently in your plays from in your novels.*

We feel time only when we see the changes of space. Unless we can catch that change of space, we cannot feel time. For example, the animal without language seems to live very much in time but in fact is controlled by time and can never control time. But human beings, because we have words, can see time as a kind of wrinkle or some shade of space. The human being has the power to imagine. By using imagination as a function of change, the human being goes beyond time. If we have only music, we wouldn't have much civilization or culture. Music is always in the form of "-ing" time. Music is to live in time but never to be able to look at time. Novels and drama, on the other hand, are forms of creativity that allow man to look at time.

Does imagination then rely much on memory?

What I have said is a form of reading space. Memory as a form of imagination is to be found in old folk stories, old folk songs. These older tales give us various kinds of time. For the past, that was fine. But the relationship we have now between time and space is much more demanding. For example, there is the law of cause and effect, the idea that the present moment is the result of the past and the future will be the result of the present. Now because the relationship between time and space has become much more complicated, it is impossible to apply the law of cause and effect to everything. The collapse of the simple belief in the law of cause and effect let modern literature suffer in the twentieth century.

I became interested in the *nouveau roman* and Robbe-Grillet precisely because such writing destroys the law of cause and effect. Robbe-Grillet used the conflict of time and space as a theme, but I think it is rather a method.

Whereas Robbe-Grillet's novels indicate this collapse of time and space as a theme, you attempt to demonstrate this collapse in the structure of your novels?

In Robbe-Grillet's static space, there are wrinkles and shades in which we can see the technique of conceiving time. I try not to overlook time. Gazing at static space very carefully, so that it seems as if no time is going on, is a process that deeply concerns me. For example, take this white wall. I must be able to gaze steadily at this white wall—that is, look at it with a special eye—if I want to make a single book about it. That is what I mean when I say the novel is a struggle against time. (pp. 439-56)

> *Abé Kōbō and Nancy S. Hardin, in an interview in* Contemporary Literature, *Vol. 15, No. 4, Autumn, 1974, pp. 439-56.*

OBITUARIES AND TRIBUTES

Myrna Oliver   (obituary date 23 January 1993)

[*In the following obituary, Oliver provides an overview of Abé's life and major works.*]

Kobo Abe, highly respected Japanese novelist and playwright whose often bizarre and allegorical themes chronicled isolation and survival in the post-World War II universe, has died in Tokyo. He was 68. . . .

He was best known for his 1962 novel *The Woman in the Dunes,* which was his first work to be translated into English. It was made into a film of the same title in 1964, and won a special jury prize at the Cannes film festival.

The story focuses on a schoolteacher and amateur entomologist who goes on a weekend insect collecting trip in lonely sand dunes, echoing Abe's childhood interest in insects and his lifelong study of identity. The hero stumbles onto a primitive tribe living in the sand pits and becomes their prisoner along with a previously imprisoned woman. He is first obsessed with the loss of his identity and with escape, but comes to realize that his sand prison gives him intellectual and spiritual freedom.

The novel was considered a contender for the Nobel Prize for literature, but was not nominated, partly because the very private Abe studiously avoided the literary spotlight.

Abe's work was often compared to that of Franz Kafka, whom he greatly admired.

Born in Tokyo and reared in Manchuria where his father practiced medicine, Abe was somewhat alienated from his country and rejoiced when Japan lost World War II.

Many critics believe that the secret of his international success was that he distanced himself from his homeland.

"He is probably the first Japanese writer whose works, having no distinctly Japanese qualities, are of interest to the Western audience because of their universal relevance," noted Hisaaki Yamanouchi in the book *The Search for Authenticity in Modern Japanese Literature.*

Abe's plays were less known in the United States and less revered. A trio of his one-acts was produced at Los Angeles' 5th Street Studio in 1980—*Suitcase, The Cliff of Time,* and *The Man Who Turned Into a Stick.* The third included program notes linking its meaning to Dante's seventh circle of hell.

"Plays that send us scurrying for obscure references to clarify what they're all about," said *Times* drama critic Sylvie Drake, "fill me with the suspicion that it's for lack of being able to tell us what they mean on their own terms."

Neither was Abe overly impressed by American writers.

He made a rare U.S. appearance in 1986 at the 48th international congress of the PEN writers group in New York, which used the theme, "Is PEN Mightier in Imagination Than the State?" Abe told the *Los Angeles Times* through an interpreter:

An excerpt from *The Woman in the Dunes*

Because winds and water currents flow over the land, the formation of sand is unavoidable. As long as the winds blew, the rivers flowed, and the seas stirred, sand would be born grain by grain from the earth, and like a living being it would creep everywhere. The sands never rested. Gently but surely they invaded and destroyed the surface of the earth.

This image of the flowing sand made an indescribably exciting impact on the man. The barrenness of sand, as it is usually pictured, was not caused by simple dryness, but apparently was due to the ceaseless movement that made it inhospitable to all living things. What a difference compared with the dreary way human beings clung together year in year out.

Certainly sand was not suitable for life. Yet, was a stationary condition absolutely indispensable for existence? Didn't unpleasant competition arise precisely because one tried to cling to a fixed position? If one were to give up a fixed position and abandon oneself to the movement of the sands, competition would soon stop. Actually, in the deserts flowers bloomed and insects and other animals lived their lives. These creatures were able to escape competition through their great ability to adjust. . . .

While he mused on the effect of the flowing sands, he was seized from time to time by hallucinations in which he himself began to move with the flow.

> *Kōbō Abé, in his* The Woman in the Dunes, *Alfred A. Knopf, 1964.*

"Generally speaking, I am not fond of attending congresses of this sort. But the theme of this congress . . . made me think that having come up with a title like this, American writers must be at a higher level than I had imagined."

Born Kimifusa Abe on March 7, 1924, Abe changed his name to the more Chinese sounding Kobo partly because of his disillusionment with Japan. He graduated from the University of Tokyo with a degree in medicine, but never practiced.

He turned instead to writing poetry, and published his first volume, *Poems of an Unknown Poet,* in 1947 at his own expense. His literary reputation was established with the publication of his novel *The Road Sign at the End of the Street* in 1948.

Abe is survived by his wife, Michiko, and a daughter, Neri.

Myrna Oliver, in an obituary in Los Angeles Times, *January 23, 1993, p. A22.*

James Sterngold   (obituary date 23 January 1993)

[*In the following obituary, Sterngold reviews Abé's life and career.*]

Kobo Abe, a literary master whose haunting visions of people senselessly trapped by modern urban life made him one of Japan's most highly acclaimed postwar authors, died today. He was 68.

After a brief illness, Mr. Abe died of heart failure in a hospital in Tokyo, hospital officials said.

Mr. Abe (pronounced AH-bay) is best known in both Japan and the United States for his 1962 novel, *The Woman in the Dunes,* a characteristically dark, surrealistic tale of a man who becomes trapped in a pit with a strange woman and struggles to make do while local villagers peer in. The movie version won a special prize at the Cannes Film Festival in 1964.

His was a threatening world of people who frequently lose their way and lose their identities, fighting against always insurmountable odds to unravel the senseless events that have left them doomed.

Although he resisted the description, he was often called a Japanese Kafka. In one story a man finds himself transformed into a plant. In another a man decides to move into a box to discover a kind of freedom he cannot find in ordinary life.

His themes shared some of the desolation of Western writers whose sensibilities were also shaped by the brutal rise of Fascism and then the devastation of World War II. His landscapes were, however, distinctively Japanese.

At least eight of Mr. Abe's novels, collections of stories and plays were translated into English, making him one of the best-known Japanese authors in the United States, along with Yukio Mishima, who was a close friend of Mr. Abe before his suicide.

Mr. Abe, an owlish figure usually pictured behind large, black-framed glasses and puffing on a cigarette, was immensely popular in Japan, especially among the generation that came of age in the 1960's. His publisher, Shinchosa, said that about nine million copies of Mr. Abe's books had been sold.

He won many of Japan's most prestigious literary awards and was occasionally mentioned as a candidate for the Nobel Prize in Literature. He founded a theater company in the 1970's and put on productions in Washington and New York.

Mr. Abe's death was announced on the front pages of every major newspaper this afternoon, and television networks immediately broadcast programs reviewing his accomplishments and themes.

Mr. Abe was born in Tokyo on March 7, 1924, but he grew up in northern China, which was being occupied by the Japanese military throughout the 1930's. (Kobo is the Chinese reading of his given name, Kimifusa.) His father was a doctor, and he eventually studied medicine at Tokyo University but was an indifferent student and never practiced.

Mr. Abe published his first short stories in the late 1940's, quickly establishing himself as a distinctly skeptical voice in a society shattered by its defeat in the war and torn from its roots. His works had none of the tragic intensity of Mishima's or the delicate explorations of feelings of the books of Yasunari Kawabata, the only Japanese to win the Nobel Prize in Literature.

At the heart of his art, ultimately, was what some critics described as a pervasive loneliness, as his characters searched for their real and spiritual homes in an inhospitable world.

As Mr. Abe wrote in **"Red Cocoon,"** one of his earliest short stories: "The day is dying, time for men to hurry home: but I have no place to go. I slowly walk along the narrow crack dividing house from house and wonder—wonder—wonder how there can be so many and none, not one, for me."

Mr. Abe was named a foreign member of the American Academy of Arts and Letters last year. He was made an honorary doctor of humane letters by Columbia University in 1975.

He is survived by his wife, Machi, an artist who collaborated on many of his theater productions, and a daughter, Neri.

James Sterngold, in an obituary in The New York Times, *January 23, 1993, p. 28.*

The Washington Post   (obituary date 23 January 1993)

[*In the following obituary, the critic summarizes Abé's life and the major themes of his work.*]

Kobo Abe, 68, a novelist and playwright who had a major influence on postwar Japanese literature and who had been celebrated around the world for his surrealist, Kafkaesque novels, died Jan. 22 at a hospital in Tokyo. He had a heart ailment.

Mr. Abe, often mentioned as a contender for the Nobel Prize for literature, was best known for his 1962 novel *Suna no Onna (The Woman in the Dunes)*. Like many of his works, the book portrayed modern man's struggle against alienation and loss of identity.

The novel was made into a 1964 movie. Its schoolteacher protagonist is hunting for insects in remote sand dunes when he is trapped in a deep pit along with a woman who is being kept there by villagers.

He first resists his captivity, but eventually realizes that his prison of sand allows him intellectual and spiritual freedom that had been denied him in the outside world.

Mr. Abe's other novels included *Tanin no Kao (The Face of Another)* and *Hako Otoko (The Box Man)*. He also wrote plays and founded a theater group.

"Of all Japanese novelists, Abe most deserved to be called Japan's Kafka," writer Takatsugu Nakano said.

Born in Tokyo, Mr. Abe spent his early life in Japanese-occupied northeast China. He was prodded into studying medicine by his physician father, but he turned to literature after graduating from medical school.

Mr. Abe, whose novels were translated into many languages, believed that the modern metropolis threatens individual human identity.

The theme underlying much of his work is the alienation of modern man in urban society, which he explored in often bizarre and allegorical situations. In his absurdist novel *The Box Man,* a man rejects the ugliness and anonymity of the city by hiding in a box.

He also was interested in the inversion of roles, when the hunter becomes the hunted and the aggressor the victim. He was much influenced by the works of Feodor Dostoevski, Franz Kafka, Edgar Allan Poe and philosopher Friedrich Nietzsche.

Politically a leftist who was critical of Japanese wartime militarism, Mr. Abe was expelled from the Japanese Communist Party for a book of scathing reportage about his travels in Eastern Europe in 1956.

Survivors include his wife, Machi, an artist who provided the illustrations for many of his works, and a daughter.

An obituary in The Washington Post, *January 23, 1993, p. C4.*

The Times, London   (obituary date 25 January 1993)

[*In the following obituary, the critic examines Abé's literary style and primary influences.*]

The literary influences on Kobo Abe were many and varied and included Dostoevsky, Edgar Allan Poe and Nietzsche. But he is, pre-eminently, the modern Japanese representative of Kafkaesque surrealism. The early short story **"Stick"**, which was published in *Japan Quarterly* and later provided the basis for a play, contains the elements of Abe's artistic procedure and of his outlook on life. Parallels with Kafka's *Metamorphosis* are inescapable. Yet the resulting piece utterly escapes the charge of derivativeness, through a philosophical dimension which is quintessentially Japanese.

Abe had severed his links with the traditions of classical Japanese literature, but he did not make the mistake of developing too uncritical an affinity with European writers. **"Stick"** is recognisably the offspring of Kafka in its selection of an idea—a man is suddenly turned into a stick and hears himself discoursed on objectively by a professor and his students. But its protagonist is, like the story's author, an intellectual hermit who feels no anger against those who control the moral no man's land in which he finds himself.

Abe had several times been a contender for the Nobel prize for Literature. But he was a deeply private man who shunned the limelight and all forms of coterie. Though he was a communist for some years, in reaction to what he had experienced of Japanese militarism, it was characteristic of him that he was unable to stay within the party fold for long. His left-wing tendency, like his lament on the dark side of Japanese industrial success, was a philosophical preoccupation rather than a political statement.

Kobo Abe spent his childhood in Japanese-occupied Manchuria, where his father, a doctor, taught at the Medical College at Mukden. He used to entertain his classmates by telling them Poe stories during the lunch breaks; when he ran out of Poe, he took to invention. Meanwhile brought up in traditional style, but against the background of an alien and hostile culture, he tried to distract himself from a fundamental unease by painting abstract pictures and collecting insects.

In 1940 he returned to Tokyo and enrolled at the Seijo High School. After recovering from tuberculosis and as he put it, "devouring Dostoevsky" in his convalescence, he began to search in contemporary Japanese literature for something to confirm his emotional opposition to his country's fascism. But he could not find it, and so turned to Nietzsche, Heidegger (a dubious influence in the circumstances) and Jaspers. The eventual result was a book of poems published in 1948 at his own expense, *Poems by an Unknown.*

At his father's insistence he had entered university in 1943 as a medical student but after a period of nervous exhaustion—during which he and a friend took each other to the same mental hospital—he escaped to Manchuria by means of a forged certificate of ill health, and spent the rest of the war in what he called "peaceful idleness."

Then in the aftermath, his father caught typhus and died and, Abe wrote, "In this way, I was released from my obligation, first to the state, and then to my father." By 1951, he had received the Akutagawa Prize for literature and his career was established.

One of the three stories which gained him this award, **"Mr S. Karuma's Crime"**, is entirely characteristic: the narrator loses his name and thus his access to normal communication with other human beings. But he is able to communicate with certain zoo animals and eventually certain inanimate objects such as shop-window mannequins which come alive to greet him. In this and other tales, such as **"Intruders"** (1951), the techniques of such French writers as Boris Vian are evidenct. By then Abe had allied himself with the group led by Kiyoteru Hamada dedicated to fusing surrealism with Marxism.

Abe was for some time a member of the Japanese Communist party, but was expelled in 1956 for writing a book of scathing reportage about travels in Eastern Europe.

His best-known work is the novel **The Woman in the Dunes** (1962), which was filmed under that title by Hiroshi Teshigahara. In it, a school-teacher discovers a strange community of people who spend their entire lives in a struggle against engulfing sands. The protagonist falls into a pit of sand and finds himself the companion and prisoner of a young widow who needs his help. He refuses to escape when chance offers it. In method and plot the book is again reminiscent of postwar French writing. But the execution is wholly Japanese and the device of slowing down the action almost to a standstill is Abe's own.

In **The Face of Another** (translated in 1966) a scientist, hideously scarred in a laboratory accident, sets out to seduce his own wife. In **The Ruined Map** (translated in 1969) a detective is transformed into the man he is hunting.

In the play **You, Too are Guilty** (translated in 1979), with which he toured the United States that year with his own theatre, he effectively experiments with the theme of a possible bond between the living and the dead.

Abe's humour and his ideas rather than his writing style—often stiff and formal—were his chief strengths. His plotting was ironically meticulous.

He is survived by his wife, Machiko, an artist, who illustrated some of his books, and by a daughter.

> *An obituary in* The Times, *London, January 25, 1993, p. 19.*

REVIEWS OF ABÉ'S RECENT WORKS

Ivan Gold   (review date 27 March 1988)

[*Gold is an American novelist, short story writer, critic, educator, and translator who is an expert on Japanese literature. In the following review, he describes* The Ark Sakura *as a badly executed—and translated—exercise in the bizarre.*]

Here's an idea for a novel. An ugly, fat man has taken up residence in an abandoned stone quarry an hour's drive from the city. He is waiting for the end. The end will be nuclear war, and the fat man, a technological wizard, has rigged his quarters to ride out the disaster. He has also boobytrapped the quarry, in the best Rube Goldberg fashion, to keep intruders from sharing in his good fortune. Things are already grisly topside: gangs of punks maraud through the garbage dump that hides the quarry, packs of wild dogs roam, and a zombie contingent of elders—they appear to have the job of policing the area, but may be a paramilitary force—compound the fat one's sense of peril.

Mole (known in his youth as "Pig," but preferring the nickname "Mole") has come to regard his underground quarters as a ship, an ark, and decides it needs a crew. Once a month he ventures forth to do his shopping (hunting down items so obscure they may not exist in English, like "faucet parking" and "large laminated dry cells"), and on one of these trips to the city he succeeds in recruiting two men and an attractive young woman to return with him and share his doomsday fantasy.

One of these recruits is a salesman, whose entire stock-in-trade consists of samples of one exotic (and possibly bogus) dried insect which survives in nature by consuming its own excrement (this closed ecosystem appeals to Mole, who buys one), and the other two are a team, a pair of professional shills in the salesman's employ. Back at the quarry, much impenetrable business goes on among these four, plus some violent interaction with the groups outside. By the end of the book, lucky to be alive at all, Mole is evicted from his underground life.

Sounds as if it might work, doesn't it? Kobo Abe has redeemed bizarre, apocalyptic materials before—his novels **The Face of Another, The Ruined Map** and **The Box Man,** all dealing with characters alienated from society, were fairly successful here. He is said by critics to owe more to Kafka (or Dostoevsky or Lewis Carroll or Beckett or Pinter or Robbe-Grillet) than to Japanese antecedents or contemporaries, although he does from time to time evince the native fondness for composing novels in journal or letter form.

But **The Ark Sakura** is a small disaster. A clumsy translation, marked by solecisms, gibberish and pseudoprose, does not sufficiently distract from the flimsiness beneath. Abe may not be at fault for tautologies like "vertical walls," nor for clodhopper similes like "ragged clouds flew by like torn shreds of threadbare cloth"—if we are asked to imagine a ragged cloud, how "torn, shredded and threadbare" does it need to get? On page one, along with "faucet parking," we have a "football," which can make sense to an American reader only as a soccer ball, and in general, plodding from the first page to the last (on which appears the sentence, "The whole town was dead, in an energetic, lifelike way") was as fraught with pain and peril, for this reader, as gaining access to Mole's sanctuary was intended to be for the world at large.

But an industrial-strength translation is perhaps appropriate for what is little more than an exercise in lunatic technology and grade-school scatology; Abe seems unable, this time out, to frame his twin obsessions with a readable novel. He does make a half-hearted effort to give the central character a usable past: Mole's father was a rapist, Mole himself was framed for rape, etc., but none of the detail resonates, connects. The centerpiece (as the jacket copy chortles) of the ark's machinery is "an extremely powerful toilet capable of flushing just about anything—not excepting people—out to sea," and when Mole gets his leg caught in the toilet we are in for nearly 100 pages of outhouse vaudeville which not even the great translator Donald Keene, I believe, could have easily salvaged. Abe has been better served (with better work) by translators in the past—Keene rendered his absurdist play, *Friends*, and E. Dale Saunders did a creditable job with *The Woman in the Dunes*, although this became a far better film than it ever was a novel.

If you prefer your foreign literature denaturalized (as well as disjointed and absurd), you might glance at *The Ark Sakura* despite these remarks. Once past the title ("sakura" means "shill," as well as "cherry blossom") there is little in it that is identifiably Japanese. An exceptional moment, when Japanese history does seem to mesh with Abe's scatological and technological concerns, comes with his aside on why the capital city had to be moved so often in ancient times: "Sewage, trash, and dead bodies . . . people's sensitivity to smell."

In the search for a perpetrator, we might begin and end with Knopf. Active for more than 30 years in bringing modern Japanese fiction to American readers, the publisher, seems to have failed to notice that the honeymoon is over, that if it plays in Tokyo in 1987, this does not necessarily mean it will play in Peoria or in Washington, D.C. Granted that Kawabatas and Tanizakis and Mishimas don't grow on trees. But even a good author may write a dreadful book, and hard choices must be made. The enormously-gifted writer Kenzaburo Oe, for one random example, is still out there alive and well, I think, and has not (or not by us) been heard from nearly enough; other first-rate talent must surely be crying out for literary translation, and the dearth of Japanese women writers available in English continues.

> Ivan Gold, "Waiting for the End of the World," in Book World—The Washington Post, *March 27, 1988, p. 10.*

Robert Garis   (review date Winter 1989)

[*Garis is an American critic and educator. In the following review of* The Ark Sakura, *he faults Abé for failing to make a meaningful work out of a number of interesting "ingredients."*]

International high style at its most stupefyingly relentless is the achievement of Kobo Abe's *The Ark Sakura*, which lays out the ingredients for some sort of fable about the nuclear age or human survival or paranoia, and then shuts down without putting anything together. The first-person narrator named Mole (also Pig, a nickname he dislikes) is looking for people to join him in his survival "ship," a many-chambered abandoned underground quarry in which his father had once imprisoned him as a punishment, but which he has now fitted out with all sorts of provisions, boobytraps against intruders and the like, as an "ark" for survival. The quarry's main feature is a huge toilet, with no seat and with immense water pressure in the flushing mechanism which makes it very inconvenient to use—it was this toilet to which his father had tied him. The candidates for survival Mole gathers (with no particular criteria) are an insect seller at a bazaar and a man and a woman who work as shills for him and whose animated

conversation about one of the insects attracts Mole's interest. This insect, an eupcaccia, feeds entirely on its own feces, moving in a perfect circle just slowly enough to keep its nutritional system functioning smoothly, except during its mating season, when it rises precariously from its circle on flimsy wings, and then "time stands still." Once Mole and his three recruits enter the Ark, there is a steady, boring action of exploration of the place itself, temporary disappearances of the male shill and the insect seller, much searching for them, suspicions that other people are hiding in the quarry, much searching for them too. Both the shill and the woman tell Mole that the other has cancer but doesn't know it. Two thirds of the way through, emissaries arrive from a group of old people called the Broom Brigade, who hope to survive in the "Kingdom of Quintessential Castoffs." In the meantime, they serve as garbage-collectors. But they have contracted out their most dangerous product, poisonous industrial wastes, to Mole and his huge toilet, and now they want him to destroy a human body for them. In the last hundred pages the action speeds up; Mole gets his leg stuck in the toilet, from which he finally releases himself by setting off an explosion which changes the pressure in the water system. He tells the other characters that the explosion is a nuclear explosion, that nuclear warfare has begun; when he afterwards tells them the truth, they prefer to believe the nuclear explanation, and when Mole leaves them behind in the Ark, he finds that the world, including his own body, has become transparent.

These are the ingredients, but no fable emerges. "Sakura" is the Japanese word for "shill": is Mole's survival ship a fake that manipulates people who are obsessed with nuclear disaster? You don't feel this as you read, and all the characters in the novel bring a kind of bland steadiness of attention to everything they do, without feeling obsessed or victimized, and you don't feel any irony about that. Apart from Mole's pleasure in little flesh contacts he makes with the flesh of the woman shill, particularly with her thighs or buttocks, and his pain when his leg is stuck in the toilet, the entire action is rendered without affect. None of the meanings promised in the action are made by the kind of connective process we are used to encountering when meaning happens. The strange insect, much discussed at the beginning of the novel, completely disappears, and we aren't given the wherewithal to connect any person or act with the insect's over-meaningful habits. Loud elements such as Mole's father's having chained him to the toilet for punishment, and the steady emphasis on the toilet and on excrement, seem continually on the verge of working up some meaning but remain inert; when we learn about Mole's job of disposing of industrial pollution, and eventually of disposing of a human body, our sense of being right on top of meaning without seeing it or feeling it generates an almost eerie emptiness which the book doesn't in any way register. The transparent outside world makes a very striking appearance formally, in a single-page final chapter, but the prose doesn't reveal either by tone or imagery what transparency means. And so on.

It is hard to guess what the novel would seem like to somebody without a reviewer's obligation to continue reading. Readers who have admired Kobo Abe in the past might

An excerpt from "The Crime of S. Karma"

I woke up. Waking up in the morning is a perfectly natural thing to do; nothing unusual about that. So what was different this morning? Something or other was definitely odd.

To know something is odd, and have no idea what it could be, is damned odd in itself—and as I washed my face and brushed my teeth, things got odder still.

To see what would happen (don't ask me why), I gave a cavernous yawn. Straight away the oddity converged in my chest. It felt as if somehow my chest were hollow.

Attributing this sensation to hunger, I went down to the building café (following my normal routine), where I breakfasted on two bowls of soup and six slices of bread. The numbers stick in my mind for a reason: normally, I would never eat so much.

But the sense of oddity only intensified, along with the sense of hollowness in my chest, so eventually I gave up. My stomach, at any rate, was full.

I went over to the register and the girl there handed me the account book to sign. For some reason I hesitated. The hesitation seemed to bear some relation to the peculiar mood I was in; I glanced over at the gray infinity beyond the window, searching for my reflection.

Suddenly I became aware of my predicament. Standing there gripping the pen, I was unable to sign my name. For the life of me, I couldn't remember what it was—that was why I was hesitating.

Still, I felt little surprise. I had read that lots of people—scholars absorbed in research, for example—often experience momentary difficulty in recalling their names. (This was in a respectable academic paper, too, not a smear of the scholars in question.)

So with perfect serenity, I took out my case of business cards. Unfortunately, it was empty. Flipping it over, I checked my ID card on the other side and saw to my amazement that my name had disappeared.

Swiftly I pulled out a letter from my father that I'd stuck in my appointment book. The address and salutation were gone.

I checked the label on the inside of my suit. Gone.

In growing alarm, I thrust my hands into every cranny of my pants and coat, scanning every scrap of paper I could find, without luck.

Every place my name had been recorded was now blank.

Frustrated, I asked the girl at the counter what my name was. We were casual acquaintances, so she must have known, but she only gave me a queer smile and made no effort to speak. I had no choice but to pay cash.

> *Kōbō Abé, in his* Beyond the Curve, *Kodansha International, 1991.*

find a positive value in what I experienced as negative: since the novel's consistent *moderato* narrative drive doesn't produce any meaning to distract us, it does bring that element of fiction—movement in time—to sharp focus. And I suppose it's possible to admire the odd skill with which Abe does in fact avoid meaningfulness—his foot never slips. When I had seen the film made from Abe's first novel, **Woman of the Dunes,** a highly regarded, portentously meaningful fable about some mysteries of sexuality, I read the novel itself to check whether the film had coarsened Abe's meaning and found that it hadn't. Abe's progress, which has led him to ever sterner renunciations of the conventional, has established him in a high place in the international literary scene. Other reviewers of this latest novel hint at the marvelous but ineffable experience they have had. For this reader there was nothing. (pp. 757-59)

> *Robert Garis, in a review of "The Ark Sakura," in* The Hudson Review, *Vol. XLI, No. 4, Winter, 1989, pp. 757-59.*

Marian Ury   (review date 17 March 1991)

[*Ury is an American critic and educator. In the following favorable review of* Beyond the Curve, *she highlights examples of Abé's main themes: human isolation, the fragility of identity, and the importance of memory.*]

One of the many attractions of the dozen ingenious stories in **Beyond the Curve,** Kobo Abe's first collection of short fiction to appear in English, is that they suggest a new parlor game: What would you do, reader, if threatened with metamorphosis into a plant? How would you react if you came home to find the corpse of an unknown man dumped behind your locked door? Or if a benevolently smiling family of nine—from tottering, toothless old lady to infant—invaded your apartment, voted it theirs, called you a "damn fascist" for trying to turn them out (majority rule, they insist), complained about the food in your refrigerator, confiscated your wallet, paycheck and the picture of your girlfriend, let you out only to go to work and imprisoned you at night in the attic? What would you do if you were an envoy from outer space and the problem was that you looked just like a human being, so that no one would believe your claim to be a Martian—just as no one believed your 32 predecessors, all of whom were carted off to a lunatic asylum? On the other hand, what would you do if you met someone claiming to be such a Martian?

. . . Oh, you would, would you?

Whatever solutions you offer, Mr. Abe can assure you they won't work—even though one of the traits of his typical protagonist (and alter ego) is boundless confidence in each new stratagem, despite the fact that it inevitably goes wrong. Take, for example, the hero of **"Intruders,"** the man whose apartment has been invaded. He appeals to the apartment-house manager, who says she doesn't care who uses the rooms and reminds him that he's behind on the rent. So he slips off to see a lawyer; but the lawyer, he discovers, is in an even worse quandary, playing unwilling host to an interloping family of 13. Eventually, the protagonist is reduced to scattering handbills from his attic window. But the intruders persuade the city government that these fliers are covered with bacteria and have them banned as a menace to public health.

In his 1962 novel, *The Woman in the Dunes,* the classic parable of entrapment for which he is best known in the West (the film version won the 1964 Special Jury Prize at the Cannes Film Festival), Mr. Abe speaks of how an apparent opening in a fence on the dunes will in reality be the final entrance to prison. And in a story in this collection, entitled **"Beguiled,"** Mr. Abe explains that the surest way of taking someone captive is to let him believe himself to be the captor. In the various stories, each protagonist's reasoning may be good, or it may be obviously bad; but, regardless of its quality, his doom is sealed.

In **"Dendrocacalia,"** the everyman who has already had intimations that he is in danger of becoming a plant receives a mysterious note that promises a rendezvous with destiny, signed with the initial K. Only an Abe hero, surely, would assume so unquestioningly and so optimistically that its writer must be some former girlfriend—for all that he cannot recall her. In fact, it is from a sinister botanist intent on (literally) potting his quarry.

In **"An Irrelevant Death,"** the man who finds the corpse assumes that no one will believe in his innocence. Thus he decides, it seems logically, to destroy the evidence that would incriminate him—only to be overwhelmed by the task, since destroying the initial evidence merely creates new evidence, which in turn must be destroyed before time runs out. As in the somber and disturbing title story, in which a man who has forgotten the past is therefore unable to imagine the future, Mr. Abe's protagonists are imprisoned in time as well as space.

Human isolation and the fragility of identity are among Mr. Abe's concerns, as is the dependence of identity upon memory. Adult Japanese carry *meishi,* for which the translation "business cards" is not quite adequate: bearing the characters for one's name, they are used rather more widely than in the West and by people (such as school-teachers and secretaries) who would not ordinarily carry them here. Typically, in Mr. Abe's stories, the business cards of a man who will be—that is to say, who is already—trapped are mysteriously missing; or they are among the first things that have been taken from him. In **"The Crime of S. Karma,"** the volume's one excerpt from a longer work, a man goes to his office and discovers that his very self has been usurped by one of his *meishi;* sitting at his desk dictating, "the other me was tracing a finger along some papers" with one hand, while with the other it is furtively caressing the typist's knee. Challenged, the business card turns belligerent. Later, thumping his own hollow chest, the narrator can only reflect on the disadvantage his lack of a name will be in the eyes of the law.

Commentators on Mr. Abe's work make much of its supposed lack of elements that are specifically Japanese. But though his themes may be admitted to be universal, there are aspects of contemporary Japanese life that might particularly elicit them.

There is the crowding. There is the isolation. Acquaint-ances who have returned from long residence in Japan sometimes complain: "You never really get to know anyone well." And there are the intrusions, however benevolent. "Does that taste *good?*" the elderly couple at the next table in a restaurant asked me, as I consumed my bowl of noodles, much as one might ask a 5-year-old with an ice-cream cone. Proselytizers from certain religious sects are reputed to station themselves immovably at a prospect's door in order to harangue him—for his own good, of course; the newly anonymous residents of urban apartment complexes are said to be especially likely converts. But whether such phenomena are distinctly Japanese rather than universal may just be a matter of degree.

The prolific Mr. Abe, who was born in 1924, has been publishing—and winning literary prizes—since he was in his early 20's. He has been fortunate in his translators throughout. Juliet Winters Carpenter's renditions here are wonderful—buoyant and full of the flavor of irritable masculinity—but I wish she, or someone, had thought of presenting the dates for the individual stories more conspicuously. (As listed on the copyright page, they span the years from 1949 to 1966.) Mr. Abe has also been active as a scriptwriter and avant-garde playwright. **"Intruders,"** for example, was rewritten as the play *Friends* in 1967 and eloquently translated by Donald Keene. In the stage version, the family members, who in the story are immediately aggressive, are sweeter, but the results of their actions are just as deadly for the hero.

> *Marian Ury, "Invasion of the Apartment Snatchers," in* The New York Times Book Review, *March 17, 1991, p. 9.*

Anthony Thwaite   (review date 21 April 1991)

[*Thwaite is a English poet, essayist, editor, and critic who has extensive knowledge of Japanese society and culture. In the following review, he praises Abé's short story collection* Beyond the Curve *for its imaginative depictions of human alienation.*]

Kobo Abe, born in 1924 in Tokyo but brought up as a child and youth in Manchuria, trained as a doctor, though he has never practiced medicine. Though he was awarded one of the most prestigious Japanese literary prizes, the Akutagawa, in 1951, his first breakthrough in the West was *The Woman in the Dunes,* the film of which won the jury prize at the Cannes Film Festival in 1963.

The Woman in the Dunes is a hypnotic story of a struggle for existence. Full of hard-edged detail and circumstantial stuff, at the same time it's a sort of parable about losing an identity and perhaps finding a new one. Abe went on to publish other strange novels, blends of matter-of-factness with wild surrealist surmises, in the '60s and '70s: *The Face of Another, The Ruined Map, Secret Rendezvous.*

One feature that distinguishes Abe from standard patterns of Japanese fiction is the sparseness of his identifiably Japanese settings. Japanese novels (like English ones, come to that) tend, and have always tended, to have a strong sense of place, of precise location, with their names attached, along with a delicately evocative descriptiveness. Abe avoids this tradition. A character is K— or A— or M—, a railway station is at S—. These features wouldn't by themselves give Abe's works their universality; they are combined with a bizarre shaping imagination, clinical, precise, often humorous in a blackish way. I have long thought that Abe's return from Manchuria to Japan at the very end of the war, a "homecoming" that must have been traumatic, must have helped shape that imagination, pushing it towards facing the problems of individuality, of identity, that lie under almost everything he has written.

Beyond the Curve contains 12 stories, ranging in date from 1951 to 1966, and in mood from the grave to what we used to call gay; or at least with a lightness of touch (as in **"Noah's Ark"**) that one could almost call whimsical. What they all have in common is a directness, even a simplicity, of procedure, that makes all the more effective the tangles of mind-bending uncertainty that follow. For example, **"An Irrelevant Death"** begins:

"He had company. The guest was lying face down with his legs stretched out neatly toward the door. Dead."

More neutrally, but equally simply, there is the opening of **"The Bet"**:

"Seated at my drawing board, I looked across at the director of general affairs at AB Company. I held myself perfectly straight, my spine a full two inches from the back of the chair, unable to relax until I heard the man's reply. He showed no sign of answering."

If these quotations suggest comparisons with Kafka, it ought to be said that Abe is not an imitator. An early reading of Kafka may have suggested possibilities, and Abe's novels and stories are often at various levels tales of metamorphosis. But one always has to remember that Abe, for all the uprootedness of his background and for all his deliberate lack of specific Japanese "color," is indeed Japanese. This gives peculiar force to his obsession with his characters' inability to be part of a group, their detachment from any sustaining togetherness or cohesion.

The contemporary literary critic Hisaaki Yamanouchi has written of Abe: "He is probably the first Japanese writer whose works, having no distinctly Japanese qualities, are of interest to the Western audience because of their universal relevance." Confusion, amnesia, an inexplicable but pervading sense of menace, haunt his fiction. For many years he has been for me (along with his contemporary Shusaku Endo—a Japanese Christian, and another isolated figure for that reason) the most interesting and impressive living Japanese writer. His imagination has no frontiers. (pp. 6, 12)

Anthony Thwaite, "Kōbō Abé's Fables of Identity," in Book World—The Washington Post, *April 21, 1991, pp. 6, 12.*

Additional coverage of Abé's life and career is contained in the following sources published by Gale Research: *Contemporary Authors,* Vols. 65-68, Vol. 140 [obituary]; *Contemporary Authors New Revision Series,* Vol. 24; *Contemporary Literary Criticism,* Vols. 8, 22, 53; and *Major 20th-Century Writers.*

Anthony Burgess

February 25, 1917—November 25, 1993

(Born John Anthony Burgess Wilson; also wrote as John Burgess Wilson and under the pseudonym Joseph Kell) English novelist, essayist, critic, playwright, translator, editor, scriptwriter, short story writer, author of children's books, and composer.

For further information on Burgess's life and works, see *CLC,* Volumes 1, 2, 4, 5, 8, 10, 13, 15, 22, 40, and 62.

INTRODUCTION

Burgess is best known for his novel *A Clockwork Orange,* which explores themes common to much of his fiction, including the nature of language and the conflicts between good and evil, free will and determinism. Set in the future in a city dominated by lawless juvenile gangs, the story centers on Alex, a maladjusted youth who, after committing a series of violent crimes, becomes the subject of a government-sponsored behavior-control experiment. The treatment causes Alex to become violently ill whenever he is tempted to engage in socially unacceptable behavior and thus prevents him from freely choosing between acts of good and evil. The novel also reveals Burgess's linguistic virtuosity through its use of the invented language *nadsat,* a crude combination of Russian and Cockney slang. Burgess began his literary career in the mid-1950s while serving as an education officer for the British Colonial Service in Malaya. Incorrectly diagnosed with an inoperable brain tumor, Burgess was given less than a year to live. Returning to England in 1959, he produced five novels over the next twelve months and subsequently became a full-time writer. In assessing Burgess's career, critics often note the wide range of his oeuvre. In addition to such dark, philosophic works as *A Clockwork Orange* and *Earthly Powers,* Burgess wrote the humorous *Enderby* novels as well as several pieces of historical fiction. *The Kingdom of the Wicked,* for example, chronicles the early years of Christianity, and *A Dead Man in Deptford* is a fictional biography of Christopher Marlowe. Burgess was also highly regarded for his works of scholarly criticism, particularly *Here Comes Everybody: An Introduction to James Joyce for the Ordinary Reader.* A composer as well as a writer, Burgess combined music and literature in *Napoleon Symphony,* a novel based on the structure of Beethoven's *Eroica* Symphony. Although his fictional worlds are sometimes disordered and often reflect his pessimism about modern society, critics agree that his inventive humor and wordplay serve to temper his cynical vision. John Updike wrote that Burgess "had the energy and the wide-ranging

interests of a dozen writers, and his love of life was of an intensity that few can produce nowadays in our post-print worlds. He seemed not only a prodigious intellect, but an affectionate spirit."

PRINCIPAL WORKS

*Time for a Tiger (novel) 1956
*The Enemy in the Blanket (novel) 1958
English Literature: A Survey for Students [as John Burgess Wilson] (criticism) 1958
*Beds in the East (novel) 1959
The Doctor Is Sick (novel) 1960
The Right to an Answer (novel) 1960
Devil of a State (novel) 1961
One Hand Clapping [as Joseph Kell] (novel) 1961
The Worm and the Ring (novel) 1961

A Clockwork Orange (novel) 1962
The Wanting Seed (novel) 1962
Honey for the Bears (novel) 1963
†*Inside Mr. Enderby* [as Joseph Kell] (novel) 1963
The Novel Today (criticism) 1963
The Eve of St. Venus (novel) 1964
Language Made Plain [as John Burgess Wilson] (nonfiction) 1964
Nothing Like the Sun: A Story of Shakespeare's Love-Life (novel) 1964
Here Comes Everybody: An Introduction to James Joyce for the Ordinary Reader (criticism) 1965; also published as *Re Joyce,* 1965
A Vision of Battlements (novel) 1965
Tremor of Intent (novel) 1966
The Novel Now: A Student's Guide to Contemporary Fiction (criticism) 1967; revised edition, 1971
†*Enderby Outside* (novel) 1968
Urgent Copy: Literary Studies (criticism) 1968
Shakespeare (biography) 1970
MF (novel) 1971
Morning in His Eyes [translator and adaptor; from the drama *Oedipus Rex* by Sophocles] (drama) 1972
Cyrano [translator and adaptor; from the drama *Cyrano de Bergerac* by Edmond Rostand] (drama) 1973
Joysprick: An Introduction to the Language of James Joyce (criticism) 1973
‡*The Clockwork Testament; or, Enderby's End* (novel) 1974
Napoleon Symphony (novel) 1974
Beard's Roman Women (novel) 1976
Abba Abba (novel) 1977
Ernest Hemingway and His World (biography) 1978
1985 (novel) 1978
Man of Nazareth (novel) 1979
Earthly Powers (novel) 1980
The End of the World News (novel) 1983
Enderby's Dark Lady; or, No End to Enderby (novel) 1984
Flame into Being: The Life and Work of D. H. Lawrence (biography) 1985
Homage to QWERT YUIOP (essays) 1985; also published as *But Do Blondes Prefer Gentlemen?*, 1986
The Kingdom of the Wicked (novel) 1985
The Pianoplayers (novel) 1986
Little Wilson and Big God (autobiography) 1988
Any Old Iron (novel) 1989
The Devil's Mode (short stories) 1989
You've Had Your Time (autobiography) 1990
Mozart and the Wolf Gang (novel) 1991; also published as *On Mozart: A Paean for Wolfgang. Being a Celestial Colloquy, an Opera Libretto, a Film Script, a Schizophrenic Dialogue, a Bewildered Rumination, a Stendahlian Transcription, and a Heartfelt Homage upon the Bicentenary of the Death of Wolfgang Amadeus Mozart,* 1991
A Mouthful of Air: Language and Languages, Especially English (nonfiction) 1992
Chatsky; or, The Importance of Being Stupid [translator; from the drama *Gore ot Uma* by Alexander Griboyedov] (drama) 1993
A Dead Man in Deptford (novel) 1993

*These works were published as *The Malayan Trilogy* in 1964 and as *The Long Day Wanes: The Malayan Trilogy* in 1965.

†These works were published as *Enderby* in 1968.

‡This work was published along with *Inside Mr. Enderby* and *Enderby Outside* as *Enderby* in 1982.

OBITUARIES AND TRIBUTES

Burt A. Folkart   (obituary date 26 November 1993)

[*In the obituary below, Folkart provides an overview of Burgess's life.*]

Anthony Burgess, the prodigious author, linguist and scholar who gazed into the future and found such quirky scenarios as ***A Clockwork Orange,*** died [this week] of cancer.

A spokeswoman for Hutchinson, his publisher, said from London that Burgess, who wrote more than 50 novels and dozens of nonfiction works, died of cancer in a London hospital. He was 76 and had been ill for some time, she added.

Burgess had left Britain in 1968 after the death of his first wife, Lynne.

From 1969 to 1974, he taught English in the United States, at Princeton and Columbia universities, the University of North Carolina and City College of New York.

He settled in the Mediterranean, first in Malta—before being driven out by censors who believed that he was a subversive and cut holes in his copies of the *Times* of London—and finally in Monte Carlo.

He was born John Anthony Burgess Wilson in Manchester. After his mother and sister died in the 1918 flu epidemic, he was brought up by his father, who was a pianist, and a coarse Irish stepmother who owned a tavern in the northern England city.

He wrote in his memoirs (***Little Wilson and Big God*** and ***You've Had Your Time***) that his parents ignored him and that he turned to sketching and writing to keep himself amused.

His father helped him learn piano and from that composing. Throughout his life, Burgess wrote a variety of songs, symphonies, concertos and sonatas.

After he became a successful novelist, he was criticized for his aloof characters that are bereft of emotion. He admitted that he found it difficult to imbue his work with affection when he had received so little himself.

In his youth, he had hoped to become a musician and became musical director of a special British Army services unit entertaining troops in Europe during World War II.

But after the war he turned to academia and work as a lecturer in phonetics for the Ministry of Education. He was named master at a grammar school near Oxford where he wrote poems and fiction in his spare time.

He next became an education officer for the Colonial Office in Malaya and Borneo. In the mid-1950s his first three novels were published: *Time for a Tiger, The Enemy in the Blanket* and *Beds in the East.*

They came to be known as *The Malayan Trilogy* and were published under one title in the United States: *The Long Day Wanes.*

That marked the beginning of a lengthy romance with American readers who were generally more forgiving of Burgess' grotesque surrealism than his fellow Britons. Burgess did not take the slight lightly. In 1984, after the *Times* of London published a list of the 100 best novels since 1939—a list that ignored Burgess' prolific work—he wrote a critique of his own: *Ninety-Nine Novels: The Best in English Since 1939.* He did not mention any of his own but left little doubt who the 100th spot belonged to.

Burgess' literary output increased mightily after 1959, when he was told, erroneously as it turned out, that a brain tumor had given him only months to live.

He set out to leave a literary legacy and enough royalties to support a widow.

"Because of hangovers," he wrote in *You've Had Your Time,* "marital quarrels, creative deadness . . . and sheer morbid gloom I was not able to achieve more than 5½ novels of very moderate size in that pseudo-terminal year." Still, he hastened to point out, "it was very nearly E. M. Forster's whole long life's output."

Although his doctors were proved wrong, Burgess seldom slackened the pace of his writing for the remainder of his life.

At one point his output was so massive that his publisher insisted on publishing two of his novels under pseudonyms for fear that the public would equate volume with mediocrity.

His work defied categorization. Considered both "elite" and "popular" by some critics, his fictional world ranged from a satiric examination of life's travails in a newly liberated East African nation (*Devil of a State*) to the sexual adventures of a Britisher trying to dump dozens of "drylon" dresses on the Soviet black market (*Honey for the Bears*).

In 1962, after successes with *Inside Mr. Enderby, The Worm and the Ring* and *One Hand Clapping,* Burgess served up what was to be his signature work, *A Clockwork Orange.*

It deals with the brutality of a psychopathic youth he called Alex and his "droogs," a gang of hoodlums who exist in a drug-saturated culture of the future.

Burgess even invented a language for the "droogs," who preferred their brutality and sexual assaults accompanied by the works of Beethoven. He called it "Nadsat," a combination of English slang and Russian words.

The author was fascinated with language. Besides English,

Burgess spoke French, Spanish, German, Russian, Italian, Mandarin Chinese and Malay and wrote a book on usage, *English Made Plain.*

Stanley Kubrick's filmed version of *A Clockwork Orange* won the New York Film Critics Award for best picture of 1971.

Baptized Roman Catholic and educated by Jesuits before receiving a degree in English at Manchester University, Burgess once told the *Guardian* newspaper that he "abandoned religion when I was young and then went back to it out of fear and later out of interest."

His stormy first marriage ended with the death of his wife from cirrhosis of the liver. Soon after, Burgess married Liliana Macellari, who introduced him to the 4-year-old son he unknowingly had from an earlier affair with her.

He spent his last years working every day from 10 a.m. to 5 p.m., producing 1,000 words at each sitting, laboring over a large architect's table. For reasons only he seemed to understand, he utilized a word processor for journalism and a typewriter for fiction.

In addition to his novels, television scripts, almost weekly journalistic contributions and literary criticism, Burgess translated a number of works, including *Cyrano de Bergerac* by Edmond Rostand from French and Sophocles' *Oedipus Rex* from Greek.

He also wrote a Broadway musical, *Cyrano,* which was performed in 1973.

Burgess was a fellow of the Royal Society of Literature and a Commandeur des Arts et des Lettres of France.

Perhaps his massive outpouring of words was best exemplified several years ago when neither his agent, his publisher, nor his entry in *Who's Who* could provide the exact number of books he had written.

> *Burt A. Folkart, in an obituary in* Los Angeles Times, *November 26, 1993, p. A44.*

Gore Vidal and others   (essay date 28 November 1993)

[*In the essay below, Vidal, an American novelist, short story writer, and critic, along with nine other writers and critics, including John Updike and George Steiner, praise Burgess for his originality, versatility, and dedication to literature and music.*]

Though in life Anthony Burgess was amiable, generous and far less self-loving than most writers, I have been disturbed, in the last few years, to read in the press that he did not think himself sufficiently admired by the literary world. It is true, of course, that he had the good fortune not to be hit, as it were, by the Swedes, but surely he was much admired and appreciated by the appreciated and admired.

In my lifetime he was one of the three 'best' novelists to come out of England (all right, the other two are the Swedised Golding, and Iris Murdoch) but he was unlike the whole lot in the sense that one never knew what he would do next. He could not be characterised.

To me this is a great virtue, and a tiny source of income for him because he was the only writer of my time whose new book I always bought and always read. On or off form, there was always something that he had come up with that I did not know—or even dream of. The *Enderby* series are even finer comedies than those by the so much admired E. Waugh.

I was both moved and alarmed that one of his own last reviews in this paper was of my collected essays in which appeared a long piece on his first volume of memoirs. In my review, I had recalled him personally with fondness; reported on his life and work; remarked, of the memoir, that he had no sense of humour.

In his review of me he quotes this, remarking that, once, he did have a sense of humour. I almost wrote him to say that I was referring only to the autobiography. Now I know that he had known for some time that he was dying of cancer, no rollicking business.

I cannot think what English book reviewing will do without him. He actually read what he wrote about, and he was always interesting on what he read. He did not suffer from the English disease of envy that tends to make most English reviewing injurious to the health of literature.

When I first came to meet him in 1964, he was about to be famous for *A Clockwork Orange.* He was, however, truly notorious because he had reviewed, pseudonymously, several of his own books in a provincial newspaper. 'At least,' I said at the time, 'he is the first novelist in England to *know* that a reviewer has actually read the book under review.'

Shakespeare, Joyce, Roman Empire (of the imagination), Malaysia; the constipated Enderby, whose fine poems were often included in the prose text. He ranged throughout language, a devoted philologist, and throughout music as a composer.

Once his first wife snarled—when it became clear that I was eight years younger than he—that I ought not to have got some Book Club selection when he had written so much more than I. Neither of us quite sober, we began to compare units of production. When it became clear that I was ahead, he said with quiet pomp, 'I am really a composer.' I was left without a single choral work, much less a fanfare, to put in the scales.

At one point when we were both living in Rome, whenever I would be offered a twelve-part television mini-series on the Medici or the Huns, I'd say, 'Get poor Burgess', and so they did. When I made the mistake of using the phrase 'poor Burgess' in an interview, he wrote, 'I can't say that I liked that "poor Burgess" bit. Happily, I left Gore out of the *Encyclopedia Britannica* on the contemporary novel.' We often indulged in *épingles,* as the French say. Then he transcended Italian television and did, for the RSC, the finest version I have ever seen of *Cyrano de Bergerac.* Many parts, not so poor Burgess.

I ended my review of Anthony's autobiography—much of it about how he lost faith in God—by making a play on the title *Little Wilson* (Burgess's real name) *and Big God.* I suggested that the book might better have been called

Little Wilson and Big Burgess, 'who did it his, if not His, way'.

I saw him a year or two ago. We were being jointly interviewed by BBC Radio. 'Odd,' he said, 'I keep looking at my watch. It's like a tic. I wonder why?' For once, I made no answer.

[American novelist and critic John Updike writes:]

> The literary world seems much more sparsely-populated with Anthony Burgess gone. He had the energy and the wide-ranging interests of a dozen writers, and his love of life was of an intensity that few can produce nowadays in our post-print worlds. He seemed not only a prodigious intellect, but an affectionate spirit, whose mind, like Ariel's, circled the globe in a few seconds.

[Samuel Schoenbaum, an American biographer of Shakespeare, writes:]

> I was extraordinarily impressed with him as a writer and a person: loquacious and witty and kind. He had such a full career and everything he did made a lasting impression. He had a forewarning when young that he might not have long to live, so he plunged into his angelic, prolific career. The nature of his work will have to be absorbed by us in the years to come. His mind was forever young. He did just about everything—and when someone does everything, you miss them all the more.

[English biographer and critic Claire Tomalin writes:]

> He could be foully bad-tempered, but he was a cheering presence as a writer. He didn't have that awful insularity of so many men-of-letters. He was a British writer who was part of the European world.

[Jonathan Kent, the joint artistic director of the Almeida Theatre in London, writes:]

> *Chatsky* was sent to us at the Almeida out of the blue towards the end of last year. Anthony had taken an impossible nineteenth-century Russian play written by a young revolutionary [Griboyedov's *Woe from Wit*] and given it all the vigour, relish and emotion of youth. We decided at once to do it. We met for breakfast at the Sherlock Holmes Hotel in Baker Street. He talked for two hours about the play, conducting a kind of tripartite conversation, with me in English, with his wife in Italian about the inadvisability of smoking or drinking more coffee, and with the bemused German waitress about making sure the coffee arrived. He was a fountain of language and energy, a heartening affirmation of life, and one of the best things to happen to our theatre because the ability of language to inspire is what the Almeida is all about.

[David Lodge, a novelist and educator, writes:]

> He was an inspiration and example to other writers, particularly younger writers, because of his enormous professionalism, tireless energy and fertility of invention. He never repeated

himself; he tried to do new things with each book. And he had a cosmopolitan view of culture—he was a world and European figure as well as a very English one. He set an example to the English literary world, which can become insular, gossipy and bland.

[English philologist Randolph Quirk writes:]

He was a friend of enormously varied talents. I think he would like to have been remembered as a great novelist, but he was a great polymath first. He was always a critic as well as a novelist, and he used the novel *Abba Abba,* for instance, to investigate something about the age of Keats. He fascinated me because he was an uneasy Catholic, and his knowledge of the Malay Peninsula used to keep me up all night. He could be a man of enormous loyalty, too: he knew perfectly well that Eric Partridge was not a great scholar but a hardworking freelancer and he had a great deal of sympathy with the way he stuck to his last; over the years he helped him to get a securer income. He was alpha minus in many areas where he could have been alpha plus if he had concentrated on them alone, but *Earthly Powers* is a major work. I shall personally miss him a great deal.

[Michael Ratcliffe, the literary editor of *The Observer,* writes:]

For at least a year Anthony Burgess had known that he was dying, and the furious productivity of his last months concealed a race against time—there were so many things he still wanted to do, things like a translation of *Finnegans Wake* into Roman dialect, for example, just for the sheer hell and fun of the thing. This was precisely the kind of virtuoso playfulness that exasperated his more solemn English critics, but it would not be too much to say that in the shadow of death his writing took on a new lease of life. One of his best novels—*Dead Man in Deptford*—was published as recently as April this year. And he retained an eagle's eye: not even the tiniest cut escaped him on Sunday mornings.

His need for work was voracious. Book reviews continued to arrive at *The Observer* with unfailing promptness, and a silence from us of more than three weeks would produce an urgent request for more: there are two waiting to be published. The joy of working with him was that we could never predict the direction in which Anthony's discoveries and interconnections would go. He led the paper's coverage of books with distinction for more than two decades. Even at his most outrageous he was a great and delightful teacher, and we shall miss him terribly.

[French-born American critic and educator George Steiner writes:]

What I want to emphasise is something very rare in the current climate. Burgess, while fiercely competitive and ambitious, almost never lacked generosity. He often went out of his way to praise and to draw attention to works which might otherwise have been overlooked. This generosity was part of a kind of playfulness

which make his writings on literature, on music, on the art of translation, among the most stimulating in our time.

[Lorna Sage, an educator and reviewer for *The Observer,* writes:]

He lived to write, ate paper and drank ink like those Shakespeare characters infatuated with literature. He worked impossibly hard, filled every day with words, stayed in love with the language all his life—exile only made him more passionate. Now he's gone, the world of English letters has lost a generous, genial and inspirational presence, who breathed his life into the words on the page.

> *Gore Vidal and others, "Not So Poor Burgess,"*
> in The Observer, *November 28, 1993, p. 2.*

Lorna Sage (essay date 17 December 1993)

[*In the essay below, Sage comments on Burgess's oeuvre and its place in modern literature.*]

The most telling memorial to Anthony Burgess would have been to leave a big white gap on the pages of the *Observer* or the *Independent* or whatever—the space his words would have filled. His death must surely supply work for a good handful of aspiring literary journalists, job opportunities galore. And that's just in the Grub Street corner of the literary A to Z. But did his many roles and his polyphonous *oeuvre*—novelist, librettist, composer, scriptwriter, reviewer, teacher—add up? Even if you concentrate on the prose, and leave out the lyrics and the music (which, being tone-deaf, I'm obliged to), it's still hard to decide whether his work is as much as the sum of its parts.

It's the kind of question he had deliberately posed, to himself as well as to his readers, at least from the 1970s on, when instead of settling down and producing books that were densely layered and epically difficult and despairing *and very far apart* in the manner of (say) Pynchon or Gaddis he started throwing off playful, complex novels—*MF* (1971), *Napoleon Symphony* (1974), *Beard's Roman Women* (1976), *ABBA ABBA* (1971),—at such indecently close intervals that they somehow disqualified themselves as canonical texts. Burgess didn't strike people as *post* anything because he wasn't troubled enough. He was too blithely at home with the promiscuous tricks of language. He throve on epistemological anxiety, took it in his stride, and so seemed to contradict the founding hypothesis about a crisis of signification. Authorship for him was a way of life in more senses than one, and when he took on the fashionable paradoxes—writing as dissemination in *Earthly Powers,* for instance (paper Onanism, recklessly spending words, echoes of Derrida)—then too his very enjoyment of his task, his ingenuity and irreverence and fluency, told against him.

Joyce was his great hero and mentor, but it's characteristic that in the second part of his autobiography, *You've Had Your Time* in 1990, thinking about what the life of letters really meant to him, he questioned even that allegiance, and bracketed Joyce with Woolf (very much not his favourite modernist). "Here I lay myself open to charges of middlebrowism. But probably the novel is a middlebrow form and both Joyce and Virginia Woolf were on the wrong track." Wordplay, self-consciousness, polyglot punning AB enjoyed beyond measure, but at the same time he liked to combine these signs of Literature with a capital L, literature squared, with a no-nonsense approach derived from Grub Street mores. He disapproved of Joyce for being a scrounger, he thought you could and should produce great art for money, in the style of Herman Wouk or—let's not be modest—Shakespeare, or Mozart. He admired Mozart for being "prolific", "a serious craftsman and a breadwinner", as he said in his bicentennial tribute-cum-travesty, ***Mozart and the Wolf Gang,*** Bloomsbury gentility and "costiveness" (Forster was the prize example) could be relied on to provoke his scorn for several reasons at once therefore: mystificatory reverence for Art, snobbish resentment of one's audience, and a kind of stinginess with one's talent which he seems Freudianly to have associated with anal retentiveness.

By contrast—though retaining the same metaphor—he was unashamed of his own logorrhoea. Pressed to explain why he wrote so much, he developed over time a number of motives. The first and most famous is the diagnosis of an inoperable brain tumour in 1959, when John Wilson was given a year to live at the most, and as a result became Anthony Burgess full-time in order to earn royalties for his prospective widow, as he put it—"I was not able to achieve more than five and a half novels of very moderate size in the pseudo-terminal year. Still, it was very nearly E. M. Forster's long life's output." It's a chillingly good story, and seems to be true, though it doesn't explain why he went on going on at such a lick once the misdiagnosis was discovered.

In fact, the reprieve hardly slowed him down at all, whereupon he produced a second strand of explanation which had to do with the childlessness of his first marriage to Lynne. Perhaps it was, he suggested, a matter of books substituting for babies—"I had converted what I termed paternity lust into art." This may sound an implausibly Platonic theory, but George Steiner gave it a convincing run for its money not long ago in *Real Presences,* and Burgess himself in *Earthly Powers* had lent it an extra colour of likelihood by making his compulsive writer-hero homosexual. Except that by the date of *Earthly Powers* (1980) he wasn't childless any longer. When Lynne died in 1968, there was a new wife-to-be, Liana, plus their son (of whose birth he'd been unaware) waiting in the wings. But this meant, of course, that now he had a wife and child to support. . . .

All of which suggests that he didn't quite know why his writing was so compulsive. It was as though the words wrote him. While other literary folk were addicted to alcohol, or sex, or drugs, he was innocently fixated on his profession. Here the book-reviewing came in handy—to fill the gaps between books—and also the script-writing. Gore Vidal recalls that he more than once passed on to Burgess lucrative jobs in that line, which were snapped up and dispatched with alacrity. The relationship between the two of them is perhaps more of a clue to "placing" Burgess

than this venal tie suggests. For though Vidal exercises more quality control, and separates out his different kinds of writing more—so that, for instance, the histories are done in lucid, ironic, discursive style, while the satires are *lusciously* vile, masterpieces of inverted decorum—they both belong to the tradition of carnivalesque adventurers, the breed of writer who (according to the school of Bakhtin) follows on from Petronius, Apuleius, Rabelais and Sterne. This kind of serio-comic writing is made up of parodies of the straight kinds. It was (says Bakhtin) "the 'journalistic' genre of antiquity . . . full of overt and hidden polemics with various philosophical, religious, ideological and scientific schools . . . seeking to unravel and evaluate the general spirit and direction of evolving contemporary life." This comes from the book on *Dostoevsky's Poetics,* so it has to be slightly edited to fit, but it does fit rather well, since it gets the sense of epic ambition, along with mock-epic tactics like (another good phrase) "slum naturalism".

So a ragbag of a book like ***The End of the World News*** in 1982—a tripartite travesty, made up of a drama-doc about Freud, a libretto for a musical about Trotsky, and a sci-fi "or futfic" story about the end of culture as we know it—does have a *genre* after all. Burgess suggests as much when he complains in the autobiography that "That term 'ragbag' is always turning up, usually when my work is at its most structured." He wasn't thinking of Bakhtin, but of structuralism and Lévi-Strauss, but in a general way the notion of programmed mayhem, or self-conscious surface disorder with an underlying pattern, can be accommodated to the carnival idea. Music, he liked to say, can aspire to universality ("Music is the Armagnac of the saved. The musician alone has access to God"), whereas the arts of words, by contrast, are local, referential, impure: "to deal in pure structure is a huge relief from peddling those impure structures called linguistic statements". Literature is in league with imperfection, and even within the Babel-world of literature, there are those who understand that comedy has the last word (like Cervantes) and those who (like Shakespeare) hanker after the glamour of tragedy. Just as he loved Joyce this side idolatry, so he adored Shakespeare but found him less myriad-minded than he's cracked up to be. That Shakespeare is the national bard had something to do with it: Burgess was all for crossing frontiers and cross-breeding cultures, an Esperantist of the spirit.

Burgess does, then, "make sense", he has a poetics. And yet there remains something resistant and idiosyncratic about his work which even the right anti-tradition can't quite accommodate. You can line him up with the correct contemporary attitudes, but there's something left over, something anachronistic about his postmodern-seeming stress on the arbitrary, shifting and ephemeral nature of words. It's as though he is trying to turn writing back into the condition of speech and set up a dialogue with his readers, a running commentary almost as continuous as breathing. This means that he doesn't go in for the double-think which finds a surreptitious sublimity in the very recognition that Literature is discredited. By the sheer quantity and continuity of his writing, he produced a real sense of the limits of what words can do. He lived that wry comedy (not a tragedy at all) and acted it out.

This involves a very special kind of modesty which almost amounts to the opposite (the devil's mode, he called it in one book)—a modesty which despises those who take themselves too seriously. Look, he's saying, I can do it just as well as you if not better, any old time, week in week out, without trying to set it in stone. This in the end, I'm sure, was why he liked literary journalism so much: the proud debasement of Grub Street, the place where you know exactly what your words are worth. So he wrote all the hours God gave. He hoped, perhaps, that if in this curious way he kept his head down, the Almighty might look the other way, and Art would creep in at the back door. If you identify writing with living so closely, you don't want to produce something too finished—after all, time will do that for you.

Lorna Sage, "In Full Spate," in The Times Literary Supplement, *No. 4733, December 17, 1993, p. 26.*

REVIEWS OF BURGESS'S RECENT WORKS

John Sutherland   (review date 26 October 1990)

[*Sutherland is a Scottish playwright and critic. In the following review, he comments favorably on Burgess's autobiographies,* Little Wilson and Big God *and* You've Had Your Time, *noting that a sense of guilt pervades both volumes.*]

Anthony Burgess is a writer about whose life one knows a lot—even without benefit of autobiography. In one of his many parts a professional journalist, Burgess has in the years of his fame kept up a stream of reviewing and incidental writing. He divulges aspects of his private life and has always been good for the indiscreet newspaper interview. He has been the subject of literary gossip and minor scandal (especially during his academic visits to America in the 1970s). Even before embarking on *You've Had Your Time*—or its predecessor *Little Wilson and Big God* (1987)—one knew him intimately. It was not necessary to work at it; Burgess simply leaks more of himself than other writers.

Various matters are common knowledge about Anthony Burgess (ie, John Burgess Wilson). He had a death sentence pronounced on him in 1960, when a brain specialist diagnosed a tumour. With a year to live he wrote five Damoclean novels to support his future widow. The tumour proved to be non-existent. But the die was cast and Burgess was a novelist for the rest of his time. This morbid episode did not render him humourless. It is one of modern literature's best jokes that, under a pseudonym, Burgess reviewed one of his own novels written under another pseudonym. In a number of places, Burgess has let it be known that the inspiration for *A Clockwork Orange* was

the assault on his wife by four GI deserters in war-time London. My original Pan copy of the novel has a final chapter which did not appear in the sensationally popular book of the film, or in Stanley Kubrick's narrative; Burgess has frequently expressed anger at the American mutilation of his text (anger too that his greatest fame should be as Kubrick's underpaid assistant). In a review of Constantine Fitz-Gibbon's book on alcoholism, Burgess reminisced publicly about the death of his first wife from cirrhosis brought on by drinking. A correspondence in the *TLS* made public the fact—already much talked about—that Burgess had enraged his American academic hosts as a visitor in the 1970s. Large gins and tonics and insults about Black Studies were vaguely involved. He wrote somewhere else that when in New York, he always carried a swordstick with him to fend off that city's droogs. In my mind's eye I see him as a cross between Zorro and Bernie Goetz dancing down the subway platforms holding the muggers at bay (in *You've Had Your Time* he reveals that he has only been required to use his weapon once). A profile in the *Evening Standard* in the mid-1970s disclosed that Burgess had been offered, and refused, Lionel Trilling's vacated chair at Columbia. It was too easy a chair for a creative writer. The same article indicated that Burgess had married an Italian aristocrat, and now lived in Italy. At this period in his life he expressed violent hatred for the British tax authorities, and regarded himself as a refugee from their cruelty. He publicly abused Harold Wilson's governments for their denigration of the art of literature and their abolition of the beautiful old coinage of England. In 1980 Burgess did an interview with his coreligionist Graham Greene, for the *Observer.* It led to public quarrels when the older novelist accused Burgess of putting words in his mouth that he had subsequently to look up in the dictionary. *Earthly Powers* was shortlisted for the Booker in a very strong year. It was put about in the newspapers that Burgess, forewarned that the prize had gone to William Golding, had absented himself from the awards ceremony out of pique. (In *You've Had Your Time* he insists it was merely that he had not brought his dinner-jacket to London.) He removed from Italy to Monaco because of kidnap threats on his young son—he has both in America and Italy publicly affronted the Mafia. A pugnacious man, Burgess habitually writes kind reviews. Here he explains that it is because he sympathizes with the pain that goes into the making of even bad books. Burgess's passions for music, for James Joyce, for the English language, permeate everything he writes, as does his detestation of the State and most things American (but not American critics, who have always been more appreciative of his fiction than we have). All this and more was in the pre-autobiographical public domain.

Little Wilson and Big God ended in 1959 with a perfect scene break. Burgess was informed by his wife—by way of a Christmas present—that the surgeons had pronounced him a dead man. Perversely he welcomed the news as twelve months of guaranteed immortality: "I had been granted something I had never had before: a whole year to live. I would not be run over by a bus tomorrow, nor knifed on the Brighton racetrack. I would not choke on a bone. If I fell in the wintry sea I would not drown." But neither could he do a proper job of work. He would have to become a professional writer so as to provide for his wife. He "sighed and put paper in the typewriter". The prognosis was wrong and the terminal year has extended to three decades of professional writing (longer, one hopes). And eight years of marriage so wretched that a brain tumour must at times have seemed preferable.

Burgess's passions for music, for James Joyce, for the English language, permeate everything he writes, as does his detestation of the State and most things American.

—John Sutherland

In *Little Wilson and Big God* Burgess gave details of the 1944 attack on his wife Lynne, but so cursorily as to suggest that forty years on, the episode was still unbearable. Unlike Alex and his droogs, the motive of the GIs was not sex but robbery. The victim, who was pregnant, was kicked unconscious and aborted. It would have been the Wilsons' first child. The injuries she sustained prevented her ever having children in future. In an otherwise expansive narrative, this traumatic episode is dealt with in a few sentences. So too in *You've Had Your Time,* the awful years of later marriage to Lynne are slipped in between extended descriptions of Burgess writing his novels and such minor matters as the couple's numerous household pets.

Lynne drank compulsively and regularly to the point of violence and physical collapse. She taunted Burgess with her infidelities, precipitating impotence within marriage and his tit-for-tat adulteries outside. She attempted suicide time and again. He drank gin as copiously as she did (but with a man's tougher constitution) and smoked eighty cigarettes a day. He developed a semi-psychosomatic paralysis in his left calf. Old men would shout across the street "All right mate?" as he limped by. Burgess glosses over bacchanalian holiday trips to Russia and Tangier with stoic comedy—both in the novels they inspired and in *You've Had Your Time.* They must have been sheer hell at the time.

All this while, as he confesses, Burgess would not let himself realize that Lynne was an alcoholic. "Few of us", as he says, "want to face reality; we kept her trouble vague, not really diagnosable." It must have been a heroic self-deception since she was drinking up to a bottle of gin and several bottles of wine a day and not holding it at all well. Her ascites (a word the pedant in Burgess relishes, deriving as it does from the distension of a Greek wine skin) he took as matronly stoutness. Her paranoid delusions—that he was a homosexual, for instance—were played down as residue from the 1944 assault. The possessiveness which meant he could never leave her side was love, in a funny kind of way. The British medical profession seems to have conspired in the protective vagueness. Finally, in 1968 she sustained a massive portal haemorrhage. "There

were not enough pots and pans in the kitchen to hold the tides of blood", Burgess recalls. Her liver had packed in. A few weeks and much gin later, she died.

Burgess was, and apparently still is, racked with guilt: "I had always persuaded her to drink drink for drink with me, ignoring the truth that women's livers are not men's. At the beginning of our relationship she had hated pubs; I taught her to love them. . . . It was right for me to feel like a murderer." Why? It was not he who kicked her in her pregnant stomach, or wrenched the wedding ring from her broken finger. Yet it is with the GIs that Burgess aligns himself, not the husband who stood by her and whose only thought, when told he must die, was how to provide for his widow. In *A Clockwork Orange,* there is a mysterious echo in the names of the characters which connects Alexander de Large (the teenage hoodlum hero) with F. Alexander the wimp author of a book called *A Clockwork Orange* and husband of Alex's rape-and-battery victim, who dies in the novel. Particularly with its last chapter attached, the narrative is friendlier to the assailant than the aggrieved husband. It's not easy to penetrate Burgess's meaning here and perhaps not decent to try. But part of his guilt seems to reside in the (understandably) homicidal feelings that his wife's illness provoked in him. "I wish to God they had killed you in 1944!" is one interpretation to be drawn from *A Clockwork Orange,* at once followed by "What a swine I must be to think that!"

Disastrous as his marriage was, Burgess's career prospered in the mid-1960s. He was in demand as a reviewer (television for the *Listener,* opera for *Queen,* drama for the *Spectator,* books everywhere). He was something of a celebrity, and appeared regularly on television. He virtually lived in a dinner-jacket. But he was not writing novels any more. He recalls that "one day a parcel arrived from Messrs Heinemann, and I said: 'Ah, the proofs of my new novel.' But I had written no new novel." Unshackled from Lynne, he resolved to travel and to write new novels again.

There were complications. In one of his casual adulteries in 1964 Burgess had made love to a young Italian student of literature, who promptly disappeared from his life. She was married to a black man but bore a white child, Andrea. Burgess was the father. The news was withheld from him, until after Lynne's death. Liana Macellari eventually became Burgess's second wife. The three of them set up initially in Malta—which turned out disastrously when it emerged that Burgess intended to work and was ineligible for the six-pence-in-the-pound tax rate that had drawn them there. The Burgesses have subsequently pitched their tent (or parked their Dormobile—their favourite mode of transport) in Italy, Switzerland and, most happily, Monaco. Their residence has not always been legal, but honest authors have always had to cheat to survive, as Burgess tells us. During this period, he has written his most ambitious fictions and composed some moderately successful music, which may have given him more satisfaction. He has also, for dollars, taught and lectured in America, a country whose irritations have been good for his fiction. Meanwhile, Burgess has churned out a mass of workmanlike incidental writing, some strange potboilers, and more and better scholarly writing (much of it on Joyce) than most full-time academics.

You would think someone who was supposed to die in 1960 might be grateful for the gift of another thirty years. "Am I happy?" Burgess asks. "Probably not." He certainly continues to stew in guilt. A writer it seems must sacrifice something—his art, his personal comfort, or care of his family. Burgess envies James Joyce whose daughter went mad and whose son became a layabout drunk; at least Joyce could console himself with the thought that he had written two undeniable masterpieces. Burgess is not sure that his artistic achievements rate the cost that his near and dear have had to pay. He feels in particular that he has done badly by his now grown-up son, dragged as he was across all of Europe and America in his childhood: "If I had been a schoolmaster in Banbury or a bank clerk in Ealing, Andrea would have had an adequate suburban education and been sensibly monoglot . . . when he attempted suicide it was clearly my fault for bringing him to Monaco. He was involved in a very nasty car accident on the road to Nice, and his left leg and thigh were converted to a bag of scrabble pieces. This was my fault again." But if Burgess had become a schoolmaster in Banbury, we would not have had *MF, Napoleon Symphony,* or *ABBA ABBA.* It is a solemn thought whether we would trade *Finnegans Wake* for a sane Lucia Joyce or *Earthly Powers* for a young man's unshattered left leg.

Burgess is incurably truculent. Time and again in *You've Had Your Time* he recalls starting fist fights in bars, airports, pubs. He is not a good man to be standing next to in a public place when he has had a drink or two. Invariably when he starts something he is overpowered and told off, or thumped. But he never seems to learn. He has, as he admits, a chip on his shoulder which he traces back to his provincial Lancashire origins. Like most brawlers, he does not expect to be liked by strangers, least of all in this volume: "it is never the object of confession, at least in the Catholic tradition, to present oneself as a likeable character. One seeks not admiration but forgiveness." What has he done that we should forgive him? Does he also feel guilt towards us, his public? In so far as a reader's absolution counts he has mine, and my admiration as well, as it happens. (pp. 1143-44)

> *John Sutherland, "An Original Sinner," in*
> The Times Literary Supplement, *No. 4569, October 26, 1990, pp. 1143-44.*

Lorna Sage   (review date 11 October 1991)

[*In the review below, Sage comments on Burgess's approach to writing about language, music, and Mozart in* Mozart and the Wolf Gang.]

[*Mozart and the Wolf Gang*] is Anthony Burgess's contribution to the chorus of bicentennial tributes to Mozart. Not content to be one voice among the many, he has produced his own cacophonous anthology, bits and pieces in diverse genres, starting with a composers' seminar in the Afterworld (Mendelssohon in charge of deathday celebrations among the immortals), and ending with a personal essay. In between, there are: an *opera buffa* rendition of

scenes from Mozart's life; a set-piece transcription of Symphony No 40 (words symphonized); some script for a parodic Mozart bio-pic (anti-*Amadeus*); and dialogues between two tetchy characters, Anthony and Burgess.

In short, *Mozart and the Wolf Gang* is at once scrappy and inordinate, throwaway and ambitious. Burgess is at his old game of demonstrating by default that words (his second love) cannot do what music (his first) can. Words deal with real things, music is "not *about* anything". On this logic, you best celebrate Mozart's achievement in words through travesty, staging comic defeats and cobbling together unlikely aphorisms. For example: "Music is the Armagnac of the saved. The musician alone has access to God." This particular line is given to Stendhal, who appears in Burgess's Heaven as an honorary musician, by virtue of his reverence for Rossini. The celestial seminar doesn't come to any very startling conclusions, though it does point up the paradox that music's universality doesn't prevent music-lovers from staying stuck in their own prejudices. It is simply that *anyone* can appropriate Mozart—the Jew in the concentration camp and the SS guard on the gate. In the background, Beethoven, Wagner, Mendelssohn and company can hear the distant boom of the guns in the Gulf, reminding us of the gulf fixed between Islamic and Judeo-Christian cultures.

Burgess wants to say that for the Western tradition Mozart remains music's Messiah, because his work embodies the noble vision of "a musical community", serious and unserious, high and low, craft and art united in a mystical marriage.

—Lorna Sage

Despite this, Burgess still wants to say that for the Western tradition Mozart remains music's Messiah, because his work embodies the noble vision of "a musical community", serious and unserious, high and low, craft and art united in a mystical marriage. His music keeps its links with dance, and so symbolizes "the union of man and woman and that larger union known as the human collective" (at least in our corner of eternity). And besides, Mozart's "prolific production" is one in the eye for all those moderns afflicted with the "costiveness . . . of Bloomsbury's gentility". He is "a serious craftsman and a breadwinner", and—here we descend from the empyrean with a bit of a thump—not, after all, so unlike wordy Anthony Burgess, who writes all the hours God gives.

The most virtuoso patch of word-spinning in the book is undoubtedly the imitation/analogy that pays tribute to Symphony No 40. Burgess may not have added much to Mozart, but there's a good deal of irreverent fun to be had out of (for instance) singing along to the opening of the second movement with the words, "The black day is coming. *What black day is coming?*" and getting to the answer

CONTEMPORARY LITERARY CRITICISM, Vol. 81

(in the fourth): "Well, the tumbrils are coming . . . ". Gibberish, comments "Anthony", or is it "Burgess"? None of this is *serious*. The trouble is, though, that in a sense it is. The whole multi-generic collage is, for me, rather like a lecture, after all. He's *preaching* lightness, rather than practising it. So that, although he avoids modernity's costiveness, he doesn't escape its other great cross, self-consciousness. Indeed, one of his many voices spells it out pretty exactly: "We feel at home with Mozart, and then suddenly realize that we're not dressed for prerevolutionary Europe. We're putting on an act."

Lorna Sage, "A Celestial Seminar," in The Times Literary Supplement, *No. 4619, October 11, 1991, p. 22.*

Fiona Maddocks (review date 19 October 1991)

[*Below, Maddocks offers a mixed review of* Mozart and the Wolf Gang, *commenting on Burgess's portrayal of Mozart.*]

The venue is heaven. 'Shalom, gentlemen, you've just arrived?', says Mendelssohn, playing the role of a sort of ecumenical St Peter. The newcomers are a string quartet from Tel Aviv, rudely interrupted in the middle of playing the slow movement of Mozart's B flat quartet K548 by one of Saddam Hussein's scud missiles and despatched, post haste, to the celestial heights. The incorporeal musicians then embark on a brief discussion of Mozart's bicentenary, the Gulf War, the fundamental cultural division between Judaism and Islam, the kinship between the skills needed for making guns and crafting musical instruments, the immortality of music, the divinity of Mozart and associated topics.

This episode comes near the end of Anthony Burgess's maddening little book, as ingenious and funny as, in many places, it is unreadable and incomprehensible. Half fantasy, half lightly veiled polemic, **Mozart and the Wolf Gang** is written as a (surely unperformable) libretto, in several scenes and with some 40 characters drawn from *Don Giovanni*, Mozart's employer Colloredo (the Archbishop of Salzburg, here puzzlingly spelled Colleredo), Schoenberg and Henry James among them. It deviates variously into film script, rhyming doggerel or straight prose. At one point, there is a fictional account of Mozart's 40th Symphony, all repeated phrases and Hopkins-esque assonance. This is from the last movement:

Well, the gumbrils are humming. The birds ingest rumbling, crumbling, blunder. Yet a thumbril is lonely, a warm start. Loud crowd the lies, lies loud for the crowd, the crowds lie loud . . .

An impossible enterprise, as Burgess himself admits (actually he calls it 'gibberish'), and a devil of a job to read.

To attempt a synopsis would be futile, if not impossible. Joyce or Sterne might have appreciated Burgess's style. Anyone else might be less tolerant, depending on their familiarity with Mozart's life and work and their taste for arch whimsy. Each page bristles with musical or musicological reference, elegantly tossed off and displaying Burgess's intimacy with the history of music and composition-

al techniques (he began his career as a self-taught composer: music is a component in many of his novels and writings). He is, too, up to date with all the latest theories as to whether Mozart was murdered by his rival Salieri (he wasn't), whether he died a pauper's death (he didn't), whether he suffered from what Burgess calls 'scatomaniacal infantilism' (no more than anyone else then or now).

The Mozart who emerges, rather—and this is the nub of Burgess's idiosyncratic bicentennial tribute—is a blunt, hard working genius who eschews the company of his toadying, less gifted colleagues, puts artistic liberty before prosperous servitude, yet is well capable of demanding his due, down to the final guilder. All of which makes him sound rather dull. In many ways, as portrayed here, he is—which is the author's point. In a conversation with his own split personality, Burgess says:

We may talk of the man, but what is the relevance of the man to the composer? The puppet Mozart I set up in the stupid little *opera buffa* libretto I contrived will do as well as any travesty. If you want the man, that is. But the music should be enough.

His friend and adversary Anthony, unconvinced, replies:

A man wrote the music . . . He had headaches and indigestion. He slept with his wife, and perhaps the rhythms of coition begot new themes.

They agree, finally, that knowledge of the man can help explain why he wrote the works he did, but not how. Elsewhere, in some other room in heaven, a gloriously pompous Henry James has a similar argument with Lorenzo Da Ponte, Mozart's librettist, who claims that *Cosi Fan Tutte* cannot be understood without knowing something of the life which was poured into it. James is unconvinced.

The book concludes with a moving essay—by an integrated Anthony Burgess, at his best, and alone worth reading the book for—on how the writer as a young man had difficulty in coming to terms with Mozart, that composer's elevation to demi-god since the 1930s when Beethoven was always considered the supreme genius, and the relationship between literature and music. In a dodgy last paragraph (far better to have stopped at the one before), he seeks an analogue amongst great writers and settles on Dante. A bizarre choice. Decidedly time to get back to the music. (pp. 36-7)

Fiona Maddocks, "Message to a Mad Deus," in The Spectator, *Vol. 267, No. 8519, October 19, 1991, pp. 36-7.*

William M. Hoffman (review date 26 April 1992)

[*An American playwright, scriptwriter, librettist, and critic, Hoffman is best known for* As Is *(1985), a controversial drama about the tragic effects of AIDS on a homosexual couple. In the review below, he describes* On Mozart *as a revisionist, "spiritual" biography.*]

Another book on Mozart? Is there anything left to write about him? During last year's commemoration of the 200th anniversary of his death, Amadeophiles delved into

The Wolf Gang of Burgess's jokey title
[*Mozart and the Wolf Gang*] are the
enemies of Amadeus: the courtly and
ecclesiastical philistines who persecuted
him while he lived; the propagandists who
appropriate or misrepresent his music
after his death.

—*Peter Conrad, in his "Sovereign Spirit
Reborn," in* The Observer, *17 November
1991.*

practically every area of his existence. So I am grateful to
report that Anthony Burgess's new book, a "heartfelt
homage" in a form combining opera, film, novel and essay,
stakes out uncharted territory. *On Mozart* provides answers to such burning questions as:

What happened to Mozart after he died and went to heav-
en?

How would you go about novelizing his Symphony No.
40?

What did Ludwig van Beethoven *really* think of Saddam
Hussein?

Mr. Burgess sets his book in heaven. The time, measured
by earthly events, is the 1991 Persian Gulf war. The premise is that a motley crew of departed composers, including
most of the biggies like Brahms, Wagner, Mendelssohn,
Gershwin and Stravinsky, is preparing to watch an opera
written by anonymous spirits for a celestial bicentennial.
The subject of the libretto is Mozart's scheme to prevent
the tyrannical Prince Archbishop Hieronymus Colloredo
from schlepping him from lively Vienna to boring old
Salzburg.

"What?" I can hear Metropolitan Opera fans cry out.
"Isn't the story similar in structure to *The Ghosts of Versailles* by John Corigliano and William Hoffman?" True,
the donnée of my libretto to *Ghosts,* which premiered at
the Metropolitan Opera last December, is that a group of
phantoms from the court of Louis XVI is eagerly waiting
for the ghost of the playwright Beaumarchais to present
his latest postmortem opus, an opera that also has as its
goal to change history. In our opus Beaumarchais plans
to have the cast of his *Figaro* trilogy rescue Marie Antoinette from the guillotine so she can run off with him to
Philadelphia.

There are other similarities: both Mr. Burgess's libretto
and mine begin with scenes of complaining servants and
contain comic Turks; in both, serious reflections on art de-
volve into farce, which turns into tragedy. Readers may
wonder what on earth—or rather, heaven—is going on
here? Is it coincidence, or is there something more dire
afoot?

The fact is that I had planned *The Ghosts of Versailles* before the end of 1982; I didn't crack the galley proofs of *On*

Mozart until about 10 years later. And to my knowledge,
Mr. Burgess could not have been familiar with my libretto
till the premiere last season. To what then, can the likeness
be attributed? Mind reading? The *Zeitgeist?*

I think I have a simpler explanation. Until recently, liberal
dogma clung to the notion that humanity was advancing
in all fields. In politics, capitalism was seen by the "progressive" vanguard of almost the entire past century as
outmoded. In painting, artists viewed themselves as
marching forever forward, proudly announcing that the
disdain of the despised middle classes was proof of their
genius. In music, the 12-tone and other avant-garde
schools claimed their legitimacy equally from the chro-
maticism of late Beethoven (which led to Wagner, whose
influence, they said, led ineluctably to who else but themselves) and the universal indifference and loathing with
which their music was greeted.

But after a century of such "advances" as the Holocaust
and the Gulag, and the almost total eclipse of serious new
music, some people have begun to question these notions
of progress. They feel that perhaps the past took a wrong
turn somewhere. What would have happened, for example, had Hitler been assassinated early in his career, or if
the French Revolution had been aborted, or if Mozart
hadn't died at the age of 35? I call this kind of revisionist
thinking "revenge therapy."

In *On Mozart* Mr. Burgess has created debates about
music that never occurred but should have. Mendelssohn,
whom the author pictures as having reconverted to his ancestral Judaism from Lutheranism as he watched the
Holocaust from his perch in heaven, accuses Wagner of
perverting music "into the service of half-baked notions
of Teutonic superiority." George Gershwin and Arnold
Schoenberg also slug it out. Says Gershwin: "You should
have dropped all that 12-tone stuff as soon as you got to
L.A. . . . All the studios wanted was straight tonic and
dominant."

But the most interesting dispute is between Mr. Burgess
and his alter ego, Anthony, on the meaning of Mozart's
music. Anthony has countered Mr. Burgess's point that
the details of Mozart's life are irrelevant to his music:

> BURGESS. We have the music, and the music is,
> if you will, divine. . . .
>
> ANTHONY. It's created by human beings.
>
> BURGESS. . . . It's not *about* anything. . . .
> Discuss Mozart's operas and we discuss how
> aptly he colors the words of da Ponte.

Nonetheless, in the end, addressing the audience *in propria
persona,* Mr. Burgess does seem to come up with an extra-
musical explanation of the art of Mozart. In a fascinating,
convincing summary, quoting Ezra Pound, he reminds us
that "poetry decays when it moves too far away from
song, and music decays when it forgets the dance," and
that in the 18th century "the spirit of the dance was raised
to its highest level."

Mr. Burgess claims that Mozart's music gained objectivity, and avoided the kind of personal, emotional content
found in the work of later composers like Mahler. He

views Mozart as a portraitist of the "static tranquility of the Austro-Hungarian Empire." "It would not be extravagant to find in him something like the serenity of Dante Alighieri."

Since he is a composer of some accomplishment himself and, in *A Clockwork Orange,* the creator of Alex, the vicious punk and ultimate Beethoven fan, this is hardly Anthony Burgess's first essay at portraying the world of music. In his *Napoleon Symphony* of 1974, he novelized Beethoven's *Eroica* Symphony, using a technique similar to that of his transfer into prose of Mozart's 40th in the present book. I'm afraid I'll have to give it the same critique that Anthony gives it in *On Mozart:* gibberish.

If you are looking for a biographically revealing work on the life of a great composer, this book most likely will not please you. This is a *spiritual* biography, similar in purpose to, but radically different in style from, J. W. N. Sullivan's classic *Beethoven: His Spiritual Development* (1927).

As much as I liked most of this brilliant rumination, I have to confess a profound dis-ease with it. We seem to be living in a silver age, content to worship the past, a time of safe art as well as safe sex. I can't help wondering what risk is there in wallowing in yesterday's masterpieces rather than in discovering today's. Good, we have a fine book to cap Mozart's bicentennial, but isn't it time to get on with it? (pp. 15-16)

> *William M. Hoffman, "He'll Always Have Vienna," in* The New York Times Book Review, *April 26, 1992, pp. 15-16.*

Joseph Epstein   (review date Autumn 1992)

[*An American nonfiction writer and critic, Epstein has been widely praised for his learned essays on American life and literature. In the excerpt below, he reviews Burgess's two-volume autobiography,* Little Wilson and Big God *and* You've Had Your Time, *commenting on the relationship between Burgess's life and art.*]

No one would accuse Anthony Burgess of either common sense or taking the small bite. But then nor does Burgess, who has lived in tax-fleeing exile from England for many years now, seem, when one gets down to it, especially English. His lineage is Irish and Catholic, for one thing. His ambitions, for another, are extra- or para-English. His productivity, of which he has himself by now doubltless heard too much, doesn't feel particularly English either. "I have written much fiction and reviewed widely and unbrophianly [a reference to the book reviews intended to maim written by Brigid Brophy], and I was sneered at for over-production and reviled for compassionate blandness." Mr. Burgess is not a man to forget a bad review, many of which he quotes, rather like showing old scars, in his [two-volume autobiography: *Little Wilson and Big God* and *You've Had You're Time*], and this, too, does not seem particularly English.

I have not myself had very good luck with Mr. Burgess' novels, only one of which, *Earthly Powers,* I have been able to read all the way through. As he puts it early in

You've Had Your Time, the second volume of his autobiography: "I was, am, trying to be a kind of comic novelist playing with a few ideas." Fair enough, except that the ideas he has chosen to play with have not, somehow, seemed much to interest me. I do read his literary journalism, and am often impressed by his erudition, his extraordinary range, his facility—when invited to review a book, it is said of him, he generally answers the invitation by providing the finished review. Mr. Burgess' talent is not in doubt; nor is his seriousness. He is a writer I rather admire without necessarily longing to read.

One comes away from his two-volume autobiography in something of the same condition: rather admiring his accomplishment of having got so much work done, of having maintained his independence without toadying to anyone, of having survived at least eleven different kinds of hell—and yet without particularly liking him. Burgess speaks at one point of Orwell's "power to ensure things," but he himself can usually be relied upon to take the smile out of Christmas. He passes Orwell's own test for autobiography by recounting many disgraceful things about himself and by tending to view his own life as, for the most part, a series of defeats.

The first of Burgess' two autobiographical volumes deals with his birth and education and horrific first marriage, and ends with him being told that he has an inoperable brain tumor that will allow him at best a year to live. His second volume deals with his wife's death and his remarriage, but it has chiefly to do with the literary life. This second volume is impressive for, among other things, its sheer comprehensiveness. Anthony Burgess has been a literary man of all work, having not only written in all the standard literary forms—poems, novels, plays, criticism, journalism—but translation for the stage and for opera, libretti, movies, television scripts, everything short of subpoenas and health-food labels. "I had become," he notes at one point of his various literary jobs, "the least fatigable of hacks." He has come through all this neither a rich man nor a cheerful one, but he has come through with all that a writer can hope for, his skill and his integrity intact. No small victory.

Certain of us go through life acquiring large grievances, and live out our days attempting to collect claims on them that can never be repaid. Mr. Burgess began life with a most serious grievance and claim of this kind. His mother and older sister died, in the great influenza epidemic of 1919, when he was only two years old. Given his rather indifferent father, who remarried to an unfeeling woman, this left poor John Anthony Burgess Wilson (for such is his full name, later shortened by a publisher) immediately alone, emotionally chilled, bereft, a twentieth-century Dickensian character in a novel that would have no happy ending. "This boy," Burgess writes of himself, "nine, going on ten, was clearly abnormal. He needed a real mother, not a surrogate one, and a real-life male model, not a mostly absent drunk who called himself a father."

Setting aside the human consequences of this sadness, for a man whose entire life is literature, the literary consequences, too, have to be calculated. No one is better fit to do this than Mr. Burgess, who, in a striking passage of self-knowledge, writes of his upbringing:

> I was not in rags and I did not starve. I was permitted an education. But I regret the emotional coldness that was established then and which, apart from other faults, has marred my work. I read of family relationships in other people's books and I envy equally the tranquility and the turbulence. *Sons and Lovers* and *Fathers and Sons* are from an alien planet which I can visit only by stretching my imagination.

This unfortunate absence of family feeling in a novelist is not a minor defect; if one believes that love and the family are two of the great—perhaps the greatest—subjects of the novel, it might just be a major defect. At a minimum, it would tend to force such a novelist to fall back upon satire, upon the schematic, upon the ideational, upon the play of language in and for itself, all of which seems to have been the result in Mr. Burgess' case.

Burgess' two volumes press the question of how deep in detail one should go in the writing of autobiography. At times Burgess himself threatens to rival Borges' poor child Ireneo Funes, in his story "Funes the Memorius," who could not forget anything and died young of what we should today call information overload. Burgess telling us that he missed his comic books in the General Strike of 1926 seems a detail if not worth forgetting then probably worth failing to record. One can't fault Burgess for want of candor. He not only fills us in on all his and his wife's love affairs, but tells us of their giving each other crabs (initially acquired elsewhere) and remarks on his own youthful propensity for premature climax ("it sounds," he remarks, "like a damn critic's rebuke"), a problem he conquered by quoting to himself from Milton, *Paradise Lost, "Book Two."* (The study of literature, it seems, has its uses after all.) Sex, as described by Burgess in these volumes, is never overly elegant.

I do not boast about the quality of my work, but I may be permitted to pride myself on the gift of steady application.

—*Anthony Burgess*

After himself, the central figure in Burgess' autobiography is his first wife, Lynne, whose infidelities to him, and his to her, on two continents he recounts in a rather matter of fact way. Their marriage, in Burgess' present view of it, was a mistake from the start. It was not much aided by her being mugged by American GIs in London, causing her to abort her pregnancy and cutting off forever the chance of her having children. Instead the Burgesses substituted cats, at one point in Brunei, where he had a teaching job, having no fewer than twenty-five of them. She added gin to this recipe for family disaster, and more than once attempted suicide. Toss in jealousy, resentment, and rivalrousness and you have quite a domestic dish. "Lynne

and I cautiously settled to a country life enlivened mostly with drunkenness and threats of suicide," Burgess writes, in a sentence of chillingly calm rhythm. Yet when Burgess' wife dies, not yet fifty, of alcoholism, he feels, yes, of course, luscious guilt, which he seems to have attempted to work off in this autobiography by demonstrating what a monstrous character she was. If raising a writer is not such a good idea, marrying one is not a less perilous proposition.

Burgess makes the most modest claims for himself as an artist in this autobiography. . . . "I do not boast about the quality of my work," he writes, "but I may be permitted to pride myself on the gift of steady application. . . . The gift of concentration stays with me, and it is perhaps my only gift." In fact, Anthony Burgess is an immensely gifted man. But one of the things that comes strongly through his autobiography is that he would have traded all his literary accomplishments for a career in serious musical composition. At one point, he refers to "the novel, the only literary genre for failed symphonists." In his first volume, he tells us that "at the age of thirteen I decided that I was to be a great composer, and I trained myself, pursuing an indulged hobby, to that end. It was an ambition that only really faded in my late thirties, and sometimes, in my late sixties, it is encouraged to re-emerge." In the 1980s, he composed a symphony that was played at the University of Iowa, and so a childhood dream was realized. It may well be that only music, in its abstraction and in its propensity to submerge to depths beneath the verbal, could have given true expression to Burgess' wounds.

The world has never been a pleasant place for Anthony Burgess, and he is not very intent on changing it—he is for the most part apolitical—or himself. He was, he reports, offered Lionel Trilling's job at Columbia, but turned it down. "Security for life, high status, the dignity of scholarship. I think, however, I made the right decision in refusing the honor. It was not really suited to one masochistically inclined to the hard knocks of the Grub Street life, not inclined to disdain vulgarity in the right place, one not averse to scandal." Liana, his second wife, he notes, "importuned me to make myself more simpatico, but I would not. Had Dante made himself simpatico?" Old mothers' wisdom impels one to reply, "Very well, but first be Dante."

Everything Anthony Burgess writes in this autobiography is believable. He cannot be accused of blowing his own tuba. There is a lifelike, inexorable dreariness to his account of his own days, relieved by flashes of wit. (To the rumor that he was living in a *ménage à trois,* with his wife and a beautiful Ethiopian secretary in Manhattan, Burgess responds that the rumor was "only two-thirds true.") Yet is his finally the true perspective? Or is it instead that writers, who not only by the nature of their occupation but because of the depression that all too often seems to have sent them into this occupation to begin with, are the least qualified for telling us what their lives have been about? Under the enchantment of their words, one is almost ready to believe them, no matter how chilling their account. Then one remembers that the world abounds in beautiful children, music, lush landscapes, friends, delightful food, and more than enough artworks to divert the mind through a lifetime, and the words, like frost on a wintry windowpane, melt away. (pp. 376-80)

Joseph Epstein, "First Person Singular," in The Hudson Review, Vol. XLV, No. 3, Autumn, 1992, pp. 367-92.

John Bossy (review date 30 April 1993)

[*In the following excerpt, Bossy favorably reviews* A Dead Man in Deptford, *commenting on Burgess's fictional portrayal of historical events.*]

A passion for anniversaries, and the publication of Charles Nicholl's account of his death, *The Reckoning,* last year, have caused a run on Christopher Marlowe, and now we have, all at once, three novels about him, and especially about it. Two of them [Robin Chapman's *Christoferus, or Tom Kyd's Revenge* and Liam Maguire's *Icarus Flying: The Tragical Story of Christopher Marlowe*] are feeble, and the third is by Anthony Burgess.

Burgess says that he has been wanting to write a novel about Marlowe since he wrote a thesis about him, fifty years ago, in Manchester. He knows what he is up to. His narrator in *A Dead Man in Deptford* is nobody we know about, a former boy actor, who has graduated from Zenocrate to the lesser male parts, and seems to be writing during the reign of Charles I. He does not claim to know what happened, only to be "supposing", which lets Burgess out of a lot of problems. At the end, the author steps out in front of his curtain and deprecates the "ill-made disguise", the "grumbling compromise" of the language he has had to use; and it is true that we should like the actor to have found a reason different from Burgess's own for putting his supposals down on paper. And, for my part, I prefer my proscenium thresholds inviolate.

However, the ignorant narrator who is really a mountain of learning will do very well if he is transparent enough to let Burgess get on with telling his story, as he does, in a powerful machine-gun rattle of direct speech, and with a composition of place for which the Jesuits (who taught him? Or was the Xaverian College in Manchester not a Jesuit institution?) ought to congratulate him. When he does Marlowe at the English College at Reims, which has pretty well everything against it (Marlowe did not go there, the town has been blown to bits, has no archives), it is not just that you suspend disbelief, but that if it was your job as a historian to write the history of the institution in that time and place (1578-1593), you would do it a great deal better if you had read Burgess.

His story, like everybody else's except the historians', presupposes that the characters involved in the scene at Deptford when Marlowe was killed at Mrs Bull's lodging-house were somehow the embodiment of his life's history. That is to say, it becomes an item not in a story but in a plot, which it is improper for history books to have. Burgess's plot has three acts. The first, running together Marlowe's Cambridge career with an introduction to spying, which takes him to Reims, to Paris and to Flushing, ends

up with the famous certificate from the Privy Council, saying that any rumour that Marlowe "was determined to have gone" to Reims and to turn Catholic was groundless, and that he has been serving the Queen and should be allowed to take his degree. Act Two: the plays; Raleigh and the School of Night, smoking (bliss) and a brief view of Shakespeare. On the public scene, Walsingham dies, Marlowe resigns the Service, Essex begins his campaign against Raleigh which, as in Nicholl, leads to Marlowe's arrest. Act Three: examination before the Privy Council, to which, when he has been dismissed, Richard Baines's "Note" about Marlowe's atheism is read. Marlowe prepares to go abroad but has to deal with his spy-supervisor, Robert Poley, whom he is to meet at Deptford. There he is surprised to find two other acquaintances, Ingram Frizer and Nicholas Skeres, who along with Poley kill him. Why? Poley's part is something to with Marlowe's having left the Service and his general bolshiness; Frizer's and Skeres's with private matters concerning the wish of their employer, the late Sir Francis Walsingham's cousin, Thomas, to put buggery behind him and marry a wife. It is also to do with the fact that Thomas Walsingham is setting himself up on the profits of usury, provided by Frizer and Skeres. It is Frizer, usurer and Puritan, who sticks the knife in Marlowe's eye.

We have been here before, and so has Burgess. Once upon a time, his younger self must have been reading his Tawney and his Belloc, and the fifty years since he wrote his thesis have not done much to dissuade him. I should have been glad of less anti-Elizabethan melodrama. Nobody is required to believe that there was an Elizabethan Secret Service; nor that Mary, Queen of Scots, was executed on forged evidence. I should also have been glad of more flexibility in Burgess's conviction that the Roman Church is *semper eadem:* it is a not quite trivial mistake to have Elizabethan Catholics addressing secular priests as "father" and using the confessional box. . . .

[Burgess, Chapman, and Maguire] have one thing in common; they all have Marlowe a victim of religious enthusiasm: another goal to Aristotle, who said that history tells you what happened, and poetry what ought to have happened.

John Bossy, "In at the Death," in The Times Literary Supplement, No. 4700, April 30, 1993, p. 21.

A Dead Man in Deptford **is not just a very good novel; it may well be Burgess' masterpiece. His grasp of the age and its angsts is profound, and his portrait of Marlowe sympathetic, critical and brilliantly imagined all at once.**

—Robert Carver, in his "Nequissimus," in New Statesman and Society, *23 April 1993.*

John Banville (review date 16 May 1993)

[*An Irish novelist, short story writer, and critic, Banville received the James Tait Black Memorial Prize for his historical novel* Doctor Copernicus (1976) *and is among the foremost contemporary writers to experiment with the format of the traditional Irish novel. In the following excerpt, he praises* A Dead Man in Deptford *for its "wonderfully dense and inventive mock-Elizabethan" language.*]

Edmund Wilson, writing many years ago on detective fiction, including the novels of Agatha Christie, called his essay 'Who Cares Who killed Roger Ackroyd?' After reading [Anthony Burgess's *A Dead Man in Deptford* and Judith Cook's *The Slicing Edge of Death: Who Killed Christopher Marlowe?*], I find myself echoing Wilson. Does it matter who killed Christopher Marlowe? The only significant fact is that this lavishly gifted poet, author of *Doctor Faustus, The Jew of Malta* and *Edward II,* died at 29, with God knows how many masterpieces unwritten.

The facts, most of them disputed, are these. On 30 May, 1593 Marlowe repaired to the house of one Widow Bull in Deptford with three cronies, Robert Poley, Ingram Frizer and Nicholas Skeres. They spent the day eating and drinking, and in the evening a dispute arose over the bill—le recknynge, as the coroner's report oddly has it—and in the resulting scuffle, Ingram Frizer stabbed Marlowe through the right eye-socket, killing him instantly.

All four men had been involved together in espionage, under Elizabeth's spymaster Walsingham, and numerous conspiracy theories have been advanced, most recently in Charles Nicholl's *The Reckoning.* There is no doubt that Marlowe had been a party to some very shady doings, and it is at least possible that his murder was ordered by Someone High Up. On the other hand, it may be that . . . oh, what the hell. The narrator did it.

A Dead Man in Deptford is Anthony Burgess's best book for a long time. It is a companion piece to his 1964 novel on the life and loves of Shakespeare, *Nothing Like the Sun,* and has the same freshness, energy and linguistic gaiety. In the later book, however, the style is more adventurous and demanding, a wonderfully dense and inventive mock-Elizabethan that bobs along on a ceaseless ripple of wordplay. Burgess's life-long love affair with the English language finds its consummation here in a rich and moving work of art.

The narrator is an anonymous actor (anonymous, that is, unless you have access to Heming and Condell's 1623 Shakespeare folio; Burgess will have his little jokes) who as a young man was occasionally used by Marlowe to ease the fleshly itch. He is inexplicably omniscient, a fact dealt with in the bravura opening paragraph: 'I must suppose that what I suppose of his doings behind the back of my viewings is of the nature of a stout link in the chain of his being, lost to my seeing, not palpable but of necessity existent. I know little.'

That little is a lot. He tells his tale briskly, with the headlong thrust of blank verse. Burgess once wrote of a schoolfriend describing the works of Shakespeare as 'all fighting and fucking', and there is a deal of both here. 'Bradley now had sword in right and dagger in left. He caught Tom Watson most bitterly in the brow with dagger, there was a wound like a mouth that spoke blood.' Constantly under all this action Burgess shows us the cauldron of language bubbling away. The book has two heroes, Marlowe, and English, and it is a question as to which of them Burgess finds most fascinating.

> John Banville, "One in the Eye," in The Observer, *May 16, 1993, p. 63.*

Additional coverage of Burgess's life and career is contained in the following sources published by Gale Research: *Authors in the News,* **Vol. 1;** *Concise Dictionary of British Literary Biography, 1960 to Present; Contemporary Authors,* **Vols. 1-4, rev. ed.;** *Contemporary Authors New Revision Series,* **Vol. 2;** *Contemporary Literary Criticism,* **Vols. 1, 2, 4, 5, 8, 10, 13, 15, 22, 40, 62;** *Dictionary of Literary Biography,* **Vol. 14; and** *Major 20th-Century Writers.*

William Golding

September 19, 1911—June 19, 1993

(Full name William Gerald Golding) English novelist, short fiction writer, playwright, essayist, poet, and nonfiction writer.

For further information on Golding's life and works, see *CLC*, Volumes 1, 2, 3, 8, 10, 17, 27, and 58.

INTRODUCTION

Best known for his acclaimed first novel *Lord of the Flies,* Golding was among the most popular and influential post-World War II British authors. Considered a moral allegory as well as an adventure tale, *Lord of the Flies* was inspired by the atrocities Golding witnessed during World War II and presents a disturbing portrait of civilization's fragility and capacity for evil. Set in the future, the novel concerns a group of British schoolboys who, after being marooned on a tropical island, organize a democratic society that eventually degenerates into primeval barbarism. Like *Lord of the Flies,* many of Golding's subsequent works have dealt with the intrinsic cruelty and depravity of humankind; *The Inheritors,* for example, concerns the destruction of Neanderthal man by Homo sapiens while *The Spire,* a novel set in the middle ages, equates the erection of a cathedral spire with the protagonist's struggle against temptation and search for religious faith. Often described as fables or parables, Golding's works are laden with symbolism, incorporate a wide variety of settings, and employ sudden shifts of perspective. In 1983 Golding received the Nobel Prize in Literature. The awarding of the prize, however, was marred by controversy when one of the judges asserted that Golding's work was not up to the Swedish Academy's standards; the controversy was further exacerbated when an English critic charged that Golding had plagiarized the idea for *Lord of the Flies.* However, as Jonathan Raban has noted: "Few novelists arouse either that sort of reverence or that sort of contempt. To be labeled simultaneously a sage and a charlatan is something that happens often to famous preachers and almost never to writers of fiction. But then, William Golding is, in his way, a famous preacher."

PRINCIPAL WORKS

Poems (poetry) 1934
Lord of the Flies (novel) 1954
The Inheritors (novel) 1955
Envoy Extraordinary (novella) 1956; published in *Sometimes, Never: Three Tales of Imagination*
Pincher Martin (novel) 1956; also published as *The Two Deaths of Christopher Martin,* 1957
*The Brass Butterfly (drama) 1958
Free Fall (novel) 1959
The Spire (novel) 1964
The Hot Gates, and Other Occasional Pieces (essays) 1965
The Pyramid (novel) 1967
†The Scorpion God (novellas) 1971
Darkness Visible (novel) 1979
‡Rites of Passage (novel) 1980
A Moving Target (essays and lectures) 1982
The Paper Men (novel) 1984
An Egyptian Journal (travel essay) 1985
‡Close Quarters (novel) 1987
‡Fire Down Below (novel) 1989

*This drama is an adaptation of the novella *Envoy Extraordinary.*

†This collection contains the novellas *Envoy Extraordinary, Clonk Clonk,* and *The Scorpion God.*

‡These works are collectively referred to as *Sea Trilogy* and were published together as *To the Ends of the Earth: A Sea Trilogy* in 1991.

OBITUARIES AND TRIBUTES

James Wood   (essay date 29 September 1991)

[*In the following excerpt from an essay written as a tribute to Golding on the occasion of his eightieth birthday, Wood describes his interview with Golding and comments on the principal characteristics of his works.*]

[Golding] looks hieratic, pharisaical, a Noah, a Moses. His white hair is sparse and flossy; but his beard prospers wirily all over the chin and neck. So much hanging down from this face, so many roots and fronds—it makes Golding's face curiously alive, yet also dead, as if frozen and framed in whiteness. His Mandarin eyes have no lashes, and slope downwards. He is somewhat godly in manner. It is clear from the beginning that he is only moderately interested in politesse. "I don't give a damn what you do," he replies to my question about a tape recorder. I'm put on edge of course; I feel the soles of my feet tighten as I follow him indoors.

Golding's writing is also somewhat godly. His prose is stony, and difficult, as if written on high-minded tablets. He has no voice, no personal tone. Though majestic and in some ways visionary, his novels are astoundingly unworldly. His fiction is a stranger to the fleshly, the robust, the contemporary. "I wouldn't know how to begin to write about contemporary society," he confesses to me at one point. Instead, he goes back into history and into closed societies—an island (*Lord Of The Flies*), a cathedral (*The Spire*), a ship (*Rites of Passage*). Moreover, his vision is curiously static. He believes, as he puts it in his essay **"Fable"**, that man produces evil as the bee produces honey. We are original sinners. He is a religious novelist, yet there is little sense in his work of dialectic, or even argument. His vision appears to be made up of blocks and formations of belief. Correspondingly, he has a weakness for the literary equivalent of such blocks—symbols. One thinks of the conch (which stands for parliamentary democracy) in *Lord Of The Flies;* or the spire in his novel of that name (which stands for hubris, knowledge, a man's phallus); or the ship in *Rites Of Passage* (which stands for nothing less than the ship of life). He has said "The important thing is not that man exists, but that God exists," which may be saintly in a believer, but is surely heretical in a novelist.

Thus his writing is strangely unwelcoming towards its characters (John Bayley has referred to the "functional evasiveness" of his writing). Can one indeed think of a Golding character whom one loves, or even knows? This may account for Golding's awkward position in English literature. He is a novelist admired but not much liked; people ingest his books but are not nourished by them. Everyone has read *Lord Of The Flies* (1954), but it is difficult to find anyone who has read the six novels that stretch between that first book and Golding's late success in *Rites Of Passage* (1980). He is armoured, formidably, in his own austerity.

> **Golding's fiction abounds in moments of vision; indeed, his fiction is essentially about vision, about finally seeing goodness, evil, and the loss of innocence.**
>
> **—James Wood**

What Golding can unquestionably do is make the reader see. If Golding's static religiosity, with its dense cruelty and elevated simplicities, is somewhat medieval, even so is his craftman's interest in the construction and functioning of things. Good in the detail, as it were. In *The Spire,* probably his best novel, we watch Dean Jocelin preside over the vast enterprise of building a cathedral spire (a teacher in Salisbury for many years, Golding could see Salisbury's great needle from the school windows). The novel rings with hammering and banging, with the creak of wood and the singing of stone. At one moment, Jocelin goes up the tower and looks out over the countryside,

> The valleys of the three rivers that met by the cathedral opened themselves up. The rivers glittered towards the tower; and you could see that all those places which had been separate to feet and only joined by an act of reason, were indeed part of the whole. To the northeast he could pick out three separate mills, three separate cascades at different levels, all joined by leagues of water that snaked towards the cathedral. The river did indeed run down hill.

Golding's fiction abounds in such moments of vision; indeed, his fiction is essentially about vision, about finally seeing goodness, evil, and the loss of innocence. Many of his characters—Ralph in *Lord Of The Flies,* Jocelin, Oliver in *The Pyramid*—have a sudden visionary access at the end of his books. "Jocelin," says Golding, "realises at the end that there is no innocent work. His spire has been erected for shabby reasons. He is a proud man. I suppose that sense of innocence polluted runs through my fiction." It may be that Golding's acute sense of this pollution has in part to do with his background. He grew up in Marlborough, in Wiltshire, a kind of rural quarantine, an innocent English idyll (it becomes the village of Stilbourne in *The Pyramid*). Golding's parents lived in an old house on the Green, next to the churchyard, and he has written powerfully about his childish discovery that bodies, stacked on the other side of his garden wall, were lying pointed into the family garden. "I made the final deduction that the dead lay, their heads under our wall, the rest of them projecting from their own place into our garden, their feet, their knees even tucked under our lawn." It is a characteristic Golding moment. I ask him about it. "At that age," he says, "our garden was the one uncontaminated place. It was innocence incarnate. I suppose death impinged for the first time in my life."

Golding is affable enough, but wary—a kind of minimum geniality, just bouncing along the bottom-floor of graciousness. He holds himself back. My sense persists that Golding wants to escape from this torture of conversation. His eyes glare. They are shrewd, and a little cold, with their naked lashless rims and tucked edges. His beard juts at me. There are tensions and reverberations in the air. We sit together inside a little chamber of hostility and awkwardness. But this does not surprise me. One of Golding's most recent novels, *The Paper Men,* was all about people like me. The book grew out of Golding's irritation with researchers, academics, and literary journalists. World famous, he felt tormented and invaded by such types. In the novel, a famous author is pursued by a crass and intrusive American academic, Rick L. Tucker (the novel barely rises above dismal caricature). The book functions as a kind of open letter of complaint: read this and stay away. Indeed, Golding is exultant about a recent triumph in France: "My wife and I were on holiday. A photographer recognised me and rushed to get his camera. So I put on my hat, pulled it down over my face, and put on a pair of dark glasses. That beat him."

The cause of all this unpleasantness is one book, *Lord Of The Flies.* Since the late fifties, the book has gone before him, waving a red flag, wherever he has gone. On campuses, in lecture halls, in interviews, Golding has elucidated its messages, unravelled its complexities. He has written many novels since *Lord Of The Flies,* but for millions of readers he exists in a kind of haze or fog of celebrity; no new information can be allowed to disturb this cloudy aura—William Golding is the author of one book. He is tired of talking about it—he wrote the essay **"Fable"** as a way of "answering some of the standard questions which students were asking me"—and yet, strangely enough, it is only when he begins to talk to me about it that he becomes at all mobile or enthusiastic. "It's gone on selling since the day it was published. God knows how many copies it's sold—10 million, 15 million?" I suppose I should be eternally grateful to those students who turned it into a campus novel in the late fifties. Because they kept on buying it. And those students, of course, are now the professors who are writing books about it."

The story of the genesis of *Lord Of The Flies* is now well known: how it was rejected by numerous publishers and plucked from the reject pile at Faber by Charles Monteith. I asked Golding if he had any sense then that he had written a classic novel. "Yes I did, I think. I'd already written three novels which no one had published, and which I knew weren't any good. I thought, this one must succeed. And so I constructed it very carefully. It sounds terribly naive, but one of my discoveries had been that in a novel something has to happen. So I went through the final manuscript with a pen, tacking each point at which some-

thing happened. This accounts for its very plotted and urgent feel . . ." But the novel was rejected again and again. "I sat down and re-read it, and said to my wife 'This is bloody good.' I also said to myself privately, 'One day this book will win me the Nobel prize'. And was instantly appalled by my pride. But you see, I knew it was good."

Talking about his early struggles, Golding comes to life. His eyes soften, the atmosphere warms. We're no longer sitting in our stiff little chamber, but in a writer's drawing-room, with a mild and unemphatic afternoon light streaming through the window and making columns and spokes of dust. Golding seems to shed some of his priestliness and to take on a humble glow. At last, a writer sits before me— the sum of his struggles, the sum of his difficult knowledge and curious isolation—not an institution, not a busy Nobel laureate. And this new humility seems right, for humility runs through Golding's work as a virtue, a prize. Humility is what the schoolboy dictators of the island in *Lord Of The Flies* learn at the end of the book; humility comes to Pincher Martin, hanging on his purgatorial rock; humility amongst broken images is the cross which Jocelin must carry at the end of *The Spire:* "Now—I know nothing at all." Golding describes Jocelin's vision to me as "wonderful ignorance. He knows nothing, but it is a splendid nothing." Some of this humility also belongs to Golding. I ask him about his work as a whole, and he says this, shifting slightly in his chair, and gazing gently into his lap: "Looking at my work, I realise what a slight and inadequate body it is. I totted my books up the other day—16 volumes after 80 years. That's my lot, essentially. It's not much is it? I envy those who have produced 30 or 40 books. I would call this body of work trivial. So naturally, I'm still looking for the ultimate novel. I have still to write my best book."

This Golding—of humility of soft grandeur and mildness—is impressive. He is no longer the bullied, hustled, and stubborn interviewed. It is a moment in which to hope, for a minute later we are back to the rule book. It is time to go after 40 minutes—Golding has made this clear. There are jerky handshakes. The photographer takes shots. Golding poses and then becomes restive. "I think it's time to stop now. You've got enough." His armour is glinting. He is utterly closed off. Suddenly, he puts his straw hat in front of his face and says commandingly, "Stop. No more photographs. That's it." He turns at the door, fierce, austere, and uncomfortably public, and walks back into his real life.

> *James Wood, "Religious Insights of a Man Apart," in* Manchester Guardian Weekly, *September 29, 1991, p. 25.*

Bruce Lambert   (obituary date 20 June 1993)

[*In the following obituary, Lambert gives an overview of Golding's life and career.*]

William Golding, the Nobel Prize-winning author of the classic *Lord of the Flies* and other disturbing novels exploring the dark side of human nature, died yesterday in his home in Perranarworthal, England. He was 81.

A heart attack was the probable cause, said Matthew Evans, chairman of Mr. Golding's publisher, Faber and Faber.

He was 73 when he won the Nobel Prize for literature in 1983, and he was knighted in 1988. Although he was primarily a novelist, his writing also included short stories, dramas, essays and poetry.

He was best known for his themes of the struggle between good and evil and for symbolism that invited interpretations on many levels. Indeed, some critics complained that he relied too heavily on symbolism that weighed down his work.

After 21 rejections, *Lord of the Flies* was finally issued in 1954 as his first published book, and it remains his most popular.

It portrays a group of proper British schoolboys who, when marooned on a deserted island by a plane crash during a global atomic war, lose their societal inhibitions and regress into blood-curdling tribal savagery.

His allegory achieved a cult status. The book inspired two films, was translated into 26 languages, sold millions of copies and became a standard on college and high school reading lists.

Sir William recalled that as a teacher he once allowed a class of boys complete freedom in a debate, but he had to intervene as mayhem broke out. That incident and his own war experiences inspired *Lord of the Flies.*

"World War II was the turning point for me," he said. "I began to see what people were capable of doing. Anyone who moved through those years without understanding that man produces evil as a bee produces honey, must have been blind or wrong in the head." Another time he said: "Look out," he said, "the evil is in us all."

He confessed that as a youth he was sometimes a spoiled brat and a bully and "I enjoyed hurting people."

For a man who once complained of his "inability to write poetry," Sir William made a major contribution to English literature.

Comparing him to Melville, the Nobel citation said: "William Golding's novels and stories are not only somber moralities and dark myths about evil and treacherous, destructive forces. They are also colorful tales of adventure which can be read as such, full of narrative joy, inventiveness and excitement."

Author Malcolm Bradbury described Sir William as "a dominant figure since the 1950's" in English letters and said that *Lord of the Flies* was a world classic. "He was a remarkable writer—his work is peculiarly timeless."

Describing his own work, Sir William said, "I am not a theologian or a philosopher. I am a story teller." Despite his reputation for pessimism on human nature, he said, "I think good will overcome evil in the end. I don't know quite how, but I have that simple faith."

Although his succeeding works never matched *Lord of the Flies* in sales, they continued to win close critical atten-

tion. They included *The Inheritors* (1955), *Pincher Martin* (1956), *Free Fall* (1958), *The Spire* (1964), *The Pyramid* (1967), *Darkness Visible* (1979) and, *Rites of Passage* (1980).

Pincher Martin describes the last moments of a drowning sailor.

Rites of Passage won Britain's premier literary award, the Booker Prize, in 1980. It describes a voyage to Australia in the 19th century, showing how a pompous cleric becomes involved in a sexual scandal and dies of shame. In 1987 Sir William completed a sequel to *Rites of Passage* called *Close Quarters.* A third novel, *Fire Down Below,* finished the series in 1989.

His own favorite was *The Inheritors,* about the destruction of Neanderthal Man by Homo sapiens.

William G. Golding was born on Sept. 19, 1911, in Cornwall. He grew up in a 14th Century house, next to a graveyard, and tried writing a novel at the age of 12.

World War II was the turning point for me. I began to see what people were capable of doing. Anyone who moved through those years without understanding that man produces evil as a bee produces honey, must have been blind or wrong in the head.

—*William Golding*

He was educated at Marlborough Grammar School, where his father taught, then studied science and later English at Oxford University's Brasenose College. He graduated in 1934 and received a master's degree in 1960.

After college, he became a settlement house worker and then joined the Royal Navy. He served as a lieutenant commanding a rocket-firing ship, took part in the 1944 Normandy landings and developed an enduring love of sailing and the sea. Early in his career he took up teaching English and philosophy, acting, directing and writing in London.

He once spoke of death: "I'd rather there wasn't an afterlife, really. I'd much rather not be me for thousands of years. Me? Hah!"

He spent his last years quietly with his wife of 54 years, the former Ann Brookfield, at their home near Falmouth in the Cornwall area on the southwest coast. They had two children, David and Judith, who also survive.

Bruce Lambert, in an obituary in The New York Times, *June 20, 1993, p. 38.*

The Times, London   (obituary date 21 June 1993)

[*In the obituary below, the critic presents an overview of Golding's life, assessing his contributions to literature.*]

William Golding was one of only four English authors (the others are Kipling, Galsworthy and Winston Churchill) to receive the Nobel Prize for Literature. Some felt it might justly have gone to Graham Greene, Anthony Powell or James Hanley, but none questioned his suitability for the award, as is so often the case.

He was a "big" novelist, most of whose work could usually carry the weight he put into it. He lived outside literary coteries, struggled with grave and ponderous themes, and took risks which lesser writers could not dare to take. As is the case with all such writers there is general disagreement about which is his masterpiece—but no doubt as to whether he produced one. Is it **Lord of the Flies** (1954), **The Inheritors** (1955), **The Spire** (1964), **Darkness Visible** (1979)—or the last trilogy consisting of **Rites of Passage, Close Quarters** and **Fire Down Below** (1981-89)? This is in any case a formidable list and some would add to it.

William Gerald Golding's father, a Quaker turned atheist, was a master at Marlborough Grammar School where William was educated. He then went on to Brasenose College, Oxford, from which he graduated in 1935. While still at Oxford he published, as "W. G. Golding", a volume **Poems** (1934) with Macmillan in London, and in New York (1935). What reviews this received were indifferent, and of the book he later declared that he made "furtive efforts to conceal, destroy, or at any rate disclaim that melancholy slim volume of my extreme youth." For some years, indeed, there was no copy of it in the British Museum Reading Room. However, slim and melancholy though it may have been, some have found in it vital clues to his later struggles and achievements.

From 1935 until 1940—and again, part-time, from 1945 to 1954—Golding worked in small theatre companies in Wiltshire as writer, actor and director. Some of his impressions of this work may be gathered from his novel **The Pyramid** (1967), not one of his best books. In 1940 he joined the Royal Navy which he admired and enjoyed "because it worked." During his service he became officer in charge of a rocket ship and (as a schoolteacher) instructed naval cadets. In 1945 he returned to Bishop Wordsworth's School, Salisbury, whose staff he had joined in 1939. He remained there until 1961 when the success of **Lord of the Flies** enabled him to resign.

This novel was the fruition of half a lifetime. Golding was 43 when he published it. Its knowledge of youth in particular and of human nature in general was immediately apparent. Yet, anthropologically, this story of boys who, isolated from adult supervision, become brutal and self-destructive is "wrong": studies have shown that boys who are actually thus isolated do not behave as Golding had them behave in **Lord of the Flies.** The force of his fable rose from its being, not based on "fact" but on what any sensitive and highly-imaginative schoolmaster might dream up while performing his duties on a wet afternoon. It was R. M. Ballantyne's charming Victorian tale, *Coral Island,* turned on its head; but its "boys" are really terrible little men—as in Kipling's *Stalky & Co.*—which Golding rewrites with the venom its author was unable to put into it.

Read like that, **Lord of the Flies** is the story of adults (at least males) in the 20th century with its politicians and its "experts" and its wars. Yet Faber's reader had originally famously said of it: "Rubbish and dull. Pointless." The public disagreed and the book quickly acquired a cult reputation, especially in the United States, where it succeeded *The Catcher in the Rye* as the most popular novel for young Americans. By the mid-1960s it had been widely translated, had sold over two million copies and had been made into a successful film (the success was part of the reason why Golding could eventually give up teaching).

Golding liked to change his style and mood with each book: his gear changes were never those of a "minor" writer and his fiction covered an enormous range of subject matter—from prehistoric man to 19th-century sea voyagers, from Ancient Egypt to Britain during the Blitz. **The Inheritors** (1955) is one of the most remarkable *tours de force* in postwar fiction of any nationality. It tells of the defeat of a group of Neanderthals at the hands of *homo sapiens.* Some would say this is Golding's greatest novel.

His work had at all times a pronounced sense of the religious, but nowhere more so than in his next magnificent novel, **The Spire** (1964) set in Medieval England: a priest, Jocelin, tries to crown his cathedral with a four-hundred foot spire, even against the laws of gravity. He, a "flesh dog", is inspired by angels and tempted by demons at every step.

Golding always waited until he was ready, and this meant long periods of comparative silence. The 15 years from 1964 to 1979 saw only the relatively minor **The Pyramid,** a collection of three novellas called **The Scorpion God** (1971), and a book of essays **The Hot Gates and other Occasional Pieces** (1966). During this period Golding had almost drowned his family and himself in the English Channel while pursuing his most beloved recreation, sailing. It was, he said: "A traumatic experience which stopped me doing anything for two or three years."

In other respects, however, he made good use of his time. He kept a journal, travelled widely and developed his love of music, particularly the piano. His reputation was by now intact: he had received a CBE in 1966, and throughout the 1960s and 1970s academic articles continued to pour out. As a novelist, however, he was silent but not forgotten.

He returned triumphantly with **Darkness Visible** (1978) and dispelled any lingering doubts among his followers that he was a one, or at most two, novel writer. **Pincher Martin** (1956) had not provoked uniformly good reviews and critics continued to quarrel over the respective merits of **Lord of the Flies** and **The Spire,** and to interpret the latter in various wild ways as anything from a Christian allegory to a Freudian phallic fantasy.

Darkness Visible is set in England from 1940 to the late 1970s. It has a relatively simple, thriller-like plot at its centre, but its complex characterisation, (of the boy Matty, in particular), its moral seriousness and dense symbolism attracted critics who, although they could not agree about it recognised that they had a real, and a really tragic, book on their hands. Golding was no help: he refused interviews and was himself profoundly disturbed by what he had produced.

Of the final trilogy and the separate novel, *The Paper Men* (1984), perhaps the latter, a grim parable about the trials and tribulations of a writer's life, is the more powerful and satisfying. The trilogy, beginning with *Rites of Passage,* is less intense and written at a lower level of energy, although it is a profoundly interesting work by a man by no means written out. Its first half is Golding's most exhuberant and humorous work, and the one which best reveals his love-hate relationship with the sea. In the work as a whole, Golding tried to express his curiosity about and sympathy with homosexuality, and to portray the nature of male sexual desire as distinct from female. It was, as always, highly unusual.

"Miss Pulkinhorn", a short story published in *Encounter* in August 1960 and adapted for radio by Golding in that year, should be mentioned as one of Golding's outstanding uncollected works.

William Golding was a private man who was careful to stay well outside the literary politics of the metropolitan world. That independence of spirit lay at the heart of his fictional achievement. But he was also genial and courteous with friends, and those who knew him spoke warmly of him.

He had been well before his sudden collapse. He leaves a widow, Ann, whom he married in 1939, and a son and a daughter.

An obituary in The Times, *London, June 21, 1993, p. 17.*

Joseph J. Feeney (essay date 31 July 1993-7 August 1993)

[*Feeney is an educator and Jesuit priest. In the essay below, he comments on the legacy and principal themes of Golding's works.*]

As a novelist, William Golding had the gift of terror. It is not the terror of a quick scare—a ghost, a scream, a slash that catches the breath—but a primal, fearsome sense of human evil and human mystery. Two of his novels, *Lord of the Flies* and *Darkness Visible,* express this gift unusually well, in scenes of primal power that show Golding's rare capacity for horror and for awe.

In *Lord of the Flies,* the emotion is horror, as a group of schoolboys, marooned on a Pacific island in World War II, learn to be cruel and discover a "beast." When they find it, the beast looks "something like a great ape . . . sitting asleep with its head between its knees. Then the wind roared in the forest, . . . and the creature lifted its head, holding towards them the ruin of a face." As horror engenders horror, the boys prepare a gift for the beast. Mounting a "dripping sow's head" on a stick, they jam it "down on the pointed end of the stick which pierced through into the mouth. . . . The head hung there, a little blood dripping down the stick," and flies buzzed "over the spilled guts." In the silence of the jungle, "the Lord of the Flies hung on his stick and grinned."

In *Darkness Visible,* the emotion—equally unforgettable—is awe. As buildings flame and collapse in the London blitz, suddenly, mysteriously, a child walks "out of a fire that is melting lead and distorting iron." The firefighters simply gape at this child in awe:

> He was naked, and the miles of light lit him variously. A child's stride is quick; but this child walked down the very middle of the street with a kind of ritual gait that in an adult would have been called solemn. . . . The brightness on his left side was not an effect of light. The burn was even more visible on the left side of his head. All his hair was gone on that side, and on the other, shrivelled to peppercorn dots. His face was so swollen he could only glimpse where he was going through the merest of slits. It was perhaps something animal that was directing him away from the place where the world was being consumed.

Such a writer is clearly primal, mythic, even ritual. Yet Golding also called himself a fable-maker—"a fabulist"—and therefore a "moralist" who "cannot make a story without a human lesson tucked away in it." In an essay called **"Fable"** he once explained *Lord of the Flies:* "Before the Second World War, I believed in the perfectibility of social man," until war showed "what one man could do to another. I am not talking of one man killing another with a gun, or dropping a bomb on him. . . . I am thinking of the vileness beyond all words that went on, year after year, in the totalitarian states." Jews were exterminated. A nation followed Hitler. Another nation followed Stalin. Realizing "that the condition of man was to be a morally diseased creation," Golding wrote his postwar fable "to trace the connection between [man's] diseased nature and the international mess he gets himself into." And the purpose of *Darkness Visible*? Here Golding kept his silence. When questioned about its sources and meaning, he refused to comment—even in private—and was profoundly disturbed by what he had created.

Who was this man who could create a book that scared even himself? Born in 1911 in England's remote and craggy Cornwall, Golding learned rationalism and scientific wonder from his father (a schoolmaster and atheist) and storytelling from his mother (a lover of ghosts and phantom ships and banshee wails). On finishing Oxford, he worked in the provincial theater, married in 1939 and served in the Royal Navy during World War II. But he mainly taught schoolboys in Salisbury until he was freed from teaching in 1961 by the success of *Lord of the Flies*—a book that shows his observation of schoolboy cruelties. Curiously, this enormously successful novel was rejected by 15 publishers—some say 21—before it was accepted, edited (to remove a framing story of a massive air battle) and published in 1954.

His second novel, *The Inheritors* (1955), was a feat of imagination, language and perspective. Written from the viewpoint of Neanderthal Man, it tells of a gentle, simple people who think in pictures instead of ideas ("I have a picture of us crossing to the island," "I do not see this picture." "Lok has no pictures in his head"). But into their peace come "the new people"—our violent breed of *homo sapiens*—who have already progressed to ideas and arrows, and who wipe out Lok and his people. It is a sad story. Yet it is highly inventive and some consider it Golding's finest novel. It was the author's personal favorite, and the novelist A. S. Byatt calls it "a tour de force which has not been equalled in my lifetime."

Nine more novels followed between 1956 and 1989 (despite the fallow years from 1967 to 1978). Of his 11 novels and eight other books, eight novels are considered major: *Lord of the Flies* (1954), *The Inheritors* (1955), *Pincher Martin* (1956), *The Spire* (1964), *Darkness Visible* (1979), and his *Sea Trilogy, Rites of Passage* (1980), *Close Quarters* (1987) and *Fire Down Below* (1989). The last three novels, revised and published together as *To the Ends of the Earth* (1991), appeared in the year of Golding's 80th birthday.

Happily, honors rewarded Golding's talent. In 1966, he was made a C.B.E. (Commander of the British Empire), and in 1980 *Rites of Passage* won the prestigious Booker Prize. He received the Nobel Prize for literature in 1983 and was knighted in 1988.

I have a much more aspirant, hopeful view of human life in the cosmos than I would dare to put in my novels.

—William Golding

When he died on June 19 at his home in Cornwall, Golding was working on a new novel and had been hardy enough to attend a dinner party the night before. His age at death was 81, and he was well loved by family and friends. Nor was his life as gloomy as his novels. He once wrote, "I have a much more aspirant, hopeful view of human life in the cosmos than I would dare to put in my novels." In his 1991 preface to the *Sea Trilogy,* he confirmed that view: "I myself am commonly thought to be a pessimist, a diagnosis with which I heartily disagree."

As for the world beyond the cosmos, Golding had a lifelong fascination with God, and though *The Independent* called him a "passionate agnostic," a good friend recalled Golding's words in a personal letter: "You see, in what I conceive to be my better moments, I believe passionately in the existence of That not this. Even the elders cast down their crowns, so what should poor Tom do but throw himself?"

William Golding was, with Graham Greene, the finest British novelist of our half-century. His fellow novelist Malcolm Bradbury memorialized him as "a writer who was both impishly difficult, and wonderfully monumental," and a teller of "primal stories—about the birth of

speech, the dawn of evil, the strange sources of art." To this I add a simpler tribute. For me, he made a mystery of horror out of a pig's head and fetid flies, and a mystery of awe out of a singed child amid the flames of London. For such terror, and such insight, I am grateful. (pp. 6-7)

> *Joseph J. Feeney, "William Golding (1911-93): Lord of Horror, Lord of Awe," in* America, *Vol. 169, No. 3, July 31-August 7, 1993, pp. 6-7.*

REVIEWS OF GOLDING'S RECENT WORKS

Blake Morrison (review date 2 March 1984)

[*Morrison is an English editor, poet, and critic. In the following review, he provides a mixed assessment of* The Paper Men, *highlighting its relation to Golding's other works and its theological subtext.*]

Few recipients of the Nobel Prize for Literature can have had as trying an inauguration as William Golding. Scarcely had the award been announced [in October 1983] when Arthur Lundkvist, one of the Swedish judges, broke ranks and judicial silence in unprecedented fashion to declare that Golding was "a little English phenomenon of no special interest", a remark he subsequently retracted, but not before at least one English commentator had unkindly endorsed it. Some weeks later the powers of Golding's imagination came under question from a different quarter when Auberon Waugh in the *Spectator* claimed that Golding's "one good novel", *Lord of the Flies,* bears a remarkable resemblance to W. L. George's little-known novel of 1926, *Children of the Morning,* which describes the violent behaviour of a group of children shipwrecked on a tropical island. Golding might not be guilty of "conscious plagiarism", Waugh argued, "but the book does seem to have had an extraordinary subliminal effect on him", and he suggested Golding donate to W. L. George's descendants at least a tin of pickled herrings out of his prize-money. Now, two months later, Golding's latest novel has appeared to almost unanimous condemnation: "a tin-eared disaster", "a hollow creation", "a gesture of humility", "out of focus", "unfunny", "irritating"—these have been some of the verdicts, while the best that others have said is that serious writers must be allowed their failures. Winning the Nobel Prize may have helped Golding's sales (*The Paper Men* is currently top of the bestseller lists, ahead of the Dick Francises and Len Deightons) but it is not clear that it has done his literary reputation any more good than it did Winston Churchill's.

The plot of *The Paper Men* is a simple and by now familiar one. Where Golding's last novel, *Rites of Passage,* hinged on events occurring in a "badger bag", his new one begins with a "badger at the bin", the badger being Professor Rick L. Tucker of the University of Astrakhan, Nebraska (hence Tucker's T-shirt emblazoned "OLE ASHCAN"), who is rooting in the dustbin of Wilfred Barclay, the famous English novelist, in the hope of finding Barclayan letters and manuscripts useful to his academic research. Barclay narrowly avoids shooting Tucker, an oversight he soon comes to regret: for as he leaves his home in rural England to take up an itinerant life abroad, crossing the patchwork of Europe ("Yurp" as Rick calls it) as restlessly as Nabokov's Humbert Humbert does North America, leaving behind him one broken relationship in England (with his wife, Liz) and then another in Italy, he finds Tucker dogging his footsteps with dreadful persistence. In Schwillen, on Lake Zurich, Tucker introduces Barclay to his lovely young wife Mary Lou; Barclay is attracted to her but flees, "determined to sear this tiny bud of the future before it was in leaf". At the Hotel Felsenblick, in the Weisswald, Tucker catches up with Barclay, asks him to appoint him as his official biographer, and apparently offers him the body of Mary Lou in return for a signed acceptance; again Barclay is tempted, and again he resists and flees, but not before an expedition through the mountain fog during which he stumbles and is saved by Tucker from falling into empty space: "It seems I owe you my life" (cf Jocelin to the dumb sculptor in *The Spire:* "I owe my life to you, it seems.")

But owing Tucker his life makes Barclay only more determined not to assign him his Life. His past, as he sketchily recalls it, has not been without interest: public school; early Eliotic days as a bank clerk; a spell as a groom; the stupendously successful first novel; a ready supply of women, including the nymphomaniac Lucinda; a scandal with a bent solicitor and some obscene letters; and travels in South America during which he ran down a native ("They say if you stop the other Indians will kill you"). But, "crusty" and private as he is—a recurrent image of him is as a "lobster"—he fears the prospect of his past being dredged up at all, let alone by a drudge like Tucker. His efforts to escape Tucker's badgering drive him to even more frenzied world travel. His heavy drinking becomes heavier, his hallucinations more hallucinatory, his black holes blacker. "Dipso-schizo", he loses track of years. In Greece he bumps into an old homosexual friend who advises him to "get rid of the armour, the exoskeleton, the carapace, before it's too late". It is advice he seems unlikely to take, but at some point afterwards he has a minor stroke and breakdown, and when he recovers determines to let Tucker "complete things"; he will offer Tucker his Life while submitting him to some "theologically witty" punishment.

As he waits for Tucker in the Weisswald, Barclay retraces their earlier walk through the mountain fog and discovers that the "abyss" Tucker saved him from was a gentle Alpine meadow "about a yard" under the path. Incensed at being (theologically) outwitted, he returns to accuse and humiliate Tucker, taunting him with the promise of the official biography but refusing signed confirmation. In the novel's last flurried chapters Barclay returns to England, to his ex-wife Liz (now dying of cancer); spurns Tucker again in a London club; prepares a bonfire of his manuscripts; and types up "this brief account"—the Life he denied Tucker, told by himself to "set over against the lying stories, the partial journals, and all the rest". As he looks up from his desk he sees Tucker peering at him "through

some instrument or other. How the devil did Rick L. Tucker manage to get hold of a gun".

A mark of Golding's fiction is that it presents us with narrators—Talbot in *Rites of Passage,* Lok in *The Inheritors*—whose limited viewpoint we have to see beyond if we are to grasp the significance of what is unfolding. But Barclay is limited in another, more fundamental sense: cruel, solipsistic, vain, tedious, cowardly, unfunny, indifferent even to those closest to him (like his dying wife and grieving daughter), he is one of the least appealing of all Golding's characters. Much of the novel's uneasiness stems from the suspicion that Golding not only does not disapprove of Barclay but regards him with the greatest affection. With his "scraggy yellow-white beard, yellow-white thatch and broken-toothed grin", he bears some physical resemblance to his creator. They share similar enthusiasms, Barclay being "something of a church fancier", for example, and an inveterate traveller. His novelistic career has followed an equivalent course: a remarkable "one off" success with a suitably nautical-sounding first novel, *Coldharbour;* another book written (like *Rites of Passage*) in "next to no time"; another still, *The Endless Plain,* troublingly dependent on the central idea of a "hopelessly bad" manuscript sent to him by a man called Prescott ("Of course it was properly treated and all that, but still! . . . *Had* I remembered? Was it wholly the work of the unconscious . . . or had I stolen the idea deliberately at some point?"). Most important of all, though, Barclay gives voice to anti-academic prejudices that can be found in the work of his inventor. In his essay **"A Moving Target"**, for example, Golding reflects on the drawbacks of serving as "the raw material of academic light industry"; this too is the burden of Barclay—he is "Rick's special subject . . . his raw material, the ore in his mine, his farm, his lobster pots". When Golding in that same essay cites the case of the female postgraduate student who wrote to him "looking for a subject for her thesis", it is hard not to see the outlines of the Barclay-Tucker relationship:

> She was not going to write a thesis on anything as dull as a dead man. She wanted fresh blood. She was going out with her critical shotgun to bring home the living. She proposed I should bare my soul, answer all her questions, do all the work, and she would write the thesis on me. But years first of reading theses on me and then more years of not reading theses on me have made me more elusive than a professor . . . I am a moving target.

On one level, Golding's novel does little more than animate the metaphor of this passage, developing it to make a general statement in defence of the individual imagination and against the threat posed to the living (English) writer by the dead hand of (American) scholarship, and also to provide the novel with its dramatic (or melodramatic) framework: the novel opens with the gun in Barclay's hand; but it ends with the moving target brought to a standstill as the relentless Tucker gets his man. And at this level one is forced to suspect that Golding is at worst merely out to get *his* man, merely settling scores with his interpreters. There are no Rick L. Tuckers in my Golding bibliography, but I might well find the name too close for comfort if I were a scholar like James R. Baker, who has been interpreting and casebooking Golding since 1964, and whose 1981 interview with him contains exchanges such as this:

> *Baker:* But again, that persistent theme in your work—the fall from innocence, or the loss of innocence.
> *Golding:* Well, it's quite a big theme, isn't it? It's rather like saying here's a novelist who writes about people.

Or, at best, Golding is earning himself a place at the butt-end of a literary tradition in which scholars are portrayed as forces of death, and American scholars as the most deadly of all. A notable example of this genre is Philip Larkin's poem "Posterity", to which **The Paper Men** bears surprising resemblances: both Golding's Tucker and Larkin's Jake Balokowsky have saddled themselves with English "old-type *natural* fouled-up guys" who don't welcome their attentions; both are under pressure from others to complete their research; both would rather be working on something else (Balokowsky on "Protest Theater", Tucker "phonetics"), were there any "future" in it. But to make the comparison is to recognize how much funnier, more economical and more incisive as satire the Larkin poem is, how much more credible the hard-bitten Balokowsky than the fawning Tucker with his talk of "the Great Pageant of English Literature". So much, indeed, does Larkin's poem both haunt and overshadow **The Paper Men** that there are two extraordinary moments in the text where Golding refers to Tucker not as "Rick" but as "Jake", as if so in debt to Larkin as to have slipped into his idiom, or as if, more plausibly, he had used the name Jake in an earlier draft, thought the better of it but neglected to strike out these two instances. Either way, the effect is to remind one how grumpy and derivative, even to an English ear, Golding's anti-academicism sounds; in America it will sound crustier and more philistine still.

It would be a very peculiar Golding novel, however, that allowed itself to operate only on one level. When Barclay and Tucker climb through the Swiss fog they hear a stream with "two voices", one a "cheerful babble, a kind of frivolity", the other "a deep meditative hum". This is an apt metaphor for a body of fiction which, even at its most social and babbling (in **The Pyramid,** for example, or the first half of **Rites of Passage**), has deeper levels of suggestion. **The Paper Men** babbles with anti-academic satire, and indeed with psychobabble (it threatens at moments to become a "dipso-schizo" case history), so that we may miss its allegorical subtext. But with the introduction of Barclay's mysterious sponsor Halliday this "hum" grows more audible. Halliday, it seems, is "the power behind the whole operation", "brooding over all", and Barclay slowly grasps that Tucker is merely an appointed representative who has been given "seven years" to complete his work and who (we learn) has sacrificed his wife to Halliday in order to appease him. Barclay endeavours to find out about Halliday but when he turns to the relevant page of *Who's Who in America* it is "bare, bare, bare, just blank white paper"; immediately afterwards, he looks across at a church and "my God he was standing at the top". Once this thread of religious metaphor is noticed even the liber-

ally sprinkled expletives—*For God's sake, My God, God knows, Christ, How the hell, Well, I'm damned*—begin to look carefully planted, and some snatches of dialogue acquire faintly absurdist metaphysical overtones:

> You don't know who I am. Nobody knows who I am.
>
> No, no. Of course not . . .
>
> Halliday now, he knows. No one else.
>
> . . . . .
>
> At some point or other you can introduce me to Halliday.
>
> That's real difficult.

Not a deep meditative hum, perhaps, but an indication that something other than satire and psychoanalysis is going on—at the very least a playful mythic rumble. Early in the novel we see Barclay ridiculing the religious conversion of his Italian "chum" (mistress): "My driving force was a passionate need for there *not* to be a miracle". Later, in the novel's most highly-charged episode, he himself undergoes a conversion when, in the middle of a Sicilian earthquake (the ground shaking in rhythm to his own DTs) he enters a cathedral and discovers "in one destroying instant that all my adult life I had believed in God and this knowledge was a vision of God". He sees himself as one of the "predestinate damned" ("I. am. sin.") and loses his shell of scepticism: "It's all in the mind" (a Barclayan—or Berkeleyan—denial of matter). Golding, it seems, has embedded in his novel two "theologically witty" possibilities: one, that Halliday is God, Barclay a sinner ("Old Filthy Rags") wandering in the desert, and Tucker the Christ-figure who offers him redemption and the promise of a Life hereafter; the other that Tucker is Satan ("Rick, you lucky young devil", "How the devil did Rick Tucker . . . ") whose temptations Barclay must refuse. Certainly Tucker, with his "stink" of deodorant and bestial physique (there is much emphasis on his hairiness, and he appears in the guise of badger, dog and shire horse) has more than a whiff of Mephistopheles. What he proposes to Barclay is in effect a Faustian pact, whereby Barclay will enjoy the earthly delights of Mary Lou (repeatedly pictured as Helen of Troy) in exchange for his Life: little wonder that Barclay should invoke Marlowe's "why this is hell, nor am I out of it", imagine that Tucker is pursuing him in a hearse, or be deluded by the end that he is himself a sort of Christ, with four stigmata/pains in his hands and feet, and a fifth wound in his side which he acquires (we presume) in the last sentence.

Since Golding invokes the spirit of "farce" and "low comedy" (as he did in **Rites of Passage**) and implies that Barclay's "autobiography" is merely "a theologically witty piece of clowning" ("*Please see the joke*"), it would be solemn and Tuckerish to take such readings any further. But even if one judges the theological overtones to be merely playful, one effect of them is to make us revalue the relationship between Barclay and Tucker, which begins to look more balanced in its sympathies, less an endorsement of Barclay *alter ego,* than a first reading might suggest. Several of Golding's novels, it is often remarked, have a

late shift of viewpoint by means of which all that has preceded is seen in a new light: the arrival of the rescue-
parties in **Lord of the Flies** and **Pincher Martin,** Colley's
letter in **Rites of Passage.** There is nothing quite like that
in **The Paper Men,** which remains within the confines of
a single narrator's mind, but the scene in which Barclay
humiliates Tucker by making him beg like a dog, lap up
Dôle from a saucer and finally burst into tears is a turning-
point of sorts: dull and dogged though he is, Tucker has
not deserved this, and as we lose our waning sympathies
for Barclay, so we find that Tucker's humiliation not only
drives him to madness but lends him a new tragic stature.

"I have always felt", Golding once said, "that a writer's
books should be as different from each other as possible",
and even his detractors would admit that he cannot fairly
be accused of repeating himself. Motifs and characters recalling other books recur none the less. Like **The Spire** and
Free Fall, The Paper Men is a novel that measures the cost
of art to human lives: Liz and Mary Lou are victims of
their husbands' obsessions much as Goody Pagnall is a
victim of Jocelin's and Beatrice of Sammy Mountjoy's.
The mutual destruction of Barclay and Tucker recalls the
similarly interlocked fates of Christopher and Nathaniel
in **Pincher Martin,** and Colley and Talbot in **Rites of Passage.** The large themes that Golding has never been afraid
to confront can be discerned through the fog: religious
faith; the evil men do to each other; above all, freedom,
which is seen here as a less desirable state of being than
it was in **Free Fall.**

Pointing to such continuities does not, of course, make
The Paper Men a better novel, nor explain why Golding's
story-telling here should be so lacking in the subtleties and
tensions we have come to expect of him. Looking back
over Golding's career, one might venture that his best novels have been those (**Lord of the Flies, The Inheritors,
Darkness Visible, Rites of Passage**) which make the
greatest demands on his powers of imaginative historical
reconstruction, and which underpin strong adventure-like
narratives with richly mythical subtexts. Where myth predominates, or where the settings are too babblingly contemporary, he writes with altogether less power. But generalizations about Golding's achievement are a precarious
business: the truth is that we are still assimilating a late
burst which, after a silence of over a decade, has produced
three novels in five years. The early critical assessments
now look redundant, and even the newly revised version
of the "standard" critical work, Mark Kinkead Weekes's
and Ian Gregor's *William Golding: A Critical Study,* just
published by Faber, looks hopelessly lopsided, cramming
into a single chapter on "The Later Golding" **The Pyramid, Darkness Visible** and **Rites of Passage,** though thirteen years separate the first from the last. All that can be
said with confidence is that Golding's previous novels,
even those that were coolly received on publication, have
stood up well to subsequent re-readings, and that **The
Paper Men** is certain to get a more patient treatment from
future explicators than it has had from its reviewers. As
for the author, he will have to console himself with Barclay's rather specious piece of reasoning on the poor reception of *Horses at the Spring:* "You have to write the bad
books if you're going to write the good ones." (pp. 215-16)

Blake Morrison, "In Death as in the Life," in
The Times Literary Supplement, *No. 4222,
March 2, 1984, pp. 215-16.*

Robert M. Adams on Golding's novels:

A convenient way to divide the novels of Mr. Golding is according to the amount of space occupied by the central figure. Probably for the novelist himself books like *Pincher
Martin* and *The Spire* in which the central figure occupies
almost the entire canvas, offer the most absorbing problems
both of construction and expression. They bring him very
close to the limits of the expressible and may well be, for the
analyst of fictional technique, the high point of Mr. Golding's achievement. But for the common reader, the road
to Mr. Golding might better start with more social fictions,
such as *Darkness Visible* or *Rites of Passage.* These novels
are not above strong dramatic effects, they involve recognizable people developing and reacting, often painfully, but
with contrast, variety and an occasional sense of open possibility. Viewing life as he does, Mr. Golding is bound somewhere to rip through the smooth texture of social pretense
with a more hideous glimpse into the pit than one had been
able to anticipate. But for a mere reader of fiction, the artful
coup de théâtre is a reward in itself—not that it precludes
a sense of the human condition but that, in conveying that
sense, it fulfills more of the tacit promises of the novel as a
form.

Robert M. Adams, in his "Partners in Damnation," in
The New York Times Book Review, *1 April 1984.*

John Ray   (review date 1 November 1985)

[*Ray is an English educator, novelist, and nonfiction
writer. In the review below, he offers a mixed assessment
of* An Egyptian Journal.]

Ancient Egypt rarely translates. When it does appear in
literature, the results tend to be either sentimental (Agatha Christie), sensational (many examples), or plain grotesque (Norman Mailer). Bernard Shaw was able to side-
step Cleopatra rather neatly, as do the authors of *Asterix,*
but that is cheating. Thomas Mann had a serious shot at
it, by avoiding specific detail and by leaning on a well-
known story, and William Golding himself has contributed a short novel, **The Scorpion God.** Golding is a self-
confessed lover of Egyptology, and had already visited the
country once before when he was asked by his publishers
to take a boat trip along the Nile in February, 1984. The
idea was good, but not its realization.

Times change, and Golding has changed with them. He
is now a Nobel prizewinner and a walking set-book, and
while he is clearly and sympathetically unaffected by this,
others are not. As his wagon clatters its way towards the
ruins of Akhenaten's capital [in **An Egyptian Journal**],
it hits a series of ruts and throws the occupants into the air
in the direction of the metal roof. A disciple chooses this
moment to ask him what he thinks of Virginia Woolf.
Thoroughly Egyptian, to be sure, but all one can do from
this sort of thing is to salvage anecdotes, which Golding

does. Egypt too, is changing, and is now suffering badly from its head-on collision with the twentieth century. Paradoxically, Egyptology gets in the way, particularly Egyptology caught young, which has the power to interfere with perceptions even sixty years later. Golding is frank in admitting these problems, most of which he had probably anticipated, but the god of confusion was planning a further surprise beyond the first bend: the boat was so small that it afforded an uninterrupted view, not of temples and biblical countryside, but of dank levees of mud. This was no doubt conducive to introspection, but one wonders if it is what the publishers had in mind. The crew of the vessel emerge as true devotees of entropy, and the result is a seedy pilgrimage along the Nile, with Leigh Hunt and Amelia Edwards firmly consigned to the hold, or rather the bilges. Golding analyses his own predicament well early on, at the end of Chapter Three: "The book I had promised to write, where was its centre, what was it all about?"

An Egyptian Journal was not about Egyptology, as it turned out. If it had been, plans would probably have been made to break the monotony of the river by visiting Abydos, or the temple of Dendera, or the rock tombs of Meir, which nobody sees. Perhaps Golding had realized that the Egypt of the mind is located in the mind, and nowhere else; certainly his visit, in a child's imagination, to the dark streets of ancient Memphis on All Souls' Night is one of the best passages; it has truth in it. The book is more important as an observation on a modern land. Egypt is probably one of the most attractive tourist destinations on earth, but Golding is determined to see beyond this, and here his status as a literary diplomat helps rather than hinders. The construction of the Aswan high dam has bought time for improvements, but has also altered the country for ill (one wonders if there is not some link between the creation of Lake Nasser and the current drought in Ethiopia and the Sudan). The tourist sees a country which is the external projection of his holiday mood, but Golding (perhaps by a parallel mental process) comes nearer to the despair which lies beneath: in Egypt there is little or no "organized" crime, no football hooliganism, and old people are not jettisoned into institutions, but there are crippling economic difficulties, and Egypt's over-extended families may well have one of the highest domestic murder rates in the world. Golding's understandable attachment to mud brick, and the romantic architecture of Hassan Fathy, comes up against the stark fact that no silt now comes through the Dam, and ugly red bricks are the only medium, other than concrete, for Egyptian villages to reconstruct themselves in.

In the end, it is his personality which wins through, and which redeems the book. He knows every splinter on a boat, and is perhaps fitter than most people half his age, and he keeps his humanity and his humour without striking poses, or wearing his heart on his nautical sleeve, or succumbing to others' beliefs in himself.

John Ray, "Change and Despair," in The Times Literary Supplement, *No. 4309, November 1, 1985, p. 1243.*

Walter Goodman   (review date 22 June 1987)

[*Goodman is an American editor, nonfiction writer, and critic. In the following review of* Close Quarters, *he argues that although the novel is well-written and entertaining, it lacks allegorical depth.*]

By literary tradition, the main cargo of a ship at sea, whether it contains fools or ghouls or whaling tools, is allegory. So when a writer with an allegorical bent like William Golding produces a book like *Close Quarters,* set on an unnamed hulk whose topmast has been destroyed by human failing and whose bottom has been ensnared in nature's weeds and whose planks are rotting, the reader may fairly assume that he is embarked shakily on the sea of life. Especially when the deck is divided—officers and upperclass passengers on one side, common folk on the other—and the author throws out such lines as: "The upshot of all is that we have no choice, you see. We can only go more or less where we are driven."

It turns out, however, that this sportive sequel to *Rites of Passage* (1980), Mr. Golding's last book before his Nobel Prize, is in a different tradition: the coming to consciousness of a young man. He is Edmund Fitzhenry Talbot, whom readers of the earlier book will remember as a somewhat stuffy aristocrat on a journey from England to Australia. This portion of the journey is a busy one. Talbot finds adventure and romance, mal de mer and hard knocks to heart and head. *Close Quarters* is like one of those overnight excursion boats that takes the reader nowhere special but fills the time pleasurably while on board.

Although the seas can be heavy, the book's pitch is light. Mr. Golding shows off his mastery of the elaborate 18th-century lingo and lore, hinting at the shakiness behind the flourishes. With the French Revolution fresh in memory, the English gentry seems to be taking shelter behind ever-fancier locutions. The language here, bubbling with boyish sentiment, becomes a running, or sailing, joke: "Hesitantly I held out my hand; and like the generous-hearted Englishman that he is, he seized it with both his own in a thrilling and manly grip. 'Edmund!' 'My dear fellow!' Still conscious as I was of a certain comical element in our situation, it was a moment at which reserve was no longer possible and I returned the pressure."

Talbot, whose diary is our guide, is afflicted with affectations. He is stubborn about deferring to shipboard usages. "We walked to the ladder—no, I refuse to be seduced—to the stairs." He is not polite to servants and gets to see himself through the eyes of a discerning seaman: "The carryon. The swaying about. The hoity-toity." The young lord receives lessons in love and friendship. His courage is tested and so are his conceptions of loyalty. "Oh," he reflects at a low-spirited point, "that self-confident young man who had come aboard, serenely determined to learn everything and control everything!"

Not only is Talbot too well born for the dictatorial democracy of a sailing vessel, he is also too tall and takes quite a beating on that account. As he laments: "Indeed, it is not easy for a man of my inches to hit off the right bearing in this world of deck beams and squabby tars. If he goes about concealing his height he is bent down like an ancient cripple whereas if he stands up straight as God meant him to and lives with his own eye level he is always cracking his skull."

Nobody who writes that way can be deeply unlikeable. When put to the test in a foggy encounter with what may be one of Boney's ships, our hero shows spunk, and when it comes to romance, he succumbs nobly to the beauteous and forthright Marion Chumley, who is on her way to the East aboard the *Alcyone,* which pauses briefly for some partying with Talbot's miserable craft. Talbot, who has always thought of himself as a prose person, is even reduced to poetry: "Brighter than moonlight, wandering maid, / By thy charms be the white seas allayed."

The book is stocked with well-told incidents that do not add up to anything very significant. The officers and men and ladies are deftly limned, but none is much developed. Mr. Golding seems to be relying on readers already having made the acquaintance of taciturn Captain Anderson, sturdy Lieutenant Summers, Talbot's "onetime inamorata" Zenobia Brocklebank, the alluring Miss Granham and all the others in *Rites of Passage.* An amusing episode on this trip is afforded by the purser who, learning that the ship may sink at any moment, scampers about trying to collect on the I.O.U.'s he holds. Missing, however, is any character as compelling as the first book's foolish and in the end, fatally abused Rev. Robert James Colley.

This time out, the winds of narrative, albeit agreeable, have little force. The extended description of the scraping of the hull, which serves as a climax, though instructive, entertaining and mildly suspenseful (there is danger that the scraping may take away part of the ship) is at best middling drama on the high seas. Perhaps we are only being prepared for the third and final book of Edmund Talbot's voyage to the Antipodes. Like the crippled ship itself, adrift for want of a mast, this part of the tale doesn't get far. Bring on the allegory.

> *Walter Goodman, in a review of "Close Quarters," in* The New York Times, *June 22, 1987, p. C15.*

[Though Golding's novels] are structurally and tonally very different, hardly any of his fictions fail to touch on a somewhat forbidding and certainly unpopular theme. They are religious parables; their recurrent theme is the innate depravity of man.

—Robert M. Adams, in his "Partners in Damnation," in The New York Times Book Review, 1 April 1984.

Frank McConnell   **(review date 12 March 1989)**

[McConnell is an American educator and critic. In the

following review of Fire Down Below, *he praises Golding for writing a truly comic novel and for capturing the sensibility of early nineteenth-century England.]*

The most remarkable thing about William Golding's new novel [*Fire Down Below*]—the conclusion to his *Sea Trilogy* begun in *Rites of Passage* and continued in *Close Quarters*—is that it is a wonderfully comic novel. Golding has written some funny things: notably *Clonk Clonk* and the priceless *Envoy Extraordinary* from *The Scorpion God.* But real comedy—that is, the mode where a joke stops a cosmic twitch and becomes part of an inclusive vision? From *Lord of the Flies* to *Darkness Visible,* he has trained us to expect from him elegant and exotic melodrama firmly mortised in the pessimism of Ecclesiastes and his beloved Euripides: Graham Greene in fancy dress and without priests.

Still, there it is—to quote, in full, the last words of *Fire Down Below:* an unmistakably Goldingesque novel that, like the trilogy it completes, increasingly explores and rejoices in the resources of the comic, not as a refutation but as a kind of final extension of the Euripidean irony that has informed all his work. Near the end of the book, Edmund Talbot, the callow, Regency-era narrator, expresses his embarrassment for the novels of Smollett and Fielding and such "moderns" as Jane Austen, "who feel that despite all the evidence from the daily life around them, a story to be veridical should have a happy ending"—and then proceeds to narrate a happy ending to his own tale that, for its suddenness and completeness, would embarrass not only Jane Austen, but the writer of any Astaire-Rogers film.

Perhaps—though I have no way of knowing—this unexpected jollity is Golding's way of avoiding the implicit doom of his 1983 Nobel Prize in literature. The worthies of Stockholm, after all, do have a penchant for rewarding writers on the solemn themes in a way that tends to lock the writers into their solemnity, to the detriment of their later work (Faulkner was a happy exception to this trap; Bellow, alas, is not). So what better way for Golding to stay alive as a writer than by producing this long, detailed, marvelously articulated *jeu d'esprit?*

The year is 1815, and a ship is sailing from England to New South Wales with a cargo of colonists: failures, convicts, social visionaries and talented young men desirous of advancement. The ship is, of course, a microcosm of society, a living, floating (and sometimes foundering) parable of the human condition.

Along its interminable voyage southward it is plagued by dissension among the passengers, incompetence among the crew, suicides, violence and intrigues, and natural disasters—culminating, in *Fire Down Below,* in a near-collision with an iceberg that is surely one of the most successfully apocalyptic passages in English sea fiction. Furthermore, the ship is dominated—by the time of the third novel—by three emblematic characters: the sullen, unapproachable Capt. Anderson (the absentee God familiar to all Golding readers), the pious, earnest and practical 1st Lt. Summers, and his countertype, the brilliant, romantic and suspiciously French Lt. Benet. While these three attempt to complete the disaster-prone voyage, their metaphysical antics and those of the other voyagers are observed—and recorded, years after the event—by Edmund FitzHenry Talbot, a young man of noble blood on his mother's side who hopes the administration of the colony will be a steppingstone to a seat in Parliament, who is a hopeless snob, a hopeless British chauvinist, a hopeless victim of Byronic ideas of romantic love and who also tends to trip over his own feet a lot—really, he seems almost always falling down, usually into someone.

Old stuff for Golding, you may say: the Voyage, the Ship of Fools, the puny ship against the Great Embracing Sea are all, at least since *The Odyssey,* the most blatant of allegories—and what is Golding if not our most consistent, rueful allegorist?

> One of Golding's distinctive talents has always been his ability to describe, *from inside,* alien states of mind. In the *Sea Trilogy* he does something harder and more brilliant, capturing with uncanny accuracy the sensibility and the language of Englishmen of the early Romantic period, a sensibility so close to our own yet so tantalizingly different.
>
> —*Frank McConnell*

But here he wears his rue with a difference. One of his distinctive talents has always been his ability to describe, *from inside,* alien states of mind: Neanderthals in *The Inheritors,* pharaonic Egyptians in *The Scorpion God,* medievals in *The Spire.* In the *Sea Trilogy* he does something harder and more brilliant, capturing with uncanny accuracy the sensibility and the language of Englishmen of the early Romantic period, a sensibility so close to our own yet so tantalizingly different. In its eurocentric, imperial arrogance, its passion for technology and "natural philosophy" (later called "science"), its literary experimentation and its cult of the personal, it is the seedtime of that worldview whose last and bitter fruits we seem now to be reaping. Golding knows this, and without a single false note, a single overemphasis, embeds that knowledge in the fabric of his narrative.

Add to that the fact that these characters, especially the gorgeously priggish Master Talbot, are literary enough to know that all voyages are types of the mythic Voyage (Talbot reads Homer in his cabin), and are much given—as are all we postmoderns—to looking for cosmic significance in the most practical, mundane details of keeping a ship afloat (Golding, like his obvious precursor Conrad, knows that there is no more mundane work). So that they are trapped in an adventure both tedious and heroic, "sparks of God," as one character describes them, exiled into a world of iron and wood (that is one of many meanings of the title, *Fire Down Below*) and trying desperately to understand, to narrate, their fate: to turn luck into destiny by an act of imagination.

And they succeed. At least, the voyage reaches its intended end, and Talbot himself, as I said, experiences an absurd, "novelistic" series of fortunate falls that enable him, years later, to record the tale. But this is true comedy. As in Shakespearean romance, just as we are exalted and delighted at everything going so finally so right after all the turmoil, we are reminded of how real the turmoil is and how fragile, how fictive, is the stuff of happy endings. This is a wonderful book: *Lord of the Flies* as written by Prospero instead of Caliban. (pp. 3, 9)

> *Frank McConnell, "William Golding's Sea Fever," in* Book World—The Washington Post, *March 12, 1989, pp. 3, 9.*

Deirdre Bair   (review date 2 April 1989)

[*Bair is an American educator and critic. In the following, she offers a negative review of* Fire Down Below.]

With *Fire Down Below,* the Nobel Laureate William Golding completes the trilogy he began in 1980 with *Rites of Passage* (winner of the Booker Prize in England) and followed with *Close Quarters* (1987). Unless you have read the first two novels, the third will be difficult going indeed.

Narrated by young Edmund FitzHenry Talbot, the trilogy recounts his voyage from England to Australia on a former man-of-war during the Napoleonic era. The last of the three novels takes the badly damaged ship through several storms, an encounter with a gigantic iceberg (actually the continent of Antarctica, but the crew doesn't know it) and finally to the safe shelter of Sydney Harbor. Mr. Golding writes in a combination of archaic period language and what he calls "tarpaulin"—a kind of seaman's slang.

Because *Fire Down Below* flounders so much at sea, with the ship most of the time beset by storms, accidents, illness and other disasters, knowledge of who the individual characters are and what they stand for is extremely important. But Mr. Golding does nothing to identify them, except as they figure in Talbot's shipboard experience. They are little more than what their titles imply—captain, midshipman, clergyman, servant or passenger. Mr. Golding also has an irritating tic—that of ending most of his sentences with an exclamation point. Somehow, that makes it even harder to keep these stock figures straight in one's mind, especially since their dialogue is both homogeneous and banal.

The author seems intent on making the ship's voyage parallel what is supposed to be Talbot's inner voyage of self-discovery, but once the ship docks, the young man is little more than the opinionated fop he was at the novel's beginning. There is one brief moment when he seems likely to join several passengers who are off on a Utopian quest once the ship is safely docked, but nothing comes of it. Instead, there is a smarmy reunion with a Miss Chumley, who figured in *Close Quarters* but is almost entirely absent from this novel.

Mr. Golding infuses *Fire Down Below* with references to

Smollet, Fielding and Jane Austen (usually in conjunction with Miss Chumley), using only their names as an attempt to enhance his period setting. The ship's travails are probably supposed to evoke overtones of Melville's dangerous journeys, but Mr. Golding's use of "tarpaulin" weakens his descriptions. Homer does yeoman service, but one of the characters cautions that although the voyage has consumed a considerable part of Talbot's young life, he should not make too much of it: "It was not an Odyssey. It is no type, emblem, metaphor of the human condition. It is, or rather *it was,* what it was. A series of events."

Unfortunately, all three novels drift in "a series of events." None stands alone: each propels the next, and then drifts wherever it is blown. Ultimately this leaves **Fire Down Below** just like the man-of-war as the novel ends: an empty, burned-out hulk.

Deirdre Bair, "At Sea in Volume Three," in The New York Times, *April 2, 1989, p. 37.*

Additional coverage of Golding's life and career is contained in the following sources published by Gale Research: *Authors and Artists for Young Adults,* **Vol. 5;** *Concise Dictionary of British Literary Biography,* **1945-1960;** *Contemporary Authors,* **Vols. 5-8, rev. ed.;** *Contemporary Authors New Revision Series,* **Vols. 13, 33;** *Contemporary Literary Criticism,* **Vols. 1, 2, 3, 8, 10, 17, 27, 58;** *DISCovering Authors; Dictionary of Literary Biography,* **Vols. 15, 100;** *Major 20th-Century Writers;* **and** *World Literature Criticism.*

John Hersey

June 17, 1914—March 24, 1993

(Full name John Richard Hersey) American novelist, nonfiction writer, short story writer, editor, and journalist.

For further information on Hersey's life and works, see *CLC*, Volumes 1, 2, 7, 9, and 40.

INTRODUCTION

Hersey is best known for his Pulitzer Prize-winning novel, *A Bell for Adano*, which details the Allied occupation of an Italian village, and for *Hiroshima*, his nonfiction account of the experiences of six residents of Hiroshima who survived the explosion of the first atomic bomb. A prolific writer, Hersey began his career as a correspondent during World War II, covering activities in the Pacific and Mediterranean, and many of his works focus on moral problems associated with war and racism. Characterized by straightforward prose, a journalist's thorough analysis of subject matter, and a novelist's attention to narrative, Hersey's works have been praised for their topical diversity, concern for humanity, and detailed rendering of setting. As David Gates has remarked: "Hersey . . . wrote best about the impact of great events on everyday lives."

PRINCIPAL WORKS

Men on Bataan (nonfiction) 1942
Into the Valley: A Skirmish of the Marines (nonfiction) 1943
A Bell for Adano (novel) 1944
Hiroshima (nonfiction) 1946
The Wall (novel) 1950
The Marmot Drive (novel) 1953
A Single Pebble (novel) 1956
The War Lover (novel) 1959
The Child Buyer (novel) 1960
Here to Stay: Studies on Human Tenacity (essays) 1962
White Lotus (novel) 1965
Too Far to Walk (novel) 1966
Under the Eye of the Storm (novel) 1967
The Algiers Motel Incident (nonfiction) 1968
Letter to the Alumni (nonfiction) 1970
The Conspiracy (novel) 1972
My Petition for More Space (novel) 1974
The President (nonfiction) 1975

The Walnut Door (novel) 1977
Aspects of the Presidency: Truman and Ford in Office (nonfiction) 1980
The Call: An American Missionary in China (novel) 1985
Blues (nonfiction) 1987
Life Sketches (sketches) 1989
Fling, and Other Stories (short stories) 1990
Antonietta (novel) 1991
Key West Tales (short stories) 1994

REVIEWS OF HERSEY'S RECENT WORKS

Helen Benedict (review date 7 May 1989)

[*Benedict is an English-born American educator, jour-*

nalist, novelist, nonfiction writer, and critic. In the following review, she offers a positive assessment of Life Sketches.]

In his 75 years, John Hersey has published 17 novels, five nonfiction books and numerous articles. *Life Sketches* is a collection of profiles and sketches published in *The New Yorker* and elsewhere, and, like most collections, it is uneven. Some of the portraits are as well crafted as a finely etched print, while others suffer from overindulgent editing—too much ponderous detail, dwelled on too lovingly. At his best, Mr. Hersey is a living tape recorder, using his excellent ear for speech to retell his sources' stories in their own tone and words. In **"Private John Daniel Ramey,"** for example, the story of a courageous illiterate who entered the Army and learned to read at the age of 30, Mr. Hersey captures the soldier's inspired teacher with a simple summary of her philosophy: "Life is too short to hurt anybody's feelings." In another of the strongest pieces, **"Varsell Pleas,"** he describes with moving accuracy the struggle of a black Mississippi family to vote in the early 1960's, and in **"Jessica Kelley"** he recounts the bravery and terror of a determined old woman caught in a violent flood. Some of his celebrity profiles, the best of which are of Sinclair Lewis and James Agee, have a pleasantly chatty quality, as if he were letting the reader in on secrets, although others are superficial or dull. Still, the skill that won Mr. Hersey a Pulitzer Prize in 1945 is more than evident. His book covers decades of memories and characters, and in doing so adds up to an important collection of lives and their lessons.

> *Helen Benedict, in a review of "Life Sketches,"*
> *in* The New York Times Book Review, *May 7, 1989, p. 25.*

Vance Bourjaily (review date 8 April 1990)

[*An American novelist, short story writer, journalist, playwright, critic, screenwriter, and editor, Bourjaily has garnered praise for his stylistic prose experiments and his examination of the divisive consequences of war on American society. In the following review, he positively assesses* Fling, and Other Stories, *noting that "the voices here are accurate, the insights convincing."*]

Throughout a long and luminous career, John Hersey has established himself as a master reporter in a great age of journalism. He has achieved equal stature as a novelist, though one cannot characterize the fiction of his times with as much certainty as its reportage. His first book, *Men on Bataan,* was published in 1942. *Fling* is his 24th, and, wonderfully enough, a departure—Mr. Hersey's first collection of short stories. Two are vintage, published in periodicals in 1947 and 1950. The other nine appeared between 1987 and 1989.

Variety is the collection's most striking overall attribute, as can be demonstrated by brief descriptions of several of the stories.

"God's Typhoon" is a first-person reminiscence of a dramatic sequence of events during an idyllic boyhood in China, where Mr. Hersey was born in 1914 and lived until he was 11. It is the only story in which we can assume narrator and author to be the same person.

"Peggety's Parcel of Shortcomings" is comic. After a bit of framing, it is told by Miss Peg, a pastry cook, to her fellow workers, and is the account of her one evening of romance, featuring a United States merchant marine who could barely get his short arms around her, and a fresh-caught Atlantic salmon, back in the days when Miss Peg "weighed scant two hundred eight pounds. . . . I was, you might say, thin as a shelf."

"Fling," the title story and crown of the collection, is some 12,000 words long. Call it a novella. In it, Venus, who is in her 70's, reviews her life in a randomly organized internal monologue. And her life (as a Gibson girl, flapper, jet-setter, beautiful person) has been a party. We are invited to the climax of the celebration, and the voice that relates it, often in a mock-royal first-person plural, is impeccably rendered:

> We like this about our Philip: he's an intelligent man, educated, one guesses, *despite* St. Paul's and Yale, the school with little wooden cubicles and the college with the great mute tomb of Scroll and Key—big men went Bones, the right men went Keys, they said, the ones who wore tails so often that they developed a bit of billiard-table green in the serge of the suit. Those were white-tie days, and here was one possible definition of the best of breeding: a slightly moldy look to your tails. But our Philip liked books even then, and always had, convention be damned. As with the cummerbund, he was a jump ahead of the pack—Henry James under his belt in 1935, long before the surge of fashion; Kafka and, yes, Kierkegaard by 1945.

Next comes a brief story called **"The Blouse,"** narrated in the author's own voice. It is rather like an O. Henry tale—but one of those in which the reversal of expectations is not mechanical but flows naturally from an experience of love.

In **"Requiescat,"** a writer, a journalist probably, plans to write a piece about the vivid life and violent death of his best and only friend, Moose Bradford. The story is set in the time when Communists were being prosecuted, and Moose, though certainly no party man himself, became notorious as the defense attorney for some of them. Let Mr. Hersey characterize:

> During the period when Moose was a frequent tenant of the gossip columns, his head was compared with those of John L. Lewis, Judge Learned Hand, Arturo Toscanini, Pablo Picasso, Wendell Willkie. When we think of such men, we speak of the lion, which, besides his huge mane, has a prodigious sack of stones between his hind legs, and indeed there was an open maleness and a hint of profligate raunchiness about all those men.

Moose is a womanizer, but he is also a man of honor, an athlete, a New England gentleman and, in some ways, an enigma. Finally, the writer tells us, he destroyed his notes, unable after all to write about Moose. But, of course, he just has, and very movingly.

The characters in **"The Captain"** are working class, hard-working class. They are lobstermen, and the weather is dangerous. The impressive thing about this story is the author's command of the details of the trade—its methods, jargon, psychology and protocol. The reader is made to feel like an insider.

In contrast, the workers in **"Mr. Quintillian"** are white collar. The time is the Depression, and what worries people are jobs and money, with the possibility of love a kind of irrelevance.

The final story, **"Affinities,"** takes place in a courtroom. There are a couple of borderline-underworld characters, one of whom is accused of stealing the other's extremely interesting and perhaps malevolent dog. The story is witty and amusing, with a fine, ironic twist.

And so in this collection we meet many characters from various backgrounds and classes, and we touch upon a number of points in American history. The voices here are accurate, the insights convincing. *Fling* is a fine performance indeed. What will Mr. Hersey show us next?

> *Vance Bourjaily, "Venus Was a Gibson Girl," in* The New York Times Book Review, *April 8, 1990, p. 24.*

Bernard Holland (review date 19 May 1991)

[*Holland is an American music critic. In the following, he provides a negative review of* Antonietta.]

A few facts, like a little learning, can be a dangerous thing. John Hersey's new novel, **Antonietta,** is enervated by them. The protagonist of Mr. Hersey's title is a violin made by Antonio Stradivari in 1699. The author has traced its subsequent travels from Italy to France to England to Switzerland and to the United States.

Tales about the adventures of this fictional violin, which Stradivari names Antonietta, accumulate along the way: its construction is inspired by a sweetheart, Mozart plays it, it is used to teach Berlioz. Mr. Hersey has polished these little barnacles of history, inflated them with air and then let them float where they will. Evidently intended as the tale of a kind of inanimate *Orlando* propelled through history, the result more nearly resembles Woody Allen's *Zelig,* except that while Zelig's nonentity was benign, Antonietta turns out to be somewhat of a pest.

Mr. Hersey, an enlightened music fan, doesn't do a very good job of getting inside the professional mind of the musician. He has tried hard to tone down even the tiniest claims for Antonietta's influence on music history, but even the hints that a violin might have inspired Mozart's composition, energized Berlioz's capacious imaginings, improved the quality of a Parisian orchestra or, in the case of "L'Histoire du Soldat," solidified the image in Stravinsky's mind of the Devil-as-fiddler are a little embarrassing.

Musicians simply don't think or respond the way the author has them do in this book.

Mr. Hersey's library time is evident. He has received impressions of Leopold Mozart (frugal, overly parental), Wolfgang Mozart (childish, obsessed with excrement), Berlioz (emotionally extravagant), Stravinsky (manipulative, skirt-chasing) and puffed them into cartoon-like portraits. Chunks of music biography have been recycled into **Antonietta;** the lore of violin construction, care and feeding has been dutifully studied; period life styles—from Stradivari's Italy to Wall Street arbitrage—are also attended to. Stradivari's son eats not just bread but "peasant bread made from a mixed meal of corn, rye, millet, and beans." Later on we are given a blow-by-blow recitation of insider trading. Mr. Hersey has done his research and, damn it, none is going to waste.

Like so much fiction bound by historical fact, **Antonietta** becomes a body of research trying vainly to invent people in its image. It is a novel without a center, for admirable as this violin undoubtedly is, wood, strings and glue do a dubious job of pulling these historical snippets together. Perhaps Mr. Hersey's view of beautiful instrument as resonant muse has been a little optimistic. **Antonietta,** like an intrusive pet, ends up snapping at the heels of music history.

> *Bernard Holland, "Mozart's Fiddle," in* The New York Times Book Review, *May 19, 1991, p. 13.*

Douglas Glover (review date 11 August 1991)

[*Glover is a Canadian short story writer, novelist, educator, and critic. In the review below, he criticizes* Antonietta *as sentimental, simplistic, and didactic.*]

John Hersey is an author forged from three constituent elements: He was born in China of missionary parents, started his writing career as a reporter for *Time* in the '30s and '40s, and then became a Pulitzer Prize-winning novelist on his first attempt at fiction.

He has carved himself a niche in the pantheon of American letters by following all three lines of attack at once—dramatizing his journalism, bulking up his novels with research, and preaching provocative homilies on modern social ills in the form of novelized parables and allegories.

This amalgam of techniques clearly has a readership: Hersey has been publishing books for nearly 50 years, often to wide acclaim. He has made himself a name as a first-rate journalist and an elegant moralizer. But literary omnidexterity has a downside.

At the muddy center of things, novels, sermons and news articles appear to share narrative elements, but at their limits, they are at war. Novels are complex, playful and ironic. Sermons and news articles tend to reduce complicated ideas to simple, easily understood formulae. News articles draw their inspiration from real life and are judged against real life; novels draw theirs from a patterning or aesthetic impulse.

An excerpt from "Fling"

"All you have to do is cross a river and you're in a foreign country?"

"That's right, Venus," Philip said.

"Let's really have one last fling. Let's go across the border. Let's go abroad."

Crossing that dirty little river to Ciudad Juárez would be, yes, a crossing. Ah, not quite a real one, not like the old days, going really abroad on the *Ile*—remember the food on the *Ile?*—sea bass *farçi* and those little paper-thin cucumber slices? That world of the heavenly ships was no more. Where had it gone? This crossing would be on foot, on a rickety bridge, in the dark of the night, and one would be trying to forget the pain. Never mind. "Let's do it tonight. I can't wait to tell Drua I've been abroad."

Every crossing, she'd once said, is an act of imagination. Walking unsteadily across that shabby bridge, tonight, to a dusty town in Mexico, one would have to try to imagine an ocean, a stateroom on the boat deck, portholes with the brass fittings shining like the hopes of all those years. She'd said that thing about crossing the ocean, she distinctly remembered, on the night of the party for Charley Trotter and Pam, their sixteenth wedding anniversary, at Cold Spring—God, how many years ago! That was also the night when that other thing happened, when nobody could persuade our Philip to rise to his feet to make the obligatory anniversary toast, and he began to rumble along seated—he was awfully tight but still he had that knack of his for the *mot juste*—and the rest of us—we were all so sozzled—scrambled out of our chairs and sat down on the floor, to establish the appropriate spacial relationship between orator and audience—the speaker pouring his words downward to his listeners—and down there we could see that Philip had his legs crossed and was kicking the upper one, showing off because during drinks Pam had suddenly gone over and curled up on his lap, and she'd reached up to her thigh and taken off that atrocious ruffled satin garter, with appliquéd hearts on it—she'd announced she could do without it because she had a garter belt on, too—and she'd given it to him, and now it was on his calf, over his trouser leg, kick kick kick as he droned on even though his audience had all disappeared under the table. On the terrace, after coffee and too many brandies, Sylvia threw Pam's slippers down the steep bank into the laurel, on account of the garter thing; Sylvia had a crush on our Philip even then, and she was jealous of Pam.

"Philip, darling," she said, "do you remember that thing of the garter?"

"You mean about Pam, that time? And Syllie? And Pam's shoes? Never forget it."

"God, how many years ago. It's all gone, darling."

John Hersey, in his Fling, and Other Stories, *Alfred A. Knopf, 1990.*

---

but in journalism—his 1946 book, *Hiroshima,* put a human face on nuclear war that has not been eclipsed in nearly 50 years. And his purely literary reputation never has been as high as his popularity might warrant.

Antonietta, Hersey's latest work of fiction, isn't a novel in the conventional sense—it's a collection of five connected stories, purporting to be the biography of a violin, the so-called Antonietta Strad, built in Cremona in 1699 by the middle-aged, lovesick Antonio Stradivari and associated with, in subsequent stories, the lives and works of Wolfgang Amadeus Mozart, Hector Berlioz, Igor Stravinsky and a tone-deaf 1980s inside trader named Spenser Ham.

Antonietta is of a piece with everything else Hersey has written. It is painstakingly researched. It is slick and intensely readable. It employs a weirdly awkward linking image as a unifying device (a magic violin that acts like a love potion—sometimes you get the idea Hersey is writing for children, then you remember that his first literary model was probably the Sunday-school story). And, at the end, it turns preachy (contemporary Americans are ruled by money and numbers).

When you finish reading this book, you feel as if you could build a violin or compose a symphony. You feel especially educated about composers. You feel you know how they think, how they make music out of ordinary human emotions like love and longing. You feel uplifted because you've absorbed some of that forbidding high culture—you can say something about Hindemith, Webern and Schoenberg without, thank God, having actually had to listen to the music.

These are all fun things to feel, and if you agree that arousing such feelings is the goal of art, then you would be forced to conclude that *Antonietta* is a terrific novel.

But the fact is there are two sorts of readers (as there are two sorts of people who listen to music): those who enjoy the work itself (listen for the interplay of melody, motif, harmony and orchestration) and those who prefer to enjoy the wash of feelings the work inspires in them. Hersey writes for the latter. Time and again in *Antonietta* he represents the experience of listening to music (and, by implication, reading a novel) as one of free-floating association—nostalgic memories, daydreams, fantasies.

Not only that, but he takes the more drastic and less defensible step of representing musical composition as the process of summoning such feelings and somehow (not clearly explained in the text) fluidly transcribing them into notes. "Music is memory. . . . Most of us have associations, usually nostalgic, that click into place when we hear certain tunes, but with Berlioz the connection is so much more intense that he states it in this extravagant way, as an absolute equivalence."

Now, I don't know if Berlioz ever said anything like this, but Hindemith, Webern and Schoenberg would have scoffed. Nor does this feeling theory explain anything about the nature of artistic genius. Instead it reduces genius to the level of everyman. It makes genius accessible by taking it to its lowest common denominator.

According to Hersey, Mozart was an emotionally imma-

The task of combining all three in perfect equilibrium in a single work is not only delicate, it is almost impossible. Hersey's greatest success has not been in the novel form

ture neurotic who wrote great music as a way of making love to whatever girl he happened to be infatuated with at the time (exactly the way a teen-ager writes poems to his sweetheart). Berlioz wrote the "Symphonie Fantastique" so he could get a date with English actress Harriet Smithson. Stravinsky said, "My ancient great-grandfather used to create by having sex. I write music." And Antonio Stradivari invented a new style of violin the day he fell in love with a black-clad widow tripping across the piazza outside his window (Hersey strains here to put the old violin/woman metaphor through its paces one more time).

This makes it easier for us to identify with greatness in a non-rigorous and patronizing way. But the truth is that Hersey's journalistic and preachy sides (sentimental, popularizing, oversimplifying) have gotten the better of the novelist in him. *Antonietta* is a mid-list entertainment pumped up with steroids to look literary and intellectual.

It's a con, and a good one—seductive, reassuring and eminently skillful. But let the reader beware: Believe nothing between these covers.

> Douglas Glover, "Hersey Strings Us Along," in Los Angeles Times Book Review, *August 11, 1991, p. 9.*

OBITUARIES AND TRIBUTES

Myrna Oliver (obituary date 25 March 1993)

[*In the following essay, Oliver surveys Hersey's life and career.*]

John Hersey, a World War II correspondent who graphically described the horrors of the world's first atomic bomb attack and won the Pulitzer Prize for his war-based novel *A Bell for Adano* died Wednesday. He was 78.

The author, who suffered a stroke a year ago and also had cancer of the colon and liver, died at 2:45 a.m. in Key West, Fla., with his family at his side, said his wife, Barbara.

Hersey first wrote his nonfiction account of *Hiroshima* as an entire issue of the *New Yorker* magazine published Aug. 31, 1946. The essay, which described the realities of the grim dawning of the atomic age, searingly traced the experiences of six Japanese survivors of the American bombing of Hiroshima on Aug. 6, 1945. The account was soon published as a book, and it was also made into a film.

Hersey covered the war for *Time* magazine and turned the experience of American soldiers occupying an Italian village into his 1944 Pulitzer Prize-winning novel. The book, describing the attempts of a well-meaning Italian-American officer named Maj. Joppolo to rebuild the occupied town, later became a play and in 1945 a film by 20th Century Fox.

"John Hersey's writing about the moral problems in

World War II was of the highest quality," author James Michener said.

As a correspondent and novelist, Hersey felt strongly that fiction could be used to advantage in depicting real life.

"Fiction is a clarifying agent. It makes truth plausible," he wrote for the *Atlantic Monthly* in 1949. "Among all the means of communication now available, imaginative literature comes closer than any other to being able to give an impression of the truth."

His other books based on World War II were *Men on Bataan* in 1942 and *Into the Valley* in 1943.

Later concentrating on subjects ranging from the U.S. presidency (particularly the administrations of Harry S. Truman and Gerald R. Ford) to the Stradivarius violin, Hersey penned more than 20 books. Among them were *The Wall* in 1950 about Jewish victims of the Holocaust, which was made into a CBS television movie in 1982; *The War Lover* in 1959, which became a movie by Columbia in 1962; *White Lotus* in 1965; *The Algiers Motel Incident* in 1968; *The President* in 1975; *Aspects of the Presidency* in 1980; *Fling and Other Stories* in 1990, and his final novel, about the violin, *Antonietta,* in 1991.

Born June 17, 1914, in Tientsin, China, as the son of American missionary parents, Hersey moved to the United States at age 10.

"I was born a foreigner," he said in a rare interview in 1985. "I was born in China, and I think in some ways I have been an outsider in America because of that."

Hersey earned a bachelor's degree at Yale University in 1936 and spent a summer as secretary and driver for writer Sinclair Lewis.

He later wrote a profile of Lewis, along with portraits of Lillian Hellman and James Agee, in a 1989 collection of essays titled *Life Sketches.* In a rare note for a writer of such stature, Hersey publicly apologized for similarities in the essay on Agee—first published in the *New Yorker* on July 18, 1988—to passages from a biography of Agee written by Laurence Bergreen in 1984.

Hersey worked for *Time* from 1937 to 1944 and then switched to its companion *Life* magazine to finish out the war coverage. He wrote for the *New Yorker* immediately after the war. Many of his books continued to reflect his war-years view of America's presence in foreign countries.

The prolific novelist lectured for 18 years at Yale and at Massachusetts Institute of Technology. He was also active in Democratic politics.

"He was an extraordinarily versatile writer and the world was his subject," Judith Jones, Hersey's editor at Albert A. Knopf Publishing, said on learning of his death.

"He believed that a writer's job was to write and not spend time doing publicity," she said. "He was a very private person."

In addition to the Pulitzer, Hersey's books garnered the Anisfield-Wolf Award and the Daroff Memorial Fiction Award from the Jewish Book Council of America in 1950, the Sidney Hillman Foundation Award in 1951, Yale's Howland Medal in 1952, the National Assn. of Independent Schools Award in 1957, the Tuition Plan Award in 1961 and the Sarah Josepha Hale Award in 1963.

Hersey married twice. With his first wife, Frances Ann Cannon, whom he married in 1940 and divorced in 1958, he had three sons, Martin, John and Baird, and one daughter, Ann. He married his second wife, Barbara Kaufman, in 1958, and with her had one daughter, Brook. Survivors also include six grandchildren.

> Myrna Oliver, "John Hersey: Won Pulitzer Prize for 'A Bell for Adano'," in Los Angeles Times, *March 25, 1993, p. A32.*

Richard Severo   (obituary date 25 March 1993)

[*Severo is an American journalist. Here, he surveys Hersey's career and comments on the critical reception of his work.*]

John Hersey, the novelist and journalist whose *A Bell for Adano* won a Pulitzer Prize for fiction in 1945 and whose nonfiction work *Hiroshima* awakened Americans to the horrors of atomic warfare, died yesterday at his home in Key West, Fla. He was 78.

The cause of death was cancer, said his family.

In the course of his five decades as a writer, Mr. Hersey emerged not only as a first-rate reporter but also as a storyteller who nurtured the idea that writers had to pursue a moral goal. He involved himself deeply in the issues of his day.

In public appearances and in work on special committees, he never hesitated to speak out on such issues as the Vietnam War, which he strongly opposed; on problems in American education, and on issues central to the craft of writing, including censorship, government intimidation of writers, copyright protection and fair taxation for those who create the nation's literature. He was a tireless worker for both the Authors League of America and the Authors Guild.

Mr. Hersey sent his latest manuscript to his publisher, Alfred A. Knopf, just six weeks ago, said Judith Jones, his editor at Knopf for the last 20 years. Entitled *Key West Tales,* it consists of short stories, set in the past and present, about people and events in his hometown. The book is to be published in the winter of 1994, Ms. Jones said.

From the beginning of his career, Mr. Hersey won praise for the directness of his style, his eye for detail and his ability to get to the heart of any situation. But most critics suggested that his past as a journalist somehow showed in his novels and that his fiction was not developed as deeply as it might have been.

This kind of criticism was heard even after the publication of *A Bell for Adano,* in 1944, Mr. Hersey's acclaimed novel about events that occurred in Licata, a small town in Sicily that was ravaged by World War II. The book used some experiences of Maj. Frank E. Toscani, the American Army officer who became Licata's military gov-

ernor and learned from townspeople that their most pressing need was the return of their bell.

The centerpiece of their community, the bell, had been taken down by the enemy and melted for the war effort against the Allies. Major Toscani became very much a part of the town's lore when he somehow succeeded in securing another bell from a Navy destroyer.

In the book, which became a best seller, Licata became Adano and Major Toscani became Major Joppolo.

Mr. Hersey had the fictional major have an affair with an Italian woman. Major Toscani promptly sued Mr. Hersey for libel, stating that the book seemed so true to so much of what happened that many people mistakenly thought that the amorous adventure was true, too. The lawsuit was finally settled amicably over dinner in New York at a restaurant named after the novel.

The novel got excellent reviews, although Diana Trilling, who reviewed it for *The Nation* and who basically liked it, wrote that Mr. Hersey's ideas, "like his prose, have undergone a process of conscious falsifying and purposeful simplification." Even so, *A Bell for Adano* won a Pulitzer Prize. In 1945, it also became a successful motion picture, starring John Hodiak in the role of Major Joppolo.

Mr. Hersey's next big project was *Hiroshima,* a major work of nonfiction that traces the lives of six people who survived the atomic bombing of Japan in 1945. It was written as a three-part series for *The New Yorker,* but the magazine's editors, Harold Ross and William Shawn, instead decided to print it in full on Aug. 31, 1946, allowing it to consume nearly all the editorial space in the issue.

The *New York Times* ran an editorial calling attention to the piece, and Lewis Gannett, writing in *The New York Herald Tribune,* called *Hiroshima* "the best reporting" of the war and *Time* magazine praised its restraint. Albert Einstein was said to have ordered a thousand copies for distribution and a great many newspapers clamored to serialize it. Mr. Hersey allowed this, provided that they made contributions to the American Red Cross, rather than pay him.

The piece was developed into a book, published by Alfred A. Knopf.

From the beginning of his career, Mr. Hersey won praise for the directness of his style, his eye for detail and his ability to get to the heart of any situation.

—*Richard Severo*

Similar praise came in 1950 with publication of *The Wall,* Mr. Hersey's novel about events in the Warsaw ghetto from November 1939, with the German occupation, to May 1943, when the last houses in the ghetto were razed. *The Wall* won the Daroff Memorial Fiction Award of the

Jewish Book Council of America and the Sidney Hillman Foundation Award. It was dramatized by Millard Lampell, produced at the Billy Rose Theater in New York in the early 1960's and filmed for television by CBS in 1982.

John Richard Hersey was born on June 17, 1914, in Tientsin, China. His father, Roscoe, worked for the Young Men's Christian Association there; his mother, the former Grace Baird, was a missionary. John, who spent most of his first 10 years in China, spoke Chinese before he spoke English. His life was eventful: at one point, he took a two-year trip around the world with his mother. But in later years he said he could recall very little of his childhood and described it as "no more exciting than the average child's."

In 1924, the family moved to Briarcliff Manor, N.Y., in Westchester County. After attending public schools there, John Hersey was enrolled in the private Hotchkiss School in Lakeville, Conn., which he attended from 1927 to his graduation in 1932. After that came Yale, from which he graduated in 1936, and then Clare College, Cambridge. By the time his college days were over, he was determined to become a journalist.

Returning to the United States in May 1937, he learned that Sinclair Lewis needed a private secretary. Mr. Hersey thus became Mr. Lewis's summertime factotum, copying pages of a play that Lewis was writing about Communism. Mr. Hersey later recalled that he worked intensively with Lewis without ever realizing that his employer had a serious drinking problem.

Later in 1937, he was hired by *Time* magazine. "*Time* seemed to me to be the liveliest enterprise of its type and I wanted more than anything to be connected with it," he later said. He talked the editors into hiring him by submitting to them an essay in which he told them what he thought was wrong with the magazine.

In 1939, *Time* sent Mr. Hersey to the Far East, where he covered the initial stages of World War II. His first book, *Men on Bataan,* was produced in 1942, and the next year he wrote *Into the Valley,* a novel about a skirmish on Guadalcanal. John Chamberlin, reviewing it for *The New York Times,* said the book gave evidence that Mr. Hersey was "a new Hemingway." Moreover, Mr. Hersey was commended by the Secretary of the Navy for his role in helping to remove wounded men from Guadalcanal.

During the years immediately after the war, as he developed his novelistic skills in such books as *The Marmot Drive* (1953), *A Single Pebble* (1956) and *The War Lover* (1959), Mr. Hersey also kept alive his interests in things that had nothing to do with his books. He joined a number of local and national educational organizations and became master of Pierson College at Yale University in 1965, holding the post for five years.

In the 1960's Mr. Hersey became an early opponent of American involvement in the Vietnam War, and in 1965 he was a sponsor of a March on Washington for Peace in Vietnam. He was no less concerned with racism in America and in 1968 wrote *The Algiers Motel Incident,* which described the killing of three black men in a Detroit motel.

Mr. Hersey became involved in a literary uproar in 1976 when an article he wrote for *The Saturday Review* was pulled by the magazine's editor, Norman Cousins. The article condemned the influence wielded by certain large corporations, and Mr. Cousins reportedly felt it was not upbeat enough.

Mr. Hersey married Frances Ann Cannon in 1940. They were divorced in 1958 and Mr. Hersey married Barbara Day Addams Kaufman that year.

He is survived by his wife; their daughter, Brook Hersey of Manhattan; three sons by his first marriage, Martin, of Eastampton, N.J., John Jr., of Millbrook, N.Y., and Baird, of Willow, N.Y.; another daughter, Ann Hersey of Cambridge, Mass.; a brother, Arthur, of Annapolis, Md., and six grandchildren.

> Richard Severo, "John Hersey, Author of 'Hiroshima', Is Dead at 78," in The New York Times, *March 25, 1993, p. B11.*

Bart Barnes   (obituary date 25 March 1993)

[*In the following essay, Barnes profiles Hersey's work, particularly* Hiroshima.]

John Hersey, 78, the celebrated writer of fact and fiction who was best known as the author of *Hiroshima,* a graphic and compelling account of the world's first atomic bomb attack, and *A Bell for Adano,* which won the 1945 Pulitzer Prize for fiction, died March 24 at his home in Key West, Fla. He had colon and liver cancer and had suffered a stroke about a year ago.

Mr. Hersey was author of more than 20 books and dozens of magazine and newspaper articles. He won critical acclaim for the passion and simplicity of his prose and the range of his subject matter, which included war, racial discrimination, politics, the student rebellion, fishing for bluefish off Martha's Vineyard and a Stradivarius violin.

His other works included *The Wall* (1950), a fictional account of life in the Warsaw ghetto during World War II, which was adapted for a CBS television film in 1982; *The War Lover* (1959), a novel about a World War II American airman who loved dropping bombs on enemy cities, which was made into a movie in 1962; and *The Algiers Motel Incident* (1968), which described the killings of three black youths in Detroit's Algiers Motel during the 1967 riots. Mr. Hersey's last book was *Antonietta* (1991), which tells the story of a Stradivarius violin and its effect on the lives of the likes of Mozart, Berlioz, Stravinsky and finally, John Hersey, a former violin student himself.

But it was in *Hiroshima* that Mr. Hersey produced a literary classic and made publishing history with a non-polemical description of the atomic blast in the Japanese city of Hiroshima on Aug. 6, 1945. He wrote a straightforward account of what happened that day and in the year afterward to the city's inhabitants and specifically to six survivors.

To write the book, Mr. Hersey visited Hiroshima and roamed through the rubble, talking to people where 100,000 had died. His story, which took up the entire issue of the *New Yorker* magazine on Aug. 31, 1946, is said to have been one of the most searing portrayals of the horrors of modern warfare.

> . . . others, because of pain, held their arms up as if carrying something in both hands. Some were vomiting as they walked. Many were naked or in shreds of clothing. On some undressed bodies, the burns had made patterns—of undershirt straps and suspenders and, on the skin of some of the women (since white repelled the heat from the bomb and dark clothes absorbed it and conducted it to the skin) the shapes of flowers they had on their kimonos . . . their faces were wholly burned, their eye sockets were hollow, the fluid from their melted eyes had run down their cheeks.

As a book, *Hiroshima* sold 118,000 copies in hardcover and more than 3.4 million in paperback.

Thirty-nine years later, Mr. Hersey updated his original in **"Hiroshima: The Aftermath,"** published first again in the *New Yorker* on July 15, 1985. Two of his six original subjects had died, one had become a prosperous physician, another a mother superior. Another had won aid from the Japanese government after years of struggle, and the fourth had toured the United States seeking help for his Protestant church. Mr. Hersey concluded the 1985 account with the observation that for one of the survivors, "his memory, like the world's, was getting spotty."

A war correspondent in Europe and the Pacific during World War II, Mr. Hersey had written three books before *Hiroshima,* including *A Bell for Adano,* which was set in the Sicilian village of Adano, occupied by American troops. It was the story of a well-meaning Italian-American officer who tried to rebuild the village near the end of the war. The book was later adapted for a stage play in New York and then made into a movie by Twentieth Century Fox.

Earlier in the war Mr. Hersey wrote *Into the Valley,* an account of the fighting on Guadalcanal, and *Men on Bataan,* the story of American soldiers trapped on the Bataan peninsula by invading Japanese early in 1942. He also had written a widely known 1944 article in the *New Yorker* describing the wartime experiences of Navy Lt. John F. Kennedy.

Mr. Hersey was born in Tianjin, China, to American missionary parents. He graduated from Yale University, then studied for a year at Clare College in Cambridge. He worked briefly as a private secretary for Sinclair Lewis, then joined the reporting staff of *Time* magazine, which in 1939 sent him to the Far East.

During the early years of the war, Mr. Hersey was assigned to the Pacific theater of operations, then in 1943 was posted in the Mediterranean.

His postwar writing included such novels as *A Single Pebble* (1956), *The Child Buyer* (1960), *White Lotus* (1965) and *The Call: An American Missionary in China* (1985). He was also author of *Aspects of the Presidency: Truman and Ford in Office* (1980) and a book about bluefishing, *Blues* (1987).

He preferred writing novels to nonfiction. "Among all the means of communication now available, imaginative literature comes closer than any other to being able to give an impression of the truth," he said in a 1949 article in *Atlantic Monthly.*

For 18 years, Mr. Hersey taught writing at Yale and the Massachusetts Institute of Technology. He was master of Pierson College, one of 12 residential colleges at Yale, for five years, ending in 1970. From this experience he wrote a book, *Letter to the Alumni.* The book attempted to explain contemporary college student attitudes to earlier generations while focusing on the 1970 May Day demonstrations at Yale in connection with a controversial Black Panther murder trial in New Haven, Conn., where Yale is located. Among the black students at Yale figuring in the book was Kurt L. Schmoke, currently the mayor of Baltimore.

Since 1976 Mr. Hersey had lived in Key West.

His marriage to the former Frances Ann Cannon ended in divorce.

Survivors include his wife of 35 years, Barbara Hersey; four children from his first marriage, Martin, John, Ann and Baird; and a daughter from his second marriage, Brook.

> Bart Barnes, " 'Hiroshima' Author John Hersey, 78, Dies," in The Washington Post, March 25, 1993, p. B5.

Steven Mufson   (essay date 25 March 1993)

[*In the following essay, Mufson recalls Hersey's dedication to teaching writing.*]

When I entered John Hersey's nonfiction writing class at Yale in the spring of 1979, I had written some high school fiction, a few amateurish, self-indulgent poems and a huge number of college newspaper articles, most of them about striking blue-collar workers.

From such meager stuff as this, John Hersey, who died yesterday at 78, tried to create writers.

Not just newspaper reporters, but people who "crafted" stories. Writing, he would say, was a bit like carpentry; the writer had to think about structure and form, and then spend hours smoothing the edges.

Carpentry was a good metaphor for what John Hersey was trying to do with us, a bunch of college juniors and seniors. Our education had focused on stuffing us with information, instead of teaching us how to take information and create something special. Hersey's class was an oasis from the dry weekly routine of speed-reading Aristotle and grinding out history papers in all-night marches.

To encourage our transformation, he assigned us a variety of readings: the nonfiction "newsreel" passages from John Dos Passos's *U.S.A.* trilogy, a Maxim Gorky profile of Leo Tolstoy, Hersey's own description of the flooding of the Mad River in Connecticut, a piece from Nora Ephron's *Crazy Salad,* as well as many works of fiction.

Use the devices of fiction to write more effective nonfiction, he preached. So instead of talking about the all-too-familiar crutches of newsrooms, such as the pyramid style, he talked to us about character, about beginnings and endings, and about detail.

Hersey's own character and appearance underlined his messages. He came to class dressed neatly, his white hair brushed back away from his forehead. His posture was erect, his personality gentle.

He was certainly not a frumpy college professor. He was a professional, and a stunningly successful professional. I couldn't help noticing then that my copy of Hersey's *Hiroshima,* which described the devastation of the atom bomb, was in its 48th printing.

Sometimes Hersey seemed embarrassed by his own success. He played down the quality of his Pulitzer Prize-winning novel, *A Bell for Adano,* which he said he wrote in three weeks. And in recalling how he wrote *Hiroshima* for *The New Yorker,* he also recalled how it coincided with his painful break with *Time* and its publisher, Henry R. Luce.

Still, he taught with the stern yet caring sense of purpose that he must have inherited from his parents, who were missionaries in China.

Each week, two or three students would turn in profiles, which were photocopied and distributed to all of us. Then the pieces were discussed and critiqued by the entire class.

We would have frequent private audiences with Hersey. In the margins of the profiles we wrote, he would make tidy little check marks. Each one signaled a flaw in grammar or word choice, a missing transition or a clumsy phrase. At times, he would reach for his copy of Fowler's English grammar and ask if you had ever heard of the book.

Though there was something remote about his manner, he gave his time generously to his students, whether in his Yale office or his home at dinner or, in later years, at his Martha's Vineyard or Key West homes. Journalism is replete with his students, who threw a 70th birthday party for him in 1985 and raised money for a scholarship fund in his honor.

In a sense, John Hersey was a practitioner of New Journalism before it became popular. But, especially as one who was both novelist and journalist, he constantly warned about the dangers of mixing fact and fiction. Integrity was a word he used often.

Later, Hersey was forced to publicly apologize for similarities in an essay he wrote about James Agee—first published in *The New Yorker* July 18, 1988—to passages from a biography of Agee written by Laurence Bergreen in 1984. This sounded nothing like the teacher we had in class, and it was something I never understood.

For us, meeting John Hersey was an introduction to what writing was really about. Not just facts, but truth. Not just arriving at the end of your column inches, but truly arriving at the end of the story.

Fourteen years after his class, I still look through the class reading selections that I keep in a cardboard box I saved from the clutches of a mother intent on cleaning out her basement. When I look at them, Hersey's admonitions and my own shortcomings in daily journalism swirl around me like dust. (pp. B5, D5)

> *Steven Mufson, "The Word Carpenter: John Hersey, Master Writer and Teacher," in* The Washington Post, *March 25, 1993, pp. B5, D5.*

David Gates   (essay date 5 April 1993)

[*Gates is an American novelist, educator, editor, and critic. In the following essay, he praises Hersey for writing about the lives of common people and for challenging popular beliefs.*]

Hersey wrote best about the impact of great events on everyday lives.

—David Gates

After 47 years, it's as powerful as ever: an opening sentence with a reporter's precision, a novelist's dramatic sense. "At exactly fifteen minutes past eight in the morning," John Hersey began his masterpiece, "on August 6, 1945, Japanese time, at the moment when the atomic bomb flashed above Hiroshima, Miss Toshiko Sasaki, a clerk in the personnel department of the East Asia Tin Works, had just sat down at her place in the plant office and was turning her head to speak to the girl at the next desk." Hersey, who died of cancer last week at 78, produced 23 books in 50 years; *Hiroshima* is the one that will live as long as there *are* books. It offers no screed against the bomb: just unforgettable details (potatoes baked in the ground, soldiers with melted eyes) and six ordinary people. That first sentence, focused on a single individual, a single gesture, contains the essential Hersey, who wrote best about the impact of great events on everyday lives.

"I was born a foreigner," he once said, to account for why he was "an outsider in America." Born in Tientsin of missionary parents, he spoke Chinese before English. Yet his prose was all-American—like his contrarian impulses. His Pulitzer Prize-winning first novel, *A Bell for Adano* (1944), with its megalomaniac American general, was startlingly subversive for a wartime work; *Hiroshima*'s account of innocent civilians in a nuclear firestorm undercut postwar moral complacency. Hersey got into scrap after scrap: the model for the *good* officer in *Adano* sued him (he dropped it after dining with Hersey); Hersey was an early opponent of the Vietnam War; in 1976, *The Saturday Review* (perhaps with an eye on advertisers) balked at running his attack on big business; in 1988, he was attacked for a *New Yorker* piece that borrowed without credit from a James Agee biography. In fact, he got his first steady job, as a *Time* reporter (in 1937), with an essay "on how rotten the magazine was."

Like many American writers, Hersey peaked early: he wrote *Adano, Hiroshima* and *The Wall,* a novel of the Warsaw ghetto, before he was 37. But he accepted this with rare equanimity. Some books, he said in 1985, "have had a life of their own, and some haven't, and that's the way things go." Reviewers found his novels less satisfactory than his reporting; naturally, he preferred them. Above all, he kept writing. Once every few books his work again took on that independent life that no writer can will into being. *The Algiers Motel Incident* (1968) gave the meticulous *Hiroshima* treatment to a racially motivated shooting in Detroit; *Blues* (1987) was a quirkily original meditation on bluefishing off Martha's Vineyard. Forty years ago he said writers most needed "dedication to the craft of writ-

ing, and bedrock character." He must have known he'd have to live up to these words. And he did.

David Gates, "An All-American Foreigner," in Newsweek, *Vol. CXXI, No. 14, April 5, 1993, p. 70.*

FURTHER READING

Garrett, George. "Fables of Florida," *The New York Times Book Review* XCIX, No. 7 (13 February 1994): 22.
    Positive review of Hersey's short story collection *Key West Tales.*

Additional coverage of Hersey's life and career is contained in the following sources published by Gale Research: *Contemporary Authors,* Vols. 17-20 (rev. ed.), 140 (obituary); *Contemporary Authors New Revision Series,* Vol. 33; *Contemporary Literary Criticism,* Vols. 1, 2, 7, 9, 40; *Dictionary of Literary Biography,* Vol. 6; *Major 20th-Century Writers;* and *Something about the Author,* Vol. 25.

Wallace Stegner

February 18, 1909—April 13, 1993

(Full name Wallace Earle Stegner) American novelist, nonfiction writer, short story writer, essayist, biographer, editor, critic, educator, and environmentalist.

For further information on Stegner's life and works, see *CLC,* Volumes 9 and 49.

INTRODUCTION

Winner of a National Book Award for Fiction, a Pulitzer Prize, and numerous O. Henry awards, Stegner was the preeminent figure in twentieth-century American western literature. In all of his writings, fiction and nonfiction, he concentrated on the relationships between the people and the land of the western United States. Stegner's realistic and subtly evocative works, critics assert, stand in sharp contrast to most western fiction, which promotes the romantic myth of the American West. For example, when Stegner wrote about cowboys—which he rarely did—he depicted them not as the Indian-fighting heroes typically found in John Wayne movies, but as "overworked, underpaid hireling[s], almost as homeless and dispossessed as modern crop worker[s]," fighting to survive in a landscape both forbidding and beautiful. Stegner's devotion to the land and the people of the West, which was the source of his lifelong commitment to environmentalism, contributed to his reputation as a strictly "regional" writer. However, as Richard W. Etulain has written, Stegner is "a western writer in the same sense that William Faulkner and Robert Frost are southern and New England authors. All use regional materials as springboards to examining wider worlds."

PRINCIPAL WORKS

Remembering Laughter   (novel)   1937
The Potter's House   (novel)   1938
On a Darkling Plain   (novel)   1940
Fire and Ice   (novel)   1941
Mormon Country   (nonfiction)   1942
The Big Rock Candy Mountain   (novel)   1943
One Nation   (nonfiction)   1945
Second Growth   (novel)   1947
The Preacher and the Slave   (novel)   1950; also published as *Joe Hill: A Biographical Novel,* 1969
The Women on the Wall   (short stories)   1950

The Writer in America   (lectures)   1951
Beyond the Hundredth Meridian: John Wesley Powell and the Second Opening of the West   (nonfiction)   1954
The City of the Living, and Other Stories   (short stories)   1956
A Shooting Star   (novel)   1961
Wolf Willow: A History, a Story, and a Memory of the Last Plains Frontier   (fiction and nonfiction)   1962
Teaching the Short Story   (nonfiction)   1965
All the Little Live Things   (novel)   1967
The Sound of Mountain Water: The Changing American West   (essays)   1969
Angle of Repose   (novel)   1971
The Uneasy Chair: A Biography of Bernard DeVoto   (biography)   1974
The Spectator Bird   (novel)   1976
Recapitulation   (novel)   1979
One Way to Spell Man   (essays)   1982
The American West as Living Space   (nonfiction)   1987
Crossing to Safety   (novel)   1987

Collected Stories of Wallace Stegner (short stories) 1990

Where the Bluebird Sings to the Lemonade Springs: Living and Writing in the West (essays) 1992

OVERVIEWS

Kenneth Whyte   (essay date April 1991)

[*In the following essay, Whyte discusses Stegner's views on nationalist literary movements, his importance to Canadian literature, and characteristic elements of his writing.*]

In 1974 the novelist Wallace Stegner, a visiting professor of American letters at the University of Toronto, was introduced to the Canadian literary scene. It stood before him in bloom of adolescence, picking at its shortcomings, quoting its clippings, fondling its national characteristics, muttering darkly about the insidious and debasing cultural influence of the United States while flirting with it. Another person might have bolted. Stegner, head of the creative-writing programme at Stanford University for most of the previous thirty years, embraced the creature and offered as a sort of confiding wink an essay entitled **"The Provincial Consciousness."**

The piece tells Canadian artists and intellectuals their fervid nationalism is just a stage they're going through—further evidence that Canada compulsively repeats American experience generations behind the pace. Stegner reminds Canadians of how Emerson and Whitman dismissed the "courtly muses of Europe" only to have their earnest prayers for an unmistakably American genius answered almost perversely with Mark Twain's barbaric backwoods yarns. Stegner's moral is that literature of universal appeal may be characteristic of a nation but is seldom self-consciously nationalistic. It is more probably "local, even colloquial in its settings, characters, morality, beliefs, in the whole backdrop of its human and environmental scenery." He concludes there's nothing wrong with CanLit that a couple of "world class" Canadian writers wouldn't cure, individuals of eloquence, perceptiveness, passion, and integrity who like Twain (or William Faulkner, Knut Hamsun, and Anton Chekhov) could make their own lives and those of their communities "meaningful to the world."

It's a wonder he wasn't stomped on for his trouble, times being as they were. It's easier today to grant him a few points: the Canadian mood was a passing one, the U.S. did suffer it first, and since 1974, as our authors have gained international recognition, the old slogan "read Canadian" has become less a dare, more an imperative. On the other side of the score sheet his arguments aren't entirely original, and he acknowledges but doesn't confront the problem of Quebec. In sum, the piece still holds its own but it's probably most interesting today for what it reveals of Stegner.

By stubbornly following his own lights through six decades of literary production he has come close to keeping the company he admires. His own locale, broadly defined, is the West. "Anything beyond the Missouri was close to home," says the hero of his autobiographical novel, *The Big Rock Candy Mountain.* He has lived, studied, or taught in more than a dozen towns and cities in the region—Great Falls, Palo Alto, Salt Lake City among them—and almost all of them appear in his fiction. None, however, is evoked with the vividness and emotion Stegner summons when writing of his "native" ground, the southern Saskatchewan town of Eastend and its surrounding prairie.

From 1914 to 1920, he spent six stable years out of an otherwise transient boyhood there. It provides the setting for his early novels and many of the better pieces in his recently released *The Collected Stories of Wallace Stegner.* A return to Eastend in middle age resulted in the multigenre work *Wolf Willow.* It uses stories, historical essays, and personal reminiscences to re-explore the region, to gauge its impact on the author's character and imagination, and to trace the region's influence on its other inhabitants, from native tribes to second- and third-generation settlers.

It is to *Wolf Willow,* perhaps the most important book yet written about the Canadian prairies, that Stegner owes his dual literary citizenship. Edna Alford, a Saskatchewan writer who defers to Stegner as "our Chekhov," calls the book "an astonishing piece of work. It made me aware that you could come from this environment and create work of significance." Rudy Wiebe cites *Wolf Willow* as a major influence and encouragement. So does Sharon Butala, who resides in Eastend (she's restoring Stegner's childhood home as a museum and authors' retreat). *Wolf Willow* is also beginning to make appearances in Western Canadian historiography, and it is in no small way responsible for recent scholarly interest in the shared cultures of plains people on either side of the forty-ninth parallel.

Stegner has made other contributions to Canadian letters, not least among which was persuading Little, Brown to publish W. O. Mitchell's *Who Has Seen the Wind* in 1947. But the author of *Wolf Willow* and twenty-six other books belongs primarily to the U.S. even though he hasn't a particularly high profile there. At least three of his novels are masterly, his biographies of the explorer John Wesley Powell and the historian Bernard Devoto are credits to the genre; he has won a Pulitzer prize and a National Book Award; but if he's at all famous it's for the creative-writing fellowship in his name at Stanford and the achievements of his students (foremost among them: Wendell Berry, Edward Abbey, N. Scott Momaday, Tillie Olsen, Robert Stone, Ken Kesey, and Larry McMurtry). On one of the few occasions on which *The New York Times* has considered his work it deemed him "the dean of Western Writers" and spelled his name wrong throughout the article. Only recently has he begun to shed the regional label. Last summer [1990] a surprised *New Republic* called him "one of the best writers of American prose in his era."

Stegner's six years in southern Saskatchewan were typical of the prairie experience on both sides of the international line. (Critics have noted parallels between his Whitemud and Willa Cather's Red Cloud, Nebraska.) Many of his memories are as pleasant as one would expect of a reasonably healthy boy set loose in a semiwild land with light weaponry and a handful of friends, but his family's story is one of failure. Wheat fields were one stop in his father's restless search for an ideal western frontier, what Stegner describes in *The Big Rock Candy Mountain* as "a wide open and unskimmed country where a man could hew his own line and not suffer for his independence."

While earlier North American frontiers had given unbounded ambition a tolerable reception the prairies answered with a hostile set of limitations: low rainfall, a short growing season, harsh temperatures, unrelieved exposure, staggering distances, a winnowed set of agricultural and entrepreneurial options. It wasn't much of a match. Most homesteaders were driven out. "More than we knew," writes Stegner, "we had our place in a human movement."

> **Stegner's cowboy is not Owen Wister's Virginian, a knight in chaps who never punched a post hole or dipped a cow. According to Stegner his cowboy's "fabled independence was and is chiefly the privilege of quitting his job in order to go looking for another just as bad."**
>
> —*Kenneth Whyte*

His family sought new opportunities south of the line and he was left "a lover but not much of a booster" of the West. He has been butting his hard head against its reigning mythologies since he started writing. His cowboy is not Owen Wister's Virginian, a knight in chaps who never punched a post hole or dipped a cow. He is an "overworked, underpaid hireling, almost as homeless and dispossessed as a modern crop worker," and his "fabled independence was and is chiefly the privilege of quitting his job in order to go looking for another just as bad." If he meets adventure, it is the sort met by the impetuous young Englishman Rusty Cullen, hero of the novella *Genesis,* perhaps Stegner's most perfect fiction (and his only major work about cowboys).

The story is set in Saskatchewan during the devastating winter of 1906-07, a season largely responsible for clearing the prairies of cattle ranchers and opening them to the stock and dirt farmers who inhabit them still. Eager for rites of passage, a free and daring life on horseback, experiences that would stand him back home with Peary and Livingstone, Rusty lands a job on a winter roundup with Ray Henry's Whitemud River outfit. In no time, his mount pile-drives him, and one of the hirelings wants to finish him off. Winter winds are blowing hard, the snow won't uncover the grass, and the range cattle have to be abandoned as the cowboys fight for their own lives. Rusty finds himself sleeping night after night in a tent in a blizzard, fully clothed, with a "numbness like freezing to death" stealing over him. He begins to think of his home and his rash decision to leave it. He is "appalled at the effectiveness of his own will."

The romantic individualist spends much of the story trudging through blowing snow literally tied to his fellows for survival. To Stegner's mind, anything less is an affront to the complexity of plains history, a denial of the real hardship, sacrifice, and tragedy of settlement.

Yet Rusty does survive, unlike most of the cattle. Stegner is an optimist in a bleak sort of way. (He just won't abide easy wins.) In **"Carrion Spring,"** an epilogue to *Genesis* (together they form the core of *Wolf Willow*), Ray Henry, the ranch foreman who hired Rusty, is taking his wife back to "civilization"—Malta, Montana—while Rusty stays behind to sell the property and the remains of the herd for its owners. En route Ray and his wife pass bloated, rotting bovine carcasses heaped in fields, floating legs-up in the river, even hanging by their horns from trees. Ray tells her there will never be a better time to buy the ranch. They fight, they have a picnic lunch, she finds a single crocus popped from the dull earth and, while she's still sick and scared and fully aware of the cruel odds and certain hardship they'll face, she enlists. That, Stegner seems to say, is what it takes.

When his fiction leaves the frontier, it often takes with it the same story line: hard fact and experience pinning enthusiasm and idealism. In *All the Little Live Things,* set in 1960s Palo Alto, a pregnant young woman named Catlin (for the American West's great romantic painter) preaches the inherent goodness of nature while slowly, painfully, dying of cancer. The counterculture founders of the University of the Free Mind are brought up on morals charges in the same book. And its crotchety narrator, a retired literary agent, rails against the "intellectual faddism and emotional anarchy and blind foolishness" of his day:

> The whole history of mankind is social, not individual. We've learned little by little to turn human energy into social order. Outside the Establishment these kids despise so much, an individual doesn't exist, he hasn't got any language, character, art, ideas, anything, that didn't come to him from society. The free individual is an untutored animal.

Stegner is a reactionary humanist. He argues against despair, absurdism, entropy, nihilism, anarchy, bohemianism, neuroticism, eroticism, utopianism, violence, depravity, and indifference—just about every radical political, economic, social, or aesthetic option this century has tossed up. (His sole indulgence, predictably, is his radical environmentalism—he flirted in the 1960s with the idea that heaven was a compost.) His reactions are not hasty dismissals. He brings to bear on the problems of his age a formidable and honest intellect grounded in the humanist tradition. He insists on the necessity of man's participation in community as a free, responsible, and progressive intellectual being. Pursuit of the good life, he admits, requires almost unbearable patience, dedication, and sacrifice but the goal is more or less achievable. (Not surprisingly, reading him, for all its rewards, can be like crossing a ploughed field in a thin coat on a cold day, comfortless if not excruciating.)

Perhaps that helps to explain why in 1974, two months back in the country, Stegner felt compelled to piss at the sacred flame of Canada's literary nationalism. It wasn't only the faddishness that bothered him. The idea itself was too easy. It was widely asserted at the time that a truly Canadian literature must of necessity begin with the land; few understood so well as Stegner that the land itself, in all its diversity, might make a single Canadian literature impossible. His essay goes on to suggest that the increasing sectionalization of North America might eventually make the search for the characteristically maritime, southern, or western more relevant than the search for the characteristically Canadian or American. He is not denying the differences between Canada and the U.S. or the impact constitutions and national politics have on people. He is insisting on recognition of the influence of shared "experience, climate, geography, occupational habit, folklore, language and vision."

That may be an extreme statement of the power of environment but the prairies of southern Saskatchewan are nothing if not extreme and powerful, and Stegner is very much of that place:

> I may not know who I am, but I know where I am from. I can say to myself that a good part of my private and social character, the kinds of scenery and weather and people and humor I respond to, the prejudices I wear like dishonorable scars, the affections that sometimes waken me from middle-aged sleep with a rush of undiminished love, the virtues I respect and the weaknesses I condemn, the code I try to live by . . . have been in good part scored into me by that little womb-village and the lovely, lonely exposed prairie of the homestead.
>
> (pp. 57-9)
>
> *Kenneth Whyte, "Prairie Patriarch," in* Saturday Night, *Vol. 106, No. 3, April, 1991, pp. 57-9.*

Jack Miles   (essay date 7 March 1993)

[*In the following essay, Miles examines the "frontier spirit" in Stegner's works and the novelist's literary aims.*]

If there is a turning point in the story of the frontier as Martin Ridge tells it in his marvelously readable and viewable *Atlas of American Frontiers,* it comes in chapter he calls "The Great American Desert." That was the name originally attached to the region we now call the Great Plains, the semi-arid region lying between the 100th meridian (roughly, Dodge City, Kan.) and the Rocky Mountains. The first explorers thought this region, in the words of Major Stephen H. Long, who visited in 1820, "almost wholly unfit for cultivation, and of course uninhabitable

by a people depending upon agriculture for their subsistence." It was John C. Fremont who corrected this view, properly noting that it was the Great Basin, lying between the Rockies and the Sierra Nevada, that was America's desert and that the high plain was suitable both for agriculture and, above all, for grazing.

If the earlier view had prevailed, perhaps the culture of the Plains Indians might have survived longer than it did. That view did not prevail, of course, but one of the most distinguished interpreters of Western life and letters has built a personal and literary synthesis around the view that the West, by its forbidding aridity, has resisted full incorporation into the common culture of the United States.

In *Where the Bluebird Sings to the Lemonade Springs: Living and Writing in the West,* Wallace Stegner puts his personal synthesis on display as never before. Writing at the top of his form in his mid-80s, Stegner, by being different and sometimes baffling, shows why the West itself is different and sometimes baffling. I began to read Stegner in 1978 when I moved to California from points east (Chicago and New York), and I found him, as I think most Eastern critics have, impressive and yet strangely unimpressive. I found his individual works of undeniably high quality, and yet somehow the whole seemed less than the sum of the parts. Stegner just didn't add up. Mormon history, a life of Bernard de Voto, essays on the environment . . . there was too much nonfiction for the serious novelist's own good, and too much fiction for the serious historian's.

In this collection, I think I see what I have been missing.

A first clue: Commenting with great subtlety on Norman Maclean's *A River Runs Through It,* Stegner writes:

> So is this a story of *hubris* in the Bitterroots, of a young god destroyed by pride? If it is, why all that other stuff the story contains . . . so much exposition of the art of fishing, so many stories of fishing expeditions, so many homilies from the preacher father, so many hints about the relations of Norman Maclean with his wife's family? An impressive story as it stands, would this be even more impressive if it were cleaned up, straightened up, and tucked in?
>
> I will tell you what I think. I only think it, I don't know it; but once when I suggested it in Norman Maclean's presence he didn't deny it. Perhaps, like Robert Frost, he thinks a writer is entitled to anything a reader can find in him.

Stegner's secret, so to call it, is that he too is a writer determined not to deny his reader anything in him to which the reader might reasonably be entitled. Not to speak of normal and abnormal, his determination is far from automatic or necessary in a writer. Where does it come from?

A second clue:

> [I]f I had been able to get to Paris I would probably have babbled with the Dadaists in the direction of total intellectual, artistic, and emotional disaffiliation. But there was one trouble. I had grown up a migrant, without history, tradition or extended family, in remote backwaters of the

West. I never saw a water closet or a lawn until I was eleven years old; I never met a person with my surname, apart from my parents and brother, until I was past thirty; I never knew, and don't know now, the first names of three of my grandparents. My family could tell me little, for neither had finished grade school, and their uprooting was the cause of mine. . . .

And so, though I was susceptible to the dialectic of those who declared their independence of custom and tradition and the dead hand of the past, I had no tradition to declare myself independent of, and had never felt the dead hand of the past in my life. If the truth were told, and it now is, I was always hungry to feel that hand on my head, to belong to some socially or intellectually or historically or literary cohesive group, some tribe, some culture, some recognizable and persistent offshoot of Western civilization. If I revolted, and I had all the appropriate temptations, I had to revolt away from what I was, and that meant *toward* something—tradition, cultural memory, shared experience, order. Even my prose felt the pull of agreed-upon grammar and syntax. Eventually, inevitably, I was drawn to what I most needed.

On my desk as I write is a work of extreme Gallic radicalism that I am, personally, unable to read without bursting into guffaws. This is *America* by the revered French sociologist Jean Baudrillard. Baudrillard wishes to devastate. His direction, to use Stegner's words, is indeed that of total intellectual, artistic and emotional disaffiliation. The central interpretive image he applies to this nation, whose soul he finds in the West far more than in the East, is that of the desert. He wishes, for the shock value of it, to show us that we are all living in a mental as well as a physical desert. What gives his work its unintentional hilarity is the writer's unawareness of how very obvious all this is to the average American, whether or not he or she disposes of anything like Baudrillard's rhetorical fluency.

Desert is central in Stegner's thinking too, but *desert* isn't the word he uses. He prefers *aridity,* precisely because that word lowers the intellectual, artistic and emotional stakes, tilts toward the pragmatic and mutes the mythic. Why not play the concept for all its worth, as Baudrillard does? Because Stegner is the son of a father who was twice literally ruined by aridity and because this harsh and broken farmer, if he didn't technically abandon his two sons, at least brought it about that their mother had to place them in an orphanage for a time. Thus was Wallace Stegner disaffiliated. Further, merely philosophical disaffiliation for such a one is all but gratuitous. . . .

Start out with a child trapped in a stifling European bourgeoisie, where everyone is measured and located in advance on the basis of family name, schools attended, accent, dress, religion and political party, and you may well end up in adulthood with an apoplectic Jean Baudrillard, screeching over scorched-earth landscapes and the prospect of scorched-earth human relationships. Start out with child on a bankrupt patch of literally scorched earth, the sun-scorched, parched earth of a ruined farm, outside a built-yesterday town where name, school, speech, religion

and party are fading memories, and you may well end up in adulthood with a Wallace Stegner rescuing a bit of this, a scrap of that, piecing things together, saving as a saver and saving as a savior, cherishing as much tradition as he can, preserving it, and then passing it on in a helpful and pleasant arrangement, for no other reason than that you are his reader and a reader is entitled to everything a writer can give. . . .

The frontier spirit that, in its twilight, shaped Wallace Stegner was a rough spirit. Stegner first fled it, then seized it and turned [it] into his art. The California of 1993, more than a century after the official closing of the frontier in 1890, may seem to suffer more from artificiality and, if you will, from a surfeit of smoothness than from any such roughness. But what a Czech visitor recently described to me as "your incredible California helpfulness" grows in us from a Stegnerian habit of saving what we can from the Western wreckage. The literary equivalent of "California helpfulness," faintly off-putting as it is to Easterners, is what, 15 years ago, made Wallace Stegner seem strange to me. He was calmly putting things together when I believed, instinctively, that what strong writers did was tear things apart. The same quality in him, I recognize with a small jolt, is what now makes him seem familiar. In the interim, I have become a Californian, and a Westerner, myself.

Jack Miles, "Frontier Spirit," in Los Angeles Times Book Review, *March 7, 1993, p. 12.*

INTERVIEW

Wallace Stegner with Steve Proffitt   (interview date 7 June 1992)

[*Proffitt frequently contributes to National Public Radio's* All Things Considered. *In the following interview, Stegner discusses the meaning of the "West" and his concern for the environment.*]

[*Proffitt*]: *Many years ago you called the West "the native home of hope." Do you feel that still applies in 1992?*

[Stegner]: No. I don't know that the decline is permanent, because these are bad times, and in bad times you can't always tell what is permanent and what is temporary. But the general course of the West is away from hope. I grew up in the West a long time ago, and I suppose I have a rather 19th-Century view of it—as opportunity—but that opportunity seems to be changing because of the serious overpopulation. Too many people. That makes hope a little harder to come by.

Someone else said California wasn't part of the West—it was west of the West. How does the state fit into your concept?

It's both within and without the West. It shares that quality of aridity that defines the territory. But it also tips toward Japan, sitting on the Pacific Rim, and is so beautifully endowed that it doesn't have the same sort of austerity that the rest of Westerners have always had to live with. So I would say that it is something of a separate region. . . .

You have battled against the myth of the West—the cowboy on the open range, man conquering nature. Is it that you see that myth as in many ways destructive?

It is. It's also very romantic, the horseman is always a romantic figure. It is destructive when it is applied, as [former President Ronald] Reagan applied it, to all the functions of life. It celebrates the ruthlessness of individualism. I think we do a good deal of harm to ourselves with this myth of pioneering self-reliance. I grew up in pretty frontier circumstances, and what let us survive was not self-reliance, but the cooperation of neighbors. Sometimes, I wish we could go back to the Middle Ages, when individualism had not yet been born.

You wrote almost 50 years ago, in **The Big Rock Candy Mountain,** *about the great American desire to get something for nothing, and about looking at the country as a big real-estate transaction. Have we learned anything in the last 50 years?*

I think some of us have, but not enough. Maybe none of us have learned enough. The people who still think of the West as a kind of warehouse, to be raided and exploited, are, I think, the people who are going to do it in. That has to change, because there is nothing in the history of the exploitation of the West that indicates any great concern for the environment or for the renewability and sustainability of the economy. Nor for the labor force used for that exploitation. Those are all serious mistakes.

You've said the West "encourages a fatal carelessness, a destructiveness, because it seems so limitless." Have we come to the limit of limitlessness?

We have. We better begin to see those limits. I think a lot of people don't want to admit that. And a lot of people don't want to give up the privileges that came with the belief that there were no limits—the cattle and sheep people who are used to the federal subsidies for cheap grazing land, and the people who are used to cheap federal water for irrigation. These are subsidies which grew up with that original carelessness, and they are running out. But the claim on the subsidies is still there.

You once wrote that before we build as much as an outhouse, we should have to file an environmental impact statement, and that we should file it with our conscience. How should we go about redeveloping our attitudes toward the land?

Well, you know, I also said that Columbus should have filed an environmental impact statement when he sailed. We really took over a continent which we assumed was empty, and which was not. We took it over by conquest, and had no sense of responsibility for it, because we hadn't lived with it long enough. The longer we do live with it, the more responsibility we are bound to develop toward it, and, in some ways, that is the grain of hope that I cling to. Because the very fact that much of the West is in feder-

al ownership—that is to say, single ownership and therefore a little more controllable—means that changes can be applied to it more easily. That's the hope. And the hope that we will learn to live in the West in some sort of sustainable way, not doing the kind of damage to the land and water and air that we have done in the past. But that's a big hope.

So this might be what you have termed "a civilization to match its scenery?"

Yeah, and it would leave the scenery pretty much alone. Any desert—and much of the West is, or is very near desert—any desert society that I know of has been either mobile, sparse or both. It's been an oasis society. What we've done is try to engineer the whole thing to fit our own notions—to transport water instead of ourselves. I don't believe in transporting water out of its own basin. Because what you are doing is creating an hydraulic society, and history tells us that these societies always collapse.

So are you saying that we are guilty of a sort of total hubris?

Oh, yes. You could say that in capital letters. It's partly because the country itself is so stimulating, and it enlarges the soul. You think, "God, anything is possible here," and so you go out and try—often with disastrous results.

The West celebrates the ruthlessness of individualism. I think we do a good deal of harm to ourselves with this myth of pioneering self-reliance. I grew up in pretty frontier circumstances, and what let us survive was not self-reliance, but the cooperation of neighbors.

—Wallace Stegner

Let's move the discussion to politics. What about Ross Perot? In some ways, he fits into the portrait you have painted—a picture you say we are to avoid—of someone who sees the world in terms of opportunities for enterprise.

Yes, he scares me because of that entrepreneurial, competitive drive of his. If by any freakish chance he should be elected, I'd bet he would be impeached within two years. He seems the kind of person who is going to be an outrage to every democratic principle, because all of his principles are about business. I think he is a very shrewd manipulator, and he has enough of the populist feel to him to scare me even more. Many demagogues have a populist feel of that kind.

How do you rate George Bush in terms of his efforts on the environment?

His claim to being the Environmental President is a farce. There has never been a President more environmentally negative.

Including Ronald Reagan?

Yes, because Bush inherited eight years of Reagan and just went on even worse. Look at the record—he fights the Clean Air Act, the Clean Water Act, he wants to drill in the last wilderness area in Alaska, he doesn't want to participate in the World Environmental Conference in Rio until he has gutted it in advance. This is no Environmental President.

Do you think a political leader can solve the sort of environmental mess we are in, or do we need some "Earth messiah?"

I think we are going to have some sort of mass conversion—it's got to take hold of more people than it has taken hold of yet. But you know, during the '70s—particularly during the Carter Administration—we had a lot of really good environmental laws passed. Most of those have been systematically subverted or undermined in the last 12 years.

I don't think we need a messiah so much as we need a change of parties—because the Republicans lately have not been good conservationists. They've been pro-business, pro-profit and not pro-environment.

Is it simply a function of capitalism to be unable to exist within a sound environmental policy?

No, I think it's the basic failure of a certain kind of capitalism—a kind which began to be restrained in the United States about 1902, with the antitrust laws. I think, over time, capitalism has learned a great deal, and there are plenty of corporations which do have a responsible attitude toward the environment, because they see their own interest in it. Like Southern California Edison and PG&E—they have power-conservation programs, which are both profitable for them and good for the environment.

What do you say to those many people in cities like Los Angeles, living desperate lives in poverty—people who find environmentalism irrelevant—who say an environmentalist will drive past miles of human suffering to save a tortoise?

There is no excuse for driving by miles of human misery to do anything. But with the increase and condensation of population, there seems to be no solution to human misery—except the control of population, and nobody wants to talk about that. Overpopulation may be one of the biggest problems we face. In the Everglades, when things get dry and the alligators get cooped up in one pool, they begin to eat each other. You have to deal with the human misery, but at the same time you have to prevent the increase of that misery. You cannot forget the environment so you can solve social problems—they must be addressed as a whole.

You have to have jobs. One could be working to clean up the environment. I really believe [Sen. David] Boren has a good idea when he wants to rejuvenate the CCC and the WPA. That will support people and do some good. It may not support profits, but it will support society. The effort to clean up is a tremendous job-making opportunity. Who pays? Either the present or the future, and I would rather see it be the present.

We began by talking about hope. Where do you look when you need to find hope for the future?

I guess to the environmental movement at large. It's much more than just an attempt to clean things up—that's just treating the symptoms. The real work is to somehow generate Earth health, rather than just patching up illnesses. And that idea seems to be very widespread among the young. Very slowly, we are creating an environmental ethic, and that is where my hope lives.

> *Wallace Stegner and Steve Proffitt, in an interview in* Los Angeles Times, *June 7, 1992, p. M3.*

REVIEWS OF STEGNER'S RECENT WORKS

Doris Grumbach   (review date 20 September 1987)

[*Grumbach is an American novelist, critic, and biographer. In the following review of* Crossing to Safety, *she praises Stegner's insights into the lives of married couples, young and old.*]

As I approach 70, I am uncomfortably aware that my generation regards very young writers with suspicion verging on indefensible dislike. We distrust the rapidity of their rise and the size of their monetary success. When blurb writers exult that those in their 20's have written an awesome or amazing or unique first novel, and then followed it, of necessity, with a collection of unmatched or brilliant short stories, we old skeptics shudder. Too fast, too early, empty of real substance, we assure one another. They cannot sustain it. Recklessly they are drawing on their capital.

So I feel great generational pleasure in celebrating the new novel by 78-year-old Wallace Stegner, who published his first novel, ***Remembering Laughter,*** 50 years ago. In the following years he published 13 works of fiction and 10 books of nonfiction. At the same time, the Iowa-born writer taught at a number of places, settling down in 1945 at Stanford University, where he remained for the rest of his academic life. He was a noted teacher of writing whose selfless devotion to his students was rewarded when Stanford named its prestigious writing fellowships for him. In the process of moving through this lifetime of achievement, Mr. Stegner won the Pulitzer Prize for his 1971 novel, ***Angle of Repose,*** and the 1977 National Book Award for ***The Spectator Bird.***

Clearly Mr. Stegner has not gone unnoticed. But neither is he a household name, as he deserves to be. What I am extolling here is the appearance of a superb book at the other end of a consistently accomplished career, heartening proof that the novelist has continued to grow, is still maturing in his late maturity, has added to his accomplishments a sympathy for his contemporaries' condition: the miseries of old age, the resentment of physical decay and, most of all, the pleasures of enduring marital love.

Crossing to Safety moves back and forward in the middle of the 20th century, from 1937 to 1972, when the narrator, Larry Morgan, and his polio-crippled wife, Sally, return after many years to the Lang family compound in Vermont to attend a farewell picnic. Charity Lang and her husband, Sid, have been friends of the Morgans since both men were instructors in English in Madison, Wis.

The couples could not have been more different. The Morgans were young, struggling and happy. "In a way, it is beautiful to be young and hard up. . . . Deprivation becomes a game," says Larry. They are from the West; the Langs are Eastern and Harvard, Sid is Jewish, both are determinedly ambitious, and their families are wealthy. The Langs are attracted to the Morgans by Larry's literary talent: during his temporary appointment at the university he has already begun to publish short stories.

The novel's fulcrum is Charity, a strong woman whose sense of how things should be done extends to everyone around her. Her husband is weakened by her strength, her friends rebel against her need to control. Larry says of her, "And with Charity it was organization, order, action, assistance to the uncertain, and direction to the wavering." When she knows she is dying of cancer, she decides to control and direct the conditions of her death. It is to this occasion that the Morgans are recalled, and her preparations for her own dying give rise to Larry's introspection:

> What ever happened to the passion we all had to improve ourselves, live up to our potential, leave a mark on the world? . . . We all hoped, in whatever way our capacities permitted, to define and illustrate the worthy life. With me it was always to be done in words. . . . Leave a mark on the world. Instead, the world has left marks on us. We got older. Life chastened us so that now we lie waiting to die. . . . And all of us, I suppose, could at least be grateful that our lives have not turned out harmful or destructive.

There is some question about Charity's life, for her determination is not so easily dismissed as harmless. The bittersweet tone of Larry's reminiscences is echoed in his thoughts about Charity's family, the Ellises:

> How do you make a book that anyone will read out of lives as quiet as these? Where are the things that novelists seize upon and readers expect? Where is the high life, the conspicuous waste, the violence, the kinky sex, the death wish? . . . Where are speed, noise, ugliness, everything that makes us who we are and makes us recognize ourselves in fiction?

Mr. Stegner's success with this story lies precisely in the absence of all these currently popular subject matters and the presence of quiet re-examination of what, close to the end, seems to have made a life not only worth living but happy and almost fulfilled. Larry realizes that "Sid Lang best understands that my marriage is as surely built on addiction and dependence as his is." Sid needed Charity's domination even as it debilitated him. Larry is tied by the inexorable chains of love to Sally, whose polio is doomed to return at the end of her life. He doubts if he can survive her, just as the reader is left to wonder, until the last lines of the book, if Sid will survive Charity.

Mr. Stegner is a wise man as well as a skilled writer. His narrator, very close to him in biographical detail as well as quality of mind, recognizes the truth that the affliction of a loved one (Sally) can be "a rueful blessing. It has made her more than she was; it has let her give me more than she would ever have been able to give me healthy; it has taught me at least the alphabet of gratitude."

John Webster (in *Westware Hoe*) said that "old lovers are soundest." Mr. Stegner has built a convincing narrative around this truth, has made survival a grace rather than a grim necessity, and enduring, tried love the test and proof of a good life. Nothing in these lives is lost or wasted, suffering becomes an enriching benediction, and life itself a luminous experience.

> *Doris Grumbach, "The Grace of Old Lovers," in* The New York Times Book Review, *September 20, 1987, p. 14.*

James R. Hepworth   (review date July-August 1990)

[*Hepworth is an American critic and educator. In the following review of the* Collected Stories of Wallace Stegner, *Hepworth praises Stegner as a master of the short story.*]

Anne Tyler recently remarked upon how much she regretted the passing of Wallace Stegner's "short story days," for clearly, she said, Stegner "never set out to write a mere short story. It was all or nothing." That statement, of course, could stand for everything Wallace Stegner has written. Nevertheless, despite his versatility as a novelist, historian, cultural and literary critic, conservationist, and biographer, Stegner's genius is nowhere better employed than in the short story form.

"It seems to me a young writer's form," he comments in his introduction, "made for discoveries and nuances and epiphanies and superbly adapted for trial syntheses." Judging by the thirty-one classic stories he chose for this volume, Stegner's own trial syntheses have resulted in the kinds of expansions and growth we might expect to find in an old growth forest of redwoods but seldom in a human life. For one thing, the range of the stories is itself extensive, not only in terms of their thematic depths and heights, but also in their genetic variety. As a species, Stegner's stories assume a number of guises within the form. At one extreme, we have novellas like *Field Guide to the Western Birds* and *Genesis;* at the other extreme, he presents us with brief flowers of the form like **"Bugle Song"** or **"The Volcano"** that burst into brilliance in a matter of five or six pages. In between those extremes, we get a variety of subspecies. The result is a tour de force in American fiction, a microcosmic history of the short story form as exemplified by a modern master of the genre.

Like Faulkner, Stegner frequently cannibalized his short stories to feed his novels. Although he published a story as recently as 1987, essentially he stopped sending stories out in 1962, the same year he published his splendid but unclassifiable book, *Wolf Willow,* from which three stories were taken for this new collection. In all, Stegner has published fifty-seven short stories, but in putting them together for this volume, he tells us that he "made no attempt to arrange" them "so that they make a nice progression from simplicity to complexity, past to present, primitive to civilized, sensuous to intellectual." On the contrary, he claims, "They lie as they fell, perhaps because I don't believe there is any clear progression to illustrate, or that this journey has any clear destination." In other words, the arrangement of *Collected Stories* strictly adheres to the arrangement of the stories in his two previous collections, *The Women on the Wall* and *The City of the Living,* to which Stegner adds uncollected stories from the pages of *Harper's, Esquire,* and the like. Still, the arrangement is anything but chronological—or haphazard. In the first third of the new book, we find a story published in 1938 ("**Bugle Song**") sandwiched between a story from 1946 ("**The Women on the Wall**") and another from 1945 ("**Balance His, Swing Yours**").

The point here, however, is that the jolt of recognition that grabs us in virtually every one of these stories is comparable to the shock from an electric fence; their charge hurts, but it's hard to let go. Stegner's truths defy any sort of logic or attempt at systematic analysis. The "progression" in the book is circular rather than linear, full of point and counterpoint, rather like a composition by Bach. For this reader's money, of the two novellas—*Field Guide to Western Birds* and *Genesis—Genesis* alone is worth the price of admission. One is not so much "better" than the other as it is different. *Field Guide* (1956) takes for its setting contemporary California and the moneyed-leisure class; *Genesis* (1959) unloads a neorealistic but parabolic tale worthy of Conrad or Melville that begins with a young man's romance with the frontier in 1909 Saskatchewan and ends a few days later inside a lineshack during a November blizzard. But as Anne Taylor put it, to call *Genesis* a western would be like calling *Anna Karenina* a romance. To compare the two novellas is like comparing sandstone and granite. "They don't give you enough time in a single life to figure anything out," Stegner's semi-reliable narrator, Joe Allston, complains at the end of *Field Guide.* And the same is true of even the shortest Stegner short story. Stegner's artifice and craft divert us with verisimilitude just long enough to hook us without our knowing it. But in due time, all hell breaks loose, at which point Stegner bluntly, and even brutally, reminds us that we are swimming in obscure waters, dealing in mysteries whose forces he evokes with extraordinary power. There is never any question about who is in control. In a matter of a few hundred words, Time itself, in a Stegner story, can come crashing down like a steel curtain.

Here I'm thinking of stories like "**The Colt**" or "**The Chink**" or "**Going to Town**," where the rites of passage sting us back into our individual childhood Edens with sweet little death-pangs: the parental lie whose truth the child perceives not in the telling, but in the experience itself, when the prized colt's "bloated, skinned body" gets glimpsed on the scrap heap as the family embarks on its exodus from home. Or, when a young Anglo boy learns a complex lesson in race and culture as the result of his passive participation in a Halloween prank that results in the death of an adult Chinese friend. In these stories

knowledge always surpasses understanding and no systematic explication of Stegner's text can ever encompass their meaning. Indeed, while analysis may personally benefit us by verifying our responses and those elements in the story that we most respond to, Stegner's artistic ambiguity will elude even the most cunning critic.

What galvanizes our respect, and what ought to prompt mainstream American publishers to include Stegner in their anthologies, can probably be reduced to a single (overused) word: *style*.

—James R. Hepworth

As with the modern short story, a typical Stegner story generally limits itself to those unified actions and characters exclusively essential to its development. It spans space and time with compression and only in passing borrowing Ibsen's century-old technique of "uncovering." Thematically, however, Stegner's stories lack the sense of alienation and spiritual malaise associated with the modern and "postmodern" periods when he composed them (or, for that matter, with contemporary experimental fiction). In many of the stories, the American frontier is still very much alive, even in Vermont. Men still split wood (but so, incidentally, do women). For the most part, though, characters and settings, the narrative points of view, and even the plots of these stories are simply too diverse to permit us to easily classify Stegner's short fiction. In "**The City of the Living**," the father vacationing in Egypt who must keep night vigil over his feverish son and, despite the "propitiating science" of "modern medicine," suffer through his parental fears, could be any American father, although there is no mistaking his individuality. The World War II army wives who queue up for mail and practice indiscretions in "**The Women on the Wall**" might just as well be the temporary widows of the Vietnam War. Likewise, in "**The Traveler**" the man whose car breaks down in sub-zero weather on a midwestern back road, who finds himself in the lonely farmboy who helps him survive, is that universal American orphan. The generosity and native hopefulness of Stegner's own personality infuses even the most recalcitrant of his protagonists with a heroic quality, setting Stegner apart even from those of his contemporaries like John Cheever and William Styron who are perhaps closest to him in terms of artistic temperament. Like Cheever, Stegner can cast a cold eye upon a scene with an uncanny instinct for rendering complex ironies.

In some ways, the publication of *Collected Stories* could not have arrived at a better time. Written long before the cool-surface terseness of minimalism caught hold in the late 1970s and formally climaxed in the so-called "sudden fiction" of the very short story, yet full of the precision that requires the total participation of both reader and writer to achieve complete meaning, Stegner's stories remind us that "progress" is a useless word in relationship to art. Over the course of sixty years, his short stories have endured at least as well as the petroglyphs hidden away in those far reaches of the southwestern canyon lands that he has helped preserve from "civilization." Alvin Toffler informs us that, "the computer operated micro printers available today on our planet can turn out 20,000 lines of verbiage every minute—which is 200 times faster than anyone on earth can read." At a time, then, when we continue to exaggerate and overvalue mechanical virtues, let me conclude with a warning: It might be very discouraging for an ambitious short story writer to read Stegner's *Collected Stories* and witness what one human being has done with only a crude instrument, a little pigment, and some stolen time. On the other hand, it might also prove to be literally inspiring.

As with Stegner's novels, a close look at the settings of his stories will deter any serious reader from imposing upon Stegner the kind of regional identification that his critics generally insist upon. Stegner's locales are largely places, as Melville might urge us to acknowledge, not on any map. True places never are. Yet out of his love for the particular, Stegner provides us with their coordinates in order to make them real: Hollywood, Vermont, Salt Lake City, California, Saskatchewan, Egypt, France, the Philippines. What galvanizes our respect, however, and what ought to prompt mainstream American publishers to include Stegner in their anthologies, can probably be reduced to a single (overused) word: *style.* Like the man himself, these stories have it in abundance.

> *James R. Hepworth, "A Crude Instrument, a Little Pigment & Some Stolen Time," in* The Bloomsbury Review, *Vol. 10, No. 4, July-August, 1990, p. 5.*

Evan S. Connell   (review date 22 March 1992)

[*Connell is an American novelist, short story writer, and critic whose works include* Mr. Bridge *(1969) and* Mrs. Bridge *(1959). In the following review, he offers a highly favorable assessment of Stegner's essay collection* Where the Bluebird Sings to the Lemonade Springs.]

Wallace Stegner feels a deep affinity with the arid western states, whose dimensions and clarity excite his senses. During the introduction to these 17 essays [in *Where the Bluebird Sings to the Lemonade Springs*] he rhetorically asks why deserts should be asked to blossom. Deserts have their own ecological systems, "including the creosote-ring clones that are the oldest living things on earth." This remarkable shrub, symbolizing continuity, is an image he employs more than once to express his anger at the damage wreaked by developers—among them the U.S. government. "The deserts were doing all right," he continues, "until we set out to reform them . . . " By reformation is meant irrigation, and he points out that most civilizations relying on irrigation have collapsed, either because of salinization or an accumulation of engineering problems. Los Angeles may be next.

Stegner has lived in much of the West. His father was a rolling-stone optimist who believed there must be a promised land where hand-outs grow on bushes and where the bluebird sings to the lemonade springs. From North Dakota the family rolled along to Washington, up to Saskatchewan, down to Montana, Utah, Nevada, California. This meant a childhood Stegner describes as culturally undernourished, so it is no great surprise that he settled in the Coast Range foothills near Stanford University, where he has spent almost five decades writing and teaching. Many honors and a long list of books including *The Big Rock Candy Mountain, Angle of Repose* and *Beyond the Hundredth Meridian* testify to his distinction as a writer, while a long list of accomplished writers who studied with him will testify to his eminence as a teacher.

His affection for remote areas of the west is never more apparent than in the essay entitled **"Crossing into Eden,"** about a pack trip to a lake high in the mountains of northeastern Utah. By the time he has taken us on a 14-mile hike through meadows bursting with flowers and icy creeks and resinous forest—up and up and farther up to an altitude of 10,000 feet—by the time Stegner reaches his campground we ourselves feel a serious urge to go there, blisters and sunburn be damned. "The land fell away at our feet . . . below us was deep water; spread out before us was an oval lake. We were between curves of blue like a clam between the valves of its shell. Nobody said a word." He then informs us that ordinarily he would not tell anybody how to get to Eden because such places cannot survive much advertising. However, he does let us know where he went, even providing the name and post office address of his guide. Unfortunately for those who are about to make plans, Stegner took that trip in 1923.

Nine essays in *Where the Bluebird Sings to the Lemonade Springs* concern western writing and writers. Just about everything he has to say on these subjects is measured and thoughtful. He might disagree with something in a book or with some writer's premise, but the commentary will be respectful; his rage or contempt is reserved for avaricious land developers, myopic politicians and bureaucrats.

There are reflections on becoming a writer—youthful uncertainty, acknowledged ignorance, the slow understanding that what is worthwhile does not depend on a calculated formula or method. Still, with his usual equipoise, he admits that whatever method enables a writer to lay bare the mystery within the rock must be legitimate.

These literary meditations include an open letter to the Kentucky novelist, essayist and farmer Wendell Berry. Stegner congratulates Berry on a recent work, *What Are People For?* "I want to praise not only the book but the man who wrote it, and it embarrasses my post-Protestant sensibilities to tell a man to his face that I admire him." Such restraint is characteristic of Stegner.

He comments on various western authors, from the relatively unknown Norman MacLean (*A River Runs Through It*) to the celebrated John Steinbeck, and in **"Walter Clark's Frontier"** he addresses one of the best.

Walter Van Tilburg Clark almost always is identified as the author of *The Ox-Bow Incident,* starring Anthony Quinn—which is inadequate. Clark wrote several very fine short stories, notably "The Wind and the Snow of Winter," "Hook," and "The Portable Phonograph." Like

Stegner, he was a teacher for many years, and one can't help wondering if the energy consumed by students might explain why he did not write more. Stegner doesn't think so, but admits to being puzzled. Clark spent a great deal of time editing the memoirs of a forgotten pioneer named Alfred Doten. Why? Stegner observes that quite a few American writers who grew up on a barely civilized frontier have turned from fiction to history: Bernard DeVoto, Paul Horgan, H. L. Davis, A. B. Guthrie. Perhaps, he suggests, after having explored the settlement of their region and the difficulties of growing up, they could find little impetus to fiction either in the past or present.

Walter Clark was a bit of a mystic, which Stegner is not, yet these two shared a common response to that vast territory they called home:

> Almost as much as he, but later in my life, I grew to hate the profane western culture, the economics and psychology of a rapacious society. I disliked it as reality and I distrusted it when it elevated itself into the western myths that aggrandized arrogance, machismo, vigilante or sidearm justice, and the oversimplified good-guy/bad-guy moralities . . .

This theme appears, disappears, and reappears like a western stream subsiding into the desert only to emerge closer to the sea.

Wallace Stegner has given us a cautionary book, full of grace, full of apprehension, carefully balanced. (pp. 1-2)

> Evan S. Connell, *"Crossing into Eden," in* Book World—The Washington Post, *March 22, 1992, pp. 1-2.*

OBITUARIES AND TRIBUTES

William H. Honan   (obituary date 15 April 1993)

[*Honan is an American editor and biographer. In the following obituary, he reviews Stegner's career and notes his commitment to the environment.*]

Wallace Stegner, the novelist and short-story writer whose work celebrated the American West and won him the country's highest literary awards, died on [13 April] at St. Vincent Hospital in Santa Fe, N. M. He was 84 and lived in Los Altos Hills, Calif.

The cause of death was respiratory failure, said Lynn Stegner, his daughter-in-law. On March 28, Mr. Stegner was seriously injured in a traffic accident in Santa Fe, where he had gone to give a lecture.

In a literary career that covered more than 50 years and produced more than two dozen novels, historical works and collections of stories and essays, Mr. Stegner found the Western frontier spirit of boundless optimism receding. But he saw in its place, as he once expressed it, "a re-

spect for the heroic virtues: fortitude, resolution, magnanimity."

His preoccupation with these upbeat qualities separated Mr. Stegner's writing from the despair and alienation in the work of many of his contemporaries. His characters seem propelled by the author's conviction "that man, even Modern Man, has some dignity if he will assume it, and that most lives are worth living even when they are lives of quiet desperation."

To appreciate the West, he once remarked, "You have to get over the color green; you have to quit associating beauty with gardens and lawns; you have to get used to an inhuman scale."

He also turned upside down the stereotypical characters of the West: the barroom beauties with hearts of gold and the lean, heroic cowboys in their chaps and Stetsons. In *Remembering Laughter,* he portrayed two sisters who are a complex mixture of youthful exuberance, penance and hatred; in *All the Little Live Things* (1967) and later in *The Spectator Bird* (1976), the recurring character Joe Allston, a fearful retired literary agent, struggles to extricate himself from a tragic past.

"The West does not need to explore its myths much further, it has already relied on them too long," he told a reporter in 1981. "The West is politically reactionary and exploitative; admit it. The West as a whole is guilty of inexplicable crimes against the land: admit that, too. The West is rootless, culturally half-baked. So be it."

Despite all this, he continued, the West remains "the New World's last chance to be something better, the only American society still malleable enough to be formed."

He won the 1972 Pulitzer Prize in fiction for *Angle of Repose,* a novel about an elderly, sickly man who learns to accept his anguish when he studies the lives of his grandparents and realizes that their lives, too, left much to be desired.

In 1977, he won a National Book Award for *The Spectator Bird.* His work has been nominated several times for the National Book Critics Circle Awards, including this year for a 1992 collection of essays, *Where the Bluebird Sings to the Lemonade Springs: Living and Writing in the West.*

Among his most popular novels was *The Big Rock Candy Mountain* (1943), a semiautobiographical work in which two sons learn to cope with life by coming to understand their father's failings. When Mr. Stegner was a child, his father had shuttled the family from North Dakota to the state of Washington, and from Saskatchewan to Montana and Utah, pursuing the dream of an easy life that was always just out of reach. The book's title is taken from the hobo song about an imaginary land where life is never less than ideal.

An important theme of that and other works was the fragility of the environment. In an essay for *The Saturday Review* in 1964, Mr. Stegner compared the way Americans were learning about the environment to the cracker-barrel joke about the boy who twisted the mule's tail and "isn't as pretty as he once was, but knows more."

"There is nothing in the history of the West that indicates any great concern for the environment or for the renewability and sustainability of the economy," he said in an interview last year. "Nor for the labor force used in that exploitation. Those are all serious mistakes."

His *Beyond the Hundredth Meridian* is a biography of John Wesley Powell, who explored the Colorado River. *Wolf Willow* is a history of Saskatchewan.

Another significant nonfiction work was *One Nation* (1945), a collection of photographs illustrating the corrosive effect of racial prejudice in the United States. The book was a co-winner of the Anisfield-Wolfe Award for the best book of the year on race relations.

Besides writing and editing, Mr. Stegner had a long career as a teacher of creative writing and literature at the University of Utah, the University of Wisconsin, Harvard University and Stanford University, where he was the director of the Creative Writing Center from 1945 until his retirement in 1971.

His students at Stanford included a number who went on to become notable writers, including Larry McMurtry.

Wallace Earle Stegner was born on Feb. 18, 1909, in Lake Mills, Iowa, the son of Scandinavian immigrants. He received a bachelor's degree from the University of Utah in 1930, a master's degree from the University of Iowa in 1932 and a doctorate from Iowa in 1935.

He then taught English at the University of Utah, and began his literary career in earnest after winning a $2,500 Little, Brown novelette contest in 1937 with *Remembering Laughter,* a tale about an adulterous triangle in Iowa farm country.

In addition to his daughter-in-law, he is survived by his wife, Mary; a son, Page Stegner, who is a novelist and professor of American literature and creative writing at the University of California at Santa Cruz, and three grandchildren.

William H. Honan, in an obituary in The New York Times, *April 15, 1993, p. B8.*

David Streitfeld   (obituary date 15 April 1993)

[*In the following article, Streitfeld profiles Stegner's life and career.*]

Maybe everyone has to die eventually, but it seems particularly cruel that Wallace Stegner did so Tuesday night via that most ubiquitous of modern death traps, the car.

Born in 1909, the novelist, historian and environmentalist hero had a ringside seat to watch the explosive growth of the automobile as a tool for settling and eventually suffocating the desert West he championed and loved. His death from injuries in a March 28 traffic accident in Santa Fe, N.M., makes it look as if the automobile has finally won.

In a novel, this wouldn't wash. The irony is too easy. During the 25 years Stegner ran the writing program at Stanford University, he would have discouraged students from using such an ending, and he certainly wouldn't have allowed it in his own work. Novels like *The Big Rock Candy Mountain, Angle of Repose* and *Crossing to Safety* disdain cheap tricks, evoking instead a world where nature is both inviting and imposing, friendship matters, marriages endure and man, for all his faults, is a relatively civilized creature.

People must be having trouble finding these qualities in the real world, because they've turned increasingly to Stegner's work. His readership grew tremendously in the last decade, and his last public appearances were as close to a revival meeting as you can get with book-toting urbanites.

Take a reading he did several years ago at Politics & Prose on upper Connecticut Avenue, the headquarters of the local Stegner fan club. During the first part, when he read a story, it was impossible even to get in the store. Those who had arrived late were reduced to standing outside, noses pressed to the glass and helpless yearning looks on their faces, like starving urchins in a remake of *Oliver Twist.*

As for the autographing segment, it went on for hours. People kept insisting on a chat. I asked Stegner about this later, and he shrugged it off. "I have a lot of former students here in Washington," he explained. Somehow, that explanation wasn't one of his more convincing ones.

Stegner once broke his life down to segments: "My first 15 years were migrant and deprived, my next 15 aspiring and academic and literary and deprived, my last 50-odd academic and literary and not so deprived."

But it was the first 15 that counted. In one of his best books, *Wolf Willow,* he describes his boyhood from a variety of viewpoints: historical, fictional, reminiscence. They shade into and reinforce each other, producing a stirring account of what it was like to live in the Cypress Hills—on the border between Montana and Saskatchewan, forsaken by God and just about everyone else—in the second decade of this century. One day, it'll be considered a classic autobiography.

The family arrived by stagecoach and struggled as subsistence farmers. For a boy, it was a wild and wonderful life. Stegner and his brother trapped the river in the summer and went ice-sailing in the winter, baked the white mud in the oven to make marbles and herded the local cows. Young Wally didn't see a lawn or a bathtub or a toilet until he was 12 and they moved to the relative metropolis of Great Falls, Mont.

In Cypress Hills, a dentist appeared once a year, "and in a week did more harm than an ordinary dentist could have done in a decade." There weren't many neighbors—just the family and the wind and the sky.

Stegner's fiction and nonfiction outlined the sometimes loving, frequently troubled relationship Americans have with their landscape—whether as majestic and complex as the Western deserts or as apparently simple as the Vermont vacation campground. He once wrote that his ne'er-do-well father, George, did in his lifetime more environmental damange than he could have repaired in another lifetime. Since his father couldn't fix things, Stegner took on the job himself.

He lobbied and wrote proclamations very effectively, but he also inspired merely by writing about the physical world as well as any American in this century. A paragraph plucked at random from *Wolf Willow,* about southern Saskatchewan:

> Across its empty miles pours the pushing and shouldering wind, a thing you tighten into as a trout tightens into fast water. It is a grassy, clean, exciting wind, with the smell of distance in it, and in its search for whatever it is looking for it turns over every wheat blade and head, every pale primrose, even the ground-hugging grass. It blows yellow-headed blackbirds and hawks and prairie sparrows around the air and ruffles the short tails of meadowlarks on fence posts. In collaboration with the light, it makes lovely and changeful what might otherwise be characterless.

Stegner's home in Saskatchewan has recently been restored. He said he intended to haunt it, "just to keep track of what goes on." It's difficult to predict these things, but it seems likely he'll be haunting a few bookstores as well. A dozen or so paperbacks are in print from Penguin, in itself a fair start on literary immortality. People who like one generally like another; if you line them up, they read like a long autobiography, which in a sense they are.

Besides *Wolf Willow* (1962), there's *The Big Rock Candy Mountain* (1943) about his steadfast mother and wandering father, who hoped to strike it rich and never did. *Recapitulation* (1979) arose out of the writer's teenage and college years in Salt Lake City, while the experience of living among the Mormons eventually produced two fine nonfiction books. *Crossing to Safety* (1987) details his young married life toward the tail end of the Depression.

That last one is particularly popular—although as Stegner pointed out, there's not a murder, divorce, gun or hot sex scene in it.

"Nothing there to strain the acting powers of Clint Eastwood or Cher," he commented. "Over the course of 30 years these couples have children, suffer disappointment and illness, make do, put one foot after the other, survive, and are bent but not broken by their experience."

That's how most people live, of course, and it's why they like Stegner. In his books, they see their own lives reflected, enhanced, given meaning. His formula was straightforward: take human experience, and just add art. (pp. C1-C2)

> *David Streitfeld, in an obituary in* The Washington Post, *April 15, 1993, pp. C1-C2.*

Bob Sipchen   (essay date 16 April 1993)

[*In the following article, several of Stegner's noted stu-dents, admirers, and colleagues reminisce about his life and work.*]

There's this image of the Wild West as the home of rugged individualists, lonely grizzled souls who got no need for no one or no dang thing.

Wallace Stegner's death [on April 13] though gives that myth perspective.

Across the United States, phones rang with word that the writer, teacher and historian had died in Santa Fe, from complications suffered in a March 28 traffic accident.

Stegner, 84, has been widely eulogized since, praised for his more than two dozen books that included the Pulitzer Prize-winning novel *Angle of Repose,* and *The Spectator Bird,* which won a National Book Award in 1977.

Many also noted that he founded the creative writing program at Stanford University, and that a number of his students went on to achieve more literary celebrity than their mentor—Ken Kesey, Larry McMurtry, Tillie Olsen and Robert Stone.

But it isn't just the unusually tight-knit community of students who took notice of "Wally's" passing. A loosely knit network of friends, professional acquaintances, mere professional admirers—some now doing the most to interpret, redefine and protect the West—pondered the loss.

Ivan Doig, author of numerous books about the Pacific Northwest including *This House of Sky: Landscapes of a Western Mind,* says

> there's a broader rainbow of work from Stegner almost than was imaginable. He wrote short stories, novels, essays, history, biography, and a magical book we can't even classify—*Wolf Willow.*
>
> There's an entire body of literature from this one homestead kid. That seems to me one of the literary miracles of all American history.

Others were equally effusive:

Novelist Robert Stone, one of Stegner's more celebrated Stanford students, says that his mentor's influence as a writer and teacher extended well beyond his academic sphere.

Stegner's writing

> reflected the changing of the West, the changing of California from the '50s, when he was first out on the West Coast, to the '90s. He was a really good recorder of all that. No one did that better. . . . He was not an eccentric stylist at all, but his writing was tremendously sound and clear and good.
>
> His work was very like him. It shows a real sense of decency. He really was a kind of mentor and parent to a whole lot of us.

Novelist and teacher William Kittredge says that "once I got it in my head that I wanted to write, Stegner was one of few models I had." Kittredge, whose *The Last Best Place* anthologizes the vast writing wealth that has come out of Montana, says Stegner "gave us all heart. His work showed reverence for the kind of place we grew up."

Before Stegner, he adds, writing about the West, painting about the West and Western movies

> all told the same kind of cowboy and Indian shootout story, the story of white men conquering the West, taking it over and making it their own possession. That was a mythological view, and to many of us who grew up here, sort of nonsensical.
>
> Stegner showed us that there were other stories to tell. We all knew that. But he made it valid to make art out of life in rural Montana.

Author Annie Dillard calls Stegner a wonderful writer. Dillard, whose *Pilgrim at Tinker Creek* won a Pulitzer Prize and whose novel *The Living* was a best seller last year, says Stegner "saw what could be done with Western history. He took 19th-Century West Coast history seriously. That meant a lot to me."

She was particularly impressed with Stegner's novel **Angle of Repose.**

> He had very few characters, very little incident, and what he did was go over it, making it deeper and deeper and deeper, dealing with the woman [his main character] again and again and again until she had a mythological stature. She became figural.

Annick Smith, a writer and filmmaker, says Stegner's reshaping of the Western myth helped make possible the telling of "an honest story about women in the West" in the film *Heartland,* for which she served as executive producer.

Smith, who co-produced the film *A River Runs Through It* and co-edited the anthology *The Last Best Place,* says that Stegner

> showed that it was possible not just to tell stories about "sturdy pioneer women and prostitutes with hearts of gold," but stories about women with specific lives and specific goals who did things that changed the country.

James Welch, a Blackfeet Indian and author of *Fools Crow* and *Indian Lawyer,* appreciates Stegner's portrayal of the West's original inhabitants:

> He created a new image of the contemporary West, complete with its problems, that was different from the romantic, Westward expansion version of Indians.
>
> He got people involved in stories about this new West. His writing was very conscious of its social issues. But he combined everything to tell terrific stories. When you're a great writer, like Wallace was, the story transcends the message in a sense.

Barry Lopez says Stegner "wrote me letters about my work that made my hair stand on end." Lopez, author of the award-winning *Arctic Dreams,* and *Crow and Weasel,* a children's book that Robert Redford has developed for the stage, says Stegner

was the only man whose compliments made me feel I had to do more. A compliment from him meant more than just a slap on the back. It meant: "Good work and you'd better keep working. . . . "

> For writers like me who never took a class with him, he taught us how to behave. He encouraged us to think hard about our responsibilities—not just to language, or, God forbid, to the literary community. But to the larger community.

Stegner's commitment to public citizenship, Lopez believes, may prove the most important part of his multifaceted legacy: "He had an effect we cannot possibly know on land policy. He was sought out by presidents, governors, and secretaries of the interior for probably 40 years."

Secretary of the Interior Bruce Babbitt was acquainted with Stegner and remains an ardent admirer. He says that he'd hoped to meet with Stegner this spring to discuss Babbitt's plan for a new U.S. Biological Survey (based on the Geological Survey).

"Stegner's **Beyond the 100th Meridian** touched my life most deeply," Babbitt recalls.

> I read it in college and it opened me up to a whole new view of the West.
>
> What he taught me with that book was to understand the love-hate relationship between Westerners and the federal government. . . . We in the West would never have made it without this relationship. We would have ruined everything. Now that I'm on the other side, I see the historical tension in that love-hate relationship. That's very important.

Poet, novelist, essayist and Kentucky farmer Wendell Berry studied in Stegner's Stanford program in 1958.

"When I first met Wally, I assumed that I would probably spend my life in some city, probably at a university, far away from my native place," Berry remembers.

> But as it happened, I later decided to return to my own part of the world to live. I became a consciously regional writer, a writer who would write about one place.
>
> At that point he became more to me than simply teacher and writer, but an example, because he is really the best example I know of a writer devoted to his region.

Essayist Gretel Ehrlich, author of the critically acclaimed *Solace of Empty Places,* arrived home Wednesday evening and found five phone messages about Stegner's death from far-flung points.

"That's one of the unusual things about writers who work out of the West—and it has a lot to do with Stegner—there's a kind of bond we have," she says. "He's given us a sense that we belong to this unique and difficult place, and that our common residence here gives us a way of connecting to each other that a lot of writers lack." (pp. E1, E6)

Bob Sipchen, "Best in the West," in Los Angeles Times, *April 16, 1993, pp. E1, E6.*

James D. Houston   (obituary date May-June 1993)

[*An American novelist, nonfiction writer, editor, biographer, educator, and past recipient of the Wallace Stegner Creative Writing Fellowship at Stanford University, Houston has written extensively about the American West. In the following essay, he extols Stegner's life and career.*]

He was the steadiest man I have ever known, steady in his habits, steady in his tastes, in his view of the world. I met him in 1961, last saw him in February 1993, and in all those years the essential things about him had not changed. He knew his mind. He answered his mail. He got his work done in a way that generated the unflagging admiration of any writer who knew the depth of his commitment to the task itself, the daily task. In his eyes there was always a look that matched the effect of his stories—probing, unswerving, humane. Like so many of his characters, Wally Stegner looked straight at the physical and social world and did not flinch at what he saw.

He had a ground-wire that ran deep and kept him anchored to the earth and to the earthly places that had been important to him. In his day-to-day living, and in all of Stegner's books, the sense of place has been essential to an understanding of life. One such place was East End, Saskatchewan, where he spent several boyhood years, a town he often circled back to—in *On a Darkling Plain* (1940), and in his first big success, *The Big Rock Candy Mountain* (1943), and in *Wolf Willow* (1962). Another is Salt Lake City, where he grew up and went to college, locale for his 1979 novel *Recapitulation,* wherein a man returns to his hometown, plays the past against the present, and brings his life full circle.

Coast Range mountainsides, like those surrounding his Los Altos Hills home for forty-five years, provided backdrops for the 1976 novel, *All the Little Live Things,* as well as for major portions of his Pulitzer-Prize winning masterpiece, *Angle of Repose* (1971). Stegner's sense of place and sense for the West as a region involved a good deal more than setting, a good deal more than the skill to evoke a landscape or the feel of a town, what they used to call "local color." Something elemental about the West emerges, comes pushing through his prose. You feel it in numerous individual works, but more impressively in the body of his work taken as a whole, the novels and short stories, the histories and biographies, together with his labors as an active conservationist—the wide-ranging output of his long and amazingly productive career.

Built into these works are levels of perception which come at you sometimes all at once, sometimes singly, like strata seen in a canyon wall. There is the physical and geological west, as an awesome stretch of the Earth's landscape. There is the legendary west, as a vast repository for illusion and fantasy and improbable hope. There is the cultural west, forever locked in its love-hate embrace with the cultural east. And there is the historical west, with its vio-lent and rapacious past that must be understood if we are to survive the present, not to mention the future.

In Stegner's world you do not find many shootouts or Apache raiders looming at the mountain rim to swoop down on a hapless wagon train. "The western past," he said in 1974, "in a lot of people's minds, is the mythic past of the horse opera, which is no past at all. It is an illusion."

Among his few cowboys is Ray Wiley, in the vintage story, **"Carrion Spring,"** (from *Wolf Willow*). Ray's adversary is not a band of outlaws. It is the weather. In the brutal Saskatchewan winter of 1907 he watches thousands of cattle freeze to death. At the taught conclusion, while carcasses rot in the spring thaw, the cowboy decides to stay on to gut it out, in spite of his disaster. Why? He can't exactly say. There is a challenge of such magnitude, he can't bear not to try again. There is also something about the land, the very look of the land. Just as winter turns to spring, the spark of hope flares one more time.

A more characteristic hero in Stegner country is John Wesley Powell, the real-life subject of his novelized biography *Beyond the Hundredth Meridian.* Powell was a naturalist, an explorer, a nineteenth century visionary whose showdown came not in the streets of Dodge City but in the Halls of Congress, where his plan for a manageable water policy for the western states was shot down by the heavy guns of expansionism and runaway development.

Published in 1954, this is essential reading for anyone who wants to understand the role of water in the evolution of western America. The sixty pages describing Powell's harrowing boat trip down the Colorado and through the Grand Canyon are in themselves worth the price of admission. And the issues Powell raised in the 1870s and 80s, raised again by Stegner in the 1950s, are still with us, supporting his contention, as both historian and novelist, that the past illuminates the present—a family's past, a river's past, a region's past—as surely as a coastline or a prairie or a mountain range can bear upon one's character, one's dreams, one's world view.

Last February some of these ideas were still on Stegner's mind. In Sacramento the Center for California Studies was holding its annual conference on the state of the state. "Reassembling California" was this year's theme, and the three-day event was dedicated to Wally, as a writer and a teacher whose work had touched just about every aspect of our western life. Knowing he would be on hand, a large crowd turned out for a Friday morning panel called "The Range of Vision: Wallace Stegner and the West." Four of us had been invited to speak: Patricia Limerick, the University of Colorado Historian; Al Young from Palo Alto, a former Stegner Fellow; Gerald Haslam, writer, and editor from Sonoma State, and me. At the end of the session Wally took the stage and talked for about ten minutes. This was one of his last public appearances, and for most of us it was the last time we would see him.

We had talked about his fiction, his historical work, about his time in Washington, D.C. when Stuart Udall was Secretary of the Interior, and about the writing program he established at Stanford. Several questions from the audi-

There was something of the minister in Wally Stegner, though not the haranguing kind, he was a scrupulously moral writer but not a moralizer. There was something of the prophet about him too, but not the Jeremiah kind. His grasp of history gave him a window on the future, but he leavened his warnings with compassion and a careful, hard-earned wisdom.

—*James D. Houston*

ence had touched upon the role of regions and places, and he came back to this, our attitudes toward the places we inhabit, invoking Mary Austin, and finally John Wesley Powell.

> He was right more than a hundred years ago when he said that in the west there is water enough for about a fifth of the land. And that means no matter what you do with it, whether you're going to have cities, going to use it for agriculture—there is water for about a fifth of the land. And thank God that will leave us some open space, I think, for quite some time.

His voice, as he said these things, was a voice I had been hearing for over thirty years, on and off the page, a voice that requires you to listen, a voice both deliberate and spirited. There was something of the minister in Wally Stegner, though not the haranguing kind, he was a scrupulously moral writer but not a moralizer. There was something of the prophet about him too, but not the Jeremiah kind. His grasp of history gave him a window on the future, but he leavened his warnings with compassion and a careful, hard-earned wisdom.

As he spoke that morning I remember thinking that he looked remarkably fit for 84. He had vigor. His eyes were bright. His newest book was in the stores—***Where the Bluebird Sings to the Lemonade Springs***—and he had readings lined up. At the time there was every reason to believe he would be with us for a good while longer. It made his untimely death in Santa Fe last month a double shock. He passed away too suddenly, and too soon. But his works live on, and they will be with us for a long time to come, a lifetime of solid prose. In six decades of writing he gave us twenty-eight books, plus countless essays, articles and stories, along with a way of looking at America and at the American west, and a way of seeing more and knowing more about ourselves. (pp. 35-6)

> *James D. Houston, in an obituary in* San Francisco Review of Books, *May-June, 1993, pp. 35-6.*

Additional coverage of Stegner's life and career is contained in the following sources published by Gale Research: *Authors in the News,* Vol. 1; *Bestsellers 1990,* Vol. 3; *Contemporary Authors,* Vols. 1-4, rev. ed.; *Contemporary Authors Autobiography Series,* Vol. 9; *Contemporary Authors New Revision Series,* Vols. 1, 21; *Contemporary Literary Criticism,* Vols. 9, 49; *Dictionary of Literary Biography,* Vol. 9; and *Major 20th-Century Writers.*

Obituaries

In addition to the authors represented in the In Memoriam section of the *Yearbook,* the following notable writers died during 1993:

Nina Nikolaevna Berberova
August 8, 1901—September 26, 1993
Russian-born American novelist, biographer, autobiographer, poet, playwright,
educator, and critic

Best known for her autobiography, *The Italics Are Mine* (1969), Berberova was a prominent figure in Russian émigré society. Leaving the Soviet Union in 1922, Berberova lived in Paris from 1925 to 1950, where she wrote for Russian-language newspapers. During this time she also produced several novels as well as the acclaimed biography *Chaikovskii* (1936; *Tchaikovsky*), which attracted widespread attention for its straightforward account of the composer's homosexuality. Berberova emigrated to the United States in 1950 and taught at both Yale and Princeton Universities. Her autobiography was lauded for its vivid and insightful portraits of such émigrés as Vladimir Nabokov and Maxim Gorky. Berberova's other works, particularly *Poems, 1922-1983* (1984) and *The Tattered Cloak, and Other Novels* (1991), have also been highly praised, with critics comparing her style with that of Ivan Turgenev and Anton Chekhov. In 1989 she was named a Chevalier of the Order of Arts and Letters by the French government.

James Bridges
February 3, 1936—June 6, 1993
American film director and screenwriter

Bridges's most famous films include *The Paper Chase* (1973) and *The China Syndrome* (1979). Initially a television actor, Bridges began writing scripts in the late 1950s, getting encouragement from Alfred Hitchcock, for whose television show he wrote several episodes, including the award-winning "The Unlocked Window." Bridges's first film as director, *The Baby Maker* (1970), which starred Barbara Hershey as a surrogate mother for a sterile couple, was followed by *The Paper Chase,* the story of an ambitious young man's journey through law school. After his next film, the small-scale and autobiographical *September 30, 1955* (1977), Bridges was asked by Tennessee Williams to direct the twenty-fifth anniversary revival of *A Streetcar Named Desire* (1947). He then directed *The China Syndrome,* which was nominated for an Academy Award for best screenplay. Bridges also directed *Urban Cowboy* (1979), *Mike's Murder* (1984), and *Bright Lights, Big City* (1988). He was honored on several occasions for his work as both a screenwriter and director.

Leslie Charteris
May 12, 1907—April 15, 1993
English-born American novelist, short story writer, screenwriter, editor, and critic

Regarded as one of the foremost writers of suspense fiction, Charteris is best known for his crime-fighting protagonist Simon Templar, otherwise known as the Saint. Born Leslie Charles Bowyer Yin, Charteris wrote numerous novels and short stories about Templar, whom many reviewers described as a suave modern-day Robin Hood, and was often instrumental in adapting these works for television and film. He was awarded the Diamond Dagger Lifetime Achievement Award by the Crime Writers' Association in 1992.

Lester del Rey
June 2, 1915—May 10, 1993
American novelist, short story writer, editor, author of children's books, and educator

One of the foremost figures of science fiction literature, del Rey wrote over forty books of fiction and nonfiction and edited numerous science fiction anthologies and magazines. Considered a superb craftsman of short fiction, del Rey often addressed themes relating to human-kind's struggle for survival and the impact of machinery and technology on society. Two of his best known novels are *Nerves* (1956), which concerns a near-disaster at a nuclear power plant, and *The Eleventh Commandment* (1962), which chronicles efforts to save humanity through the implementation of a postatomic war breeding program. Some of del Rey's other works include the novels *Day of the Giants* (1959) and *Pstalemate* (1971), as well as the short story collections *Robots and Changelings: Eleven Science Fiction Stories* (1957), *Mortals and Monsters: Twelve Science Fiction Stories* (1965), and *The Best of Lester del Rey* (1978). Until his retirement in 1992, del Rey served as fantasy editor for Del Rey Books, a science fiction imprint that he and his fourth wife, Judy-Lynn Benjamin, established in 1977. Born Ramon Felipe San Juan Mario Silvio Enrico Smith Harcourt-Brace Sierra y Alvarez-del Rey de los Verdes, del Rey published under a variety of pseudonyms, including Philip James, Wade Kaempfert, Philip St. John, Erik van Lhin, and Kenneth Wright.

Peter De Vries
February 27, 1910—September 28, 1993
American novelist, short story writer, poet, and editor

Considered one of America's best comic writers, De Vries is known for his editorial contributions to *The New Yorker* and for such novels as *The Tunnel of Love* (1954), which hilariously chronicles the misadventures of an art editor for a major magazine; *The Mackerel Plaza* (1958), which follows the plight of a widowed minister who faces opposition from his congregation when he expresses an interest in remarrying; and *The Blood of the Lamb* (1962), which traces the suffering of Don Wanderhope, whose belief in God is challenged by the death of his child from leukemia. Employing puns, parodies, aphorisms, and burlesque, De Vries satirized various aspects of modern American society, focusing on characters who recognize the absurdity of their lives yet courageously search for meaning in a purposeless, disordered world. His works often suggest that conformity and domesticity are essential to surviving the chaos of modern life. Several of De Vries's works, including *The Tunnel of Love, Reuben, Reuben* (1964), *Let Me Count the Ways* (1965), and *Witch's Milk* (1968), have been adapted for film. [For further information on De Vries's life and works, see *CLC,* Volumes 1, 2, 3, 7, 10, 28, and 46.]

Federico Fellini
January 20, 1920—October 31, 1993
Italian director, screenwriter, cartoonist, and actor

Considered one of the most influential and original filmmakers of his generation, Fellini is noted for the surreal and perversely lyrical quality of his films. Fellini was initially influenced by the techniques of neorealist filmmakers, which he later expanded to incorporate personal themes and flamboyant imagery often derived from circuses, carnivals, parades, and television. A mixture of fantasy and autobiography characterizes his works, which have been interpreted by critics as exaggerated or distorted reflections of the filmmaker's personal experiences, perceptions, and dreams. Among Fellini's best known films are *La strada* (1954); *La dolce vita* (1960; *La dolce vita*); *Giulietta degli spiriti* (1965; *Juliet of the Spirits*); and *Satyricon* (1969). In addition to the numerous European and American film awards he garnered throughout his career, Fellini won an Academy Award for Lifetime Achievement in 1993. [For further information on Fellini's life and career, see *CLC,* Volume 16.]

Daniel Fuchs
June 25, 1909—July 26, 1993
American novelist, short story writer, and screenwriter

Fuchs contributed significantly to the American-Jewish literary tradition and earned praise from such prominent critics as Irving Howe and Alfred Kazin for his novels *Summer in Williamsburg* (1934), *Homage to Blenholt* (1936), and *Low Company* (1937). Set in the Brooklyn slum where Fuchs was raised, these works, collectively known as *The Williamsburg Trilogy,* depict—with irony, humor, and pathos—the lives of Jewish immigrants who struggled to survive in a world of limited financial and emotional resources. In 1937 Fuchs moved to Hollywood where he became a screenwriter and won an Academy Award for best original story for *Love Me or Leave Me* (1955). Fuchs is also the author of the novel *West of the Rockies* (1971) and *The Apathetic Bookie Joint* (1979), a collection of short stories. [For further information on Fuchs's life and works, see *CLC,* Volumes 8 and 22.]

Karen Gershon
August 29, 1923—March 24, 1993
German-born English poet, novelist, and editor

Gershon, whose real name was Karen Tripp, was best known for her poetry and prose about the Holocaust and the children who survived it. In her first collection, *Selected Poems* (1966), she lamented her sudden separation from her parents, who sent her to England in 1938 as part of the Kindertransport operation, and the guilt she associated with surviving World War II. She attracted further attention as editor of *We Came as Children* (1966), a collection of autobiographical accounts of over two hundred children who survived the Holocaust as refugees. Praised for her insightful verse investigation of a painful and distressing topic, Gershon received the British Arts Council Award for poetry in 1967. Some of her other poetry collections include *Legacies and Encounters* (1972), *My Sisters, My Daughters* (1975), and *Coming Back from Babylon* (1979).

Penelope Ann Douglass Gilliatt
March 25, 1932—May 9, 1993
English novelist, short story writer, screenwriter, film critic, and dramatist

A highly regarded film reviewer for *The Observer* and *The New Yorker,* Gilliatt wrote the critically acclaimed screenplay *Sunday, Bloody Sunday* (1971). Nominated for an Academy Award, the screenplay earned praise for its sensitive treatment of an English man and woman who both fall in love with the same man. Like *Sunday, Bloody Sunday,* Gilliatt's novels and short stories often deal with the shifting sexual and social mores of postwar England and the difficulties involved in initiating and maintaining relationships. Noted for their understated prose style, terse dialogue, and sparse settings, Gilliatt's best-known fiction includes the novels *One by One* (1965), *A State of Change* (1967), and *The Cutting Edge* (1978), and the short story collections *What's It Like Out?* (1968; *Come Back If It Doesn't Get Better*) and *They Sleep without Dreaming* (1985). [For further information on Gilliatt's life and works, see *CLC,* Volumes 2, 10, 13, and 53.]

MacDonald Harris
September 7, 1921—July 24, 1993
American novelist, short story writer, educator, and critic

Harris, whose real name was Donald William Heiney, frequently used such popular genres as the historical novel, the war-adventure novel, and the crime-thriller as frameworks for his fiction. Noted for their irony and humor, Harris's works often focus on the conflict between illusion and reality and have been praised for their thorough attention to historical detail. Additionally a scholar of comparative literature, Harris wrote sixteen novels during his lifetime and received the American Academy and Institute of Arts and Sciences Award for Literature in 1982. Some of his best known novels include *Herma* (1981), *Hemingway's Suitcase* (1991), and *The Balloonist* (1976), which was nominated for a National Book Award. [For further information on Harris's life and works, see *CLC,* Volume 9.]

Jerry Gustav Hasford
November 28, 1947—January 29, 1993
American novelist, screenwriter, and journalist

Best known for his semi-autobiographical novel *The Short-Timers* (1979), which served as the basis for the Stanley Kubrick film *Full Metal Jacket* (1987), Hasford led a colorful, itinerant life devoted primarily to researching subjects for future books. For *The Short-Timers* he drew on his experiences as a combat correspondent with the First Marine Division in Vietnam during the Tet offensive. Hasford was nominated for an Academy Award along with Kubrick and Michael Herr for the *Full Metal Jacket* screenplay. His other books include *The Phantom Blooper* (1990), a sequel to *The Short-Timers,* and *A Gypsy Good Time* (1992).

357

Eleanor Alice Burford Hibbert
1906?—January 18, 1993
English novelist

A prolific and immensely popular romance novelist, Hibbert wrote over a hundred books under several pseudonyms, including Jean Plaidy, Victoria Holt, and Phillippa Carr. As Plaidy, Hibbert focused on English history and royalty, authoring such novels as *Beyond the Blue Mountains* (1947), *The Captive Queen of Scots* (1963), and *The Widow of Windsor* (1974). As Holt, she turned to Gothic themes and settings with such works as *Mistress of Mellyn* (1960) and *The Bride of Pendorric* (1963). Throughout her career, Hibbert remained unforthcoming concerning details of her personal life and claimed that she wrote merely to entertain. [For further information on Hibbert's life and works, see *CLC,* Volume 7.]

Irving Howe
June 11, 1920—May 5, 1993
American critic, essayist, editor, historian,
nonfiction writer, biographer, and autobiographer

Equally well known as a literary critic and political commentator, Howe was one of the "New York Intellectuals," a group of writers and critics who became nationally prominent in the 1940s. As a political activist, he promoted a socialism rooted in the American democratic tradition and founded *Dissent,* a quarterly journal devoted to democratic socialism, in 1953. As a literary critic, he pursued a humanistic approach to literature and was well known for such critical works as *William Faulkner* (1952), *Politics and the Novel* (1957), *Thomas Hardy* (1967), and *The Critical Point: On Literature and Culture* (1973). Concerned over the decline of the Yiddish language, Howe edited several volumes of Yiddish poetry and fiction, introducing English-speaking readers to the work of Isaac Bashevis Singer. His historical work on Eastern European Jewish immigrants, *World of Our Fathers: The Journey of the Eastern European Jews to America and the Life They Found and Made* (1976), received a National Book Award in 1976.

Masuji Ibuse
February 15, 1898—July 10, 1993
Japanese novelist, short story writer, essayist, and poet

Ibuse is best known for *Kuroi ame* (1966; *Black Rain*), a novel about the atomic bombing of Hiroshima. Characterized by a nonjudgmental, observant approach, *Black Rain* compassionately elegizes the victims of the bombing and addresses the problems faced by the survivors. A popular and critically acclaimed writer, Ibuse also wrote several historical novels about Japan before the Meiji restoration—two of which, *Sazanami gunki* (1930-38) and *Wabisuke* (1946), have been collected in *Waves: Two Short Novels* (1986)—and numerous pieces of short fiction. Ibuse was awarded Japan's Order of Cultural Merit in 1966 for *Black Rain* and is considered one of Japan's chief literary figures. [For further information on Ibuse's life and works, see *CLC,* Volume 22.]

Fletcher Knebel
October 1, 1911—February 26, 1993
American novelist, journalist, and nonfiction writer

Best known for the novel *Seven Days in May* (1962), which he co-wrote with Charles W. Bailey II, Knebel was a journalist in Washington, D. C., for over twenty-five years and the author of the well-known syndicated column "Potomac Fever." *Seven Days in May,* which was adapted for film in 1964, concerns an attempt by the American military to take over the United States government and has been praised as one of American literature's most successful depictions of the corruption of power at the national level. In subsequent novels, Knebel treated such political topics as the perplexing issue of a "mentally ill" president in *Night of Camp David* (1965) and black American militancy in *Trespass* (1969). Knebel's works are noted for incorporating elements of adventure and espionage, highly credible political settings, and complex character studies. [For further information on Knebel's life and works, see *CLC,* Volume 14.]

Eugene T. Maleska
January 6, 1916—August 3, 1993
American editor and educator

The crossword puzzle editor at the *New York Times,* Maleska was credited with increasing the difficulty of the daily puzzles and inventing the word games Stepquotes, Diagonograms, and Cryptoquotes. For most of his professional career he was an English teacher and public school administrator in New Jersey and New York. Constructing his first puzzle in 1933, he began supplementing his income by selling his crosswords to local newspapers. His puzzles are noted for their exactitude and their playful sense of humor.

Joseph Leo Mankiewicz
February 11, 1909—February 5, 1993
American screenwriter, film director, and producer

Mankiewicz wrote and directed such classic films as *A Letter to Three Wives* (1949), *All About Eve* (1950), *Julius Caesar* (1953), and *Sleuth* (1972). He began his career as a screenwriter, working on such films as the Oscar-nominated W. C. Fields vehicle *Skippy* (1931), for which he coined the phrase "my little chickadee." His ambition to direct was first realized with *Dragonwyck* (1946), a Gothic thriller, and subsequently with such highly regarded films as *The Ghost and Mrs. Muir* (1947), *Guys & Dolls* (1955), and the Elizabeth Taylor hit *Suddenly, Last Summer* (1959). In addition to the Oscars he won for *A Letter to Three Wives* and *All About Eve,* Mankiewicz was honored by the Directors Guild of America with a D. W. Griffith Award for lifetime achievement.

Robert Clyve Maynard
June 17, 1937—August 17, 1993
Barbadian-born American journalist, editor, and publisher

One of America's most prominent African-American journalists, Maynard was the editor, owner, and publisher of the *Oakland Tribune* from 1983 to 1992. Under his leadership, the newspaper won numerous awards for editorial excellence, including a Pulitzer Prize for photo coverage of the 1989 San Francisco earthquake. Maynard was also known for founding the Institute for Journalism Education at Berkeley, California, a nonprofit organization that has trained more than 600 minority students. Early in his career, Maynard won a fellowship to Harvard's Nieman education program for journalists and later became a reporter for *The Washington Post,* where he won praise for his coverage of the 1968 urban riots. In 1986 Maynard became a regular commentator on the television news program "This Week with David Brinkley." He also served on the boards of the Associated Press, the American Society of Newspaper Editors, and the National News Council.

Norman Vincent Peale
May 31, 1898—December 24, 1993
American preacher, lecturer, nonfiction writer, editor, and essayist

The author of over forty books, many of them on religious and motivational themes, Peale is best known for *The Power of Positive Thinking* (1952), the self-help book that established the genre. In this work Peale stressed that people "manufacture [their] own unhappiness" and that faith in God and themselves—positive thinking—was the key to success and contentment. Though often criticized as somewhat simplistic and promoting egoism, the book was a bestseller for three years and is still in print.

Harrison Evans Salisbury
November 14, 1908—July 5, 1993
American journalist and nonfiction writer

A renowned authority on the Soviet Union and Asia, Salisbury was a Pulitzer Prize-winning foreign correspondent for *The New York Times* and the author of numerous nonfiction books. He won the Pulitzer Prize in 1955 for a series of articles covering Soviet politics which he wrote following his five years as a correspondent based in Moscow. Salisbury's dauntless coverage of the Vietnam War incited the ire of the Johnson Administration when he began reporting that American bombing was causing a horrifying number of civilian deaths and injuries. Although he was publicly accused of treason, his reportage contributed significantly to the escalating anti-War sentiment in America. Salisbury is also noted for being one of several top editors at *The New York Times* who, in 1971, made the historic decision to publish the Pentagon Papers, which disclosed classified information concerning U.S. involvement in Vietnam. The Supreme Court upheld the newspaper's right to publish the documents despite the objections of President Richard Nixon. Salisbury is additionally recognized for such journalistic innovations as the implementation of the *Times* Op-Ed page.

Severo Sarduy
February 25, 1937—August 1993
Cuban novelist, poet, dramatist, essayist, and critic

Sarduy is known for experimental, linguistically complex fiction and poetry in which he explored Cuban culture and the ways in which language creates and transforms reality. A resident of France since leaving Cuba in 1959, Sarduy studied with Roland Barthes and applied structuralism to his critical treatises on Latin American literature. His best known novel *Cobra* (1972; *Cobra*), for which he received the French *Prix Médicis étranger,* follows the transformations of the novel's transsexual protagonist as well as the evolving meanings of the word "cobra" through a series of disjointed images and dialogue. Some of his other works include the novels *Gestos* (1963) and *Maitreya* (1978; *Maitreya*); the novella *De donde son los cantantes* (1967; *From Cuba with a Song*); and the essay collections *Barroco* (1974) and *La simulación* (1982). [For further information on Sarduy's life and works, see *CLC,* Volume 6.]

William Lawrence Shirer
February 23, 1904—December 1993
American journalist, memoirist, novelist, and historian

Shirer is best known for *Berlin Diary: The Journal of a Foreign Correspondent, 1934-1941* (1941) and *The Rise and Fall of the Third Reich: A History of Nazi Germany* (1960). Hoping to become a novelist and poet, Shirer traveled to Paris in 1925, where he eventually served as a foreign correspondent for the *Chicago Tribune.* Later, reporting from Berlin, Vienna, and Prague for the Universal News Service and the Columbia Broadcasting System, he covered events in Nazi Germany and kept a record of his experiences which formed the basis for his *Berlin Diary.* Blacklisted as a Communist sympathizer, Shirer left journalism in 1950. After ten years of research and writing, he published what is considered his best work, *The Rise and Fall of the Third Reich,* for which he received a National Book Award. Some of his other works include *The Traitor* (1950), a novel about an American journalist who joins the Nazis; *The Collapse of the Third Republic: An Inquiry into the Fall of France in 1940* (1969), a study of France's international decline between 1920 and 1940; and *Twentieth-Century Journey: A Memoir of a Life and the Times—The Start, 1904-1930* (1976).

James Radcliffe Squires
May 23, 1917—February 14, 1993
American poet, critic, biographer, editor, and educator

In his verse Squires often drew on his extensive knowledge of Greek mythology to address problems and concerns of modern existence. He also focused on personal themes in such volumes as *Waiting in the Bone* (1973), contemplating such topics as love, loss of innocence, and humanity's relationship to nature. In addition to his poetry collections, which include *Cornar* (1940), *Where the Compass Spins* (1951), and *Fingers of Hermes* (1965), he authored the critical studies *The Major Themes of Robert Frost* (1963) and *Allen Tate: A Literary Biography* (1971). [For further information on Squires's life and works, see *CLC,* Volume 51.]

Robert Atkinson Westall
October 7, 1929—April 15, 1993
English author of children's books, short story writer, critic, and educator

Best known for *The Machine-Gunners* (1975), the story of five British teenagers who find and set up a machine gun in their own private gun-emplacement during World War II, Westall attracted praise and controversy for his mature treatment of violence, sexuality, language, and family tensions in his novels for adolescents. His works often address the power struggle between children and adults and range from realistic stories to time-travel adventures infused with elements of history, mystery, and the supernatural. Noted for his insightful depictions of adolescent characters and the dynamics of children's gangs, Westall received Carnegie Medals, Britain's most prestigious award for children's books, for *The Machine-Gunners* and *Scarecrows* (1980). Some of his other works include *The Wind Eye* (1976), *The Kingdom by the Sea* (1990), and *Antique Dust* (1989), a collection of ghost stories for adults. [For further information on Westall's life and works, see *CLC*, Volume 17.]

Topics in Literature: 1993

AIDS in Literature

INTRODUCTION

First recognized in the early 1980s, AIDS (acquired immunodeficiency syndrome) is an incurable disease caused by the human immunodeficiency virus (HIV). HIV attacks the body's immune system and renders the affected individual highly susceptible to life-threatening infections and diseases. Although the virus can remain dormant for an indefinite period, the disease has thus far always proven fatal to those who develop its advanced symptoms. Transmitted through body fluids, AIDS has tremendously impacted, though is not exclusive to, such "high-risk groups" as intravenous drug users and homosexual men. As a literary topic, AIDS has given rise to a diverse multitude of responses, particularly from gay men, concerning the effects of the disease on infected and healthy individuals, the gay community, and society at large. Most critics therefore have focused on works by gay men, and some, such as Emmanuel Nelson, have argued that "though heterosexual writers have responded to the AIDS crisis with imaginative works . . . their fictions tend to lack the power and poignancy of gay male writing on the subject."

AIDS literature has generally focused on themes of alienation, homophobia, remembrance, and affirmation. The isolation and fear associated with AIDS is particularly explicit in Robert Chesley's drama *Jerker: or, The Helping Hand,* in which Chesley depicts masturbation and phone sex as logical, but ultimately unfulfilling, responses to the anxiety that characterizes homosexual relations in the age of AIDS. Other writers have focused on the interactions between heterosexuals and homosexuals. In the novel *A Cry in the Desert,* for example, Jed A. Bryan describes a fictional research lab in the Nevada desert where gay men are taken to undergo medical experiments before being executed. Despite the horror and despondency associated with AIDS, most literature on the disease has been positive. For instance, in Harvey Fierstein's drama, *On Tidy Evenings,* the wife and gay lover of a man who has died of AIDS learn to respect each other despite their initial hostility. In other works, such as Paul Reed's *Facing It: A Novel of AIDS* and William Hoffman's *As Is,* a gay lover's imminent death becomes the occasion for the renewal of love and commitment. Another prominent theme is the affirmation of the gay experience through remembrance. In their respective novels *The Swimming-Pool Library* and *The Beautiful Room Is Empty,* Alan Hollinghurst and Edmund White reaffirm the value of homosexual love by focusing on the erotic experiences of their protagonists prior to the advent of the disease. In *Afterlife* Paul Monette confronts the problem of AIDS directly, suggesting that love remains possible despite an uncertain future.

As critics have noted, AIDS literature is intimately linked with popular and biomedical discourses about the disease. In examining these discourses, such commentators as Lee Edelman and Susan Sontag have highlighted the social and cultural assumptions that underlie discussions about AIDS. Edelman has argued that discourses on AIDS are inherently homophobic, linking homosexuality with disease and death, while Sontag has pointed out parallels between current metaphoric descriptions of AIDS and earlier depictions of such diseases as syphilis. Overall, critical reaction to AIDS literature has been favorable. While commentators have criticized numerous works for lacking subtlety and sophistication, they have praised many others as highly imaginative works of art that attempt to aestheticize the AIDS experience and find something positive in it. As Shaun O'Connell has remarked: "Though much of the literature that responds to AIDS . . . is pedestrian, repetitive, or special-pleading, all of it resonates with the shock of recognition of the power of AIDS to alter our collective consciousness, to change *all* our lives."

REPRESENTATIVE WORKS DISCUSSED BELOW

Becker, Bill
  An Intimate Desire to Survive (poetry) 1985
Borgman, C. F.
  River Road (novel) 1988
Boucheron, Robert
  Epitaphs for the Plague Dead (poetry) 1985
Bryan, Jed A.
  A Cry in the Desert (novel) 1987
Champagne, John
  The Blue Lady's Hand (novel) 1988
Chesley, Robert
  Jerker: or, The Helping Hand (drama) 1985
Cowen, Ronald
  An Early Frost [with Daniel Lipman] (television drama) 1985
Curzon, Daniel
  The World Can Break Your Heart (novel) 1984
D'Allesandro, Sam
  "Nothing Ever Just Disappears" (short story)

1986; published in *Men on Men: Best New Gay Fiction*

Davis, Christopher
  Valley of the Shadow (novel) 1988

Duplechan, Larry
  Tangled Up in Blue (novel) 1989

Feinberg, David
  Eighty-Sixed (novel) 1989

Ferro, Robert
  Second Son (novel) 1988

Fierstein, Harvey
  *Safe Sex (drama) 1987

FitzGerald, Frances
  Cities on a Hill: A Journey through Contemporary American Culture (nonfiction) 1986

Graham, Clayton
  Tweeds (novel) 1987

Hadas, Rachel
  Unending Dialogue: Voices from an Aids Poetry Workshop [editor] (poetry) 1991

Hoffman, Alice
  At Risk (novel) 1988

Hoffman, William M.
  As Is (drama) 1985

Holleran, Andrew
  "Friends at Evening" (short story) 1986; published in *Men on Men: Best New Gay Fiction*

Hollinghurst, Alan
  The Swimming-Pool Library (novel) 1988

Johnson, Toby
  Plague: A Novel about Healing (novel) 1987

Klass, Perri
  Other Women's Children (novel) 1990

Klein, Michael
  Poets for Life: Seventy-Six Poets Respond to AIDS [editor] (poetry) 1989

Kramer, Larry
  The Normal Heart (drama) 1985
  The Destiny of Me (drama) 1993

Kushner, Tony
  †Millennium Approaches (drama) 1991
  †Perestroika (drama) 1992

Miklovitz, Gloria
  Good-bye, Tomorrow (novel) 1987

Monette, Paul
  Borrowed Time (memoir) 1988
  Love Alone: 18 Elegies for Rog (poetry) 1988
  Afterlife (novel) 1990
  Halfway Home (novel) 1991

Money, J. W.
  To All the Girls I've Loved Before: An AIDS Diary (essays) 1987

Oberndorf, Charles
  Sheltered Lives (novel) 1992

Osborn, Elizabeth M.
  The Way We Live Now: American Plays & the AIDS Crisis [editor] (drama) 1990

Peck, Dale
  Martin and John (novel) 1993

Puccia, Joseph
  The Holy Spirit Dance Club (novel) 1988

Ranson, Rebecca
  Higher Ground (drama) 1990

Reed, Paul
  Facing It: A Novel of AIDS (novel) 1984
  Longing (novel) 1988

Shewey, Don
  Out Front: Contemporary Gay and Lesbian Plays [editor] (drama) 1988

Shilts, Randy
  And the Band Played On: Politics, People, and the AIDS Epidemic (nonfiction) 1987

Sontag, Susan
  "The Way We Live Now" (short story) 1986; published in journal *The New Yorker*

Weir, John
  The Irreversible Decline of Eddie Socket (novel) 1989

White, Edmund
  A Boy's Own Story (novel) 1982
  The Beautiful Room Is Empty (novel) 1988
  The Darker Proof: Stories from a Crisis [editor, with Adam Mars-Jones] (short stories) 1988

*This trilogy comprises the dramas: *Manny and Jake, Safe Sex,* and *On Tidy Evenings.*

†These works are performed as parts one and two of the two-part drama entitled *Angels in America: A Gay Fantasia on National Themes.*

CRITICISM

Shaun O'Connell (essay date 1988)

[*O'Connell is a specialist in Irish and American literature. In the following excerpt, which originally appeared in the* New England Journal of Public Policy *in 1988, he surveys journalism, poetry, and fiction dealing with AIDS.*]

Gradually, the belletristic writing on AIDS has come to terms with the cultural and literary implications of the disease. The sudden appearance of AIDS challenges the abilities of our imaginations to *know.* Writers in various fields and forms have registered their surprise in many ways. The literature of the AIDS era is high-minded, didactic, and direct, though also often comic. This literature documents and articulates a major shift of consciousness which accompanies the disease. Much of the writing that responds to AIDS, literature that describes its effects upon the male homosexual community, is raw, unpolished, angry, contentious, as though shouting might break through the walls of ignorance and indifference surrounding the affected. As we might expect from writings on such a horrific topic, much of the fiction on AIDS presents simple characterizations, types who embody positions in didactic designs, and predictable themes: insistence that attention must be paid to AIDS victims, for we are all, directly or indirectly, AIDS victims. (Many writers urge the use of the more oblique description "person with AIDS," but there is no way to deflect the power of AIDS to create victims.) Many works of fiction on AIDS have the feel of thinly disguised autobiographical testimonies: cries in the gathering darkness. No doubt, in time, given the projected progress of the disease and the growing sophistication of those who seek to translate its implications into art, we will have a distinguished literature on the topic, as we have, say, on the Holocaust. There is yet, however, no work of fiction on AIDS to match Leslie Epstein's novel on the Holocaust, *King of the Jews* (1979), a work that mixes modes, comic and tragic, that deals with personal and ethnic identity—what is a Jew?—in complex and subtle ways, a novel that is sustained by a fully articulated sense of irony.

The best literature on AIDS is found in the theater, for several reasons. Not only has the world of the theater been shaken by the disease, but the theater has long been the proper medium to bear bad tidings in artful designs to affected communities in times of crisis. As the early Abbey Theatre sought to raise Irish consciousness and mobilize its energies; as the Group Theater sought to articulate Depression grievances before audiences of the grieved; so too does AIDS theater seek, sometimes in wonderfully inventive fashions, to shock its audiences with the recognition of its human bond with those stage characters who suffer and find symbolic triumphs over AIDS. However, worthy works on AIDS appear, with increasing frequency, in a variety of other forms: journalism, poetry, and fiction.

In the midst of crises—wars and other disasters, natural and man-made—the documentary impulse is strong. One of the most insightful records of the effects of AIDS upon the male homosexual community can be found in Frances FitzGerald's *Cities on a Hill*. Her book examines several utopian or visionary subcultures in America, ranging from Florida's Sun City to Jerry Falwell's Liberty Baptist Church in Lynchburg, Virginia. Her study of the gay male community focuses on the Castro, an area of San Francisco where, in the mid-1970s, homosexual men established their own cultural identity, and where they eventually, in the 1980s, saw their lives and community divide under the threat of plague. FitzGerald approaches her subject with the eye of a cultural anthropologist, aware of the shifts in values and alterations of sensibilities which accompany this decade of change. Men had traveled far, geographically and personally, to come into their own sexual identities—which often meant sexual promiscuity in the Castro's gay bars and bathhouses—only to discover that they had to adapt to a scourge that challenged their personal and community existences. Suddenly, "the Castro became a city of moral dramas—dramas that involved not only the victims but their lovers, their parents, and their friends." The Castro, then, became an allegorical landscape; its citizens were passionate pilgrims who had to confront the new implications of their actions.

> In the Castro those who had spent a good part of their lives in the struggle against the sexual taboo now had to acknowledge that the sexual liberation they had fought for so strenuously—and on which they had laid their claims of being the avant-garde of a national revolution—had

deadly consequences. What was more, they had to face the fact that they were giving the disease to one another.

Life in the Castro changed when its residents acknowledged this *memento mori* in their midst. (pp. 490-91)

By far the most comprehensive and moving work of journalism on the AIDS crisis, Randy Shilts's *And the Band Played On* is driven by similar impulses of grief, protest, and the celebration of courage and heroism among those who fought the good "fight for acceptance and equality, against ignorance and fear," first in establishing a gay male community and later in protesting that the Reagan administration and state and local agencies were criminally negligent in dealing with the killing disease. Where FitzGerald had placed the life and death cycle in the Castro in the context of other fringe communities in American culture, Shilts's massive and impassioned book, which catalogues nearly a decade of the growth of the disease and the recognition of its threat, establishes AIDS and its implications at the heart and soul of American life.

Shilts structures *And the Band Played On* on a time line of ever increasing dramatic occasions; ironic juxtaposition sets the AIDS crisis in relation to major public events in American life. For example, at the bicentennial celebration in New York City, in 1976, tall ships from fifty-five nations brought sailors, some of whom may have been carrying the AIDS virus, to America. In November 1984, Ronald Reagan, who had never spoken out on AIDS, was reelected president, an occasion upon which Shilts casts a cold eye. "When claiming victory on election night, President Reagan told a cheering crowd, 'America's best days lie ahead.' It was during the month of Reagan's reelection that the nation's AIDS caseload surpassed 7,000." Shilts notes that by the time Reagan tentatively spoke out on AIDS, in mid-1987, 36,058 Americans had been diagnosed with the disease and 20,849 had died. The two Americans portrayed in *Band*—Reagan's myth of morning in America and the dark night of the soul created by AIDS—are traced in lines that, eventually, converge.

And the Band Played On is at once a chronicle—jump-cuts intersect moments of medical research, political infighting, and case histories of those affected—and a polemic, a work of vivid advocacy journalism, an indictment of national bigotry. Shilts details the various ways in which Americans respond to what some of them ironically call "gay cancer." . . . Particularly fascinating is Shilts's tracing of the florid sexual career and finally horrid death of Gaetan Dugas, an airline steward from Canada, who was one of the first North Americans diagnosed with AIDS. Knowing he was infected, Dugas continued coupling in bathhouses; after sex he would taunt his partners, telling them they too would surely die. After sexual encounters, Dugas would turn on the lights, point to the purple lesions on his chest, then say to his shocked lover, "Gay cancer. Maybe you'll get it too." Poe's gothic story "The Masque of the Red Death" had turned real.

> There's no doubt that Gaetan played a key role in spreading the new virus from one end of the United States to the other. The bathhouse controversy, peaking so dramatically in San Fran-

cisco on the morning of his death [March 30, 1984], was also linked directly to Gaetan's own exploits in those sex palaces and his recalcitrance in changing his ways. At one time, Gaetan had been what every man wanted from gay life; by the time he died, he had become what every man feared.

Yet Shilts celebrates more than he denigrates. Particular praise is reserved for social activists. Shilts praises Cleve Jones, famous for his memorial marches in San Francisco in memory of Harvey Milk, member of the city's Board of Supervisors and gay rights activist, and George Moscone, the city's mayor—both of whom had been killed by a deranged politician; later, Jones founded the Kaposi's Sarcoma Research and Education Foundation. Shilts also praises Larry Kramer, writer and organizer of Gay Men's Health Crisis in New York City. It was Kramer's article in March 1983, "1,112 and Counting," argues Shilts, which "irrevocably altered the context in which AIDS was discussed in the gay community and, hence, in the nation." Kramer attacked the medical community, especially the Centers for Disease Control, for its hesitancy; the political community, particularly Mayor Ed Koch of New York, for its callous disregard; and the gay male community, for its refusal to change its ways: "Unless we fight for our lives we shall die. In all the history of homosexuality we have never been so close to death and extinction before. Many of us are dying or dead already."

When the novelists and playwrights examined those who suffer, directly or obliquely, from AIDS, they too found enormous strengths. Occasionally these writers match and surpass, in fiction, poetry, or drama, the level of conviction and sense of crisis achieved in documentaries. Whatever the form, some writers who emerge from the gay male community to tell the story of AIDS have the authenticity and the passion of some Holocaust testimony, from Anne Frank to Elie Wiesel. "I had the energy to do my book because I'm gay," Randy Shilts told *Newsweek,* "AIDS wasn't somebody else's problem. I live every day with the knowledge that friends will be dead in five years. I had to write the book, or go crazy." (pp. 491-93)

Poetry on AIDS tends to be traditional in form and moral in intent: direct and didactic. Robert Boucheron, in *Epitaphs for the Plague Dead,* invokes Tennyson's *In Memoriam* as his model. Boucheron draws his technique—testimonies from those killed by AIDS—from Edgar Lee Master's *Spoon River Anthology,* Thornton Wilder's *Our Town,* and A. E. Housman's *A Shropshire Lad,* by writers who also composed epitaphs as dramatic monologues. Boucheron's volume, however, owes more in form than in achievement to those predecessors. Rather than devise a new form to fit this new threat to our health and consciousness, Boucheron has forced a contemporary horror into the rigidities of Victorian verse, all the better to instruct. Still, some of his poems convey the shock of sudden awareness of the threatening ways of this plague, as in "Epitaph for an Innocent":

> I got it from my mother's breasts,
> unknowing, as an infant sips.
> She got it from my father's lips,
> conceiving in my interest.

> He got it lying still in bed,
> his arm connected to a sack
> that, as a hemophiliac,
> he needed any time he bled.

> A small, unhappy family,
> we shared more than a common cold.
> For my part, the sum is soon told:
> nine months I lived, dying in three.

In another collection of AIDS poetry, *An Intimate Desire to Survive,* Bill Becker keeps a diary in poetic form during the eighteen months in which he suspected he had contracted AIDS. Both poets obey a documentary impulse: Boucheron moves through a range of characters for his AIDS chronicle, while Becker moves through time. Becker, too, dramatizes the plight of the victim who cannot imagine what has happened to him. Like Job, Becker asks, "Why me?" However, Becker poses his questions and finds his working metaphors in more original poetic forms, which, in turn, convey more complex impressions, as does this entry of choppy lines and patterned associations which records the disease cycle, "5 Feb 85":

> The body collapses
> into itself
> Structured demolition
> surface unseen
> Candid eruption
> doing havoc on nerve
> Nuclear fission
> on a human scale—

> Cellular chain reaction
> An immunity implosion
> Self interest
> Self pity
> Schizophrenic optimism
> Relapse—

Poetry in the AIDS crisis is commemorative and dedicatory, written in memoriam. It is the verbal equivalent of the "performance art" emblem displayed at the October 1987 gay rights march on Washington: a giant quilt, composed of three-by-six-foot, hand-made panels, each containing the name of a person who had died of AIDS. (pp. 496-97)

Fiction on AIDS can be loosely grouped in two categories: first, horrific cautionary tales of fascist responses to the AIDS crisis: dystopias, in the manner of *1984,* in which writers posit scenarios of massive retaliation against homosexuals by a society—set some time in the near future, or in the reconfigured immediate past—which seeks a Final Solution to the plague; second, documentary, largely autobiographical records of case histories of persons with AIDS, along with the ramifications of the disease for the victim's immediate family and loved ones. In *Plagues and People,* William H. McNeill makes the distinction between external and internal threats to man's survival: "One can properly think of most human lives as caught in a precarious equilibrium between the microparasitism of disease organisms and the macroparasitism of large-bodied predators, chief among which have been other human beings." The social and science fiction fantasies on AIDS move from lethal microparasites, fostered by the AIDS virus, to speculations upon the form of lethal macroparasites: those who seek the Final Solution against AIDS through elimination of its carriers.

The AIDS crisis has stirred fears—paranoia, unfounded hysteria, justly founded anxieties—in the male homosexual community over social isolation and retaliation. Testing for AIDS was advocated by the Reagan administration; some police wore masks in the presence of male homosexuals; and a Florida boy with AIDS was assaulted, his family's house burned. Where will all this lead? Two novelists, Jed A. Bryan and Toby Johnson, fear they know.

Bryan's *A Cry in the Desert* imagines a "pogrom" against male homosexuals in Nevada, in the early 1980s, a genocide that began with AIDS testing. It is an insistent example of message literature. As Bryan notes, in a brief preface, "the message is clear. AIDS is not a *gay plague*. It is a very real danger to us all." The novel is driven and sustained by a sense of threat and betrayal. Its epigraph is from Luke (21:16), a passage that could serve as the epigraph for many illustrative works on the AIDS crisis.

> And ye shall be betrayed both by parents and brethren and kinfolk and friends; and some of you shall they cause to be put to death.

Bryan construes Luke's text into a wild parable. Alfred Botts, himself a repressed homosexual, heads up Project ERAD (Emergency Research and Development), on two thousand acres of Nevada desert, near a nuclear plant, and works for a new Emergency Quarantine Act, under which he seizes homosexuals, then brings them to ERAD, where they undergo experiments, then are eliminated. Botts is aided by the Reverend Theophilis Stokeswood, a radio minister, who preaches on the scourge of God: AIDS as God's punishment against male homosexuals. Industrialist Kurt Stakl bankrolls Botts's research project, hoping to patent an AIDS cure through which he seeks world control! Arrayed against this powerful triumvirate are a few journalists, doctors, and others who are fighting for the rights of homosexual men. Incredibly, despite many lurid assaults—one homosexual man is nailed to a cross, another is dehydrated to death!—this group of citizens, working together, brings down Botts and his nefarious associates. *A Cry in the Desert* is a model of improbable fiction.

So too is Toby Johnson's *Plague: A Novel About Healing*. Johnson, a psychotherapist who has worked with AIDS victims and has sought to educate the public about preventive measures, contrives an equally unlikely, melodramatic parable of warning. Like Bryan, Johnson sees his fantastic story—the planned use of nuclear weapons against AIDS carriers—as reasonable. "The projections for the resolution of the plague that haunts us in 1987 are reasonable extrapolations of current medical fact." Set in "Early Autumn, in the Possible Near Future," *Plague* imagines evil men, Dr. Strangeloves and Dr. Frankensteins, who are repressed homosexuals; they manipulate the crisis, developing and withholding an AIDS antidote so that they can seize money and power. Arrayed, once again, against them are various high-minded gay males who struggle within encompassing plots. The AIDS crisis, in this dystopia, reveals the homophobic depths of American culture: "Curiously, at the very heart of this discussion was

the notion that pinko-leaning homosexuals were undermining American morality." AIDS, we are told, allows fag-bashing fascists to come out of the closet and do their damndest, though they, in turn, are done in by noble gay males and their fellow travelers. While all literature tends toward mythic reductions, these fictions tend toward the simplifications of comic strips.

Though one can easily understand the sense of psychic dread that motivates the writing of *A Cry in the Desert* and *Plague,* it is difficult to take them seriously as analyses or as predictive models. In both works, AIDS is seized upon to settle old scores—hostility to homosexual men comes from those who repress their own homosexual inclinations—and imagine fantastic political scenarios, in the manner of the suspense fiction of Robert Ludlum, Ken Follett, or Tom Clancy. But then, it might be argued, until recently AIDS itself would have seemed to most people an imaginative extravagance, a science fiction. Jed A. Bryan and Toby Johnson have tried to think about the unthinkable in implausible but haunting fictions. Voices crying in the wilderness don't have perfect pitch!

It is as difficult to plot a plausible mystery on the AIDS topic as it is to contrive happy endings for an AIDS story, for the same reason: because persons with AIDS die. As soon as a lesion appears, sadly, we know the rest of the story. Some writers, as we have seen, shift readers' attentions to plot against homosexual men either by the disease itself or by those who want to gain wealth or power through their extinction. Other writers take the AIDS story head-on, without embellishment or imaginative contrivance. They resort to plain-style prose and accessible plots to bear witness to the devastation of AIDS. Either these writers are dying or their loved ones have died. Their books are records that implicate the reader in the victim's suffering and in the impact of the victim's suffering upon his lovers, his friends, and his family. Most of these autobiographical works avoid artful indirection: they make their claim for the victim's humanity with the blunt insistence of a heart's cry.

J. W. Money's *To All the Girls I've Loved Before* has the artless authenticity of dying words, for that is just what they are: brief, self-reflective essays written, during March 1986, while the author suffered high fevers that kept him up at night. He wrote his entries on the bathroom floor to keep from disturbing his companion. This, then, is a version of prison literature, though the author was to be released from his sentence only by death. Many of Money's reflections—notes, memories, whimsies, farewell missives, and thank-you notes—are not on AIDS, but on music, fashion, people, and places he has loved. He thanks his mother for introducing him to opera; she died of cancer at age forty-three, the same age he would contract AIDS. He recalls his crushes on media stars: Bette Davis, Natalie Wood, and Joan Baez. He tries to construe his life as an allegory in a stiff, jingly poem about Prudence and Folly. He, of course, assumed the role of Folly, who "was last seen somewhere near the docks" with a sailor. That is, he blames himself for AIDS, but defends his choices. "I have AIDS in part, because I was promiscuous. I'm not complaining: If God's punishing me, He's certainly allowed me to have a lot of pleasure." At that point, words fail Money and he invokes a sentimental song to speak for him: "Kiss the day goodbye, and I won't regret what I did for love."

J. W. Money died in October 1986. His lover, who had stood vigil over him during his illness, died a few months later. All that remains is this fragmentary, flawed, but moving work, written in feverish conviction, when he knew that time was running out.

In *The World Can Break Your Heart,* Daniel Curzon tells the familiar story of a sensitive young man (Benjamin Vance) who grew up in a tough environment (Detroit), with a sense of his difference and a need to discover his own place in the wider world: "I'm gonna be a movie star like Sonja Henie!" declares the boy. Though he is shamed by adults and Catholic clergy, Benjamin accepts his identity as a homosexual, then goes to Hollywood in search of fame. There he meets gay men who celebrate their sexuality: "Leave Detroit behind, sweetie," says one. Benjamin learns to turn tricks, but, when one of his partners contracts AIDS, Benjamin quickly grows up; he learns love and compassion. Here, as in other AIDS-related literature, the disease concentrates the mind upon Final Things and intensifies the humanity of those affected. As in Money's commitment to writing during his last days, Curzon's Benjamin affirms art over deteriorating life: "Life may be a 'long disease', as Hamlet said. But a work of art, I see now, is the cure!"

Of course, this asks too much of art. In *The Renewal of Literature,* Richard Poirier questions the powers and responsibilities of literature to address the problem of culture. "Literature is a very restricted passage into life, if it is one at all." At its best, said Auden, writing on Yeats, "poetry makes nothing happen." Even granting that art has limited powers, *The World Can Break Your Heart* is not the best art: the novel seems hasty, episodic, undeveloped, with no detailed sense of its Detroit and Hollywood settings. In form, it is a conventional novel of coming out with the consciousness of AIDS tacked on, as Curzon's own words imply: he dedicates his novel "to all straight readers so that they will know what it felt like to grow up gay and for all gay people so they won't forget." Still, this novel follows the pattern of direct appeal for the sad plight of those who struggle to accept and have accepted their sexual identities only to discover that their lives are threatened by AIDS. These writers are correct in insisting that this story must be told and told again, whatever the effects or achievements of their art. Fiction, too, as Auden said of poetry, "survives in the valley of its saying."

Paul Reed's *Facing It: A Novel of AIDS* is a romance of sorts, with a love story in the foreground and AIDS looming in the background. In the summer of 1981, Andy Stone, a handsome young worker for gay rights in Manhattan, grows ill. His macho father rejects his dying, homosexual son. Andy finds support from his elected, gay male "family." His lover, David, is ennobled through suffering. A writer for various gay presses, David had been "waiting for something to write about, something worth the effort; he knew inspiration would hit him in time." Andy's illness and the wider threat of AIDS give David a worthy personal mission and a significant public topic for his writing. He investigates the AIDS disease, in search of explanations. David finds some dedication in the medical profession but also uncovers much callousness—"Fags are big news nowadays, and dead ones are even better news," says one calculating researcher—and evil. As in *A Cry in the Desert* and *Plague,* the villain in *Facing It* is a closet homosexual man. Dr. Arthur Maguire won't release funds for the dedicated Dr. Branch's research: "What with the homosexual element and all—well, it's all delicate and avoidable," says Maguire. It turns out that obese Maguire had been Kinder-Mann's lover in medical school, that he had used a woman, Carolyn, who later became Branch's rich wife, as his cover. However, now Carolyn threatens Maguire with exposure if he does not release funds. That is, the novel descends to soap opera villainy and intrigue to make its point. In *Facing It,* the AIDS crisis renews the bonding not only of gay male lovers but of this married couple. Like every other work in the genre, this novel sets out to raise the consciousness of its readers and to renew the covenant between gay men, even in the face of AIDS. The disease is, it seems, a great teacher as well as a great killer.

The most subtle and moving fiction on AIDS that I have read appears in George Stambolian's anthology *Men on Men: Best New Gay Fiction.* Despite its flaunting title, many stories in this anthology do more than celebrate coming-out parties for young men, though that pattern appears. As Stambolian notes, AIDS-era fiction is likely to be even more controversial, particularly descriptions of sexual practices. "This situation partly explains why many stories involving erotically unrestrained behavior are now habitually set in the years preceding the advent of AIDS." It is the turn away from scenes of explicit sexuality and the turn toward mature and eloquent confrontation with disease, death, and the effects of death upon the living which distinguish these stories. Paradoxically, but justly, as the gay male community suffers its Holocaust, its fiction has increasingly been accepted by mainstream publishers and readers. Gay male literature has gone past the stage of either justifying itself to American straight culture or shocking the bourgeoisie; rather, at its best, it portrays characters who are confronting the meaning of their lives and the mystery of death.

John Fox's "Choice" is a poignant tale of a gay antihero, Jimmy Abooz, who suppresses his lusts out of the fear of AIDS, though his caution has so far protected him and given him a wry humor. "He doesn't know a single person with AIDS and hopes he never does. . . . The previous summer he wore shorts almost every day to show off his lesion-free legs." Still, he does not know which way to turn. He still does not get along with his family, though they drink chi-chis (piña coladas with vodka) together during a dreary Christmas day. Jimmy, weary of his family, afraid of sexual encounters, stays in his room, alone. "He decided to start saving for a video-cassette player so he could watch porn videos in the privacy of his own home." Fox catches the AIDS-era state of personal paralysis: isolation and masturbation.

The central character in Edmund White's "An Oracle" resists changing his life. Though he has buried his lover, Ray feels "dying would be easier than figuring out a new way of living." In Greece, Ray reads Homer, weeps over Achilles' death, and confronts his own fragile mortality. "He thought it very likely that he was carrying death inside him, that it was ticking inside him like a time bomb but one he couldn't find because it had been secreted by an unknown terrorist." Still, he cannot keep his hands off a local boy. However, no longer able to see other men as sex objects, Ray falls in love with the Greek boy, who, wary of involvement, rejects him. The old wanton ways of Ray's gay days are long gone.

In Andrew Holleran's fine story "Friends at Evening," mourners gather for the funeral of Louis, an AIDS victim. Louis is a symbolic figure who stands for all the friends and lovers they have lost. Unlike Clifford Odets's Lefty or Samuel Beckett's Godot, chimeras of hope and rescue, Holleran's Louis presents only an occasion for mourning. The narrator gathers Louis's friends for the occasion. One cites Walt Whitman: "It is enough to be with friends at evening."

The gathering turns into an extended elegy. "We're all going, in sequence, at different times. And will the last person please turn out the lights?" says one mourner. Another, who refuses to detach his identity as a homosexual man from sexual practices, complains, *The wrong people are dying.* The city has become a cemetery through which this group of sad men passes, like a funeral procession. "More Than You Know" serves as their plaintive theme song: "Oh how I'd die. Oh, how I'd cry, if you got tired and said good-bye." Romance is gone. Yet their friendships are intensified and narrowed, their lives reaffirmed in their ceremonial mourning.

In Sam D'Allesandro's "Nothing Ever Just Disappears," a survivor grieves for his lost lover in similarly plaintive yet oddly affirming terms. "Someone said the pain would go away, but I'm not sure that's where I want it to go. It's how I feel him most sharply." In Robert Ferro's "Second Son," a tough antiromantic note is struck when a son dying of AIDS wards off his father's bluff reassurances. "The bottom line is that there's no cure," the wise child tells his stunned father. The wise children of AIDS have much to tell us all.

The literature of AIDS, then, is

- divided between conflicting impulses: realistic and antiromantic or satiric and fantastic;

- more concerned with death than sex, though nostalgic for the lost old days of wine and roses;

- family-centered, whether that means a reconciliation with the victim's biological family, the affirmation of one's elected family, or both: fellowship and family renewal in the face of death are the constant themes of these works;

- antibourgeois; evil and indifferent men from the social establishment exploit the crisis;

- self-reflective: these works raise questions about the nature, form, and substance of gay male literature and ask members of the male homosexual community to question what it means to be gay;

- committed to the proposition that most victims and their loved ones are ennobled through suffering;

- intensely, bleakly humorous; thoughtful, inward, plaintive, eloquent; often artless or excessive;

- cautionary: AIDS affects us all; no man is an island.

The AIDS crisis has already produced a considerable body of literature, though not yet a great work of art. In a provocative survey ["La Cage au Dull," *Boston Review* (1987)], Daniel Harris dismisses most recent gay male fiction. "It's a literature caught in limbo between the hell of outlandish grotesques and the heaven of recipes and salads, one twisted and misshapen by its own extreme ideological tensions." Certainly it is true that AIDS has shaken the identity of the gay male community, but Harris's objections to new gay male literature are excessive. Though much of the literature that responds to AIDS—most of which emerges from or studies the male homosexual community—is pedestrian, repetitious, or special-pleading, all of it resonates with the shock of recognition of the power of AIDS to alter our collective consciousness, to change *all* our lives. Some writings on this topic are achieved works of literature: the journalism of FitzGerald and Shilts; the plays of Kramer [*The Normal Heart*], [William M.] Hoffman [*As Is*], and [Harvey] Fierstein [*Safe Sex*], the fiction of Holleran and a few others who have raised gay male literature from the celebration of uncloseted sexuality to the level of a requiem. AIDS literature will expand and, in time, will find its genius, as AIDS increasingly finds its place at the center of the American mind.

On Tidy Endings, Harvey Fierstein's brief play, is the most successful treatment of the AIDS crisis in literature which I have read. It meets the challenge of incorporating the horrific fact of AIDS—*memento mori,* masque of death, plague—in a drama that, without resort to theatrical tricks, teaches us how to see, prods us to feel our way to new levels of understanding. In the play, a recent widow, Marion, confronts Arthur, her deceased husband's lover, in the cooperative apartment in which Arthur had cared for Collin, the man they both loved, who has died of AIDS-related disease. Marion had sent her son, Jim, away before her meeting with Arthur, who is hurt that the boy blames him for Collin's death. Marion and Arthur are each wary and jealous. "He died in my arms, not yours," cries Arthur. They bicker over mementos of Collin: a teapot that had been given to Collin and Marion as a wedding gift, though Arthur tells her it is a replacement for the burnt-out original, bought by Collin and Arthur in the Village. Marion and Arthur cannot acknowledge each other. They savage each other so thoroughly that, at last, nothing is left but compassion. Arthur tells Marion of Collin's final moments.

> ARTHUR. Marion, you've got your life and his son. All I have is an intangible place in a man's history. Leave me that. Respect that.

MARION. I understand.

Here Marion comes a long way, from the role of the conventional, aggrieved wife, to stand before and understand her dead husband's lover. Moved by his pain, she asks Arthur how he is. Arthur is not infected, he says, but when he asks how *she* is, Marion admits that she has AIDS antibodies in her blood. No one, then, is free from the threat of infection, so no one can remove himself/herself from the human family, which has no choice but to stand together in the face of this awesome threat.

Marion calls her son, Jim, back into the room and insists that the boy tell Arthur what his father had told him. Reluctantly, Jim speaks:

> JIM. He said that after me and Mommy he loved you the most. . . . And that I should love you too. And make sure that you're not lonely or very sad.
>
> ARTHUR. Thank you.

At the end of *On Tidy Endings,* Marion and her son are on one side of a door; Arthur is on the other side. That separation symbolically acknowledges the social division between those who choose either heterosexual or homosexual relationships in America. However, the real story of Fierstein's fine play is that doors have been opened and thresholds of understanding have been crossed between different kinds of people who have been affected and infected by a family death caused by AIDS. Indeed, AIDS, in this play, knows no barriers; it has forced characters to acknowledge each other's humanity and to accept each other's love. The common threat posed by AIDS may redefine and restore our idea of the American family. (pp. 497-503)

> Shaun O'Connell, "The Big One: Literature Discovers AIDS," in The AIDS Epidemic: Private Rights and the Public Interest, *edited by Padraig O'Malley, Beacon Press, 1989, pp. 485-506.*

George Newtown   (essay date Spring 1989)

[*In the following essay, Newtown examines how sex and its consequences have been portrayed in literature throughout history and maintains that by imitating some of the techniques of classical drama, AIDS plays express universal themes.*]

AIDS has increased the tension between gay and straight society in America. Before AIDS, homosexual sex was worrisome for the heterosexual population primarily in symbolic terms: in lacking procreative possibilities, homosexuality seems close to pure sexual urge and therefore threatens the hegemony of the myth of the stable heterosexual family. While the symbolic dimension remains important, the advent of AIDS makes the sexuality of gays no longer biologically inconsequential; sex becomes a matter of death, if not life. Although much of the straight American populace was initially able to ignore AIDS because the disease seemed to affect only gays, now that AIDS can clearly be transmitted heterosexually, sex and death threaten to become entwined for everyone. In the wave of fear that has accompanied this realization, gays have been held accountable for the disease, as if it resulted from a lifestyle rather than from a virus.

Fundamentalist preachers invoke AIDS to prove that God is angry about sexual misconduct, even as the secret sex lives of the preachers themselves enter the news. Evidence of pastoral hypocrisy may not cause all Christians to accept gays as brothers, but such revelations do affirm that Christianity, at least since Augustine, continues to be preoccupied with sex. Of course we knew *that* (in a deconstructive sense): the sacred text of sexual prohibition masks (and therefore reveals) an intense sexual preoccupation. As Michel Foucault argues in his *History of Sexuality,* the discourse of sexuality resounded in the Victorian era, even though the *repression* of sexuality might seem the major Victorian mode. For Foucault, Victorian attention to sex takes a step in the historical progression toward today's "Faustian pact" through which we exchange "life in its entirety" for "the truth and sovereignty of sex." Gays who die of AIDS rather than give up sex behave just like any other moderns for whom sex is more important than life itself. The argument derives a particular poignancy from the observation that Foucault himself, despite his clearsighted analysis of the modern Faustian pact, died of AIDS.

George Stambolian on AIDS and gay culture:

Almost everyone is aware of the changes that have occurred within the gay community in recent years: the weakening of urban ghettos; the decline in importance of bars, baths, and discos as focal institutions; the rise to greater prominence of other institutions such as political groups, community centers, health and charitable organizations. Although these changes have usually been attributed to the AIDS crisis, it would be more accurate to say that AIDS has accelerated changes that had already begun.

Gay culture of the 1970s was largely established by a generation which after decades of repression could celebrate its new consciousness and the very fact that it was creating a new culture on its own terms. This process continues, but much that was culturally new in the 1970s is now understandably seen as a *given* both by a younger generation and by many who were earlier engaged in gay life. We are also witnessing another familiar pattern of cultural change: After a revolutionary ingathering, a movement outward toward the rest of society is taking place. This movement is less the result of disillusionment caused by AIDS than a manifestation of confidence based on the fact that a certain psychological, social, and artistic ground has been secured against the continued onslaughts of antigay discrimination and violence.

These developments partly explain why some writers with established reputations in gay fiction are now venturing to treat other subjects, whereas writers previously known for their nongay work are turning to gay fiction for the first time.

George Stambolian, in his introduction to Men on Men 2: Best New Gay Fiction, *1988.*

Sex became indispensable—paradoxically—when we were able to separate it from its biological effects and thereby raise ourselves to the level of divinity. We moderns cultivated the capacity to use our power for our merest pleasure: we believed we could enjoy passion without consequence (through, say, the use of contraceptives) as even the gods cannot do. As we made our Faustian bargain, it seems we arrogated to ourselves prerogatives greater than the divine and imagined we could declare gods dead; instead, the gods selectively kill us for our arrogance, lest we forget that we are powerless. This conclusion resonates with the arguments not only of fundamentalist Christian preachers, but of the fatalistic religion of ancient Greece, where a prophylactic drama developed to respond to the terrors that belief in such arbitrary and retributive divinities fostered.

Modern Western drama began in the Athenian preoccupation with the confluence of sex, death, and divinity. In rites of spring, Greeks copulated amid the mess of spilled wine and sacrificial blood; the fluids honored the gods, especially the wine-god Dionysus, whose ritual required orgiastic drunkenness and ecstatic frenzy, and whose ceremonies sometimes concluded, as we see reflected overtly in Euripides' *The Bacchae,* in the sacrifice of a scapegoat king. The spilling of wine, semen, and blood symbolically fertilized the ground and ensured, in a representative way, that the crops would be successful in the next growing season. Clearly, the fertilization had to be symbolic, as not enough of these vital fluids could be spilled to provide actual fertilizer. Just as clearly, the human sacrifice—if not necessarily the spilling of the seed—had to be representative, or the entire population would have been at risk. Drama became possible when the representative and symbolic dimensions of the ritual were extended toward the representational: where the king had died so that his people might live, the player-king pretended to die so that his people might vicariously cleanse themselves of their inadequacies through his supposed sacrifice. The ritual of scapegoating was rendered less socially harmful because drama created an apparently life-threatening reality during the three-hour traffic on the stage, and thereby averted threats to life off-stage.

The dramatic genres of comedy and tragedy grew in different directions from the preoccupation with sex and death. In comedy, sex is the device that thwarts death: the essentially interchangeable figures in the *gamos* or ritual coupling at the end of the play bring the conservative message that society will survive, even though its individual members may have been temporarily incommoded. In tragedy, death itself thwarts death; sex may speed or slow its progress, but the inevitable death of the hero keeps us alive a little longer. The ritual scapegoating of tragic heroes caused the onlookers not to reject their kings, but to sigh in relief that the representational destruction of great, if flawed, heroes wards off the evil eye. Thus, tragedy only seems to suggest social revolution, even as it seems, from an anachronistic modern perspective, to focus on individual uncertainties about sexuality and identity. If we can believe Greek accounts of the importance of their political organization, we conclude that members of the Athenian audience cried not because Oedipus suffered, or even because he killed his father and married his mother; instead, they trembled because they saw in the sufferings of the king the potential downfall of their city and of life as they knew it. So, too, with the deaths of Agamemnon and of Pentheus, or the sorrows of the Trojan women: individual suffering was subsumed under the suffering of the *polis.* The representative king died, so that the political organization (and therefore the people) might live.

When the thinkers of the Renaissance, nearly two thousand years after the golden age of Athenian Greece, sought to return attention to the classical civilizations, they did so from a very different perspective. No longer, as had been the case with the Greeks or with the medieval guilds of artists, did anonymous artists perform to the glory of the god or to the benefit of the collective. Eventually, through the agency of the bourgeois revolution, dramatic conflict and the dominant literary themes of sex and death came to embody "merely" existential questions: sexual encounters, and sometimes even deaths, became personal expressions or at most ways to establish individual identity. Modern heroes have copulated and died as if in total isolation—as if their random encounters evinced no causes, no effects, no connections, and no responsibilities.

Flaubert's *Madame Bovary* shows a result of the bourgeois emphasis on the individual. Emma may be a woman, but she acts like a man, who thinks he is able to have sex without consequences to himself. (Within sexist bourgeois morality, male freedoms are limited only by lack of funds; and in the solipsistic bourgeois universe, unencumbered freedom seems to imply promiscuity.) Flaubert hints that Emma's irresponsible sexuality will kill her: as the carriage containing Emma and her lover careens through an entire afternoon, the odor of death fills the lurching cab, "more tightly sealed than a tomb," even as Leon and Emma make love in it. Finally, Emma's sexuality *does* have consequences: she comes to her death through the symbolic pregnancy of a debt that grows until it can no longer be hidden. In a last ugly irony, she is laid out like an innocent bride reclining on a sweet marriage bed, after she has died struggling in the vomit and blood of a parody of the labor of childbirth. If Flaubert has Emma die the death that fallen women have had to die in generations of "moral" literary works, she nevertheless demonstrates that members of the bourgeoisie cannot find freedom, as long as freedom is equated with attaining individual self-expression. The freed bourgeois of either sex, with no other values and no membership in a supportive community, is just an irresponsible (and still isolated) bourgeois.

Emma's mistaken view that her most personal acts will have no social consequence places her in a literary genealogy that includes such "free" individuals as the Nietzschean superman and the Sartrean existentialist. Willie Loman in Arthur Miller's *Death of a Salesman* seems an even less likely candidate than Emma Bovary to share a tradition with the Nietzschean superman. Yet Willie, too, wanted to make his own existential choices. He is most like the superman—and paradoxically (although the paradox is more apparent than real) most like the pettiest of bourgeois—because he wants his acts judged only in terms of his own emotions and perceptions. When he tries to convince his son that the woman in his hotel room meant "nothing to me," he says, "I was lonely, I was terribly lonely." Anonymous sex in a hotel room fulfills a deeply felt personal need. If no one knows, what possible repercussions are there? Because he is unable to see the effects on those beyond himself, Willie makes the final existential choice of suicide, without regard to the feelings of his family. In the meantime he has helped destroy his son's will.

Willie probably never in his life worried about his sexual orientation, nor did he imagine that anyone would know the secrets of his private sex life. Even in claiming a right to promiscuity, modern gays have acted rather more responsibly than poor ignorant Willie. In pre-AIDS gay literature, "who will know" became the most important question. In literature as in life, as gays "came out of the closet," the private was rendered public for a political end: gays risked the misunderstanding of their society and families to defend their right to exercise personal freedom.

In addition to "coming out," the other main theme of recent gay drama before AIDS was also a political one: gays were to be viewed as more feeling, more loving, more sympathetic, more endearingly neurotic than straights, and, since they were admirable (however unorthodox and shocking their language or practices), they would be rendered acceptable to the audience that viewed them. Unfortunately for the proponents of this political agenda, the audience for pre-AIDS gay plays was largely made up of gays; only one exception among these dramas, Harvey Fierstein's *Torchsong Trilogy* (1981), garnered marked success among a general American audience. *Torchsong Trilogy* is an outrageously funny play, whose political import is tied to creating a world in which personal preference can find its expression. The themes are those that had come to be expected in the Gay Sweatshop plays of the preceding decade: the main characters are a neurotic drag queen obsessed with finding the perfect relationship and his bisexual lover unwilling to come out of the closet. Together, once the bisexual has left his pasty wife for the last time, they adopt a flaming fourteen-year old whose education into gay pride becomes their parental mission. In their love for their son, they see a glimmer of immortality and of worthwhile human experience for themselves.

AIDS, of course, changes the stakes. Immortal longings stand aside for mortality. Sex can no longer be considered a personal expression. In fact, AIDS makes a purely personal sexual expression dangerous. The dark plague redirects our preoccupations toward the most primitive conjunction of sex and death and toward our most primitive instincts for scapegoating. Almost immediately, the process of scapegoating has been directed into literature, in a process through which a representative dramatic hero can deflect those primitive instincts onto himself. Since 1984 several AIDS dramas have appeared; although all of them to date have contained dramatic flaws, they represent an important body of work.

The best known of the AIDS dramas are Larry Kramer's *The Normal Heart* (1985), William Hoffman's *As Is* (1985), Ronald Cowen's and Daniel Lipman's television drama, *An Early Frost* (1985), and Harvey Fierstein's *Safe Sex* (1987). In *The Normal Heart*, Kramer angrily recre-

ates the story of his efforts to enlist the support of New York city officials for generalized AIDS treatment and to reform sex practices within the New York gay community. His high-minded crusades were rejected both by timid city officials and by his gay confreres who thought he represented an anti-revolutionary swing back to guilt about homosexual sexuality. When Kramer's play fails, it is generally in its preachy moments—when he tries, for example, to equate the treatment of AIDS sufferers with the extermination of Jews in Nazi Germany. There is a shrillness here that not even the caring relationship between the principled main character Ned Weeks and his dying lover can fully overcome. Hoffman's *As Is* is a cleverer view of the relationship between gay lovers, one who also has AIDS, and the other who returns to nurse him. The very jocularity of the play reveals the anxiety in it, although it pulls back from confronting the final ugliness of Rich's death. In its fluid scenes and overlapping dialogue, *As Is* is artistically more innovative than *The Normal Heart*. The Emmy-winning television drama, *An Early Frost*, shows yet another noble gay hero—this one himself the primary victim of AIDS. Perhaps because the audience for television is composed primarily of straight families, "An Early Frost" focuses less on the sexuality of the son than on the soul-searching of his parents who struggle to accept their son's medical and sexual "conditions." Harvey Fierstein's *Safe Sex* is a somewhat disjunct trilogy, in which the first two playlets, *Manny and Jake* and *Safe Sex,* are stylized allegories that show how gay interactions have been constrained now that AIDS has destroyed gay innocence. The third one-act, *On Tidy Endings,* is at once the best and the most conventional (in the tradition of Neil Simon's *Plaza Suite*); it is largely an extended bitchy dialogue between the two "wives" of a recent AIDS victim—Marion and Arthur—who must agree to a division of his effects. Arthur is another principled gay male, who has rejoined his lover/husband even after learning that he has AIDS, and has invested in "rubber futures" in order to engage in safe sex.

To judge from the examples of the woman doctor in *The Normal Heart* and the actress Lily in *As Is,* AIDS plays continue to be as hard-pressed to present many-faceted female characters as earlier gay drama; the major exception to date may be Marion in *On Tidy Endings.* Fierstein draws his audience toward real sympathy for Marion through a *coup de théâtre* in which it is revealed that *she* carries the virus; because she fears to hurt her new husband or the unborn children that they desperately want to have, she, like her gay counterpart, must also invest in "rubber futures." In some ways *On Tidy Endings* represents a sad conclusion to Fierstein's earlier *Torchsong Trilogy*. The flamboyant fourteen-year-old adoptee of *Torchsong Trilogy* regresses to become the tense pre-pubescent eleven-year-old of *On Tidy Endings.* Even though they once got on well, Jimmy now fears and loathes his homosexual "uncle," who, in the boy's view, has killed his father. Fierstein attempts to reconcile them with a kiss at the end of the play, but when the boy leaves with his mother, the scene marks the failure of the hopeful vision contained in *Torchsong Trilogy:* because of AIDS, gays are denied the dream of immortality that the nuclear family and the education of adoptive offspring might have brought. Marion shares in the pathos because she carries the "gay disease"; her inability to have children reflects and expands an essentially male tragedy.

The principled (and—apart from Marion—usually male) main characters of the AIDS dramas help to make sense of a senseless disease on behalf of audiences both male and female. Because of the AIDS plague, contemporary gay dramas seem universal in ways seldom experienced in modern dramatic works since the individual replaced the representative hero. The heroes of AIDS dramas face a mortality larger than just their own. They function as surrogates for the rest of society. They are helpless, they are moral, they are sympathetic, they are in pain. Beyond the Aristophanic comic rhythms of *As Is,* AIDS dramas carry other reminders of ancient Greece and of themes and treatments that have been considered universal since the Athenian era. Joseph Papp, the original director of *The Normal Heart,* writes in his foreword to the play, "In taking a burning social issue and holding it up to public and private scrutiny so that it reverberates with the social and personal implications of that issue, *The Normal Heart* reveals its origins in the theater of Sophocles, Euripides, and Shakespeare." Its essence, says Papp, is the universal preoccupation of "love . . . overcoming our greatest fear: death."

Concepts of "universality" are almost always culturally imposed; perhaps I would be on firmer footing to suggest, not that contemporary gay dramatists have found a new avenue to universality, but merely that they have approached closer to the dramatic ideal held by the Athenian Greeks. It might be argued that gay drama simply bears the imprint of a peculiar Athenian pathology, in which a homophilic and misogynist subculture replicates its values in formulaic dramatic patterns; in fact, however, contemporary gay drama is no more a copy of a Greek model than is modern gay sexual expression. In at least one important respect modern male homosexuality has run counter to the prevailing mode of the Greeks, who placed value on moderation, not on promiscuity. In elevating love between men and boys, the Greeks elaborated, in Michel Foucault's terms, an "ethics of abstention" or an "ethics of domination"; the urge to dominate found some expression in relation to subjugated sex objects such as slaves, women, and male and female prostitutes, but for the most part it was directed toward domination of the self over forces of desire. Sexual control was one of several lessons men sought to teach youth by example. Few acts were, in themselves, evil; instead, failure came in lack of mastery. "Effeminacy" was manifested not in limpwristedness or homosexual inclination, but in lack of control. Some modern gays, among other observers, have misunderstood this aspect of Greek homosexuality; even in Hoffman's *As Is,* Saul's characterization of the "good ship *Socrates,*" as if that were the vehicle that carried Rich into his arms, suggests a physicality at odds with the cerebral Socrates shown in the testimony of his contemporaries. While Plato may have falsified some of the evidence in order to play down Socrates' relation to the turncoat Alcibiades, enough support for an "ethics of abstention" remains. Evidently, unrestrained profligacy is not a universal element in homosexual experience through the ages.

The ancient Greek and the modern gay theaters do display a shared fascination—even if it may not be a universal preoccupation—with characters beyond conventional morality. Although the Greek society did not regard the "unnatural" acts of dramatic heroes with the same levels of prudish judgment that modern heterosexual American audiences might demonstrate, many Greek dramas do direct attention to perversions of the "natural" procreative order: Oedipus kills his father and sleeps with his mother, and together they produce some ill-fated, if not quite idiot children; Agamemnon sacrifices his daughter for the sake of a wind; as a consequence Clytemnestra kills her husband, who is the father of her children; Medea and Phaedra each cause the deaths of their children, one of whom, Hippolytus, is offensively proud of his celibacy. Despite the interest in unconventional sexuality, the "tragic flaw" of the scapegoat king of Greek drama was seldom directly equated with an evident sexual perversion, nor was the flaw considered the fault of the hero, who was the best champion his society had to offer. We might contend that the flaw was imposed upon him by the society for whom he had to suffer, or that he possessed it unwittingly as a part of his psychological nature. Oedipus, for example, pursues his own downfall because of a characteristic haughtiness and pig-headedness, which, it might be argued, he inherited from his father Laius. "Fate" contained the usual Greek explanation of the tragic flaw; "fault" (and, more evidently, "sin") is a more Christian concept, which became particularly useful after Calvin applied bourgeois teleology to Protestant theology. The dour philosophers of predestination saw no contradiction in blaming the indigent or the sinners for insufficiencies that the religious leaders believed had been ordained before time. In the bourgeois schema, one's state and one's status gave clear indication of one's worth before God; those who fell short could be held blameworthy on their own account, as God must not bear reproach.

Though their record may be better than the Calvinists', the Athenians were not blameless in their treatment of minority figures, women, and foreigners, who were regarded as probable extremists and perverts, unbounded by civilized laws. A focus on the tragic flaw draws our attention to Greek kings; if we are to determine the "universals" involved in the scapegoating of homosexuals in our own society, we might better look at how Greece treated its queens. No one really blamed Oedipus, even though his pride prevented him from seeing that he was powerless to thwart his fate. Perhaps no one really blamed his wife-mother Jocasta either, although she was quicker than Oedipus to blame herself. In the eyes of Aeschylus's audience, Agamemnon might render himself remotely blameworthy when he takes a sybaritic step onto the "effeminate" Persian carpet. In contrast, the "evil" in Clytemnestra as she usurps his power is more pervasive and more destructive, even if it may be of defensible origin in her outrage at seeing her daughter sacrificed, in her loneliness as a young wife whose husband was away at the wars, in her jealousy when that husband brings another woman home with him, and in the greater satisfaction she feels in the sexuality of the lover whom she can dominate. Clytemnestra, Medea, and Phaedra embody terrifying evil, while their spouses Agamemnon, Jason, and Theseus stand accused at worst of inconsiderate self-absorption. Greek society, as Philip Slater has demonstrated in *The Glory of Hera* (1968) by putting the society (through its literature) onto the psychiatrist's couch, was seriously misogynist. Since the men, who composed the in-group, wrote the plays, it is hardly a surprise that the "universal" Greek tragic heroes are members of the dominant gender. While our own society is as seriously homophobic as Athens was misogynist, members of the gay out-group have written many of the early plays about AIDS.

The concept of "universality" has seemed problematic to gay, feminist, and other minority critics on the fringes of mainstream society. Too often the "universal" has seemed "what applies to the world of straight white men." Nevertheless, some gay critics have worked the concept into their criticism. In his *Literary Visions of Homosexuality* (1983), Stuart Kellogg saw some of the earlier modern gay literature in terms of the universal theme of forbidden knowledge: to know oneself and one's own sexuality involves the blasphemy of having discovered the secrets of the gods; further, in imagining that one is free, one attempts to possess divine power. Kellogg's examples of gays becoming like the gods (like Odin, who gave his eye in order to obtain knowledge) detail the comparatively trivial gestures of a first sexual experience or a coming out. How much more significant—and how much more like the austere, ancient parables—is the insight that in the enormity of the destruction of AIDS—almost as if it is fated from the gods—the social deviancy of one individual (or even of one class of individuals) becomes insignificant; and yet, if one's acts can kill, the decision to act (or not to act) becomes full of meaning. Perhaps universality and meaningful heroism arise only in the face of impossible odds and irresolvable dilemmas. In this context, the act of Saul, as he enters Rich's hospital bed at the end of *As Is,* is a heroic (as well as a loving) act—the act of one who knows the risks and accepts whatever his incomprehensible fate might deal him, in a grand gesture much like that of the noble scapegoats of Greek tragedies.

Even if it is not universal, drama that releases tension through symbolic scapegoating is too widespread to result solely from Athenian homophilia or misogyny. It engages processes that work not only for Greeks (and, I would argue, for modern American gays) but for many other cultural groups over the globe. In the *gisaro* ceremony of the Kaluli dancers of Papua New Guinea, for instance, as Edward L. Schieffelin describes it in *The Sorrow of the Lonely and the Burning of the Dancers* (1976), a representative artist suffers so that the society's fears of death may be eased. In the form of a bird, considered the repository of the spirit returning from the spirit world, the dancer sings of specific places that will remind members of the audience of lost family and friends. The images of isolation and loneliness are judged a success if a weeping audience member grabs a torch and rams it into the back of the dancer. The purpose is evidently satisfied less by the burning than by the grieving, since the pain of those who grieve requires additional (monetary) compensation from the performers. Just as clearly, the ceremony contributes to the health of the society, as the dancers attest when they shout at their departure, "It looks like your souls will stay with you; you

won't be dying." How does the *gisaro* ensure the health of the society? In Schieffelin's view, the ceremony affirms that one will receive return for the things in life that have been lost. That is, the ceremony gives power to the victim over insurmountable forces, even over death. In a sense, the dancer returns from the other world to bring the deserved compensation.

In another sense, the *gisaro* ceremony reknots the centrifugal forces of antagonism into a social bond by reinforcing, on a symbolic level, the orderly form of social processes. Without the *gisaro,* Kaluli aggressions might find more antisocial outlets, such as more frequent witch-hunts. In the Kaluli world-view, a *sei,* an evil being who takes over the body of an unwitting victim, causes others to die; the ritual killing of a *sei*—the Kaluli equivalent of actually sacrificing a flesh-and-blood scapegoat—is much more destructive than the ceremony of burning the dancers, since only after the Kaluli kill a purported *sei* can they see whether his heart is the yellow organ of an evil spirit or the healthy organ of an innocent victim. Though their beliefs may lead them to the antisocial conclusion of killing their fellows, the Kaluli would rather believe that evil spirits inhabit unknowing human hosts than recognize that their anguish could have no explanation. The *gisaro* helps dissipate their anger by giving them another source of power over death. Athenian drama, as we have seen, apparently arose from a similar impulse and took a similar course.

Even as I stress the geographic distance between Athens and Papua New Guinea, I must, in all honesty, mention that homophilic (and some misogynist) elements of Kaluli culture bear uncanny resemblances to their Athenian counterparts: Kaluli fathers arrange an extended homosexual liaison for their pubescent sons to provide them the invigoration they need for adult sexuality (in the same way, Schieffelin posits, that the *gisaro* prepares them for the afterlife). While I would not contend that homophilia or misogyny pervade all cultures, the dramatic rituals of the Kaluli, as well as those of the Athenians and the AIDS dramatists, do reflect a widespread rhythm that Victor Turner identifies in rituals that are prophylactic against conflict. Turner argues in *From Ritual to Theatre: The Human Seriousness of Play* (1982) that an interdependent, possibly even dialectic, relationship between social dramas and genres of cultural performance exists in "perhaps all societies." According to Turner, it is all the more necessary to develop this relationship in situations where historical life becomes too complex, when narrative and cultural drama must take over the task of making cultural sense. A play is—in the context of the Protestant ethic of work—something we indulge in, like sex. Ergo, dramas introduce a moral laxness into society. The connection between moral uncertainty and redressive public ritual is not accidental; rather, it is essential in the process of social healing. In that process, marginal or liminal characters form a separate egalitarian and usually short-lived *communitas;* the secrets shared in the private enclave serve to heal the greater society when the liminal figures are reintegrated into the social structure.

For American gays in the atmosphere of political self-expression during the post–Viet Nam and Watergate era, promiscuous homosexuality came to represent an egalitarian *communitas,* in which all gay men could find brotherhood in their essence as bodies bearing sex organs. (Even if the liminal state is often sexless, liminal experience—as is evident in the license during the carnival celebration at Mardi Gras—can include sexual freedom; the sexual act can be the sacramental act of *communitas.*) It is ironic that homosexuals attempted to found their *communitas* on the bourgeois ideal of total, apparently inalienable individuality, including insistence on a right to promiscuity. Clearly, to judge from the incidence of AIDS in Africa, the widespread expression of promiscuity does not result solely from Western individualistic cosmogony. (To argue otherwise would exaggerate the effects of colonialism.) On the other hand, however much the drives that can lead to promiscuity may be inherent, a belief in the right to promiscuity is not genetic, but is culturally conditioned. An apparent right to promiscuity presents a perceptual problem for Western heterosexuals as well as homosexuals: Emma Bovary and Willie Loman also err when they imagine that their rights guarantee them a liberty that must or can be absolute. When they are exposed to public scrutiny, they discover that there is no communal support for the erring individual, even if the individualistic society shares their errors in private.

The gay "community" sought to supply the supportive network so that individual proclivities would become acceptable personal expressions rather than aberrant "sins." Unfortunately, the structural imposition of a past and a future is usually enough to change (and often destroy) the *communitas;* through AIDS, the gay *communitas,* with its central doctrine of sexual freedom, is given a past and a future. In terms of their participation in this ritual process, gays have a right—beyond their hurt and dismay at the effects of the actual disease—to feel betrayed about the failure of their public ritual of "coming out." If things had remained unchanged, "coming out" might have represented, in Victor Turner's terms, a liminal victory that would have reinvigorated society. At the very least, the gesture could have remained an initiatory or confirmatory act for new members of the *communitas.* Instead, because the scale has become, in Turner's language, more "global and species-threatening," the ritual gesture of "coming out" is no longer meaningful. Perhaps because they have felt themselves in a perpetual liminal existence, gay playwrights have been able to respond almost immediately to AIDS with another public ritual that may have an effect on the health of our society.

In the state of modern existential *anomie,* the intrusion of AIDS might seem the final alienating blow. Can AIDS dramas cure, not the disease of AIDS, but the disease of our separation from one another? I cling to the hope that the representative and symbolic scapegoating in the AIDS dramas can help reduce actual scapegoating of gays by restoring a unity to our collective selves. It is perhaps encouraging that AIDS has become a topic for drama in the mass media (even though most of the television plays, other than *An Early Frost,* have involved more "sympathetic"—because they can be considered more "innocent"—victims, such as recipients of blood transfusions).

Yet, there is no reason to believe that drama, even television drama, can affect our huge and diverse society today in the way theatrical events affected a few thousand Athenians or a few hundred Kaluli. I do find it auspicious that playwrights are once again taking sex and death, the main themes of dramatic literature, beyond the realm of purely personal choice.

The AIDS dramatists help raise consideration of sex (by both gays and straights) to the level of social responsibility: a responsible choice about sex can help remove the specter of death from the entire society. Saul's act in entering Rich's bed becomes a responsible—as well as a loving and heroic—act if he subsequently refuses to place others in jeopardy; indeed, Rich supplied an example when he insisted on telling his would-be lovers that he had the disease. The AIDS dramatists act responsibly in a direct way by increasing the awareness of the society. In an indirect way, they provide the society with representative scapegoats, who, because of the awesome scope and the incomprehensible threat of the plague, take on the suffering of the whole society and may help reintegrate their liminal brothers into it.

The recent new York openings of *Buddies, Zero Positive, Positive Me,* and a variety of workshop productions suggest that the subject of AIDS will continue to attract playwrights and audiences. It should. AIDS dramas directly confront a threat to all of modern humanity. Indirectly, they help us deal with age-old forces we can overcome in no other way. (pp. 209-22)

> *George Newtown, "Sex, Death, and the Drama of AIDS," in* The Antioch Review, *Vol. 47, No. 2, Spring, 1989, pp. 209-22.*

Susan Sontag   (essay date 1989)

[*An American critic, novelist, short story writer, and script writer, Sontag is the author of* Illness as Metaphor *(1978) and is a renowned scholar of modernist literature and Western culture. In the following excerpt from* AIDS and Its Metaphors, *she compares the metaphoric qualities of cancer, syphilis, and AIDS and describes the characteristics of AIDS that inform its potential use as a metaphor.*]

Just as one might predict for a disease that is not yet fully understood as well as extremely recalcitrant to treatment, the advent of this terrifying new disease, new at least in its epidemic form, has provided a large-scale occasion for the metaphorizing of illness.

Strictly speaking, AIDS—acquired immune deficiency syndrome—is not the name of an illness at all. It is the name of a medical condition, whose consequences are a spectrum of illnesses. In contrast to syphilis and cancer, which provide prototypes for most of the images and metaphors attached to AIDS, the very definition of AIDS requires the presence of other illnesses, so-called opportunistic infections and malignancies. But though not in *that* sense a single disease, AIDS lends itself to being regarded as one—in part because, unlike cancer and like syphilis, it is thought to have a single cause.

AIDS has a dual metaphoric genealogy. As a micro-process, it is described as cancer is: an invasion. When the focus is transmission of the disease, an older metaphor, reminiscent of syphilis, is invoked: pollution. (One gets it from the blood or sexual fluids of infected people or from contaminated blood products.) But the military metaphors used to describe AIDS have a somewhat different focus from those used in describing cancer. With cancer, the metaphor scants the issue of causality (still a murky topic in cancer research) and picks up at the point at which rogue cells inside the body mutate, eventually moving out from an original site or organ to overrun other organs or systems—a domestic subversion. In the description of AIDS the enemy is what causes the disease, an infectious agent that comes from the outside:

> The invader is tiny, about one sixteen-thous-andth the size of the head of a pin. . . . Scouts of the body's immune system, large cells called macrophages, sense the presence of the diminu-tive foreigner and promptly alert the immune system. It begins to mobilize an array of cells that, among other things, produce antibodies to deal with the threat. Single-mindedly, the AIDS virus ignores many of the blood cells in its path, evades the rapidly advancing defenders and homes in on the master coordinator of the im-mune system, a helper T cell. . . .

This is the language of political paranoia, with its characteristic distrust of a pluralistic world. A defense system consisting of cells "that, among other things, produce antibodies to deal with the threat" is, predictably, no match for an invader who advances "single-mindedly." And the science-fiction flavor, already present in cancer talk, is even more pungent in accounts of AIDS—this one comes from *Time* magazine in late 1986—with infection described like the high-tech warfare for which we are being prepared (and inured) by the fantasies of our leaders and by video entertainments. In the era of Star Wars and Space Invaders, AIDS has proved an ideally comprehensible illness:

> On the surface of that cell, it finds a receptor into which one of its envelope proteins fits perfectly, like a key into a lock. Docking with the cell, the virus penetrates the cell membrane and is stripped of its protective shell in the process. . . .

Next the invader takes up permanent residence, by a form of alien takeover familiar in science-fiction narratives. The body's own cells *become* the invader. With the help of an enzyme the virus carries with it,

> the naked AIDS virus converts its RNA into . . . DNA, the master molecule of life. The molecule then penetrates the cell nucleus, inserts itself into a chromosome and takes over part of the cellular machinery, directing it to produce more AIDS viruses. Eventually, overcome by its alien product, the cell swells and dies, releasing a flood of new viruses to attack other cells. . . .

As viruses attack other cells, runs the metaphor, so "a host of opportunistic diseases, normally warded off by a healthy immune system, attacks the body," whose integri-ty and vigor have been sapped by the sheer replication of "alien product" that follows the collapse of its im-munological defenses. "Gradually weakened by the on-slaught, the AIDS victim dies, sometimes in months, but almost always within a few years of the first symptoms." Those who have not already succumbed are described as "under assault, showing the telltale symptoms of the dis-ease," while millions of others "harbor the virus, vulnera-ble at any time to a final, all-out attack."

Cancer makes cells proliferate; in AIDS, cells die. Even as this original model of AIDS (the mirror image of leuke-mia) has been altered, descriptions of how the virus does its work continue to echo the way the illness is perceived as infiltrating the society. "AIDS Virus Found to Hide in Cells, Eluding Detection by Normal Tests" was the head-line of a recent front-page story in *The New York Times* announcing the discovery that the virus can "lurk" for years in the macrophages—disrupting their disease-fighting function without killing them, "even when the macrophages are filled almost to bursting with virus," and without producing antibodies, the chemicals the body makes in response to "invading agents" and whose pres-ence has been regarded as an infallible marker of the syn-drome. That the virus isn't lethal for *all* the cells where it takes up residence, as is now thought, only increases the illness-foe's reputation for wiliness and invincibility.

What makes the viral assault so terrifying is that contami-nation, and therefore vulnerability, is understood as per-manent. Even if someone infected were never to develop any symptoms—that is, the infection remained, or could by medical intervention be rendered, inactive—the viral enemy would be forever within. In fact, so it is believed, it is just a matter of time before something awakens ("trig-gers") it, before the appearance of "the telltale symp-toms." Like syphilis, known to generations of doctors as "the great masquerader," AIDS is a clinical construction, an inference. It takes its identity from the presence of *some* among a long, and lengthening, roster of symptoms (no one has everything that AIDS could be), symptoms which "mean" that what the patient has is this illness. The con-struction of the illness rests on the invention not only of AIDS as a clinical entity but of a kind of junior AIDS, called AIDS-related complex (ARC), to which people are assigned if they show "early" and often intermittent symp-toms of immunological deficit such as fevers, weight loss, fungal infections, and swollen lymph glands. AIDS is pro-gressive, a disease of time. Once a certain density of symp-toms is attained, the course of the illness can be swift, and brings atrocious suffering. Besides the commonest "pre-senting" illnesses (some hitherto unusual, at least in a fatal form, such as a rare skin cancer and a rare form of pneu-monia), a plethora of disabling, disfiguring, and humiliat-ing symptoms make the AIDS patient steadily more in-firm, helpless, and unable to control or take care of basic functions and needs.

The sense in which AIDS is a slow disease makes it more like syphilis, which is characterized in terms of "stages," than like cancer. Thinking in terms of "stages" is essential to discourse about AIDS. Syphilis in its most dreaded form is "tertiary syphilis," syphilis in its third stage. What is called AIDS is generally understood as the last of three stages—the first of which is infection with a human immunodeficiency virus (HIV) and early evidence of inroads on the immune system—with a long latency period between infection and the onset of the "telltale" symptoms. (Apparently not as long as syphilis, in which the latency period between secondary and tertiary illness might be decades. But it is worth noting that when syphilis first appeared in epidemic form in Europe at the end of the fifteenth century, it was a rapid disease, of an unexplained virulence that is unknown today, in which death often occurred in the second stage, sometimes within months or a few years.) Cancer *grows* slowly: it is not thought to be, for a long time, latent. (A convincing account of a process in terms of "stages" seems invariably to include the notion of a normative delay or halt in the process, such as is supplied by the notion of latency.) True, a cancer is "staged." This is a principal tool of diagnosis, which means classifying it according to its gravity, determining how "advanced" it is. But it is mostly a spatial notion: that the cancer advances through the body, traveling or migrating along predictable routes. Cancer is first of all a disease of the body's geography, in contrast to syphilis and AIDS, whose definition depends on constructing a temporal sequence of stages.

Syphilis is an affliction that didn't have to run its ghastly full course, to paresis (as it did for Baudelaire and Maupassant and Jules de Goncourt), and could and often did remain at the stage of nuisance, indignity (as it did for Flaubert). The scourge was also a cliché, as Flaubert himself observed. "SYPHILIS. Everybody has it, more or less" reads one entry in the *Dictionary of Accepted Opinions,* his treasury of mid-nineteenth-century platitudes. And syphilis did manage to acquire a darkly positive association in late-nineteenth- and early-twentieth-century Europe, when a link was made between syphilis and heightened ("feverish") mental activity that parallels the connection made since the era of the Romantic writers between pulmonary tuberculosis and heightened emotional activity. As if in honor of all the notable writers and artists who ended their lives in syphilitic witlessness, it came to be believed that the brain lesions of neurosyphilis might actually inspire original thought or art. Thomas Mann, whose fiction is a storehouse of early-twentieth-century disease myths, makes this notion of syphilis as muse central to his *Doctor Faustus,* with its protagonist a great composer whose voluntarily contracted syphilis—the Devil guarantees that the infection will be limited to the central nervous system—confers on him twenty-four years of incandescent creativity. E. M. Cioran recalls how, in Romania in the late 1920s, syphilis-envy figured in his adolescent expectations of literary glory: he would discover that he had contracted syphilis, be rewarded with several hyperproductive years of genius, then collapse into madness. This romanticizing of the dementia characteristic of neurosyphilis was the forerunner of the much more persistent fantasy in this century about mental illness as a source of artistic creativity or spiritual originality. But with AIDS—though dementia is also a common, late symptom—no compensatory mythology has arisen, or seems likely to arise. AIDS, like cancer, does not allow romanticizing or sentimentalizing, perhaps because its association

with death is too powerful. In Krzysztof Zanussi's film *Spiral* (1978), the most truthful account I know of anger at dying, the protagonist's illness is never specified; therefore, it *has* to be cancer. For several generations now, the generic idea of death has been a death from cancer, and a cancer death is experienced as a generic defeat. Now the generic rebuke to life and to hope is AIDS. (pp. 16-24)

. . . . .

The emergence of a new catastrophic epidemic, when for several decades it had been confidently assumed that such calamities belonged to the past, would not be enough to revive the moralistic inflation of an epidemic into a "plague." It was necessary that the epidemic be one whose most common means of transmission is sexual.

Cotton Mather called syphilis a punishment "which the Just Judgment of God has reserved for our Late Ages." Recalling this and other nonsense uttered about syphilis from the end of the fifteenth to the early twentieth centuries, one should hardly be surprised that many want to view AIDS metaphorically—as, plague-like, a moral judgment on society. Professional fulminators can't resist the rhetorical opportunity offered by a sexually transmitted disease that is lethal. Thus, the fact that AIDS is predominantly a heterosexually transmitted illness in the countries where it first emerged in epidemic form has not prevented such guardians of public morals as Jesse Helms and Norman Podhoretz from depicting it as a visitation specially aimed at (and deservedly incurred by) Western homosexuals, while another Reagan-era celebrity, Pat Buchanan, orates about "AIDS and Moral Bankruptcy," and Jerry Falwell offers the generic diagnosis that "AIDS is God's judgment on a society that does not live by His rules." What is surprising is not that the AIDS epidemic has been exploited in this way but that such cant has been confined to so predictable a sector of bigots; the official discourse about AIDS invariably includes admonitions against bigotry.

The pronouncements of those who claim to speak for God can mostly be discounted as the rhetoric regularly prompted by sexually transmitted illness—from Cotton Mather's judgment to recent statements by two leading Brazilian clerics, Bishop Falcão of Brasilia, who declares AIDS to be "the consequence of moral decadence," and the Cardinal of Rio de Janeiro, Eugenio Sales, who wants it both ways, describing AIDS as "God's punishment" and as "the revenge of nature." More interesting, because their purposes are more complex, are the secular sponsors of this sort of invective. Authoritarian political ideologies have a vested interest in promoting fear, a sense of the imminence of takeover by aliens—and real diseases are useful material. Epidemic diseases usually elicit a call to ban the entry of foreigners, immigrants. And xenophobic propaganda has always depicted immigrants as bearers of disease (in the late nineteenth century: cholera, yellow fever, typhoid fever, tuberculosis). It seems logical that the political figure in France who represents the most extreme nativist, racist views, Jean-Marie Le Pen, has attempted a strategy of fomenting fear of this new alien peril, insisting that AIDS is not just infectious but contagious, and calling for mandatory nationwide testing and the quarantine of everyone carrying the virus. And AIDS is a gift to the present regime in South Africa, whose Foreign Minister declared recently, evoking the incidence of the illness among the mine workers imported from neighboring all-black countries: "The terrorists are now coming to us with a weapon more terrible than Marxism: AIDS."

The AIDS epidemic serves as an ideal projection for First World political paranoia. Not only is the so-called AIDS virus the quintessential invader from the Third World. It can stand for any mythological menace. In this country, AIDS has so far evoked less pointedly racist reactions than in Europe, including the Soviet Union, where the African origin of the disease is stressed. Here it is as much a reminder of feelings associated with the menace of the Second World as it is an image of being overrun by the Third. Predictably, the public voices in this country most committed to drawing moral lessons from the AIDS epidemic, such as Norman Podhoretz, are those whose main theme is worry about America's will to maintain its bellicosity, its expenditures on armaments, its firm anticommunist stance, and who find everywhere evidence of the decline of American political and imperial authority. Denunciations of "the gay plague" are part of a much larger complaint, common among antiliberals in the West and many exiles from the Russian bloc, about contemporary permissiveness of all kinds: a now-familiar diatribe against the "soft" West, with its hedonism, its vulgar sexy music, its indulgence in drugs, its disabled family life, which have sapped the will to stand up to communism. AIDS is a favorite concern of those who translate their political agenda into questions of group psychology: of national self-esteem and self-confidence. Although these specialists in ugly feelings insist that AIDS is a punishment for deviant sex, what moves them is not just, or even principally, homophobia. Even more important is the utility of AIDS in pursuing one of the main activities of the so-called neoconservatives, the Kulturkampf against all that is called, for short (and inaccurately), the 1960s. A whole politics of "the will"—of intolerance, of paranoia, of fear of political weakness—has fastened on this disease.

AIDS is such an apt goad to familiar, consensus-building fears that have been cultivated for several generations, like fear of "subversion"—and to fears that have surfaced more recently, of uncontrollable pollution and of unstoppable migration from the Third World—that it would seem inevitable that AIDS be envisaged in this society as something total, civilization-threatening. And raising the disease's metaphorical stature by keeping alive fears of its easy transmissibility, its imminent spread, does not diminish its status as, mainly, a consequence of illicit acts (or of economic and cultural backwardness). That it is a punishment for deviant behavior and that it threatens the innocent—these two notions about AIDS are hardly in contradiction. Such is the extraordinary potency and efficacy of the plague metaphor: it allows a disease to be regarded both as something incurred by vulnerable "others" and as (potentially) everyone's disease.

Still, it is one thing to emphasize how the disease menaces everybody (in order to incite fear and confirm prejudice), quite another to argue (in order to defuse prejudice and reduce stigma) that eventually AIDS will, directly or indirectly, affect everybody. Recently these same mythologists who have been eager to use AIDS for ideological mobilization against deviance have backed away from the most panic-inspiring estimates of the illness. They are among the most vocal of those who insist that infection will *not* spread to "the general population" and have turned their attention to denouncing "hysteria" or "frenzy" about AIDS. Behind what they now consider the excessive publicity given the disease, they discern the desire to placate an all-powerful minority by agreeing to regard "their" disease as "ours"—further evidence of the sway of nefarious "liberal" values and of America's spiritual decline. Making AIDS everyone's problem and therefore a subject on which everyone needs to be educated, charge the antiliberal AIDS mythologists, subverts our understanding of the difference between "us" and "them"; indeed, exculpates or at least makes irrelevant moral judgments about "them." (In such rhetoric the disease continues to be identified almost exclusively with homosexuality, and specifically the practice of sodomy.) "Has America become a country where classroom discussion of the Ten Commandments is impermissible but teacher instructions in safe sodomy are to be mandatory?" inquires Pat Buchanan, protesting the "foolish" proposal made in the report of the recent Presidential Commission on the epidemic, chaired by Admiral Watkins, to outlaw discrimination against people with AIDS. Not the disease but the appeals heard from the most official quarters "to set aside prejudice and fear in favor of compassion" (the words of the Watkins Report) have become a principal target, suggesting as they do a weakening of this society's power (or willingness) to punish and segregate through judgments about sexual behavior.

More than cancer, but rather like syphilis, AIDS seems to foster ominous fantasies about a disease that is a marker of both individual and social vulnerabilities. The virus invades the body; the disease (or, in the newer version, the fear of the disease) is described as invading the whole society. In late 1986 President Reagan pronounced AIDS to be spreading—"insidiously" of course—"through the length and breadth of our society." But AIDS, while the pretext for expressing dark intimations about the body politic, has yet to seem credible as a political metaphor for internal enemies, even in France, where AIDS—in French *le sida*—was quickly added to the store of political invective. Le Pen has dismissed some of his opponents as "AIDS-ish" (*sidatique*), and the antiliberal polemicist Louis Pauwels said that lycée students on strike last year were suffering from "mental AIDS" (*sont atteint d'un sida mental*). Neither has AIDS proved of much use as a metaphor for international political evil. True, Jeane Kirkpatrick once couldn't resist comparing international terrorism to AIDS, but such sallies are rare—perhaps because for that purpose the cancer metaphor has proved so fecund.

This doesn't mean that AIDS is not used, preposterously, as a metaphor, but only that AIDS has a metaphoric potential different from that of cancer. When the movie director in Alain Tanner's film *La Vallée Fantôme* (1987)

> **Even more promising than its connection with latency is the potential of AIDS as a metaphor for contamination and mutation.**
>
> —*Susan Sontag*

muses, "Cinema is like a cancer," and then corrects himself, "No, it's infectious, it's more like AIDS," the comparison seems lumberingly self-conscious as well as a decided underuse of AIDS. Not its infectiousness but its characteristic latency offers a more distinctive use of AIDS as a metaphor. Thus, the Palestinian Israeli writer Anton Shammas in the Jerusalem weekly *Kol Ha'ir,* in a fit of medical, sexual, and political fantasy, recently described Israel's Declaration of Independence of 1948 as

> the AIDS of "the Jewish State in the Land of Israel," whose long incubation has produced Gush Emunim and . . . [Rabbi Meir] Kahane. That is where it all began, and that is where it all will end. AIDS, I am sorry to say, despite my sympathy for homosexuals, affects mainly mono-erotics, and a mononational Jewish State contains by definition the seeds of its own destruction: the collapse of the political immune system that we call democracy. . . . Rock Hudson, who once was as beautiful as a Palmachnik, now lies dying long after the dissolution of the Palmach. The State of Israel (for Jews, of course) was indeed once beautiful. . . .

And even more promising than its connection with latency is the potential of AIDS as a metaphor for contamination and mutation. Cancer is still common as a metaphor for what is feared or deplored, even if the illness is less dreaded than before. If AIDS can eventually be drafted for comparable use, it will be because AIDS is not only invasive (a trait it shares with cancer) or even because it is infectious, but because of the specific imagery that surrounds viruses.

Virology supplies a new set of medical metaphors independent of AIDS which nevertheless reinforce the AIDS mythology. It was years before AIDS that William Burroughs oracularly declared, and Laurie Anderson echoed, "Language is a virus." And the viral explanation is invoked more and more often. Until recently, most of the infections recognized as viral were ones, like rabies and influenza, that have very rapid effects. But the category of slow-acting viral infections is growing. Many progressive and invariably fatal disorders of the central nervous system and some degenerative diseases of the brain that can appear in old age, as well as the so-called auto-immune diseases, are now suspected of being, in fact, slow virus diseases. (And evidence continues to accumulate for a viral cause of at least some human cancers.) Notions of conspiracy translate well into metaphors of implacable, insidious, infinitely patient viruses. In contrast to bacteria, which are relatively complex organisms, viruses are described as an extremely primitive form of life. At the same

time, their activities are far more complex than those envisaged in the earlier germ models of infection. Viruses are not simply agents of infection, contamination. They transport genetic "information," they transform cells. And they themselves, many of them, evolve. While the smallpox virus appears to stay constant for centuries, influenza viruses evolve so rapidly that vaccines need to be modified every year to keep up with changes in the "surface coat" of the virus. The virus or, more accurately, viruses thought to cause AIDS are at least as mutable as the influenza viruses. Indeed, "virus" is now a synonym for change. Linda Ronstadt, recently explaining why she prefers doing Mexican folk music to rock 'n' roll, observed: "We don't have any tradition in contemporary music except change. Mutate, like a virus."

So far as "plague" still has a future as a metaphor, it is through the ever more familiar notion of the virus. (Perhaps no disease in the future caused by a bacillus will be considered as plague-like.) Information itself, now inextricably linked to the powers of computers, is threatened by something compared to a virus. Rogue or pirate programs, known as software viruses, are described as paralleling the behavior of biological viruses (which can capture the genetic code of parts of an organism and effect transfers of alien genetic material). These programs, deliberately planted onto a floppy disk meant to be used with the computer or introduced when the computer is communicating over telephone lines or data networks with other computers, copy themselves onto the computer's operating system. Like their biological namesakes, they won't produce immediate signs of damage to the computer's memory, which gives the newly "infected" program time to spread to other computers. Such metaphors drawn from virology, partly stimulated by the omnipresence of talk of AIDS, are turning up everywhere. (The virus that destroyed a considerable amount of data at the student computer center at Lehigh University in Bethlehem, Pennsylvania, in 1987, was given the name PC AIDS. In France, computer specialists already speak of the problem of *le sida informatique.*) And they reinforce the sense of the omnipresence of AIDS.

It is perhaps not surprising that the newest transforming element in the modern world, computers, should be borrowing metaphors drawn from our newest transforming illness. Nor is it surprising that descriptions of the course of viral infection now often echo the language of the computer age, as when it is said that a virus will normally produce "new copies of itself." In addition to the mechanistic descriptions, the way viruses are animistically characterized—as a menace in waiting, as mutable, as furtive, as biologically innovative—reinforces the sense that a disease can be something ingenious, unpredictable, novel. These metaphors are central to ideas about AIDS that distinguish this illness from others that have been regarded as plague-like. For though the fears AIDS represents are old, its status as that unexpected event, an entirely new disease—a new judgment, as it were—adds to the dread. (pp. 60-71)

Susan Sontag, in her AIDS and Its Metaphors, *Farrar, Straus and Giroux, 1989, 95 p.*

Lee Edelman   (essay date 1989)

[A professor of English, Edelman has written widely on gay literature. In the following essay, he examines the relationship between the literal and figurative in AIDS discourse.]

In an article titled "The Metaphor of AIDS," published for a popular audience in the Sunday magazine of the *Boston Globe,* Lee Grove, an instructor of creative writing and American literature at the University of Massachusetts, reflects on the ways in which the AIDS epidemic has altered his understanding of literary texts and his relation to the teaching of literature. Referring specifically to the Renaissance pun that brought together, at least linguistically, the experiences of orgasm and death, Grove writes:

> "To die," "to have sex"—that coupling has always been figurative, metaphorical, sophisticated wordplay, a literary conceit, one of those outrageous paradoxes dear to the heart of a racy divine like John Donne.

> Outrageous no longer. The coupling isn't figurative anymore. It's literal.

I want to consider the highly charged relation between the literal and the figural as it informs the discussion of AIDS in America and to explore the political uses to which the ideological framing of that relationship has been put. Toward that end my subtitle locates "literary theory" between the categories of "politics" and "AIDS" to indicate my belief that both of those categories produce, and are produced as, historical discourses susceptible to analysis by the critical methodologies associated with literary theory.

This is not to say that literary theory occupies some unproblematic or privileged position; to the contrary, literature, including that form of literature that is literary theory, is by no means distinct from political discourse, and thus from either the discourse on AIDS, or the politics that governs the discourse on AIDS. By the same token, politics and AIDS cannot be disentangled from their implication in the linguistic or the rhetorical. Indeed, one of the ideological oppositions I would call into question is that whereby the biological, associated with the literal or the "real," is counterposed against the literary, associated with the figural or the fictive. That opposition is already deeply and unavoidably political, which is to say, it bespeaks an ideologically determined hierarchy of values in which power—the power to speak seriously, to speak with authority, and thereby to influence policy—is very much at stake in the claim to be able to speak literally.

The AIDS epidemic, then, is not to be construed, as Grove asserts, in terms of its defiguralizing literality, but rather, and more dangerously, as the breeding ground for all sorts of figural associations whose virulence derives from their presentation under the aspect of literality. Indeed, one of the most disturbing features that characterizes the discourse on AIDS in America is the way in which the literal is recurrently and tendentiously produced as a figure whose figurality remains strategically occluded—a figure that thus has the potential to be used toward the most politically repressive ends. The often hysterical terms within which the Western discussion of AIDS has been conducted reflect an untenable, but politically manipulable, belief that we can separate biological science, and therefore the social policy based on that science, from the instability and duplicity that literary theory has increasingly identified as inherent in the operations of language.

Though my subject necessarily involves literature and AIDS, my focus falls not on those literary works wherein the urgency of AIDS achieves thematic inscription, but rather on the inevitable inscriptions of the literary that mark the discourse on AIDS. The text that provides the occasion for my analysis, the text on which my remarks will turn or trope, is a relatively brief one, "Silence = Death." This slogan has achieved wide currency, particularly—though by no means exclusively—within the gay community, both as a challenge to the murderously delayed and cynically inadequate official responses to AIDS and as a rallying cry for those who have borne the burden of death and suffering, calling upon them to defend themselves against the dangerous discourse of mastery produced by medical or legislative authorities in order to defend their *own* vested interests in the face of this epidemic. Significantly, issues of defense achieve an inevitable centrality in discussions of AIDS in ways that critically distinguish this epidemic from many others. Because the syndrome attacks the body's defensive mechanisms; because once it does so, science as yet can offer no defense against it; because in the West it has appeared primarily among groups already engaged in efforts to defend themselves against the intolerance of the dominant culture; because modern science and the national political institutions funding modern science feel called upon to defend their prestige against the assault on medical know-how represented by this disease; because individuals and groups, often irrationally, seek ways to defend themselves against contact with this disease; and because some politicians, in order to defend against political opposition, deploy the AIDS issue strategically to ensure their own political survival: for all of these reasons the question of defense is inextricably and distinctively inscribed in the discourse on AIDS. And as this preliminary formulation of the issues suggests, my focus is on the interrelations among the notions of discourse, defense, and disease—particularly as they intersect with the already activated ideologies of homosexuality and homophobia in the West to converge at the virulent site of discursive contention that is AIDS.

> **The often hysterical terms within which the Western discussion of AIDS has been conducted reflect an untenable, but politically manipulable, belief that we can separate biological science from the instability and duplicity that literary theory has increasingly identified as inherent in the operations of language.**
>
> **—Lee Edelman**

These last words seem to define AIDS in a way that few in the medical profession would recognize, so let me present a definition of AIDS at the outset that will seem more literal, or as students of rhetoric would say, more "proper." According to current scientific understanding, and I hasten to add that it is not my intention necessarily to endorse or validate that understanding, AIDS results from infection with some quantity of HIV or Human Immunodeficiency Virus, which attacks the cells of the immune system, particularly the T-helper or T-4 cells, and impairs the body's ability to defend itself against viral, fungal, and parasitic infections. Medical researchers would thus accept a characterization of AIDS as an infectious condition in which the stake is "literally" the possibility of defense. As David Black puts it simply in *The Plague Years,* his "chronicle" of AIDS, "the immune system is the body's complex and still imperfectly understood defense mechanism. Its job is to tell the difference between Self and Not-Self." I will come back to the Emersonian implications of this description of the immune response, but for now I want to examine the notion of defense and its importance not only in the bio-logic articulated within the body by AIDS, but also in the reactive or defensive discourse embodied in the slogan Silence = Death. For if that slogan challenges those in the communities most affected by AIDS to defend themselves, it does so by appealing to defensive properties that it implicitly identifies as inherent in discourse. The slogan, after all, which most frequently appears in a graphic configuration that positions the letters of its text, in white, beneath a pink triangle on a field of black, alludes to the Nazi campaign against homosexuals (identified in the concentration camps by the pink triangle they were required to wear) in order to propose a gay equivalent to the post-Holocaust rallying cry of Jewish activists: "Never again." At the same time, Silence = Death can be read as a post-AIDS revision of a motto popular among gay militants not long ago—"Out of the closets and into the streets"—and as such it similarly implies that language, discourse, public manifestations are necessary weapons of defense in a contemporary strategy of gay survival. For if we assert that Silence = Death, then one corollary to this theorem in the geometry that governs the relationship among discourse, defense, and disease must be that Discourse = Defense, that language, articulation, the intervention of voice, is salutary, vivifying, since discourse can defend us against the death that must result from the continuation of our silence.

But to speak of mechanisms of defense, particularly in terms of linguistic operations, is necessarily to invoke the specter of Freud, who offered us a taxonomy of psychic defenses in his studies of the unconscious and its operations. And here, as always, Freud calls into question the basis for any naive optimism about the success of our defensive maneuvers. Here is a passage from H. D.'s memoir [*Tribute to Freud,* 1974] of her psychoanalysis by Freud that speaks to the relation between discourse and defense in a particularly telling way: only once, according to H. D., did Freud ever "lay down the law" and that was when he said "never—I mean, never at any time, in any circumstance, endeavor to defend me, if and when you hear abusive remarks made about me and my work." H. D. then goes on to recall:

He explained it carefully. He might have been giving a lesson in geometry or demonstrating the inevitable course of a disease once the virus has entered the system. At this point, he seemed to indicate (as if there were a chart of the fever patient, pinned on the wall before us), at the least suggestion that you may be about to begin a counterargument in my defense, the anger or frustration of the assailant will be driven deeper. You will do no good to the detractor by mistakenly beginning a logical defense. You will drive the hatred or the fear or the prejudice in deeper.

Defense of this sort is necessarily failed defense; far from being salubrious, it serves only to compromise further one's immunity and to stimulate greater virulence. Interestingly enough, this corresponds to the process whereby, according to some medical researchers, HIV moves from a state of latency in an infected cell to active reproduction. The defensive "stimulation of an immune response" seems to be one of "the conditions that activates the production of new" HIV that can then go on to infect other cells. Since defensive maneuvers may have the unintended effect of disseminating or intensifying infection, the relationship between the two can be rearticulated in the formula: Defense = Disease.

Freud's argument in warning H. D. against engaging in defensive interventions significantly echoes the logic sounded centuries earlier by Plato in the *Timaeus.* Writing specifically about the wisdom of medical interventions to defend the body against the ravages of disease, Plato offers a cautionary note: "diseases unless they are very dangerous should not be irritated by medicines, since every form of disease is in a manner akin to the living being, whose complex frame has an appointed term of life. . . . And this holds also of the constitution of diseases; if any one regardless of the appointed time tries to subdue them by medicine, he only aggravates and multiplies them." The word here translated as "medicine" derives, as Jacques Derrida argues in "Plato's Pharmacy," [in his *Dissemination,* 1981], from the Greek word *pharmakon* signifying a drug or philter that occupies an ambiguous position as remedy and poison at once. Commenting on this passage from Plato, Derrida observes: "Just as health is autonomous and auto-matic, 'normal' disease demonstrates its autarky by confronting the pharmaceutical aggression with *metastatic* reactions which displace the site of the disease, with the eventual result that the points of resistance are reinforced and multiplied." Thus for Plato, as for Freud, gestures of defense can aggravate rather than ameliorate one's condition. Freud, of course, is referring explicitly to language or discourse as a mechanism of defense against one's enemies or detractors; H. D.'s reference to the "course of a disease once the virus has entered the system" is clearly presented only as a figural embellishment. Plato, on the other hand, is referring explicitly to medical defenses against disease, but considerations of discourse are decisively at issue in his discussion as well.

In the long and complicated argument unfolded in "Plato's Pharmacy," Derrida shows how Plato identifies writing with the *pharmakon,* thus rendering it simultaneously a poison, a remedy, a fantastic or magical philter, and a rational medical technology. If writing as *pharmakon* is already, at the beginning of Western culture, producing an entanglement of literary and medical discourse, its antithesis, the true voice of speech, is identified by Plato in the *Phaedrus* with the vital force of *logos.* Thus Derrida characterizes Plato's notion of *logos* in the following words:

> *Logos* is a *zoon.* An animal that is born, grows, belongs to the *phusis.* Linguistics, logic, dialectics, and zoology are all in the same camp.
>
> In describing *logos* as a *zoon,* Plato is following certain rhetors and sophists before him who, as a contrast to the cadaverous rigidity of writing, had held up the living spoken word.

Derrida's strategy in deconstructing the opposition between speech and writing is to show how the living word of speech is already informed by or predicated upon a form of writing or an *archi-écriture.* But of particular importance for my purposes is the way in which Derrida's reading of Plato insists upon the inextricability of the textual and the biological even as it uses rhetorical or literary techniques to subvert or dismantle the rational edifice of the Western philosophical tradition.

Consider again Derrida's gloss on Plato's wariness about the *pharmakon* in *Timaeus:* "Just as health is autonomous and auto-matic, 'normal' disease demonstrates its autarky by confronting the pharmaceutical aggression with *metastatic* reactions which displace the site of the disease, with the eventual result that the points of resistance are reinforced or multiplied." Bearing in mind that Derrida's reading of the *pharmakon* explicitly invokes the critical conjunction of discourse and biology informing the platonic opposition between writing as supplement and speech as living word, his gloss suggests that defensive strategies deployed—in the realm of discourse or disease—to combat agencies of virulence may themselves be informed by the virulence they are seeking to efface, informed by it in ways that do not produce the immunizing effect of a vaccine, but that serve, instead, to reinforce and even multiply the dangerous sites of infection. Derrida makes explicit this pathology of rhetoric when, elsewhere in "Plato's Pharmacy," he remarks that "metaphoricity is the contamination of logic and the logic of contamination." In other words, Disease = Discourse. Derrida's diagnosis of metaphor as contamination makes clear that the rationalism of philosophical logic—a rationalism that provides the foundation for Western medical and scientific practice—is not untainted by the figurality that philosophy repudiates as literary, and, in consequence, as deceptive, inessential, and expendable. Both logic and contamination are very much at stake in the unfolding of these infectiously multiplying equations. Perhaps by returning to the germ of these remarks it will be possible to see how the logic of equations distinctively contaminates the discourse on AIDS.

Against my initial text, Silence = Death, let me juxtapose a passage from an open letter written by Larry Kramer, AIDS activist and author of, among other things, *The Normal Heart,* a play about the difficulties of getting Americans—gay and straight alike—to pay serious atten-

Larry Kramer.

tion to the AIDS epidemic. Outraged by dilatory and inadequate responses at the early stages of the medical crisis, Kramer is quoted as having addressed the following words to both the press and the leaders of the gay rights movement: "That all of you . . . continue to refuse to transmit to the public the facts and figures of what is happening *daily* makes you, in my mind, equal to murderers." Beside Kramer's remark I would place a graffito that David Black describes as having been scrawled on a wall at New York University: "Gay Rights = AIDS." A somewhat less overtly homophobic but no less insidious version of this notion is offered by Frances Fitzgerald in her analysis of the effects of AIDS on San Francisco's Castro Street community ["The Castro—II," *The New Yorker* (1986)]: "The gay carnival, with its leather masks and ball gowns, had thus been the twentieth-century equivalent of the Masque of the Red Death." And finally, here is a quotation from a "26-year-old-never-married woman" cited by Masters and Johnson in *Newsweek* magazine's excerpt from their controversial book on AIDS: "No sex, no worries. No sex, no AIDS. It's really a very simple equation, isn't it?" Even this brief list indicates that it is by no means a "simple equation," but rather a complex pattern of equations that must lead us to consider just what is at issue in this effort to translate differences (such as silence/death, leaders/murderers, gay rights/AIDS) into identities through a language that invokes the rhetorical form of mathematical or scientific inevitability (A = B), a language of equations that can be marshaled in the service of homophobic (Gay Rights = AIDS) or antihomophobic (Silence = Death) discourse.

In thinking about this we would do well to recall that it is precisely the question of equality, the post-Stonewall demand for equal rights for gays, that has mobilized in unprecedented ways both of these discursive fields. Indeed, the already complex matter of AIDS is exponentially complicated by the fact that the homophobic response to the demands for gay equality, long *before* the phenomenon of AIDS, was largely predicated on the equation of homosexuality with the unnatural, the irrational, and the diseased. The logic of homophobia thus rests upon the very same binary that enables Plato in the *Phaedrus* to value speech at the expense of writing—and lest this assertion seem too frivolous or far-fetched an association, let me cite another passage from Derrida's reading of Plato: "the conclusion of the *Phaedrus* is less a condemnation of writing in the name of present speech than a preference for one sort of writing over another, for the fertile trace over the sterile trace, for a seed that engenders because it is planted inside over a seed scattered wastefully outside: at the risk of *dissemination*." If Derrida displaces the opposition between speech and writing by identifying speech itself as just another "sort of writing," he thereby calls into question the logic of the Western philosophical tradition that claims to be able to identify and distinguish the true from the false, the natural from the unnatural. In so doing he enacts the law of transgression that he sees as operative in "both the writing *and* the pederasty of a young man named Plato," a "transgression . . . not thinkable within the terms of classical logic but only within the graphics of the supplement or of the *pharmakon*." Deconstruction, as a disseminative project, then, can be subsumed beneath the rubric of the homosexual and one can read, by contrast, in the emphatic equations cited earlier as politically antithetical responses to the AIDS epidemic, an insistence on the possibility of recuperating truth, of knowing absolutely, even mathematically, some literal identity unmarked by the logic of the supplement or the indeterminacy of the *pharmakon*. So homophobic and antihomophobic forces alike find themselves producing, as defensive reactions to the social and medical crisis of AIDS, discourses that reify and absolutize identities, discourses that make clear the extent to which both groups see the AIDS epidemic as threatening the social structures through which they have constituted their identities for themselves.

Of course heterosexual culture in the West has long interpreted homosexuality as a threat to the security or integrity of heterosexual identity. In our dauntingly inconsistent mythology of homosexuality, "the love that dared not speak its name" was long known as the crime "inter Christianos non nominandum," and it was so designated not only because it was seen as lurid, shameful, and repellent, but also, and contradictorally, because it was, and is, conceived of as being potentially so attractive that even to speak about it is to risk the possibility of tempting some innocent into a fate too horrible—and too seductive—to imagine. One corollary of this fear of seduction through nomination is the still pervasive homophobic misperception of gay sexuality as contagious—as something one can catch through contact with, for instance, a teacher who is

lesbian or gay. Thus even before the historical accident of the outbreak of AIDS in the gay communities of the West, homosexuality was conceived as a contagion, and the homosexual as parasitic upon the heterosexual community. One chilling instance that may synecdochically evoke the insidious logic behind this homophobic ideology was produced in 1977 in a dissent written by William Rehnquist, now chief justice of the United States, in response to the Court's refusal to grant certiorari in the case of *Gay Lib v. University of Missouri*. As an essay in the *Harvard Law Review* described the case,

> the university had refused to recognize a gay students' organization on the ground that such recognition would encourage violation of Missouri's anti-sodomy statute. In support of the university's position, Justice Rehnquist argued that permitting the exercise of first amendment rights of speech and association in this instance would undercut a legitimate state interest, just as permitting people with the measles to associate freely with others would undercut the states's interest in imposing a quarantine.

Here, in 1977, the ideological configuration of both homosexuality and discourse in relation to disease, and the invocation, albeit in metaphor, of quarantine as an acceptable model for containment, is offered as an argument against the right to produce a nonhomophobic public discourse on homosexuality.

If such a context suggests the bitter urgency of the activists' assertion that Silence = Death, it does not suffice as a reading of the slogan or of the slogan's relation to the historically specific logic that governs the interimplication of discourse, defense, and disease. For what is striking about Silence = Death as the most widely publicized, gay-articulated language of response to the AIDS epidemic is its insistence upon the therapeutic property of discourse without specifying in any way what should or must be said. Indeed, as a text produced in response to a medical and political emergency, Silence = Death is stunningly self-reflexive. It takes the form of a rallying cry, but its call for resistance is no call to arms; rather, it calls for the production of discourse, the production of more text, as a mode of defense against the opportunism of medical and legislative responses to the epidemic. But what can be said beyond the need to speak? What discourse can this call to discourse desire? Just what *is* the discourse of defense that will immunize the gay body politic against the opportunistic infections of demagogic rhetoric?

An answer to this question can be discerned in Kramer's accusation: "That all of you . . . continue to refuse to transmit to the public the facts and figures of what is happening *daily* makes you, in my mind, equal to murderers." Kramer's charge explicitly demands the production of texts in order to defend against the transmission of disease. In so doing it makes clear that the defensive discourse is a discourse of "facts and figures," a discourse that resists the rhetoric of homophobic ideologues by articulating a truth that it casts in the form of mathematical or scientific data beyond the disputations of rhetoric. In a similar fashion, the textual prescription offered in Silence = Death takes the form of a formula that implies for it the status of a mathematical axiom, a given, a literal truth that is not susceptible to figural evasions and distortions. In this light, the pink triangle that appears above the slogan in the graphic representations of the text functions not only as an emblem of homosexual oppression, but also, and crucially, as a geometrical shape—a triangle *tout court*—that produces a sort of cognitive rhyme with the equation mark inscribed in the text, thus reinforcing semiotically the scientific or geometric inevitability of the textual equation.

At the same time, however, the very formula of mathematical discourse (A = B) that appeals to the prestige of scientific fact evokes the paradigmatic formulation or figure of metaphoric substitution. A = B, after all, is a wholly conventional way of representing the process whereby metaphor improperly designates one thing by employing the name of another. Though Silence = Death is cast in the rhetorical form of geometric equation, and though it invokes, by means of that form, the necessity of articulating a truth of "facts and figures," the fact remains that the equation takes shape as a figure, that it enacts a metaphorical redefinition of "silence" as "death." What this means, then, is that the equations that appear to pronounce literal, scientifically verifiable truth cannot be distinguished from the disavowed literariness of the very figural language those equations undertake to repudiate or exclude. The truth of such equations can only pass for truth so long as we ignore that the literal must itself be produced by a figural sleight of hand.

The rhetorical form of Silence = Death thereby translates the mathematical into the poetic, the literal into the figural, by framing the call to discourse in terms that evoke the distinctive signature of metaphoric exchange. It would be useful in this context to recall for a moment Harold Bloom's identification of trope and defense and to cite yet one more equation, this one actually a series of equations proposed by Bloom in his essay "Freud and the Sublime" [in his *Agon: Towards a Theory of Revisionism,* 1982]: "Literal meaning equals anteriority equals an earlier state of meaning equals an earlier state of things equals death equals literal meaning." Silence = Death, read in light of this, would gesture metaphorically toward the process of tropological substitution that resists or defends against the literality that Bloom, following Freud, identifies with death and sees as producing the reductive absolutism that informs the reality principle. Indeed, Silence = Death would seem to cast itself as that most heroic of all texts: a text whose metaphoric invocation of textuality, a text whose defensive appeal to discourse would have the power "literally" to counteract the agencies of death by exposing the duplicity inherent in the false equations that pass for "literal" truth and that make possible, as a result, such virulent formulations as Gay Rights = AIDS. In this case, for trope to operate as defense would involve, in part, the repudiation of what passes for the "literal truth" of AIDS by attending to the ideological investments that inform the scientific and political discourse about it and by articulating the inevitable construction of the disease within a massively overdetermined array of figural associations.

But such a defensive discourse can claim no immunity against contamination by the figural—a contamination that is nowhere more evident than in its defensive production of the figure of literality, the figure of mathematically precise calculation implicit in the equation Silence = Death. For the politics of language governing the claim of absolute identity in such a formula as Silence = Death aligns that formula, despite its explicitly antihomophobic import, with the logic of natural self-identity implicit in Plato's binary oppositions, a logic that provides the ideological support for the homophobic terrorism Plato himself endorsed in order to defend the "law of restricting procreative intercourse to its natural function by abstention from congress with our own sex, with its deliberate murder of the race and its wasting of the seed of life on a stony and rocky soil, where it will never take root and bear its natural fruit."

The proliferating equations that mark the discourse on AIDS, then, suggest that in the face of the terrifying epistemological ambiguity provoked by this epidemic, in the face of so powerful a representation of the force of what we do not know, the figure of certainty, the figure of literality, is itself ideologically constructed and deployed as a defense, if not as a remedy. (Note one manifestation of this deployment of the figure of knowledge or certainty in the way that political debate about AIDS in America has been counterproductively fixated on proposals to divert millions of dollars from necessary research toward compulsory testing of various populations for the presence of HIV antibodies. Given the persistence of the identification in America of AIDS with the gay male community, it is hard not to see this fixation as part and parcel of the desire to combat uncertainty not only about who has been infected by the so-called "AIDS virus," but also, and perhaps more deeply and irrationally, about how it is possible to determine who is straight and who is gay.) Precisely because the defensive appeal to literality in a slogan like Silence = Death must produce the literal *as a figure* of the need and desire for the shelter of certain knowledge, such a discourse is always necessarily a dangerously contaminated defense—contaminated by the Derridean logic of metaphor so that its attempt to achieve a natural or literal discourse beyond rhetoricity must reproduce the suspect ideology of reified (and threatened) identity marking the reactionary medical and political discourse it would counteract. The discursive logic of Silence = Death thus contributes to the ideologically motivated confusion of the literal and the figural, the proper and the improper, the inside and the outside, and in the process it recalls the biology of the human immunodeficiency virus as it attacks the mechanism whereby the body is able, in David Black's words, to distinguish between "Self and Not-Self."

HIV, scientists tell us, is a retrovirus that reproduces by a method involving an enzyme called reverse transcriptase. This "allows the virus to copy its genetic information into a form that can be integrated into the host cell's own genetic code. Each time a host cell divides, viral copies are produced along with more host cells, each containing the viral code." At issue in the progress of the disease, then, is the question of inscription and transcription, the question of reproduction and substitution. The virus endangers precisely because it produces a code, or speaks a language,

> Any discourse on AIDS must inscribe itself in a volatile and uncontrollable field of metaphoric contention in which its language will necessarily find itself at once appropriating AIDS for its own tendentious purposes and becoming subject to appropriation by the contradictory logic of homophobic ideology.
>
> —*Lee Edelman*

that can usurp or substitute for the genetic discourse of certain cells in the human immune system. AIDS thus inscribes within the biology of the human organism the notion of parasitic transcription. And this metastatic or substitutive transcription of the cell is particularly difficult to counteract because HIV, like metaphor, operates to naturalize, or present as proper, that which is improper or alien or imported from without. Subsequent to the metonymy, the contiguous transmission, of infection, the virus establishes itself as part of the essence or essential material of the invaded cell through a version of metaphoric substitution. It changes the meaning of the cellular code so that each reproduction or articulation of the cell disseminates further the altered genetic message. Moreover, one of the properties of HIV is that it can change the "genetic structure of [the] external proteins" that constitute the outer coat by which the immune system is able to recognize it; thus it can evade the agents of the immune system that attempt to defend against what is alien or improper. Even worse, since HIV attacks the immune system itself, depleting the T-4 or T-helper cells, it prevents the immune system from being able to "recognize foreign substances (antigens) and . . . eliminate them from the body." Even as it works its tropological wiles within the infected cells, HIV is subverting the capacity of the immune system to read the difference between what is proper to the body, what is "literally" its own, and what is figural or extrinsic.

But these metaphoric flights of fancy that are at work in the scientific discourse on AIDS, just as they are at work in my own metaphorizing discourse, the flights of fancy in which the failures of discourse as defense are already inscribed within disease, have no literal warrant in "nature." Reverse transcriptase and immune defense systems are metaphoric designations that determine the way we understand the operations of the body; they are readings that metastasize the metabolic by infecting it with a strain of metaphor that can appear to be so natural, so intrinsic to our way of thinking, that we mistake it for the literal truth of the body, as if our rhetorical immune system were no longer operating properly, or as if the virus that is metaphor had mutated so successfully as to evade the antibodies that would differentiate between the inside and the outside, between the proper and the improper. This once again brings to mind Derrida's analysis of the parasitic relation of writing to Plato's living word of speech: "In order to cure the latter of the *pharmakon* and rid it of the para-

site, it is thus necessary to put the outside back in its place. To keep the outside out. This is the inaugural gesture of 'logic' itself, of good 'sense' insofar as it accords with the self-identity of *that which is:* being is what it is, the outside is outside and the inside inside." But since, as Derrida says, "metaphoricity is the logic of contamination and the contamination of logic," no discourse can ever achieve the logic of self-identity, the logic of scientific equations, without the infection of metaphor that finds the enemy or alien always already within. As Emily Dickinson [in "A Word Dropped Careless on a Page," in *The Complete Poems of Emily Dickinson,* 1960] declared in anticipation of Derrida's reading of the *pharmakon,* "infection in the sentence breeds." And in the case of AIDS, infection endlessly breeds sentences—sentences whose implication in a poisonous history of homophobic constructions assures that no matter what explicit ideology they serve, they will carry within them the virulent germ of the dominant cultural discourse.

If my conclusion presents the somber circularity of Discourse = Defense = Disease = Discourse, I cannot conclude without trying to locate the zone of infection within these remarks. What I have been suggesting is that any discourse on AIDS must inscribe itself in a volatile and uncontrollable field of metaphoric contention in which its language will necessarily find itself at once appropriating AIDS for its own tendentious purposes and becoming subject to appropriation by the contradictory logic of homophobic ideology. This essay is not exempt from those necessities. As much as I would insist on the value and urgency of examining the figural inscriptions of AIDS, I am sufficiently susceptible to the gravity of the literal to feel uneasy, as a gay man, about producing a discourse in which the horrors experienced by my own community, along with other communities in America and abroad, become the material for intellectual arabesques that inscribe those horrors within the neutralizing conventions of literary criticism. Yet as painfully as my own investment in the figure of literality evokes for me the profound inhumanity implicit in this figural discourse on AIDS, I am also aware that any discourse on AIDS must inevitably reproduce that tendentious figurality. At the same time, I would argue that the appeal of the literal can be an equally dangerous seduction; it is, after all, the citation of the pressing literality of the epidemic with its allegedly "literal" identification of homosexuality and disease, that fuels the homophobic responses to AIDS and demands that we renounce what are blithely dismissed as figural embellishments upon the "real," material necessities of human survival—embellishments such as civil rights and equal protection under the law. We must be as wary, then, of the temptations of the literal as we are of the ideologies at work in the figural; for discourse, alas, is the only defense with which we can counteract discourse, and there is no available discourse on AIDS that is not itself diseased. (pp. 289-304)

Lee Edelman, "The Plague of Discourse: Politics, Literary Theory, and AIDS," in Displacing Homophobia: Gay Male Perspectives in Literature and Culture, *Ronald R. Butters,*

John M. Clum, Michael Moon, eds., Duke University Press, 1989, pp. 289-305.

Carol Muske   (essay date 1989)

[*Muske is an American poet, novelist, educator, and critic. In the following essay, she comments on the poems collected in* Poets for Life: Seventy-Six Poets Respond to AIDS, *noting that the poets in the volume have reinvigorated and transformed the elegiac form.*]

Perhaps the single positive contribution of AIDS to our culture is a politics of death. That is to say, AIDS (like the Right to Die movement) has made dying itself—in bed, away from the battlefield—a political act. Death remains as personal as ever, but now everyone must bear witness to the rapid, brutal, sweeping disappearances of human beings. Everyone must hear (because we have a government that refuses to listen) what the dying have to say about how they will die, where they will die, what their right to treatment encompasses, how they wish the living to care for them, how they wish to be let go. To paraphrase Auden, we must pay attention, or die.

I feel the newness of this politics throughout this collection of poems [*Poets for Life: Seventy-Six Poets Respond to AIDS*]. The dying have voices, finally: angry, intuitive, dreamy, fearful, eloquent, funny. Listening to them changes the way we write about death. Perhaps, as editor Michael Denneny has suggested, we will see in the growing body of AIDS literature, including this anthology, a literary "renaissance." The community of the dead and the dying and those who sit by the beds in homes and hospices and transient hotels, writing, will change forever how we imagine death. It seems to me that we have left behind us the tradition of "let the dead bury their dead." *These* dead will not lie quiet in their graves.

> At the wake, the tension broke
> when someone guessed
>
> the casket was closed because
> "he was in there in a big wig
> and heels," and someone said,
>
> "You know he was always late,
> he probably wasn't there yet—
> he's still fixing his makeup."
>
> Mark Doty, "Tiara"

Certainly death has been our most political enemy, a master strategist when blocked and, with the advent of AIDS, reverting to archetype: the unconquerable primitive specter, leaping handily over the immunological beachheads of the twentieth century, trailing its centuries-long cape of fevers, cancers, bacilli.

Now death has advanced its politics to all-out war, or plague, undermining the body's defenses, exploding the autoimmune system, replacing it with a primary, staggering medical irony (a disease which destroys the destroyers of disease) as well as ironies philosophical and literary. We make love and death at the same time. It is literally possible to die of love.

> the elegies are writing themselves

> on desire's sheets, passion and suffering
> are fusing their etymological roots
> into a single trunk. *Yet why should they not embrace,*
> *these beautiful two?* They are, after all, part
> of the oldest story in the world—before God,
> before microbes, before the sea had licked
> the earth and the air clean with its long tongue.
>
> Michael Blumenthal, "No More Kissing—
> AIDS Everywhere"

Or as Heather McHugh puts it: " . . . Nobody knows / how your disease is spread; it came / from love, or some / such place."

As passion and suffering fuse, we think of Keats, half in love with easeful death—but the angle is sharper, crueler.

> My thoughts are crowded with death
> and it draws so oddly on the sexual
> that I am confused to be attracted
> by, in effect, my own annihilation.
>
> Thom Gunn, "In Time of Plague"

Facing death has given these poems a common urgency, but without a collective viewpoint. Poets with vastly different sensibilities and styles have responded with similar rhetorical intent—to mobilize the reader to pity, to anger or compassion. Mallarmé said that everything in the world exists to end in a book. Writers are all too familiar with the daily implacability of this literary dictum, as their lives routinely become the substance of their art. In writing about AIDS, the mind reels: Can all this death be a like substance? The mind *resists:* Is it possible that this monolith, this unspeakable *wall* of grief, will be scribbled on too? With gravestone graffiti? Survivor ego?

But these poems are not the glib eulogies of survivors, millers of literary grist, they are the stunned words of the bloodied. They neither diminish *nor* sensationalize the horror. They eschew the falseness of the *natur morte;* they haven't the rigid, glossy beauties of the still life; they seem, in fact, to stagger under the burdensome cliché of the natural order, of death's sanctimonious inevitability. There is collective amazement that this is how death is entering our bodies—that the disease is *not* a technological invention, a sci-fi plot, a nightmare. What is conveyed, in poem after poem, is wonder that these words ever got written. There is an uncharacteristic (for contemporary poetry) lack of self-absorption; and thus, the poems seem oddly, attractively, unfinished, in the sense of a literary finish: Mallarmé's perfunctory poetic end to all existence.

Despite their varying tones, the poems in this anthology seem to hit the page at the same velocity. A fast slow-motion. We move in a terrible false parallel motion with those dying of AIDS, we struggle to keep up at the same time as we outdistance them.

> Terror has made us real enough
> to touch
> almost intimate . . .
>
> Deborah Digges, "Faith-Falling"

People who have AIDS turn the mirror we hold to their lips around to our terrified faces. In an eerily transparent moment in a poem about his friend's blindness, Paul Monette leads Roger down the sidewalk and asks him what fragment he still sees of the world.

> you stop peer impish intent as a hawk
> and say *I see you* just like that . . .

> Paul Monette, "Your Sightless Days"

The startled fixity of that gaze is on every page of this book. The dying see us. The faces looking out are not the legions of Munch-like "death had undone so many" phantoms, but are real as Roger, intent as hawks watching us, lovers, friends, parents, children.

The elegy itself is changing. It has always been a competent traditional vessel to hold grief and praise of the dead. Now it seems to overflow, shatter, reform.

> Back from what he could neither
> Accept, as one opposed,
> Nor, as a life-long breather,
> Consentingly let go,
> The tube his mouth enclosed
> In an astonished O.

> Thom Gunn, "Still Life"

> You are not the target, you're the arrow
> and the dirty wind that hits
> your face on summer streets these
> too-long evenings means you're moving
> faster than you know, a shrill
> projectile through the neutral air
> above a world war . . .

> Tim Dlugos, "Retrovir"

The elegiac form, like a graveside path, has been worn smooth in places by the years, but the language of these poems is direct and unsparing in detail; it refuses literary phrasing or the phrasing of the eulogy. Part of what fuels the unconventional response is the incongruousness of the dying themselves. The young and strong are disappearing, people at the height of their careers and talents. Children are dying. It is a monumental task to find words for any elegy. To describe the loss of so many who should have lived into the next century strains all our notions of composition.

I knew Roger Horwitz, Paul Monette's friend. It is inconceivable to me that he is dead. Yet I stood at his funeral and witnessed his burial. It is also inconceivable to me that five-year-old Zachary Jacob Fried, who attended the same pre-school as my daughter, is dead. Zack died of AIDS, having received at birth an "infiltrated" transfusion from the Cedars Sinai blood bank.

Zack's name is on a quilt that travels the country like a postdated letter from the dead.

> We are all made of
> our own people
> laying names on the ground

> Michael Klein, "Naming the Elements"

The AIDS quilt keeps Zack looking back at us—a small, pale, gifted child who drew beautiful pictures for his friends. Zack even offered a kind of elegy for himself,

when he wondered aloud to his mother during the height of his suffering what it would be like to be a "let go balloon."

I would like to add Zack's elegy to this collection. It is tempting to think of the book itself as a kind of "let go balloon," rising away from suffering. But it isn't. Certainly, as Deborah Digges says in her poem "Faith-Falling," "on earth you can say goodbye." This anthology of poems must belong to this time on earth. It is both testimony and triumph—what elegy can be when we find the right words to match our grief. (pp. 6-10)

> Carol Muske, "Rewriting the Elegy," in Poets for Life: Seventy-Six Poets Respond to AIDS, edited by Michael Klein, Crown Publishers, Inc., 1989, pp. 6-10.

Emmanuel S. Nelson   (essay date Spring 1990)

[*In the following essay, Nelson outlines the range of responses that the AIDS crisis has elicited from American male homosexual novelists.*]

While answering an interviewer's query regarding the rather scant literary response to the AIDS crisis, Michael Denneny—co-founder of *Christopher Street* and editor at St. Martin's Press—asserted in 1987,

> The real question is how come so many people *are* writing about AIDS. It's like Vietnam. If you consider the peak of the war around 1966, it was a good decade and a half before you got any books. The same with the world wars. Normally there is this lag because the creative imagination can't comprehend the scope of the problem. It has to sink, to some extent. The amazing thing is that the writers are now rising to it with a vengeance, and we are on the verge of getting a literature out of this that will be renaissance. [David Kaufman, "AIDS: The Creative Response," *Horizon* (1987)]

There is nothing romantic, nothing sentimental—not even anything *more* frightening—about dying of AIDS. It is not, as Susan Sontag might point out, a metaphor for anything. It is like all death: a painful hard end to the painful and sometimes hard act of living.

—*Michael Bronski, in his "Death and the Erotic Imagination," in* Personal Dispatches: Writers Confront AIDS, *edited by John Preston, 1989.*

AIDS made its frightening and dramatic entry into the American consciousness in 1981 when it first manifested itself in the form of rare types of cancer and pneumonia among urban gay men. Since then it has evolved into one of the major medical disasters of the modern era. The initial literary response to the crisis was a reluctant one: stunned, confused silence. By the late eighties, however, writers have begun to respond in a variety of ways. And indeed Michael Denneny's prediction of a renaissance is rapidly becoming a reality.

Numerous creative works dealing with aspects of the AIDS crisis have appeared in the last few years. There are, for example, several plays that examine, often with considerable success, the impact of AIDS on individual lives: William Hoffman's *As Is,* Larry Kramer's *Normal Heart,* Harvey Fierstein's *Safe Sex,* Robert Chesley's *Jerker,* Alan Bowne's *Beirut,* among others. There are poignant memoirs: Paul Monette's *Borrowed Time,* Andrew Holleran's *Ground Zero,* George Whitmore's *Someone Was Here.* There are anthologies of short stories and poems, such as Adam Mars-Jones and Ed White's *The Darker Proof,* Cindy Ruskin's *Quilt* and Paul Monette's *Love Alone: Eighteen Elegies for Rog.* And more than a dozen novels that deal with AIDS, either centrally or marginally, have appeared since Paul Reed's *Facing It*—the first major work of fiction in the AIDS genre—was published in 1984.

My commentary is limited to these American novels of AIDS; the focus of my discussion, specifically, is on gay male fiction. Though heterosexual writers have responded to the AIDS crisis with imaginative works—Alice Hoffman's *At Risk* and Gloria Miklowitz's *Good-bye Tomorrow* are prime examples—their fictions tend to lack the power and poignancy of gay male writing on the subject.

At Risk and *Good-bye Tomorrow* are somewhat similar texts: both center around middle-class suburban children from loving, in-tact, nuclear families. Amanda, Hoffman's protagonist, is an eleven-year-old, a promising member of her school's gymnastics team; Alex, Miklowitz's central character, is a good-looking, popular student who is also a star of his high school's swim team. Neither is gay or bisexual; neither is an intravenous drug abuser. Both are exposed to the AIDS virus through transfusion of infected blood during routine surgeries and both eventually develop AIDS-related complications. Their parents are distraught; insensitive friends and neighbors ostracize them. The children face various forms of harassment: there is, for example, an organized attempt to expel Amanda from school; Alex is encouraged to quit the swim team because his teammates fear he will infect the pool.

While both narratives at times are moving, neither one fully explores the complex thematic demands that AIDS poses. In Hoffman's novel, for instance, AIDS is reduced to a metaphor, a universal symbol of the random nature of death; it becomes merely "a vehicle to explore the issues of death and dying" [John Preston, "New Words for a New Reality," *Advocate* (1988)]. An inadequately researched text, *At Risk* contains obvious medical inaccuracies: there are errors in Hoffman's handling of the diagnostic as well as therapeutic aspects of AIDS. And *Good-bye Tomorrow,* as all other novels by Miklowitz, is intended for an adolescent audience; its didactic intent is evident throughout, since one of the objectives of the author is to educate her readers on the subject of AIDS.

Since both works are geared to accommodate the tastes of mainstream, heterosexual audiences, the authors locate their novels' action in "safe" settings: close-knit homes in the affluent suburbia. Homosexuality is not an issue here; the protagonists are heterosexual and, therefore, will be perceived by the mainstream readers to be entirely underserving of their tragic fates. But AIDS is a highly politicized malady; its connections with sexuality are too real to be so conveniently ignored. Both texts avoid the larger cultural and ideological concerns caused by the perceived link between homosexuality and AIDS, despite the fact that AIDS continues to strike, at least in the United States, most fiercely in the gay community—a historically marginalized and stigmatized community. The value of Hoffman's and Miklowitz's works, then, is rather limited because of their eagerness to accommodate mainstream sensitivities, their tendency toward the metaphoric, and their retreat from confronting not only the medical but also the political uniqueness of AIDS and the enormously complex personal, social, sexual and moral dilemmas it has spawned.

Not surprisingly, the responses of gay male writers to the AIDS crisis differ significantly from those of heterosexual writers, such as Hoffman and Miklowitz. Gay writers, as one would expect, bring with them a fundamentally different set of perspectives, assumptions and experiences which shape their creative constructions. Their response to AIDS, inevitably, is deeply personal. AIDS to them is too real to be merely a metaphor. They do not have to imagine the horror; they live in the midst of the holocaust.

Moreover, the political significance of AIDS to gay writers and their community is radically different from what it is to heterosexual artists and their society. While AIDS has merely scared the larger American society, it has profoundly traumatized the gay community. The ranks of gay America are being decimated at an alarming pace and in a gruesome manner. AIDS has crushed the relative freedom of the seventies—freedom that was won after many bitter generations of repression and secrecy. It has doubled the burdens of the American homosexual male: in the pre-AIDS era, for example, his sexuality was the target of social stigma; now he is additionally stigmatized because he is also assumed to be an agent of an infectious, fatal disease. This perceived connection between his sexuality and an incurable illness has helped reinforce traditional anti-gay hostility. AIDS has provided a convenient and hideous excuse for a variety of bigots—from reactionary politicians to bible-thumping fundamentalists—to grant pseudolegitimacy to their nearly pathological intolerance.

The ironies that AIDS has engendered are tragic. Promiscuity was once thought by many gays as a valid, even necessary component of urban gay male identity. Many a gay activist eloquently advocated it; it was viewed as a form of sexual rebellion against the repressive heterosexual establishment, as a means of personal and sexual liberation. And promiscuity did indeed provide the urban gay male with a sense of community. The sexual arenas, often *terra incognita* to heterosexuals, provided a spacious theater for sexual self-discovery through unlimited supplies of sexual partners and for emotional bonding—even if the connections made were only transient and frequently anonymous. By the late seventies promiscuity had become a core characteristic of urban gay culture. It is precisely this cultural trait that in the eighties, ironically, has proved to be the primary reason for the disastrously rapid spread of AIDS infection among gay men. The significant weakening of this core cultural characteristic in the last few years, caused largely by the basic changes in gay lifestyle as a necessary response to AIDS, has, therefore, disrupted a core dimension in the contemporary urban gay male identity. The familiar structures of metropolitan gay life—bars, baths, movie houses and other sexual playing grounds which were once so vital to forging personal and communal identities—have now become killing fields.

Gay male literary responses to the massive crisis that AIDS has generated fall into three categories. The first form of response is silence. It is a silence that is chillingly meaningful and piercingly loud. Perhaps to some writers the burden of creating art out of the horror seems too heavy to bear, the proportions of the calamity too large to be contained within the boundaries of fiction. Just as some post-WWII Jewish writers have resolutely avoided imaginative confrontation with the Holocaust, many contemporary gay writers have tended to shy away from the plague that rages around them. AIDS to them is too dreadful to be aestheticized. [In *Ground Zero,* 1988] Andrew Holleran, for example, asserts,

> Novels weren't needed; one only had to read the series of interviews carried in the *Washington Blade* with a man named Engebretsen, who allowed a reporter to visit him periodically as he withered away. The truth was quite enough; there was no need to make it up. To attempt to imagine such scenes seemed impertinence of the worst kind.

Holleran, the author of two critically acclaimed novels, is yet to approach the topic of AIDS in his fiction. Even more remarkable is the silence of John Rechy. A pioneer in gay fiction, Rechy is one of the most incisive analysts of the gay sensibilities and a powerfully authentic interpreter of the American homosexual underground. Angry and radical, but always honest and forthright, Rechy has in the past celebrated the promiscuous homosexual as "a sexual revolutionary." He once suggested that a mass homosexual orgy should be globally televised to shock heterosexuals and to defy their social, cultural, religious and sexual mores. While many of the novels he wrote prior to the AIDS era insistently and explicitly dealt with gay life, his two post-AIDS novels—*Bodies and Souls* (1983) and *Marilyn's Daughter* (1988)—deal with homosexuality only marginally. Neither one even alludes to AIDS. While Rechy eschews the subject of AIDS by choosing non-gay themes, there are other gay writers who avoid it by setting their novels in the pre-AIDS era. The action of Edmund White's recent quasi-autobiographical novel *The Beautiful Room Is Empty,* for example, is set entirely in the age before AIDS, mid-fifties through late sixties. George Whitmore's *Nebraska,* too, is set at a time prior to the arrival of the plague.

This silence also manifests itself in a subtle way as contemporary gay fiction increasingly begins to focus on a new theme, the "theme of family formation." As Richard Hall argues [in "Gay Fiction Comes Home," *The New York Times Book Review* (1988)], several recent works of gay fiction—he cites Christopher Bram's *Surprising Myself* and David Leavitt's *The Lost Language of Cranes* as classic examples—seem intent on reinventing the traditional family by rearranging that social unit and building it "on friendship, common interests and choice rather than on sacraments and sex." Anonymous sex, once an obsessive theme in gay fiction, is a matter of considerably less interest, as Rechy's celebrated sexual outlaw begins to give way to the "sexual in-law." And there is an increased affirmation of monogamy, commitment, rootedness and permanence—values that were once dismissed as too vulgarly traditional and boringly heterosexual.

The second category of gay literary responses to AIDS includes works which acknowledge the menacing presence of the plague but avoid direct, full-scale confrontation with it. Some works in this category merely allude to the epidemic. In some others the presence of AIDS is so palpable that it defines the mood. Yet in all of these works the central characters are not infected (or, perhaps, are unaware of their antibody status). The protagonists continue to live and love, although with fear and anxiety.

Paul Reed's *Longing* (1988) is a lyrical tale of a young man's initiatory journey toward self-discovery, a classic story of coming of age in gay America. Fleeing the repressiveness of his rural home he arrives in San Francisco, in the early eighties, with visions of finding love and sexual freedom in the gay mecca. AIDS is never mentioned by its name; its threatening presence, nevertheless, is a vague but disturbing part of the young narrator-protagonist's consciousness and his social milieu. He arrives in San Francisco just before the city succumbs "to Change, the result of the terror of death," when people in Castro "still danced," "still fucked," just before "several thousand men became fatally infected." He begins his quest for love "amidst the consternation of panic and confusion." His search, initially, entails the familiar routine: multiple, fleeting, anonymous sexual encounters. The increasingly frantic nature of his search is accompanied by alarmingly visible signs that the world around him is falling apart. He hears reports of rare skin cancers and pneumonias. At bars he overhears conversations about a "gay cancer." The rumors multiply, intensifying his anxiety. He begins to witness the transformation of Castro. When he first arrived the streets were full of men in tight jeans displaying their flesh defiantly. But now he notices "fear and caution . . . women and children, and men not clad in tight jeans . . . women wearing masks of white hankies over their noses and mouth as they stood awaiting the 24 Divisadero." In the midst of such change and creeping terror, he falls madly in love with Cole. The sweetness of their relationship lulls his awareness of the contagion that is beginning to rage outside. But the romance soon begins to collapse, just as the world around him starts to disintegrate. The troubled Castro provides a grim backdrop to his private hell; it defines his loss. The novel, nevertheless, ends on a hopeful note as the narrator catches an epiphanic, transcendent glimpse of the larger meaning of his longing.

Quest for meaning, for a liberating, redemptive vision, is also at the center of Joseph Puccia's *The Holy Spirit Dance Club.* Set in New York City of the early eighties, Puccia's novel, like Reed's, documents the beginning of the Change. Here, as in Reed's work, AIDS is an encroaching feature of the milieu; it informs the mood of the novel. *The Holy Spirit Dance Club* is a bittersweet testament of its protagonist, Harold Fenestere, to "the last day of the circuit . . . the last and loudest beat of liberal lifestyles and an ethic of pleasure." He is initiated into the drug-and-dance culture of gay Manhattan in the year "when some of the men started to disappear, when the ranks thinned just a bit," just "before the beginning of the end of New York City, the year before several thousand men were missing, the year before any of us knew what a rubber looked like." There is sweet nostalgia for the seventies when sex was safe and available in superabundance but the remembrance of the hedonistic past is tempered by bitter knowledge of the sweeping change. But a reconciliation with this change—an awareness that change is not only inevitable but even necessary—becomes part of the new vision of life that Harold gains at the end of his journey.

John Champagne's *The Blue Lady's Hand,* too, deals with living and loving homosexually in the eighties. The setting is Manhattan; the presence of AIDS is pervasive. Signs of change are everywhere: JO Clubs, decrease in promiscuity, trend toward monogamy, emphasis on safe sex. Amid this sexual minefield, the narrator-protagonist seeks love and commitment. He longs for a relationship that is similar to the one that his parents share but he is conscious of the futility of such a desire. Simultaneously, he is not comfortable with the life his gay friends lead: an endless series of fleeting, anonymous sexual contacts. He falls in love with Daniel only to find that Daniel does not believe in monogamy. Initially jealous and insecure, he eventually reaches an understanding that "sexual fidelity is only one kind of fidelity" and that there are "other, more important kinds." He concludes that "Maybe Daniel needs to love more than one man. It is a good thing, to be able to love many people. Maybe his heart is big enough to love many people. And mine is big enough to let him." One may appreciate the protagonist's practical approach to his romantic dilemma and his seeming magnanimity. But one also wonders about the wisdom of such a philosophy in the age of the plague.

C. F. Borgman's remarkable debut novel, *River Road,* traces the development of its bisexual protagonist, Eugene Goessler, from his boyhood in Ohio in the nineteen-fifties, his emergence as an avant-garde artist in the eighties and concludes with a glimpse of his life with his Brazilian lover, Octavio, during the early decades of the twenty-first century. Borgman's handling of the AIDS theme is especially interesting, given the projection of the novel's plot well into the next century. AIDS enters the narrative, and the protagonist's consciousness, in the mid-eighties. In 1985 he hears that Scott, with whom he has had a brief affair, is dead of AIDS. But by then Eugene had personally known at least eight individuals who had died of it and, in fact, he had written eulogies for four of them. Increasingly he finds himself growing "numb to AIDS news," but his sobering awareness of the plague makes him anxious

about his own and Octavio's safety. However, AIDS in *River Road* is not a malady peculiar to gay men. In the year 2006, one of the female characters in the novel, has a facelift done to counter "the scarring she'd gotten from her bout with AIDS, which she's gotten from Tobey 'Too Tall' Thomas, or so she assumed." The implication here is that AIDS will be around even in the twenty-first century but, like many other major medical conditions, it can be remedied or at least managed. Life and love endure.

One of the most powerful texts in the second category of gay literary response to AIDS, and certainly one of the best novels in the entire genre of AIDS literature, is David Feinberg's *Eighty-Sixed* (1989). It is divided into two segments, "1980: Ancient History" and "1986: Learning How to Cry." The narrator is B. J. Rosenthal who, in the process of telling his one private tale, bears witness to gay life in New York before and after the arrival of the plague. The quest motif, a staple of gay American fiction, is central to *Eighty-Sixed:* B.J.'s search for enduring love, for stability, for wholeness. The record of his search also becomes a memorable document of the sad contrast between the gay life of the seventies and that of the eighties. The first part deals with the young narrator's coming of age, his frenetic search for *agape* through *eros* in the bars, parks, bathhouses and streets of Manhattan. Witty, at times satirical, the first part is a brilliantly realistic evocation of pre-AIDS gay life in New York City at its carnivalesque peak. "The only shadows of [this] world, other than being turned down by a gorgeous stud, are the temporary nuisances of venereal warts and being eighty-sixed from a hot club" [Catherine Texier, "When Sex Was All That Mattered," *The New York Times Book Review* (1989)]. But the shadows that cast their darkness in the second section of the novel, however, are of a different kind. AIDS, unforgiving and fatal, has arrived. "By the time you read this," cautions the narrator, "I may in all likelihood be dead." Death, not sex, begins to dominate his consciousness. News reports scream the latest statistics on AIDS-related casualty. Anxiety about his antibody status begins to intensify as death begins to hit close to him. Bob, a former trick, is diagnosed with AIDS; he subsequently dies. B.J.'s ex-lover, Richard, develops symptoms of the disease. But even as he fearfully trends the wasteland of gay Manhattan, he learns to use his sense of humor and penchant for irony to sustain his journey. And death tolls keep mounting. At the end of the novel, when Gordon, a phone buddy, calls to say that he has tested positive, B.J. begins to learn to cry. The final lines of the novel are as much a revelation of B.J.'s emotional state as they are a summation of gay life in the late eighties:

> It [tear] begins as gentle rain. Just a drop, for each illness, each death. And with each passing it gets worse. Now a downpour. Now a torrent. And there is no likelihood of its ever ending.

The third category of gay literary responses to AIDS includes novels in which it is directly confronted. The plague in these works does not merely provide a menacing shadow as the uninfected (or untested) central character continues to live and love, but it plays a role that is much more integral to the plot: one or more of the main characters themselves are dying of AIDS. Here the nagging anxieties of becoming infected are replaced by the terrors of actual infection, of devastating opportunistic diseases, of facing the sure prospects of imminent incapacitation and agonizing death. To the novelists, some of whom are dying of AIDS themselves, the subject poses grave personal and artistic challenges. Despite the problems inherent in aestheticizing material so distressing and in achieving artistic distance from themes so painfully personal, some of the novels in this category rank among the best imaginative works in the eighties.

Facing It (1984), Paul Reed's first novel, is the first major creative work to take AIDS out of the realms of scientific discourse and locate it in a human context through artistic rendering. Though stylistically sometimes awkward—perhaps because Reed, a newcomer to the craft of fiction, occasionally falters in the face of having to tackle so demanding a subject—it is, unlike Hoffman's *At Risk,* a carefully researched work. The narrative centers around Andrew Stone, a twenty-eight-year-old gay activist and "one of the most handsome men in Manhattan," who is among the very first individuals in the United States to be diagnosed with AIDS-related ailments. Reed explores Andy's private tragedy while placing it in a larger context of the politics of AIDS. But Reed's attacks on the pettiness of some medical professionals and on the criminal apathy of the government in the initial stages of the AIDS crisis do not distract him from effectively rendering Andy's personal battle with his illness. *Facing It,* as the title implies, is a heroic story of individuals confronting, with remarkable dignity, the terrifying realities of their lives. Despite the grimness of the action, the novel, ultimately, emerges as a celebration of love, loyalty and friendship: though Andy is abandoned by his family, his lover, David Markman, supports and sustains him through the final moments. Though their "Love does not triumph, in the sense of preventing death or averting tragedy . . . it succeeds by making 'facing it' possible" [Joseph Bean, "Prescriptions for the Here and Now," *Advocate* (1988)]. The novel affirms life, even as it depicts death. As Andy's disease-ravaged body deteriorates, he grows morally. In his death bed he asserts to David that his life has indeed been meaningful:

> You know, David, we were there! We were there! We were at the forefront of something new, something hopeful. How many people can say that? How many people have been out there—in the parades, in the papers, in the political offices—doing something that makes it easier for others to come out, to be fully gay and fully human, to have men like you to love. . . .

His gayness, Andy realizes, has been a "most compelling force" in his life that has given him the strength to lead an authentic existence. Such a death-bed awareness gives him a sense of "a great harmony, a consonance. He had made his armistice with the world."

Similar gallantry also characterizes Andrew Ellis's response to death in Christopher Davis' *Valley of the Shadow.* A poignant and poetic novel of remembrance, it is narrated in the first-person by Andrew, a Wall Street banker in his late twenties, from his death-bed. He calls his narrative "a final gift" to the memory of his recently dead lover, Ted Erikson, but it is also his final attempt to recall, exam-

ine, accept, and affirm his own life as it nears extinction. Remembering, even as his memory falters because of advancing illness, becomes redemptive. It helps heal the mind, if not the dying body. The novel begins with Andrew's recollection of his childhood in an upper middle-class Connecticut home; he relates his sexual self-discovery, his relationship with his disappointed but supportive family, his fast life in gay Manhattan, his stormy but intensely passionate love affair with Ted. Infidelity, at times mutual, destroys Andrew's relationship with Ted; the latter moves to San Francisco. Five years later, when Andrew accidentally spots Ted on a Manhattan street, Ted is dying of AIDS. Andrew's reunion with Ted is soon followed by his discovery that he, too, is developing AIDS-related complications. Despite his own failing health, Andrew takes care of Ted until Ted's death. Neither does Andrew die alone; he has the supportive presence of friends and family as he faces death. His crisp narrative, till the end, is honest, unsentimental and free of self-pity. He does not regret the life he has led; he does not blame anyone for its premature closure. His final act, the articulation of his memory of Ted and remembrance of his own life, is a tender act of love, made all the more poignant by its defiant rendering in the face of death.

Clayton Graham's *Tweeds* offers a different approach to the theme. Rather than focus on an individual suffering from AIDS, he explores its impact on the healthy lover of a man with AIDS. Corey Reese's love for his boyhood friend—Scott Sommerfeld, who is now dying of AIDS, helps Corey to grow from an inauthentic existence toward a healing and liberating sense of self. Unable to accept his sexual self, Corey, even after moving to the relatively enlightened Chicago from his home in rural Iowa, continues to hide his sexuality from others. His tendency to concoct and project a series of false identities is symptomatic of his inability to accept himself and to connect with others on any authentic level. Though Corey has always loved Scott, he does not reveal his feelings to Scott—until Scott, now suffering from AIDS, declares his love for him. The relationship they forge nourishes and sustains both. Corey creates a supportive environment for Scott; Scott's love helps Corey to step out of the prison of his self, to shed his false set of identities, to connect meaningfully with another individual. When Scott's illness becomes grave, Corey marries him—on television! The event becomes not only an open declaration of his love for Scott but also a public acknowledgment of his own homosexual identity. Concealment gives way to defiant and honest self-acceptance. Corey learns to care, to share, to love. Thus his encounter with Scott—an encounter in which AIDS is as tragic as it is a major part—proves, in an ultimate sense, to be redemptive.

Robert Ferro's *Second Son* (1988), written when Ferro and his lover, Michael Grumley, were fighting their own private, losing battles with AIDS, is about two men with AIDS who fall in love. AIDS is never mentioned by name; it is always alluded to as the ominous, unspeakable "It." In *Second Son* Ferro evokes a world in crisis. The references to acts of terrorism (*Achille Lauro*), nuclear accidents (Chernobyl) and space disasters (Challenger Shuttle) create images of our collective vulnerability to random violence. It is against such a backdrop Mark Valarian and his lover, Bill Mackey, face the uncertainties of their lives as they cope with AIDS. Breaking under enormous pressures and awaiting experimental therapy, both begin to dream about a distant planet, Splendora, where life can be lived free of illness. Unwilling to die, helpless in the face of a disease with no cure, they desperately hope to travel to the magical planet. The impossibility of their dream only serves to accent the reality of their horror. The shattering final scene which reveals the two lovers holding each other as closely as they hold their dreams of Splendora offers a haunting picture of the very real vulnerabilities of the human heart and the sad stubbornness of hope.

Larry Duplechan's *Tangled Up in Blue* (1989), one of the most recent novels on AIDS, provides a fresh perspective. The plot centers on three characters: Daniel Sullivan, who is bisexual; Crockett Miller, who is homosexual; and Maggie Sullivan, who is a heterosexual woman married to Daniel. Maggie accidentally finds out that her husband has tested for AIDS antibody and, subsequently, discovers not only his bisexuality but also the fact that he and their best friend, Crockett, were once lovers. The ensuing crisis nearly destroys the Sullivans' marriage and Crockett's close friendship with Maggie. Ultimately, however, love and friendship triumph. While the development of the plot is not always convincing, Duplechan's novel is indeed an important addition to the genre; it broadens the literary representation of AIDS by exploring the complex connections among gay, bisexual and straight characters who are at risk.

More works of fiction, gay as well as straight, are certain to appear. The direction and concerns of gay American writing, in particular, have been and continue to be altered fundamentally by AIDS. A good deal of gay fiction in the seventies tended to be rather shallow: the protagonists often seemed to be eternally searching for an ideal lover while keeping themselves amused and busy with a string of casual tricks. But AIDS has rearranged the priorities; it has necessitated a new direction; and it has forced new concerns. While the eerie silence of some writers, such as John Rechy and Andrew Holleran, haunts the gay literary landscape, in the works of other writers, such as Joseph Puccia, John Champagne, C. F. Borgman and David Feinberg, AIDS has become a dominant determinant of tone and mood. In the daring texts of Clayton Graham, Christopher Davis, Paul Reed, Robert Ferro and Larry Duplechan, the authors unflinchingly face the demon in the eye and articulate the terror. The catharsis can strengthen the spirit, even if it cannot heal the dying.

Though death is at the core of the literature of AIDS, many of the works in the genre, ultimately, prove to be life-giving. They affirm life, even as they explore the human consciousness on the verge of entering the Void. The characters confront death with grace. They endure to the end. While AIDS creates only meaningless suffering, the dignity and heroism with which the human spirit faces the terrifying odds are indeed meaningful. Themes of betrayal and cruelty are present, but these works also celebrate resilience of friendship and love in a world of flimsy connections. Often these novels are more about love and

loyalty than about death and dying. And more so than ever before, gay writers have begun to affirm and articulate a sense of community, the need for connectedness and cultural cohesion.

Yet some pre-AIDS traits of gay fiction persist. The preoccupation with casual sex is still there, for example, though the obsession, for good reasons, is less intense. Almost all protagonists in post-AIDS fiction, as before, continue to be impossibly good-looking—so much so that one has to wonder if they are not merely fond projections of their authors' pornographic imaginations. And American gay fiction, as always, continues to be solidly middle-class, concerned largely with the lives of white, urban professionals. Poor whites, Blacks, Asians and Hispanics, curiously, remain largely invisible. AIDS has not altered the demographics of gay fiction.

In the absence of a cure, AIDS is bound to influence profoundly gay life and letters. The literary responses are likely to follow the present patterns. Some writers will probably maintain their stance of silence, unable or unwilling to speak of the nightmare that refuses to cease. Others may acknowledge its dangerous presence but allow their characters to go on with their lives and loves. Some will choose to speak the unspeakable. Even if AIDS eventually becomes curable, it is likely to haunt the American homosexual literary consciousness for a long time. AIDS, after all, has become the central tragedy in the history of gay America, a holocaust with far-reaching historical consequences. But, meanwhile, some of the most gifted and cou-

---

D. S. Lawson on the reaction of playwrights to AIDS:

As the incidence of Acquired Immune Deficiency Syndrome has spread, the literature dealing with or focusing on the disease has burgeoned. Ironically, at the same time that the virus is killing many men and women around the world, the body of literature surrounding AIDS seems to be growing with alacrity; as people sicken and die, the words flourish and live.

Early on in the plague, two plays—Larry Kramer's *The Normal Heart* and William Hoffman's *As Is*—established twin avenues of dramatic reaction to the situation. Borrowing terms from the subtitle of gay American composer John Corigliano's first symphony, I call these reactions rage and remembrance. Kramer's invective typifies the rage many feel at this microscopic killer and at the society that for so long ignored (and continues to ignore) the health and destiny of its gay brothers and sons and fathers and friends. Hoffman's nostalgic play defines a mode of remembrance, of sadness over freedom and innocence and pleasure lost; it is a wistful elegy for a world we can now only remember and hope to recapture. Of course, often these modes of dramatic reaction are mixed together in any given play, but . . . many plays are primarily either rage or remembrance plays.

D. S. Lawson, in his "Rage and Remembrance: The AIDS Plays," in AIDS: The Literary Response, *edited by Emmanuel S. Nelson, 1992.*

rageous writers of our times continue to give voice and form to our collective distress. (pp. 47-53)

Emmanuel S. Nelson, "AIDS and the American Novel," in Journal of American Culture, *Vol. 13, No. 1, Spring, 1990, pp. 47-53.*

Edmund White on art and AIDS:

If art is to confront AIDS more honestly than the media has done, it must begin in tact, avoid humor, and end in anger.

Begin in tact, I say, because we must not reduce individuals to their deaths; we must not fall into the trap of replacing the afterlife with the moment of dying. How someone dies says nothing about how he lived. And tact because we must not let the disease stand for other things. AIDS generates complex and harrowing reflections, but it is not caused by moral or intellectual choices. We are witnessing at long last the end of illness as metaphor and metonym.

Avoid humor, because humor seems grotesquely inappropriate to the occasion. Humor puts the public (indifferent when not uneasy) on cosy terms with what is an unspeakable scandal: death. Humor domesticates terror, lays to rest misgivings that should be intensified. Humor suggests that AIDS is just another calamity to befall Mother Camp, whereas in truth AIDS is not one more item in a sequence, but a rupture in meaning itself. Humor, like melodrama, is an assertion of bourgeois values; it falsely suggests that AIDS is all in the family. Baudelaire reminded us that the wise man laughs only with fear and trembling.

End in anger, I say, because it is only sane to rage against the dying of the light, because strategically anger is a political response, because psychologically anger replaces despondency, and because existentially anger lightens the solitude of frightened individuals.

Edmund White, in his "Esthetics and Loss," in Personal Dispatches: Writers Confront AIDS, *edited by John Preston, 1989.*

Katie Hogan (essay date Spring-Summer 1993)

[*In the following essay, Hogan examines the portrayal of women in literary works dealing with AIDS, particularly Alice Hoffman's* At Risk *(1988) and Perri Klass's* Other Women's Children *(1990).*]

> [W]hy should the task of moral and social transformation be laid on women's doorstep and not on everyone's. . . . It is as though women don't really believe they are entitled to full citizenship unless they can make a special claim to virtue. Why isn't being human enough?
>
> —Katha Pollitt

The topic of women and AIDS is often curiously absent from AIDS discourse. When images of women and concepts of gender do appear, they recall traditional narratives of "woman" as nurturer, as caretaker, as facilitator of virtuous feeling. As Katha Pollitt observes [in "Marooned on Gilligan's Island: Are Women Morally Superior to Man?" *The Nation* (December 1992)], women seem

to be required to show exceptional virtue to claim public life. Pollitt's observation illuminates the haunting images of women that tend to appear in AIDS discourse. For instance, female characters in AIDS literature are often confined to the work of mourning while male characters brazenly express anger and sexual desire even as their bodies give way to physical deterioration. Why is AIDS still conceptualized as a male disease? Why is it assumed that AIDS literature tells us about gay male culture and practices? By the same token, what does the absence of women as people with AIDS teach us about women's predicament in our culture? How is this silence incorporated into our discourses on AIDS? What is missing in AIDS discourse in relation to women and what are the political implications?

Along with absences and silences, I find deeply distorted constructions of women entrenched in AIDS discourse. Moreover, when I look at a specific kind of AIDS discourse—a literary AIDS, for example—I find very little sense of any sort of feminist history or consciousness even though most AIDS literature is promoted as "political," "activist," an artistic form of cultural dissent.

I will explore some of these questions through brief readings of two AIDS novels: Alice Hoffman's *At Risk* and Perri Klass's *Other Women's Children.* I begin with the assumption that "woman" has appeared in literary, medical, and popular discourse as either the site of disease and pathology, or as a symbol of affect and virtue, and that the latter of these rhetorical traditions surface in some American AIDS literature with a vengeance.

For at least a decade, creative writers, intellectuals, activists and academics have been responding to the AIDS crisis with critical force and creativity. In particular, they have responded to the politics of blame and stigma, homophobia and racism, sexism, and classism that characterize much AIDS commentary in the United States. But there has been no developed analysis of women and AIDS nor of the conceptual gap itself until the late 1980s. One finds in much AIDS literature (and certainly in the AIDS literature that I discuss here) the time-worn narrative of what Judith Williamson [in "Every Virtue Tells a Story: The Meaning of HIV and AIDS," in *Taking Liberties* (1989)] calls the "Ministering Angel." That is, women are cast as caretakers and nurturers of men and children, as if their genuine activity in life is their self-sacrificing service to others. Rarely, if ever, do we encounter richly developed, autonomous female characters who are themselves at risk for HIV infection—unless the female character can be depicted as an "innocent" (read asexual) victim. Most images of women in AIDS literature cast them as playing the impossible, privatized caretaker role. As "Bev" remarks in [*Positive Women: Voices of Women Living with AIDS*, edited by Andrea Rudd and Darien Taylor (1992)], "little account is taken of the fact that women are still the major nurturers in society and that many [HIV] infected women still have to fulfill this role in relation to their own children and partners, often to the detriment of their own health."

From Paul Monette's *Halfway Home* to Tony Kushner's Pulitzer prize-winning *Angels in America,* female charac-

Roger Horwitz (left) and Paul Monette (right).

ters appear in AIDS writing as ancillary: their main activity is to grieve, mourn and attend to the emotional needs and dying processes of men or children. Even a play as sprawling, and as historically informed and as politically aware, as the award winning *Angels in America* overlooks the gender politics of the very history Kushner employs. The most prominent female character, Harper, intuitively connects to the other male characters' complex emotional states more so than to her own needs and rights. Her child-like fragility resembles Tennessee Williams's asexual and frightened Laura from *The Glass Menagerie* in contrast to Prior, the gay man dying of AIDS, who experiences a "hard on" each time he hears the mysterious angel's voice. And when Kushner's long awaited angel of history appears wearing glorious wings and a flowing white gown, some feminist spectators may painfully recall that insidious "angel in the house" that Virginia Woolf wrote about with fierce passion and rage.

Now this may seem like a harsh line of reasoning, an ugly attempt to erect a hierarchy of oppression. Let me repeat that my argument is a call for an oppositional feminist "sensibility," one that assumes an interlocking oppression of gender, sexuality, race and class. And one that neither eschews politics in favor of the mysteries of "artistic expression" nor sacrifices the imagination and vision of literary creation to the needs and demands of political urgency. In fact, what confuses me as a person embroiled in the long, unrelenting process of loss and grief due to AIDS is the political imperative most creative writers attach to their artistic renderings, yet a visionary feminist consciousness seems painfully absent from most of this literary/political writing.

My purpose is neither to compete with or downplay the hardships of gay men, nor to exacerbate the historical tensions between gay men and lesbian feminists that have been partially healed in response to the AIDS crisis. This speculative essay is my contribution to the now-growing dialogue on women and AIDS, and this writing expresses the anger I feel about what the particular treatment of women in the AIDS epidemic tells us, reveals to us, and

teaches us about the economic, social and political predicament of many women in the United States. In addition, I have personal stakes in this particular representation of women as the "Ministering Angel," a story I'll spare you for now, but one that has shown me that these images have material effects and hurt people.

I experience contradictory and conflicted feelings when sitting in the theatre watching *Angels in America* or reading Adam Mars Jones's and Edmund White's *The Darker Proof*, or Allan Barnett's beautiful collection of stories, *The Body and Its Dancers;* or when I watch a film such as *Longtime Companion* and my gut-level identification with the expression of deep loss, and depression and grief, my appreciation of the artistry is compromised by the absence of women characters on the one hand, or the tenacious, entrenched image of child-like women on the other. I can grieve for men and children with AIDS, I can identify with the emotional accuracy of the writing, but the silence and distortions about women, class, and race in major artistic productions disturb me and hurt me for deeply personal as well as manifestly critical reasons.

Writing about images of women in AIDS literature gives me permission to find a form for my own complex emotional suffering caused by the reality of AIDS—a suffering inextricably linked to the devastating effects of sexism. To this end, I chose a speculative approach rather than a discussion of how AIDS challenges our systems of thought, although I think that the reality of AIDS allows us to engage in these philosophical questions. Rather I want to begin to name what is missing in AIDS literature by drawing from a dialogue already begun by feminist theorists, creative writers, and lesbian feminist political activists (Cindy Patton, The ACT UP Women and AIDS Book Group, The New Jersey Women and AIDS Network, Donna Haraway, Gena Corea, Darrien Taylor and Andrea Rudd, Kate Thompson, Ruth L. Schwartz, Paula Treichler, Sander Gilman, Amber Hollibaugh, Beth E. Schneider, Jackie Winnow, Sybil Claiborne and Paula Martinac). These fiction writers, activists and academics offer models for investigating how women and AIDS are constructed in literary discourse and suggest what this may indicate about the condition of women in this country who are living with or greatly affected by AIDS.

I also maintain that the issue is not whether AIDS literature is written by men or women. The issue here is the gender politics of the narratives of women in AIDS literature—no matter how "minor"—and the "cultural work" that these narratives perform. For instance, in order to complicate our culture's understanding of "sentimentality," Jane Tompkins argues in *Sensational Designs* that nineteenth century literary productions by women—what we would call sentimental—"articulat[e] and propos[e] solutions for the problems that shape a particular moment." In other words, sentimentality is not necessarily pernicious or salutary and, despite our bias against it, Tompkins finds it does useful work. However, in the case of contemporary American literature on AIDS, I find that these persistent sentimental images of angelic women and children render women invisible and therefore have a decidedly negative political impact. When sentimentality appears in AIDS literature it tends to depict female characters in a distorted, limited, and stereotypical way. In the meantime, these literary occlusions in AIDS literature appear as women worldwide are experiencing the fastest rise in the rate of HIV infection.

When Alice Hoffman's *At Risk* was presented in 1988 at the American Bookseller's Association conference with glitzy lights and a glossy cover, best-selling novelist David Leavitt intimated that its public reception was linked to the politics of the innocent victim. Other gay male writers echo Leavitt's feelings and point to *Newsweek*'s mixed review of Paul Monette's memoir *Borrowed Time* while praising Hoffman's *At Risk* for its heartfelt qualities. The argument set forth by Leavitt and others is that *At Risk* feeds into "mainstream" readers' homophobia, racism, classism and contempt for IV drug users by parading a white, blonde, eleven year old suburban girl who is dying of AIDS as the novel's central focus.

Judith Laurence Pastore argues [in "Suburban AIDS: Alice Hoffman's *At Risk*," in *AIDS: The Literary Response* (1992)] that *At Risk* aggressively asserts inclusiveness, as Hoffman smashes the "risk group"/"general population" construction by creating a character, Amanda Farrell, who experiences "the same" prejudices as other people with AIDS—marginalized gay men, IV drug users and "inner city" minorities. I think there is some truth to Pastore's argument: Hoffman's Amanda Farrell and the entire Farrell family do experience "shunning," isolation, depression, anger and an intense fear of mortality. But *At Risk* swerves to an extreme in its pubescent, virginal "innocent victim" who resembles Harriet Beecher Stowe's "Little Eva" or the recent high-profile dying of virginal Kimberly Bergalis.

Pastore reasons that Hoffman purposely created this "Little Eva" character to demonstrate how even innocents suffer the brutalities of ignorance, prejudice and fear. On the contrary, HIV and AIDS continues to highlight the inequalities among various communities, genders, races, classes and sexualities; HIV infection and AIDS illuminates injustices that are deeply disturbing and culturally reinforced. To repeat, the studies and testimony that are emerging about women's experiences in this crisis tell us disturbing truths about women's invisibility in our culture at large. In other words, if Hoffman truly wished to employ the transformative powers of fiction to challenge the "innocent victim" label, why not dramatize the politics of this very category itself? Why create a paragon of innocence, Amanda Farrell, and redeem the only bisexual male character with AIDS in the novel as also "noble" by constructing him with similar images of sentimental purity used to describe Amanda?

Again, by rendering Brian as "innocent" as Amanda, Hoffman sidesteps the more complex issue of the politics of the "innocent victim" which would have been a far more interesting and honest literary and political effort. I want to emphasize that Hoffman's artistic desire for alliance and connection between a white presumably straight girl and a white bisexual man does not disturb me—besides, Amanda and Brian share similar middle-class entitlements. Instead, I question how Hoffman forges this alliance: with a sentimental expression of sameness. Hoffman presents Brian, a bisexual man and former IV drug user and musician as both the composite of several "outcast" identities on the one hand and then casts him as overwhelmingly acceptable on the other. Again I return to David Leavitt's argument that *At Risk*'s success and notoriety was mostly due to its ideological palatability: no transgressive gay male sex; a bisexual man with AIDS who seems saint-like and unearthly in a novel that flirts with a problematic use of sentimental death. For instance, Hoffman rids her text of Brian's problematic body by describing him as "dissolving," as "barely there," as "already looking at something far away, something in another dimension no one else can see." Significantly, Amanda is similarly portrayed as "one made up not of flesh but of points of brilliant light."

Curiously, however, while Leavitt exposes the politics of Amanda's character in terms of gay male sexuality, he seems unaffected by the invisibility of women's sexuality and complex experiences with HIV or AIDS, or the ways in which gender and sexuality get constructed. That is, the objections to *At Risk* have mostly been articulated from a still male, patriarchical perspective, with little feminist awareness. What is the connection between Amanda Farrell, the paragon of innocence and physical virtue (she is a promising gymnast), the politics of Brian's characterization, and the occlusion of women's sexuality and complex experiences with HIV and AIDS? In an essay that explores how gender, race and class constitute lesbian desire ["Sexual Practice and Changing Lesbian Identities," in *Destabalizing Theory: Contemporary Feminist Debates* (1992)], Biddy Martin observes that "one ironic effect of AIDS [is] . . . an opening up of public discussions of sexuality, even in the face of renewed repressions." Martin's analyses help illuminate the erotophobia that characterizes *At Risk,* an ideology that explains Hoffman's investment in the "innocent victim" rhetoric as well as her attraction to sentimental rhetoric and imagery—the blond haired, non-urban, athletic girl-child, dying of a stigmatized disease which she acquires "innocently" through a blood transfusion.

The point is that the potential for public discussions of sexuality is policed and contained in *At Risk* through the uncritical use of "innocence" and sentimentality, which is used to carry out this surveillance. As I argued earlier, there is nothing "innately" repressive about sentimental rhetoric; its repressiveness arises from its relationship to the context in which it is used. As Eve Kosofsky Sedgwick argues in *Epistemology of the Closet,* sentimentality is a structure of relations between books and readers, or performers and audiences, rather than as a fixed subject or thematic associated with women's culture."

The effects of this angelic sentimental girl in a contemporary AIDS novel similarly determines the presentation of several adult female characters in Hoffman's writing. From the "New Age," asexual, blonde, Laurel Smith who intuitively guides Amanda to the next world, to the creation of Polly Farrell, Amanda's defeated and long-suffering mother, Hoffman casts her female characters as women without complex needs, women who exist in order to serve others. The novel breaks this pattern when Amanda's contentedly married mother collapses into Ned Reardon's (Amanda's doctor's) arms at which time the two exhausted grown-ups kiss and notice that their body heat is steaming up the car windows.

But my interpretation of this scene is that here Hoffman clearly wants her readers to understand Polly's desire as irregular, as caused by the enormous stress and depletion associated with her child's dying from AIDS. The embrace and kiss are portrayed as warm, cuddly, affectionate, nonthreatening: it both unleashes and contains our culture's unconscious belief that AIDS is linked to every imaginable form of chaos—the demise of traditional families, the rise of non-monogamy, promiscuity and deviant sexual practices—while reassuring its readers that nothing of the sort will happen to them, even if one of their own should become ill and die.

At Risk is not interested in presenting complex women characters who experience genuine and clear sexual arousal, making women's sexuality almost invisible. Further, it fails to consider the fact that women have HIV infection and AIDS, let alone presenting a female character with the disease. In fact, *At Risk* is not truly concerned with AIDS, despite the fact that the multiple literacies of AIDS comprise much of its content. In effect, *At Risk* is about our culture's fear of AIDS, fear of women's sexuality, gay male sexuality, non-traditional gender roles, and any other cultural practices linked to the breakdown of boundaries. For this reason, Hoffman constructs a fictional world that often resembles the erotophobia of nineteenth century sentimental writing by women. Accordingly, she writes for readers who are comforted by women and "feminized" men who earn their right to public approval through their commitment to exceptional moral and social virtue. Therefore, the potentially "transgressive" aspects of their lives—sexual desire, non-monogamy, IV drug use, nontraditional roles and experiences for female characters—are either absent, dismissed as threatening, or rendered insignificant.

Hoffman does not ask her readers to deconstruct AIDS stigma nor does she offer a fictional vision of how this process might occur. Judith Laurence Pastore puts it well: "[A]s to whether *At Risk* does much to combat the mounting homophobia in our society, I would have to say it does little." It also does little to confront sexism, classism and heterosexism, cultural systems that the politics of AIDS thrives on.

Perri Klass's *Other Women's Children,* although similar to Hoffman's novel in that Klass focuses on ill children, one of whom is a three year old boy dying of AIDS, and similar in that it conveys conservative panic about the breakdown of the nuclear family, nevertheless serves as a powerful alternative to Hoffman's vision.

Other Women's Children's inside jacket describes this novel as articulating "the tension between a woman's commitment to her family and the demands of her professional responsibilities." Yet what I find most astonishing about this novel is its fictional exploration of the ways in which its main protagonist's professional responsibilities

as a pediatrician mirror her motherly and wifely activities. In other words, the real tension in this novel is that even a female character as "exceptional" as Klass's Amelia Stern cannot escape traditional gender role expectations. And that when the intensity of a crisis like AIDS, childhood poverty, and inadequate medical care enters a particular woman's life, she experiences cultural pressure to perform unexceptioned selfless service to others.

As I look back over the margin notes I made the first two times I read Klass's novel, I can see that I didn't know what to think of this text so I penned in complaints: it's bad the way that Klass confuses HIV with AIDS, the way that she incorrectly and insensitively refers to the test for HIV that Amelia Stern administers to her patients as the "AIDS test"; the way that Klass's Amelia conveys such a smug attitude towards IV drug users. In short, I hunted down places in this complex and sometimes wild text where Klass employed politically problematic language. At that time, I could only envision a certain kind of "political" novel, one with scenes of demonstrations and long ideological passages. And it's not that I now believe that my observations are not valid or unworthy of mention. It's that they seem also to signal my desperate attempt to find some way to engage in a novel that I didn't really understand.

There are aspects of Klass's fictional vision that still anger me. For all of Klass's brave critique of "domesticity" and her relentless exploration of the politics of the Victorian dying innocent, she ends this novel with a picture of family that is aggressively heterosexist and problematically romantic. For all of this, however, *Other Women's Children* is in my view a brave, complex novel, one that unwittingly exposes the damage done to an accomplished, independent, thoughtful and talented woman: the type of woman most equipped to overthrow the "Ministering Angel."

In addition to being a skilled pediatrician and medical researcher, Amelia Stern is a writer, which, in her case, translates into a deep, engaged, critical thoughtfulness about life. Still, none of the powerful aspects of her personality, her creative writing, her scientific knowledge and doctor skills, her education and economic security, her cozy, milky intimacy with her delightful four year old, Alexander, protect her from the painful ironies, conflicts and human suffering that haunt her life.

A typical day for Amelia Stern includes attending to the medical needs of a poor, black three year old boy named Darren who is dying of AIDS to seeing mostly lower middle class "clinic" children. These experiences are glaringly contrasted with a visit to an expensive, posh, "independent" school where her four year old son may attend if he gets "accepted." Amelia understands that her days shift between a privileged, white, upper-middle-class world and family life and the limited, grim lives of the children she takes care of. "How can I go back and forth, how can I hold these two realities in my mind at the same time?"

In an act of desperation, she turns to nineteenth century literature to find solace, a philosophy, a "representation" mapped out for those who want to comprehend the senseless suffering and death of children. Instead of comfort,

Amelia grows more and more agitated and angry as she rereads the books of her childhood, *Little Women* (which she knows by heart) and *Uncle Tom's Cabin.* Amelia's reactions to these novels betray her newfound critical reading of what she calls the manipulative construction of the Victorian ideal of the dying innocent. What Amelia sees as repulsive and insensitive is the "waste of baby": "I'll take a random accident any day over a manufactured plot twist. The children of nineteenth-century literature really ought to strike for safer working conditions." And, "Dying children are the sweet creamy centers of literature."

To add to Amelia's frustration is the contradictory effect these literary models have on her ability to express her feelings: "I can't even talk about the worst parts of my work because it would just seem like bad soap opera." And yet talking about her pain is exactly what Amelia needs to do: "The death scenes in books make me cry and then I feel like I've been had." But as a writer herself, Amelia confesses "the possibility of killing off a child, especially a loved and beautiful child, a child who is the heart of his parents, is very tempting from a literary point of view." Isn't this how one elevates writing into art, Amelia bitterly concludes.

Stated differently, *Other Women's Children,* unlike *At Risk,* contains its own powerful critique as Amelia Stern, in the act of writing the novel we are reading, discovers her deep ambivalence towards the politics of sentimental death—a discourse she finds both repulsive and yet the only writing that attempts to express emotional grief. This repulsion and attraction becomes one of the crucial issues in her struggle to find an adequate language for conveying her experience as a witness to children, death, AIDS, and poverty.

The novel is also the story of Amelia's socialization and at the same time awareness of the pitfalls of the moral and social reformer: "Amelia is mildly suspicious of herself whenever she finds herself doing anything that echoes her mother's somewhat simpleminded us-against-them do-gooding; she has wondered from time to time whether she became a doctor to be irreproachably beneficent." Amelia begins to realize, in a way that she had never realized before, how her life differs from Darren's and the other clinic children (differs not just in terms of her being healthy and HIV negative, but in the sense that she has escaped many injustices). She begins to examine her entire world: her social, familial, political, and economic positions. The politics of the "literary" language used to convey childhood death, especially literary sentimentality, all come under her scrutiny. It's not just that Amelia's awareness of these children's lives bring her sadness, which it does; it's that Amelia allows her relationship with Darren and with the other "clinic" children to challenge the way that she thinks about every aspect of her life.

Yet, while Klass's writing expresses a vibrant feminist awareness of Amelia Stern's exhausting moral predicament and provides a more complex discussion of sentimentality and childhood death than Alice Hoffman's writing, Klass's novel sadly portrays Amelia Stern's witnessing and critical thinking in the most privatized, isolated

manner. As a result, her novel suggests that Amelia's alienation expresses an individual, moral failing rather than a reflection of structural and institutional sexism and hypocrisy. In other words, Amelia begins to think that she is a bad mother because she fails to balance the demands of her professional life with the demands of her family. In the end, Amelia's husband, Matt leaves her (he takes their son with him but eventually the family is reunited) because he feels she puts the needs of "other women's children" before the less dramatic needs—but still most important needs—of their healthy and happy son. Amelia repents. She begins to understand how difficult it must have been for Matt to be with a woman whose mind is overflowing with sadness, anger and observations concerning the social and political injustices she encounters every day of her working life. Amelia's retreat suggests that when an unusually thoughtful, talented, skilled, creative and educated woman begins to piece together the systems of sexism, racism and classism, she is reigned back in with the threat of loss.

The intensity of suffering, loss, and panic that ensues because of AIDS can lead to a nostalgia for supposedly less ambiguous times—when women were always available to nurture the afflicted. Even early twentieth century lesbians, as Lillian Faderman has argued [in *Odd Girls and Twilight Lovers: A History of Lesbian Life in Twentieth-Century America* (1991)], gained prominence "because what they did could often be seen as housekeeping on a large scale—teaching, nurturing, healing—domestic duties brought into the public sphere." The desire for this ministering image of women can short circuit our ability to read AIDS literature "against the grain." Reading against the grain and with an enabling cynicism can be very painful indeed. But many readers, myself included, come to AIDS literature looking for a place to go with isolation and sadness, and it is particularly alienating either to find their pain rendered invisible or constructed in the most predictable traditional forms. Women should not have to strive for exceptional moral and social nobility in order to be heard. Nor should anyone else. (pp. 84-93)

Katie Hogan, "Speculation on Women and AIDS," in The Minnesota Review, *n.s. No. 40, Spring-Summer, 1993, pp. 84-93.*

John M. Clum   (essay date 1993)

[*In the essay below, Clum examines the treatment of the "lost past" in AIDS literature.*]

As it was during the Vietnam War, the most important writing during the various battles being waged in the age of AIDS is historical and political. AIDS has raised so many unanswered questions that getting the facts seems paramount. Yet AIDS is the cause of thousands—millions—of personal tragedies, and more personal literary forms—the memoir, poetry, and written, staged, and filmed fictions—have focused on the effects of AIDS on individuals touched by the virus. These AIDS narratives have so far been a series of variations on a few themes. Most mainstream narratives, aimed at the popular media's mythical, cohesive, all-heterosexual audience, have usually focused on homosexual characters with AIDS but move the spotlight early in the story from the person with AIDS to his family's problems in coping with the news that he is homosexual, for homosexuality is usually equated with and presented as the cause of AIDS. However much such cultural productions claim tolerance, AIDS becomes a sign of past sexual transgressions. AIDS narratives written by gay writers have a far more complex, more troubled causality. They often focus not on coping with the disease itself, but on the character's changed relationship to their past sexual activity.

What links mainstream and gay AIDS narratives are their affluent setting and their sense that AIDS has threatened both the American dream of the good life and the sense of protection from menaces to that insular life. When AIDS comes close to heterosexuals thrown into the position of caregiver to a loved one with AIDS, it leads to emotional and spiritual crises as the linked threats of AIDS/homosexuality force people to question the assumptions of the Reagan era—that people were soundly buttressed by their affluence, freedom, technology, and carefully marketed illusions of eternal youth and health. In gay-created AIDS narratives, AIDS also transforms a world of affluence and pleasure. Paul Monette's memory in his poem "Half Life" that "once I had it all" refers not only to his beloved Rog, now dead from HIV-related infections, but also to the affluent world he and Rog once luxuriously shared. That world now seems invaded, compromised as AIDS throws into question the values of the 1970s, what Paul Monette calls "the time before the war."

While "outside" heterosexist narratives tend to place the sexual activity which can be the mode of transmission for the AIDS virus into a murky, almost unspeakable past, a crucial issue for gay writers is how to recollect the pleasure principle that allowed urban gay communities to become a breeding ground for the AIDS virus. Even gay-authored works that critique the promiscuity of the pre-AIDS era attempt to resist self-hating explanations of AIDS. In either case, a major theme of gay AIDS literature is what to do with a lost past, which was both affluent and carefree.

Two typical outside, heterosexual AIDS narratives that seem to offer tolerance, compassion, and understanding actually reinforce aspects of the virulent AIDS mythology. In these fictions, the physical signs of AIDS not only come from the other, the homosexual, they are invasions of the ideal, affluent world of the "me generation" from someplace outside that socio-economic location.

Early in the 1991 ABC telefilm *Our Sons* (written by William Hanley), we see the extremely successful Audrey Grant (Julie Andrews) wake up in her opulent San Diego beachfront home and begin dictating messages. This total workaholic is used to being in control professionally and emotionally. We follow Audrey to her executive office, where she dials her son James's phone number, which is eighth on her list of calls for the day. The telefilm then cuts to her son's answering machine announcing that the spacious apartment we see is the home of two men, James and Donald, who "have no secrets from each other." The camera follows handsome young James through the large liv-

ing room to a hallway where his lover Donald, who bears television's signs of AIDS—thinning, eerily orange-colored hair, an unnaturally pale complexion, and KS lesions—is being carried on a stretcher. In the ten years since his mother threw him out of their Arkansas mobile home, Donald, we discover, has become an enormously successful young California architect. James is a pianist/singer at a chic cocktail lounge.

Our Sons presents a conventional television AIDS narrative with an extremely mixed message. In a medium in which cosmetic perfection equals success and virtue, the disfigured face and frail body of the [Person with AIDS (PWA)] is the horror usually unseen except on occasional newscasts or documentaries. Such disfiguration seems out of place on sanitized television fiction, which must be virtually indistinguishable from the commercials that pay for the program. The horror of the appearance of television's PWA contains complex codes. Donald's first line in *Our Sons*, when he is placed in his hospital bed and holds his lover's hand, is "Toto, I don't think we're in Kansas anymore." The allusion to Judy Garland codes Donald as television's generic homosexual. He bears the marks not only of the opportunistic infections and medical treatments he has endured (after all, the thinning hair and pallid complexion are as much a function of the treatments as the infections) but also the marks of his openly gay "condition." While *Our Sons* does not, as earlier telefilms about AIDS did, turn an AIDS story into a coming-out saga, it does once again link AIDS and homosexuality into one parental problem. While James's mother bravely faces the possibility that her son may be HIV-positive, she has never fully accepted his sexuality. Donald's mother, Luanne (Ann-Margret), who rejected her son because of his homosexuality, sees AIDS as its natural outcome. Both mothers spend most of their on-screen time fighting over which one has most realistically dealt with her son's sexuality. *Our Sons*, then, reinforces the notion that AIDS is ultimately equatable with if not a cause of homosexuality.

Donald comes from a working-class background far from the designer world of James and his mother (though in ten years he gained the training and connections to be a successful, fashionable southern California architect). While James's chic executive mother tries to cure Donald's brash, Southern working-class mother of her virulent bigotry, the telefilm perpetuates narrative constructions that show that affluent, handsome James is endangered, infected, by this outsider to his world.

While Donald's mother literally hates his homosexuality, James's mother has avoided dealing with James's relationship with Donald. As James describes it: "Enter Donald Barnes to share my home and hearth. . . . What could you do but distance yourself from so perversely domestic an arrangement." The perversion here is domesticity, what British politicians refer to as a "pretended family relationship." James and Donald's home is presented as virtually windowless (disconnected from the outside world?), yet we hear a constant thunderstorm rumbling outside (in drought-plagued San Diego!) to emphasize the gay household's frailty and vulnerability to natural disaster—like lightning, flood, or nature's avenger, HIV infection.

It is worth beginning this discussion with television because there one sees most vividly how the committees of producers and writers try to accommodate their audience. The purpose of television is to make its audience feel good about itself and about television. Compassion, perhaps pity, for certain PWAs is evoked, but television is more interested in creating empathy and sympathy for their parents, those representatives of a "normal" world who suffer the invasion of homosexuality into their families. Moreover, homosexuality may be the cause of AIDS, but television must also imply causes for homosexuality. In *Our Sons,* both young men are fatherless; their mothers are tough, determined, independent women. Is the absence of a father the cause of homosexuality and thus AIDS? Is James's strong, ambivalent relationship with his tough, domineering mother the cause of his homosexuality? Does the focus on the mother's sympathetic, loving attempts to care for her son assume that fathers shouldn't have to deal with gay sons or HIV-infected sons who have obviously transgressed the Law of the Father? Causality is always assumed, even if not directly discussed, on television AIDS dramas.

The image of disfigured Donald and the presage that James will soon look like that exemplify British video artist Stuart Marshall's observations about the link of homosexuality and AIDS: "Via the relay of AIDS, the image of the gay man has been woven through with some of the most terrifying representations of degenerative disease. Death and homosexuality are now inseparably linked in the public consciousness" ["Picturing Deviancy," in *Ecstatic Antibodies: Resisting the AIDS Mythology,* edited by Tessa Boffin and Sunil Gupta, 1990]. Donald, in fact, does die in the course of the program. When James first tells his mother that Donald has AIDS and will die soon, she asks: "How long do you have?" Critic Simon Watney connects such representations, examples of what he calls "The Spectacle of AIDS," to the dominant heterosexist "truth" about homosexuality:

> The spectacle of AIDS operates as a public masque in which we witness the corporal punishment of the "homosexual body," identified as the enigmatic and indecent source of an incomprehensible, voluntary resistance to the unquestionable governance of marriage, parenthood, and property. ["The Spectacle of AIDS" in *AIDS: Cultural Analysis, Cultural Activism,* edited by Don Crimp, (1988)]

Our Sons is a version of that masque.

In Elizabeth Cox's memoir, *Thanksgiving: An AIDS Journal,* we see not only another version of the virulent coding that undergirds television AIDS narratives but a heterosexual version of the threat to the 1970s dream of affluence and pleasure. In *Thanksgiving,* AIDS has touched a seemingly ideal young American family—handsome, talented husband, beautiful wife, lovely baby. When AIDS touches their lives, it poisons the blissful innocence Elizabeth has enjoyed: "The age of innocence is over and the world seems crueler and sicker than I could ever have imagined." Like the typical wife/mother in television AIDS fantasies, Elizabeth finds her world poisoned by various forms of otherness that become embedded in her husband,

specifically through his closeted homosexual activity and the HIV infection it makes possible.

In Cox's memoir, her handsome musician husband, Keith Avedon, a composer and arranger of music for glossy commercials, develops *Pneumocystis carinii* pneumonia while on a business trip to England. Though it is never specifically mentioned, Elizabeth is extremely lucky—she has the money to fly to London with her child to be with her husband, and her mother and his sister have the money to fly over at short notice to join her and offer support. This is a family without financial constraints.

In one revealing sequence, Elizabeth gives us the book's most horrible picture of her husband's physical condition as he recovers in a London hospital from his bout with pneumonia:

> He sat sunken into himself, his head nodding on his chest, like an old man past death, a skeleton covered with skin—a vision of Keith as he would have been at 110, an ancient Keith, a sight that must be a ghastly vision, an apparition, because my Keith is thirty-eight.

Keith's looks are gone, and so is the illusion of eternal youth. The specific numbers—110 presented as three digits, thirty-eight spelled out—suggest the importance of Keith's youth to Elizabeth. His sudden aging is something alien, horrifying. Age cannot wither Keith, but AIDS can. Like something in a 1950s horror movie, a vision of American youthfulness has been blasted in a weekend.

There must be a reason for this virus, and in outside AIDS narratives the mode of transmission is the real problem. Keith, after all, is another actor in "The Spectacle of AIDS," in which AIDS must have a behavioral cause as well as an epidemiological one. The night Elizabeth saw her suddenly aged husband, Keith's sister tells Elizabeth that "Keith has had a homosexual past"—a fascinating construction. "Keith is bisexual" seems to be more accurate, but it wouldn't place Keith's present illness within the proper equation of AIDS = homosexuality = disfiguration and death. Elizabeth's first response is to identify Keith's background—his family—as the other. "Why is your family so crazy?" Elizabeth screams at Keith's sister, "Why is there nothing normal?" Elizabeth places insane, abnormal, homosexual onto the "other," Keith's troubled, artistic, half-Catholic–half-Jewish family. Narratives of causality continue to emerge, not only of the possible sexual liaisons that could have caused infection, but of the childhood traumas that could have led to the homosexual activity: "I knew it would be impossible for anyone to escape the repercussions of a childhood like Keith's. I knew that much of Keith's life was a reaction to his past." Homosexual activity could not possibly have been simply the expression of a naturally occurring desire among men but must be interpreted as the outcome of childhood trauma and abuse.

Further details about Keith's past homosexual activity are couched in descriptions of a loathsome addiction and become themselves the problems Elizabeth must wrestle with: "He had been having anonymous sex with men. He couldn't help himself. He wanted to stop. It made him hate himself." Elizabeth never mentions that the affairs she was having with men could have put her and her family at risk. HIV infection thus is once again connected with homosexual activity, which is a hated, fatal compulsion. Elizabeth tells us, "Keith feels guilty, marked," as if only such Hester Prynne-like shame could justify and forgive him.

Throughout her memoir, Elizabeth catches herself and her husband in a double bind. On one hand, she despises intrusions of the AIDS = homosexuality equation and the causality it assumes:

> It seems that everyone I tell asks how Keith got AIDS. Why? What are they responding to, the disease or what it represents? I hate being asked how Keith got AIDS. . . . My own feeling is that nothing can explain such complete devastation of a person's life.

The vagueness, yet precision, of "what it represents" is fascinating. While there is denial in that euphemism, there is also a knowledge that it represents precisely homosexuality. Elizabeth seems to want to explode that equation, but she is more strongly driven to stereotypical causality, which leads her to focus on the homosexual past that is for her the cause of Keith's illness.

Elizabeth labors over her memories of the summer six years before when Keith "couldn't help" having sex with men and Elizabeth was also "staying out all night": "This is changing the way I see my past. What I thought of at the time as high-spirited recklessness I'm now being asked to see as desperation. I can't do it. It's too scary to change my memories." Yet she continues to ask, "Why did he do it?" It is fascinating throughout Elizabeth's memoir to see the changes from active to passive voice and her unquestioning perpetuation of the mythology of AIDS and various mythologies of homosexuality. What is the "it" Keith did? He sullied Elizabeth's memories by spending the night with men instead of women, thus turning "carefree" sex into "desperation"? The horror isn't a virus: it is ultimately Keith's "homosexual past."

Sexual history is particularly important in AIDS literature, since a sexually transmitted disease has, for many, replaced the sex = life equation of gay liberation with the equation of sex = death and the causal linking of the disease with the sexual playground of the 1970s. Gay men are sick because of sex, an unnatural causality that empowers all sorts of metaphors of disease already associated with homosexuality. Paula Treichler, in her superb essay on AIDS, homophobia, and biomedical discourse, calls AIDS "an epidemic of signification." Lee Edelman goes one step further and calls it a "plague of discourse," a notion Susan Sontag also developed in *AIDS and Its Metaphors*. It is the linkings of sex = disease, homosexuality = disease, promiscuity = disease, and, finally, homosexuality = promiscuity = disease that enchain people with AIDS and, by association, all gay men.

Yet Elizabeth also sees, and tries to deny, that AIDS throws her behavior into question as well. The pinpointing of that summer of sexual experimentation six years before, of testing and affirming their liberated marriage, has led both of them to this moment. "I had loved that summer while we were living it, but now it represents Keith's downfall." Keith's illnesses are not only debilitation; they are also his "downfall." AIDS has also destroyed her dream world. The first sentence of the book is "There is no space in this apartment," as if a limitless world of affluence and happiness has been contracted into a cell.

Space is central to such mainstream AIDS works, because AIDS came from outside the "normal" world and makes that world smaller and more vulnerable. Mainstream AIDS works therefore ask who brought this into "our" world and why. "When" becomes even more important as a question, as if AIDS were caused by not only a moment of seroconversion that must be pinpointed, but also by an era, a time of social and personal permissiveness for which one must atone. Historian Jeffrey Weeks has noted [in his 1991 *Against Nature: Essays on History, Sexuality, and Identity*] that AIDS mythology thus expresses "deeply rooted fears about the unprecedented rate of change in sexual behavior and social mores in the past two generations."

In gay-created narratives, to be sure, one is still dealing with a paradise threatened by the encroachment of AIDS, with poisoning of the present by a past that seemed paradisiacal. While in mainstream narratives, "AIDS came to represent the fruits of permissiveness" [Jeffrey Weeks, "Post-modern AIDS," in *Ecstatic Antibodies*], gay narratives show a complex relationship to the same construction. Gay AIDS literature must deal with the past sexuality = present disease issue in a way that either breaks the chain or affirms the past in a healing way. In other words, it must avoid the self-hating causalities that poisoned Keith Avedon's sense of self and the oppressive constructions that taint his wife's journal.

At the opening of the 1990 film *Longtime Companion*, it is July 1981. A handsome, perfectly built young man jogs down a beach, stops, strips off his clothes, and runs naked into the surf in a moment of carefree isolation. This scene is followed by scenes of beautiful young men, mostly coupled, discovering through the *New York Times* that a new disease is attacking numbers of gay men. The young men we see live in roomy, expensive Manhattan apartments and Fire Island beach houses. They are either rich or, through their beauty, charm, and availability, friends of the rich. The men work in advertising or show business. One writes episodes of a soap opera in which another stars. These men see the new "gay cancer" as something that couldn't touch them. It must be attacking men who are sleazier, more promiscuous, dirtier than they would ever be.

In *Longtime Companion* the audience sees the encroachment of AIDS on the American dream of beauty, affluence, and immortality, the dream created and sustained by the writer, actor, advertising executive, show-business lawyer, and gym worker we see in *Longtime Companion*. Fire Island in 1981, as it had been for years before, is the setting for the best of gay life—happiness, money, fellowship, male beauty, la dolce vita. But this isn't decadence, this is truly the American dream of television commercials and glossy magazine ads. Gay men in *Longtime Compan-*

ion represent the leisure class, a group with which American society carries on an ardent love-hate relationship. For screenwriter Craig Lucas, director Norman René, and their characters, Fire Island in the days before AIDS was heaven. The AIDS-changed world the film depicts is one of fear, debilitating illness, loss, anger, action—and nostalgia. In the final scene, eight years later, Willy, whose beautiful body ran into the waves at the film's opening, Fuzzy, the lover he met in Fire Island in 1981, and Fuzzy's sister Lisa walk the desolate beach of Fire Island in 1989. All are now AIDS activists. As they look longingly from the beach to the empty houses, Willy says, "I just want to be there. If they ever do find a cure." The film cuts to the boardwalk and stairs, now filled with hundreds of men, including Willy's friends who have died in the past eight years. Willy's dream of a world without AIDS is a dream of recapturing the past, of bringing his beloved friends back to life. It is also a dream of restoring the "carnival" of the Fire Island summers he remembers, of restoring the carefree leisure class. This is one gay version of AIDS, attacked by many critics for confining itself to white, affluent, privileged gay men, but still a leitmotiv of gay AIDS-era literature.

Willy's nostalgia is a convention of gay AIDS fiction. In a gay culture now rightfully obsessed with a plague, remembering becomes a central act, and it is how and what one remembers that defines much of AIDS literature, art, and film. That focus on memory is a central feature of the landscape of the wasteland described by AIDS-age gay writers. In this world, memory and desire take on new meaning as new links to the past must be forged, the present is sad and terrifying, and the future is drastically foreshortened. To affirm the past is to affirm the power of sexual desire; affirming the foreshortened, uncertain future is to affirm the possibility of love in the face of death.

Preston Wallace, the central character in the late Allen Barnett's story "Philostorgy, Now Obscure," responds to his diagnosis of full-blown AIDS by focusing on sorting and discarding memories and more tangible remnants of his past. As he burns his mementos he realizes, "He needed to do the same with old friends, affect their memory of him, introduce himself anew and say, 'This is me now.'" As he looks at a letter from his first lover, Jim Stoller, Preston realizes "what Eliot had meant by mixing memory and desire, a combination so intoxicating, Preston feared the room would begin to spin, that he might need help out of his clothes and into bed, and his head held if he was to sleep." What Preston remembers most strongly, since "the body can recall things on its own," is Jim Stoller's body, though it is ten years since he and Jim have been together. Impelled to see him once more, Preston seeks Jim out, hoping he can "arouse old feelings in Jim Stoller." After Preston tells Jim he has AIDS and shares his memories of Jim, Jim offers to take Preston home to bed:

> "It's too dangerous," Preston said.
>
> "I'm not afraid of you anymore," Jim said. "And I want some say in how you remember me."

Jim, living in affluence in Chicago, has not been touched by AIDS. His complacency and self-absorption lead him to misread Preston's warning of physical danger. It is Jim who should be concerned about how he remembers Preston, whose life has been foreshortened, but Jim has neither the wit nor depth to see that. For that kind of caring, Preston has his friends. He is wise enough to cherish Jim as a physical experience: "The smell of Jim was still on his beard, the taste of him under his tongue."

In a world in which philostorgy, meaning natural affection, is now obscure, Barnett's story is an assertion of the power of physical desire and physical memory, reflections of the power of the body itself. Preston understands Blanche DuBois's belief that "the opposite of death is desire." Yet the allusion to Eliot's "The Wasteland" is a reminder as well that a way of life has been compromised, reduced, by AIDS.

The paradigmatic writer in this new barren land of displacement, pain, and loss is Paul Monette, whose memoir *Borrowed Time,* volume of poems *Love Alone: Eighteen Elegies for Rog,* and novel *Afterlife* define both the sweetness and the horror of what AIDS means to a gay man touched tragically by the disease. Lamenting the loss of his beloved Roger Horwitz, who fell to the "opportunistic infections" (how inopportune that word *opportunistic* is) that HIV allowed to poison his system over nineteen months of suffering, Monette, HIV-positive himself, waits for the time bomb to turn his body into another Beirut. "I don't know if I will live to finish this," Monette says on the first page of *Borrowed Time:* "All I know is this, the virus ticks in me." "This" is aptly vague—is it the memoir on which he labors, an act of grief, celebration, and therapy—or is it his now incomplete and drastically curtailed life as the time bomb virus "ticks" away?

Monette's memoir is not just of him and Rog: it is a memoir of AIDS itself and how it is decimating a culture. The memoir begins, perforce, not with Rog's diagnosis, but, like *Longtime Companion,* with the insertion of AIDS into their lives: "The fact is, no one knows where to start with AIDS. Now, in the seventh year of the calamity my friends in L.A. can hardly recall what it felt like any longer, the time before the sickness." The "insertion" begins with phone calls from friends telling of others sick and dying, then the friends themselves become the bravely ill others. And what is forever changed is—was—paradise, the cozy world of affluent, gay southern California, seemingly untouched by the plague riddling New York and San Francisco (though, ironically, it was in Los Angeles that a physician started drawing conclusions from the five cases of *Pneumocystis carinii* he was treating). An affluent couple, lawyer and writer, beautifully, devotedly in love, in a beautiful house-cum-pool in the L.A. suburbs, wealthy enough to give to the right causes, seemed untouchable. The invasion of the home of Paul Monette and Roger Horwitz by HIV is not only an invasion of one loving couple, one household, or of gay culture; it is an invasion of the American dream itself.

The first pages of *Borrowed Time* introduce the refrain: "Equally difficult, of course, is knowing where to start." The fascination of Monette's work, like so much of AIDS literature, is that every phrase becomes an omen. Why does that "of course" jump out so ominously? Monette is aware that in eschatology, language gains new power: "The world around me is defined by endings and closures—the date on the grave that follows the hyphen," and for Monette, life has become circumscribed by two dates, the day Rog died, and the day of the Diagnosis, "the day we began to live on the moon." Anything before March 1985 is a brief glimpse of a lost past, but even those glimpses become tainted, yellowed with what will become intimations of mortality. The past before March 1985 has been lost, as has the cozy, loving world of Rog and Paul.

What is shattered in *Borrowed Time* is a gay version of the American dream of suburban, married bliss: a beautiful house emptied of the marriage that gave it meaning, a grief-stricken man lying huddled, alone on the bed he shared with his partner. Monette and Horwitz lived the dream liberal television and filmmakers gave gay men, when they showed us at all, in the 1980s—beautiful, tasteful surroundings in which a sensitive, frightened man is bolstered by his love of a strong, brave, sweet lover/friend. The reality is more complex and tragic. Tragedy brings pain and insight: Monette, the writer of novelizations and unsold Whoppi Goldberg scripts, becomes an anguished, eloquent Jeremiah, angry at the insensitivity of many doctors, in whose cold hands people with AIDS become dependent patients, angry at the disease itself, but possessed, articulate, and gifted with the ability to forge a harrowing beauty out of pain, grief, and fury. Monette becomes the bard of AIDS.

In the memoir, as in the poems, Monette begins fastidiously with details: "I sift through these details now because they are so concrete, still here in the house, evidence of all the roads of our lives in the time before the war." But the "time before the war" is irretrievable, and therein lies the real pain. Not only are men lost, but a culture is waning. Monette refers to his state as "half life," because he has lost half of what made life meaningful. Searching through remnants of the past to retrieve that past, he occasionally finds Rog:

> how is it you spring full-blown
> from a thousand fragments it's like picking up
> a shard of red-black vase off a Greek hillside
> looks like part of a sandal and a girl's long hair
> in a flash the white-stone city rises entire
> around you full of just men who live to be
> 90 the buried pieces fit

As Rog emerges in Paul's imagination from concrete remnants of their past together, so does an idealized past in which men were not blasted prematurely. Now Rog is "Proof of the end / of all gentle men." But Paul's "Half Life" also means that the remaining half will, like radioactive substances themselves, disintegrate. Soon he will be no more.

Paul Monette is in his mid-forties, one of a generation who "came of age" during the era of "gay liberation" that followed the 1969 Stonewall riots, a generation for whom sexual appetite could be joyfully sated. Gay men were at the vanguard of the sexual revolution, ironically supported by the protection of medicine: "Contraception and the assurance by medicine of the easy curability of sexual-

ly transmitted diseases (as of almost all infectious diseases) made it possible to regard sex as an adventure without consequences" [Susan Sontag, *AIDS and Its Metaphors*, 1989]. The effect of this brave new sexual world on a generation of gay men is depicted in the history of Mark in Robert Ferro's novel, *Second Son:*

> His generation had made love in great numbers, not from a sense of disobeying rules or smashing traditional morality but because moral, social reasons for abstinence no longer obtained against this sudden bursting of physical beauty and exuberance into their lives; it was the result of natural forces magnified by great numbers, into a phenomenon. Tandem notions of attachment and sex were meticulously, scrupulously disentangled. For them, as for no other generation, it could be either, instead of both or neither one.

This is the past that lights the memories in AIDS literature, the unabashed enjoyment of erotic pleasure: "So many men, so little time." Even the ideal marriage of Roger and Paul involved fashioning "a sexual ethics just for us" that excluded monogamy. Although Roger "was comfortable with relative monogamy, even at a time when certain quarters of the gay world found the whole idea trivial and bourgeois," Paul "would go after a sexual encounter as if it were an ice cream cone—casual, quick, good-bye." Yet Paul knows that promiscuity is not the issue: "But the disease wasn't drawn to obsessive sex or meaningless sex. Sex itself, pure and simple, was the medium and the world out there was ravenous for it." But times have drastically changed: AIDS has made the sexual past fearful:

> The fear of AIDS imposes on an act whose ideal is an experience of pure presentness (and a creation of the future), a relation to the past to be ignored at one's peril. Sex no longer withdraws its partners, if only for a moment, from the social. It cannot be considered just a coupling: it is a chain, a chain of transmission, from the past. [Susan Sontag, *AIDS and Its Metaphors*, 1989]

Or, as B. J., the narrator of David Feinberg's *Eighty-Sixed*, describes it: "Erica Jong's zipless fuck has gone the way of the Edsel. There is no such thing as sex without angst anymore. The specter of death cannot be ignored, forgotten." The past is not just the glorious memories of Whitmanesque, celebratory male coupling; it is also the possibly poisonous sexual/immunological past of you, your partner, his partners, even unto the beginning of time.

For the generation that lived through the erotic age, finding a meaningful present in an age in which sex has become not only de-eroticized but terrifying involves retrieving and affirming the past and purging it of the stigma of guilt, sin, and corruption with which AIDS and homophobia have embossed it. For men of Monette's generation, remembering is not only answering what Edmund White calls "the urge to memorialize the dead, to honor their lives," nor is it only remembering lost loves. It can also be a means of recalling the vanished past of a drastically changed society by remembering, or trying to remember, the orgiastic time before AIDS.

Some AIDS-era literature affirms the past by staying in it and ignoring the fraught present. Alan Hollinghurst's brilliant 1988 novel, *The Swimming Pool Library,* takes place in the summer of 1983, which the narrator calls "the last summer of its kind there was ever to be." The novel compares the "present" experience of a young civil servant who lives for his erotic experience with those of an eighty-year-old gay man who has entrusted his memoirs to our young central character. Beginning five years before the novel's publication and moving back in time, the novel purposely ignores, and to some extent defies, AIDS. Edmund White's *The Beautiful Room Is Empty* is a memoir of a young man's pre-Stonewall erotic experiences. The novel follows his own sense of the value of the past for gay men—and particular for gay writers: "There is an equally strong urge to record one's own past—one's own life—before it vanishes." White's novel/memoir, a sequel to his earlier AIDS-age work, *A Boy's Own Story,* offers not only individual experience, but typical experiences for gay men of his generation who have lived through a series of rapid changes:

> To have been oppressed in the fifties, freed in the sixties, exalted in the seventies, and wiped out in the eighties is a quick itinerary for a whole culture to follow. For we are witnessing not just the death of individuals but a menace to an entire culture. All the more reason to bear witness to the cultural moment.

In *The Beautiful Room Is Empty,* White, through the experience of one character, presents the early chapters of a paradigmatic history of gay men who grew up in the 1940s and 1950s, lived through the glory days, and now watch their society dwindle away in a grim performance of the "Farewell Symphony." If nothing else survives, there will at least be an imaginative record of the past in all its erotic subversiveness and subversive eroticism.

Even for some of White's characters, though, the past is not enough. Mark, the central character in White's story "Palace Days," not only partied, but made a career out of staging gay parties:

> He was the president of the Bunyonettes, a gay travel agency that arranged all-male tours. Forty gay guys would float down the Nile from Aswan to Luxor, impressing the Egyptians with their muscles and moustaches. . . . Or Mark would charter a small liner that would cruise the Caribbean and surprise the port town of Curacao when two hundred fellows, stocky, cheerful and guiltless, would ransack the outdoor clothes market looking for bits of female finery to wear to the Carmen Miranda ball scheduled for the high seas tomorrow night.

AIDS imperils Mark's business and his health. He and his lover Ned flee to Europe to avoid the epidemic and to continue the party in a supposedly safe place. Europe, of course, is no escape. Mark eventually tests positive, which leads him to mourn more fervently the lost past that was, for him, home. Mark sits with Ned in a Paris theater watching a poor performance of a Balanchine ballet and

remembers when "the lobby of the New York State Theater had been the drawing room of America and that we, yes, *we* Americans saw in the elaborate *enchainements* on stage a radiant vision of society." But this world of elegance, unwittingly parodied by this inferior Parisian performance, is, like Balanchine himself, gone. Mark becomes homesick for a lost culture:

> His muscles registered the word "home" with a tensing, as though to push himself up out of the chair and head back towards home, to . . . stingers at the Riv and the wild nights of sex and dance, but then he relaxed back into his seat, since he knew that "home" wasn't there anymore.

Time and space are conflated into this notion of home, a place one can never be again. But the enemy is not the past. As Harvey Fierstein's Ghee proclaims in *Safe Sex,* the enemy is "now": "We can never touch as before. We can never be as before. 'Now' will always define us. Different times. Too late." For young writers who came of age in the age of AIDS, there is no blissful past to remember, only a sad present.

David B. Feinberg's novel *Eighty-Sixed* mixes the sadness of the age of AIDS with recollections of a brief, less-than-golden "time before the war" experienced by the younger generation of gay men who came of age after Stonewall. "Ancient History," the first of the book's two parts and written in the past tense, recounts month-by-month the sexual exploits of its narrator and central character, B. J. Rosenthal. B. J. tells the reader that "the first man I slept with demonstrated the difference between love and sex quite vividly." The brief encounters of 1980 only reinforce B. J.'s first impression. Although B. J. claims both lust and love, both feelings seem destined to be aimed at "lost causes." The many sexual encounters are described in language that is far from erotic and seem to lead inevitably to venereal disease (the smorgasbord of venereal diseases of part 1 is eclipsed by AIDS in the second part). Love is nonexistent, as it inevitably would be for a man whose ambition is to "blend into a crowd of clones and disappear." Like many narrators in contemporary fiction, B. J. seems most identified with his ambition *not to feel,* for his overwhelming emotion in 1980 is a desperation not slaked by the constant, meaningless, usually pleasureless sexual activity.

Ironically, what often characterizes B. J.'s memories is his inability to remember names and sexual encounters. The first sexual encounter he describes in his book is indescribable because it has been forgotten: "Anyway, we were in the middle of some act that discretion requires I don't describe in too much detail; the fact of the matter is I don't even remember it." Nor does he remember having sex with Bob Broome, whom he met at a Juilliard concert: "What happened next I don't recall. I'm not absolutely sure what transpired." Yet Bob Broome looms large in the second, present-tense, half of the novel, "Learning How to Cry," which takes place in 1986 and centers on B. J.'s reaction to Bob's AIDS.

The news of Bob's illness throws B. J.'s memory into high gear:

Bob. Bob. Bob. Who do I know named Bob? There's Robert Walker. Bob. Bob. Bob. Was he the one—? No, that's someone else. Arthur. Think. It'll come to me. Bob. Bob. Broome! That's it. Bob Broome. Wait a sec, he was the one from the Juilliard concert, wasn't he? Shit, we tricked. It must have been four, five years ago. What did we do?

Bob Broome may not inspire many memories, but New York City itself evokes sad memories of past brief encounters:

At Forty-second Street stand the twin apartment towers of Manhattan Plaza, grim reminders of two more miserable affairs. In the west tower resides Jefferson Peters, an ignoble lout who tortured me with his massive member and malign indifference for several months last autumn; in the east Luigi Porcelli, who kept his focus on the tv as I did him, watching for his alias and phone number to flash on the screen of the gay cable-show personals, back in June of '82.

The dominant features of the architectural landscape now, though, are hospitals: "To the north, on Fifty-eighth, is Roosevelt Hospital, where John Lennon died in 1980" (Lennon's death is the capstone of part 1), and across the street is "St. Claire's, where Bob Broome is beginning to lose his mind." B. J. dutifully visits Bob Broome regularly and cares for him. Yet when Bob dies, B. J. tries "to forget the Bob in the hospital and remember the Bob I knew before," an impossibility, since B. J. has virtually no memory of that Bob. Nor does B. J. have a present:

Dave Johnson calls me and asks me what I'm doing with my time now that Bob has died and I don't go over to the hospital every other night. I don't know what to say. Maybe the worst thing is that life goes on.

There is considerable doubt whether life before AIDS was any more meaningful for B. J. than life in the age of AIDS. Only the illness of a former trick seems to offer structure, meaning. Like a Beckett character, B. J. finds living painful and meaningless, especially since living now means dealing again and again with AIDS. Bob is dead, and now Gordon, another friend, phones to say that he has it: "'OK.' I'm practically choking. 'I'm really sorry. Stay well,' I say," a nonsensical response—"Stay well"—but what does one say? A meaningless past, a present filled with AIDS; and could the future be any different?

B. J.'s present is filled not with the numb desperation of 1980 but with choking back the tears that are certain to flow endlessly: "I am afraid that once I start crying, I will be on a jag that won't end for days. I will never stop; I will cry and cry and cry." Finally, though, the tears do flow:

It begins as a gentle rain. Just a drop, for each illness, each death. And with each passing day it gets worse. Now a downpour. Now a torrent. And there is no likelihood of its ever ending.

The tears of the "almost choking" man who has learned how to cry will only be quenched in one way: "By the time you read these words I may in all likelihood be dead." The

year 1986 offers a real desperation—the desperation of a man, paralyzed by loss and fear, by using his calculator to "figure the odds," who cannot even find affirmation in the memory or fantasy of a joyous, orgiastic past.

B. J. is in his early twenties in 1980 and turns thirty in 1986. He missed the real glory days celebrated by writers who came of age in the Stonewall generation. He does not have the same past to celebrate, which might account for the numbness he feels. Like chain-smoking, sex is an addiction that has ceased to offer much except the desire to have more.

John Weir's Eddie Socket, a.k.a. Wallie Jeffers, is younger still, in his late twenties when he contracts and dies with AIDS. In *The Irreversible Decline of Eddie Socket*, we watch the interactions of gay men of three different decades: Eddie; the forty-five-year-old Merrit Mather; his estranged lover, thirty-six-year-old Saul Isenberg; and the young Wall Street trader, Brag Voleslavski, who, luckily, prefers masturbating on his sexual partners.

Saul and Merrit are in a state of crisis. Their friends are almost systematically dying, and their social life is composed of ominous phone calls, viewings, and funerals: "But listen, everyone does not get asked to viewings twice a week, unless they're eighty-seven or living in London in the plague of 1592, or fighting in a war. Or a New York homosexual at 6:00 A.M. this Friday, at the end of March."

While Saul would like to maintain the relationship as a means of security and order in a chaotic world, Merrit has other needs: "This week he's feeling forty-five, and all his friends are dying, and he thinks he wants a virgin boy to make him feel innocent again." So Merrit has a brief liaison with Eddie, then runs off to Europe with Brag Voleslavski, of whom he quickly, predictably, tires. Saul is left with memories of making love with Merrit, appropriately in a patch of pink narcissus, but AIDS encroaches even on this romantic recollection:

I held him very tight and said that we were cosmic twins, and he said, "Saul, if I get AIDS and die, will you die, too?" And this was very early on, before we knew we couldn't take each other in our mouths, an innocent time, it's funny to think of it now as an innocent time, innocent because we believed that if we slept only with each other, we couldn't get sick.

Now Saul and Merrit have no relationship, and worse, their world is gone:

I didn't have to end that relationship, because everybody died. Oh, Merrit didn't die, and I didn't die. But everybody else. We were just the last two remaining pieces of the puzzle. We fit together, but it didn't matter anymore; we had no context, no landscape, no frame.

Without a gay culture and society to support their life together, the relationship of Merrit and Saul becomes meaningless, and they finally, irrevocably, part, another loss in a world that is all loss: "Even grief is lost, finally, and then you mourn the loss of that." Young Eddie, the representative of what Saul calls "the blank generation," dies with

AIDS without ever really living. For most of the novel, Eddie seems to have nothing to lose. At the beginning, we are told, "he was still waiting for whatever miracle he thought it would take for his real life to begin." Ironically, that miracle is AIDS. Miserably ill and on the run, he calls his mother from a Los Angeles phone booth and finally springs to life:

> I'm thinking that I want my life. . . . I want it whole, and I want it complete, I want its texture and its spirit. I want its internal rhythms and its external shape. I want it all at once and forever, and I want it now. I want it now that it's going, Mom, and that's the final reversal.

Eddie, who "hated men and liked dicks," had little chance of being lucky in sex or in love. Sex "was either a performance or a disappointment" and "being held" was what he really wanted. Nor was there any sense of identity or belonging gained from his gayness: "There was nothing to define himself against, no lover, no family, no community, only New York, and his homosexuality, and he had not emerged in one, and he had not taken pleasure in the other."

The world John Weir creates offers loss for the older generation, and, for Eddie and his peers, a tangential link to a world never really experienced. Saul works at an auction house handling the artifacts of gay celebrities who have died with AIDS. His life is a round of funerals, of loss. Merrit is insulated by his self-centeredness and will live alone, unable to sustain a relationship. Eddie is dead, but without the tragic insight that would have made death meaningful, an insight that would have come from experience, from a past:

> Because it's not convincing, not dramatically, it doesn't play for all these twenty-eight-year-olds to die. They have to learn about their lives, they have to have catharsis, something has to come from their despair, some kind of knowledge, maybe wisdom. . . . So if you're learning wisdom from a tragedy, what happens when you suffer terminal disease and death, and all you learn is that you're falling in a dream?

For a generation that knows only numbness, the generation of B. J. Rosenthal and Eddie Socket, there is no past to lament, no future to dream of, no lover to embrace. There is nothing to remember. For Saul's generation, all that is left is the possibility of memory in a lost world: "I move around the room as if to memorize the final setting, the placement of objects."

Despite this overwhelming sense of loss, *The Irreversible Decline of Eddie Socket* manages to be an uplifting, touching book, an antidote to the bleakness of *Eighty-Sixed,* for it is also a celebration of the remnants of gay culture and imagination in its playfulness and sense of irony; chapter titles that echo opera, Sondheim, and Lorenz Hart lyrics; and Eddie's and Saul's camp sense of humor. In chronicling the loss of culture, the novel evokes that lost gay world and fixes it. That, too, is a crucial form of remembering. There remains, also, the voice of Saul, which contains both comic desperation and a sense of tragic insight that has come from its losses.

At the end of his poem "Half Life," Paul Monette cries, "and once I had it all." That memory, for him, brings pain, when the "all" wasn't fully appreciated or acknowledged. Now there is but half life. In AIDS literature, one cry of anguish comes from the "Stonewall generation," who once thought they had found paradise, and lost it through AIDS; another comes from a sadder, younger generation experiencing pain and loss without saving memories, present love, or dreams of a future. The older generation affirms the saving possibility of love to make present and future bearable, a possibility younger gay men seem never to have believed. For both generations the urge to remember and affirm remains as a culture fights the threats from the virus and from its enemies outside. That almost obsessive focus on memory—memory of desire—is a central characteristic of gay literature in the age of AIDS as gay men fight the inroads of the virus and the oppressive constructions that could rob them of the freedom and pride gained in that now-compromised past.

Sander L. Gilman has pointed out [in "AIDS and Syphilis: The Iconography of Disease," in *AIDS: Cultural Analysis/Cultural Activism,* edited by Don Crimp, 1988] that in the popular media, pictures of people with AIDS present their subject in poses echoing the classical iconography of melancholy ("elbow on knee, head on hand, a gesture of passive submission and reflection as well as despair"):

> The iconography of depression, with its emphasis on the body, stresses the age-old association of the nature of the mind (here, homosexuality as "mental illness") with the image of the body (here, homosexuality as sexual deviance). The image of the body is made to "portray" the state of mind. The person with AIDS remains the suffering, hopeless male, shown as depressed and marginal.

This is also the picture many AIDS narratives have shown or described. Television's picture of the wan, sensitive young man, shoulders sagging, staring out the window, or lying inert, helpless in a bed a few sizes too large; or prose fiction's depiction of a character paralyzed into anomie by the plague, like Feinberg's B. J.; memoirs' records of the baffled voices of those witnessing the wasting away and loss of loved ones. The image is of passivity. At best, one can control how one is remembered.

Many AIDS narratives have tended to be elegiac. As mainstream narratives have equated AIDS and homosexuality, so gay AIDS narratives have, not without cause, maintained the AIDS = death equation. In a way, this tendency climaxed in the creation and display of the AIDS quilt, so movingly recorded in the television documentary, *Common Threads: Stories from the Quilt* (1989). The sight of this giant tribute to people who have died of HIV-related opportunistic infections is not only a site for celebration and grief but also an incitement to anger.

While gay fiction has in the last few years tried to incorporate the dark design of AIDS into a larger tapestry of gay life, other cultural productions have recorded the second wave of response to AIDS, that of fighting for a future for PWAs. AIDS activism is a counter to the anguished, passive responses we have seen, in which endurance is the only available sign of strength.

The counter to the melancholia of gay people with AIDS and their loved ones seen in teleplays like *Our Sons* and films like *Longtime Companion* is the productive anger at work in the 1991 documentary, *Stop the Church* (directed by Robert Hilferty), in which the viewer sees the members of ACT UP, the Women's Health Action Mobilization, and related groups plan and stage the December 1989 demonstration against Cardinal John O'Connor during a service at Saint Patrick's Cathedral in New York. The vision of Cardinal O'Connor, who has become the symbol of the unrealistic, destructive intransigence of the Catholic church on the subject of AIDS education and homosexuality, improvising a homily on the sadness of hate while AIDS activists protesting his bigotry are dragged bodily out of the cathedral, followed by the reactions of his parishioners, who share O'Connor's desire to keep his cathedral a sanctuary from reality and compassion, is chillingly powerful, and more effective as a call to arms than AIDS fictions have been. *Stop the Church* shows another, more vital war that counters the victim mentality of many AIDS narratives.

In *Stop the Church,* we see not isolated, sad young men but a supportive, productive community that has managed to have a strong impact on how AIDS is treated in this country and that wants as strong a voice in how AIDS is prevented and how the rights and dignity of people with AIDS are protected. *Stop the Church* focuses not on grief or nostalgia but on anger. It shows anger and incites anger.

One sees the same determination in Michael Callen's memoir, *Surviving AIDS,* the account of a gay man who has lived with AIDS for nine years. Callen's argument is that just as the heterosexual, heterosexist world has educated gay men into a negative self-image that has often led to self-destructive behaviors, so that world is educating people with AIDS to see themselves as hopelessly doomed by HIV infection:

> If I believed everything I was told—if I believed that tiresome boilerplate lie that AIDS is 100 percent fatal—I'd probably be dead by now. If I didn't arm myself with information—facts, statistics, and diverse views—I wouldn't be able to defend myself against the madness and gibberish that daily assault those of us who have AIDS.

That daily assault is waged by editors who will not print pictures of healthy-looking people with AIDS and photographers who want picturesque shots: "When he [a *Newsweek* editor] arrived, he looked me over and then snorted contemptuously: 'Where are your lesions? I need someone with lesions!' " It is also waged by the "apocalyptic" language of television reporting.

Like many earlier AIDS writers, Callen sees his condition as a by-product of his past sexual hyperactivity. Without attacking the ethos of the 1970s, he wants to show that a host of venereal infections had already made their way into the gay community: "Unwittingly, and with the best of revolutionary intentions, a small subset of gay men

managed to create disease settings equivalent to those of poor third-world nations in one of the richest nations on earth." In this environment, it is not surprising that a lethal virus could be transmitted so widely.

For Callen, the issue now is not to focus on the past but to combat hopelessness and offer practical, if medically controversial, advice. Callen, for instance, argues against taking the highly toxic AZT, the drug of choice of many medical practitioners. He believes that prophylaxis against common opportunistic infections, particularly *Pneumocystis carinii* pneumonia, and avoidance of highly toxic drugs is crucial. More important, however, he says, is attitude. Central to survival is refusing "to believe AIDS is an 'automatic death sentence.' " Equally important, "Survivors are passionately committed to living and have a sense of 'meaningfulness and purpose in life,' of 'unmet goals.' Often the diagnosis itself enables them to find 'new meaning in life.' "

As the makers of *Stop the Church* celebrate political activism to end the stigmas against people with AIDS and to fight for AIDS research, education, and proper health care, so Michael Callen calls for personal activism on the part of people with AIDS as a counter to what has seemed an inevitable passivity.

Twelve years into the age of AIDS, fictions seem less important than active encounters with and vivid records of reality. Few gay people have not experienced the loss and grief associated with AIDS. Few have not at least confronted for themselves the question, "to test or not to test." Recently, a gay New York theatrical producer, John Glines, proclaimed [in Michael LaSalle's "Broadway Loses Talent to AIDS," *The Advocate* (8 October 1991)] that he wouldn't produce plays about AIDS:

> One third of my audience will have AIDS and another third will have tested positive. They don't want to come to the theater at night, hear how horrible this disease is, and weep. We do that during the day. What I'm producing is entertainment for the troops during the war.

There is no need for more depictions of loss and grief. There is no longer time for nostalgia for "the time before the war," which is receding farther into the past. Nor do those sagas of the encroachment of AIDS into the consumer's paradise of the Reagan era seem to fit the 1990s. There is, after all, a younger generation of gay men who know only the Age of AIDS, the war. While a *Village Voice* article once quipped that the principal theatrical event of the 1980s was the memorial service, AIDS literature of the 1990s will be a record of battles waged.

> *John M. Clum, " 'And Once I Had it All':*
> *AIDS Narratives and Memories of an American Dream," in* Writing AIDS: Gay Literature, Language, and Analysis, *edited by Timothy F. Murphy and Suzanne Poirier, Columbia University Press, 1993, pp. 200-221.*

James W. Jones   (essay date 1993)

[*An American critic and educator, Jones has written ex-*

*tensively on gay and lesbian literature. In the following
essay, he explores the thematic implications of refusing
to use the term "AIDS" in short stories and novels about
homosexuality and AIDS.*]

The application of a name carries with it cultural connotations. "AIDS" especially conveys cultural biases and stigmas, since the majority of those who now have the syndrome in the United States and Western Europe are either gay males or intravenous drug users—two groups already stigmatized by definitions of sexual "normalcy" and of narcotic legality. The act of naming imprints values upon the body of the named. As Susan Sontag has shown in her works *Illness as Metaphor* and *AIDS and Its Metaphors,* each culture interprets disease according to its view of the group or the individual who is diseased. AIDS has particular meanings within the United States because American culture needs to punish groups of persons who "choose" to engage in culturally proscribed behaviors. AIDS acquires meaning because it still largely affects people who are socially marginalized, and thus it evokes questions of stereotyping, scapegoating, retribution for "unnatural" lives, and the pathology of proscribed sex. Thus, certain meanings of AIDS permit the further marginalization of gay men, drug users, and prostitutes, to name but three groups.

AIDS has particular meaning for gay male American authors especially, because of the ways they are directly affected by it. Either they themselves have the syndrome or HIV infection (Robert Ferro and Sam D'Allesandro, for example, have died with it), or they accompany friends and lovers through the paths of the disease(s) and the social reactions to AIDS. I sketch here only briefly and in broad strokes some chief aspects of the way American authors writing about gay men are influenced by the health crisis, and the way they respond to the public discourses about AIDS in the United States, especially those that configure AIDS as morally synonymous with homosexuality.

According to a pervasive and powerful interpretation, AIDS is acquired because one is a certain kind of person, namely one who refuses to obey social, legal, religious, or moral restrictions on behavior. People with AIDS are often divided into two groups: innocent victims ("innocent" because they have broken no rule) and those deserving the disease. Even methods of education and treatment reinforce this division. For example, as Deb Whippen describes it [in "Science Fictions: The Making of a Medical Model for AIDS," *Radical America* (1986)], "hetero-AIDS" mandates the use of a condom for heterosexual intercourse, but "homoAIDS" demands that all gay sex cease. Stephen Johnson, who has done statistical research on the attitudes of American fundamentalists towards people with AIDS, explains [in "Factors Related to Intolerance of AIDS Victims," *Journal for the Scientific Study of Religion* (1987)] "that homosexuals, and by association AIDS victims, may serve as scapegoats for conservative fundamentalists, so that they might blame someone for the moral decay they see all around them." Richard Poirier observes [in "AIDS and Traditions of Homophobia," *Social Research* (1988)] "that the designation of the virus as the primary cause of the disease . . . has created an oppor-

tunity for a most primitive designation of homosexuality as the criminal mode of its transmission." Thus, "the need to eradicate homosexuality, even as homosexuals lie dying, takes precedence over the need to eradicate disease. . . . AIDS has become the metaphor for the *sin* of homosexuality and, more generally I think, the *sin* of sexual pleasure."

Such a description of AIDS is clearly just one aspect of the discourses about the epidemic in America. Another, the "enlightened" or "liberal" discourse, maintains that AIDS is an "equal opportunity destroyer." This discourse seems to break the links established between morality and disease but in fact reinforces it for gays, precisely because the discourse aims at keeping the majority (i.e., heterosexuals) healthy and confining HIV to "risk groups" of the socially marginalized and politically disenfranchised. And thus again does AIDS = homosexuality. This point has been made a number of times: "What distinguishes AIDS as it has been constructed in the United States from other diseases is the centrality of sexuality, specifically homosexuality, to its etiology and spread." [Robert Padgug, "More Than the Story of a Virus: Gay History, Gay Communities, and AIDS," *Radical America* (1987)]. The packaging of AIDS ostensibly aims at controlling contagion. In fact, it also, often overtly (as in William F. Buckley's call for tattooing gays on the buttocks), more often covertly (as in repeated denials of federal funding for publishing "safe sex" educational materials that use "explicit" language), seeks to reinforce the link between disease and homosexuality, so that homosexuality becomes the death that aberrance calls upon itself.

Gay men recognized early on that "in this country, how we think about disease determines who lives and who dies" [Evelynn Hammonds, "Race, Sex, AIDS: The Construction of 'Other'," *Radical America* (1986)]. They have therefore fought to create a counterdiscourse to defend against efforts to cordon off the sick by labeling them and to empower those living "at risk." Thus, one finds competing terms such as "Persons with AIDS" used to supplant the unfortunate and common term of "AIDS victims." Drug companies and the medical establishment develop new modes of profit and control while activist groups such as ACT UP seek to redistribute power by creating new processes of social empowerment. The discourses compete over the questions of who will be the subjects and who the objects of their speech: who may say "I," and who will become the "they" whom the "I" regulates.

AIDS continues to exist as a developing social construction. In it, as Deb Whippen writes, fact and fiction clearly (at least to the constructors and the constructed) intersect. The "fact" of HIV infection, or of certain "opportunistic" diseases, is given meaning through an interpretation that is in many cases itself *fictive.* She describes how the homophobia of scientists determined what questions they asked about the "facts" of the epidemic, and how this made them see what they wanted to find: a "lifestyle" and not a virus. The effect of such psychological blinders occurs often, but the public discourses on AIDS often cloak their speech in the authenticity and validity of science, making the facts they proclaim appear to be the truth—

whereas they clearly are someone's fictions. Estimates of numbers of infected persons and prognostications of numbers of sick, for example, are accepted as inevitable truths, whereas these numbers are speculative. But from them one is expected to deduce the fact that HIV = AIDS = death. The facts of modes of transmission make "unprotected" anal and, to some "experts," oral sex probably lethal. But the description of such modes of transmission can be—and has been—used to titillate and to stir up disgust on the part of nongays, thus creating an often equally lethal fiction for gays who are the recipients of this homophobia based on fact. These facts also turn all sex outside of the proscribed limits of monogamous heterosexual marriage into anonymous sex behind which, as Allan Brandt shows [in "AIDS and Metaphor," *Social Research* (1988)], stands the deathly specter of homosexual sex. What the cultural crisis of AIDS makes quite evident is that the distinction between fact and fiction has become extremely blurred and has been in many instances completely erased. In the end, many facts of the epidemic have been shown to be merely convenient fictions to describe a threatening reality/morality.

Is it possible, however, to break the equation in which AIDS = homosexuality = general moral decay = death? Literature presents one way to do so. Many authors have created stories in which gay men have AIDS; yet, surprisingly, the name AIDS is not often mentioned. Instead, narrators and characters speak of "my terrible news," "it," "this horrible disease," "my illness." But the various illnesses that afflict these characters or their context make it clear that the unnamed disease is AIDS. For example, in Robert Ferro's novel *Second Son,* Mark develops purplish lesions, and his lover, Bill, becomes ill with pneumonia. Neither illness is named, but the symptoms and treatments mark them as those two common diseases, Kaposi's sarcoma and *Pneumocystis carinii* pneumonia, that among others signify AIDS. The symptomatology of AIDS traces itself throughout the stories: weight loss, diarrhea, night sweats, cytomegalovirus, dementia. The reactions to illness in oneself and in others make it possible to understand that AIDS is what is meant. "The test," "immune systems," guilt about past anonymous sex, and the "plague" make up the semiotics of this language of indirection, which, because the characters are gay men living in the present and because the signs placed into the text are found in everyday discourses of AIDS, is easily decoded.

The name AIDS evokes certain images that circumscribe the ability to transcend the limits they impose. By refusing to utter or write the name AIDS in these stories, as in the case of *Second Son,* the author pushes the disease to the edge of fiction; it is the effects upon the lives of individuals and the life of the community that form the centers of these stories, rather than the disease itself and its public mythology. In Susan Sontag's short story "The Way We Live Now," many friends, women and men, talk to each other about their mutual friend, a gay man with AIDS. Each friend is named, but the name of the man with AIDS is never given. The story consists of a series of paragraphs that use indirect discourse to report on the man's pneumonia and on his friends' reaction and accommodations to

it. Sontag is concerned with the ways in which AIDS is changing relationships and behavior between friends: They vie to spend time with him and arrange their schedules to suit him, which may just be "a way of our trying to define ourselves more firmly and irrevocably as the well, those who aren't ill, who aren't going to fall ill." As one of them says, "Even *we* are all side effects." Yet, he, the friend with AIDS, is able to say the name of the disease, an act that is a sign of health, "a sign that one has accepted being who one is, mortal, vulnerable, not exempt." His friends, however, cannot. They view themselves as exempt because of good health, even when one of them, Max, another gay man, suddenly falls ill and is put on a respirator. They are the ones who declare that "the way he had lived until now" is finished. The incessant chatter of the story expresses the overwhelming flood of news about AIDS and friends with AIDS that is the lived reality for gay men and their friends today, as well as the inability of many of these friends to come to terms with it. As Michael Bronski observes [in "Death and the Erotic Imagination," *Radical America* (1987)]: "It is impossible to be a gay male today and not think of AIDS all the time."

And it is impossible to read a piece of fiction about gay men in the present and not assume AIDS is going to make its presence felt one way or another. Writings by and about gay men must henceforth assume that the reader bears in mind precisely that culturally determined equation of homosexuality = AIDS. That is why the name does not need to be invoked specifically and yet the reader can be expected to be able to decode the signs that signify AIDS within the text. That is also why readers can understand the significance of *refusing* to use that name. Only where the name is expected can its absence be made significant. What will become evident in the following is the nature of that significance.

Sontag's story demonstrates one way in which, as Paula Treichler describes it, AIDS has become an epidemic of signification. The unnamed thing that remains always the Other for these friends retains a power of signification that their chatter cannot mute, much less break. Here the equation merely restates its meaning (homosexuality = AIDS = death), and not naming AIDS becomes merely another capitulation to the signification a homophobic culture has already ascribed to AIDS.

The focus is quite different in Andrew Holleran's "Friends at Evening," in which several men gather to talk about a friend with AIDS, a friend who has already died. Four friends meet to go to his funeral, and the story centers on the effect of AIDS upon the gay community in general as represented in this group: Mister Lark, Ned, Curtis, and the first-person narrator (who mostly reports what the others say and do). The effect of AIDS upon the gay community, in Holleran's view, has been the end of a gay identity that drew men together in sexual community. Louis died because, as Ned puts it, "he came into his penis" and "realized the value of what he had." That is, he pursued his identity sexually. Ned now feels guilty about his own promiscuity; he has retreated to Ohio to nurse his invalid father and believes gays should have known better. Mister Lark berates such remorse as the misplaced angst of middle age: "The virus is merely a tragic accident that has nothing to do with either Africa, or our sex lives. . . . It does not invalidate the thing which still persists in the midst of all this horror—I mean . . . the incalculable, the divine, the overwhelming, godlike beauty of the . . . male body."

Mister Lark continues to find beauty and inspiration in men, but only because he never has sex with them. For the others, sex has become dangerous and lethal, and this danger has shaken the foundations of gay identity. Ned has given up sex; he can conjure a romantic fantasy only by setting it in a place he believes untouched by AIDS: "Budapest, in a light snow." A stranger calls Mister Lark on a pay phone and wants him to watch while the stranger exhibits himself and masturbates in his apartment window above. Sex separated by a street and a sheet of glass, love in a city imagined from films and novels—this is what Holleran suggests gay erotic possibility and, thus, identity threatens to become.

AIDS has sundered the gay community in Holleran's story. Louis has died, Ned lives in Ohio, Curtis is being evicted from his apartment. The old gay life that has a history in these men's friendships and loves, that even has a literary tradition in the story's title, taken from Walt Whitman, appears at an end. It appears to be in the evening of its existence, and what it will become remains unclear. At the time of writing this story, Holleran was very pessimistic about the future of gay community and identity. As a gay man writing for gay men, he faced the dilemma: "How could one write truthfully of the horror when part of one's audience was experiencing that horror?" [*Ground Zero,* 1988] In particular, he did not see how literature could help define the future: "Literature could not heal or explain this catastrophe. . . . Someday writing about this plague may be read with pleasure, by people for whom it is a distant catastrophe, but I suspect the best writing will be nothing more, nor less, than a lament: 'We are as wanton flies [sic] to the gods; they kill us for their sport.' "

Despite the melancholy tone of this story and the pessimistic attitude of these statements, there is something nonetheless in Holleran's writing that affirms a gay spirit, a refusal to concede desire altogether in the face of disease. At the story's conclusion, the friends climb into a cab to go to Louis's funeral, a moment in which it seems "as if one renews one's life each time a meter switches on," and Mister Lark strikes up a conversation with the Argentinean cab driver. The possibility inherent in simply *being* gay opens itself even in the darkness.

In three other short stories, the unspoken disease is the silence that continually speaks. In so doing, its language alters forever the lives of those who hear it. Sam D'Allesandro's "Nothing Ever Just Disappears" provides an interior monologue by "S" about his lover "J" in which he describes how they met and became involved and what has happened to him since J's death. Through a spare language full of unstated meanings, D'Allesandro shows how love develops incongruously, in spurts. His simple, short sentences take the reader swiftly through the prose sections: "Here's what I found out that afternoon: He was a

painter. He was a waiter. He was thirty. It was enough to know." The conversations he relates, on the other hand, contain inscrutable exchanges that ask to be explained: " 'Your way is not bad. I do the same thing. We're not the same.' 'No, we're not.' 'Maybe you're right.' "

A break in the story (not the first) after their relationship has been established separates S's and J's lives before and after AIDS. The next sentence comes as a shock then: "When the time came I wasn't waiting for him to die." D'Allesandro provides none of the usual signs that other stories use to indicate that death has been caused by AIDS, though he does supply a possible hint early in the third section of the story, when S tells how J "said a lot of things that I didn't exactly understand, or that seemed to carry connotations other than those most obvious." At J's hospital bedside the narrator mentions "tubes that sucked at his arms like hungry little snakes, trying to put life back in" and doctors discussing J "like some kind of textbook experiment." But the fact of one gay man writing about the death of his lover at this time in history forces us, whether we want to or not, to fill that break in the text with the name AIDS, especially when the author does *not* fill that break with another cause of death.

D'Allesandro's silence about the cause of the death, even about the course of the disease, makes us focus on the effect J's death has upon his lover. His repetition of certain sentences and phrases makes us ask what they mean, leading us to interpret them according to our experience of love, of gay love, of gay love in the age of AIDS. When D'Allesandro states, before we know that J dies, "there is such a thing as the tyranny of fate," the sentence's meaning is vague; but when he repeats it after his lover's death, we can read this as a response to the argument that AIDS is a just punishment for an unnatural life. In the final paragraphs, S's incantation of "Everything's OK" and "I'm OK" become a mantra, a chant to free himself of the past while continually invoking it. He knows he can never leave that past because it is always the present, in some form, because "nothing ever just disappears," not J, not their love, and not AIDS, whether spoken or not.

An unspoken name also shapes the lives of gay men in Edmund White's "Palace Days." Mark and Ned, lovers who no longer have sex with each other, have left New York for Paris. Their relationship began in 1981, a time "when the official line had been 'Limit the number of your partners. Know their names.' " In Europe, where the effects of and consciousness about AIDS developed somewhat later than in the United States, they attempt to continue the hedonism they had enjoyed on the other side of the Atlantic. They believe themselves protected by their relationship and their life made secure by the money flowing from their gay tour business. Using their pet name for one another, they ask: " 'Aren't we cosy here, Peters?' That was their word for happy: 'cosy.' " As the ravages of the epidemic became more clear, it also meant "free of disease."

As time passes and the disease draws nearer, Mark begins to fear their dependence upon outsiders for sex. He wonders whether "they might already be harboring this lazy seed, this century plant of death." Nonetheless, Mark becomes involved with a health-conscious German, Hajo,

Edmund White.

and they are "passionate but cautious," not exchanging "those fluids that had once been the gush of life but that now seemed the liquid drained off a fatal infection." When Mark confesses that he had been promiscuous, Hajo demands more and more precautions be used in what little sex they do have. Their relationship ends as their friends begin to die in the United States and as Mark's supply of money dwindles. Mark eventually tests positive. White does not specify what the test is, but the entire context and discourse of the story make this abundantly clear. He returns to Ned, who has enjoyed his own affairs, and "they both expected to die." Reunited with his lover with whom he shares everything except sex, Mark realizes "Ned was the only home he had." The unspoken disease shapes desire and destroys life, but in White's story it also creates a community of love and of strength.

That silence about AIDS does literally speak in another story by Edmund White, "An Oracle." Ray's lover, George, has died of AIDS before the story begins. The reader can interpret "George's disease" as AIDS through such signs as "the virus," the "blood test," and a dentist's refusal to treat George. The impact of AIDS upon the sexual relationships of gay men today makes itself evident in the relationship Ray forms with a young Greek man, Marco. No longer is it possible to take part in the Greek tradition or to lose oneself in the Greek history of homosexuality. Now, it is the younger man wearing a condom who sodomizes the older partner. Ray further breaks the tradition by falling in love with Marco. When he offers to

quit his life in New York and move to Greece, a more circumspect Marco replies, "I won't see you again. You must look out for yourself." And yet something in that Greek past of men loving men still lives today. George, to whom Ray has clung even since his death, seems to have used Marco as an oracle through which to set Ray free.

Robert Ferro's *Second Son* and Christopher Davis's *Valley of the Shadow* provide further evidence of how not naming the disease enables the authors to push AIDS, as culturally defined and defining, to the edge of the work and place the relationships of gay men affected by the epidemic at the center. Ferro's novel focuses on the relationships of its central character, Mark Valerian, the second son, to his family and to Bill Mackey, the lover he finds in the course of the novel. Like his mother who recently died, Mark seeks to hold the family together by hanging on to the family's summer home. His father and older brother do not understand why he will not agree to sell the house when the family business desperately needs money.

At the beginning of the relationship, both lovers have Kaposi's sarcoma but are relatively healthy. When Bill becomes ill with pneumonia, the feeling grows that something must be done—about their health (even though Bill recovers and Mark's health remains stable) and about the house. Letters from Mark's friend Matthew, an author, describe a possible way out of this dilemma. The "Lambda Project," a group of gay men searching for a haven, has discovered beings from the planet Sirius (which the Sirians call "Splendora"), who are willing to help them emigrate; AIDS seems not to present a problem there; it may be that the Sirians have a cure or that the escape itself represents a cure. The reality of this is never entirely assured, however, especially since it may just be a product of Matthew's fantasy. Bill is willing to believe the emigration can happen, and Mark slowly accepts it as a possibility. Before they must decide whether to go, there is time to take one more measure. Mark enters a drug protocol, which he had previously refused to do. Should it fail or should their illnesses get worse, then they can seize this last chance.

Ferro slowly makes it clear that Mark is sick: he is "ill, dying perhaps" and then "apparently dying" of "the medical thing" later referred to as "It." His illness is linked to his "inverted sexuality" and to the distance he now feels from desire for men. Handsome men, his erotic ideals and masturbatory fantasies, exist at first only on the other side of panes of glass in his bedroom or in taxicabs. Descriptions of Mark's lesions, theories as to the etiology of "the disease" (germ warfare, infected plasma in gamma globulin shots for hepatitis B, something in the pools at gay bathhouses), as well as descriptions of the social responses to this disease (the search for a vaccine, the attitude of letting the sick die off and seeking to protect the healthy) all make it evident that AIDS is the subject not being named outright. It is not named because the family does not want to hear it, and Mark does not want to invite its presence by invoking it. Perhaps most importantly for the structure of this novel, AIDS is not named because its reality would undermine the elements of fantasy in the possibility of Splendora and in the metaphor of a haven and safe vessel that the house, built in the form of a ship, represents.

Letters, mostly from Matthew to Mark, maintain a fantasy element that deprives AIDS of its power to define reality. They evade its power by using a premodern literary form largely associated with women, and they also maintain a kind of gay identity by employing camp humor. Matthew and Mark close their letters with remarks that might be made by the women whose names they sign ("[Mrs.] Edward R. Murrow," "Mark's teacher [Mrs.]," "[Mrs.] Neil Armstrong").

Fantasy provides the realm where the tyranny of "science" can—if anywhere—perhaps be overthrown. A clairvoyant in Rome tells Mark that radiation will cure him, that his disease is not fatal. The love he shares with Bill reinvigorates and renews him. Emigration to another planet represents a possibility for survival (just as the drug protocol does). All these nonrational elements offer other answers to the lockstep equation that determines so much of our concept of AIDS in reality, as well as the possibility that love—in particular and, here, of necessity, between two men who have AIDS—may break that equation.

Valley of the Shadow by Christopher Davis is another novel that places relationships rather than disease at its center. A memory book written by the narrator, Andy, in the first person as a way to take control of his disease, it is by his own description, "a story of just one gay man who enjoyed being gay, who loved his lover as much as one man can love another, and who will die before he is thirty." As a student at Columbia University, Andy meets Ted, who leads him into an assured, political gay identity and who becomes his lover. Their stormy relationship ends, however, and Andy immerses himself in the wide variety of gay erotic experiences available in New York. Some years after their breakup, Andy meets Ted by chance and notices he is wearing makeup—to hide the lesions on his face. Andy forces Ted, who is alone and without money, to move in with him, and the two build a new relationship as loving friends. Three weeks after Ted's death, Andy is himself diagnosed with pneumonia, and within a short time he dies. He writes about the loving support of his family and friends. The novel concludes with his obituary.

As with Ferro's novel, hints are given from the beginning that the main character is gay and ill. These two pieces of information ("I no longer have the strength," "I would masturbate, and when I had I usually thought about boys") become linked in the story. Moreover, because they are also linked in the extratextual discourse of AIDS, the reader deciphers the following remarks as referring to AIDS: "[Ted] always looked so good, not at the end, of course"; "I am not ashamed of the kind of sex I had." Without the extratextual discourse of AIDS, such remarks could refer to any sort of death from disease or even old age, for the sex is not explicitly linked to death. But the relationship that exists inside that discourse (AIDS = homosexuality) determines as well as enables this reading—and writing—about gay men with AIDS.

In this novel, the narrator *does* at one point name AIDS as his disease. In a defiant, angry statement Andy declares: "I *have* AIDS, I *am* dying, and the result *will* be death." But that single sentence is the only identification of AIDS as his disease. The term is also mentioned three other times: in reference to Ted, to a gay man who is alone and embittered because of his illness, and to an acquaintance from the small town in which Andy and his family celebrate holidays. Perhaps these direct mentions of AIDS ought to disqualify this novel from consideration here. They are, however, isolated, and only a single direct mention is made late in the novel with respect to the illness of the narrator. Indeed, once may be more than enough where AIDS is concerned, but throughout the novel Andy typically mentions not AIDS but "this horrible disease" or "this damned disease."

Davis employs the term AIDS sparingly and instead chooses euphemisms and metaphors for two significant reasons. He wants to resist the popular conception, even among gay people, that AIDS is a gay disease, that it somehow punishes gays justly for their unjust desires:

> "Why is it so much a part of *gay* life!" I cried, and Teddy held my hand and told me that it was important to remember that this damned disease is just a virus. It is not our *fault* that it infects us; it is just an organism that happens to flourish in the free-sex culture we developed. That does not mean that our culture was wrong; it only means that some insidious little organism has, in some kind of perverse Darwinist survival-of-the-fittest way, found us a physical medium in which to thrive.

Deconstructing that mythology strips the power from discourses of stereotyping and scapegoating. Secondly, Davis refuses to characterize AIDS as a disease with a name and a process proceeding inevitably to death because he refuses to portray these gay men with AIDS as victims. Again, he is responding to the image, evoked under the popular discourse, of people with AIDS as powerless over the destiny of their lives. Andy's telling of his story is an act of empowerment. He refuses to speak of AIDS and instead describes the joys of being gay and loving men and the sorrow of dying.

The form of Davis's novel is perfectly suited to these intents. The first-person narrator of this fictional autobiography draws the reader into the text, creating a familiarity with this fearful Other, be it AIDS or homosexuality. It evokes identification with the narrator and makes his life, his love, and his death sympathetic and understandable. The politics of *Valley of the Shadow* refute popular (mis)conceptions of gay men with AIDS in that Andy feels no remorse for his sexual life. On the contrary, he maintains a vigorous erotic life until he becomes too sick to do so. In the novel, gay men create their own families, and, while some families of blood break all ties with their gay sons because of AIDS, Andy's family stands by him.

While Ferro uses fantasy or nonrational elements to counteract the oppressive reality of the disease, Davis explores the intricacies of memory in order to evade the determining grip of AIDS. Memories reshaped by what has been learned and what has occurred since then form the basis of the novel. The process of memory, obstructed by the dementia that sometimes accompanies AIDS, provides a style that acts as a metaphor for the disease itself. The obituary that ends this memory book is like a wall the reader strikes, leaving him/her with the imprint of the memory of this text and the need to react to it.

Refusing to name enables all these authors to particularize and to universalize the effects of AIDS upon those characters and their communities. Because of the discourse on AIDS outside the text, both possibilities occur: it is necessary to demystify AIDS by individualizing it, and it is necessary to demonstrate the commonality of experiences and the possibility of community in the face of a disease that often isolates the diseased. These works use the space created by not naming to make readers familiar with the feelings and experiences of people with AIDS, which are both individual to these particular characters and also representative of the ways gay men and their lovers, friends, and family are responding to AIDS. An exception to this intertwining of individualization and universalization is Susan Sontag's "The Way We Live Now." The second-hand reports of what the gay man's friends say about him focus the story upon the diversity of responses among the *healthy,* linking them within a common experience and separating them from the sick individual. Of course, that is exactly Sontag's point: the way we (or at least a good number of us) live now is shaped by our responses to those with AIDS, responses that draw ever more sharply the division between health and illness.

In demonstrating the universality of AIDS as it affects gay men, these stories combat efforts to marginalize gays further because of their sexuality or their erotic practices. They draw new lines around a gay identity that is threatened by a society that would like to use AIDS as an excuse to erase the existence of gays. Because of this process of particularization and universalization, individual gay characters or the interplay between several gay characters speaks for common gay experience at this point in time. The contradictory opinions of Ned and Mister Lark as to the "reasons" for AIDS among gays are an example in point. This division of opinion occurs even in such disparate forms as the interior monologue of "Nothing Ever Just Disappears," the third-person narrative of *Second Son,* and the first-person "autobiography" of *Valley of the Shadow.* In the two novels, the individuality of each man's disease and of his reactions to being ill are depicted along with the commonality of the diseases and their symptomatology.

Falling in and being in love are described as experiences shared by all, experienced in the same way whether gay or straight. In "Nothing Ever Just Disappears" S describes his relationship with J: "Let's just say things were fine. Some usual things happened, some unusual. That's normal." Andy in *Valley of the Shadow* addresses the reader: "In Love. I know that sounds foolish and trite and sentimental and banal and like a horrible cliché, but when you are experiencing this, and every person—man or woman, gay or straight—has, I hope, experienced it at least once, it does not seem banal or trite or any of the other disparaging things: It is wonderful." What makes these loves unique, however, is precisely the facts that the men in love *are* gay and that, through sexual contact with other men, they have become infected. Through the love

relationships in these three works, the individuals (gay men with AIDS and a gay man whose lover dies of AIDS) are set within a common framework of experience with only individual permutations. In depicting the relationships in this way, the stories create for them a universality available to the reader.

Not naming AIDS represents a process of empowerment for these gay authors. By refusing to succumb to AIDS they are able to define death *and* life.

—James W. Jones

The "gay space" that critic Jacob Stockinger mentioned over a decade ago in "Homotextuality: A Proposal" [in *The Gay Academic,* edited by Louie Crew, 1978] requires a new definition because of AIDS. The division between interior and exterior has long been central to gay texts, but now its meanings vary. Interiors confine the disease and the diseased in White's "Palace Days," forcing gay men to come to terms with it; even the walled city of West Berlin becomes such an interior, "an emblem of their endangered, quarantined happiness." With D'Allesandro, the interiority of the monologue form itself contains both the sense of refuge S had found in his relationship with J ("In his apartment I always became very relaxed. I didn't do a lot of thinking there. When I entered I stopped making plans") and the emptiness he feels.

Interior space in *Second Son* supplies safe haven from the threats of AIDS. But the defenses are breached. Rome falls under the radioactive cloud from Chernobyl. The cabin's lack of heat intensifies Bill's pneumonia. The family home, built in the form of a ship, seems ready to depart at the order of its owner, but its safety is threatened by the mortgage his family has taken upon it. That space is complemented by the expanse of the heavens, which represent a possible salvation, even a return to a home never seen but long felt: "For it seemed that what they would do together—what would be done to them in the hospital—was a kind of trip, a voyage home. As with Matthew, the ship had become their metaphor, something to look for by day over the horizon, by night among the stars." Even space, too, is compromised: earlier, Matthew had written about the explosion of the Challenger and the uncertainty of future space travel.

Without benefit of social approval and example, gay men must create their own homes and their own communities to overcome their exile from the community of the majority, an exile whose borders have been drawn tighter with the advent of AIDS. [In *Borrowed Time: An AIDS Memoir* (1988)] Paul Monette describes the situation as he and his lover experienced it: "It begins in a country beyond tears. Once you have your arms around your friend with his terrible news, your eyes are too shut to cry." Robert Ferro writes of Mark as an exile continually seeking admittance to his own family: "It was not that it didn't exist, this idea of family, but that it did not seem to exist always, and never as Mark saw it; or if it did, which he saw it did, it was really only among each of them and for their very own. Meaning that he was not a member, in each case, of *their very own.*" In this regard, *Second Son* does not permit the resolution found in the TV drama *An Early Frost* (1985). Whereas the family in the latter rethinks its attitudes toward the gay son because of his AIDS, here the gay son rethinks his attitude toward his family because of his illness. Gay men and heterosexual women bridge the exile of many of these men with AIDS, but the links are tenuous. The friends die; the women are involved with their own families. The gay men are left, like Mark and Bill or Ned and Mark, to make their own "home" with each other.

Christopher Davis's novel presents yet another view. Andy has never had to struggle for acceptance from his family, and although he works in a conservative business, he never mentions having faced discrimination. But precisely that economic status and social integration enable Davis to infuse AIDS with his own meanings. Because the characters here do not have to deal with jobs, rent, disapproving parents, and fearful friends, Davis can focus upon the relationship between AIDS and gays in terms of the influence AIDS has on gay identity and gay community. Although there are family tensions around Mark's sexuality, the gay characters in Ferro's novel similarly do not face difficulties with money or jobs, with the mundane necessities of life beyond that so crucial: health. As Richard Goldstein writes [in "Till Death Do Us Part: Love and Loyalty in the Age of AIDS," *Voice Literary Supplement* (1988)], because they are simultaneously privileged and oppressed, they are "therefore acutely aware of the gap between perception and power" that AIDS has widened. AIDS does not succeed in destroying identity and community; on the contrary, gays themselves redefine identity and expand community.

Not naming AIDS represents a process of empowerment for these gay authors. By refusing to succumb to AIDS they are able to define death *and* life. While the numbing chatter of the friends in "The Way We Live Now" reflects their inability to affect the disease itself or its effects on them, most of the other stories and novels reflect attempts to define death on gay men's terms, that is, not as the end of gay identity or gay community but as leading both in new directions. The definitions vary among the stories. The pessimism of Holleran's "Friends at Evening" is tempered by the optimism of Mister Lark's desire to meet new men. Gay eroticism takes new forms, but it never disappears, not even in White's melancholy "Running on Empty." As George Stambolian writes [in *Men on Men: Best New Gay Fiction,* 1986], "It is death that has had the most troubled history in gay fiction." The response of these writers to that awfully troubled present is to state plainly and boldly "that the gay community exists and will survive."

These fictions about gay men with AIDS find ways for gays to create new spaces, new interiors and exteriors, according to their own definitions; thus, they continue to ex-

plore the homosexual space Stockinger described. Not by ignoring its presence, but by refusing the definitions American culture has loaded into AIDS, these fictions also radically alter the portrayal of gays in American fiction generally. The homosexual male character in American literature had until only very recently been defined according to the medical-psychological discourse that created the very category of "the homosexual" in the late nineteenth and early twentieth centuries. His assigned lot remained unhappiness, suffering, and death (ideally by his own hand). These were the necessary corollaries of the equation homosexuality = illness. With the gay liberation movement of the 1970s, that equation was broken, and a much wider variety of gay realities, experiences, and lives found expression within American literature.

AIDS elicited, however, a forceful restatement of the link that never entirely disappeared in American culture: homosexuality = illness. And since illness = AIDS, it follows as a matter of course that homosexuality = AIDS. While other works within the growing genre of AIDS literature may indeed ultimately reinforce that link, the works discussed here break that chain of signification and continue the project of gay liberation by moving the representation of gays within literature onto radically different avenues by defusing the power of oppressive discourse, by refusing the name. While the gay character in American fiction until the 1970s was defined by a majority, nongay, homophobic society within a literature written primarily for members of that society, these characters can discover methods of empowerment within a minority, gay society. These stories build on the achievements of a gay liberation tradition created over the past two decades, refusing to cede the power gained in moving from a discourse of disease to a discourse of desire, from being the objects of speech to the subjects of speaking.

The gay men depicted in AIDS literature are often indeed physically ill, and their illness has indeed followed the physical love of men. But that illness does not throw these gay characters back into the arms of physicians waiting to cure them of their "real" illness (homosexuality) or to attend them as they experience the just reward of their aberrance (death). Instead, they turn to the welcoming arms of other gay men and of nongay friends to find new kinds of gay community and gay identity. To refuse to name is to resist a power that seeks to strengthen and protect itself by classifying and by excluding. That refusal has become a dynamic theme within the literary response to AIDS. It empowers both sick and healthy to move beyond the language of AIDS and to speak to one another with the words of their shared humanity. (pp. 225-41)

James W. Jones, "Refusing the Name: The Absence of AIDS in Recent American Gay Male Fiction," in Writing AIDS: Gay Literature, Language, and Analysis, *edited by Timothy F. Murphy and Suzanne Poirier, Columbia University Press, 1993, pp. 225-43.*

FURTHER READING

Bibliography

Brooks, Franklin, and Murphy, Timothy F. "Annotated Bibliography of AIDS Literature, 1982-91." In *Writing AIDS: Gay Literature, Language, and Analysis,* edited by Timothy F. Murphy and Suzanne Poirier, pp. 321-39. New York: Columbia University Press, 1993.

Lists fiction, poetry, dramas, autobiographies, biographies, and criticism concerning AIDS and literature.

Criticism

Cady, Joseph, and Hunter, Kathryn Montgomery. "Making Contact: The AIDS Plays." In *The Meaning of AIDS: Implications for Medical Science, Clinical Practice, and Public Health Policy,* edited by Eric T. Juengst and Barbara A. Koenig, pp. 42-9. New York: Praeger, 1989.

Argues that despite differences in form and content both Larry Kramer's *The Normal Heart* and William M. Hoffman's *As Is* depict divisions within society.

Callow, Simon. "In Times of Plague and Pestilence." *The Observer: Review* (26 September 1993): 8-9.

Remarks on the works of dramatists Larry Kramer and Tony Kushner and on how AIDS has affected gay theater in general.

Gross, Gregory D. "Coming Up for Air: Three AIDS Plays." *Journal of American Culture* 15, No. 2 (Summer 1992): 63-7.

Discusses William Hoffman's *As Is,* Larry Kramer's *The Normal Heart,* and Harvey Fierstein's *Safe Sex,* noting that each play "gives us characters who struggle with the suffocation of alienation and loneliness."

Levin, James. "The Enigmatic Eighties." In his *The Gay Novel in America,* pp. 317-63. New York: Garland Publishing, 1991.

Surveys fiction about homosexuality published during the 1980s. Levin observes that despite the centrality of AIDS to gay men, the disease rarely figures in the fiction produced during the period.

The Minnesota Review, Special Issue: The Politics of AIDS, No. 40 (Spring-Summer 1993): 1-159.

Contains fiction, poetry, and critical essays concerning AIDS.

Nelson, Emmanuel S., ed. *AIDS: The Literary Response.* New York: Twayne Publishers, 1992, 233 p.

Collection of critical essays dealing with various aspects of AIDS fiction, poetry, and drama.

Nunokawa, Jeff. " 'All the Sad Young Men': AIDS and the Work of Mourning." *The Yale Journal of Criticism* 4, No. 2 (Spring 1991): 1-12.

Examines past and present depictions of gay males, arguing that homosexuality has long been associated with early death.

Preston, John, ed. *Personal Dispatches: Writers Confront AIDS.* New York: St. Martin's Press, 1989, 184 p.

Collection of essays in which writers discuss AIDS, its effects on society, and how the disease should be presented in literature.

Román, David. " 'It's My Party and I'll Die If I Want To!': Gay Men, AIDS, and the Circulation of Camp in U.S. Theatre." *Theatre Journal* 44, No. 3 (October 1992): 305-27.

Speculates on the discourses gay men construct to define themselves and their relationships in the context of the AIDS epidemic through an examination of camp in Terrence McNally's *The Lisbon Traviata,* John Epperson's *I Could Go on Lip-Synching,* and *AIDS! The Musical!,* written by Wendell Jones and David Stanley.

Treichler, Paula A. "AIDS, Gender, and Biomedical Discourse: Current Contests for Meaning." In *AIDS: The Burdens of History,* edited by Elizabeth Fee and Daniel M. Fox, pp. 190-266. Berkeley: University of California Press, 1988.

Analyzes medical discourse on AIDS, particularly the way in which "words . . . enact and reinforce deeply entrenched, pervasive, and often conservative cultural 'narratives' about gender."

———. "AIDS, Homophobia, and Biomedical Discourse: An Epidemic of Signification." In *AIDS: Cultural Analysis/Cultural Activism,* edited by Douglas Crimp, pp. 31-70. Cambridge, Mass.: MIT Press, 1988.

Discusses the social dimensions of popular and biomedical discourses on AIDS.

The Philip Larkin Controversy

The following entry presents critical commentary on *The Selected Letters of Philip Larkin, 1940-1985* and *Philip Larkin: A Writer's Life,* a biography of Larkin by Andrew Motion. For further discussion of Larkin's literary career, see *CLC,* Volumes 3, 5, 8, 9, 13, 18, 33, 39, and 64.

INTRODUCTION

Larkin was one of England's most popular and acclaimed poets. Although he declined the position of poet laureate offered by former Prime Minister Margaret Thatcher, he was widely considered England's unofficial laureate and praised for his remarkable ability to give voice to the sentiments of many English people. "The voice was unmistakable," observed Clive James. "It made misery beautiful." With the publication of *The Selected Letters of Philip Larkin, 1940-1985* in 1992, however, many of Larkin's former devotees were shocked to discover what appeared to be a malevolent side to the poet—Larkin's private correspondence contains numerous racist and misogynist statements, as well as insulting comments about his friends and literary rivals. The 1993 publication of Andrew Motion's biography of Larkin, *Philip Larkin: A Writer's Life,* also contributed to the poet's unsavory public image with its discussion of such topics as Larkin's proclivity for pornography and his dubious treatment of women. The British media responded with a barrage of commentary in which critics and the public scrutinized Larkin's life and challenged his elevated status as one of England's most accomplished poets. Martin Amis lamented: "The word 'Larkinesque' used to evoke the wistful, the provincial, the crepuscular, the sad, the unloved; now it evokes the scabrous and the supremacist. The word 'Larkinism' used to stand for a certain sort of staid, decent, wary Englishness; now it refers to the articulate far right."

Many critics have answered the outraged reaction to the publication of *Selected Letters* and *A Writer's Life* by questioning the validity and appropriateness of moralistic commentary on Larkin's life and complaining that Larkin's deserved reputation as a great poet has been unjustly damaged. Amis commented: "The reaction against Larkin has been unprecedentedly violent, as well as unprecedentedly hypocritical, tendentious, and smug. Its energy does not—could not—derive from literature: it derives from ideology, or from the vaguer promptings of a new ethos." Although most commentators concede that Larkin was guilty of such human failings as hypocrisy and xenophobia, some have defended Larkin, arguing that his personal faults are irrelevant in relation to his art and that his poems should remain the sole focus of critical attention. Geoffrey Wheatcroft asserted: "If Philip Larkin survives, it will be because of what he wrote rather than anything the rest of us have written about him."

PRINCIPAL WORKS DISCUSSED BELOW

Thwaite, Anthony, ed.
  The Selected Letters of Philip Larkin, 1940 to 1985
    (letters) 1992
Motion, Andrew
  Philip Larkin: A Writer's Life (biography) 1993

CRITICISM

Ian Hamilton (review date 22 October 1992)

[*Hamilton is an English poet, critic, and the founder and editor of the poetry journal* New Review. *In the following review of* The Selected Letters of Philip Larkin, *he focuses on Larkin's treatment of his literary rivals and the poet's pessimistic outlook.*]

There is a story that when William F. Buckley Jr sent a copy of his essays to Norman Mailer, he pencilled a welcoming 'Hi, Norman!' in the Index, next to Mailer's name. A similar tactic might happily have been ventured by the publishers of Philip Larkin's *Letters:* the book's back pages are going to be well-thumbed. 'Hi, Craig' . . . you 'mad sod'; 'Hi, John' . . . you 'arse-faced trendy'; 'Hi, David' . . . you 'deaf cunt', and so on. Less succinct salutations will be discovered by the likes of Donald Davie ('droning out his tosh'), Ted Hughes ('boring old monolith, no good at all—not a single solitary bit of good') and Anthony Powell, aka 'the horse-face dwarf'. There is even a 'Hi, Ian': he calls me 'the Kerensky of poetry'. Not too bad, I thought at first. Alas, though, the book's editor advises me that Larkin almost certainly meant to say Dzerzhinsky, or somebody—some murderer—like that. He had probably misread a communication from Robert (*The Great Terror*) Conquest.

Anyway, it is already pretty clear that one of the chief excitements of this publication will be in finding out who has been dumped on, and how badly. Few well-known names escape the Larkin lash and although Anthony Thwaite seems in this area to have been abundantly forthcoming, we can surmise that he must have done *some* toning down. After all, this is merely a *Selected Letters* and there are over three hundred [. . .]'s sprinkled throughout.

Apart from Thwaite himself, the few who are spared include figures like Vernon Watkins, Gavin Ewart, Barbara Pym: allies who are genuinely liked and admired but who are nonetheless junior to Larkin in talent and repute. The really big hates tend to be reserved for sizable poetic rivals. Ted Hughes is a recurrent, near-obsessive target, with S. Heaney advancing on the rails. Even John Betjeman is given a few slap-downs here and there. All in all, I think it is true to say that Larkin has not a kind word for any contemporary writer who might be thought of as a threat to his preeminence. Kingsley Amis seems to be the exception but actually isn't, quite: in this complicated case, the kind words are often double-edged. And as Larkin got older, he became increasingly disposed to downgrade the literary heroes of his youth. Auden, once worshipped, becomes a 'cosmopolitan lisping no-good'; Yeats turns into 'old gyre-and-grumble'. Only Lawrence, Larkin's earliest 'touchstone against the false', survives more or less intact.

It would be easy enough, then, to argue that—fun and games aside—the really important revelation of these letters is that Larkin, the above-it-all curmudgeon and recluse, the arch-self-deprecator, was in truth nursing a champ-sized fixation on matters of literary rank—a fixation perhaps Maileresque in its immensity and scope. The settings, we might say, are different, drabber, Hull not Brooklyn, and so on, but the ache for supremacy is much the same. Mailer, in his *Advertisements for Myself,* set out to annihilate the opposition, rather as Larkin seems to here. The American made a show of his megalomania; he overplayed it, with a grin. Larkin, being English, being Larkin, chose a public stance that was meant to disguise the ferocity of his ambition.

This sounds plausible, and could be backed up with some fairly unappealing extracts from these once-private letters. Larkin *was* surprisingly alert to questions of literary-world status and to the encroachments of his rivals. No attempt to account for his lifelong unhappiness can now possibly pretend that he was not. But his ambition, as its largely dismal narrative unwinds, seems anything but Maileresque. There is no zest in it, no Tarzan-calls, no muscle-flexing self-delusion, no . . . well, no ambition, really, as somebody like Mailer would define it. The yearned-for bays are withered; they may even turn out to be made of plastic—*withered plastic,* if this boy's luck runs true to form. Larkin knew himself to be the champ—but he knew also that he was a small-time, local sort of champ. He was unlikely to make it in the heavyweight division, nor was he a serious contender for world titles. He was at best perhaps a bantam-weight or—ho ho ho—a cruiser. But then, God bugger me blue, what did *that* make all the other craps and shags—the Wains, Davies, *Hugheses,* for

Christ's sake? At least he, Larkin, didn't show up for readings in a *leather jacket.*

'You've become what I dreamed of becoming,' Larkin wrote to Kingsley Amis at a point quite late on in their careers, seeming to mean by this that Amis was an esteemed, successful novelist and that he himself was a mere poet. But there were other ways in which he envied Amis—or rather there were other ways in which he measured himself against what Amis seemed to represent.

In a very early letter—not to Amis—Larkin finds himself brooding, as he often does, on 'ways of life', and he ends up contrasting two types of literary artist: there is the 'ivory tower cunt . . . who denies all human relationships, either through disgust, shyness, or weakness, or inability to deal with them', and there is 'the solid man with plenty of roots in everyday living by which his spiritual and mental existence is nourished'. Although Larkin would surely have guffawed later on had Amis proposed himself as an example of the second type, he knew that he, Larkin, had grown into a pretty fair example of the first. What was it that had made him stay put, miss out, cave in, while his comrade voyaged out to grasp the goodies?

'After comparing lives with you for years / I see how I've been losing,' Larkin wrote, in a poem which was not published in his lifetime but which he tinkered with for two decades. The addressee may not have been Amis but one's guess is that it was. Even after the pair of them have become grand figures, Larkin still has the Amis model on his mind. When the *Oxford Book of 20th-Century Verse* clocks up sales of 85,000, this is 'chickenfeed compared with *Lucky Jim*'. On the other hand, Larkin is delighted to find that his entries in the *Oxford Dictionary of Quotations* outnumber Amis's by five to one.

Twenty years' worth of the Amis-Larkin correspondence has gone missing, so it is not easy to track their rivalry in detail. From what there is, though, we get the sense that Amis's worldly success had some significant bearing on Larkin's precocious sourness, his posture of exclusion and defeat, the sense even that without the Amis irritation Larkin may not so readily have found his subject, his unlucky Jim. At the beginning of their friendship, Larkin took it for granted that he was the more serious, the more loftily-destined of the two. On the face of it, in 1941, the two were neck and neck, a couple of randy bachelor types who didn't give a bugger, partners in pornography, swapping smut, comparing readings on their ever-active masturbation charts, and all the rest of it. Each of them was working on a novel, and although we don't know what Amis thought of his own work at this time (or, come to that, of Larkin's) we are in no doubt of Larkin's intensity of purpose.

'I so badly want to write novels,' he wrote (again, though, not to Amis), novels that would be 'a mix of Lawrence, Thomas Hardy and George Eliot'. In order to achieve this aim, he is already shaping up to distance himself from enfeebling human attachments: 'I find that once I "give in" to another person . . . there is a slackening and dulling of the peculiar artistic fibres.' As early as 1943, he is looking forward to a 'lonely bachelorhood interspersed with buggery and strictly monetary fornication'. At this stage, such resolutions are for art's sake and are anyway half-joking. Amis's readiness to get sexually involved is to be envied in some ways but it also suggests a failure of essential seriousness. On the very few occasions when Larkin does address Amis solemnly, as writer to writer, the tone is close to condescending: 'You know that the putting down of good words about good things is the mainspring of my endeavours.'

By the age of 25, Larkin had published two novels and one book of poems, with another book of poems ready, as he thought, for publication. Amis had managed but one volume of his verse; none of his fiction had appeared. Six years later, Larkin had one further publication to his credit—the privately-printed *XX Poems*—and Amis had come out with *Lucky Jim,* a novel that had its comic roots in the ribald world which he and Larkin had once shared and which (so Larkin may have thought) they had invented. Its spectacular success, coming when it did, must have been hard for Larkin to endure. Or maybe he didn't give a toss. Come in, Andrew Motion.

It is unusual for a writer's letters—all foreground and virtually no background—to come out in advance of a biography (Motion's Life will be coming out next year), and the Amis connection is just one of several areas on which conjecture is rather teasingly encouraged. More familiar, perhaps, than the idea of Larkin-the-careerist is the idea of Larkin-the depressive but here also we have to many gaps in the life-story, too many possible crisis-points, too many relationships that are insufficiently explained. Even so, as a chronicle of ever-deepening wretchedness, this book has weight enough. From 1945, when he takes his first job as a librarian in Leicester (having already written his two novels) until his death forty years later, the pattern of complaint remains more or less the same: the job is boring, the writing is going badly or not going at all, the relationship he is in—if there is one—is dreary, futureless and guilt-inducing, the world—and England in particular—is going to pot, thanks usually to lefties, foreigners and niggers.

Pornography, cricket, jazz, gin, Mrs Thatcher and the occasional spring day provide relief but even these cases are eventually discovered to be tainted. Pornography is all very well but where—in real life—do you get to see 'schoolgirls suck each other off while you whip them'? Test matches have to be avoided because there are 'too many fucking niggers about', too many 'Caribbean germs'. Even good jazz gets boring in late middle age and the trouble with spring is that you're *supposed* to like it. Gin, he's advised, is killing him. Only Mrs Thatcher (along with D. H. Lawrence) fails in the end to disappoint, but Larkin lashes himself for having disappointed *her:* he refuses the offered Laureateship because, he says, he has become 'a turned-off tap'.

Larkin stopped writing altogether in 1977, the year his mother died, and in his last years the routine misery takes on a sharper, more urgently self-loathing edge, as if the one thing that had made the rest just about possible to bear had, by withdrawing, left him exposed—to the world, and to himself—as an impostor, a grotesque: 'In the old days,

depression wasn't too bad because I could write about it. Now writing has left me, and only depression remains': 'So now we face 1982, 16 stone six, gargantuanly paunched, helplessly addicted to alcohol, tired of livin' and scared of dyin', world-famous unable-to-write poet.'

Now and then, Larkin's misery sounds clinical, there from the start, as when he writes that 'depression hangs over me as if I were Iceland' or (in 1949) that he feels as if he has been 'doctored in some way, and my central core dripped on with acid'. At other times, of course, it comes across as Larkinesque, the act he opted for because it was so easy to perform, so 'true to life'. What might have made a difference? In 1944, he wrote:

> You see, my trouble is that I simply can't understand anybody doing anything but write, paint, compose music—I can understand their doing things as a means to these ends, but I can't see what a man is up to who is satisfied to follow a profession in the normal way. If I hadn't the continual knowledge that 'when all this bloody work is through for today I can start work again' or 'this half-hour is simply ghastly, but one day it will have been digested sufficiently to be written about'—if I didn't think that, I don't what I should do. And all the people who don't think it, what do they do? What are they striving for?

The great novel never happened and perhaps Larkin recognised—and hated to recognise—how little of the true novelist's generosity, or curiosity, of spirit he could actually muster or sustain. But he was proud of what he did write, even though it was in the nature of his gift that its appearances would be intermittent, and it is unlikely that he was all that tormented by his failure to write fiction. He may have wanted to *be* Kingsley Amis (now and then) but it seems doubtful that he would have wanted to swap oeuvres.

The love of a good woman? Larkin's misogyny was well entrenched by his early twenties—all women are stupid, he would say, they make scenes, they cling, they are forever parading their 'emotional haberdashery', they want babies—but who knows how things might have turned out if he had been luckier in his liaisons? Or, he would no doubt have retorted, more courageous, better-looking, or more ready to fork out for endless boring dinners (with no money back when it's all over)? In the early Fifties, there was one affair (described by the editor as 'passionate') which seems to have made more than the usual impact. Patsy Strang, a married woman, actually has Larkin addressing her as 'sugarbush' and 'honeybear'. The episode is short-lived but the recollection of it somehow hangs over all subsequent involvements. When it ended Larkin wrote to her:

> You are the sort of person one can't help feeling (in a carping sort of way) *ought* to come one's way *once* in one's life—without really expecting she will—and since you did, I feel I mustn't raise a howl when circumstances withdraw you, however much I miss you—it would be ungrateful to fortune, if you see what I mean . . . do you? At least, that's what I try to feel! But oh dear, oh dear! You were so wonderful!

There is no other moment quite like this in the book. To turn the screw, Patsy Strang died—of alcoholic poisoning—in 1977, two months before old Mrs Larkin died. This was, of course, the year of Larkin's 'retirement' from writing poetry, and the year, too, in which he finally completed the poem 'Aubade': 'the good not done, the love not given, time / torn off unused'.

Postscript, Patsy Strang, we learn, was the only person who got to read Larkin's notorious journals, the ones that were destroyed, on his instructions, at his death. In Larkin's letters of 1975, though, he speaks of 'my old diaries (which I am now destroying)' and again 'I am all right but not writing anything, except slowly boiling down my diaries: the idea is that I shall then burn them. I'm on 1940 at the moment.' Does this mean that the journals shredded after his death were actually digests of the originals perused by Strang? (pp. 3-4)

Ian Hamilton, "Bugger Me Blue," in London Review of Books, *Vol. 14, No. 20, October 22, 1992, pp. 3-4.*

Mick Imlah (review date 23 October 1992)

[*In the following review, Imlah evaluates the scope and format of* The Selected Letters of Philip Larkin *and discusses the private personality Larkin revealed in his correspondence.*]

Philip Larkin's executors and publishers have made an odd decision in [publishing Larkin's *Selected Letters* before his biography]. Anthony Thwaite promises in his introduction to the former that Andrew Motion's biography—due out next year [1993]—"will fill in some of the apparent gaps". Which is one way of putting it. Meanwhile, we read the *Letters* as inefficient biography, and they do serve up some mysterious fragmentary evidence: the sudden switch of addressee from "Colin and Patsy Strang" to Patsy alone ("Dearest Honeybear . . ."); and the unexplained break in Larkin's regular correspondence with his oldest friend, J. B. Sutton, which then goes unmended for thirty years. Through what the poet himself called the "Larkin Drama"—his illness and death—the letters are naturally muted; and so are the footnotes. Thwaite, presumably anxious not to steal the biographer's thunder, has left such gaps honourably vacant.

His introduction acknowledges gaps of another kind. This "selection" amounts to more than 700 letters, which—given the nature of the life, its single mood and almost constant non-event—feels far too many. But then, Larkin wrote a lot of letters, and the editor has tried to balance the requirements of the lay reader with those of (say) Larkin's *next* biographer. (One is reminded of the conflict of interests in Thwaite's edition of the *Collected Poems*—reviewed in the *TLS,* October 14, 1988—which sacrificed the integrity of the finished volumes for a scholarly inclusiveness.)

And yet three significant groups of letters are noted as missing: those to Bruce Montgomery, Larkin's closest correspondent for many years (lodged in the Bodleian by Montgomery's widow); those withheld by George Hart-ley, the unyielding publisher of *The Less Deceived,* with whom Larkin's disaffection ("I don't say Hartley is a phoney, exactly—well, I do") is never as thorough as you'd expect; and those to his mother. We're told that Larkin wrote "regularly" to her through the last three decades of her life (he refers himself to "daily" letters), but Thwaite chooses to exclude this correspondence on the grounds that it "would have swelled the book to unmanageable proportions". Most of it must be very dull, but something could surely have been salvaged to represent the subject's family life.

Half-a-dozen favoured correspondents are represented by fifty letters or more. The first of these is the invisible Sutton, whom Larkin used through his university years and beyond as a sounding-board for ideas about himself ("It's hard to say whether I improve or not with keeping and living"). The most inventive letters are those to Kingsley Amis, conducted in a private mutation of Greyfrairs style, with its own conventions like their method of signing off—a phrase from any sphere of life with the last word replaced by "bum" ("Smoking can damage your bum, *Philip*", etc). The high spirits of this exchange endure over four decades, though schoolgirls gradually yield place to strikers and immigrants ("keep up the cracks about niggers and wogs"). The correspondence with another politically like mind, Robert Conquest, is built on bawdy verses and a shared pursuit of pornography; sending Conquest the poem entitled "Annus Mirabilis" was asking for the parody it got. Barbara Pym, by contrast, generates parsonical fan letters of a unique gentleness and generosity: after a typical outburst to Amis about what the Permissive Society hadn't delivered, "LIKE WATCHING SCHOOLGIRLS SUCK EACH OTHER OFF WHILE YOU WHIP THEM", the note of "My Dear Barbara" falls with a sort of comic grace.

With each of these, Larkin enjoyed, for some time, satisfactory postal relations; and the products have the literary interest of things that he wanted to write. But there is another style of letter to women, intermittently represented here, which seems to have been squeezed from him as a guilty substitute for the sort of relationship he preferred to do without. A sour, unfinished poem of August 1953 analyses this phenomenon:

> letters of a kind I now
> Feel most of my spare time is going on:
>
> I mean, letters to women—no,
> Not of the sort
> The papers tell us get read out in court,
> Leading directly to or from the bed.
> Love-letters only in a sense: they owe
> Too much elsewhere to come under that head.
> Too much to kindness, for a start. . . .

But the effect of this kindness is to disgust the kind:

> Another evening wasted! I begin
> Writing the envelope, and a bitter smoke
> Of self-contempt, of boredom too, ascends.
> What use is an endearment and a joke?

At which the poem is abandoned. Thwaite prints two letters to women written in the same month as these lines.

The more trivial and laborious is to Winifred Arnott, the girl behind "Maiden Name" and other poems, to whose virginity Larkin laid unsuccessful siege ("Wish I had some of the money back I spent on her, and *the time*", he moans later). Winifred doggedly kept up the correspondence after she married, and would eventually get replies with less-than-urgent sentiments like "I'm sorry you had such a dreary winter, and hope you aren't having another". The other August letter is to Patsy Strang (with whom Larkin was still having a sort of affair); this mocks Winifred as "Miss Mouse". Reviewing Evelyn Waugh's letters critically at a later date, Larkin finds himself wondering "how my own wd rank for 'charity'—not very highly, I should imagine"; and in cases like Winifred's, his chief "kindness" seems to have been to disguise the boredom or unkindness he really felt.

The "Miss Mouse" / "Winifred dear" effect is a common one in the book, especially in Larkin's Belfast period (1950-5): on one page, we read about "horrible craps like Arthur", on the next it's "My Dear Arthur". The poet was to dramatize such a slide nearly twenty years later in "Vers de Société" where the poet's gut response to a dreary invitation—*"Dear Warlock-Williams, I'm afraid"*—is transformed by lonely fears into hapless acceptance (*"Dear Warlock-Williams: Why, of course"*). The poem and its real-life counterparts—the more furtive or disengaged of Larkin's social letters—show an essential selfishness doing its penance.

One of Anthony Thwaite's dilemmas is that the last major correspondent of Larkin's life seems to have been Anthony Thwaite. Larkin's praise of his future editor's poems and personality is here in full; in one place, he chastises him for leaving himself out of his book on *Contemporary Poetry*. One can hardly blame Thwaite for printing this; it is, after all, a letter from Larkin about poetry. But a message to Thwaite from Larkin's secretary, even if it is about the poet's final illness, ought not to be here.

The most questionable aspect of Thwaite's editing at the local level is the way he omits parts of letters without indicating how much material has gone, or of what sort, or why. Some cuts are evidently to avoid libel ("In my experience it's easier to [. . . .] than to get a publisher to accept anything he doesn't like"); others look as if they have been made to protect Larkin himself. The footnoting, kept deliberately "light", is sometimes too reticent: when Larkin, reading Virginia Woolf's *A Writer's Diary,* exclaims, "What a sentence about Isherwood!", it would be easy and helpful to supply that sentence, especially as it appears to be a very rare instance of Larkin approving another writer.

Indeed, in all these pages, there is hardly anything to supplement the astonishingly meagre list of approved reading that Larkin used to offer interviewers. His student passion for D. H. Lawrence burns surprisingly brightly—"the greatest writer of this century, and in many things the greatest writer of all time"—but is renounced at the age of twenty-four, by which time he was already unreceptive to new writing ("My mind has stopped at 1945", as he wrote later, "like some cheap wartime clock"). Among poets of his own generation, only Betjeman, Amis, Gavin

Ewart, and *Patience Strong* merit praise, along with a few poems each by J. C. Hall and Jonathan Price. Everyone else—from Sidney Keyes in the 1940s, through Lowell, Gunn and Hughes in the 50s and 60s, to Heaney in the 70s (" 'the best poet since Seamus Heaney' which is like saying the best Chancellor since Jim Callaghan")—is entertainingly dispatched. Larkin confronts the idea of new writing with wicked structures of horrified multiple abuse:

> Today I bought *The Breaking of Bumbo* by Andrew Sinclair at a Boots' chuck-out—Good God, every "new young" writer I read seems worse than the last. John Braine—there couldn't be anyone worse than him. Oh yes there could: John Osborne. And now Andrew Sinclair: soft-headed hysterical guardee. Like an upper-class John Wain.

The editorship of the *Oxford Book of Twentieth-Century English Verse* involved Larkin in some especially fruitless reading: the likes of W. W. Gibson (*"never wrote a good poem in his life.* . . . People like this make Rupert Brooke seem colossal"); or Laurie Lee ("Xt, he's absolutely no good whatsoever"); and Alun Lewis ("not really so good as some would have you think . . . ") or MacDiarmid ("Is there any bit . . . that's noticeably less morally repugnant and aesthetically null than the rest?"). The chief value of most other writers for Larkin is the understanding that they aren't "any good"—no elaboration needed—as the basis for other jokes: of T. F. Griffin, "Of course I don't mean that he is any real *good,* just that he seemed well up to publishing standard"; or of a conversation with George MacBeth, "He replied to my question 'Do you think William Golding is any good' with 'I prefer to bypass that aspect of his work'. Rather nice, don't you think?" (His self-criticism is only a modification of this rule of thumb; as he told the *Paris Review,* "My 'secret flaw' is just not being very good, like everyone else.")

What is most unusual about this monumental correspondence is how—since Larkin so soon recognized his need for stable employment and domestic solitude—its concerns and attitudes remain so much the same. Just as he laughs with Amis about those life-changing letters he never received—"Something starting 'I am directed to inform you that under the will of the late Mr Getty . . . ' or 'Dear Philip, You'll be interested to know that old Humpley is at last giving up the library at Windsor, and HM . . . ' or 'Dear Mr Larkin, I expect you'll think it jolly cheeky for a schoolgirl to—' "—so his own seldom have any news to break or passion to declare or end to achieve. What they restate, richly and poorly, are: the impossibility of letting another person into his life; his depression at writing so much less than he wished; his innate meanness, which characteristically places the cost of his pleasures before them ("I spent 7 /- yesterday on [two art books]", involves him in long disputes with publishers over halves of one per cent, and makes nastily plain sense of that ambiguous adjective at the end of "The Building"—"With *wasteful,* weak, propitiatory flowers"; and, above all, his consuming fear of ageing and death. The refrain "What have I done to be [gives his age]? / It isn't fair" recurs with variations from twenty-six to sixty. And even the death of his former lover, Patsy Strang, from an overdose of Cointreau and Benedictine elicits only a hard joke ("Fascinating mixture, what? . . . ") before leading him anew to the subject of his *own* mortality. Still, self was his life (of which more later); and in it he made not only—incidentally—hundreds of sharp and sad and funny letters to others, but also (and this was the paradoxical point of it) dozens of the most generally enjoyed English poems of the century.

> Mick Imlah, "Selfishly Yours, Philip," in The Times Literary Supplement, *No. 4673, October 23, 1992, p. 13.*

With fantastic rigour, with the clarity of genius, Larkin accepted that, for himself, happiness was out of the question, and his poetry, which celebrates the possibility of happiness, comes to seem even more poignant and magnificent after reading his biography.

—P. N. Furbank, in The London Review of Books, *22 July, 1993.*

James Wood   (review date 15 November 1992)

[*Below, Wood discusses Thwaite's* Selected Letters, *noting Larkin's deprecating and perceptive commentary on English society and himself.*]

"I like the general prevailing atmosphere of irreverent irritation that prevails, the creative grossness," writes Philip Larkin in 1952, of Henry de Montherlant's *Les Jeunes Filles,* almost the only foreign bloom to be found in this nursery of English provincialism. What will dismay any lover of Larkin's poetry is precisely the monotonous "creative grossness" of these letters. Small-minded and foul-mouthed, they have a rawness, an unprotectedness, a proximity, as if they had not been allowed enough time in the world since Larkin's death for posterity to put a skin on them. Here is what Larkin would call in a famous poem "unfenced existence"—and the reader does not always want to see its bare acres.

What saves them from victimhood, and the reader from voyeurism, is not just their wit, but the quality of Larkin's self-understanding. Actually, these two are almost the same: Larkin's deepest wit is always self-ironic—"I went to the local Austin Reed on Saturday and brought some dreary clothes, real chartered-accountant stuff"; "yes, I'm settling down in Hull all right. Every day I sink a little further". Larkin had hardened into his adulthood by the age of 24, and was sending his friends proleptic self-assessments. "I aim at increased negativeness, a kind of infinite recession in the face of the world," he writes at the age of 22, as if already preparing for the loneliness of life in Hull, the librarianship, the two trips abroad he would make in the next 40 years.

"I shan't be a scholar," he wrote at the age of 20, or even have really much delight in the classics . . . literature is a very tiny thing compared with one's own life (and of course one's own literature). Nor shall I ever have much taste." There is something ghoulish about these predictions, as if Larkin were plotting his disappearance. How accurate! For even as his life shrank—he boasted to Jonathan Raban that he had reduced his life in Hull to a convenient triangle: his house, the library, and the corner shop—it swelled, like a toad of his own making, huge and immovable, filling his emptiness. Literature was truly "a very tiny thing" compared to the enormous renunciations of his life; the tragedy is that Larkin's *own* literature, which started out as big as his life, part of its very continuance, grew tiny too. As most readers know, Larkin was unable to write poetry in his last 10 years. The letters show that it is at this point that something like clinical depression and near-alcoholism began their steady drip.

He was, of course, a master-critic of his own writing—how could a perfectionism so exquisitely self-rejecting not be? So he could see the decline of his talent into simplicity and brutishness. "Thin ranting conventional dogma," he writes of his ranting patriotic poem "Going, Going"; "the death-throes of a talent" is how he describes the over-literal late poem "Aubade," about his fear of death. Looking again at the poems, one sees how short-lived was Larkin's genius. *High Windows* (1974) records its death. It is markedly inferior to Larkin's earlier volume *The Whitsun Weddings* (1964), and has too much thin ranting in it. The old lyricism and sublimity gives way to flatness of statement, only half-excused by its coarse irony: "Next year we shall be living in a country / That brought its soldiers home for lack of money" ("Homage To A Government"); "Their kids are screaming for more / — More houses, more parking allowed, / More caravan sites, more pay." The poem "High Windows" itself is a rant dignified by a last-minute escape into mystery. Even the swoony pastoral "Show Saturday," about an agricultural show, ends with a feebly patriotic "Let it always be there."

The letters of the last twenty years (and a few of them before) are full of this. Racism ("got a nigger for a neighbour"), tedious hearty references to "Coonland", "Wopland", "Yankland", to masturbation and pornography. An example: Larkin on the poet Elizabeth Jennings winning a travel grant: "Elizabeth Jennings getting 400 nicker to go and get stuffed in Wopland?" Certainly, the coarseness, or rather the coarse *obviousness,* of these letters is a shock. Yet like much in Evelyn Waugh's letters, many of these outbursts, though not all, have an ambiguous status, produced for literary effect, or to stretch the permissible (one thinks of Nietzsche's reference to "my old beloved *wicked* thoughts" at the end of *Beyond Good And Evil*). But the difference between Waugh and Larkin is importantly sociological. Larkin belonged to the first generation of writers allowed to speak like this. Before this, writers were prohibited either by society, or by their idea of their standing in society (Waugh, for instance, rebuked Henry Green for using the word "cunt"). Larkin uses this freedom too strenuously just because it is still new. And yet it is still a *private* freedom, confined to letters, and confined to letters addressed to men (Larkin's correspondence with women is much more genteel).

This is not unimportant, because much of Larkin's greatness as a poet lies in his peculiar, sad, sociological acuteness. He brings the novel into the poem. Think of Mr Bleaney in his furnished room and "his preference for sauce to gravy"; or the perfection of "Not quite your class, I'd say, dear, on the whole"; or the last two words of the tiny poem "Home Is So Sad"—"that vase"—which demand a certain accent and drawl. This ability to squeeze new, sometimes "coarse" material into romantic, even Georgian forms, was new in English poetry, and had much to do with the relative freedom of Larkin's social origins. Likewise in these letters, the details and poeticisms that glint have a social weight—such as Larkin's description of his "aldermanic belly" (his father was a City Treasurer), or the "Jaguar-haunted hotel in Bournemouth" he took his aged mother to, or the "Woolworth-baroque" architecture of Oxford. His rigid, petty, provincial aesthetic was a *morality,* and a social morality—the rebelliousness against social superiority, as a letter here makes explicit: "I am getting to the stage when I HATE anybody who does anything UNUSUAL AT ALL, whether it's make a lot of MONEY or dress in silly CLOTHES or read books of foreign WORDS or know a lot about anything . . . THEY ARE SHOWING OFF."

There are jokes on every page of this book, and a marvellous contempt for most of Larkin's contemporaries: "Roy Fuller HE SHOULDN'T BE REVIEWING POETRY EVEN FOR THE BLOODY SCHOOL MAGAZINE)", Ted Hughes ("Ted The Incredible Hulk"), Laurie Lee ("Christ, he's absolutely no good whatsoever"), William Golding ("nice Wm Golding not being shortlisted, isn't it? I've never thought much of him")—and so on. Hull takes a battering too ("The village smells of chips. The town smells of fish"). But the book as a whole is terribly sad, chronicling as it does an English version of a poetic model one had come to see as traditionally 20th-century-American—drinking, depression, loneliness, talent-drought. Some words of Auden come to mind: "Worse things can befall a poet than an early death," said Auden at Louis MacNeice's funeral. "At least MacNeice was spared that experience of being condemned to go on living with the knowledge that the Muse has abandoned them."

> James Wood, *"Filling the Emptiness,"* in Manchester Guardian Weekly, *November 15, 1992, p. 28.*

Lisa Jardine   (essay date 8 December 1992)

[*In the following essay, Jardine argues that Larkin should be considered a marginal figure in British literature because his writing was informed by prejudiced views.*]

The students in my University Department of English are for the most part neither Anglo-Saxon nor male. Furthermore, the Anglo-Saxons and the young men belong to a generation whose face is turned towards the new Europe, and for whom comfortable British insularity holds no romance. The publication of the *Selected Letters Of Philip Larkin 1940-1985,* edited by Anthony Thwaite, has therefore landed my lecturer colleagues and myself with a problem. It is a more vivid and immediate one than the issue being hotly debated in the "quality" press as to whether or not the more than 700 letters have been expurgated—trimmed of remarks even more banally offensive than some of those that have been allowed to stand.

Our problem concerns the place Larkin's poetry occupies at the heart of the traditional canon of English Literature. Its place, that is, within that body of works cherished by defenders of British culture as the repository of the Best of British—those sentiments and ideas which allow our culture to reflect the standards and values which the educated world considers universally valid. Can we continue to present the poetic writings of Larkin as self-evidently "humane" when the student who consults the selected Larkin Letters in the college library confronts a steady stream of casual obscenity, throwaway derogatory remarks about women, and arrogant disdain for those of different skin colour or nationality?

This question cannot be answered simply by advising us to keep our students away from such "supplementary" material, and to concentrate on the poems. "What matters about Larkin," a recent Times leader reassures us, "is the handful of melancholy and funny poems that captured the mood of his times." We encourage our students to "read around" their key literary texts. A significant part of their training consists in juxtaposing careful reading of the text with equally careful exploration of the life and thought of the period which produced it. The work is the product of its times; its author's preoccupations are those of a generation, a class and a nation. Thwaite's edition of Larkin's Letters, coming as it does ahead of fellow literary executor Andrew Motion's biography, offers invaluable material for the curious and conscientious student. What she or he finds there has to be confronted as an intrinsic part of the study of "Larkin". And what the curious and conscientious student will discover is a Philip Larkin who is not the benevolent, modest, librarian with an extraordinary ear for a quintessentially British kind of detail of A-level anthologies, but rather a casual, habitual racist, and an easy misogynist. Not to mention a malicious gossip, who relished savagely caricaturing fellow authors and critics, and abusing acquaintances.

I am not proposing that we ought to have expected Larkin to be a nice man, because he wrote "dozens of the most generally enjoyed English poems of the century" (as the reviewer of the Larkin Letters in the *TLS* observes). It is rather that the Letters alert us to a cultural frame within which Larkin writes, one which indeed takes racism and sexism for granted as crucially a part of the British national heritage. The trouble with our encounter with the Larkin Letters, in fact, is that we are not a bit surprised by them. They are part of the fabric of everyday British life. Written against a background of everyday discrimination, everyday assumptions of white British superiority, Larkin's poems, likewise, leave familiar prejudices intact. They do not engage with them, in spite of their own resolutely everyday texture and quality. The very familiarity of the poetic tone, its easy reference to what we know and love, masks its implications for those who "don't belong". Larkin's poetry carries a baggage of attitudes which the *Selected Letters* now make explicit.

Actually, we don't tend to teach Larkin much now in my Department of English. The Little Englandism he celebrates sits uneasily within our revised curriculum, which seeks to give all of our students, regardless of background, race or creed, a voice within British culture. The vigorous debates I and my colleagues had over how to teach attitudes and values had already led us to reorganise our English Studies around a core of texts which included works by women, by Asian and Afro-Caribbean writers, by non-British writers in English. That much-loved tone of Larkin, with its comfortable cultural assumptions, and its anticipation of a readership alert to the nuances of a particular way of life, edged him from centre to margin. He is now included in third year special options like Poetry In The Fifties, no longer as a set text in the first year course in 20th-century literature.

The furore over Larkin (censored or uncensored) is a row about cherished values. Tom Paulin thinks we are no longer allowed Larkin (or Virginia Woolf), because their writings are structured by key beliefs to which we can no longer subscribe. To acknowledge their beliefs and still to promote the cultural centrality of their works is, in his view, at best dishonest, at worst viciously corrupting. Anthony Thwaite's commitment to the continuing importance and centrality of Larkin's work means that be regards Larkin's more unfortunate observations in the Letters as just that unfortunate, but occasional, unimportant, temporary distractions from the major objective which is the poetic oeuvre. In our secondary school class rooms English may be reduced by the exigencies of the National Curriculum and testing to a shortlist of dull texts, and rigorous instruction in grammar and spelling. In universities we still pride ourselves, with that residual humanism which all committed teachers share, on providing a "preparation for life" which includes an aptitude for considered thought, the ability to frame measured judgments, to evaluate an issue, to make choices, and intellectually to assess an argument. Above all we teach our students to read with care, and to take account of the nuanced opinions that careful reading reveals. In 1992 that means teaching our students to see through the even texture of Larkin's verse, to the parochial beliefs which lie behind them.

The row over the Larkin Letters is in the end about whether we are right to turn our attention to a cultural centre which reflects the diversity and richness of contemporary multi-racial Britain, and to draw our contemporary values from that rich vein. Or whether to dig in with nostalgic memories of a "great" Britain that (perhaps) once was, and to spend the fading years of British imperial glory trying to persuade our children that everything of value lies behind us. In his inaugural lecture as Professor of English at the University of Oxford last week, Terry Eagleton referred to the traditional canon of English literature as increasingly an ancient monument, a cultural Stonehenge. Professors of English "might as well hand over responsibility for its preservation to the National Trust right now". For the sake of the new, forward-looking, plural and multicultural British nation, we must stop teaching the old canon as the repository of authentically "British values" and as a monument to a precious "British way of life".

> *Lisa Jardine, "Saxon Violence," in* The Guardian, *December 8, 1992, p. G2.*

A. L. Rowse   (review date March 1993)

[*Rowse is an English historian and critic whose works have been praised for their lively prose style and exhaustive coverage of social and political life in Elizabethan England. In the following review of* Selected Letters, *he discusses Larkin's habitual negativism and its relation to his work as a poet.*]

A technical difficulty arises in reviewing Larkin's Letters: in all my experience I have never seen or read such foul-mouthed language, the whole virtuoso gamut of bawdry, swear-words often in every line, particularly in the earlier letters and to male cronies like Kingsley Amis. This makes it impossible to do justice to Larkin's idiom, since one cannot quote it.

The pity of it is that underneath the smelly swamp of such verbiage there is the firm ground of Larkin's thinking about poetry, again in the earlier letters where he is forming his creed and poetic persona. He told me that he was very careful of his persona. Fancy anybody bothering in such a society! However, Eliot did, so did Housman, and Hardy wrote his own biography under his (second) wife's name. Perhaps it was worth while in their society's day.

Did this stance on Larkin's part come from the undergraduate pose he and his friends took up? The crass Philistinism: 'Jazz is better than Beethoven', 'Books are a load of crap'. Of course they were clever boys, and some of it was pose. When not, they are flagrantly silly. All dons are put down as mediocre. Larkin's examiners at Oxford were Lord David Cecil, C. S. Lewis, Nichol Smith, Tolkien—each one a man of distinction. They gave Larkin a First, much to his surprise: in spite of his perverseness, they perceived his quality.

The complex goes much further back, to his 'unspent childhood'. On the very first page, on glancing at the gravestones of his family in the churchyard at Lichfield: 'Major think. I reeled away conscious of a desire to vomit into a homburg hat.' When Coventry was so heavily bombed he was given refuge by an uncle and aunt at Warwick. They are cruelly caricatured for their pains. Is childhood all 'boredom'? He gives Coventry a sour acquittance: 'it's not the place's fault'.

Why does everybody, everything, every place, have to be demeaned, disparaged, insulted? Especially his fellow writers, if not every one—Barbara Pym was a notable exception. But his friend, Ted Hughes, is 'no good, no good at all'. William Golding's *Lord of the Flies* 'I didn't find it convincing, a 'literary idea' dressed up as realistically as possible but not realistically enough'. Still, years later it is 'I've never thought very much of him'. Did he ever think very much of anybody? For myself I noticed how supercilious he was in person.

When young he had hero-worshipped Auden and D. H. Lawrence. Eventually everything that Auden wrote after 1940, i.e. in America, is condemned. This is undiscriminating—I agree that much of it is inferior, but not all. And often Larkin's criticism, ruthless as it is, hits the target and one has to agree with it. The cantankerous Grigson, who was so nasty about everybody else, especially his old friend Betjeman, gets his comeuppance: 'how rotten his poems were and his criticism and his manners and his judgement'. What about Larkin's manners, though his judgement was sound, if too severe.

He did not spare his own publishers. He saw that, after Eliot's death, 'Faber's imprint isn't what it was'. His successors' judgement in poetry became very erratic, 'Faber's crap is as usual'. My own experience confirms Larkin in this, when my name was dropped from the list for a number of people who have never been much heard of since.

Places similarly: Hull is constantly disparaged, it is 'the a–hole of the East Riding'. Now Hull is fascinating historically, with one of the grandest parish churches in England, besides much else of interest to anyone of perception. On the threshold is Beverley, with a Minster the North Country equivalent of Westminster Abbey, the Percy tomb in it has the finest of medieval sculpture. To persons of any cultural sensibility, even common sense appreciation of the past, the East Riding is a paradise of pleasures. Nothing of all this anywhere in Larkin, plenty about jazz and seedy squalor.

Larkin was miserable, and made himself more so. His letters are full of whining and moaning. 'Wifeless, childless'—that was by his own choice, which we must respect: then why complain about it? He admits at one point what was wrong—he could not give himself to anyone. We cannot blame him for that: that was the way he was made. Conventional people think him 'diseased'; but that is not right, they do not understand the psychology of genius (for he was one). Writers of genius write out of the tangle of their complexes, it is for critics to estimate the product. Larkin agreed with Hardy's definition of poetry—words from the heart expressed rhythmically in such a way as to move other hearts. Not much of that in Larkin, the overall message is—as Eliot's widow has said—enough to make one drown oneself.

Even so, he was a good poet, technically a perfectionist. He had no use for the uncooked, uneducated outpourings patronised by the media today. Interestingly he compared himself with Housman—though no such scholar (except for Jazz), and Housman did speak straight from the heart to other hearts. A professor of English—of whom Philip would not have approved—calls him 'the best poet of the century'. What about Yeats or Eliot, Bridges, whom Housman, no easy critic, thought best; or Hardy, who would have been Philip's choice? The professor thought these Letters the best of any poet he had ever read. Has he never read Byron's, or Keats's, Shelley's, or the incomparable letters of Swift?

Anthony Thwaite has done a fine job in editing these—thorough and conscientious, the notes are most useful and properly fair. There is a fascinating paradox about Larkin.

Why is he so popular, when he hated the society of our day?—Because he was its laureate. (pp. 162-63)

A. L. Rowse, *"What Was Wrong with Larkin?" in* Contemporary Review, *Vol. 262, No. 1526, March, 1993, pp. 162-63.*

Esther B. Fein (review date 10 March 1993)

[*Below, Fein comments on the disclosure of Larkin's racial and sexual prejudices in his published letters and biography.*]

Two new books about Philip Larkin [*Selected Letters of Philip Larkin* and *Philip Larkin: A Writer's Life*], one of Britain's best-loved and most renowned modern poets, who died in 1985 at the age of 63, reveal that he was an anti-Semite and a racist and that his poetic ambivalence about love masked a vicious streak of misogyny.

Although Larkin cultivated, and indeed seemed somewhat to revel in, an image of himself as a right-wing curmudgeon, a selection of letters and a biography by his friend and literary executor, Andrew Motion, both of which are to be published later this year by Farrar, Straus & Giroux, show a far more sinister aspect to his conservatism.

Larkin's father, Sydney, was openly sympathetic to Hitler, Mr. Motion says, and while the son's views never reached that extreme, he, after an initial embarrassment about his father, "adopted and adapted" his anti-Semitism and racism.

"These findings are important, as unpleasant as they might be, to say the least," Mr. Motion said in a telephone interview from London. "I would be sorry if in the final analysis, these revelations overwhelmed his poems. I have very great devotion to Philip as a poet. But the beautiful flower of art grows on a long stem out of often murky material."

Two letters included in Larkin's *Selected Letters of Philip Larkin, 1940 to 1985,* which were selected and edited by Anthony Thwaite, Larkin's other literary executor, and have already been published in England by Faber & Faber, give some idea of Larkin's overt racism.

In a letter to Robert Conquest, the eminent historian and poet, dated June 19, 1970, Larkin included a ditty he composed titled "How to Win the Next Election": "Prison for the strikers / Bring back the cat / Kick out the niggers / How about that?"

In a letter to Colin Gunner, a childhood friend, dated Oct. 18, 1985, less than two months before he died, Mr. Larkin wrote: "I find the 'state of the nation' quite terrifying. In 10 years' time we shall *all* be cowering under our beds as hordes of blacks steal anything they can lay their hands on."

The revelations about Larkin will surely be surprising as well to readers of poetry in the United States, where he was one of the best-selling modern poets, known for his ruminations on loneliness, death, aging and the encroaching vulgarity of the modern.

Even after his death, his works sold phenomenally well here: a 1989 volume, *Collected Poems,* edited by Mr. Thwaite and published by Farrar, Straus & Giroux, sold over 22,000 copies and is among the best-selling poetry books for the publisher. To put the book's success in perspective, the average poetry volume has about a 3,000-copy first printing and is lucky if it sells out in two years, so the collection's sales can be thought of as the rough equivalent of a novel selling about 200,000 copies.

Mr. Motion said the conclusions in his biography, titled *Philip Larkin: A Writer's Life* were drawn not only from reading the full trove of Larkin's letters, but also from other interviews and research.

"One of the most striking things I discovered is that he felt very unrepentant about his attitudes," said Mr. Motion, a writer who met Larkin at the University of Hull, where Larkin was librarian and he was a professor of English. "He didn't take enormous opportunity to go banging on about it, but nor did he avoid the subjects, unless like me, you drew a line around it and said that our friendship had to exist outside of those discussions."

Mr. Motion observed that Larkin's sentiments "were commoner then than they are now, especially for men of his generation" and that Larkin had not been politically active or vitriolic as, for example, Ezra Pound had been. But that "hardly forgives him," he added.

Jonathan Galassi, the editor in chief of Farrar, Straus & Giroux and himself an accomplished poet, said that he had known of Larkin's general conservatism but that he had been taken aback when he read the Motion biography. "He made no bones about his xenophobia," Mr. Galassi said. "He hated foreigners and he once said, 'I loathe abroad.' He was clearly a man of prejudices. But I was surprised at the degree of it and I think others surely will be."

Esther B. Fein, "A Dark Side to Larkin," in *The New York Times, March 10, 1993, p. 20.*

Alan Bennett   (review date 25 March 1993)

[*Bennett is an English playwright, scriptwriter, actor, and nonfiction writer. In the following review of* Philip Larkin: A Writer's Life *by Andrew Motion, Bennett presents an overview of Larkin's life and career and examines the poet's views on various subjects.*]

'My mother is such a bloody rambling fool,' wrote Philip Larkin in 1965, 'that half the time I doubt her sanity. Two things she said today, for instance, were that she had "thought of getting a job in Woolworth's" and that she wanted to win the football pools so that she could "give cocktail parties".' Eva Larkin was 79 at the time so that to see herself presiding over the Pick'n'Mix counter was a little unrealistic and her chances of winning the football pools were remote as she didn't go in for them. Still, mothers do get ideas about cocktail parties, or mine did anyway, who'd never had a cocktail in her life and couldn't even pronounce the word, always laying the emphasis (maybe out of prudery) on the tail rather than the cock. I always assumed she got these longings from women's magazines or off the television and maybe Mrs Larkin did

too, though 'she never got used to the television'—which in view of her son's distrust of it is hardly surprising.

Mrs Larkin went into a home in 1971, a few months after her son had finished his most notorious poem, 'They fuck you up, your mum and dad'. She never read it (Larkin didn't want to 'confuse her with information about books') but bloody rambling fool or not she shared more of her son's life and thoughts than do most mothers, or at any rate the version he gave her of them in his regular letters, still writing to her daily when she was in her eighties. By turns guilty and grumbling ('a perpetual burning bush of fury in my chest'), Larkin's attitude towards her doesn't seem particularly unusual, though his dutifulness does. Even so, Woolworth's would hardly have been her cup of tea. The other long-standing lady in Larkin's life (and who stood for a good deal), Monica Jones, remarks that to the Larkins the least expenditure of effort was 'something heroic': 'Mrs Larkin's home was one in which if you'd cooked lunch you had to lie down afterwards to recover.' Monica, one feels, was more of a Woolworth's supervisor than a counter assistant. 'I suppose,' wrote Larkin, 'I shall become free [of mother] at 60, three years before the cancer starts. What a bloody, sodding awful life.' His, of course, not hers. Eva died in 1977 aged 91, after which the poems more or less stopped coming. Andrew Motion thinks this is no coincidence.

Larkin pinpointed 63 as his probable departure date because that was when his father went, turned by his mother into 'the sort of closed, reserved man who would die of something internal'. Sydney Larkin was the City Treasurer of Coventry. He was also a veteran of several Nuremberg rallies, a pen-pal of Schacht's, and had a statue of Hitler on the mantelpiece that gave the Nazi salute. Sydney made no secret of his sympathies down at the office: 'I see that Mr Larkin's got one of them swastika things up on his wall now. Whatever next?' Next was a snip in the shape of some cardboard coffins that Sydney had cannily invested in and which came in handy when Coventry got blitzed, the Nazi insignia down from the wall by this time (a quiet word from the Town Clerk). But he didn't change his tune, still less swap the swastika for a snap of Churchill, who had, he thought, 'the face of a criminal in the dock'.

To describe a childhood with this grotesque figure at the centre of it as 'a forgotten boredom' seems ungrateful of Larkin, if not untypical, even though the phrase comes from a poem not an interview, so Larkin is telling the truth rather than the facts. Besides, it would have been difficult to accommodate Sydney in a standard Larkin poem, giving an account of his peculiar personality before rolling it up into a general statement in the way Larkin liked to do. Sylvia Plath had a stab at that kind of thing with her 'Daddy', though she had to pretend he was a Nazi, while Larkin's dad was the real thing. Still, to anyone (I mean me) whose childhood was more sparsely accoutred with characters, Larkin's insistence on its dullness is galling, if only on the 'I should be so lucky' principle.

As a script, the City Treasurer and his family feels already half-written by J. B. Priestley; were it a film Sydney (played by Raymond Huntley) would be a domestic tyrant, making the life of his liberal and sensitive son a misery, thereby driving him to Art. Not a bit of it. For a start the son was never liberal ('true blue' all his life, Monica says) and with a soft spot for Hitler himself. Nor was the father a tyrant; he introduced his son to the works of Hardy and, more surprisingly, Joyce, did not regard jazz as the work of the devil, bought him a subscription to the magazine *Downbeat* (a signpost here) and also helped him invest in a drum-kit. What if anything he bought his daughter Kitty and what Mrs Larkin thought of it all is not recorded. Perhaps she was lying down. The women in the Larkin household always took second place, which, in Motion's view, is half the trouble. Kitty, Larkin's older sister ('the one person in the world I am confident I am superior to'), scarcely figures at all. Hers would, I imagine, be a dissenting voice, more brunt-bearing than her brother where Mrs Larkin was concerned and as undeceived about the poet as were most of the women in his life.

Whatever reservations Larkin had about his parents ('days spent in black, twitching, boiling HATE!!!'), by Oxford and adulthood they had modulated, says Motion, into 'controlled but bitter resentment'. This doesn't stop Larkin sending poems to his father ('I crave / The gift of your courage and indifference') and sharing his thoughts with his mother ('that obsessive snivelling pest') on all manner of things; in a word treating them as people rather than parents. It's nothing if not 'civilised' but still slightly creepy and it might have come as a surprise to Kingsley Amis, in view of their intimate oath-larded letters to one another, that Larkin, disappointed of a visit, should promptly have complained about him ('He is a wretched type') to his *mother*.

'Fearsome and hard-driving', Larkin senior is said never to have missed the chance of slipping an arm round a secretary and though Larkin junior took a little longer about it (twenty-odd years in one case), it is just one of the ways he comes to resemble his father as he grows older, in the process getting to look less like Raymond Huntley and more like Francis L. Sullivan and 'the sort of person that democracy doesn't suit'.

Larkin's choice of profession is unsurprising because from an early age libraries had been irresistible.

> I was an especially irritating kind of borrower, who brought back in the evening the books he had borrowed in the morning and read in the afternoon. This was the old Coventry Central Library, nestling at the foot of the unbombed cathedral, filled with tall antiquated bookcases (blindstamped Coventry Central Libraries after the fashion of the time) with my ex-schoolfellow Ginger Thompson . . . This was my first experience of the addictive excitement a large open-access public library generates.

When he jumped over the counter, as it were, things were rather different though father's footsteps come into this too: if you can't be a gauleiter being a librarian's the next best thing. When called upon to explain his success as a librarian, Larkin said: 'A librarian can be one of a number of things . . . a pure scholar, a technician . . . an administrator or he . . . can be just a nice chap to have around,

which is the role I vaguely thought I filled.' Motion calls this a 'typically self-effacing judgment' but it's also a bit of a self-deluding one. It's a short step from the jackboot to the book-jacket and by all accounts Larkin the librarian could be a pretty daunting figure. Neville Smith remembers him at Hull stood at the entrance to the Brynmor Jones, scanning the faces of the incoming hordes, the face heavy and expressionless, the glasses gleaming and the hands, after the manner of a soccer player awaiting a free-kick on the edge of the penalty area, clasped over what is rumoured to have been a substantial package. 'FUCK OFF, LARKIN, YOU CUNT' might have been the cheery signing-off in a letter from Kingsley Amis: it was actually written up on the wall of the library lifts, presumably by one of those 'devious, lazy and stupid' students who persisted in infesting the librarian's proper domain and reading the books.

It hadn't always been like that, though, and Larkin's first stint at Wellington in Shropshire, where in 1943 he was put in charge of the municipal library, was a kind of idyll. Bitterly cold, gas-lit and with a boiler Larkin himself had to stoke, the library had an eccentric collection of books and a readership to match. Here he does seem to have been the type of librarian who was 'a nice chap to have around', one who quietly got on with improving the stock while beginning to study for his professional qualifications by correspondence course. Expecting 'not to give a zebra's turd' for the job he had hit upon his vocation.

Posts at Leicester and Belfast followed until in 1965 he was appointed Librarian at the University of Hull with the job of reorganising the library and transferring it to new premises. Moan as Larkin inevitably did about his job, it was one he enjoyed and which he did exceptionally well. The students may have been intimidated by him but he was popular with his staff and particularly with the women. Mary Judd, the librarian at the issue desk at Hull, thought that 'most women liked him more than most men because he could talk to a woman and make her feel unique and valuable.' In last year's *Selected Letters* there is a photo of him with the staff of the Brynmor Jones and, Larkin apart, there is not a man in sight. Surrounded by his beaming middle-aged assistants—with two at least he was having or would have an affair—he looks like a walrus with his herd of contented cows. There was contentment here for him, too, and one of his last poems, written when deeply depressed, is about a library.

> New eyes each year
> Find old books here,
> And new books, too,
> Old eyes renew;
> So youth and age
> Like ink and page
> In this house join,
> Minting new coin.

Much of Motion's story is about sex, not getting it, not getting enough of it or getting it wrong. For a time it seemed Larkin could go either way and there are a few messy homosexual encounters at Oxford, though not *Brideshead* by a long chalk, lungings more than longings and not the stuff of poetry except as the tail-end of 'these incidents last night'. After Oxford Larkin's homosexual feelings 'evaporated' (Motion's word) and were henceforth seemingly confined to his choice of socks. At Wellington he starts walking out with Ruth Bowman, 'a 16-year-old schoolgirl and regular borrower from the library'. This period of Larkin's life is quite touching and reads like a Fifties novel of provincial life, though not one written by him so much as by John Wain or Keith Waterhouse. Indeed Ruth sounds (or Larkin makes her sound) like Billy Liar's unsatisfactory girlfriend, whose snog-inhibiting Jaffa Billy hurls to the other end of the cemetery. Having laid out a grand total of 15s. 7d. on an evening with Ruth, Larkin writes to Amis:

> Don't you think it's ABSOLUTELY SHAMEFUL that men have to pay for women without BEING ALLOWED TO SHAG the women afterwards AS A MATTER OF COURSE? I do: simply DISGUSTING. It makes me ANGRY. Everything about the ree-lay-shun-ship between men and women makes me angry. It's all a fucking balls-up. It might have been planned by the army or the Ministry of Food.

To be fair, Larkin's foreplay could be on the funereal side. In the middle of one date with Ruth, Larkin (22) lapsed into silence. Was it something she'd said? 'No, I have just thought what it would be like to be old and have no one to look after you.' This was what Larkin would later refer to as 'his startling youth'. 'He could,' says Ruth, 'be a draining companion.'

In the end one's sympathies, as always in Larkin's affairs, go to the woman and one is glad when Ruth finally has him sized up and decides that he's no hubby-to-be. And he's glad too, of course. Ruth has Amis well sussed besides. 'He wanted,' she says, 'to turn Larkin into a "love 'em and lose 'em type",' and for a moment we see these two leading lights of literature as what they once were, the Likely Lads, Larkin as Bob, Amis as Terry and Ruth at this juncture the terrible Thelma.

Looking back on it now Ruth says: 'I was his first love and there's something special about a first love, isn't there?' Except that love is never quite the right word with Larkin, 'getting involved' for once not a euphemism for the tortuous process it always turns out to be. 'My relations with women,' he wrote, 'are governed by a shrinking sensitivity, a morbid sense of sin, a furtive lechery. Women don't just sit still and back you up. They want children; they like scenes; they want a chance of parading all the empty haberdashery they are stocked with. Above all they like feeling they own you—or that you own them—a thing I hate.' A. C. Benson, whose medal Larkin was later to receive from the Royal Society of Literature, put it more succinctly, quoting (I think) Aristophanes: 'Don't make your house in my mind.' Though with Larkin it was 'Don't make your house in my house either,' his constant fear being that he will be moved in on, first by his mother and then, when she's safely in a home, some other scheming woman. When towards the finish Monica Jones does manage to move in it's because she's ill and can't look after herself, and so the cause of a great deal more grumbling. With hindsight (Larkin's favourite vantage-point) it would have been wiser to have persisted with the messy homosexual fumblings, one of the advantages of boys that

they're more anxious to move on than in. Not, of course, that one has a choice, 'something hidden from us' seeing to that.

Larkin's earliest poems were published by R. A. Caton of the Fortune Press. Caton's list might have been entitled 'Poetic Justice', as besides the poetry it included such titles as *Chastisement Across the Ages* and an account of corporal punishment as meted out to women in South German prisons; since Larkin's tastes ran to both poetry and porn there is poetic justice in that too. He found that he shared his interest in dirty books with 'the sensitive and worldly-wise' Robert Conquest and together they went on expeditions, trawling the specialist shops for their respective bag in a partnership that seems both carefree and innocent. Unusual, too, as I had always thought that porn, looking for it and looking at it, was something solo. Conquest would also send him juicy material through the post and on one occasion conned the fearful Larkin into thinking the law was on his tracks and ruin imminent; he made him sweat for two or three days before letting him off the hook. That Larkin forgave him and bore no ill-will seems to me one of the few occasions outside his poetry when he comes close to real generosity of spirit.

I imagine women will be less shocked by the Larkin story, find it not all that different from the norm than will men, who don't care to see their stratagems mapped out as sedulously as Motion has done with Larkin's.

—Alan Bennett

Timorous though Larkin was he was not shamefaced and made no secret of his predilections. Just as Elsie, secretary to his father, took her bottom-pinching Führer-friendly boss in her stride, so Betty, the secretary to the son, never turned a hair when she came across his lunchtime reading in the shape of the splayed buttocks of some gym-slipped tot, just covering it briskly with a copy of the *Library Association Record* and carrying on cataloguing. One of the many virtues of Motion's book is that it celebrates the understanding and tolerance of the average British secretary and the forbearance of women generally. As, for instance, the friend to whom Larkin showed a large cupboard in his office, full of both literary and photographic porn. 'What is it for?' she asked. 'To wank to, or with, or at' was Larkin's reply, which Motion calls embarrassed, though it doesn't sound so, the question, or at any rate the answer, presumably giving him a bit of a thrill. Like the other documents of his life and his half-life, the magazines were carefully kept, if not catalogued, in his desolate attic, though after twenty-odd years' perusal they must have been about as stimulating as *Beowulf*.

One unremarked oddity in the *Selected Letters* is a note from Larkin to Conquest in 1976 mentioning a visit to

Cardiff where he had 'found a newsagent with a good line in Yank homo porn, in quite a classy district too. Didn't dare touch it.' I had assumed that in the matter of dirty magazines, be it nurses, nuns or louts in leather, you found whatever knocked on your particular box and stuck to it. So what did Larkin want with 'this nice line in homo porn'? Swaps? Or hadn't all that messy homosexuality really evaporated? Certainly pictured holidaying on Sark in 1955 he looks anything but butch. One here for Jake Balokowsky.

I am writing this before the book is published, but Larkin's taste for pornography is already being touted by the newspapers as something shocking. It isn't but, deluded liberal that I am, I persist in thinking that those with a streak of sexual unorthodoxy ought to be more tolerant of their fellows than those who lead an entirely godly, righteous and sober life. Illogically I tend to assume that if you dream of caning schoolgirls' bottoms it disqualifies you from dismissing half the nation as work-shy. It doesn't, of course; more often it's the other way round but when Larkin and Conquest rant about the country going to the dogs there's a touch of hypocrisy about it. As an undergraduate Larkin had written two facetious novels set in a girls' school under the pseudonym of Brunette Coleman. It's tempting to think that his much advertised adoration of Mrs Thatcher ('What a superb creature she is, right and beautiful!') owes something to the sadistic headmistress of St Bride's, Miss Holden.

> As Pam finally pulled Marie's tunic down over her black-stockinged legs Miss Holden, pausing only to snatch a cane from the cupboard in the wall, gripped Marie by her hair and, with strength lent by anger, forced down her head till she was bent nearly double. Then she began thrashing her unmercifully, her face a mask of ferocity, caring little where the blows fell, as long as they found a mark somewhere on Marie's squirming body. At last a cry was wrung from her bloodless lips and Marie collapsed on the floor, twisting in agony, her face hidden by a flood of amber hair.

Whether Mr Heseltine is ever known as Marie is a detail; that apart it could be a verbatim extract from A History of Cabinet Government 1979-90.

Meeting Larkin at Downing Street in 1980 Mrs Thatcher gushed that she liked his wonderful poem about a girl. 'You know,' she said, " 'Her mind was full of knives" ' The line is actually 'All the unhurried day / Your mind lay open like a drawer of knives,' but Larkin liked to think that Madam knew the poem or she would not have been able to misquote it. Inadequate briefing seems a likelier explanation and anyway, since the line is about an open mind it's not surprising the superb creature got it wrong.

Mrs Thatcher's great virtue, Larkin told a journalist, 'is saying that two and two makes four, which is as unpopular nowadays as it always has been'. What Larkin did not see was that it was only by banking on two and two making five that institutions like the Brynmor Jones Library could survive. He lived long enough to see much of his work at the library dismantled; one of the meetings he was putting off before his death was with the Vice-Chancellor designate, who was seeking ways of saving a quarter of a million pounds and wanted to shrink the library by having off some of its rooms. That was two and two making four.

Andrew Motion makes most of these points himself but without rancour or the impatience this reader certainly felt. Honest but not prurient, critical but also compassionate, Motion's book could not be bettered. It is above all patient and with no trace of the condescension or irritation that are the hazards of biography. He is a sure guide when he relates the poetry to the life, even though the mystery of where the poetry came from, and why, and when, sometimes defeats him. But then it defeated Larkin or his writing would not have petered out when it did. For all that, it's a sad read and Motion's patience with his subject is often hard to match. Larkin being Larkin, though, there are lots of laughs and jokes never far away. Before he became a celebrity (and wriggle though he did that was what he became) and one heard gossip about Larkin it was generally his jokes and his crabbiness that were quoted. 'More creakings from an old gate', was his dedication in Patrick Garland's volume of *High Windows* and there were the PCs (which were not PC at all) he used to send to Charles Monteith, including one not quoted here or in the *Selected Letters*. Along with other Faber authors Larkin had been circularised asking what events, if any, he was prepared to take part in to mark National Libraries Week. Larkin wrote back saying that the letter reminded him of the story of Sir George Sitwell being stopped by someone selling flags in aid of National Self-Denial Week: 'For some of us,' said Sir George, 'every week is self-denial week.' 'I feel,' wrote Larkin, 'exactly the same about National Libraries Week.' The letters are full of jokes. 'I fully expect', he says of 'They fuck you up, your mum and dad', 'to hear it recited by 1000 Girl Guides before I die'; he gets 'a letter from a whole form of Welsh schoolgirls, seemingly inviting mass coition. Where were they when I wanted them?' And in the cause of jokes he was prepared to dramatise himself, heighten his circumstances, darken his despair, claim to have been a bastard in situations where he had actually been all charm. What one wants to go on feeling was that, the poems apart, the jokes were the man and the saddest thing about this book and the *Selected Letters* is to find that they weren't, that beyond the jokes was a sphere of gloom, fear and self-pity that nothing and no one touched. And so far from feeling compassion for him on this score, as Motion always manages to do, I just felt impatient and somehow conned.

Trying to locate why takes one back to Auden:

> A writer, or at least a poet, is always being asked by people who should know better: 'Whom do you write for?' The question is, of course, a silly one, but I can give it a silly answer. Occasionally I come across a book which I feel has been written especially for me and for me only. Like a jealous lover I don't want anybody else to hear of it. To have a million such readers, unaware of each other's existence, to be read with passion and never talked about, is the daydream, surely, of every author.

Larkin was like that, certainly after the publication of *The Less Deceived* and even for a few years after *The Whitsun*

Weddings came out. Because his poems spoke in an ordinary voice and boasted his quiescence and self-deprecation one felt that here was someone to like, to take to and whose voice echoed one's inner thoughts and that he was, as he is here engagingly indexed (under his initials), a PAL. So that in those days, certainly until the mid-Seventies, Larkin seemed always a shared secret. The great and unexpected outpouring of regret when he died showed this sentiment to have been widespread and that through the public intimacy of his poetry he had acquired a constituency as Betjeman, partly through being less introspective and more available, never entirely did. And while we did not quite learn his language or make him a pattern to live and to die, what one is left with now is a sense of betrayal which is quite difficult to locate and no less palpable for the fact that he never sought to mislead the public about his character, particularly as he got older.

They were deceived, though. When Anthony Thwaite published the *Selected Letters* last year the balance of critical opinion was disposed to overlook—or at any rate excuse—his racist and reactionary sentiments as partly a joke, racism more pardonable these days in the backlash against political correctness. Besides it was plain that in his letters Larkin exaggerated; he wasn't really like that. Motion's book closes down this escape route. 'You'll be pleased to see the black folk go from the house over the way,' he says in a 1970 letter, and were it written to Amis or Conquest it might get by as irony, wit even, a voice put on. But he is writing to his mother for whom he did not put on a voice, or not that voice anyway. Did it come with the flimsiest of apologies it would help ('I'm sorry,' as I once heard someone say, 'but I have a blind spot with black people'). How were the blacks across the way different from 'Those antique negroes' who blew their 'flock of notes' out of 'Chicago air into / A huge remembering pre-electric horn / The year after I was born'? Well, they were in Chicago for a start, not Loughborough. Wanting so much for him to be other, one is forced against every inclination to conclude that, in trading bigotries with an eighty-year-old, Larkin was sincere; he was being really himself:

> I want to see them starving
> The so-called working class
> Their weekly wages halving
> Their women stewing grass.

The man who penned that might have been pleased to come up with the slogan of the 1968 Smethwick by-election, 'If you want a nigger neighbour, Vote Labour.' Larkin refused the Laureateship because he couldn't turn out poetry to order. But if he could churn out this stuff for his letters and postcards he could have turned an honest penny on the *Sun* any day of the week.

Then there is Larkin, the Hermit of Hull. Schweitzer in the Congo did not derive more moral credit than Larkin did for living in Hull. No matter that of the four places he spent most of his life, Hull, Coventry, Leicester and Belfast, Hull is probably the most pleasant; or that poets are not and never have been creatures of the capital: to the newspapers, as Motion says, remoteness is synonymous with integrity. But Hull isn't even particularly remote.

Ted Hughes, living in Devon, is further from London (as the crow flies, of course) than Larkin ever was but that he gets no credit for it is partly the place's fault, Devon to the metropolitan crowd having nothing on the horrors of Hull. Hughes, incidentally, gets much the same treatment here as he did in the *Selected Letters,* more pissed on than the back wall of the Batley Working Men's club before a Dusty Springfield concert.

Peter Cook once did a sketch when, dressed as Garbo, he was filmed touring the streets in an open-topped limousine shouting through a megaphone 'I want to be alone'. Larkin wasn't quite as obvious as that but poetry is a public address system too and that his remoteness was so well publicised came about less from his interviews or personal pronouncements than from the popularity of poems like 'Here' and 'The Whitsun Weddings' which located Larkin, put him on (and off) the map and advertised his distance from the centre of things.

That Hull was the back of beyond in the Fifties wasn't simply a London opinion; it prevailed in Hull itself. In 1959 I tentatively applied there for a lectureship in medieval history and the professor kicked off the interview by emphasising that train services were now so good that Hull was scarcely four hours from King's Cross. It wasn't that he'd sensed in me someone who'd feel cut off from the vivifying currents of capital chic, rather that my field of study was the medieval exchequer, the records of which were then at Chancery Lane. Still, there was a definite sense that a slow and stopping train southwards was some kind of lifeline and that, come a free moment, there one was going to be aimed. Even Larkin himself was aimed there from time to time, and though his social life was hardly a hectic round, he put himself about more than he liked to think.

Until I read Motion's book I had imagined that Larkin was someone who had largely opted out of the rituals of literary and academic life, that he didn't subscribe to them and wasn't taken in by them. Not a bit of it. There are umpteen formal functions, the poet dutifully getting on the train to London for the annual dinner of the Royal Academy, which involves a visit to Moss Bros ('and untold expense'); there's at least one party at Buckingham Palace, a Foyle's Literary Luncheon at which he has to give a speech, there are dinners at his old college and at All Souls and while he does not quite go to a dinner up a yak's arse he does trundle along to the annual festivities of the Hull Magic Circle. Well, the chairman of the library committee was an enthusiastic conjuror, Larkin lamely explains. When Motion says that Larkin had reluctantly to accept that his emergence as a public man would involve more public duties it's the 'reluctantly' one quibbles with. Of course there's no harm in any of these occasions if you're going to enjoy yourself. But Larkin seemingly never does; or never admits that he does. But if he didn't, why did he go? Because they are not difficult to duck. Amis has recorded how much pleasanter life became when he realised he could refuse invitations simply by saying 'don't do dinners'—a revelation comparable to Larkin's at Oxford when it dawned on him he could walk out of a play at the interval and not come back. But Larkin did do dinners and not just dinners. He did the Booker Prize, he did the Royal Society of Literature, he did the Shakespeare Prize; he even did a dinner for the Coventry Award of Merit. Hermit of Hull or not, he dutifully turns up to collect whatever is offered to him, including a sackful of honours and seven honorary degrees. He was going to call a halt at six only Oxford then came through with 'the big one', the letter getting him seriously over-excited. 'He actually ran upstairs,' says Monica. And this is a recluse. Fame-seeking, reputation-hugging, he's about as big a recluse as the late Bubbles Rothermere.

Motion says that institutional rewards for his work annoyed him, but there's not much evidence of it. Still, to parade in a silly hat, then stand on a platform to hear your virtues recited followed by at least one formal dinner is no fun at all, as Larkin is at pains to point out, particularly when you've got sweaty palms and are frightened you're going to pass out. His account of the Oxford ceremony makes it fun, of course. His new suit looks like 'a walrus maternity garment' and the Public Orator's speech was 'a bit like a review in *Poetry Tyneside*', so he gets by, as ever, on jokes. But if to be celebrated is such a burden why does he bother with it while still managing to suggest that his life is a kind of Grand Refusal? Because he's a public figure is Motion's kindly explanation. Because he's a man is nearer the point.

A crucial text here is 'The Life with a Hole in it' (1974):

> When I throw back my head and howl
> People (women mostly) say
> *But you've always done what you want*
> *You always get your own way*
> —A perfectly vile and foul
> Inversion of all that's been.
> What the old ratbags mean
> Is that I've never done what I don't.

It's a set-up, though, that repeats itself so regularly in Larkin's life, Larkin wanting his cake but not wanting it to be thought he enjoys eating it, that it's hard to go on sympathising as Monica and Maeve (and indeed Motion) are expected to do, as well as any woman who would listen. Not the men, of course. Larkin knows that kind of stuff just bores the chaps so they are fed the jokes, the good ladies his dizziness and sweaty palms, thus endearing him to them because it counts as 'opening up'.

About the only thing Larkin consistently didn't do were poetry readings ('I don't like going about pretending to be myself') and television. On the 1982 *South Bank Show* he allowed his voice to be recorded but refused to appear in person and it's to Patrick Garland's credit that he managed to persuade the then virtually unknown Larkin to take part in a 1965 *Monitor* film, which happily survives. He was interviewed, or at any rate was talked at, by Betjeman and typically, of course, it's Larkin who comes out of it as the better performer. Like other figures on the right, Paul Johnson, Michael Wharton and the *Spectator* crowd, Larkin regarded television as the work of the devil, or at any rate the Labour Party, and was as reluctant to be pictured as any primitive tribesman. Silly, I suppose I think this is, and also self-regarding. Hughes has done as little TV as Larkin and not made such a song and dance

about it. There is always the danger for a writer of becoming a pundit, or turning into a character, putting on a performance of oneself as Betjeman did. But there was little danger of that with Larkin. He claimed he was nervous of TV because he didn't want to be recognised, but one appearance on the *South Bank Show* doesn't start a stampede in Safeways as other authors could regretfully have told him.

If sticking in Hull seemed a deprivation but wasn't quite, so were the circumstances in which Larkin chose to live, a top-floor flat in Pearson Park rented from the University and then an 'utterly undistinguished modern house' he bought in 1974, 'not quite the bungalow on the by-pass' but 'not the kind of dwelling that is eloquent of the nobility of the human spirit'. It's tempting to think Larkin sought out these uninspiring places because for him they weren't uninspiring, and settings appropriate to the kind of poems he wrote. But he seems never to have taken much pleasure in the look of things—furniture, pictures and so on. His quarters weren't particularly spartan or even Wittgenstein-minimalist (deckchairs and porridge), just dull. The implication of living like this is that a choice has been made, another of life's pleasures foregone in the cause of art, part of Larkin's strategy for a stripped down sort of life, a traveller without luggage.

'I do believe,' he wrote to Maeve Brennan, 'that the happiest way to get through life is to want things and get them; now I don't believe I've ever wanted anything in the sense of a . . . Jaguar Mark IX . . . I mean, although there's always plenty of things I couldn't do with, there's never been anything I couldn't do without and in consequence I "have" very little.' But the truth is, surely, he wasn't all that interested and if he kept his flat like a dentist's waiting-room it was because he preferred it that way. He wanted his jazz records after all and he 'had' those. In one's own choosier circumstances it may be that reading of a life like this one feels by implication criticised and got at. And there is with Larkin an air of virtue about it, a sense that a sacrifice has been made. After all Auden's idea of the cosy was other people's idea of the squalid but he never implied that living in a shitheap was a precondition of his writing poetry; it just happened to be the way he liked it.

Still, Larkin never wanted to be one of those people with 'specially-chosen junk, / The good books, the good bed, / And my life, in perfect order' or indeed to live, as he said practically everyone he knew did, in something called The Old Mill or The Old Forge or The Old Rectory. All of them, I imagine, with prams in the hall. Cyril Connolly's strictures on this point may have been one of the reasons Larkin claimed *The Condemned Playground* as his sacred book and which led him, meeting Connolly, uncharacteristically to blurt out: 'You formed me.' But if his definition of possessions seems a narrow one (hard to see how he could feel encumbered by a house, say, but not by half a dozen honorary degrees), his version of his life, which is to some extent Motion's also, was that if he had lived a more cluttered life then Art, 'that lifted rough tongued bell', would cease to chime. When it did cease to chime, rather earlier than he'd thought, ten years or so before he died, he went on living as he'd always lived, saying it was all he knew.

Striding down the library in the *Monitor* film Larkin thought he looked like a rapist. Garland reassured him, but walking by the canal in the same film there is no reassurance; he definitely does. Clad in his doleful raincoat with pebble glasses, cycle-clips and oceanic feet, he bears more than a passing resemblance to Reginald Halliday Christie. Haunting his cemeteries and churchyards he could be on the verge of exposing himself, and whether it's to a grim, head-scarved wife from Hessle or in a slim volume from Faber and Faber seems a bit of a toss-up. Had his diary survived, that 'sexual log-book', one might have learned whether this shy, tormented man ever came close to the dock, the poetry even a safety valve. As it was, lovers on the grass in Pearson Park would catch among the threshing chestnut trees the dull glint of binoculars and on campus errant borrowers, interviewed by the Librarian, found themselves eyed up as well as dressed down.

> Day by day your estimation clocks up
> Who deserves a smile and who a frown,
> And girls you have to tell to pull their socks up
> Are those whose pants you'd most like to pull
>   down.

Motion's hardest task undoubtedly has been to cover, to understand and somehow enlist sympathy for Larkin and his women. Chief among them was his mother, whose joyless marriage put him off the institution long before poetry provided him with the excuse; Monica Jones, lecturer in English at Leicester, whom he first met in 1946 and who was living with him when he died; Maeve Brennan, an assistant librarian at Hull with whom he had a 17-year fling which overlapped with another, begun in 1975, with his long-time secretary at the library, Betty Mackereth. All of them he clubbed with sex, though Maeve was for a long time reluctant to join the clubbed and Betty escaped his notice until, after 17 years as his secretary, there was presumably one of those 'When-you-take-off-your-glasses-you're-actually-quite-pretty' moments. Though the library was the setting for so much of this heavy breathing, propriety seems to have been maintained and there was no slipping down to the stacks for a spot of beefjerky.

Of the three Monica, one feels, could look after herself and though Larkin gave her the runaround over many years she was never in any doubt about the score. 'He cared,' she told Motion, 'a tenth as much about what happened around him as what was happening inside him.' Betty, too, had him taped and besides had several other strings to her bow, including some spot-welding which she'd picked up in Leeds. It's only Maeve Brennan, among his later ladies anyway, for whom one feels sorry. Maeve knew nothing of the darker side of his nature, the porn for instance coming as a posthumous revelation as did his affair with Betty. If only for her sake one should be thankful the diaries did not survive. A simpler woman than the other two, she was Larkin's sweetheart, her love for him romantic and innocent, his for her companionable and protective. Dull you might even say,

> If that is what a skilled,
> Vigilant, flexible,

> Unemphasised, enthralled
> Catching of happiness is called.

A fervent Catholic (trust his luck), Maeve took a long time before she would sleep with him, keeping the poet-librarian at arm's length. Her arms were actually quite hairy, this, Motion says, adding to her attraction. Quite what she will feel when reading this is hard to figure and she's perhaps even now belting down to Hull's Tao Clinic. While Maeve held him off the romance flourished but as soon as she does start to sleep with him on a regular basis her days are numbered. Larkin, having made sure of his options with Betty, drops Maeve, who is desolate, and though he sees her every day in the Library and they evolve 'a distant but friendly relationship', no proper explanation is ever offered.

There is, though, a lot of other explanation on the way, far too much for this reader, with Monica being pacified about Maeve, Maeve reassured about Monica and Mother given edited versions of them both. And so much of it is in letters. When the *Selected Letters* came out there was general gratitude that Larkin was old-fashioned enough still to write letters, but there's not much to be thankful for in his correspondence with Maeve and Monica. 'One could say,' wrote Kafka, 'that all the misfortunes in my life stem from letters . . . I have hardly ever been deceived by people, but letters have deceived me without fail . . . not other people's letters, but my own.' So it is with Larkin, who as a young man took the piss out of all the twaddle he now in middle age writes about ree-lay-shun-ships.

The pity is that these three women never got together to compare notes on their lover, preferably in one of those siderooms in the Library Mrs T's cuts meant had to be hived off. But then women never do get together except in French comedies. Besides the conference would have had to include the now senile Eva Larkin, whose spectre Larkin detected in all the women he had anything to do with, or had sex to do with. Motion identifies Larkin's mother as his muse, which I suppose one must take on trust if only out of gratitude to Motion for ploughing through all their correspondence.

What makes one impatient with a lot of the stuff Larkin writes to Monica and Maeve is that it's plain that what he really wants is just to get his end away on a regular basis and without obligation. 'Sex is so difficult,' he complained to Jean Hartley. 'You ought to be able to get it and pay for it monthly like a laundry bill.' The impression the public had from the poems was that Larkin had missed out on sex, and this was corroborated by occasional interviews ('Sexual recreation was a socially remote thing, like baccarat or clog-dancing'). But though Motion calls him 'a sexually disappointed Eyore', in fact he seems to have had a pretty average time, comparing lives with Amis ('staggering skirmishes / in train, tutorial and telephone booth') the cause of much of his dissatisfaction. He needed someone to plug him into the fleshpots of Hull, the 'sensitive and worldly-wise conquest' the likeliest candidate, except that Larkin didn't want Conquest coming to Hull, partly because he was conscious of the homeliness of Maeve. On the other hand, there must have been plenty of ladies who would have been willing to oblige, even in Hull; ready to drop everything and pop up to Pearson Park, sucking off the great poet at least a change from gutting herrings.

I imagine women will be less shocked by the Larkin story, find it not all that different from the norm than will men, who don't care to see their stratagems mapped out as sedulously as Motion has done with Larkin's. To will his own discomfort then complain about it, as Larkin persistently does, makes infuriating reading but women see it every day. And if I have a criticism of this book it is that Motion attributes to Larkin the poet faults I would have said were to do with Larkin the man. It's true Larkin wanted to keep women at a distance, fend off family life because he felt that writing poetry depended on it. But most men regard their life as a poem that women threaten. They may not have two spondees to rub together but they still want to pen their saga untrammelled by life-threatening activities like trailing round Sainsbury's, emptying the dishwasher or going to the nativity play. Larkin complains to Judy Egerton about Christmas and having to

> buy six simple inexpensive presents when there are rather more people about than usual . . . No doubt in yours it means seeing your house given over to hordes of mannerless middle-class brats and your good food and drink vanishing into the quacking tooth-equipped jaws of their alleged parents. Yours is the harder course, I can see. On the other hand, mine is happening to me.

'And' (though he doesn't say this) 'I'm the poet.' Motion comments: 'As in "Self's the Man", Larkin here angrily acknowledges his selfishness hoping that by admitting it he will be forgiven.' 'Not that old trick!' wives will say, though sometimes they have to be grateful just for that, and few ordinary husbands would get away with it. But Larkin wasn't a husband and that he did get away with it was partly because of that and because he had this fall-back position as Great Poet. Monica, Maeve and even Betty took more from him, gave him more rope because this was someone with a line to posterity.

In all this the writer he most resembles—though, 'falling over backwards to be thought philistine' (as was said at All Souls), he would hardly relish the comparison—is Kafka. Here is the same looming father and timid, unprotesting mother, a day job meticulously performed with the writing done at night and the same-dithering on the brink of marriage with art the likely casualty. Larkin's letters analysing these difficulties with girls are as wearisome to read as Kafka's and as inconclusive. Both played games with death, Larkin hiding, Kafka seeking and when they were called in it got them both by the throat.

Like Kafka it was only as a failure that Larkin could be a success. 'Striving to succeed he had failed; accepting failure he had begun to triumph.' Not that this dispersed the gloom then or ever. Motion calls him a Parnassian Ron Glum and A. L. Rowse (not usually a fount of common sense) remarks: 'What the hell was the matter with him? He hadn't much to complain about. He was *tall!'*

The publication of the *Selected Letters* and now the biography is not, I fear, the end of it. This is early days for Larkin plc as there's a hoard of material still unpublished,

the correspondence already printed just a drop in the bucket, and with no widow standing guard packs of post-graduates must already be converging on the grave. May I toss them a bone?

In 1962 Monica Jones bought a holiday cottage at Haydon Bridge, near Hexham in Northumberland. Two up, two down it's a bleakish spot with the Tyne at the back and the main Newcastle-Carlisle road at the front and in Motion's account of his visit there to rescue Larkin's letters it sounds particularly desolate. However Jones and Larkin spent many happy holidays at the cottage and on their first visit in 1962 they

> lazed, drank, read, pottered round the village and amused themselves with private games. Soon after the move, for instance, they began systematically defacing a copy of Iris Murdoch's novel *The Flight from the Enchanter,* taking it in turns to interpolate salacious remarks and corrupt the text. Many apparently innocent sentences are merely underlined ('Today it seemed likely to be especially hard'). Many more are altered ('her lips were parted and he had never seen her eyes so wide open' becomes 'Her legs were parted and he had never seen her cunt so wide open'). Many of the numbered chapter-headings are changed ('Ten' is assimilated into I Fuck my STENographer). Even the list of books by the same author is changed to include UNDER THE NET her Garments.

Something to look forward to after a breezy day on Hadrian's Wall or striding across the sands at Lindisfarne this 'childishly naughty game' was continued over many years.

As a librarian Larkin must have derived a special pleasure from the defacement of the text but he and Miss Jones were not the first. Two other lovers had been at the same game a year or so earlier only, more daring than our two pranksters, they had borrowed the books they planned to deface from a public library and then, despite the scrutiny of the staff, had managed to smuggle them back onto the shelves. But in 1962 their luck ran out and Joe Orton and Kenneth Halliwell were prosecuted for defacing the property of Islington Borough Council. Was it this case, plentifully written up in the national press, that gave Philip and Monica their wicked idea? Or did he take his cue from the more detailed account of the case published the following year in the *Library Association Record,* that delightful periodical which was his constant study? It's another one for Jake Balokowsky.

At 45 Larkin had felt himself 'periodically washed over by waves of sadness, remorse, fear and all the rest of it, like the automatic flushing of a urinal.' By 60 the slide towards extinction is unremitting, made helpless by the dead weight of his own self. His life becomes so dark that it takes on a quality of inevitability: when a hedgehog turns up in the garden you know, as you would know in a film, that the creature is doomed. Sure enough he runs over it with the lawnmower and comes running into the house wailing. He had always predicted he would die at 63 as his father did and when he falls ill at 62 it is of the cancer he is most afraid of. He goes into the Nuffield to be operated on, the surgeon telling him he will be a new man 'when

I was quite fond of the old one'. One of the nurses is called Thatcher, another Scargill ('They wear labels'). A privilege of private medicine is that patients have ready access to drink and it was a bottle of whisky from an unknown friend that is thought to have led him to swallow his own vomit and go into a coma. In a crisis in a private hospital the patient is generally transferred to a National Health unit, in this case the Hull Royal Infirmary, for them to clear up the mess. 'As usual' I was piously preparing to write but then I read how Louis MacNeice died. He caught a chill down a pothole in Yorkshire while producing a documentary for the BBC and was taken into University College Hospital. He was accustomed at this time to drinking a bottle of whisky a day but being an NHS patient was not allowed even a sip, whereupon the chill turned to pneumonia and he died, his case almost the exact converse of Larkin's. Larkin came out of the coma, went home but not to work and returned to hospital a few months later, dying on 2 December 1985.

Fear of death had been the subject of his last major poem, 'Aubade', finished in 1977, and when he died it was much quoted and by implication his views endorsed, particularly perhaps the lines

> Courage is no good:
> It means not scaring others. Being brave
> Lets no one off the grave.
> Death is no different whined at than withstood.

The poem was read by Harold Pinter at a memorial meeting at Riverside Studios in the following March and I wrote it up in my diary:

3 March 1986

A commemorative programme for Larkin at Riverside Studios, arranged by Blake Morrison. Arrive late as there is heavy rain and the traffic solid, nearly two hours to get from Camden Town to Hammersmith. I am to read with Pinter, who has the beginnings of a moustache he is growing in order to play Goldberg in a TV production of *The Birthday Party.* My lateness and the state of the traffic occasions some disjointed conversation between us very much in the manner of his plays. I am told this often happens.

Patrick Garland, who is due to compere the programme, is also late so we kick off without him, George Hartley talking about Larkin and the Marvell Press and his early days in Hull. Ordering *The Less Deceived* no one ever got the title right, asking for 'Alas! Deceived', 'The Lass Deceived' or 'The Less Received' and calling the author Carkin, Lartin, Lackin, Laikin and Lock. I sit in the front row with Blake Morrison, Julian Barnes and Andrew Motion. There are more poems and reminiscences but it's all a bit thin and jerky. Now Patrick G. arrives, bringing the video of the film he made of Larkin in 1965 but there is further delay because while the machine works there is no sound. Eventually we sit and watch it like a silent film with Patrick giving a commentary and saying how Larkinesque this situation is (which it isn't particularly) and how when he was stuck in the unending traffic-jam he

had felt that was Larkinesque too and how often the word Larkinesque is used and now it's part of the language. Pinter, whose own adjective is much more often used, remains impassive. Patrick, as always, tells some good stories, including one I hadn't heard of how Larkin used to cheer himself up by looking in the mirror and saying the line from *Rebecca,* 'I am Mrs de Winter now!'

Then Andrew Motion, who is tall elegant and fair, a kind of verse Heseltine, reads his poem on the death of Larkin which ends with his last glimpse of the great man, staring out of the hospital window, his fingers splayed out on the glass, watching as Motion drives away. In the second half Pinter and I are to read with an interlude about the novels by Julian Barnes. Riverside had earlier telephoned to ask what furniture we needed and I had suggested a couple of reading-desks. These have been provided but absurdly with only one microphone so both desks are positioned centre stage, an inch or so apart with the mike between them. This means that when I read Pinter stands silently by and when he reads I do the same. Except that there is a loose board on my side and every time I shift my feet while Pinter is reading there is an audible creak. Were it Stoppard reading or Simon Gray I wouldn't care a toss: it's only because it's Pinter the creak acquires significance and seems somehow *meant.*

We finish at half-past ten and I go straight to Great Ormond Street where Sam is in Intensive Care. See sick children (and in particular one baby almost hidden under wires and apparatus) and Larkin's fear of death seems self-indulgent. Sitting there I find myself wondering what would have happened had he worked in a hospital once a week like (dare one say it?) Jimmy Saville.

A propos Pinter I thought it odd that in the *Selected Letters* almost alone of Larkin's contemporaries he escaped whipping—given that neither his political views nor his poetry seemed likely to commend him to Larkin. But Pinter is passionate about cricket and, as Motion reveals, sponsored Larkin for the MCC so it's just a case of the chaps sticking together.

This must have been a hard book to write and I read it with growing admiration for the author and, until his pitiful death, mounting impatience with the subject. Motion, who was a friend of Larkin's must have been attended throughout by the thought, by the sound even, of his subject's sepulchral disclaimers. Without ever having known Larkin I feel, as I think many readers will, that I have lost a friend. I found myself and still find myself not wanting to believe that Larkin was really like this, the unpacking of that 'really', which Motion has done, what so much of the poetry is about. The publication of the *Selected Letters* before the biography was criticised but as a marketing strategy, which is what publishing is about these days, it can't be faulted. The Letters may sell the Life; the Life, splendid though it is, is unlikely to sell the Letters: few readers coming to the end of this book would want to know more. Different, yes, but not more.

There remain the poems, without which there would be no biography. Reading it I could not see how they would emerge unscathed. But I have read them again and they do, just as with Auden and Hardy, who have taken a similar biographical battering. Auden's epitaph on Yeats explains why:

> Time that is intolerant
> Of the brave and innocent
> And indifferent in a week
> To a beautiful physique
>
> Worships language and forgives
> Everyone by whom it lives;
> Pardons cowardice, conceit,
> Lays its honours at their feet
>
> Time that with this strange excuse
> Pardoned Kipling and his views,
> And will pardon Paul Claudel,
> Pardons him for writing well.

The black-sailed unfamiliar ship has sailed on, leaving in its wake not a huge birdless silence but an armada both sparkling and intact. Looking at this bright fleet you see there is a man on the jetty, who might be anybody. (pp. 3, 5-9)

> Alan Bennett, "Alas! Deceived," in London Review of Books, *Vol. 15, No. 6, March 25, 1993, pp. 3, 5-9.*

Larkin in a letter to J.B. Sutton dated January 26, 1950:

I had been wondering what you were doing & am sorry to hear life has had you by the balls. It is a grim business, & I do sympathise: it is also a business that appears differently to every man. To me it appears like the floor of some huge Stock Exchange, full of men quarreling & fighting & shouting & fucking & drinking & making plans and scheming to carry them out, experiencing desires & contriving to gratify them, and in general acting & being acted upon: I sit shuddering at the side, out of the fray, too much of a funk to fight or contrive, imagining I am living a full life when I pick up an old bottle & toss it back into the mêlée. But let a whizzing tomato spread over my face & I yelp for the complete & utter solitude so necessary for any worthwhile artistic creation &c. My relations with women are governed by a shrinking sensitivity, a morbid sense of sin, a furtive lechery & a deplorable flirtatiousness—all of which are menaced by the clear knowledge that I should find marriage a trial. 'One hates the person one lives with.'

Philip Larkin, in The Selected Letters of Philip Larkin, *edited by Anthony Thwaite, 1992.*

John Bayley   (essay date 25 March 1993)

[*Bayley is a highly respected English critic, poet, and novelist. In the following essay, he discusses the role of women and sexual fantasy in Larkin's writings, focusing on Larkin's 1947 novel* A Girl in Winter.]

It may be off-putting to think that great artists create to excite themselves sexually; yet in some degree this is probably the case. At least with quite a number. Although the obvious danger would then be including almost every artistic effect under the heading of the pornographic ('everything he does is so artistic,' as Anthony Powell remarked of Lawrence's gamekeeper, quoting a song of Marie Lloyd's), it might be tempting to construct a General Theory of Pornography in Art along these lines. Lawrence himself, oddly enough, would not qualify; certainly not in the context of *Lady Chatterley*. One of the many not quite right things about that novel is the way Lawrence tries to distance sexual excitement from himself and his readers, making it a matter of the higher impulse: the feel in the blood and not the sex in the head. Being, in one sense, a better artist in this context than he wished to be, Lawrence none the less succeeded, as we know, in exciting many of his readers.

One of them was Philip Larkin, who always liked and admired Lawrence, considering him a criterion for the literary 'non-bogus'. But Lawrence would not at all have cared for Larkin's own use of the pornographic, in its higher or its lower manifestations. For Larkin, like Housman, excited himself on two levels, one of which may seem to have been the impulse behind his best and most characteristic art. The other was plain pornography, of the dirty mackintosh kind, corresponding to Housman's relish for sex jokes. The relation of the two levels is not easy to determine, but the higher seems connected with a yearning to escape the compulsive repulsiveness of the lower: to escape into art and the mysterious sexual excitement of creation, the world of the Shropshire Lad and of Larkin's 'dear translucent bergs: / Silence and space'. The escape is palpably disingenuous, for the reader still feels and can participate in the kind of excitement the writer is giving himself. In the poem 'Dry-Point' Larkin specifically contrasts the exasperatingly mechanical repetitiveness of sexual desire with 'that bare and sun-scrubbed room . . . Where you, we dream, obtain no right of entry'—'you' being the diurnal sexual itch. 'We dream' shows that the poet himself does not believe it—nor does his poem intend we should. The cube of light, the sun-scrubbed room, like those 'dear translucent bergs', are for Larkin sexual properties by other means, as Wenlock Edge and dead soldier lads and nettles dancing on suicides' graves were for Housman. It is there that for the poet sex in the head most excitingly takes place.

I started to reflect on Larkin and pornography when reading James Booth's highly effective and detailed study of his poems, [*Philip Larkin: Writer*], though the subject had been put into my head by Anthony Thwaite's selection of the poet's letters. [*The Selected Letters of Philip Larkin*]. Booth, together with Barbara Everett, is among the few critics who have produced real illumination about the way the poems work: ways of working which notoriously have become more and more indefinable the more public and popular a figure the poet has become—and indeed the more he has become a new industry for the critics. The point to hold onto might well be that such a popularity occurs on the rare occasions when a highly idiosyncratic writer like Larkin or Housman manages unexpectedly to strike an all-responsive chord; when, in fine, as Henry

435

James would say, by exciting themselves they excite others. Like the higher pornography, the higher self-pity—vital to any bestseller—is an important ingredient in Larkin's popularity.

There is nothing specialised about the excitement. One does not have to share homoerotic feelings to be excited by Housman; or, when moved by Larkin, to share his fantasies about schoolgirls. The higher pornography does not work that way, for its erotic charge is not only generalised into art but disseminated among mysterious and apparently neutral properties, to which it transmits an excitement which can always none the less be traced straight back to the poet's own sex feelings. This is particularly true of the masterpiece which is one of Larkin's two youthful attempts at fiction, *A Girl in Winter*, which should more properly be known by the title Larkin wanted, *The Kingdom of Winter*, and then changed at the publisher's request. Both novels' titles thus have a faint air of Soho about them; the first, *Jill*, is reported by Kingsley Amis to have been found located next to *High-Heeled Yvonne*, on a shelf of such works.

With some justification, for the fantasies about Jill Bradley at her school Willow Gables do come close to what Booth calls 'an unusual kind of pornography, despite, or rather because of, their "complicated sexless" quality'. As Larkin explained in an introduction to the American edition, the original publisher divided his activity between poetry 'and what then passed for pornography'. 'Then' is the significant word, for what is old-fashioned is important to Larkin in this context: the girl in his oddly moving poem 'Broadcast' has 'slightly outmoded shoes'. Jill's 'super-soft porn undertones', in Amis's phrase quoted by Booth, are of course not at all what that phrase would lead one to expect, and yet the connection is clear: 'All my kirbigrips have vanished for a start this morning (yes, and WHO took them?), so what with searching for them and trying to find a slide, I hadn't time to get my hymn-book before prayers—and of course the Badger had to choose today to inspect them, as she said she's seen too many girls sharing recently. I suppose she thinks I *like* sharing with Molly.' In *A Girl in Winter* the technique has been taken much further and is far more artifically sophisticated, though the novelist was still only 21. As Booth crisply puts it, the Pygmalion myth 'is repeated *within* the story with the gender roles reversed . . . Katherine acts as the creative Pygmalion rather than the created statue.' Robin—the youthful 'hero'—'is her work of art, her "Jill Bradley and Willow Gables" fantasy. She is no longer merely the object of male creative fantasy; she has become a subject in her own right, creating her own artistic object.' In this masterly attempt at making a novel out of what he called 'diffused poetry', the young Larkin succeeded by imagining himself into the role of the girl who is doing the imagining: more important, all the properties in the story, those outside her imagination, are polarised by the process, as they will be in the poems he was to write later by the kinds of excitement in which they began. (In 'Broadcast' the girl at the concert excites his tenderness and desire as a result of her helplessness inside his imagination of it—'Your hands, tiny in all that air, applauding'.)

'Diffused poetry' works so well here because it is so intimately attached to the high plane of fantasy: desire by means of poetical self-identification. This is far more effective than, say, Virginia Woolf's fantasy in *Orlando,* which only seems poetic, because the sexual transposition is done with skittish amusement rather than the right true sexual devotion. Oddly enough, the novels of Barbara Pym, which struck an immediate chord with the older Larkin, have something of his own skill in creating sexual fantasy wholly devoid of overt sex, and in which characters excite themselves by creating each other in their heads. In *A Girl in Winter* Larkin can even achieve a perfect transposed 'family' fantasy—it is also marvellously funny—by means of a visit to the dentist. Katherine, the fantasy girl in the poet's head who is also creating a young man in her own, becomes in the scene, as it were, the mother of a young colleague, Miss Green: the dentist who pulls the latter's tooth becoming in the act a temporary fantasy father. For the author the scene clearly displaces the 'unsatisfactory' (a favourite word) nature of a real family relationship, adding a sexual dimension to it as well. Even the pink mouthwash tablet the dentist drops in a glass of water for his patient 'sinks furiously to the bottom'—a hilarious visual emblem of domestic tantrums and paternal frustration. When the tooth has been pulled, and Miss Green is still unconscious, Katherine and the dentist, who care nothing about her, involuntarily stand back for a moment and see her as if she were a little girl. Only in the displaced sex of fantasy can she be 'a real girl in a real place'. Real, that is, in terms of the curious quality of Larkinian art. 'The impulse to preserve,' Larkin wrote to D. J. Enright in 1955, 'lies at the bottom of all art.' For Larkin the preservation of the moment itself involved a transposition of sex, as with the trilby hat in a snapshot of the girl from 'Lines on a Young Lady's Photograph Album'—'(Faintly disturbing, that, in several ways)'. In *A Girl in Winter* winter itself becomes the groper and voyeur, as the girls leave the library where they work to go to the dentist, the time being carefully noted. 'They stood for a second on the top of the steps, the cold rising up their skirts, and began to walk down as a clock struck ten-fifteen . . . Katherine looked disproportionately strong and dark beside Miss Green.' Viewpoint and selection of detail all enhance the slightly eerie nature of, as it were, transvestised fact. Katherine is strong and dark because she is not really a girl at all; or, alternatively, being inside the poet's head, she is so much of a girl that she has a transposed sexual awareness no real girl would bother to have. She feels winter fingering her; and it is to winter and not to her tiresome young man that she gives herself at the novel's conclusion, an ending which makes sex a tiresome triviality, like the ticking of a watch on your partner's wrist, but the possession by sleep and winter, with its visions of bergs white and slow-approaching, a deeply satisfying artistic (or sexual) experience.

It is certainly a remarkably intense one. Katherine, as Booth says, becomes 'a resigned subject of the kingdom of winter', and the author at the time wrote to a friend that 'it is a deathly book and has for theme the relinquishing of live response to life.' For Larkin, as he was no doubt gloomily but also satisfyingly aware, that is what sex was all about. One cannot help being struck by the ways in which Larkin quietly turns his hero-author Lawrence inside out, adapting Lawrence's vivid perception of things but displacing them to the spirit of something more like the Fin de Siècle. Where Gerald at the end of *Women in Love* is condemned for not being 'on the side of life' to a death in snow and ice, Katherine welcomes her seduction by winter, and the whole novel endorses her doing so. Lawrence detested preservation, but for Larkin it is the essence of sex in art (even the plural 'skirts' in those sentences from the novel is a subtle reminder of this sex's old-fashionedness, 'as if all summer settled there and died'). Perhaps the only point on which Larkin intensifies instead of reversing Lawrence is in his tacit emphasis on the absolute difference between the sexes, a difference further emphasised by the artistic feat of realising sex—'the wonderful feel of girls'—and in preserving such a moment by becoming a girl himself.

Desire to preserve is not, no doubt, a novelist's ideal frame of mind. Larkin, whistling in the dark, assured a friend that his third novel 'will pick up where Katherine left off and develop *logically* back to life again'. As Booth remarks, that 'logically' rather gives the game away. Larkin was no Lawrentian phoenix, and the resurrection of Katherine or of himself in novel form was naturally not to be. The two pieces of fiction, like many of the later poems, end in the comfort of snow and ice, in eloquent emptiness, however much Larkin professed to hope that 'the north ship will come back instead of being bogged up there in a glacier.' What you desire is not yourself, because your self is still haplessly if hopelessly alive and ongoing, but the absence which mysteriously becomes sex itself, preserved in Katherine who is all the more female for being foreign, a foreignness suggested by Larkin with an extraordinary and unobtrusive skill. Perhaps, when one comes to think of it, that is one more positive bond with Lawrence, who always fancied foreign females himself. And yet his females really were foreign, whereas Katherine is only foreign by imaginative suggestion, by the peculiar sexual intensity of Larkin/winter.

Probably the purely negative aspect of Larkin's imagination can be dwelt on too heavily. Even his intensities have a light touch; and though his wry modesty about himself is as unconvincing as that of any other artist, it can still be convincing enough, as when he writes that the last line of the brief poem about sea and sky, 'Absences' ('Such attics cleared of me! Such absences!'), 'sounds like a slightly-unconvincing translation from a French symbolist. I wish I could write like this more often.' Booth appositely comments that like Shelley's Mont Blanc Larkin's seascape is 'sublimely unobserved'; and the poet wrote that he was 'always thrilled by the thought of what places look like when I am not there'. The word 'thrilled' is again significant: Larkinian pornography is an affair of absences, the arts of imagining without being there.

This relish for negativism is balanced by the odd ways in which Larkin is none the less 'on the side of life'. Like the poems that came later, *A Girl in Winter* is unobtrusively full of human feelings for the troubles, regrets and rewards of human beings. Even the poet's misogyny, which has nothing hard about it, is a kind of wistfulness. As Booth

shrewdly observes, Larkin is quite capable of 'coming near to launching a female attack on his own misogyny'. Hardy the novelist could do that too, but with less sense of the basic untenability of his own fantasies: Larkin is always sardonically aware that the idea of a 'girl' (like Hardy's 'pure woman') can only exist in the male imagination. Our General Theory of the Pornographic in Art would probably have to stipulate that the artist exciting himself by means of whatever he fancies must—to qualify for the definition—be doing so consciously. The pornographer has few if any illusions about his techniques, and yet if he is as good an artist as Larkin he cannot end-stop them: they meet and mingle with the whole interest of life, and as Henry James so passionately declared, 'art *makes* life, *makes* interest.' So of course does sex.

> *John Bayley, "Becoming a Girl," in* London Review of Books, *Vol. 15, No. 6, March 25, 1993, p. 10.*

Peter Conrad   (review date 28 March 1993)

[*In the following positive review of* Philip Larkin: A Writer's Life, *Conrad focuses on the importance of solitude and emotional detachment in Larkin's life.*]

Andrew Motion's superb biography of Philip Larkin has a quietly provocative subtitle—'A Writer's Life'. Socially reclusive, emotionally recessive—it might be asked whether Larkin had any life at all; the student radicals at Hull who daubed denunciations of him in the university lavatories presumably thought that he should have got himself one. Motion warns us against expecting adventures or events: there will be 'no games of Russian roulette, no shark-fishing expeditions'. But despite his self-denials, Larkin had the kind of life a writer should have—a life spent guarding his gift.

Yeats proposed a choice between perfection of the life or of the work. For Larkin, the work demanded virtual abstention from life. The central moral struggle in Motion's narrative is between the susceptible, galumphingly passionate man and the stringently self-sufficient poet; its emotional drama derives from Larkin's efforts to hold on to several lovers simultaneously while maintaining his independence from them. 'How will I be able to write', he demanded when the first of these women badgered him to marry her, 'when I have to be thinking about you?'

Larkin once fulsomely thanked Cyril Connolly for having been his conscience. Presumably he was remembering Connolly's citation of 'the pram in the hall' as the deadliest enemy of literary promise. The wedded state remained a synonym for any entanglement which Larkin felt might thwart his poems. He was aghast when offered a contract to review regularly for *The Observer* and made the literary editor Blake Morrison feel as if he had proposed marriage.

His objection to domesticity was metaphysical: it invested in a deceptive security, and Larkin preferred the terrifying knowledge of temporariness. 'To think of myself owning furniture', he said, 'gives me a sinking feeling.' The same austerity compelled his resignation from the form to which he entrusted his first and most earnest ambitions, the novel.

The heroine of *A Girl in Winter* volunteers, as Motion remarks, 'for permanent exile in the snow-covered landscape of her own self'; Larkin's subsequent, unfinished novels tried 'to forgive the world' and to imagine a social life which would not disrupt that lonely, chilling integrity, but eventually despaired of making the compromise work.

Larkin opted for solitude, and for the anonymity of a drab profession (conscientiously worked at: Motion makes clear what an excellent librarian he was) in a nondescript provincial city. Grumpy, obstinate withdrawal was his equivalent of what Keats, wondering at Wordsworth's autonomy, called 'the egotistical sublime'. In retrospect, this choice of life confers a certain moral heroism on him, reproaching our own era when writers have become celebrities, not always for their books.

With a martyr's zealotry, Larkin submitted himself to the humbling dailiness of existence. After moving his mother to a nursing home, he faithfully wrote to her every day. His letters did not mention the books he was publishing or the honours he was collecting; instead he chronicled the toings and froings of a fluffy toy frog she had given him, and described his panic when he left two dishcloths to boil and burn in a pan on the stove.

Public renown, when it came, signalled the approach of extermination, as the poems set about detaching themselves from the downcast, ailing man who once wrote them. Meanwhile, tragically, the gift which had vetoed the chance of conventional happiness took its whimsical leave, mocking his protective stratagems. 'It's awful to have lost whatever talent one may have had,' Larkin said in 1978. 'I could no more write a poem than achieve levitation.'

Although Larkin was a repressed romantic, the repression was never absolute. While he moaned that sexual intercourse began in 1963, 'rather too late for me', Motion reveals that it began for Larkin in 1945, with the young woman who was later jilted to make room for the poems. Motion sympathetically characterises a succession of would-be muses, but judges that Larkin's most intimate alliance was with his mother, who 'preceded him through life, loading him down with constraints he dreaded but also embraced'.

His ardour had to seek other ways of venting itself—in his jazz records, and his private archive of pornography. Also in his larkiness, often surrealist in its impish fantasticality. Like Orton defacing library books, Larkin scatologically annotated a copy of Irish Murdoch's *Flight from the Enchanter,* licentiously warping its story with superscriptions and marginal graffiti. Not surprisingly, his family name is akin to 'larrikin'.

This hilariously mischievous underside of Larkin is better represented in Anthony Thwaite's selection of his letters. Motion understandably emphasises grief and glumness—the muffled anguish of his drinking, the occasional howl of unappeasable pain as when, in an episode of gruesome farce, he butchered a hedgehog while mowing his lawn. Perhaps he defers too much to what Larkin, speaking of

Stevie Smith, called 'the authority of sadness'. Suffering has authority and is right to claim prerogatives for itself, but what eminence can mere sadness legitimately pretend to? Larkin's gloom was a mask, a calculated affront to intruders.

I have other worries about the contagious appeal of his self-pity. Motion finely comments that Larkin's voice became 'one of the means by which his country recognised itself'. That is true, but also depressing. Larkin became the laureate of national failure, as well as of personal disappointment.

He presented himself as a doddering Prufrock with a shopping bag of string and a bus pass, too timid to contemplate the consumption of a peach. One letter frets about whether he can afford to buy another Marks & Spencer sweater and about whether there will be any left in stock when he gets to the shop; another confesses his fear of buying steak in Fine Fare, because he's convinced that the butcher sees him coming and substitutes horse meat.

Motion sensibly dismisses the fuss about the illicit prejudices of the letters, but there are moments when a flailing anger maddens Larkin as he tallies the doom of his class and the decline of his country. His father, to Larkin's shame, naively sympathised with Hitler's Germany; Larkin himself, to Motion's dismay, adored Mrs Thatcher.

Like his friend Betjeman, Larkin was invidiously turned into a political icon. The former personified the cuddly quaintness of old England, the latter the dispirited retrenchment of little England. Larkin was even photographed on the Scottish border, lolling on a sign which announces 'England'. It is good to learn from Motion that, before settling into his demure pose, the impudent Larkin 'had urinated copiously just behind the word'.

Auden, writing about the ideological credulity of Yeats, decided 'your gift survived it all'. So did Larkin's, jealous-

---

Larkin in a letter to Kingsley Amis dated June 18, 1976:

The hay-bloody fever season is arriving, one of the things in life that never lets you down (like triple gins), so I am likely to be even less amusing than I might have been in propria persona what what.

It was nice having a letter, especially from you dalling; I don't get many letters now, except ones threatening to cut off the gas or the telephone, or wanting £5,000 by 1st July 1976; what I want is something starting 'I am directed to inform you that under the will of the late Mr Getty . . .' or 'Dear Philip, You'll be interested to know that old Humbleby is at last giving up the Library at Windsor, and HM . . . of course, only £10,000 but there's a rather jolly little g & f Georgian dower house in the Great Park that seems to go with the job . . .' or 'Dear Mr Larkin, I expect you think it's jolly cheeky for a schoolgirl to—'

Philip Larkin, in The Selected Letters of Philip Larkin, *edited by Anthony Thwaite, 1992.*

ly sequestered from temptation. A gift is a donation from elsewhere, fragile and unaccountable, as Larkin discovered when his quit him. Like the children he refused to have, it is merely loaned, and must be handled with superstitious care. Never exploiting or perjuring it, disavowing all else for its sake, Larkin lived a quietly noble and exemplary version of the writer's life; Motion—affectionate but undeceived about the man's frailties, a diligent researcher and a deft reader of poetry—has written an equally exemplary *Life* of him.

Peter Conrad, "The Laureate of Our Failure," in The Observer, *March 28, 1993, p. 61.*

Christopher Hitchens   (essay date April 1993)

[*In the following excerpt, Hitchens argues that Larkin's achievements as a poet remain untarnished despite his unpopular political views.*]

The frisson which attended publication of the *Selected Letters* extended beyond the reaction to insular, foul-mouthed baiting and into the realm of intimate, private vendetta. Some critics had deduced Larkin's conservative and sometimes chauvinist growl from his very occasional reviews and interviews, but they were unprepared to find, let alone to defuse, the time bombs he left for comrades and colleagues. Of his best friend, Kingsley Amis (and this in a letter to his next-best friend, Robert Conquest): "The only reason I hope I predecease him is that I'd find it next to impossible to say anything nice about him at his memorial service." Of Anthony Burgess: "a kind of Batman of contemporary letters." Of his old chum Anthony Powell, author of *A Dance to the Music of Time:* "the horse-faced dwarf."

This was England's best-loved poet speaking, a man who was quoted and esteemed even in mass-circulation papers, and honored in different ways by Mrs Thatcher and Her Majesty the Queen. (Though he never became poet laureate, very probably because one of his best-known poems concerned family values and kicked off with the pregnant line "They fuck you up, your mum and dad.") So the exposure of the squalid recesses in his character was a grand opportunity for the confrontation between political correctness and literature, or perhaps better say between the literal and the ironic mind.

As indeed it proved. Writing in *The Times Literary Supplement,* the Irish poet and essayist Tom Paulin opened the bidding with an allegation about the "open sewer" over which the "national monument" of English letters was hypocritically raised. (As well as being a superb writer and critic, and as well as having an Indian wife, Paulin is that rare and valuable thing an Ulster Protestant Republican, and may or may not have been influenced by Larkin's pungent evocation of the Ulster accent as sounding like "a Glaswegian, after a short stay in the USA, whining for mercy.") Paulin went on to make the yet more serious observation that the *Letters,* as edited, contain numerous ellipses. What could the editor, fellow poet Anthony Thwaite, have left out? Was there even worse abuse and savagery being kept from the Brits? Ought we not to be told? The dark question gained point and weight when it

was revealed that Larkin had mandated the burning of much of his archive, an auto-da-fé which included his great trove of ultra-English flagellant pornography.

Philip Larkin lived almost all his adult life as a provincial-university librarian (in the grim port of Hull, which led to many jokes about "Hull on wheels" and "Hull is other people"), and he managed to essentialize in his poems the deep, sarcastic, self-deprecating pessimism with which Englishmen of his class and kind faced the loss of empire, the decline of Britain, the erosion of the countryside, and the rise of a mass culture of cleverness and greed. He wrote about churchyards, cricket, coastlines, small market towns. He hymned creeping age, crapulous ailments, dull meetings, petty irritants. One of his least fine but most effective poems was titled "Going, Going," and foresaw the swamping of the sceptered isle by junk modernism— "First slum of Europe . . . "

> And that will be England gone,
> The shadows, the meadows, the lanes,
> The guildhalls, the carved choirs.
> There'll be books; it will linger on
> In galleries; but all that remains
> For us will be concrete and tyres.

Amputated of one verse, which attacked greedy corporations, by the *other* sort of politically correct, this poem appeared on the front of a Tory-government white paper on the environment. Even so, how Larkin would have scorned the very idea of being "green." He was just too *noticeable,* too challenging, too emblematic of the national psyche, to escape the eager attention of the strict P.C. patrol (in which I do not include Tom Paulin).

Seizing on the fresh fodder of his letters, Professor Lisa Jardine of the University of London described them in *The Guardian* as "a steady stream of casual obscenity, throwaway derogatory remarks about women, and arrogant disdain for those of different skin colour and nationality . . . a cultural frame within which Larkin writes, one which indeed takes racism and sexism for granted as crucially a part of the British national heritage." La Jardine then added the much more serious assertion that "Larkin's poetry carries a baggage of attitudes which the *Selected Letters* now make explicit." It is *that* connection which defines the ideological practice of modern P.C.—the same mental connection that indicts Thomas Jefferson's prose because it was written by a slaveholder.

"All right then," said novelist Julian Barnes, taking up this challenge. "Go on. Point to any of the poems that are diminished by this new knowledge." Barnes is one of the very few Larkin correspondents to whom—and about whom—the old brute was consistently friendly and civil, so I pressed him further. "Well, the other night I read Philip's poem 'Breadfruit' at an AIDS benefit. Now, you *could* say, if you had no sense of humor at all, that here's Larkin writing like an exploiting colonialist about dusky maidens bringing breadfruit. But actually it's obvious that the poem is rather a touching satire on the silliness of male sexual fantasy, both in youth and in old age."

As I spoke to those who were mentioned less kindly in Larkin's dispatches, I found a similar reluctance to draw

P.C. conclusions. Salman Rushdie (dismissed in a 1982 letter as "wogs like Salmagundi or whatever his name is") told me, "Well, my first reaction, since I'd never even met the man, was 'What am I doing in your *letters?* Let me out of here!' But I think it's an excess of egg in the pudding to talk about 'open sewers.' And when Larkin writes about jazz, for example, he's quite engaging." Martin Amis, whose brother was Larkin's godson and who appears in a 1981 letter ("Martin's book sounds piss"), was similarly staunch. "There's only one *really* horrible bit, where he describes a cricket match and writes about 'those black scum kicking up a din on the boundary—a squad of South African police would have sorted them out to my satisfaction,' and that's written to someone who's boringly likely to agree. You could never get from there to the poems. But I can feel a huge fiesta of false consciousness about to get under way—just what we don't need now."

Robert Conquest, who used to furnish Larkin with the occasional consoling dirty mag, took a robustly defensive position. He said that the notorious and contentious ellipses were the result of the editor cutting "tedious stuff " only, and to prove his point read me the missing sentence from one of Larkin's published epistles to himself. It did indeed contain a nugatory and pointless observation about a forgotten university appointment. "Anyway," added Conquest, "anyone who's a member of the united front against bullshit can see that Philip's foul mouth was a form of subversiveness. Saying the unsayable because it's unsayable."

The poet Andrew Motion, who is also Larkin's about-to-be biographer, was more fastidious. "Larkin, like Wordsworth, has two voices. One is of the street, so to say, and one is of Parnassus. It's true that in the letters you get the same *tension* as in the poetry—the temptations of slang and obscenity versus the yearning for language. Combined very strongly with the longing *to be elsewhere.*"

It was the first direct allusion I encountered to one of the few tropes that are present in both the letters and the poems: Larkin's awkwardly managed wish for death, balanced against his thwarted hunger for love. "I used to think," said Motion, "that Philip was the greatest poet in modern English of death and dying. Increasingly, though, I look upon him as the great verse critic of marriage and females."

This summer in America, Farrar, Straus & Giroux will do an intelligent and necessary thing by releasing Andrew Motion's biography first and the *Selected Letters* second, obviating some of the needless expenditure of ink that occurred in the London reviews. Motion has known for some time where the real problem lies. It lies somewhere among Larkin's repressed homosexuality (barely mentioned in the surviving letters), his latent anti-Semitism (only glancing in the letters), and the formative effect of his much-missed father, who died when Larkin was young and who was an active pre-war sympathizer of Nazism.

The P.C. warriors are so fixated on such frantically earnest "now" terms as "racismsexismisogyny," and so set on employing Larkin's case to discredit Englishness, that they have failed to register his most salient and atypical delinquency. As far as the letters can speak, they instruct us

that, in the period 1940 to 1945, Larkin expected Hitler to win the war or half hoped he would, or both. Absent from all the quick and easy citations of modern thought crime are such early-manhood bursts as this, from December 20, 1940: "Germany will win this war like a dose of salts, and if [saying] that gets me into gaol, a bloody good job too. Balls to the war. Balls to a good many things, events, people, and institutions." Or this, from April 7, 1942: "I agree we don't deserve to win." Or this, from July 6, 1942: "If there is any new life in the world today, it is in Germany. True, it's a vicious and blood-brutal kind of affair—the new shoots are rather like bayonets. It won't suit me. By 'new' life I don't mean better life, but a change, a new direction. Germany has revolted back too far, into the other extremes. But I think they may have many valuable new habits. Otherwise, how could [D. H. Lawrence] be called Fascist?"

Pretty un-English for 1942, and even the careful ambiguities have their element of relish. Elsewhere, and far too numerous to quote, are incessant bitter lampoons from Larkin about the British war effort, many of them written to a lifelong crony and reactionary cynic named Colin Gunner. Larkin himself, who made exactly two voyages "abroad" after 1945, had been taken by his father on two trips to see "the new Germany" before 1939. One has to inquire, of the father and son: did the apple fall very far from the tree? ("They fuck you up," all right.)

But it's at just this point that Larkin becomes more legible, more intelligible. A quarter of a century ago, and unknown to the P.C. practitioners, John Harrison published a book called *The Reactionaries.* It was a study of the overt sympathy for Fascism expressed by T. S. Eliot, Ezra Pound, W. B. Yeats, D. H. Lawrence, and Wyndham Lewis.

In an introduction, William Empson wrote of these warped, brilliant colossi, "May it not be that their curses are still operating, or their confusions adding to the fog, in some preventable way? Mr. Harrison feels that the political scandal of their weakness for Fascism is what most needs to be faced; and the great merit of his book is to present the evidence about that aspect of them coolly, with justice and understanding."

It wasn't at all simple for Harrison to theorize the Catholic anti-Semitism of Eliot, the mystical folk nationalism of Yeats, the dingbat currency and conspiracy schemes of Pound, the blood obsession of Lawrence, or the hatred of enlightenment manifested by Lewis. But he located the core quotation in *The Meaning of Culture,* by a now forgotten English author named John Cowper Powys, who in 1930 wrote, "Outworn, misused, misapplied for so long, the aristocratic ideal is now quite dead. There is no escape from machinery and modern inventions; no escape from city vulgarity and money power, no escape from the dictatorship of the uncultured."

Powys found his own solution: "An individual man or woman, carrying to a comfortless job through clanging streets the cheapest editions of some immortal book, can mount the stairs of his secret psychic watch-tower and think the whole ant heap into invisibility."

A real shock of recognition here—recognition of the crabbed, rancorous old librarian retreating behind his bound volumes to snarl and bark at the lapping tides of democracy and modernity. And the coincidence is not purely textual or biographical. Larkin's letters breathe a continual admiration for Powys ("Picking up the trails of Powys is a thing I'd dearly love to do") as well as for Lawrence, and especially for Lawrence's emphasis on blood, and on thinking with the blood at that. It is thus quite possible to place the reactionary poet from Hull within the classical tradition of European literary Fascism, though I doubt that either the Queen or Mrs. Thatcher was dimly or fully aware (respectively) of the fact.

Yet, just as the jaws of P.C. are about to clamp together, they spring apart. Because even at his most foul and spoiled and twisted, during his period of sniping cheaply from behind the lines at his own country's fight for survival, Larkin tried with every sinew of his imagination to be worthy of comparison to W. H. Auden ("It's no use short circuiting myself in an effort to out-Auden Auden"— December 31, 1941) and at a time when Auden was in his most leftist and anti-Fascist phase. Therefore, the most generous verdict is arguably the most durable. In his imperishable poetic obituary for Yeats, Auden dissolved the transient political differences between them by writing that

> Time that is intolerant
> Of the brave and innocent,
> And indifferent in a week
> To a beautiful physique,
>
> Worships language and forgives
> Everyone by whom it lives.

It forgives, you notice, rather than forgets. (No one is so dense as to argue that you can't discern the base prejudices of Pound and Eliot in their poems.) As if anticipating later stupidities on precisely this point, Auden was yet more explicit in adding:

> Time that with this strange excuse
> Pardoned Kipling and his views,
> And will pardon Paul Claudel,
> Pardons him for writing well.

To consider Larkin in this light is to appreciate that, perhaps paradoxically, what will survive of him is certainly not love but, equally certainly, art, and that poetry and language will always outlive the merely political, barely even registering the politically correct. Of course, it's not without interest that England's premier and preferred poet should have been such a prey to hatefulness. It even suggests that there may be a teensy *cultural* problem. That doesn't alter the point that the crude mixture of literature and politics is the problem in the first place. (pp. 82, 86, 88)

> *Christopher Hitchens, "D.W.E.M. Seeks to R.I.P.," in Vanity Fair, Vol. 56, No. 4, April, 1993, pp. 80, 82, 86, 88.*

Alan Brownjohn   (review date 2 April 1993)

[*Brownjohn is an English poet, novelist, and critic. In the*

following review, he focuses on the positive aspects of Larkin's life presented in Andrew Motion's biography of Larkin.]

The full-face dust-jacket photograph of the poet on the Larkin *Selected Letters* (1992) is much bigger than the one on the *Collected Poems* (1988). On Andrew Motion's biography the image expands even further, to a huge, eerie half-head: one spectacled eye, seven-eighths of the nose, large impassive mouth, jowl starting a five o'clock shadow. This horror—one can imagine the sort of sardonic comment Larkin might have passed on it—suggests not just his powerful personality (appropriately enough) but also a life still too close to focus. But the biographer's achievement in this deeply absorbing year-by-year history is to focus Larkin with authoritative clarity, and place him in perspective as a writer among a wide range of other public and private activities. At the same time, in the way of so many modern biographers, it tries to leave nothing to conjecture, and spares none of the warts on those droll, correct features.

A Writer's Life pushes forward by several stages the change in the reader's impression of Larkin effected by the *Letters*. Larkin the recluse, slowly writing the poems while he held down the routine library job, now transforms into Larkin the genial boss and brilliant administrator, creator at Hull of the finest modern university library, the diligent (and mostly unpaid) servant of a dozen literary committees and causes, the regular reviewer of books and jazz records who never missed a deadline.

His closer acquaintances saw all this outgoing industry. His closest friends knew also about his long, dutiful devotion to his widowed mother, his 40-year partnership with Monica Jones, his deep drinking, his health terrors. One or two even knew about the now notorious diaries, shredded on his death-bed instructions (Motion takes them to be "sexual logbooks, and a gigantic repository for bile, resentment, envy and misanthropy"). But no one could have counted at least four other important love affairs, conducted with a mixture of joy, agony, guilt and chronic, rationalising indecision.

We know from this book that one famous poem certainly does not sum up Larkin's views of his parents, Eva and Sydney. Larkin's devotion to Eva, maddening as she was, remained profound until her death; in her declining years he wrote her a letter a day. The faults she had, principally her complaining and hesitations (recurrently stressed by Motion, who gives a fairly harsh account of her) came out as virtues in the son: a "vivacious melancholy" (his own words) in his personality, and the ability in his poems to make something eloquent and resonant out of his own diffidence.

But Sydney was, to say the least, a complex parent. Ostensibly severe and dictatorial (attending Nuremberg rallies and amazingly keeping Nazi regalia in his Treasurer's office in Coventry City Hall) he was nevertheless a wide reader (Hardy, Wilde, Shaw, Lawrence) and tolerant, even indulgent and encouraging, about his son's taste in books, music, dress, and drink. From Sydney, Larkin took his administrative skills and his outward puritanism, more advantages than faults. Philip was admittedly too shy to challenge his parents by producing girl friends. But there is a remarkable ease, candour and fullness about the letters to Eva and Sydney quoted here which belies any assumption of simple remoteness or resentment. He largely got on with his Mum and Dad, confiding in them his ambitions, fears and failures where most of us would not.

They obviously approved of his literary hopes. Did they fully realise that their tall, stammering young man with the Oxford. First put the literary vocation before anything else? All his life he was unable to reconcile it with money-earning work, or domestic living, and absolutely not with the notion of marriage. At Oxford, and from Wellington to Leicester to Belfast, Larkin worked determinedly on his writing in his spare time. First it was to be fiction (the unpublished soft porn fantasies under the name "Brunette Coleman", then the real, extraordinary, published novels *Jill* and *A Girl in Winter*). And when the fiction dried up—two further novels were planned but never went beyond a few drafts—he concentrated on the rueful, poignant, fastidiously-crafted poems, which eventually, after a decade of discouragement and false starts, won him high praise.

All that time he lived in awful austere, not very private lodgings, a "Mr Bleaney" by choice. When circumstances finally rushed him (in Hull) into buying the house he could have afforded long before, he sat in the drab, conventional residence with blinds drawn, an acclaimed celebrity, feeling trapped and finished, cohabiting with Monica only when sickness made them mutually dependent.

When certain bizarre and shocking facts about a famous life become available, no biographer, let alone a publisher, would nowadays dare not to use them. So biographies become faithful and disappointing—or worse—about their subjects. With writers, there is the risk (which Motion gladly runs) of tethering the revealed sorrows and oddities of the sex life too tightly to the work. Nagging questions arise: Do we really need to know these things to appreciate Larkin's poems? Are the connections actually important to establish, or might they not undermine our enjoyment of the writing?

Where there is no provable or guessable connection Motion sometimes suggests a vaguer association. Thus, Larkin's poems "Wild Oats," "Sunny Prestatyn", "The Large Cool Store", and even "An Arundel Tomb" are cited as deriving (since Larkin read pornographic magazines) from "a masturbatory impulse and an addiction to solitude."

Well yes, if you want to be *that* psychological about them and have one's attention diverted from what really matters in those singularly moving and arresting poems.

Similarly, if one chooses to be shocked by the racist remarks displayed in a few of the *Letters,* and have that reduce the pleasure of the poetry, one may. The point there, surely, is that these objectionable prejudices, and other kinds of Larkin bile, remained private, a currency used with certain friends (and regrettably his mother), not showing themselves in public, or in actions of any kind. The editor of the *Letters,* Anthony Thwaite, found Larkin the *funniest* man he had ever met. Larkin's correspondence (how did he organise the time for that?) revealed

warm enthusiasms (as well as melancholy grouches), exuberant humour and a zest for friendship—right up to the end.

Did Andrew Motion, setting out to research the biography, imagine a shortish record of a quiet life? His work, which has taken seven years, has expanded into a long and magisterial account of the complex and fascinating man who was incomparably our best post-war poet, a work of immense narrative skill. Hardly a page seems dull or unnecessary.

> *Alan Brownjohn, "Close up on Life," in* The Times Educational Supplement, *No. 4005, April 2, 1993, p. 10.*

Larkin in a letter to Kingsley Amis dated August 20, 1943:

As far as I can see, all women are stupid beings. What is more, marriage seems a revolting institution, unless the parties have enough money to keep reasonably distant from each other—imagine sharing a bedroom with a withered old woman!

No, *sir.* A lonely bachelorhood interspersed with buggery and strictly-monetary fornication seems to me preferable. Still, I don't want to be a bore. I know perfectly well I shall get married—probably by someone who'll call me a 'funny, silly creature'.

Philip Larkin, in The Selected Letters of Philip Larkin, *edited by Anthony Thwaite, 1992.*

Kingsley Amis   (review date 3 April 1993)

[*A distinguished English novelist, poet, essayist, and editor, Amis was one of the "Angry Young Men," a group of British writers of the 1950s whose writings expressed bitterness and disillusionment with society. He and Larkin maintained a lifelong friendship. Below, Amis presents a negative assessment of Motion's biography of Larkin.*]

The author of this book consulted me repeatedly while preparing and writing it, and last year sent me a draft to check for factual accuracy where I could. If, as seems likely, Andrew Motion was as scrupulous with all his sources as he was with what I provided, then this must be one of the most truthful of modern biographies. Truthful, as I said, to fact; interpretation is a different matter.

As a volume of nearly 600 large pages, *Philip Larkin* is uncomfortable to hold on the lap, and, thanks to the method of binding, those pages will not stay lying down. The jacket design is repulsive. It consists mostly of a black-and-white photograph of about half of Larkin's face, blown up to about twice life-size and tilted over to one side, like a smart movie shot of about 50 years ago. Few would call him a handsome man, but he deserves better than such a distortion.

This is a critical biography, which is to say that it offers to explain and pass judgment on the subject's works as well as recounting events in his life, sometimes linking the two. As in biographies of other poets, to link the two tends to trivialise and de-universalise individual poems. Motion does not always avoid this danger:

> The precise source for 'Lines on a Young Lady's Photograph Album' is easy to trace, though Larkin altered some details. 'I mean,' says Winifred Arnott, 'there were in fact two albums, not one; there's not a picture of me wearing a trilby hat . . . ' Behind such details, and behind the feelings which make them precious, lies another, less obvious, source. By covertly admitting to the pleasure it takes in fantasy, the poem connects with the other pictures Larkin liked to gaze at: the photographs in pornographic magazines.

Of which more later. At other times a poem simply disappears under an avalanche of biographical detail:

> Begun on 14 February and completed after 15 pages of drafts on 28 March, 'Dockery and Son' describes a visit Larkin had made to his old college at Oxford, St John's, on the way back from the funeral of Agnes Cuming, his predecessor as librarian at Hull, almost exactly a year earlier. [Agnes Cuming had died on 8 March 1962, and her funeral had taken place on the 12th]. The precise circumstances help to explain why Larkin describes himself as 'death-suited' in the poem, as well as illuminating larger questions of theme and mood . . . [The poem] was a good last choice for the manuscript Larkin was preparing to send Monteith. On 11 June he made his final decision . . .

In the same literalising, diminishing way, 'Reference Back', a poem which in characteristic Larkin fashion moves from a particular moment to a general view of life and age, and a chilling one, is taken as merely the record of a single incident on a datable holiday from Hull. When connections or contrasts between poems or novels are suggested, they sink to the transatlantic-thesis level of the observation that 'mouths, which yearned for fulfilment in *Jill,* are here [in *A Girl in Winter*] punished,' meaning simply that there is an unsuccessful kiss in the one and a visit to the dentist in the other.

It will be seen that the argument keeps shifting from the work to the life, and it is the life or the supposed character of Philip Larkin that Motion, no doubt properly, is most concerned with. The current popularity of biographies testifies to the existence of a large public interested only tepidly in what a famous person achieved in public, like climbing a mountain or writing a book, but avidly in what he or she got up to in private and was 'really' like. Unfortunately, in the present case the famous person, like most writers, led a rather dull life among rather dull people and, more unusually, wrote thousands of extant letters illustrating the fact.

This might not matter so much if Motion added to his qualities of diligence and conscientiousness others, almost as desirable, such as skill, dash, ability to select, above all humour. By a second stroke of ill luck, he is deficient in

all of them. These shortcoming, or others, see to it that the portraits of some minor figures in the story, like Patsy Strang, seem woefully out of drawing. But perhaps in cases like this what should rather be stressed is the danger of reconstructing a character entirely from letters and second-hand information.

No such lack of personal contact extenuates Motion's almost complete failure to understand and convey the large part that jazz played in Larkin's life. Here, as well as a whole book of reviews of jazz records (*All What Jazz,* 1970) and scattered references elsewhere, he could observe and discuss at first hand. But he appears not even to have looked at all closely when Larkin was listening to a favourite record, describing him for instance as capering round his Hull sitting-room with a spilling gin and tonic in one hand 'while the other mimed the drummer's part'. Philip spill an expensive drink like gin? Mime the drummer's 'part' with one hand? Boy, will you get off?

At least Motion mostly avoids taking any high moral tone on the jazz question. So much cannot be said for his treatment of Larkin's fondness for 'pornography', as it is invariably and tendentiously called here. In fact what Larkin was buying in the Fifties and later was porn only by courtesy, pinups, girlie photos, tit magazines with nothing pubic ever shown, page-three stuff on a good day. But Motion draws in his skirt in pious horror every time the subject comes up, talking about it with the shocked disapproval he otherwise reserves for Larkin's 'racist' political effusions. He goes further in an interview he gave in the *Bookseller* of 26 February 1993.

First suggesting in his insightful way that the women in Larkin's poems are 'cleaned-up' versions of what he drooled over in less right-minded moments, Motion reveals that the day he uncovered Larkin's cache of 'pornography'

Larkin in a letter to J.B. Sutton dated October 30, 1949:

My views are very simple and childish. I think we are born, & grow up, & die. I think our view of life is formed before the age of 5 & any subsequent major alteration is partial & unsatisfying. Everything we do is done with the motive of pleasure & if we are unhappy it is because we are such silly bastards for thinking we should like whatever it is we find we don't like, or because events run counter to our plans, or because of the inevitable inroads of illness, death & time. Imagination & sensitivity are also great bringers of distress & are capacities for which no adequate function seems to have been provided.

If we seriously contemplate life it appears an agony too great to be supported, but for the most part our minds gloss such things over & until the ice finally lets us through we skate about merrily enough. Most people, I'm convinced, don't think about life at all. They grab what they think they want and the subsequent consequences keep them busy in an endless chain till they're carried out feet first.

Philip Larkin, in The Selected Letters of Philip Larkin, *edited by Anthony Thwaite, 1992.*

was the most important day in the writing of the book, because it was then that I realised that I had the opportunity to talk about a general truth, that the beautiful flower of art grows, on a long stalk, out of some very murky stuff.

Oh, so it was only *then* that he realised it, was it? Pfui! It seems we are supposed to regard Motion with awed respect for having intrepidly ventured into the very depths of squalor and infamy on our behalf. So be it. If he has never leered, or even looked, at a photograph of a naked female, he is some kind of freak. If he ever has, then he is no worse than a medium-sized hypocrite. (pp. 25-6)

> Kingsley Amis, "Simple Truth His Utmost Skill," in The Spectator, Vol. 270, No. 8595, April 3, 1993, pp. 25-6.

John Bayley   (essay date 22 April 1993)

[*In the following essay, Bayley disputes the assessment of Larkin's life and personality presented in Motion's biography as negative and moralistic, and argues that Larkin's character is best discovered in his poetry.*]

In 1974, with *High Windows* about to appear, Larkin lamented in a letter that critics would have passed the word around—*Donnez la côtelette à Larquin*—gave Larkin the chop. Of course he was wrong. The chorus of praise swelled higher than ever: with each slim volume the certainty and authority of the poems and their unique feel of personality left readers dazzled. Larkin first; the rest nowhere. And though no one said so—perhaps fellow-poets were too envious—they showed how indispensable rhyme-schemes as subtle yet as traditional as his could still be.

Now, with the letters and biography it is the personality that has got the chop. Clearly it was not PC; but amongst all that has been written about him that seems hardly relevant, though Doctors Eagleton, Paulin and Jardine have rubbed home the point that poetry is politics, and that Larkin's is now shown to be fundamentally out of order—'English' therefore bad. The establishment they represent takes for granted that poets now bring the right assumptions to their work, a point that struck me forcibly in the summer when acting as a judge for the Forward Poetry Prize, an admirable new scheme for giving some money to good poets, not necessarily young ones. As it turned out, Thom Gunn, once associated with Larkin in the 'Movement', was the chief beneficiary. But what struck me most about the numerous entries, all of which had been published in magazines or in booklet form, was that they were poems with the right attitudes, demonstrating subliminally or openly that their creators conformed, and had their hearts in the right place.

It seemed a bit like the Augustan ideal, or the Victorian convention. However wild and woolly their form and language, the poems had an underlying correctness, an unconscious wish to be ideologically sound. Mavericks were common, but true outsiders not. Augustan conformity had its Collins and its Blake and Smart: its mad poets who kicked over the traces. Victorian poetry had to have its nonsense and its horror writers, its Lears and Carrolls and Cities of Dreadful Night. Our version of this today might be Larkinian lugubriousness and derision, defeatism, irresponsibility—sentiments to which every bosom is capable of returning an echo, particularly in an era of national and social decline.

Might be, but isn't: there was no sign of a Larkin or of Larkinism among the entries for the poetry prize. Perhaps this was natural, considering the recent outcry against him: indeed from a social point of view it might even be considered a good sign. Much as the Augustans wanted remoralisation and tranquillity after the upheavals of civil war and restoration, so today we seem to desire a universally accepted morale-bestowing conformity. The arts acquiesce in this more than they seem to know. Indeed, such internal conformity often strikes one as virtually a product of its apparent opposite: widespread social and sexual toleration. We approve empowerment and being nonjudgmental. But as the Foucault camp used to say—from a rather different angle—such tolerance is itself insidiously repressive. It is not the bourgeois who exercise it today, but the wider and more indeterminate class of the ideologically sound.

So there was no question of being nonjudgmental about Larkin. Not just because he was not PC but because his whole personality, as openly and flagrantly revealed in his letters and by his biographer, was seen to constitute a kind of outrage. Paulin and Jardine were quite right that the poetry reveals it all: it had already done so to anyone who had really read it and delighted in its personality. The personality was what mattered; and the fact that Larkin brought no ready-made outside attitudes to it—good or bad. Like his hero Lawrence he was shamelessly himself.

The attack on Larkin is thus fundamentally an attack on the idea of personality—personality devoid of the appropriate ideological trimmings. For Larkin that was what art was all about. He declined to enter into any discussions about it, merely saying that he knew what got him, what for him was 'thrilling'. All forms of contemporary academic criticism reject such simple absoluteness, principally because English departments must ultimately be dedicated, even if only by the logic of their present-day organisation, to an ideas-centred pursuit of togetherness, a uniformity of response. Hence all official or quasi-official writing on Larkin gets him wrong. Larkin despised English departments (he got a First in one himself) and made no secret of his hilarity and contempt. They do not forgive him, however cleverly and enthusiastically they may have admired and dissected his poems; and publication of the letters and biography gives them a chance to show it.

The only comment on the subject which Larkin himself seems to have thoroughly approved of, and quotes in a letter, was by Clive James in his collection *The Metropolitan Critic*. 'Just now and again James says something really penetrating: "originality is not an ingredient of poetry, it is poetry"—I've been feeling that for years.' This suggests, among other things, how deep was his instinct for not bringing anything in from outside when he wrote: no *idées reçues*, no second-hand emotional baggage. He only 'thrilled' to the kind of poetry which did not do that, although he began by using other styles as models—Auden, Yeats, Hardy. He judged other poets of his time as phonies who used, not other styles but whatever attitudes were lying about, and were anxious to be in the swim. This in itself makes him an intractable subject for criticism's comparative techniques.

Much deeper than any ideological objection, however, is our assumption today about the language of art, or rather language in art. Since Adorno's and George Steiner's assertions that the horrors of the concentration-camps and the German final solution had made the language of poetry impossible, there has existed a lack of confidence in the potential of language to do more than stand by and wring its hands, as it does with each new atrocity in the utterances on radio and TV. Geoffrey Hill's poetry has made something of a speciality in distrusting language in this way; inventing, as it were, a precise and searching idiom of distrust. But the real poet of these horrors, Paul Celan, had no such distrust. His vision of them is wholly individual, wholly his own; so that his words exist not beside the thing they describe but have become it. The language of real poetry can do that; and in so doing, as R. P. Blackmur put it, 'adds to the sum of available reality'.

It is significant that no fewer than three reviewers of the Larkin biography quoted Auden's epitaph on Yeats. Time, says Auden, 'Worships language and forgives / Everyone by whom it lives.' 'With this strange excuse' it pardons Yeats and Kipling, and will even, seemingly, pardon Paul Claudel; and Larkin as well no doubt. But why the whole question of pardon, deployed with ironic lightness by Auden but now accepted dead seriously, should come into the matter is not easy to see. You do not pardon an aardvark for being an aardvark. Larkin, Celan, Auden himself, are all in their different ways originals. Their poetry is itself, and not another thing; with no trace of what the post-war German poet Günter Eich called 'controlled language'.

In this context the idea of disapproval seems engrained in contemporary social attitude: all the odder, as I remarked, because in so many other contexts we are adjured not to be 'judgmental'. Even Alan Bennett in this journal, friendliest of Larkin's reviewers, found Larkin's family situation and father 'grotesque' because of the father's pro-Nazi views. But in those days eccentrics flourished, and views of all kinds were taken to be one's own affair. It was not exactly toleration, more a kind of innocence, an instinctive respect for individuality. Post-war events have certainly seen that off. Anthony Burgess remembered in his review of the Larkin biography attending a fancy-dress party in 1941 dressed as an SS officer. Nobody took much notice. Today it would seem a vicious provocation or an act of tasteless bravado. Humour and ridicule, antidote and disinfectant, have all become politicised.

Larkin's independence, or irresponsibility, is all the more striking because it was always there. Amis, Wain, even Conquest, were once conventionally of the left, as the thing to be: Larkin gave it all the cold shoulder. And they remained politicised in a way that he did not. He made fun of it all in his own way, as the late poem 'Aubade' makes

a joke and a pose out of his horror of dying. Nothing in the proprieties can be more serious than a joke; and his certainly do not need the pardon and patronage that his biographer, or even the friendly reviewer, have given him. All tightly compressed poetry, Blake's or Celan's, makes a joke where ordinary language waffles or euphemises. 'Der Tod ist ein Meister aus Deutschland sein Auge ist blau.' Celan's joke is the best, or the worst, of all.

Since the biography and the letters the correct attitude to Larkin seems to have become a version of the rather snooty though reverberant epitaph which Mallarmé made for Poe. 'Tel qu'en lui-même enfin l'éternité le change.' But death and immortal fame have not turned this poet into pure essence, nor his writings. Larkin was his own Boswell, and the letters are just as much a work of art as the poems, with the same power of eliciting fascination, curiosity, hilarity. Who but Larkin would have signed off to one correspondent 'Ogokuo (what happens if you type Philip one space along)'. Postmen, like doctors, carried such jests from house to house. 'What use is an endearment and a joke?' he ended an early unpublished poem about letter-writing. Of course he knew that in the best poetry, as in the best letters, they are of paramount use. Kidding on the level was his natural sport, as Dr Johnson said that comedy was Shakespeare's.

No doubt he really did have 'a huge contempt for all "groups" that listen to or discuss poetry'; but he revelled in all kinds of ceremonial, because ceremony was both traditional and moving, and next door to farce. The Great Comedian rejoiced in the wickedly explicit ('my own mind is so shallow that I can only respond to lighter poems, written in total explicit style') because it concealed the fact that he really was a Good Egg, if not necessarily 'one of the best'. When he had to move from the High Windows flat his despair was characteristically comical. 'Abbey National bum. Neighbours bum. Rates bum. Retirement bum. Pension bum. Emergency bum. Cause for concern bum. After a long illness bravely borne bum. In his day thought to be representative of bum . . . ' Bum—including his own and Mrs Thatcher's—was the time-honoured way of signing off a letter to Kingsley Amis. Childish stuff ? His last letter to Amis ends: 'You will excuse the absence of the usual valediction.'

The valediction, like the poetry, works by a sort of uncovenanted reversal. Grandeur comes out of diminishment in poem after poem—'Absences', 'Days', 'Coming', 'Ignorance', 'Sad Steps', 'Dockery and Son', 'The Old Fools', 'Going', 'Love Songs in Age'—all of them. Like the ill-tempered priest and doctor in 'Days', running over the fields in their long coats, the heroic and the sublime make their reluctant appearance willy-nilly. It is the paradox of great art distrusted by Adorno and yet manifested in Celan: poetry becoming another thing—its language transforming the place of horror or the place of boredom. Can readers really feel depressed and lowered by Larkin? He seems to me to uplift, to be in a comic sense 'too good for this life', like the desecrated lady on the poster advertisement for Sunny Prestatyn. Even his fear of death can calm and satisfy ours. (After 'Aubade', he had a letter from a lady of 72 'saying she felt as I did once but now doesn't mind'.) But, as happens with other great writers, everyone has their own Larkin. Mine is not that of his biographer Andrew Motion, whose good intentions seem to speak from beyond too great a gap in culture and time.

John Bayley, "Aardvark," in London Review of Books, *Vol. 15, No. 8, April 22, 1993, p. 11.*

Stuart Wright   (review date Summer 1993)

[*Below, Wright evaluates* Selected Letters, *commenting "through these letters we do get a splendid kaleidoscopic self-portrait of" Larkin.*]

Kingsley Amis wrote in a tribute to Philip Larkin on his sixtieth birthday in 1982 that he was the "best letter-writer" Amis had ever known. "To this day a glimpse of the Hull postmark brings that tiny tingle of excitement and optimism, like a reminder of youth." Amis repeated this assessment nearly verbatim in his *Memoirs* (1991). Larkin's own view on letters is expressed in a poem he abandoned in August 1953: "I know, none better, / The eyelessness of days without a letter."

Philip Larkin was a prodigious and often highly entertaining correspondent. This generous selection of over seven hundred letters from the thousands that he wrote between 1940 and his death in December 1985 amplifies much of what we already know about Larkin the man from reading his poetry, critical work, and interviews. I would argue with Donald Davie's recent (qualified) appraisal, for this is the sort of person he chose to *seem* to be. So be forewarned: this book will not make pleasant reading for the humorless politically correct. If, on the other hand, you do not object to a misanthrope's self-deprecating good humor, his bilious verbal assaults on friends and enemies alike, and his sharp jabs at contemporary institutions and mores, university education, and the like, then prepare yourself for a delightful romp through Larkinland.

Was Philip Larkin a xenophobe and racist? Very probably. He refers to Frogland, Hunland, and Coonland; only rarely to France, Germany, and Africa. And, yes, he uses the N—word, but usually in the Anglo-Indian sense of Kipling's time to refer to all dark-skinned peoples. I noted only one exception to this rule, when he added "and wogs," undoubtedly for the sake of clarity and inclusion. Larkin's dislike of places abroad is well known. Writing from Belfast in 1951 he observed that the "Irish are rotten with drink in my opinion—drivelling slack jawed blackguards." Just over a year later, writing this time from Dublin, he noted the "collection of baboon-faced rogues, & provincial patriotisms, and shoddy shops full of shoddy goods," advising his correspondent that "if you want to eat cleanly cheaply & enjoyably in Dublin," then you must "TAKE SANDWICHES FROM BELFAST." (I wonder if his feelings toward the Irish were at this time hardened by the fact that, however incredible it must now seem, the manuscript of *The Less Deceived* had been turned down by the Dolmen Press.) But, soon after returning to England from Ireland to take a library post at the University of Hull in 1955, Larkin complained to the wife of the Irish poet Richard Murphy that the Mackeson-swilling English "are miles uglier and noisier than the Irish."

Was he a misogynist? Every tribute I have ever read by a female member of Larkin's 100-plus library staff at Hull was uniformly laudatory in her estimation of his personal regard for all of them. He was praised by one and all for the respectful professional treatment he exhibited. Larkin was twice (at least) engaged, and he conducted a regular and affectionate correspondence with his women friends, among them his former fiancées, and rarely if ever vacationed alone. Larkin addressed them variously as, for example, Honeybird, Dearest Honeybear, and Sugarbush (Patsy Avis Strang Murphy), or Dearest Bun (short for bunny rabbit), and a simple Dearest (Monica Jones). Indeed we learn from an excerpt from Andrew Motion's forthcoming biography of Larkin that, although rarely separated by great physical distance, he and Monica Jones wrote letters to each other or spoke on the telephone—sometimes both—almost daily from 1955 until mid-1983, when he took her into his own home to nurse her back to health after a debilitating (and lingering) case of shingles. In fact Jones never fully recovered and Larkin, until the final painful weeks preceding his own death, continued to look after her, despite his own rapid and painful deterioration after surgery for esophageal cancer. As for the other woman in his life, his mother, who was widowed in 1948 but who lived almost three decades longer, dying in 1977 at the age of ninety-one, Larkin traveled to visit her every weekend from the time he moved to Hull in 1955, wrote frequently, and telephoned her often. From the evidence of his letters to others, he was extremely solicitous about her health and well-being (although he rarely shows his concern with much affection).

My hunch is that, for Philip Larkin, it was more a matter of misogamy than of misogyny. His wish to be alone was complimented by his pence-pinching nature. In his *Memoirs* Kingsley Amis recalls, from a letter that Larkin wrote him, probably in the mid-1950s, how he hated taking girls out and wasting money on them. The letter is not published in this selection (Amis lost a number of them between moves and marriages), but he recollects Larkin's stating emphatically that "I don't—I *don't*—want to [do that] and spend circa £5 when I can toss off in five minutes, free, and have the rest of the evening to myself." Given the choice then, it was money over girls; a life to himself, solitude self-imposed. Marriage to Larkin, Amis recalls, meant "you promise to give someone half your money for the rest of your life and not to fuck anyone else." Aside from this Larkin's half-joking notion on the subject of sex is simple: "Sex is too wonderful to be shared with anybody else."

Larkin's closeness with money is also evident in his business affairs. He was extremely careful with book contracts and frequently sought free advice from the Society of Authors (he dispensed with Literary agents after his second novel was published in 1947). Although he published exclusively with Faber and Faber from 1964 onward, he squeezed from that house every extra little half-percent royalty possible. His love-hate relationship with George Hartley, founder and publisher of the Marvell Press, is largely based, I believe, on Hartley's hard-headed and tenacious good business sense in holding on to the republication rights to the poems published in *The Less Deceived*

(1955); his press is listed on the title page with Faber and Faber as copublisher of Larkin's *Collected Poems* (1988). And, although Larkin refers to Hartley as "the ponce of Hessle" and "The Thing from Outer Hessle," he nevertheless admired Hartley's ability to extract greater reprint fees than did Faber. Hartley's wilfulness and tenacity prevented publication of Larkin's selected poems during the poet's lifetime, but these letters suggest that, despite his complaints, the poet did not mind so much—just so long as he got his penceworth for his poems.

Philip Larkin seems to have had a lifelong interest in pornography (news to many of us). These letters, especially those to Kingsley Amis and Robert Conquest, are full of references to specific issues of girlie magazines, whips-and-chains movies (real and imaginary), and nostalgic references to the porn shops of yesteryear. Just short of his sixtieth birthday Larkin complained in a letter to Amis about the poor quality of programming on the BBC. "Why," he asked, why "don't they show NAKED WOMEN, or PROS AND CONS OF CORPORAL PUNISHMENT IN GIRLS' SCHOOLS?" No harm done, I suppose, and doubtless old Kingsley chuckled, just as he was meant to do. It is clear that Philip Larkin, "half-drunk" (see "Aubade") on gin or beer, or an "expensive bottle or cheap port" (letter to Conquest, 2 May 1974), alone and late on many an evening, adored writing his friends to amuse them as well as himself. And in a significant way, I suppose, letterwriting also filled the void when poems simply did not come, as was frequently the case after the early 1960s.

Was Larkin a misopedist? Did he play W. C. Fields to his friends' young children, the Baby LaRoys of his life? Consider this advice to his close friend Judy Egerton in 1958: "Have a happy Christmas. Drop laudanum on the children's plum pudding, for a happy Xmas afternoon." A few years later, again writing to Mrs. Egerton, announcing his time of arrival at her London flat as 8 P.M., he says: "Trust children will be chloroformed by then." (Maybe he did not like the Egerton children.) Martin Amis reports that as a child he feared Uncle Philip and dreaded his visits. Martin's father Kingsley records that Larkin once told him that when he was growing up he thought he disliked everybody, but that when he got older he realized it was only children he disliked. And yet Larkin wrote a lovely poem for the infant Sally Amis, "Born Yesterday," which is reminiscent of the "potent music" of Yeats's "A Prayer for My Daughter." (See Larkin's introduction to the 1966 reprint of *The North Ship*.) The poet addresses the newborn Sally: "Tightly-folded bud, / I have wished for you something / None of the others would"; then he moves through "the usual stuff" others would wish for her; and he concludes with his own, purely Larkinesque wish that, "may you be dull— / If that is what a skilled, / Vigilant, flexible, / Unemphasised, enthralled / Catching of happiness is called."

As most readers of Larkin's criticism already know, he did not think well of much that was modern or of the work of his contemporaries, especially their fiction or poetry. He was not being altogether disingenuous when he wrote this to Anthony Thwaite at the end of 1973: "Personally I should need only 2 words to describe English poetry since 1960 ('horse-shit'—Monica says that is actually one word)."

Robert Conquest must have shared many of Larkin's views on other writers, especially John Wain, who proved a favorite and frequent target caught in the crossfire. In one of his earliest letters to Conquest, 24 July 1955, Larkin established the Wain pattern when he asked, "Have you read John's new book. I loved it . . . till about p. 13." And there is a humorous description of Wain (who always seems to have attempted originality in his attire), "dressed in a beret and leather flying jacket," sporting a "chestnut walking stick." Larkin adds: "I have a photograph of him looking like a sexual maniac utterly out of control standing outside a lady's underwear shop in Castle Lane." (Larkin's photograph is reproduced in this volume, and be sure to compare the complete verbal description to the photograph.)

Nor did Larkin ever seem to have warmed up to Ted Hughes, his fellow northerner. (He may have been mildly envious of Hughes's early recognition and success.) Larkin delighted in reporting to Conquest in June 1975 that at a recent poetry festival "a woman shrieked and vomited during a Ted Hughes reading," adding a personal note: "I must say that I've never felt like shrieking." Larkin and his friends could not abide the theatrics of the Sitwells. In 1984, responding to Patrick Taylor-Martin for sending him Osbert Sitwell's *Left Hand, Right Hand!*, Larkin relates how "many years ago Kingsley & I devised a literary award for the book of the year combining the greatest pretension and the least talent: it was called the Osbert."

Not all of these letters are mean-spirited. There is a tender, deeply moving note to the Scottish poet Douglas Dunn, who worked for Larkin at the university library, on the death of his young wife, not yet thirty years old. Larkin begins by saying that he does not "know whether it is harder to speak or write" to Dunn, because "whichever I am doing seems the more difficult." He goes on to mention his last visit to Mrs. Dunn's bedside, and thanks Dunn for allowing it. "I shall always remember her composure and courage," Larkin writes, "and even the gaiety with which she made it, incredibly, a happy occasion." He goes on to mention the celebratory nature of the funeral service, noting that it "quite transcended the wretchedness that was inevitably there too." He then closes: "Please don't bother to answer this, but when you would like an hour or two of talk, drink, jass, just ring me. . . . Then we'll fix something up."

The editor, Anthony Thwaite, himself a poet of some standing, Larkin's longtime friend, and coexecutor of his literary estate as well as editor of the *Collected Poems,* for the most part has done a good job. His stated purpose, in addition to providing this selection, has been to annotate the letters "lightly and usefully, not pedantically." The book is too large. There are too many of the artist-as-a-young-man letters to James Sutton, Larkin's childhood friend. The Sutton letters comprise nearly 90 percent of the first 175 pages.

No letters to Larkin's parents have been included, even

though he wrote his mother regularly. Much critical commentary has been given to these lines from Larkin's "This Be The Verse" (1971), first published in *High Windows:* "They fuck you up, your mum and dad. / They may not mean to, but they do." Thwaite's odd rationale for excluding this highly important and potentially revealing correspondence is that these letters "would have swelled the book to unmanageable proportions." By any reckoning this is unsound editorial accounting.

Beyond the editor's control, however, is the absence of letters to Bruce Montgomery, the writer of detective fiction Edmund Crispin, who was Larkin's Oxford chum and the dedicatee of *A Girl in Winter.* Montgomery's papers are on sealed deposit at the Bodleian Library until 2035. George Hartley withheld his letters from publication pending their sale. (Much useful information on this particular relationship may be found in Jean Hartley's *Philip Larkin, The Marvell Press, and Me.*) Otherwise the most important dramatis personae seem to be represented. Thwaite also provides a generous list of recipients whose letters he examined but did not include owing to repetitiveness. Informative individual biographies of Larkin's correspondents precede the text, as does a helpful chronology of Larkin's life.

For a book of this sort to be useful, its index must be inclusive. The thirty-page, double-columned general index appears solid until one begins to seek out specific information in the letters. There are many omissions of named individuals (other than recipients). Infinitely more troublesome, however, is the lack of a general index entry for *Larkin, Philip:* on women, on children, on poetry, and so on.

Finally there is a curious mix of too much and too little in the editor's annotations. Too much, for example, includes his dutiful (and tiresome) identification by full name and instrument, dozens of them, of every jazz musician Larkin mentions in the letters of the 1940s written to James Sutton and others. Thwaite probably got hold of a good biographical dictionary for jazz and went to town with it. One inclusive note might well have done the job, with a simple reference to Larkin's delightful *All What Jazz* and its index. If, on the other hand, Larkin mentions the name *Coleman,* then it would be well to distinguish Coleman *Hawkins* (he made the index) from *Ornette* Coleman (he didn't make it).

A reliable medical dictionary would have helped Thwaite out with *chondromalacia patellae,* Andrew Motion's knee complaint, which Thwaite inexplicably renders in a note into some sort of pidgin Spanish or Portuguese. And besides which, if he wanted to footnote this at all, then the words *softening of the kneecap cartilage* would have sufficed to satisfy the lay reader and kept Thwaite out of trouble.

In a letter dealing with poetry, is it necessary for the editor to identify by name in separate footnotes "that posturing old ass W.B.Y." and "that cosmopolitan lisping no-good W.H.A."? Thwaite has attempted to cover both sides of the Atlantic in his annotations: the American edition of this

book is inevitable. He is inconsistent in degree and manager in his annotations.

More troublesome, perhaps, are the deficiencies in the annotation. One example will suffice. In April 1969 when writing to Robert Conquest, Larkin asks: "Why is Kingsley sueing (suing?) the BBC? Full details please." One month and one page of text later, he again asks Conquest about the suit. The editor never explains what, if anything, happened.

I suppose these complaints are mostly niggling. Anthony Thwaite mainly has done a good job—by letting Philip Larkin do most of the work. And in so doing, he has succeeded in showing how consistently Larkin emerges from behind all his masks as, finally, neither completely philistine nor as narrowly insular as Larkin himself would have you think he is. Philip Larkin wrote letters for his own enjoyment, for the sheer pleasure of writing, as well as to amuse his correspondent. I heartily and unequivocally agree with Thwaite that through these letters we do get a splendid kaleidoscopic self-portrait of the man: "the lonely, gregarious, exuberant, desolate, close-fisted, generous, intolerant, compassionate, eloquent, foul-mouthed, harsh and humorous Philip Larkin"—surely England's most popular poet, and one of the finest poets, of our time. (pp. 427-33)

Stuart Wright, "Larkin's Outgoing Mail," in The Sewanee Review, *Vol. CI, No. 3, Summer, 1993, pp. 427-33.*

Martin Amis   (essay date 12 July 1993)

[*Amis is a popular English novelist, critic, and satirist of contemporary life. In the following essay, he analyzes the goals and assumptions of "politically correct" commentators in evaluations of Larkin's life and faults Andrew Motion's treatment of Larkin as impatient and judgmental.*]

When poets die, there is usually a rush to judgment: a revaluation, a retaliation—a reaction, anyway. We know how these things go, with the poets. He who was praised and popular is suddenly found to be facile and frictionless. He who was mocked and much remaindered is suddenly found to be "strangely" neglected. In 1985, the year of his death, Philip Larkin was unquestionably England's unofficial laureate, our best-loved poet since the war: better loved, qua poet, than John Betjeman, who was loved also for his charm, his famous giggle, his patrician bohemianism, and his televisual charisma, all of which Larkin notably lacked. Now, in 1993, Larkin is something like a pariah, or an untouchable. He who was beautiful is suddenly found to be ugly.

The word "Larkinesque" used to evoke the wistful, the provincial, the crepuscular, the sad, the unloved; now it evokes the scabrous and the supremacist. The word "Larkinism" used to stand for a certain sort of staid, decent, wary Englishness; now it refers to the articulate far right. In the early eighties, the common mind imagined Larkin as a reclusive yet twinkly drudge—bald, bespectacled, bicycle-clipped, slumped in a shabby library gaslit against the dusk. In the early nineties, we see a fuddled Scrooge and bigot, his singlet-clad form barely visible through a mephitis of alcohol, anality, and spank magazines. The reaction against Larkin has been unprecedentedly violent, as well as unprecedentedly hypocritical, tendentious, and smug. Its energy does not—could not—derive from literature: it derives from ideology, or from the vaguer promptings of a new ethos. In a sense, none of this matters, because only the poems matter. But the spectacle holds the attention. This is critical revisionism in an eye-catching new outfit. The reaction, like most reactions, is just an overreaction. To get an overreaction, you need plenty of overreactors. Somebody has to do it. And here they all are, busy overreacting.

There are those who believe that the trouble began with the *Collected Poems,* in 1988. Its editor, Anthony Thwaite, who also edited Larkin's *Selected Letters,* decided not to segregate the published poems from the unpublished. So instead of the three volumes of clearly finished work—*The Less Deceived* (1955), *The Whitsun Weddings* (1964), and *High Windows* (1974)—with all the other stuff tucked away at the back, we get a looser and more promiscuous corpus, containing squibs and snippets, rambling failures later abandoned, lecherous doggerel, and confessional curiosities like the frightening late poem "Love Again":

> Love again: wanking at ten past three
> (Surely he's taken her home by now?),
> The bedroom hot as a bakery,
> The drink gone dead, without showing how
> To meet tomorrow, and afterwards,
> And the usual pain, like dysentery.
>
> Someone else feeling her breasts and cunt,
> Someone else drowned in that lashwide
> stare . . .

You could say that the editorial decision had a clouding effect on the poems. You could even argue that it went against Larkin's spirit. Larkin left a lot of good things out. His œuvre (like his taste) was narrow, but it was crystallized; he could circle around a poem for years, in drafts, before completing or rejecting it. In any event, Larkin the man had started to look a little stranger. The *Collected Poems* didn't open him to attack. But it might have softened him up.

The frontal assault began in the autumn of 1992, with the English publication of the *Selected Letters.* The charge was led by Tom Paulin, who is well known, in the U.K., for his literary criticism, his poetry, his controversialism, and his small-screen losses of temper. In the correspondence columns of the *Times Literary Supplement* (and on television) Paulin articulated the case against. It centered on accusations of "race hatred": "racism, misogyny and quasi-fascist views." He suggested that the editor, Thwaite, had doctored the letters with ellipses to suppress even more "violently racist" passages than those he was prepared to include. Paulin summarized: "For the present, this selection stands as a distressing and in many ways revolting compilation which imperfectly reveals and conceals the sewer under the national monument Larkin became."

I remember thinking, when I saw the fiery Paulin's opening shot: We're not really going to do this, are we? But the new ethos was already emplaced—and, yes, we really were going to do this. On Paulin's terms, too: his language set the tone for the final assault, and mop-up, which came this spring with the publication of Andrew Motion's *Philip Larkin: A Writer's Life . . . Revolting, sewer:* such language is essentially unstable; it calls for a contest of the passions, and hopes that the fight will get dirty. (Blake Morrison, another poet, welcomed Paulin's intervention, with its summoning of the cloacal and the diseased, as—of all things—"salutary." Look that word up.) Thus the reception of the "Life" was marked by the quivering nostril, and by frequent recourse to the pomaded hanky, the smelling salts, and the sick bag. Writing in the London *Times,* Peter Ackroyd attributed "a rancid and insidious philistinism" to the "foul-mouthed bigot." Similarly, Bryan Appleyard saw, or nosed, "a repellent, smelly, inadequate masculinity" in "this provincial grotesque." ("To the objective eye he seems to have been almost wholly repulsive.") A. N. Wilson, in a piece graciously entitled "Larkin: the old friend I never liked," said that "Larks" was a "really rather nasty, prematurely aged man," and "really a kind of petty-bourgeois fascist," and "really a nutcase."

We get an idea of the breadth of the debate when we see that it extended to the normally tranquil pages of the Library Association *Record,* alongside headlines like "New approach to DNH PL review" and "Funding blow to NVQ Lead Body." Here an unnamed columnist called the Commoner compared Larkin to David Irving (the historian who keeps discovering that the Holocaust never happened, and who, whether by accident or design, looks more like Hitler every year); the Commoner also said, in conclusion, that Larkin's books "should be banned." The more senior commentators in the mainstream press are, of course, not so impetuous. But offended senses rouse the will; and the will looks around for something to do about it. They can't ban—or burn—Larkin's books. What they can embark on is the more genteel process of literary disposal. A third alternative would be to group Larkin with the multitude of other major writers who harbored undemocratic (or predemocratic) opinions; but they're too stirred up for that—the offense is too rank and too immediate. So: "a sporadically excellent minor poet who has been raised to an undeserved monumentality" (Appleyard); "essentially a minor poet who, for purely local and temporary reasons, acquired a large reputation" (Ackroyd); "he seems to me more and more minor. . . . [The poems] are good—yes—but not *that* good, for Christ's sake" (Wilson).

In late April, when the smoke was clearing after the appearance of the biography, Andrew Motion reviewed the controversy in his column in the London *Observer.* Sadder and wiser—not shocked, just disappointed—Motion identified several regrettable tendencies in the anti-Larkin crusade: the lack of sociohistorical context (Larkin, "alas," was pretty typical of his time and place); the failure to distinguish private from public utterance ("We need to remind ourselves that we are dealing with Dr Larkin here, not Dr Goebbels"); "the evidence of people struggling in the straitjacket of political correctness"; and the naïve "conflation of life and art." Such a conflation, he went on:

> rest[s] on the assumption that art is merely a convulsive expression of personality. Sometimes in its purest lyric moments, it may be. More generally, it is a suppression of personality . . . an adaptation, an enlargement. It's intensely disappointing to read literary commentators who write as if they don't understand that art exists at a crucial distance from its creator.

Which sounds—and is—very sensible. But what we can also hear is the whirr of bicycle spokes: for the *Observer* piece is in fact a Tour de France of backpedalling. Unstridently, often rather hesitantly, and even sensitively, Motion's book commits all the sins that he is now wryly shaking his head over. It is not a position so much as an attitude, or just a tone. *Philip Larkin: A Writer's Life* is confidently managed, and chasteningly thorough; it is also an anthology of the contemporary tendencies toward the literal, the conformist, and the amnesiac. Future historians of taste wishing to study the Larkin fluctuation will not have to look very much further.

The book—the life—is rich in the authentic poetry of dowdiness and deprivation, although Motion hears it faintly or not at all. Hardly anything in Larkin's letters is as thrillingly grim as the little clump of words and numerals in their top right-hand corners: Flat 13, 30 Elmwood Avenue, Belfast; 200 Hallgate, Cottingham, East Yorkshire; 192A Hallgate, Cottingham, Yorks; 172 London Road, Leicestershire ("I am established in an attic with a small window, a bed, an armchair, a basket chair, a carpet, a reading lamp THAT DOESN'T WORK, a small electric fire THAT DOESN'T WORK, and a few books"); Glentworth, King St, Wellington, Salop. Even his holiday spots sound far from festive: for example, Dixcart Hotel, Sark. No, the place-names don't help. "I envy you your visit to Sledmere," he writes to an intrepid acquaintance. When his girlfriend's mother gets her fatal heart attack, she does so "at her home in Stourport-on-Severn." Watch the sap rising as Larkin contemplates his summer break:

> My holidays loom like fearful obstacle-races: Mallaig-Weymouth with no sleeper (probably) & no reserve seats: they reserve seats, it seems, only on days when there will be enough to go around. On July 25 & Aug. 1—two busiest days in the year—*they don't*. I'M TRAVELLING ON BOTH.

One significant address was 73 Coten End, Warwick. This was the house that contained Larkin's parents, Sydney and Eva. Motion is quietly persuasive about the feel of the household, with its airlessness and constraint. Nor does he make too much of various sexy discoveries about Sydney Larkin's pro-German—even pro-Nazi—bent. It seems that Sydney attended several Nuremberg rallies in the thirties; bizarrely, he kept some sort of mechanical statue of Hitler on his mantelpiece, "which at the touch of a button leapt into a Nazi salute." Even a Nazi might have found that mannequin a little too kitsch, and insufficiently serious. Old Sydney, a city treasurer, sounds like a miserably typical eccentric of the prewar English provinces: a mood tyrant, a man who set the emotional barometer, and

set it low, for everyone around him. In an unpublished autobiographical fragment cited by Motion, Larkin wrote, "When I try to tune into my childhood, the dominant emotions I pick up are, overwhelmingly, fear and boredom. . . . I never left the house without the sense of walking into a cooler, cleaner, saner and pleasanter atmosphere." Sydney died in 1948, when Larkin was in his midtwenties; and Eva then began a widowhood that was to last almost as long as her marriage. During those twenty-nine years, Larkin wrote to her several times a week. None of these letters appears in the *Letters* (there are presumably many thousands of them), but from Motion's quotes we see that they were candid and detailed, and were not dashed off in a couple of minutes. Her letters to him are almost artistic in their flair for the trivial. Here is an especially lively extract:

> I do hope you achieved some warmth after loading all your apparel upon the bed like that. Of course you ought not to have changed those pants—remember that I thought it very unwise at the time.

Larkin's life, Motion writes in his introduction, was not "much diversified by event." This is one way of putting it. What he gives us, then, is chronic inactivity in an epic frame (five hundred and seventy pages in the British edition). This is one way of doing it. Larkin grew up, studied at Oxford, had a series of jobs as a librarian (and as nothing else), grew fat, grew frail, and died. War, travel, marriage, children: none of this ever happened to him. The poverty of event is best illustrated by the kinds of nonevent that Motion finds himself including. When Larkin attends a wedding or a musical ("he took Monica to London to see *The Boy Friend*"), when he involves himself in the expansion of the Hull University Library ("The existing plans consisted of two stages—Stage 1 and Stage 2—the first of which envisaged a central administrative three-storey block with a two-storey wing of the same height joined to it on the south side"), when in the course of his duties he is sent on a short tour of northern universities to study "issue desk layouts," we get to hear about it. No, nothing happened. Larkin worked nine to five, then wrote, then drank; he coped with his mother, he corresponded with his friends, and he had perhaps half a dozen love affairs. And that was all.

The attics-digs-lodgings period lasted from 1943, when Larkin left home, to 1955, when he arrived at Hull (where he would dourly remain). It was in 1955 that he commemorated those years in "Mr Bleaney":

> "This was Mr Bleaney's room . . . "
>
> So it happens that I lie
> Where Mr Bleaney lay, and stub my fags
> On the same saucer-souvenir, and try
> Stuffing my ears with cotton-wool, to drown
> The jabbering set he egged her on to buy.
> I know his habits—what time he came down,
> His preference for sauce to gravy, why
>
> He kept on plugging at the four aways—
> Likewise their yearly frame: the Frinton folk
> Who put him up for summer holidays,
> And Christmas at his sister's house in Stoke.

But if he stood and watched the frigid wind
Tousling the clouds, lay on the fusty bed
Telling himself that this was home, and grinned,
And shivered, without shaking off the dread

That how we live measures our own nature,
And at his age having no more to show
Than one hired box should make him pretty sure
He warranted no better, I don't know.

In such habitats, Larkin's nature was being measured.
And his sexuality was fermenting, or congealing. Earlier,
at Oxford, he had briefly kept a dream journal. This is Motion:

> Dreams in which he is in bed with men (friends
> in St John's, a "negro") outnumber dreams in
> which he is trying to seduce a woman, but the
> world in which these encounters occur is uni-
> formly drab and disagreeable. Nazis, black dogs,
> excrement and underground rooms appear time
> and time again, and so do the figures of parents,
> aloof but omnipresent.

Which sure looks like a mess. He had also devoted a ridiculous amount of time and energy to the composition,
under the pseudonym Brunette Coleman, of prose fictions
about schoolgirls ("As Pam finally pulled Marie's tunic
down over her black stockinged legs, Miss Holden, paus-
ing only to snatch a cane from the cupboard . . . ").
Along the way, he was developing a set of sexual attitudes
as an obvious and understandable defense against his shyness (bad stammer), his unattractiveness ("My baldness
seems to be keeping its end up well": he was twenty-six),
and his fear of failure and of unrequited expense (he was
always psychopathically cheap). Thus: "Women . . .
repel me inconceivably. They are shits." Or "All women
are stupid beings." To his old childhood friend
J. B. Sutton he confessed to feelings of anxiety and cow-
ardliness (he worried that he "had been 'doctored' in some
way"), but to his own peer group he liked to sound defiant:

> Don't you think it's ABSOLUTELY SHAMEFUL
> that men have to pay for women without BEING
> ALLOWED TO SHAG the women afterwards AS A
> MATTER OF COURSE? I do: simply DISGUSTING.
> It makes me ANGRY. Everything about the ree-
> lay-shun-ship between men and women makes
> me *angry*. It's all a fucking balls up. It might
> have been planned by the army, or the Ministry
> of Food.

On another occasion, he confided, "I *don't* want to take
a girl out, and spend *circa* £5 when I can toss off in five
minutes, free, and have the rest of the evening to myself."

Those five minutes, it seems, would normally be spent
under the auspices of pornography, or what passed for
pornography at the time. Once, loitering around a sex
shop in London, Larkin was approached by the owner,
who quietly asked, "Was it bondage, sir?" Actually it *was*
bondage: bondage, spanking, intertwined schoolgirls. He
was mightily gratified when he first got his hands on a
copy of a magazine called *Swish*. "Jolly good stuff, *Swish*,"
wrote Larkin in his thank-you letter to the friend who had
sent it to him. ("Also I wanted to know if the head master
stuck his cock up her bum or up her cunt but no doubt

I shall go to the grave unsatisfied.") This area of fantasy
is referred to in the correspondence when Larkin complains about the kind of letter he *isn't* getting. Extracts
from Larkin's dream mail:

> Dear Mr Larkin, I expect you think it's jolly
> cheeky for a schoolgirl to—
>
> Dear Dr Larkin, My friend and I had an argu-
> ment as to which of us has the biggest breasts
> and we wondered if you would act as—
>
> My youngest, she's fourteen and quite absurdly
> stuck on your poems—but then she's advanced
> in all ways—refuses to wear a—

Today, we all know how we feel, or how we're supposed
to feel, about such "attitudes" or "mind-sets," especially
when we have shorn them of individuality and self-
mockery. Motion duly reaches for the nearest words: "misogyny," which at least in theory describes a real condition, and the still more problematic "sexism." He spots "a
masturbatory impulse" behind several of Larkin's poems:
"Wild Oats," "Sunny Prestatyn," "The Large Cool
Store," and, he writes, "even 'An Arundel Tomb.'"
("Even" is certainly the mot juste.) Of "Lines on a Young
Lady's Photograph Album" Motion says, "The poem connects with the other pictures Larkin liked to gaze at: the
photographs in pornographic magazines. The sex life they
entail—solitary, exploitative—is a crude version of the
pleasure he takes in the album." "Exploitative" is the key
word here. It suggests that, while you are free to be as sexually miserable as you like, the moment you exchange
hard cash for a copy of *Playboy* you are in the pornogra-
phy-perpetuation business and your misery becomes political. The truth is that pornography is just a sad affair all
round (and its industrial dimensions are an inescapable
modern theme). It is there because men—in their hundreds of millions—want it to be there. Killing pornography is like killing the messenger. The extent to which
Larkin was "dependent" on it should be a measure of our
pity, or even our sympathy. But Motion hears the beep of
his political pager, and he stands to attention. The two
poems he specifically convicts of sexism were written in
1965, at which point "sexism" had no currency and no
meaning. This is a mild enough incidence, but one wonders how the literary revisionists and canon-cleansers can
bear to take the money. Imagine a school of sixteenth-
century art criticism that spent its time contentedly jeering at the past for not knowing about perspective.

***Philip Larkin: A Writer's Life* is
confidently managed, and chasteningly
thorough; it is also an anthology of the
contemporary tendencies toward the
literal, the conformist, and the amnesiac.**

—Martin Amis

Applied to the individual, "sexism" has always been a

non-clarifier. Unlike the relationship between the races ("racism" describes a much simpler hostility), the relationship between the sexes is based on biological interdependency, which takes complex forms. Still, the biological imperative was something Larkin never felt. A virgin himself until the age of twenty-three, he was excited by virginity in women. His first love, Ruth Bowman, was not much more than a girl when he took up with her, and in appearance remained avianchildlike into middle age. (In a marvellously depressing coda to their relationship, Larkin offered Ruth "some money to help pay for a hip-replacement operation.") His other—comparatively—great romantic love, Maeve Brennan (this is not *The New Yorker*'s Maeve Brennan, needless to say), was principled and religious and took many years to wear down. Larkin's thing with Maeve was accommodated within, and balanced against, a steadier relationship with his long-term companion, Monica Jones. The two women knew about each other: Larkin expended a lot of effort managing to hang on to both.

Thus the reader is almost as scandalized as Andrew Motion when, after so much temporizing, after so many survived ultimatums, Larkin starts an affair (significantly, soon after Maeve's surrender) with a *third* woman: Betty Mackereth, his secretary.

Now, you might perhaps feel that having one girlfriend is happenstance, having two girlfriends is coincidence, but having three girlfriends is enemy action. After registering his astonishment at this latest turn, Motion quickly decides that "it is all of a piece with [Larkin's] previous behaviour." There is selfishness and duplicity; there is even a touch of seigneurism. One can almost hear Motion begging Larkin to seek professional help. Why can't he be more . . . sensible, caring, normal? But, of course, Larkin, at fifty-two, didn't have three women: he had four. He had Eva Larkin, who just went on and on living. "My mother," he wrote in 1977, "not content with being motionless, deaf and speechless, is now going blind. That's what you get for not dying, you see." It has been pointed out in a London paper that of the score or so major reviews of the biography none was written by a woman. (Were the literary editors feeling protective? Stand back, my dear: this won't be a pretty sight.) The job was left to the hardy menfolk, with their insecurities, their contemporary amour propre. It occurs to you that women may be less inclined to be baffled or repelled by Larkin's peculiar chaos, and less inclined to reach for the buzzwords of the hour. Just as a "philistine" does not, on the whole, devote his life to his art (however clumsily), so a "misogynist" does not devote his inner life to women (however messily). Larkin's men friends devolved into pen pals. Such intimacies as he shared he shared with women.

Before moving on to the charge of racial hatred, it will be necessary to answer to younger readers (those under about seventy) the following question: What is a correspondence? Younger readers know what a phone message is, and what a fax is. They probably know what a letter is. But they don't know what a correspondence is. Words are not deeds. In published poems (we think first of Eliot's Jew), words edge closer to deeds. In Céline's anti-Semitic textbooks, words get as close to deeds as words can get. Blood libels scrawled on front doors *are* deeds. In a correspondence, words are hardly even words. They are soundless cries and whispers; "gouts of bile," as Larkin characterized his political opinions; ways of saying "Gloomy old sod, aren't I?" or, more simply, "Grrr." Correspondences are self-dramatizations. Above all, a word in a letter is never your *last* word on any subject. Although in Larkin's writings on jazz (collected in *All What Jazz*) admiration and nostalgia for black musicians are sometimes tinged with condescension, there is no public side to Larkin's prejudices, and nothing that could be construed as a racist act.

The racial hatred—and fear—in the *Selected Letters* is insistent; and very ugly it often looks to the contemporary eye. " 'Sidney Keyes is already outstanding' says Stephen Spender. . . . So is the rock of Gibraltar & a negro's cock" (Larkin at nineteen). "This Cambridge Guide looks pretty bad to me: explaining Scott's plots for niggers" (at sixty). "Too many fucking niggers about" and "I can hear fat Caribbean germs pattering after me in the Underground"—such remarks are pitched to what each correspondent is felt likely to indulge. Colin Gunner, an old school friend, brings out the worst in him: "And as for those black scum kicking up a din on the boundary—a squad of South African police would have sorted them out to my satisfaction." In this case, words are *about* deeds. (Still, there is some justice here. Gunner ended up in a house trailer: this is not much of a destiny.) For Motion, the rambling rubbish of Larkin's prejudice comes under the heading of "racism"; he even has a little subentry on it under "Larkin" in his (brilliant) index: "racism 65, 309, 400, 409-10." The word suggests a system of thought, rather than an absence of thought, which would be closer to the reality—closer to the jolts and twitches of stock response. Like mood-clichés, Larkin's racial snarls were inherited propositions, shamefully unexamined, humiliatingly average. These were his "spots of commonness," in George Eliot's sense. He failed to shed them.

"Politically correct" is a better designation than *"bien pensant"*: both bespeak a strong commitment to the herd instinct, but P.C. suggests the necessary regimentation. Although it is French in its philosophical origins, P.C. begins with the very American—and attractive and honorable—idea that no one should feel ashamed of what he was born as, of what he is. Of what he does, of what he says, yes; but not ashamed of what he is. Viewed at its grandest, P.C. is an attempt to accelerate evolution. To speak truthfully, while that's still O.K., everybody is "racist," or has racial prejudices. This is because human beings tend to like the similar, the familiar, the familial. I am a racist; I am not as racist as my parents; my children will not be as racist as I am. (Larkin was less racist than his parents; his children would have been less racist than he.) Freedom from racial prejudice is what we hope for, down the line. Impatient with this hope, this process, P.C. seeks to get the thing done right now—in a generation. To achieve this, it will need a busy executive wing, and much invigilation. What it will actually entrain is another ton of false consciousness, to add to the megatons of false consciousness already aboard, and then a backlash. Still. Here it is.

In Andrew Motion's book we have the constant sense that Larkin is somehow falling short of the cloudless emotional health enjoyed by (for instance) Andrew Motion. Also the sense, as Motion invokes his like-minded contemporaries, that Larkin is being judged by a newer, cleaner, braver, saner world. In the 1968 poem "Posterity" Larkin envisages "Jake Balokowsky, my biographer." "I'm stuck with this old fart at least a year," says Jake, not bothering "to hide / Some slight impatience with his destiny." "What's he like? / Christ, I just told you. . . . One of those old-type *natural* fouled-up guys." Jake, then, is hardly ideal for the job; but in the space of a few lines he gets further than Motion gets. He is asking himself the right questions, and neutrally: What is the difference between being like him and being like me? What is the difference between living then and living now? Motion maintains the tone of an over-worked psychotherapist dealing with a hidebound depressive who, exasperatingly, keeps failing to respond to the latest modern treatments. There is nothing visceral in it. The mood of the book is one of impatience: mounting impatience.

It sometimes seems that the basis of the vexation is that Larkin was born in 1922, rather than more recently. Not only is he not well adjusted; he *doesn't want to do anything about it.* There are no serious shots at self-improvement, at personal growth. Larkin left it too late to "change his ways." Even when he spots the difficulty, he "gives little sign of wanting to make analysis part of a process of change." He doesn't show a healthy enjoyment of positive experiences like sex and travel. Of Larkin's first love: "The best he could do in the way of celebrating physical tenderness was to say 'Her hands intend no harm.' " Of a late (and rare) trip abroad: "The best he could manage was a grudging admission that he had '*survived.*' " With women generally, Larkin morbidly refuses to be caring and upfront: he is "deceitful," a "self-tormenting liar," and his affairs are characterized by "indecisions, lies and contradictions." After a while, the book starts to feel like some kind of folie à deux: Motion is extremely irritated by Larkin's extreme irritability; he is always complaining that Larkin is always complaining. One thinks of a remark in the *Letters* when Larkin is commiserating with (and complaining to) a woman friend about the inconveniences of Christmas: "Yours is the harder course, I can see. On the other hand, mine is happening to me." Motion is only writing the "Life." Larkin had to live it.

Toward the end, even Larkin's fear of death—so central, so formative, so remorseless—has come to strike Motion as just another skein of unsalubrious egotism. After seeing the *Times* obituary for Bruce Montgomery, "a really close friend," Larkin said in a letter that "it makes it all sort of realler." Motion continues: "Larkin aired the same sorrowful but self-interested feelings in a letter to Robert Conquest. 'Funeral was today,' he reported. 'All very sad, and makes the world seem very temporary.' " Since when are intimations of mortality, at a friend's graveside, "self-interested"? But perhaps all such thoughts, and perhaps mortality itself, are now suspect. Don't dwell on death. It's anti-life.

Motion is so shamanistically sensitive to self-interest that you wonder whether this is a personal quirk or whether it somehow fits in with the new-ethos picture. Sober materialism and machine careerism, in response to the incontinence of the eighties? In any event, you have to warp your mind into novel contortions as Motion monitors Larkin's "self-interest," and identifies this or that apparently straightforward remark as a "pretense" or a "tactic." The friendship with Kingsley Amis, for example, was not as warm as it seemed to "the wide world," for "both men went to some lengths to publicize it as a way of consolidating their literary reputations." My filial reluctance to make much of this (it might look like a "tactic") disappeared thirty-odd pages later, when Motion repeats his depressing strophe with regard to John Betjeman: their friendship was "affectionate but not . . . intimate"; for Larkin there was "something self-protective" in it. ("By extolling Betjeman's virtues he helped to create the taste by which he wished his own work to be judged.") And he played the same angle, according to Motion, when he edited the *Oxford Book of Twentieth Century English Verse* (a seven-year job): "Larkin used the *Oxford* book to define and promote the taste by which he wished to be relished." Even the friendship with Barbara Pym, which comes across in the *Letters* as a jewel of delicacy and disinterestedness (in fact, Larkin did more than anyone to help resuscitate Pym's ailing career), is mysteriously found wanting: despite "a genuine warmth," Larkin "nevertheless addressed her as if he knew an audience was listening"; he "projects," he "parades." Motion says, "To the extent that Larkin ever shouldered Pym's worries, he did so knowing he would never be crushed by them." What test is Larkin failing here? It is a pity that Pym never held out to him the promise of a free hardback or a bottle of milk, so that Motion could call the friendship "self-interested." O brave new superego world, where you shoulder each other's worries, where men never lie to women, where people will, of course, be marvellous when they are old and dying, where everyone is so incredibly interested in self-interest.

Biography, besides being a lowly trade, may also be attritional. Perhaps Motion (who knew Larkin, who knew Hull, and who is a poet) had his empathic powers blunted rather than sharpened by the years of (dedicated) research and (womanlike) composition. Certainly his perspectives become fatally erratic. In his *Observer* piece, which contained more about-faces than a battalion parade ground, Motion spoke of the relationship between art and life: "All good biographers insist on separation, as well as connection." No, what they do, or what they end up doing, is insist on connection. And Motion connects and nauseam: "obviously the spur," "the message for Ruth in these poems," "put these fears into the mouth of," "the precise source . . . is easy to trace," "arising from the continuing wrangle," "prompted by Maeve," "released the rage he had been storing," "feeding off his suppressed rage with Eva," "the only begetters of many of his poems," and so on. Only begetters, however, are a romantic convention: poems don't have only begetters. At one point, Motion says that the influence of one of Larkin's women friends "extended beyond the poems in which she appears"— appears, just as Marla Maples appears in "The Will Rogers Follies." Biographers may claim separation, but what they helplessly insist on is connection. They have to. Or what are they about? What the hell are they doing day after day, year after year (gossiping? ringing changes on the Zeitgeist?), if the life doesn't somehow account for the art?

"You know I was never a child," wrote Larkin, at the age of fifty-seven. "I really feel somewhat at the last gasp. Carry me from the spot, Time, with thy all forgiving wave," he wrote at the age of twenty-seven. Arriving in Hull, aged thirty-two, he wrote to his mother, "Oh dear, the future now seems very bleak and difficult." It is in the word "difficult" that we hear the authentic quaver of the valetudinarian. "I'm so finished," he wrote to a woman friend when the end really was getting closer. When it was closer still, he told Monica, with "a fascinated horror," that he was "spiralling down towards extinction." His last words were spoken to a woman—to the nurse who was holding his hand. Perhaps we all have the last words ready when we go into the last room. Perhaps the thing about last words is not how good they are but whether you can get them out. What Larkin said (faintly) was "I am going to the inevitable."

Inevitable in the sense that death could never be avoided—as a fate, and as a fixation. "I don't want to write anything at present. In fact, thinking it over, I want to die. I am very impressed by this sort of unrealised deathwish of mine," Larkin wrote at eighteen. They probably have a name for it now, something like Early Death-Awareness Syndrome. What we get at forty or forty-five he had all along. He never did anything about it (you didn't then); he seemed to nurture this adolescent lassitude; he made it his own patch of melancholy, and tried to write the poetry that belonged there. Humanly, it turned him into an old woman—like his mother. "I bought a pair of shoes and they don't even *try* to keep the water out." "I have an insensate prejudice against people who go abroad AT ANY TIME OF THE YEAR, but PARTICULARLY at Easter & Christmas." Given his opportunities for variety and expansion, he makes Mr. Woodhouse, in "Emma," look like Evel Knievel. "This is a hell of a week. Must get a haircut. Wanted to get another dark sweater from M and S"—Marks & Spencer—"but doubt if there'll be time or if they'll have one." He was so worried about his weight that he took his bathroom scales on holiday. "I've just returned from Hamburg," he wrote in 1976 (it was his first trip abroad in twenty-four years). "They were all very kind, but oh the strain! The best thing was a little 'mini-bar,' a kind of locked drink-cupboard in my hotel room." Colloquialisms as audacious as "news," "deal," "make my bed," "deep freeze," and "embarrassing" similarly had him reaching for his inverted commas. "How very bold of you to buy an electric typewriter," he wrote to a friend in 1985.

What redeems and monumentalizes this slow drizzle—what makes the "Letters" a literary experience and the "Life" just one thing after another—is the comedy of candor. Here melancholy still hurts, but it embodies its own comic relief; and dignity is not needed. "The US edition of [*High Windows*] is out, with a photograph of me that cries out for the caption 'FAITH HEALER OR HEARTLESS FRAUD?'" "And then my sagging face, an egg sculpted in lard, with goggles on." "None of my clothes fit either: when I sit down my tongue comes out." A Life is one kind of biography, and the *Letters* are another kind of Life; but the internal story, the true story, is in the *Collected Poems*. The recent attempts, by Motion and others, to pass judgment on Larkin look awfully green and pale compared with the self-examinations of the poetry. They think they judge him? No. He judges them. His indivisibility judges their hedging and trimming. His honesty judges their watchfulness:

> If my darling were once to decide
> Not to stop at my eyes,
> But to jump, like Alice, with floating skirt into
> my head . . .
>
> She would find herself looped with the creep of
> varying light,
> Monkey-brown, fish-grey, a string of infected
> circles
> Loitering like bullies, about to coagulate . . .
> —"If, My Darling."
>
> For something sufficiently toad-like
> Squats in me, too;
> Its hunkers are heavy as hard luck,
> And cold as snow . . .
> —"Toads."

Larkin the man is separated from us, historically, by changes in the self. For his generation, you were what you were, and that was that. It made you unswervable and adamantine. My father has this quality. I don't. None of us do. There are too many forces at work on us. There are too many fronts to cover. In the age of self-improvement, the self is inexorably self-conscious. Still, a price has to be paid for not caring what others think of you, and Larkin paid it. He couldn't change the cards he was dealt ("What poor hands we hold, / When we face each other honestly!"). His poems insist on this helplessness:

> And I meet full face on dark mornings
> The bestial visor, bent in
> By the blows of what happened to happen.
> —"Send No Money."
>
> Most things are never meant.
> —"Going, Going."
>
> The unbeatable slow machine
> That brings what you'll get.
> —"The Life with a Hole in It."
>
> Life is first boredom, then fear.
> Whether or not we use it, it goes,
> And leaves what something hidden from us
> chose,
> And age, and then the only end of age.
> —"Dockery and Son."

My most enduring memory of Larkin is a composite one, formed from the many visits he paid to the series of flats and houses where I spent my first ten years, in Swansea, South Wales. My elder brother was Larkin's godson and namesake, and Larkin's visits were doubly welcome: it was the custom then for godfathers to give money to their godsons (and to their godsons' brothers); in our family we called it "tipping the boys." *My* godfather was Bruce

Montgomery, who makes frequent—and decreasingly jovial—appearances in both the biography and the letters (thin talent; alcohol). When I was a child, Bruce was always jovial, and ridiculously generous. There was one occasion—it was November 5th (Bonfire Night), in perhaps 1955—when Bruce gave my brother and me the usual florin or half crown, plus a *ten-shilling note:* for fireworks. We couldn't believe it. We were like the brides' fathers in *The Whitsun Weddings,* never having known "Success so huge and wholly farcical."

It was different with Larkin. We were told that Larkin "didn't really like children" ("children / With their shallow violent eyes"), and we tended to stay out of his way. When it came time for him to tip the boys, we would stand there tremulously with our palms outturned, quite flattered to think of ourselves as representatives of a menacing subgroup: children. The tip, always in the form of big, black old pennies, would be doled out in priestly silence. Threepence for Martin, fourpence for Philip (a year my senior). Later, sixpence for me, ninepence for him. The money still meant a lot to us, because we intuited what it had cost Larkin to part with it. (He was, by the way, a genuine miser. In his last weeks, he lived off "cheap red wine and Complan." He left over a quarter of a million pounds.) No, Larkin did not come out and gambol with us in the garden. (Neither, to be sure, did Bruce.) He did not tell us magical bedtime stories. But when I readdress my eager, timid, childish feelings in his presence, I find solidity as well as oddity, and tolerant humor (held in reserve, in case it was needed) as well as the given melancholy. "When will it get dark? When will it get dark?" I kept asking, that Bonfire Night. The answer in Swansea, in that vanished world, was three o'clock in the afternoon—even earlier than in Hull, where "the lights come on at four / At the end of another year." And it was always raining, whatever the season. I remember Larkin coming in from the rain, or preparing to go out in it: slightly fussy, cumbrous, long-suffering.

Rain, as an element and an ambience, provides a backdrop to the life and to this very English story. "On 13 November Larkin travelled through heavy rain to Wellington for his interview, clutching his green-bound copy of *The Public Library System of Great Britain.*" "Heavy rain," "driving rain," "torrential rain." Under the heading "FIVE DON'TS FOR OLD CREATURES" Larkin wrote to his mother: "4. Don't waste time worrying about *rain.* This is a wettish country. Lots of it falls. It always has done, and always will." What was Hull? Hull was as dull as rain. Rain was what Larkin felt marriages turned into; rain was what love and desire eventually became. *The Whitsun Weddings* describes a rail journey to London in which the poet witnesses the aftermaths of wedding parties as, at every stop, the train fills up with "fresh couples" about to begin their honeymoons and the rest of their lives. London approaches:

> and it was nearly done, this frail
> Travelling coincidence; and what it held
> Stood ready to be loosed with all the power
> That being changed can give. We slowed again,
> And as the tightened brakes took hold, there
> swelled

> A sense of falling, like an arrow-shower
> Sent out of sight, somewhere becoming rain.

Everybody knows "They fuck you up, your mum and dad" and the thrilled finality of that poem's closing stanza ("This Be the Verse"):

> Man hands on misery to man.
> It deepens like a coastal shelf.
> Get out as early as you can,
> And don't have any kids yourself.

But there is always a sense of romantic balance in Larkin, however reluctant, however thwarted. "This Be the Verse" has a sister poem, called "The Trees." After finishing it, Larkin wrote "Bloody awful tripe" at the foot of the manuscript. But the last lines stand:

> Yet still the unresting castles thresh
> In fullgrown thickness every May.
> Last year is dead, they seem to say,
> Begin afresh, afresh, afresh.

(pp. 74-82)

Martin Amis, "Don Juan in Hull," in The New Yorker, *Vol. LXIX, No. 21, July 12, 1993, pp. 74-82.*

Robert Richman (review date September 1993)

[*In the following review, Richman disputes Motion's portrayal of Larkin's life as unfairly negative and judgmental.*]

Andrew Motion met Philip Larkin, the greatest of postwar English poets, in 1977, the year Motion went to teach at the University of Hull, where Larkin had been librarian. Motion had defended Larkin's verse in numerous essays, a book, and in a 1982 memoir, "On the Plain of Holderness," in which he said of Larkin: "He's certainly helped me more than anyone else to clarify the kind of poetry I want to write, and been marvellous company—often profound, and sometimes extremely funny."

Motion, who was named one of the executors of Larkin's estate, also wrote a poignant poem for the *Times Literary Supplement* in the days following Larkin's death of esophageal cancer in December 1985. The poem was important because Larkin's amusing side can be found almost everywhere in it. Furthermore, it repudiated a caricature popular among the free-verse dogmatists and the chic radicals who have been governing English cultural life since the 1960s: that Larkin was a bitter misogynist and child-hater who cared for nothing except himself and his work. It comes as a shock, then, to find Larkin's former friend retracting in his new biography many revisionist claims he spent the better part of a decade formulating.

Granted, even politically incorrect readers of *Philip Larkin: A Writer's Life* and *The Selected Letters of Philip Larkin, 1940-1985* may be surprised by Larkin's occasional private deriding of blacks, immigrants, Jews, and women. In one letter Larkin includes mock policy recommendations in a poem:

> Prison for Strikers,
> Bring back the cat,

Kick out the niggers,
How about that?

And in a 1946 letter to Kingsley Amis, whom Larkin often tried to outdo in epistolary outrageousness, he writes:

> Don't you think it's ABSOLUTELY SHAMEFUL that men have to pay for women without BEING ALLOWED TO SHAG the woman afterwards AS A MATTER OF COURSE? I do: simply DISGUSTING. It makes me ANGRY. Everything about the ree-lay-shun-ship between men and women makes me ANGRY . . . It's all a f—ing balls up. It might have been planned by the army, or the Ministry of Food.

But Larkin's sporadic lapses of taste, which have renewed the cries for his head in the literary world, are nothing compared to Motion's distortions and deceptions, his blatant lack of balance, his determination to give as little weight as possible to people and events that might cast Larkin in a better light.

Philip Larkin was born in Coventry in 1922, the second child of Eva and Sydney Larkin. Sydney, the Treasurer of Coventry, was, Motion claims, "autocratic" and given to "extreme political views."

Motion holds that Sydney was a Nazi sympathizer during the 1930s. (His documentation: one essay by Noel Hughes, from which Hughes retracted the assertion, and another essay by John Kenyon—which, Motion tells us in a footnote, is unpublished and in his sole possession.)

Sydney certainly valued the intellect. His home was filled with books, and Sydney impressed on his son that reading should be an autonomous activity divorced from school. Eva, for her part, was, in Motion's words, "mousy," "whining," and "scared almost into hysterics by thunderstorms." Their marriage was "bloody hell," Philip himself said, and instilled in him permanent doubts about the institution.

A sister, Kittie, was eight years older than Philip, so he grew up feeling like an only child. His eyes were weak, he was ungainly, and at age four he developed a stammer that wasn't cured until he was an adult. His parents bequeathed to him their own diffidence and social awkwardness. "You don't know what shyness is," Sydney once said "very crushingly" (Larkin's words) to his son when he complained about his own. The result was few friends for Philip, and no friends at all of the opposite sex.

Larkin was exempted from war service because of bad eyes, and attended Oxford from 1940 to 1944. His troubles with girls continued, but one male friend he met remained close for life: Kingsley Amis, the novelist and poet, whose *Lucky Jim* is dedicated to Larkin. Amis, whose father was an export clerk for Colman's Mustard, shared Larkin's love of jazz, and both men hated public school boys and all forms of social pretension. (Larkin later distanced himself from the Symbolist-styled poems that appeared in his first collection, *The North Ship* (1945), but never tried to disown the two fine novels he published fresh from school and in amazingly quick succession: *Jill* (1946) and *A Girl in Winter* (1947). The former had as its subject the very social dislocation he had felt at Oxford.)

Larkin's reputation grew slowly, with four volumes of poetry coming out roughly one a decade. *The Less Deceived* (1955) got a slew of favorable reviews, and orders inundated the Marvell Press, the tiny husband-and-wife outfit that had published the book. (Weeks after signing his contract, an editor at Faber & Faber—T. S. Eliot's house and the pinnacle of British poetry publishing—asked Larkin if he had a manuscript to consider. Larkin told him he was too late.) *The Whitsun Weddings* (1964), in Motion's words, "did more than confirm Larkin's reputation; it turned his voice into one of the means by which his country recognized itself." *High Windows* (1974), Larkin's last book of his own poems, sold 18,000 copies—a feat given the anti-formalist esthetic climate of the time—and made Larkin "a national monument."

Larkin graduated with a First, but his stammer made teaching impossible. He was also rejected by the Civil Service. Motion doesn't speculate why, but Larkin's social standing may have had something to do with it. Larkin landed a library job in Shropshire where he did everything from stoke the boiler to serve the children. In an interview, Larkin later said about this job, in a broad Yorkshire accent for effect, "I'm fond of saying, *'I started at the bottom.'*" It was here that Larkin finally met a girl who would sleep with him: Ruth Bowman.

In 1948, on the heels of his father's death, Larkin got engaged to Ruth, "making it clear," as Motion writes, "that marriage would not automatically follow." Larkin told a friend that he proposed because he didn't want to "desert the only girl I have met who doesn't instantly frighten me away." In the months to come, Motion writes, Larkin "slowly but surely . . . crushed Ruth's happiness beneath his own worries." Finally Larkin made an offer of marriage, only to withdraw it. Ruth returned the ring and refused to see him.

As a librarian at Leicester University, Larkin met Monica Jones, a teacher of English. The independent-minded Jones, who would become the poet's closest friend, claimed to have no interest in marriage. Nor did she mind the distance between her and Larkin after he took a series of jobs in remote areas, beginning in 1950 at the library of Queen's University in Belfast. "She suited his selfishness in virtually every respect," Motion writes. From this point on, in fact, and until Jones moved in with Larkin in 1982, they saw each other only on weekends and holidays. "I wasn't much trouble," Jones says, "and then I'd go and cook the supper."

At Belfast, Larkin had the best writing conditions of his life, working every weekday evening from 8 to 10 p.m., then going out for drinks and cards until 1 or 2 a.m. Four years later, when he was about to take a new job at the University of Hull, he told Robert Conquest: "I feel terribly regretful at leaving Belfast."

Larkin's first impression of Hull, written on a postcard to his mother, was dour: "It's a bit chilly here and smells of fish." Situated at the junction of the Hull and Humber rivers, Hull not only reeked of fish, but was less interesting and less attractive than Belfast, and even more remote: "on the way to nowhere," as Larkin wrote. But for someone who was fast becoming the laureate of the dismal side of England, Hull was perfect. He stayed until his death thirty years later.

At Hull, Larkin started to see Maeve Brennan, a co-worker at the library. Motion is tough on Larkin about this "affair," and its supposedly calamitous emotional impact on Monica, but his anger seems misplaced. For one thing, Larkin did not sleep with Maeve for seventeen years. ("I'm extremely faithful by nature," Larkin wrote to Maeve, and nothing here disputes that.) Both women knew about each other almost from the start, and Larkin was more honest with them than most men in his position would be. And anyway, if this seventeen-year "triangle" was as unbearable as Maeve and Monica now claim, they are as much at fault for perpetuating it as was Larkin.

In 1961 Larkin began corresponding with—and championing—the novelist Barbara Pym, who had fallen out of favor after publishing a string of acclaimed books in the 1950s. It was his unselfish devotion to her novels, in fact, that succeeded in resuscitating her reputation. Pym and Larkin also saw eye to eye politically. When planning to meet for the first time at an Oxford hotel in 1975, Larkin told Pym that he would be able to deduce who she was by "progressive elimination—i.e., eliminating all the progressives."

After a Labour victory in 1964, Motion writes, Larkin began to air his "political prejudices more and more freely." After students locked a campus building, Larkin complained to Conquest: "We're off the boil at present, having licked the blacking off the boots of all students in sight." And to Amis he wrote: "F— the whole lot of them, I say, the decimal-loving, nigger-mad, army-cutting, abortion-promoting, murderer-pardoning, daylight-hating ponces."

His sagging spirits were lifted briefly by Margaret Thatcher's victory in 1979: "Oh, I adore Mrs. Thatcher," he remarked. "At last politics makes sense to me. . . . Recognizing that if you haven't got the money for something you can't have it—this is a concept that's vanished for many years." Motion, for his part, calls the Larkin of these years "narrowly defensive and nationalistic," impugns him for supporting the Falklands war, and reproves him for venting his ire in letters to Amis after finding scrawled on the walls of an elevator: "F—OFF LARKIN YOU C–T."

In 1982 the essay collection *Required Writing* was published, in Motion's words, "to universal acclaim." Two years later Larkin declined Thatcher's offer of the Laureateship, in part because he had more or less stopped writing poetry. But when Ted Hughes was chosen instead, Larkin wrote to Amis that "the thought of being the cause of Ted's being buried in Westminster Abbey is hard to live with. 'There is regret. Always, there is regret.'"

In 1985 Larkin's health deteriorated. He had no appetite: his tongue, he said, felt "like an autumn leaf." When inoperable cancer was discovered, Monica chose not to tell him. Just days after surgery, while still at the hospital, Larkin drank some whiskey someone had smuggled in, vomited, flooded his lungs, and almost died. On returning home, he rewrote his will, leaving his $500,000 estate to

Monica, the Society of Authors, and the Royal Society for the Prevention of Cruelty to Animals. A bequest to Maeve Brennan was cancelled. In late November, he collapsed in his bathroom with his face pressed against the heating pipes. Monica called an ambulance. When it arrived "he looked up at her wildly, begging her to destroy his diaries." (He always intended to do this himself; his final wish was carried out not by Monica but by Betty Hesketh, his secretary, who fed the thirty-odd books into the university shredder.) Three days later Larkin died, turning to a hospital nurse to say: "I am going to the inevitable."

"The obituaries generally agreed," Motion writes, that Larkin

> had been "the greatest living poet in our language," the writer who spoke most intimately to an enormous range of people, and the personality who for all his reticence "cared most for what we all care about.". . . He had produced poems that spoke exactly as he—and Samuel Johnson—believed art should: helping people endure life, as well as enjoy it. . . .
>
> This was a cold comfort to Monica, [who didn't attend the funeral]. Isolated . . . ill, virtually unknown to the outside world . . . she felt her life disintegrate. She had no existence without Larkin. She was a widow without even the consolation of that title. . . . Drinking heavily, not bothering to change out of her nightdress and dressing-gown during the day, she surrendered to her sorrow.

Motion has relied on three main sources: Monica Jones, Maeve Brennan, and the cache of letters that became available under the terms of Larkin's contradictory will. And it is doubtful that Monica Jones is worthy of the total trust Motion places in her. Her irritation with Larkin is expected, and some of it may even be warranted, but that doesn't mean that Motion should accept everything she says. "He cared a tenth as much about what happened around him as he did what was happening inside him," is a typical remark. Maeve Brennan, too, has an axe to grind, and Motion accepts everything she says: "I wonder whether I really knew him at all," Maeve observes at one point. "He had feet of clay, didn't he? Huge feet of clay." And Motion is not content simply to iterate her claims:

> The indecision, lies, and contradictions which often characterized his life with Maeve and Monica . . .
> He was too self-absorbed to respond to [Monica's] grief.
>
> The modesty of Larkin's letters to Maeve [modest, that is, because they "conceal" the "true" vicious self Larkin reserved for Conquest and Amis] makes them seem—in their well-meaning way—deceitful.
>
> In a letter Larkin sent to Maeve . . . it is clear that he was not so much a reformed character as a more [sic] self-tormenting liar.

Motion relies heavily on the letters, but the ones he quotes showing the poet's smutty and repellant side are atypical—an effort, it seems, to "prove" that Larkin was a creep all along. Larkin wrote his mother two loving letters a week; at one point, when she was sick, he wrote every day. All except one are ignored by Motion. Motion's reason for slighting this important group of letters? Because they are "doting," "trivial," and show an "amiable banality." (Larkin's letters to his mother are also completely ignored by Thwaite in the *Selected Letters*.) The letters to Monica showing warmth and affection, and there are plenty, are kept to a minimum; the same goes for the hundreds of congenial letters to Maeve. The dozens of extant letters from Maeve to Larkin—and they are, by Motion's own admission, "affectionate, tender, enthusiastic, and gossipy"—are also disregarded. The correspondence with Pym gets short shrift.

Such letters are downplayed to make room for those that show Larkin at his most lascivious ("I agree *Bamboo & Frolic* are tops, or rather the bottoms; do pass on any that have ceased to stimulate"), juvenile ("Sod and bollocks anyway. Not to mention c–t and f—. Omitting bugger and s–t"), or rightwing ("Term starts soon; you can guess how I look forward to it. Little subsidised socialist sods. See you on the breadline").

Another low blow is Motion's equating of the bigotry found in a handful of letters written mainly when Larkin was drunk, and only to those who wouldn't be offended, with a real, substantive politics. Larkin organized no marches, campaigned for no candidates, wrote no editorials, joined no racist clubs, and was above reproach in his dealings with people. (The only time he voiced any political views was in two interviews done late in life and in a couple of poems.) As a fulltime librarian he spent countless hours with women, "Pakis," and Jews, and not a single incident of intolerance, obnoxiousness, or political rancor is reported. The great affection Larkin's female colleagues at Hull felt for him belies Motion's claim that his "hostility to women would sometimes soften but never entirely disappear." Without real meanness or real political activism to bash Larkin with, Motion is forced to equate juvenile opinions expressed by a half-soused poet in a few private letters never intended for public consumption with political activity itself. It is one of the more disgraceful deeds in the history of literary biography.

Monica and Maeve are not the only ones whose facts are suspect. The third-hand testimony of Patsy Murphy, who died in 1977 of alcohol poisoning, appears unreliable, yet Motion reports it without so much as a raised eyebrow. Evidently Murphy told her ex-husband, the Irish poet Richard Murphy, that she had read portions of Larkin's diaries years before and without permission while at Larkin's house. Paraphrasing the Murphys, Motion describes them as a

> sexual log book . . . full of fantasies . . . a repository for his rage against the world. . . . Patsy opened the secret drawer in Larkin's life and glimpsed his grimmest, sexiest, most angry thoughts. . . . Even his most candid letters only hint at their intensity. To gauge them we might think of some of the seethingly bitter things he

wrote to [school friend Jim] Sutton as a young man, then multiply them.

Poor Larkin: he is rebuked for shrinking from action, for denying his mother an active role in his life, for being unable to write love poems when young, for criticizing his parents in a youthful memoir, for being controlled in his letters to Maeve but uncontrolled in those to Amis, for being a "prisoner of the past," for being motivated solely by the "cold drops of self-interest," for being jealous, rude, self-deprecating, self-absorbed, self-promoting, and lazy. (The last is my favorite: Larkin oversaw the transformation of the Hull library from a tiny backwater collection into one of the great provincial libraries.) "His moment had passed; his life was ending," writes Motion near the end of his narrative, and one can't help but read into the line a certain degree of relish. (pp. 72-4)

> *Robert Richman, "Philip Larkin: A Writer's Life," in* The American Spectator, *Vol. 26, No. 9, September, 1993, pp. 72-4.*

Larkin in a letter to Norman Iles dated July 4, 1972:

I'm glad you feel satisfied with your life—no reason why you shouldn't. When I look back on mine I think it has changed very little—ever since leaving Oxford I've worked in a library & tried to write in my spare time. For the last 16 years I've lived in a small flat, washing in the sink, & not having central heating or double glazing or fitted carpets or the other things everyone has, & of course I haven't any biblical things such as a wife, children, house, land, cattle, sheep etc. To me I seem very much an outsider, yet I suppose 99% of people wd say I'm very establishment & conventional. Funny, isn't it? Of course I can't say I'm satisfied with it. Terrible waste of time.

Philip Larkin, in The Selected Letters of Philip Larkin, *edited by Anthony Thwaite, 1992.*

Geoffrey Wheatcroft   (review date September 1993)

[*In the following review of* Philip Larkin: A Writer's Life, *Wheatcroft attempts to determine the validity of allegations that Larkin harbored racist and sexist beliefs.*]

Despite hints to the contrary (see the poem "Talking in Bed"), part of the Larkin myth had been the hermit bachelor, the hopeless sexual and emotional cripple, the author of "Annus Mirabilis": "Sexual intercourse began / In nineteen sixty-three / (Which was rather late for me)—." Letters and biography do reveal a man who was sexually complicated and awkward, and in some dispiriting ways. We learn that he and Robert Conquest (yes, that Robert Conquest, the famous Sovietologist) haunted the dirty-book shops of Soho together. Spanking magazines were Larkin's specialty, and he was candid about the purpose of pornography: to help him masturbate. More surprising is to discover from Motion just how far this solitary avocation was from being his only sexual activity. He may not have gone to bed with a woman until he was twenty-three—sexual intercourse began for him in 1945, to be precise—but after that he had a regular succession of women, sometimes two at once, and for a time three.

For the best part of forty years he had an on-and-off relationship with Monica Jones, the dedicatee of *The Less Deceived.* She emerges as a kindly, long-suffering, embarrassing woman. (Kingsley Amis's first novel, *Lucky Jim,* was partly inspired by Larkin's circumstances, and Monica appears in it as a portrait straight from life, her voice, looks, clothes, "ridiculed on page after page"; in the first draft Amis even called this character "Margaret Beale," just in case Monica Margaret Beale Jones didn't get the point.) Larkin's relationship with her is itself embarrassing to read about. Other people's sex lives are usually easier to condemn than to understand, and in any case Larkin described himself ruthlessly enough: "too selfish, withdrawn, / And easily bored to love." Even so, forty years does seem a long time to string someone along. He two-timed Monica with, among others, Maeve Brennan, who herself felt betrayed because he had "given little in return" for "all the anguish he has caused me." But in the end it was Monica who was with Larkin when he died—when, as Motion grimly says, she was left "a widow without even the consolation of that title."

Heartlessness toward women and love of pornography are not, however, what have most exercised Larkin's critics. They are more disgusted—though, one suspects, also gratified—by the confirmation in his letters that Larkin was a casual bigot. He told one friend that his political anthem would be "Prison for strikers, / Bring back the cat, / Kick out the niggers— / How about that?" That might be seen as an ironic, self-parodying joke, but it is harder to make that excuse when he told another friend that he no longer enjoyed going to watch cricket at Lord's, in London, because there were "too many fucking niggers about." All this is powerful evidence for the Larkin-bashing brigade. Their brigadier is the poet and critic Tom Paulin, a man who combines left-wing political correctness with dour Ulster Protestant humorlessness (and that's some combination). He has called Larkin's letters "a distressing and in many ways revolting compilation which imperfectly reveals and conceals the sewer under the national monument Larkin became."

This is strong language, but obviously Paulin has a prima facie case (legal language seems appropriate). It is true that he is peculiarly ill-equipped to understand this or to understand Larkin, being himself a man for whom light and shade, nuance and irony, are closed books. All the same, let us state the obvious: even making allowances for the fact that Larkin was showing off and letting off steam when he wrote to friends (through the continual schoolboy obscenity as much as the politically incorrect language), letters and life do reveal a very dark side to him, of which his meanness, his prejudices, his envious denigration of friends as well as foes, and his unsatisfactory dealings with women were all manifestations. I should record that Larkin was a surprisingly likable man to meet, charming, courteous, and companionable. But it isn't easy to like him more after reading Motion's book.

Indeed, I can't help thinking that the PC police have

missed a trick by concentrating on Larkin's taste for ethnic slurs. As often with writers, what is most damning to Larkin is the contrast between his public attitudes and his private conduct. Odious as those ethnic slurs are, Larkin had never pretended to be any kind of progressive multiracialist. But look at another contrast. He turned eighteen, coming of military age, in 1940, the year of his country's greatest crisis and trial. Philip Larkin's own finest hour was to spend three years at Oxford and then become a librarian, after failing his army medical with intense relief; "I was fundamentally," as he put it, "uninterested in the war." This was the man who twenty-seven years later (see his feeble 1969 squib "Homage to a Government") railed interminably at the idleness, greed, and treason of Labour politicians who cut defense spending. *Tu quoque,* chicken-hawk!

> Larkin's racial bigotry was a by-product of an inner rage. . . . His fulminations against "coloured immigrants" were fear of the new, and misery at some private loss.
>
> —*Geoffrey Wheatcroft*

Given what he wrote in private, it might seem perverse to defend him on a charge of racism. And yet the very word is at once so loaded and so general that it misses the point. Well aware as I am that complacency and self-congratulation are another two symptoms of the English disease, I call as witness Janet Daley, an American journalist who has been living in London for twenty-eight years. She said recently that in her view—and in specific comparison with her fellow countrymen—the English weren't really racist, just arrogant and xenophobic. I think that verdict is fair and accurate, and that Larkin illustrates it very well. Larkin's racial bigotry was a by-product of an inner rage. He was quite capable of showing kindness to, for example, individual Indian scholars, as one has recently testified, and I don't think that he really hated black people in the way that the true racist does. His fulminations against "coloured immigrants" were fear of the new, and misery at some private loss.

Yes, Larkin was an icon of Englishry, and a fine specimen of its complexes and neuroses: not only arrogant and xenophobic but also inward-looking, frightened, and depressive. The continual impression Motion's book leaves is not only of bleakness but of emptiness and unresponsiveness, too. For a highly intelligent man and a subtle poet, Larkin's artistic and intellectual interests were remarkably limited. His reading was relentlessly middlebrow, and although his hatred of abroad may have become self-parodic ("Who's Jorge Luis Borges?"), it was real enough in the first place. Apart from his adolescent visits to Germany, and a school trip to Belgium, he appears to have gone to the Continent just twice in forty-five years, to Paris for a few days in 1952, and to Germany again in

1976, to receive a prize in Hamburg. Ah, well. There is no point in trying to persuade his shade that one of the consolations of living in our damp little island is its proximity to Europe, fine food, delicious wines, and pretty pictures.

But then, he seems to have had no feeling whatever for visual art. Judy Egerton, an old friend from Belfast, became a curator at the Tate Gallery, in London, where she arranged a wonderful exhibition of one of the greatest of English painters, George Stubbs. Larkin went to see the show, and afterward wrote politely to Egerton, remarking on the pictures' "super-fine finish." It's a wonder he didn't say that the horses' eyes followed you around the room. Again, given his general disposition, he ought to have shared the hostility to modern architecture which is nowadays a touchstone of aesthetic fogeyism in England (see the Prince of Wales on the subject). As it was, Larkin cheerfully presided over the construction of the Brynmor Jones Library, in Hull, a foursquare Stalinist barracks of such gruesome ugliness that no sane follower of Wright or Mies could admire it. He was clearly a man who did not even begin to notice his physical surroundings.

Then there was music. Larkin and his Oxford friends made a cult of jazz, which Larkin kept up all his life. He was the jazz critic of the *Daily Telegraph* from 1961 to 1971, and set himself up as a standard-bearer for anti-modernism; his reviews were collected in *All What Jazz*, whose introduction reappears in *Required Writing*. Charlie Parker is linked with Picasso and Pound as the loathsome modern age incarnate, destroyers of order and beauty. On top of that Larkin wrote about jazz in painful terms: "[Far] from using music to entertain the white man, the Negro had moved to hating him with it. . . . The Negro is in a paradoxical position: he is looking for the jazz that isn't jazz."

Rereading *All What Jazz*, I think I see the problem. It was not that Larkin was a reactionary or a racist. He just wasn't musical. There was no reason why he should have liked John Coltrane—that was a matter of taste—but his loathing of all contemporary jazz was revealing. The musicologist Wilfrid Mellers hit the nail on the head when he reviewed the book: Larkin's inability to respond to any jazz played after 1945 casts doubt on the genuineness of his response to any played before. It might seem surprising to say this of someone who made such a parade of his music-loving, but to imagine that you love music while you are in fact unmusical is a much more common condition than is generally realized. Larkin seems, significantly, to have had almost no interest in other music: just one visit to the opera is recorded, to hear *Tristan und Isolde* (in Dublin, oddly enough), and he never went to concerts. Even jazz he described in essentially trite and unmusical terms. He complained that it had ceased to be what it had been in the 1920s, "the music of happy men," forgetting not only a few facts about black American life seventy years ago but also what Schubert supposedly once said when he was asked at a party to "play some jolly music": "There is no jolly music, dear lady. All music is sad."

And from all this numbness and emptiness came those poems. His detractors dismiss them as grossly overrated and symptomatic of English decline. The accusation was foreshadowed in 1973, when Larkin published his anthology *The Oxford Book of Twentieth Century English Verse*, edited in a defiantly conservative spirit. Donald Davie pilloried it for its "perverse triumph of philistinism, the cult of the amateur, the wrong kind of postmodernism, the weakest kind of Englishry," which looked like a veiled attack on Larkin's own verse. To a degree the charge is circular: there is a sense in which Larkin's literary conservatism makes him almost willfully "minor" and "marginal." His poems speak for themselves. They don't need explaining, studying, or teaching, which may upset English lit professors like Davie, but not us who still read for pleasure rather than academic duty. They are there to be read and enjoyed or not, as the reader chooses. Their deliberate avoidance of experiment and blatant technical virtuosity disguises their very great skill, which was recognized by other poets as diverse as Auden, Betjeman, and Lowell. Larkin knew exactly what he was doing, and he understood just what defines poetry: the tension between the formality of meter and the informal rhythm of speech, which tension disappears when all semblance of metrical rules is abandoned. Several dozen of his poems are masterly, and however they stand in the canon of the ages, I suspect they are about as good as it was possible to write in his time and place. Cultures and civilizations do rise and fall, and if the best that could be done in England in the second half of the twentieth century was marginal or minor, then maybe the country and its culture were also by then in a silver or even a bronze age.

If Larkin's enemies misunderstand him, there is something ludicrous about the "Larkin industry" of his devotees. Far from needing expansion into a "collected" edition of more than 300 pages, Larkin's published work needed pruning back to those few dozen masterpieces, from "If, My Darling," in 1950, to "Aubade," in 1977. There is something even more preposterous about the way his four little books are completely overshadowed and outweighed by the 790 pages of the letters and by Motion's 570 pages. His biography is very good of its kind, though I am inclined to add, like the man in an old cartoon, "but goddamn its kind." It is thoroughly researched and sympathetic. All the same, it illustrates the truth that great artists have always been less and done more than the public wishes to believe. If Philip Larkin survives, it will be because of what he wrote rather than anything the rest of us have written about him. (pp. 108-11)

> *Geoffrey Wheatcroft, "An Icon of Englishry,"*
> in The Atlantic Monthly, *Vol. 272, No. 3, September, 1993, pp. 104, 106, 108-11.*

Christopher Carduff   (review date September 1993)

[*In the following review, Carduff maintains that an appreciation of Larkin's poetry need not be adversely affected by the negative image of the poet presented in Andrew Motion's biography or Anthony Thwaite's edition of Larkin's letters.*]

They are creatures of the moment, and they've created an end-of-the-century literary genre all their own. If you haven't actually read their books, you've surely skimmed their reviews or perhaps even seen them on the afternoon television talk-show circuit. Their story is always the same, these writers, and it's always delivered with the same straightforward, controlled, and terrible bitterness: *I loved him, he was in many ways a great man, but Daddy wasn't the little tin angel he led us to believe he was.*

Andrew Motion, though he is also a distinguished poet, critic, and editor, is, in his new biography of Philip Larkin, just another such writer. His book is the high-art critical-bio version of *Daddy, Dearest,* but it's *Daddy, Dearest* all the same, and the English-language audience for poetry has been snapping it up like some sort of hardcover tabloid, clucking their tongues with condescending pleasure over just how bad the Old Man really was. Nugget-diggers will find the excellent index invaluable, especially, under "Larkin, Philip Arthur" (1922-1985), the subheadings SEX ("attitude to women . . . complains about expense . . . sexual log books . . . pornography") and ATTITUDES AND OPINIONS ("dislike of children . . . fear of marriage . . . loathing of abroad . . . right-wing politics . . . racism"). It's a map to what Tom Paulin, the British press's foreman nugget-digger, calls "the sewer under the national monument Larkin became."

In his introduction, Motion, sketching the connections among Larkin's art, life, and public persona, lays out the major theme of the book in three memorable sentences: "[M]any of Larkin's inner conflicts evolved in ways his work can only hint at. When he found his authentic voice in the late 1940s, the beautiful flowers of his poetry were already growing on long stalks out of pretty dismal ground. Describing this ground must necessarily alter the image of Larkin that he prepared so carefully for his readers." In other words: How perfect the art. How imperfect the life. And oh what a sham all that charming, curmudgeonly, "Hermit of Hull" crap he served up on a pub-lunch platter. Motion's chief aim as biographer is not to devalue Larkin's *oeuvre*—on the contrary, most of his reading of it is appreciative—but to make us marvel at the paradox of its very existence: for Motion, it's the improbably gorgeous product of a wholly loathsome mind. "To follow [Larkin's] development"—and here Motion means emotional and ideological development, not artistic—"is to have our sense of his achievement sharply increased."

Motion, of course, is not Larkin's son—not, that is, in the literal sense. But to Motion's generation of poets, Larkin was the father-figure, the standard-setter. To Motion himself, as to much of the public, he was the greatest contemporary English poet—indeed, "one of the great poets of the century." And Motion was Larkin's protégé—if Larkin can be said ever to have had one. Thirty years Larkin's junior, Motion first met the poet in 1976 when he, Motion, was twenty-four and newly appointed a lecturer in English at the University of Hull. Larkin was then fifty-three, and had been the university's librarian for over twenty years. The two became good friends, and in 1983, not long before his death, Larkin asked Motion to become one of his literary executors. "At no time during the nine years of our friendship did we discuss his biography," Motion writes. "He did not ask me to write this book."

Neither did Larkin ask another of his executors, his old friend Anthony Thwaite, to collect and edit his letters. (Whether he wished the letters to be collected at all is uncertain; his will, which has much vexed the trustees of his estate, is contradictory on this and other matters pertaining to the posthumous fate of his unpublished writings.) [Thwaite's eight-hundred-page selection] is very much a companion piece to Motion's *Life* in that it gives us, in great detail and at great length, the same "new" picture of Larkin. This Larkin is not the public Larkin of the published interviews, who, with self-deprecating humor, presented us with a highly attractive case of stiff-upper-lip in the face of life's shortcomings and of self-sacrifice in the name of art. This Larkin is the private Larkin, and his picture is painted in darker tones of "racism, misogyny and quasi-fascis[m]" (Tom Paulin again). Both the *Life* and the *Letters* may have been begun by friends wishing to do honor to Larkin's achievement, but in the end, and on the bookshelf together, their fourteen hundred pages seem intended to crush the three skinny books of poems—*The Less Deceived, The Whitsun Weddings,* and *High Windows*—that remain the heart of his *oeuvre.* More exactly, the books seem intended to vandalize—and certainly have had the popular effect of vandalizing—the familiar, shyly smiling image that peered out at us from Larkin's jacket photos. Like the idealized girl on the poster in "Sunny Prestatyn," this image of the poet was too good for this life. It proved an irresistible target to Motion and Paulin and all the other conflicted scribblers who both take excitement from Larkin's work and, consciously or not, hate him for it.

"You know," Larkin once wrote to Thwaite, "I was never a child: my life began at 21, or 31 more likely. Say with the publication of *The Less Deceived.*" This was one of Larkin's many ways of saying that only his art really mattered; all else, including the "biographical sources" of that art, was dross. But Larkin was, of course, a child once, and he remained forever his parents' son. Motion is at his most sympathetic when writing of Larkin's early years and the ways they shaped his sensibility.

Larkin's father, Sydney, a government accountant in Coventry, filled his son with the faults he had, but also imparted his virtues. He was, in Motion's words, "intolerant to the point of perversity, contemptuous of women, careless of other people's feelings or fates, yet at the same time excitingly intellectual [and] inspirationally quick-witted." Larkin's mother, Eva, a cosseting parent and a cowed wife, was passive, snobbish, and forever bewailing her lot. In an unpublished memoir, Larkin wrote that "the marriage left me with two convictions: that human beings should not live together, and that children should be taken from their parents at an early age."

According to Motion, Sydney Larkin's chief legacy to his son was twofold: a taste for literature, especially Thomas Hardy, and a tendency toward what Motion calls "reactionary politics." (Sydney was a Nazi sympathizer, may have been part of a British para-Nazi organization called the Link, and kept a mechanical statuette of Hitler on the mantelpiece at home that, at the touch of a button, sprang into the "Sieg Heil!" salute.) He died in 1948, when Larkin was twenty-five. Eva Larkin's legacy was a good deal more complicated. Motion makes her out to be both Larkin's deepest emotional attachment and, more than any other woman in his life, his muse. "Although [she] was often silly," he writes, "although she often drove Larkin into agonies of boredom and frenzies of rage, the ties which bound her to her son were not merely comforting but inspirational. They connected Larkin to his past, to memories of hope and excitement, and to the creative 'sense of being young.' Until the end of her life"—she lived on to the age of ninety-one, and Larkin didn't long survive her—"Eva . . . crucially influenced the accents and attitudes of his poems." Indeed, says Motion, "many of his best [poems] were either triggered by her or about her: 'Love Songs in Age,' 'Reference Back,' 'To the Sea,' 'The Building,' 'The Old Fools,' " and, finally, "Aubade." This said, it strikes one as decidedly odd that Larkin's letters to his mother—there are several hundred extant, for after his father died, he wrote her at least twice a week—are scarcely quoted by Motion and don't figure into Thwaite's collection at all.

After Coventry came Oxford, where Larkin struck out with the girls, flirted with at least one young man, and, at the prompting of his friend Kingsley Amis, began to write imaginative prose—mock-lesbian romances, mostly, set in a girl's school. Despite his best efforts to play the Bad Boy—to keep his reading strictly off the syllabus and to spend his nights in jazz cellars—Larkin took a First. He left Oxford without plans, longing to become a great writer and hunting for a trade that would both complement that desire and suit his temperament. Quite by accident, while paging through the Help Wanted section of the *Birmingham Post,* he discovered an opening for a librarian position in Wellington, Shropshire. He applied for the job and got it, beginning a distinguished career in librarianship that would take him, in 1955, to the University of Hull.

By that time—he was then thirty-two—he had already completed the bulk of his writing. There had been two remarkably accomplished novels, *Jill* and *A Girl in Winter,* and the beginnings of a never-to-be-completed third. He had brought out a book of poems, *The North Ship,* and found a publisher for his first mature collection, *The Less Deceived.* In an interview with the London *Observer,* Larkin would later call this "probably the 'interest' time of my life"; for Andrew Motion, who once remarked that "obviously I regret not having known him when he was writing more fluently," they were also his most admirable. What followed, much to Motion's "obvious regret," were three decades of fame, frustrated creativity, and, consequently, lack of authenticity. "All the faces, voices, attitudes, beliefs, jokes and opinions that had evolved during his growth to maturity were," with the popular success of his second book of poems, "suddenly enshrined in the personality which the public decided was 'him.' Like the characteristics he later described in 'Dockery and Son,' they hardened into all he'd got." Larkin suddenly became "Larkin," a character of whom his biographer disapproves.

"Fame," writes Motion, "endangered [Larkin's] poems by threatening the delicate balance between a desire for pri-

vate rumination and a longing for a public hearing. He wondered how he could continue to 'be himself' if his self depended on remoteness and disappointment, neither of which he could truly be said to possess any more." Here and elsewhere throughout the latter half of the book, Motion is arguing that Larkin, by winning what every poet hopes for (readers, reviews, and respect) and yet rejecting all the perks of the modern poet's "profession" (writer-in-residence sinecures, television appearances, public readings, book tours, etc.), was being hypocritical or even clinically perverse. All that poet-of-deprivation stuff should have been abandoned after 1955, and Larkin should have "developed" beyond it, moved on to other and perhaps sunnier incarnations. He should have "improved" himself, but instead he patented "Larkinism," a private-label poetic shtick. Increasingly, "he was tempted to freeze his life in postures of continuing unhappiness. As far as his work was concerned, this meant making things out to be worse than they actually were, and at the same time denying that there was anything redemptively strange or unique involved in writing about them."

Even worse, Larkin's fame justified him in his selfishness. "The success of *The Less Deceived* strengthened his resolve to live alone," to have no obligations but to himself and his art. "Never mind that his rate of production was so low (only two poems in 1956)—he now regarded every [positive] development in his career as proof that he was right to behave as he did." And, Motion argues, Larkin behaved very badly, especially toward his women.

In his adult life, there were four. There were Patsy Strang, the free-spirited wife of an acquaintance in Belfast; Maeve Brennan, a member of his staff at Hull; and Betty Mackereth, his personal secretary. But first and foremost there was Monica Jones, whom he met in 1947, when he was a librarian at the University College of Leicester and she a lecturer in English. Except for his mother, she was the most important person in Larkin's life, and she survives him as co-trustee of his estate and, with Thwaite and Motion, one of his literary executors. Although I'm certain the author doesn't see it this way, she emerges as the true heroine of Motion's book when, after being asked by the dying Larkin to do so, she arranges to have his diaries fed to the Hull University Library shredder. She also appears to have been admirably stingy about sharing her most intimate letters from Larkin with her fellow-executors.

What did Larkin get out of these relationships with women, none of which, he was adamant, would ever end in marriage, and three of which, those with Monica, Maeve, and Betty, he juggled at one time? Beyond providing the pleasures of sexual companionship, these love affairs "activated," Motion argues, "a dramatic struggle between life and work on which his personality [and his poems] depended." By dividing his affections among two or more women at once, Larkin ensured emotional disappointment for every party involved, disappointment he could then (sometimes) turn into poetry. Furthermore, his candid acknowledgments of faithlessness, like his openness about his habit of masturbating to pornography, made it clear to would-be wives that he was promised to no one but himself.

Larkin's taste in pornography, like his taste in everything else, was essentially conventional. (His friend Robert Conquest called it "really very unchallenging. Perhaps a bit of spanking, that's all.") Unchallenging or not, that Larkin had *any* kind of taste for it clearly unsettles Motion, as does the wildly abusive language about women (and "wogs" and "socialists" and so on) that peppers many of Larkin's letters, especially those to old schoolmates such as Kingsley Amis. That Larkin the letter-writer was often playing to his recipients' expectations—that he was trying to keep a wartime schoolchum camaraderie and a damn-the-world adolescent's worldview alive for old time's sake—is cold comfort to Motion. For Larkin to have used such language in his youth, back when the world was less enlightened about "the other," is one thing. For him to have used such language even into the 1980s is unforgivable.

This is why Motion saves his most severe blasts for the last years of Larkin's life, the years between the publication of his final book of poems, *High Windows* (1974), and his death, at age sixty-three, in 1985. It was during these years, when the poems were no longer coming, that his "anger and sense of futility kept pace with each other, driving the comedy out of his extravagant opinions and clouding the pleasures that remained to him." In other words, "his frustration as a writer had by now affected all his judgements." That Larkin professed in an interview to "adore" Margaret Thatcher is offered up as definitive proof of his jadedness, of his having gone totally beyond the pale. Motion cites this tidbit no fewer than four times, with the word "adore" always in scare quotes.

Martin Amis, writing about the *Life* in a recent issue of *The New Yorker,* wrote that "in Andrew Motion's book we have the constant sense that Larkin is somehow falling short of the cloudless emotional health enjoyed by (for instance) Andrew Motion." As an effort to catch the between-the-lines condescension of biographer to subject, this sentence can scarcely be improved. But Motion is not merely condescending, he is, by the book's final pages, wholly out-of-sympathy, unable or unwilling to imagine Larkin from the inside out. Larkin saw him coming, or someone very much like him, when he dreamed up "Jake Balokowsky, my biographer," in the poem "Posterity." Balokowsky is the jeaned-and-sneakered embodiment of the Sixties-generation literary professional, a careerist who laments that, in writing Larkin's life, "I'm stuck with this old fart at least a year." "Just let me put this bastard on the skids," he says, "I'll get a couple of semesters leave / To work on Protest Theater." What's Larkin *really* like? a friend enquires. "Christ, I just told you," he replies:

> "Oh, you know the thing,
> That crummy textbook stuff from Freshman
>   Psych,
> Not out of kicks or something happening—
> One of those old-type *natural* fouled-up guys."

At the end of his *Observer* interview, Larkin says: "I should hate anybody to read my work because he's been told to and told what to think about it." For my part, I should hate anybody *not* to read Larkin because he's been told what to think about the man and so thinks he needn't

bother. There's a brand new generation of readers that believes, and is being instructed to believe, that flowers grown from dismal ground are not worth picking. Well, Larkin's flowers are of a hardy strain, and they will survive the present miasma in which they must live, the poisonous and obscuring atmosphere created by the *Letters* and the *Life* and the Paulins among their reviewers. "Church Going," "Dockery and Son," "The Whitsun Weddings," "An Arundel Tomb," "Aubade": go read them again, now, and *aloud*. To do so is to be moved by them afresh and to drown out all the irrelevant noise about the "unfortunate" circumstances of their composition. (pp. 83-7)

Christopher Carduff, "Just Let Me Put This Bastard on the Skids," in The New Criterion, *Vol. XII, No. 1, September, 1993, pp. 83-7.*

FURTHER READING

Eder, Richard. "Eluding Himself." *The Los Angeles Times Book Review* (25 July 1993): 3, 10.
    Discusses Motion's account of Larkin's life and asserts that "Larkin was a recurring set of intensely small-scaled contradictions; Motion circles round and round the same contradictions, detailing the slight variations of a hesitant, depressive and utterly self-absorbed temperament."

Gioia, Dana. "The Still, Sad Music of Philip Larkin." *The Washington Post Book World* XXIII, No. 33 (15 August 1993): 1, 9.
    Positive review of *Philip Larkin: A Writer's Life.* Gioia comments: "Reading Motion's detailed biography, one realizes how reductive it is to label Larkin politically incorrect."

Griffiths, Sian. "The Brilliance of Failure." *The Times Higher Education Supplement,* No. 1038 (25 September 1993): 15.
    Interview with Andrew Motion about the process of writing his biography of Larkin.

Horovitz, Michael. "An Undeveloped Heart." *New Statesman & Society* 6, No. 246 (2 April 1993): 24-5.
    Negative assessment of Andrew Motion's biography of Larkin, in which Horovitz comments: "Motion provides an all too formulaic summary."

Powell, Anthony. "The Narrow Road to Hull." *The Spectator* 269, No. 8572 (24 October 1992): 39.
    Presents a positive review of *Selected Letters of Philip Larkin* and discusses Larkin's views on literature and his contemporaries.

Raban, Jonathan. "The Idea of Elsewhere." *The New Republic* 209, Nos. 3-4 (19-26 July 1993): 30-6.
    Praises Andrew Motion's attention to the paradoxical elements of Larkin's life and art in *Philip Larkin: A Writer's Life.*

Ratcliffe, Michael. "Friday Lunch Blues." *The Observer,* No. 10,492 (November 1992): 64.

Predominantly positive review of *Selected Letters of Philip Larkin.*

Additional coverage of Larkin's life and career is contained in the following sources published by Gale Research: *Concise Dictionary of British Literary Biography, 1960 to Present; Contemporary Authors,* Vols. 5-8 (rev. ed.), 117 (obituary); *Contemporary Authors New Revision Series,* Vol. 24; *Contemporary Literary Criticism,* Vols. 3, 5, 8, 9, 13, 18, 33, 39, 64; *Dictionary of Literary Biography,* Vol. 27; and *Major 20th-Century Writers.*

Revising the Literary Canon

INTRODUCTION

A literary canon is a list of "great books" with which, it is believed, one must be familiar in order to participate meaningfully in the prevailing culture. The current debate about revising the Western literary canon so that it includes works by women, ethnic, and minority writers is part of a larger political and cultural dispute in contemporary education. The question of selecting the books a society should deem great—"the best that was thought and said," in Andrew Marvell's frequently quoted words—is an ancient one. As commentators point out, the first major debate over a canon occurred when compilers of the Old and New Testaments decided which books to include in the Bible and which to relegate to the Apocrypha. Today, the issue is not one of divine inspiration but political power, ethnicity, gender, and sexual orientation.

Critics favoring revision argue for diversity, faulting the traditional canon for representing only the works of "dead white European males." These commentators often support progressive and sometimes radical social and literary theories—for example, Marxism and deconstruction—as well as aggressive approaches to redefining the curriculum to reflect multicultural and interdisciplinary interests. Comparatively, scholars who uphold the traditional canon argue that the "great books" are still relevant. Propounding a conservative, classical form of education, they claim that the revisionist position entails distasteful, even absurd implications: namely that women cannot learn from men, one ethnic group cannot learn from another, and the past has no lessons for the future. Recent studies warning of a crisis in American education and such interrelated and controversial issues as multiculturalism, postcolonialism, cultural literacy, and the merits of deconstructionism have fueled debate over the canon. Recognizing the controversy's pervasiveness, some educators have suggested that discussion of the canon should be incorporated into the curriculum as a way of revitalizing an issue and set of books from which many students feel increasingly removed.

HISTORICAL OVERVIEW

David H. Richter (essay date 1989)

[*Richter is an American educator and critic. In the following essay, he discusses the history of the debate about literary canons and examines the perspectives embodied in absolutist and relativistic arguments.*]

Which texts shall be accepted into the canon and which shall be relegated to the apocrypha? This was the question that both the compilers of the Masoretic text of the Old Testament in the first and second centuries and the patristic fathers establishing the New Testament in the third century had to answer. In those days, the books of Daniel and Esther were accepted into the canon, while the prophecies of Baruch ben Sirach and the chronicles of the Maccabees were exiled to the apocrypha; the gospels of Matthew and Luke were given canonical authority while the gospel of Nicodemus was discarded. Today, the equivalent question concerns a less well codified canon of texts: the major works of imaginative literature. While everyone knows that the canon of major Western writers includes Homer, Dante, Shakespeare, Molière, Tolstoy, . . . and so on down the list, below that level the consensus dissolves into controversy, and it is less clear who will survive and who will perish, whose reputation is beyond question and whose is vulnerable to challenge.

The one undeniable truth is that most works of the imagination do perish. Robert Escarpit, the French sociologist of literature, estimated that no more than one book in two hundred is read—read by a genuine public, that is, beyond the occasional burrower in libraries—ten years after its publication. Fewer still last twenty years or thirty; almost none survive a century. A century was the measure Samuel Johnson used to define a classic. In the preface to his 1763 edition of Shakespeare, he explained that since the plays had survived a century—nearly a hundred and fifty years, in fact—and had lost their topical interest, they seemed meant for all time and might be criticized judicially against the other classics of drama that had also outlasted their age. It should hardly be surprising that "instant classics"—works that seem upon publication to be destined for a long life—most often surprise us by their premature decease: Thomas Wolfe was a great novelist in the 1930s but is almost unread today; even a recent biography (1987) failed to touch off a Wolfe revival.

But even long survival carries no guarantee of indefinite tenure. An important group of American poets, including John Greenleaf Whittier, Henry Wadsworth Longfellow,

Sidney Lanier, and James Russell Lowell, were classics to the generation of Americans who entered school before World War II but are virtually unknown to the generation of Americans entering school today. Textbooks that once enshrined them as classics no longer have room for them. The same is true for English literature. Not long ago, the poetry of Walter Scott was thought worthy of memorization; today readers have little time even for his prose. Poets like Matthew Prior and George Crabbe, novelists like Elizabeth Manley, Robert Bage, and Charles Reade, and playwrights like Arthur Pinero have all dropped in esteem to near the vanishing point. Their works are out of print, exiled from most of the newest school anthologies, and can only be found in better university libraries and used bookshops. A glance through older catalogues of the Modern Library in America or the Everyman's Library or World's Classics editions in England confirms the difference between the canon of an earlier day and that of our own.

Survival is a risky business. The lists of required reading a culture prescribes for its educated elite have to be tailored to the short span of a human life. Like nature, therefore, literature has an ecology that forbids unlimited expansion; when something is added, something else must go. In a sense, the debate over the canon began when poets realized that they were competing for fame not merely with their coevals but with all of their predecessors. Hence Horace's remark, "I hate it when a book is condemned, not for being bad but for being new," which has been echoed by poet-critics for centuries thereafter. But the contemporary debate over the canon is not entirely parallel with the poets' long-standing complaint that there cannot be room on Parnassus for everyone. The new interest is not in the *facts* of literary ecology but in the *process* by which certain texts achieve canonical status, particularly the relationship between literary value and the more sordid matters of literary economics and politics.

The debate over the canon has evolved, like the canon itself. As late as the mid-nineteenth century, in essays like Sainte-Beuve's "What Is a Classic?" or Arnold's "The Study of Poetry," literary value was assumed ultimately to be a function of human nature. "A true classic," says Sainte-Beuve,

> is an author who has enriched the human spirit, who has truly increased its treasure, who has caused it to take a step forward, who has discovered some unequivocal moral truth or laid fresh hold on some eternal passion in that heart where all seemed known and explored; who has conveyed his thought, his observation, or his discovery in whatever form, only let it be liberal and grand, choice and judicious, intrinsically wholesome and seemly; who has spoken to all men in a style of his own which at the same time turns out to be every man's style, a style which is new without neologism, at once new and old, easily contemporaneous with every age.

Arnold appeals to "the best that has been thought and said" as though it could be true for all time. T. S. Eliot speaks of the "tradition" as an "eternal order"—a club to which new members, agreeable to the charter founders,

are always welcome. For such critics, though beauty is necessarily subjective—not the object's possession of a quantum of Platonic essence but a conformity or relation between the object of art and human nature—quality is in effect absolute because human nature is presumed constant. The ecology of literature is seen as a winnowing process: Time destroys the worst and leaves the best, and time will do this, apparently, without any help from literary critics. Absolutists are operating nowadays as well. Hans-Georg Gadamer, the mentor of the reception theorists Iser and Jauss, defends the classic [in *Truth and Method* (1988)] as "a truly historical category, a consciousness of something enduring, of significance that cannot be lost and is independent of all the circumstances of time." Like Hegel, who understood the classic as "that which signifies itself and hence also interprets itself," Gadamer feels that the timelessness of the classic is in itself "a mode of historical being."

On the other side are the relativists who believe that literary quality is a function of the current interests of the reading public; each public revises the short list drawn up by publics of the past to accord with its own cultural needs. This is the perspective of Jane Tompkins's *Sensational Designs: The Cultural Work of American Fiction, 1790-1860* (1985), which suggests that imaginative texts are admired in a society to the extent that they meet its cultural needs. Thus, Susan Warner's didactic *The Wide Wide World* (1850) was immensely popular in its day because its sentimental melodrama defined cultural stereotypes in an intelligible way for a public adrift because of rapid social change.

Novels like *The Wide Wide World* are of undoubted historical interest, and certainly writers like Warner (and Harriet Beecher Stowe) more closely defined the interests and tastes of the American public of their time than did writers like Hawthorne or Melville, Emerson or Thoreau. But Tompkins wishes to go further. She denigrates Hawthorne's early survival as due primarily to his connections in New England editorial and publishing circles, which kept his works alive through biographies and new editions for twenty years after his death. Tompkins recognizes that no conspiracy of editors could have kept Hawthorne before the public for a hundred and thirty years, but she does not allow his fame since the 1870s to result from his classical timelessness. Rather, she claims, each generation of readers has *redefined* Hawthorne's greatness according to its own terms, and therefore nothing intrinsic to the author's work has preserved his reputation. The "classic" Hawthorne thus splinters, in this analysis, into different facets, each of which has, for assorted social, political, economic, and cultural reasons, been the darling of successive interpretive communities and interest groups.

Tompkins's analysis of Hawthorne translates the concept of aesthetic quality into ideology. Her ultimate end is to show how cultural politics may alter the literary canon—how feminists may displace Hawthorne and Melville in favor of currently neglected writers like Warner and Stowe. But critics have long tried to influence the canon, and it is difficult to know how far they have ever succeeded. Jeremy Collier's "Short View of the Profanity . . .

of the English Stage" (1698) is sometimes credited with having cleaned up the nastiness of Restoration comedy, although recent stage historians have suggested that the most offensive plays were written in the 1670s and that the stage had been cleaning up its own act for two decades before Collier wrote. And despite the prestige of Samuel Johnson, the "Great Cham of Literature" in eighteenth-century England, his preference for Richardson over Fielding ("a barren rascal") has not been echoed by succeeding generations.

Perhaps the closest equivalent to a Johnson in our own day was F. R. Leavis. It is hard to think of a twentieth-century critic of greater moral weight and prestige. Unlike Sainte-Beuve, Leavis conceived of literature as a manifestation of culture and of culture itself as something molded by the forces of history. This may be how one must treat his claim, in Chapter I of *The Great Tradition,* that "the great novelists are Jane Austen, George Eliot, Henry James, and Joseph Conrad" (with D. H. Lawrence included as an addendum). For this sociocultural savant, the novel was a genre designed to speak of man and society, of the individual and his consciousness, against the backdrop of the social forces that shaped them and conflicted with them. For this reason, the greatest novelists were those for whom these issues were paramount. Mere humorists like Fielding and Sterne in the eighteenth century, or Thackeray in the nineteenth, need not apply. At the same time, contemporary modernists like Woolf and Joyce—for whom society did not exist as a separable force but as something implicit within individual consciousness—did not appeal to Leavis. As a result, his list of favorites, while certainly enshrined in today's canon, seems quirky rather than inexorably ordained, a quirkiness that to later eyes seems a common characteristic of all lists drawn up by magisterial critics.

If magisterial critics like Johnson, Arnold, Eliot, and Leavis cannot dictate the canon, then who does? Perhaps it is a mistake to look to individuals; perhaps institutional factors should be explored, as Barbara Herrnstein Smith has done in "Contingencies of Value." To begin with, it seems clear that social change produces audiences with new and varied interests. The politics of feminism over the past twenty years has sparked a growth of interest in previously neglected female authors. But although it appears that society has changed rapidly over the past half-century, the canon has not. Strong conservative forces (including the very *idea* of a canon) are operating to keep the canon constant. Institutional education is arguably the strongest of these conservative forces. The most widely read texts are those read in schools, where teachers are likely to teach the texts that were valued during their own education. Furthermore, some texts may survive precisely because they are useful to educators: Xenophon's *Memorabilia* may have endured not because of its intellectual quality but because it was a perfect vehicle for teaching children the principles of Greek syntax; and some poems may be extant today because they are perfect examples of prosody or symbolism.

Also to be considered are other classes of people who are responsible for altering the literary canon. Since education is an important conservative force, those who compile textbooks and anthologies function, more and more self-consciously these days, as both the preservers and the re-shapers of a tradition. Today the editors of anthologies are indeed tastemakers, but given the institutional framework of publishing, their individual tastes are seldom any more decisive than those of the magisterial critics. When an editor compiles a list of texts to be included in a book, the editor's voice does not sing solo. The project editor assigned by the publisher will make suggestions for inclusion and exclusion, and after these are assimilated, the list will be sent out to a number of experts who will express their own preferences. Meanwhile, editors have their own institutional reasons for repressing the quirks of personal taste. Most of them want their books to sell, and they will do so only if they provide what the teachers who assign textbooks want.

In this process we can identify initiators (the authors of texts), mediators (editors, publishers, marketers, teachers), and ultimately, consumers. This structure also exists for trade books, although here, book reviewers (and the editors who give prominence to certain books and not to others, who assign books to reviewers likely to be friendly or hostile) have an important mediating role. In the nineteenth century, the editors of magazines determined which novels would be serialized—an important determinant of sales and reputation, while the heads of circulating libraries (and some of these, like Mudie's, were large and influential) could often make or break reputations by including authors on or excluding authors from their lists. All these mediators between author and reader operate under capitalism: They may indulge their personal taste, but at the risk that the market may disagree and put them out of business.

These factors, along with others, are cited in Smith's essay, which makes the best possible case for relativism. Smith feels that the evaluation of a work is not influenced by any absolute quality it possesses but by whether or not it meets the cultural needs of a public. (For Smith, "aesthetic value" is an aspect of economics, broadly conceived.) As society changes, the work takes one of two trajectories: downward to oblivion or upward toward canonical status. Smith recognizes that even canonical works can "always move into a trajectory of extinction" under unfavorable circumstances. But canonical status works to protect a text from this path because "features that would, in a noncanonical work, be found alienating . . . technically crude, philosophically naive, or narrowly topical—will be glozed over or backgrounded." If a work is bigoted or chauvinistic, "there will be a tendency among humanistic scholars and academic critics to 'save the text' by transferring the locus of its interest to more formal or structural features."

Smith's paradigm of the relationship between a culture and its canon is also fascinating on the question of how the generic categorization of cultural objects follows from society's changing interests and purposes. An illuminating example of these dynamic relations in action can be found in Houston Baker's "Generational Shifts and the Recent Criticism of Afro-American Literature." Here Baker shows, from an explicitly Marxist perspective, how shifts in the class interests of three "generations" of critics of Afro-American literature have changed not only the language of criticism but also their evaluations of the primary texts of that tradition.

It is obvious that the middle ground between canonical absolutism and relativism will be difficult to defend philosophically; at the same time, many critics have found it hard to believe firmly in either extreme. The indubitable fact that once-canonized texts can disappear into oblivion undermines any idea of absolute quality. Yet, despite Smith's arguments, the fact that Homer and Shakespeare have been revered over the centuries seems to be the result of more than accident or the inertia of literary institutions. A psychological explanation of this may be found in Kant's notion that the judgment of taste is subjective but absolute, that the disinterested apprehension of beauty we experience makes us *feel* (whatever our empirical knowledge to the contrary) that everyone ought to agree with us, that our judgment is true for everyone and for all time.

Few critics have mediated between absolutism and relativism with the deftness of Frank Kermode. In *The Classic,* Kermode accepts the relativist position in principle but also holds that "the survival of the classic" depends on its having "a surplus of the signifier"—what might be called the sort of very rich economy that lends it use and value in a large variety of cultural systems. Classics like *King Lear* or *Wuthering Heights* "must always signify more than is needed by any one interpreter or any one generation of interpreters." By richness texts endure: Ripeness is all. (pp. 1285-91)

> *David H. Richter, "Issue Under Debate: The Canon," in* The Critical Tradition: Classic Texts and Contemporary Trends, *edited by David H. Richter, St. Martin's Press, 1989, pp. 1285-91.*

CRITICISM

Hugh Kenner (essay date Spring 1984)

[*Kenner is the foremost American critic and chronicler of literary Modernism. He is best known for* The Pound Era *(1971), a comprehensive study of the Modernist movement, and for his influential works on T. S. Eliot, James Joyce, Samuel Beckett, and Wyndham Lewis. In the following essay, he examines the factors that influence the formation of a canon.*]

Your whimsical thoughts, if you live long enough, will be back haunting you. I am now beset by a notion that crossed my mind twenty years ago. Then it seemed only a mild historical fancy. Now it resembles a cognitive Black Hole. It is simply this: that *no Englishman alive in 1600 was living in the Age of Shakespeare.* For there was no Age of Shakespeare in 1600. That age was invented long afterwards.

Partly, I was thinking of Borges' famous statement that writers invent their predecessors; partly, I was pondering angry speculations rife in those years, when it was held, if you remember, that the Beatles, if you remember them, might be unacknowledged Mozarts. We were all of us being reproved for not celebrating their genius. Moreover genius, we were being told, never does get properly celebrated. It goes to a premature and quicklimed grave, after which posterity's accolades need cost posterity exactly nothing.

We are talking about psychic money: that was the currency bourgeoisiedom denied the Beatles while they were intact. Yes, yes, mere dollars came fluttering down abundantly upon Ringo and George and Paul and John. But not for them a reward that was withheld from Mozart also while he lived: assimilation into the musical canon. It is like the withholding of a full professorship.

I was set to wondering, when did Shakespeare get assimilated into the canon? Moreover, was there any inherent scandal in his not having been assimilated while he lived? And to the second question the ready answer was no. In 1600 there was no canon, literary history not yet having been invented. Nor, save in theater circles, was Will Shakespeare even so much as a celebrity. Not only no canvasclimber of Drake's, but no learned fellow of the court had any reason to suppose he would some day be envied for having been Shakespeare's coeval, privileged to stand in the pit at the Globe while Burbage, reciting words about seas of troubles, sawed the air with his hand thus. The canvasclimber, for that matter, could have told Burbage a thing or two first-hand about seas and trouble.

How did it ever become obvious that about 1600 Englishmen were living in the Age of Shakespeare? And is it even obvious now? Roland Barthes would have said it is not; he would have had us believe that such determinations were reversible, were in fact at bottom political, serving as they did to advantage a custodial class whose livelihood was bound up with the preeminence of Shakespeare: a class apt to be relegated to janitorial status should anyone make college deans believe that in 1600 men lived in the Age of—oh, Tom Dekker. It is, of course, professors such as myself who have a fiscal stake in Shakespeare. One Marxist gambit is to make innocents doubt whether there is any other stake.

Meanwhile such fin-de-siècle Englishmen as thought about it—fin, I mean, du seizième siècle—doubtless thought they were living in the age of Queen Elizabeth, not thinking to define their good fortune in literary categories at all. I could as well attribute my presence here to the fact that we live in the age of sterile surgery and penicillin.

By the 18th century vernacular literature had accumulated a long enough history to be thought about historically. By 1783 Dr. Johnson had collected his *Lives of the English Poets,* working from a canon established, interestingly enough, not by himself but by a syndicate of booksellers. It included no poet born earlier than 16xx: none, in short, whose conventions of spelling, syntax and image would be apt to strike an Augustan browser as odd. It was possible to wonder about the present state of literature. If that means, to ask with what names posterity might associate one's own time, then it concedes that our posterity will know us in ways we do not.

Where did our present canonical list come from? That is unwritten history. How canons are determined is in general unwritten history.

—Hugh Kenner

So in what age did a literate man about 1810 suppose he was living? Why, in the age of Samuel Rogers, Thomas Campbell, Robert Southey. Those are the names that would have come to mind: names we no longer hear. Our present canonical list is Wordsworth, Coleridge, Byron, Keats, Shelley, to which add Blake: and where did it come from? That is unwritten history. How canons are determined is in general unwritten history.

Let me therefore throw what light I can on one canon I have a little knowledge of. The canon of literary modernism: how did that get made? Is it made yet?

As recently as 1931, a year I can just remember, it was not made, was not even adumbrated. That was the year F. R. Leavis published *New Bearings in English Poetry,* and felt obliged, before he disclosed the new bearings, to dispose of pseudo-bearings, the likes of Alfred Noyes and Walter de la Mare. Noyes had lately undertaken a long poem about the great astronomers of history, and Leavis even felt required to deal with that; his dealing was formal in syntax but paraphrasable as a snort. Nor was he overcome by William Butler Yeats, whose intelligence he called "magnificent" but much of whose poetry he described as meditation on the events of the poet's life: an *Irish* life, moreover. Leavis identified one *English* modern poet, G. M. Hopkins; one naturalized English one, the American-born T. S. Eliot (who would later advert to Leavis's "rather lonely battle for literacy"); finally one *echt* American, Ezra Pound. Pound was the author of just one good poem, *Hugh Selwyn Mauberley* (1920); the rest, before and after, was enamel and polish and the doing of inorganic will; such "limited interest" as the *Cantos* had was "technical." Dead 42 years but organic, G. M. Hopkins was O.K. Alive 43 years, T. S. Eliot was more than O.K.; the hope of the time, it was clear, lay with Mr. Eliot.

Whatever else *New Bearings* was, it was an intelligent start at canon-defining, given the state of knowledge in '31. Pointless now to ironize at the expense of Leavis's later career: his disenchantment with Eliot, his growing obsession with Lawrence, his virtual dismissal of Joyce, his grotesque determination that what at bottom had prevented Eliot from being a major poet was American birth. The state of knowledge in 1931, that is the thing to concentrate on. What do you need to know to define a canon?

Wrong question, since there's no generic answer. Better: what did Leavis in 1931 not know? Two things at least of great scope. One was the unprecedented interdependence of prose modernism and verse modernism. Though his magazine *Scrutiny* was later to deal with *Wuthering Heights* and *Hard Times* in a series it called "The Novel as Dramatic Poem," still how *Ulysses* had been the necessary forerunner of *The Waste Land* was something never clear to Leavis, nor how Henry James's habits of diction were refracted throughout a poem Leavis nowhere mentions, Pound's *Homage to Sextus Propertius.* That was a central modernist discovery, that distinctions between "prose" and "verse" vanish before distinctions between firm writing and loose; there is no more dramatic moment in the *Cantos* than the one that affixes to the poem's page scraps of so-called "prose" that have been extracted and Englished, with neither meter nor ragged right margins, from the contents of Sigismundo Malatesta's post-bag. "Hang it all, Robert Browning," commences *Canto II,* and when Robert Browning had processed old Italian letters he'd felt constrained to put them into blank verse, thus marking the frontier across which they were fetched: from "out there," where prose is, into a genuine *poem.*

But we no longer think language must vest itself in measure when it is brought into a poem. "Give me my robe, put on my crown"—that is a formula it need no longer intone. One test of a sensibility that acknowledges this new bearing is hospitality to Marianne Moore, who can pick her brisk way through unmetered though counted lines that are open to scraps of actual prose, and not the prose of Gibbon or Pater either, but corporation pamphlets about the Icosasphere. Of her, despite T. S. Eliot's firm endorsement, Leavis could make nothing: a defeat of a great critic so humiliating it has vanished from the Index to the reprinted *Scrutiny.* Another test is William Carlos Williams, who comes as close as any real poet does to validating the philistine complaint that modernist verse misrepresents mere prose by "lines." *Scrutiny* was not alone in ignoring Williams in England; he was not even published there until after his ex-compatriot Eliot had died, and even today so unabashed a British pro-modernist as Donald Davie confesses to making little of him.

And of course when we're in Donald Davie's company we may feel sure we're remote from prose/verse naivete. No, it's something else about Williams, his American-ness, the cisatlantic tang of his cadence, that still eludes John Bull. And now we are ready for the second cardinal fact that was hidden from Leavis in 1931: the fact that the English language had split four ways, leaving English natives in control of but a fraction. No Englishman will contemplate this with any zest, so if you get your literary news from England you'll hear little of it.

Since Chaucer, the domain of English literature had been a country, England. Early in the 20th century its domain commenced to be a language, English. By about 1925 it was clear that three countries, Ireland, America and England, were conducting substantial national literatures in this language. Common words had deceptively different meanings in these three different literatures, and divergences of idiom were guaranteed by the fact that the three literatures drew on radically different traditions and on different intuitions of what literature might be for. It was no longer feasible to retain for the canon only what readers in England were prepared to like, the way they had once liked the songs of the Scotsman, Bobbie Burns, and the Irishman, Tom Moore. ("Bobbie"; "Tom"; they condescend when they accept.)

And by mid-century it was also clear, if not to everyone, that the decentralization of "English" was not the whole story: that there was arguably a new center, locatable in books but on no map. English was the language not only of the Three Provinces but also of several masterpieces best located in a supranational movement called International Modernism.

Such a modernism flourished in conjunction with other modernisms, painted, sculpted, danced. These in turn acknowledged new environments created by new technologies: notably, the invasion of the city by the rhythms of the machine (subways and the crowds they brought, motorcars, pavement drills like the Rock Drill Epstein sculpted).

Looking back, Virginia Woolf said whimsically that late in 1910 "human nature changed." She meant that by 1910 you could see International Modernism coming, which is true though an observer thenabouts would have expected its literary language to be French. That it proved to be English instead was largely the doing of James Joyce, whose *Ulysses* helps us define the very concept of an International work. To what literature does it belong?

Not to Irish, though its events are set in Dublin. Joyce had explicitly rejected the Irish Literary Revival as provincial, and had not only left Ireland—many Irishmen have done that—but had adduced alien canons of which his systematic parallel with a Greek epic is probably the least radical. Not to English, though most of its words are in English dictionaries and Shakespeare is an adduced presence. No, the parts of *Ulysses* that resemble a novel resemble continental, not Victorian, narratives, and its sense of what business a large work of fiction ought to be about is continuously alien to English expectations. Its fit reader is not someone schooled in a tradition it augments, as the best reader of Dickens will be grounded in Fielding and Smollett; rather, anyone willing to master the book's language, its procedures, its Dublin materials, must do so all on the book's own terms. In Ireland, peevishness about its authenticity is apt to fasten on the claim that most of its devotees are American, and indeed many of them are, though anyone's current list of six *Ulysses* authorities would include one Australian, one German, and one Swiss.

Though the language of International Modernism, like that of air control towers, proved to be English, none of its canonical works came either out of England or out of any mind formed there. International Modernism was the work of Irishmen and Americans. Its masterpieces include *Ulysses, The Waste Land,* the first thirty *Cantos.*

After 1910 it flourished for some forty years. Its last masterpiece was *Waiting for Godot,* which an Irishman living in Paris wrote in English after having first detached himself from English by writing the first version in French.

One reason Modernism's primary language was English was the emergence in this century of Irish and American self-confidence, affording to no other Indo-European language so rich a variety of social and cultural experience. And International Modernism was not restricted to language; it drew on a variety of 20th century activities which transcend the need for translators: on cubist and non-representational painting, which though mostly done in Paris owed little to any specifically French tradition; on renovations in music, inseparable from the impact (enabled by the railway) of the Russian ballet on three capitals; on the fact that the first century of world travel has also been the century of world wars; above all on the popularization, through technology, of a science which knows no frontiers and sets down its austere oracles in equations exactly as accessible to a Muscovite as to a New Yorker.

Via technology, science has shaped our century. Three events of 1895 might have foreshadowed the shape had anyone known how to correlate them. The first American gasoline-powered car was designed; an Italian named Marconi sent messages more than a mile with no wires at all; a German named Roentgen discovered that rays his apparatus was emitting passed clean through materials opaque to light.

The automobile was to end the domination of the railroad, the 19th century's triumphant cultural and economic symbol; post-Ford, all men chugged on their own, and a decent car soon meant more than a decent house.

Wireless, transmitting sounds and later pictures, was to terminate printed fiction and live drama as the normative media for entertainment; the play, the short story, in part the novel, became "art forms," art being the name we give an abandoned genre. (So television turns old movies into an art called "cinema.")

And X-rays heralded the bending of learned attention on the technology of the invisible, a change with analogies as striking as they are difficult to reckon. When early in our century John Donne's poems began to be revived after more than a century of total neglect, the eye-beams of his lovers in "The Ecstasie" no longer seemed remote from physical reality as they had when everything real was made of brick.

Hard on the discovery of the electron in 1898 came Max Planck's discovery that energy is radiated not in a continuous stream but in discrete packets, called quanta, which are never fractional, always intact, and can be counted like chromosomes. More: when a quantum of energy was emitted, its electron jumped to a new orbit, without occupying even for an instant any of the space between. Mysterious energies, sudden transitions, are as congenial to the 20th-century mind as they would have been unthinkable to our great-grandfathers. It is pointless to ask whether Eliot, who made Planck-like transitions in *The Waste Land,* did so on any scientific analogy (probably not) or had heard at all of the relevant physics (perhaps). The life of the mind in any age coheres thanks to shared assumptions both explicit and tacit, between which lines of causality may not be profitably traceable.

Before the first war the life of the English-speaking mind

emanated from London, the last of the great capitals. The skeptical Joseph Conrad, a Pole, walked its streets (and his son became a motor-car salesman). He was England's most distinguished practising novelist in the century's early decades. The principal novelist of an earlier generation was also foreign: Henry James. He lived in Rye and came up to London for the winters. London, he said ecstatically, could always give you exactly what you sought. And England's principal poet was W. B. Yeats, a man who made a symbol of his Irish identity though from 1895 to 1919 he preferred to live at 18 Woburn Buildings, London WC1. That the principal resident talent in those years was foreign in origin and often in allegiance should arrest us: London was attracting world talent the way Rome had in Augustan times when the world had a smaller circumference, and like Rome it was seeing its cultural affairs preempted by the talent it had attracted. (Vergil, Cicero, Horace, Propertius, Ovid: none was native to the Rome that claims them. Ovid had come from wild hills now called the Abruzzi, as alien to Rome as any Idaho.)

And yet another wave came. Ezra Pound, born in Idaho, reached London in 1908 from Pennsylvania via Venice, partly to learn from Yeats, whose skill in fitting the sentence exactly into the stanza was one of the signs of mastery he discerned. His old Pennsylvania classmate Hilda Doolittle ("H. D.") arrived a little later. In 1914 Tom Eliot, of St. Louis and Harvard, became a Londoner too. By contrast the native talent is apt to seem unimportant, or else proves not to be native: even Wyndham Lewis, who went to an English public school (Rugby), had been born near a dock at Amherst, Nova Scotia, on his American father's yacht.

So early modernism (say 1910-1920) was the work of a foreign coterie, the first literary generation to come to maturity in the 20th century, in awareness of Marconi and radium and Picasso, in awareness too of the French poetic avant-garde of the 1880's and '90's. Their work was either written in London or disseminated from there; Eliot brought *Prufrock* in his luggage; Joyce mailed installments of his *Portrait of the Artist as a Young Man* from Trieste as fast as he could have them typed, for serialization in a London feminist paper called *The Egoist*. London was the place to come to: Mecca: the center of the world's sophistication and prosperity, the great inexhaustible settled capital. When Pound and Lewis in 1914 named the whole modern movement "The Great London Vortex," one thing they had in mind was the ingathering power of vortices. *The Waste Land*'s occasion was the failure of that vortex. Eliot wrote in 1921 that London "only shrivels, like a little bookkeeper grown old." The same year Lewis discerned " . . . a sort of No Man's Land atmosphere. The dead never rise up, and men will not return to the Past, whatever else they may do. But as yet there is Nothing, or rather the corpse of the past age, and the sprinkling of children of the new."

A while back we left F. R. Leavis, from whom was hidden, all his life, the truth that England had become, linguistically speaking, a province. Thus American literature was no longer English literature that had happened to get written somewhere else. And the history of England, its cli-

mate, its customs, its local pieties, no longer afforded, by sheer impalpable presence, a test for the genuineness of a piece of writing in the language called English. And the capital, a "torture" for Wordsworth, was not England, but a magnet for polyglot talent including Polish and American talent. As late as the 1930's, Faber & Faber's letterhead was designating one of the firm's directors, T. S. Eliot, as "U.S.A. Origin." He was also known as "Tom (Missouri) Eliot." The capital had lured him but not whelmed him.

As the capital ingathered, the provinces stirred. Poems were mailed to *The Egoist* by William Carlos Williams from New Jersey and by Marianne Moore from New York. Williams had known Pound at college; Miss Moore revered the example of James. Though they stayed settled in America all their lives they were never tempted to make easy rhymes for the natives. Their generation, aware of emissaries in London—Pound, Eliot, H.D.—could look toward London for contact with more than mere Englishness. The next American generation, that of Hemingway, Fitzgerald and Faulkner, also drew profit from the transatlantic example. By the time of its apprenticeship there were modern masterworks to study, notably *Ulysses* and *The Waste Land*. However rootedly local, American writing, thanks to some twenty years of looking abroad, has enjoyed ever since an inwardness with the international, the technological century. Today young poets in Germany or Norway expect that it will be Americans who will understand them.

Analogously, in England, Virginia Woolf, hating *Ulysses*, still made haste to exploit its riches. She is not part of International Modernism; she is an English novelist of manners, writing village gossip from a village called Bloomsbury for her English readers (though *cultivated* readers; that distinction had become operative between Dickens's time and hers, and Bloomsbury was a village with a good library). She and they share shrewd awarenesses difficult to specify; that is always the provincial writer's strength. And she pertains to the English province, as Faulkner and Dr. Williams to the American: craftily knowing, in a local place, about mighty things afar: things of the order of *Ulysses*, even. It is normal for the writers of the Three Provinces to acknowledge International Modernism and take from it what they can; normal, intelligent, and wise. Seamus Heaney and John Montague would not be the authentic Irish poets they are but for International Modernism; Montague is especially instructive in having absorbed it, for his Irish purposes, at second hand from Williams, who had learned from Joyce and Pound and had also innovated, locally, on his own. Montague has learned the way of that. A thing writers can learn from one another is how to learn.

I have been describing the view from 1983. I have also been describing it as seen by myself. Other people have seen it quite differently, and from earlier years it has looked almost unrecognizably other. I can next enlighten you best by being personal and specific. It was in 1947, under Marshall McLuhan's informal tutelage, that I first became aware of my own century. Such a lag was perhaps possible only in Canada. By then an American movement called the New Criticism was enjoying its heyday. Like most critical stirrings on this self-improving continent, it was almost wholly a classroom movement. Stressing as it did Wit, Tension and Irony, it enabled teachers to say classroom things about certain kinds of poems. Donne was a handy poet for its purposes; so was Eliot; so too was the post-1916 Yeats. Thus Eliot and the later Yeats became living poets, and a few Americans such as Richard Eberhart, also a few Englishmen, e.g. William Empson. The Pound of *Mauberley* was (barely) part of the canon, 1920 having been Pound's brief moment of being almost like Eliot, tentative and an ironist. But when Pound was working in his normal way, by lapidary *statement,* New Critics could find nothing whatever to say about him. Since "Being-able-to-say-about" is a pedagogic criterion, he was largely absent from a canon pedagogues were defining. So was Williams, and wholly. What can Wit, Tension, Irony enable you to say about The Red Wheelbarrow? "So much depends . . .", says the poem, and seems to *mean* it; for a New Critic that was too naive for words. I can still see Marshall chucking aside a mint copy of *Paterson I,* with the words "pretty feeble."

In those years we couldn't see the pertinence of *Ulysses* either. *Ulysses* had been blighted, ever since 1930, by Stuart Gilbert's heavy-handed crib. Nothing as mechanical as that could be organic. Frank Budgen's 1936 book, which might have helped, was too biographical to survive New Critical scrutiny. (The tears Old Critics dropped in Keats's Urn got prompted by his tuberculosis, not his words. So a pox on biographers.) Richard Kain's *Fabulous Voyager,* the first book about *Ulysses* in more than a decade, looked like brave pioneering; as, in the circumstances, it was. Not that it took us the distance we needed to go, if we were to see *Ulysses* as pivotal.

Nor to see Pound as the central figure he was. The chain of accidents that brought Marshall McLuhan and me into his presence on 4 June 1948 I'll detail some other time. The *Pisan Cantos* were then newly published. Later I reviewed them for the *Hudson Review,* another connection masterminded by Marshall. I'd read them, ecstatic, with Pound's remembered voice in my ear. Soon, thanks to New Directions' well-timed one-volume reprint, I could read to the surge of the same spoken cadences the rest of the poem he'd begun in 1916 or before. Its authority, after what my Toronto mentors used to call poetry, was as if great rocks were rolling. I was 25, and about to become a Yale graduate student under Cleanth Brooks's mentorship. That fall the dismal Bollingen fuss broke—a forgotten minor poet named Robert Hillyer assembling three installments of invective in the equally forgotten *Saturday Review*—and literati in pulpit after pulpit would do no more than affirm the purity of their own political motives. Enthralled by the master, I resolved that if no one else would make the case for Ezra Pound the poet, then I would. Having no reputation whatever, I had nothing to lose. I was naive enough not to guess that I was mortgaging my future; it is sometimes liberating not to know how the world works. So in six weeks in the summer of 1949, on a picnic table in Canada, aided by books from the University of Toronto library, I banged out on a flimsy Smith-Corona the 308 typescript pages of *The Poetry of Ezra*

Pound . . . which to my wonderment was instantly accepted by New Directions and by Faber & Faber. By 1951 they got it out. Though most of the reviews were put-downs, Pound before long was a stock on the academic exchange: a safe "subject." What that means is not that I'd "discovered" him, or been magnetically persuasive concerning his virtues. What I'd done, unwittingly, at the threshold of two decades' academic expansion—people peering under every cabbage-leaf for "topics"—was show how this new man with his large and complex oeuvre might plausibly be written about. Whether that was a service to him or to anyone I have never been sure.

In 1956, *annus mirabilis,* I visited Williams, Lewis, and Eliot, with introductions from Pound. He had told me that you have an obligation to visit the great men of your own time. Amid those visits and conversations a book to be called *The Pound Era* first began to shimmer hazily in my mind. Its typescript would not be complete for 13 years during which nothing stood still. Many were making the place of *Ulysses* clearer and clearer; Beckett was defining the trajectory of International Modernism; much attention to Pound was bringing one thing clearly into focus: that what he had always demanded was old-fashioned source-hunting scholarship, the very kind of thing the New Criticism had made disreputable for a generation. Part of a canon is the state and history of the relevant criticism.

For a canon is not a list but a narrative of some intricacy, depending on places and times and opportunities. Any list—a mere curriculum—is shorthand for that. The absence of Wallace Stevens from the canon I use has somehow been made to seem notorious. I account for it by his unassimilability into the only story that I find has adequate explanatory power: a story of capitals, from which he was absent. Like Virginia Woolf of Bloomsbury or Faulkner of Oxford, he seems a voice from a province, quirkily enabled by the International Modernism of which he was never a part, no more than they. His touch is uncertain; fully half his work is rhythmically dead. The life of the live part is generally the life of whimsy. And when, as in "Idea of Order at Key West," he commands a voice of unexpected resonance, then it is a voice unmistakably American, affirming that it finds around itself a wildering chaos in which minds empowered not culturally but cosmically can discern (or make) precarious order. Whence order may stem, how nearly there is none, is Stevens's obsessive theme. Some splendid poems affirm this. They get lost in the shuffle of *Collected Poems* and *Opus Posthumous,* where, "ideas" being close to every surface, the seminars find gratification. His proponents seem not willing, perhaps not able, to distinguish his live poems from his stillborn: a sign, I think, that he is rather a counter on their board-game than an active force.

The rumor has been put about that Pound despised him. Let me place on record therefore that the night Stevens died, Ezra Pound, having gleaned the news from the blurry TV in a recreation lounge at St Elizabeths, wrote an urgent letter to *Poetry.* In those days I was his contact with *Poetry,* so he addressed it to me. *"Poetry,"* he said, "owes him a memorial issue." He hoped that someone, preferably ol' Doc Wms, would explain in that issue what Stevens had been writing *about*. I passed the word to Henry Rago, who solicited Doc Williams, who complied. Williams did not say what Stevens had been writing about; sick and old himself, he was content to affirm a commonality with Stevens in being mortal.

The question, though, was characteristically Poundian. In the story I have been elaborating for 35 years, everything innovative in our century was a response to something outside of literature. Pound's way of putting that is famous: "It is not man / Made courage, or made order, or made grace." Nor was it Joyce who made Dublin, nor Eliot London. Nor I, for that matter, the canon. I have tried to reconstruct an intricate story, continually guided by my judgment of six people I saw face to face, and listened to intently, never taking notes. They were Pound, Williams, Eliot, Lewis, Beckett, Miss Moore. I'm aware that I never met Stevens: nor, for that matter, Yeats or Joyce.

Heminge and Condell saw Shakespeare face to face. They subsequently enabled the First Folio of 1623, such a homage, observe, as no other dramatist of the time received. That was the beginning of Shakespeare's canonization. For 350 years this year, we have been confirming the judgment of Heminge and Condell. Something a contemporary can speak to is the aliveness of a man, his power to invest the air with forms. My own testimony, for what it has been worth, is that of a privileged contemporary. Yeats was able to proclaim, of Synge and Lady Gregory, "And say my glory was, I had such friends." I cannot pretend to such intimacy. I can hope, like Spence with his anecdotes of Pope, to have left some reasonably faithful portraits, and remember how, despite the smug confidence of Arnold, Spence's evaluation of Pope is no longer thought wrong.

The Modernist canon has been made in part by readers like me; in part in Borges' way by later writers choosing and inventing ancestors; chiefly though, I think, by the canonized themselves, who were apt to be aware of a collective enterprise, and repeatedly acknowledged one another. For our age has been canon-minded. One way to make a canon has been by explicit homages: imitation, translation. Pound made pedagogic lists of dead authors, and translated their texts. To the suggestion that he tended to list what he had translated, he replied that on the contrary he translated what he thought alive enough to list.

Poets translate to get into the language something that was not there before, some new possibility. In our century they have been especially apt to be incited by a sense of communing, in an ancient author, with otherness: with a coherent sense of the world for which we and our words are unprepared. If a translation turns out to resemble the sort of poem we are used to, it is probably unnecessary. Critics and historians (which all of us are informally, even when we may think we are simply reading) are similarly guided: we deplore the unnecessary. Pound discovered that the way for a poet to write the poem he wants to write, life having prompted some chemistry of desire, may be to co-opt an alien precursor whose sense of the world, in

wholly foreign words, may guide English words today. Such a poet, the "Seafarer" poet for instance, became part of Pound's canon. Our canon likewise, when our eyes are not on pedagogic expedience, is something we shape by our needs and our sense of what is complexly coherent: what accords with the facts, and folds them into a shapely story, and brings us news from across Pound's godly sea, which is also the sea beside which the girl in Key West sang. (pp. 49-61)

Hugh Kenner, "The Making of the Modernist Canon," in Chicago Review, *Vol. 34, No. 2, Spring, 1984, pp. 49-61.*

Robert Scholes   (essay date Fall 1986)

[*Scholes is an eminent American educator, editor, and critic who has written widely on literature and literary theory. In the following essay, he argues against creating a fixed literary canon, placing his arguments in opposition to those of E. D. Hirsch, the author of* Cultural Literacy: What Every American Needs to Know *(1987), and William J. Bennett, the former Secretary of Education in the Reagan administration.*]

The pun in my title ["Aiming a Canon at the Curriculum"] is both more and less than a pun, as a brief etymological excursion will demonstrate.

In ancient Greek the word $\kappa\alpha\nu\nu\alpha$ was used to refer to certain types of reeds. A related word, $\kappa\alpha\nu\omega\nu$ was used for various metaphoric and metonymic extensions of the word for reed. According to Liddell and Scott's *Greek-English Lexicon,* 1961, these meanings included straight rod, bar, ruler, reed (of a wind organ), rule, standard, model, severe critic, metrical scheme, astrological table, limit, boundary, and assessment for taxation.

In Latin each of the Greek words has a descendant. The Latin *canna* carries the more restricted meanings of reed, cane, and reed pipe or flute, while *canon* (according to Lewis and Short's *A Latin Dictionary,* 1980), like its Greek predecessor, bears the extensions: a marking or measuring line, a rule, canon, model, a wooden channel in hydraulic instruments, an annual tribute in grain, gold, silver; in Church Latin a catalogue of sacred writings, as admitted by the rule, the Canon; and in late Latin, from their shape, in the plural *cannones, cannonum,* meaning cannon or guns. We still use cannon, in the plural, without the s, to mean guns.

In English we find a similar division of lexical burdens. Our word *cane* means the hollow jointed stem of giant reeds or grasses, according to the *OED.* This word clearly derives from Latin *Canna* and Greek $\kappa\alpha\nu\nu\alpha$ However, we appear to have two other words, *cannon* and *canon,* carrying the more extended significations derived from the Latin *canon.* The spelling of *cannon* as our word for an artillery piece, however, was not settled until the latter half of the nineteenth century, by which time the guns clearly insisted on a spelling of their own, and, as guns usually do, they prevailed. The meanings once attached to this word, of tube or cylindrical bore, derived from the Latin hydraulic uses, are now obsolete, though they may well have once hovered over John Donne's vision of being Canoniz'd for love.

Our other modern word, *canon,* now refers primarily to a law, rule or edict, and, when capitalized as *Canon,* to the collection or list of the books of the Bible accepted by the Christian Church as genuine and inspired. By extension, Canon with a capital C also refers to any set of sacred books (See the *OED,* 1971). Both modern words—*cannon* with two n's and *canon* with one—can be traced back to the properties of the reed: its tubular inner structure, its flat outer edges, its regular jointed stem, and its consequent straightness and rigidity. The metaphorical extensions of the word for reed were already highly developed in the ancient Greek language and have been further extended in Latin and English. The ability of a hollow tube to shape the dimensions of sound waves, to control the flow of water, and to aim an object propelled by an explosion led to the word for reed being used in musical, engineering, and military discourse by 1600. The properties of a straight edge with regular joints lent themselves to measuring, limiting, and controlling—properties still linked in the diverse meanings of our word "ruler"—a measuring stick and a potentate or dictator. Britain imposed its will on the world and became an imperial power by means of the cannon and the cane, subduing the foreigners by the cannon of its navy and controlling its own sailors by liberal use of the cane. Law and power: the gun, the cane, and, of course, the book. Where the Empire went, the cannon and the Canon went too.

I mention all this because the current attempt to impose a canon on all humanistic study in this country presents itself in rhetoric designed to conceal its ideological bases. This attempt is most powerfully embodied in recent writings of E. D. Hirsch (Kenan Professor of English at the University of Virginia) and William J. Bennett (who published his views when he was chairman of the National Endowment for the Humanities and is now U.S. Secretary of Education). It has the support of the [Reagan administration] and of powerful foundations. It is anything but trivial. I am opposed to the establishment of a canon in humanistic studies because I believe such a move to be fundamentally undemocratic: a usurpation of curricular power by the federal government. I also believe, and hope to show why in the following discussion, that the establishment of a canon such as that proposed by William Bennett would entail severe restrictions upon the way that the canonical texts should be approached: restrictions of a quasireligious sort designed to stifle any genuinely critical attitude toward the canonized texts. It is with these concerns in mind that I undertake a critical examination of the proposals of Bennett and Hirsch.

For both Hirsch and Bennett American education is presently in a state of crisis which they explain as a decline. Exactly what it is a decline *from* is somewhat less clear, but the rhetoric of their discourse is structured around the topics of present crisis and the myth of an earlier golden age. Their theme is *"O tempora, O mores,"* as Rome's greatest rhetorician put it, complaining about the decline of everything a few decades before the Augustan age. Their use of the notion of crisis is certainly understandable

and thus perhaps forgiveable though hardly believable. In this country, at this time, we act only upon crises, just as we eat only olives that are large—or larger. We live, most certainly, in an age of inflation, of bloated rhetoric, or, to use our own word for it, of hype. None of us can escape this: not the Secretary of Education, nor you, nor I.

The myth of decline, however, is far less inevitable, which makes the choice of it by Bennett and Hirsch more interesting. They, of course, regard it as a fact not a myth, which will make it a key in the debate I am proposing. I see the myth of decline as a standard element in conservative ideology, just as the myth of progress is fundamental to liberal ideology. If we are to get beyond the repetitive confrontations of Tweedledum and Tweedledee on this matter, we shall have to get beyond both of these myths to the extent that we can. This means that on the present occasion we must subject the myth of decline to critical scrutiny. For Bennett this decline presents itself in terms of legal and economic metaphors. The "rightful heirs," as he calls them, have been deprived of "their heritage." The title of his report on the humanities in education is "To Claim a Legacy." A Victorian plot from the fertile brain of Dickens or Wilkie Collins underlies this version of the myth. Who is the guilty party? Who has deprived the rightful heirs of their heritage? You and I are the guilty parties, brothers and sisters, but most guilty are those who should have led us:

> The decline in learning in the humanities was caused in part by a failure of nerve and faith on the part of many college faculties and administrators, and persists because of a vacuum in educational leadership. A recent study of college presidents found that only 2 percent are active in their institutions' academic affairs. ("To Reclaim a Legacy," *Chronicle of Higher Education,* Nov. 28, 1984)

The logic of this is at best elusive. One implication seems to be that the bosses went fishing and the employees, without supervision, sat around goofing off. Is it, in fact, self evident that greater involvement by college presidents would improve education in the humanities? It would depend, I should think, upon who they were and what they did. Over the past few decades the office of college president, like that of university president, has become politicized, bureaucratized, and economized. Presidents mostly raise funds and negotiate with various constituencies that have funding power. This is a full-time job, necessitated by the socio-economic position of these schools in this historical situation. Mr. Bennett ought to know this. In fact, there is usually another officer whose job it is to take a lead in academic affairs, though this leadership normally involves some negotiation with faculty, other administrators, and trustees. Mr. Bennett must know this, too. Then why is he counting the number of presidents who double as deans of academic affairs? Why does he suggest this figure is so significant? Partly for rhetorical effect, no doubt, but also because he is bemused by a vision of the powerful leader, plentifully equipped with "nerve" and "faith," who can as he puts it, "reclaim a legacy," restore a lost heritage, "reverse the decline."

The leader who will reclaim a legacy is a potent image,

ranging in Western cultural history from the Once and Future King drawing Excalibur from its stone scabbard to Adolf Hitler reviving the spirit of a fallen people by finding suitable scapegoats upon whom to blame their fall. William Bennett's cry for strong leadership from those on top, combined with the charge that the loss of our legacy is the fault of a "failure of nerve and faith" strongly suggests that the first move of an educational leader should be a purge of those lacking in nerve and faith. This implication of Bennett's position can be glossed by a personal anecdote. At my thirty-fifth college reunion last spring I participated in a panel discussion led by my classmate William F. Buckley and taped for his TV show, *Firing Line*. The panel was about college education. The panelists, including a couple of people whose political positions are somewhat to the right of Buckley's, wandered from irrelevance to irrelevancy, but I was struck at one point by the introduction of a phrase that I soon realized has become a commonplace of the new intellectual right: one of my classmates referred to "a new treason of the clerks." What is meant by this phrase is a betrayal of the values of this country on behalf of a discredited Marxism that is either foolish or wicked. The young are being led astray by teachers who have lost their faith in God and country. This overtly political critique of America meshes perfectly with Bennett's apparently non-political critique of the same system and the same people. The remedy in both cases is strong leadership imposed from the top. It is ironic, of course, that the phrase "new treason of the clerks" should be employed by partisans of a particular ideology. The phrase is borrowed from Julien Benda's essay of 1928, *La Trahison des clercs*. What Benda meant by "trahison" was a falling away from devotion to abstract principles, such as "justice," on the part of intellectuals, in order to adopt partisan positions on behalf of a nation, a class, or a race. Benda specifically repudiated those who denounce their compatriots as "traitors to the nation" because these compatriots have retained sufficient liberty of mind and speech to be critical of their own country. This bullying phrase, then, "the *new* treason of the clerks," advanced in the name of patriotism, is precisely what Benda decried, and those who use it are in fact behaving as just what he meant by treasonous clerks in the first place. But let us hear his own words (in Richard Aldington's translation, republished by Norton in 1969):

> For twenty centuries the "clerks" preached that the State should be just; now they proclaim that the State should be strong and should care nothing about being just. . . . Convinced that the strength of the State depends upon authority, they defend autocratic systems, arbitrary government, the reason of State, the religions which teach blind submission to authority, and they cannot sufficiently denounce all institutions based on liberty and discussion.

There is no need to worry about a *new* treason of the clerks. The old one is clearly embodied in the notion of strong, authoritarian leadership in education. The college president as leader of a particular school is visualized as a local version of a national leader in education, one who has the faith and nerve to take charge of the whole country and tell everyone what they must read. This is, of course, what Mr. Bennett himself has done, and we shall give his proposed canon some scrutiny a bit further on. For the moment, however, it will be appropriate to pause and consider the theme of strong leadership. Hirsch, too, echoes this theme, but he proposes a "National Board of Education on the pattern of the New York State Board of Regents." This more modest proposal avoids the theme of the powerful individual as leader but again argues for strong central leadership of a hierarchical sort. The general point that I am making here is that concern for our cultural heritage or "legacy" is closely linked to a vision of a powerful hierarchical structure, with or without an individual leader.

Such thinking is of course typical of the political "right," which now calls itself "conservative," though it might more properly be named reactionary. In this connection it is interesting to listen to some thoughts on education from fifty years ago:

> The first task of anyone who might be imagined as occupying a dictatorial position in the education of a country should obviously be to see that elementary education is as good as it can be made; and then proceeding forward make sure that no one received *too much* education, limiting the numbers treated to "higher education" to a third (let us say) of those receiving that treatment to-day. (I do not want a dictator, even in education, but it is sometimes convenient to employ a hypothetical dictator in illustration.)

This "hypothetical dictator" is the work of T. S. Eliot. His disclaimer indicates only too plainly that he at least tried on the idea of being an educational dictator, though he seems to have rejected it by 1936, when he revised this essay for publication.

In this essay Eliot was arguing for the restoration of a heritage, the reclamation of a legacy. Things have reached such a pass, he said, that "one might almost speak of a *crisis* of education." The parallels with Bennett and Hirsch should be clear, but Eliot's position differs from theirs in a number of respects. When the rhetoric of nostalgia and decline is brought to bear on the situation of humanistic education, the problem and the solution fit together with breathtaking precision. We have declined because we have lost our cultural heritage (or, we have lost our cultural heritage because we have declined—the cause and effect relationship can be presented either way); therefore, we need only become familiar with certain texts (the canon) and we will have our heritage back and will be better citizens too. We will also, adds Professor Hirsch, write better. It seems to be very simple. But T. S. Eliot did not think so.

I wish to digress here for a moment to consider Eliot's thinking in this matter for two reasons. First, because he is neither unable nor afraid to follow his reactionary line of thought to its logical conclusions. (In short, he has both faith and nerve in plentiful supply.) And, second, because in doing so, as in the case of his dictatorial musings, he makes explicit certain dimensions of this line of thought that seem to me present but suppressed (or repressed) in the arguments of Bennett and Hirsch. Here is the opening paragraph of Eliot's essay on "Modern Education and the Classics":

> Questions of education are frequently discussed as if they bore no relation to the social system in which and for which the education is carried on. This is one of the commonest reasons for the unsatisfactoriness of the answers. It is only within a particular social system that a system of education has any meaning. If education to-day seems to deteriorate, if it seems to become more and more chaotic and meaningless, it is primarily because we have no settled and satisfactory arrangement of society, and because we have both vague and diverse opinions about the kind of society we want. Education is a subject which cannot be discussed in a void: our questions raise other questions, social, economic, financial, political. And the bearings are on more ultimate problems even than these: to know what we want in education we must know what we want in general, we must derive our theory of education from our philosophy of life. The problem turns out to be a religious problem.

I could not agree more with this posing of the problem. The question of what education should be can only be discussed fruitfully within some consensus about what society should be, and, indeed, what life should be, which latter clause I offer as a legitimate interpretation of the word "religious" in Eliot's text. Eliot himself indicates that communism and Christianity are both religious, or as he also puts it, "There are two and only two finally tenable hypotheses about life: the Catholic and the materialistic." You know which one he chooses. I personally, if those were the only options, would choose the other, but I hope those are not the only options. I hope so for a number of reasons: primarily because that particular binary opposition eliminates the space in which this country has existed for two centuries. It is a totalizing opposition, which, if we cannot transcend it, will doom us to a totalitarian existence.

Eliot himself takes up the question of a middle ground. He calls it liberalism and he finds it despicable. He despises its shabby pluralism that considers all subjects equal, despising it because he *knows* that they are not. His views on the relative merits of the disciplines are too quaint to be considered seriously, but it is worth nothing that he considers the study of *"English Literature,* or, to be more comprehensive, the literature of one's own language" to be "bad for reasons of its own." Eliot's canon, then, is not the same as Bennett's. His notion of our heritage is truly classical. All students should study Latin and Greek language and literature, partly because these studies are the keys to "power over [such] other subjects" as English, modern languages, and history, and partly because they are difficult. Liberal pluralism in education is despicable, then, because it considers all subjects equal, *and* because it believes "that the student who advances to the university should take up the subject that interests him most," whereas the proper view is that "no one can become really educated without having pursued some study in which he took no interest—for it is a part of education to *learn to*

interest ourselves in subjects for which we have no aptitude."

If liberalism is soft, letting people do what they want, conservatism will be hard, forcing them to do what they don't want, because it is good for people to do what they don't want to do. Education is partly learning to do things we don't want to do. This is a far cry from Bennett's rhetoric of the lost legacy. It is the really conservative—or, as Eliot would say, the *Catholic*—position. And it is by no means a foolish educational attitude, though not without its problems. Eliot himself has italicized the crucial phrase. It is "a part of education," he says, "to *learn to interest ourselves*" in unpalatable subjects. He does not present this simply as a matter of "taking," as we say, such subjects, but as something much more complex: *interesting ourselves* in these subjects. In this little gap between "taking" a subject and "interesting oneself" in it lies the essence of pedagogy, for it is the teacher who must move the student toward that interest. The traditional British way toward establishing the proper level of interest has been corporal punishment, which led Dr. Johnson to his famous comment: "There is now less flogging in our great schools than formerly, but then less is learned there; so that what the boys get at one end they lose at the other" [James Boswell, *Life of Johnson*].

This is no joke. The decline of classical study in England has marched hand in hand with the decline of corporal punishment—for over two centuries. I do not wish to endorse the logic of Johnson's position in this matter, but I must observe that this logic is far superior to most of what is proposed by Hirsch and Bennett as causes for the "declines" that interest them. Johnson at least had the consistency to note that his own strong grasp of the classics was based on pain: when asked to explain his own command of Latin, he replied, "My master whipt me very well." Eliot holds no brief for whipping, so far as I know, but he does not take student interest for granted:

> Anyone who has taught children even for a few weeks knows that the size of a class makes an immense difference to the amount you can teach. Fifteen is an ideal number; twenty is the maximum; with thirty much less is done; with more than thirty most teachers' first concern is simply to keep order, and the clever children creep at the pace of the backward.

Small classes and good teaching before college, and then admission to college of a very small highly-motivated group: that is his recipe for generating student interest in the unpalatable. Fifty years ago, Eliot advocated reducing the number of students at British universities by two thirds, and in his argument for this he presented America as the horrible example of what might happen in England. He was appalled by the fact that one American university "boasted an enrollment of 18,000 students—including, I must explain, evening classes." Extrapolating from this figure, Eliot would want our present university enrollments reduced by over 90%, though he was quite well aware of the social and economic reasons why American universities could make no such reductions (and said so). The point, however, is that Eliot's illiberal attitude toward required subjects makes sense only in the context of his illiberal attitude toward college admissions, and his assumption that the problem of elementary and secondary education would be attended to first.

Bennett's interest in classroom practice is limited but revealing. He believes that senior professors are the best teachers (the strong leader motif in another guise) and should be used to lure students into humanistic study, and he argues strongly against "the tendency of some humanities professors to present their subjects in a tendentious, ideological manner." Nothing makes him more indignant than what we may call, using his words, this tendency toward tendentiousness. He is furious to think that "sometimes the humanities are used as if they were the handmaiden of ideology, subordinated to particular prejudices and valued or rejected on the basis of their relation to a certain social stance." He wants the classroom to be exciting and value free, and he believes the great humanistic texts to be exciting and value free also, as if Dante, Vergil, Karl Marx and T. S. Eliot (to name four from his list of classics) were ideological innocents, sharing a common humanistic view of the world. Mr. Bennett is not innocent either, and nowhere is this more apparent than in his taking the hotly debated question of the ideological component of humanistic texts as a matter already settled to the effect that they have none—or if they do it should not influence our regard for them.

Bennett's concern for teaching is in fact almost entirely ideological. Such matters as the size of classes, which seemed so important to Eliot, are not important to Bennett. Hirsch, on the other hand, has for some time taken a serious interest in pedagogical technique, which he uses as a point of departure for his curricular argument [as he writes in his essay "Cultural Literacy"]:

> For the past twelve years I have been pursuing technical research in the teaching of reading and writing. I now wish to emerge from my closet to declare that technical research is not going to remedy the decline in our literacy that is documented in the decline of verbal SAT scores. We already know enough about methodology to do a good job of teaching reading and writing.

Twelve years in that particular closet is a long time, and I am glad that Hirsch has come out of it, but I must confess to some scepticism as to whether anyone who has spent the last twelve years *in there* will be a reliable guide through out cultural perplexities. Hirsch seems to be saying that twelve years of technical research have persuaded him that technical research is inconsequential. Having thoroughly discredited his own recent enterprise, he then proposes to enlist us in his next one. This is, to say the least, a curious rhetorical strategy. The logic of his argument is equally curious.

Hirsch argues that steady but modest declines in SAT scores are symptoms of a national decline in what he calls "literacy." That is, lower scores are *caused by* a decline in students' ability to read, write, and understand the English language. He argues further that the decline in SAT scores has *"accompanied"* a decline in our use of common, nationwide materials in the subject most closely connected with literacy, 'English'. The decline in scores, Hirsch ar-

gues, has been caused by the decline in use of a common national curriculum. In moving from "accompanied" to "caused" Hirsch has introduced a new logical fallacy into argumentation. Even more fallacious than *post hoc, ergo propter hoc,* we now have *simul cum hoc, propter hoc.* This fallacy, however, is not the most serious weakness in Hirsch's argument. The real problems lie in the relationship between the test scores and what those scores are supposed to represent, that is, in the notion of literacy itself.

Hirsch claims that "the decline in our literacy and the decline in *the commonly shared knowledge that we acquire in school* are causally related facts" (my italics). His way of demonstrating the truth of this proposition is essentially to redefine literacy as a matter of culturally shared knowledge. For instance, he cites an elaborate experiment in which American and Indian students read and were tested upon two syntactically comparable texts, each of which described a wedding: one in India and one in the U.S. The test demonstrated conclusively that students read the description of the familiar wedding better than they read the other text. The test showed, in other words, that reading is not a pure skill but depends upon cultural information. But the cultural information used by the students in this test was not based upon their school curricula in English, nor, indeed, upon any school subjects. We learn about such customs as weddings from a cultural web of textuality in which school plays only a minor part. Surely, the ability to understand a description of a modern wedding does not depend upon having read such works as *Romeo and Juliet* or *The Taming of the Shrew,* which offer us a glimpse of cultural systems that are doubly (or trebly) removed from our own, being Elizabethan English versions of Renaissance Italian codes of behavior.

Part of the problem in arguments like Hirsch's is that they use words like "culture" in two quite different and even opposed senses. In the anthropological sense, "culture" means the textual web that young people enter as they are born and raised in any particular time and place. But "culture" also means "high culture," the "classics," or monuments of the past that have a quasi-religious or "canonical" status within a given society. Performing a verbal shell game with the two meanings of "culture," Hirsch argues that something called "cultural literacy" can be improved by having a common, classical curriculum taught throughout these United States.

A common curriculum would certainly make life easier for the compilers of the SAT. It might even produce higher scores, because everyone would now be teaching to the test. But this efficiently closed system would be effectively cut off from our actual culture, and would tell us nothing about literacy in *that* culture. If "cultural literacy" is our goal, we shall first have to decide what we mean by culture as well as what we mean by literacy. The end result of Hirsch's proposals, if they were enacted, might be more efficient testing of less significant behavior. Higher test scores would not in this case indicate a higher degree of literacy but only a more efficient test. All of which suggests that Hirsch may not have come far enough out of his educationist closet, since his proposals seem likely to benefit the makers of tests more than the students, the teachers, or the citizens of this country.

The arguments for "cultural literacy" are presented in the name of improved education, but education is never far from politics. Hirsch claims, for instance, that his proposal for a national curriculum established by a National Board of Education is free of political considerations and based merely upon his professional "expertise." He admits that politics would enter into the selection of the canon itself, but claims that the *need* for a canon has been established by arguments that are not in themselves political. I do not believe him. His arguments are deeply political and in the service of the same ideology that motivates the proposals of William J. Bennett for a curricular core that would restore its lost legacy to liberal education.

We shall turn to Bennett's proposals in a moment, but first we must consider one more dimension of Hirsch's case. If by "literacy" we were to mean mastery of a wide vocabularly and a broad range of syntactic structures, there is absolutely no reason why we should believe that a common national curriculum would lead students to achieve this result better than an eclectic set of curricula established locally to suit local conditions. There is no way to argue for a unified national curriculum except upon political grounds. If we wish to say, for instance, that a certain cultural competence is desirable for every person in order to exercise effectively their rights and responsibilities as *citizens*—that seems to me an entirely valid and proper argument. But, as Eliot pointed out, we need to discuss such possibilities within the framework of some consensus "about the kind of society we want." At its deepest level, beneath the absurd notion of making a great educational effort in order to raise the national median score on the SAT, lies the idea that a common curriculum—*any* common curriculum—would have a unifying effect upon a society that suffers from an excess of "pluralism," and this unifying effect, an achieved cultural consensus, would in itself be a good thing for the country socially and politically. This is sound conservative doctrine and I acknowledge its appeal, but I am keenly aware of the difficulties attendant upon enacting it. Hirsch says, essentially, let us decide to do it and then worry about exactly what we will do and how we will do it. I say, no, let us consider the problems first and then decide what action to take. The problems are posed vigorously by the proposals of William Bennett.

Bennett in fact cites Hirsch with approval and sees his own proposals as developing Hirsch's notion of "cultural literacy," but his argument is somewhat different. He sees Western Civilization as a consistent and coherent enterprise, a great tradition that has achieved what he calls a "lasting vision." We should, he asserts, "want all students to know a common culture rooted in civilization's lasting vision, its highest shared ideals and aspirations, and its heritage." It is hard not to respond to such rhetoric, and doubly hard to criticize it without appearing to join the ranks of the bad teachers, whom Bennett characterizes (in the words of David Riesman) as sophisticated cynics who are "witty, abrasive, and sometimes engrossing" but "really lifeless." Yet criticize it I must, for I believe Ben-

nett is wrong in his assumptions and his proposals for American education.

> **The trouble with establishing a canon—the great, insuperable problem—is that it removes the chosen texts from history and from human actualities, placing them forever behind a veil of pieties.**
>
> **—Robert Scholes**

He is wrong, first of all, in speaking of Western Civilization as a joint stock-company, in which we are all "shareholders." He is especially wrong in speaking of something he calls "civilization's lasting vision." I agree that we have a cultural heritage, and I agree further that it is satisfying and even useful to know as much as possible about it, but I see no evidence whatsoever to suggest that there is any such entity as "civilization" or that our cultural history embodies or expresses any single, durable vision. Bennett sees Western Civilization as a single coherent object, constructed of masterpieces built by geniuses. He sees teaching as the presentation of these masterpieces to students "with insight and appreciation." The students are to read these masterpieces "because an important part of education is learning to read, and the highest purpose of reading is to be in the company of great souls." Other masterpieces in other media are important for the same reason: "Great souls do not express themselves by the written word only: they also paint, sculpt, build, and compose." One wonders if they make movies? Probably not.

This justification for studying the humanities strikes me as deeply, disastrously wrong: designed to promote false emotions and to make actual engagement with important texts almost impossible. The trouble with establishing a canon—the great, insuperable problem—is that it removes the chosen texts from history and from human actualities, placing them forever behind a veil of pieties. This soulful rhetoric is guaranteed to drain the life out of the texts studied, because it permits only worship and forbids all criticism. These may indeed be texts that every young American should be studying in 1990; I am quite prepared to accept that as a possibility; but not for Mr. Bennett's reasons and, above all, not for study in the way that his reasons would compel.

He has the courage (or should I say the "nerve and faith") to propose a list of works and authors that, in his view, "virtually define the development of the Western mind." This list includes twenty-seven writers from Europe: five Greeks, one Roman, two Italians, three Frenchmen, three Germans, two Russians, nine Englishmen, and two English women. There are also some texts from American history and literature, including four novelists, no poets, no playwrights, and no women. It would be easy to criticize this list upon all sorts of grounds, including the exclusion of the Iberian peninsula and all of Latin America from "the Western mind," but I do not wish to make too much of its lacunae, noting only the persistent exclusion of such comic and satiric writers as Aristophanes, Petronius, Lucian, Boccaccio, Rabelais, Cervantes, Moliere, Fielding, Voltaire, Shaw, and Joyce; the stunning omission of Emily Dickinson and Virginia Woolf, and the (Freudian?) omission of Sigmund Freud himself, whose life and work were described recently by the philosopher Richard Wollheim [in *On Art and Mind* (1974)] as "the most exciting, the most courageous, the most poignant adventure in the history of Western ideas." The Western mind without Hegel I can possibly understand, but without Freud? Well, there are minds and minds: every canon has its apocrypha, every faith its heretics. This is how books and people get burned and buried.

The list has its problems, but any list would—which is one argument against making them. But there are other problems that transcend those of list-making. They have to do with *how* the list is to be taught. We have touched on these problems briefly but they need further consideration. We can tackle them concretely be asking how one should teach a work on Bennett's list that is clearly appropriate for any study of our cultural heritage: the Bible, which, as Bennett says, must be mentioned "because it is the basis for so much subsequent history, literature, and philosophy." How, in this society, at this time, should the Bible be taught? Is there an approach to Biblical study that is not tendentious and ideological? Who, for instance, are the authors? Should we give the Apocrypha equal weight? What translations and commentaries should we use? And so on endlessly through one ideological crux after another. If the "classics" are to become a canon, what will become of the Canon. Will we read the Bible as "literature" or will we read literature as the Bible?

Let me make my position as clear as possible. I hold no brief against studying the Bible or any other text that can be shown to be important from our present historical situation. But I want the right as a teacher to study and teach every text critically, guided by such learning and methods as I have generated in a life devoted largely to these very matters. To be told that I must teach *any* text in a reverent manner would be to drain the very life blood from my practice as a teacher. I have similar feelings about the superficial study that I know results from most attempts to "cover" a set body of texts. This superficiality is acknowledged and even accepted by Bennett. He praises certain institutions for instituting courses that cover parts of his proposed canon, but notes that "these institutions do not expect undergraduates to read most of the major works of these authors. They have learned, however, that it is not unreasonable to expect students to read works by some of them and to know who the others were and why they are important." Is this not a recipe for precisely the sort of trivial knowledge that Socrates condemned in the *Phaedrus,* saying, "it is not true wisdom that you offer your disciples, but only its semblance, for by telling them of many things without teaching them you will make them seem to know much, while for the most part they know nothing, and as men filled, not with wisdom, but with the conceit of wisdom, they will be a burden to their fellows"? And is it not also a recipe for enormous financial success for the

producers of those "Notes" that even now act as substitutes for actual texts in required courses?

What I am opposing is the learning of a set of pious cliches about a set of sacred texts. What I advocate in its place I have presented and will continue to develop elsewhere, but it can be summarized as the critical study of texts in their full historical context. At the heart of my belief— separating me by a great distance from Hirsch and Bennett—is the conviction that *no text* is so trivial as to be outside the bounds of humanistic study. The meanest graffito, if fully understood in its context, can be a treasure of human expressiveness. The purpose of humanistic study is to learn what it has meant to be human in other times and places, what it means now, and to speculate about what it ought to mean and what it might mean in the human future. The best texts for this purpose should be determined locally, by local conditions, limited and facilitated by local wisdom. Above all, they should not be imposed and regulated by a central power. (pp. 101-16)

> *Robert Scholes, "Aiming a Canon at the Curriculum," in* Salmagundi, *No. 72, Fall, 1986, pp. 101-17.*

Gerald Graff   (essay date Autumn 1990)

[*Graff is an American educator who has written extensively on trends in literary studies. In the following excerpt from an essay that originally appeared in the Autumn 1990 issue of* New Literary History, *he describes two sides of the debate on revising the literary canon and suggests how the controversy itself could be usefully incorporated into contemporary school curricula.*]

In the faculty lounge the other day, a dispute arose between a couple of my colleagues that typifies the warfare currently agitating the educational world. It began when one of our older male professors complained that he had just come from teaching Matthew Arnold's "Dover Beach" and had been appalled to discover that the poem was virtually incomprehensible to his class. Why, can you believe it, said the older male professor (let us call him OMP for short), my students were at a loss as to what to make of Arnold's famous concluding lines, which he proceeded to recite with slightly self-mocking grandiloquence:

> Ah, love, let us be true
> To one another! For the world, which seems
> To lie before us like a land of dreams,
> So various, so beautiful, so new,
> Hath really neither joy, nor love, nor light,
> Nor certitude, nor peace, nor help for pain;
> And we are here as on a darkling plain
> Swept with confused alarms of struggle and
>   flight
> Where ignorant armies clash by night.

My other colleague, a young woman who has just recently joined our department (let us call her YFP), replied that she could appreciate the students' reaction. She recalled that she had been forced to study "Dover Beach" in high school and had consequently formed a dislike for poetry that had taken her years to overcome. Why teach "Dover Beach" anyway? YFP asked.

Furiously stirring his Coffee-mate, OMP replied that in *his* humble opinion—reactionary though he supposed it now was—"Dover Beach" was one of the great masterpieces of the Western tradition, a work that, until recently at least, every seriously educated person took for granted as part of the cultural heritage. YFP retorted that while that might be so, it was not altogether to the credit of the cultural heritage. Take those lines addressed to the woman by the speaker, she said: "Ah, love, let us be true / To one another . . . ," and so on. In other words, protect and console me, my dear—as we know it's the function of your naturally more spiritual sex to do—from the "struggle and flight" of politics and history that we men have regrettably been assigned the unpleasant duty of dealing with. YFP added that she would have a hard time finding a better example of what feminists mean when they speak of the ideological construction of the feminine as by nature private and domestic and therefore justly disqualified from sharing male power. Here, however, she paused and corrected herself: "Actually," she said, "we *should* teach 'Dover Beach.' We should teach it as the example of phallocentric discourse that it is."

OMP responded that YFP seemed to be treating "Dover Beach" as if it were a piece of political propaganda rather than a work of art. To take Arnold's poem as if it were a species of "phallocentric discourse," whatever that is, misses the whole point of poetry, OMP said, which is to rise above such local and transitory problems by transmuting them into universal structures of language and image. Arnold's poem is no more about gender politics, declared OMP, than *Macbeth* is about the Stuart monarchical succession.

But *Macbeth is* about the Stuart monarchical succession, retorted YFP—or so its original audience may well have thought. It's about gender politics too—why else does Lady Macbeth need to "unsex" herself before she can participate in murdering Duncan? Not to mention all the business about men born of woman and from their mother's womb untimely ripped. The fact is, Professor OMP, that what you presume to be the universal human experience in Arnold and Shakespeare is male experience presented as if it were universal. You don't need to notice the politics of sexuality because for you patriarchy is the normal state of affairs. You can afford to ignore the sexual politics of literature, or to "transmute" them, as you put it, onto a universal plane, but that's a luxury I don't enjoy.

From an educational point of view, the classics have less to fear from newfangled ideological hostility than from old-fashioned indifference.

—*Gerald Graff*

There are many possible ways to describe what happened here, but one of them would be to say that "theory" had broken out. What we have come to call "theory," I would suggest, is the kind of reflective discourse about practices that is generated when a consensus that was once taken for granted in a community breaks down. When this happens, assumptions that previously had gone without saying as the "normal state of affairs"—in this case OMP's assumption that literature is above sexual politics—have to be explicitly formulated and argued about.

OMP would probably complain that this trend diverts attention from literature itself. But YFP could reply that literature itself was not being ignored in their debate but discussed in a new way. It was not that she and OMP stopped talking about poetry and started talking theory. It was rather that, because their conflicting theoretical assumptions differed about how to talk about poetry, they had to talk about it in a way that highlighted those theories.

The recent prominence of theory, then, is the result of a climate of radical disagreement, and the complaint that theory is pervasive finally reduces to the complaint that literature and criticism have become too controversial. Yet the complaint only has the effect of generating more theory and more of the theoretical disagreement being deplored. Forced by the disagreement to articulate his principles, OMP, the traditional humanist, was "doing theory" just as much as was YFP, articulating assumptions that previously he could have taken as given. For this reason, the belief that the theory trend is a mere passing fad is likely to be wishful thinking.

The question is: Who and what are hurt by this situation? Who and what are damaged by conflicts like the one in the faculty lounge? The obvious answer would seem to be "Dover Beach." But just how well was "Dover Beach" doing in college (and high school) literature classes before radical teachers like YFP came along? We need only look at the complaint by OMP that triggered the lounge debate to be reminded that such classics have often inspired deep apathy in students even when taught in the most reverential fashion—perhaps especially when taught in that fashion.

Considered in this light, one might argue that "Dover Beach" has little to lose from the debate between OMP and YFP and a good deal to gain. In an odd way, YFP is doing "Dover Beach" a favor: In treating Arnold's poem as a significant instance of ideological mystification, her critique does more to make the poem *a live issue* in the culture again than does the respectful treatment of traditionalist teachers like OMP, which, as he himself complains, fails to arouse his class.

What the debate between OMP and YFP really threatens is not "Dover Beach," I think, but OMP's conception of "Dover Beach" as a repository of universal values that transcend the circumstances of its creation and reception. Whereas this decontextualized concept of culture was once axiomatic in humanistic education, it has now become one theory among others, a proposition that has to be argued for rather than taken as given. What is threatened by the canon controversy, in other words, is not the classics but their unquestioned status. But again, when the classics enjoyed that unquestioned status there is little evidence that it made them seem more compelling to students than they seem now. In short, from an educational point of view, the classics have less to fear from newfangled ideological hostility than from old-fashioned indifference.

What is most unfortunate about the conflict between OMP and YFP is not *that* it is taking place but *where* it is taking place, behind the educational scenes where students cannot learn anything from it. My thought as I watched OMP and YFP go back and forth in the faculty lounge was that if OMP's students could witness this debate they would be more likely to get worked up over "Dover Beach" than they are now. They might even find it easier to gain access to the poem, for the controversy over it might give them a context for reading it that they do not now possess.

Then again, it might not. The controversy would have to be presented in a way that avoids pedantry, obscurity, and technicality, and this is difficult to do. And even when it is done, many students will still have as much trouble seeing why they should take an interest in critical debates over "Dover Beach" as they do seeing why they should take an interest in "Dover Beach" itself. The alienation of students from academic culture runs deep, and it may deepen further as the terms of that culture become more confusingly in dispute than in the past.

In such a situation, helping students gain access to academic discourse means clarifying conflicts like the one between OMP and YFP (and numerous others not so neatly polarized). If the goal is to help students become interested participants in the present cultural conversation instead of puzzled and alienated spectators, the aim should be to *organize* such conflicts of principle in the curriculum itself. They are, after all, only an extension of the real-life conflicts that students experience every day.

Just opening reading lists to noncanonical works—necessary as that step is—will not in itself solve the problem. Replacing "Dover Beach" with *The Color Purple* does not necessarily help the student who has difficulty with the intellectual vocabularies in which both texts are discussed in the academic environment. What makes reading and interpretation difficult for many students is not the kind of text being read, whether canonical or noncanonical, highbrow or popular, but the heavily thematic and symbolic ways in which all texts, irrespective of status, are discussed in the academic setting. (The student phrase for it is "looking for 'hidden meaning.'") If the practice of looking for hidden meaning seems strange to you, it will seem no less strange to look for it in *The Color Purple* than in *Hamlet*.

This last point needs underscoring, because educational progressives have been too quick to blame student alienation from academic literacy on the elitist or conservative aspects of that literacy. But students can be as alienated from democratized forms of academic literacy as from conservative forms. What alienates these students is academic literacy *as such*, with its unavoidably abstract and

analytical ways of talking and writing, regardless of whether that literacy is traditional or populist.

There is no question of occupying a neutral position here: In my view, the shift from the traditionalist to the revisionist view of culture is very much a change for the better. But from the vantage point of students who feel estranged from the intellectual life as such, revisionist culture can easily seem like the same old stuff in a new guise. To such students a feminist theorist and an Allan Bloom would seem far more similar to each other than to people like themselves, their parents, and friends. In the students' eyes, the feminist and Bloom would be just a couple of intellectuals speaking a very different language from their own about problems the students have a hard time regarding as problems.

The new climate of ideological contention in the university seems to me a sign of democratic vitality rather than the symptom of "disarray," relativism, and declining standards that the critics on the Right take it to be. But so far the university *has* failed to make a focused curriculum out of its contentiousness. For this reason, it is failing to tap its full potential for drawing students into its culture.

The best way to do this is to make the conflicts themselves part of the object of study. There are worse things that could happen to literature than having a passionate controversy erupt over it. (pp. 31-2, 34-5)

> *Gerald Graff, "Debate the Canon in Class," in* Harper's, *Vol. 282, No. 1691, April, 1991, pp. 31-2, 34-5.*

Reed Way Dasenbrock   (essay date 1990)

[*Dasenbrock is an American educator and critic. In the following excerpt, he advocates not simply "opening up the canon" but revising its nationalist preconceptions, thereby forcing educators to focus on "literature in English" rather than "English and American literature."*]

The established canon of English and American literature as received and taught has been seen to be a very partial representation, biased toward men from privileged classes and races. Advocates of literature by women and by marginalized social and economic groups have pressed to open up the canon, to move toward a more expansive, pluralistic view of literature with room for all sectors of society. But there is a problem with this movement, or at least with the way it has been conceptualized: in a number of important senses, the canon can't open. There are demonstrable and important constraints on the number of writers, especially from the past, that we can study and teach. The move to open up the canon has been primarily additive, adding works by women and minorities to the canon. One concrete result of this can be seen in the standard anthologies used in survey courses, especially anthologies of American literature, which keep getting longer and longer. But our courses aren't getting any longer, and I don't suspect that our students read more for their classes or outside of class, so an ever-growing percentage of these massive anthologies is going unread. This is not a trivial fact. Unless our students take more courses or do more reading in or beyond their courses, the amount of material they will encounter is a fixed quantity. As Marjorie Perloff has pointed out [in "An Intellectual Impasse," *Salmagundi* (Fall 1986)]:

> For every X that is added to a given syllabus or anthology, a Y must, after all, be withdrawn. The class that reads Chopin's *Awakening* will not, in all likelihood, have time for Henry James' *Portrait of a Lady*. I am not saying that this is necessarily a bad thing, but we should be under no illusion that we have replaced a 'closed' and narrow canon with an 'open' and flexible one.

So the logical end result of "opening up the canon" may well be a contradiction. Scholars investigating our literature are finding more and more writers whom they urge upon our attention. Our collective sense of our literature is becoming more complex, more variegated, and much richer (this is particularly true in American literature, where the movement toward canon-revision has been strongest, but it is true elsewhere as well). And I certainly welcome this development. Yet when we come to present this material to our students, our additive rhetoric of "opening up the canon" meets hard, subtractive logic. We can't teach the new literature in addition to the old canon: something has to give, substitutions have to be made, in the classroom the canon inexorably closes down.

The language of opening up the canon therefore needs rethinking. The new material being added to the canon as it opens up risks being left out of the canon as it closes back down, in just the way minorities newly hired under affirmative action programs tend to be fired first during layoffs because of their lack of seniority. Last in, first out may be the order of the day in curricula as well as in fire departments and police forces. The reason will be the same: seniority. When hard choices have to be made and justified, "central" figures will always win out over "marginal" figures. "These are the central texts our students need to know," so the argument will always run, and the figures perceived to be central are likely to be those who have long been considered central.

This can be seen clearly enough in the recent calls to teach a core. Those concerned with opening up the canon have, of course, strongly opposed the contrasting call to return to a core and have pointed out that the core called for by the Bennett Report, for example, is almost exclusively a core of texts by European males; it is, in short, the old canon we are trying to move away from. But the call to return to a core has been made more persuasive by the inability of the other side to contest the received vision of the core. "Opening up the canon" implies dilation without a reordering within the opened-up canon, and this failure to confront the issue of centrality head-on will, I think, prove costly in the confrontation over centrality that must necessarily follow the opening up of the canon. What will we teach when the canon closes down, as it must? What we feel to be central, of course. So if we wish to avoid returning to the older vision of the core of central texts that we have sought to move away from, we need to contest the older vision of centrality. (pp. 64-5)

What I would like to suggest is that to teach, to prescribe

a curriculum, to assign one book for class as opposed to another, is ineluctably to call certain texts central, to create a canon, to create a hierarchy, in short, to be an essentialist. And the seemingly attractive argument made to the effect that we should move away from canon-formation toward canonical "heterodoxy" is simply a utopian notion that cannot be realized. We can't read everything, we can't teach everything, we can't study everything. And this means that there is no escaping the task of selection, no escaping the task of canon-formation, and no escaping essentialism. Deconstruction helped dislodge the old essentialism, but it can't give us what we need now. If we want to contest the old essentialism successfully, we need a vision of what we do that would valorize as central precisely what the old essentialism and the old canon marginalized and devalued. We need, not the by now familiar decentering, but a new recentering. We need, in short, a new essentialism. Without a new essentialism, our curriculum will continue to be shaped by the old. With a new essentialism, and only with a new essentialism, will the material recently added to the canon stay put, redefined as central, when the canon closes down. (pp. 67-8)

The determinate canon . . . is the canon of English and American literature, and that phrase perfectly represents the map of English literature held by most professors of English and enshrined in all our institutions. The literature anthologies . . . serve a basic building block in the curriculum of virtually every English department: the lower-division surveys. The surveys divide literature into three parts: American, English, and World. World literature is in languages other than English, read in translation, and English and American literature are therefore understood to divide the world of literature in English between them. And though these anthologies and the courses they are designed to serve offer the most clear-cut example, literature in English is similarly divided between the English and the Americans in all our institutions and ways of representing literature. This is true, somewhat surprisingly, even for most of those trying to open up the canon. This movement has been stronger in the study of American literature than anywhere else, but the effort has been to rethink the canon of American literature rather than to rethink the need for an organizing concept such as "American literature."

Why is this so? It certainly was not always so, for the origins of the study of literature were never narrowly nationalistic. Aristotle didn't refuse to comment on Homer even though Homer probably wasn't an Athenian; Longinus didn't ignore the Book of Genesis even though it was the product of an alien people and culture; Horace certainly didn't ignore the Greek poets, though he wrote in Latin. There has always been a tendency to consider literature in a given language as a cohesive unity, but that posits language communities—not nation-states—as the logical way to subdivide the world of literature. There is, moreover, a broad understanding in our era of the dysfunctional nature of nationalism, yet English professors hold onto the values of nationalism as stoutly as politicians calling for protectionist legislation, immigration controls, and preemptive strikes against nations whose systems of government they dislike. Unfortunately, this is also largely true of professors of other languages, who just as vehemently are professors of Italian or Peruvian or German literature. Even among scholars of comparative literature, the institutional antidote to nationalistic categories, it is the exception who doesn't say, "I do comparative work, but my real field is Italian or French or whatever." What has happened to the international impulse of Renaissance humanism in which Erasmus, More, Linacre, and others had a broadly shared international culture?

That was based on Latin, one response might run, and Latin disappeared as an international language a long time ago. True enough, but English has taken its place and now functions as a broad international language with, moreover, an important role inside nearly one-quarter of the world's countries. English is also an important international literary language, and English and American literature emphatically do not divide the world of English literature between them. Important writing in English is being done all over the world in more than thirty countries. This development is something those calling for a return to the old essentialism generally fail to recognize. J. Hillis Miller, for example, in the essay ["The Return of Historical Study at the Present Time," *ADE Bade-in* (1979)] in which he develops his credo about English and American literature, seems to be arguing for a return to studying literature in English as opposed to work in other languages. But he states this as "English and American literature," seemingly unaware of any other literatures in the English language. Similarly, E. D. Hirsch's focus in *Cultural Literacy* is unabashedly on national cultures, as the subtitle of his book, *What Every American Needs to Know,* transparently reveals. Hirsch, unlike Hillis Miller, at least recognizes that other countries, such as Australia and India, use English, but his stress is even more nationalistic than Hillis Miller's: "To teach the ways of one's own community has always been and still remains the essence of the education of our children, who enter neither a narrow tribal culture nor a transcendent world culture but a national literate culture."

But that is not to say that simply expanding the number of national categories will solve the problem. The problem is our reliance upon nationalistic categories in the first place. Our nationalistic emphasis on English and American literature misses a lot because much of the most interesting writing being done in English today comes from outside England and America. But even if we move toward an awareness of the other national literatures in English, such as Nigerian literature in English (a country not found in Hirsch's list of nations using English), we are still going to miss a lot because national categories seem curiously blunt instruments for the representation of the international character of literature in English today. Once we use a category like "American literature," as any Derridean or Wittgensteinian would tell us, the temptation is to look for the essence of that category, to look for the truly American in American literature. (William Spengemann has acutely criticized this tendency in the study of American literature, which he calls the "exceptionalist claims" made for American literature.) What we do is divide the concept internally, privileging the pure case over the marginal or problematic. So William Carlos Williams

is seen as more of an American writer than Ezra Pound or T. S. Eliot, since he stayed home while they went to Europe. Willa Cather is seen as a more American writer than Ole Rölvaag, since her descriptions of the settling of the Plains are in English, not Norwegian. And John Cheever is seen as a more American writer than Leslie Marmon Silko or Maxine Hong Kingston because he comes from a more mainstream community than Native or Chinese Americans. Comparably, Buchi Emecheta's *In the Ditch,* set in London, is the most striking portrayal of the Welfare State gone disastrously astray that I know, yet Emecheta's Nigerian origin tends to disqualify her from consideration as an English writer. These are precisely the kinds of exclusions and hierarchies that critics opening up the canon struggle against, but I would argue that as long as we organize our literature around value-laden terms such as "American" and "English," these exclusions and hierarchies are inescapable. To ask if something is part of American literature or not can never be a neutral act of description, and in the resulting struggle much of what is most interesting in American literature is not going to meet someone's criterion of "Americanness." Thus our reliance upon the national categories of English and American literature not only causes us to miss much that lies clearly outside English and American literature, but it also causes us to miss much that lies not so clearly inside.

There is a simple solution to this: we should declare that it is literature in English, not English and American literature, that we study; the language should be seen as the thread that holds us together. All professors of English teach in departments of English, after all, and we should understand a concern with the language as more fundamental than a concern with any given national categories.

Important consequences follow or would follow from this subtle shift in terminology and emphasis. The history of English is, of course, not a history of two discrete nation-states, England and America. The United States of America has been an independent nation for just about half of its recorded history (even if one ignores everything prior to the European "discovery" and settlement), and England has not been a discrete nation-state for 385 years. The history of English is rather a history of a gradual expansion of the language beyond its home in England to encompass the entire world. A full history of this expansion would of course be the subject of a book, but it can be divided into four partially overlapping stages. In the first, encompassing the period up to the early seventeenth century, English became the dominant language of the British Isles, not just England, and the "Celtic periphery" was brought under (a somewhat unstable) English political and linguistic hegemony. The second phase can be roughly placed during the seventeenth and eighteenth centuries, the period of the "First British Empire," as it has been called, in which the British settlements in America flourished and then broke away. The third stage has been called the "Second British Empire," that far more imposing imperial edifice with India as its core that rose on the ruins of the first and lasted into the second half of this century. The fourth stage is the current stage of implosion, in which Britain has divested itself of its colonies but a dual legacy of empire remains in the worldwide spread of English and in the minorities from the former colonies who now live in Britain.

Each of these periods has left a political and social legacy that causes problems for anyone thinking of literature in English as a combination of English and American literature. The English domination of the Celtic periphery raises a host of problems in definition and categories: are Irish, Welsh, and Scottish literature part of English literature, or should they be considered independent entities? The argument for coherence is a powerful one, given the influence of English literature on Celtic writers, yet any specialist in the Celtic literatures will tell one, justly, that Celtic writers draw on their own heritage as well as that of the English and that they don't receive proper recognition in courses on English literature. And this is not an issue that has been faced squarely, particularly in the design of our curriculum. We tend to call our historical and survey courses "English literature," throwing in Sheridan, Scott, Yeats, and others without providing an adequate explanation of their differing cultural backgrounds and contexts. The lasting legacy of the first British Empire is, of course, the United States. The concept of American literature would seem to have handled that legacy well enough, but our habit of dichotomizing English and American literature causes problems as well as solves them: we have a hard time dealing with mixed cases, with English writers like Auden or Isherwood who came here or with American writers such as James or Eliot who moved to England. And William Spengemann has recently argued [in "American Writers and English Literature," *BLH* (1985)] that we should abandon the very concept of American literature, given the amount of American literature we have misunderstood by "keeping it separate from the rest of the world, especially Britain." Far more complexity was introduced by the second British Empire, during which English spread all over the world. Writers from the West Indies, Africa, Asia, and the Pacific are English rather than American in some trivial senses: they spell color with a *u,* and they play cricket rather than baseball. But their cultural and political frames of reference are far more variegated than that and can only be misread by dividing literature in English between the English and the Americans. The initial reaction to such complexity was simply to ignore the plethora of world writing in English, but this has been challenged most directly by the changing shape of writing coming from England, by the preeminence in English literature of writers originally from around the world such as V. S. Naipaul and Salman Rushdie. It has become impossible to continue to ignore the fact that English literature is no longer very English, at least by F. R. Leavis's standards. Comparable issues are raised in American literature by the increasingly powerful work of writers from marginalized immigrant or indigenous communities, such as Asian Americans, Native Americans, and Chicanos.

But if we say that the English language and its spread provides our thread of coherence, these marginal examples that threaten the coherence of English and American literature become just the opposite, central examples of the spread of English into new lands and communities. Each moment of expansion breaks or risks the coherence of the

nation-based category, but that moment is central in a model based on the expansion of the language. Let me take the eighteenth century as a convenient example. Most traditional England-centered models of English literary history would define Fielding and Richardson as central figures in the novel, Pope as the central poet, and Johnson as the central poet-critic. It should be easy to see the parallel between this list of central figures and an England-centered notion of English literature. But if we make the expansion of English—not England itself—central to our conception of English literature, our sense of what is central changes. An astonishingly high percentage of the great writers and thinkers in English in the eighteenth century comes from the "Celtic periphery," preeminently from Scotland, though the Ireland that produced Berkeley, Goldsmith, Burke, and Sheridan and gave a home to Swift isn't to be ignored. The nonnationalistic model would see this not as a curious anomaly to be ignored, but as the beginning of a decisive shift in English-language culture away from England that should be emphasized. Moreover, there is at least an interesting homology between our sense of Fielding and Richardson as initiators of the tradition of the English novel and their role as initiators of the domestic novel, the novel about people staying at home, in England. Other novelists, including Defoe and Smollett, were intimately linked to the spread of English and wrote novels depicting that spread. Though academics teach and write about Fielding and Richardson far more often than Defoe, it is Defoe who remains the central novelist of the century for world writers in English, as his narratives of the world outside England remain potent images, in many cases images to be struggled against. I cannot imagine a contemporary novelist rewriting *Joseph Andrews* or *Clarissa* in the way J. M. Coetzee grapples with *Robinson Crusoe* in his recent *Foe.* And of course, the cultural renaissance of the Celtic periphery and the spread of the empire are closely linked phenomena: the British Empire could almost be called the Scottish Empire, so important were the Scots in the expansion of the Empire. And this link finds its literal embodiment in Smollett's *Roderick Random,* as well as, more obliquely, in *Gulliver's Travels.*

So in place of the centripetal canon oriented toward the England of Pope, Fielding, Richardson, and Johnson, a centrifugal canon might focus on Swift, Defoe, Smollett, and Boswell. This is a slight change, perhaps, as all these figures are recognized to be important and are placed in the canon somewhere. But as one moves closer and closer to the present, a centripetal, England-centered canon captures fewer and fewer of the important figures, whereas a centrifugal canon focused on the totality of writing in English has no difficulty at all in representing the panorama of world writing in English. The same is true within the study of American literature. It took considerable energy to get American literature recognized as a distinct entity in the first place, so powerful were the centripetal tendencies of the English tradition. But once established, the study of American literature has by and large replicated the same centripetal tendencies, privileging those at the defined center over the margins. This is the context in which it has been so difficult to open up the canon to work by minorities and women, since they have been perceived to be at the margins. But if we replace the category of nationalism with the category of language, just the opposite happens. And the now dynamically defined center is not England, but instead whatever new group is acquiring English or beginning to write in it at that moment.

This simple reversal of emphasis in redefining the center does everything we need, I think, to keep the canon from closing down in the wrong way. Much that was central in the old canon remains central in this one, but not always for the same reasons. By anyone's standards Spenser is a great poet, the greatest nondramatic poet of the Elizabethan era. But in a centrifugal history, he takes on renewed emphasis as someone involved in the expansion of the Empire, directly in Ireland and through his connection with Raleigh, and indirectly in a variety of ways in his poetry and poetics. *The Tempest* becomes a central play of Shakespeare's, central for its representation of colonization and discovery rather than for its return to the romance wellsprings of literature, as Northrop Frye—himself a child of empire—would have it. *The Tempest* just as much as *Robinson Crusoe* has been a text writers from once-colonized countries have reacted against and rewritten, as can be seen in George Lamming's *The Pleasures of Exile*. As great as they are, both Defoe's and Shakespeare's works stand revealed in this context as the voice of the colonizer depicting the colonized; we also need to find a place in what we teach for Caliban's response to Prospero and Friday's response to Crusoe. Only a centrifugal conception of literature in English that embraces Lamming and Coetzee as well as Shakespeare and Defoe can place all these works in the juxtapositions they deserve.

So opening up the canon, though important, is not enough. We also need to rethink the field in order to find a central—not marginal—place for the work added to the canon as it opens up. Until this is achieved, that work will remained marginalized and insufficiently appreciated, always in danger of losing its place as the canon closes down. In this essay, I have offered my sketch of how to

rethink the field, and I offer it in an unabashedly essentialist mode of thought. For the only way to resist the essentializing move back to the "classics of English and American literature" is to redefine the essence of our concerns, from the literature of the English and the Americans to English literature in its entirety, from a nationalist conception of English literature to an acceptance of its internationalism. (pp. 68-74)

> *Reed Way Dasenbrock, "What to Teach When the Canon Closes Down: Toward a New Essentialism," in* Reorientations: Critical Theories and Pedagogies, *edited by Bruce Henricksen and Thais E. Morgan, University of Illinois Press, 1990, pp. 63-76.*

Robert Alter   (essay date Spring 1991)

[*Alter is an American critic and educator. In the following essay, he discusses recent developments in academic literary criticism, assesses the underlying principles behind academic movements to revise the literary canon, and then examines two highly regarded examples of recent literary criticism which attempt to "devalue" James Joyce's canonical novel* Ulysses.]

One of the most disquieting features of contemporary American academic culture is the growing chasm between the study of literature in the university and the reading practices of educated people outside the academy. Proponents of the sundry varieties of new academic criticism will of course argue that those very reading practices are naive, intellectually otiose, unwittingly complicit with the manipulative pressures of regnant ideologies. I would counter that claims of this sort are more institutionally self-serving than, as those who make them contend, culturally soul-searching, and that the peculiar treatment literature is now widely accorded in the academy is dictated far more by an inner momentum of academic life than by a serious critical engagement with the larger culture.

It becomes increasingly clear that the 1960s were the great watershed in the evolution of the university in this country. This is most obvious in the continuing legacy of what some French circles now dismissively call "the thought of '68," which is manifested in American critical trends like deconstruction, radical feminism, neo-Marxism, and the critique of colonial discourse. Before 1968, however, and ultimately underlying all these trends, is the sheer fact of the immense expansion of the university—new campuses mushrooming, old ones multiplied in size—that took place in the early sixties. That expansion triggered a crisis of professional identity both for those already in the academy and for those preparing to enter it, especially in the humanities, and a criticism that insists on the ultimately ideological character of both literature and criticism is at least in part an uneasy solution to this crisis of identity. This new criticism is of course actuated by political concerns as well, but certain of its underlying motives are strongly linked to internal developments of the university as an institution.

Let me offer a rough sketch of three successive waves of American literary scholarship. The first, going back to the

---

The effect of "deconstruction" on the nature of contemporary canon revision:

[The] effect of deconstruction has not been to widen inquiry but to narrow it. Not content with the perfectly sensible idea that much besides high literature is worthy of scrutiny, deconstructionists would obliterate the differences between Roger Rabbit and Henry James. The function of criticism is reduced to description and analysis; the task of evaluating works of art is left undone. Abandoned is one of criticism's foremost responsibilities: the making and revising of critical discriminations. The determination of a canon, a syllabus, a reading list of any kind, is stripped of all but political considerations, with results that are nothing if not arrogant. For most educated persons it would be difficult to dismiss the masterworks of Homer, Dante, Shakespeare, Cervantes, Milton, Goethe, Tolstoi—but not for the deconstructionist.

David Lehman, in his Signs of the Times: Deconstruction and the Fall of Paul de Man, *1991.*

early decades of the century, was positivist and historical in its assumptions and philological in its methodology (at this point, philology, long unjustly maligned, may begin to seem not such a bad idea). Here you would encounter the kind of scholar who could spend hours prowling through the antique weapons sections of museums in an effort to discover an original model for Milton's "two-handed engine of destruction." This group of Germanic-style researchers was leavened by a healthy admixture of quite a different group, especially in departments of English—gentlemen-scholars, men (of course, there were scarcely any women) who were cultivated readers, Anglophiles, "appreciators" of literary values, and on the whole nonpublishing teachers. A striking change occurred in the 1940s and 50s, at least at many elite institutions, with the entrance into the academy of people who were more critics than scholars in the old sense. These new teachers of literature were more likely to publish in the *Partisan Review* or *The Kenyon Review* than in the *Journal of English and Germanic Philology.* Many of them came to their academic jobs from work as literary journalists, editors, freelance writers, in some notable instances without the benefit of graduate-school training and a Ph.D. As evaluative critics, some of whom were also practicing poets and novelists, they were keenly concerned with contemporary literature and its urgent antecedents in High Modernism and the nineteenth century, and often raised questions in their essayistic manner about the moral, political, and cognitive uses of literature. This wave of literary scholars might on occasion be faulted for self-conscious phrase-making, pontification, facile generalization, but it represents a moment of optimal closeness between the academic scrutiny of literature and the kind of attention devoted to serious literature by an educated public outside the academy. Whatever their errors and limitations, the makers of the so-called Age of Criticism in the middle decades of the century brought to the academic study of literature a liveliness, a sense of vital engagement in the experiential dynamics of reading, that it did not have before and has not had since.

Now, it is common to designate the third wave of literary studies, the one that engulfs us at this moment, as the wave of theory, but that is in part a misnomer. It should be noted that the very term "theory" has been turned into a club with which to beat down the opposition, as one can see, for example, in the recent fulminations of Gerald Graff. "Theory," in this acceptation, is assumed to be intellectually serious, conceptually daring, boldly adversary to established opinion, while everything else is mere time-serving. Every other person in a department of literature these days claims to be a theorist. The problem, as Louis Menand has shrewdly observed in a recent article in *The New Republic,* is not that they are theorists but that they are conformists, repeating certain fashionable formulas and strategies of argumentation.

A literary theorist is someone with a certain capacity for original abstract thinking who proposes categories to define the nature of literature, its connections with and differences from other modes of expression, its organizing dynamics, its possible links with extraliterary reality. In making these propositions, the theorist performs a valuable service by obliging us to rethink our unexamined as-

sumptions about the body of texts we study. Mikhail Bakhtin, Roland Barthes, Kenneth Burke, Northrop Frye, Roman Jakobson are all strong and salutary instances of literary theorists, however much one might want to debate any of their views. There is only intermittent evidence, however, among the scholars waving the banner of theory today, of people capable, like the writers in my brief list, of thinking through basic assumptions about literature and of articulating new conceptual frameworks. What qualifies them as "theorists" is a high dosage of abstraction in their prose, an avoidance of sustained readings of specific literary texts, and, above all, a constant ritual invocation of theoretical phrases and formulas struck by others—usually by figures more removed from the actual study of literature than those on my list, like Jacques Derrida, Jacques Lacan, or Edward Said.

The defining feature of the third wave of literary scholarship is not theory but professional consolidation as a guild—or rather a series of sometimes competing sub-guilds—of intellectual technocrats. In the vastness of the new university world first shaped in the early 60s, with no possibility of sustaining the illusion that this was an elite profession of cultivated amateurs or secluded researchers, academicians sought to differentiate themselves as much as possible from other readers and to give themselves a sense of distinctive vocational solidarity. The easiest way to effect this end was on the level of terminology, though the need for differentiation goes much deeper than terminology. If instead of talking about the novel in the old homespun terms of plot and character and point of view, one insisted on diagesis and analepsis, subject position and discursive strategy, one could savor the superiority of belonging to a privileged class of specialists who grasped things more profoundly than the common reader. Indeed, as with any kind of dialect—ethnic, regional, generational, class—the special language served to confirm membership in the group and to exclude the uninitiated.

This general movement of aggressive esotericism is intimately allied with an unprecedented preoccupation with power on several levels. It has proved, first of all, to be a highly effective means for consolidating power within the academy. If you are, say, a Marxisant critic or a deconstructionist, you belong to a highly defined prestige network of likeminded critics in which status is established by the persuasive emulation in phrase and intellectual gesture of one or two or three models. With a little luck, you may be able to stack a department with adherents of the same sectarian trend, enabling you to dominate the curriculum, influence students, isolate or marginalize colleagues who do not follow the party line. And since the academic market responds rapidly and sensitively to what is fashionable in the eyes of its faculty constituency, the material rewards of dedicated trendiness can be substantial. It is perhaps not even ironic that literary Marxists have become some of the great entrepreneurs of the American academy, commanding three or four times the salary of the academic proletariat (the assistant professors, the "conventional" scholars at less prestigious institutions), enjoying endowed chairs with generous perks and in some instances their own journals or research institutes.

> **Whether the angle is feminist or Foucauldian or anticolonial or deconstructionist, literature is construed again and again as an instrument for the exercise of power, with the much-reviled canon as the supreme expression of ugly or sinister "hegemonic" forces.**
>
> *—Robert Alter*

From the standpoint of the larger society—say, a Wall Street law firm or a large corporation—power of this sort is very small potatoes. Proponents of the new wave of literary scholarship are themselves keenly aware of the disparity, and in a variety of ways what they have to say about literature is obsessed with the idea of power, even to the point of totally submerging literature in power. Whether the angle is feminist or Foucauldian or anticolonial or deconstructionist, literature is construed again and again as an instrument for the exercise of power, with the much-reviled canon as the supreme expression of ugly or sinister "hegemonic" forces. Shakespeare is no longer a revealer of dizzying breadths and awesome depths of character and psychology or a shaper of some of the most beautiful verbal artifacts our culture has known but is rather a manifestation of British imperialism, patriarchy, European racism, logocentrism, or what you will. And there is no intrinsic value to literary works; value is rather fixed by the subtly coercive power of "communities of interpretation," which change in the course of time.

What goes hand-in-glove with the conception of literature as an epiphenomenon of political power is an assumption—really, an illusion—that criticism or "theory" provides a tremendous lever of power against the oppressive structures of the surrounding society. The various academic sectarians, by their very use of a specialized dialect and a closed set of orthodox principles of political faith, can actually address only members of their own ideological sub-group, but they cherish the notion that through their writing they will "deconstruct" the language of society at large, expose its oppressive aims, effect a radical transformation in general consciousness, and bring about a new age of liberation. The revolution will come not from the barrel of a gun but from a reversal of hermeneutic practice, a fusillade of labored puns, the subversive introduction of parentheses in the middle of ordinary English words. The addiction to this odd but seductive illusion may explain in part why Marxism continues to flourish luxuriantly on our campuses a year after the wholesale collapse of communism in Europe. The academic Marxists, after all, continue, as they have always done, to speak to each other and to pretend they are addressing the concerns of the general culture. What happens in the realm of history, of real political events, hardly matters because the internal academic discussion from the start had only a suppositious relation to political realities.

The current academic preoccupation with power mani-

fests itself on one other level, which is the critic's assertion of power over the work of literature under consideration. Behind this assertion lies a fear or at least a certain leeriness, of what Walter Benjamin once quite reverently called "the power of the text." An element of generational rebellion may also be involved in this feeling, a reaction against the perceived excesses of the New Critics (decades after the fact, still the most popular whipping-boys) or the mid-century New York Critics, who variously saw the literary text as a crystallization of immense imaginative insight and uncanny complexity. The reign of the idolatry of the text has been followed by the era of the hermeneutics of suspicion. A degree of suspicion is no doubt a healthy component of intellectual life, but suspicion, too, has its excesses, and in the current climate every critic with the vehement will to brandish terms like "reification," "phallogocentric," and "oppressive discourse" can place himself or herself in a position of powerful superiority to Shakespeare and Tolstoy.

This last point touches on an essential aspect of difference between literature as it is now often expounded in the university and the expectations of literature among educated readers outside the academy. Reading itself, as has often been proposed, may be an endangered activity in our society, and perhaps the actual distaste for literature that begins to find expression in some academic circles could itself be a reflection of this cultural pathology. But for the many thousands of Americans who still read works of literature more challenging than formula-fiction and the daily newspaper, there are good indications that they seek in literature not only entertainment but something like a better understanding of things, an order of insight not available to them through the popular media or even through other intellectual disciplines.

A couple of years ago, I was invited to give a talk to a local association of psychiatrists on any literary topic of my choice. I decided to speak on the mimetic persuasiveness of fictional character. Especially because my framework was not in the least psychoanalytic, I was apprehensive, with my profession-bound academic assumptions, that I would be challenged in the question-period for the naivete of my approach, my failure to consider primary-process thinking, sublimation, and so forth. Most of the responses proved instead to be not challenges but testimonials to the illuminating power of fiction. Some of my principal examples had been drawn from Stendhal, and one woman analyst announced that since her first reading of Stendhal when she was twenty her understanding of human nature had been permanently changed and deepened. Needless to say, a professor of literature making such a declaration would be exposed to ridicule—an ironic disparity that suggests how much the teaching of literature has come to serve the internal vocational needs of an academic technocracy, how little it is in touch with the serious cultural needs of the larger society.

It would be easy to cite rather silly examples from current academic criticism in which the critic breezily condescends to the text or quickly leaves it behind in pursuit of bigger game like late capitalism, the early formation of the ego, the phallus as ultimate signifier, or the "discursive strategies" of a whole cultural era. I think it will be more instructive, however, to look at specimens of fashionable criticism at its assumed best. Let me propose for consideration two recent devaluations of Joyce's *Ulysses,* one by Fredric Jameson, who is I suppose the leading American Marxist critic, and the other by Leo Bersani, one of the most independent-minded of the poststructuralist critics, whose general orientation is psychoanalytic and metapsychological.

Joyce's novel, of course, is a central canonical text of High Modernism (a fact that in itself is likely to raise suspicion in the minds of third-wave critics), and was regularly celebrated as such by the nonacademic and essayistic critics who wrote for literary journals in this country during the first three or four decades after the publication of *Ulysses.* Since, it has also notoriously become the subject of a formidable academic industry, as was entirely predictable. Joyce, one of the most pedantic as well as one of the most inventive of great novelists, knew perfectly well that he was providing an endless vista of work for the professors in his elaborate edifice of allusion and cross-references and recondite lore. One should not condescend to all this scholarly activity. It has produced some illuminating commentary on Joyce. (As Frederick Crews recently observed, there is a good deal of fine scholarship done by single-author specialists, including young ones, that tends to be overlooked by nonspecialists, who have their eyes on the prestige network, which is decidedly elsewhere.) Bersani imagines the captains of the Joyce industry as participants in a modern "culture of redemption," conceiving literature as the vehicle of redemption, though I should think most of them were rather library-bound addicts of erudition, responding to the arcane learning of the master, and thereby making a modest academic career for themselves. In any case, both Bersani and Jameson look askance at all the Joyceans and raise questions about whether *Ulysses* is really the sort of masterwork our culture needs.

Jameson illustrates with particular vividness how the adversaries of the traditional canon are themselves actuated by a zeal for canon-formation on unbending principles that would make the arbiters of taste of all previous eras look like models of flexibility. *Ulysses* is an extravagantly symbolic novel, and Jameson announces early in his essay that "we have learned this particular lesson fairly well: . . . that for us, any art which practices symbolism is already discredited before the fact." The identity of the "we" who have learned this lesson is unspecified, an ambiguity that reflects the problem of audience to which I have already referred. Presumably, the "we" embraces all sophisticated students of literature after Derrida. However, the tenor of the essay as a whole would in fact restrict the first-person plural to American academic Marxists who are followers or associates of Jameson. Having condemned Joyce for the cardinal sin of "facile affirmation that the existent also means that things are symbols," Jameson attempts to rescue something for readerly attention by construing *Ulysses* as an authentic reflection of alienation under capitalism—a strategy that does not distinguish the novel very clearly from, say, newspaper and magazine advertisements.

Jameson's initial interpretive maneuver is to insist on both an isomorphism and a causal connection between formal features of the novel and industrial processes, social patterns, economic constellations, and so forth. Fragmentation, manifested in "the meaningless yet efficient segments of mass industrial production," is also a key to Joyce's novel, in which "time, experience, and storytelling . . . are inexorably atomised and broken down into their most minimal unities." This reductive analogy confuses fragmentation and microscopic detail, atomization and elliptic free association. The great interior monologues of *Ulysses* weave memories and perceived images and recurring phrases into ever-thickening webs of extraordinary tensile strength; this powerfully integrative process of mimetic art is virtually the opposite of the assembly-line alienation of labor ritually invoked, as by Jameson, in Marxist analysis. In a related move, Jameson contends that "point of view" narration—roughly, *style indirect libre*—which predominates in Part One of the novel, is, in historical terms, "the quasi-material expression of a fundamental social development itself, namely the increasing social fragmentation and monadisation of late capitalist society, the intensifying privatisation and isolation of its subjects." This bold and agile leap from social history to novelistic form leaves beneath it a vast field strewn with unanswered questions. Is interest in subjective experience necessarily dictated by social fragmentation? Why are there anticipations of point-of-view narration in the Hebrew Bible, composed in the early Iron Age? Why do the first subtle articulations of the technique in the European novel occur in the *Princesse de Clèves,* a book written in the court of Louis XIV? Does the fact that this method of narration was brought to a mature perfection in the novels of Stendhal have even a remote connection with the monadization of the subject under late capitalism? Why is it that in the age of still later capitalism, in fiction written since World War II, point-of-view narration has so often been displaced by first-person narration or flamboyantly omniscient narration?

But sensing that to reduce Joyce to an unwitting reflection of social forces is scarcely a rehabilitation. Jameson, a poststructuralist as well as a Marxist, tries to find some redeeming value in this gross purveyor of symbols by arguing that *Ulysses* reacts against the capitalist wasteland by carrying out a conscious "dereification." In his reading, the two concluding chapters before Molly's soliloquy enact a salutary "radical depersonalisation" that "also removes the reader, and finally that unifying and organising mirage or afterimage of both author and reader which is the 'character,' or better still, 'point of view.'" With the withdrawal of these organizing categories of the reading experience, all that is left is "a form of material unity . . . , the printed book itself," the letters on the bound pages and their self-reflexive interlinks. Jameson's language sounds sophisticated but the idea behind it is entirely untenable. Any appreciable distinction between the late chapters of *Ulysses* and the novels of Alain Robbe-Grillet dissolves. In order to make his point, Jameson characterizes the "Ithaca" chapter, which is done with catechistic query and response in scientifically factual language, as one of the two most boring sections of the novel. (For whatever reason, he doesn't even mention the "Oxen of the Sun" as a source of tedium.) I don't want to dispute

Jameson's right to be bored by what he chooses, but in my own reading experience, Ithaca is one of the most haunting pieces of writing in modern fiction. This is so for me because I find nothing in the chapter that tempts me to imagine Bloom's—or Stephen's—disappearance as a character or my own as a reader. On the contrary, the scientific catechism is a means of beautifully defusing pathos while inviting the reader to contemplate Bloom's pathetic circumstances, the sorry but ever hopeful tangle of his existence, under the aspect of eternity. "Alone," the catechistic asks, "what did Bloom feel?" The response is not a dissolution of the subject but the poignant representation of a human being under the immense vault of the stars, those scary distances of which Pascal wrote: "The cold of interstellar space, thousands of degrees below freezing point or the absolute zero of Fahrenheit, Centigrade, or Réaumur: the incipient intimations of proximate dawn."

At the beginning of his essay, Jameson observes dismissively that the Joycean parallel to Odysseus's absence from Penelope is a "ten-year period" during which Bloom practices "coitus interruptus or anal intercourse" with Molly. This is perhaps a small error but one that is strikingly symptomatic of the predisposition to impose a pattern on the work of literature rather than attend to its minute and instructive details. The sexual practices Jameson refers to are familiar ones in life and literature but do not occur in the Bloom household. Molly in her soliloquy is quite explicit about the substitute for vaginal intercourse adopted by her husband during the ten and a half years since the death of their infant son. Bloom ejaculates by pressing himself against her buttocks ("the last time he came on my bottom"), probably in the odd bedtime position he favors of head to Molly's feet. Neither the anus nor the vagina is involved. To imagine Bloom penetrating Molly, as Jameson does, is to misconceive something important about Bloom's character as Joyce represents it. His response to the traumatic loss of his son is not merely a fear of further paternity but a sad surrender of any full claim to conjugal possession. He may in fact be impotent ever since the death of Rudi, at least in regard to actual penetration (the novel is ambiguous about this because the explicit references to impotence occur in the fantasy of Nighttown). In any case, Molly is the promised land that he, Bloom-Moses, now cannot enter. He nevertheless continues to long for this unattainable bourne. He has sexual fantasies aplenty that wander elsewhere, but he still loves Molly in his complicated way and, however hopelessly, still passionately desires her. The habit of consummation by pressing against her buttocks is a nice indication of this terrible, self-subverting ambiguity that he has made of his married life. It is also a small intimation that between Jameson's impossible poles of spurious symbolism and reduction to mere printed artifact lies a large middle ground—where, I think, most readers really respond to the novel—in which the full concreteness of individual lives is persuasively imagined. This mimetic enterprise is no doubt meant to be reinforced and extended in meaning by the novel's structure of symbols and archetypes, but it is not strictly dependent on the symbolic references, as one may reasonably infer from the telling image of Bloom in bed with Molly, which exerts its revelatory mimesis even if one puts entirely out of mind both Ulysses and Moses.

Leo Bersani's devaluative essay is considerably more interesting than Jameson's because it does not attempt to force the book into prefabricated ideological formulas. He has some thought-provoking ideas to propose about the novel, like his intriguing if enigmatic notion that the Aristotelian Joyce came in *Ulysses* to imagine that "literature could quote being independently of any particular being's point of view." He also evinces a lively sense of what is going on in *Ulysses,* as when he writes that "the text . . . is transformed into a kind of electrical board with innumerable points of light connected to one another in elaborate, crisscrossing patterns." Bersani has a keen appreciation of Joyce's architectonic virtuosity—indeed, in one respect, as I shall argue momentarily, he rather overestimates its effect. The concomitant, however, of this appreciation is an odd lack of responsiveness to the novel's mimetic aims that is akin to the related failure of perception in Jameson.

As he approaches the conclusion of his essay, he announces that "*Ulysses* is a text to be deciphered but not read. . . . The exegetical work to be done is enormous, but it has already been done by the author and we simply have to catch up with him." The meaning of the novel, that is, will totally manifest itself once we are able, through the exercise of "a nearly superhuman memory," to turn on every possible light on the crisscrossing circuits of its great electric board. Escaping "the reader's dangerous freedom," the novel "asks that we be nothing but the exegetical machinery necessary to complete its sense." Bersani also suggests, in keeping with the larger argument of his book, that the surrender of one's freedom to this magisterially preemptive text is an affirmation of belonging to a community of (spurious) redemption, though I cannot see where or how the novel makes redemptive claims, or how anyone outside a tiny group of Joyce cultists actually reads *Ulysses* that way.

The point is that we do read *Ulysses,* not merely decipher it, and that the process of deciphering, however amusing as an intellectual pastime or however useful as a means of orienting oneself in the novel, is very far from determining the meanings of the book. Leopold and Molly Bloom are two of the most compelling characters in modern literature not because they are Ulysses and Penelope, or Elijah and Gea-Tellus, but because they are such splendidly individual, experientially substantial representations of an *homme moyen sensuel* and a *femme moyenne sensuelle.* Their lives, extravagantly different—one hopes—from the lives of most of us, succeed in touching something deep in our lives as we read. I will resist quoting a passage without allusions and cross-references, of which there are, after all, many in the novel, and instead cite a paragraph in which both occur, in order to test whether the effect is the displacement of reading by deciphering. Here is Bloom coming out of the cemetery after attending Paddy Digman's funeral at the end of the Hades episode:

> The gates glimmered in front: still open. Back to the world again. Enough of this place. Brings you a bit nearer every time. Last time I was here was Mrs. Sinico's funeral. Poor papa too. The love that kills. And even scraping up the earth at night with a lantern like that case I read of to

get at fresh buried females or even putrefied with running gravesores. Give you the creeps after a bit. I will appear to you after death. You will see my ghost after death. My ghost will haunt you after death. There is another world after death named hell. I do not like that other world she wrote. No more do I. Plenty to see and hear and feel yet. Feel live warm beings near you. Let them sleep in their maggoty beds. They are not going to get me this innings. Warm beds: warm fullblooded life.

The glimmering gates at the beginning of course are an allusion to the gates of Hades in Book X of the *Odyssey.* The reverberation of the moment is amplified by the mythic allusion, a procedure that has been employed by writers of all sorts again and again through the ages. It is hard to see, though, how the here-and-now specificity of Bloom's experience at the Prospect Cemetery is in any way engulfed, subverted, or even defined in meaning by the invocation of Homeric Hades. The warm beds at the end probably refer both to the bed of Calypso that Bloom has left at the beginning of his morning and the bed of Penelope it will become at the end of the novel. In any event, the obvious force of the image is concrete rather than mythic, and it takes no feat of memory to recall the marriage bed in which somnolent Molly sprawls that dominates Bloom's first chapter. At a couple of other points in the passage, memory is more severely taxed. Mrs. Sinico's funeral alludes to "A Painful Case," a story in *Dubliners.* Such coy self-reference goes back in fiction at least to Balzac, and I hardly think it matters for our sense of the meaning of the passage whether we can identify Mrs. Sinico. The "she" who wrote, "I do not like that other world" is Martha, Bloom's romantic correspondent, and the sentence occurs in the letter from her he read in the previous chapter. Perhaps we may recall the letter, but does it make a great deal of difference if we fail this small memory-quiz, if, say, we imagine the sentence cited was written by a younger Molly? Poor papa hardly needs elucidation. The fact that he was a suicide, as we have recently learned, makes the fragmentary reference all the more poignant. I am not sure whether the appearance of the father's ghost—which actually will occur in Nighttown—is also a garbled reference by Bloom to Hamlet, or a citation of some piece of popular Gothic literature.

The imaginative effectiveness, in any case, of the passage, transcends all such citational and cross-referencing activity that may reinforce its meanings. What stands at the center is the vivid representation of a man on the border between the realm of the living and the dead, himself full of stubborn life, his quirky, irrepressibly prurient imagination constantly working away at the stuff of experience—as when in these grave circumstances he recalls reading an article about necrophilia. Bloom is preeminently a Sancho to Stephen's Quixote in his adherence to Sancho's motto, *hasta la muerta todo es vida,* until death everything is life. "They are not going to get me this innings," he says, thinking of the warm refuge of Molly's bed as his intimately personal—not just archetypal—image of life. "Plenty to see and hear and feel yet." All that kaleidoscopic plenty of the senses is the substance of Joyce's novel, the driving-force and justification for its interior monologues and its

other narrative techniques. It is the narrative realization of life's plenty to see and hear and feel that makes this book a great novel for readers, not only for exegetes, despite all its extravagant show of learning and the convolute loops of its formal design.

Leo Bersani is one of the best of the third-wave academic critics because he has the intellectual élan to work out his own challenging categories of analysis. He shares, however, with the many lesser figures a predisposition to submit literature to a new canonical inquisition, banning or blessing on the basis of criteria that belong to an extraliterary agenda. Though it is of course true that no reading is entirely innocent, that everyone brings to the text a range of concerns and predispositions fostered by the world outside the text, there is a crucial difference between possessing an agenda and a value. My own reading of *Ulysses* no doubt presupposes the essential value of the self and its experience—as, I would argue, Joyce himself did. Adherence to this particular value may dispose me to particularly sympathetic response to certain kinds of literature but it does not prevent me from enjoying other kinds as well and it does not compel me to make categorical decisions about what is authentic and inauthentic in literary expression. To have an agenda, on the other hand, which is to say, a sweeping program for evaluating and transforming human existence, leads to a canon-making mindset that judges each work of art quite inexorably in regard to whether it contributes to or deflects from the urgent program.

Jameson's agenda, at least on the level of rhetorical gesture, is the destruction of the bourgeois world. Bersani's more complicated agenda is the pulverization of the unitary self, to which, in much of his recent writing, he attributes our sundry political, moral, and social ills. For him, as for many postmodern critics, the individual subject itself (himself? herself?) has become ideologically suspect, somehow implicated in those sinister concentrations of political power that oppress anarchic spirits and prepare the instruments for nuclear apocalypse. Only a literature that breaks down what Bersani calls the "myth of personality" can inoculate consciousness against the killing illusions of our culture. I am not sure if I understand what Bersani actually means by his repeated celebrations of the dissolution of the self, but it is worth noting that his argument to that effect in his essay on Pynchon, which he is careful to place in immediate sequence with his devaluation of Joyce, just as the two appeared when they were published periodically, points to the conclusion that Pynchon is a better writer, or at any rate a more authentic writer, than Joyce. Even before the publication of the unfortunate *Vineland,* that is hardly a judgment that a critic of Bersani's intelligence should want even to imply.

I do not mean to sound unduly bleak. If there have been three waves of literary scholarship in recent memory, we may yet live to see a fourth, and better, wave. And there are certainly still many people of all ages teaching at our universities who are passionately devoted to literature and capable of conveying something of their passion and their informed understanding to the young. For the moment, however, such people are likely to feel embattled, perhaps isolated. In far too many instances, political concerns, the explicit preoccupation with power on the several levels we have seen, tend to push the reading of literature to the margins. Even some astute critics strenuously resist the idea that literature may offer a unique experiential density, perhaps even a deepened apprehension of life. Outside the academy, this is still why many readers care about books. (pp. 282-94)

> Robert Alter, "The Revolt Against Tradition: Readers, Writers, and Critics," in Partisan Review, *Vol. LVIII, No. 2, Spring, 1991, pp. 282-94.*

Cleanth Brooks　(essay date Spring 1991)

[*Brooks is the most prominent proponent of The New Criticism, an influential movement in American criticism that included Allen Tate, John Crowe Ransom, and Robert Penn Warren and paralleled a critical movement in England led by I. A. Richards, T. S. Eliot, and William Empson. Brooks's criticism strongly influenced critical writing and the teaching of literature in the United States during the 1940s and 1950s. In the following excerpt, he characterizes the attempt to revise the canon as issuing from a misunderstanding of the value of literature, regarding this revisionism as an abandonment of the pursuit of knowledge and discipline in favor of "social therapy."*]

The present dissatisfaction with the canon has nothing to do with the charge that it lacks literary merit. The point urged is that none of us can make a case for his judgments of literary merit in any objective sense, for there is no such thing as literary merit in the present attack. The claim is made that the texts included in any canon were put there, not because they possessed any special literary merit or any philosophical wisdom. Not at all. Richard Johnson has put matters thus: "Analysts need to abandon once and for all both of the two main models of the critical reader: the primarily evaluative reading (is this a good/bad text?) and the aspiration to text-analysis as an 'objective science.' "

It is plain where such a notion leaves Matthew Arnold's praise of the "best that has been thought and written." The argument is that there is simply no way of measuring literary worth. Any textual analysis is simply a subjective fiddling with the text and has no objective value. Therefore, the choice of what texts we ought to have our students study must be made on very different sorts of grounds. Those grounds are frankly political. Although the new revolutionaries undertake to overturn common sense and a centuries-old tradition, their radical notions do fit certain popular ideas so well that they are easily accepted without much thought and do not require any profound verification. But what is meant by "objective science"? If the writer means the kind of verification demanded by the physicist or the chemist, for example, he will certainly not find it in any instance of literary analysis, but then think of what else he will not find capable of this kind of proof. How many of the principles by which we live can be proved with scientific exactness?

In a highly interesting essay entitled "The Frontiers and Limits of Science," Professor Victor Weisskopf, a distinguished physicist at M.I.T., sums up as follows:

> . . . important parts of human experience cannot be reasonably evaluated within the scientific system. There cannot be an all-encompassing scientific definition of good and evil, of compassion, of rapture, or tragedy or humor, or hate, love, or faith, of dignity, and humiliation, or of concepts like the quality of life and happiness.

Indeed, outside the "hard sciences," very little discourse could qualify as verifiable truth, including, let me repeat, the major laws and customs under which most of us conduct our lives. The newest critics, then, having rejected literary merit as the basis for any canon, frankly accept political concerns as the warrant for selecting our great books and go on to indicate the aim of their own political concerns: they want to create a new, more democratic society. America is increasingly multicultural. Why not then require cultural courses that will recognize this fact and include elements of Asiatic, African, Amerindian, Hispanic, as well as European culture? (But the culture of the Iberian Peninsula is European, is it not? Yes, indeed. But I am not trying to be logical here. I am simply using the terms actually used by our New Revolutionaries.) This new plan is indeed democratic in the sense that it sees that everybody gets represented. Everyone (or at least most of us) will find something in his studies that should make him feel at home.

The sentiment is indeed generous in spirit. Who wants anyone to feel left out? But as for culture and education, the scheme is hopeless, for it rests on a complete misunderstanding of what literature can give and needs to give to any culture. It shifts the issue from the acquisition of knowledge and disciplines to that of social therapy. It can be argued that such a notion is un-American. Indeed, Professor Arthur Schlesinger, Jr., as a social scientist, has made just this point. Professor Diane Ravitch, of Teachers College, Columbia University, has also stated her sharp objections to this kind of multicultural teaching. It should be of interest that the folly of such programs is thoroughly apparent to many more scholars than simply a few old-fashioned English professors, like myself. A number of recent tests have shown how little many of our students know about American history or even about world geography. They have evidently been fed on a very thin cultural soup. To add to it a few extra bits of cultural information will not suffice. Rather than informing and clarifying, this procedure will simply confuse. Students do need more information. They need to learn true facts about our world, but they require most of all some pattern of reference—some way to understand how these facts hold together in a comprehensible scheme. But a multicultural course or series of courses will hardly supply a significant pattern. In sum, the positive suggestions of our newest literary critics do not seem promising or persuasive. They amount to abandoning as meaningless what might be called literary study. If we want to use literary works at all—and for a start, better call them simply texts—they would teach them for what they might yield of political, historical, and sociological information.

As for the negative accomplishments of our newest literary critics, they are mostly exercises in debunking. This poem can be shown to mean just the opposite of what it has always been thought to mean; the novel, properly read, seems to have no definite meaning at all. But most of what is claimed by these newest critics to be new often represents no more than an extreme distortion of something that is not at all new but rather that has been known for a long time: for example, the varying senses of certain terms or the ambiguity of certain phrases. Obviously debunking carries with it a good deal of excitement and generates comment—even fame. But in view of the exaggerated claims made by some of our critics and their frequent violations of common sense, it seems likely that this new cult of destruction will wear itself out and that matters will settle down once more. Perhaps they will, but it is possible that something deeper, something promising continuation, is at the bottom of what had seemed to be not much more than a temporary fad. I am thinking here of a loss of interest in literature—even a certain contempt for it. Instances in my personal notice of these traits go back over forty years.

In the late 1940s I was at a small scholars' meeting in New England. I met there a bright young instructor, or assistant professor, who was teaching at Harvard. He was intelligent, somewhat unhappy, and his unhappiness clearly included his feelings toward his profession. Later we got into conversation. It turned out that he had become something of a Communist. Clearly he found his profession of teaching English literature unsatisfactory. Literature seemed to him to do nothing and to be going nowhere. It was a rather absurd by-product of a decadent civilization. But one could use it, he had come to realize, in order to teach Marxism. It turned out to be a way to get some good out of a rather useless body of knowledge. I don't remember the young man's name, but I do recall this thinking well enough to be sure that I caught a certain note of sarcasm with which he referred to his profession as an English teacher. I wonder whether he is still alive and, if so, he has read Frank Lentricchia's recent statement, "Literature is inherently nothing, or it is a body of rhetorical strategies waiting to be seized." The young man I met had the point long before and had seized upon it for his own purposes.

A few months after this episode, I gave a lecture in Atlanta and met a married couple who were insistent that I dine with them that evening. They were both teachers of English, enthusiastic, lively, eager to tell me their story. They, too, had come into difficulties—with their jobs and with their marriage—but then they had discovered Sigmund Freud. His work had saved their marriage and given them a satisfactory life work. While their subject was officially literature, what they really were teaching was Freud. It was really easy to do. His theories gave them something to talk about in almost any novel or poem that they had to teach. In short, their profession earlier had come to mean nothing to them, but now literature could be meaningful. They were almost deliriously happy with what they had discovered. But they were now teaching in effect psychology, though they were officially teaching literature.

I wonder how many people get trapped into teaching English and then find the job not particularly interesting, but refuse to remain stuck in what seems to them a meaningless enterprise. Some of them, obviously, have sought and discovered a way to use it—not necessarily to promote Marxism or Freudianism, but to promote some other movement that they believed needed promotion as they moved along the pathway toward the proper ideal society. I say, I wonder, for I certainly do not know, but I have been aware for a long, long time, of English teachers who find their work dreadfully dull. Such, however, I concede, are personal observations. One must be careful not to generalize too readily from them.

One need not, however. There are current movements that are highly visible and that may indeed bear upon our problem. I want to mention one in particular. We live in a highly technological society. It has devised for mankind some of the most intricate and beautifully discriminating machines ever seen as well as some of the most powerful. What modern medicine has been able to do to cope with certain diseases would have seemed to earlier generations truly miraculous. But the range of accomplishments has gone far beyond medicine or any other particular art or science. Whatever the horrors of the nuclear weapon, its invention and development represent in terms of pure fabrication an enormous extension of man's powers. Or consider our having put men on the moon and bringing them back alive and well. It was truly a marvelous event and, quite apart from what good it may or may not have accomplished, as a technical feat it was superb. It is no wonder then that we have been deeply impressed by such accomplishments. We have been profoundly affected by them and, most of us, affected in ways that we have not fully understood. We have, for instance, been confirmed in our belief that at last man is truly the master of nature—or soon will become so: that his ability to use nature and sometimes even reshape nature is immense; and that at least theoretically man has found, or can soon devise, the means to do almost anything he seriously wants to do.

Yet, what about the problem of ends? Our command of means has become very great: there is no doubt of that, but where do we stand on purposes, values and ends? Has science or its application as technology prescribed not only the means but the proper ends for human beings? Indeed, can it? I am thinking here of the passage I quoted to you earlier from Weisskopf's essay, "The Frontiers and Limits of Science," that there can be no scientific definition of good and evil or of the quality of life and happiness. However, it is verification by scientific tests that actually determines what many of us regard as genuinely true. That is to say, the world of means can be verified rather accurately. If we don't know the quickest way to get from Boston to Tokyo, we are confident we can quickly find out. The proper way to prevent an attack of gout has been found out for us if we are patients of a competent physician. But the realm of ends is much more problematic, more subjective, indeed largely a matter of taste, as many of us have come to feel.

How do we choose what we want to be and how we want to live? Many say, let me make enough money and I'll know better than anyone else how to spend it. The earliest universities were primarily concerned with ends. Today universities, or their students at least, are preoccupied with means. More and more students go to college to learn how to get a good job. At least that is what the statistical reports tell us. Since 1970 the number of students enrolled in the humanities has dropped by half. For the humanities have historically been concerned with ends, not means. They have taught (or at least been thought to teach) not how to make a living but how to live. Yet in our day most people seem to believe that our mighty advertising industry will best teach us how to live—what kind of house to own, what kind of car to buy, what kind of spouse to marry, and so on.

So it may be no accident that when our technological studies flourish most vigorously, it is then that our humane studies have become distracted, confused, and often are admitted to be in themselves just rhetoric, meaning nothing. In sum, our increasing confidence in our knowledge of means and our uncertainty about any objective basis for choosing ends may have had something to do with the notion that literature is mere rhetoric and that any one interpretation of a poem or story is just as good—or as little good—as any other.

I am even tempted to see the present disarray in literary affairs as a residue (or, if one prefers, a blossoming) of ideas that have been with us for a very long time. I am not thinking here particularly of the Greek Sophists but of the beginnings of the Enlightenment. A book entitled *From Enlightenment to Revolution,* written by the late brilliant scholar, Eric Voegelin, makes the point quite sharply. In his chapter on Bossuet and Voltaire he writes that Voltaire:

> . . . was deficient in spiritual substance and he was vulgarly irreverent. His surprising range of solid knowledge was coupled with an equally surprising ignorance concerning the more intricate questions of philosophy and religion; as a result his judgment was frequently superficial, though delivered with authority. He has set the style for brilliantly precise misinformation, as well as for the second-rater's smart detraction of the better man. He was ever ready to sacrifice intellectual solidity to a clever witticism. He introduced to the European scene the unhappy persuasion that a good writer can talk about everything, that every unsound utterance has to be considered an opinion, and that irresponsibility of thought is synonymous with freedom of thought. In short: he has done more than anybody else to make the darkness of enlightened reason descend on the Western world.

Yet Voegelin goes on to say, "Still, Voltaire is not superficial. There is in him a quality which is praised in such terms as his spirit of tolerance, his common sense, his indignation at scholastic obscurantism and at bigotry, his hatred of oppression and persecution, his advocacy of freedom of speech and thought." One is caught by the phrase "the unhappy persuasion that a good writer can talk about everything. . . . " Our contemporary intellectuals are very articulate and often use the language well, but their utterances are often not intellectually sound. One is

caught also by the phrase "the darkness of enlightened reason." It very well describes one of the principal features of our present culture in which there is vast information about certain aspects of our world coupled with a firm dismissal of other important aspects of the human condition.

The philosophers of the Enlightenment went on to dismiss knowledge that was not useful. Scientific knowledge was valued but contemplative knowledge was set aside as useless. "The acquisition of useful knowledge," Voegelin goes on to say, was "considered quite intelligible, but why should men devote their energies to the acquisition of useless knowledge?" What Voegelin calls the *bios theoretikos,* the contemplative life, disappeared from the calculations of these heralds of positivism. They ignored, or else did not know, "that the life of man does not exhaust its meaning on the level of utilitarian desires and needs, and that the life of contemplation, resulting in the understanding of man himself and of his place in the universe, is a fundamental spiritual obligation quite independent of its contribution to 'useful' activities." So here, I take it, again appears in slightly different terminology the point I was making a few minutes ago about the present-day attack on activities that concern the ends of human life rather than the study of means. Means are obviously useful and knowledge about them can be acquired. But literature may indeed easily seem to be in itself nothing, and its only useful role to teach us modes of persuasion that might be put to some really useful service in recommending something else.

Such a view seems to me woefully wrong. To reduce literature to something relatively meaningless—to an exercise that has as little to do with serious concerns as, say, has contract bridge or chess, is to make a ruinous mistake. Thus, I have chosen to make literature the principal matter of my defense. For various reasons it is certainly the most vulnerable item for attack. Millions of our citizens who have never heard of Derrida and who will never read a line written by J. Hillis Miller have no use for literature. They never read it. They would concede that a man like Shakespeare, safely dead, might attract tourists to his birthplace and thus become an economic asset, but a poet sitting in the next room is a joke.

Can students of one culture learn from the masters of another culture? Will they remain always alien? The question has been pushed even further in our time. Can a woman learn from a man? Or a man from a woman? I see no reason why one can't answer generally, yes.

—Cleanth Brooks

If one can make a case for literature, one has made a case for the arts generally. And there is a case. If we can observe through great literature how human beings behave, how they succeed and how they fail—how they justify their lives or how they fail to do so, we may enrich our own lives. Literature engages us in the total human situation often much more deeply and powerfully than philosophy or even history does. Yet I must not in concluding lead any of you to feel that I would play down the other great thinkers of the past. If we are to talk of some sort of canon, any version of it must include such names as Plato, Aristotle, Sophocles, Virgil, Julius Caesar, and so on down the ages. . . . Can students of one culture learn from the masters of another culture? Will they remain always alien? The question has been pushed even further in our time. Can a woman learn from a man? Or a man from a woman? An honest answer will depend on a number of conditions and circumstances. But I see no reason why one can't answer generally, yes. It is foolish to assume that each of us is sealed up in some private and impenetrable envelope.

The Dean of Yale College has recently spoken on this point with eloquent authority. A few weeks ago, in addressing the newly-arrived freshmen, Dean Kagan spoke as follows:

> In response to those who claim that Western culture is relevant only to a limited group, it is enough to quote W. E. B. Du Bois, the African-American intellectual and political leader, writing at the turn of the century in a Jim Crow America: "I sit with Shakespeare and he winces not. Across the color line I walk arm in arm with Balzac and Dumas, where smiling men and welcoming women glide in gilded halls. From out of the caves of the evening that swing between the strong-limbed earth and the tracery of the stars, I summon Aristotle and Aurelius and what soul I will, and they come all graciously with no scorn or condescension. So, wed with truth, I dwell above the veil." For him the wisdom of the West's great writers was valuable for all, and he would not allow himself or others to be deprived of it because of the accident of race.

(pp. 353-60)

Cleanth Brooks, "The Remaking of the Canon," in Partisan Review, *Vol. LVIII, No. 2, Spring, 1991, pp. 350-60.*

Jim Burke   (essay date February 1993)

[*Burke is a high school English teacher. In the following essay, he argues for expanding the canon to include literature written after* Lord of the Flies *(1954) on the grounds that the classical canon no longer addresses students' concerns and does not nurture their enthusiasm for reading.*]

Literature explores and makes sense of the mystery of the human condition in all its varied and twisted configurations. Each novel or play seems another page in an unfolding story that drives me on, hungry to see what happens next, eager to imagine all the different possible resolutions that could transpire by the story's end. But the story doesn't end—not in this modern, constantly transforming society in which we live—as novels and plays do; rather,

the story of our society, indeed our civilization, continues, the plot and theme constantly rewriting themselves. And though the literature available in bookstores offers the questing reader a constantly growing and improving fare of books that portray accurately and insightfully the reality of today's reader, the books in the schools do not. The stacks of Dickens, *A Separate Peace,* the Brontës, and other important writers and their works stand like bricks in a wall that bar today's increasingly diverse and disaffected students from reaching the literature that would speak to their own experience.

Richard Ford's novel, *The Sportswriter,* reminded me recently how serious this problem of what Ford calls "literary permanence" is, or can be if taken to its worst extreme. In this book the main character says upon leaving a college where he was a guest lecturer for a semester,

> What I did hate, though, . . . was that with the exception of Selma [a teacher at the university], the place was all anti-mystery types right to the core—men and women both—all expert in the arts of explaining, explicating and dissecting, and by these means promoting permanence.

This character's ruminations on the problem of teachers promoting permanence insofar as they hold steadfastly to the canon echoed my own disillusionment of two years ago. Having just finished my studies, I came to the schools after studying under Dorothy Petit, a professor whose ideas and teaching greatly influenced me. Petit talked to us about new and exciting books that were being written, books such as Ntozake Shange's *Betsey Brown,* books that were alive and current and showed, most important, that literature was a living, breathing thing that did not die after Harper Lee wrote *To Kill a Mockingbird.* Yet, upon beginning my teaching at a nationally recognized school in San Francisco, I found myself locked into a bookroom filled with thousands of books, few if any of them written within the last twenty years. Surrounded by these volumes, I heard Petit's steady and fervent refrain echoing in the back of my mind: *"There are no sacred books!"*

What is at issue is not the quality of these books: I do not mean to slander any of the books that belong to the esteemed canon. I would only say that there are no such things as sacred books when it comes to works of literature, no particular books that are truly mandatory reading for one to claim to be a whole person. I say this as a writer of fiction, an avid reader, and a teacher who loves teaching literature. For what we are doing by offering such old, used goods is saying to students that nothing has been written since *Lord of the Flies* that is worth reading; we are saying that life as we know it in the United States has not changed since *A Separate Peace.* We imply this, in spite of the fact that the growing majority of the students in our classes bring with them experiences that cannot be found in the literature we offer them. Again, I go back to Ford's novel.

> Everything about the place was meant to be lasting—life no less than the bricks in the library and books of literature, especially when seen through the keyhole of their incumbent themes: eternal returns, the domination of man by the

machine, the continuing saga of choosing middling life over zesty death, on and on to a wormy stupor. Real mystery—the very reason to read (and certainly write) any book—was to them a thing to dismantle, distill and mine out into rubble they could tyrannize into sorry but more permanent explanations; monuments to themselves, in other words. In my view all teachers should be required to stop teaching at age thirty-two and not allowed to resume until they're sixty-five, so that they can *live* their lives, not teach them away—live lives full of ambiguity and transience and regret and wonder, be asked to explain nothing in public until very near the end when they can't do anything else.

The last lines sound a particularly cynical note, and I do not agree with what Ford says there—at least not for public-school teachers. But I would say that during those years indicated, the English teacher must read, and read steadily. I know many if not most do read; but we must challenge ourselves to keep abreast of the field so that we can lobby effectively to get the latest books into the schools, so that we can be convinced that there *is* a book worth using in lieu of *Catcher in the Rye*. Surely it would be easier to cement into the framework those "classics" for which we have developed all the appropriate materials and lesson plans. But literature, the act of reading quality works, will then become increasingly practiced only by those rare students who prefer "the old way," or who see themselves as belonging to a part of the past that they can only visit through books; meanwhile, the others will give up on reading completely, the growing antiquity of the books in schools having convinced them that books are not relevant to them.

Students look to literature, as we all do, to discover themselves in it, and to experience different dimensions of the human condition that they may or may not realize they are a part of. What the majority of students see is that their world, their reality, is not worthy of literature, is not worthy of study. Nearly every work they encounter puts them on the outside, forces them to feel that it is irrelevant to their lives. Yet the bookstores team with excellent novels and plays and stories that would speak to them, if only given the chance. Furthermore, this distance from the material only exacerbates the students' view of teachers as totally removed, locked into the past, unable to understand the present.

Lest I offend the many teachers who read avidly and widely—for I know many do—or the few who are lucky enough to have incorporated into their curriculum such books as Amy Tan's *Joy Luck Club*, for instance, I say that I know there are those out there who are working at this important task. Some may say that there is simply no money; and this claim has merit. But when I look at the amount of money spent on ten-pound textbooks full of stories I sometimes have a hard time enjoying, stories provided because they are great "examples of the use of theme" or character development, I can't help thinking how many copies of Gary Soto's *A Summer Life* could have been purchased, or some novel that teachers could have decided is the "must read" of this year. And to those who say that books get ruined and don't last because they are paperbacks, I say so what: books are not bricks to be cemented into a wall that never wears down. They are meant to be kept with you, so you can learn to *enjoy* reading—in the sun at the beach, or in the park, or while you are waiting in the dentist's office. It is what is in the books that must be given a chance to last. In these times of growing economic hardship one might also look to the option of forcing students to buy their own copies of books: the books would mean more to them; they would appreciate the *feel* of real books in their hands and probably take better care of them.

What we cannot do, though, is give students the impression that literature is dead, that it is static. Never before have the bookshelves of good bookstores been so filled with such a range of quality literature covering the range of human experience in all of its conditions. Frustration out there is serious and high, I know that. The fight is an important one, though, and must be waged steadily and professionally. (pp. 56-9)

Jim Burke, "Canon Fodder," in English Journal, *Vol. 82, No. 2, February, 1993, pp. 56-9.*

A negative view of contemporary canon revisionists:

[What] most distinguishes the critics of today from those of earlier generations is not their frank interest in demystifying the process of canon making, but their insistence that power is the whole of the game—that power is what criticism is all about. No canon is or should be sacred, fixed once forever, beyond revision, but the canon revisionists now at work are perhaps unique in their readiness to subordinate literary and aesthetic values to a political standard. Acquiescing in the notion that disinterested inquiry is an impossibility and that every value judgment is necessarily a power play before it is anything else, they make their decisions by applying ideological litmus tests and determining the sexist and racist quotient in any piece of writing, from Plato to the present. This is, at bottom, a conception of the literary critic as an agent of the thought police, single-minded, obsessively concerned to enforce the party line, willing to subject chosen works to a violent form of interrogation, and more than happy to eliminate literature altogether in favor of pure theory.

David Lehman, in his Signs of the Times: Deconstruction and the Fall of Paul de Man, *1991.*

Kenneth Warren   (essay date June 1993)

[*In the following essay, which was part of a published debate on the issue of which works to include in new literary anthologies, Warren argues for a historically and culturally sensitive canon that addresses the needs of student populations.*]

At present one suspects that the appropriate response to W. E. B. Du Bois's claim that he can sit with a Shakespeare who "winces not" ["I sit with Shakespeare and he winces not. Across the color line I walk arm in arm with Balzac and Dumas. . . . So, wed with truth, I dwell above the veil."] would be, "Dead white men don't wince." This riposte, however, signals less an irreverence for Du Bois's admiration for European writers than an acknowledgment that politics, even of the textual kind, vary with circumstances. If imagining a literary utopia where readers and writers of every race, color, and gender could amiably rub elbows might once have served to point up the irrationality of our Jim Crow nation, similar invocations now tend to underpin arguments that can, paradoxically, leave Du Bois's *The Souls of Black Folk* out of the pantheon of Great Books because the canon itself is said already to speak to the questions that so troubled the austere New Englander.

If this irony were not sufficient, from elsewhere along the cultural politics spectrum come at least two other reminders to blunt the force of Du Bois's Shakespearean gambit. First, we are cautioned to remember that books are not bodies and that the presence of a European text in the hands of a black scholar is no particular cause for celebration; nor (which is more to the point) is the placement of "black" and "ethnic" texts in the hands of "white" readers any necessary advance on the front of social tolerance and equity. Books can go where certain people can't or won't, and it is literature's capacity to move across social boundaries that is invoked to keep literary study above the fray of politics and protest.

We are also urged to keep in mind that despite the attempt of anthologies, in Paul Lauter's words, "to represent as fully as possible the varied cultures of the United States," representation in anthologies, on reading lists, and in curricula is not the same as either political representation outside the academy or numerical representation within it. "Political representation," says Henry Louis Gates Jr. (echoing John Guillory), "has been confused with the 'representation' of various ethnic identities in the curriculum, while debates about the nature of the humanities and core curricula have become marionette theaters for larger political concerns."

Behind these reminders, however, is often a great deal of second guessing of the cultural Left, which, it is feared, may have mistaken the game at hand and ended up looking at best a little foolish and at worst like cultural extremists who have created, according to Gates, "a politics that is, in the worst sense, purely academic."

But even these avuncular reminders seem now to be wearing a little thin. After all, whatever the excesses and misrepresentations that have attended arguments for changing "the canon," there is in these various demands a principle worth reiterating: people of color and women of European descent ought to have a say in determining what is taught, read, and discussed on campuses and in classrooms. To argue that culture is fixed and that those now entering the conversation cannot, despite the conscientiousness and rigor of their formulations, make arguments for revision or change is to make an argument that won't withstand much scrutiny.

In this context, multicultural anthologies and curricula, if they do nothing else, serve to index the degree to which "new" voices have prompted observable changes in the way business is conducted on curricular committees and on the boards of publishing houses. That these changes strike some cultural conservatives as curriculum by plebiscite rather than by merit should not be cause for too much worry. Critical standards, especially in the case of American literature where "botches" litter the landscape of classic texts, are generally planted in the sand. Whatever the criteria, arguing individual cases on their merits seems in most instances an acceptable challenge.

But when we face the question of what we really want new anthologies to do other than mark the extent of previous successes in admissions offices, hiring committees, and editorial meetings, we confront something of an impasse. For a variety of reasons it is not enough to hope that teaching a multicultural curriculum based on multicultural anthologies will either make all students more aware, appreciative, and tolerant of diversity or will empower students from the groups whose writers are now being represented. Suffice it to say that effectiveness along these lines depends largely on anecdotal evidence, which is presumably as plentiful in favor of a traditional canon as against it.

Nor is it enough to hope that by setting "straight" a heretofore falsified or suppressed cultural record that we will effectively disable the oppressive practices that caused or were in some sense abetted by such falsifications. This latter hope rests heavily on the assumption that good old American racism at present is, in the main, what Kwame Anthony Appiah terms "extrinsic"—that is, based on a "belief that members of different races differ in respects that *warrant* the differential treatment." To believe that revising the "cultural record" will significantly oppose contemporary racism we would then have to argue that Enlightenment assumptions about the relation of literary originality to a people's intellectual capacity—assumptions that, according to Gates, were decisive in shaping early "black" letters—still play a significant role in underpinning current racist practices. And while there exists significant evidence that many Americans—both black and white—believe that blacks are inherently less intelligent than whites, there does not seem to be as yet substantial evidence to indicate that the reading of "good" literature by racial and ethnic minorities and European women will go a long way towards providing the kinds of facts that would presumably be effective in undermining extrinsic racism.

Yet if anthologies are uncertain tools for combatting racism and sexism, their various headnotes, introductions, and explanatory footnotes do begin to point to what these texts actually do—and that is to alert students to the importance and necessity of thinking historically about literature. Rather than placing before students the single text—be it poem, play, or novel—the anthology materializes the truism that all interpretation is intertextually mediated. If Fredric Jameson's "always historicize" remains the first move in a political critique of literary and critical texts, anthologies, by placing texts in relation to one another and in relation to their historical "context," begin the task of historicization, in part by corroding the specious authority that clings to "canonical" works. This beginning, however, is necessarily tenuous because of the way that anthologies, by their very nature, arrest the de-mystifying process even as they set it in motion.

The mass-produced reassemblage that is the contemporary anthology stands opposite the solitary paperback bestseller in the same way that, for Walter Benjamin, the original artistic masterpiece stands opposite the photographic copy. That is, paradoxically, the cut-and-paste operation of the anthology, unlike the cutting-room assemblage of motion picture, acts to confer "aura" upon a work and to embed it in, rather than detach it from, tradition. The ephemeral nature of the cheap trade paperbacks which make it into the classroom only on mass culture reading lists throws into relief the extent to which anthologies, even revisionist ones, reinscribe a rather traditional relationship of Literature to audience, managing reception by (in Benjamin's phrase) "graduated hierarchical mediation." In that relationship, trained cultural priests initiate willing novices into the mysteries of the process of reading and understanding the sacred texts. To this extent it makes little difference what the texts being read actually are, provided they are approached with due reverence and respect. One imagines that could "canonical" authors get a peek into the contemporary editorial rooms and professorial offices, their initial shock at the "diversity" of faces they saw would be short-lived—for uniting these newcomers would be a seriousness, conscientiousness, and regard for the literary texts that any author would find gratifying. It would appear not that the "Kingdom of heaven has been taken by storm and that the violent bear it away," but rather that the meek have inherited the earth.

The rude awakening that revision hopes to give to tradition may not be possible if we ourselves set limits that do not allow rude and relatively untutored hands to shape and reshape the order we have so laboriously wrought. Our task may not be so much a matter of following Gerald Graff's dictum to "teach the conflict" (which we ought to do anyway) but to continue reminding ourselves of the extent to which our students embody the conflicts we face in attempting to mediate between text and audience, between "history" and the people of the present. What we teach is inextricably linked to those whom we teach and our impressions of their deficiencies and needs; and our sense of what we ought to teach has changed, and will change, with our shifting student populations.

The biblical weight and size of anthologies—their almost exclusive presence in the classroom as opposed to the newsstand—indicates how fixed we are in the traditional practices we hope to modify or overturn. Against the palpable weight of a tradition in the form of anthology whose making is removed from the site/sight of the classroom, we perhaps ought to make some rather mundane moves.

Imagine that instead of sending our students off to purchase two-volume sets on American literature we gave them large ring binders into which could be inserted, modular fashion, the excerpts, introductions, and other textual apparatus that currently constitute anthologies. Many of us already use photocopied course readers, which we often view as anthologies-in-the-making, or as what we wish some enterprising publisher had already done for us. What I'm suggesting is slightly different—something along the line of the course reader as a commonly held commonplace book. In this case, students would not merely read these collections but during and at the conclusion of the course would be encouraged to remove, reshuffle, or add texts (including their own creative work) to the binder, with the proviso that they also insert commentary explaining their reasoning for any changes they have made. The binders and their contents would stay with the course, being randomly passed on to individuals in succeeding classes who would have the same right of revision. We (and our students) would in essence be teaching and confronting the history of our courses and our students; and by drawing some rough equation between canonical authors and student authors we might go a little way towards dimming literature's aura.

I make this suggestion in part tongue-in-cheek. New marketing techniques are, after all, new marketing techniques. And I don't think that the answers to the problems facing us are merely matters to be solved by the technologies of literary dissemination. I do think, however, that we ought to meditate more seriously about what it would take and what it would mean to wrest tradition from the well-trained (but now more diverse) hands that still hold it quite firmly, and to re-examine the possibility of establishing a truly democratic culture. (pp. 338-42)

> *Kenneth Warren, "The Problem of Anthologies, or Making the Dead Wince," in* American Literature, *Vol. 65, No. 2, June, 1993, pp. 338-42.*

Eva T. H. Brann (essay date October 1993)

[*Brann is a German-born American scholar, educator, critic, and translator. In the following essay, she proposes a number of arguments supporting the pedagogical necessity of the Western canon of great books.*]

I intend to mount the strongest defense, no punches pulled, for the Canon of the Western Tradition. To be perfectly up front about my allegiances: I shall be making my case from two sources, from principles that articulate my intellectual convictions and from experiences gathered in the course of one-third of a century's teaching at St. John's College, where my ideas were formed.

By "the canon" I shall mean a list of books held in high, even reverent, regard by a stable community of readers; by "the Western Tradition," a sequence of books, beginning with the Homeric epics, that stand to each other in a dialectical tradition of mutual response; by "a defense," a cluster of claims, arguing that faculties of universities and colleges should assign these books to themselves and to their students for common study.

It goes without saying that I could not mean that teachers or students should read these books exclusively. I think that we should all read, at our choice, whatever book is fine in itself and of consequence to the world, in any language and by an author of any sort. Zest for all books and allegiance to a few is a natural consequence of a good education. My claim is only that a first reading of the books of the canon is a *sine qua non* of literacy.

I am, moreover, acutely aware of the fact that none of my arguments is conclusive. Each has a rational counterargument worth listening to. That is what gives the "canon controversy" such life as it has. Naturally I think that the preponderance of principle and pedagogy is on the side of the canonical books. It must, however, be said that as more mental energy goes into these wars, less is left for those studies that make us competent to fight them. Some of the hubbub is, I begin to suspect, diversionary activity. In the time spent arguing which books to read, all the books could be read, especially since the number of books cited as replacements is not vast and the suggested texts are not inherently difficult. I cannot get over the impression that *accedia,* the sin of intellectual sloth, does have some part in this affair. Otherwise we could resolve it simply, as eager students always do, by reading beyond the assignment. That seems to be what our students, bred on great books, often do. Quite a few are avid for topical reading and good at finding what speaks to their particular condition. Hence they discover early the revisionist standbys long before they achieve cult status. For example, a decade ago, one of my students, Laura Nakatsuka, gave me as a present a copy of Maxine Hong Kingston's *The Warrior Woman,* somewhat before it became a standard feminist reference. She set me on a course of Anglo-Asian reading and alerted me to a literature that may be the salvation of the English language. Disciplined formal reading seems to engender adventurous personal reading.

· · · · ·

Typing. In the canon controversy, books are too frequently cited *en masse,* by genres and types. There is, for example, Literature, the superset, and then there are Black (or African American), Ethnic, Feminist, Women's, and other subsets of books. "Literature" is produced by authors, and the subsets are produced by African American, ethnic, feminist, or women authors.

I am not merely expressing a teacher's irritation with a lack of specificity, with the lack of reference to actual books in the public debate, especially the "multicultural" debate. That is very American—I cannot resist citing Tocqueville, who repeatedly points to our democratic propensity for vague generalities and large abstractions.

There is, however, a deeper issue here, a "hermeneutic" issue—that is to say, a question concerning the nature of books and readings. It seems to me that after reading many books one might conclude that Literature (or Art) designates a legitimate class of objects, and the terms "novel," "poem," "essay," and even "fiction" likewise. Or one might have misgivings. But these typings ought to be conclusions, and they ought to be postponed as long as possible. Unfortunately, they are built as assumptions into the course announcements of our schools. The consequence is that typological abstractions are taken as antecedent to individual, unique, untyped works, whereas these generalizations might better be introduced problematically, *ex post facto.* It is at the end of the course that a teacher might ask, "Is what we have read a mere or a meaningful collection?" Whether there is, for example, such a thing as "women's literature" should be a question, not an assumption; and it cannot become a question when the works in question are from the beginning segregated by external criteria.

Suspicion. I realize that these dicta are fighting words and require more detailed argumentation, some of which I shall offer as I go. What I maintain, however, is that pre-classifications of works on nonintrinsic grounds, such as the author's biography, are intellectually debilitating. I realize that the claim is that the personal and social circumstances of the writer are very much an intrinsic part of a book, and I shall not dispute that there must be some truth in the point. I question, however, whether it is a valuable or even a usable principle of selection. Taken seriously, it presents too subtle a hermeneutic problem for practical use; taken polemically, it floats too far above concrete reading and the particularities of books. It is the cause of willful inattention. In fact, the critics of the canon are not notably faithful readers of texts; some glory in creative construals.

The unwillingness to treat books as the individual creatures of individual authors has this, to my mind bad, consequence: the "hermeneutics of suspicion." The suspicion of ulterior motives, conscious or unconscious, of dominance assumed or independence surrendered, is the perfectly legitimate prerogative of a canny reader—but surely it will not do as an initial stance, as a prescription for beginning students! Toward books, as toward people, the beginning imputation should be one of good faith, of full self-consciousness, of staunch independence. That is all the authority an author has. In young readers especially, suspicion should surely be allowed to arise, but it should not be preinduced.

Subversiveness. The chief evidence in favor of the attribution of intellectual independence to the authors of the canon (who they are will be discussed below) is their endemic contentious subversiveness. There is no opinion I have heard in the recent debate that is not somewhere represented in the books under attack. I shall make the point later that this argumentativeness, this dialectic, is what makes our canon coherent. And it is not merely intellectual opposition to the opinions of their time, but deep social subversion that characterizes a portion of these books. It is no use casting around much for the best examples, for they are legion. Is not Euripides an author of the canon who depicts the catastrophe brought on by the pseudorational contempt displayed by a man and a legitimate king for the power of women's extrapolitical ecstasy and that of their transvestite god? Is not Marx a subversive? To be sure, one can always shape the historical setting and the psychobiography of authors so as to make them unwitting propagandists for some cause, but why would we do something to our writers that is indecent to do to our friends?

Mortality. It is undeniable that most of the authors of what I shall distinguish below as the Western canon are, as is nowadays much emphasized, white, male, European, and dead. To hold their mortality against writers is an unspeakable absurdity, for mortality at least is what we all do share, wildly diverse as we may be. As in individuals so in a tradition, the passage of time is needed to confirm excellence, and while an experienced reader can sometimes tell great quality in a page, it will have taken years for the book to become known or for the general reader to be ready. Those who make death an oblivion are consigning themselves to ephemerality. Think of all the aging professors who once preached "Don't trust anyone over thirty."

Gender. Most of the books of the canon are indeed written by men; many are about men, but few (I would argue, none) are written *for* men. Some of those works, like the *Critique of Pure Reason,* elevate the human soul to a universal genderless "it"; Kant's transcendental subject is not a "he." Some writers, like Aristotle, but not Plato, think women are the lesser sex. The question then should be whether and why they are either right or wrong. In my opinion some authors simply have a false opinion of women's capabilities. So what? These opinions are rarely of the essence to their theses, and no books ought, in any case, to be read without mental reservation, for, like persons, they will have shortcomings. We should trash neither the one nor the other for their failings. We should not vilify these books; we should study them.

Trashings are to be avoided because experience teaches that there are no winners. For example, the classical liberal arts curriculum was trashed in this country to make way for universal science education; the result is less Latin but little physics. I mention in passing that routine insults couched as charges, such as sexism, chauvinism, racism, and cultural imperialism, are not to be dignified with notice.

Take my favorite Toni Morrison novel, *Song of Solomon.* It is above all a book of names, allusion-freighted names. The Bible, Homer, Joyce, Faulkner—all are part of proper preparation for reading this text with appreciation.

—Eva T. H. Brann

Race. Concerning the race of the writers, it seems to me very shortsighted to emphasize it. In the short run it deflects students' learning by setting up resentment against what, I will argue, is inescapably the dominant tradition, but over time it grinds in the fact that this tradition is not nonwhite, an inessentiality raised to a stumbling block. Color blindness is not a politically correct principle these days, but it is both the most principled and the most advantageous way of reading.

It is most principled because until it is proved (not by social research but by public experience) that race is really a radical determinant of a person's perspective on life, economy requires the minimum hypothesis, which is that the intellect is universal. It is the most advantageous to the writers in question, because by the same token by which their own racial groups appropriate them exclusively, they withdraw them from the arena of books considered accessible to the general reader. The predominantly Black at-

tendance at Afrocentric studies is a case in point. Moreover, the self-esteem supposedly engendered by segregated studies is surely fragile and easily shattered in the unsheltered world. It is unlikely that the pride of students can be created from intellectual parochialism; it seems to come rather from being well-grounded in large contexts.

What is more, I question the very notion of Black, women, or gay writers. There are certainly writers who have special empathy for, and inside knowledge of, certain kinds of people and their settings, and these writers take, say, Blacks, women, or gays as their subject. Usually a reader can guess their origins because one supposes that writers know most about their own. But could a reader, for example, of *Middlemarch* be sure of George Eliot's sex? In taking this view I may have an ally in W. E. B. Dubois, who wrote in *The Soul of Black Folk* (1903),

> I sit with Shakespeare and he winces not. Across the color line I move arm in arm with Balzac and Dumas, where smiling men and welcoming women glide in gilded halls. From out the caves of evening that swing between the strong-limbed earth and the tracery of the stars, I summon Aristotle and Aurelius and what soul I will, and they come all graciously with no scorn nor condescension.

Furthermore, the writers I am familiar with, the older generation of Black men, the new generation of Black women, the new Asian American writers, are unmistakably Anglo-American first and last, and they clearly write for me who, they hope, will buy their books (and who does). They are Anglo-American in having mastered the craft of the novel in English, which has always included the loving use of dialect. They also have command of the Western literary tradition, which calls for referential and allusive writing. Take my favorite Toni Morrison novel, *Song of Solomon.* It is above all a book of names, allusion-freighted names: Omar, Calvin, Luther, and Solomon of Shalimar. The story culminates in a catalogue of names, in the Homeric and the African tradition: "Names they got from yearnings, gestures, flaws, events, mistakes, weaknesses. Names that bore witness. Macon Dead, Sing Byrd, Crowell Byrd, Pilate, Reba, Hajor, Magdalene, Guitar . . . Circe, Moon, Nero." The Bible, Homer, Joyce, Faulkner—all are part of proper preparation for reading this text with appreciation.

Background. In general, I doubt that I am obligated, or even entitled, to pay attention to the lives of writers whose books I buy. If a book cannot speak for itself it was delivered prematurely and should go back to the incubator. A conscientious author worth reading tries for a certain completeness of the textual world, and in return the reader is honor-bound neither to suspect nor to second-guess the text. In time, when the author's book has worked its way into my intellectual makeup, I might indulge my intellectual nosiness, from love or puzzlement. I might delve into author's private affairs, expose their social class, read around in the history of their time.

"In time"—if I have the time—I may acquire all sorts of information, but not first, not before the initial reading. There are questions—concerning age, family, handicap—

we may not ask prospective employees, and authors have at least equal rights. The practical implication for under-graduate education is that students should not be kept from good texts by backgrounds, biographies, or interpre-tations, or even explications. It seems to me that the acad-emy laid itself open to the present rage for ideological in-termediations and special-interest readings by the some-what self-serving insistence that every book should be in-troduced by the professor. Of course, it was inevitable that such scene-setting would at some moment turn into un-abashed propaganda. The directness of reading I am rec-ommending is again a minimum hypothesis; it gives to the teacher least control over the student's understanding and to the student the greatest responsibility. The counterar-gument, that students need academic introductions, is simply false, as our experience tells. They are capable of direct initial confrontation with most texts of stature. The good-faith reading of such texts consequently brings with it certain modes of nondirective teaching, of which more below.

Canonicity. These critical reflections now bring me to the question of a canon in the most general sense. I shall not go into the history of book lists, West or East, because my knowledge is sketchy. An excellent reference is Ernst Rob-ert Curtius's *European Literature and the Latin Middle Ages.* It is a broad fact that in the West lists of recom-mended, required or, indeed, proscribed or indexed books, go back to antiquity. I have before me Quintilian's list in the *Institutio Oratoria,* which starts with Homer and Vir-gil, the books with which our freshman and sophomore seminars, respectively, begin. The word "canon" for such reading lists first appears in the fourth century A.D. There were diverse canons, canons of pagan literature, of juris-prudence, and of Christian scripture. The canon, then, is a set of books meeting certain criteria of excellence or au-thenticity. Insofar as a canon is of sacred texts, the rever-ence it commands is scarcely surprising; but other books, too, undergo a sort of secular canonization, merely by rea-son of being on a list.

Canon-making is an unavoidable and, in fact, a pedagogi-cally useful byproduct of communal reading. The books many have read in common, found hard but very profit-able to crack, and seriously conversed about attract a cer-tain reverence. Even the most withdrawn bookworms turn into implacable hierarchists about their reading; the urge to establish degrees of greatness is a part of connoisseur-ship. So much is just human nature.

Nor is the necessity of canons in schools very controver-sial. If the community does not supply a book list the indi-vidual professor will. What is questioned is whether the canonical books should be high-class, classical. One argu-ment says that the books chosen should be representative rather than excellent. Then it divides. One branch says that the new candidates are in any case fully as good as the traditional works. I have already argued that these books are in fact members of that tradition; no doubt some are first-rate. Here time will tell. The tendentious book must be given time to fade—recall the sixties, for example, when the wisdom of the age was thought to be located in the media writings of Marshall McLuhan—and then these

quiet classics will emerge. That process is the life of liter-ate communities. Wherever people read—and reading is always first—books gather a penumbra of opinion, as peo-ple do reputation; excellence will out. Another branch ad-mits that books might vary in quality but claims that an affirmative effort should be made to include books by (not so much about) members of minorities to compensate for past neglect and to mirror the inclusiveness of this coun-try. This principle of representivity will be taken up below.

Excellence. A third branch of the argument denies that there are discernible differences in quality. Excellence is an elitist, an exclusionary, notion. This last is an absurdity that will wither on the vine. If by elitism is meant the in-vidious exclusion of certain people from a community, then standing between the people and the best is as arro-gant and as elitist as anything can be. That teachers would impose on their students readings in which they cannot see any intrinsic merit, and whose value consequently requires that ideological enhancements be provided by the profes-sor, seems just deplorable. Many of these books will come under my all-solvent principle of reading everything in time—but they should not be assigned to students, whose temporal economy is often so infirm!

I want to make a claim that needs more defense and differ-entiation that it can get here. It is that the four-year-long companionship of the best makes for the soundest sort of education. It stretches students' scope and capacities: their informed sense that the realm of human artifice superadds interpretable wonders to the intelligible wonders of the natural world, their detailed sense of the inexhaustible sig-nificance of human affairs, their justified sense of having access to the *mundus intellectualis,* and above all their sense of knowing a refuge in times of dearth or danger. Consider what a course of reading large amounts of medi-ocre books with special agendas leaves in its wake: a vague sense of least effort, of universal hokum, of being had, of being excluded and exposed. Of course, in commerce with excellence there are also dangers: pretentiousness, cliqu-ishness, name-dropping, discouragement, surfeit, fatigue. But it is worth the risk.

Community. I am working up to two points concerning the idea of a canon of books. One is that canons are made, quite unavoidably, by communities of readers, people who are brought up with books, introduced to more by friends and teachers, and engaged in companionable argument with each other. The converse is just as true. Common reading makes communities. It makes communities that are contentious, that is to say, intellectually engaged com-munities. The effort to compose a canon from individual books actually read brings people together—though the attempt to include, or exclude, types of books before they are read drives them apart.

I might go so far as to assert that there is no more powerful bond—of affection or enmity—than the bond of books dis-cussed in common. In fact, the elevation of book lists into canons is one of the preservative activities schools engage in. Just as Lincoln advises in his speech on "The Perpetua-tion of Our Political Institutions" (1838) that, to preserve a democratic nation, reverence for our founding docu-ments be taught as a "political religion" in the schools, so a critical reverence for great books, a sort of intellectual faith engendered by living daily in their presence, preserves the intellectual institutions, the communities of learning.

At St. John's the canon keeps us together, students and teachers, some of whom are reading now what all will have read in time. These readings lay the predicate of a conversation that all can join. It is the condition for diverse opinions to emerge just as it is the common ground that makes rational opposition possible. It incidentally hones temperamental biases and intellectual bends. To discover diversity of opinion read identical books; to uncover ultimate diversities of human nature read identical great books. But always there is this antecedent condition, whose logic would seem self-evident: the books have to get themselves truly read and actually discussed.

Immediacy. This brings me to my second point concerning the canon, the mode of reading canonical books. What are the appropriate approaches? I have already suggested my answer: with the minimum of pomp and circumstances, directly, immediately, the sooner the better.

But is that approachless approach possible? Are our students prepared? The answer is no, shading into yes. It is no, because when students arrive their buckets of learning are fairly dry. The first splash nearly evaporates before the second drops in. But soon the liquid of learning accumulates, and now each drop finds an element to sustain it; the level of preparation rises with the activity for which it is the preparation. It is undeniable that some verbal and mathematical literacy is required, but very little learning. Our students begin, as I did, with Homer. They cannot pronounce "Achaea" or locate Troy or spell "Ilium," but they learn all these concomitants of literacy as they think and talk about a hero their own age who is, like them, at once quite certain of his own preeminence and in great need of public esteem. In general, though they may never have the learning to get a literary reference, they become alert to the fact that it *is* a reference, and that is half the game.

The canonical books themselves, moreover, obviate the need for special preparation. I won't try to list here the numerous indices of canonicity that readers have gathered from books ex post facto and then turned into criteria. The American great books tradition abounds in such check lists, and I will mention some of the items below. A recent one from Europe, with which I am in tune, comes from Italo Calvino's *The Uses of Literature.* Number six says: "A classic is a book that has never finished saying what it has to say." This feature seems to me to be the symptom of a more determinate characteristic: a classic is a book that carries within itself all that it needs to be understood. Shallow and careless authors are borne along, more or less innocently, by established or disestablished opinions and by their own predilections. They write books that are, simply put, deficient and groundless, hence unintelligible without outside information, explanation, or interpretation. Deep and careful books are, as I suggested, self-sufficient. They provide the knowledge—or the references—needed to approach them and they contain the foundations on which they are framed, though it may take

some work to expose them. That is, incidentally, why great books manage to be at once intellectually positive and nonideological. Their authors are able and willing to write with candor; they know to the depths what they mean and they intend to be understood.

Consequently, the patience born of desire and the vicinity of friendly fellow readers are all students need—any students. The friendliness of the community has one cause and one expression, its *sine qua non:* sympathetic listening. Just as books should initially be construed to their best advantage, so students and teachers should listen to each other as if they could be speaking reason. They should question each other about meaning but never about motive. Canonical books, in our experience, promote such listening, as tendentious books block it.

Authority. Let this be my defense of accepting a canon in general and of reading it directly. Before going on to recommend the canon of the *Western* tradition (meaning a fairly definite and well-known sequence of books), a claim far more embattled than the mere notion of a canon, let me anticipate an inevitable challenge. Who has the authority to adopt such a list? Who shall judge? The answer is that the faculties shall judge—who else? Who in our tradition of intellectual freedom should tell a liberal arts school what to teach but the teachers?

But what if sectarian and individual interests have so balkanized the teachers that the only peace seems to be in mutual indifference? What if the center does not hold, and rights are sooner granted than arguments? When every attempt to reach a commonality of reason is taken as a sly attempt to impose the domination of a faction? I do think that abstaining from determinate judgment means surrendering to the tyranny of tendentious drift. Yet I also think that it is sometimes right to retreat into the more ardent study and the more intimate teaching of the books in question, to prepare for the turning of the tide—I mean the tide of political ideology, programmatic suspicion, and literary theory.

. . . . .

My defense of the use of Western books seems to have these three, not completely separable, aspects: pedagogical practicalities, civic purposes, and intellectual principles.

A. *Pedagogical Practicalities*

Our students have four years to learn where they stand. That translates into 256 seminar readings and discussions. Let it be granted, for present purposes, that they are to read from a canon, a communally established book list of highly esteemed texts. Then which one of the many, belonging to different disciplines, countries, civilizations, should be chosen?

At St. John's we have chosen to skim the canon of the West. It is a largely inherited but continually fine-tuned list of well over a hundred books. It appears to stem remotely from a list made up by Sir John Lubbock, published in 1895, and designed for the continuing education of English working men. So much for the elitism of the Great Books—they have in fact populist roots. They have always been, and are now, closer to the Chautauqua than to the Ivy League. The driving thought of the movement has always been that excellence is popularly accessible.

We use a series of books from Homer to Flannery O'Connor and from Plato to Heidegger. They belong exclusively to the so-called Western tradition, the line of texts that begins with a double origin, sometimes designated as "Athens and Jerusalem." Why this elective exclusiveness? The answer is practical but shades over into principle: time and cohesion.

Time. Had we but world enough and time we would include first of all two subtraditions that are, almost perversely, left out: the postbiblical Jewish and the Islamic texts. The inclusion of these traditions would in no way destroy the coherence of our readings; they would simply be interleaved with our present list.

But there is no time, in our judgment. We have learned over and over what pedagogues have always known: that it takes time to digest reading—mere, extended, uncluttered time devoted to a few texts, and that more reading does not mean more learning. We have already pruned and curtailed our works past respectability and cannot find significant stretches for additions. This we know: packing is pedagogically worthless. If we had a fifth year we might well decide to read some contemporary works of emergent stature. More likely, we would try to read in the classics of India and China: the Upanishads and the Bhagavad-Gita, Lao-Tse and Confucius.

There is another difficulty, again mostly temporal. Although I have alleged above that the best books can be faced quite directly, there is one sort of background preparation that is very desirable: the liberal arts, the skills of learning. We pick these up with our students, in a modest and unsophisticated way, as we read through the canon. They study Greek and French as paradigm languages through which to practice the "trivial," that is, the verbal skills of translation, of rhetorical analysis, and of stylistic appreciation. They study mathematics, for example Euclid and Lobachevsky, to learn about demonstration, axiomatization, and mathematical elegance. The comparable communal preparation for non-Western literature is beyond our means (though some colleagues are even now studying Sanskrit and Chinese). As far as I can tell, there is not even the slightest acknowledgment, on the part of the people who blithely recommend global learning, of these time-consuming prerequisites to understanding.

Cohesion. Cohesiveness is our second constraint. All teachers know that, just as learning takes time, it requires cohesion and reiteration, that it must have a chance to build on itself, that connection is essential to retention.

Just as a common program builds a human community of learning, so the unity of the tradition makes for an intellectual complex of understandings. In staying within one tradition we join a conversation, "the great conversation," as the phrase goes, among authors who implicitly and explicitly take account of each other and respond to each other: Dante to Virgil, Aristotle to Plato, Kant to Hume, Milton to Homer, Hegel to Aristotle—or, just as plausibly, the inverse. The temporal relation of these interlocutors is not necessarily linear—at least that is a hypothesis

we ask our students to entertain. Finally, we do not care so much that students should know authors as that they should participate in their dialectic, that they should hear and respond to their own intellectual forebears, great names aside.

It would, we think, be disruptive and undignified to treat our reading list like a Greek new year's cake, into which one kneads this or that alien piece of gold. We might insert some Upanishads next, say, to the *Republic* because they display remarkable similarities to Plato's three parts of the soul and the three castes derived from them. To what purpose? We would distract ourselves from delving into the meaning of one text by comparing two, and from asking about the truth of both by worrying about the priority of either. And we would be starting down a slippery slope of grab bag incoherence. As one of our students, who has been carrying on with me a keen correspondence in favor of Eastern books, has pointed out, we do breach the principle of excellence here, since some of these excluded Eastern books are surely better than some included Western books. We do it, in the first instance, in the interest of cohesion. But we do it also from a respect for alien classics, a respect that warns: not to be casually approached!

B. *Civic Purposes*

A liberal education, by its ancient definition, is not a direct preparation for a livelihood, but it is purposefully concerned with the students' lives as citizens. Since the Western books are read in the context of an American liberal arts college, the argument must be made that they, rather than others, are good reading for American citizens.

Let me make the argument under four rubrics. The West should be the mainstay of study because it is (1) universal, (2) ours, (3) endangered, and (4) beautiful. These arguments seem to me convincing in descending order.

Universalism. The books of the West are universal in two peculiar and related ways. Universality is claimed for other classics. For example, Gandhi says of the *Bhagavad-Gita,* "A knowledge of its teaching leads to the realization of all human aspirations." The peculiar universalism of the West is not that of one source of wisdom but that of deliberate universalization, be it by appeal to types, forms, noumena, principles, abstractions, or laws. This propensity, especially when applied to the immediate world so as to convert it into law-governed nature, turns out to be irresistibly powerful, both because it is intellectually engaging and because it is practically potent. Hence intellectual universalism achieves practical dominance. The world, our earth, is now universally westernized in crucial respects.

We should, incidentally, not forget that it is in this universalist tradition that there arises the notion of multiculturalism, that is, of an intellectually mandated interest in the variety of human communities. Witness Herodotus, the first anthropologist, who defines the Greeks by the non-Greeks.

The universalism of the West imposes on every contemporary the obligation to ask whether the fact that this universalist knowledge is power implies that the converse holds: that power is truth. Behind this formulation is a complex of old and current questions to which our students simply must have an approach or they will flit helplessly to the periphery of our problems. The Western canon is that approach.

Roots. This tradition is also peculiarly ours, particularly ours as Americans. America is the mother of individualistic democracy and the father of theory-grounded technology. Americans of all subgroups have willy-nilly a peculiarly intimate relation to these universal features of contemporary life: human rights and the mathematicization of nature. Whoever is a user of machines is a participant in this tradition. Whoever has democratic feelings belongs to it. Its roots outrun those of blood, race, and (I would add) gender:

> If they look back through this history, to trace their connection with those days [of the Revolution] by blood, they find they have none: they cannot carry themselves back into that glorious epoch and make themselves feel that they are part of us; but when they look through that old Declaration of Independence, they find that those old men say that "we hold these truths to be self-evident, that all men are created equal," and then they feel that that moral sentiment taught in that day evidences their relation to those men, that it is the father of all moral principle in them, and that they have a right to claim it as though they were blood of the blood, and flesh of the flesh, of the men who wrote that Declaration; and so they are. (Lincoln, July 10, 1858)

The Declaration is, of course, a part of the tradition and its roots go back through Jefferson and Locke to the Greek political philosophers, as natural science reaches back to the Ionian physicists. Not to know the main moments of this tradition is to float in a cloud of ignorance, to know civil rights as a phrase and science as a fetish. Moreover, we think that there is really no abbreviated way to reach the inwardness of these two great facts of our life. They are developments and bear their beginnings within; so to the beginnings, the principles, we must go.

Endangerment. The tradition is endangered—and endangering. What is endangered is the wisdom of the West. Hostile and hasty readings present the tradition as rabidly rationalistic and aggressively dominating. But these are provably desiccated and derivative readings. The sources should be allowed to speak for themselves.

There is now a notion abroad that the dangers inherent in Western ways—the domination of mankind by machines, the conversion of nature into new material, the atomization of human beings, the bureaucratization of human relations, all the rubrics of anxiety—might be cured by a wisdom newly learned from the East, from Africa, from American Indians. It is a possibility but not a likelihood. For one thing, in the absence of a mature practice of translation, the meaning-laden Eastern terms tend to go over into Western categories whose significance escapes the enthusiasts while their use makes the text into something very derivative. (It is, incidentally, a source of surprise that the same people who preach the contextuality of meaning, the relativity of truth, and the untranslatability

of terms, sometimes show little appreciation of the lifelong devotion to the study of, say, Sanskrit, that is needed to work one's way into Hindu texts. At least our students have a year and a half of Greek.) And, more generally, I offer it as an *obiter dictum* that the cures for the ills of the West can and will largely come out of the West. Often they will come from a reconsideration of more original understandings of, for example, Aristotle's claim that nature first appears in the individual animate being.

Beauty. The defense of the Western canon that derives from the beauty and magnificence of the works—particularly of the literature, the music, and the visual arts of the West—is the weakest. All civilizations appear to have works of surpassing beauty, a beauty which, although it is the efflorescence of their particular life, nevertheless captures even an alien's imagination quite directly.

Yet it makes sense to choose the works of art from the same tradition as the works of philosophy. For one thing, the imaginative sensibility and truth-seeking reason are in a peculiarly close and tense relation in the West. Again, the high art of the West takes some getting used to and sometimes requires some theoretical knowledge. A hearing of the *Matthew Passion,* for example, is helped not only by the habit of active listening but also by some knowledge of theology and some skill in musical analysis. That is one reason why all our students study the elements of music in the year when they read theology, having previously had the experience of singing together for a year. In sum, we think that there is some value in the cultivation of a common sensibility, a shared intimacy with one related set of works, chosen from a tradition of staggering richness.

But the world urges diversity, and this claim must now be considered.

Representation. One argument for diversifying the canon is to make it representative. There is a multitude of American authors that should be heard, especially since the country is growing increasingly diverse. Two specially urgent points are that the self-esteem of minorities is at stake and that as fellow citizens we should know each other.

Here is the first problem. In this large nation there is no group that cannot specify itself into a minority by some criterion: ethnicity, femininity, negritude, challengedness, even WASPishness. If representation is to be a principle, all must have a voice. I understand that there are more than twenty Asian American national groups who resent being lumped together. Most of the ethnic groups are fiercely ethnocentric—as opposed to the supraethnic universalism of the tradition I am defending. A university with an expansible and *ad hoc* curriculum can accommodate the most pressing local demands. But how is a college with finite resources to make rational choices? Inclusivity is surely impossible, and exclusion now becomes invidious. Moreover, even at a university as sumptuously stocked as the food basement of a Japanese department store, each student can feed at only a few counters.

Another problem is that while the minorities demand sympathy, they deny empathy. The claim is often made that only a woman can understand women, only an African American, African Americans. Whether true or false, it certainly undercuts the argument for mutual understanding. And, in fact, the courses built around this view are directed to and attended by members of the group that is being studied. Perhaps such activity should take place, but perhaps not at a university, an institution shaped to support the Western tradition of free and open inquiry.

Here are further misgivings: Does the inclusion, under political pressure, of multicultural selections do right by this country and by the students? Does the country want it? America is at present still predominantly European-descended. Should this fact be so readily set aside in favor of futuristic statistics? Should we overlook the actual present to accommodate ourselves to a projected future? Should we destroy a tradition which is still that of the majority—and as I argue, indeed, also that of all minorities? Do we really know that particularism fosters pride?

When I was an immigrant child in Brooklyn the school establishment quashed signs of sensitivity to slights and nursings of resentment in the public arena. Here we were to be bright little Americans. At home, on weekends, we separated and went with our own in those quasi-public associations that Tocqueville describes as the counterweights to American conformism. Some went to study Torah and Talmud, some went to learn the Catholic catechism, some went to Greek school. This was American pluralism, a wrenching but rich experience. Do we know that, the academy apart, this is not what the communities would still prefer—to get semiprivately together about what is close to them and to preserve a public realm for what takes them out of themselves? There is a self-esteem that comes from having been made free of the universe.

Individualism. The tradition I am defending is the very one that can obviate the need for group representation—by means of its currently much maligned individualism. The individualism of the tradition is maligned because it is misread as self-aggrandizing atomization, incompatible with community. Such harsh egotism, to my mind, is not what the great texts of individualism intend, though it is an arguable interpretation. Another charge brought against the individualistic tradition is that in its parochial logocentrism it excludes most of mankind: women and nonwhites. Such retrospective charges are in equal parts undeniable and not in very good faith. Though by and large the truths told by these authors are meant to be universal—for they hold that reason is generally human—their circumstances determined where their attention and their allegiance went. Why would Lincoln speak of women when his audience consisted of men? Why should Pericles speak of Africans when his world stretched from Greater Greece to Asia Minor? Why should we fix on what the author regarded as peripheral? Do I stop reading English novels because of their pervasive semiconscious anti-Semitism?

The great books are almost all concerned with the individual human soul, creature, or person, which is, in the first instance, genderless, colorless, and classless. And that sort of individualism is what makes the books ours in common, as incarnate spirits and rational animals. It is possible to argue that this universal individualism too is a bias, an ideology. But in America, at least, it is within this transcir-

cumstantial republic of radical individuals that the factions and sects are defined and that rebels and revolutionaries make their claims. So let individualism be acknowledged as a premise, a falsifiable premise, but let its origins and ramifications be studied in their deepest presentations, difficult though they may be. A prime example: the *Critique of Practical Reason.*

Corroboration comes from a counterexample. St. John's has a Graduate Institute, originally meant mainly for teachers. When grant money was more plentiful, we had a good number of Black inner-city school teachers. One of the readings was and is Aristotle's *Politics,* which presents an argument for natural slavery, that is, for the defectiveness of certain souls. This chapter never failed to ignite the intellect of our students. Is an argument for natural slavery not an implicit argument against racial slavery? But is it not also an argument against the universality of the human constitution, against equality? Why does equality appeal to us so powerfully? These were questions raised through Aristotle's text and passionately yet objectively discussed. Objective passion is, in fact, what such texts are able to induce, because whatever their specific claims, they address the reader's human reason, and the reason has more tenacious passions than the heart.

Stature. Finally, the most convincing argument, though not the one most often given, for widening the Western canon is that unknown works of great stature, previously "marginalized," should be allowed to take center stage, or at least to become known.

Of course they should. I have already argued that a number of those works, by women, African American, and Asian American writers, are in the tradition anyhow and will be so regarded when the ideological excitement has passed. Those that are superlative will simply enter the perennial canon. Others will be discovered by lovers of literature over a lifetime, as are all the fine minor masterpieces (a classification perfectly intelligible to devoted readers; it means wholly absorbing and admired books that don't quite achieve Calvino's infinity of significance).

But recognition is wanted now, and should be and, in fact, is given now; it is given by all the individual readers who make up the republic of letters. What would life be without the women novelists from Fanny Burney on? And there is, in fact, one of those Anglo-Asian novels I find so enchanting, by Ishiguru, now sitting on the shelf awaiting the end of my engagement with the canon controversy. I should say that our students read such works in "guerilla seminars" that they organize.

So the idea of multiculturalism as an encouragement to wide reading poses no danger, no competition to the canon, unless it is officially enforced. But there are two modes of reading that do pose such a danger.

Victims. Victim-readings seem to rest on two notions. One is that the very idea of excellence is repugnant to egalitarian principles and oppressive because exclusionary and marginalizing: every claim of excellence involves an arrogation of authority. All books are social documents, and especially those written by oppressed minorities must be brought to the attention of the academy. I doubt that many students will have the social sympathy to live in the barrios of literature for any length of time and to engage in affirmative action reading exclusively.

The second notion is the oppressiveness of the high tradition. Insofar as this implication of cultural imperialism is an implicit acknowledgement of the potency of these books, the counter plea is *nolo contendere*. But insofar as the claim is that these books, being largely by dead, white European males, are full of oppressive opinions, I do contend that a closer reading may show otherwise. Again, the academy brought such interpretations on itself by engaging in the bad intellectual habit called "history of ideas," that is, ideas divorced from the particular texts that give them their subtle shading and their intellectual context, hence ideas exposed to ideological appropriation. Similarly the notion, most explicitly worked out by Marxist critics, that all texts are so enmeshed in the author's social allegiances as to make them in some sense semi-conscious automatic writings, prepared the way for regarding the biography of the author as more revealing than the argument of the text.

But let it be an open question whether the young should be led to impose on themselves what the harsh world will always finally regard as the stigma of victimization. Let it, by all means, also be an open question whether the canon has elements of exclusionary arrogance, or whether all texts need demographic contexts. It remains our conviction that a teacher's business is not to ideologize or even to interpret texts. It is to say "Read this!" or to ask "What does it mean?" "Is it true?" "Can you defend your opinion?" and then to watch helpfully over students' attempts to answer. That, incidentally, is why at St. John's we call ourselves "tutors"—protectors, and not professors. Of course, students may ask their teachers' opinions or teachers may wish to enter their own readings, but they should always be on a footing of equality with the students. That is the egalitarianism we think appropriate in the face of great books.

Hermeneutics. This brings me to the second mode of reading that is a danger to the Western canon, and actually to all books intending to signify originally and determinately. This mode was introduced to the academy through hermeneutics, which deals with problems of interpretation in general. It is based on the theory that textual meanings are essentially construals, that there is no single discoverable textual significance, and that the reader is therefore the final author. This way with texts is a subject of the postmodern conviction that the whole *mundus intellectualis* is a free human invention. Although these construals, or deconstructions, are most often worked on canonical authors such as Rousseau, there is ultimately not much reason why the next generation should not pick just any text on which to exercise its idiosyncratic brilliance. Certainly these theories foreclose the communal establishment of a reading list and the common search for meaning and truth. But that such a search is a possible and sensible undertaking is yet another promise of reading great books, a working hypothesis, no more and no less. The positive proof of its possibility comes from the actuality of our pedagogic practice. The negative proof comes from the ennui and the drift of study in its absence.

Nor are we daunted by the fact that in our conversations conflicting meanings and convictions of truth emerge. I have never understood why from a profusion of interpretations should be deduced the absence of meaning, and from a multitude of convictions the impossibility of truth. It seems to me that the same evidence can be cited in favor of the unquenchable desire human beings have to extract meaning and to establish truth, and as proof of a common universe of agreements and oppositions, whose very possibility lends plausibility to the desire to know. But such speculations bring me to the third part of my defense of Western readings.

C. *Intellectual Principles*

The recommendation of the Western canon can be grounded in certain intellectual principles, principles that seem to govern the composition of the great Western texts, particularly the philosophical books. It is useful to hold these principles in mind while reading the texts. It is not, however, necessary to subscribe to them in order to read in the canon with profit. Most of them have already emerged in the part on the pedagogical practice of St. John's. But although I think I see them at work there, their formulation is more mine than my school's. The rubrics are: (1) originality, (2) dialectic, (3) truth-telling, and (4) self-knowledge.

Originality. The books of the canon are original. Originality is eventually a criterion of choice, but it is initially a characteristic of composition. By the originality of the books I mean their double character: first as root inquiries, as articulations of an attempt to be radical, to ground—or undercut—traditional opinions by finding their true origins, sources, and geneses; and second as authorized texts, as speaking with the impersonal yet individual authority of a writer who has discovered the hitherto hidden. I am not sure that non-Western books ever make precisely these claims.

Since books in the Western tradition do make them, there are failed or flawed (as distinct from insignificant or intentionally secondary) works in this respect, and "greatness," superlativeness, becomes an intelligible issue. But while authors through their books join a critical competition, these same books are also in some sense isolated by incomparability, as each strives to speak both newly and ultimately. In this third millennium of philosophy, Kant advises the metaphysically inclined reader that it is "inevitably necessary . . . to regard all that has happened up to now as not having happened, and before everything first to raise the question whether such a thing as metaphysics is generally even possible" (*Prolegomena to Any Future Metaphysics*). It is their originality that makes the immediacy of reading, the approachless directness defended above, possible and preferable.

Each book attempts to be elementary, to begin at the beginning, and to be self-sufficient, to lead the reader on in its own chosen way. Many open a primordial world as it was antecedent to the present organization of the intellectual world into disciplines; for example, the world as it was before physics was divorced from theology, and mathematics from philosophy.

Another consequence of the originality of these books is the need for having the texts always present, but not only because they are peculiarly provocative third parties in any conversation. The more telling reason is that they are particularly vulnerable to travesty through retelling and epitome, because they so often originate their own terms and develop their thought organically. It is to prevent ourselves from dealing in the academic coin of conventional vocabulary and predetermined ideas that we try to keep close to the text in seminars. Consequently our community's estimation of a book may vary as widely from its academic reputation as the picture a family has of a famous member may differ from his public persona. To put it another way, texts are not textbooks—it is impossible to extract the kernel of topical truth while discarding the textual shell. Canonical books require and elicit close reading.

A further concomitant of the principle of originality is the notion of contemplative learning, a learning that is, at least in the first instance, for the sake of illumination rather than performance. Many of these books are locked in battle over the question of efficacy. Is there substantial knowledge worth having for its own sake or is all learning for the sake of doing? The engaged distance, the liberation, that comes from at least once conceiving the notion of pursuing things to their origins simply for the sake of being enlightened—that is a frame of mind these books induce by their originality.

At its inception, liberal education was understood to be nonutilitarian. The battle between the original conception that, though learning often has as an incidental outcome intellectual readiness for all contingencies and a sense of civic responsibility, it is essentially to be done for its own sake, and the idea that the training of the young should be focused on specific competence and secular success is as old in America as the republic and is raging now. The canon bears on it in this way. Originality in the sense in which I have been using it, as radical inquiry, implies contemplative theory as antecedent to practical application. In its readers it encourages intellectual venturesomeness and playfulness. Free speculation is the element of the canon.

Dialectic. From its beginning, the Western tradition, especially in its philosophical books, has been dialectical. I mean that it is not so much handed down in a collection of dicta and commentaries as developed in a sequence of claims and counterclaims. *Traditio* means "handing over"—as in preservation *and* in betrayal. Heraclitus, one of the avatars of the tradition, has a revealing figure for the cosmic counterpart of the human argumentative mode. "People," he says "do not take in how the Logos, being different from itself, agrees with itself. There is a resistant joining as in bow or lyre" (Fragment D).

The tradition is like a recursive system of such recalcitrant coherences. Each book is in high-strung opposition directly to its chronological neighbor, while the subtraditions are again related in a long flexed arc, texts to remote texts: Plato to Aristotle, the Ancients to the Moderns.

The reflection of this principle in selecting the teaching canon is its peculiar coherence. It is not only a collection of superlative and self-sufficient texts, but a sequence. It is its own context, a system of cohesion and recoil. That is why not every great book can be fitted in and some not so great books are included, sometimes as needed complements. The intellectual principle of tensile connection turns out to be a pedagogical principle of selection.

The reflection of the principle in the sequence of reading is chronology. A chronological arrangement is a minimum ordering principle; it introduces the fewest prejudgments concerning themes and affinities, but it also takes account of the dialectic relation, by which I mean the fact that many books cite forerunners and antagonists and lean on them in their arguments.

The reflection of the principle in teaching the canon is conversation. The books are mutually responsive, dialectical, argumentative, and so should their readers be. Neither discipleship nor esotericism (though some individual books invite both) is the appropriate mode of learning from the tradition as a whole; open and responsible declarative speech supported by reasons is. Passive learning in the philosophical tradition is a contradiction in terms. Hence the teacher must give the students room to speak, to fumble, to be outrageous. That means no lectures, by now for two reasons. First, as was said above, so as not to skew the approaches, and now so as not to steal time, that one great limiting factor of learning.

The incessant dialectical onslaught is sometimes stupefying to students—and tutors. But the swirl of opinions has a salutary effect too. It invites the exercise of objective judgment, of the cool consideration of alternative opinions. The notion of an objectivity that is nevertheless passionately interested is deep-rooted in the tradition (as is, incidentally, the idea of an objectivity divorced from persons, from subjective pleas). Heraclitus, once more, asks us to listen "not to me but to my argument [*logos*]" (Fragment D).

Does dialectic operate in the imaginative tradition, in poetry, fiction, music, and the visual arts? Since these are said to have developments, since—as I said before—their authors are often learned in philosophy, scripture, and theology, and since the works are often full of references to and rebellions against antecedent works, the imaginative tradition too can be said to be dialectical. Certainly poetry as an enterprise stands in an embattled relation to philosophy, a relation first explicitly entered into the tradition as "that ancient quarrel between poetry and philosophy" in Plato's *Republic*. Nonetheless, because at least in modern times the arts arrogate to themselves a "creative," that is, a radically inventive, mode, singular works can quite legitimately be approached in isolation. And in general, as I have mentioned, the arguments for coherence in the imaginative canon are much weaker and the canon itself is much more difficult to fix for fictions of all sorts.

Truth-Telling. No principle is more ingrained in the Western works than that truth is to be found and told. These books are written to reveal the truth that has been discovered or revealed to their author and to initiate readers into it—although the price of admission may be very hard work. Almost by definition, the canon, a tradition of publication, is antithetical to the keeping of mysteries; even the mysteries of religion are the subject of public discussion. "Theology" means a "rational account," a *logos,* of divinity.

The books of the West try to tell something to the anonymous reader, and what they try to tell is truth. They ask, What is *Truth?* and stay to answer. They ask what is *the* Truth? and give a reply. From the founder of our tradition, "Father" Parmenides, who tells of being carried by his sun chariot to learn "in the untrembling heart of well-rounded Truth" (Fragment 1), that is the claim of these books: that they lay out the truth directly or lead readers to it indirectly. It is the claim even of those authors who deny that truth is untrembling, well-rounded, or even possible. They too argue their case as being so.

The studied indifferentism of the academy is the mildew that has most damaged the canon. Teachers feel obliged to put distance between the students and the books by avoiding the blunt question: Does this text tell truth? But without the possibility of truth the whole tradition becomes musty and antiquarian. Why labor to understand antiquated opinions? No wonder the choice of reading lists is dominated by the "relevance" question, for if the question of truth is forestalled, reading these texts is in fact relevant to nothing. It is an academic exercise. As I argued above, the easy despair concerning the possibility of true speech should be reconsidered in the face of these canonical readings. Authors that make the claim to tell truth should be given the courtesy of having it tested.

The principle of reading that complements the truth-*telling* of the book is the truth-*seeking* of the readers. It goes without saying that in a nonsectarian school there is no institutional truth, no school dogma beyond the common faith in the search. But that faith has a strong and refreshing effect on classes where no one retells an author's system or plot in the neutral and distant tone of being beyond and above the text, or begins by attributing ulterior or unconscious motives to the authors. Instead there is immediate engagement with the book; it is an aspect of the immediacy of reading discussed above. For example, the eponymous text of Western metaphysics opens with the claim that "All human beings have by their nature an appetite for knowing" (Aristotle, *Metaphysics*). Is this true, the students will ask themselves. Is it our experience? Is the desire to know an appetite like any other? (When they read, twelve books on in the *Metaphysics,* about a divinity that moves the world by the attraction of intelligibility, they will perhaps ask whether the opening assertion was a free observation or a necessary premise.) The next sentence tells them that "a sign of this is our fondness for sensation." They have just read Platonic dialogues in which Socrates vehemently denies that sensation is or leads to knowledge, and now they take on this battle, as do their tutors. For what is this or any text, if it is not allowed to be true or false? Of course, it goes without saying that the expectation that a text will have discernible meaning is even prior to the hope for truth. The possibility of the search for truth is our most powerful principle of

reading and the reason why life at St. John's has (in the long run) not gone stale.

Self-Knowledge. The investigation of humanity, be it as being, person, existence, soul, self, mind, animal, or body, is a principal preoccupation of the Western tradition. Socrates refuses to interest himself in mythological particulars, and declines "to investigate irrelevant things. And so I dismiss these matters and accepting the customary belief about them, as I was saying just now, I investigate not these things, but myself, to know whether I am a monster more complicated and more furious than Typhon or a gentler and simpler creature, to whom a divine and quiet lot is given by nature" (*Phaedrus*).

Under the aegis of authors from Plato to Freud, students learn that self-knowledge can be the antithesis of self-involvement. They raise the possibility that they might harbor within themselves hopelessly alien spaces, that they might be separated from their most intimate friend by an impassable distance, but also that in the face of human individuality the barriers of nation, race, and gender might not be so insuperable. They ask what human beings have in common. Is it their intellect, their passionate constitution, their animality? They ask whether self-expression or self-inhibition is more conducive to sanity. Is thinking an action or a passion? Is gender accidental, essential, or perhaps essentially accidental to human nature?

Besides raising questions concerning their own human nature, reading in the tradition initiates students into a wider sort of self-knowledge, into the roots of their present condition, as mentioned above. Human being is temporally strung out over the generations, and the public tradition is the transindividual genesis of our students' present conditions and opinions, whatever their private antecedents may be. I have broached this argument earlier.

But should we, instead of tracing our intellectual genesis back in time, not widen our knowledge over the contemporary globe? No, for these reasons: The nations of our globe will not thank us for coming to them with a skewed smattering of their ways that is based on forgetfulness of our own. The treasuries of alien civilizations are opened up most readily to those who bring something in exchange. Those who are shallowly rooted experience otherness as quaintness and miss the rebuff in a first familiarity. Certainly civilized persons will want to be versed in world literature—but first comes the home tradition.

But, as I said before, most globalism is in any case preached without serious intention. Serious intention would be evidenced by a call for the study of a foreign language, a near impossibility with students who are not very literate in their own.

It is the peculiar condition of our civilization—not, as far as I know, duplicated in any other high civilization or any culture—that its children are raised in an ambience of received opinion which its higher education is intended not to confirm but to controvert. Our rites of initiation into adulthood are invitations to a critique of the common wisdom. A liberal education is a second birth into a larger world. It is, or ought to be, a slow and somewhat painful delivery. Four years are usually thought to be barely sufficient. The reading of the canon is, however, the most natural course of self-parturition. (pp. 193-218)

Eva T. H. Brann, "The Canon Defended," in Philosophy and Literature, *Vol. 17, No. 2, October, 1993, pp. 193-218.*

William E. Cain (essay date October 1993)

[*In the following excerpt, Cain argues that attempting to delimit the literary canon is futile.*]

In their contributions to *Wild Orchids and Trotsky*—a series of "intellectual autobiographies" by academic critics—William Kerrigan and Harold Bloom assail the attention paid in current scholarship to "race, class, and gender," lament the spread of theory and the decay of prose style, and condemn efforts to make literary studies "political." Both testily dwell in particular upon the expansion of the literary canon. Kerrigan states that while the reasons for including works by "women, nonwhites, and postcolonial authors" sound plausible, "the educational program they support is a prescription for mediocrity": "Nothing I have ever read or heard has made me doubt for a moment that the greatest figures in English literature are Chaucer, Shakespeare, Donne, Milton, Swift, Pope, Johnson, Austen, the Romantic poets, Dickens, Emerson, Melville, Whitman, and so on." Bloom in turn maintains that "gender and power freaks" have foolishly concluded that literature can be made to function as "an instrument of social change or an instrument for social reform." They have lost sight of aesthetic principles, are too ill-equipped and tone-deaf to understand major authors, and have incarcerated one another and their students behind the bars of political correctness—"Stalinism without Stalin."

Yet Kerrigan and Bloom are optimistic. "Quality will out," Kerrigan prophesies: "Great literature, I guarantee, will one day bury theory, and its scandals will outlive all the political correctness in this confused world." Bloom says with a rumbling chuckle that in fact "the intolerance, the self-congratulation, smugness, sanctimoniousness, the retreat from imaginative values, the flight from the aesthetic" are "not worth being truly outraged about": "eventually these people will provide their own antidote, because they will perish of boredom. I will win in the end."

Many will find Kerrigan's and Bloom's views compelling, because these seem briskly to straighten out a complex, confusing, often exasperating state of affairs in academic criticism and scholarship today. But it is important to resist the temptation to echo Kerrigan and Bloom. Major authors matter: all can agree about *that*. But who are the major authors? Who belongs on the list and who does not? These are the questions that are harder now to answer.

And it is easy to understand why by glancing at Kerrigan's list with its revealing "and so on." To it one could add: Spenser, Johnson, Marlowe, Marvell, Richardson, Hawthorne, Henry James, Yeats, Frost, Lawrence, and Joyce. And Jefferson, Lincoln, Henry Adams, William James. One could also cite Charlotte and Emily Brontë, George

Eliot, Dickinson, Cather, and Woolf, and Du Bois, Hurston, Richard Wright, and Ellison. And so on.

Perhaps it was formerly the case that a list like Kerrigan's could settle the argument. But the critiques and revisions of the canon have shown that however attractive is the naming of imposing names—I am almost swayed myself—it is a rhetorical gesture. It reassures the like-minded, but not others, especially not women and minorities whom the profession has excluded and whose authors have been omitted from roll-calls of the Greats.

Most persons are aware, or should be, of the shortcomings of past pedagogy and criticism. Every one of the chapters in the 1,511-page *Literary History of the United States* (3rd ed., 1963), for instance, was written by a white male. Senator Stephen Douglas is mentioned four times in it, Frederick Douglass not at all. The most important postwar anthology of American poetry, the *Oxford Book of American Verse,* edited by F. O. Matthiessen, published in 1950, does not include a single African American; Matthiessen in fact deleted the one poem by Paul Laurence Dunbar that Bliss Carman had included in the earlier edition published in 1927. As late as 1967, the widely used anthology, *The American Tradition in Literature,* included two poems by the African American poet LeRoi Jones at the tail-end of its 3,500 pages of literature by whites. Black writers from Douglass to W. E. B. Du Bois and Zora Neale Hurston were typically ignored because their conception of literary values and contexts differed from the one to which white writers subscribed; and yet still others (e.g., Jean Toomer, Richard Wright) remained invisible in the academy even when their writerly idiom and procedure were roughly the same.

The anthologies, textbooks, and scholarly studies published today are far more capacious. This does not mean that every one of the new writers will endure or reward rereadings. There will be sifting, winnowing, sorting out, and recombining, as has always been true. It is worth remembering, after all, that plenty of renowned figures of bygone eras, such as Longfellow, Holmes, and Whittier, have lost their luster, and that not everything that Swift and Pope, and Melville and Whitman, wrote is equally good or has been identified *as* good for the same reasons from one generation to the next.

Consider the figures whom Perry Miller included in his two-volume *Major Writers of America,* published in 1962: Bradford, Taylor, Franklin, Edwards, Irving, Cooper, Bryant, Poe, Emerson, Thoreau, Hawthorne, Longfellow, Lowell, Melville, Whitman, Dickinson, Twain, James, Adams, Crane, Dreiser, O'Neill, Frost, Anderson, Fitzgerald, Hemingway, Eliot, Faulkner. A fine list as far as it goes, but one that could be questioned for its inclusions and exclusions alike without even making reference to African Americans or women: Longfellow and Lowell but not Whittier? Dreiser but not Howells? Frost and Eliot but neither Williams nor Stevens?

Writers and their works are always in the midst of revaluation and reassessment, and frequently have proven richer and more intricate because of new authors, texts, and contexts brought forward for the study and appreciation of them. *Moby-Dick* and *Benito Cereno* are charged, complicated texts when read alongside Emerson and Hawthorne. They are even more so when to Emerson and Hawthorne are added Stowe, Douglass, Harriet Jacobs, Martin Delany, and other writers, black as well as white, whose literary work intersected with the slavery crisis and the Civil War. Why limit the literary contexts in which important works might be interpreted?

The expansion and readjustment of the canon will continue, despite the protests by Kerrigan and Bloom. In the decades ahead, in fact, as more women and minorities enter the profession, as more nonwhite and female authors are discovered, as the formalist values of the past are even more intensively scrutinized, and as "the literature of the Americas" replaces the English-dominated and European-directed category of "English and American literature," the array of books that *now* seems diverse will surely be judged incomplete and partial. Scholars will then maintain that canonical change must be taken still further, and they will regret the limits of the revision performed in the 1980s and early 1990s. (pp. 302-305)

William E. Cain, "Canons, Critics, Theorists, Classrooms," in Philosophy and Literature, *Vol. 17, No. 2, October, 1993, pp. 302-14.*

☐ Contemporary
Literary Criticism

Indexes

Literary Criticism Series
Cumulative Author Index
Cumulative Topic Index
Cumulative Nationality Index
Title Index, Volume 81

How to Use This Index

The main references

Calvino, Italo
1923-1985.....CLC **5, 8, 11, 22, 33, 39,**
73; SSC 3

list all author entries in the following Gale Literary Criticism series:

BLC = Black Literature Criticism
CLC = Contemporary Literary Criticism
CLR = Children's Literature Review
CMLC = Classical and Medieval Literature Criticism
DA = DISCovering Authors
DC = Drama Criticism
HLC = Hispanic Literature Criticism
LC = Literature Criticism from 1400 to 1800
NCLC = Nineteenth-Century Literature Criticism
PC = Poetry Criticism
SSC = Short Story Criticism
TCLC = Twentieth-Century Literary Criticism
WLC = World Literature Criticism, 1500 to the Present

The cross-references

See also CANR 23; CA 85-88;
obituary CA 116

list all author entries in the following Gale biographical and literary sources:

AAYA = Authors & Artists for Young Adults
AITN = Authors in the News
BEST = Bestsellers
BW = Black Writers
CA = Contemporary Authors
CAAS = Contemporary Authors Autobiography Series
CABS = Contemporary Authors Bibliographical Series
CANR = Contemporary Authors New Revision Series
CAP = Contemporary Authors Permanent Series
CDALB = Concise Dictionary of American Literary Biography
CDBLB = Concise Dictionary of British Literary Biography
DLB = Dictionary of Literary Biography
DLBD = Dictionary of Literary Biography Documentary Series
DLBY = Dictionary of Literary Biography Yearbook
HW = Hispanic Writers
JRDA = Junior DISCovering Authors
MAICYA = Major Authors and Illustrators for Children and Young Adults
MTCW = Major 20th-Century Writers
SAAS = Something about the Author Autobiography Series
SATA = Something about the Author
YABC = Yesterday's Authors of Books for Children

Literary Criticism Series
Cumulative Author Index

A.
See Arnold, Matthew

A. E. . . . . **TCLC 3, 10**
See also Russell, George William
See also DLB 19

A. M.
See Megged, Aharon

A. R. P-C
See Galsworthy, John

Abasiyanik, Sait Faik 1906-1954
See Sait Faik
See also CA 123

Abbey, Edward 1927-1989 . . . . . . **CLC 36, 59**
See also CA 45-48; 128; CANR 2, 41

Abbott, Lee K(ittredge) 1947- . . . . . . **CLC 48**
See also CA 124; DLB 130

Abe, Kobo 1924-1993 . . . . . **CLC 8, 22, 53, 81**
See also CA 65-68; 140; CANR 24; MTCW

Abelard, Peter c. 1079-c. 1142 . . . **CMLC 11**
See also DLB 115

Abell, Kjeld 1901-1961 . . . . **CLC 15**
See also CA 111

Abish, Walter 1931- . . . . **CLC 22**
See also CA 101; CANR 37; DLB 130

Abrahams, Peter (Henry) 1919- . . . . . **CLC 4**
See also BW; CA 57-60; CANR 26;
DLB 117; MTCW

Abrams, M(eyer) H(oward) 1912- . . . **CLC 24**
See also CA 57-60; CANR 13, 33; DLB 67

Abse, Dannie 1923- . . . . **CLC 7, 29**
See also CA 53-56; CAAS 1; CANR 4;
DLB 27

Achebe, (Albert) Chinua(lumogu)
1930- . . . . . **CLC 1, 3, 5, 7, 11, 26, 51, 75;**
BLC 1; DA; WLC
See also BW; CA 1-4R; CANR 6, 26;
CLR 20; DLB 117; MAICYA; MTCW;
SATA 38, 40

Acker, Kathy 1948- . . . . **CLC 45**
See also CA 117; 122

Ackroyd, Peter 1949- . . . . **CLC 34, 52**
See also CA 123; 127

Acorn, Milton 1923- . . . . **CLC 15**
See also CA 103; DLB 53

Adamov, Arthur 1908-1970 . . . . . . **CLC 4, 25**
See also CA 17-18; 25-28R; CAP 2; MTCW

Adams, Alice (Boyd) 1926- . . **CLC 6, 13, 46**
See also CA 81-84; CANR 26; DLBY 86;
MTCW

Adams, Douglas (Noel) 1952- . . . **CLC 27, 60**
See also AAYA 4; BEST 89:3; CA 106;
CANR 34; DLBY 83; JRDA

Adams, Francis 1862-1893 . . . . **NCLC 33**

Adams, Henry (Brooks)
1838-1918 . . . . **TCLC 4, 52; DA**
See also CA 104; 133; DLB 12, 47

Adams, Richard (George)
1920- . . . . **CLC 4, 5, 18**
See also AITN 1, 2; CA 49-52; CANR 3,
35; CLR 20; JRDA; MAICYA; MTCW;
SATA 7, 69

Adamson, Joy(-Friederike Victoria)
1910-1980 . . . . **CLC 17**
See also CA 69-72; 93-96; CANR 22;
MTCW; SATA 11, 22

Adcock, Fleur 1934- . . . . **CLC 41**
See also CA 25-28R; CANR 11, 34;
DLB 40

Addams, Charles (Samuel)
1912-1988 . . . . **CLC 30**
See also CA 61-64; 126; CANR 12

Addison, Joseph 1672-1719 . . . . **LC 18**
See also CDBLB 1660-1789; DLB 101

Adler, C(arole) S(chwerdtfeger)
1932- . . . . **CLC 35**
See also AAYA 4; CA 89-92; CANR 19,
40; JRDA; MAICYA; SAAS 15;
SATA 26, 63

Adler, Renata 1938- . . . . **CLC 8, 31**
See also CA 49-52; CANR 5, 22; MTCW

Ady, Endre 1877-1919 . . . . **TCLC 11**
See also CA 107

Aeschylus
525B.C.-456B.C. . . . . **CMLC 11; DA**

Afton, Effie
See Harper, Frances Ellen Watkins

Agapida, Fray Antonio
See Irving, Washington

Agee, James (Rufus)
1909-1955 . . . . **TCLC 1, 19**
See also AITN 1; CA 108;
CDALB 1941-1968; DLB 2, 26

Aghill, Gordon
See Silverberg, Robert

Agnon, S(hmuel) Y(osef Halevi)
1888-1970 . . . . **CLC 4, 8, 14**
See also CA 17-18; 25-28R; CAP 2; MTCW

Aherne, Owen
See Cassill, R(onald) V(erlin)

Ai 1947- . . . . **CLC 4, 14, 69**
See also CA 85-88; CAAS 13; DLB 120

Aickman, Robert (Fordyce)
1914-1981 . . . . **CLC 57**
See also CA 5-8R; CANR 3

Aiken, Conrad (Potter)
1889-1973 . . . **CLC 1, 3, 5, 10, 52; SSC 9**
See also CA 5-8R; 45-48; CANR 4;
CDALB 1929-1941; DLB 9, 45, 102;
MTCW; SATA 3, 30

Aiken, Joan (Delano) 1924- . . . . **CLC 35**
See also AAYA 1; CA 9-12R; CANR 4, 23,
34; CLR 1, 19; JRDA; MAICYA;
MTCW; SAAS 1; SATA 2, 30, 73

Ainsworth, William Harrison
1805-1882 . . . . **NCLC 13**
See also DLB 21; SATA 24

Aitmatov, Chingiz (Torekulovich)
1928- . . . . **CLC 71**
See also CA 103; CANR 38; MTCW;
SATA 56

Akers, Floyd
See Baum, L(yman) Frank

Akhmadulina, Bella Akhatovna
1937- . . . . **CLC 53**
See also CA 65-68

Akhmatova, Anna
1888-1966 . . . . **CLC 11, 25, 64; PC 2**
See also CA 19-20; 25-28R; CANR 35;
CAP 1; MTCW

Aksakov, Sergei Timofeyvich
1791-1859 . . . . **NCLC 2**

Aksenov, Vassily . . . . **CLC 22**
See also Aksyonov, Vassily (Pavlovich)

Aksyonov, Vassily (Pavlovich)
1932- . . . . **CLC 37**
See also Aksenov, Vassily
See also CA 53-56; CANR 12

Akutagawa Ryunosuke
1892-1927 . . . . **TCLC 16**
See also CA 117

Alain 1868-1951 . . . . **TCLC 41**

Alain-Fournier . . . . **TCLC 6**
See also Fournier, Henri Alban
See also DLB 65

Alarcon, Pedro Antonio de
1833-1891 . . . . **NCLC 1**

Alas (y Urena), Leopoldo (Enrique Garcia)
1852-1901 . . . . **TCLC 29**
See also CA 113; 131; HW

Albee, Edward (Franklin III)
1928- . . . . . . **CLC 1, 2, 3, 5, 9, 11, 13, 25,**
53; DA; WLC
See also AITN 1; CA 5-8R; CABS 3;
CANR 8; CDALB 1941-1968; DLB 7;
MTCW

Alberti, Rafael 1902- . . . . **CLC 7**
See also CA 85-88; DLB 108

Alcala-Galiano, Juan Valera y
See Valera y Alcala-Galiano, Juan

Alcott, Amos Bronson 1799-1888 . . **NCLC 1**
See also DLB 1

Alcott, Louisa May
1832-1888 . . . . **NCLC 6; DA; WLC**
See also CDALB 1865-1917; CLR 1;
DLB 1, 42, 79; JRDA; MAICYA;
YABC 1

Aldanov, M. A.
See Aldanov, Mark (Alexandrovich)

Aldanov, Mark (Alexandrovich)
1886(?)-1957 . . . . **TCLC 23**
See also CA 118

Aldington, Richard 1892-1962 . . . . . . **CLC 49**
See also CA 85-88; DLB 20, 36, 100

Aldiss, Brian W(ilson)
1925- . . . . **CLC 5, 14, 40**
See also CA 5-8R; CAAS 2; CANR 5, 28;
DLB 14; MTCW; SATA 34

Alegria, Claribel 1924- . . . . **CLC 75**
See also CA 131; CAAS 15; HW

Alegria, Fernando 1918- . . . . **CLC 57**
See also CA 9-12R; CANR 5, 32; HW

Aleichem, Sholom . . . . **TCLC 1, 35**
See also Rabinovitch, Sholem

Aleixandre, Vicente 1898-1984 . . . **CLC 9, 36**
See also CA 85-88; 114; CANR 26;
DLB 108; HW; MTCW

Alepoudelis, Odysseus
See Elytis, Odysseus

Aleshkovsky, Joseph 1929-
See Aleshkovsky, Yuz
See also CA 121; 128

Aleshkovsky, Yuz . . . . **CLC 44**
See also Aleshkovsky, Joseph

Alexander, Lloyd (Chudley) 1924- . . **CLC 35**
See also AAYA 1; CA 1-4R; CANR 1, 24,
38; CLR 1, 5; DLB 52; JRDA; MAICYA;
MTCW; SATA 3, 49

Alfau, Felipe 1902- . . . . **CLC 66**
See also CA 137

Alger, Horatio, Jr. 1832-1899 . . . . . **NCLC 8**
See also DLB 42; SATA 16

Algren, Nelson 1909-1981 . . . . **CLC 4, 10, 33**
See also CA 13-16R; 103; CANR 20;
CDALB 1941-1968; DLB 9; DLBY 81,
82; MTCW

Ali, Ahmed 1910- . . . . **CLC 69**
See also CA 25-28R; CANR 15, 34

Alighieri, Dante 1265-1321 . . . . **CMLC 3**

Allan, John B.
See Westlake, Donald E(dwin)

Allen, Edward 1948- . . . . **CLC 59**

Allen, Roland
See Ayckbourn, Alan

Allen, Sarah A.
See Hopkins, Pauline Elizabeth

Allen, Woody 1935- . . . . **CLC 16, 52**
See also AAYA 10; CA 33-36R; CANR 27,
38; DLB 44; MTCW

Allende, Isabel 1942- . . . **CLC 39, 57; HLC 1**
See also CA 125; 130; HW; MTCW

Alleyn, Ellen
See Rossetti, Christina (Georgina)

Allingham, Margery (Louise)
1904-1966 . . . . **CLC 19**
See also CA 5-8R; 25-28R; CANR 4;
DLB 77; MTCW

Allingham, William 1824-1889 . . . **NCLC 25**
See also DLB 35

Allison, Dorothy E. 1949- . . . . **CLC 78**
See also CA 140

Allston, Washington 1779-1843 . . . . **NCLC 2**
See also DLB 1

Almedingen, E. M. . . . . **CLC 12**
See also Almedingen, Martha Edith von
See also SATA 3

Almedingen, Martha Edith von 1898-1971
See Almedingen, E. M.
See also CA 1-4R; CANR 1

Almqvist, Carl Jonas Love
1793-1866 . . . . **NCLC 42**

Alonso, Damaso 1898-1990 . . . . **CLC 14**
See also CA 110; 131; 130; DLB 108; HW

Alov
See Gogol, Nikolai (Vasilyevich)

Alta 1942- . . . . **CLC 19**
See also CA 57-60

Alter, Robert B(ernard) 1935- . . . . . . **CLC 34**
See also CA 49-52; CANR 1

Alther, Lisa 1944- . . . . **CLC 7, 41**
See also CA 65-68; CANR 12, 30; MTCW

Altman, Robert 1925- . . . . **CLC 16**
See also CA 73-76; CANR 43

Alvarez, A(lfred) 1929- . . . . **CLC 5, 13**
See also CA 1-4R; CANR 3, 33; DLB 14,
40

Alvarez, Alejandro Rodriguez 1903-1965
See Casona, Alejandro
See also CA 131; 93-96; HW

Amado, Jorge 1912- . . . . **CLC 13, 40; HLC 1**
See also CA 77-80; CANR 35; DLB 113;
MTCW

Ambler, Eric 1909- . . . . **CLC 4, 6, 9**
See also CA 9-12R; CANR 7, 38; DLB 77;
MTCW

Amichai, Yehuda 1924- . . . . . . **CLC 9, 22, 57**
See also CA 85-88; MTCW

Amiel, Henri Frederic 1821-1881 . . **NCLC 4**

Amis, Kingsley (William)
1922- . . **CLC 1, 2, 3, 5, 8, 13, 40, 44; DA**
See also AITN 2; CA 9-12R; CANR 8, 28;
CDBLB 1945-1960; DLB 15, 27, 100;
MTCW

Amis, Martin (Louis)
1949- . . . . **CLC 4, 9, 38, 62**
See also BEST 90:3; CA 65-68; CANR 8,
27; DLB 14

Ammons, A(rchie) R(andolph)
1926- . . . . **CLC 2, 3, 5, 8, 9, 25, 57**
See also AITN 1; CA 9-12R; CANR 6, 36;
DLB 5; MTCW

Amo, Tauraatua i
See Adams, Henry (Brooks)

Anand, Mulk Raj 1905- . . . . **CLC 23**
See also CA 65-68; CANR 32; MTCW

Anatol
See Schnitzler, Arthur

Anaya, Rudolfo A(lfonso)
1937- . . . . **CLC 23; HLC 1**
See also CA 45-48; CAAS 4; CANR 1, 32;
DLB 82; HW 1; MTCW

Andersen, Hans Christian
1805-1875 . . **NCLC 7; DA; SSC 6; WLC**
See also CLR 6; MAICYA; YABC 1

Anderson, C. Farley
See Mencken, H(enry) L(ouis); Nathan,
George Jean

Anderson, Jessica (Margaret) Queale
. . . . **CLC 37**
See also CA 9-12R; CANR 4

Anderson, Jon (Victor) 1940- . . . . **CLC 9**
See also CA 25-28R; CANR 20

Anderson, Lindsay (Gordon)
1923- . . . . **CLC 20**
See also CA 125; 128

Anderson, Maxwell 1888-1959 . . . . . **TCLC 2**
See also CA 105; DLB 7

Anderson, Poul (William) 1926- . . . . **CLC 15**
See also AAYA 5; CA 1-4R; CAAS 2;
CANR 2, 15, 34; DLB 8; MTCW;
SATA 39

Anderson, Robert (Woodruff)
1917- . . . . **CLC 23**
See also AITN 1; CA 21-24R; CANR 32;
DLB 7

Anderson, Sherwood
1876-1941 . . . . **TCLC 1, 10, 24; DA;**
SSC 1; WLC
See also CA 104; 121; CDALB 1917-1929;
DLB 4, 9, 86; DLBD 1; MTCW

Andouard
See Giraudoux, (Hippolyte) Jean

Andrade, Carlos Drummond de . . . . . . **CLC 18**
See also Drummond de Andrade, Carlos

Andrade, Mario de 1893-1945 . . . . . **TCLC 43**

Andrewes, Lancelot 1555-1626 . . . . **LC 5**

Andrews, Cicily Fairfield
See West, Rebecca

Andrews, Elton V.
See Pohl, Frederik

Andreyev, Leonid (Nikolaevich)
1871-1919 . . . . **TCLC 3**
See also CA 104

Andric, Ivo 1892-1975 . . . . **CLC 8**
See also CA 81-84; 57-60; CANR 43;
MTCW

Angelique, Pierre
See Bataille, Georges

Angell, Roger 1920- . . . . **CLC 26**
See also CA 57-60; CANR 13

Angelou, Maya
1928- . . . **CLC 12, 35, 64, 77; BLC 1; DA**
See also AAYA 7; BW; CA 65-68;
CANR 19, 42; DLB 38; MTCW;
SATA 38

Annensky, Innokenty Fyodorovich
1856-1909 . . . . **TCLC 14**
See also CA 110

Anon, Charles Robert
See Pessoa, Fernando (Antonio Nogueira)

Anouilh, Jean (Marie Lucien Pierre)
1910-1987 . . . . . . **CLC 1, 3, 8, 13, 40, 50**
See also CA 17-20R; 123; CANR 32;
MTCW

Anthony, Florence
See Ai

Anthony, John
See Ciardi, John (Anthony)

Anthony, Peter
See Shaffer, Anthony (Joshua); Shaffer,
Peter (Levin)

Anthony, Piers 1934- . . . . **CLC 35**
See also CA 21-24R; CANR 28; DLB 8;
MTCW

Author Index

Antoine, Marc
See Proust, (Valentin-Louis-George-Eugene-)
Marcel

Antoninus, Brother
See Everson, William (Oliver)

Antonioni, Michelangelo 1912- ..... **CLC 20**
See also CA 73-76

Antschel, Paul 1920-1970....... **CLC 10, 19**
See also Celan, Paul
See also CA 85-88; CANR 33; MTCW

Anwar, Chairil 1922-1949 .... **TCLC 22**
See also CA 121

Apollinaire, Guillaume .. **TCLC 3, 8, 51; PC 7**
See also Kostrowitzki, Wilhelm Apollinaris
de

Appelfeld, Aharon 1932- .... **CLC 23, 47**
See also CA 112; 133

Apple, Max (Isaac) 1941-........ **CLC 9, 33**
See also CA 81-84; CANR 19; DLB 130

Appleman, Philip (Dean) 1926- ..... **CLC 51**
See also CA 13-16R; CAAS 18; CANR 6,
29

Appleton, Lawrence
See Lovecraft, H(oward) P(hillips)

Apteryx
See Eliot, T(homas) S(tearns)

Apuleius, (Lucius Madaurensis)
125(?)-175(?) .... **CMLC 1**

Aquin, Hubert 1929-1977......... **CLC 15**
See also CA 105; DLB 53

Aragon, Louis 1897-1982........ **CLC 3, 22**
See also CA 69-72; 108; CANR 28;
DLB 72; MTCW

Arany, Janos 1817-1882........ **NCLC 34**

Arbuthnot, John 1667-1735.......... **LC 1**
See also DLB 101

Archer, Herbert Winslow
See Mencken, H(enry) L(ouis)

Archer, Jeffrey (Howard) 1940- .... **CLC 28**
See also BEST 89:3; CA 77-80; CANR 22

Archer, Jules 1915- .... **CLC 12**
See also CA 9-12R; CANR 6; SAAS 5;
SATA 4

Archer, Lee
See Ellison, Harlan

Arden, John 1930- .... **CLC 6, 13, 15**
See also CA 13-16R; CAAS 4; CANR 31;
DLB 13; MTCW

Arenas, Reinaldo
1943-1990 .... **CLC 41; HLC 1**
See also CA 124; 128; 133; HW

Arendt, Hannah 1906-1975 .... **CLC 66**
See also CA 17-20R; 61-64; CANR 26;
MTCW

Aretino, Pietro 1492-1556 .... **LC 12**

Arghezi, Tudor.................... **CLC 80**
See also Theodorescu, Ion N.

Arguedas, Jose Maria
1911-1969 .... **CLC 10, 18**
See also CA 89-92; DLB 113; HW

Argueta, Manlio 1936-............ **CLC 31**
See also CA 131; HW

Ariosto, Ludovico 1474-1533........ **LC 6**

Aristides
See Epstein, Joseph

Aristophanes
450B.C.-385B.C.... **CMLC 4; DA; DC 2**

Arlt, Roberto (Godofredo Christophersen)
1900-1942 .... **TCLC 29; HLC 1**
See also CA 123; 131; HW

Armah, Ayi Kwei 1939-.. **CLC 5, 33; BLC 1**
See also BW; CA 61-64; CANR 21;
DLB 117; MTCW

Armatrading, Joan 1950-.......... **CLC 17**
See also CA 114

Arnette, Robert
See Silverberg, Robert

Arnim, Achim von (Ludwig Joachim von
Arnim) 1781-1831 .... **NCLC 5**
See also DLB 90

Arnim, Bettina von 1785-1859.... **NCLC 38**
See also DLB 90

Arnold, Matthew
1822-1888 ..... **NCLC 6, 29; DA; PC 5;**
WLC
See also CDBLB 1832-1890; DLB 32, 57

Arnold, Thomas 1795-1842 ...... **NCLC 18**
See also DLB 55

Arnow, Harriette (Louisa) Simpson
1908-1986 .... **CLC 2, 7, 18**
See also CA 9-12R; 118; CANR 14; DLB 6;
MTCW; SATA 42, 47

Arp, Hans
See Arp, Jean

Arp, Jean 1887-1966............... **CLC 5**
See also CA 81-84; 25-28R; CANR 42

Arrabal
See Arrabal, Fernando

Arrabal, Fernando 1932- ... **CLC 2, 9, 18, 58**
See also CA 9-12R; CANR 15

Arrick, Fran..................... **CLC 30**

Artaud, Antonin 1896-1948 ..... **TCLC 3, 36**
See also CA 104

Arthur, Ruth M(abel) 1905-1979.... **CLC 12**
See also CA 9-12R; 85-88; CANR 4;
SATA 7, 26

Artsybashev, Mikhail (Petrovich)
1878-1927 .... **TCLC 31**

Arundel, Honor (Morfydd)
1919-1973 .... **CLC 17**
See also CA 21-22; 41-44R; CAP 2;
SATA 4, 24

Asch, Sholem 1880-1957 .... **TCLC 3**
See also CA 105

Ash, Shalom
See Asch, Sholem

Ashbery, John (Lawrence)
1927- ...... **CLC 2, 3, 4, 6, 9, 13, 15, 25,**
41, 77
See also CA 5-8R; CANR 9, 37; DLB 5;
DLBY 81; MTCW

Ashdown, Clifford
See Freeman, R(ichard) Austin

Ashe, Gordon
See Creasey, John

Ashton-Warner, Sylvia (Constance)
1908-1984 .... **CLC 19**
See also CA 69-72; 112; CANR 29; MTCW

Asimov, Isaac
1920-1992 ...... **CLC 1, 3, 9, 19, 26, 76**
See also BEST 90:2; CA 1-4R; 137;
CANR 2, 19, 36; CLR 12; DLB 8;
DLBY 92; JRDA; MAICYA; MTCW;
SATA 1, 26, 74

Astley, Thea (Beatrice May)
1925- .... **CLC 41**
See also CA 65-68; CANR 11, 43

Aston, James
See White, T(erence) H(anbury)

Asturias, Miguel Angel
1899-1974 .... **CLC 3, 8, 13; HLC 1**
See also CA 25-28; 49-52; CANR 32;
CAP 2; DLB 113; HW; MTCW

Atares, Carlos Saura
See Saura (Atares), Carlos

Atheling, William
See Pound, Ezra (Weston Loomis)

Atheling, William, Jr.
See Blish, James (Benjamin)

Atherton, Gertrude (Franklin Horn)
1857-1948 .... **TCLC 2**
See also CA 104; DLB 9, 78

Atherton, Lucius
See Masters, Edgar Lee

Atkins, Jack
See Harris, Mark

Atticus
See Fleming, Ian (Lancaster)

Atwood, Margaret (Eleanor)
1939- ..... **CLC 2, 3, 4, 8, 13, 15, 25, 44;**
DA; PC 8; SSC 2; WLC
See also BEST 89:2; CA 49-52; CANR 3,
24, 33; DLB 53; MTCW; SATA 50

Aubigny, Pierre d'
See Mencken, H(enry) L(ouis)

Aubin, Penelope 1685-1731(?)........ **LC 9**
See also DLB 39

Auchincloss, Louis (Stanton)
1917- .... **CLC 4, 6, 9, 18, 45**
See also CA 1-4R; CANR 6, 29; DLB 2;
DLBY 80; MTCW

Auden, W(ystan) H(ugh)
1907-1973 ...... **CLC 1, 2, 3, 4, 6, 9, 11,**
14, 43; DA; PC 1; WLC
See also CA 9-12R; 45-48; CANR 5;
CDBLB 1914-1945; DLB 10, 20; MTCW

Audiberti, Jacques 1900-1965 ...... **CLC 38**
See also CA 25-28R

Auel, Jean M(arie) 1936-.......... **CLC 31**
See also AAYA 7; BEST 90:4; CA 103;
CANR 21

Auerbach, Erich 1892-1957 .... **TCLC 43**
See also CA 118

Augier, Emile 1820-1889 .... **NCLC 31**

August, John
See De Voto, Bernard (Augustine)

Augustine, St. 354-430 .... **CMLC 6**

Aurelius
See Bourne, Randolph S(illiman)

Baroja (y Nessi), Pio
    1872-1956 . . . . **TCLC 8; HLC 1**
    See also CA 104

Baron, David
    See Pinter, Harold

Baron Corvo
    See Rolfe, Frederick (William Serafino
        Austin Lewis Mary)

Barondess, Sue K(aufman)
    1926-1977 . . . . **CLC 8**
    See also Kaufman, Sue
    See also CA 1-4R; 69-72; CANR 1

Baron de Teive
    See Pessoa, Fernando (Antonio Nogueira)

Barres, Maurice 1862-1923 . . . . **TCLC 47**
    See also DLB 123

Barreto, Afonso Henrique de Lima
    See Lima Barreto, Afonso Henrique de

Barrett, (Roger) Syd 1946- . . . . **CLC 35**
    See also Pink Floyd

Barrett, William (Christopher)
    1913-1992 . . . . **CLC 27**
    See also CA 13-16R; 139; CANR 11

Barrie, J(ames) M(atthew)
    1860-1937 . . . . **TCLC 2**
    See also CA 104; 136; CDBLB 1890-1914;
        CLR 16; DLB 10; MAICYA; YABC 1

Barrington, Michael
    See Moorcock, Michael (John)

Barrol, Grady
    See Bograd, Larry

Barry, Mike
    See Malzberg, Barry N(athaniel)

Barry, Philip 1896-1949 . . . . **TCLC 11**
    See also CA 109; DLB 7

Bart, Andre Schwarz
    See Schwarz-Bart, Andre

Barth, John (Simmons)
    1930- . . . . . . **CLC 1, 2, 3, 5, 7, 9, 10, 14,
                        27, 51; SSC 10**
    See also AITN 1, 2; CA 1-4R; CABS 1;
        CANR 5, 23; DLB 2; MTCW

Barthelme, Donald
    1931-1989 . . . . . . **CLC 1, 2, 3, 5, 6, 8, 13,
                        23, 46, 59; SSC 2**
    See also CA 21-24R; 129; CANR 20;
        DLB 2; DLBY 80, 89; MTCW; SATA 7,
        62

Barthelme, Frederick 1943- . . . . **CLC 36**
    See also CA 114; 122; DLBY 85

Barthes, Roland (Gerard)
    1915-1980 . . . . **CLC 24**
    See also CA 130; 97-100; MTCW

Barzun, Jacques (Martin) 1907- . . . . **CLC 51**
    See also CA 61-64; CANR 22

Bashevis, Isaac
    See Singer, Isaac Bashevis

Bashkirtseff, Marie 1859-1884 . . . **NCLC 27**

Basho
    See Matsuo Basho

Bass, Kingsley B., Jr.
    See Bullins, Ed

Bass, Rick 1958- . . . . **CLC 79**
    See also CA 126

Bassani, Giorgio 1916- . . . . **CLC 9**
    See also CA 65-68; CANR 33; DLB 128;
        MTCW

Bastos, Augusto (Antonio) Roa
    See Roa Bastos, Augusto (Antonio)

Bataille, Georges 1897-1962 . . . . **CLC 29**
    See also CA 101; 89-92

Bates, H(erbert) E(rnest)
    1905-1974 . . . . **CLC 46; SSC 10**
    See also CA 93-96; 45-48; CANR 34;
        MTCW

Bauchart
    See Camus, Albert

Baudelaire, Charles
    1821-1867 . . . . . **NCLC 6, 29; DA; PC 1;
                        WLC**

Baudrillard, Jean 1929- . . . . **CLC 60**

Baum, L(yman) Frank 1856-1919 . . . **TCLC 7**
    See also CA 108; 133; CLR 15; DLB 22;
        JRDA; MAICYA; MTCW; SATA 18

Baum, Louis F.
    See Baum, L(yman) Frank

Baumbach, Jonathan 1933- . . . . . . **CLC 6, 23**
    See also CA 13-16R; CAAS 5; CANR 12;
        DLBY 80; MTCW

Bausch, Richard (Carl) 1945- . . . . . . **CLC 51**
    See also CA 101; CAAS 14; CANR 43;
        DLB 130

Baxter, Charles 1947- . . . . **CLC 45, 78**
    See also CA 57-60; CANR 40; DLB 130

Baxter, George Owen
    See Faust, Frederick (Schiller)

Baxter, James K(eir) 1926-1972 . . . . **CLC 14**
    See also CA 77-80

Baxter, John
    See Hunt, E(verette) Howard, Jr.

Bayer, Sylvia
    See Glassco, John

Beagle, Peter S(oyer) 1939- . . . . **CLC 7**
    See also CA 9-12R; CANR 4; DLBY 80;
        SATA 60

Bean, Normal
    See Burroughs, Edgar Rice

Beard, Charles A(ustin)
    1874-1948 . . . . **TCLC 15**
    See also CA 115; DLB 17; SATA 18

Beardsley, Aubrey 1872-1898 . . . . . **NCLC 6**

Beattie, Ann
    1947- . . . . **CLC 8, 13, 18, 40, 63; SSC 11**
    See also BEST 90:2; CA 81-84; DLBY 82;
        MTCW

Beattie, James 1735-1803 . . . . **NCLC 25**
    See also DLB 109

Beauchamp, Kathleen Mansfield 1888-1923
    See Mansfield, Katherine
    See also CA 104; 134; DA

Beaumarchais, Pierre-Augustin Caron de
    1732-1799 . . . . **DC 4**

**Beauvoir, Simone (Lucie Ernestine Marie
        Bertrand) de**
    1908-1986 . . . . **CLC 1, 2, 4, 8, 14, 31, 44,
                        50, 71; DA; WLC**
    See also CA 9-12R; 118; CANR 28;
        DLB 72; DLBY 86; MTCW

Becker, Jurek 1937- . . . . **CLC 7, 19**
    See also CA 85-88; DLB 75

Becker, Walter 1950- . . . . **CLC 26**

Beckett, Samuel (Barclay)
    1906-1989 . . . . . . **CLC 1, 2, 3, 4, 6, 9, 10,
                        11, 14, 18, 29, 57, 59; DA; WLC**
    See also CA 5-8R; 130; CANR 33;
        CDBLB 1945-1960; DLB 13, 15;
        DLBY 90; MTCW

Beckford, William 1760-1844 . . . . **NCLC 16**
    See also DLB 39

Beckman, Gunnel 1910- . . . . **CLC 26**
    See also CA 33-36R; CANR 15; CLR 25;
        MAICYA; SAAS 9; SATA 6

Becque, Henri 1837-1899 . . . . **NCLC 3**

Beddoes, Thomas Lovell
    1803-1849 . . . . **NCLC 3**
    See also DLB 96

Bedford, Donald F.
    See Fearing, Kenneth (Flexner)

Beecher, Catharine Esther
    1800-1878 . . . . **NCLC 30**
    See also DLB 1

Beecher, John 1904-1980 . . . . **CLC 6**
    See also AITN 1; CA 5-8R; 105; CANR 8

Beer, Johann 1655-1700 . . . . **LC 5**

Beer, Patricia 1924- . . . . **CLC 58**
    See also CA 61-64; CANR 13; DLB 40

Beerbohm, Henry Maximilian
    1872-1956 . . . . **TCLC 1, 24**
    See also CA 104; DLB 34, 100

Begiebing, Robert J(ohn) 1946- . . . . . **CLC 70**
    See also CA 122; CANR 40

Behan, Brendan
    1923-1964 . . . . **CLC 1, 8, 11, 15, 79**
    See also CA 73-76; CANR 33;
        CDBLB 1945-1960; DLB 13; MTCW

Behn, Aphra
    1640(?)-1689 . . . . **LC 1; DA; DC 4; WLC**
    See also DLB 39, 80, 131

Behrman, S(amuel) N(athaniel)
    1893-1973 . . . . **CLC 40**
    See also CA 13-16; 45-48; CAP 1; DLB 7,
        44

Belasco, David 1853-1931 . . . . **TCLC 3**
    See also CA 104; DLB 7

Belcheva, Elisaveta 1893- . . . . **CLC 10**

Beldone, Phil "Cheech"
    See Ellison, Harlan

Beleno
    See Azuela, Mariano

Belinski, Vissarion Grigoryevich
    1811-1848 . . . . **NCLC 5**

Belitt, Ben 1911- . . . . **CLC 22**
    See also CA 13-16R; CAAS 4; CANR 7;
        DLB 5

Bell, James Madison
    1826-1902 . . . . **TCLC 43; BLC 1**
    See also BW; CA 122; 124; DLB 50

Bell, Madison (Smartt) 1957- . . . . . . **CLC 41**
    See also CA 111; CANR 28

Bell, Marvin (Hartley) 1937- . . . . . **CLC 8, 31**
    See also CA 21-24R; CAAS 14; DLB 5;
        MTCW

Bell, W. L. D.
See Mencken, H(enry) L(ouis)

Bellamy, Atwood C.
See Mencken, H(enry) L(ouis)

Bellamy, Edward 1850-1898 ...... **NCLC 4**
See also DLB 12

Bellin, Edward J.
See Kuttner, Henry

Belloc, (Joseph) Hilaire (Pierre)
1870-1953 .... **TCLC 7, 18**
See also CA 106; DLB 19, 100; YABC 1

Belloc, Joseph Peter Rene Hilaire
See Belloc, (Joseph) Hilaire (Pierre)

Belloc, Joseph Pierre Hilaire
See Belloc, (Joseph) Hilaire (Pierre)

Belloc, M. A.
See Lowndes, Marie Adelaide (Belloc)

Bellow, Saul
1915- ...... **CLC 1, 2, 3, 6, 8, 10, 13, 15,
25, 33, 34, 63, 79; DA; SSC 14; WLC**
See also AITN 2; BEST 89:3; CA 5-8R;
CABS 1; CANR 29; CDALB 1941-1968;
DLB 2, 28; DLBD 3; DLBY 82; MTCW

Belser, Reimond Karel Maria de
1929- .... **CLC 14**

Bely, Andrey .... **TCLC 7**
See also Bugayev, Boris Nikolayevich

Benary, Margot
See Benary-Isbert, Margot

Benary-Isbert, Margot 1889-1979... **CLC 12**
See also CA 5-8R; 89-92; CANR 4;
CLR 12; MAICYA; SATA 2, 21

Benavente (y Martinez), Jacinto
1866-1954 .... **TCLC 3**
See also CA 106; 131; HW; MTCW

Benchley, Peter (Bradford)
1940- .... **CLC 4, 8**
See also AITN 2; CA 17-20R; CANR 12,
35; MTCW; SATA 3

Benchley, Robert (Charles)
1889-1945 .... **TCLC 1**
See also CA 105; DLB 11

Benedikt, Michael 1935- .... **CLC 4, 14**
See also CA 13-16R; CANR 7; DLB 5

Benet, Juan 1927- .... **CLC 28**

Benet, Stephen Vincent
1898-1943 .... **TCLC 7; SSC 10**
See also CA 104; DLB 4, 48, 102; YABC 1

Benet, William Rose 1886-1950 ... **TCLC 28**
See also CA 118; DLB 45

Benford, Gregory (Albert) 1941-.... **CLC 52**
See also CA 69-72; CANR 12, 24;
DLBY 82

Bengtsson, Frans (Gunnar)
1894-1954 .... **TCLC 48**

Benjamin, David
See Slavitt, David R(ytman)

Benjamin, Lois
See Gould, Lois

Benjamin, Walter 1892-1940 ...... **TCLC 39**

Benn, Gottfried 1886-1956........ **TCLC 3**
See also CA 106; DLB 56

Bennett, Alan 1934- .... **CLC 45, 77**
See also CA 103; CANR 35; MTCW

Bennett, (Enoch) Arnold
1867-1931 .... **TCLC 5, 20**
See also CA 106; CDBLB 1890-1914;
DLB 10, 34, 98

Bennett, Elizabeth
See Mitchell, Margaret (Munnerlyn)

Bennett, George Harold 1930-
See Bennett, Hal
See also BW; CA 97-100

Bennett, Hal .... **CLC 5**
See also Bennett, George Harold
See also DLB 33

Bennett, Jay 1912- .... **CLC 35**
See also AAYA 10; CA 69-72; CANR 11,
42; JRDA; SAAS 4; SATA 27, 41

Bennett, Louise (Simone)
1919- .... **CLC 28; BLC 1**
See also DLB 117

Benson, E(dward) F(rederic)
1867-1940 .... **TCLC 27**
See also CA 114; DLB 135

Benson, Jackson J. 1930-......... **CLC 34**
See also CA 25-28R; DLB 111

Benson, Sally 1900-1972 .... **CLC 17**
See also CA 19-20; 37-40R; CAP 1;
SATA 1, 27, 35

Benson, Stella 1892-1933........ **TCLC 17**
See also CA 117; DLB 36

Bentham, Jeremy 1748-1832 ..... **NCLC 38**
See also DLB 107

Bentley, E(dmund) C(lerihew)
1875-1956 .... **TCLC 12**
See also CA 108; DLB 70

Bentley, Eric (Russell) 1916-....... **CLC 24**
See also CA 5-8R; CANR 6

Beranger, Pierre Jean de
1780-1857 .... **NCLC 34**

Berger, Colonel
See Malraux, (Georges-)Andre

Berger, John (Peter) 1926- ..... **CLC 2, 19**
See also CA 81-84; DLB 14

Berger, Melvin H. 1927- .... **CLC 12**
See also CA 5-8R; CANR 4; CLR 32;
SAAS 2; SATA 5

Berger, Thomas (Louis)
1924- .... **CLC 3, 5, 8, 11, 18, 38**
See also CA 1-4R; CANR 5, 28; DLB 2;
DLBY 80; MTCW

Bergman, (Ernst) Ingmar
1918- .... **CLC 16, 72**
See also CA 81-84; CANR 33

Bergson, Henri 1859-1941 .... **TCLC 32**

Bergstein, Eleanor 1938- .... **CLC 4**
See also CA 53-56; CANR 5

Berkoff, Steven 1937-............. **CLC 56**
See also CA 104

Bermant, Chaim (Icyk) 1929- ...... **CLC 40**
See also CA 57-60; CANR 6, 31

Bern, Victoria
See Fisher, M(ary) F(rances) K(ennedy)

Bernanos, (Paul Louis) Georges
1888-1948 .... **TCLC 3**
See also CA 104; 130; DLB 72

Bernard, April 1956- .... **CLC 59**
See also CA 131

Bernhard, Thomas
1931-1989 .... **CLC 3, 32, 61**
See also CA 85-88; 127; CANR 32;
DLB 85, 124; MTCW

Berrigan, Daniel 1921-............. **CLC 4**
See also CA 33-36R; CAAS 1; CANR 11,
43; DLB 5

Berrigan, Edmund Joseph Michael, Jr.
1934-1983
See Berrigan, Ted
See also CA 61-64; 110; CANR 14

Berrigan, Ted.................... **CLC 37**
See also Berrigan, Edmund Joseph Michael,
Jr.
See also DLB 5

Berry, Charles Edward Anderson 1931-
See Berry, Chuck
See also CA 115

Berry, Chuck.................... **CLC 17**
See also Berry, Charles Edward Anderson

Berry, Jonas
See Ashbery, John (Lawrence)

Berry, Wendell (Erdman)
1934- .... **CLC 4, 6, 8, 27, 46**
See also AITN 1; CA 73-76; DLB 5, 6

Berryman, John
1914-1972 ...... **CLC 1, 2, 3, 4, 6, 8, 10,
13, 25, 62**
See also CA 13-16; 33-36R; CABS 2;
CANR 35; CAP 1; CDALB 1941-1968;
DLB 48; MTCW

Bertolucci, Bernardo 1940- .... **CLC 16**
See also CA 106

Bertrand, Aloysius 1807-1841 .... **NCLC 31**

Bertran de Born c. 1140-1215 ..... **CMLC 5**

Besant, Annie (Wood) 1847-1933 ... **TCLC 9**
See also CA 105

Bessie, Alvah 1904-1985........... **CLC 23**
See also CA 5-8R; 116; CANR 2; DLB 26

Bethlen, T. D.
See Silverberg, Robert

Beti, Mongo.............. **CLC 27; BLC 1**
See also Biyidi, Alexandre

Betjeman, John
1906-1984 .... **CLC 2, 6, 10, 34, 43**
See also CA 9-12R; 112; CANR 33;
CDBLB 1945-1960; DLB 20; DLBY 84;
MTCW

Bettelheim, Bruno 1903-1990 ...... **CLC 79**
See also CA 81-84; 131; CANR 23; MTCW

Betti, Ugo 1892-1953............. **TCLC 5**
See also CA 104

Betts, Doris (Waugh) 1932-.... **CLC 3, 6, 28**
See also CA 13-16R; CANR 9; DLBY 82

Bevan, Alistair
See Roberts, Keith (John Kingston)

Beynon, John
See Harris, John (Wyndham Parkes Lucas)
Beynon

Bialik, Chaim Nachman
1873-1934 .... **TCLC 25**

Bickerstaff, Isaac
See Swift, Jonathan

Bidart, Frank 1939- .... **CLC 33**
See also CA 140

Bienek, Horst 1930-............ **CLC 7, 11**
See also CA 73-76; DLB 75

Bierce, Ambrose (Gwinett)
1842-1914(?) ...... **TCLC 1, 7, 44; DA;**
SSC 9; WLC
See also CA 104; 139; CDALB 1865-1917;
DLB 11, 12, 23, 71, 74

Billings, Josh
See Shaw, Henry Wheeler

Billington, Rachel 1942-........... **CLC 43**
See also AITN 2; CA 33-36R

Binyon, T(imothy) J(ohn) 1936- .... **CLC 34**
See also CA 111; CANR 28

Bioy Casares, Adolfo
1914- .... **CLC 4, 8, 13; HLC 1**
See also CA 29-32R; CANR 19, 43;
DLB 113; HW; MTCW

Bird, C.
See Ellison, Harlan

Bird, Cordwainer
See Ellison, Harlan

Bird, Robert Montgomery
1806-1854 .... **NCLC 1**

Birney, (Alfred) Earle
1904- .... **CLC 1, 4, 6, 11**
See also CA 1-4R; CANR 5, 20; DLB 88;
MTCW

Bishop, Elizabeth
1911-1979 ...... **CLC 1, 4, 9, 13, 15, 32;**
DA; PC 3
See also CA 5-8R; 89-92; CABS 2;
CANR 26; CDALB 1968-1988; DLB 5;
MTCW; SATA 24

Bishop, John 1935-............... **CLC 10**
See also CA 105

Bissett, Bill 1939-................ **CLC 18**
See also CA 69-72; CANR 15; DLB 53;
MTCW

Bitov, Andrei (Georgievich) 1937-... **CLC 57**
See also CA 142

Biyidi, Alexandre 1932-
See Beti, Mongo
See also BW; CA 114; 124; MTCW

Bjarme, Brynjolf
See Ibsen, Henrik (Johan)

Bjornson, Bjornstjerne (Martinius)
1832-1910 .... **TCLC 7, 37**
See also CA 104

Black, Robert
See Holdstock, Robert P.

Blackburn, Paul 1926-1971 ...... **CLC 9, 43**
See also CA 81-84; 33-36R; CANR 34;
DLB 16; DLBY 81

Black Elk 1863-1950 .... **TCLC 33**

Black Hobart
See Sanders, (James) Ed(ward)

Blacklin, Malcolm
See Chambers, Aidan

Blackmore, R(ichard) D(oddridge)
1825-1900 .... **TCLC 27**
See also CA 120; DLB 18

Blackmur, R(ichard) P(almer)
1904-1965 .... **CLC 2, 24**
See also CA 11-12; 25-28R; CAP 1; DLB 63

Black Tarantula, The
See Acker, Kathy

Blackwood, Algernon (Henry)
1869-1951 .... **TCLC 5**
See also CA 105

Blackwood, Caroline 1931- .... **CLC 6, 9**
See also CA 85-88; CANR 32; DLB 14;
MTCW

Blade, Alexander
See Hamilton, Edmond; Silverberg, Robert

Blaga, Lucian 1895-1961 .... **CLC 75**

Blair, Eric (Arthur) 1903-1950
See Orwell, George
See also CA 104; 132; DA; MTCW;
SATA 29

Blais, Marie-Claire
1939- .... **CLC 2, 4, 6, 13, 22**
See also CA 21-24R; CAAS 4; CANR 38;
DLB 53; MTCW

Blaise, Clark 1940-............... **CLC 29**
See also AITN 2; CA 53-56; CAAS 3;
CANR 5; DLB 53

Blake, Nicholas
See Day Lewis, C(ecil)
See also DLB 77

Blake, William
1757-1827 ..... **NCLC 13, 37; DA; WLC**
See also CDBLB 1789-1832; DLB 93;
MAICYA; SATA 30

Blasco Ibanez, Vicente
1867-1928 .... **TCLC 12**
See also CA 110; 131; HW; MTCW

Blatty, William Peter 1928-........ **CLC 2**
See also CA 5-8R; CANR 9

Bleeck, Oliver
See Thomas, Ross (Elmore)

Blessing, Lee 1949-.............. **CLC 54**

Blish, James (Benjamin)
1921-1975 .... **CLC 14**
See also CA 1-4R; 57-60; CANR 3; DLB 8;
MTCW; SATA 66

Bliss, Reginald
See Wells, H(erbert) G(eorge)

Blixen, Karen (Christentze Dinesen)
1885-1962
See Dinesen, Isak
See also CA 25-28; CANR 22; CAP 2;
MTCW; SATA 44

Bloch, Robert (Albert) 1917-....... **CLC 33**
See also CA 5-8R; CANR 5; DLB 44;
SATA 12

Blok, Alexander (Alexandrovich)
1880-1921 .... **TCLC 5**
See also CA 104

Blom, Jan
See Breytenbach, Breyten

Bloom, Harold 1930- .... **CLC 24**
See also CA 13-16R; CANR 39; DLB 67

Bloomfield, Aurelius
See Bourne, Randolph S(illiman)

Blount, Roy (Alton), Jr. 1941- ..... **CLC 38**
See also CA 53-56; CANR 10, 28; MTCW

Bloy, Leon 1846-1917............ **TCLC 22**
See also CA 121; DLB 123

Blume, Judy (Sussman) 1938-... **CLC 12, 30**
See also AAYA 3; CA 29-32R; CANR 13,
37; CLR 2, 15; DLB 52; JRDA;
MAICYA; MTCW; SATA 2, 31

Blunden, Edmund (Charles)
1896-1974 .... **CLC 2, 56**
See also CA 17-18; 45-48; CAP 2; DLB 20,
100; MTCW

Bly, Robert (Elwood)
1926-.......... **CLC 1, 2, 5, 10, 15, 38**
See also CA 5-8R; CANR 41; DLB 5;
MTCW

Bobette
See Simenon, Georges (Jacques Christian)

Boccaccio, Giovanni 1313-1375
See also SSC 10

Bochco, Steven 1943-............. **CLC 35**
See also CA 124; 138

Bodenheim, Maxwell 1892-1954 ... **TCLC 44**
See also CA 110; DLB 9, 45

Bodker, Cecil 1927-.............. **CLC 21**
See also CA 73-76; CANR 13; CLR 23;
MAICYA; SATA 14

Boell, Heinrich (Theodor) 1917-1985
See Boll, Heinrich (Theodor)
See also CA 21-24R; 116; CANR 24; DA;
DLB 69; DLBY 85; MTCW

Boerne, Alfred
See Doeblin, Alfred

Bogan, Louise 1897-1970..... **CLC 4, 39, 46**
See also CA 73-76; 25-28R; CANR 33;
DLB 45; MTCW

Bogarde, Dirk .... **CLC 19**
See also Van Den Bogarde, Derek Jules
Gaspard Ulric Niven
See also DLB 14

Bogosian, Eric 1953- .... **CLC 45**
See also CA 138

Bograd, Larry 1953-.............. **CLC 35**
See also CA 93-96; SATA 33

Boiardo, Matteo Maria 1441-1494 .... **LC 6**

Boileau-Despreaux, Nicolas
1636-1711 .... **LC 3**

Boland, Eavan 1944-........... **CLC 40, 67**
See also DLB 40

Boll, Heinrich (Theodor)
1917-1985 .... **CLC 2, 3, 6, 9, 11, 15, 27,**
39, 72; WLC
See also Boell, Heinrich (Theodor)
See also DLB 69; DLBY 85

Bolt, Lee
See Faust, Frederick (Schiller)

Bolt, Robert (Oxton) 1924-........ **CLC 14**
See also CA 17-20R; CANR 35; DLB 13;
MTCW

Bomkauf
See Kaufman, Bob (Garnell)

Bonaventura.................... NCLC 35
See also DLB 90

Bond, Edward 1934-....... CLC 4, 6, 13, 23
See also CA 25-28R; CANR 38; DLB 13;
MTCW

Bonham, Frank 1914-1989........ CLC 12
See also AAYA 1; CA 9-12R; CANR 4, 36;
JRDA; MAICYA; SAAS 3; SATA 1, 49,
62

Bonnefoy, Yves 1923-........ CLC 9, 15, 58
See also CA 85-88; CANR 33; MTCW

Bontemps, Arna(ud Wendell)
1902-1973 .... CLC 1, 18; BLC 1
See also BW; CA 1-4R; 41-44R; CANR 4,
35; CLR 6; DLB 48, 51; JRDA;
MAICYA; MTCW; SATA 2, 24, 44

Booth, Martin 1944-.............. CLC 13
See also CA 93-96; CAAS 2

Booth, Philip 1925-.............. CLC 23
See also CA 5-8R; CANR 5; DLBY 82

Booth, Wayne C(layson) 1921- ..... CLC 24
See also CA 1-4R; CAAS 5; CANR 3, 43;
DLB 67

Borchert, Wolfgang 1921-1947 ..... TCLC 5
See also CA 104; DLB 69, 124

Borel, Petrus 1809-1859........ NCLC 41

Borges, Jorge Luis
1899-1986 ... CLC 1, 2, 3, 4, 6, 8, 9, 10,
13, 19, 44, 48; DA; HLC 1; SSC 4; WLC
See also CA 21-24R; CANR 19, 33;
DLB 113; DLBY 86; HW; MTCW

Borowski, Tadeusz 1922-1951 ..... TCLC 9
See also CA 106

Borrow, George (Henry)
1803-1881 .... NCLC 9
See also DLB 21, 55

Bosman, Herman Charles
1905-1951 .... TCLC 49

Bosschere, Jean de 1878(?)-1953... TCLC 19
See also CA 115

Boswell, James
1740-1795 .... LC 4; DA; WLC
See also CDBLB 1660-1789; DLB 104

Bottoms, David 1949-............. CLC 53
See also CA 105; CANR 22; DLB 120;
DLBY 83

Boucicault, Dion 1820-1890...... NCLC 41

Boucolon, Maryse 1937-
See Conde, Maryse
See also CA 110; CANR 30

Bourget, Paul (Charles Joseph)
1852-1935 .... TCLC 12
See also CA 107; DLB 123

Bourjaily, Vance (Nye) 1922- .... CLC 8, 62
See also CA 1-4R; CAAS 1; CANR 2;
DLB 2

Bourne, Randolph S(illiman)
1886-1918 .... TCLC 16
See also CA 117; DLB 63

Bova, Ben(jamin William) 1932-.... CLC 45
See also CA 5-8R; CAAS 18; CANR 11;
CLR 3; DLBY 81; MAICYA; MTCW;
SATA 6, 68

Bowen, Elizabeth (Dorothea Cole)
1899-1973 ...... CLC 1, 3, 6, 11, 15, 22;
SSC 3
See also CA 17-18; 41-44R; CANR 35;
CAP 2; CDBLB 1945-1960; DLB 15;
MTCW

Bowering, George 1935-........ CLC 15, 47
See also CA 21-24R; CAAS 16; CANR 10;
DLB 53

Bowering, Marilyn R(uthe) 1949-... CLC 32
See also CA 101

Bowers, Edgar 1924- .... CLC 9
See also CA 5-8R; CANR 24; DLB 5

Bowie, David..................... CLC 17
See also Jones, David Robert

Bowles, Jane (Sydney)
1917-1973 .... CLC 3, 68
See also CA 19-20; 41-44R; CAP 2

Bowles, Paul (Frederick)
1910- .... CLC 1, 2, 19, 53; SSC 3
See also CA 1-4R; CAAS 1; CANR 1, 19;
DLB 5, 6; MTCW

Box, Edgar
See Vidal, Gore

Boyd, Nancy
See Millay, Edna St. Vincent

Boyd, William 1952-........ CLC 28, 53, 70
See also CA 114; 120

Boyle, Kay
1902-1992 ..... CLC 1, 5, 19, 58; SSC 5
See also CA 13-16R; 140; CAAS 1;
CANR 29; DLB 4, 9, 48, 86; MTCW

Boyle, Mark
See Kienzle, William X(avier)

Boyle, Patrick 1905-1982.......... CLC 19
See also CA 127

Boyle, T. Coraghessan 1948-.... CLC 36, 55
See also BEST 90:4; CA 120; DLBY 86

Boz
See Dickens, Charles (John Huffam)

Brackenridge, Hugh Henry
1748-1816 .... NCLC 7
See also DLB 11, 37

Bradbury, Edward P.
See Moorcock, Michael (John)

Bradbury, Malcolm (Stanley)
1932- .... CLC 32, 61
See also CA 1-4R; CANR 1, 33; DLB 14;
MTCW

Bradbury, Ray (Douglas)
1920- ... CLC 1, 3, 10, 15, 42; DA; WLC
See also AITN 1, 2; CA 1-4R; CANR 2, 30;
CDALB 1968-1988; DLB 2, 8; MTCW;
SATA 11, 64

Bradford, Gamaliel 1863-1932..... TCLC 36
See also DLB 17

Bradley, David (Henry, Jr.)
1950- .... CLC 23; BLC 1
See also BW; CA 104; CANR 26; DLB 33

Bradley, John Ed 1959-........... CLC 55

Bradley, Marion Zimmer 1930-..... CLC 30
See also AAYA 9; CA 57-60; CAAS 10;
CANR 7, 31; DLB 8; MTCW

Bradstreet, Anne 1612(?)-1672 ... LC 4; DA
See also CDALB 1640-1865; DLB 24

Bragg, Melvyn 1939- .... CLC 10
See also BEST 89:3; CA 57-60; CANR 10;
DLB 14

Braine, John (Gerard)
1922-1986 .... CLC 1, 3, 41
See also CA 1-4R; 120; CANR 1, 33;
CDBLB 1945-1960; DLB 15; DLBY 86;
MTCW

Brammer, William 1930(?)-1978 .... CLC 31
See also CA 77-80

Brancati, Vitaliano 1907-1954..... TCLC 12
See also CA 109

Brancato, Robin F(idler) 1936-..... CLC 35
See also AAYA 9; CA 69-72; CANR 11;
CLR 32; JRDA; SAAS 9; SATA 23

Brand, Max
See Faust, Frederick (Schiller)

Brand, Millen 1906-1980.......... CLC 7
See also CA 21-24R; 97-100

Branden, Barbara .... CLC 44

Brandes, Georg (Morris Cohen)
1842-1927 .... TCLC 10
See also CA 105

Brandys, Kazimierz 1916-........ CLC 62

Branley, Franklyn M(ansfield)
1915- .... CLC 21
See also CA 33-36R; CANR 14, 39;
CLR 13; MAICYA; SAAS 16; SATA 4,
68

Brathwaite, Edward (Kamau)
1930- .... CLC 11
See also BW; CA 25-28R; CANR 11, 26;
DLB 125

Brautigan, Richard (Gary)
1935-1984 .... CLC 1, 3, 5, 9, 12, 34, 42
See also CA 53-56; 113; CANR 34; DLB 2,
5; DLBY 80, 84; MTCW; SATA 56

Braverman, Kate 1950- .... CLC 67
See also CA 89-92

Brecht, Bertolt
1898-1956 ...... TCLC 1, 6, 13, 35; DA;
DC 3; WLC
See also CA 104; 133; DLB 56, 124; MTCW

Brecht, Eugen Berthold Friedrich
See Brecht, Bertolt

Bremer, Fredrika 1801-1865 ..... NCLC 11

Brennan, Christopher John
1870-1932 .... TCLC 17
See also CA 117

Brennan, Maeve 1917-............ CLC 5
See also CA 81-84

Brentano, Clemens (Maria)
1778-1842 .... NCLC 1

Brent of Bin Bin
See Franklin, (Stella Maraia Sarah) Miles

Brenton, Howard 1942-........... CLC 31
See also CA 69-72; CANR 33; DLB 13;
MTCW

Breslin, James 1930-
See Breslin, Jimmy
See also CA 73-76; CANR 31; MTCW

Breslin, Jimmy .... CLC 4, 43
See also Breslin, James
See also AITN 1

Bresson, Robert 1907- .... **CLC 16**
See also CA 110

Breton, Andre 1896-1966... **CLC 2, 9, 15, 54**
See also CA 19-20; 25-28R; CANR 40;
CAP 2; DLB 65; MTCW

Breytenbach, Breyten 1939(?)- .. **CLC 23, 37**
See also CA 113; 129

Bridgers, Sue Ellen 1942- .... **CLC 26**
See also AAYA 8; CA 65-68; CANR 11,
36; CLR 18; DLB 52; JRDA; MAICYA;
SAAS 1; SATA 22

Bridges, Robert (Seymour)
1844-1930 .... **TCLC 1**
See also CA 104; CDBLB 1890-1914;
DLB 19, 98

Bridie, James.................... **TCLC 3**
See also Mavor, Osborne Henry
See also DLB 10

Brin, David 1950-................ **CLC 34**
See also CA 102; CANR 24; SATA 65

Brink, Andre (Philippus)
1935-.................... **CLC 18, 36**
See also CA 104; CANR 39; MTCW

Brinsmead, H(esba) F(ay) 1922- .... **CLC 21**
See also CA 21-24R; CANR 10; MAICYA;
SAAS 5; SATA 18

Brittain, Vera (Mary)
1893(?)-1970 .... **CLC 23**
See also CA 13-16; 25-28R; CAP 1; MTCW

Broch, Hermann 1886-1951....... **TCLC 20**
See also CA 117; DLB 85, 124

Brock, Rose
See Hansen, Joseph

Brodkey, Harold 1930-........... **CLC 56**
See also CA 111; DLB 130

Brodsky, Iosif Alexandrovich 1940-
See Brodsky, Joseph
See also AITN 1; CA 41-44R; CANR 37;
MTCW

Brodsky, Joseph .... **CLC 4, 6, 13, 36, 50**
See also Brodsky, Iosif Alexandrovich

Brodsky, Michael Mark 1948- ..... **CLC 19**
See also CA 102; CANR 18, 41

Bromell, Henry 1947-............. **CLC 5**
See also CA 53-56; CANR 9

Bromfield, Louis (Brucker)
1896-1956 .... **TCLC 11**
See also CA 107; DLB 4, 9, 86

Broner, E(sther) M(asserman)
1930-...................... **CLC 19**
See also CA 17-20R; CANR 8, 25; DLB 28

Bronk, William 1918-............ **CLC 10**
See also CA 89-92; CANR 23

Bronstein, Lev Davidovich
See Trotsky, Leon

Bronte, Anne 1820-1849......... **NCLC 4**
See also DLB 21

Bronte, Charlotte
1816-1855 ... **NCLC 3, 8, 33; DA; WLC**
See also CDBLB 1832-1890; DLB 21

Bronte, (Jane) Emily
1818-1848 .... **NCLC 16, 35; DA; PC 8;
WLC**
See also CDBLB 1832-1890; DLB 21, 32

Brooke, Frances 1724-1789 .... **LC 6**
See also DLB 39, 99

Brooke, Henry 1703(?)-1783 .... **LC 1**
See also DLB 39

Brooke, Rupert (Chawner)
1887-1915 .... **TCLC 2, 7; DA; WLC**
See also CA 104; 132; CDBLB 1914-1945;
DLB 19; MTCW

Brooke-Haven, P.
See Wodehouse, P(elham) G(renville)

Brooke-Rose, Christine 1926- ...... **CLC 40**
See also CA 13-16R; DLB 14

Brookner, Anita 1928- ...... **CLC 32, 34, 51**
See also CA 114; 120; CANR 37; DLBY 87;
MTCW

Brooks, Cleanth 1906- .... **CLC 24**
See also CA 17-20R; CANR 33, 35;
DLB 63; MTCW

Brooks, George
See Baum, L(yman) Frank

Brooks, Gwendolyn
1917-.... **CLC 1, 2, 4, 5, 15, 49; BLC 1;
DA; PC 7; WLC**
See also AITN 1; BW; CA 1-4R; CANR 1,
27; CDALB 1941-1968; CLR 27; DLB 5,
76; MTCW; SATA 6

Brooks, Mel...................... **CLC 12**
See also Kaminsky, Melvin
See also DLB 26

Brooks, Peter 1938-.............. **CLC 34**
See also CA 45-48; CANR 1

Brooks, Van Wyck 1886-1963...... **CLC 29**
See also CA 1-4R; CANR 6; DLB 45, 63,
103

Brophy, Brigid (Antonia)
1929-.................. **CLC 6, 11, 29**
See also CA 5-8R; CAAS 4; CANR 25;
DLB 14; MTCW

Brosman, Catharine Savage 1934-.... **CLC 9**
See also CA 61-64; CANR 21

Brother Antoninus
See Everson, William (Oliver)

Broughton, T(homas) Alan 1936- ... **CLC 19**
See also CA 45-48; CANR 2, 23

Broumas, Olga 1949-.......... **CLC 10, 73**
See also CA 85-88; CANR 20

Brown, Charles Brockden
1771-1810 .... **NCLC 22**
See also CDALB 1640-1865; DLB 37, 59,
73

Brown, Christy 1932-1981........ **CLC 63**
See also CA 105; 104; DLB 14

Brown, Claude 1937- ...... **CLC 30; BLC 1**
See also AAYA 7; BW; CA 73-76

Brown, Dee (Alexander) 1908- .. **CLC 18, 47**
See also CA 13-16R; CAAS 6; CANR 11;
DLBY 80; MTCW; SATA 5

Brown, George
See Wertmueller, Lina

Brown, George Douglas
1869-1902 .... **TCLC 28**

Brown, George Mackay 1921-.... **CLC 5, 48**
See also CA 21-24R; CAAS 6; CANR 12,
37; DLB 14, 27; MTCW; SATA 35

Brown, (William) Larry 1951-...... **CLC 73**
See also CA 130; 134

Brown, Moses
See Barrett, William (Christopher)

Brown, Rita Mae 1944-..... **CLC 18, 43, 79**
See also CA 45-48; CANR 2, 11, 35;
MTCW

Brown, Roderick (Langmere) Haig-
See Haig-Brown, Roderick (Langmere)

Brown, Rosellen 1939-............ **CLC 32**
See also CA 77-80; CAAS 10; CANR 14

Brown, Sterling Allen
1901-1989 .... **CLC 1, 23, 59; BLC 1**
See also BW; CA 85-88; 127; CANR 26;
DLB 48, 51, 63; MTCW

Brown, Will
See Ainsworth, William Harrison

Brown, William Wells
1813-1884 ...... **NCLC 2; BLC 1; DC 1**
See also DLB 3, 50

Browne, (Clyde) Jackson 1948(?)-... **CLC 21**
See also CA 120

Browning, Elizabeth Barrett
1806-1861 ..... **NCLC 1, 16; DA; PC 6;
WLC**
See also CDBLB 1832-1890; DLB 32

Browning, Robert
1812-1889 .... **NCLC 19; DA; PC 2**
See also CDBLB 1832-1890; DLB 32;
YABC 1

Browning, Tod 1882-1962 .... **CLC 16**
See also CA 141; 117

Bruccoli, Matthew J(oseph) 1931- .. **CLC 34**
See also CA 9-12R; CANR 7; DLB 103

Bruce, Lenny..................... **CLC 21**
See also Schneider, Leonard Alfred

Bruin, John
See Brutus, Dennis

Brulls, Christian
See Simenon, Georges (Jacques Christian)

Brunner, John (Kilian Houston)
1934-.................... **CLC 8, 10**
See also CA 1-4R; CAAS 8; CANR 2, 37;
MTCW

Brutus, Dennis 1924- ...... **CLC 43; BLC 1**
See also BW; CA 49-52; CAAS 14;
CANR 2, 27, 42; DLB 117

Bryan, C(ourtlandt) D(ixon) B(arnes)
1936-...................... **CLC 29**
See also CA 73-76; CANR 13

Bryan, Michael
See Moore, Brian

Bryant, William Cullen
1794-1878 .... **NCLC 6; DA**
See also CDALB 1640-1865; DLB 3, 43, 59

Bryusov, Valery Yakovlevich
1873-1924 .... **TCLC 10**
See also CA 107

Buchan, John 1875-1940 .... **TCLC 41**
See also CA 108; DLB 34, 70; YABC 2

Buchanan, George 1506-1582 .... **LC 4**

Buchheim, Lothar-Guenther 1918- ... **CLC 6**
See also CA 85-88

Buchner, (Karl) Georg
1813-1837 .... **NCLC 26**

Buchwald, Art(hur) 1925- .... **CLC 33**
See also AITN 1; CA 5-8R; CANR 21;
MTCW; SATA 10

Buck, Pearl S(ydenstricker)
1892-1973 .... **CLC 7, 11, 18; DA**
See also AITN 1; CA 1-4R; 41-44R;
CANR 1, 34; DLB 9, 102; MTCW;
SATA 1, 25

Buckler, Ernest 1908-1984........ **CLC 13**
See also CA 11-12; 114; CAP 1; DLB 68;
SATA 47

Buckley, Vincent (Thomas)
1925-1988 .... **CLC 57**
See also CA 101

Buckley, William F(rank), Jr.
1925- .... **CLC 7, 18, 37**
See also AITN 1; CA 1-4R; CANR 1, 24;
DLBY 80; MTCW

Buechner, (Carl) Frederick
1926- .... **CLC 2, 4, 6, 9**
See also CA 13-16R; CANR 11, 39;
DLBY 80; MTCW

Buell, John (Edward) 1927-........ **CLC 10**
See also CA 1-4R; DLB 53

Buero Vallejo, Antonio 1916- ... **CLC 15, 46**
See also CA 106; CANR 24; HW; MTCW

Bufalino, Gesualdo 1920(?)-........ **CLC 74**

Bugayev, Boris Nikolayevich 1880-1934
See Bely, Andrey
See also CA 104

Bukowski, Charles 1920- .... **CLC 2, 5, 9, 41**
See also CA 17-20R; CANR 40; DLB 5,
130; MTCW

Bulgakov, Mikhail (Afanas'evich)
1891-1940 .... **TCLC 2, 16**
See also CA 105

Bulgya, Alexander Alexandrovich
1901-1956 .... **TCLC 53**
See also Fadeyev, Alexander
See also CA 117

Bullins, Ed 1935- ...... **CLC 1, 5, 7; BLC 1**
See also BW; CA 49-52; CAAS 16;
CANR 24; DLB 7, 38; MTCW

Bulwer-Lytton, Edward (George Earle Lytton)
1803-1873 .... **NCLC 1**
See also DLB 21

Bunin, Ivan Alexeyevich
1870-1953 .... **TCLC 6; SSC 5**
See also CA 104

Bunting, Basil 1900-1985.... **CLC 10, 39, 47**
See also CA 53-56; 115; CANR 7; DLB 20

Bunuel, Luis
1900-1983 .... **CLC 16, 80; HLC 1**
See also CA 101; 110; CANR 32; HW

Bunyan, John 1628-1688 .. **LC 4; DA; WLC**
See also CDBLB 1660-1789; DLB 39

Burford, Eleanor
See Hibbert, Eleanor Alice Burford

Burgess, Anthony
CLC 1, 2, 4, 5, 8, 10, 13, 15, 22, 40, 62,
81
See also Wilson, John (Anthony) Burgess
See also AITN 1; CDBLB 1960 to Present;
DLB 14

Burke, Edmund
1729(?)-1797 .... **LC 7; DA; WLC**
See also DLB 104

Burke, Kenneth (Duva) 1897- .... **CLC 2, 24**
See also CA 5-8R; CANR 39; DLB 45, 63;
MTCW

Burke, Leda
See Garnett, David

Burke, Ralph
See Silverberg, Robert

Burney, Fanny 1752-1840 .... **NCLC 12**
See also DLB 39

Burns, Robert
1759-1796 ...... **LC 3; DA; PC 6; WLC**
See also CDBLB 1789-1832; DLB 109

Burns, Tex
See L'Amour, Louis (Dearborn)

Burnshaw, Stanley 1906- ..... **CLC 3, 13, 44**
See also CA 9-12R; DLB 48

Burr, Anne 1937- .... **CLC 6**
See also CA 25-28R

Burroughs, Edgar Rice
1875-1950 .... **TCLC 2, 32**
See also CA 104; 132; DLB 8; MTCW;
SATA 41

Burroughs, William S(eward)
1914- .... **CLC 1, 2, 5, 15, 22, 42, 75;**
DA; WLC
See also AITN 2; CA 9-12R; CANR 20;
DLB 2, 8, 16; DLBY 81; MTCW

Burton, Richard F. 1821-1890.... **NCLC 42**
See also DLB 55

Busch, Frederick 1941- ... **CLC 7, 10, 18, 47**
See also CA 33-36R; CAAS 1; DLB 6

Bush, Ronald 1946- .... **CLC 34**
See also CA 136

Bustos, F(rancisco)
See Borges, Jorge Luis

Bustos Domecq, H(onorio)
See Bioy Casares, Adolfo; Borges, Jorge
Luis

Butler, Octavia E(stelle) 1947- ..... **CLC 38**
See also BW; CA 73-76; CANR 12, 24, 38;
DLB 33; MTCW

Butler, Robert Olen (Jr.) 1945-..... **CLC 81**
See also CA 112

Butler, Samuel 1612-1680 .... **LC 16**
See also DLB 101, 126

Butler, Samuel
1835-1902 ...... **TCLC 1, 33; DA; WLC**
See also CA 104; CDBLB 1890-1914;
DLB 18, 57

Butler, Walter C.
See Faust, Frederick (Schiller)

Butor, Michel (Marie Francois)
1926- .... **CLC 1, 3, 8, 11, 15**
See also CA 9-12R; CANR 33; DLB 83;
MTCW

Buzo, Alexander (John) 1944-...... **CLC 61**
See also CA 97-100; CANR 17, 39

Buzzati, Dino 1906-1972 .... **CLC 36**
See also CA 33-36R

Byars, Betsy (Cromer) 1928-....... **CLC 35**
See also CA 33-36R; CANR 18, 36; CLR 1,
16; DLB 52; JRDA; MAICYA; MTCW;
SAAS 1; SATA 4, 46

Byatt, A(ntonia) S(usan Drabble)
1936- .... **CLC 19, 65**
See also CA 13-16R; CANR 13, 33;
DLB 14; MTCW

Byrne, David 1952-.............. **CLC 26**
See also CA 127

Byrne, John Keyes 1926-......... **CLC 19**
See also Leonard, Hugh
See also CA 102

Byron, George Gordon (Noel)
1788-1824 ...... **NCLC 2, 12; DA; WLC**
See also CDBLB 1789-1832; DLB 96, 110

C.3.3.
See Wilde, Oscar (Fingal O'Flahertie Wills)

Caballero, Fernan 1796-1877..... **NCLC 10**

Cabell, James Branch 1879-1958 ... **TCLC 6**
See also CA 105; DLB 9, 78

Cable, George Washington
1844-1925 .... **TCLC 4; SSC 4**
See also CA 104; DLB 12, 74

Cabral de Melo Neto, Joao 1920-... **CLC 76**

Cabrera Infante, G(uillermo)
1929- .... **CLC 5, 25, 45; HLC 1**
See also CA 85-88; CANR 29; DLB 113;
HW; MTCW

Cade, Toni
See Bambara, Toni Cade

Cadmus
See Buchan, John

Caedmon fl. 658-680............. **CMLC 7**

Caeiro, Alberto
See Pessoa, Fernando (Antonio Nogueira)

Cage, John (Milton, Jr.) 1912- ..... **CLC 41**
See also CA 13-16R; CANR 9

Cain, G.
See Cabrera Infante, G(uillermo)

Cain, Guillermo
See Cabrera Infante, G(uillermo)

Cain, James M(allahan)
1892-1977 .... **CLC 3, 11, 28**
See also AITN 1; CA 17-20R; 73-76;
CANR 8, 34; MTCW

Caine, Mark
See Raphael, Frederic (Michael)

Calasso, Roberto 1941- .... **CLC 81**

Calderon de la Barca, Pedro
1600-1681 .... **LC 23; DC 3**

Caldwell, Erskine (Preston)
1903-1987 .... **CLC 1, 8, 14, 50, 60**
See also AITN 1; CA 1-4R; 121; CAAS 1;
CANR 2, 33; DLB 9, 86; MTCW

Caldwell, (Janet Miriam) Taylor (Holland)
1900-1985 .... **CLC 2, 28, 39**
See also CA 5-8R; 116; CANR 5

Calhoun, John Caldwell
1782-1850 .... NCLC **15**
See also DLB 3

Calisher, Hortense 1911-.... CLC **2, 4, 8, 38**
See also CA 1-4R; CANR 1, 22; DLB 2;
MTCW

Callaghan, Morley Edward
1903-1990 .... CLC **3, 14, 41, 65**
See also CA 9-12R; 132; CANR 33;
DLB 68; MTCW

Calvino, Italo
1923-1985 ..... CLC **5, 8, 11, 22, 33, 39,
73; SSC 3**
See also CA 85-88; 116; CANR 23; MTCW

Cameron, Carey 1952- .... CLC **59**
See also CA 135

Cameron, Peter 1959-............. CLC **44**
See also CA 125

Campana, Dino 1885-1932....... TCLC **20**
See also CA 117; DLB 114

Campbell, John W(ood, Jr.)
1910-1971 .... CLC **32**
See also CA 21-22; 29-32R; CANR 34;
CAP 2; DLB 8; MTCW

Campbell, Joseph 1904-1987 .... CLC **69**
See also AAYA 3; BEST 89:2; CA 1-4R;
124; CANR 3, 28; MTCW

Campbell, (John) Ramsey 1946- .... CLC **42**
See also CA 57-60; CANR 7

Campbell, (Ignatius) Roy (Dunnachie)
1901-1957 .... TCLC **5**
See also CA 104; DLB 20

Campbell, Thomas 1777-1844 .... NCLC **19**
See also DLB 93

Campbell, Wilfred............... TCLC **9**
See also Campbell, William

Campbell, William 1858(?)-1918
See Campbell, Wilfred
See also CA 106; DLB 92

Campos, Alvaro de
See Pessoa, Fernando (Antonio Nogueira)

Camus, Albert
1913-1960 .... CLC **1, 2, 4, 9, 11, 14, 32,
63, 69; DA; DC 2; SSC 9; WLC**
See also CA 89-92; DLB 72; MTCW

Canby, Vincent 1924-............. CLC **13**
See also CA 81-84

Cancale
See Desnos, Robert

Canetti, Elias 1905- ...... CLC **3, 14, 25, 75**
See also CA 21-24R; CANR 23; DLB 85,
124; MTCW

Canin, Ethan 1960-............... CLC **55**
See also CA 131; 135

Cannon, Curt
See Hunter, Evan

Cape, Judith
See Page, P(atricia) K(athleen)

Capek, Karel
1890-1938 ..... TCLC **6, 37; DA; DC 1;
WLC**
See also CA 104; 140

Capote, Truman
1924-1984 ...... CLC **1, 3, 8, 13, 19, 34,
38, 58; DA; SSC 2; WLC**
See also CA 5-8R; 113; CANR 18;
CDALB 1941-1968; DLB 2; DLBY 80,
84; MTCW

Capra, Frank 1897-1991.......... CLC **16**
See also CA 61-64; 135

Caputo, Philip 1941-.............. CLC **32**
See also CA 73-76; CANR 40

Card, Orson Scott 1951- .... CLC **44, 47, 50**
See also CA 102; CANR 27; MTCW

Cardenal (Martinez), Ernesto
1925- .... CLC **31; HLC 1**
See also CA 49-52; CANR 2, 32; HW;
MTCW

Carducci, Giosue 1835-1907...... TCLC **32**

Carew, Thomas 1595(?)-1640....... LC **13**
See also DLB 126

Carey, Ernestine Gilbreth 1908-.... CLC **17**
See also CA 5-8R; SATA 2

Carey, Peter 1943-............. CLC **40, 55**
See also CA 123; 127; MTCW

Carleton, William 1794-1869...... NCLC **3**

Carlisle, Henry (Coffin) 1926-...... CLC **33**
See also CA 13-16R; CANR 15

Carlsen, Chris
See Holdstock, Robert P.

Carlson, Ron(ald F.) 1947-........ CLC **54**
See also CA 105; CANR 27

Carlyle, Thomas 1795-1881 .. NCLC **22; DA**
See also CDBLB 1789-1832; DLB 55

Carman, (William) Bliss
1861-1929 .... TCLC **7**
See also CA 104; DLB 92

Carnegie, Dale 1888-1955 .... TCLC **53**

Carossa, Hans 1878-1956........ TCLC **48**
See also DLB 66

Carpenter, Don(ald Richard)
1931- .... CLC **41**
See also CA 45-48; CANR 1

Carpentier (y Valmont), Alejo
1904-1980 .... CLC **8, 11, 38; HLC 1**
See also CA 65-68; 97-100; CANR 11;
DLB 113; HW

Carr, Emily 1871-1945........... TCLC **32**
See also DLB 68

Carr, John Dickson 1906-1977 ...... CLC **3**
See also CA 49-52; 69-72; CANR 3, 33;
MTCW

Carr, Philippa
See Hibbert, Eleanor Alice Burford

Carr, Virginia Spencer 1929-....... CLC **34**
See also CA 61-64; DLB 111

Carrier, Roch 1937-........... CLC **13, 78**
See also CA 130; DLB 53

Carroll, James P. 1943(?)-........ CLC **38**
See also CA 81-84

Carroll, Jim 1951- .... CLC **35**
See also CA 45-48; CANR 42

Carroll, Lewis .... NCLC **2; WLC**
See also Dodgson, Charles Lutwidge
See also CDBLB 1832-1890; CLR 2, 18;
DLB 18; JRDA

Carroll, Paul Vincent 1900-1968.... CLC **10**
See also CA 9-12R; 25-28R; DLB 10

Carruth, Hayden 1921- .... CLC **4, 7, 10, 18**
See also CA 9-12R; CANR 4, 38; DLB 5;
MTCW; SATA 47

Carson, Rachel Louise 1907-1964... CLC **71**
See also CA 77-80; CANR 35; MTCW;
SATA 23

Carter, Angela (Olive)
1940-1992 ...... CLC **5, 41, 76; SSC 13**
See also CA 53-56; 136; CANR 12, 36;
DLB 14; MTCW; SATA 66;
SATA-Obit 70

Carter, Nick
See Smith, Martin Cruz

Carver, Raymond
1938-1988 ... CLC **22, 36, 53, 55; SSC 8**
See also CA 33-36R; 126; CANR 17, 34;
DLB 130; DLBY 84, 88; MTCW

Cary, (Arthur) Joyce (Lunel)
1888-1957 .... TCLC **1, 29**
See also CA 104; CDBLB 1914-1945;
DLB 15, 100

Casanova de Seingalt, Giovanni Jacopo
1725-1798 .... LC **13**

Casares, Adolfo Bioy
See Bioy Casares, Adolfo

Casely-Hayford, J(oseph) E(phraim)
1866-1930 .... TCLC **24; BLC 1**
See also CA 123

Casey, John (Dudley) 1939-........ CLC **59**
See also BEST 90:2; CA 69-72; CANR 23

Casey, Michael 1947-.............. CLC **2**
See also CA 65-68; DLB 5

Casey, Patrick
See Thurman, Wallace (Henry)

Casey, Warren (Peter) 1935-1988... CLC **12**
See also CA 101; 127

Casona, Alejandro................. CLC **49**
See also Alvarez, Alejandro Rodriguez

Cassavetes, John 1929-1989........ CLC **20**
See also CA 85-88; 127

Cassill, R(onald) V(erlin) 1919-... CLC **4, 23**
See also CA 9-12R; CAAS 1; CANR 7;
DLB 6

Cassity, (Allen) Turner 1929- .... CLC **6, 42**
See also CA 17-20R; CAAS 8; CANR 11;
DLB 105

Castaneda, Carlos 1931(?)-......... CLC **12**
See also CA 25-28R; CANR 32; HW;
MTCW

Castedo, Elena 1937- .... CLC **65**
See also CA 132

Castedo-Ellerman, Elena
See Castedo, Elena

Castellanos, Rosario
1925-1974 .... CLC **66; HLC 1**
See also CA 131; 53-56; DLB 113; HW

Castelvetro, Lodovico 1505-1571..... LC **12**

Castiglione, Baldassare 1478-1529 ... LC **12**

Castle, Robert
See Hamilton, Edmond

Castro, Guillen de 1569-1631........ LC **19**

Castro, Rosalia de 1837-1885 ..... NCLC **3**

Cather, Willa
See Cather, Willa Sibert

Cather, Willa Sibert
1873-1947 .... **TCLC 1, 11, 31; DA;**
SSC 2; WLC
See also CA 104; 128; CDALB 1865-1917;
DLB 9, 54, 78; DLBD 1; MTCW;
SATA 30

Catton, (Charles) Bruce
1899-1978 .... **CLC 35**
See also AITN 1; CA 5-8R; 81-84;
CANR 7; DLB 17; SATA 2, 24

Cauldwell, Frank
See King, Francis (Henry)

Caunitz, William J. 1933- .... **CLC 34**
See also BEST 89:3; CA 125; 130

Causley, Charles (Stanley) 1917- ..... **CLC 7**
See also CA 9-12R; CANR 5, 35; CLR 30;
DLB 27; MTCW; SATA 3, 66

Caute, David 1936- .... **CLC 29**
See also CA 1-4R; CAAS 4; CANR 1, 33;
DLB 14

Cavafy, C(onstantine) P(eter) ...... **TCLC 2, 7**
See also Kavafis, Konstantinos Petrou

Cavallo, Evelyn
See Spark, Muriel (Sarah)

Cavanna, Betty .... **CLC 12**
See also Harrison, Elizabeth Cavanna
See also JRDA; MAICYA; SAAS 4;
SATA 1, 30

Caxton, William 1421(?)-1491(?) ..... **LC 17**

Cayrol, Jean 1911- .... **CLC 11**
See also CA 89-92; DLB 83

Cela, Camilo Jose
1916- .... **CLC 4, 13, 59; HLC 1**
See also BEST 90:2; CA 21-24R; CAAS 10;
CANR 21, 32; DLBY 89; HW; MTCW

Celan, Paul .... **CLC 53**
See also Antschel, Paul
See also DLB 69

Celine, Louis-Ferdinand
.... **CLC 1, 3, 4, 7, 9, 15, 47**
See also Destouches, Louis-Ferdinand
See also DLB 72

Cellini, Benvenuto 1500-1571 .... **LC 7**

Cendrars, Blaise
See Sauser-Hall, Frederic

Cernuda (y Bidon), Luis
1902-1963 .... **CLC 54**
See also CA 131; 89-92; DLB 134; HW

Cervantes (Saavedra), Miguel de
1547-1616 ..... **LC 6, 23; DA; SSC 12;**
WLC

Cesaire, Aime (Fernand)
1913- .... **CLC 19, 32; BLC 1**
See also BW; CA 65-68; CANR 24, 43;
MTCW

Chabon, Michael 1965(?)- .... **CLC 55**
See also CA 139

Chabrol, Claude 1930- .... **CLC 16**
See also CA 110

Challans, Mary 1905-1983
See Renault, Mary
See also CA 81-84; 111; SATA 23, 36

Challis, George
See Faust, Frederick (Schiller)

Chambers, Aidan 1934- .... **CLC 35**
See also CA 25-28R; CANR 12, 31; JRDA;
MAICYA; SAAS 12; SATA 1, 69

Chambers, James 1948-
See Cliff, Jimmy
See also CA 124

Chambers, Jessie
See Lawrence, D(avid) H(erbert Richards)

Chambers, Robert W. 1865-1933... **TCLC 41**

Chandler, Raymond (Thornton)
1888-1959 .... **TCLC 1, 7**
See also CA 104; 129; CDALB 1929-1941;
DLBD 6; MTCW

Chang, Jung 1952- .... **CLC 71**
See also CA 142

Channing, William Ellery
1780-1842 .... **NCLC 17**
See also DLB 1, 59

Chaplin, Charles Spencer
1889-1977 .... **CLC 16**
See also Chaplin, Charlie
See also CA 81-84; 73-76

Chaplin, Charlie
See Chaplin, Charles Spencer
See also DLB 44

Chapman, George 1559(?)-1634 ...... **LC 22**
See also DLB 62, 121

Chapman, Graham 1941-1989 ...... **CLC 21**
See also Monty Python
See also CA 116; 129; CANR 35

Chapman, John Jay 1862-1933 ..... **TCLC 7**
See also CA 104

Chapman, Walker
See Silverberg, Robert

Chappell, Fred (Davis) 1936-.... **CLC 40, 78**
See also CA 5-8R; CAAS 4; CANR 8, 33;
DLB 6, 105

Char, Rene(-Emile)
1907-1988 .... **CLC 9, 11, 14, 55**
See also CA 13-16R; 124; CANR 32;
MTCW

Charby, Jay
See Ellison, Harlan

Chardin, Pierre Teilhard de
See Teilhard de Chardin, (Marie Joseph)
Pierre

Charles I 1600-1649 .... **LC 13**

Charyn, Jerome 1937- .... **CLC 5, 8, 18**
See also CA 5-8R; CAAS 1; CANR 7;
DLBY 83; MTCW

Chase, Mary (Coyle) 1907-1981 ...... **DC 1**
See also CA 77-80; 105; SATA 17, 29

Chase, Mary Ellen 1887-1973 .... **CLC 2**
See also CA 13-16; 41-44R; CAP 1;
SATA 10

Chase, Nicholas
See Hyde, Anthony

Chateaubriand, Francois Rene de
1768-1848 .... **NCLC 3**
See also DLB 119

Chatterje, Sarat Chandra 1876-1936(?)
See Chatterji, Saratchandra
See also CA 109

Chatterji, Bankim Chandra
1838-1894 .... **NCLC 19**

Chatterji, Saratchandra .... **TCLC 13**
See also Chatterje, Sarat Chandra

Chatterton, Thomas 1752-1770 .... **LC 3**
See also DLB 109

Chatwin, (Charles) Bruce
1940-1989 .... **CLC 28, 57, 59**
See also AAYA 4; BEST 90:1; CA 85-88;
127

Chaucer, Daniel
See Ford, Ford Madox

Chaucer, Geoffrey
1340(?)-1400 .... **LC 17; DA**
See also CDBLB Before 1660

Chaviaras, Strates 1935-
See Haviaras, Stratis
See also CA 105

Chayefsky, Paddy .... **CLC 23**
See also Chayefsky, Sidney
See also DLB 7, 44; DLBY 81

Chayefsky, Sidney 1923-1981
See Chayefsky, Paddy
See also CA 9-12R; 104; CANR 18

Chedid, Andree 1920- .... **CLC 47**

Cheever, John
1912-1982 ...... **CLC 3, 7, 8, 11, 15, 25,**
64; DA; SSC 1; WLC
See also CA 5-8R; 106; CABS 1; CANR 5,
27; CDALB 1941-1968; DLB 2, 102;
DLBY 80, 82; MTCW

Cheever, Susan 1943-.......... **CLC 18, 48**
See also CA 103; CANR 27; DLBY 82

Chekhonte, Antosha
See Chekhov, Anton (Pavlovich)

Chekhov, Anton (Pavlovich)
1860-1904 .... **TCLC 3, 10, 31; DA;**
SSC 2; WLC
See also CA 104; 124

Chernyshevsky, Nikolay Gavrilovich
1828-1889 .... **NCLC 1**

Cherry, Carolyn Janice 1942-
See Cherryh, C. J.
See also CA 65-68; CANR 10

Cherryh, C. J. .... **CLC 35**
See also Cherry, Carolyn Janice
See also DLBY 80

Chesnutt, Charles W(addell)
1858-1932 .. **TCLC 5, 39; BLC 1; SSC 7**
See also BW; CA 106; 125; DLB 12, 50, 78;
MTCW

Chester, Alfred 1929(?)-1971....... **CLC 49**
See also CA 33-36R; DLB 130

Chesterton, G(ilbert) K(eith)
1874-1936 .... **TCLC 1, 6; SSC 1**
See also CA 104; 132; CDBLB 1914-1945;
DLB 10, 19, 34, 70, 98; MTCW;
SATA 27

Chiang Pin-chin 1904-1986
See Ding Ling
See also CA 118

Cohen, Matt 1942- . . . . CLC 19
See also CA 61-64; CAAS 18; CANR 40;
DLB 53

Cohen-Solal, Annie 19(?)- . . . . CLC 50

Colegate, Isabel 1931- . . . . CLC 36
See also CA 17-20R; CANR 8, 22; DLB 14;
MTCW

Coleman, Emmett
See Reed, Ishmael

Coleridge, Samuel Taylor
1772-1834 . . . . NCLC 9; DA; WLC
See also CDBLB 1789-1832; DLB 93, 107

Coleridge, Sara 1802-1852 . . . . . . NCLC 31

Coles, Don 1928- . . . . CLC 46
See also CA 115; CANR 38

Colette, (Sidonie-Gabrielle)
1873-1954 . . . . . . TCLC 1, 5, 16; SSC 10
See also CA 104; 131; DLB 65; MTCW

Collett, (Jacobine) Camilla (Wergeland)
1813-1895 . . . . NCLC 22

Collier, Christopher 1930- . . . . CLC 30
See also CA 33-36R; CANR 13, 33; JRDA;
MAICYA; SATA 16, 70

Collier, James L(incoln) 1928- . . . . . CLC 30
See also CA 9-12R; CANR 4, 33; JRDA;
MAICYA; SATA 8, 70

Collier, Jeremy 1650-1726 . . . . LC 6

Collins, Hunt
See Hunter, Evan

Collins, Linda 1931- . . . . CLC 44
See also CA 125

Collins, (William) Wilkie
1824-1889 . . . . NCLC 1, 18
See also CDBLB 1832-1890; DLB 18, 70

Collins, William 1721-1759 . . . . LC 4
See also DLB 109

Colman, George
See Glassco, John

Colt, Winchester Remington
See Hubbard, L(afayette) Ron(ald)

Colter, Cyrus 1910- . . . . CLC 58
See also BW; CA 65-68; CANR 10; DLB 33

Colton, James
See Hansen, Joseph

Colum, Padraic 1881-1972 . . . . CLC 28
See also CA 73-76; 33-36R; CANR 35;
MAICYA; MTCW; SATA 15

Colvin, James
See Moorcock, Michael (John)

Colwin, Laurie (E.)
1944-1992 . . . . CLC 5, 13, 23
See also CA 89-92; 139; CANR 20;
DLBY 80; MTCW

Comfort, Alex(ander) 1920- . . . . CLC 7
See also CA 1-4R; CANR 1

Comfort, Montgomery
See Campbell, (John) Ramsey

Compton-Burnett, I(vy)
1884(?)-1969 . . . . . . CLC 1, 3, 10, 15, 34
See also CA 1-4R; 25-28R; CANR 4;
DLB 36; MTCW

Comstock, Anthony 1844-1915 . . . . TCLC 13
See also CA 110

Conan Doyle, Arthur
See Doyle, Arthur Conan

Conde, Maryse . . . . CLC 52
See also Boucolon, Maryse

Condon, Richard (Thomas)
1915- . . . . CLC 4, 6, 8, 10, 45
See also BEST 90:3; CA 1-4R; CAAS 1;
CANR 2, 23; MTCW

Congreve, William
1670-1729 . . . LC 5, 21; DA; DC 2; WLC
See also CDBLB 1660-1789; DLB 39, 84

Connell, Evan S(helby), Jr.
1924- . . . . CLC 4, 6, 45
See also AAYA 7; CA 1-4R; CAAS 2;
CANR 2, 39; DLB 2; DLBY 81; MTCW

Connelly, Marc(us Cook)
1890-1980 . . . . CLC 7
See also CA 85-88; 102; CANR 30; DLB 7;
DLBY 80; SATA 25

Connor, Ralph . . . . TCLC 31
See also Gordon, Charles William
See also DLB 92

Conrad, Joseph
1857-1924 . . . . . . TCLC 1, 6, 13, 25, 43;
DA; SSC 9; WLC
See also CA 104; 131; CDBLB 1890-1914;
DLB 10, 34, 98; MTCW; SATA 27

Conrad, Robert Arnold
See Hart, Moss

Conroy, Pat 1945- . . . . CLC 30, 74
See also AAYA 8; AITN 1; CA 85-88;
CANR 24; DLB 6; MTCW

Constant (de Rebecque), (Henri) Benjamin
1767-1830 . . . . NCLC 6
See also DLB 119

Conybeare, Charles Augustus
See Eliot, T(homas) S(tearns)

Cook, Michael 1933- . . . . CLC 58
See also CA 93-96; DLB 53

Cook, Robin 1940- . . . . CLC 14
See also BEST 90:2; CA 108; 111;
CANR 41

Cook, Roy
See Silverberg, Robert

Cooke, Elizabeth 1948- . . . . CLC 55
See also CA 129

Cooke, John Esten 1830-1886 . . . . . NCLC 5
See also DLB 3

Cooke, John Estes
See Baum, L(yman) Frank

Cooke, M. E.
See Creasey, John

Cooke, Margaret
See Creasey, John

Cooney, Ray . . . . CLC 62

Cooper, Henry St. John
See Creasey, John

Cooper, J. California . . . . CLC 56
See also BW; CA 125

Cooper, James Fenimore
1789-1851 . . . . NCLC 1, 27
See also CDALB 1640-1865; DLB 3;
SATA 19

Coover, Robert (Lowell)
1932- . . . . CLC 3, 7, 15, 32, 46
See also CA 45-48; CANR 3, 37; DLB 2;
DLBY 81; MTCW

Copeland, Stewart (Armstrong)
1952- . . . . CLC 26
See also Police, The

Coppard, A(lfred) E(dgar)
1878-1957 . . . . TCLC 5
See also CA 114; YABC 1

Coppee, Francois 1842-1908 . . . . . . TCLC 25

Coppola, Francis Ford 1939- . . . . CLC 16
See also CA 77-80; CANR 40; DLB 44

Corbiere, Tristan 1845-1875 . . . . . NCLC 43

Corcoran, Barbara 1911- . . . . CLC 17
See also CA 21-24R; CAAS 2; CANR 11,
28; DLB 52; JRDA; SATA 3

Cordelier, Maurice
See Giraudoux, (Hippolyte) Jean

Corelli, Marie 1855-1924 . . . . TCLC 51
See also Mackay, Mary
See also DLB 34

Corman, Cid . . . . CLC 9
See also Corman, Sidney
See also CAAS 2; DLB 5

Corman, Sidney 1924-
See Corman, Cid
See also CA 85-88

Cormier, Robert (Edmund)
1925- . . . . CLC 12, 30; DA
See also AAYA 3; CA 1-4R; CANR 5, 23;
CDALB 1968-1988; CLR 12; DLB 52;
JRDA; MAICYA; MTCW; SATA 10, 45

Corn, Alfred 1943- . . . . CLC 33
See also CA 104; DLB 120; DLBY 80

Cornwell, David (John Moore)
1931- . . . . CLC 9, 15
See also le Carre, John
See also CA 5-8R; CANR 13, 33; MTCW

Corrigan, Kevin . . . . CLC 55

Corso, (Nunzio) Gregory 1930- . . . CLC 1, 11
See also CA 5-8R; CANR 41; DLB 5, 16;
MTCW

Cortazar, Julio
1914-1984 . . . . . . CLC 2, 3, 5, 10, 13, 15,
33, 34; HLC 1; SSC 7
See also CA 21-24R; CANR 12, 32;
DLB 113; HW; MTCW

Corwin, Cecil
See Kornbluth, C(yril) M.

Cosic, Dobrica 1921- . . . . CLC 14
See also CA 122; 138

Costain, Thomas B(ertram)
1885-1965 . . . . CLC 30
See also CA 5-8R; 25-28R; DLB 9

Costantini, Humberto
1924(?)-1987 . . . . CLC 49
See also CA 131; 122; HW

Costello, Elvis 1955- . . . . CLC 21

Cotter, Joseph S. Sr.
See Cotter, Joseph Seamon Sr.

Cotter, Joseph Seamon Sr.
1861-1949 . . . . TCLC 28; BLC 1
See also BW; CA 124; DLB 50

Couch, Arthur Thomas Quiller
See Quiller-Couch, Arthur Thomas

Coulton, James
See Hansen, Joseph

Couperus, Louis (Marie Anne)
1863-1923 .... TCLC 15
See also CA 115

Court, Wesli
See Turco, Lewis (Putnam)

Courtenay, Bryce 1933- .... CLC 59
See also CA 138

Courtney, Robert
See Ellison, Harlan

Cousteau, Jacques-Yves 1910- ...... CLC 30
See also CA 65-68; CANR 15; MTCW;
SATA 38

Coward, Noel (Peirce)
1899-1973 .... CLC 1, 9, 29, 51
See also AITN 1; CA 17-18; 41-44R;
CANR 35; CAP 2; CDBLB 1914-1945;
DLB 10; MTCW

Cowley, Malcolm 1898-1989 .... CLC 39
See also CA 5-8R; 128; CANR 3; DLB 4,
48; DLBY 81, 89; MTCW

Cowper, William 1731-1800...... NCLC 8
See also DLB 104, 109

Cox, William Trevor 1928- ... CLC 9, 14, 71
See also Trevor, William
See also CA 9-12R; CANR 4, 37; DLB 14;
MTCW

Cozzens, James Gould
1903-1978 .... CLC 1, 4, 11
See also CA 9-12R; 81-84; CANR 19;
CDALB 1941-1968; DLB 9; DLBD 2;
DLBY 84; MTCW

Crabbe, George 1754-1832...... NCLC 26
See also DLB 93

Craig, A. A.
See Anderson, Poul (William)

Craik, Dinah Maria (Mulock)
1826-1887 .... NCLC 38
See also DLB 35; MAICYA; SATA 34

Cram, Ralph Adams 1863-1942.... TCLC 45

Crane, (Harold) Hart
1899-1932 .... TCLC 2, 5; DA; PC 3;
WLC
See also CA 104; 127; CDALB 1917-1929;
DLB 4, 48; MTCW

Crane, R(onald) S(almon)
1886-1967 .... CLC 27
See also CA 85-88; DLB 63

Crane, Stephen (Townley)
1871-1900 .... TCLC 11, 17, 32; DA;
SSC 7; WLC
See also CA 109; 140; CDALB 1865-1917;
DLB 12, 54, 78; YABC 2

Crase, Douglas 1944- .... CLC 58
See also CA 106

Crashaw, Richard 1612(?)-1649...... LC 24
See also DLB 126

Craven, Margaret 1901-1980....... CLC 17
See also CA 103

Crawford, F(rancis) Marion
1854-1909 .... TCLC 10
See also CA 107; DLB 71

Crawford, Isabella Valancy
1850-1887 .... NCLC 12
See also DLB 92

Crayon, Geoffrey
See Irving, Washington

Creasey, John 1908-1973.......... CLC 11
See also CA 5-8R; 41-44R; CANR 8;
DLB 77; MTCW

Crebillon, Claude Prosper Jolyot de (fils)
1707-1777 .... LC 1

Credo
See Creasey, John

Creeley, Robert (White)
1926- ..... CLC 1, 2, 4, 8, 11, 15, 36, 78
See also CA 1-4R; CAAS 10; CANR 23, 43;
DLB 5, 16; MTCW

Crews, Harry (Eugene)
1935- .... CLC 6, 23, 49
See also AITN 1; CA 25-28R; CANR 20;
DLB 6; MTCW

Crichton, (John) Michael
1942- .... CLC 2, 6, 54
See also AAYA 10; AITN 2; CA 25-28R;
CANR 13, 40; DLBY 81; JRDA;
MTCW; SATA 9

Crispin, Edmund .... CLC 22
See also Montgomery, (Robert) Bruce
See also DLB 87

Cristofer, Michael 1945(?)- .... CLC 28
See also CA 110; DLB 7

Croce, Benedetto 1866-1952 ...... TCLC 37
See also CA 120

Crockett, David 1786-1836 .... NCLC 8
See also DLB 3, 11

Crockett, Davy
See Crockett, David

Croker, John Wilson 1780-1857 .. NCLC 10
See also DLB 110

Crommelynck, Fernand 1885-1970 .. CLC 75
See also CA 89-92

Cronin, A(rchibald) J(oseph)
1896-1981 .... CLC 32
See also CA 1-4R; 102; CANR 5; SATA 25,
47

Cross, Amanda
See Heilbrun, Carolyn G(old)

Crothers, Rachel 1878(?)-1958..... TCLC 19
See also CA 113; DLB 7

Croves, Hal
See Traven, B.

Crowfield, Christopher
See Stowe, Harriet (Elizabeth) Beecher

Crowley, Aleister................. TCLC 7
See also Crowley, Edward Alexander

Crowley, Edward Alexander 1875-1947
See Crowley, Aleister
See also CA 104

Crowley, John 1942-.............. CLC 57
See also CA 61-64; CANR 43; DLBY 82;
SATA 65

Crud
See Crumb, R(obert)

Crumarums
See Crumb, R(obert)

Crumb, R(obert) 1943-........... CLC 17
See also CA 106

Crumbum
See Crumb, R(obert)

Crumski
See Crumb, R(obert)

Crum the Bum
See Crumb, R(obert)

Crunk
See Crumb, R(obert)

Crustt
See Crumb, R(obert)

Cryer, Gretchen (Kiger) 1935-...... CLC 21
See also CA 114; 123

Csath, Geza 1887-1919.......... TCLC 13
See also CA 111

Cudlip, David 1933- .... CLC 34

Cullen, Countee
1903-1946 ..... TCLC 4, 37; BLC 1; DA
See also BW; CA 108; 124;
CDALB 1917-1929; DLB 4, 48, 51;
MTCW; SATA 18

Cum, R.
See Crumb, R(obert)

Cummings, Bruce F(rederick) 1889-1919
See Barbellion, W. N. P.
See also CA 123

Cummings, E(dward) E(stlin)
1894-1962 ...... CLC 1, 3, 8, 12, 15, 68;
DA; PC 5; WLC 2
See also CA 73-76; CANR 31;
CDALB 1929-1941; DLB 4, 48; MTCW

Cunha, Euclides (Rodrigues Pimenta) da
1866-1909 .... TCLC 24
See also CA 123

Cunningham, E. V.
See Fast, Howard (Melvin)

Cunningham, J(ames) V(incent)
1911-1985 .... CLC 3, 31
See also CA 1-4R; 115; CANR 1; DLB 5

Cunningham, Julia (Woolfolk)
1916- .... CLC 12
See also CA 9-12R; CANR 4, 19, 36;
JRDA; MAICYA; SAAS 2; SATA 1, 26

Cunningham, Michael 1952- .... CLC 34
See also CA 136

Cunninghame Graham, R(obert) B(ontine)
1852-1936 .... TCLC 19
See also Graham, R(obert) B(ontine)
Cunninghame
See also CA 119; DLB 98

Currie, Ellen 19(?)-.............. CLC 44

Curtin, Philip
See Lowndes, Marie Adelaide (Belloc)

Curtis, Price
See Ellison, Harlan

Cutrate, Joe
See Spiegelman, Art

Czaczkes, Shmuel Yosef
See Agnon, S(hmuel) Y(osef Halevi)

D. P.
See Wells, H(erbert) G(eorge)

Dabrowska, Maria (Szumska)
1889-1965 .... **CLC 15**
See also CA 106

Dabydeen, David 1955- .... **CLC 34**
See also BW; CA 125

Dacey, Philip 1939- .... **CLC 51**
See also CA 37-40R; CAAS 17; CANR 14,
32; DLB 105

Dagerman, Stig (Halvard)
1923-1954 .... **TCLC 17**
See also CA 117

Dahl, Roald 1916-1990..... **CLC 1, 6, 18, 79**
See also CA 1-4R; 133; CANR 6, 32, 37;
CLR 1, 7; JRDA; MAICYA; MTCW;
SATA 1, 26, 73; SATA-Obit 65

Dahlberg, Edward 1900-1977... **CLC 1, 7, 14**
See also CA 9-12R; 69-72; CANR 31;
DLB 48; MTCW

Dale, Colin.................... **TCLC 18**
See also Lawrence, T(homas) E(dward)

Dale, George E.
See Asimov, Isaac

Daly, Elizabeth 1878-1967........ **CLC 52**
See also CA 23-24; 25-28R; CAP 2

Daly, Maureen 1921- .... **CLC 17**
See also AAYA 5; CANR 37; JRDA;
MAICYA; SAAS 1; SATA 2

Daniel, Samuel 1562(?)-1619........ **LC 24**
See also DLB 62

Daniels, Brett
See Adler, Renata

Dannay, Frederic 1905-1982 .... **CLC 11**
See also Queen, Ellery
See also CA 1-4R; 107; CANR 1, 39;
MTCW

D'Annunzio, Gabriele
1863-1938 .... **TCLC 6, 40**
See also CA 104

d'Antibes, Germain
See Simenon, Georges (Jacques Christian)

Danvers, Dennis 1947-............ **CLC 70**

Danziger, Paula 1944- .... **CLC 21**
See also AAYA 4; CA 112; 115; CANR 37;
CLR 20; JRDA; MAICYA; SATA 30,
36, 63

Dario, Ruben 1867-1916 ... **TCLC 4; HLC 1**
See also CA 131; HW; MTCW

Darley, George 1795-1846........ **NCLC 2**
See also DLB 96

Daryush, Elizabeth 1887-1977.... **CLC 6, 19**
See also CA 49-52; CANR 3; DLB 20

Daudet, (Louis Marie) Alphonse
1840-1897 .... **NCLC 1**
See also DLB 123

Daumal, Rene 1908-1944........ **TCLC 14**
See also CA 114

Davenport, Guy (Mattison, Jr.)
1927- .... **CLC 6, 14, 38**
See also CA 33-36R; CANR 23; DLB 130

Davidson, Avram 1923-
See Queen, Ellery
See also CA 101; CANR 26; DLB 8

Davidson, Donald (Grady)
1893-1968 .... **CLC 2, 13, 19**
See also CA 5-8R; 25-28R; CANR 4;
DLB 45

Davidson, Hugh
See Hamilton, Edmond

Davidson, John 1857-1909....... **TCLC 24**
See also CA 118; DLB 19

Davidson, Sara 1943- .... **CLC 9**
See also CA 81-84

Davie, Donald (Alfred)
1922- .... **CLC 5, 8, 10, 31**
See also CA 1-4R; CAAS 3; CANR 1;
DLB 27; MTCW

Davies, Ray(mond Douglas) 1944- .. **CLC 21**
See also CA 116

Davies, Rhys 1903-1978.......... **CLC 23**
See also CA 9-12R; 81-84; CANR 4

Davies, (William) Robertson
1913- ..... **CLC 2, 7, 13, 25, 42, 75; DA;**
WLC
See also BEST 89:2; CA 33-36R; CANR 17,
42; DLB 68; MTCW

Davies, W(illiam) H(enry)
1871-1940 .... **TCLC 5**
See also CA 104; DLB 19

Davies, Walter C.
See Kornbluth, C(yril) M.

Davis, Angela (Yvonne) 1944-...... **CLC 77**
See also BW; CA 57-60; CANR 10

Davis, B. Lynch
See Bioy Casares, Adolfo; Borges, Jorge
Luis

Davis, Gordon
See Hunt, E(verette) Howard, Jr.

Davis, Harold Lenoir 1896-1960.... **CLC 49**
See also CA 89-92; DLB 9

Davis, Rebecca (Blaine) Harding
1831-1910 .... **TCLC 6**
See also CA 104; DLB 74

Davis, Richard Harding
1864-1916 .... **TCLC 24**
See also CA 114; DLB 12, 23, 78, 79

Davison, Frank Dalby 1893-1970 ... **CLC 15**
See also CA 116

Davison, Lawrence H.
See Lawrence, D(avid) H(erbert Richards)

Davison, Peter (Hubert) 1928- ..... **CLC 28**
See also CA 9-12R; CAAS 4; CANR 3, 43;
DLB 5

Davys, Mary 1674-1732............. **LC 1**
See also DLB 39

Dawson, Fielding 1930- .... **CLC 6**
See also CA 85-88; DLB 130

Dawson, Peter
See Faust, Frederick (Schiller)

Day, Clarence (Shepard, Jr.)
1874-1935 .... **TCLC 25**
See also CA 108; DLB 11

Day, Thomas 1748-1789............ **LC 1**
See also DLB 39; YABC 1

Day Lewis, C(ecil)
1904-1972 .... **CLC 1, 6, 10**
See also Blake, Nicholas
See also CA 13-16; 33-36R; CANR 34;
CAP 1; DLB 15, 20; MTCW

Dazai, Osamu .... **TCLC 11**
See also Tsushima, Shuji

de Andrade, Carlos Drummond
See Drummond de Andrade, Carlos

Deane, Norman
See Creasey, John

de Beauvoir, Simone (Lucie Ernestine Marie
Bertrand)
See Beauvoir, Simone (Lucie Ernestine
Marie Bertrand) de

de Brissac, Malcolm
See Dickinson, Peter (Malcolm)

de Chardin, Pierre Teilhard
See Teilhard de Chardin, (Marie Joseph)
Pierre

Dee, John 1527-1608 .... **LC 20**

Deer, Sandra 1940-............... **CLC 45**

De Ferrari, Gabriella .... **CLC 65**

Defoe, Daniel
1660(?)-1731 .... **LC 1; DA; WLC**
See also CDBLB 1660-1789; DLB 39, 95,
101; JRDA; MAICYA; SATA 22

de Gourmont, Remy
See Gourmont, Remy de

de Hartog, Jan 1914-............. **CLC 19**
See also CA 1-4R; CANR 1

de Hostos, E. M.
See Hostos (y Bonilla), Eugenio Maria de

de Hostos, Eugenio M.
See Hostos (y Bonilla), Eugenio Maria de

Deighton, Len .... **CLC 4, 7, 22, 46**
See also Deighton, Leonard Cyril
See also AAYA 6; BEST 89:2;
CDBLB 1960 to Present; DLB 87

Deighton, Leonard Cyril 1929-
See Deighton, Len
See also CA 9-12R; CANR 19, 33; MTCW

Dekker, Thomas 1572(?)-1632....... **LC 22**
See also CDBLB Before 1660; DLB 62

de la Mare, Walter (John)
1873-1956 .. **TCLC 4, 53; SSC 14; WLC**
See also CDBLB 1914-1945; CLR 23;
DLB 19; SATA 16

Delaney, Franey
See O'Hara, John (Henry)

Delaney, Shelagh 1939-........... **CLC 29**
See also CA 17-20R; CANR 30;
CDBLB 1960 to Present; DLB 13;
MTCW

Delany, Mary (Granville Pendarves)
1700-1788 .... **LC 12**

Delany, Samuel R(ay, Jr.)
1942- .... **CLC 8, 14, 38; BLC 1**
See also BW; CA 81-84; CANR 27, 43;
DLB 8, 33; MTCW

De La Ramee, (Marie) Louise 1839-1908
See Ouida
See also SATA 20

de la Roche, Mazo 1879-1961 ...... **CLC 14**
See also CA 85-88; CANR 30; DLB 68;
SATA 64

Delbanco, Nicholas (Franklin)
1942- .... **CLC 6, 13**
See also CA 17-20R; CAAS 2; CANR 29;
DLB 6

del Castillo, Michel 1933- .... **CLC 38**
See also CA 109

Deledda, Grazia (Cosima)
1875(?)-1936 .... **TCLC 23**
See also CA 123

Delibes, Miguel .... **CLC 8, 18**
See also Delibes Setien, Miguel

Delibes Setien, Miguel 1920-
See Delibes, Miguel
See also CA 45-48; CANR 1, 32; HW;
MTCW

DeLillo, Don
1936- ..... **CLC 8, 10, 13, 27, 39, 54, 76**
See also BEST 89:1; CA 81-84; CANR 21;
DLB 6; MTCW

de Lisser, H. G.
See De Lisser, Herbert George
See also DLB 117

De Lisser, Herbert George
1878-1944 .... **TCLC 12**
See also de Lisser, H. G.
See also CA 109

Deloria, Vine (Victor), Jr. 1933- .... **CLC 21**
See also CA 53-56; CANR 5, 20; MTCW;
SATA 21

Del Vecchio, John M(ichael)
1947- .... **CLC 29**
See also CA 110; DLBD 9

de Man, Paul (Adolph Michel)
1919-1983 .... **CLC 55**
See also CA 128; 111; DLB 67; MTCW

De Marinis, Rick 1934- .... **CLC 54**
See also CA 57-60; CANR 9, 25

Demby, William 1922- ..... **CLC 53; BLC 1**
See also BW; CA 81-84; DLB 33

Demijohn, Thom
See Disch, Thomas M(ichael)

de Montherlant, Henry (Milon)
See Montherlant, Henry (Milon) de

de Natale, Francine
See Malzberg, Barry N(athaniel)

Denby, Edwin (Orr) 1903-1983 ..... **CLC 48**
See also CA 138; 110

Denis, Julio
See Cortazar, Julio

Denmark, Harrison
See Zelazny, Roger (Joseph)

Dennis, John 1658-1734 .... **LC 11**
See also DLB 101

Dennis, Nigel (Forbes) 1912-1989 .... **CLC 8**
See also CA 25-28R; 129; DLB 13, 15;
MTCW

De Palma, Brian (Russell) 1940- .... **CLC 20**
See also CA 109

De Quincey, Thomas 1785-1859 ... **NCLC 4**
See also CDBLB 1789-1832; DLB 110

Deren, Eleanora 1908(?)-1961
See Deren, Maya
See also CA 111

Deren, Maya .... **CLC 16**
See also Deren, Eleanora

Derleth, August (William)
1909-1971 .... **CLC 31**
See also CA 1-4R; 29-32R; CANR 4;
DLB 9; SATA 5

de Routisie, Albert
See Aragon, Louis

Derrida, Jacques 1930- .... **CLC 24**
See also CA 124; 127

Derry Down Derry
See Lear, Edward

Dersonnes, Jacques
See Simenon, Georges (Jacques Christian)

Desai, Anita 1937- .... **CLC 19, 37**
See also CA 81-84; CANR 33; MTCW;
SATA 63

de Saint-Luc, Jean
See Glassco, John

de Saint Roman, Arnaud
See Aragon, Louis

Descartes, Rene 1596-1650 .... **LC 20**

De Sica, Vittorio 1901(?)-1974 ..... **CLC 20**
See also CA 117

Desnos, Robert 1900-1945 .... **TCLC 22**
See also CA 121

Destouches, Louis-Ferdinand
1894-1961 .... **CLC 9, 15**
See also Celine, Louis-Ferdinand
See also CA 85-88; CANR 28; MTCW

Deutsch, Babette 1895-1982 .... **CLC 18**
See also CA 1-4R; 108; CANR 4; DLB 45;
SATA 1, 33

Devenant, William 1606-1649 .... **LC 13**

Devkota, Laxmiprasad
1909-1959 .... **TCLC 23**
See also CA 123

De Voto, Bernard (Augustine)
1897-1955 .... **TCLC 29**
See also CA 113; DLB 9

De Vries, Peter
1910-1993 .... **CLC 1, 2, 3, 7, 10, 28, 46**
See also CA 17-20R; 142; CANR 41;
DLB 6; DLBY 82; MTCW

Dexter, Martin
See Faust, Frederick (Schiller)

Dexter, Pete 1943- .... **CLC 34, 55**
See also BEST 89:2; CA 127; 131; MTCW

Diamano, Silmang
See Senghor, Leopold Sedar

Diamond, Neil 1941- .... **CLC 30**
See also CA 108

di Bassetto, Corno
See Shaw, George Bernard

Dick, Philip K(indred)
1928-1982 .... **CLC 10, 30, 72**
See also CA 49-52; 106; CANR 2, 16;
DLB 8; MTCW

Dickens, Charles (John Huffam)
1812-1870 ...... **NCLC 3, 8, 18, 26; DA**
See also CDBLB 1832-1890; DLB 21, 55,
70; JRDA; MAICYA; SATA 15

Dickey, James (Lafayette)
1923- .... **CLC 1, 2, 4, 7, 10, 15, 47**
See also AITN 1, 2; CA 9-12R; CABS 2;
CANR 10; CDALB 1968-1988; DLB 5;
DLBD 7; DLBY 82; MTCW

Dickey, William 1928- .... **CLC 3, 28**
See also CA 9-12R; CANR 24; DLB 5

Dickinson, Charles 1951- .... **CLC 49**
See also CA 128

Dickinson, Emily (Elizabeth)
1830-1886 .. **NCLC 21; DA; PC 1; WLC**
See also CDALB 1865-1917; DLB 1;
SATA 29

Dickinson, Peter (Malcolm)
1927- .... **CLC 12, 35**
See also AAYA 9; CA 41-44R; CANR 31;
CLR 29; DLB 87; JRDA; MAICYA;
SATA 5, 62

Dickson, Carr
See Carr, John Dickson

Dickson, Carter
See Carr, John Dickson

Didion, Joan 1934- ..... **CLC 1, 3, 8, 14, 32**
See also AITN 1; CA 5-8R; CANR 14;
CDALB 1968-1988; DLB 2; DLBY 81,
86; MTCW

Dietrich, Robert
See Hunt, E(verette) Howard, Jr.

Dillard, Annie 1945- .... **CLC 9, 60**
See also AAYA 6; CA 49-52; CANR 3, 43;
DLBY 80; MTCW; SATA 10

Dillard, R(ichard) H(enry) W(ilde)
1937- .... **CLC 5**
See also CA 21-24R; CAAS 7; CANR 10;
DLB 5

Dillon, Eilis 1920- .... **CLC 17**
See also CA 9-12R; CAAS 3; CANR 4, 38;
CLR 26; MAICYA; SATA 2, 74

Dimont, Penelope
See Mortimer, Penelope (Ruth)

Dinesen, Isak .... **CLC 10, 29; SSC 7**
See also Blixen, Karen (Christentze
Dinesen)

Ding Ling .... **CLC 68**
See also Chiang Pin-chin

Disch, Thomas M(ichael) 1940- ... **CLC 7, 36**
See also CA 21-24R; CAAS 4; CANR 17,
36; CLR 18; DLB 8; MAICYA; MTCW;
SAAS 15; SATA 54

Disch, Tom
See Disch, Thomas M(ichael)

d'Isly, Georges
See Simenon, Georges (Jacques Christian)

Disraeli, Benjamin 1804-1881 .. **NCLC 2, 39**
See also DLB 21, 55

Ditcum, Steve
See Crumb, R(obert)

Dixon, Paige
See Corcoran, Barbara

Dixon, Stephen 1936- .... **CLC 52**
See also CA 89-92; CANR 17, 40; DLB 130

Dobell, Sydney Thompson
1824-1874 . . . . **NCLC 43**
See also DLB 32

Doblin, Alfred . . . . **TCLC 13**
See also Doeblin, Alfred

Dobrolyubov, Nikolai Alexandrovich
1836-1861 . . . . **NCLC 5**

Dobyns, Stephen 1941- . . . . **CLC 37**
See also CA 45-48; CANR 2, 18

Doctorow, E(dgar) L(aurence)
1931- . . . . . **CLC 6, 11, 15, 18, 37, 44, 65**
See also AITN 2; BEST 89:3; CA 45-48;
CANR 2, 33; CDALB 1968-1988; DLB 2,
28; DLBY 80; MTCW

Dodgson, Charles Lutwidge 1832-1898
See Carroll, Lewis
See also CLR 2; DA; MAICYA; YABC 2

Dodson, Owen (Vincent)
1914-1983 . . . . **CLC 79; BLC 1**
See also BW; CA 65-68; 110; CANR 24;
DLB 76

Doeblin, Alfred 1878-1957 . . . . **TCLC 13**
See also Doblin, Alfred
See also CA 110; 141; DLB 66

Doerr, Harriet 1910- . . . . **CLC 34**
See also CA 117; 122

Domecq, H(onorio) Bustos
See Bioy Casares, Adolfo; Borges, Jorge
Luis

Domini, Rey
See Lorde, Audre (Geraldine)

Dominique
See Proust, (Valentin-Louis-George-Eugene-)
Marcel

Don, A
See Stephen, Leslie

Donaldson, Stephen R. 1947- . . . . **CLC 46**
See also CA 89-92; CANR 13

Donleavy, J(ames) P(atrick)
1926- . . . . **CLC 1, 4, 6, 10, 45**
See also AITN 2; CA 9-12R; CANR 24;
DLB 6; MTCW

Donne, John
1572-1631 . . . . **LC 10, 24; DA; PC 1**
See also CDBLB Before 1660; DLB 121

Donnell, David 1939(?)- . . . . **CLC 34**

Donoso (Yanez), Jose
1924- . . . . **CLC 4, 8, 11, 32; HLC 1**
See also CA 81-84; CANR 32; DLB 113;
HW; MTCW

Donovan, John 1928-1992 . . . . **CLC 35**
See also CA 97-100; 137; CLR 3;
MAICYA; SATA 29

Don Roberto
See Cunninghame Graham, R(obert)
B(ontine)

Doolittle, Hilda
1886-1961 . . . . . **CLC 3, 8, 14, 31, 34, 73;
DA; PC 5; WLC**
See also H. D.
See also CA 97-100; CANR 35; DLB 4, 45;
MTCW

Dorfman, Ariel 1942- . . . **CLC 48, 77; HLC 1**
See also CA 124; 130; HW

Dorn, Edward (Merton) 1929- . . . **CLC 10, 18**
See also CA 93-96; CANR 42; DLB 5

Dorsan, Luc
See Simenon, Georges (Jacques Christian)

Dorsange, Jean
See Simenon, Georges (Jacques Christian)

Dos Passos, John (Roderigo)
1896-1970 . . . . . . **CLC 1, 4, 8, 11, 15, 25,
34; DA; WLC**
See also CA 1-4R; 29-32R; CANR 3;
CDALB 1929-1941; DLB 4, 9; DLBD 1;
MTCW

Dossage, Jean
See Simenon, Georges (Jacques Christian)

Dostoevsky, Fedor Mikhailovich
1821-1881 . . . . . . **NCLC 2, 7, 21, 33, 43;
DA; SSC 2; WLC**

Doughty, Charles M(ontagu)
1843-1926 . . . . **TCLC 27**
See also CA 115; DLB 19, 57

Douglas, Ellen
See Haxton, Josephine Ayres

Douglas, Gavin 1475(?)-1522 . . . . **LC 20**

Douglas, Keith 1920-1944 . . . . **TCLC 40**
See also DLB 27

Douglas, Leonard
See Bradbury, Ray (Douglas)

Douglas, Michael
See Crichton, (John) Michael

Douglass, Frederick
1817(?)-1895 . . . . . **NCLC 7; BLC 1; DA;
WLC**
See also CDALB 1640-1865; DLB 1, 43, 50,
79; SATA 29

Dourado, (Waldomiro Freitas) Autran
1926- . . . . **CLC 23, 60**
See also CA 25-28R; CANR 34

Dourado, Waldomiro Autran
See Dourado, (Waldomiro Freitas) Autran

Dove, Rita (Frances)
1952- . . . . **CLC 50, 81; PC 6**
See also BW; CA 109; CANR 27, 42;
DLB 120

Dowell, Coleman 1925-1985 . . . . **CLC 60**
See also CA 25-28R; 117; CANR 10;
DLB 130

Dowson, Ernest Christopher
1867-1900 . . . . **TCLC 4**
See also CA 105; DLB 19, 135

Doyle, A. Conan
See Doyle, Arthur Conan

Doyle, Arthur Conan
1859-1930 . . . . . . **TCLC 7; DA; SSC 12;
WLC**
See also CA 104; 122; CDBLB 1890-1914;
DLB 18, 70; MTCW; SATA 24

Doyle, Conan 1859-1930
See Doyle, Arthur Conan

Doyle, John
See Graves, Robert (von Ranke)

Doyle, Roddy 1958(?)- . . . . **CLC 81**

Doyle, Sir A. Conan
See Doyle, Arthur Conan

Doyle, Sir Arthur Conan
See Doyle, Arthur Conan

Dr. A
See Asimov, Isaac; Silverstein, Alvin

Drabble, Margaret
1939- . . . . **CLC 2, 3, 5, 8, 10, 22, 53**
See also CA 13-16R; CANR 18, 35;
CDBLB 1960 to Present; DLB 14;
MTCW; SATA 48

Drapier, M. B.
See Swift, Jonathan

Drayham, James
See Mencken, H(enry) L(ouis)

Drayton, Michael 1563-1631 . . . . **LC 8**

Dreadstone, Carl
See Campbell, (John) Ramsey

Dreiser, Theodore (Herman Albert)
1871-1945 . . . . **TCLC 10, 18, 35; DA;
WLC**
See also CA 106; 132; CDALB 1865-1917;
DLB 9, 12, 102; DLBD 1; MTCW

Drexler, Rosalyn 1926- . . . . **CLC 2, 6**
See also CA 81-84

Dreyer, Carl Theodor 1889-1968 . . . . **CLC 16**
See also CA 116

Drieu la Rochelle, Pierre(-Eugene)
1893-1945 . . . . **TCLC 21**
See also CA 117; DLB 72

Drop Shot
See Cable, George Washington

Droste-Hulshoff, Annette Freiin von
1797-1848 . . . . **NCLC 3**
See also DLB 133

Drummond, Walter
See Silverberg, Robert

Drummond, William Henry
1854-1907 . . . . **TCLC 25**
See also DLB 92

Drummond de Andrade, Carlos
1902-1987 . . . . **CLC 18**
See also Andrade, Carlos Drummond de
See also CA 132; 123

Drury, Allen (Stuart) 1918- . . . . **CLC 37**
See also CA 57-60; CANR 18

Dryden, John
1631-1700 . . . **LC 3, 21; DA; DC 3; WLC**
See also CDBLB 1660-1789; DLB 80, 101,
131

Duberman, Martin 1930- . . . . **CLC 8**
See also CA 1-4R; CANR 2

Dubie, Norman (Evans) 1945- . . . . . . **CLC 36**
See also CA 69-72; CANR 12; DLB 120

Du Bois, W(illiam) E(dward) B(urghardt)
1868-1963 . . . . **CLC 1, 2, 13, 64; BLC 1;
DA; WLC**
See also BW; CA 85-88; CANR 34;
CDALB 1865-1917; DLB 47, 50, 91;
MTCW; SATA 42

Dubus, Andre 1936- . . . . **CLC 13, 36**
See also CA 21-24R; CANR 17; DLB 130

Duca Minimo
See D'Annunzio, Gabriele

Ducharme, Rejean 1941- . . . . **CLC 74**
See also DLB 60

Duclos, Charles Pinot 1704-1772 ..... **LC 1**

Dudek, Louis 1918- .... **CLC 11, 19**
See also CA 45-48; CAAS 14; CANR 1;
DLB 88

Duerrenmatt, Friedrich
.... **CLC 1, 4, 8, 11, 15, 43**
See also Duerrenmatt, Friedrich
See also DLB 69, 124

Duerrenmatt, Friedrich
1921-1990 ...... **CLC 1, 4, 8, 11, 15, 43**
See also Duerrenmatt, Friedrich
See also CA 17-20R; CANR 33; DLB 69,
124; MTCW

Duffy, Bruce (?)- .... **CLC 50**

Duffy, Maureen 1933- .... **CLC 37**
See also CA 25-28R; CANR 33; DLB 14;
MTCW

Dugan, Alan 1923- .... **CLC 2, 6**
See also CA 81-84; DLB 5

du Gard, Roger Martin
See Martin du Gard, Roger

Duhamel, Georges 1884-1966 .... **CLC 8**
See also CA 81-84; 25-28R; CANR 35;
DLB 65; MTCW

Dujardin, Edouard (Emile Louis)
1861-1949 .... **TCLC 13**
See also CA 109; DLB 123

Dumas, Alexandre (Davy de la Pailleterie)
1802-1870 .... **NCLC 11; DA; WLC**
See also DLB 119; SATA 18

Dumas, Alexandre
1824-1895 .... **NCLC 9; DC 1**

Dumas, Claudine
See Malzberg, Barry N(athaniel)

Dumas, Henry L. 1934-1968 ..... **CLC 6, 62**
See also BW; CA 85-88; DLB 41

du Maurier, Daphne
1907-1989 .... **CLC 6, 11, 59**
See also CA 5-8R; 128; CANR 6; MTCW;
SATA 27, 60

Dunbar, Paul Laurence
1872-1906 .... **TCLC 2, 12; BLC 1; DA;
PC 5; SSC 8; WLC**
See also BW; CA 104; 124;
CDALB 1865-1917; DLB 50, 54, 78;
SATA 34

Dunbar, William 1460(?)-1530(?) .... **LC 20**

Duncan, Lois 1934- .... **CLC 26**
See also AAYA 4; CA 1-4R; CANR 2, 23,
36; CLR 29; JRDA; MAICYA; SAAS 2;
SATA 1, 36, 75

Duncan, Robert (Edward)
1919-1988 .... **CLC 1, 2, 4, 7, 15, 41, 55;
PC 2**
See also CA 9-12R; 124; CANR 28; DLB 5,
16; MTCW

Dunlap, William 1766-1839 .... **NCLC 2**
See also DLB 30, 37, 59

Dunn, Douglas (Eaglesham)
1942- .... **CLC 6, 40**
See also CA 45-48; CANR 2, 33; DLB 40;
MTCW

Dunn, Katherine (Karen) 1945- .... **CLC 71**
See also CA 33-36R

Dunn, Stephen 1939- .... **CLC 36**
See also CA 33-36R; CANR 12; DLB 105

Dunne, Finley Peter 1867-1936.... **TCLC 28**
See also CA 108; DLB 11, 23

Dunne, John Gregory 1932-........ **CLC 28**
See also CA 25-28R; CANR 14; DLBY 80

**Dunsany, Edward John Moreton Drax
Plunkett** 1878-1957
See Dunsany, Lord; Lord Dunsany
See also CA 104; DLB 10

Dunsany, Lord.................... **TCLC 2**
See also Dunsany, Edward John Moreton
Drax Plunkett
See also DLB 77

du Perry, Jean
See Simenon, Georges (Jacques Christian)

Durang, Christopher (Ferdinand)
1949- .... **CLC 27, 38**
See also CA 105

Duras, Marguerite
1914- ...... **CLC 3, 6, 11, 20, 34, 40, 68**
See also CA 25-28R; DLB 83; MTCW

Durban, (Rosa) Pam 1947-........ **CLC 39**
See also CA 123

Durcan, Paul 1944- .... **CLC 43, 70**
See also CA 134

Durrell, Lawrence (George)
1912-1990 .... **CLC 1, 4, 6, 8, 13, 27, 41**
See also CA 9-12R; 132; CANR 40;
CDBLB 1945-1960; DLB 15, 27;
DLBY 90; MTCW

Dutt, Toru 1856-1877.......... **NCLC 29**

Dwight, Timothy 1752-1817...... **NCLC 13**
See also DLB 37

Dworkin, Andrea 1946- .... **CLC 43**
See also CA 77-80; CANR 16, 39; MTCW

Dwyer, Deanna
See Koontz, Dean R(ay)

Dwyer, K. R.
See Koontz, Dean R(ay)

Dylan, Bob 1941- ...... **CLC 3, 4, 6, 12, 77**
See also CA 41-44R; DLB 16

Eagleton, Terence (Francis) 1943-
See Eagleton, Terry
See also CA 57-60; CANR 7, 23; MTCW

Eagleton, Terry .... **CLC 63**
See also Eagleton, Terence (Francis)

Early, Jack
See Scoppettone, Sandra

East, Michael
See West, Morris L(anglo)

Eastaway, Edward
See Thomas, (Philip) Edward

Eastlake, William (Derry) 1917-..... **CLC 8**
See also CA 5-8R; CAAS 1; CANR 5;
DLB 6

Eberhart, Richard (Ghormley)
1904- .... **CLC 3, 11, 19, 56**
See also CA 1-4R; CANR 2;
CDALB 1941-1968; DLB 48; MTCW

Eberstadt, Fernanda 1960-........ **CLC 39**
See also CA 136

Echegaray (y Eizaguirre), Jose (Maria Waldo)
1832-1916 .... **TCLC 4**
See also CA 104; CANR 32; HW; MTCW

Echeverria, (Jose) Esteban (Antonino)
1805-1851 .... **NCLC 18**

Echo
See Proust, (Valentin-Louis-George-Eugene-)
Marcel

Eckert, Allan W. 1931- .... **CLC 17**
See also CA 13-16R; CANR 14; SATA 27,
29

Eckhart, Meister 1260(?)-1328(?) .. **CMLC 9**
See also DLB 115

Eckmar, F. R.
See de Hartog, Jan

Eco, Umberto 1932-........... **CLC 28, 60**
See also BEST 90:1; CA 77-80; CANR 12,
33; MTCW

Eddison, E(ric) R(ucker)
1882-1945 .... **TCLC 15**
See also CA 109

Edel, (Joseph) Leon 1907-...... **CLC 29, 34**
See also CA 1-4R; CANR 1, 22; DLB 103

Eden, Emily 1797-1869 .... **NCLC 10**

Edgar, David 1948-............... **CLC 42**
See also CA 57-60; CANR 12; DLB 13;
MTCW

Edgerton, Clyde (Carlyle) 1944- .... **CLC 39**
See also CA 118; 134

Edgeworth, Maria 1767-1849...... **NCLC 1**
See also DLB 116; SATA 21

Edmonds, Paul
See Kuttner, Henry

Edmonds, Walter D(umaux) 1903- .. **CLC 35**
See also CA 5-8R; CANR 2; DLB 9;
MAICYA; SAAS 4; SATA 1, 27

Edmondson, Wallace
See Ellison, Harlan

Edson, Russell .... **CLC 13**
See also CA 33-36R

Edwards, G(erald) B(asil)
1899-1976 .... **CLC 25**
See also CA 110

Edwards, Gus 1939- .... **CLC 43**
See also CA 108

Edwards, Jonathan 1703-1758.... **LC 7; DA**
See also DLB 24

Efron, Marina Ivanovna Tsvetaeva
See Tsvetaeva (Efron), Marina (Ivanovna)

Ehle, John (Marsden, Jr.) 1925-.... **CLC 27**
See also CA 9-12R

Ehrenbourg, Ilya (Grigoryevich)
See Ehrenburg, Ilya (Grigoryevich)

Ehrenburg, Ilya (Grigoryevich)
1891-1967 .... **CLC 18, 34, 62**
See also CA 102; 25-28R

Ehrenburg, Ilyo (Grigoryevich)
See Ehrenburg, Ilya (Grigoryevich)

Eich, Guenter 1907-1972 .... **CLC 15**
See also CA 111; 93-96; DLB 69, 124

Eichendorff, Joseph Freiherr von
1788-1857 .... **NCLC 8**
See also DLB 90

Eigner, Larry. CLC 9
 See also Eigner, Laurence (Joel)
 See also DLB 5

Eigner, Laurence (Joel) 1927-
 See Eigner, Larry
 See also CA 9-12R; CANR 6

Eiseley, Loren Corey 1907-1977 . . . . . CLC 7
 See also AAYA 5; CA 1-4R; 73-76;
 CANR 6

Eisenstadt, Jill 1963- . . . . CLC 50
 See also CA 140

Eisner, Simon
 See Kornbluth, C(yril) M.

Ekeloef, (Bengt) Gunnar
 1907-1968 . . . . CLC 27
 See also Ekelof, (Bengt) Gunnar
 See also CA 123; 25-28R

Ekelof, (Bengt) Gunnar. . . . . CLC 27
 See also Ekeloef, (Bengt) Gunnar

Ekwensi, C. O. D.
 See Ekwensi, Cyprian (Odiatu Duaka)

Ekwensi, Cyprian (Odiatu Duaka)
 1921- . . . . CLC 4; BLC 1
 See also BW; CA 29-32R; CANR 18, 42;
 DLB 117; MTCW; SATA 66

Elaine. . . . . TCLC 18
 See also Leverson, Ada

El Crummo
 See Crumb, R(obert)

Elia
 See Lamb, Charles

Eliade, Mircea 1907-1986 . . . . CLC 19
 See also CA 65-68; 119; CANR 30; MTCW

Eliot, A. D.
 See Jewett, (Theodora) Sarah Orne

Eliot, Alice
 See Jewett, (Theodora) Sarah Orne

Eliot, Dan
 See Silverberg, Robert

Eliot, George
 1819-1880 . . . . NCLC 4, 13, 23, 41; DA;
 WLC
 See also CDBLB 1832-1890; DLB 21, 35, 55

Eliot, John 1604-1690 . . . . LC 5
 See also DLB 24

Eliot, T(homas) S(tearns)
 1888-1965 . . . . . CLC 1, 2, 3, 6, 9, 10, 13,
 15, 24, 34, 41, 55, 57; DA; PC 5; WLC 2
 See also CA 5-8R; 25-28R; CANR 41;
 CDALB 1929-1941; DLB 7, 10, 45, 63;
 DLBY 88; MTCW

Elizabeth 1866-1941 . . . . TCLC 41

Elkin, Stanley L(awrence)
 1930- . . . CLC 4, 6, 9, 14, 27, 51; SSC 12
 See also CA 9-12R; CANR 8; DLB 2, 28;
 DLBY 80; MTCW

Elledge, Scott. . . . . CLC 34

Elliott, Don
 See Silverberg, Robert

Elliott, George P(aul) 1918-1980. . . . . CLC 2
 See also CA 1-4R; 97-100; CANR 2

Elliott, Janice 1931- . . . . CLC 47
 See also CA 13-16R; CANR 8, 29; DLB 14

Elliott, Sumner Locke 1917-1991 . . . CLC 38
 See also CA 5-8R; 134; CANR 2, 21

Elliott, William
 See Bradbury, Ray (Douglas)

Ellis, A. E. . . . . CLC 7

Ellis, Alice Thomas. . . . . CLC 40
 See also Haycraft, Anna

Ellis, Bret Easton 1964- . . . . CLC 39, 71
 See also AAYA 2; CA 118; 123

Ellis, (Henry) Havelock
 1859-1939 . . . . TCLC 14
 See also CA 109

Ellis, Landon
 See Ellison, Harlan

Ellis, Trey 1962- . . . . CLC 55

Ellison, Harlan
 1934- . . . . CLC 1, 13, 42; SSC 14
 See also CA 5-8R; CANR 5; DLB 8;
 MTCW

Ellison, Ralph (Waldo)
 1914- . . . . CLC 1, 3, 11, 54; BLC 1; DA;
 WLC
 See also BW; CA 9-12R; CANR 24;
 CDALB 1941-1968; DLB 2, 76; MTCW

Ellmann, Lucy (Elizabeth) 1956- . . . . CLC 61
 See also CA 128

Ellmann, Richard (David)
 1918-1987 . . . . CLC 50
 See also BEST 89:2; CA 1-4R; 122;
 CANR 2, 28; DLB 103; DLBY 87;
 MTCW

Elman, Richard 1934- . . . . CLC 19
 See also CA 17-20R; CAAS 3

Elron
 See Hubbard, L(afayette) Ron(ald)

Eluard, Paul. . . . . TCLC 7, 41
 See also Grindel, Eugene

Elyot, Sir Thomas 1490(?)-1546 . . . . . LC 11

Elytis, Odysseus 1911- . . . . CLC 15, 49
 See also CA 102; MTCW

Emecheta, (Florence Onye) Buchi
 1944- . . . . CLC 14, 48; BLC 2
 See also BW; CA 81-84; CANR 27;
 DLB 117; MTCW; SATA 66

Emerson, Ralph Waldo
 1803-1882 . . . . . . NCLC 1, 38; DA; WLC
 See also CDALB 1640-1865; DLB 1, 59, 73

Eminescu, Mihail 1850-1889 . . . . . NCLC 33

Empson, William
 1906-1984 . . . . . . CLC 3, 8, 19, 33, 34
 See also CA 17-20R; 112; CANR 31;
 DLB 20; MTCW

Enchi Fumiko (Ueda) 1905-1986. . . . CLC 31
 See also CA 129; 121

Ende, Michael (Andreas Helmuth)
 1929- . . . . CLC 31
 See also CA 118; 124; CANR 36; CLR 14;
 DLB 75; MAICYA; SATA 42, 61

Endo, Shusaku 1923- . . . . . CLC 7, 14, 19, 54
 See also CA 29-32R; CANR 21; MTCW

Engel, Marian 1933-1985. . . . . CLC 36
 See also CA 25-28R; CANR 12; DLB 53

Engelhardt, Frederick
 See Hubbard, L(afayette) Ron(ald)

Enright, D(ennis) J(oseph)
 1920- . . . . CLC 4, 8, 31
 See also CA 1-4R; CANR 1, 42; DLB 27;
 SATA 25

Enzensberger, Hans Magnus
 1929- . . . . CLC 43
 See also CA 116; 119

Ephron, Nora 1941- . . . . CLC 17, 31
 See also AITN 2; CA 65-68; CANR 12, 39

Epsilon
 See Betjeman, John

Epstein, Daniel Mark 1948- . . . . CLC 7
 See also CA 49-52; CANR 2

Epstein, Jacob 1956- . . . . CLC 19
 See also CA 114

Epstein, Joseph 1937-. . . . . CLC 39
 See also CA 112; 119

Epstein, Leslie 1938- . . . . CLC 27
 See also CA 73-76; CAAS 12; CANR 23

Equiano, Olaudah
 1745(?)-1797 . . . . LC 16; BLC 2
 See also DLB 37, 50

Erasmus, Desiderius 1469(?)-1536. . . . LC 16

Erdman, Paul E(mil) 1932- . . . . CLC 25
 See also AITN 1; CA 61-64; CANR 13, 43

Erdrich, Louise 1954- . . . . CLC 39, 54
 See also AAYA 10; BEST 89:1; CA 114;
 CANR 41; MTCW

Erenburg, Ilya (Grigoryevich)
 See Ehrenburg, Ilya (Grigoryevich)

Erickson, Stephen Michael 1950-
 See Erickson, Steve
 See also CA 129

Erickson, Steve . . . . CLC 64
 See also Erickson, Stephen Michael

Ericson, Walter
 See Fast, Howard (Melvin)

Eriksson, Buntel
 See Bergman, (Ernst) Ingmar

Eschenbach, Wolfram von
 See Wolfram von Eschenbach

Eseki, Bruno
 See Mphahlele, Ezekiel

Esenin, Sergei (Alexandrovich)
 1895-1925 . . . . TCLC 4
 See also CA 104

Eshleman, Clayton 1935- . . . . CLC 7
 See also CA 33-36R; CAAS 6; DLB 5

Espriella, Don Manuel Alvarez
 See Southey, Robert

Espriu, Salvador 1913-1985 . . . . CLC 9
 See also CA 115; DLB 134

Espronceda, Jose de 1808-1842 . . . NCLC 39

Esse, James
 See Stephens, James

Esterbrook, Tom
 See Hubbard, L(afayette) Ron(ald)

Estleman, Loren D. 1952- . . . . CLC 48
 See also CA 85-88; CANR 27; MTCW

Eugenides, Jeffrey 1960(?)- . . . . CLC 81

Euripides c. 485B.C.-406B.C. . . . . DC 4
 See also DA

Evan, Evin
See Faust, Frederick (Schiller)

Evans, Evan
See Faust, Frederick (Schiller)

Evans, Marian
See Eliot, George

Evans, Mary Ann
See Eliot, George

Evarts, Esther
See Benson, Sally

Everett, Percival
See Everett, Percival L.

Everett, Percival L. 1956- .... **CLC 57**
See also CA 129

Everson, R(onald) G(ilmour)
1903- .... **CLC 27**
See also CA 17-20R; DLB 88

Everson, William (Oliver)
1912- .... **CLC 1, 5, 14**
See also CA 9-12R; CANR 20; DLB 5, 16;
MTCW

Evtushenko, Evgenii Aleksandrovich
See Yevtushenko, Yevgeny (Alexandrovich)

Ewart, Gavin (Buchanan)
1916- .... **CLC 13, 46**
See also CA 89-92; CANR 17; DLB 40;
MTCW

Ewers, Hanns Heinz 1871-1943 ... **TCLC 12**
See also CA 109

Ewing, Frederick R.
See Sturgeon, Theodore (Hamilton)

Exley, Frederick (Earl)
1929-1992 .... **CLC 6, 11**
See also AITN 2; CA 81-84; 138; DLBY 81

Eynhardt, Guillermo
See Quiroga, Horacio (Sylvestre)

Ezekiel, Nissim 1924- .... **CLC 61**
See also CA 61-64

Ezekiel, Tish O'Dowd 1943- .... **CLC 34**
See also CA 129

Fadeyev, A.
See Bulgya, Alexander Alexandrovich

Fadeyev, Alexander .... **TCLC 53**
See also Bulgya, Alexander Alexandrovich

Fagen, Donald 1948- .... **CLC 26**

Fainzilberg, Ilya Arnoldovich 1897-1937
See Ilf, Ilya
See also CA 120

Fair, Ronald L. 1932- .... **CLC 18**
See also BW; CA 69-72; CANR 25; DLB 33

Fairbairns, Zoe (Ann) 1948- .... **CLC 32**
See also CA 103; CANR 21

Falco, Gian
See Papini, Giovanni

Falconer, James
See Kirkup, James

Falconer, Kenneth
See Kornbluth, C(yril) M.

Falkland, Samuel
See Heijermans, Herman

Fallaci, Oriana 1930- .... **CLC 11**
See also CA 77-80; CANR 15; MTCW

Faludy, George 1913- .... **CLC 42**
See also CA 21-24R

Faludy, Gyoergy
See Faludy, George

Fanon, Frantz 1925-1961 ... **CLC 74; BLC 2**
See also BW; CA 116; 89-92

Fanshawe, Ann .... **LC 11**

Fante, John (Thomas) 1911-1983 ... **CLC 60**
See also CA 69-72; 109; CANR 23;
DLB 130; DLBY 83

Farah, Nuruddin 1945- ..... **CLC 53; BLC 2**
See also CA 106; DLB 125

Fargue, Leon-Paul 1876(?)-1947 ... **TCLC 11**
See also CA 109

Farigoule, Louis
See Romains, Jules

Farina, Richard 1936(?)-1966 .... **CLC 9**
See also CA 81-84; 25-28R

Farley, Walter (Lorimer)
1915-1989 .... **CLC 17**
See also CA 17-20R; CANR 8, 29; DLB 22;
JRDA; MAICYA; SATA 2, 43

Farmer, Philip Jose 1918- .... **CLC 1, 19**
See also CA 1-4R; CANR 4, 35; DLB 8;
MTCW

Farquhar, George 1677-1707 .... **LC 21**
See also DLB 84

Farrell, J(ames) G(ordon)
1935-1979 .... **CLC 6**
See also CA 73-76; 89-92; CANR 36;
DLB 14; MTCW

Farrell, James T(homas)
1904-1979 .... **CLC 1, 4, 8, 11, 66**
See also CA 5-8R; 89-92; CANR 9; DLB 4,
9, 86; DLBD 2; MTCW

Farren, Richard J.
See Betjeman, John

Farren, Richard M.
See Betjeman, John

Fassbinder, Rainer Werner
1946-1982 .... **CLC 20**
See also CA 93-96; 106; CANR 31

Fast, Howard (Melvin) 1914- ...... **CLC 23**
See also CA 1-4R; CAAS 18; CANR 1, 33;
DLB 9; SATA 7

Faulcon, Robert
See Holdstock, Robert P.

Faulkner, William (Cuthbert)
1897-1962 ..... **CLC 1, 3, 6, 8, 9, 11, 14,
18, 28, 52, 68; DA; SSC 1; WLC**
See also AAYA 7; CA 81-84; CANR 33;
CDALB 1929-1941; DLB 9, 11, 44, 102;
DLBD 2; DLBY 86; MTCW

Fauset, Jessie Redmon
1884(?)-1961 ...... **CLC 19, 54; BLC 2**
See also BW; CA 109; DLB 51

Faust, Frederick (Schiller)
1892-1944(?) .... **TCLC 49**
See also CA 108

Faust, Irvin 1924- .... **CLC 8**
See also CA 33-36R; CANR 28; DLB 2, 28;
DLBY 80

Fawkes, Guy
See Benchley, Robert (Charles)

Fearing, Kenneth (Flexner)
1902-1961 .... **CLC 51**
See also CA 93-96; DLB 9

Fecamps, Elise
See Creasey, John

Federman, Raymond 1928- ...... **CLC 6, 47**
See also CA 17-20R; CAAS 8; CANR 10,
43; DLBY 80

Federspiel, J(uerg) F. 1931- .... **CLC 42**

Feiffer, Jules (Ralph) 1929- .... **CLC 2, 8, 64**
See also AAYA 3; CA 17-20R; CANR 30;
DLB 7, 44; MTCW; SATA 8, 61

Feige, Hermann Albert Otto Maximilian
See Traven, B.

Fei-Kan, Li
See Li Fei-kan

Feinberg, David B. 1956- .... **CLC 59**
See also CA 135

Feinstein, Elaine 1930- .... **CLC 36**
See also CA 69-72; CAAS 1; CANR 31;
DLB 14, 40; MTCW

Feldman, Irving (Mordecai) 1928- .... **CLC 7**
See also CA 1-4R; CANR 1

Fellini, Federico 1920-1993 ..... **CLC 16**
See also CA 65-68; CANR 33

Felsen, Henry Gregor 1916- .... **CLC 17**
See also CA 1-4R; CANR 1; SAAS 2;
SATA 1

Fenton, James Martin 1949- .... **CLC 32**
See also CA 102; DLB 40

Ferber, Edna 1887-1968 .... **CLC 18**
See also AITN 1; CA 5-8R; 25-28R; DLB 9,
28, 86; MTCW; SATA 7

Ferguson, Helen
See Kavan, Anna

Ferguson, Samuel 1810-1886 ..... **NCLC 33**
See also DLB 32

Ferling, Lawrence
See Ferlinghetti, Lawrence (Monsanto)

Ferlinghetti, Lawrence (Monsanto)
1919(?)- .... **CLC 2, 6, 10, 27; PC 1**
See also CA 5-8R; CANR 3, 41;
CDALB 1941-1968; DLB 5, 16; MTCW

Fernandez, Vicente Garcia Huidobro
See Huidobro Fernandez, Vicente Garcia

Ferrer, Gabriel (Francisco Victor) Miro
See Miro (Ferrer), Gabriel (Francisco
Victor)

Ferrier, Susan (Edmonstone)
1782-1854 .... **NCLC 8**
See also DLB 116

Ferrigno, Robert 1948(?)- .... **CLC 65**
See also CA 140

Feuchtwanger, Lion 1884-1958 ..... **TCLC 3**
See also CA 104; DLB 66

Feydeau, Georges (Leon Jules Marie)
1862-1921 .... **TCLC 22**
See also CA 113

Ficino, Marsilio 1433-1499 .... **LC 12**

Fiedeler, Hans
See Doeblin, Alfred

Fiedler, Leslie A(aron)
   1917- . . . . **CLC 4, 13, 24**
   See also CA 9-12R; CANR 7; DLB 28, 67;
   MTCW

Field, Andrew 1938- . . . . **CLC 44**
   See also CA 97-100; CANR 25

Field, Eugene 1850-1895 . . . . **NCLC 3**
   See also DLB 23, 42; MAICYA; SATA 16

Field, Gans T.
   See Wellman, Manly Wade

Field, Michael . . . . **TCLC 43**

Field, Peter
   See Hobson, Laura Z(ametkin)

Fielding, Henry
   1707-1754 . . . . **LC 1; DA; WLC**
   See also CDBLB 1660-1789; DLB 39, 84,
   101

Fielding, Sarah 1710-1768 . . . . **LC 1**
   See also DLB 39

Fierstein, Harvey (Forbes) 1954- . . . **CLC 33**
   See also CA 123; 129

Figes, Eva 1932- . . . . **CLC 31**
   See also CA 53-56; CANR 4; DLB 14

Finch, Robert (Duer Claydon)
   1900- . . . . **CLC 18**
   See also CA 57-60; CANR 9, 24; DLB 88

Findley, Timothy 1930- . . . . **CLC 27**
   See also CA 25-28R; CANR 12, 42;
   DLB 53

Fink, William
   See Mencken, H(enry) L(ouis)

Firbank, Louis 1942-
   See Reed, Lou
   See also CA 117

Firbank, (Arthur Annesley) Ronald
   1886-1926 . . . . **TCLC 1**
   See also CA 104; DLB 36

Fisher, M(ary) F(rances) K(ennedy)
   1908-1992 . . . . **CLC 76**
   See also CA 77-80; 138

Fisher, Roy 1930- . . . . **CLC 25**
   See also CA 81-84; CAAS 10; CANR 16;
   DLB 40

Fisher, Rudolph
   1897-1934 . . . . **TCLC 11; BLC 2**
   See also BW; CA 107; 124; DLB 51, 102

Fisher, Vardis (Alvero) 1895-1968 . . . . **CLC 7**
   See also CA 5-8R; 25-28R; DLB 9

Fiske, Tarleton
   See Bloch, Robert (Albert)

Fitch, Clarke
   See Sinclair, Upton (Beall)

Fitch, John IV
   See Cormier, Robert (Edmund)

Fitgerald, Penelope 1916- . . . . **CLC 61**

Fitzgerald, Captain Hugh
   See Baum, L(yman) Frank

FitzGerald, Edward 1809-1883 . . . . **NCLC 9**
   See also DLB 32

Fitzgerald, F(rancis) Scott (Key)
   1896-1940 . . . . . **TCLC 1, 6, 14, 28; DA;**
   SSC 6; WLC
   See also AITN 1; CA 110; 123;
   CDALB 1917-1929; DLB 4, 9, 86;
   DLBD 1; DLBY 81; MTCW

Fitzgerald, Penelope 1916- . . . . . . **CLC 19, 51**
   See also CA 85-88; CAAS 10; DLB 14

Fitzgerald, Robert (Stuart)
   1910-1985 . . . . **CLC 39**
   See also CA 1-4R; 114; CANR 1; DLBY 80

FitzGerald, Robert D(avid)
   1902-1987 . . . . **CLC 19**
   See also CA 17-20R

Fitzgerald, Zelda (Sayre)
   1900-1948 . . . . **TCLC 52**
   See also CA 117; 126; DLBY 84

Flanagan, Thomas (James Bonner)
   1923- . . . . **CLC 25, 52**
   See also CA 108; DLBY 80; MTCW

Flaubert, Gustave
   1821-1880 . . . . **NCLC 2, 10, 19; DA;**
   SSC 11; WLC
   See also DLB 119

Flecker, (Herman) James Elroy
   1884-1915 . . . . **TCLC 43**
   See also CA 109; DLB 10, 19

Fleming, Ian (Lancaster)
   1908-1964 . . . . **CLC 3, 30**
   See also CA 5-8R; CDBLB 1945-1960;
   DLB 87; MTCW; SATA 9

Fleming, Thomas (James) 1927- . . . . **CLC 37**
   See also CA 5-8R; CANR 10; SATA 8

Fletcher, John Gould 1886-1950 . . . **TCLC 35**
   See also CA 107; DLB 4, 45

Fleur, Paul
   See Pohl, Frederik

Flooglebuckle, Al
   See Spiegelman, Art

Flying Officer X
   See Bates, H(erbert) E(rnest)

Fo, Dario 1926- . . . . **CLC 32**
   See also CA 116; 128; MTCW

Fogarty, Jonathan Titulescu Esq.
   See Farrell, James T(homas)

Folke, Will
   See Bloch, Robert (Albert)

Follett, Ken(neth Martin) 1949- . . . . **CLC 18**
   See also AAYA 6; BEST 89:4; CA 81-84;
   CANR 13, 33; DLB 87; DLBY 81;
   MTCW

Fontane, Theodor 1819-1898 . . . . . **NCLC 26**
   See also DLB 129

Foote, Horton 1916- . . . . **CLC 51**
   See also CA 73-76; CANR 34; DLB 26

Foote, Shelby 1916- . . . . **CLC 75**
   See also CA 5-8R; CANR 3; DLB 2, 17

Forbes, Esther 1891-1967 . . . . **CLC 12**
   See also CA 13-14; 25-28R; CAP 1;
   CLR 27; DLB 22; JRDA; MAICYA;
   SATA 2

Forche, Carolyn (Louise) 1950- . . . . . **CLC 25**
   See also CA 109; 117; DLB 5

Ford, Elbur
   See Hibbert, Eleanor Alice Burford

Ford, Ford Madox
   1873-1939 . . . . **TCLC 1, 15, 39**
   See also CA 104; 132; CDBLB 1914-1945;
   DLB 34, 98; MTCW

Ford, John 1895-1973 . . . . **CLC 16**
   See also CA 45-48

Ford, Richard 1944- . . . . **CLC 46**
   See also CA 69-72; CANR 11

Ford, Webster
   See Masters, Edgar Lee

Foreman, Richard 1937- . . . . **CLC 50**
   See also CA 65-68; CANR 32

Forester, C(ecil) S(cott)
   1899-1966 . . . . **CLC 35**
   See also CA 73-76; 25-28R; SATA 13

Forez
   See Mauriac, Francois (Charles)

Forman, James Douglas 1932- . . . . . **CLC 21**
   See also CA 9-12R; CANR 4, 19, 42;
   JRDA; MAICYA; SATA 8, 70

Fornes, Maria Irene 1930- . . . . . . **CLC 39, 61**
   See also CA 25-28R; CANR 28; DLB 7;
   HW; MTCW

Forrest, Leon 1937- . . . . **CLC 4**
   See also BW; CA 89-92; CAAS 7;
   CANR 25; DLB 33

Forster, E(dward) M(organ)
   1879-1970 . . . . . **CLC 1, 2, 3, 4, 9, 10, 13,**
   15, 22, 45, 77; DA; WLC
   See also AAYA 2; CA 13-14; 25-28R;
   CAP 1; CDBLB 1914-1945; DLB 34, 98;
   DLBD 10; MTCW; SATA 57

Forster, John 1812-1876 . . . . **NCLC 11**

Forsyth, Frederick 1938- . . . . . . **CLC 2, 5, 36**
   See also BEST 89:4; CA 85-88; CANR 38;
   DLB 87; MTCW

Forten, Charlotte L. . . . . **TCLC 16; BLC 2**
   See also Grimke, Charlotte L(ottie) Forten
   See also DLB 50

Foscolo, Ugo 1778-1827 . . . . **NCLC 8**

Fosse, Bob . . . . **CLC 20**
   See also Fosse, Robert Louis

Fosse, Robert Louis 1927-1987
   See Fosse, Bob
   See also CA 110; 123

Foster, Stephen Collins
   1826-1864 . . . . **NCLC 26**

Foucault, Michel
   1926-1984 . . . . **CLC 31, 34, 69**
   See also CA 105; 113; CANR 34; MTCW

Fouque, Friedrich (Heinrich Karl) de la Motte
   1777-1843 . . . . **NCLC 2**
   See also DLB 90

Fournier, Henri Alban 1886-1914
   See Alain-Fournier
   See also CA 104

Fournier, Pierre 1916- . . . . **CLC 11**
   See also Gascar, Pierre
   See also CA 89-92; CANR 16, 40

Fowles, John
   1926- . . . . **CLC 1, 2, 3, 4, 6, 9, 10, 15, 33**
   See also CA 5-8R; CANR 25; CDBLB 1960
   to Present; DLB 14; MTCW; SATA 22

Fox, Paula 1923-............... **CLC 2, 8**
See also AAYA 3; CA 73-76; CANR 20,
36; CLR 1; DLB 52; JRDA; MAICYA;
MTCW; SATA 17, 60

Fox, William Price (Jr.) 1926-..... **CLC 22**
See also CA 17-20R; CANR 11; DLB 2;
DLBY 81

Foxe, John 1516(?)-1587 .... **LC 14**

Frame, Janet .... **CLC 2, 3, 6, 22, 66**
See also Clutha, Janet Paterson Frame

France, Anatole .... **TCLC 9**
See also Thibault, Jacques Anatole Francois
See also DLB 123

Francis, Claude 19(?)- .... **CLC 50**

Francis, Dick 1920-......... **CLC 2, 22, 42**
See also AAYA 5; BEST 89:3; CA 5-8R;
CANR 9, 42; CDBLB 1960 to Present;
DLB 87; MTCW

Francis, Robert (Churchill)
1901-1987 .... **CLC 15**
See also CA 1-4R; 123; CANR 1

Frank, Anne(lies Marie)
1929-1945 .... **TCLC 17; DA; WLC**
See also CA 113; 133; MTCW; SATA 42

Frank, Elizabeth 1945-............ **CLC 39**
See also CA 121; 126

Franklin, Benjamin
See Hasek, Jaroslav (Matej Frantisek)

Franklin, (Stella Maraia Sarah) Miles
1879-1954 .... **TCLC 7**
See also CA 104

Fraser, Antonia (Pakenham)
1932- .... **CLC 32**
See also CA 85-88; MTCW; SATA 32

Fraser, George MacDonald 1925-.... **CLC 7**
See also CA 45-48; CANR 2

Fraser, Sylvia 1935-.............. **CLC 64**
See also CA 45-48; CANR 1, 16

Frayn, Michael 1933-...... **CLC 3, 7, 31, 47**
See also CA 5-8R; CANR 30; DLB 13, 14;
MTCW

Fraze, Candida (Merrill) 1945-..... **CLC 50**
See also CA 126

Frazer, J(ames) G(eorge)
1854-1941 .... **TCLC 32**
See also CA 118

Frazer, Robert Caine
See Creasey, John

Frazer, Sir James George
See Frazer, J(ames) G(eorge)

Frazier, Ian 1951-................ **CLC 46**
See also CA 130

Frederic, Harold 1856-1898...... **NCLC 10**
See also DLB 12, 23

Frederick, John
See Faust, Frederick (Schiller)

Frederick the Great 1712-1786 ...... **LC 14**

Fredro, Aleksander 1793-1876..... **NCLC 8**

Freeling, Nicolas 1927- .... **CLC 38**
See also CA 49-52; CAAS 12; CANR 1, 17;
DLB 87

Freeman, Douglas Southall
1886-1953 .... **TCLC 11**
See also CA 109; DLB 17

Freeman, Judith 1946-........... **CLC 55**

Freeman, Mary Eleanor Wilkins
1852-1930 .... **TCLC 9; SSC 1**
See also CA 106; DLB 12, 78

Freeman, R(ichard) Austin
1862-1943 .... **TCLC 21**
See also CA 113; DLB 70

French, Marilyn 1929-...... **CLC 10, 18, 60**
See also CA 69-72; CANR 3, 31; MTCW

French, Paul
See Asimov, Isaac

Freneau, Philip Morin 1752-1832.. **NCLC 1**
See also DLB 37, 43

Freud, Sigmund 1856-1939 ...... **TCLC 52**
See also CA 115; 133; MTCW

Friedan, Betty (Naomi) 1921-...... **CLC 74**
See also CA 65-68; CANR 18; MTCW

Friedman, B(ernard) H(arper)
1926- .... **CLC 7**
See also CA 1-4R; CANR 3

Friedman, Bruce Jay 1930-.... **CLC 3, 5, 56**
See also CA 9-12R; CANR 25; DLB 2, 28

Friel, Brian 1929-........... **CLC 5, 42, 59**
See also CA 21-24R; CANR 33; DLB 13;
MTCW

Friis-Baastad, Babbis Ellinor
1921-1970 .... **CLC 12**
See also CA 17-20R; 134; SATA 7

Frisch, Max (Rudolf)
1911-1991 ..... **CLC 3, 9, 14, 18, 32, 44**
See also CA 85-88; 134; CANR 32;
DLB 69, 124; MTCW

Fromentin, Eugene (Samuel Auguste)
1820-1876 .... **NCLC 10**
See also DLB 123

Frost, Frederick
See Faust, Frederick (Schiller)

Frost, Robert (Lee)
1874-1963 .... **CLC 1, 3, 4, 9, 10, 13, 15,
26, 34, 44; DA; PC 1; WLC**
See also CA 89-92; CANR 33;
CDALB 1917-1929; DLB 54; DLBD 7;
MTCW; SATA 14

Froude, James Anthony
1818-1894 .... **NCLC 43**
See also DLB 18, 57

Froy, Herald
See Waterhouse, Keith (Spencer)

Fry, Christopher 1907-....... **CLC 2, 10, 14**
See also CA 17-20R; CANR 9, 30; DLB 13;
MTCW; SATA 66

Frye, (Herman) Northrop
1912-1991 .... **CLC 24, 70**
See also CA 5-8R; 133; CANR 8, 37;
DLB 67, 68; MTCW

Fuchs, Daniel 1909-1993 .... **CLC 8, 22**
See also CA 81-84; 142; CAAS 5;
CANR 40; DLB 9, 26, 28

Fuchs, Daniel 1934-.............. **CLC 34**
See also CA 37-40R; CANR 14

Fuentes, Carlos
1928-...... **CLC 3, 8, 10, 13, 22, 41, 60;
DA; HLC 1; WLC**
See also AAYA 4; AITN 2; CA 69-72;
CANR 10, 32; DLB 113; HW; MTCW

Fuentes, Gregorio Lopez y
See Lopez y Fuentes, Gregorio

Fugard, (Harold) Athol
1932-.... **CLC 5, 9, 14, 25, 40, 80; DC 3**
See also CA 85-88; CANR 32; MTCW

Fugard, Sheila 1932-............. **CLC 48**
See also CA 125

Fuller, Charles (H., Jr.)
1939-...........**CLC 25; BLC 2; DC 1**
See also BW; CA 108; 112; DLB 38;
MTCW

Fuller, John (Leopold) 1937-....... **CLC 62**
See also CA 21-24R; CANR 9; DLB 40

Fuller, Margaret .... **NCLC 5**
See also Ossoli, Sarah Margaret (Fuller
marchesa d')

Fuller, Roy (Broadbent)
1912-1991 .... **CLC 4, 28**
See also CA 5-8R; 135; CAAS 10; DLB 15,
20

Fulton, Alice 1952-............... **CLC 52**
See also CA 116

Furphy, Joseph 1843-1912........ **TCLC 25**

Fussell, Paul 1924-.............. **CLC 74**
See also BEST 90:1; CA 17-20R; CANR 8,
21, 35; MTCW

Futabatei, Shimei 1864-1909...... **TCLC 44**

Futrelle, Jacques 1875-1912 ...... **TCLC 19**
See also CA 113

G. B. S.
See Shaw, George Bernard

Gaboriau, Emile 1835-1873...... **NCLC 14**

Gadda, Carlo Emilio 1893-1973 .... **CLC 11**
See also CA 89-92

Gaddis, William
1922-........ **CLC 1, 3, 6, 8, 10, 19, 43**
See also CA 17-20R; CANR 21; DLB 2;
MTCW

Gaines, Ernest J(ames)
1933-........... **CLC 3, 11, 18; BLC 2**
See also AITN 1; BW; CA 9-12R; CANR 6,
24, 42; CDALB 1968-1988; DLB 2, 33;
DLBY 80; MTCW

Gaitskill, Mary 1954-............. **CLC 69**
See also CA 128

Galdos, Benito Perez
See Perez Galdos, Benito

Gale, Zona 1874-1938 .... **TCLC 7**
See also CA 105; DLB 9, 78

Galeano, Eduardo (Hughes) 1940-... **CLC 72**
See also CA 29-32R; CANR 13, 32; HW

Galiano, Juan Valera y Alcala
See Valera y Alcala-Galiano, Juan

Gallagher, Tess 1943-.......... **CLC 18, 63**
See also CA 106; DLB 120

Gallant, Mavis
1922-........... **CLC 7, 18, 38; SSC 5**
See also CA 69-72; CANR 29; DLB 53;
MTCW

Gallant, Roy A(rthur) 1924-....... **CLC 17**
See also CA 5-8R; CANR 4, 29; CLR 30;
MAICYA; SATA 4, 68

Gallico, Paul (William) 1897-1976 ... **CLC 2**
See also AITN 1; CA 5-8R; 69-72;
CANR 23; DLB 9; MAICYA; SATA 13

Gallup, Ralph
See Whitemore, Hugh (John)

Galsworthy, John
1867-1933 .... **TCLC 1, 45; DA; WLC 2**
See also CA 104; 141; CDBLB 1890-1914;
DLB 10, 34, 98

Galt, John 1779-1839 .... **NCLC 1**
See also DLB 99, 116

Galvin, James 1951- .... **CLC 38**
See also CA 108; CANR 26

Gamboa, Federico 1864-1939 ..... **TCLC 36**

Gann, Ernest Kellogg 1910-1991 .... **CLC 23**
See also AITN 1; CA 1-4R; 136; CANR 1

Garcia, Cristina 1958- .... **CLC 76**
See also CA 141

Garcia Lorca, Federico
1898-1936 .... **TCLC 1, 7, 49; DA;
DC 2; HLC 2; PC 3; WLC**
See also CA 104; 131; DLB 108; HW;
MTCW

Garcia Marquez, Gabriel (Jose)
1928- .... **CLC 2, 3, 8, 10, 15, 27, 47, 55;
DA; HLC 1; SSC 8; WLC**
See also Marquez, Gabriel (Jose) Garcia
See also AAYA 3; BEST 89:1, 90:4;
CA 33-36R; CANR 10, 28; DLB 113;
HW; MTCW

Gard, Janice
See Latham, Jean Lee

Gard, Roger Martin du
See Martin du Gard, Roger

Gardam, Jane 1928- .... **CLC 43**
See also CA 49-52; CANR 2, 18, 33;
CLR 12; DLB 14; MAICYA; MTCW;
SAAS 9; SATA 28, 39

Gardner, Herb .... **CLC 44**

Gardner, John (Champlin), Jr.
1933-1982 ..... **CLC 2, 3, 5, 7, 8, 10, 18,
28, 34; SSC 7**
See also AITN 1; CA 65-68; 107;
CANR 33; DLB 2; DLBY 82; MTCW;
SATA 31, 40

Gardner, John (Edmund) 1926- ..... **CLC 30**
See also CA 103; CANR 15; MTCW

Gardner, Noel
See Kuttner, Henry

Gardons, S. S.
See Snodgrass, W(illiam) D(e Witt)

Garfield, Leon 1921- .... **CLC 12**
See also AAYA 8; CA 17-20R; CANR 38,
41; CLR 21; JRDA; MAICYA; SATA 1,
32

Garland, (Hannibal) Hamlin
1860-1940 .... **TCLC 3**
See also CA 104; DLB 12, 71, 78

Garneau, (Hector de) Saint-Denys
1912-1943 .... **TCLC 13**
See also CA 111; DLB 88

Garner, Alan 1934- .... **CLC 17**
See also CA 73-76; CANR 15; CLR 20;
MAICYA; MTCW; SATA 18, 69

Garner, Hugh 1913-1979 .... **CLC 13**
See also CA 69-72; CANR 31; DLB 68

Garnett, David 1892-1981 .... **CLC 3**
See also CA 5-8R; 103; CANR 17; DLB 34

Garos, Stephanie
See Katz, Steve

Garrett, George (Palmer)
1929- .... **CLC 3, 11, 51**
See also CA 1-4R; CAAS 5; CANR 1, 42;
DLB 2, 5, 130; DLBY 83

Garrick, David 1717-1779 .... **LC 15**
See also DLB 84

Garrigue, Jean 1914-1972 .... **CLC 2, 8**
See also CA 5-8R; 37-40R; CANR 20

Garrison, Frederick
See Sinclair, Upton (Beall)

Garth, Will
See Hamilton, Edmond; Kuttner, Henry

Garvey, Marcus (Moziah, Jr.)
1887-1940 .... **TCLC 41; BLC 2**
See also BW; CA 120; 124

Gary, Romain .... **CLC 25**
See also Kacew, Romain
See also DLB 83

Gascar, Pierre .... **CLC 11**
See also Fournier, Pierre

Gascoyne, David (Emery) 1916- .... **CLC 45**
See also CA 65-68; CANR 10, 28; DLB 20;
MTCW

Gaskell, Elizabeth Cleghorn
1810-1865 .... **NCLC 5**
See also CDBLB 1832-1890; DLB 21

Gass, William H(oward)
1924- ... **CLC 1, 2, 8, 11, 15, 39; SSC 12**
See also CA 17-20R; CANR 30; DLB 2;
MTCW

Gasset, Jose Ortega y
See Ortega y Gasset, Jose

Gautier, Theophile 1811-1872 ..... **NCLC 1**
See also DLB 119

Gawsworth, John
See Bates, H(erbert) E(rnest)

Gaye, Marvin (Penze) 1939-1984 ... **CLC 26**
See also CA 112

Gebler, Carlo (Ernest) 1954- .... **CLC 39**
See also CA 119; 133

Gee, Maggie (Mary) 1948- .... **CLC 57**
See also CA 130

Gee, Maurice (Gough) 1931- .... **CLC 29**
See also CA 97-100; SATA 46

Gelbart, Larry (Simon) 1923- ... **CLC 21, 61**
See also CA 73-76

Gelber, Jack 1932- .... **CLC 1, 6, 14, 79**
See also CA 1-4R; CANR 2; DLB 7

Gellhorn, Martha Ellis 1908- ... **CLC 14, 60**
See also CA 77-80; DLBY 82

Genet, Jean
1910-1986 ... **CLC 1, 2, 5, 10, 14, 44, 46**
See also CA 13-16R; CANR 18; DLB 72;
DLBY 86; MTCW

Gent, Peter 1942- .... **CLC 29**
See also AITN 1; CA 89-92; DLBY 82

Gentlewoman in New England, A
See Bradstreet, Anne

Gentlewoman in Those Parts, A
See Bradstreet, Anne

George, Jean Craighead 1919- ...... **CLC 35**
See also AAYA 8; CA 5-8R; CANR 25;
CLR 1; DLB 52; JRDA; MAICYA;
SATA 2, 68

George, Stefan (Anton)
1868-1933 .... **TCLC 2, 14**
See also CA 104

Georges, Georges Martin
See Simenon, Georges (Jacques Christian)

Gerhardi, William Alexander
See Gerhardie, William Alexander

Gerhardie, William Alexander
1895-1977 .... **CLC 5**
See also CA 25-28R; 73-76; CANR 18;
DLB 36

Gerstler, Amy 1956- .... **CLC 70**

Gertler, T. .... **CLC 34**
See also CA 116; 121

Ghalib 1797-1869 .... **NCLC 39**

Ghelderode, Michel de
1898-1962 .... **CLC 6, 11**
See also CA 85-88; CANR 40

Ghiselin, Brewster 1903- .... **CLC 23**
See also CA 13-16R; CAAS 10; CANR 13

Ghose, Zulfikar 1935- .... **CLC 42**
See also CA 65-68

Ghosh, Amitav 1956- .... **CLC 44**

Giacosa, Giuseppe 1847-1906 ...... **TCLC 7**
See also CA 104

Gibb, Lee
See Waterhouse, Keith (Spencer)

Gibbon, Lewis Grassic .... **TCLC 4**
See also Mitchell, James Leslie

Gibbons, Kaye 1960- .... **CLC 50**

Gibran, Kahlil 1883-1931 .... **TCLC 1, 9**
See also CA 104

Gibson, William 1914- .... **CLC 23; DA**
See also CA 9-12R; CANR 9, 42; DLB 7;
SATA 66

Gibson, William (Ford) 1948- ... **CLC 39, 63**
See also CA 126; 133

Gide, Andre (Paul Guillaume)
1869-1951 .... **TCLC 5, 12, 36; DA;
SSC 13; WLC**
See also CA 104; 124; DLB 65; MTCW

Gifford, Barry (Colby) 1946- .... **CLC 34**
See also CA 65-68; CANR 9, 30, 40

Gilbert, W(illiam) S(chwenck)
1836-1911 .... **TCLC 3**
See also CA 104; SATA 36

Gilbreth, Frank B., Jr. 1911- .... **CLC 17**
See also CA 9-12R; SATA 2

Gilchrist, Ellen 1935- .. **CLC 34, 48; SSC 14**
See also CA 113; 116; CANR 41; DLB 130;
MTCW

Giles, Molly 1942- .... **CLC 39**
See also CA 126

Gill, Patrick
See Creasey, John

Gilliam, Terry (Vance) 1940-....... **CLC 21**
See also Monty Python
See also CA 108; 113; CANR 35

Gillian, Jerry
See Gilliam, Terry (Vance)

Gilliatt, Penelope (Ann Douglass)
1932-1993 .... **CLC 2, 10, 13, 53**
See also AITN 2; CA 13-16R; 141; DLB 14

Gilman, Charlotte (Anna) Perkins (Stetson)
1860-1935 .... **TCLC 9, 37; SSC 13**
See also CA 106

Gilmour, David 1949-............. **CLC 35**
See also Pink Floyd
See also CA 138

Gilpin, William 1724-1804....... **NCLC 30**

Gilray, J. D.
See Mencken, H(enry) L(ouis)

Gilroy, Frank D(aniel) 1925-........ **CLC 2**
See also CA 81-84; CANR 32; DLB 7

Ginsberg, Allen
1926- ...... **CLC 1, 2, 3, 4, 6, 13, 36, 69;**
DA; PC 4; WLC 3
See also AITN 1; CA 1-4R; CANR 2, 41;
CDALB 1941-1968; DLB 5, 16; MTCW

Ginzburg, Natalia
1916-1991 .... **CLC 5, 11, 54, 70**
See also CA 85-88; 135; CANR 33; MTCW

Giono, Jean 1895-1970......... **CLC 4, 11**
See also CA 45-48; 29-32R; CANR 2, 35;
DLB 72; MTCW

Giovanni, Nikki
1943- ..... **CLC 2, 4, 19, 64; BLC 2; DA**
See also AITN 1; BW; CA 29-32R;
CAAS 6; CANR 18, 41; CLR 6; DLB 5,
41; MAICYA; MTCW; SATA 24

Giovene, Andrea 1904-............. **CLC 7**
See also CA 85-88

Gippius, Zinaida (Nikolayevna) 1869-1945
See Hippius, Zinaida
See also CA 106

Giraudoux, (Hippolyte) Jean
1882-1944 .... **TCLC 2, 7**
See also CA 104; DLB 65

Gironella, Jose Maria 1917-....... **CLC 11**
See also CA 101

Gissing, George (Robert)
1857-1903 .... **TCLC 3, 24, 47**
See also CA 105; DLB 18, 135

Giurlani, Aldo
See Palazzeschi, Aldo

Gladkov, Fyodor (Vasilyevich)
1883-1958 .... **TCLC 27**

Glanville, Brian (Lester) 1931-...... **CLC 6**
See also CA 5-8R; CAAS 9; CANR 3;
DLB 15; SATA 42

Glasgow, Ellen (Anderson Gholson)
1873(?)-1945 .... **TCLC 2, 7**
See also CA 104; DLB 9, 12

Glassco, John 1909-1981 .... **CLC 9**
See also CA 13-16R; 102; CANR 15;
DLB 68

Glasscock, Amnesia
See Steinbeck, John (Ernst)

Glasser, Ronald J. 1940(?)-........ **CLC 37**

Glassman, Joyce
See Johnson, Joyce

Glendinning, Victoria 1937-........ **CLC 50**
See also CA 120; 127

Glissant, Edouard 1928-........ **CLC 10, 68**

Gloag, Julian 1930- .... **CLC 40**
See also AITN 1; CA 65-68; CANR 10

Gluck, Louise (Elisabeth)
1943- .... **CLC 7, 22, 44, 81**
See also Glueck, Louise
See also CA 33-36R; CANR 40; DLB 5

Glueck, Louise. .... **CLC 7, 22**
See also Gluck, Louise (Elisabeth)
See also DLB 5

Gobineau, Joseph Arthur (Comte) de
1816-1882 .... **NCLC 17**
See also DLB 123

Godard, Jean-Luc 1930-........... **CLC 20**
See also CA 93-96

Godden, (Margaret) Rumer 1907-... **CLC 53**
See also AAYA 6; CA 5-8R; CANR 4, 27,
36; CLR 20; MAICYA; SAAS 12;
SATA 3, 36

Godoy Alcayaga, Lucila 1889-1957
See Mistral, Gabriela
See also CA 104; 131; HW; MTCW

Godwin, Gail (Kathleen)
1937- .... **CLC 5, 8, 22, 31, 69**
See also CA 29-32R; CANR 15, 43; DLB 6;
MTCW

Godwin, William 1756-1836...... **NCLC 14**
See also CDBLB 1789-1832; DLB 39, 104

Goethe, Johann Wolfgang von
1749-1832 .... **NCLC 4, 22, 34; DA;**
PC 5; WLC 3
See also DLB 94

Gogarty, Oliver St. John
1878-1957 .... **TCLC 15**
See also CA 109; DLB 15, 19

Gogol, Nikolai (Vasilyevich)
1809-1852 .... **NCLC 5, 15, 31; DA;**
DC 1; SSC 4; WLC

Goines, Donald
1937(?)-1974 .... **CLC 80; BLC 2**
See also AITN 1; BW; CA 124; 114;
DLB 33

Gold, Herbert 1924-....... **CLC 4, 7, 14, 42**
See also CA 9-12R; CANR 17; DLB 2;
DLBY 81

Goldbarth, Albert 1948-........ **CLC 5, 38**
See also CA 53-56; CANR 6, 40; DLB 120

Goldberg, Anatol 1910-1982 .... **CLC 34**
See also CA 131; 117

Goldemberg, Isaac 1945- .... **CLC 52**
See also CA 69-72; CAAS 12; CANR 11,
32; HW

Golden Silver
See Storm, Hyemeyohsts

Golding, William (Gerald)
1911-1993 .... **CLC 1, 2, 3, 8, 10, 17, 27,**
58, 81; DA; WLC
See also AAYA 5; CA 5-8R; 141;
CANR 13, 33; CDBLB 1945-1960;
DLB 15, 100; MTCW

Goldman, Emma 1869-1940...... **TCLC 13**
See also CA 110

Goldman, Francisco 1955-......... **CLC 76**

Goldman, William (W.) 1931-.... **CLC 1, 48**
See also CA 9-12R; CANR 29; DLB 44

Goldmann, Lucien 1913-1970 ...... **CLC 24**
See also CA 25-28; CAP 2

Goldoni, Carlo 1707-1793 .... **LC 4**

Goldsberry, Steven 1949-.......... **CLC 34**
See also CA 131

Goldsmith, Oliver
1728-1774 .... **LC 2; DA; WLC**
See also CDBLB 1660-1789; DLB 39, 89,
104, 109; SATA 26

Goldsmith, Peter
See Priestley, J(ohn) B(oynton)

Gombrowicz, Witold
1904-1969 .... **CLC 4, 7, 11, 49**
See also CA 19-20; 25-28R; CAP 2

Gomez de la Serna, Ramon
1888-1963 .... **CLC 9**
See also CA 116; HW

Goncharov, Ivan Alexandrovich
1812-1891 .... **NCLC 1**

Goncourt, Edmond (Louis Antoine Huot) de
1822-1896 .... **NCLC 7**
See also DLB 123

Goncourt, Jules (Alfred Huot) de
1830-1870 .... **NCLC 7**
See also DLB 123

Gontier, Fernande 19(?)- .... **CLC 50**

Goodman, Paul 1911-1972.... **CLC 1, 2, 4, 7**
See also CA 19-20; 37-40R; CANR 34;
CAP 2; DLB 130; MTCW

Gordimer, Nadine
1923- .... **CLC 3, 5, 7, 10, 18, 33, 51, 70;**
DA
See also CA 5-8R; CANR 3, 28; MTCW

Gordon, Adam Lindsay
1833-1870 .... **NCLC 21**

Gordon, Caroline
1895-1981 .... **CLC 6, 13, 29**
See also CA 11-12; 103; CANR 36; CAP 1;
DLB 4, 9, 102; DLBY 81; MTCW

Gordon, Charles William 1860-1937
See Connor, Ralph
See also CA 109

Gordon, Mary (Catherine)
1949- .... **CLC 13, 22**
See also CA 102; DLB 6; DLBY 81;
MTCW

Gordon, Sol 1923-................ **CLC 26**
See also CA 53-56; CANR 4; SATA 11

Gordone, Charles 1925-.......... **CLC 1, 4**
See also BW; CA 93-96; DLB 7; MTCW

Gorenko, Anna Andreevna
See Akhmatova, Anna

Gorky, Maxim. .... **TCLC 8; WLC**
See also Peshkov, Alexei Maximovich

Goryan, Sirak
See Saroyan, William

Gosse, Edmund (William)
1849-1928 .... **TCLC 28**
See also CA 117; DLB 57

Gotlieb, Phyllis Fay (Bloom)
1926- . . . . **CLC 18**
See also CA 13-16R; CANR 7; DLB 88

Gottesman, S. D.
See Kornbluth, C(yril) M.; Pohl, Frederik

Gottfried von Strassburg
fl. c. 1210- . . . . **CMLC 10**

Gould, Lois . . . . **CLC 4, 10**
See also CA 77-80; CANR 29; MTCW

Gourmont, Remy de   1858-1915 . . . . **TCLC 17**
See also CA 109

Govier, Katherine   1948- . . . . **CLC 51**
See also CA 101; CANR 18, 40

Goyen, (Charles) William
1915-1983 . . . . **CLC 5, 8, 14, 40**
See also AITN 2; CA 5-8R; 110; CANR 6;
DLB 2; DLBY 83

Goytisolo, Juan
1931- . . . . **CLC 5, 10, 23; HLC 1**
See also CA 85-88; CANR 32; HW; MTCW

Gozzi, (Conte) Carlo   1720-1806 . . **NCLC 23**

Grabbe, Christian Dietrich
1801-1836 . . . . **NCLC 2**
See also DLB 133

Grace, Patricia   1937- . . . . **CLC 56**

Gracian y Morales, Baltasar
1601-1658 . . . . **LC 15**

Gracq, Julien . . . . **CLC 11, 48**
See also Poirier, Louis
See also DLB 83

Grade, Chaim   1910-1982 . . . . **CLC 10**
See also CA 93-96; 107

Graduate of Oxford, A
See Ruskin, John

Graham, John
See Phillips, David Graham

Graham, Jorie   1951- . . . . **CLC 48**
See also CA 111; DLB 120

Graham, R(obert) B(ontine) Cunninghame
See Cunninghame Graham, R(obert)
B(ontine)
See also DLB 98, 135

Graham, Robert
See Haldeman, Joe (William)

Graham, Tom
See Lewis, (Harry) Sinclair

Graham, W(illiam) S(ydney)
1918-1986 . . . . **CLC 29**
See also CA 73-76; 118; DLB 20

Graham, Winston (Mawdsley)
1910- . . . . **CLC 23**
See also CA 49-52; CANR 2, 22; DLB 77

Grant, Skeeter
See Spiegelman, Art

Granville-Barker, Harley
1877-1946 . . . . **TCLC 2**
See also Barker, Harley Granville
See also CA 104

Grass, Guenter (Wilhelm)
1927- . . . . . **CLC 1, 2, 4, 6, 11, 15, 22, 32,
49; DA; WLC**
See also CA 13-16R; CANR 20; DLB 75,
124; MTCW

Gratton, Thomas
See Hulme, T(homas) E(rnest)

Grau, Shirley Ann   1929- . . . . **CLC 4, 9**
See also CA 89-92; CANR 22; DLB 2;
MTCW

Gravel, Fern
See Hall, James Norman

Graver, Elizabeth   1964- . . . . **CLC 70**
See also CA 135

Graves, Richard Perceval   1945- . . . . **CLC 44**
See also CA 65-68; CANR 9, 26

Graves, Robert (von Ranke)
1895-1985 . . . . . . **CLC 1, 2, 6, 11, 39, 44,
45; PC 6**
See also CA 5-8R; 117; CANR 5, 36;
CDBLB 1914-1945; DLB 20, 100;
DLBY 85; MTCW; SATA 45

Gray, Alasdair   1934- . . . . **CLC 41**
See also CA 126; MTCW

Gray, Amlin   1946- . . . . **CLC 29**
See also CA 138

Gray, Francine du Plessix   1930- . . . . **CLC 22**
See also BEST 90:3; CA 61-64; CAAS 2;
CANR 11, 33; MTCW

Gray, John (Henry)   1866-1934 . . . . **TCLC 19**
See also CA 119

Gray, Simon (James Holliday)
1936- . . . . **CLC 9, 14, 36**
See also AITN 1; CA 21-24R; CAAS 3;
CANR 32; DLB 13; MTCW

Gray, Spalding   1941- . . . . **CLC 49**
See also CA 128

Gray, Thomas
1716-1771 . . . . . . **LC 4; DA; PC 2; WLC**
See also CDBLB 1660-1789; DLB 109

Grayson, David
See Baker, Ray Stannard

Grayson, Richard (A.)   1951- . . . . **CLC 38**
See also CA 85-88; CANR 14, 31

Greeley, Andrew M(oran)   1928- . . . . **CLC 28**
See also CA 5-8R; CAAS 7; CANR 7, 43;
MTCW

Green, Brian
See Card, Orson Scott

Green, Hannah
See Greenberg, Joanne (Goldenberg)

Green, Hannah . . . . **CLC 3**
See also CA 73-76

Green, Henry . . . . **CLC 2, 13**
See also Yorke, Henry Vincent
See also DLB 15

Green, Julian (Hartridge)   1900-
See Green, Julien
See also CA 21-24R; CANR 33; DLB 4, 72;
MTCW

Green, Julien . . . . **CLC 3, 11, 77**
See also Green, Julian (Hartridge)

Green, Paul (Eliot)   1894-1981 . . . . . . **CLC 25**
See also AITN 1; CA 5-8R; 103; CANR 3;
DLB 7, 9; DLBY 81

Greenberg, Ivan   1908-1973
See Rahv, Philip
See also CA 85-88

Greenberg, Joanne (Goldenberg)
1932- . . . . **CLC 7, 30**
See also CA 5-8R; CANR 14, 32; SATA 25

Greenberg, Richard   1959(?)- . . . . **CLC 57**
See also CA 138

Greene, Bette   1934- . . . . **CLC 30**
See also AAYA 7; CA 53-56; CANR 4;
CLR 2; JRDA; MAICYA; SAAS 16;
SATA 8

Greene, Gael . . . . **CLC 8**
See also CA 13-16R; CANR 10

Greene, Graham
1904-1991 . . . . **CLC 1, 3, 6, 9, 14, 18, 27,
37, 70, 72; DA; WLC**
See also AITN 2; CA 13-16R; 133;
CANR 35; CDBLB 1945-1960; DLB 13,
15, 77, 100; DLBY 91; MTCW; SATA 20

Greer, Richard
See Silverberg, Robert

Greer, Richard
See Silverberg, Robert

Gregor, Arthur   1923- . . . . **CLC 9**
See also CA 25-28R; CAAS 10; CANR 11;
SATA 36

Gregor, Lee
See Pohl, Frederik

Gregory, Isabella Augusta (Persse)
1852-1932 . . . . **TCLC 1**
See also CA 104; DLB 10

Gregory, J. Dennis
See Williams, John A(lfred)

Grendon, Stephen
See Derleth, August (William)

Grenville, Kate   1950- . . . . **CLC 61**
See also CA 118

Grenville, Pelham
See Wodehouse, P(elham) G(renville)

Greve, Felix Paul (Berthold Friedrich)
1879-1948
See Grove, Frederick Philip
See also CA 104; 141

Grey, Zane   1872-1939 . . . . **TCLC 6**
See also CA 104; 132; DLB 9; MTCW

Grieg, (Johan) Nordahl (Brun)
1902-1943 . . . . **TCLC 10**
See also CA 107

Grieve, C(hristopher) M(urray)
1892-1978 . . . . **CLC 11, 19**
See also MacDiarmid, Hugh
See also CA 5-8R; 85-88; CANR 33;
MTCW

Griffin, Gerald   1803-1840 . . . . **NCLC 7**

Griffin, John Howard   1920-1980 . . . . **CLC 68**
See also AITN 1; CA 1-4R; 101; CANR 2

Griffin, Peter . . . . **CLC 39**

Griffiths, Trevor   1935- . . . . **CLC 13, 52**
See also CA 97-100; DLB 13

Grigson, Geoffrey (Edward Harvey)
1905-1985 . . . . **CLC 7, 39**
See also CA 25-28R; 118; CANR 20, 33;
DLB 27; MTCW

Grillparzer, Franz   1791-1872 . . . . . . **NCLC 1**
See also DLB 133

Grimble, Reverend Charles James
See Eliot, T(homas) S(tearns)

Grimke, Charlotte L(ottie) Forten
1837(?)-1914
See Forten, Charlotte L.
See also BW; CA 117; 124

Grimm, Jacob Ludwig Karl
1785-1863 . . . . **NCLC 3**
See also DLB 90; MAICYA; SATA 22

Grimm, Wilhelm Karl 1786-1859 . . **NCLC 3**
See also DLB 90; MAICYA; SATA 22

Grimmelshausen, Johann Jakob Christoffel
von 1621-1676 . . . . **LC 6**

Grindel, Eugene 1895-1952
See Eluard, Paul
See also CA 104

Grossman, David 1954- . . . . **CLC 67**
See also CA 138

Grossman, Vasily (Semenovich)
1905-1964 . . . . **CLC 41**
See also CA 124; 130; MTCW

Grove, Frederick Philip . . . . **TCLC 4**
See also Greve, Felix Paul (Berthold
Friedrich)
See also DLB 92

Grubb
See Crumb, R(obert)

Grumbach, Doris (Isaac)
1918- . . . . **CLC 13, 22, 64**
See also CA 5-8R; CAAS 2; CANR 9, 42

Grundtvig, Nicolai Frederik Severin
1783-1872 . . . . **NCLC 1**

Grunge
See Crumb, R(obert)

Grunwald, Lisa 1959- . . . . **CLC 44**
See also CA 120

Guare, John 1938- . . . . **CLC 8, 14, 29, 67**
See also CA 73-76; CANR 21; DLB 7;
MTCW

Gudjonsson, Halldor Kiljan 1902-
See Laxness, Halldor
See also CA 103

Guenter, Erich
See Eich, Guenter

Guest, Barbara 1920- . . . . **CLC 34**
See also CA 25-28R; CANR 11; DLB 5

Guest, Judith (Ann) 1936- . . . . **CLC 8, 30**
See also AAYA 7; CA 77-80; CANR 15;
MTCW

Guild, Nicholas M. 1944- . . . . **CLC 33**
See also CA 93-96

Guillemin, Jacques
See Sartre, Jean-Paul

Guillen, Jorge 1893-1984 . . . . **CLC 11**
See also CA 89-92; 112; DLB 108; HW

Guillen (y Batista), Nicolas (Cristobal)
1902-1989 . . **CLC 48, 79; BLC 2; HLC 1**
See also BW; CA 116; 125; 129; HW

Guillevic, (Eugene) 1907- . . . . **CLC 33**
See also CA 93-96

Guillois
See Desnos, Robert

Guiney, Louise Imogen
1861-1920 . . . . **TCLC 41**
See also DLB 54

Guiraldes, Ricardo (Guillermo)
1886-1927 . . . . **TCLC 39**
See also CA 131; HW; MTCW

Gunn, Bill . . . . **CLC 5**
See also Gunn, William Harrison
See also DLB 38

Gunn, Thom(son William)
1929- . . . . **CLC 3, 6, 18, 32, 81**
See also CA 17-20R; CANR 9, 33;
CDBLB 1960 to Present; DLB 27;
MTCW

Gunn, William Harrison 1934(?)-1989
See Gunn, Bill
See also AITN 1; BW; CA 13-16R; 128;
CANR 12, 25

Gunnars, Kristjana 1948- . . . . **CLC 69**
See also CA 113; DLB 60

Gurganus, Allan 1947- . . . . **CLC 70**
See also BEST 90:1; CA 135

Gurney, A(lbert) R(amsdell), Jr.
1930- . . . . **CLC 32, 50, 54**
See also CA 77-80; CANR 32

Gurney, Ivor (Bertie) 1890-1937 . . . **TCLC 33**

Gurney, Peter
See Gurney, A(lbert) R(amsdell), Jr.

Gustafson, Ralph (Barker) 1909- . . . . **CLC 36**
See also CA 21-24R; CANR 8; DLB 88

Gut, Gom
See Simenon, Georges (Jacques Christian)

Guthrie, A(lfred) B(ertram), Jr.
1901-1991 . . . . **CLC 23**
See also CA 57-60; 134; CANR 24; DLB 6;
SATA 62; SATA-Obit 67

Guthrie, Isobel
See Grieve, C(hristopher) M(urray)

Guthrie, Woodrow Wilson 1912-1967
See Guthrie, Woody
See also CA 113; 93-96

Guthrie, Woody . . . . **CLC 35**
See also Guthrie, Woodrow Wilson

Guy, Rosa (Cuthbert) 1928- . . . . **CLC 26**
See also AAYA 4; BW; CA 17-20R;
CANR 14, 34; CLR 13; DLB 33; JRDA;
MAICYA; SATA 14, 62

Gwendolyn
See Bennett, (Enoch) Arnold

H. D. . . . . **CLC 3, 8, 14, 31, 34, 73; PC 5**
See also Doolittle, Hilda

Haavikko, Paavo Juhani
1931- . . . . **CLC 18, 34**
See also CA 106

Habbema, Koos
See Heijermans, Herman

Hacker, Marilyn 1942- . . . . **CLC 5, 9, 23, 72**
See also CA 77-80; DLB 120

Haggard, H(enry) Rider
1856-1925 . . . . **TCLC 11**
See also CA 108; DLB 70; SATA 16

Haig, Fenil
See Ford, Ford Madox

Haig-Brown, Roderick (Langmere)
1908-1976 . . . . **CLC 21**
See also CA 5-8R; 69-72; CANR 4, 38;
CLR 31; DLB 88; MAICYA; SATA 12

Hailey, Arthur 1920- . . . . **CLC 5**
See also AITN 2; BEST 90:3; CA 1-4R;
CANR 2, 36; DLB 88; DLBY 82; MTCW

Hailey, Elizabeth Forsythe 1938- . . . **CLC 40**
See also CA 93-96; CAAS 1; CANR 15

Haines, John (Meade) 1924- . . . . **CLC 58**
See also CA 17-20R; CANR 13, 34; DLB 5

Haldeman, Joe (William) 1943- . . . . . **CLC 61**
See also CA 53-56; CANR 6; DLB 8

Haley, Alex(ander Murray Palmer)
1921-1992 . . . **CLC 8, 12, 76; BLC 2; DA**
See also BW; CA 77-80; 136; DLB 38;
MTCW

Haliburton, Thomas Chandler
1796-1865 . . . . **NCLC 15**
See also DLB 11, 99

Hall, Donald (Andrew, Jr.)
1928- . . . . **CLC 1, 13, 37, 59**
See also CA 5-8R; CAAS 7; CANR 2;
DLB 5; SATA 23

Hall, Frederic Sauser
See Sauser-Hall, Frederic

Hall, James
See Kuttner, Henry

Hall, James Norman 1887-1951 . . . **TCLC 23**
See also CA 123; SATA 21

Hall, (Marguerite) Radclyffe
1886(?)-1943 . . . . **TCLC 12**
See also CA 110

Hall, Rodney 1935- . . . . **CLC 51**
See also CA 109

Halliday, Michael
See Creasey, John

Halpern, Daniel 1945- . . . . **CLC 14**
See also CA 33-36R

Hamburger, Michael (Peter Leopold)
1924- . . . . **CLC 5, 14**
See also CA 5-8R; CAAS 4; CANR 2;
DLB 27

Hamill, Pete 1935- . . . . **CLC 10**
See also CA 25-28R; CANR 18

Hamilton, Clive
See Lewis, C(live) S(taples)

Hamilton, Edmond 1904-1977 . . . . **CLC 1**
See also CA 1-4R; CANR 3; DLB 8

Hamilton, Eugene (Jacob) Lee
See Lee-Hamilton, Eugene (Jacob)

Hamilton, Franklin
See Silverberg, Robert

Hamilton, Gail
See Corcoran, Barbara

Hamilton, Mollie
See Kaye, M(ary) M(argaret)

Hamilton, (Anthony Walter) Patrick
1904-1962 . . . . **CLC 51**
See also CA 113; DLB 10

Hamilton, Virginia 1936- . . . . **CLC 26**
See also AAYA 2; BW; CA 25-28R;
CANR 20, 37; CLR 1, 11; DLB 33, 52;
JRDA; MAICYA; MTCW; SATA 4, 56

Hammett, (Samuel) Dashiell
1894-1961 .... **CLC 3, 5, 10, 19, 47**
See also AITN 1; CA 81-84; CANR 42;
CDALB 1929-1941; DLBD 6; MTCW

Hammon, Jupiter
1711(?)-1800(?) .... **NCLC 5; BLC 2**
See also DLB 31, 50

Hammond, Keith
See Kuttner, Henry

Hamner, Earl (Henry), Jr.   1923- ... **CLC 12**
See also AITN 2; CA 73-76; DLB 6

Hampton, Christopher (James)
1946- .... **CLC 4**
See also CA 25-28R; DLB 13; MTCW

Hamsun, Knut .... **TCLC 2, 14, 49**
See also Pedersen, Knut

Handke, Peter   1942- .. **CLC 5, 8, 10, 15, 38**
See also CA 77-80; CANR 33; DLB 85,
124; MTCW

Hanley, James   1901-1985 ... **CLC 3, 5, 8, 13**
See also CA 73-76; 117; CANR 36; MTCW

Hannah, Barry   1942- .... **CLC 23, 38**
See also CA 108; 110; CANR 43; DLB 6;
MTCW

Hannon, Ezra
See Hunter, Evan

Hansberry, Lorraine (Vivian)
1930-1965 .... **CLC 17, 62; BLC 2; DA;
DC 2**
See also BW; CA 109; 25-28R; CABS 3;
CDALB 1941-1968; DLB 7, 38; MTCW

Hansen, Joseph   1923- .... **CLC 38**
See also CA 29-32R; CAAS 17; CANR 16

Hansen, Martin A.   1909-1955 ..... **TCLC 32**

Hanson, Kenneth O(stlin)   1922- .... **CLC 13**
See also CA 53-56; CANR 7

Hardwick, Elizabeth   1916- .... **CLC 13**
See also CA 5-8R; CANR 3, 32; DLB 6;
MTCW

Hardy, Thomas
1840-1928 ...... **TCLC 4, 10, 18, 32, 48,
53; DA; PC 8; SSC 2; WLC**
See also CA 104; 123; CDBLB 1890-1914;
DLB 18, 19, 135; MTCW

Hare, David   1947- .... **CLC 29, 58**
See also CA 97-100; CANR 39; DLB 13;
MTCW

Harford, Henry
See Hudson, W(illiam) H(enry)

Hargrave, Leonie
See Disch, Thomas M(ichael)

Harlan, Louis R(udolph)   1922- ..... **CLC 34**
See also CA 21-24R; CANR 25

Harling, Robert   1951(?)- .... **CLC 53**

Harmon, William (Ruth)   1938- ..... **CLC 38**
See also CA 33-36R; CANR 14, 32, 35;
SATA 65

Harper, F. E. W.
See Harper, Frances Ellen Watkins

Harper, Frances E. W.
See Harper, Frances Ellen Watkins

Harper, Frances E. Watkins
See Harper, Frances Ellen Watkins

Harper, Frances Ellen
See Harper, Frances Ellen Watkins

Harper, Frances Ellen Watkins
1825-1911 .... **TCLC 14; BLC 2**
See also BW; CA 111; 125; DLB 50

Harper, Michael S(teven)   1938- .. **CLC 7, 22**
See also BW; CA 33-36R; CANR 24;
DLB 41

Harper, Mrs. F. E. W.
See Harper, Frances Ellen Watkins

Harris, Christie (Lucy) Irwin
1907- .... **CLC 12**
See also CA 5-8R; CANR 6; DLB 88;
JRDA; MAICYA; SAAS 10; SATA 6, 74

Harris, Frank   1856(?)-1931 .... **TCLC 24**
See also CA 109

Harris, George Washington
1814-1869 .... **NCLC 23**
See also DLB 3, 11

Harris, Joel Chandler   1848-1908 ... **TCLC 2**
See also CA 104; 137; DLB 11, 23, 42, 78,
91; MAICYA; YABC 1

**Harris, John (Wyndham Parkes Lucas)
Beynon**   1903-1969 .... **CLC 19**
See also CA 102; 89-92

Harris, MacDonald
See Heiney, Donald (William)

Harris, Mark   1922- .... **CLC 19**
See also CA 5-8R; CAAS 3; CANR 2;
DLB 2; DLBY 80

Harris, (Theodore) Wilson   1921- .... **CLC 25**
See also BW; CA 65-68; CAAS 16;
CANR 11, 27; DLB 117; MTCW

Harrison, Elizabeth Cavanna   1909-
See Cavanna, Betty
See also CA 9-12R; CANR 6, 27

Harrison, Harry (Max)   1925- ...... **CLC 42**
See also CA 1-4R; CANR 5, 21; DLB 8;
SATA 4

Harrison, James (Thomas)
1937- .... **CLC 6, 14, 33, 66**
See also CA 13-16R; CANR 8; DLBY 82

Harrison, Kathryn   1961- .... **CLC 70**

Harrison, Tony   1937- .... **CLC 43**
See also CA 65-68; DLB 40; MTCW

Harriss, Will(ard Irvin)   1922- ...... **CLC 34**
See also CA 111

Harson, Sley
See Ellison, Harlan

Hart, Ellis
See Ellison, Harlan

Hart, Josephine   1942(?)- .... **CLC 70**
See also CA 138

Hart, Moss   1904-1961 .... **CLC 66**
See also CA 109; 89-92; DLB 7

Harte, (Francis) Bret(t)
1836(?)-1902 .... **TCLC 1, 25; DA;
SSC 8; WLC**
See also CA 104; 140; CDALB 1865-1917;
DLB 12, 64, 74, 79; SATA 26

Hartley, L(eslie) P(oles)
1895-1972 .... **CLC 2, 22**
See also CA 45-48; 37-40R; CANR 33;
DLB 15; MTCW

Hartman, Geoffrey H.   1929- .... **CLC 27**
See also CA 117; 125; DLB 67

Haruf, Kent   19(?)- .... **CLC 34**

Harwood, Ronald   1934- .... **CLC 32**
See also CA 1-4R; CANR 4; DLB 13

Hasek, Jaroslav (Matej Frantisek)
1883-1923 .... **TCLC 4**
See also CA 104; 129; MTCW

Hass, Robert   1941- .... **CLC 18, 39**
See also CA 111; CANR 30; DLB 105

Hastings, Hudson
See Kuttner, Henry

Hastings, Selina .... **CLC 44**

Hatteras, Amelia
See Mencken, H(enry) L(ouis)

Hatteras, Owen .... **TCLC 18**
See also Mencken, H(enry) L(ouis); Nathan,
George Jean

Hauptmann, Gerhart (Johann Robert)
1862-1946 .... **TCLC 4**
See also CA 104; DLB 66, 118

Havel, Vaclav   1936- .... **CLC 25, 58, 65**
See also CA 104; CANR 36; MTCW

Haviaras, Stratis .... **CLC 33**
See also Chaviaras, Strates

Hawes, Stephen   1475(?)-1523(?) ..... **LC 17**

Hawkes, John (Clendennin Burne, Jr.)
1925- ...... **CLC 1, 2, 3, 4, 7, 9, 14, 15,
27, 49**
See also CA 1-4R; CANR 2; DLB 2, 7;
DLBY 80; MTCW

Hawking, S. W.
See Hawking, Stephen W(illiam)

Hawking, Stephen W(illiam)
1942- .... **CLC 63**
See also BEST 89:1; CA 126; 129

Hawthorne, Julian   1846-1934 ..... **TCLC 25**

Hawthorne, Nathaniel
1804-1864 ...... **NCLC 39; DA; SSC 3;
WLC**
See also CDALB 1640-1865; DLB 1, 74;
YABC 2

Haxton, Josephine Ayres   1921- .... **CLC 73**
See also CA 115; CANR 41

Hayaseca y Eizaguirre, Jorge
See Echegaray (y Eizaguirre), Jose (Maria
Waldo)

Hayashi Fumiko   1904-1951 .... **TCLC 27**

Haycraft, Anna
See Ellis, Alice Thomas
See also CA 122

Hayden, Robert E(arl)
1913-1980 .... **CLC 5, 9, 14, 37; BLC 2;
DA; PC 6**
See also BW; CA 69-72; 97-100; CABS 2;
CANR 24; CDALB 1941-1968; DLB 5,
76; MTCW; SATA 19, 26

Hayford, J(oseph) E(phraim) Casely
See Casely-Hayford, J(oseph) E(phraim)

Hayman, Ronald   1932- .... **CLC 44**
See also CA 25-28R; CANR 18

Haywood, Eliza (Fowler)
1693(?)-1756 .... **LC 1**

Hazlitt, William 1778-1830 ...... **NCLC 29**
See also DLB 110

Hazzard, Shirley 1931- .... **CLC 18**
See also CA 9-12R; CANR 4; DLBY 82;
MTCW

Head, Bessie
1937-1986 .... **CLC 25, 67; BLC 2**
See also BW; CA 29-32R; 119; CANR 25;
DLB 117; MTCW

Headon, (Nicky) Topper 1956(?)- ... **CLC 30**
See also Clash, The

Heaney, Seamus (Justin)
1939- .... **CLC 5, 7, 14, 25, 37, 74**
See also CA 85-88; CANR 25;
CDBLB 1960 to Present; DLB 40;
MTCW

Hearn, (Patricio) Lafcadio (Tessima Carlos)
1850-1904 .... **TCLC 9**
See also CA 105; DLB 12, 78

Hearne, Vicki 1946- .... **CLC 56**
See also CA 139

Hearon, Shelby 1931- .... **CLC 63**
See also AITN 2; CA 25-28R; CANR 18

Heat-Moon, William Least .... **CLC 29**
See also Trogdon, William (Lewis)
See also AAYA 9

Hebbel, Friedrich 1813-1863 ..... **NCLC 43**
See also DLB 129

Hebert, Anne 1916- .... **CLC 4, 13, 29**
See also CA 85-88; DLB 68; MTCW

Hecht, Anthony (Evan)
1923- .... **CLC 8, 13, 19**
See also CA 9-12R; CANR 6; DLB 5

Hecht, Ben 1894-1964 .... **CLC 8**
See also CA 85-88; DLB 7, 9, 25, 26, 28, 86

Hedayat, Sadeq 1903-1951 .... **TCLC 21**
See also CA 120

Heidegger, Martin 1889-1976 ...... **CLC 24**
See also CA 81-84; 65-68; CANR 34;
MTCW

Heidenstam, (Carl Gustaf) Verner von
1859-1940 .... **TCLC 5**
See also CA 104

Heifner, Jack 1946- .... **CLC 11**
See also CA 105

Heijermans, Herman 1864-1924 ... **TCLC 24**
See also CA 123

Heilbrun, Carolyn G(old) 1926- ..... **CLC 25**
See also CA 45-48; CANR 1, 28

Heine, Heinrich 1797-1856 .... **NCLC 4**
See also DLB 90

Heinemann, Larry (Curtiss) 1944- .. **CLC 50**
See also CA 110; CANR 31; DLBD 9

Heiney, Donald (William)
1921-1993 .... **CLC 9**
See also CA 1-4R; 142; CANR 3

Heinlein, Robert A(nson)
1907-1988 ...... **CLC 1, 3, 8, 14, 26, 55**
See also CA 1-4R; 125; CANR 1, 20;
DLB 8; JRDA; MAICYA; MTCW;
SATA 9, 56, 69

Helforth, John
See Doolittle, Hilda

Hellenhofferu, Vojtech Kapristian z
See Hasek, Jaroslav (Matej Frantisek)

Heller, Joseph
1923- .... **CLC 1, 3, 5, 8, 11, 36, 63; DA;
WLC**
See also AITN 1; CA 5-8R; CABS 1;
CANR 8, 42; DLB 2, 28; DLBY 80;
MTCW

Hellman, Lillian (Florence)
1906-1984 ...... **CLC 2, 4, 8, 14, 18, 34,
44, 52; DC 1**
See also AITN 1, 2; CA 13-16R; 112;
CANR 33; DLB 7; DLBY 84; MTCW

Helprin, Mark 1947- ..... **CLC 7, 10, 22, 32**
See also CA 81-84; DLBY 85; MTCW

Helyar, Jane Penelope Josephine 1933-
See Poole, Josephine
See also CA 21-24R; CANR 10, 26

Hemans, Felicia 1793-1835 ...... **NCLC 29**
See also DLB 96

Hemingway, Ernest (Miller)
1899-1961 .... **CLC 1, 3, 6, 8, 10, 13, 19,
30, 34, 39, 41, 44, 50, 61, 80; DA; SSC 1;
WLC**
See also CA 77-80; CANR 34;
CDALB 1917-1929; DLB 4, 9, 102;
DLBD 1; DLBY 81, 87; MTCW

Hempel, Amy 1951- .... **CLC 39**
See also CA 118; 137

Henderson, F. C.
See Mencken, H(enry) L(ouis)

Henderson, Sylvia
See Ashton-Warner, Sylvia (Constance)

Henley, Beth .... **CLC 23**
See also Henley, Elizabeth Becker
See also CABS 3; DLBY 86

Henley, Elizabeth Becker 1952-
See Henley, Beth
See also CA 107; CANR 32; MTCW

Henley, William Ernest
1849-1903 .... **TCLC 8**
See also CA 105; DLB 19

Hennissart, Martha
See Lathen, Emma
See also CA 85-88

Henry, O. .... **TCLC 1, 19; SSC 5; WLC**
See also Porter, William Sydney

Henryson, Robert 1430(?)-1506(?).... **LC 20**

Henry VIII 1491-1547 .... **LC 10**

Henschke, Alfred
See Klabund

Hentoff, Nat(han Irving) 1925- ..... **CLC 26**
See also AAYA 4; CA 1-4R; CAAS 6;
CANR 5, 25; CLR 1; JRDA; MAICYA;
SATA 27, 42, 69

Heppenstall, (John) Rayner
1911-1981 .... **CLC 10**
See also CA 1-4R; 103; CANR 29

Herbert, Frank (Patrick)
1920-1986 .... **CLC 12, 23, 35, 44**
See also CA 53-56; 118; CANR 5, 43;
DLB 8; MTCW; SATA 9, 37, 47

Herbert, George 1593-1633 .... **LC 24; PC 4**
See also CDBLB Before 1660; DLB 126

Herbert, Zbigniew 1924- .... **CLC 9, 43**
See also CA 89-92; CANR 36; MTCW

Herbst, Josephine (Frey)
1897-1969 .... **CLC 34**
See also CA 5-8R; 25-28R; DLB 9

Hergesheimer, Joseph
1880-1954 .... **TCLC 11**
See also CA 109; DLB 102, 9

Herlihy, James Leo 1927- .... **CLC 6**
See also CA 1-4R; CANR 2

Hermogenes fl. c. 175- .... **CMLC 6**

Hernandez, Jose 1834-1886 ...... **NCLC 17**

Herrick, Robert 1591-1674 ..... **LC 13; DA**
See also DLB 126

Herring, Guilles
See Somerville, Edith

Herriot, James 1916- .... **CLC 12**
See also Wight, James Alfred
See also AAYA 1; CANR 40

Herrmann, Dorothy 1941- .... **CLC 44**
See also CA 107

Herrmann, Taffy
See Herrmann, Dorothy

Hersey, John (Richard)
1914-1993 .... **CLC 1, 2, 7, 9, 40, 81**
See also CA 17-20R; 140; CANR 33;
DLB 6; MTCW; SATA 25

Herzen, Aleksandr Ivanovich
1812-1870 .... **NCLC 10**

Herzl, Theodor 1860-1904 .... **TCLC 36**

Herzog, Werner 1942- .... **CLC 16**
See also CA 89-92

Hesiod c. 8th cent. B.C.- .... **CMLC 5**

Hesse, Hermann
1877-1962 .... **CLC 1, 2, 3, 6, 11, 17, 25,
69; DA; SSC 9; WLC**
See also CA 17-18; CAP 2; DLB 66;
MTCW; SATA 50

Hewes, Cady
See De Voto, Bernard (Augustine)

Heyen, William 1940- .... **CLC 13, 18**
See also CA 33-36R; CAAS 9; DLB 5

Heyerdahl, Thor 1914- .... **CLC 26**
See also CA 5-8R; CANR 5, 22; MTCW;
SATA 2, 52

Heym, Georg (Theodor Franz Arthur)
1887-1912 .... **TCLC 9**
See also CA 106

Heym, Stefan 1913- .... **CLC 41**
See also CA 9-12R; CANR 4; DLB 69

Heyse, Paul (Johann Ludwig von)
1830-1914 .... **TCLC 8**
See also CA 104; DLB 129

Hibbert, Eleanor Alice Burford
1906-1993 .... **CLC 7**
See also BEST 90:4; CA 17-20R; 140;
CANR 9, 28; SATA 2; SATA-Obit 74

Higgins, George V(incent)
1939- .... **CLC 4, 7, 10, 18**
See also CA 77-80; CAAS 5; CANR 17;
DLB 2; DLBY 81; MTCW

Higginson, Thomas Wentworth
1823-1911 .... **TCLC 36**
See also DLB 1, 64

Hopkins, Pauline Elizabeth
1859-1930 .... **TCLC 28; BLC 2**
See also CA 141; DLB 50

Hopley-Woolrich, Cornell George   1903-1968
See Woolrich, Cornell
See also CA 13-14; CAP 1

Horatio
See Proust, (Valentin-Louis-George-Eugene-)
Marcel

Horgan, Paul   1903- .... **CLC 9, 53**
See also CA 13-16R; CANR 9, 35;
DLB 102; DLBY 85; MTCW; SATA 13

Horn, Peter
See Kuttner, Henry

Hornem, Horace Esq.
See Byron, George Gordon (Noel)

Horovitz, Israel   1939- .... **CLC 56**
See also CA 33-36R; DLB 7

Horvath, Odon von
See Horvath, Oedoen von
See also DLB 85, 124

Horvath, Oedoen von   1901-1938... **TCLC 45**
See also Horvath, Odon von
See also CA 118

Horwitz, Julius   1920-1986........ **CLC 14**
See also CA 9-12R; 119; CANR 12

Hospital, Janette Turner   1942- ..... **CLC 42**
See also CA 108

Hostos, E. M. de
See Hostos (y Bonilla), Eugenio Maria de

Hostos, Eugenio M. de
See Hostos (y Bonilla), Eugenio Maria de

Hostos, Eugenio Maria
See Hostos (y Bonilla), Eugenio Maria de

Hostos (y Bonilla), Eugenio Maria de
1839-1903 .... **TCLC 24**
See also CA 123; 131; HW

Houdini
See Lovecraft, H(oward) P(hillips)

Hougan, Carolyn   1943- .... **CLC 34**
See also CA 139

Household, Geoffrey (Edward West)
1900-1988 .... **CLC 11**
See also CA 77-80; 126; DLB 87; SATA 14,
59

Housman, A(lfred) E(dward)
1859-1936 ...... **TCLC 1, 10; DA; PC 2**
See also CA 104; 125; DLB 19; MTCW

Housman, Laurence   1865-1959 ..... **TCLC 7**
See also CA 106; DLB 10; SATA 25

Howard, Elizabeth Jane   1923- ... **CLC 7, 29**
See also CA 5-8R; CANR 8

Howard, Maureen   1930- ..... **CLC 5, 14, 46**
See also CA 53-56; CANR 31; DLBY 83;
MTCW

Howard, Richard   1929- ...... **CLC 7, 10, 47**
See also AITN 1; CA 85-88; CANR 25;
DLB 5

Howard, Robert Ervin   1906-1936... **TCLC 8**
See also CA 105

Howard, Warren F.
See Pohl, Frederik

Howe, Fanny   1940- .... **CLC 47**
See also CA 117; SATA 52

Howe, Julia Ward   1819-1910 ..... **TCLC 21**
See also CA 117; DLB 1

Howe, Susan   1937- .... **CLC 72**
See also DLB 120

Howe, Tina   1937- .... **CLC 48**
See also CA 109

Howell, James   1594(?)-1666 .... **LC 13**

Howells, W. D.
See Howells, William Dean

Howells, William D.
See Howells, William Dean

Howells, William Dean
1837-1920 .... **TCLC 7, 17, 41**
See also CA 104; 134; CDALB 1865-1917;
DLB 12, 64, 74, 79

Howes, Barbara   1914- .... **CLC 15**
See also CA 9-12R; CAAS 3; SATA 5

Hrabal, Bohumil   1914-........ **CLC 13, 67**
See also CA 106; CAAS 12

Hsun, Lu .... **TCLC 3**
See also Shu-Jen, Chou

Hubbard, L(afayette) Ron(ald)
1911-1986 .... **CLC 43**
See also CA 77-80; 118; CANR 22

Huch, Ricarda (Octavia)
1864-1947 .... **TCLC 13**
See also CA 111; DLB 66

Huddle, David   1942- .... **CLC 49**
See also CA 57-60; DLB 130

Hudson, Jeffrey
See Crichton, (John) Michael

Hudson, W(illiam) H(enry)
1841-1922 .... **TCLC 29**
See also CA 115; DLB 98; SATA 35

Hueffer, Ford Madox
See Ford, Ford Madox

Hughart, Barry   1934-............. **CLC 39**
See also CA 137

Hug⬛Colin
See Creasey, John

Hughes, David (John)   1930- .... **CLC 48**
See also CA 116; 129; DLB 14

Hughes, (James) Langston
1902-1967 ..... **CLC 1, 5, 10, 15, 35, 44;
BLC 2; DA; DC 3; PC 1; SSC 6; WLC**
See also BW; CA 1-4R; 25-28R; CANR 1,
34; CDALB 1929-1941; CLR 17; DLB 4,
7, 48, 51, 86; JRDA; MAICYA; MTCW;
SATA 4, 33

Hughes, Richard (Arthur Warren)
1900-1976 .... **CLC 1, 11**
See also CA 5-8R; 65-68; CANR 4;
DLB 15; MTCW; SATA 8, 25

Hughes, Ted
1930- .... **CLC 2, 4, 9, 14, 37; PC 7**
See also CA 1-4R; CANR 1, 33; CLR 3;
DLB 40; MAICYA; SATA 27,
49

Hugo, Richard F(ranklin)
1923-1982 .... **CLC 6, 18, 32**
See also CA 49-52; 108; CANR 3; DLB 5

Hugo, Victor (Marie)
1802-1885 .. **NCLC 3, 10, 21; DA; WLC**
See also DLB 119; SATA 47

Huidobro, Vicente
See Huidobro Fernandez, Vicente Garcia

Huidobro Fernandez, Vicente Garcia
1893-1948 .... **TCLC 31**
See also CA 131; HW

Hulme, Keri   1947- .... **CLC 39**
See also CA 125

Hulme, T(homas) E(rnest)
1883-1917 .... **TCLC 21**
See also CA 117; DLB 19

Hume, David   1711-1776............. **LC 7**
See also DLB 104

Humphrey, William   1924-........ **CLC 45**
See also CA 77-80; DLB 6

Humphreys, Emyr Owen   1919-..... **CLC 47**
See also CA 5-8R; CANR 3, 24; DLB 15

Humphreys, Josephine   1945-.... **CLC 34, 57**
See also CA 121; 127

Hungerford, Pixie
See Brinsmead, H(esba) F(ay)

Hunt, E(verette) Howard, Jr.
1918- .... **CLC 3**
See also AITN 1; CA 45-48; CANR 2

Hunt, Kyle
See Creasey, John

Hunt, (James Henry) Leigh
1784-1859 .... **NCLC 1**

Hunt, Marsha   1946-............. **CLC 70**

Hunt, Violet   1866-1942 .... **TCLC 53**

Hunter, E. Waldo
See Sturgeon, Theodore (Hamilton)

Hunter, Evan   1926- .... **CLC 11, 31**
See also CA 5-8R; CANR 5, 38; DLBY 82;
MTCW; SATA 25

Hunter, Kristin (Eggleston)   1931-... **CLC 35**
See also AITN 1; BW; CA 13-16R;
CANR 13; CLR 3; DLB 33; MAICYA;
SAAS 10; SATA 12

Hunter, Mollie   1922- .... **CLC 21**
See also McIlwraith, Maureen Mollie
Hunter
See also CANR 37; CLR 25; JRDA;
MAICYA; SAAS 7; SATA 54

Hunter, Robert   (?)-1734............. **LC 7**

Hurston, Zora Neale
1903-1960 ...... **CLC 7, 30, 61; BLC 2;
DA; SSC 4**
See also BW; CA 85-88; DLB 51, 86;
MTCW

Huston, John (Marcellus)
1906-1987 .... **CLC 20**
See also CA 73-76; 123; CANR 34; DLB 26

Hustvedt, Siri   1955-............... **CLC 76**
See also CA 137

Hutten, Ulrich von   1488-1523....... **LC 16**

Huxley, Aldous (Leonard)
1894-1963 ..... **CLC 1, 3, 4, 5, 8, 11, 18,
35, 79; DA; WLC**
See also CA 85-88; CDBLB 1914-1945;
DLB 36, 100; MTCW; SATA 63

Jeffers, (John) Robinson
1887-1962 .... **CLC 2, 3, 11, 15, 54; DA;
WLC**
See also CA 85-88; CANR 35;
CDALB 1917-1929; DLB 45; MTCW

Jefferson, Janet
See Mencken, H(enry) L(ouis)

Jefferson, Thomas 1743-1826 .... **NCLC 11**
See also CDALB 1640-1865; DLB 31

Jeffrey, Francis 1773-1850...... **NCLC 33**
See also DLB 107

Jelakowitch, Ivan
See Heijermans, Herman

Jellicoe, (Patricia) Ann 1927-...... **CLC 27**
See also CA 85-88; DLB 13

Jen, Gish .... **CLC 70**
See also Jen, Lillian

Jen, Lillian 1956(?)-
See Jen, Gish
See also CA 135

Jenkins, (John) Robin 1912-....... **CLC 52**
See also CA 1-4R; CANR 1; DLB 14

Jennings, Elizabeth (Joan)
1926-...................... **CLC 5, 14**
See also CA 61-64; CAAS 5; CANR 8, 39;
DLB 27; MTCW; SATA 66

Jennings, Waylon 1937-........... **CLC 21**

Jensen, Johannes V. 1873-1950.... **TCLC 41**

Jensen, Laura (Linnea) 1948-...... **CLC 37**
See also CA 103

Jerome, Jerome K(lapka)
1859-1927 .... **TCLC 23**
See also CA 119; DLB 10, 34, 135

Jerrold, Douglas William
1803-1857 .... **NCLC 2**

Jewett, (Theodora) Sarah Orne
1849-1909 .... **TCLC 1, 22; SSC 6**
See also CA 108; 127; DLB 12, 74;
SATA 15

Jewsbury, Geraldine (Endsor)
1812-1880 .... **NCLC 22**
See also DLB 21

Jhabvala, Ruth Prawer
1927-................... **CLC 4, 8, 29**
See also CA 1-4R; CANR 2, 29; MTCW

Jiles, Paulette 1943-........... **CLC 13, 58**
See also CA 101

Jimenez (Mantecon), Juan Ramon
1881-1958 ...... **TCLC 4; HLC 1; PC 7**
See also CA 104; 131; DLB 134; HW;
MTCW

Jimenez, Ramon
See Jimenez (Mantecon), Juan Ramon

Jimenez Mantecon, Juan
See Jimenez (Mantecon), Juan Ramon

Joel, Billy .... **CLC 26**
See also Joel, William Martin

Joel, William Martin 1949-
See Joel, Billy
See also CA 108

John of the Cross, St. 1542-1591 .... **LC 18**

Johnson, B(ryan) S(tanley William)
1933-1973 .... **CLC 6, 9**
See also CA 9-12R; 53-56; CANR 9;
DLB 14, 40

Johnson, Benj. F. of Boo
See Riley, James Whitcomb

Johnson, Benjamin F. of Boo
See Riley, James Whitcomb

Johnson, Charles (Richard)
1948-........... **CLC 7, 51, 65; BLC 2**
See also BW; CA 116; CAAS 18;
CANR 42; DLB 33

Johnson, Denis 1949-............. **CLC 52**
See also CA 117; 121; DLB 120

Johnson, Diane 1934-........ **CLC 5, 13, 48**
See also CA 41-44R; CANR 17, 40;
DLBY 80; MTCW

Johnson, Eyvind (Olof Verner)
1900-1976 .... **CLC 14**
See also CA 73-76; 69-72; CANR 34

Johnson, J. R.
See James, C(yril) L(ionel) R(obert)

Johnson, James Weldon
1871-1938 .... **TCLC 3, 19; BLC 2**
See also BW; CA 104; 125;
CDALB 1917-1929; CLR 32; DLB 51;
MTCW; SATA 31

Johnson, Joyce 1935-............. **CLC 58**
See also CA 125; 129

Johnson, Lionel (Pigot)
1867-1902 .... **TCLC 19**
See also CA 117; DLB 19

Johnson, Mel
See Malzberg, Barry N(athaniel)

Johnson, Pamela Hansford
1912-1981 .... **CLC 1, 7, 27**
See also CA 1-4R; 104; CANR 2, 28;
DLB 15; MTCW

Johnson, Samuel
1709-1784 .... **LC 15; DA; WLC**
See also CDBLB 1660-1789; DLB 39, 95,
104

Johnson, Uwe
1934-1984 .... **CLC 5, 10, 15, 40**
See also CA 1-4R; 112; CANR 1, 39;
DLB 75; MTCW

Johnston, George (Benson) 1913-... **CLC 51**
See also CA 1-4R; CANR 5, 20; DLB 88

Johnston, Jennifer 1930-.......... **CLC 7**
See also CA 85-88; DLB 14

Jolley, (Monica) Elizabeth 1923-... **CLC 46**
See also CA 127; CAAS 13

Jones, Arthur Llewellyn 1863-1947
See Machen, Arthur
See also CA 104

Jones, D(ouglas) G(ordon) 1929-.... **CLC 10**
See also CA 29-32R; CANR 13; DLB 53

Jones, David (Michael)
1895-1974 .... **CLC 2, 4, 7, 13, 42**
See also CA 9-12R; 53-56; CANR 28;
CDBLB 1945-1960; DLB 20, 100; MTCW

Jones, David Robert 1947-
See Bowie, David
See also CA 103

Jones, Diana Wynne 1934- .... **CLC 26**
See also CA 49-52; CANR 4, 26; CLR 23;
JRDA; MAICYA; SAAS 7; SATA 9, 70

Jones, Edward P. 1950-........... **CLC 76**
See also CA 142

Jones, Gayl 1949-........ **CLC 6, 9; BLC 2**
See also BW; CA 77-80; CANR 27;
DLB 33; MTCW

Jones, James 1921-1977.... **CLC 1, 3, 10, 39**
See also AITN 1, 2; CA 1-4R; 69-72;
CANR 6; DLB 2; MTCW

Jones, John J.
See Lovecraft, H(oward) P(hillips)

Jones, LeRoi .... **CLC 1, 2, 3, 5, 10, 14**
See also Baraka, Amiri

Jones, Louis B. .... **CLC 65**
See also CA 141

Jones, Madison (Percy, Jr.) 1925- ... **CLC 4**
See also CA 13-16R; CAAS 11; CANR 7

Jones, Mervyn 1922- .... **CLC 10, 52**
See also CA 45-48; CAAS 5; CANR 1;
MTCW

Jones, Mick 1956(?)- .... **CLC 30**
See also Clash, The

Jones, Nettie (Pearl) 1941- .... **CLC 34**
See also CA 137

Jones, Preston 1936-1979 .... **CLC 10**
See also CA 73-76; 89-92; DLB 7

Jones, Robert F(rancis) 1934-....... **CLC 7**
See also CA 49-52; CANR 2

Jones, Rod 1953- .... **CLC 50**
See also CA 128

Jones, Terence Graham Parry
1942-....................... **CLC 21**
See also Jones, Terry; Monty Python
See also CA 112; 116; CANR 35; SATA 51

Jones, Terry
See Jones, Terence Graham Parry
See also SATA 67

Jones, Thom 1945(?)-............. **CLC 81**

Jong, Erica 1942-.......... **CLC 4, 6, 8, 18**
See also AITN 1; BEST 90:2; CA 73-76;
CANR 26; DLB 2, 5, 28; MTCW

Jonson, Ben(jamin)
1572(?)-1637 .... **LC 6; DA; DC 4; WLC**
See also CDBLB Before 1660; DLB 62, 121

Jordan, June 1936-.......... **CLC 5, 11, 23**
See also AAYA 2; BW; CA 33-36R;
CANR 25; CLR 10; DLB 38; MAICYA;
MTCW; SATA 4

Jordan, Pat(rick M.) 1941-........ **CLC 37**
See also CA 33-36R

Jorgensen, Ivar
See Ellison, Harlan

Jorgenson, Ivar
See Silverberg, Robert

Josipovici, Gabriel 1940-........ **CLC 6, 43**
See also CA 37-40R; CAAS 8; DLB 14

Joubert, Joseph 1754-1824 .... **NCLC 9**

Jouve, Pierre Jean 1887-1976...... **CLC 47**
See also CA 65-68

Kenyon, Robert O.
　See Kuttner, Henry

Kerouac, Jack . . . . . CLC **1, 2, 3, 5, 14, 29, 61**
　See also Kerouac, Jean-Louis Lebris de
　See also CDALB 1941-1968; DLB 2, 16;
　DLBD 3

Kerouac, Jean-Louis Lebris de 1922-1969
　See Kerouac, Jack
　See also AITN 1; CA 5-8R; 25-28R;
　CANR 26; DA; MTCW; WLC

Kerr, Jean 1923- . . . . CLC **22**
　See also CA 5-8R; CANR 7

Kerr, M. E. . . . . CLC **12, 35**
　See also Meaker, Marijane (Agnes)
　See also AAYA 2; CLR 29; SAAS 1

Kerr, Robert . . . . CLC **55**

Kerrigan, (Thomas) Anthony
　1918- . . . . CLC **4, 6**
　See also CA 49-52; CAAS 11; CANR 4

Kerry, Lois
　See Duncan, Lois

Kesey, Ken (Elton)
　1935- . . . . . . CLC **1, 3, 6, 11, 46, 64; DA;**
　　　　　　　　　　　　　　　　　　　　　　　　WLC
　See also CA 1-4R; CANR 22, 38;
　CDALB 1968-1988; DLB 2, 16; MTCW;
　SATA 66

Kesselring, Joseph (Otto)
　1902-1967 . . . . CLC **45**

Kessler, Jascha (Frederick) 1929- . . . . CLC **4**
　See also CA 17-20R; CANR 8

Kettelkamp, Larry (Dale) 1933- . . . . CLC **12**
　See also CA 29-32R; CANR 16; SAAS 3;
　SATA 2

Keyber, Conny
　See Fielding, Henry

Keyes, Daniel 1927- . . . . CLC **80; DA**
　See also CA 17-20R; CANR 10, 26;
　SATA 37

Khayyam, Omar
　1048-1131 . . . . CMLC **11; PC 8**

Kherdian, David 1931- . . . . CLC **6, 9**
　See also CA 21-24R; CAAS 2; CANR 39;
　CLR 24; JRDA; MAICYA; SATA 16, 74

Khlebnikov, Velimir . . . . TCLC **20**
　See also Khlebnikov, Viktor Vladimirovich

Khlebnikov, Viktor Vladimirovich 1885-1922
　See Khlebnikov, Velimir
　See also CA 117

Khodasevich, Vladislav (Felitsianovich)
　1886-1939 . . . . TCLC **15**
　See also CA 115

Kielland, Alexander Lange
　1849-1906 . . . . TCLC **5**
　See also CA 104

Kiely, Benedict 1919- . . . . CLC **23, 43**
　See also CA 1-4R; CANR 2; DLB 15

Kienzle, William X(avier) 1928- . . . . CLC **25**
　See also CA 93-96; CAAS 1; CANR 9, 31;
　MTCW

Kierkegaard, Soren 1813-1855 . . . . NCLC **34**

Killens, John Oliver 1916-1987 . . . . . CLC **10**
　See also BW; CA 77-80; 123; CAAS 2;
　CANR 26; DLB 33

Killigrew, Anne 1660-1685 . . . . LC **4**
　See also DLB 131

Kim
　See Simenon, Georges (Jacques Christian)

Kincaid, Jamaica
　1949- . . . . CLC **43, 68; BLC 2**
　See also BW; CA 125

King, Francis (Henry) 1923- . . . . . CLC **8, 53**
　See also CA 1-4R; CANR 1, 33; DLB 15;
　MTCW

King, Stephen (Edwin)
　1947- . . . . CLC **12, 26, 37, 61**
　See also AAYA 1; BEST 90:1; CA 61-64;
　CANR 1, 30; DLBY 80; JRDA; MTCW;
　SATA 9, 55

King, Steve
　See King, Stephen (Edwin)

Kingman, Lee . . . . CLC **17**
　See also Natti, (Mary) Lee
　See also SAAS 3; SATA 1, 67

Kingsley, Charles 1819-1875 . . . . . NCLC **35**
　See also DLB 21, 32; YABC 2

Kingsley, Sidney 1906- . . . . CLC **44**
　See also CA 85-88; DLB 7

Kingsolver, Barbara 1955- . . . . . . CLC **55, 81**
　See also CA 129; 134

Kingston, Maxine (Ting Ting) Hong
　1940- . . . . CLC **12, 19, 58**
　See also AAYA 8; CA 69-72; CANR 13,
　38; DLBY 80; MTCW; SATA 53

Kinnell, Galway
　1927- . . . . CLC **1, 2, 3, 5, 13, 29**
　See also CA 9-12R; CANR 10, 34; DLB 5;
　DLBY 87; MTCW

Kinsella, Thomas 1928- . . . . CLC **4, 19**
　See also CA 17-20R; CANR 15; DLB 27;
　MTCW

Kinsella, W(illiam) P(atrick)
　1935- . . . . CLC **27, 43**
　See also AAYA 7; CA 97-100; CAAS 7;
　CANR 21, 35; MTCW

Kipling, (Joseph) Rudyard
　1865-1936 . . . . . . TCLC **8, 17; DA; PC 3;**
　　　　　　　　　　　　　　　　　　　　SSC 5; WLC
　See also CA 105; 120; CANR 33;
　CDBLB 1890-1914; DLB 19, 34;
　MAICYA; MTCW; YABC 2

Kirkup, James 1918- . . . . CLC **1**
　See also CA 1-4R; CAAS 4; CANR 2;
　DLB 27; SATA 12

Kirkwood, James 1930(?)-1989 . . . . . . CLC **9**
　See also AITN 2; CA 1-4R; 128; CANR 6,
　40

Kis, Danilo 1935-1989 . . . . CLC **57**
　See also CA 109; 118; 129; MTCW

Kivi, Aleksis 1834-1872 . . . . NCLC **30**

Kizer, Carolyn (Ashley)
　1925- . . . . CLC **15, 39, 80**
　See also CA 65-68; CAAS 5; CANR 24;
　DLB 5

Klabund 1890-1928 . . . . TCLC **44**
　See also DLB 66

Klappert, Peter 1942- . . . . CLC **57**
　See also CA 33-36R; DLB 5

Klein, A(braham) M(oses)
　1909-1972 . . . . CLC **19**
　See also CA 101; 37-40R; DLB 68

Klein, Norma 1938-1989 . . . . CLC **30**
　See also AAYA 2; CA 41-44R; 128;
　CANR 15, 37; CLR 2, 19; JRDA;
　MAICYA; SAAS 1; SATA 7, 57

Klein, T(heodore) E(ibon) D(onald)
　1947- . . . . CLC **34**
　See also CA 119

Kleist, Heinrich von 1777-1811 . . . . NCLC **2**
　See also DLB 90

Klima, Ivan 1931- . . . . CLC **56**
　See also CA 25-28R; CANR 17

Klimentov, Andrei Platonovich 1899-1951
　See Platonov, Andrei
　See also CA 108

Klinger, Friedrich Maximilian von
　1752-1831 . . . . NCLC **1**
　See also DLB 94

Klopstock, Friedrich Gottlieb
　1724-1803 . . . . NCLC **11**
　See also DLB 97

Knebel, Fletcher 1911-1993 . . . . CLC **14**
　See also AITN 1; CA 1-4R; 140; CAAS 3;
　CANR 1, 36; SATA 36; SATA-Obit 75

Knickerbocker, Diedrich
　See Irving, Washington

Knight, Etheridge
　1931-1991 . . . . CLC **40; BLC 2**
　See also BW; CA 21-24R; 133; CANR 23;
　DLB 41

Knight, Sarah Kemble 1666-1727 . . . . . LC **7**
　See also DLB 24

Knowles, John
　1926- . . . . CLC **1, 4, 10, 26; DA**
　See also AAYA 10; CA 17-20R; CANR 40;
　CDALB 1968-1988; DLB 6; MTCW;
　SATA 8

Knox, Calvin M.
　See Silverberg, Robert

Knye, Cassandra
　See Disch, Thomas M(ichael)

Koch, C(hristopher) J(ohn) 1932- . . . CLC **42**
　See also CA 127

Koch, Christopher
　See Koch, C(hristopher) J(ohn)

Koch, Kenneth 1925- . . . . CLC **5, 8, 44**
　See also CA 1-4R; CANR 6, 36; DLB 5;
　SATA 65

Kochanowski, Jan 1530-1584 . . . . LC **10**

Kock, Charles Paul de
　1794-1871 . . . . NCLC **16**

Koda Shigeyuki 1867-1947
　See Rohan, Koda
　See also CA 121

Koestler, Arthur
　1905-1983 . . . . CLC **1, 3, 6, 8, 15, 33**
　See also CA 1-4R; 109; CANR 1, 33;
　CDBLB 1945-1960; DLBY 83; MTCW

Kogawa, Joy Nozomi 1935- . . . . CLC **78**
　See also CA 101; CANR 19

Kohout, Pavel 1928- . . . . CLC **13**
　See also CA 45-48; CANR 3

Koizumi, Yakumo
See Hearn, (Patricio) Lafcadio (Tessima Carlos)

Kolmar, Gertrud 1894-1943...... **TCLC 40**

Konrad, George
See Konrad, Gyoergy

Konrad, Gyoergy 1933- ...... **CLC 4, 10, 73**
See also CA 85-88

Konwicki, Tadeusz 1926-..... **CLC 8, 28, 54**
See also CA 101; CAAS 9; CANR 39;
MTCW

Koontz, Dean R(ay) 1945-......... **CLC 78**
See also AAYA 9; BEST 89:3, 90:2;
CA 108; CANR 19, 36; MTCW

Kopit, Arthur (Lee) 1937- .... **CLC 1, 18, 33**
See also AITN 1; CA 81-84; CABS 3;
DLB 7; MTCW

Kops, Bernard 1926-.............. **CLC 4**
See also CA 5-8R; DLB 13

Kornbluth, C(yril) M. 1923-1958.... **TCLC 8**
See also CA 105; DLB 8

Korolenko, V. G.
See Korolenko, Vladimir Galaktionovich

Korolenko, Vladimir
See Korolenko, Vladimir Galaktionovich

Korolenko, Vladimir G.
See Korolenko, Vladimir Galaktionovich

Korolenko, Vladimir Galaktionovich
1853-1921 .... **TCLC 22**
See also CA 121

Kosinski, Jerzy (Nikodem)
1933-1991 .... **CLC 1, 2, 3, 6, 10, 15, 53,
70**
See also CA 17-20R; 134; CANR 9; DLB 2;
DLBY 82; MTCW

Kostelanetz, Richard (Cory) 1940- .. **CLC 28**
See also CA 13-16R; CAAS 8; CANR 38

Kostrowitzki, Wilhelm Apollinaris de
1880-1918
See Apollinaire, Guillaume
See also CA 104

Kotlowitz, Robert 1924-............ **CLC 4**
See also CA 33-36R; CANR 36

Kotzebue, August (Friedrich Ferdinand) von
1761-1819 .... **NCLC 25**
See also DLB 94

Kotzwinkle, William 1938- ... **CLC 5, 14, 35**
See also CA 45-48; CANR 3; CLR 6;
MAICYA; SATA 24, 70

Kozol, Jonathan 1936-............. **CLC 17**
See also CA 61-64; CANR 16

Kozoll, Michael 1940(?)- .... **CLC 35**

Kramer, Kathryn 19(?)- .... **CLC 34**

Kramer, Larry 1935- .... **CLC 42**
See also CA 124; 126

Krasicki, Ignacy 1735-1801....... **NCLC 8**

Krasinski, Zygmunt 1812-1859 .... **NCLC 4**

Kraus, Karl 1874-1936........... **TCLC 5**
See also CA 104; DLB 118

Kreve (Mickevicius), Vincas
1882-1954 .... **TCLC 27**

Kristeva, Julia 1941- .... **CLC 77**

Kristofferson, Kris 1936-.......... **CLC 26**
See also CA 104

Krizanc, John 1956-.............. **CLC 57**

Krleza, Miroslav 1893-1981........ **CLC 8**
See also CA 97-100; 105

Kroetsch, Robert 1927- ...... **CLC 5, 23, 57**
See also CA 17-20R; CANR 8, 38; DLB 53;
MTCW

Kroetz, Franz
See Kroetz, Franz Xaver

Kroetz, Franz Xaver 1946- .... **CLC 41**
See also CA 130

Kroker, Arthur 1945-............. **CLC 77**

Kropotkin, Peter (Aleksieevich)
1842-1921 .... **TCLC 36**
See also CA 119

Krotkov, Yuri 1917-............. **CLC 19**
See also CA 102

Krumb
See Crumb, R(obert)

Krumgold, Joseph (Quincy)
1908-1980 .... **CLC 12**
See also CA 9-12R; 101; CANR 7;
MAICYA; SATA 1, 23, 48

Krumwitz
See Crumb, R(obert)

Krutch, Joseph Wood 1893-1970.... **CLC 24**
See also CA 1-4R; 25-28R; CANR 4;
DLB 63

Krutzch, Gus
See Eliot, T(homas) S(tearns)

Krylov, Ivan Andreevich
1768(?)-1844 .... **NCLC 1**

Kubin, Alfred 1877-1959 .... **TCLC 23**
See also CA 112; DLB 81

Kubrick, Stanley 1928-........... **CLC 16**
See also CA 81-84; CANR 33; DLB 26

Kumin, Maxine (Winokur)
1925-.................. **CLC 5, 13, 28**
See also AITN 2; CA 1-4R; CAAS 8;
CANR 1, 21; DLB 5; MTCW; SATA 12

Kundera, Milan
1929-........... **CLC 4, 9, 19, 32, 68**
See also AAYA 2; CA 85-88; CANR 19;
MTCW

Kunitz, Stanley (Jasspon)
1905-.................. **CLC 6, 11, 14**
See also CA 41-44R; CANR 26; DLB 48;
MTCW

Kunze, Reiner 1933-............. **CLC 10**
See also CA 93-96; DLB 75

Kuprin, Aleksandr Ivanovich
1870-1938 .... **TCLC 5**
See also CA 104

Kureishi, Hanif 1954(?)-.......... **CLC 64**
See also CA 139

Kurosawa, Akira 1910-........... **CLC 16**
See also CA 101

Kushner, Tony 1957(?)- .... **CLC 81**

Kuttner, Henry 1915-1958........ **TCLC 10**
See also CA 107; DLB 8

Kuzma, Greg 1944-............... **CLC 7**
See also CA 33-36R

Kuzmin, Mikhail 1872(?)-1936 .... **TCLC 40**

Kyd, Thomas 1558-1594...... **LC 22; DC 3**
See also DLB 62

Kyprianos, Iossif
See Samarakis, Antonis

La Bruyere, Jean de 1645-1696..... **LC 17**

Lacan, Jacques (Marie Emile)
1901-1981 .... **CLC 75**
See also CA 121; 104

**Laclos, Pierre Ambroise Francois Choderlos
de** 1741-1803 .... **NCLC 4**

Lacolere, Francois
See Aragon, Louis

La Colere, Francois
See Aragon, Louis

La Deshabilleuse
See Simenon, Georges (Jacques Christian)

Lady Gregory
See Gregory, Isabella Augusta (Persse)

Lady of Quality, A
See Bagnold, Enid

**La Fayette, Marie (Madelaine Pioche de la
Vergne Comtes** 1634-1693....... **LC 2**

Lafayette, Rene
See Hubbard, L(afayette) Ron(ald)

Laforgue, Jules 1860-1887........ **NCLC 5**

Lagerkvist, Paer (Fabian)
1891-1974 .... **CLC 7, 10, 13, 54**
See also Lagerkvist, Par
See also CA 85-88; 49-52; MTCW

Lagerkvist, Par
See Lagerkvist, Paer (Fabian)
See also SSC 12

Lagerloef, Selma (Ottiliana Lovisa)
1858-1940 .... **TCLC 4, 36**
See also Lagerlof, Selma (Ottiliana Lovisa)
See also CA 108; CLR 7; SATA 15

Lagerlof, Selma (Ottiliana Lovisa)
See Lagerloef, Selma (Ottiliana Lovisa)
See also CLR 7; SATA 15

La Guma, (Justin) Alex(ander)
1925-1985 .... **CLC 19**
See also BW; CA 49-52; 118; CANR 25;
DLB 117; MTCW

Laidlaw, A. K.
See Grieve, C(hristopher) M(urray)

Lainez, Manuel Mujica
See Mujica Lainez, Manuel
See also HW

Lamartine, Alphonse (Marie Louis Prat) de
1790-1869 .... **NCLC 11**

Lamb, Charles
1775-1834 .... **NCLC 10; DA; WLC**
See also CDBLB 1789-1832; DLB 93, 107;
SATA 17

Lamb, Lady Caroline 1785-1828.. **NCLC 38**
See also DLB 116

Lamming, George (William)
1927-............. **CLC 2, 4, 66; BLC 2**
See also BW; CA 85-88; CANR 26;
DLB 125; MTCW

L'Amour, Louis (Dearborn)
1908-1988 . . . . CLC 25, 55
See also AITN 2; BEST 89:2; CA 1-4R;
125; CANR 3, 25, 40; DLBY 80; MTCW

Lampedusa, Giuseppe (Tomasi) di . . . TCLC 13
See also Tomasi di Lampedusa, Giuseppe

Lampman, Archibald 1861-1899 . . NCLC 25
See also DLB 92

Lancaster, Bruce 1896-1963. . . . . . . CLC 36
See also CA 9-10; CAP 1; SATA 9

Landau, Mark Alexandrovich
See Aldanov, Mark (Alexandrovich)

Landau-Aldanov, Mark Alexandrovich
See Aldanov, Mark (Alexandrovich)

Landis, John 1950- . . . . CLC 26
See also CA 112; 122

Landolfi, Tommaso 1908-1979. . . CLC 11, 49
See also CA 127; 117

Landon, Letitia Elizabeth
1802-1838 . . . . NCLC 15
See also DLB 96

Landor, Walter Savage
1775-1864 . . . . NCLC 14
See also DLB 93, 107

Landwirth, Heinz 1927-
See Lind, Jakov
See also CA 9-12R; CANR 7

Lane, Patrick 1939- . . . . CLC 25
See also CA 97-100; DLB 53

Lang, Andrew 1844-1912. . . . . TCLC 16
See also CA 114; 137; DLB 98; MAICYA;
SATA 16

Lang, Fritz 1890-1976 . . . . CLC 20
See also CA 77-80; 69-72; CANR 30

Lange, John
See Crichton, (John) Michael

Langer, Elinor 1939- . . . . CLC 34
See also CA 121

Langland, William
1330(?)-1400(?) . . . . LC 19; DA

Langstaff, Launcelot
See Irving, Washington

Lanier, Sidney 1842-1881 . . . . NCLC 6
See also DLB 64; MAICYA; SATA 18

Lanyer, Aemilia 1569-1645 . . . . LC 10

Lao Tzu . . . . CMLC 7

Lapine, James (Elliot) 1949- . . . . CLC 39
See also CA 123; 130

Larbaud, Valery (Nicolas)
1881-1957 . . . . TCLC 9
See also CA 106

Lardner, Ring
See Lardner, Ring(gold) W(ilmer)

Lardner, Ring W., Jr.
See Lardner, Ring(gold) W(ilmer)

Lardner, Ring(gold) W(ilmer)
1885-1933 . . . . TCLC 2, 14
See also CA 104; 131; CDALB 1917-1929;
DLB 11, 25, 86; MTCW

Laredo, Betty
See Codrescu, Andrei

Larkin, Maia
See Wojciechowska, Maia (Teresa)

Larkin, Philip (Arthur)
1922-1985 . . . . CLC 3, 5, 8, 9, 13, 18, 33,
39, 64
See also CA 5-8R; 117; CANR 24;
CDBLB 1960 to Present; DLB 27;
MTCW

Larra (y Sanchez de Castro), Mariano Jose de
1809-1837 . . . . NCLC 17

Larsen, Eric 1941- . . . . CLC 55
See also CA 132

Larsen, Nella 1891-1964 . . . CLC 37; BLC 2
See also BW; CA 125; DLB 51

Larson, Charles R(aymond) 1938-. . . CLC 31
See also CA 53-56; CANR 4

Latham, Jean Lee 1902-. . . . . CLC 12
See also AITN 1; CA 5-8R; CANR 7;
MAICYA; SATA 2, 68

Latham, Mavis
See Clark, Mavis Thorpe

Lathen, Emma . . . . CLC 2
See also Hennissart, Martha; Latsis, Mary
J(ane)

Lathrop, Francis
See Leiber, Fritz (Reuter, Jr.)

Latsis, Mary J(ane)
See Lathen, Emma
See also CA 85-88

Lattimore, Richmond (Alexander)
1906-1984 . . . . CLC 3
See also CA 1-4R; 112; CANR 1

Laughlin, James 1914- . . . . CLC 49
See also CA 21-24R; CANR 9; DLB 48

Laurence, (Jean) Margaret (Wemyss)
1926-1987 . . CLC 3, 6, 13, 50, 62; SSC 7
See also CA 5-8R; 121; CANR 33; DLB 53;
MTCW; SATA 50

Laurent, Antoine 1952- . . . . CLC 50

Lauscher, Hermann
See Hesse, Hermann

Lautreamont, Comte de
1846-1870 . . . . NCLC 12; SSC 14

Laverty, Donald
See Blish, James (Benjamin)

Lavin, Mary 1912- . . . . . . CLC 4, 18; SSC 4
See also CA 9-12R; CANR 33; DLB 15;
MTCW

Lavond, Paul Dennis
See Kornbluth, C(yril) M.; Pohl, Frederik

Lawler, Raymond Evenor 1922- . . . . CLC 58
See also CA 103

Lawrence, D(avid) H(erbert Richards)
1885-1930 . . . . TCLC 2, 9, 16, 33, 48;
DA; SSC 4; WLC
See also CA 104; 121; CDBLB 1914-1945;
DLB 10, 19, 36, 98; MTCW

Lawrence, T(homas) E(dward)
1888-1935 . . . . TCLC 18
See also Dale, Colin
See also CA 115

Lawrence of Arabia
See Lawrence, T(homas) E(dward)

Lawson, Henry (Archibald Hertzberg)
1867-1922 . . . . TCLC 27
See also CA 120

Lawton, Dennis
See Faust, Frederick (Schiller)

Laxness, Halldor. . . . . CLC 25
See also Gudjonsson, Halldor Kiljan

Layamon fl. c. 1200-. . . . . CMLC 10

Laye, Camara
1928-1980 . . . . CLC 4, 38; BLC 2
See also BW; CA 85-88; 97-100; CANR 25;
MTCW

Layton, Irving (Peter) 1912- . . . . . CLC 2, 15
See also CA 1-4R; CANR 2, 33, 43;
DLB 88; MTCW

Lazarus, Emma 1849-1887. . . . . NCLC 8

Lazarus, Felix
See Cable, George Washington

Lazarus, Henry
See Slavitt, David R(ytman)

Lea, Joan
See Neufeld, John (Arthur)

Leacock, Stephen (Butler)
1869-1944 . . . . TCLC 2
See also CA 104; 141; DLB 92

Lear, Edward 1812-1888 . . . . NCLC 3
See also CLR 1; DLB 32; MAICYA;
SATA 18

Lear, Norman (Milton) 1922- . . . . . . CLC 12
See also CA 73-76

Leavis, F(rank) R(aymond)
1895-1978 . . . . CLC 24
See also CA 21-24R; 77-80; MTCW

Leavitt, David 1961- . . . . CLC 34
See also CA 116; 122; DLB 130

Leblanc, Maurice (Marie Emile)
1864-1941 . . . . TCLC 49
See also CA 110

Lebowitz, Fran(ces Ann)
1951(?)- . . . . CLC 11, 36
See also CA 81-84; CANR 14; MTCW

le Carre, John . . . . CLC 3, 5, 9, 15, 28
See also Cornwell, David (John Moore)
See also BEST 89:4; CDBLB 1960 to
Present; DLB 87

Le Clezio, J(ean) M(arie) G(ustave)
1940- . . . . CLC 31
See also CA 116; 128; DLB 83

Leconte de Lisle, Charles-Marie-Rene
1818-1894 . . . . NCLC 29

Le Coq, Monsieur
See Simenon, Georges (Jacques Christian)

Leduc, Violette 1907-1972. . . . . CLC 22
See also CA 13-14; 33-36R; CAP 1

Ledwidge, Francis 1887(?)-1917 . . . TCLC 23
See also CA 123; DLB 20

Lee, Andrea 1953- . . . . CLC 36; BLC 2
See also BW; CA 125

Lee, Andrew
See Auchincloss, Louis (Stanton)

Lee, Don L.. CLC 2
See also Madhubuti, Haki R.

Lee, George W(ashington)
1894-1976 . . . . CLC 52; BLC 2
See also BW; CA 125; DLB 51

Lewis, (Harry) Sinclair
1885-1951 . . . . . **TCLC 4, 13, 23, 39; DA;**
WLC
See also CA 104; 133; CDALB 1917-1929;
DLB 9, 102; DLBD 1; MTCW

Lewis, (Percy) Wyndham
1884(?)-1957 . . . . **TCLC 2, 9**
See also CA 104; DLB 15

Lewisohn, Ludwig 1883-1955 . . . . . . **TCLC 19**
See also CA 107; DLB 4, 9, 28, 102

Lezama Lima, Jose 1910-1976 . . . **CLC 4, 10**
See also CA 77-80; DLB 113; HW

L'Heureux, John (Clarke) 1934- . . . . **CLC 52**
See also CA 13-16R; CANR 23

Liddell, C. H.
See Kuttner, Henry

Lie, Jonas (Lauritz Idemil)
1833-1908(?) . . . . **TCLC 5**
See also CA 115

Lieber, Joel 1937-1971 . . . . **CLC 6**
See also CA 73-76; 29-32R

Lieber, Stanley Martin
See Lee, Stan

Lieberman, Laurence (James)
1935- . . . . **CLC 4, 36**
See also CA 17-20R; CANR 8, 36

Lieksman, Anders
See Haavikko, Paavo Juhani

Li Fei-kan 1904- . . . . **CLC 18**
See also CA 105

Lifton, Robert Jay 1926- . . . . **CLC 67**
See also CA 17-20R; CANR 27; SATA 66

Lightfoot, Gordon 1938- . . . . **CLC 26**
See also CA 109

Lightman, Alan P. 1948- . . . . **CLC 81**
See also CA 141

Ligotti, Thomas 1953- . . . . **CLC 44**
See also CA 123

Liliencron, (Friedrich Adolf Axel) Detlev von
1844-1909 . . . . **TCLC 18**
See also CA 117

Lima, Jose Lezama
See Lezama Lima, Jose

Lima Barreto, Afonso Henrique de
1881-1922 . . . . **TCLC 23**
See also CA 117

Limonov, Eduard . . . . **CLC 67**

Lin, Frank
See Atherton, Gertrude (Franklin Horn)

Lincoln, Abraham 1809-1865 . . . . . **NCLC 18**

Lind, Jakov . . . . **CLC 1, 2, 4, 27**
See also Landwirth, Heinz
See also CAAS 4

Lindsay, David 1878-1945 . . . . **TCLC 15**
See also CA 113

Lindsay, (Nicholas) Vachel
1879-1931 . . . . **TCLC 17; DA; WLC**
See also CA 114; 135; CDALB 1865-1917;
DLB 54; SATA 40

Linke-Poot
See Doeblin, Alfred

Linney, Romulus 1930- . . . . **CLC 51**
See also CA 1-4R; CANR 40

Linton, Eliza Lynn 1822-1898 . . . . **NCLC 41**
See also DLB 18

Li Po 701-763 . . . . **CMLC 2**

Lipsius, Justus 1547-1606 . . . . **LC 16**

Lipsyte, Robert (Michael)
1938- . . . . **CLC 21; DA**
See also AAYA 7; CA 17-20R; CANR 8;
CLR 23; JRDA; MAICYA; SATA 5, 68

Lish, Gordon (Jay) 1934- . . . . **CLC 45**
See also CA 113; 117; DLB 130

Lispector, Clarice 1925-1977 . . . . . . **CLC 43**
See also CA 139; 116; DLB 113

Littell, Robert 1935(?)- . . . . **CLC 42**
See also CA 109; 112

Littlewit, Humphrey Gent.
See Lovecraft, H(oward) P(hillips)

Litwos
See Sienkiewicz, Henryk (Adam Alexander
Pius)

Liu E 1857-1909 . . . . **TCLC 15**
See also CA 115

Lively, Penelope (Margaret)
1933- . . . . **CLC 32, 50**
See also CA 41-44R; CANR 29; CLR 7;
DLB 14; JRDA; MAICYA; MTCW;
SATA 7, 60

Livesay, Dorothy (Kathleen)
1909- . . . . **CLC 4, 15, 79**
See also AITN 2; CA 25-28R; CAAS 8;
CANR 36; DLB 68; MTCW

Livy c. 59B.C.-c. 17 . . . . **CMLC 11**

Lizardi, Jose Joaquin Fernandez de
1776-1827 . . . . **NCLC 30**

Llewellyn, Richard . . . . **CLC 7**
See also Llewellyn Lloyd, Richard Dafydd
Vivian
See also DLB 15

Llewellyn Lloyd, Richard Dafydd Vivian
1906-1983 . . . . **CLC 80**
See also Llewellyn, Richard
See also CA 53-56; 111; CANR 7;
SATA 11, 37

Llosa, (Jorge) Mario (Pedro) Vargas
See Vargas Llosa, (Jorge) Mario (Pedro)

Lloyd Webber, Andrew 1948-
See Webber, Andrew Lloyd
See also AAYA 1; CA 116; SATA 56

Llull, Ramon c. 1235-c. 1316 . . . . . **CMLC 12**

Locke, Alain (Le Roy)
1886-1954 . . . . **TCLC 43**
See also BW; CA 106; 124; DLB 51

Locke, John 1632-1704 . . . . **LC 7**
See also DLB 101

Locke-Elliott, Sumner
See Elliott, Sumner Locke

Lockhart, John Gibson
1794-1854 . . . . **NCLC 6**
See also DLB 110, 116

Lodge, David (John) 1935- . . . . **CLC 36**
See also BEST 90:1; CA 17-20R; CANR 19;
DLB 14; MTCW

Loennbohm, Armas Eino Leopold 1878-1926
See Leino, Eino
See also CA 123

Loewinsohn, Ron(ald William)
1937- . . . . **CLC 52**
See also CA 25-28R

Logan, Jake
See Smith, Martin Cruz

Logan, John (Burton) 1923-1987 . . . . . **CLC 5**
See also CA 77-80; 124; DLB 5

Lo Kuan-chung 1330(?)-1400(?) . . . . . . **LC 12**

Lombard, Nap
See Johnson, Pamela Hansford

London, Jack . . **TCLC 9, 15, 39; SSC 4; WLC**
See also London, John Griffith
See also AITN 2; CDALB 1865-1917;
DLB 8, 12, 78; SATA 18

London, John Griffith 1876-1916
See London, Jack
See also CA 110; 119; DA; JRDA;
MAICYA; MTCW

Long, Emmett
See Leonard, Elmore (John, Jr.)

Longbaugh, Harry
See Goldman, William (W.)

Longfellow, Henry Wadsworth
1807-1882 . . . . **NCLC 2; DA**
See also CDALB 1640-1865; DLB 1, 59;
SATA 19

Longley, Michael 1939- . . . . **CLC 29**
See also CA 102; DLB 40

Longus fl. c. 2nd cent. - . . . . **CMLC 7**

Longway, A. Hugh
See Lang, Andrew

Lopate, Phillip 1943- . . . . **CLC 29**
See also CA 97-100; DLBY 80

Lopez Portillo (y Pacheco), Jose
1920- . . . . **CLC 46**
See also CA 129; HW

Lopez y Fuentes, Gregorio
1897(?)-1966 . . . . **CLC 32**
See also CA 131; HW

Lorca, Federico Garcia
See Garcia Lorca, Federico

Lord, Bette Bao 1938- . . . . **CLC 23**
See also BEST 90:3; CA 107; CANR 41;
SATA 58

Lord Auch
See Bataille, Georges

Lord Byron
See Byron, George Gordon (Noel)

Lord Dunsany . . . . **TCLC 2**
See also Dunsany, Edward John Moreton
Drax Plunkett

Lorde, Audre (Geraldine)
1934-1992 . . . . **CLC 18, 71; BLC 2**
See also BW; CA 25-28R; 142; CANR 16,
26; DLB 41; MTCW

Lord Jeffrey
See Jeffrey, Francis

Lorenzo, Heberto Padilla
See Padilla (Lorenzo), Heberto

Loris
See Hofmannsthal, Hugo von

Loti, Pierre . . . . **TCLC 11**
See also Viaud, (Louis Marie) Julien
See also DLB 123

MacLennan, (John) Hugh
1907-1990 . . . . **CLC 2, 14**
See also CA 5-8R; 142; CANR 33; DLB 68;
MTCW

MacLeod, Alistair 1936- . . . . **CLC 56**
See also CA 123; DLB 60

MacNeice, (Frederick) Louis
1907-1963 . . . . **CLC 1, 4, 10, 53**
See also CA 85-88; DLB 10, 20; MTCW

MacNeill, Dand
See Fraser, George MacDonald

Macpherson, (Jean) Jay 1931- . . . . . . **CLC 14**
See also CA 5-8R; DLB 53

MacShane, Frank 1927- . . . . **CLC 39**
See also CA 9-12R; CANR 3, 33; DLB 111

Macumber, Mari
See Sandoz, Mari(e Susette)

Madach, Imre 1823-1864 . . . . **NCLC 19**

Madden, (Jerry) David 1933- . . . . **CLC 5, 15**
See also CA 1-4R; CAAS 3; CANR 4;
DLB 6; MTCW

Maddern, Al(an)
See Ellison, Harlan

Madhubuti, Haki R.
1942- . . . . **CLC 6, 73; BLC 2; PC 5**
See also Lee, Don L.
See also BW; CA 73-76; CANR 24; DLB 5,
41; DLBD 8

Madow, Pauline (Reichberg) . . . . **CLC 1**
See also CA 9-12R

Maepenn, Hugh
See Kuttner, Henry

Maepenn, K. H.
See Kuttner, Henry

Maeterlinck, Maurice 1862-1949 . . . **TCLC 3**
See also CA 104; 136; SATA 66

Maginn, William 1794-1842 . . . . . . **NCLC 8**
See also DLB 110

Mahapatra, Jayanta 1928- . . . . **CLC 33**
See also CA 73-76; CAAS 9; CANR 15, 33

Mahfouz, Naguib (Abdel Aziz Al-Sabilgi)
1911(?)-
See Mahfuz, Najib
See also BEST 89:2; CA 128; MTCW

Mahfuz, Najib . . . . **CLC 52, 55**
See also Mahfouz, Naguib (Abdel Aziz
Al-Sabilgi)
See also DLBY 88

Mahon, Derek 1941- . . . . **CLC 27**
See also CA 113; 128; DLB 40

Mailer, Norman
1923- . . . . . . **CLC 1, 2, 3, 4, 5, 8, 11, 14,
28, 39, 74; DA**
See also AITN 2; CA 9-12R; CABS 1;
CANR 28; CDALB 1968-1988; DLB 2,
16, 28; DLBD 3; DLBY 80, 83; MTCW

Maillet, Antonine 1929- . . . . **CLC 54**
See also CA 115; 120; DLB 60

Mais, Roger 1905-1955 . . . . **TCLC 8**
See also BW; CA 105; 124; DLB 125;
MTCW

Maitland, Sara (Louise) 1950- . . . . . . **CLC 49**
See also CA 69-72; CANR 13

Major, Clarence
1936- . . . . **CLC 3, 19, 48; BLC 2**
See also BW; CA 21-24R; CAAS 6;
CANR 13, 25; DLB 33

Major, Kevin (Gerald) 1949- . . . . **CLC 26**
See also CA 97-100; CANR 21, 38;
CLR 11; DLB 60; JRDA; MAICYA;
SATA 32

Maki, James
See Ozu, Yasujiro

Malabaila, Damiano
See Levi, Primo

Malamud, Bernard
1914-1986 . . . . . **CLC 1, 2, 3, 5, 8, 9, 11,
18, 27, 44, 78; DA; WLC**
See also CA 5-8R; 118; CABS 1; CANR 28;
CDALB 1941-1968; DLB 2, 28;
DLBY 80, 86; MTCW

Malaparte, Curzio 1898-1957 . . . . . **TCLC 52**

Malcolm, Dan
See Silverberg, Robert

Malherbe, Francois de 1555-1628 . . . . . **LC 5**

Mallarme, Stephane
1842-1898 . . . . **NCLC 4, 41; PC 4**

Mallet-Joris, Francoise 1930- . . . . . . **CLC 11**
See also CA 65-68; CANR 17; DLB 83

Malley, Ern
See McAuley, James Phillip

Mallowan, Agatha Christie
See Christie, Agatha (Mary Clarissa)

Maloff, Saul 1922- . . . . **CLC 5**
See also CA 33-36R

Malone, Louis
See MacNeice, (Frederick) Louis

Malone, Michael (Christopher)
1942- . . . . **CLC 43**
See also CA 77-80; CANR 14, 32

Malory, (Sir) Thomas
1410(?)-1471(?) . . . . **LC 11; DA**
See also CDBLB Before 1660; SATA 33, 59

Malouf, (George Joseph) David
1934- . . . . **CLC 28**
See also CA 124

Malraux, (Georges-)Andre
1901-1976 . . . . . . **CLC 1, 4, 9, 13, 15, 57**
See also CA 21-22; 69-72; CANR 34;
CAP 2; DLB 72; MTCW

Malzberg, Barry N(athaniel) 1939-... **CLC 7**
See also CA 61-64; CAAS 4; CANR 16;
DLB 8

Mamet, David (Alan)
1947- . . . . **CLC 9, 15, 34, 46; DC 4**
See also AAYA 3; CA 81-84; CABS 3;
CANR 15, 41; DLB 7; MTCW

Mamoulian, Rouben (Zachary)
1897-1987 . . . . **CLC 16**
See also CA 25-28R; 124

Mandelstam, Osip (Emilievich)
1891(?)-1938(?) . . . . **TCLC 2, 6**
See also CA 104

Mander, (Mary) Jane 1877-1949 . . . **TCLC 31**

Mandiargues, Andre Pieyre de . . . . . . **CLC 41**
See also Pieyre de Mandiargues, Andre
See also DLB 83

Mandrake, Ethel Belle
See Thurman, Wallace (Henry)

Mangan, James Clarence
1803-1849 . . . . **NCLC 27**

Maniere, J.-E.
See Giraudoux, (Hippolyte) Jean

Manley, (Mary) Delariviere
1672(?)-1724 . . . . **LC 1**
See also DLB 39, 80

Mann, Abel
See Creasey, John

Mann, (Luiz) Heinrich 1871-1950... **TCLC 9**
See also CA 106; DLB 66

Mann, (Paul) Thomas
1875-1955 . . . . **TCLC 2, 8, 14, 21, 35, 44;
DA; SSC 5; WLC**
See also CA 104; 128; DLB 66; MTCW

Manning, David
See Faust, Frederick (Schiller)

Manning, Frederic 1887(?)-1935 . . . **TCLC 25**
See also CA 124

Manning, Olivia 1915-1980 . . . . . . **CLC 5, 19**
See also CA 5-8R; 101; CANR 29; MTCW

Mano, D. Keith 1942- . . . . **CLC 2, 10**
See also CA 25-28R; CAAS 6; CANR 26;
DLB 6

Mansfield, Katherine
. . . . **TCLC 2, 8, 39; SSC 9; WLC**
See also Beauchamp, Kathleen Mansfield

Manso, Peter 1940- . . . . **CLC 39**
See also CA 29-32R

Mantecon, Juan Jimenez
See Jimenez (Mantecon), Juan Ramon

Manton, Peter
See Creasey, John

Man Without a Spleen, A
See Chekhov, Anton (Pavlovich)

Manzoni, Alessandro 1785-1873 . . **NCLC 29**

Mapu, Abraham (ben Jekutiel)
1808-1867 . . . . **NCLC 18**

Mara, Sally
See Queneau, Raymond

Marat, Jean Paul 1743-1793 . . . . **LC 10**

Marcel, Gabriel Honore
1889-1973 . . . . **CLC 15**
See also CA 102; 45-48; MTCW

Marchbanks, Samuel
See Davies, (William) Robertson

Marchi, Giacomo
See Bassani, Giorgio

Margulies, Donald . . . . **CLC 76**

Marie de France c. 12th cent. - . . . . **CMLC 8**

Marie de l'Incarnation 1599-1672 . . . . **LC 10**

Mariner, Scott
See Pohl, Frederik

Marinetti, Filippo Tommaso
1876-1944 . . . . :. . **TCLC 10**
See also CA 107; DLB 114

Marivaux, Pierre Carlet de Chamblain de
1688-1763 . . . . **LC 4**

Markandaya, Kamala . . . . **CLC 8, 38**
See also Taylor, Kamala (Purnaiya)

Markfield, Wallace 1926-.......... **CLC 8**
See also CA 69-72; CAAS 3; DLB 2, 28

Markham, Edwin 1852-1940 ...... **TCLC 47**
See also DLB 54

Markham, Robert
See Amis, Kingsley (William)

Marks, J
See Highwater, Jamake (Mamake)

Marks-Highwater, J
See Highwater, Jamake (Mamake)

Markson, David M(errill) 1927-.... **CLC 67**
See also CA 49-52; CANR 1

Marley, Bob..................... **CLC 17**
See also Marley, Robert Nesta

Marley, Robert Nesta 1945-1981
See Marley, Bob
See also CA 107; 103

Marlowe, Christopher
1564-1593 ..... **LC 22; DA; DC 1; WLC**
See also CDBLB Before 1660; DLB 62

Marmontel, Jean-Francois
1723-1799 .... **LC 2**

Marquand, John P(hillips)
1893-1960 .... **CLC 2, 10**
See also CA 85-88; DLB 9, 102

Marquez, Gabriel (Jose) Garcia...... **CLC 68**
See also Garcia Marquez, Gabriel (Jose)

Marquis, Don(ald Robert Perry)
1878-1937 .... **TCLC 7**
See also CA 104; DLB 11, 25

Marric, J. J.
See Creasey, John

Marrow, Bernard
See Moore, Brian

Marryat, Frederick 1792-1848 .... **NCLC 3**
See also DLB 21

Marsden, James
See Creasey, John

Marsh, (Edith) Ngaio
1899-1982 .... **CLC 7, 53**
See also CA 9-12R; CANR 6; DLB 77;
MTCW

Marshall, Garry 1934-............ **CLC 17**
See also AAYA 3; CA 111; SATA 60

Marshall, Paule
1929- .... **CLC 27, 72; BLC 3; SSC 3**
See also BW; CA 77-80; CANR 25;
DLB 33; MTCW

Marsten, Richard
See Hunter, Evan

Martha, Henry
See Harris, Mark

Martin, Ken
See Hubbard, L(afayette) Ron(ald)

Martin, Richard
See Creasey, John

Martin, Steve 1945-.............. **CLC 30**
See also CA 97-100; CANR 30; MTCW

Martin, Violet Florence
1862-1915 .... **TCLC 51**

Martin, Webber
See Silverberg, Robert

Martindale, Patrick Victor
See White, Patrick (Victor Martindale)

Martin du Gard, Roger
1881-1958 .... **TCLC 24**
See also CA 118; DLB 65

Martineau, Harriet 1802-1876.... **NCLC 26**
See also DLB 21, 55; YABC 2

Martines, Julia
See O'Faolain, Julia

Martinez, Jacinto Benavente y
See Benavente (y Martinez), Jacinto

Martinez Ruiz, Jose 1873-1967
See Azorin; Ruiz, Jose Martinez
See also CA 93-96; HW

Martinez Sierra, Gregorio
1881-1947 .... **TCLC 6**
See also CA 115

Martinez Sierra, Maria (de la O'LeJarraga)
1874-1974 .... **TCLC 6**
See also CA 115

Martinsen, Martin
See Follett, Ken(neth Martin)

Martinson, Harry (Edmund)
1904-1978 .... **CLC 14**
See also CA 77-80; CANR 34

Marut, Ret
See Traven, B.

Marut, Robert
See Traven, B.

Marvell, Andrew
1621-1678 .... **LC 4; DA; WLC**
See also CDBLB 1660-1789; DLB 131

Marx, Karl (Heinrich)
1818-1883 .... **NCLC 17**
See also DLB 129

Masaoka Shiki................... **TCLC 18**
See also Masaoka Tsunenori

Masaoka Tsunenori 1867-1902
See Masaoka Shiki
See also CA 117

Masefield, John (Edward)
1878-1967 .... **CLC 11, 47**
See also CA 19-20; 25-28R; CANR 33;
CAP 2; CDBLB 1890-1914; DLB 10;
MTCW; SATA 19

Maso, Carole 19(?)- .... **CLC 44**

Mason, Bobbie Ann
1940-............. **CLC 28, 43; SSC 4**
See also AAYA 5; CA 53-56; CANR 11,
31; DLBY 87; MTCW

Mason, Ernst
See Pohl, Frederik

Mason, Lee W.
See Malzberg, Barry N(athaniel)

Mason, Nick 1945-.............. **CLC 35**
See also Pink Floyd

Mason, Tally
See Derleth, August (William)

Mass, William
See Gibson, William

Masters, Edgar Lee
1868-1950 ...... **TCLC 2, 25; DA; PC 1**
See also CA 104; 133; CDALB 1865-1917;
DLB 54; MTCW

Masters, Hilary 1928-............ **CLC 48**
See also CA 25-28R; CANR 13

Mastrosimone, William 19(?)-...... **CLC 36**

Mathe, Albert
See Camus, Albert

Matheson, Richard Burton 1926-... **CLC 37**
See also CA 97-100; DLB 8, 44

Mathews, Harry 1930-.......... **CLC 6, 52**
See also CA 21-24R; CAAS 6; CANR 18,
40

Mathias, Roland (Glyn) 1915-...... **CLC 45**
See also CA 97-100; CANR 19, 41; DLB 27

Matsuo Basho 1644-1694........... **PC 3**

Mattheson, Rodney
See Creasey, John

Matthews, Greg 1949-............ **CLC 45**
See also CA 135

Matthews, William 1942-.......... **CLC 40**
See also CA 29-32R; CAAS 18; CANR 12;
DLB 5

Matthias, John (Edward) 1941-...... **CLC 9**
See also CA 33-36R

Matthiessen, Peter
1927- .... **CLC 5, 7, 11, 32, 64**
See also AAYA 6; BEST 90:4; CA 9-12R;
CANR 21; DLB 6; MTCW; SATA 27

Maturin, Charles Robert
1780(?)-1824 .... **NCLC 6**

Matute (Ausejo), Ana Maria
1925-...................... **CLC 11**
See also CA 89-92; MTCW

Maugham, W. S.
See Maugham, W(illiam) Somerset

Maugham, W(illiam) Somerset
1874-1965 ...... **CLC 1, 11, 15, 67; DA;
SSC 8; WLC**
See also CA 5-8R; 25-28R; CANR 40;
CDBLB 1914-1945; DLB 10, 36, 77, 100;
MTCW; SATA 54

Maugham, William Somerset
See Maugham, W(illiam) Somerset

Maupassant, (Henri Rene Albert) Guy de
1850-1893 .... **NCLC 1, 42; DA; SSC 1;
WLC**
See also DLB 123

Maurhut, Richard
See Traven, B.

Mauriac, Claude 1914-............. **CLC 9**
See also CA 89-92; DLB 83

Mauriac, Francois (Charles)
1885-1970 .... **CLC 4, 9, 56**
See also CA 25-28; CAP 2; DLB 65;
MTCW

Mavor, Osborne Henry 1888-1951
See Bridie, James
See also CA 104

Maxwell, William (Keepers, Jr.)
1908- .... **CLC 19**
See also CA 93-96; DLBY 80

May, Elaine 1932- .... **CLC 16**
See also CA 124; 142; DLB 44

Mayakovski, Vladimir (Vladimirovich)
1893-1930 .... **TCLC 4, 18**
See also CA 104

Mayhew, Henry 1812-1887 ...... **NCLC 31**
See also DLB 18, 55

Maynard, Joyce 1953- .... **CLC 23**
See also CA 111; 129

Mayne, William (James Carter)
1928- .... **CLC 12**
See also CA 9-12R; CANR 37; CLR 25;
JRDA; MAICYA; SAAS 11; SATA 6, 68

Mayo, Jim
See L'Amour, Louis (Dearborn)

Maysles, Albert 1926- .... **CLC 16**
See also CA 29-32R

Maysles, David 1932- .... **CLC 16**

Mazer, Norma Fox 1931- .... **CLC 26**
See also AAYA 5; CA 69-72; CANR 12,
32; CLR 23; JRDA; MAICYA; SAAS 1;
SATA 24, 67

Mazzini, Guiseppe 1805-1872 .... **NCLC 34**

McAuley, James Phillip
1917-1976 .... **CLC 45**
See also CA 97-100

McBain, Ed
See Hunter, Evan

McBrien, William Augustine
1930- .... **CLC 44**
See also CA 107

McCaffrey, Anne (Inez) 1926- ...... **CLC 17**
See also AAYA 6; AITN 2; BEST 89:2;
CA 25-28R; CANR 15, 35; DLB 8;
JRDA; MAICYA; MTCW; SAAS 11;
SATA 8, 70

McCann, Arthur
See Campbell, John W(ood, Jr.)

McCann, Edson
See Pohl, Frederik

McCarthy, Cormac, Jr. .... **CLC 4, 57**
See also McCarthy, Charles, Jr.
See also DLB 6

McCarthy, Mary (Therese)
1912-1989 ... **CLC 1, 3, 5, 14, 24, 39, 59**
See also CA 5-8R; 129; CANR 16; DLB 2;
DLBY 81; MTCW

McCartney, (James) Paul
1942- .... **CLC 12, 35**

McCauley, Stephen (D.) 1955- ..... **CLC 50**
See also CA 141

McClure, Michael (Thomas)
1932- .... **CLC 6, 10**
See also CA 21-24R; CANR 17; DLB 16

McCorkle, Jill (Collins) 1958- ...... **CLC 51**
See also CA 121; DLBY 87

McCourt, James 1941- .... **CLC 5**
See also CA 57-60

McCoy, Horace (Stanley)
1897-1955 .... **TCLC 28**
See also CA 108; DLB 9

McCrae, John 1872-1918 .... **TCLC 12**
See also CA 109; DLB 92

McCreigh, James
See Pohl, Frederik

McCullers, (Lula) Carson (Smith)
1917-1967 .... **CLC 1, 4, 10, 12, 48; DA;
SSC 9; WLC**
See also CA 5-8R; 25-28R; CABS 1, 3;
CANR 18; CDALB 1941-1968; DLB 2, 7;
MTCW; SATA 27

McCulloch, John Tyler
See Burroughs, Edgar Rice

McCullough, Colleen 1938(?)- ...... **CLC 27**
See also CA 81-84; CANR 17; MTCW

McElroy, Joseph 1930- .... **CLC 5, 47**
See also CA 17-20R

McEwan, Ian (Russell) 1948- ... **CLC 13, 66**
See also BEST 90:4; CA 61-64; CANR 14,
41; DLB 14; MTCW

McFadden, David 1940- .... **CLC 48**
See also CA 104; DLB 60

McFarland, Dennis 1950- .... **CLC 65**

McGahern, John 1934- .... **CLC 5, 9, 48**
See also CA 17-20R; CANR 29; DLB 14;
MTCW

McGinley, Patrick (Anthony)
1937- .... **CLC 41**
See also CA 120; 127

McGinley, Phyllis 1905-1978 ...... **CLC 14**
See also CA 9-12R; 77-80; CANR 19;
DLB 11, 48; SATA 2, 24, 44

McGinniss, Joe 1942- .... **CLC 32**
See also AITN 2; BEST 89:2; CA 25-28R;
CANR 26

McGivern, Maureen Daly
See Daly, Maureen

McGrath, Patrick 1950- .... **CLC 55**
See also CA 136

McGrath, Thomas (Matthew)
1916-1990 .... **CLC 28, 59**
See also CA 9-12R; 132; CANR 6, 33;
MTCW; SATA 41; SATA-Obit 66

McGuane, Thomas (Francis III)
1939- .... **CLC 3, 7, 18, 45**
See also AITN 2; CA 49-52; CANR 5, 24;
DLB 2; DLBY 80; MTCW

McGuckian, Medbh 1950- .... **CLC 48**
See also DLB 40

McHale, Tom 1942(?)-1982 .... **CLC 3, 5**
See also AITN 1; CA 77-80; 106

McIlvanney, William 1936- .... **CLC 42**
See also CA 25-28R; DLB 14

McIlwraith, Maureen Mollie Hunter
See Hunter, Mollie
See also SATA 2

McInerney, Jay 1955- .... **CLC 34**
See also CA 116; 123

McIntyre, Vonda N(eel) 1948- ..... **CLC 18**
See also CA 81-84; CANR 17, 34; MTCW

McKay, Claude ... **TCLC 7, 41; BLC 3; PC 2**
See also McKay, Festus Claudius
See also DLB 4, 45, 51, 117

McKay, Festus Claudius 1889-1948
See McKay, Claude
See also BW; CA 104; 124; DA; MTCW;
WLC

McKuen, Rod 1933- .... **CLC 1, 3**
See also AITN 1; CA 41-44R; CANR 40

McLoughlin, R. B.
See Mencken, H(enry) L(ouis)

McLuhan, (Herbert) Marshall
1911-1980 .... **CLC 37**
See also CA 9-12R; 102; CANR 12, 34;
DLB 88; MTCW

McMillan, Terry (L.) 1951- ..... **CLC 50, 61**
See also CA 140

McMurtry, Larry (Jeff)
1936- .... **CLC 2, 3, 7, 11, 27, 44**
See also AITN 2; BEST 89:2; CA 5-8R;
CANR 19, 43; CDALB 1968-1988;
DLB 2; DLBY 80, 87; MTCW

McNally, Terrence 1939- ...... **CLC 4, 7, 41**
See also CA 45-48; CANR 2; DLB 7

McNamer, Deirdre 1950- .... **CLC 70**

McNeile, Herman Cyril 1888-1937
See Sapper
See also DLB 77

McPhee, John (Angus) 1931- ...... **CLC 36**
See also BEST 90:1; CA 65-68; CANR 20;
MTCW

McPherson, James Alan
1943- .... **CLC 19, 77**
See also BW; CA 25-28R; CAAS 17;
CANR 24; DLB 38; MTCW

McPherson, William (Alexander)
1933- .... **CLC 34**
See also CA 69-72; CANR 28

McSweeney, Kerry .... **CLC 34**

Mead, Margaret 1901-1978 .... **CLC 37**
See also AITN 1; CA 1-4R; 81-84;
CANR 4; MTCW; SATA 20

Meaker, Marijane (Agnes) 1927-
See Kerr, M. E.
See also CA 107; CANR 37; JRDA;
MAICYA; MTCW; SATA 20, 61

Medoff, Mark (Howard) 1940- ... **CLC 6, 23**
See also AITN 1; CA 53-56; CANR 5;
DLB 7

Meged, Aharon
See Megged, Aharon

Meged, Aron
See Megged, Aharon

Megged, Aharon 1920- .... **CLC 9**
See also CA 49-52; CAAS 13; CANR 1

Mehta, Ved (Parkash) 1934- .... **CLC 37**
See also CA 1-4R; CANR 2, 23; MTCW

Melanter
See Blackmore, R(ichard) D(oddridge)

Melikow, Loris
See Hofmannsthal, Hugo von

Melmoth, Sebastian
See Wilde, Oscar (Fingal O'Flahertie Wills)

Meltzer, Milton 1915- .... **CLC 26**
See also AAYA 8; CA 13-16R; CANR 38;
CLR 13; DLB 61; JRDA; MAICYA;
SAAS 1; SATA 1, 50

Melville, Herman
1819-1891 .... **NCLC 3, 12, 29; DA;
SSC 1; WLC**
See also CDALB 1640-1865; DLB 3, 74;
SATA 59

Menander
c. 342B.C.-c. 292B.C. .... **CMLC 9; DC 3**

Mencken, H(enry) L(ouis)
1880-1956 . . . . TCLC 13
See also CA 105; 125; CDALB 1917-1929;
DLB 11, 29, 63; MTCW

Mercer, David 1928-1980. . . . . CLC 5
See also CA 9-12R; 102; CANR 23;
DLB 13; MTCW

Merchant, Paul
See Ellison, Harlan

Meredith, George 1828-1909 . . . TCLC 17, 43
See also CA 117; CDBLB 1832-1890;
DLB 18, 35, 57

Meredith, William (Morris)
1919- . . . . CLC 4, 13, 22, 55
See also CA 9-12R; CAAS 14; CANR 6, 40;
DLB 5

Merezhkovsky, Dmitry Sergeyevich
1865-1941 . . . . TCLC 29

Merimee, Prosper
1803-1870 . . . . NCLC 6; SSC 7
See also DLB 119

Merkin, Daphne 1954- . . . . CLC 44
See also CA 123

Merlin, Arthur
See Blish, James (Benjamin)

Merrill, James (Ingram)
1926- . . . . CLC 2, 3, 6, 8, 13, 18, 34
See also CA 13-16R; CANR 10; DLB 5;
DLBY 85; MTCW

Merriman, Alex
See Silverberg, Robert

Merritt, E. B.
See Waddington, Miriam

Merton, Thomas
1915-1968 . . . . CLC 1, 3, 11, 34
See also CA 5-8R; 25-28R; CANR 22;
DLB 48; DLBY 81; MTCW

Merwin, W(illiam) S(tanley)
1927- . . . . . . CLC 1, 2, 3, 5, 8, 13, 18, 45
See also CA 13-16R; CANR 15; DLB 5;
MTCW

Metcalf, John 1938- . . . . CLC 37
See also CA 113; DLB 60

Metcalf, Suzanne
See Baum, L(yman) Frank

Mew, Charlotte (Mary)
1870-1928 . . . . TCLC 8
See also CA 105; DLB 19, 135

Mewshaw, Michael 1943- . . . . CLC 9
See also CA 53-56; CANR 7; DLBY 80

Meyer, June
See Jordan, June

Meyer, Lynn
See Slavitt, David R(ytman)

Meyer-Meyrink, Gustav 1868-1932
See Meyrink, Gustav
See also CA 117

Meyers, Jeffrey 1939- . . . . CLC 39
See also CA 73-76; DLB 111

Meynell, Alice (Christina Gertrude Thompson)
1847-1922 . . . . TCLC 6
See also CA 104; DLB 19, 98

Meyrink, Gustav . . . . TCLC 21
See also Meyer-Meyrink, Gustav
See also DLB 81

Michaels, Leonard 1933- . . . . CLC 6, 25
See also CA 61-64; CANR 21; DLB 130;
MTCW

Michaux, Henri 1899-1984 . . . . . CLC 8, 19
See also CA 85-88; 114

Michelangelo 1475-1564. . . . . LC 12

Michelet, Jules 1798-1874 . . . . . . NCLC 31

Michener, James A(lbert)
1907(?)- . . . . CLC 1, 5, 11, 29, 60
See also AITN 1; BEST 90:1; CA 5-8R;
CANR 21; DLB 6; MTCW

Mickiewicz, Adam 1798-1855 . . . . . NCLC 3

Middleton, Christopher 1926- . . . . . . CLC 13
See also CA 13-16R; CANR 29; DLB 40

Middleton, Stanley 1919- . . . . CLC 7, 38
See also CA 25-28R; CANR 21; DLB 14

Migueis, Jose Rodrigues 1901- . . . . . CLC 10

Mikszath, Kalman 1847-1910 . . . . . TCLC 31

Miles, Josephine
1911-1985 . . . . CLC 1, 2, 14, 34, 39
See also CA 1-4R; 116; CANR 2; DLB 48

Militant
See Sandburg, Carl (August)

Mill, John Stuart 1806-1873 . . . . . NCLC 11
See also CDBLB 1832-1890; DLB 55

Millar, Kenneth 1915-1983 . . . . CLC 14
See also Macdonald, Ross
See also CA 9-12R; 110; CANR 16; DLB 2;
DLBD 6; DLBY 83; MTCW

Millay, E. Vincent
See Millay, Edna St. Vincent

Millay, Edna St. Vincent
1892-1950 . . . . . . TCLC 4, 49; DA; PC 6
See also CA 104; 130; CDALB 1917-1929;
DLB 45; MTCW

Miller, Arthur
1915- . . . . CLC 1, 2, 6, 10, 15, 26, 47, 78;
DA; DC 1; WLC
See also AITN 1; CA 1-4R; CABS 3;
CANR 2, 30; CDALB 1941-1968; DLB 7;
MTCW

Miller, Henry (Valentine)
1891-1980 . . . . CLC 1, 2, 4, 9, 14, 43;
DA; WLC
See also CA 9-12R; 97-100; CANR 33;
CDALB 1929-1941; DLB 4, 9; DLBY 80;
MTCW

Miller, Jason 1939(?)- . . . . CLC 2
See also AITN 1; CA 73-76; DLB 7

Miller, Sue 1943- . . . . CLC 44
See also BEST 90:3; CA 139

Miller, Walter M(ichael, Jr.)
1923- . . . . CLC 4, 30
See also CA 85-88; DLB 8

Millett, Kate 1934- . . . . CLC 67
See also AITN 1; CA 73-76; CANR 32;
MTCW

Millhauser, Steven 1943- . . . . CLC 21, 54
See also CA 110; 111; DLB 2

Millin, Sarah Gertrude 1889-1968 . . CLC 49
See also CA 102; 93-96

Milne, A(lan) A(lexander)
1882-1956 . . . . TCLC 6
See also CA 104; 133; CLR 1, 26; DLB 10,
77, 100; MAICYA; MTCW; YABC 1

Milner, Ron(ald) 1938- . . . . . CLC 56; BLC 3
See also AITN 1; BW; CA 73-76;
CANR 24; DLB 38; MTCW

Milosz, Czeslaw
1911- . . . . . . CLC 5, 11, 22, 31, 56; PC 8
See also CA 81-84; CANR 23; MTCW

Milton, John 1608-1674 . . . LC 9; DA; WLC
See also CDBLB 1660-1789; DLB 131

Minehaha, Cornelius
See Wedekind, (Benjamin) Frank(lin)

Miner, Valerie 1947- . . . . CLC 40
See also CA 97-100

Minimo, Duca
See D'Annunzio, Gabriele

Minot, Susan 1956- . . . . CLC 44
See also CA 134

Minus, Ed 1938- . . . . CLC 39

Miranda, Javier
See Bioy Casares, Adolfo

Miro (Ferrer), Gabriel (Francisco Victor)
1879-1930 . . . . TCLC 5
See also CA 104

Mishima, Yukio
. . . . CLC 2, 4, 6, 9, 27; DC 1; SSC 4
See also Hiraoka, Kimitake

Mistral, Frederic 1830-1914 . . . . . . TCLC 51
See also CA 122

Mistral, Gabriela. . . . . TCLC 2; HLC 2
See also Godoy Alcayaga, Lucila

Mistry, Rohinton 1952- . . . . CLC 71
See also CA 141

Mitchell, Clyde
See Ellison, Harlan; Silverberg, Robert

Mitchell, James Leslie 1901-1935
See Gibbon, Lewis Grassic
See also CA 104; DLB 15

Mitchell, Joni 1943- . . . . CLC 12
See also CA 112

Mitchell, Margaret (Munnerlyn)
1900-1949 . . . . TCLC 11
See also CA 109; 125; DLB 9; MTCW

Mitchell, Peggy
See Mitchell, Margaret (Munnerlyn)

Mitchell, S(ilas) Weir 1829-1914 . . TCLC 36

Mitchell, W(illiam) O(rmond)
1914- . . . . CLC 25
See also CA 77-80; CANR 15, 43; DLB 88

Mitford, Mary Russell 1787-1855. . NCLC 4
See also DLB 110, 116

Mitford, Nancy 1904-1973. . . . . CLC 44
See also CA 9-12R

Miyamoto, Yuriko 1899-1951 . . . . . TCLC 37

Mo, Timothy (Peter) 1950(?)- . . . . . . CLC 46
See also CA 117; MTCW

Modarressi, Taghi (M.) 1931- . . . . . . CLC 44
See also CA 121; 134

Modiano, Patrick (Jean) 1945- . . . . . CLC 18
See also CA 85-88; CANR 17, 40; DLB 83

Moerck, Paal
See Roelvaag, O(le) E(dvart)

Mofolo, Thomas (Mokopu)
1875(?)-1948 . . . . **TCLC 22; BLC 3**
See also CA 121

Mohr, Nicholasa　1935-. . . . **CLC 12; HLC 2**
See also AAYA 8; CA 49-52; CANR 1, 32;
CLR 22; HW; JRDA; SAAS 8; SATA 8

Mojtabai, A(nn) G(race)
1938- . . . . **CLC 5, 9, 15, 29**
See also CA 85-88

Moliere　1622-1673 . . . . . . **LC 10; DA; WLC**

Molin, Charles
See Mayne, William (James Carter)

Molnar, Ferenc　1878-1952. . . . . . . **TCLC 20**
See also CA 109

Momaday, N(avarre) Scott
1934- . . . . **CLC 2, 19; DA**
See also CA 25-28R; CANR 14, 34;
MTCW; SATA 30, 48

Monroe, Harriet　1860-1936. . . . . . . **TCLC 12**
See also CA 109; DLB 54, 91

Monroe, Lyle
See Heinlein, Robert A(nson)

Montagu, Elizabeth　1917- . . . . **NCLC 7**
See also CA 9-12R

Montagu, Mary (Pierrepont) Wortley
1689-1762 . . . . **LC 9**
See also DLB 95, 101

Montagu, W. H.
See Coleridge, Samuel Taylor

Montague, John (Patrick)
1929- . . . . **CLC 13, 46**
See also CA 9-12R; CANR 9; DLB 40;
MTCW

Montaigne, Michel (Eyquem) de
1533-1592 . . . . **LC 8; DA; WLC**

Montale, Eugenio　1896-1981 . . . **CLC 7, 9, 18**
See also CA 17-20R; 104; CANR 30;
DLB 114; MTCW

Montesquieu, Charles-Louis de Secondat
1689-1755 . . . . **LC 7**

Montgomery, (Robert) Bruce　1921-1978
See Crispin, Edmund
See also CA 104

Montgomery, L(ucy) M(aud)
1874-1942 . . . . **TCLC 51**
See also CA 108; 137; CLR 8; DLB 92;
JRDA; MAICYA; YABC 1

Montgomery, Marion H., Jr.　1925- . . **CLC 7**
See also AITN 1; CA 1-4R; CANR 3;
DLB 6

Montgomery, Max
See Davenport, Guy (Mattison, Jr.)

Montherlant, Henry (Milon) de
1896-1972 . . . . **CLC 8, 19**
See also CA 85-88; 37-40R; DLB 72;
MTCW

Monty Python . . . . **CLC 21**
See also Chapman, Graham; Cleese, John
(Marwood); Gilliam, Terry (Vance); Idle,
Eric; Jones, Terence Graham Parry; Palin,
Michael (Edward)
See also AAYA 7

Moodie, Susanna (Strickland)
1803-1885 . . . . **NCLC 14**
See also DLB 99

Mooney, Edward　1951- . . . . **CLC 25**
See also CA 130

Mooney, Ted
See Mooney, Edward

Moorcock, Michael (John)
1939- . . . . **CLC 5, 27, 58**
See also CA 45-48; CAAS 5; CANR 2, 17,
38; DLB 14; MTCW

Moore, Brian
1921- . . . . **CLC 1, 3, 5, 7, 8, 19, 32**
See also CA 1-4R; CANR 1, 25, 42; MTCW

Moore, Edward
See Muir, Edwin

Moore, George Augustus
1852-1933 . . . . **TCLC 7**
See also CA 104; DLB 10, 18, 57, 135

Moore, Lorrie . . . . **CLC 39, 45, 68**
See also Moore, Marie Lorena

Moore, Marianne (Craig)
1887-1972 . . . . **CLC 1, 2, 4, 8, 10, 13, 19,
47; DA; PC 4**
See also CA 1-4R; 33-36R; CANR 3;
CDALB 1929-1941; DLB 45; DLBD 7;
MTCW; SATA 20

Moore, Marie Lorena　1957-
See Moore, Lorrie
See also CA 116; CANR 39

Moore, Thomas　1779-1852. . . . . . . **NCLC 6**
See also DLB 96

Morand, Paul　1888-1976 . . . . **CLC 41**
See also CA 69-72; DLB 65

Morante, Elsa　1918-1985. . . . . . . **CLC 8, 47**
See also CA 85-88; 117; CANR 35; MTCW

Moravia, Alberto . . . . **CLC 2, 7, 11, 27, 46**
See also Pincherle, Alberto

More, Hannah　1745-1833 . . . . **NCLC 27**
See also DLB 107, 109, 116

More, Henry　1614-1687. . . . . **LC 9**
See also DLB 126

More, Sir Thomas　1478-1535 . . . . **LC 10**

Moreas, Jean . . . . **TCLC 18**
See also Papadiamantopoulos, Johannes

Morgan, Berry　1919- . . . . **CLC 6**
See also CA 49-52; DLB 6

Morgan, Claire
See Highsmith, (Mary) Patricia

Morgan, Edwin (George)　1920- . . . . . **CLC 31**
See also CA 5-8R; CANR 3, 43; DLB 27

Morgan, (George) Frederick
1922- . . . . **CLC 23**
See also CA 17-20R; CANR 21

Morgan, Harriet
See Mencken, H(enry) L(ouis)

Morgan, Jane
See Cooper, James Fenimore

Morgan, Janet　1945- . . . . **CLC 39**
See also CA 65-68

Morgan, Lady　1776(?)-1859. . . . . . **NCLC 29**
See also DLB 116

Morgan, Robin　1941- . . . . **CLC 2**
See also CA 69-72; CANR 29; MTCW

Morgan, Scott
See Kuttner, Henry

Morgan, Seth　1949(?)-1990 . . . . **CLC 65**
See also CA 132

Morgenstern, Christian
1871-1914 . . . . **TCLC 8**
See also CA 105

Morgenstern, S.
See Goldman, William (W.)

Moricz, Zsigmond　1879-1942 . . . . . **TCLC 33**

Morike, Eduard (Friedrich)
1804-1875 . . . . **NCLC 10**
See also DLB 133

Mori Ogai . . . . **TCLC 14**
See also Mori Rintaro

Mori Rintaro　1862-1922
See Mori Ogai
See also CA 110

Moritz, Karl Philipp　1756-1793 . . . . . . **LC 2**
See also DLB 94

Morland, Peter Henry
See Faust, Frederick (Schiller)

Morren, Theophil
See Hofmannsthal, Hugo von

Morris, Bill　1952-. . . . . **CLC 76**

Morris, Julian
See West, Morris L(anglo)

Morris, Steveland Judkins　1950(?)-
See Wonder, Stevie
See also CA 111

Morris, William　1834-1896 . . . . **NCLC 4**
See also CDBLB 1832-1890; DLB 18, 35, 57

Morris, Wright　1910-. . . **CLC 1, 3, 7, 18, 37**
See also CA 9-12R; CANR 21; DLB 2;
DLBY 81; MTCW

Morrison, Chloe Anthony Wofford
See Morrison, Toni

Morrison, James Douglas　1943-1971
See Morrison, Jim
See also CA 73-76; CANR 40

Morrison, Jim . . . . **CLC 17**
See also Morrison, James Douglas

Morrison, Toni
1931- . . . . **CLC 4, 10, 22, 55, 81; BLC 3;
DA**
See also AAYA 1; BW; CA 29-32R;
CANR 27, 42; CDALB 1968-1988;
DLB 6, 33; DLBY 81; MTCW; SATA 57

Morrison, Van　1945- . . . . **CLC 21**
See also CA 116

Mortimer, John (Clifford)
1923- . . . . **CLC 28, 43**
See also CA 13-16R; CANR 21;
CDBLB 1960 to Present; DLB 13;
MTCW

Mortimer, Penelope (Ruth)　1918- . . . . **CLC 5**
See also CA 57-60

Morton, Anthony
See Creasey, John

Mosher, Howard Frank　1943- . . . . . . **CLC 62**
See also CA 139

Mosley, Nicholas　1923- . . . . **CLC 43, 70**
See also CA 69-72; CANR 41; DLB 14

Newbound, Bernard Slade 1930-
See Slade, Bernard
See also CA 81-84

Newby, P(ercy) H(oward)
1918- .... **CLC 2, 13**
See also CA 5-8R; CANR 32; DLB 15;
MTCW

Newlove, Donald 1928- .... **CLC 6**
See also CA 29-32R; CANR 25

Newlove, John (Herbert) 1938-..... **CLC 14**
See also CA 21-24R; CANR 9, 25

Newman, Charles 1938-.......... **CLC 2, 8**
See also CA 21-24R

Newman, Edwin (Harold) 1919- .... **CLC 14**
See also AITN 1; CA 69-72; CANR 5

Newman, John Henry
1801-1890 .... **NCLC 38**
See also DLB 18, 32, 55

Newton, Suzanne 1936- .... **CLC 35**
See also CA 41-44R; CANR 14; JRDA;
SATA 5

Nexo, Martin Andersen
1869-1954 .... **TCLC 43**

Nezval, Vitezslav 1900-1958 ...... **TCLC 44**
See also CA 123

Ng, Fae Myenne 1957(?)-.......... **CLC 81**

Ngema, Mbongeni 1955- .... **CLC 57**

Ngugi, James T(hiong'o)........ **CLC 3, 7, 13**
See also Ngugi wa Thiong'o

Ngugi wa Thiong'o 1938-... **CLC 36; BLC 3**
See also Ngugi, James T(hiong'o)
See also BW; CA 81-84; CANR 27;
DLB 125; MTCW

Nichol, B(arrie) P(hillip)
1944-1988 .... **CLC 18**
See also CA 53-56; DLB 53; SATA 66

Nichols, John (Treadwell) 1940-.... **CLC 38**
See also CA 9-12R; CAAS 2; CANR 6;
DLBY 82

Nichols, Leigh
See Koontz, Dean R(ay)

Nichols, Peter (Richard)
1927- .... **CLC 5, 36, 65**
See also CA 104; CANR 33; DLB 13;
MTCW

Nicolas, F. R. E.
See Freeling, Nicolas

Niedecker, Lorine 1903-1970.... **CLC 10, 42**
See also CA 25-28; CAP 2; DLB 48

Nietzsche, Friedrich (Wilhelm)
1844-1900 .... **TCLC 10, 18**
See also CA 107; 121; DLB 129

Nievo, Ippolito 1831-1861 .... **NCLC 22**

Nightingale, Anne Redmon 1943-
See Redmon, Anne
See also CA 103

Nik.T.O.
See Annensky, Innokenty Fyodorovich

Nin, Anais
1903-1977 ...... **CLC 1, 4, 8, 11, 14, 60;**
SSC 10
See also AITN 2; CA 13-16R; 69-72;
CANR 22; DLB 2, 4; MTCW

Nissenson, Hugh 1933-.......... **CLC 4, 9**
See also CA 17-20R; CANR 27; DLB 28

Niven, Larry .... **CLC 8**
See also Niven, Laurence Van Cott
See also DLB 8

Niven, Laurence Van Cott 1938-
See Niven, Larry
See also CA 21-24R; CAAS 12; CANR 14;
MTCW

Nixon, Agnes Eckhardt 1927-...... **CLC 21**
See also CA 110

Nizan, Paul 1905-1940........... **TCLC 40**
See also DLB 72

Nkosi, Lewis 1936-....... **CLC 45; BLC 3**
See also BW; CA 65-68; CANR 27

Nodier, (Jean) Charles (Emmanuel)
1780-1844 .... **NCLC 19**
See also DLB 119

Nolan, Christopher 1965-.......... **CLC 58**
See also CA 111

Norden, Charles
See Durrell, Lawrence (George)

Nordhoff, Charles (Bernard)
1887-1947 .... **TCLC 23**
See also CA 108; DLB 9; SATA 23

Norfolk, Lawrence 1963-.......... **CLC 76**

Norman, Marsha 1947- .... **CLC 28**
See also CA 105; CABS 3; CANR 41;
DLBY 84

Norris, Benjamin Franklin, Jr.
1870-1902 .... **TCLC 24**
See also Norris, Frank
See also CA 110

Norris, Frank
See Norris, Benjamin Franklin, Jr.
See also CDALB 1865-1917; DLB 12, 71

Norris, Leslie 1921-.............. **CLC 14**
See also CA 11-12; CANR 14; CAP 1;
DLB 27

North, Andrew
See Norton, Andre

North, Anthony
See Koontz, Dean R(ay)

North, Captain George
See Stevenson, Robert Louis (Balfour)

North, Milou
See Erdrich, Louise

Northrup, B. A.
See Hubbard, L(afayette) Ron(ald)

North Staffs
See Hulme, T(homas) E(rnest)

Norton, Alice Mary
See Norton, Andre
See also MAICYA; SATA 1, 43

Norton, Andre 1912- .... **CLC 12**
See also Norton, Alice Mary
See also CA 1-4R; CANR 2, 31; DLB 8, 52;
JRDA; MTCW

Norway, Nevil Shute 1899-1960
See Shute, Nevil
See also CA 102; 93-96

Norwid, Cyprian Kamil
1821-1883 .... **NCLC 17**

Nosille, Nabrah
See Ellison, Harlan

Nossack, Hans Erich 1901-1978 ..... **CLC 6**
See also CA 93-96; 85-88; DLB 69

Nosu, Chuji
See Ozu, Yasujiro

Nova, Craig 1945-.............. **CLC 7, 31**
See also CA 45-48; CANR 2

Novak, Joseph
See Kosinski, Jerzy (Nikodem)

Novalis 1772-1801 .... **NCLC 13**
See also DLB 90

Nowlan, Alden (Albert) 1933-1983 .. **CLC 15**
See also CA 9-12R; CANR 5; DLB 53

Noyes, Alfred 1880-1958 .... **TCLC 7**
See also CA 104; DLB 20

Nunn, Kem 19(?)-................ **CLC 34**

Nye, Robert 1939- .... **CLC 13, 42**
See also CA 33-36R; CANR 29; DLB 14;
MTCW; SATA 6

Nyro, Laura 1947- .... **CLC 17**

Oates, Joyce Carol
1938- ...... **CLC 1, 2, 3, 6, 9, 11, 15, 19,**
33, 52; DA; SSC 6; WLC
See also AITN 1; BEST 89:2; CA 5-8R;
CANR 25; CDALB 1968-1988; DLB 2, 5,
130; DLBY 81; MTCW

O'Brien, E. G.
See Clarke, Arthur C(harles)

O'Brien, Edna
1936- ... **CLC 3, 5, 8, 13, 36, 65; SSC 10**
See also CA 1-4R; CANR 6, 41;
CDBLB 1960 to Present; DLB 14;
MTCW

O'Brien, Fitz-James 1828-1862... **NCLC 21**
See also DLB 74

O'Brien, Flann........ **CLC 1, 4, 5, 7, 10, 47**
See also O Nuallain, Brian

O'Brien, Richard 1942- .... **CLC 17**
See also CA 124

O'Brien, Tim 1946-.......... **CLC 7, 19, 40**
See also CA 85-88; CANR 40; DLBD 9;
DLBY 80

Obstfelder, Sigbjoern 1866-1900... **TCLC 23**
See also CA 123

O'Casey, Sean
1880-1964 .... **CLC 1, 5, 9, 11, 15**
See also CA 89-92; CDBLB 1914-1945;
DLB 10; MTCW

O'Cathasaigh, Sean
See O'Casey, Sean

Ochs, Phil 1940-1976............ **CLC 17**
See also CA 65-68

O'Connor, Edwin (Greene)
1918-1968 .... **CLC 14**
See also CA 93-96; 25-28R

O'Connor, (Mary) Flannery
1925-1964 .... **CLC 1, 2, 3, 6, 10, 13, 15,**
21, 66; DA; SSC 1; WLC
See also AAYA 7; CA 1-4R; CANR 3, 41;
CDALB 1941-1968; DLB 2; DLBY 80;
MTCW

O'Connor, Frank.......... **CLC 23; SSC 5**
See also O'Donovan, Michael John

Paglia, Camille (Anna) 1947- .... **CLC 68**
See also CA 140

Paige, Richard
See Koontz, Dean R(ay)

Pakenham, Antonia
See Fraser, Antonia (Pakenham)

Palamas, Kostes 1859-1943 .... **TCLC 5**
See also CA 105

Palazzeschi, Aldo 1885-1974 .... **CLC 11**
See also CA 89-92; 53-56; DLB 114

Paley, Grace 1922- .... **CLC 4, 6, 37; SSC 8**
See also CA 25-28R; CANR 13; DLB 28;
MTCW

Palin, Michael (Edward) 1943- ..... **CLC 21**
See also Monty Python
See also CA 107; CANR 35; SATA 67

Palliser, Charles 1947- .... **CLC 65**
See also CA 136

Palma, Ricardo 1833-1919 .... **TCLC 29**

Pancake, Breece Dexter 1952-1979
See Pancake, Breece D'J
See also CA 123; 109

Pancake, Breece D'J .... **CLC 29**
See also Pancake, Breece Dexter
See also DLB 130

Panko, Rudy
See Gogol, Nikolai (Vasilyevich)

Papadiamantis, Alexandros
1851-1911 .... **TCLC 29**

Papadiamantopoulos, Johannes 1856-1910
See Moreas, Jean
See also CA 117

Papini, Giovanni 1881-1956 .... **TCLC 22**
See also CA 121

Paracelsus 1493-1541 .... **LC 14**

Parasol, Peter
See Stevens, Wallace

Parfenie, Maria
See Codrescu, Andrei

Parini, Jay (Lee) 1948- .... **CLC 54**
See also CA 97-100; CAAS 16; CANR 32

Park, Jordan
See Kornbluth, C(yril) M.; Pohl, Frederik

Parker, Bert
See Ellison, Harlan

Parker, Dorothy (Rothschild)
1893-1967 .... **CLC 15, 68; SSC 2**
See also CA 19-20; 25-28R; CAP 2;
DLB 11, 45, 86; MTCW

Parker, Robert B(rown) 1932- ..... **CLC 27**
See also BEST 89:4; CA 49-52; CANR 1,
26; MTCW

Parkes, Lucas
See Harris, John (Wyndham Parkes Lucas)
Beynon

Parkin, Frank 1940- .... **CLC 43**

Parkman, Francis, Jr.
1823-1893 .... **NCLC 12**
See also DLB 1, 30

Parks, Gordon (Alexander Buchanan)
1912- .... **CLC 1, 16; BLC 3**
See also AITN 2; BW; CA 41-44R;
CANR 26; DLB 33; SATA 8

Parnell, Thomas 1679-1718 .... **LC 3**
See also DLB 94

Parra, Nicanor 1914- .... **CLC 2; HLC 2**
See also CA 85-88; CANR 32; HW; MTCW

Parrish, Mary Frances
See Fisher, M(ary) F(rances) K(ennedy)

Parson
See Coleridge, Samuel Taylor

Parson Lot
See Kingsley, Charles

Partridge, Anthony
See Oppenheim, E(dward) Phillips

Pascoli, Giovanni 1855-1912 ...... **TCLC 45**

Pasolini, Pier Paolo
1922-1975 .... **CLC 20, 37**
See also CA 93-96; 61-64; DLB 128;
MTCW

Pasquini
See Silone, Ignazio

Pastan, Linda (Olenik) 1932- ...... **CLC 27**
See also CA 61-64; CANR 18, 40; DLB 5

Pasternak, Boris (Leonidovich)
1890-1960 ...... **CLC 7, 10, 18, 63; DA;**
PC 6; WLC
See also CA 127; 116; MTCW

Patchen, Kenneth 1911-1972 ... **CLC 1, 2, 18**
See also CA 1-4R; 33-36R; CANR 3, 35;
DLB 16, 48; MTCW

Pater, Walter (Horatio)
1839-1894 .... **NCLC 7**
See also CDBLB 1832-1890; DLB 57

Paterson, A(ndrew) B(arton)
1864-1941 .... **TCLC 32**

Paterson, Katherine (Womeldorf)
1932- .... **CLC 12, 30**
See also AAYA 1; CA 21-24R; CANR 28;
CLR 7; DLB 52; JRDA; MAICYA;
MTCW; SATA 13, 53

Patmore, Coventry Kersey Dighton
1823-1896 .... **NCLC 9**
See also DLB 35, 98

Paton, Alan (Stewart)
1903-1988 ...... **CLC 4, 10, 25, 55; DA;**
WLC
See also CA 13-16; 125; CANR 22; CAP 1;
MTCW; SATA 11, 56

Paton Walsh, Gillian 1937-
See Walsh, Jill Paton
See also CANR 38; JRDA; MAICYA;
SAAS 3; SATA 4, 72

Paulding, James Kirke 1778-1860 .. **NCLC 2**
See also DLB 3, 59, 74

Paulin, Thomas Neilson 1949-
See Paulin, Tom
See also CA 123; 128

Paulin, Tom .... **CLC 37**
See also Paulin, Thomas Neilson
See also DLB 40

Paustovsky, Konstantin (Georgievich)
1892-1968 .... **CLC 40**
See also CA 93-96; 25-28R

Pavese, Cesare 1908-1950 .... **TCLC 3**
See also CA 104; DLB 128

Pavic, Milorad 1929- .... **CLC 60**
See also CA 136

Payne, Alan
See Jakes, John (William)

Paz, Gil
See Lugones, Leopoldo

Paz, Octavio
1914- .... **CLC 3, 4, 6, 10, 19, 51, 65;**
DA; HLC 2; PC 1; WLC
See also CA 73-76; CANR 32; DLBY 90;
HW; MTCW

Peacock, Molly 1947- .... **CLC 60**
See also CA 103; DLB 120

Peacock, Thomas Love
1785-1866 .... **NCLC 22**
See also DLB 96, 116

Peake, Mervyn 1911-1968 .... **CLC 7, 54**
See also CA 5-8R; 25-28R; CANR 3;
DLB 15; MTCW; SATA 23

Pearce, Philippa .... **CLC 21**
See also Christie, (Ann) Philippa
See also CLR 9; MAICYA; SATA 1, 67

Pearl, Eric
See Elman, Richard

Pearson, T(homas) R(eid) 1956- .... **CLC 39**
See also CA 120; 130

Peck, Dale 1968(?)- .... **CLC 81**

Peck, John 1941- .... **CLC 3**
See also CA 49-52; CANR 3

Peck, Richard (Wayne) 1934- ...... **CLC 21**
See also AAYA 1; CA 85-88; CANR 19,
38; JRDA; MAICYA; SAAS 2; SATA 18,
55

Peck, Robert Newton 1928- .... **CLC 17; DA**
See also AAYA 3; CA 81-84; CANR 31;
JRDA; MAICYA; SAAS 1; SATA 21, 62

Peckinpah, (David) Sam(uel)
1925-1984 .... **CLC 20**
See also CA 109; 114

Pedersen, Knut 1859-1952
See Hamsun, Knut
See also CA 104; 119; MTCW

Peeslake, Gaffer
See Durrell, Lawrence (George)

Peguy, Charles Pierre
1873-1914 .... **TCLC 10**
See also CA 107

Pena, Ramon del Valle y
See Valle-Inclan, Ramon (Maria) del

Pendennis, Arthur Esquir
See Thackeray, William Makepeace

Pepys, Samuel
1633-1703 .... **LC 11; DA; WLC**
See also CDBLB 1660-1789; DLB 101

Percy, Walker
1916-1990 .... **CLC 2, 3, 6, 8, 14, 18, 47,**
65
See also CA 1-4R; 131; CANR 1, 23;
DLB 2; DLBY 80, 90; MTCW

Perec, Georges 1936-1982 .... **CLC 56**
See also CA 141; DLB 83

Pereda (y Sanchez de Porrua), Jose Maria de
1833-1906 .... **TCLC 16**
See also CA 117

Pereda y Porrua, Jose Maria de
See Pereda (y Sanchez de Porrua), Jose
Maria de

Peregoy, George Weems
　　See Mencken, H(enry) L(ouis)

Perelman, S(idney) J(oseph)
　　1904-1979 . . . **CLC 3, 5, 9, 15, 23, 44, 49**
　　See also AITN 1, 2; CA 73-76; 89-92;
　　CANR 18; DLB 11, 44; MTCW

Peret, Benjamin　1899-1959 . . . . **TCLC 20**
　　See also CA 117

Peretz, Isaac Loeb　1851(?)-1915 . . . **TCLC 16**
　　See also CA 109

Peretz, Yitzkhok Leibush
　　See Peretz, Isaac Loeb

Perez Galdos, Benito　1843-1920 . . . **TCLC 27**
　　See also CA 125; HW

Perrault, Charles　1628-1703 . . . . **LC 2**
　　See also MAICYA; SATA 25

Perry, Brighton
　　See Sherwood, Robert E(mmet)

Perse, St.-John . . . . **CLC 4, 11, 46**
　　See also Leger, (Marie-Rene Auguste) Alexis
　　Saint-Leger

Peseenz, Tulio F.
　　See Lopez y Fuentes, Gregorio

Pesetsky, Bette　1932- . . . . **CLC 28**
　　See also CA 133; DLB 130

Peshkov, Alexei Maximovich　1868-1936
　　See Gorky, Maxim
　　See also CA 105; 141; DA

Pessoa, Fernando (Antonio Nogueira)
　　1888-1935 . . . . **TCLC 27; HLC 2**
　　See also CA 125

Peterkin, Julia Mood　1880-1961 . . . . **CLC 31**
　　See also CA 102; DLB 9

Peters, Joan K.　1945- . . . . **CLC 39**

Peters, Robert L(ouis)　1924- . . . . **CLC 7**
　　See also CA 13-16R; CAAS 8; DLB 105

Petofi, Sandor　1823-1849 . . . . **NCLC 21**

Petrakis, Harry Mark　1923- . . . . **CLC 3**
　　See also CA 9-12R; CANR 4, 30

Petrarch　1304-1374 . . . . **PC 8**

Petrov, Evgeny . . . . **TCLC 21**
　　See also Kataev, Evgeny Petrovich

Petry, Ann (Lane)　1908- . . . . . . **CLC 1, 7, 18**
　　See also BW; CA 5-8R; CAAS 6; CANR 4;
　　CLR 12; DLB 76; JRDA; MAICYA;
　　MTCW; SATA 5

Petursson, Halligrimur　1614-1674 . . . . **LC 8**

Philipson, Morris H.　1926- . . . . **CLC 53**
　　See also CA 1-4R; CANR 4

Phillips, David Graham
　　1867-1911 . . . . **TCLC 44**
　　See also CA 108; DLB 9, 12

Phillips, Jack
　　See Sandburg, Carl (August)

Phillips, Jayne Anne　1952- . . . . . **CLC 15, 33**
　　See also CA 101; CANR 24; DLBY 80;
　　MTCW

Phillips, Richard
　　See Dick, Philip K(indred)

Phillips, Robert (Schaeffer)　1938- . . . **CLC 28**
　　See also CA 17-20R; CAAS 13; CANR 8;
　　DLB 105

Phillips, Ward
　　See Lovecraft, H(oward) P(hillips)

Piccolo, Lucio　1901-1969 . . . . **CLC 13**
　　See also CA 97-100; DLB 114

Pickthall, Marjorie L(owry) C(hristie)
　　1883-1922 . . . . **TCLC 21**
　　See also CA 107; DLB 92

Pico della Mirandola, Giovanni
　　1463-1494 . . . . **LC 15**

Piercy, Marge
　　1936- . . . . **CLC 3, 6, 14, 18, 27, 62**
　　See also CA 21-24R; CAAS 1; CANR 13,
　　43; DLB 120; MTCW

Piers, Robert
　　See Anthony, Piers

Pieyre de Mandiargues, Andre　1909-1991
　　See Mandiargues, Andre Pieyre de
　　See also CA 103; 136; CANR 22

Pilnyak, Boris . . . . **TCLC 23**
　　See also Vogau, Boris Andreyevich

Pincherle, Alberto　1907-1990 . . . **CLC 11, 18**
　　See also Moravia, Alberto
　　See also CA 25-28R; 132; CANR 33;
　　MTCW

Pinckney, Darryl　1953- . . . . **CLC 76**

Pindar　518B.C.-446B.C. . . . . **CMLC 12**

Pineda, Cecile　1942- . . . . **CLC 39**
　　See also CA 118

Pinero, Arthur Wing　1855-1934 . . . **TCLC 32**
　　See also CA 110; DLB 10

Pinero, Miguel (Antonio Gomez)
　　1946-1988 . . . . **CLC 4, 55**
　　See also CA 61-64; 125; CANR 29; HW

Pinget, Robert　1919- . . . . **CLC 7, 13, 37**
　　See also CA 85-88; DLB 83

Pink Floyd . . . . **CLC 35**
　　See also Barrett, (Roger) Syd; Gilmour,
　　David; Mason, Nick; Waters, Roger;
　　Wright, Rick

Pinkney, Edward　1802-1828 . . . . . **NCLC 31**

Pinkwater, Daniel Manus　1941- . . . . **CLC 35**
　　See also Pinkwater, Manus
　　See also AAYA 1; CA 29-32R; CANR 12,
　　38; CLR 4; JRDA; MAICYA; SAAS 3;
　　SATA 46

Pinkwater, Manus
　　See Pinkwater, Daniel Manus
　　See also SATA 8

Pinsky, Robert　1940- . . . . **CLC 9, 19, 38**
　　See also CA 29-32R; CAAS 4; DLBY 82

Pinta, Harold
　　See Pinter, Harold

Pinter, Harold
　　1930- . . . . . **CLC 1, 3, 6, 9, 11, 15, 27, 58,
　　　　　　　　　　　　　　　　　　73; DA; WLC**
　　See also CA 5-8R; CANR 33; CDBLB 1960
　　to Present; DLB 13; MTCW

Pirandello, Luigi
　　1867-1936 . . . . . . **TCLC 4, 29; DA; WLC**
　　See also CA 104

Pirsig, Robert M(aynard)
　　1928- . . . . **CLC 4, 6, 73**
　　See also CA 53-56; CANR 42; MTCW;
　　SATA 39

Pisarev, Dmitry Ivanovich
　　1840-1868 . . . . **NCLC 25**

Pix, Mary (Griffith)　1666-1709 . . . . . . **LC 8**
　　See also DLB 80

Pixerecourt, Guilbert de
　　1773-1844 . . . . **NCLC 39**

Plaidy, Jean
　　See Hibbert, Eleanor Alice Burford

Planche, James Robinson
　　1796-1880 . . . . **NCLC 42**

Plant, Robert　1948- . . . . **CLC 12**

Plante, David (Robert)
　　1940- . . . . **CLC 7, 23, 38**
　　See also CA 37-40R; CANR 12, 36;
　　DLBY 83; MTCW

Plath, Sylvia
　　1932-1963 . . . . . **CLC 1, 2, 3, 5, 9, 11, 14,
　　　　　　　　　　17, 50, 51, 62; DA; PC 1; WLC**
　　See also CA 19-20; CANR 34; CAP 2;
　　CDALB 1941-1968; DLB 5, 6; MTCW

Plato　428(?)B.C.-348(?)B.C. . . . . **CMLC 8; DA**

Platonov, Andrei . . . . **TCLC 14**
　　See also Klimentov, Andrei Platonovich

Platt, Kin　1911- . . . . **CLC 26**
　　See also CA 17-20R; CANR 11; JRDA;
　　SAAS 17; SATA 21

Plick et Plock
　　See Simenon, Georges (Jacques Christian)

Plimpton, George (Ames)　1927- . . . . . **CLC 36**
　　See also AITN 1; CA 21-24R; CANR 32;
　　MTCW; SATA 10

Plomer, William Charles Franklin
　　1903-1973 . . . . **CLC 4, 8**
　　See also CA 21-22; CANR 34; CAP 2;
　　DLB 20; MTCW; SATA 24

Plowman, Piers
　　See Kavanagh, Patrick (Joseph)

Plum, J.
　　See Wodehouse, P(elham) G(renville)

Plumly, Stanley (Ross)　1939- . . . . . . **CLC 33**
　　See also CA 108; 110; DLB 5

Plumpe, Friedrich Wilhelm
　　1888-1931 . . . . **TCLC 53**
　　See also CA 112

Poe, Edgar Allan
　　1809-1849 . . . . . **NCLC 1, 16; DA; PC 1;
　　　　　　　　　　　　　　　　　SSC 1; WLC**
　　See also CDALB 1640-1865; DLB 3, 59, 73,
　　74; SATA 23

Poet of Titchfield Street, The
　　See Pound, Ezra (Weston Loomis)

Pohl, Frederik　1919- . . . . **CLC 18**
　　See also CA 61-64; CAAS 1; CANR 11, 37;
　　DLB 8; MTCW; SATA 24

Poirier, Louis　1910-
　　See Gracq, Julien
　　See also CA 122; 126

Poitier, Sidney　1927- . . . . **CLC 26**
　　See also BW; CA 117

Polanski, Roman　1933- . . . . **CLC 16**
　　See also CA 77-80

Poliakoff, Stephen　1952- . . . . **CLC 38**
　　See also CA 106; DLB 13

Police, The...................... CLC 26
See also Copeland, Stewart (Armstrong);
Summers, Andrew James; Sumner,
Gordon Matthew

Pollitt, Katha 1949- .... CLC 28
See also CA 120; 122; MTCW

Pollock, (Mary) Sharon 1936-...... CLC 50
See also CA 141; DLB 60

Pomerance, Bernard 1940-........ CLC 13
See also CA 101

Ponge, Francis (Jean Gaston Alfred)
1899-1988 .... CLC 6, 18
See also CA 85-88; 126; CANR 40

Pontoppidan, Henrik 1857-1943 ... TCLC 29

Poole, Josephine .... CLC 17
See also Helyar, Jane Penelope Josephine
See also SAAS 2; SATA 5

Popa, Vasko 1922- .... CLC 19
See also CA 112

Pope, Alexander
1688-1744 .... LC 3; DA; WLC
See also CDBLB 1660-1789; DLB 95, 101

Porter, Connie (Rose) 1959(?)- ..... CLC 70
See also CA 142

Porter, Gene(va Grace) Stratton
1863(?)-1924 .... TCLC 21
See also CA 112

Porter, Katherine Anne
1890-1980 ...... CLC 1, 3, 7, 10, 13, 15,
27; DA; SSC 4
See also AITN 2; CA 1-4R; 101; CANR 1;
DLB 4, 9, 102; DLBY 80; MTCW;
SATA 23, 39

Porter, Peter (Neville Frederick)
1929- .... CLC 5, 13, 33
See also CA 85-88; DLB 40

Porter, William Sydney 1862-1910
See Henry, O.
See also CA 104; 131; CDALB 1865-1917;
DA; DLB 12, 78, 79; MTCW; YABC 2

Portillo (y Pacheco), Jose Lopez
See Lopez Portillo (y Pacheco), Jose

Post, Melville Davisson
1869-1930 .... TCLC 39
See also CA 110

Potok, Chaim 1929- .... CLC 2, 7, 14, 26
See also AITN 1, 2; CA 17-20R; CANR 19,
35; DLB 28; MTCW; SATA 33

Potter, Beatrice
See Webb, (Martha) Beatrice (Potter)
See also MAICYA

Potter, Dennis (Christopher George)
1935- .... CLC 58
See also CA 107; CANR 33; MTCW

Pound, Ezra (Weston Loomis)
1885-1972 ...... CLC 1, 2, 3, 4, 5, 7, 10,
13, 18, 34, 48, 50; DA; PC 4; WLC
See also CA 5-8R; 37-40R; CANR 40;
CDALB 1917-1929; DLB 4, 45, 63;
MTCW

Povod, Reinaldo 1959-........... CLC 44
See also CA 136

Powell, Anthony (Dymoke)
1905- .... CLC 1, 3, 7, 9, 10, 31
See also CA 1-4R; CANR 1, 32;
CDBLB 1945-1960; DLB 15; MTCW

Powell, Dawn 1897-1965 .... CLC 66
See also CA 5-8R

Powell, Padgett 1952-............. CLC 34
See also CA 126

Powers, J(ames) F(arl)
1917- .... CLC 1, 4, 8, 57; SSC 4
See also CA 1-4R; CANR 2; DLB 130;
MTCW

Powers, John J(ames) 1945-
See Powers, John R.
See also CA 69-72

Powers, John R. .... CLC 66
See also Powers, John J(ames)

Pownall, David 1938-............. CLC 10
See also CA 89-92; CAAS 18; DLB 14

Powys, John Cowper
1872-1963 .... CLC 7, 9, 15, 46
See also CA 85-88; DLB 15; MTCW

Powys, T(heodore) F(rancis)
1875-1953 .... TCLC 9
See also CA 106; DLB 36

Prager, Emily 1952-............. CLC 56

Pratt, E(dwin) J(ohn)
1883(?)-1964 .... CLC 19
See also CA 141; 93-96; DLB 92

Premchand..................... TCLC 21
See also Srivastava, Dhanpat Rai

Preussler, Otfried 1923-........... CLC 17
See also CA 77-80; SATA 24

Prevert, Jacques (Henri Marie)
1900-1977 .... CLC 15
See also CA 77-80; 69-72; CANR 29;
MTCW; SATA 30

Prevost, Abbe (Antoine Francois)
1697-1763 .... LC 1

Price, (Edward) Reynolds
1933- .... CLC 3, 6, 13, 43, 50, 63
See also CA 1-4R; CANR 1, 37; DLB 2

Price, Richard 1949- .... CLC 6, 12
See also CA 49-52; CANR 3; DLBY 81

Prichard, Katharine Susannah
1883-1969 .... CLC 46
See also CA 11-12; CANR 33; CAP 1;
MTCW; SATA 66

Priestley, J(ohn) B(oynton)
1894-1984 ....CLC 2, 5, 9, 34
See also CA 9-12R; 113; CANR 33;
CDBLB 1914-1945; DLB 10, 34, 77, 100;
DLBY 84; MTCW

Prince 1958(?)-.................. CLC 35

Prince, F(rank) T(empleton) 1912-.. CLC 22
See also CA 101; CANR 43; DLB 20

Prince Kropotkin
See Kropotkin, Peter (Aleksieevich)

Prior, Matthew 1664-1721.......... LC 4
See also DLB 95

Pritchard, William H(arrison)
1932- .... CLC 34
See also CA 65-68; CANR 23; DLB 111

Pritchett, V(ictor) S(awdon)
1900- .... CLC 5, 13, 15, 41; SSC 14
See also CA 61-64; CANR 31; DLB 15;
MTCW

Private 19022
See Manning, Frederic

Probst, Mark 1925- .... CLC 59
See also CA 130

Prokosch, Frederic 1908-1989.... CLC 4, 48
See also CA 73-76; 128; DLB 48

Prophet, The
See Dreiser, Theodore (Herman Albert)

Prose, Francine 1947-............. CLC 45
See also CA 109; 112

Proudhon
See Cunha, Euclides (Rodrigues Pimenta) da

Proulx, E. Annie 1935- .... CLC 81

**Proust, (Valentin-Louis-George-Eugene-)
Marcel**
1871-1922 ... TCLC 7, 13, 33; DA; WLC
See also CA 104; 120; DLB 65; MTCW

Prowler, Harley
See Masters, Edgar Lee

Prus, Boleslaw.................. TCLC 48
See also Glowacki, Aleksander

Pryor, Richard (Franklin Lenox Thomas)
1940- .... CLC 26
See also CA 122

Przybyszewski, Stanislaw
1868-1927 .... TCLC 36
See also DLB 66

Pteleon
See Grieve, C(hristopher) M(urray)

Puckett, Lute
See Masters, Edgar Lee

Puig, Manuel
1932-1990 .... CLC 3, 5, 10, 28, 65;
HLC 2
See also CA 45-48; CANR 2, 32; DLB 113;
HW; MTCW

Purdy, A(lfred Wellington)
1918-................ CLC 3, 6, 14, 50
See also CA 81-84; CANR 42

Purdy, Al
See Purdy, A(lfred Wellington)
See also CAAS 17; DLB 88

Purdy, James (Amos)
1923- .... CLC 2, 4, 10, 28, 52
See also CA 33-36R; CAAS 1; CANR 19;
DLB 2; MTCW

Pure, Simon
See Swinnerton, Frank Arthur

Pushkin, Alexander (Sergeyevich)
1799-1837 ...... NCLC 3, 27; DA; WLC
See also SATA 61

P'u Sung-ling 1640-1715 .... LC 3

Putnam, Arthur Lee
See Alger, Horatio, Jr.

Puzo, Mario 1920-........ CLC 1, 2, 6, 36
See also CA 65-68; CANR 4, 42; DLB 6;
MTCW

Reiner, Max
See Caldwell, (Janet Miriam) Taylor
(Holland)

Reis, Ricardo
See Pessoa, Fernando (Antonio Nogueira)

Remarque, Erich Maria
1898-1970 . . . . **CLC 21; DA**
See also CA 77-80; 29-32R; DLB 56;
MTCW

Remizov, A.
See Remizov, Aleksei (Mikhailovich)

Remizov, A. M.
See Remizov, Aleksei (Mikhailovich)

Remizov, Aleksei (Mikhailovich)
1877-1957 . . . . **TCLC 27**
See also CA 125; 133

Renan, Joseph Ernest
1823-1892 . . . . **NCLC 26**

Renard, Jules   1864-1910 . . . . **TCLC 17**
See also CA 117

Renault, Mary . . . . **CLC 3, 11, 17**
See also Challans, Mary
See also DLBY 83

Rendell, Ruth (Barbara)   1930- . . **CLC 28, 48**
See also Vine, Barbara
See also CA 109; CANR 32; DLB 87;
MTCW

Renoir, Jean   1894-1979 . . . . **CLC 20**
See also CA 129; 85-88

Resnais, Alain   1922- . . . . **CLC 16**

Reverdy, Pierre   1889-1960 . . . . **CLC 53**
See also CA 97-100; 89-92

Rexroth, Kenneth
1905-1982 . . . . . . **CLC 1, 2, 6, 11, 22, 49**
See also CA 5-8R; 107; CANR 14, 34;
CDALB 1941-1968; DLB 16, 48;
DLBY 82; MTCW

Reyes, Alfonso   1889-1959 . . . . **TCLC 33**
See also CA 131; HW

Reyes y Basoalto, Ricardo Eliecer Neftali
See Neruda, Pablo

Reymont, Wladyslaw (Stanislaw)
1868(?)-1925 . . . . **TCLC 5**
See also CA 104

Reynolds, Jonathan   1942- . . . . **CLC 6, 38**
See also CA 65-68; CANR 28

Reynolds, Joshua   1723-1792 . . . . **LC 15**
See also DLB 104

Reynolds, Michael Shane   1937- . . . . **CLC 44**
See also CA 65-68; CANR 9

Reznikoff, Charles   1894-1976 . . . . **CLC 9**
See also CA 33-36; 61-64; CAP 2; DLB 28,
45

Rezzori (d'Arezzo), Gregor von
1914- . . . . **CLC 25**
See also CA 122; 136

Rhine, Richard
See Silverstein, Alvin

Rhodes, Eugene Manlove
1869-1934 . . . . **TCLC 53**

R'hoone
See Balzac, Honore de

Rhys, Jean
1890(?)-1979 . . . . **CLC 2, 4, 6, 14, 19, 51**
See also CA 25-28R; 85-88; CANR 35;
CDBLB 1945-1960; DLB 36, 117; MTCW

Ribeiro, Darcy   1922- . . . . **CLC 34**
See also CA 33-36R

Ribeiro, Joao Ubaldo (Osorio Pimentel)
1941- . . . . **CLC 10, 67**
See also CA 81-84

Ribman, Ronald (Burt)   1932- . . . . **CLC 7**
See also CA 21-24R

Ricci, Nino   1959- . . . . **CLC 70**
See also CA 137

Rice, Anne   1941- . . . . **CLC 41**
See also AAYA 9; BEST 89:2; CA 65-68;
CANR 12, 36

Rice, Elmer (Leopold)
1892-1967 . . . . **CLC 7, 49**
See also CA 21-22; 25-28R; CAP 2; DLB 4,
7; MTCW

Rice, Tim   1944- . . . . **CLC 21**
See also CA 103

Rich, Adrienne (Cecile)
1929- . . . . **CLC 3, 6, 7, 11, 18, 36, 73, 76;**
PC 5
See also CA 9-12R; CANR 20; DLB 5, 67;
MTCW

Rich, Barbara
See Graves, Robert (von Ranke)

Rich, Robert
See Trumbo, Dalton

Richards, David Adams   1950- . . . . . . **CLC 59**
See also CA 93-96; DLB 53

Richards, I(vor) A(rmstrong)
1893-1979 . . . . **CLC 14, 24**
See also CA 41-44R; 89-92; CANR 34;
DLB 27

Richardson, Anne
See Roiphe, Anne Richardson

Richardson, Dorothy Miller
1873-1957 . . . . **TCLC 3**
See also CA 104; DLB 36

Richardson, Ethel Florence (Lindesay)
1870-1946
See Richardson, Henry Handel
See also CA 105

Richardson, Henry Handel . . . . **TCLC 4**
See also Richardson, Ethel Florence
(Lindesay)

Richardson, Samuel
1689-1761 . . . . **LC 1; DA; WLC**
See also CDBLB 1660-1789; DLB 39

Richler, Mordecai
1931- . . . . **CLC 3, 5, 9, 13, 18, 46, 70**
See also AITN 1; CA 65-68; CANR 31;
CLR 17; DLB 53; MAICYA; MTCW;
SATA 27, 44

Richter, Conrad (Michael)
1890-1968 . . . . **CLC 30**
See also CA 5-8R; 25-28R; CANR 23;
DLB 9; MTCW; SATA 3

Riddell, J. H.   1832-1906 . . . . **TCLC 40**

Riding, Laura . . . . **CLC 3, 7**
See also Jackson, Laura (Riding)

Riefenstahl, Berta Helene Amalia   1902-
See Riefenstahl, Leni
See also CA 108

Riefenstahl, Leni . . . . **CLC 16**
See also Riefenstahl, Berta Helene Amalia

Riffe, Ernest
See Bergman, (Ernst) Ingmar

Riley, James Whitcomb
1849-1916 . . . . **TCLC 51**
See also CA 118; 137; MAICYA; SATA 17

Riley, Tex
See Creasey, John

Rilke, Rainer Maria
1875-1926 . . . . **TCLC 1, 6, 19; PC 2**
See also CA 104; 132; DLB 81; MTCW

Rimbaud, (Jean Nicolas) Arthur
1854-1891 . . . . . **NCLC 4, 35; DA; PC 3;**
WLC

Rinehart, Mary Roberts
1876-1958 . . . . **TCLC 52**
See also CA 108

Ringmaster, The
See Mencken, H(enry) L(ouis)

Ringwood, Gwen(dolyn Margaret) Pharis
1910-1984 . . . . **CLC 48**
See also CA 112; DLB 88

Rio, Michel   19(?)- . . . . **CLC 43**

Ritsos, Giannes
See Ritsos, Yannis

Ritsos, Yannis   1909-1990 . . . . . **CLC 6, 13, 31**
See also CA 77-80; 133; CANR 39; MTCW

Ritter, Erika   1948(?)- . . . . **CLC 52**

Rivera, Jose Eustasio   1889-1928 . . . **TCLC 35**
See also HW

Rivers, Conrad Kent   1933-1968 . . . . . . **CLC 1**
See also BW; CA 85-88; DLB 41

Rivers, Elfrida
See Bradley, Marion Zimmer

Riverside, John
See Heinlein, Robert A(nson)

Rizal, Jose   1861-1896 . . . . **NCLC 27**

Roa Bastos, Augusto (Antonio)
1917- . . . . **CLC 45; HLC 2**
See also CA 131; DLB 113; HW

Robbe-Grillet, Alain
1922- . . . . . . **CLC 1, 2, 4, 6, 8, 10, 14, 43**
See also CA 9-12R; CANR 33; DLB 83;
MTCW

Robbins, Harold   1916- . . . . **CLC 5**
See also CA 73-76; CANR 26; MTCW

Robbins, Thomas Eugene   1936-
See Robbins, Tom
See also CA 81-84; CANR 29; MTCW

Robbins, Tom . . . . **CLC 9, 32, 64**
See also Robbins, Thomas Eugene
See also BEST 90:3; DLBY 80

Robbins, Trina   1938- . . . . **CLC 21**
See also CA 128

Roberts, Charles G(eorge) D(ouglas)
1860-1943 . . . . **TCLC 8**
See also CA 105; DLB 92; SATA 29

Roberts, Kate   1891-1985 . . . . **CLC 15**
See also CA 107; 116

Roberts, Keith (John Kingston)
    1935- .... CLC 14
    See also CA 25-28R

Roberts, Kenneth (Lewis)
    1885-1957 .... TCLC 23
    See also CA 109; DLB 9

Roberts, Michele (B.) 1949- .... CLC 48
    See also CA 115

Robertson, Ellis
    See Ellison, Harlan; Silverberg, Robert

Robertson, Thomas William
    1829-1871 .... NCLC 35

Robinson, Edwin Arlington
    1869-1935 .... TCLC 5; DA; PC 1
    See also CA 104; 133; CDALB 1865-1917;
    DLB 54; MTCW

Robinson, Henry Crabb
    1775-1867 .... NCLC 15
    See also DLB 107

Robinson, Jill 1936- .... CLC 10
    See also CA 102

Robinson, Kim Stanley 1952- ...... CLC 34
    See also CA 126

Robinson, Lloyd
    See Silverberg, Robert

Robinson, Marilynne 1944- .... CLC 25
    See also CA 116

Robinson, Smokey .... CLC 21
    See also Robinson, William, Jr.

Robinson, William, Jr. 1940-
    See Robinson, Smokey
    See also CA 116

Robison, Mary 1949- .... CLC 42
    See also CA 113; 116; DLB 130

Rod, Edouard 1857-1910 .... TCLC 52

Roddenberry, Eugene Wesley 1921-1991
    See Roddenberry, Gene
    See also CA 110; 135; CANR 37; SATA 45

Roddenberry, Gene .... CLC 17
    See also Roddenberry, Eugene Wesley
    See also AAYA 5; SATA-Obit 69

Rodgers, Mary 1931- .... CLC 12
    See also CA 49-52; CANR 8; CLR 20;
    JRDA; MAICYA; SATA 8

Rodgers, W(illiam) R(obert)
    1909-1969 .... CLC 7
    See also CA 85-88; DLB 20

Rodman, Eric
    See Silverberg, Robert

Rodman, Howard 1920(?)-1985 ..... CLC 65
    See also CA 118

Rodman, Maia
    See Wojciechowska, Maia (Teresa)

Rodriguez, Claudio 1934- .... CLC 10
    See also DLB 134

Roelvaag, O(le) E(dvart)
    1876-1931 .... TCLC 17
    See also CA 117; DLB 9

Roethke, Theodore (Huebner)
    1908-1963 ...... CLC 1, 3, 8, 11, 19, 46
    See also CA 81-84; CABS 2;
    CDALB 1941-1968; DLB 5; MTCW

Rogers, Thomas Hunton 1927- ..... CLC 57
    See also CA 89-92

Rogers, Will(iam Penn Adair)
    1879-1935 .... TCLC 8
    See also CA 105; DLB 11

Rogin, Gilbert 1929- .... CLC 18
    See also CA 65-68; CANR 15

Rohan, Koda .... TCLC 22
    See also Koda Shigeyuki

Rohmer, Eric .... CLC 16
    See also Scherer, Jean-Marie Maurice

Rohmer, Sax .... TCLC 28
    See also Ward, Arthur Henry Sarsfield
    See also DLB 70

Roiphe, Anne Richardson 1935- ... CLC 3, 9
    See also CA 89-92; DLBY 80

Rojas, Fernando de 1465-1541 ...... LC 23

Rolfe, Frederick (William Serafino Austin
    Lewis Mary) 1860-1913 ..... TCLC 12
    See also CA 107; DLB 34

Rolland, Romain 1866-1944 ...... TCLC 23
    See also CA 118; DLB 65

Rolvaag, O(le) E(dvart)
    See Roelvaag, O(le) E(dvart)

Romain Arnaud, Saint
    See Aragon, Louis

Romains, Jules 1885-1972 .... CLC 7
    See also CA 85-88; CANR 34; DLB 65;
    MTCW

Romero, Jose Ruben 1890-1952 ... TCLC 14
    See also CA 114; 131; HW

Ronsard, Pierre de 1524-1585 .... LC 6

Rooke, Leon 1934- .... CLC 25, 34
    See also CA 25-28R; CANR 23

Roper, William 1498-1578 .... LC 10

Roquelaure, A. N.
    See Rice, Anne

Rosa, Joao Guimaraes 1908-1967 ... CLC 23
    See also CA 89-92; DLB 113

Rosen, Richard (Dean) 1949- .... CLC 39
    See also CA 77-80

Rosenberg, Isaac 1890-1918 ...... TCLC 12
    See also CA 107; DLB 20

Rosenblatt, Joe .... CLC 15
    See also Rosenblatt, Joseph

Rosenblatt, Joseph 1933-
    See Rosenblatt, Joe
    See also CA 89-92

Rosenfeld, Samuel 1896-1963
    See Tzara, Tristan
    See also CA 89-92

Rosenthal, M(acha) L(ouis) 1917- ... CLC 28
    See also CA 1-4R; CAAS 6; CANR 4;
    DLB 5; SATA 59

Ross, Barnaby
    See Dannay, Frederic

Ross, Bernard L.
    See Follett, Ken(neth Martin)

Ross, J. H.
    See Lawrence, T(homas) E(dward)

Ross, Martin
    See Martin, Violet Florence
    See also DLB 135

Ross, (James) Sinclair 1908- .... CLC 13
    See also CA 73-76; DLB 88

Rossetti, Christina (Georgina)
    1830-1894 ... NCLC 2; DA; PC 7; WLC
    See also DLB 35; MAICYA; SATA 20

Rossetti, Dante Gabriel
    1828-1882 .... NCLC 4; DA; WLC
    See also CDBLB 1832-1890; DLB 35

Rossner, Judith (Perelman)
    1935- .... CLC 6, 9, 29
    See also AITN 2; BEST 90:3; CA 17-20R;
    CANR 18; DLB 6; MTCW

Rostand, Edmond (Eugene Alexis)
    1868-1918 .... TCLC 6, 37; DA
    See also CA 104; 126; MTCW

Roth, Henry 1906- .... CLC 2, 6, 11
    See also CA 11-12; CANR 38; CAP 1;
    DLB 28; MTCW

Roth, Joseph 1894-1939 .... TCLC 33
    See also DLB 85

Roth, Philip (Milton)
    1933- ...... CLC 1, 2, 3, 4, 6, 9, 15, 22,
                    31, 47, 66; DA; WLC
    See also BEST 90:3; CA 1-4R; CANR 1, 22,
    36; CDALB 1968-1988; DLB 2, 28;
    DLBY 82; MTCW

Rothenberg, Jerome 1931- .... CLC 6, 57
    See also CA 45-48; CANR 1; DLB 5

Roumain, Jacques (Jean Baptiste)
    1907-1944 .... TCLC 19; BLC 3
    See also BW; CA 117; 125

Rourke, Constance (Mayfield)
    1885-1941 .... TCLC 12
    See also CA 107; YABC 1

Rousseau, Jean-Baptiste 1671-1741 ... LC 9

Rousseau, Jean-Jacques
    1712-1778 .... LC 14; DA; WLC

Roussel, Raymond 1877-1933 ..... TCLC 20
    See also CA 117

Rovit, Earl (Herbert) 1927- .... CLC 7
    See also CA 5-8R; CANR 12

Rowe, Nicholas 1674-1718 .... LC 8
    See also DLB 84

Rowley, Ames Dorrance
    See Lovecraft, H(oward) P(hillips)

Rowson, Susanna Haswell
    1762(?)-1824 .... NCLC 5
    See also DLB 37

Roy, Gabrielle 1909-1983 .... CLC 10, 14
    See also CA 53-56; 110; CANR 5; DLB 68;
    MTCW

Rozewicz, Tadeusz 1921- .... CLC 9, 23
    See also CA 108; CANR 36; MTCW

Ruark, Gibbons 1941- .... CLC 3
    See also CA 33-36R; CANR 14, 31;
    DLB 120

Rubens, Bernice (Ruth) 1923- ... CLC 19, 31
    See also CA 25-28R; CANR 33; DLB 14;
    MTCW

Rudkin, (James) David 1936- ...... CLC 14
    See also CA 89-92; DLB 13

Rudnik, Raphael 1933- .... CLC 7
    See also CA 29-32R

Ruffian, M.
    See Hasek, Jaroslav (Matej Frantisek)

Ruiz, Jose Martinez . . . . CLC 11
   See also Martinez Ruiz, Jose

Rukeyser, Muriel
   1913-1980 . . . . CLC 6, 10, 15, 27
   See also CA 5-8R; 93-96; CANR 26;
   DLB 48; MTCW; SATA 22

Rule, Jane (Vance)   1931- . . . . CLC 27
   See also CA 25-28R; CAAS 18; CANR 12;
   DLB 60

Rulfo, Juan   1918-1986 . . . CLC 8, 80; HLC 2
   See also CA 85-88; 118; CANR 26;
   DLB 113; HW; MTCW

Runeberg, Johan   1804-1877 . . . . . . NCLC 41

Runyon, (Alfred) Damon
   1884(?)-1946 . . . . TCLC 10
   See also CA 107; DLB 11, 86

Rush, Norman   1933- . . . . CLC 44
   See also CA 121; 126

Rushdie, (Ahmed) Salman
   1947- . . . . CLC 23, 31, 55
   See also BEST 89:3; CA 108; 111;
   CANR 33; MTCW

Rushforth, Peter (Scott)   1945- . . . . . CLC 19
   See also CA 101

Ruskin, John   1819-1900 . . . . TCLC 20
   See also CA 114; 129; CDBLB 1832-1890;
   DLB 55; SATA 24

Russ, Joanna   1937- . . . . CLC 15
   See also CA 25-28R; CANR 11, 31; DLB 8;
   MTCW

Russell, George William   1867-1935
   See A. E.
   See also CA 104; CDBLB 1890-1914

Russell, (Henry) Ken(neth Alfred)
   1927- . . . . CLC 16
   See also CA 105

Russell, Willy   1947- . . . . CLC 60

Rutherford, Mark . . . . TCLC 25
   See also White, William Hale
   See also DLB 18

Ruyslinck, Ward
   See Belser, Reimond Karel Maria de

Ryan, Cornelius (John)   1920-1974 . . . CLC 7
   See also CA 69-72; 53-56; CANR 38

Ryan, Michael   1946- . . . . CLC 65
   See also CA 49-52; DLBY 82

Rybakov, Anatoli (Naumovich)
   1911- . . . . CLC 23, 53
   See also CA 126; 135

Ryder, Jonathan
   See Ludlum, Robert

Ryga, George   1932-1987 . . . . CLC 14
   See also CA 101; 124; CANR 43; DLB 60

S. S.
   See Sassoon, Siegfried (Lorraine)

Saba, Umberto   1883-1957 . . . . TCLC 33
   See also DLB 114

Sabatini, Rafael   1875-1950 . . . . TCLC 47

Sabato, Ernesto (R.)
   1911- . . . . CLC 10, 23; HLC 2
   See also CA 97-100; CANR 32; HW;
   MTCW

Sacastru, Martin
   See Bioy Casares, Adolfo

Sacher-Masoch, Leopold von
   1836(?)-1895 . . . . NCLC 31

Sachs, Marilyn (Stickle)   1927- . . . . . CLC 35
   See also AAYA 2; CA 17-20R; CANR 13;
   CLR 2; JRDA; MAICYA; SAAS 2;
   SATA 3, 68

Sachs, Nelly   1891-1970 . . . . CLC 14
   See also CA 17-18; 25-28R; CAP 2

Sackler, Howard (Oliver)
   1929-1982 . . . . CLC 14
   See also CA 61-64; 108; CANR 30; DLB 7

Sacks, Oliver (Wolf)   1933- . . . . CLC 67
   See also CA 53-56; CANR 28; MTCW

Sade, Donatien Alphonse Francois Comte
   1740-1814 . . . . NCLC 3

Sadoff, Ira   1945- . . . . CLC 9
   See also CA 53-56; CANR 5, 21; DLB 120

Saetone
   See Camus, Albert

Safire, William   1929- . . . . CLC 10
   See also CA 17-20R; CANR 31

Sagan, Carl (Edward)   1934- . . . . CLC 30
   See also AAYA 2; CA 25-28R; CANR 11,
   36; MTCW; SATA 58

Sagan, Francoise . . . . CLC 3, 6, 9, 17, 36
   See also Quoirez, Francoise
   See also DLB 83

Sahgal, Nayantara (Pandit)   1927- . . . CLC 41
   See also CA 9-12R; CANR 11

Saint, H(arry) F.   1941- . . . . CLC 50
   See also CA 127

St. Aubin de Teran, Lisa   1953-
   See Teran, Lisa St. Aubin de
   See also CA 118; 126

Sainte-Beuve, Charles Augustin
   1804-1869 . . . . NCLC 5

Saint-Exupery, Antoine (Jean Baptiste Marie
   Roger) de   1900-1944 . . . TCLC 2; WLC
   See also CA 108; 132; CLR 10; DLB 72;
   MAICYA; MTCW; SATA 20

St. John, David
   See Hunt, E(verette) Howard, Jr.

Saint-John Perse
   See Leger, (Marie-Rene Auguste) Alexis
   Saint-Leger

Saintsbury, George (Edward Bateman)
   1845-1933 . . . . TCLC 31
   See also DLB 57

Sait Faik . . . . TCLC 23
   See also Abasiyanik, Sait Faik

Saki . . . . TCLC 3; SSC 12
   See also Munro, H(ector) H(ugh)

Salama, Hannu   1936- . . . . CLC 18

Salamanca, J(ack) R(ichard)
   1922- . . . . CLC 4, 15
   See also CA 25-28R

Sale, J. Kirkpatrick
   See Sale, Kirkpatrick

Sale, Kirkpatrick   1937- . . . . CLC 68
   See also CA 13-16R; CANR 10

Salinas (y Serrano), Pedro
   1891(?)-1951 . . . . TCLC 17
   See also CA 117; DLB 134

Salinger, J(erome) D(avid)
   1919- . . . . . . CLC 1, 3, 8, 12, 55, 56; DA;
                                        SSC 2; WLC
   See also AAYA 2; CA 5-8R; CANR 39;
   CDALB 1941-1968; CLR 18; DLB 2, 102;
   MAICYA; MTCW; SATA 67

Salisbury, John
   See Caute, David

Salter, James   1925- . . . . CLC 7, 52, 59
   See also CA 73-76; DLB 130

Saltus, Edgar (Everton)
   1855-1921 . . . . TCLC 8
   See also CA 105

Saltykov, Mikhail Evgrafovich
   1826-1889 . . . . NCLC 16

Samarakis, Antonis   1919- . . . . CLC 5
   See also CA 25-28R; CAAS 16; CANR 36

Sanchez, Florencio   1875-1910 . . . . . TCLC 37
   See also HW

Sanchez, Luis Rafael   1936- . . . . CLC 23
   See also CA 128; HW

Sanchez, Sonia   1934- . . . . CLC 5; BLC 3
   See also BW; CA 33-36R; CANR 24;
   CLR 18; DLB 41; DLBD 8; MAICYA;
   MTCW; SATA 22

Sand, George
   1804-1876 . . . . . . NCLC 2, 42; DA; WLC
   See also DLB 119

Sandburg, Carl (August)
   1878-1967 . . . . CLC 1, 4, 10, 15, 35; DA;
                                        PC 2; WLC
   See also CA 5-8R; 25-28R; CANR 35;
   CDALB 1865-1917; DLB 17, 54;
   MAICYA; MTCW; SATA 8

Sandburg, Charles
   See Sandburg, Carl (August)

Sandburg, Charles A.
   See Sandburg, Carl (August)

Sanders, (James) Ed(ward)   1939- . . . CLC 53
   See also CA 13-16R; CANR 13; DLB 16

Sanders, Lawrence   1920- . . . . CLC 41
   See also BEST 89:4; CA 81-84; CANR 33;
   MTCW

Sanders, Noah
   See Blount, Roy (Alton), Jr.

Sanders, Winston P.
   See Anderson, Poul (William)

Sandoz, Mari(e Susette)
   1896-1966 . . . . CLC 28
   See also CA 1-4R; 25-28R; CANR 17;
   DLB 9; MTCW; SATA 5

Saner, Reg(inald Anthony)   1931- . . . . CLC 9
   See also CA 65-68

Sannazaro, Jacopo   1456(?)-1530 . . . . . . LC 8

Sansom, William   1912-1976 . . . . CLC 2, 6
   See also CA 5-8R; 65-68; CANR 42;
   MTCW

Santayana, George   1863-1952 . . . . . TCLC 40
   See also CA 115; DLB 54, 71

Santiago, Danny . . . . CLC 33
   See also James, Daniel (Lewis); James,
   Daniel (Lewis)
   See also DLB 122

Scum
See Crumb, R(obert)

Scumbag, Little Bobby
See Crumb, R(obert)

Seabrook, John
See Hubbard, L(afayette) Ron(ald)

Sealy, I. Allan   1951- . . . . **CLC 55**

Search, Alexander
See Pessoa, Fernando (Antonio Nogueira)

Sebastian, Lee
See Silverberg, Robert

Sebastian Owl
See Thompson, Hunter S(tockton)

Sebestyen, Ouida   1924- . . . . **CLC 30**
See also AAYA 8; CA 107; CANR 40;
CLR 17; JRDA; MAICYA; SAAS 10;
SATA 39

Secundus, H. Scriblerus
See Fielding, Henry

Sedges, John
See Buck, Pearl S(ydenstricker)

Sedgwick, Catharine Maria
1789-1867 . . . . **NCLC 19**
See also DLB 1, 74

Seelye, John   1931- . . . . **CLC 7**

Seferiades, Giorgos Stylianou   1900-1971
See Seferis, George
See also CA 5-8R; 33-36R; CANR 5, 36;
MTCW

Seferis, George . . . . **CLC 5, 11**
See also Seferiades, Giorgos Stylianou

Segal, Erich (Wolf)   1937- . . . . **CLC 3, 10**
See also BEST 89:1; CA 25-28R; CANR 20,
36; DLBY 86; MTCW

Seger, Bob   1945- . . . . **CLC 35**

Seghers, Anna . . . . **CLC 7**
See also Radvanyi, Netty
See also DLB 69

Seidel, Frederick (Lewis)   1936- . . . . . **CLC 18**
See also CA 13-16R; CANR 8; DLBY 84

Seifert, Jaroslav   1901-1986 . . . . . **CLC 34, 44**
See also CA 127; MTCW

Sei Shonagon   c. 966-1017(?) . . . . . . **CMLC 6**

Selby, Hubert, Jr.   1928- . . . . . **CLC 1, 2, 4, 8**
See also CA 13-16R; CANR 33; DLB 2

Selzer, Richard   1928- . . . . **CLC 74**
See also CA 65-68; CANR 14

Sembene, Ousmane
See Ousmane, Sembene

Senancour, Etienne Pivert de
1770-1846 . . . . **NCLC 16**
See also DLB 119

Sender, Ramon (Jose)
1902-1982 . . . . **CLC 8; HLC 2**
See also CA 5-8R; 105; CANR 8; HW;
MTCW

Seneca, Lucius Annaeus
4B.C.-65. . . . . **CMLC 6**

Senghor, Leopold Sedar
1906- . . . . **CLC 54; BLC 3**
See also BW; CA 116; 125; MTCW

Serling, (Edward) Rod(man)
1924-1975 . . . . **CLC 30**
See also AITN 1; CA 65-68; 57-60; DLB 26

Serna, Ramon Gomez de la
See Gomez de la Serna, Ramon

Serpieres
See Guillevic, (Eugene)

Service, Robert
See Service, Robert W(illiam)
See also DLB 92

Service, Robert W(illiam)
1874(?)-1958 . . . . . . **TCLC 15; DA; WLC**
See also Service, Robert
See also CA 115; 140; SATA 20

Seth, Vikram   1952- . . . . **CLC 43**
See also CA 121; 127; DLB 120

Seton, Cynthia Propper
1926-1982 . . . . **CLC 27**
See also CA 5-8R; 108; CANR 7

Seton, Ernest (Evan) Thompson
1860-1946 . . . . **TCLC 31**
See also CA 109; DLB 92; JRDA; SATA 18

Seton-Thompson, Ernest
See Seton, Ernest (Evan) Thompson

Settle, Mary Lee   1918- . . . . **CLC 19, 61**
See also CA 89-92; CAAS 1; DLB 6

Seuphor, Michel
See Arp, Jean

Sevigne, Marie (de Rabutin-Chantal) Marquise
de   1626-1696 . . . . **LC 11**

Sexton, Anne (Harvey)
1928-1974 . . . . **CLC 2, 4, 6, 8, 10, 15, 53;
DA; PC 2; WLC**
See also CA 1-4R; 53-56; CABS 2;
CANR 3, 36; CDALB 1941-1968; DLB 5;
MTCW; SATA 10

Shaara, Michael (Joseph Jr.)
1929-1988 . . . . **CLC 15**
See also AITN 1; CA 102; DLBY 83

Shackleton, C. C.
See Aldiss, Brian W(ilson)

Shacochis, Bob . . . . **CLC 39**
See also Shacochis, Robert G.

Shacochis, Robert G.   1951-
See Shacochis, Bob
See also CA 119; 124

Shaffer, Anthony (Joshua)   1926- . . . . **CLC 19**
See also CA 110; 116; DLB 13

Shaffer, Peter (Levin)
1926- . . . . **CLC 5, 14, 18, 37, 60**
See also CA 25-28R; CANR 25;
CDBLB 1960 to Present; DLB 13;
MTCW

Shakey, Bernard
See Young, Neil

Shalamov, Varlam (Tikhonovich)
1907(?)-1982 . . . . **CLC 18**
See also CA 129; 105

Shamlu, Ahmad   1925- . . . . **CLC 10**

Shammas, Anton   1951- . . . . **CLC 55**

Shange, Ntozake
1948- . . **CLC 8, 25, 38, 74; BLC 3; DC 3**
See also AAYA 9; BW; CA 85-88; CABS 3;
CANR 27; DLB 38; MTCW

Shanley, John Patrick   1950- . . . . **CLC 75**
See also CA 128; 133

Shapcott, Thomas William   1935- . . . **CLC 38**
See also CA 69-72

Shapiro, Jane . . . . **CLC 76**

Shapiro, Karl (Jay)   1913- . . **CLC 4, 8, 15, 53**
See also CA 1-4R; CAAS 6; CANR 1, 36;
DLB 48; MTCW

Sharp, William   1855-1905 . . . . **TCLC 39**

Sharpe, Thomas Ridley   1928-
See Sharpe, Tom
See also CA 114; 122

Sharpe, Tom . . . . **CLC 36**
See also Sharpe, Thomas Ridley
See also DLB 14

Shaw, Bernard . . . . **TCLC 45**
See also Shaw, George Bernard

Shaw, G. Bernard
See Shaw, George Bernard

Shaw, George Bernard
1856-1950 . . . . **TCLC 3, 9, 21; DA; WLC**
See also Shaw, Bernard
See also CA 104; 128; CDBLB 1914-1945;
DLB 10, 57; MTCW

Shaw, Henry Wheeler
1818-1885 . . . . **NCLC 15**
See also DLB 11

Shaw, Irwin   1913-1984 . . . . . . **CLC 7, 23, 34**
See also AITN 1; CA 13-16R; 112;
CANR 21; CDALB 1941-1968; DLB 6,
102; DLBY 84; MTCW

Shaw, Robert   1927-1978 . . . . **CLC 5**
See also AITN 1; CA 1-4R; 81-84;
CANR 4; DLB 13, 14

Shaw, T. E.
See Lawrence, T(homas) E(dward)

Shawn, Wallace   1943- . . . . **CLC 41**
See also CA 112

Sheed, Wilfrid (John Joseph)
1930- . . . . **CLC 2, 4, 10, 53**
See also CA 65-68; CANR 30; DLB 6;
MTCW

Sheldon, Alice Hastings Bradley
1915(?)-1987
See Tiptree, James, Jr.
See also CA 108; 122; CANR 34; MTCW

Sheldon, John
See Bloch, Robert (Albert)

Shelley, Mary Wollstonecraft (Godwin)
1797-1851 . . . . **NCLC 14; DA; WLC**
See also CDBLB 1789-1832; DLB 110, 116;
SATA 29

Shelley, Percy Bysshe
1792-1822 . . . . **NCLC 18; DA; WLC**
See also CDBLB 1789-1832; DLB 96, 110

Shepard, Jim   1956- . . . . **CLC 36**
See also CA 137

Shepard, Lucius   1947- . . . . **CLC 34**
See also CA 128; 141

Shepard, Sam
1943- . . . . **CLC 4, 6, 17, 34, 41, 44**
See also AAYA 1; CA 69-72; CABS 3;
CANR 22; DLB 7; MTCW

Shepherd, Michael
See Ludlum, Robert

Sherburne, Zoa (Morin) 1912- ...... **CLC 30**
See also CA 1-4R; CANR 3, 37; MAICYA;
SATA 3

Sheridan, Frances 1724-1766 .... **LC 7**
See also DLB 39, 84

Sheridan, Richard Brinsley
1751-1816 ... **NCLC 5; DA; DC 1; WLC**
See also CDBLB 1660-1789; DLB 89

Sherman, Jonathan Marc .... **CLC 55**

Sherman, Martin 1941(?)- .... **CLC 19**
See also CA 116; 123

Sherwin, Judith Johnson 1936- ... **CLC 7, 15**
See also CA 25-28R; CANR 34

Sherwood, Frances 1940- .... **CLC 81**

Sherwood, Robert E(mmet)
1896-1955 .... **TCLC 3**
See also CA 104; DLB 7, 26

Shiel, M(atthew) P(hipps)
1865-1947 .... **TCLC 8**
See also CA 106

Shiga, Naoya 1883-1971 .... **CLC 33**
See also CA 101; 33-36R

Shimazaki Haruki 1872-1943
See Shimazaki Toson
See also CA 105; 134

Shimazaki Toson .... **TCLC 5**
See also Shimazaki Haruki

Sholokhov, Mikhail (Aleksandrovich)
1905-1984 .... **CLC 7, 15**
See also CA 101; 112; MTCW; SATA 36

Shone, Patric
See Hanley, James

Shreve, Susan Richards 1939- ...... **CLC 23**
See also CA 49-52; CAAS 5; CANR 5, 38;
MAICYA; SATA 41, 46

Shue, Larry 1946-1985 .... **CLC 52**
See also CA 117

Shu-Jen, Chou 1881-1936
See Hsun, Lu
See also CA 104

Shulman, Alix Kates 1932- ...... **CLC 2, 10**
See also CA 29-32R; CANR 43; SATA 7

Shuster, Joe 1914- .... **CLC 21**

Shute, Nevil .... **CLC 30**
See also Norway, Nevil Shute

Shuttle, Penelope (Diane) 1947- ..... **CLC 7**
See also CA 93-96; CANR 39; DLB 14, 40

Sidney, Mary 1561-1621 .... **LC 19**

Sidney, Sir Philip 1554-1586 .... **LC 19; DA**
See also CDBLB Before 1660

Siegel, Jerome 1914- .... **CLC 21**
See also CA 116

Siegel, Jerry
See Siegel, Jerome

Sienkiewicz, Henryk (Adam Alexander Pius)
1846-1916 .... **TCLC 3**
See also CA 104; 134

Sierra, Gregorio Martinez
See Martinez Sierra, Gregorio

Sierra, Maria (de la O'LeJarraga) Martinez
See Martinez Sierra, Maria (de la
O'LeJarraga)

Sigal, Clancy 1926- .... **CLC 7**
See also CA 1-4R

Sigourney, Lydia Howard (Huntley)
1791-1865 .... **NCLC 21**
See also DLB 1, 42, 73

Siguenza y Gongora, Carlos de
1645-1700 .... **LC 8**

Sigurjonsson, Johann 1880-1919 ... **TCLC 27**

Sikelianos, Angelos 1884-1951 .... **TCLC 39**

Silkin, Jon 1930- .... **CLC 2, 6, 43**
See also CA 5-8R; CAAS 5; DLB 27

Silko, Leslie Marmon
1948- .... **CLC 23, 74; DA**
See also CA 115; 122

Sillanpaa, Frans Eemil 1888-1964 ... **CLC 19**
See also CA 129; 93-96; MTCW

Sillitoe, Alan
1928- .... **CLC 1, 3, 6, 10, 19, 57**
See also AITN 1; CA 9-12R; CAAS 2;
CANR 8, 26; CDBLB 1960 to Present;
DLB 14; MTCW; SATA 61

Silone, Ignazio 1900-1978 .... **CLC 4**
See also CA 25-28; 81-84; CANR 34;
CAP 2; MTCW

Silver, Joan Micklin 1935- .... **CLC 20**
See also CA 114; 121

Silver, Nicholas
See Faust, Frederick (Schiller)

Silverberg, Robert 1935- .... **CLC 7**
See also CA 1-4R; CAAS 3; CANR 1, 20,
36; DLB 8; MAICYA; MTCW; SATA 13

Silverstein, Alvin 1933- .... **CLC 17**
See also CA 49-52; CANR 2; CLR 25;
JRDA; MAICYA; SATA 8, 69

Silverstein, Virginia B(arbara Opshelor)
1937- .... **CLC 17**
See also CA 49-52; CANR 2; CLR 25;
JRDA; MAICYA; SATA 8, 69

Sim, Georges
See Simenon, Georges (Jacques Christian)

Simak, Clifford D(onald)
1904-1988 .... **CLC 1, 55**
See also CA 1-4R; 125; CANR 1, 35;
DLB 8; MTCW; SATA 56

Simenon, Georges (Jacques Christian)
1903-1989 .... **CLC 1, 2, 3, 8, 18, 47**
See also CA 85-88; 129; CANR 35;
DLB 72; DLBY 89; MTCW

Simic, Charles 1938- ... **CLC 6, 9, 22, 49, 68**
See also CA 29-32R; CAAS 4; CANR 12,
33; DLB 105

Simmons, Charles (Paul) 1924- ..... **CLC 57**
See also CA 89-92

Simmons, Dan 1948- .... **CLC 44**
See also CA 138

Simmons, James (Stewart Alexander)
1933- .... **CLC 43**
See also CA 105; DLB 40

Simms, William Gilmore
1806-1870 .... **NCLC 3**
See also DLB 3, 30, 59, 73

Simon, Carly 1945- .... **CLC 26**
See also CA 105

Simon, Claude 1913- .... **CLC 4, 9, 15, 39**
See also CA 89-92; CANR 33; DLB 83;
MTCW

Simon, (Marvin) Neil
1927- .... **CLC 6, 11, 31, 39, 70**
See also AITN 1; CA 21-24R; CANR 26;
DLB 7; MTCW

Simon, Paul 1942(?)- .... **CLC 17**
See also CA 116

Simonon, Paul 1956(?)- .... **CLC 30**
See also Clash, The

Simpson, Harriette
See Arnow, Harriette (Louisa) Simpson

Simpson, Louis (Aston Marantz)
1923- .... **CLC 4, 7, 9, 32**
See also CA 1-4R; CAAS 4; CANR 1;
DLB 5; MTCW

Simpson, Mona (Elizabeth) 1957- ... **CLC 44**
See also CA 122; 135

Simpson, N(orman) F(rederick)
1919- .... **CLC 29**
See also CA 13-16R; DLB 13

Sinclair, Andrew (Annandale)
1935- .... **CLC 2, 14**
See also CA 9-12R; CAAS 5; CANR 14, 38;
DLB 14; MTCW

Sinclair, Emil
See Hesse, Hermann

Sinclair, Iain 1943- .... **CLC 76**
See also CA 132

Sinclair, Iain MacGregor
See Sinclair, Iain

Sinclair, Mary Amelia St. Clair 1865(?)-1946
See Sinclair, May
See also CA 104

Sinclair, May .... **TCLC 3, 11**
See also Sinclair, Mary Amelia St. Clair
See also DLB 36, 135

Sinclair, Upton (Beall)
1878-1968 ...... **CLC 1, 11, 15, 63; DA;
WLC**
See also CA 5-8R; 25-28R; CANR 7;
CDALB 1929-1941; DLB 9; MTCW;
SATA 9

Singer, Isaac
See Singer, Isaac Bashevis

Singer, Isaac Bashevis
1904-1991 .... **CLC 1, 3, 6, 9, 11, 15, 23,
38, 69; DA; SSC 3; WLC**
See also AITN 1, 2; CA 1-4R; 134;
CANR 1, 39; CDALB 1941-1968; CLR 1;
DLB 6, 28, 52; DLBY 91; JRDA;
MAICYA; MTCW; SATA 3, 27;
SATA-Obit 68

Singer, Israel Joshua 1893-1944 ... **TCLC 33**

Singh, Khushwant 1915- .... **CLC 11**
See also CA 9-12R; CAAS 9; CANR 6

Sinjohn, John
See Galsworthy, John

Sinyavsky, Andrei (Donatevich)
1925- .... **CLC 8**
See also CA 85-88

Sirin, V.
See Nabokov, Vladimir (Vladimirovich)

Sissman, L(ouis) E(dward)
1928-1976 . . . . **CLC 9, 18**
See also CA 21-24R; 65-68; CANR 13;
DLB 5

Sisson, C(harles) H(ubert)   1914- . . . . . **CLC 8**
See also CA 1-4R; CAAS 3; CANR 3;
DLB 27

Sitwell, Dame Edith
1887-1964 . . . . **CLC 2, 9, 67; PC 3**
See also CA 9-12R; CANR 35;
CDBLB 1945-1960; DLB 20; MTCW

Sjoewall, Maj   1935- . . . . **CLC 7**
See also CA 65-68

Sjowall, Maj
See Sjoewall, Maj

Skelton, Robin   1925- . . . . **CLC 13**
See also AITN 2; CA 5-8R; CAAS 5;
CANR 28; DLB 27, 53

Skolimowski, Jerzy   1938- . . . . **CLC 20**
See also CA 128

Skram, Amalie (Bertha)
1847-1905 . . . . **TCLC 25**

Skvorecky, Josef (Vaclav)
1924- . . . . **CLC 15, 39, 69**
See also CA 61-64; CAAS 1; CANR 10, 34;
MTCW

Slade, Bernard . . . . **CLC 11, 46**
See also Newbound, Bernard Slade
See also CAAS 9; DLB 53

Slaughter, Carolyn   1946- . . . . **CLC 56**
See also CA 85-88

Slaughter, Frank G(ill)   1908- . . . . . . **CLC 29**
See also AITN 2; CA 5-8R; CANR 5

Slavitt, David R(ytman)   1935- . . . . **CLC 5, 14**
See also CA 21-24R; CAAS 3; CANR 41;
DLB 5, 6

Slesinger, Tess   1905-1945 . . . . **TCLC 10**
See also CA 107; DLB 102

Slessor, Kenneth   1901-1971 . . . . **CLC 14**
See also CA 102; 89-92

Slowacki, Juliusz   1809-1849 . . . . . **NCLC 15**

Smart, Christopher   1722-1771 . . . . **LC 3**
See also DLB 109

Smart, Elizabeth   1913-1986 . . . . **CLC 54**
See also CA 81-84; 118; DLB 88

Smiley, Jane (Graves)   1949- . . . . **CLC 53, 76**
See also CA 104; CANR 30

Smith, A(rthur) J(ames) M(arshall)
1902-1980 . . . . **CLC 15**
See also CA 1-4R; 102; CANR 4; DLB 88

Smith, Betty (Wehner)   1896-1972 . . . **CLC 19**
See also CA 5-8R; 33-36R; DLBY 82;
SATA 6

Smith, Charlotte (Turner)
1749-1806 . . . . **NCLC 23**
See also DLB 39, 109

Smith, Clark Ashton   1893-1961 . . . . **CLC 43**

Smith, Dave . . . . **CLC 22, 42**
See also Smith, David (Jeddie)
See also CAAS 7; DLB 5

Smith, David (Jeddie)   1942-
See Smith, Dave
See also CA 49-52; CANR 1

Smith, Florence Margaret
1902-1971 . . . . **CLC 8**
See also Smith, Stevie
See also CA 17-18; 29-32R; CANR 35;
CAP 2; MTCW

Smith, Iain Crichton   1928- . . . . **CLC 64**
See also CA 21-24R; DLB 40

Smith, John   1580(?)-1631 . . . . **LC 9**

Smith, Johnston
See Crane, Stephen (Townley)

Smith, Lee   1944- . . . . **CLC 25, 73**
See also CA 114; 119; DLBY 83

Smith, Martin
See Smith, Martin Cruz

Smith, Martin Cruz   1942- . . . . **CLC 25**
See also BEST 89:4; CA 85-88; CANR 6,
23, 43

Smith, Mary-Ann Tirone   1944- . . . . . **CLC 39**
See also CA 118; 136

Smith, Patti   1946- . . . . **CLC 12**
See also CA 93-96

Smith, Pauline (Urmson)
1882-1959 . . . . **TCLC 25**

Smith, Rosamond
See Oates, Joyce Carol

Smith, Sheila Kaye
See Kaye-Smith, Sheila

Smith, Stevie . . . . **CLC 3, 8, 25, 44**
See also Smith, Florence Margaret
See also DLB 20

Smith, Wilbur A(ddison)   1933- . . . . . **CLC 33**
See also CA 13-16R; CANR 7; MTCW

Smith, William Jay   1918- . . . . **CLC 6**
See also CA 5-8R; DLB 5; MAICYA;
SATA 2, 68

Smith, Woodrow Wilson
See Kuttner, Henry

Smolenskin, Peretz   1842-1885 . . . . **NCLC 30**

Smollett, Tobias (George)   1721-1771 . . **LC 2**
See also CDBLB 1660-1789; DLB 39, 104

Snodgrass, W(illiam) D(e Witt)
1926- . . . . **CLC 2, 6, 10, 18, 68**
See also CA 1-4R; CANR 6, 36; DLB 5;
MTCW

Snow, C(harles) P(ercy)
1905-1980 . . . . **CLC 1, 4, 6, 9, 13, 19**
See also CA 5-8R; 101; CANR 28;
CDBLB 1945-1960; DLB 15, 77; MTCW

Snow, Frances Compton
See Adams, Henry (Brooks)

Snyder, Gary (Sherman)
1930- . . . . **CLC 1, 2, 5, 9, 32**
See also CA 17-20R; CANR 30; DLB 5, 16

Snyder, Zilpha Keatley   1927- . . . . . . **CLC 17**
See also CA 9-12R; CANR 38; CLR 31;
JRDA; MAICYA; SAAS 2; SATA 1, 28,
75

Soares, Bernardo
See Pessoa, Fernando (Antonio Nogueira)

Sobh, A.
See Shamlu, Ahmad

Sobol, Joshua . . . . **CLC 60**

Soderberg, Hjalmar   1869-1941 . . . . **TCLC 39**

Sodergran, Edith (Irene)
See Soedergran, Edith (Irene)

Soedergran, Edith (Irene)
1892-1923 . . . . **TCLC 31**

Softly, Edgar
See Lovecraft, H(oward) P(hillips)

Softly, Edward
See Lovecraft, H(oward) P(hillips)

Sokolov, Raymond   1941- . . . . **CLC 7**
See also CA 85-88

Solo, Jay
See Ellison, Harlan

Sologub, Fyodor . . . . **TCLC 9**
See also Teternikov, Fyodor Kuzmich

Solomons, Ikey Esquir
See Thackeray, William Makepeace

Solomos, Dionysios   1798-1857 . . . **NCLC 15**

Solwoska, Mara
See French, Marilyn

Solzhenitsyn, Aleksandr I(sayevich)
1918- . . . . . . **CLC 1, 2, 4, 7, 9, 10, 18, 26,**
34, 78; DA; WLC
See also AITN 1; CA 69-72; CANR 40;
MTCW

Somers, Jane
See Lessing, Doris (May)

Somerville, Edith   1858-1949 . . . . . . **TCLC 51**
See also DLB 135

Somerville & Ross
See Martin, Violet Florence; Somerville,
Edith

Sommer, Scott   1951- . . . . **CLC 25**
See also CA 106

Sondheim, Stephen (Joshua)
1930- . . . . **CLC 30, 39**
See also CA 103

Sontag, Susan   1933- . . . **CLC 1, 2, 10, 13, 31**
See also CA 17-20R; CANR 25; DLB 2, 67;
MTCW

Sophocles
496(?)B.C.-406(?)B.C. . . . . . **CMLC 2; DA;**
DC 1

Sorel, Julia
See Drexler, Rosalyn

Sorrentino, Gilbert
1929- . . . . **CLC 3, 7, 14, 22, 40**
See also CA 77-80; CANR 14, 33; DLB 5;
DLBY 80

Soto, Gary   1952- . . . . **CLC 32, 80; HLC 2**
See also AAYA 10; CA 119; 125; DLB 82;
HW; JRDA

Soupault, Philippe   1897-1990 . . . . . . **CLC 68**
See also CA 116; 131

Souster, (Holmes) Raymond
1921- . . . . **CLC 5, 14**
See also CA 13-16R; CAAS 14; CANR 13,
29; DLB 88; SATA 63

Southern, Terry   1926- . . . . **CLC 7**
See also CA 1-4R; CANR 1; DLB 2

Southey, Robert   1774-1843 . . . . **NCLC 8**
See also DLB 93, 107; SATA 54

Southworth, Emma Dorothy Eliza Nevitte
1819-1899 . . . . **NCLC 26**

Souza, Ernest
See Scott, Evelyn

Soyinka, Wole
1934- . . . . . **CLC 3, 5, 14, 36, 44; BLC 3;
DA; DC 2; WLC**
See also BW; CA 13-16R; CANR 27, 39;
DLB 125; MTCW

Spackman, W(illiam) M(ode)
1905-1990 . . . . **CLC 46**
See also CA 81-84; 132

Spacks, Barry 1931- . . . . **CLC 14**
See also CA 29-32R; CANR 33; DLB 105

Spanidou, Irini 1946- . . . . **CLC 44**

Spark, Muriel (Sarah)
1918- . . . . **CLC 2, 3, 5, 8, 13, 18, 40;
SSC 10**
See also CA 5-8R; CANR 12, 36;
CDBLB 1945-1960; DLB 15; MTCW

Spaulding, Douglas
See Bradbury, Ray (Douglas)

Spaulding, Leonard
See Bradbury, Ray (Douglas)

Spence, J. A. D.
See Eliot, T(homas) S(tearns)

Spencer, Elizabeth 1921- . . . . **CLC 22**
See also CA 13-16R; CANR 32; DLB 6;
MTCW; SATA 14

Spencer, Leonard G.
See Silverberg, Robert

Spencer, Scott 1945- . . . . **CLC 30**
See also CA 113; DLBY 86

Spender, Stephen (Harold)
1909- . . . . **CLC 1, 2, 5, 10, 41**
See also CA 9-12R; CANR 31;
CDBLB 1945-1960; DLB 20; MTCW

Spengler, Oswald (Arnold Gottfried)
1880-1936 . . . . **TCLC 25**
See also CA 118

Spenser, Edmund
1552(?)-1599 . . . . **LC 5; DA; PC 8; WLC**
See also CDBLB Before 1660

Spicer, Jack 1925-1965 . . . . . . **CLC 8, 18, 72**
See also CA 85-88; DLB 5, 16

Spiegelman, Art 1948- . . . . **CLC 76**
See also AAYA 10; CA 125; CANR 41

Spielberg, Peter 1929- . . . . **CLC 6**
See also CA 5-8R; CANR 4; DLBY 81

Spielberg, Steven 1947- . . . . **CLC 20**
See also AAYA 8; CA 77-80; CANR 32;
SATA 32

Spillane, Frank Morrison 1918-
See Spillane, Mickey
See also CA 25-28R; CANR 28; MTCW;
SATA 66

Spillane, Mickey . . . . **CLC 3, 13**
See also Spillane, Frank Morrison

Spinoza, Benedictus de 1632-1677 . . . . **LC 9**

Spinrad, Norman (Richard) 1940- . . . **CLC 46**
See also CA 37-40R; CANR 20; DLB 8

Spitteler, Carl (Friedrich Georg)
1845-1924 . . . . **TCLC 12**
See also CA 109; DLB 129

Spivack, Kathleen (Romola Drucker)
1938- . . . . **CLC 6**
See also CA 49-52

Spoto, Donald 1941- . . . . **CLC 39**
See also CA 65-68; CANR 11

Springsteen, Bruce (F.) 1949- . . . . . . **CLC 17**
See also CA 111

Spurling, Hilary 1940- . . . . **CLC 34**
See also CA 104; CANR 25

Squires, (James) Radcliffe
1917-1993 . . . . **CLC 51**
See also CA 1-4R; 140; CANR 6, 21

Srivastava, Dhanpat Rai 1880(?)-1936
See Premchand
See also CA 118

Stacy, Donald
See Pohl, Frederik

Stael, Germaine de
See Stael-Holstein, Anne Louise Germaine
Necker Baronn
See also DLB 119

Stael-Holstein, Anne Louise Germaine Necker
Baronn 1766-1817 . . . . **NCLC 3**
See also Stael, Germaine de

Stafford, Jean 1915-1979 . . . **CLC 4, 7, 19, 68**
See also CA 1-4R; 85-88; CANR 3; DLB 2;
MTCW; SATA 22

Stafford, William (Edgar)
1914-1993 . . . . **CLC 4, 7, 29**
See also CA 5-8R; 142; CAAS 3; CANR 5,
22; DLB 5

Staines, Trevor
See Brunner, John (Kilian Houston)

Stairs, Gordon
See Austin, Mary (Hunter)

Stannard, Martin 1947- . . . . **CLC 44**
See also CA 142

Stanton, Maura 1946- . . . . **CLC 9**
See also CA 89-92; CANR 15; DLB 120

Stanton, Schuyler
See Baum, L(yman) Frank

Stapledon, (William) Olaf
1886-1950 . . . . **TCLC 22**
See also CA 111; DLB 15

Starbuck, George (Edwin) 1931- . . . . **CLC 53**
See also CA 21-24R; CANR 23

Stark, Richard
See Westlake, Donald E(dwin)

Staunton, Schuyler
See Baum, L(yman) Frank

Stead, Christina (Ellen)
1902-1983 . . . . **CLC 2, 5, 8, 32, 80**
See also CA 13-16R; 109; CANR 33, 40;
MTCW

Stead, William Thomas
1849-1912 . . . . **TCLC 48**

Steele, Richard 1672-1729 . . . . **LC 18**
See also CDBLB 1660-1789; DLB 84, 101

Steele, Timothy (Reid) 1948- . . . . **CLC 45**
See also CA 93-96; CANR 16; DLB 120

Steffens, (Joseph) Lincoln
1866-1936 . . . . **TCLC 20**
See also CA 117

Stegner, Wallace (Earle)
1909-1993 . . . . **CLC 9, 49, 81**
See also AITN 1; BEST 90:3; CA 1-4R;
141; CAAS 9; CANR 1, 21; DLB 9;
MTCW

Stein, Gertrude
1874-1946 . . . . . . **TCLC 1, 6, 28, 48; DA;
WLC**
See also CA 104; 132; CDALB 1917-1929;
DLB 4, 54, 86; MTCW

Steinbeck, John (Ernst)
1902-1968 . . . . . . **CLC 1, 5, 9, 13, 21, 34,
45, 75; DA; SSC 11; WLC**
See also CA 1-4R; 25-28R; CANR 1, 35;
CDALB 1929-1941; DLB 7, 9; DLBD 2;
MTCW; SATA 9

Steinem, Gloria 1934- . . . . **CLC 63**
See also CA 53-56; CANR 28; MTCW

Steiner, George 1929- . . . . **CLC 24**
See also CA 73-76; CANR 31; DLB 67;
MTCW; SATA 62

Steiner, K. Leslie
See Delany, Samuel R(ay, Jr.)

Steiner, Rudolf 1861-1925 . . . . **TCLC 13**
See also CA 107

Stendhal 1783-1842 . . . . **NCLC 23; DA; WLC**
See also DLB 119

Stephen, Leslie 1832-1904 . . . . **TCLC 23**
See also CA 123; DLB 57

Stephen, Sir Leslie
See Stephen, Leslie

Stephen, Virginia
See Woolf, (Adeline) Virginia

Stephens, James 1882(?)-1950 . . . . . . **TCLC 4**
See also CA 104; DLB 19

Stephens, Reed
See Donaldson, Stephen R.

Steptoe, Lydia
See Barnes, Djuna

Sterchi, Beat 1949- . . . . **CLC 65**

Sterling, Brett
See Bradbury, Ray (Douglas); Hamilton,
Edmond

Sterling, Bruce 1954- . . . . **CLC 72**
See also CA 119

Sterling, George 1869-1926 . . . . **TCLC 20**
See also CA 117; DLB 54

Stern, Gerald 1925- . . . . **CLC 40**
See also CA 81-84; CANR 28; DLB 105

Stern, Richard (Gustave) 1928- . . . **CLC 4, 39**
See also CA 1-4R; CANR 1, 25; DLBY 87

Sternberg, Josef von 1894-1969 . . . . . **CLC 20**
See also CA 81-84

Sterne, Laurence
1713-1768 . . . . **LC 2; DA; WLC**
See also CDBLB 1660-1789; DLB 39

Sternheim, (William Adolf) Carl
1878-1942 . . . . **TCLC 8**
See also CA 105; DLB 56, 118

Stevens, Mark 1951- . . . . **CLC 34**
See also CA 122

Stevens, Wallace
1879-1955 . . . . **TCLC 3, 12, 45; DA;**
PC 6; WLC
See also CA 104; 124; CDALB 1929-1941;
DLB 54; MTCW

Stevenson, Anne (Katharine)
1933- . . . . **CLC 7, 33**
See also CA 17-20R; CAAS 9; CANR 9, 33;
DLB 40; MTCW

Stevenson, Robert Louis (Balfour)
1850-1894 . . . . **NCLC 5, 14; DA;**
SSC 11; WLC
See also CDBLB 1890-1914; CLR 10, 11;
DLB 18, 57; JRDA; MAICYA; YABC 2

Stewart, J(ohn) I(nnes) M(ackintosh)
1906- . . . . **CLC 7, 14, 32**
See also CA 85-88; CAAS 3; MTCW

Stewart, Mary (Florence Elinor)
1916- . . . . **CLC 7, 35**
See also CA 1-4R; CANR 1; SATA 12

Stewart, Mary Rainbow
See Stewart, Mary (Florence Elinor)

Stifter, Adalbert 1805-1868 . . . . . . **NCLC 41**
See also DLB 133

Still, James 1906- . . . . **CLC 49**
See also CA 65-68; CAAS 17; CANR 10,
26; DLB 9; SATA 29

Sting
See Sumner, Gordon Matthew

Stirling, Arthur
See Sinclair, Upton (Beall)

Stitt, Milan 1941- . . . . **CLC 29**
See also CA 69-72

Stockton, Francis Richard 1834-1902
See Stockton, Frank R.
See also CA 108; 137; MAICYA; SATA 44

Stockton, Frank R. . . . . **TCLC 47**
See also Stockton, Francis Richard
See also DLB 42, 74; SATA 32

Stoddard, Charles
See Kuttner, Henry

Stoker, Abraham 1847-1912
See Stoker, Bram
See also CA 105; DA; SATA 29

Stoker, Bram . . . . **TCLC 8; WLC**
See also Stoker, Abraham
See also CDBLB 1890-1914; DLB 36, 70

Stolz, Mary (Slattery) 1920- . . . . **CLC 12**
See also AAYA 8; AITN 1; CA 5-8R;
CANR 13, 41; JRDA; MAICYA;
SAAS 3; SATA 10, 71

Stone, Irving 1903-1989 . . . . **CLC 7**
See also AITN 1; CA 1-4R; 129; CAAS 3;
CANR 1, 23; MTCW; SATA 3;
SATA-Obit 64

Stone, Oliver 1946- . . . . **CLC 73**
See also CA 110

Stone, Robert (Anthony)
1937- . . . . **CLC 5, 23, 42**
See also CA 85-88; CANR 23; MTCW

Stone, Zachary
See Follett, Ken(neth Martin)

Stoppard, Tom
1937- . . . . . . **CLC 1, 3, 4, 5, 8, 15, 29, 34,**
63; DA; WLC
See also CA 81-84; CANR 39;
CDBLB 1960 to Present; DLB 13;
DLBY 85; MTCW

Storey, David (Malcolm)
1933- . . . . **CLC 2, 4, 5, 8**
See also CA 81-84; CANR 36; DLB 13, 14;
MTCW

Storm, Hyemeyohsts 1935- . . . . **CLC 3**
See also CA 81-84

Storm, (Hans) Theodor (Woldsen)
1817-1888 . . . . **NCLC 1**

Storni, Alfonsina
1892-1938 . . . . **TCLC 5; HLC 2**
See also CA 104; 131; HW

Stout, Rex (Todhunter) 1886-1975 . . . **CLC 3**
See also AITN 2; CA 61-64

Stow, (Julian) Randolph 1935- . . **CLC 23, 48**
See also CA 13-16R; CANR 33; MTCW

Stowe, Harriet (Elizabeth) Beecher
1811-1896 . . . . **NCLC 3; DA; WLC**
See also CDALB 1865-1917; DLB 1, 12, 42,
74; JRDA; MAICYA; YABC 1

Strachey, (Giles) Lytton
1880-1932 . . . . **TCLC 12**
See also CA 110; DLBD 10

Strand, Mark 1934- . . . . . . **CLC 6, 18, 41, 71**
See also CA 21-24R; CANR 40; DLB 5;
SATA 41

Straub, Peter (Francis) 1943- . . . . . . **CLC 28**
See also BEST 89:1; CA 85-88; CANR 28;
DLBY 84; MTCW

Strauss, Botho 1944- . . . . **CLC 22**
See also DLB 124

Streatfeild, (Mary) Noel
1895(?)-1986 . . . . **CLC 21**
See also CA 81-84; 120; CANR 31;
CLR 17; MAICYA; SATA 20, 48

Stribling, T(homas) S(igismund)
1881-1965 . . . . **CLC 23**
See also CA 107; DLB 9

Strindberg, (Johan) August
1849-1912 . . . . . . **TCLC 1, 8, 21, 47; DA;**
WLC
See also CA 104; 135

Stringer, Arthur 1874-1950 . . . . . . **TCLC 37**
See also DLB 92

Stringer, David
See Roberts, Keith (John Kingston)

Strugatskii, Arkadii (Natanovich)
1925-1991 . . . . **CLC 27**
See also CA 106; 135

Strugatskii, Boris (Natanovich)
1933- . . . . **CLC 27**
See also CA 106

Strummer, Joe 1953(?)- . . . . **CLC 30**
See also Clash, The

Stuart, Don A.
See Campbell, John W(ood, Jr.)

Stuart, Ian
See MacLean, Alistair (Stuart)

Stuart, Jesse (Hilton)
1906-1984 . . . . **CLC 1, 8, 11, 14, 34**
See also CA 5-8R; 112; CANR 31; DLB 9,
48, 102; DLBY 84; SATA 2, 36

Sturgeon, Theodore (Hamilton)
1918-1985 . . . . **CLC 22, 39**
See also Queen, Ellery
See also CA 81-84; 116; CANR 32; DLB 8;
DLBY 85; MTCW

Sturges, Preston 1898-1959 . . . . . . **TCLC 48**
See also CA 114; DLB 26

Styron, William
1925- . . . . **CLC 1, 3, 5, 11, 15, 60**
See also BEST 90:4; CA 5-8R; CANR 6, 33;
CDALB 1968-1988; DLB 2; DLBY 80;
MTCW

Suarez Lynch, B.
See Bioy Casares, Adolfo; Borges, Jorge
Luis

Suarez Lynch, B.
See Borges, Jorge Luis

Su Chien 1884-1918
See Su Man-shu
See also CA 123

Sudermann, Hermann 1857-1928 . . **TCLC 15**
See also CA 107; DLB 118

Sue, Eugene 1804-1857 . . . . **NCLC 1**
See also DLB 119

Sueskind, Patrick 1949- . . . . **CLC 44**

Sukenick, Ronald 1932- . . . . . **CLC 3, 4, 6, 48**
See also CA 25-28R; CAAS 8; CANR 32;
DLBY 81

Suknaski, Andrew 1942- . . . . **CLC 19**
See also CA 101; DLB 53

Sullivan, Vernon
See Vian, Boris

Sully Prudhomme 1839-1907 . . . . . . **TCLC 31**

Su Man-shu . . . . **TCLC 24**
See also Su Chien

Summerforest, Ivy B.
See Kirkup, James

Summers, Andrew James 1942- . . . . . **CLC 26**
See also Police, The

Summers, Andy
See Summers, Andrew James

Summers, Hollis (Spurgeon, Jr.)
1916- . . . . **CLC 10**
See also CA 5-8R; CANR 3; DLB 6

Summers, (Alphonsus Joseph-Mary Augustus)
Montague 1880-1948 . . . . **TCLC 16**
See also CA 118

Sumner, Gordon Matthew 1951- . . . . **CLC 26**
See also Police, The

Surtees, Robert Smith
1803-1864 . . . . **NCLC 14**
See also DLB 21

Susann, Jacqueline 1921-1974 . . . . **CLC 3**
See also AITN 1; CA 65-68; 53-56; MTCW

Suskind, Patrick
See Sueskind, Patrick

Sutcliff, Rosemary 1920-1992 . . . . . . **CLC 26**
See also AAYA 10; CA 5-8R; 139;
CANR 37; CLR 1; JRDA; MAICYA;
SATA 6, 44; SATA-Obit 73

Thakura, Ravindranatha
See Tagore, Rabindranath

Tharoor, Shashi 1956- . . . . **CLC 70**
See also CA 141

Thelwell, Michael Miles 1939- . . . . . **CLC 22**
See also CA 101

Theobald, Lewis, Jr.
See Lovecraft, H(oward) P(hillips)

Theodorescu, Ion N. 1880-1967
See Arghezi, Tudor
See also CA 116

The Prophet
See Dreiser, Theodore (Herman Albert)

Theriault, Yves 1915-1983 . . . . **CLC 79**
See also CA 102; DLB 88

Theroux, Alexander (Louis)
1939- . . . . **CLC 2, 25**
See also CA 85-88; CANR 20

Theroux, Paul (Edward)
1941- . . . . **CLC 5, 8, 11, 15, 28, 46**
See also BEST 89:4; CA 33-36R; CANR 20;
DLB 2; MTCW; SATA 44

Thesen, Sharon 1946- . . . . **CLC 56**

Thevenin, Denis
See Duhamel, Georges

Thibault, Jacques Anatole Francois
1844-1924
See France, Anatole
See also CA 106; 127; MTCW

Thiele, Colin (Milton) 1920- . . . . **CLC 17**
See also CA 29-32R; CANR 12, 28;
CLR 27; MAICYA; SAAS 2; SATA 14,
72

Thomas, Audrey (Callahan)
1935- . . . . **CLC 7, 13, 37**
See also AITN 2; CA 21-24R; CANR 36;
DLB 60; MTCW

Thomas, D(onald) M(ichael)
1935- . . . . **CLC 13, 22, 31**
See also CA 61-64; CAAS 11; CANR 17;
CDBLB 1960 to Present; DLB 40;
MTCW

Thomas, Dylan (Marlais)
1914-1953 . . . **TCLC 1, 8, 45; DA; PC 2;**
SSC 3; WLC
See also CA 104; 120; CDBLB 1945-1960;
DLB 13, 20; MTCW; SATA 60

Thomas, (Philip) Edward
1878-1917 . . . . **TCLC 10**
See also CA 106; DLB 19

Thomas, Joyce Carol 1938- . . . . **CLC 35**
See also BW; CA 113; 116; CLR 19;
DLB 33; JRDA; MAICYA; MTCW;
SAAS 7; SATA 40

Thomas, Lewis 1913- . . . . **CLC 35**
See also CA 85-88; CANR 38; MTCW

Thomas, Paul
See Mann, (Paul) Thomas

Thomas, Piri 1928- . . . . **CLC 17**
See also CA 73-76; HW

Thomas, R(onald) S(tuart)
1913- . . . . **CLC 6, 13, 48**
See also CA 89-92; CAAS 4; CANR 30;
CDBLB 1960 to Present; DLB 27;
MTCW

Thomas, Ross (Elmore) 1926- . . . . . . **CLC 39**
See also CA 33-36R; CANR 22

Thompson, Francis Clegg
See Mencken, H(enry) L(ouis)

Thompson, Francis Joseph
1859-1907 . . . . **TCLC 4**
See also CA 104; CDBLB 1890-1914;
DLB 19

Thompson, Hunter S(tockton)
1939- . . . . **CLC 9, 17, 40**
See also BEST 89:1; CA 17-20R; CANR 23;
MTCW

Thompson, James Myers
See Thompson, Jim (Myers)

Thompson, Jim (Myers)
1906-1977(?) . . . . **CLC 69**
See also CA 140

Thompson, Judith . . . . **CLC 39**

Thomson, James 1700-1748 . . . . **LC 16**

Thomson, James 1834-1882 . . . . . **NCLC 18**

Thoreau, Henry David
1817-1862 . . . . . . **NCLC 7, 21; DA; WLC**
See also CDALB 1640-1865; DLB 1

Thornton, Hall
See Silverberg, Robert

Thurber, James (Grover)
1894-1961 . . . **CLC 5, 11, 25; DA; SSC 1**
See also CA 73-76; CANR 17, 39;
CDALB 1929-1941; DLB 4, 11, 22, 102;
MAICYA; MTCW; SATA 13

Thurman, Wallace (Henry)
1902-1934 . . . . **TCLC 6; BLC 3**
See also BW; CA 104; 124; DLB 51

Ticheburn, Cheviot
See Ainsworth, William Harrison

Tieck, (Johann) Ludwig
1773-1853 . . . . **NCLC 5**
See also DLB 90

Tiger, Derry
See Ellison, Harlan

Tilghman, Christopher 1948(?)- . . . . . **CLC 65**

Tillinghast, Richard (Williford)
1940- . . . . **CLC 29**
See also CA 29-32R; CANR 26

Timrod, Henry 1828-1867 . . . . **NCLC 25**
See also DLB 3

Tindall, Gillian 1938- . . . . **CLC 7**
See also CA 21-24R; CANR 11

Tiptree, James, Jr. . . . . **CLC 48, 50**
See also Sheldon, Alice Hastings Bradley
See also DLB 8

Titmarsh, Michael Angelo
See Thackeray, William Makepeace

Tocqueville, Alexis (Charles Henri Maurice
Clerel Comte) 1805-1859 . . . . . **NCLC 7**

Tolkien, J(ohn) R(onald) R(euel)
1892-1973 . . . . **CLC 1, 2, 3, 8, 12, 38;**
DA; WLC
See also AAYA 10; AITN 1; CA 17-18;
45-48; CANR 36; CAP 2;
CDBLB 1914-1945; DLB 15; JRDA;
MAICYA; MTCW; SATA 2, 24, 32

Toller, Ernst 1893-1939 . . . . **TCLC 10**
See also CA 107; DLB 124

Tolson, M. B.
See Tolson, Melvin B(eaunorus)

Tolson, Melvin B(eaunorus)
1898(?)-1966 . . . . **CLC 36; BLC 3**
See also BW; CA 124; 89-92; DLB 48, 76

Tolstoi, Aleksei Nikolaevich
See Tolstoy, Alexey Nikolaevich

Tolstoy, Alexey Nikolaevich
1882-1945 . . . . **TCLC 18**
See also CA 107

Tolstoy, Count Leo
See Tolstoy, Leo (Nikolaevich)

Tolstoy, Leo (Nikolaevich)
1828-1910 . . . . . . **TCLC 4, 11, 17, 28, 44;**
DA; SSC 9; WLC
See also CA 104; 123; SATA 26

Tomasi di Lampedusa, Giuseppe 1896-1957
See Lampedusa, Giuseppe (Tomasi) di
See also CA 111

Tomlin, Lily . . . . **CLC 17**
See also Tomlin, Mary Jean

Tomlin, Mary Jean 1939(?)-
See Tomlin, Lily
See also CA 117

Tomlinson, (Alfred) Charles
1927- . . . . **CLC 2, 4, 6, 13, 45**
See also CA 5-8R; CANR 33; DLB 40

Tonson, Jacob
See Bennett, (Enoch) Arnold

Toole, John Kennedy
1937-1969 . . . . **CLC 19, 64**
See also CA 104; DLBY 81

Toomer, Jean
1894-1967 . . . . **CLC 1, 4, 13, 22; BLC 3;**
PC 7; SSC 1
See also BW; CA 85-88;
CDALB 1917-1929; DLB 45, 51; MTCW

Torley, Luke
See Blish, James (Benjamin)

Tornimparte, Alessandra
See Ginzburg, Natalia

Torre, Raoul della
See Mencken, H(enry) L(ouis)

Torrey, E(dwin) Fuller 1937- . . . . **CLC 34**
See also CA 119

Torsvan, Ben Traven
See Traven, B.

Torsvan, Benno Traven
See Traven, B.

Torsvan, Berick Traven
See Traven, B.

Torsvan, Berwick Traven
See Traven, B.

Torsvan, Bruno Traven
See Traven, B.

Torsvan, Traven
See Traven, B.

Tournier, Michel (Edouard)
1924- . . . . **CLC 6, 23, 36**
See also CA 49-52; CANR 3, 36; DLB 83;
MTCW; SATA 23

Tournimparte, Alessandra
See Ginzburg, Natalia

Towers, Ivar
See Kornbluth, C(yril) M.

Townsend, Sue 1946- . . . . **CLC 61**
See also CA 119; 127; MTCW; SATA 48,
55

Townshend, Peter (Dennis Blandford)
1945- . . . . **CLC 17, 42**
See also CA 107

Tozzi, Federigo 1883-1920 . . . . **TCLC 31**

Traill, Catharine Parr
1802-1899 . . . . **NCLC 31**
See also DLB 99

Trakl, Georg 1887-1914 . . . . **TCLC 5**
See also CA 104

Transtroemer, Tomas (Goesta)
1931- . . . . **CLC 52, 65**
See also CA 117; 129; CAAS 17

Transtromer, Tomas Gosta
See Transtroemer, Tomas (Goesta)

Traven, B. (?)-1969 . . . . **CLC 8, 11**
See also CA 19-20; 25-28R; CAP 2; DLB 9,
56; MTCW

Treitel, Jonathan 1959- . . . . **CLC 70**

Tremain, Rose 1943- . . . . **CLC 42**
See also CA 97-100; DLB 14

Tremblay, Michel 1942- . . . . **CLC 29**
See also CA 116; 128; DLB 60; MTCW

Trevanian (a pseudonym) 1930(?)- . . . **CLC 29**
See also CA 108

Trevor, Glen
See Hilton, James

Trevor, William
1928- . . . . **CLC 7, 9, 14, 25, 71**
See also Cox, William Trevor
See also DLB 14

Trifonov, Yuri (Valentinovich)
1925-1981 . . . . **CLC 45**
See also CA 126; 103; MTCW

Trilling, Lionel 1905-1975 . . . . **CLC 9, 11, 24**
See also CA 9-12R; 61-64; CANR 10;
DLB 28, 63; MTCW

Trimball, W. H.
See Mencken, H(enry) L(ouis)

Tristan
See Gomez de la Serna, Ramon

Tristram
See Housman, A(lfred) E(dward)

Trogdon, William (Lewis) 1939-
See Heat-Moon, William Least
See also CA 115; 119

Trollope, Anthony
1815-1882 . . . . . . **NCLC 6, 33; DA; WLC**
See also CDBLB 1832-1890; DLB 21, 57;
SATA 22

Trollope, Frances 1779-1863 . . . . . **NCLC 30**
See also DLB 21

Trotsky, Leon 1879-1940 . . . . **TCLC 22**
See also CA 118

Trotter (Cockburn), Catharine
1679-1749 . . . . **LC 8**
See also DLB 84

Trout, Kilgore
See Farmer, Philip Jose

Trow, George W. S. 1943- . . . . **CLC 52**
See also CA 126

Troyat, Henri 1911- . . . . **CLC 23**
See also CA 45-48; CANR 2, 33; MTCW

Trudeau, G(arretson) B(eekman) 1948-
See Trudeau, Garry B.
See also CA 81-84; CANR 31; SATA 35

Trudeau, Garry B. . . . . **CLC 12**
See also Trudeau, G(arretson) B(eekman)
See also AAYA 10; AITN 2

Truffaut, Francois 1932-1984 . . . . . . **CLC 20**
See also CA 81-84; 113; CANR 34

Trumbo, Dalton 1905-1976 . . . . **CLC 19**
See also CA 21-24R; 69-72; CANR 10;
DLB 26

Trumbull, John 1750-1831 . . . . . . **NCLC 30**
See also DLB 31

Trundlett, Helen B.
See Eliot, T(homas) S(tearns)

Tryon, Thomas 1926-1991 . . . . . **CLC 3, 11**
See also AITN 1; CA 29-32R; 135;
CANR 32; MTCW

Tryon, Tom
See Tryon, Thomas

Ts'ao Hsueh-ch'in 1715(?)-1763 . . . . . . **LC 1**

Tsushima, Shuji 1909-1948
See Dazai, Osamu
See also CA 107

Tsvetaeva (Efron), Marina (Ivanovna)
1892-1941 . . . . **TCLC 7, 35**
See also CA 104; 128; MTCW

Tuck, Lily 1938- . . . . **CLC 70**
See also CA 139

Tunis, John R(oberts) 1889-1975 . . . **CLC 12**
See also CA 61-64; DLB 22; JRDA;
MAICYA; SATA 30, 37

Tuohy, Frank . . . . **CLC 37**
See also Tuohy, John Francis
See also DLB 14

Tuohy, John Francis 1925-
See Tuohy, Frank
See also CA 5-8R; CANR 3

Turco, Lewis (Putnam) 1934- . . . **CLC 11, 63**
See also CA 13-16R; CANR 24; DLBY 84

Turgenev, Ivan
1818-1883 . . . . . . **NCLC 21; DA; SSC 7;
WLC**

Turner, Frederick 1943- . . . . **CLC 48**
See also CA 73-76; CAAS 10; CANR 12,
30; DLB 40

Tusan, Stan 1936- . . . . **CLC 22**
See also CA 105

Tutu, Desmond M(pilo)
1931- . . . . **CLC 80; BLC 3**
See also BW; CA 125

Tutuola, Amos
1920- . . . . **CLC 5, 14, 29; BLC 3**
See also BW; CA 9-12R; CANR 27;
DLB 125; MTCW

Twain, Mark
. . . **TCLC 6, 12, 19, 36, 48; SSC 6; WLC**
See also Clemens, Samuel Langhorne
See also DLB 11, 12, 23, 64, 74

Tyler, Anne
1941- . . . . **CLC 7, 11, 18, 28, 44, 59**
See also BEST 89:1; CA 9-12R; CANR 11,
33; DLB 6; DLBY 82; MTCW; SATA 7

Tyler, Royall 1757-1826 . . . . **NCLC 3**
See also DLB 37

Tynan, Katharine 1861-1931 . . . . . . **TCLC 3**
See also CA 104

Tytell, John 1939- . . . . **CLC 50**
See also CA 29-32R

Tyutchev, Fyodor 1803-1873 . . . . . **NCLC 34**

Tzara, Tristan . . . . **CLC 47**
See also Rosenfeld, Samuel

Uhry, Alfred 1936- . . . . **CLC 55**
See also CA 127; 133

Ulf, Haerved
See Strindberg, (Johan) August

Ulf, Harved
See Strindberg, (Johan) August

Unamuno (y Jugo), Miguel de
1864-1936 . . **TCLC 2, 9; HLC 2; SSC 11**
See also CA 104; 131; DLB 108; HW;
MTCW

Undercliffe, Errol
See Campbell, (John) Ramsey

Underwood, Miles
See Glassco, John

Undset, Sigrid
1882-1949 . . . . **TCLC 3; DA; WLC**
See also CA 104; 129; MTCW

Ungaretti, Giuseppe
1888-1970 . . . . **CLC 7, 11, 15**
See also CA 19-20; 25-28R; CAP 2;
DLB 114

Unger, Douglas 1952- . . . . **CLC 34**
See also CA 130

Unsworth, Barry (Forster) 1930- . . . . **CLC 76**
See also CA 25-28R; CANR 30

Updike, John (Hoyer)
1932- . . . . . . **CLC 1, 2, 3, 5, 7, 9, 13, 15,
23, 34, 43, 70; DA; SSC 13; WLC**
See also CA 1-4R; CABS 1; CANR 4, 33;
CDALB 1968-1988; DLB 2, 5; DLBD 3;
DLBY 80, 82; MTCW

Upshaw, Margaret Mitchell
See Mitchell, Margaret (Munnerlyn)

Upton, Mark
See Sanders, Lawrence

Urdang, Constance (Henriette)
1922- . . . . **CLC 47**
See also CA 21-24R; CANR 9, 24

Uriel, Henry
See Faust, Frederick (Schiller)

Uris, Leon (Marcus) 1924- . . . . **CLC 7, 32**
See also AITN 1, 2; BEST 89:2; CA 1-4R;
CANR 1, 40; MTCW; SATA 49

Urmuz
See Codrescu, Andrei

Ustinov, Peter (Alexander) 1921- . . . . **CLC 1**
See also AITN 1; CA 13-16R; CANR 25;
DLB 13

V
See Chekhov, Anton (Pavlovich)

Watkins, Gerrold
See Malzberg, Barry N(athaniel)

Watkins, Paul 1964- .... **CLC 55**
See also CA 132

Watkins, Vernon Phillips
1906-1967 .... **CLC 43**
See also CA 9-10; 25-28R; CAP 1; DLB 20

Watson, Irving S.
See Mencken, H(enry) L(ouis)

Watson, John H.
See Farmer, Philip Jose

Watson, Richard F.
See Silverberg, Robert

Waugh, Auberon (Alexander) 1939- .. **CLC 7**
See also CA 45-48; CANR 6, 22; DLB 14

Waugh, Evelyn (Arthur St. John)
1903-1966 ...... **CLC 1, 3, 8, 13, 19, 27,**
44; DA; WLC
See also CA 85-88; 25-28R; CANR 22;
CDBLB 1914-1945; DLB 15; MTCW

Waugh, Harriet 1944- .... **CLC 6**
See also CA 85-88; CANR 22

Ways, C. R.
See Blount, Roy (Alton), Jr.

Waystaff, Simon
See Swift, Jonathan

Webb, (Martha) Beatrice (Potter)
1858-1943 .... **TCLC 22**
See also Potter, Beatrice
See also CA 117

Webb, Charles (Richard) 1939- ...... **CLC 7**
See also CA 25-28R

Webb, James H(enry), Jr. 1946- .... **CLC 22**
See also CA 81-84

Webb, Mary (Gladys Meredith)
1881-1927 .... **TCLC 24**
See also CA 123; DLB 34

Webb, Mrs. Sidney
See Webb, (Martha) Beatrice (Potter)

Webb, Phyllis 1927- .... **CLC 18**
See also CA 104; CANR 23; DLB 53

Webb, Sidney (James)
1859-1947 .... **TCLC 22**
See also CA 117

Webber, Andrew Lloyd .... **CLC 21**
See also Lloyd Webber, Andrew

Weber, Lenora Mattingly
1895-1971 .... **CLC 12**
See also CA 19-20; 29-32R; CAP 1;
SATA 2, 26

Webster, John 1579(?)-1634(?) .... **DC 2**
See also CDBLB Before 1660; DA; DLB 58;
WLC

Webster, Noah 1758-1843 .... **NCLC 30**

Wedekind, (Benjamin) Frank(lin)
1864-1918 .... **TCLC 7**
See also CA 104; DLB 118

Weidman, Jerome 1913- .... **CLC 7**
See also AITN 2; CA 1-4R; CANR 1;
DLB 28

Weil, Simone (Adolphine)
1909-1943 .... **TCLC 23**
See also CA 117

Weinstein, Nathan
See West, Nathanael

Weinstein, Nathan von Wallenstein
See West, Nathanael

Weir, Peter (Lindsay) 1944- .... **CLC 20**
See also CA 113; 123

Weiss, Peter (Ulrich)
1916-1982 .... **CLC 3, 15, 51**
See also CA 45-48; 106; CANR 3; DLB 69,
124

Weiss, Theodore (Russell)
1916- .... **CLC 3, 8, 14**
See also CA 9-12R; CAAS 2; DLB 5

Welch, (Maurice) Denton
1915-1948 .... **TCLC 22**
See also CA 121

Welch, James 1940- .... **CLC 6, 14, 52**
See also CA 85-88; CANR 42

Weldon, Fay
1933(?)- .... **CLC 6, 9, 11, 19, 36, 59**
See also CA 21-24R; CANR 16;
CDBLB 1960 to Present; DLB 14;
MTCW

Wellek, Rene 1903- .... **CLC 28**
See also CA 5-8R; CAAS 7; CANR 8;
DLB 63

Weller, Michael 1942- .... **CLC 10, 53**
See also CA 85-88

Weller, Paul 1958- .... **CLC 26**

Wellershoff, Dieter 1925- .... **CLC 46**
See also CA 89-92; CANR 16, 37

Welles, (George) Orson
1915-1985 .... **CLC 20, 80**
See also CA 93-96; 117

Wellman, Mac 1945- .... **CLC 65**

Wellman, Manly Wade 1903-1986 .. **CLC 49**
See also CA 1-4R; 118; CANR 6, 16;
SATA 6, 47

Wells, Carolyn 1869(?)-1942 ...... **TCLC 35**
See also CA 113; DLB 11

Wells, H(erbert) G(eorge)
1866-1946 .... **TCLC 6, 12, 19; DA;**
SSC 6; WLC
See also CA 110; 121; CDBLB 1914-1945;
DLB 34, 70; MTCW; SATA 20

Wells, Rosemary 1943- .... **CLC 12**
See also CA 85-88; CLR 16; MAICYA;
SAAS 1; SATA 18, 69

Welty, Eudora
1909- ...... **CLC 1, 2, 5, 14, 22, 33; DA;**
SSC 1; WLC
See also CA 9-12R; CABS 1; CANR 32;
CDALB 1941-1968; DLB 2, 102;
DLBY 87; MTCW

Wen I-to 1899-1946 .... **TCLC 28**

Wentworth, Robert
See Hamilton, Edmond

Werfel, Franz (V.) 1890-1945 ...... **TCLC 8**
See also CA 104; DLB 81, 124

Wergeland, Henrik Arnold
1808-1845 .... **NCLC 5**

Wersba, Barbara 1932- .... **CLC 30**
See also AAYA 2; CA 29-32R; CANR 16,
38; CLR 3; DLB 52; JRDA; MAICYA;
SAAS 2; SATA 1, 58

Wertmueller, Lina 1928- .... **CLC 16**
See also CA 97-100; CANR 39

Wescott, Glenway 1901-1987....... **CLC 13**
See also CA 13-16R; 121; CANR 23;
DLB 4, 9, 102

Wesker, Arnold 1932- .... **CLC 3, 5, 42**
See also CA 1-4R; CAAS 7; CANR 1, 33;
CDBLB 1960 to Present; DLB 13;
MTCW

Wesley, Richard (Errol) 1945-....... **CLC 7**
See also BW; CA 57-60; CANR 27; DLB 38

Wessel, Johan Herman 1742-1785 .... **LC 7**

West, Anthony (Panther)
1914-1987 .... **CLC 50**
See also CA 45-48; 124; CANR 3, 19;
DLB 15

West, C. P.
See Wodehouse, P(elham) G(renville)

West, (Mary) Jessamyn
1902-1984 .... **CLC 7, 17**
See also CA 9-12R; 112; CANR 27; DLB 6;
DLBY 84; MTCW; SATA 37

West, Morris L(anglo) 1916-..... **CLC 6, 33**
See also CA 5-8R; CANR 24; MTCW

West, Nathanael
1903-1940 .... **TCLC 1, 14, 44**
See also CA 104; 125; CDALB 1929-1941;
DLB 4, 9, 28; MTCW

West, Owen
See Koontz, Dean R(ay)

West, Paul 1930- .... **CLC 7, 14**
See also CA 13-16R; CAAS 7; CANR 22;
DLB 14

West, Rebecca 1892-1983 .. **CLC 7, 9, 31, 50**
See also CA 5-8R; 109; CANR 19; DLB 36;
DLBY 83; MTCW

Westall, Robert (Atkinson)
1929-1993 .... **CLC 17**
See also CA 69-72; 141; CANR 18;
CLR 13; JRDA; MAICYA; SAAS 2;
SATA 23, 69; SATA-Obit 75

Westlake, Donald E(dwin)
1933- .... **CLC 7, 33**
See also CA 17-20R; CAAS 13; CANR 16

Westmacott, Mary
See Christie, Agatha (Mary Clarissa)

Weston, Allen
See Norton, Andre

Wetcheek, J. L.
See Feuchtwanger, Lion

Wetering, Janwillem van de
See van de Wetering, Janwillem

Wetherell, Elizabeth
See Warner, Susan (Bogert)

Whalen, Philip 1923- .... **CLC 6, 29**
See also CA 9-12R; CANR 5, 39; DLB 16

Wharton, Edith (Newbold Jones)
1862-1937 ...... **TCLC 3, 9, 27, 53; DA;**
SSC 6; WLC
See also CA 104; 132; CDALB 1865-1917;
DLB 4, 9, 12, 78; MTCW

Wharton, James
See Mencken, H(enry) L(ouis)

Wharton, William (a pseudonym)
.... CLC 18, 37
See also CA 93-96; DLBY 80

Wheatley (Peters), Phillis
1754(?)-1784 .... LC 3; BLC 3; DA;
PC 3; WLC
See also CDALB 1640-1865; DLB 31, 50

Wheelock, John Hall 1886-1978 .... CLC 14
See also CA 13-16R; 77-80; CANR 14;
DLB 45

White, E(lwyn) B(rooks)
1899-1985 .... CLC 10, 34, 39
See also AITN 2; CA 13-16R; 116;
CANR 16, 37; CLR 1, 21; DLB 11, 22;
MAICYA; MTCW; SATA 2, 29, 44

White, Edmund (Valentine III)
1940- .... CLC 27
See also AAYA 7; CA 45-48; CANR 3, 19,
36; MTCW

White, Patrick (Victor Martindale)
1912-1990 .. CLC 3, 4, 5, 7, 9, 18, 65, 69
See also CA 81-84; 132; CANR 43; MTCW

White, Phyllis Dorothy James 1920-
See James, P. D.
See also CA 21-24R; CANR 17, 43; MTCW

White, T(erence) H(anbury)
1906-1964 .... CLC 30
See also CA 73-76; CANR 37; JRDA;
MAICYA; SATA 12

White, Terence de Vere 1912- ...... CLC 49
See also CA 49-52; CANR 3

White, Walter F(rancis)
1893-1955 .... TCLC 15
See also White, Walter
See also CA 115; 124; DLB 51

White, William Hale 1831-1913
See Rutherford, Mark
See also CA 121

Whitehead, E(dward) A(nthony)
1933- .... CLC 5
See also CA 65-68

Whitemore, Hugh (John) 1936- ..... CLC 37
See also CA 132

Whitman, Sarah Helen (Power)
1803-1878 .... NCLC 19
See also DLB 1

Whitman, Walt(er)
1819-1892 ..... NCLC 4, 31; DA; PC 3;
WLC
See also CDALB 1640-1865; DLB 3, 64;
SATA 20

Whitney, Phyllis A(yame) 1903- .... CLC 42
See also AITN 2; BEST 90:3; CA 1-4R;
CANR 3, 25, 38; JRDA; MAICYA;
SATA 1, 30

Whittemore, (Edward) Reed (Jr.)
1919- .... CLC 4
See also CA 9-12R; CAAS 8; CANR 4;
DLB 5

Whittier, John Greenleaf
1807-1892 .... NCLC 8
See also CDALB 1640-1865; DLB 1

Whittlebot, Hernia
See Coward, Noel (Peirce)

Wicker, Thomas Grey 1926-
See Wicker, Tom
See also CA 65-68; CANR 21

Wicker, Tom .... CLC 7
See also Wicker, Thomas Grey

Wideman, John Edgar
1941- .... CLC 5, 34, 36, 67; BLC 3
See also BW; CA 85-88; CANR 14, 42;
DLB 33

Wiebe, Rudy (Henry) 1934-... CLC 6, 11, 14
See also CA 37-40R; CANR 42; DLB 60

Wieland, Christoph Martin
1733-1813 .... NCLC 17
See also DLB 97

Wieners, John 1934- .... CLC 7
See also CA 13-16R; DLB 16

Wiesel, Elie(zer)
1928- .... CLC 3, 5, 11, 37; DA
See also AAYA 7; AITN 1; CA 5-8R;
CAAS 4; CANR 8, 40; DLB 83;
DLBY 87; MTCW; SATA 56

Wiggins, Marianne 1947-.......... CLC 57
See also BEST 89:3; CA 130

Wight, James Alfred 1916-
See Herriot, James
See also CA 77-80; SATA 44, 55

Wilbur, Richard (Purdy)
1921- .... CLC 3, 6, 9, 14, 53; DA
See also CA 1-4R; CABS 2; CANR 2, 29;
DLB 5; MTCW; SATA 9

Wild, Peter 1940- .... CLC 14
See also CA 37-40R; DLB 5

Wilde, Oscar (Fingal O'Flahertie Wills)
1854(?)-1900 .... TCLC 1, 8, 23, 41; DA;
SSC 11; WLC
See also CA 104; 119; CDBLB 1890-1914;
DLB 10, 19, 34, 57; SATA 24

Wilder, Billy .... CLC 20
See also Wilder, Samuel
See also DLB 26

Wilder, Samuel 1906-
See Wilder, Billy
See also CA 89-92

Wilder, Thornton (Niven)
1897-1975 ...... CLC 1, 5, 6, 10, 15, 35;
DA; DC 1; WLC
See also AITN 2; CA 13-16R; 61-64;
CANR 40; DLB 4, 7, 9; MTCW

Wilding, Michael 1942-.......... CLC 73
See also CA 104; CANR 24

Wiley, Richard 1944-............. CLC 44
See also CA 121; 129

Wilhelm, Kate .... CLC 7
See also Wilhelm, Katie Gertrude
See also CAAS 5; DLB 8

Wilhelm, Katie Gertrude 1928-
See Wilhelm, Kate
See also CA 37-40R; CANR 17, 36; MTCW

Wilkins, Mary
See Freeman, Mary Eleanor Wilkins

Willard, Nancy 1936-.......... CLC 7, 37
See also CA 89-92; CANR 10, 39; CLR 5;
DLB 5, 52; MAICYA; MTCW;
SATA 30, 37, 71

Williams, C(harles) K(enneth)
1936- .... CLC 33, 56
See also CA 37-40R; DLB 5

Williams, Charles
See Collier, James L(incoln)

Williams, Charles (Walter Stansby)
1886-1945 .... TCLC 1, 11
See also CA 104; DLB 100

Williams, (George) Emlyn
1905-1987 .... CLC 15
See also CA 104; 123; CANR 36; DLB 10,
77; MTCW

Williams, Hugo 1942-............ CLC 42
See also CA 17-20R; DLB 40

Williams, J. Walker
See Wodehouse, P(elham) G(renville)

Williams, John A(lfred)
1925- .... CLC 5, 13; BLC 3
See also BW; CA 53-56; CAAS 3; CANR 6,
26; DLB 2, 33

Williams, Jonathan (Chamberlain)
1929- .... CLC 13
See also CA 9-12R; CAAS 12; CANR 8;
DLB 5

Williams, Joy 1944-.............. CLC 31
See also CA 41-44R; CANR 22

Williams, Norman 1952- .... CLC 39
See also CA 118

Williams, Tennessee
1911-1983 ..... CLC 1, 2, 5, 7, 8, 11, 15,
19, 30, 39, 45, 71; DA; DC 4; WLC
See also AITN 1, 2; CA 5-8R; 108;
CABS 3; CANR 31; CDALB 1941-1968;
DLB 7; DLBD 4; DLBY 83; MTCW

Williams, Thomas (Alonzo)
1926-1990 .... CLC 14
See also CA 1-4R; 132; CANR 2

Williams, William C.
See Williams, William Carlos

Williams, William Carlos
1883-1963 .... CLC 1, 2, 5, 9, 13, 22, 42,
67; DA; PC 7
See also CA 89-92; CANR 34;
CDALB 1917-1929; DLB 4, 16, 54, 86;
MTCW

Williamson, David (Keith) 1942-.... CLC 56
See also CA 103; CANR 41

Williamson, Jack................. CLC 29
See also Williamson, John Stewart
See also CAAS 8; DLB 8

Williamson, John Stewart 1908-
See Williamson, Jack
See also CA 17-20R; CANR 23

Willie, Frederick
See Lovecraft, H(oward) P(hillips)

Willingham, Calder (Baynard, Jr.)
1922- .... CLC 5, 51
See also CA 5-8R; CANR 3; DLB 2, 44;
MTCW

Willis, Charles
See Clarke, Arthur C(harles)

Willy
See Colette, (Sidonie-Gabrielle)

Willy, Colette
See Colette, (Sidonie-Gabrielle)

Wilson, A(ndrew) N(orman) 1950- .. **CLC 33**
See also CA 112; 122; DLB 14

Wilson, Angus (Frank Johnstone)
1913-1991 .... **CLC 2, 3, 5, 25, 34**
See also CA 5-8R; 134; CANR 21; DLB 15;
MTCW

Wilson, August
1945- ..... **CLC 39, 50, 63; BLC 3; DA;**
DC 2
See also BW; CA 115; 122; CANR 42;
MTCW

Wilson, Brian 1942- .... **CLC 12**

Wilson, Colin 1931- .... **CLC 3, 14**
See also CA 1-4R; CAAS 5; CANR 1, 22,
33; DLB 14; MTCW

Wilson, Dirk
See Pohl, Frederik

Wilson, Edmund
1895-1972 .... **CLC 1, 2, 3, 8, 24**
See also CA 1-4R; 37-40R; CANR 1;
DLB 63; MTCW

Wilson, Ethel Davis (Bryant)
1888(?)-1980 .... **CLC 13**
See also CA 102; DLB 68; MTCW

Wilson, John 1785-1854.......... **NCLC 5**

Wilson, John (Anthony) Burgess 1917-1993
See Burgess, Anthony
See also CA 1-4R; CANR 2; MTCW

Wilson, Lanford 1937- .... **CLC 7, 14, 36**
See also CA 17-20R; CABS 3; DLB 7

Wilson, Robert M. 1944- .... **CLC 7, 9**
See also CA 49-52; CANR 2, 41; MTCW

Wilson, Robert McLiam 1964- ..... **CLC 59**
See also CA 132

Wilson, Sloan 1920- .... **CLC 32**
See also CA 1-4R; CANR 1

Wilson, Snoo 1948-................ **CLC 33**
See also CA 69-72

Wilson, William S(mith) 1932- ..... **CLC 49**
See also CA 81-84

Winchilsea, Anne (Kingsmill) Finch Counte
1661-1720 .... **LC 3**

Windham, Basil
See Wodehouse, P(elham) G(renville)

Wingrove, David (John) 1954-...... **CLC 68**
See also CA 133

Winters, Janet Lewis .... **CLC 41**
See also Lewis, Janet
See also DLBY 87

Winters, (Arthur) Yvor
1900-1968 .... **CLC 4, 8, 32**
See also CA 11-12; 25-28R; CAP 1;
DLB 48; MTCW

Winterson, Jeanette 1959-......... **CLC 64**
See also CA 136

Wiseman, Frederick 1930-......... **CLC 20**

Wister, Owen 1860-1938 .... **TCLC 21**
See also CA 108; DLB 9, 78; SATA 62

Witkacy
See Witkiewicz, Stanislaw Ignacy

Witkiewicz, Stanislaw Ignacy
1885-1939 .... **TCLC 8**
See also CA 105

Wittig, Monique 1935(?)-.......... **CLC 22**
See also CA 116; 135; DLB 83

Wittlin, Jozef 1896-1976 .... **CLC 25**
See also CA 49-52; 65-68; CANR 3

Wodehouse, P(elham) G(renville)
1881-1975 ... **CLC 1, 2, 5, 10, 22; SSC 2**
See also AITN 2; CA 45-48; 57-60;
CANR 3, 33; CDBLB 1914-1945;
DLB 34; MTCW; SATA 22

Woiwode, L.
See Woiwode, Larry (Alfred)

Woiwode, Larry (Alfred) 1941-... **CLC 6, 10**
See also CA 73-76; CANR 16; DLB 6

Wojciechowska, Maia (Teresa)
1927-........................ **CLC 26**
See also AAYA 8; CA 9-12R; CANR 4, 41;
CLR 1; JRDA; MAICYA; SAAS 1;
SATA 1, 28

Wolf, Christa 1929- .... **CLC 14, 29, 58**
See also CA 85-88; DLB 75; MTCW

Wolfe, Gene (Rodman) 1931-....... **CLC 25**
See also CA 57-60; CAAS 9; CANR 6, 32;
DLB 8

Wolfe, George C. 1954-........... **CLC 49**

Wolfe, Thomas (Clayton)
1900-1938 ... **TCLC 4, 13, 29; DA; WLC**
See also CA 104; 132; CDALB 1929-1941;
DLB 9, 102; DLBD 2; DLBY 85; MTCW

Wolfe, Thomas Kennerly, Jr. 1931-
See Wolfe, Tom
See also CA 13-16R; CANR 9, 33; MTCW

Wolfe, Tom .... **CLC 1, 2, 9, 15, 35, 51**
See also Wolfe, Thomas Kennerly, Jr.
See also AAYA 8; AITN 2; BEST 89:1

Wolff, Geoffrey (Ansell) 1937- ..... **CLC 41**
See also CA 29-32R; CANR 29, 43

Wolff, Sonia
See Levitin, Sonia (Wolff)

Wolff, Tobias (Jonathan Ansell)
1945- .... **CLC 39, 64**
See also BEST 90:2; CA 114; 117; DLB 130

Wolfram von Eschenbach
c. 1170-c. 1220 .... **CMLC 5**

Wolitzer, Hilma 1930-........... **CLC 17**
See also CA 65-68; CANR 18, 40; SATA 31

Wollstonecraft, Mary 1759-1797...... **LC 5**
See also CDBLB 1789-1832; DLB 39, 104

Wonder, Stevie .... **CLC 12**
See also Morris, Steveland Judkins

Wong, Jade Snow 1922-........... **CLC 17**
See also CA 109

Woodcott, Keith
See Brunner, John (Kilian Houston)

Woodruff, Robert W.
See Mencken, H(enry) L(ouis)

Woolf, (Adeline) Virginia
1882-1941 ...... **TCLC 1, 5, 20, 43; DA;**
SSC 7; WLC
See also CA 104; 130; CDBLB 1914-1945;
DLB 36, 100; DLBD 10; MTCW

Woollcott, Alexander (Humphreys)
1887-1943 .... **TCLC 5**
See also CA 105; DLB 29

Woolrich, Cornell 1903-1968....... **CLC 77**
See also Hopley-Woolrich, Cornell George

Wordsworth, Dorothy
1771-1855 .... **NCLC 25**
See also DLB 107

Wordsworth, William
1770-1850 .... **NCLC 12, 38; DA; PC 4;**
WLC
See also CDBLB 1789-1832; DLB 93, 107

Wouk, Herman 1915-......... **CLC 1, 9, 38**
See also CA 5-8R; CANR 6, 33; DLBY 82;
MTCW

Wright, Charles (Penzel, Jr.)
1935- .... **CLC 6, 13, 28**
See also CA 29-32R; CAAS 7; CANR 23,
36; DLBY 82; MTCW

Wright, Charles Stevenson
1932- .... **CLC 49; BLC 3**
See also BW; CA 9-12R; CANR 26;
DLB 33

Wright, Jack R.
See Harris, Mark

Wright, James (Arlington)
1927-1980 .... **CLC 3, 5, 10, 28**
See also AITN 2; CA 49-52; 97-100;
CANR 4, 34; DLB 5; MTCW

Wright, Judith (Arandell)
1915- .... **CLC 11, 53**
See also CA 13-16R; CANR 31; MTCW;
SATA 14

Wright, L(aurali) R. 1939-......... **CLC 44**
See also CA 138

Wright, Richard (Nathaniel)
1908-1960 .... **CLC 1, 3, 4, 9, 14, 21, 48,**
74; BLC 3; DA; SSC 2; WLC
See also AAYA 5; BW; CA 108;
CDALB 1929-1941; DLB 76, 102;
DLBD 2; MTCW

Wright, Richard B(ruce) 1937- ...... **CLC 6**
See also CA 85-88; DLB 53

Wright, Rick 1945-............... **CLC 35**
See also Pink Floyd

Wright, Rowland
See Wells, Carolyn

Wright, Stephen 1946-............ **CLC 33**

Wright, Willard Huntington 1888-1939
See Van Dine, S. S.
See also CA 115

Wright, William 1930-........... **CLC 44**
See also CA 53-56; CANR 7, 23

Wu Ch'eng-en 1500(?)-1582(?)........ **LC 7**

Wu Ching-tzu 1701-1754 .... **LC 2**

Wurlitzer, Rudolph 1938(?)- ... **CLC 2, 4, 15**
See also CA 85-88

Wycherley, William 1641-1715 .... **LC 8, 21**
See also CDBLB 1660-1789; DLB 80

Wylie, Elinor (Morton Hoyt)
1885-1928 .... **TCLC 8**
See also CA 105; DLB 9, 45

Wylie, Philip (Gordon) 1902-1971... **CLC 43**
See also CA 21-22; 33-36R; CAP 2; DLB 9

Wyndham, John
See Harris, John (Wyndham Parkes Lucas)
Beynon

Wyss, Johann David Von
1743-1818 . . . . **NCLC 10**
See also JRDA; MAICYA; SATA 27, 29

Yakumo Koizumi
See Hearn, (Patricio) Lafcadio (Tessima Carlos)

Yanez, Jose Donoso
See Donoso (Yanez), Jose

Yanovsky, Basile S.
See Yanovsky, V(assily) S(emenovich)

Yanovsky, V(assily) S(emenovich)
1906-1989 . . . . **CLC 2, 18**
See also CA 97-100; 129

Yates, Richard 1926-1992 . . . . . **CLC 7, 8, 23**
See also CA 5-8R; 139; CANR 10, 43;
DLB 2; DLBY 81, 92

Yeats, W. B.
See Yeats, William Butler

Yeats, William Butler
1865-1939 . . . . . **TCLC 1, 11, 18, 31; DA;
WLC**
See also CA 104; 127; CDBLB 1890-1914;
DLB 10, 19, 98; MTCW

Yehoshua, A(braham) B.
1936- . . . . **CLC 13, 31**
See also CA 33-36R; CANR 43

Yep, Laurence Michael 1948- . . . . . . **CLC 35**
See also AAYA 5; CA 49-52; CANR 1;
CLR 3, 17; DLB 52; JRDA; MAICYA;
SATA 7, 69

Yerby, Frank G(arvin)
1916-1991 . . . . **CLC 1, 7, 22; BLC 3**
See also BW; CA 9-12R; 136; CANR 16;
DLB 76; MTCW

Yesenin, Sergei Alexandrovich
See Esenin, Sergei (Alexandrovich)

Yevtushenko, Yevgeny (Alexandrovich)
1933- . . . . **CLC 1, 3, 13, 26, 51**
See also CA 81-84; CANR 33; MTCW

Yezierska, Anzia 1885(?)-1970 . . . . . **CLC 46**
See also CA 126; 89-92; DLB 28; MTCW

Yglesias, Helen 1915- . . . . **CLC 7, 22**
See also CA 37-40R; CANR 15; MTCW

Yokomitsu Riichi 1898-1947 . . . . . . **TCLC 47**

Yonge, Charlotte (Mary)
1823-1901 . . . . **TCLC 48**
See also CA 109; DLB 18; SATA 17

York, Jeremy
See Creasey, John

York, Simon
See Heinlein, Robert A(nson)

Yorke, Henry Vincent 1905-1974 . . . **CLC 13**
See also Green, Henry
See also CA 85-88; 49-52

Young, Al(bert James)
1939- . . . . **CLC 19; BLC 3**
See also BW; CA 29-32R; CANR 26;
DLB 33

Young, Andrew (John) 1885-1971 . . . . **CLC 5**
See also CA 5-8R; CANR 7, 29

Young, Collier
See Bloch, Robert (Albert)

Young, Edward 1683-1765 . . . . **LC 3**
See also DLB 95

Young, Neil 1945- . . . . **CLC 17**
See also CA 110

Yourcenar, Marguerite
1903-1987 . . . . **CLC 19, 38, 50**
See also CA 69-72; CANR 23; DLB 72;
DLBY 88; MTCW

Yurick, Sol 1925- . . . . **CLC 6**
See also CA 13-16R; CANR 25

Zabolotskii, Nikolai Alekseevich
1903-1958 . . . . **TCLC 52**
See also CA 116

Zamiatin, Yevgenii
See Zamyatin, Evgeny Ivanovich

Zamyatin, Evgeny Ivanovich
1884-1937 . . . . **TCLC 8, 37**
See also CA 105

Zangwill, Israel 1864-1926 . . . . **TCLC 16**
See also CA 109; DLB 10, 135

Zappa, Francis Vincent, Jr. 1940-
See Zappa, Frank
See also CA 108

Zappa, Frank . . . . **CLC 17**
See also Zappa, Francis Vincent, Jr.

Zaturenska, Marya 1902-1982 . . . . **CLC 6, 11**
See also CA 13-16R; 105; CANR 22

Zelazny, Roger (Joseph) 1937- . . . . . **CLC 21**
See also AAYA 7; CA 21-24R; CANR 26;
DLB 8; MTCW; SATA 39, 57

Zhdanov, Andrei A(lexandrovich)
1896-1948 . . . . **TCLC 18**
See also CA 117

Zhukovsky, Vasily 1783-1852 . . . . **NCLC 35**

Ziegenhagen, Eric . . . . **CLC 55**

Zimmer, Jill Schary
See Robinson, Jill

Zimmerman, Robert
See Dylan, Bob

Zindel, Paul 1936- . . . . **CLC 6, 26; DA**
See also AAYA 2; CA 73-76; CANR 31;
CLR 3; DLB 7, 52; JRDA; MAICYA;
MTCW; SATA 16, 58

Zinov'Ev, A. A.
See Zinoviev, Alexander (Aleksandrovich)

Zinoviev, Alexander (Aleksandrovich)
1922- . . . . **CLC 19**
See also CA 116; 133; CAAS 10

Zoilus
See Lovecraft, H(oward) P(hillips)

Zola, Emile (Edouard Charles Antoine)
1840-1902 . . . . . . **TCLC 1, 6, 21, 41; DA;
WLC**
See also CA 104; 138; DLB 123

Zoline, Pamela 1941- . . . . **CLC 62**

Zorrilla y Moral, Jose 1817-1893 . . **NCLC 6**

Zoshchenko, Mikhail (Mikhailovich)
1895-1958 . . . . **TCLC 15**
See also CA 115

Zuckmayer, Carl 1896-1977 . . . . **CLC 18**
See also CA 69-72; DLB 56, 124

Zuk, Georges
See Skelton, Robin

Zukofsky, Louis
1904-1978 . . . . **CLC 1, 2, 4, 7, 11, 18**
See also CA 9-12R; 77-80; CANR 39;
DLB 5; MTCW

Zweig, Paul 1935-1984 . . . . **CLC 34, 42**
See also CA 85-88; 113

Zweig, Stefan 1881-1942 . . . . **TCLC 17**
See also CA 112; DLB 81, 118

Literary Criticism Series
Cumulative Topic Index

This index lists all topic entries in the Gale Literary Criticism Series *Classical and Medieval Literature Criticism, Contemporary Literary Criticism, Literature Criticism from 1400 to 1800, Nineteenth-Century Literature Criticism,* and *Twentieth-Century Literary Criticism.*

Topic Index

CLC Cumulative Nationality Index

589

Nationality Index

Nationality Index

Nationality Index

Nationality Index

Nationality Index

CLC-81 Title Index

Title Index

ISBN 0-8103-4989-2